CW01064645

The Reason Why

A History of the
Masonic Province
of South Wales

Y Rheswm Pam

Hanes
Talaith Seiri Rhyddion
De Cymru

The Reason Why

A History of the
Masonic Province of South Wales

Published by the South Wales Masonic History Group

First Published January 2012

Printed by HSW Print,
Tonypandy, South Wales

ISBN 978-0-9571282-0-0

Contents

Contents

Contents

Alphabetical List of Lodges

Alphabetical List of Lodges

Alphabetical List of Lodges

Foreword

It is with the utmost pleasure that I commend to you this History of the Province of South Wales. When the possibility of such a project was first discussed in 2005 it was assumed that it would take a few years to compile but, covering a period of over 200 years and having 170 Lodges in our area which embraces the whole of the 'old' Counties of Glamorganshire, Breconshire and Radnorshire, it was bound to take time.

An informal meeting of the Committee of the Guildford Gazette (previous name for Y Dalaith, our Provincial magazine) first mooted the idea but there were fears about cost and likely demand. The Committee however were encouraged in the knowledge that WBro Denis Woods, PPrJGW, of Caerphilly had already started to piece together some histories some seventeen years earlier and so there was a start. My predecessor, RWBro Hywel Davies, gave his blessing subject to assurances being made that the project would be viable. We could not afford to have lots of unsold books on our shelves. Happily, Brethren's support has been sufficient for it to go ahead.

Looking back, I doubt if the Committee realised the full extent of the work involved, including compilation and collation by the Lodges with research and expansion by the Editing team. Each Lodge was asked to give an account of its history. Some replied with very bare facts (chiefly a list of Founders and Consecrating Teams) while others wrote so much that they warranted a book of their own! Some could not find the relevant data, so members of the Committee had to act as historians, editors, researchers and proof readers.

The result is an account of every Lodge, including pictures of at least its Banner, Past Master's Jewel and a photograph of the Temple or Masonic Centre where it meets, together with Profiles of the most prominent Members of our Province over the years.

Such a project has not been done before in South Wales and we now have the definitive account of our whole Province. It will be a source of reference, information and interest for many years to come and not only to Freemasons but to all who are interested in people and events in Welsh history. I suspect that many will be surprised at the significant contribution to society that Brethren have made over the years, all of which has helped to shape the pattern of life today.

The Province is indebted to the dedication of the Publication Committee under the able leadership of WBro Peter Davies, ProvJGW, Chairman; WBro Brian Langley, PGStB, ProvSGW, Secretary; WBro Don Jones, PProvSGD, Graphic Designer; and WBro Anthony Howell, PPrJGW, Photographer. The full composition of this Committee can be seen at the end of the book. Gratitude is also due to the printer, WBro David Hackman, PSGD, AProvGM, and all those listed in the acknowledgements.

This is a book which you can read right through or more likely dip into from time to time. Enjoy.

Captain Sir Norman Lloyd-Edwards, ProvGM.

Rhagair

Pleser o'r mwyaf i fi yw cyflwyno i chi Hanes Talaith De Cymru. Pan drafodwyd y posibilrwydd o gynllun o'r fath yn ôl yn 2005 cymerwyd yn ganiataol y byddai'n cymryd ychydig o flynyddoedd i'w gwblhau ond, gan ei fod yn cynnwys cyfnod o dros 200 o flynyddoedd a 170 o Gyfrinfeydd yn ein hardal, sef yr hen siroedd Morgannwg, Brycheiniog a Maesyfed, yn naturiol ddigon yr oedd yn mynd i gymryd amser.

Cynhaliwyd cyfarfod anffurfiol o bwyllgor y Guildford Gazette (yr hen enw am Y Dalaith, ein cylchgrawn Taleithiol) i drafod y syniad ond 'roedd pryderon ynglyn a'r gôst a'r galwad tebygol amdano. Calonogwyd y pwyllgor fodd bynnag gan y wybodaeth fod Yr HFd Denis Woods, PPrJGW, o Gaerffili wedi dechrau casglu rhai hanesion rhyw ddwy flynedd ar bymtheg yn gynharach ac felly yr oedd yn ddechreuad. Rhoddodd Y Gwir HFd Hywel Davies, fy rhagflaenydd, ei sêl bendith ar yr amod y byddai'r cynllun yn ymarferol. Ni allem fforddio gael llyfrau heb eu gwerthu ar ein silffoedd. Yn ffodus y mae cefnogaeth y Brodyr wedi bod yn ddigon i barhau â'r syniad.

Wrth edrych yn ôl, rwy'n amau'n fawr bod y Pwyllgor wedi sylweddoli maint y gwaith gan gynnwys crynhoad a chymhariad gan y cyfrinfeydd ac ymchwil ac ymestyniad gan y tîm golygyddol. Gofynnwyd i bob cyfrinfa i roi disgrifiad o'i hanes. Ymateb rhai oedd rhoi manylion moel (yn bennaf rhestr o'r Sylfaenwyr a'r Timau Cysegru) tra ysgrifennodd eraill ddigon i gyhoeddi llyfrau eu hunain! Methodd rhai ddod o hyd i ddata pwrpasol, felly 'roedd rhaid i aelodau'r pwyllgor weithredu fel haneswyr, golygyddion, ymchwilwyr a darllenwyr y proflenni.

Y canlyniad yw adroddiad o bob Cyfrinfa gan gynnwys lluniau, o leiaf o'r Faner, Tlws y Cynfeistr, a'r Deml neu Ganolfan y Seiri Rhyddion lle y maent yn cyfarfod, ac hefyd bywgraffiadau byr o Aelodau mwyaf blaenllaw ein Talaith dros y blynyddoedd.

Ni chafwyd cynllun o'i fath o'r blaen yn Ne Cymru ac yn awr mae gennym adroddiad pendant o'r holl Dalaith. Fe fydd yn ffynhonell gwybodaeth a diddordeb am flynyddoedd maith i ddod ac nid yn unig i Seiri Rhyddion ond i bawb sy'n ymddiddori mewn pobl a digwyddiadau yn hanes Cymru. Rwy'n tybio y bydd llawer yn synnu at faint o gyfraniad y mae'r Brodyr wedi'i wneud i gymdeithas dros y blynyddoedd ac sydd wedi helpu ffurfio patrwm bywyd heddiw.

Mae'r Dalaith yn ddyledus i'r Pwyllgor Cyhoeddi am eu hymroddiad o dan arweiniad Yr HFd Peter Davies, ProvJGW, Cadeirydd; Yr HFd Brian Langley, PGStB, ProvSGW, Ysgrifenydd; Yr HFd Don Jones, PProvSGD, Cynllunydd Graffeg; a'r HFd Anthony Howell, PPrJGW, Ffotograffydd. Gwelir rhestr lawn o'r pwyllgor ar ddiwedd y llyfr. Mae ein dyled yn fawr hefyd i'r argraffwr Yr HFd David Hackman, PGSD, AProvGM, a phawb sydd wedi'u rhestru yn y cydnabyddiaethau.

Llyfr yw hwn y gellir ei ddarllen ar ei hyd neu, yn fwy tebygol, i bori ynddo yn achlysurol. Mwynhewch.

Y Capten Syr Norman Lloyd-Edwards, ProvGM.

Acknowledgements

First and foremost, I wish to thank all those Brethren throughout the Province who have acted as historians for the various Lodges and who have co-operated with the Provincial History Book Committee in providing all the required information. Without their input, this book would not have been possible.

The Provincial History Book Committee was formed as a section of the 'Provincial Education and Communications Committee', initially under the superintendence of WBro Brian Eveleigh, PAProvGM and, latterly, WBro Roy Woodward, AProvGM. I greatly value the freedom of operation they both afforded me, yet within the knowledge that they were there to support if and when necessary. WBro Roy Woodward was most helpful in assisting with the Swansea Lodges and he has proved to be invaluable in promoting the book.

Gratitude must also be expressed to the staff at the Library and Museum of Freemasonry, Freemasons' Hall, London, for their patience and readiness to assist with numerous requests for information and for permitting access to a range of documents from the archives. I am grateful in particular to Martin Cherry, Librarian; Peter Aitkenhead, Assistant Librarian; and Susan Snell, Archivist. Also, I wish to acknowledge the kindness of VWBro Terry Haunch, MA, PDepGSuptWks, former Librarian and Curator, Grand Lodge Library and Museum, who unhesitatingly gave me permission to refer to his article 'Early Freemasonry in South Wales'.

I have been fortunate in having the assistance of a most enthusiastic band of editors who have given loyal support and tremendous commitment throughout the project. They have been a delight to work with, and their friendship and determination to complete the book have been a continuous source of encouragement.

The high quality of this publication would not have been possible without the professionalism and dedication of WBro Don Jones, who has spent untold hours in compiling the pages and preparing the photographic images for printing. I am also extremely grateful to WBro Anthony Howell for agreeing to be part of the team. His ability as a photographer is second to none, and his numerous photographs reproduced in the book are a testimony to his undoubted talent.

The onerous task of proof reading was undertaken by WBro David Murphy, who has been meticulous in his approach. His attention to detail, his suggestions for amendments to the text, and his emphasis on consistency in phrasing and presentation, have added significantly to the final narrative.

The business side of the venture has been admirably dealt with by WBro Graham Wilcox, Treasurer. Knowing that this aspect of the project was in such capable hands, enabled me to concentrate on my editing duties.

It has also been a pleasure to work with WBro David Hackman, of HSW Print, who agreed to be responsible for the printing of the book. His sound financial advice allowed us to proceed smoothly and effectively with the marketing and facilitated the successful defraying of all the publishing costs.

Throughout the five years it has taken to bring this project to fruition, I have been extremely fortunate in having the loyal support of WBro Brian Langley. My task would have been impossible without his assistance. His wisdom, commitment and determination have been a constant source of inspiration and reassurance; nothing was ever too much trouble for him.

A very special thank you is due to my wife, Mari, for her patience, understanding and support throughout the preparation of this book, which has made enormous demands on our free time together. She has given a warm welcome to the Committee members who have met in our home for our almost monthly meetings during the last five years; and she has provided much needed refreshments, which I know have been greatly appreciated. Indeed, without the interest and support of all the Committee members' wives, this book definitely would not have been produced – a great debt of gratitude is owed to all of them, and I thank them wholeheartedly for their tremendous support.

Finally, I wish to express my gratitude to RWBro Captain Sir Norman Lloyd-Edwards, ProvGM, for his unstinting support, interest, enthusiasm and encouragement. One could not have wished for a finer ambassador.

WBro Peter M Davies, ProvJGW, Chairman.

A Guide to the Provincial History Book

The Lodge histories are arranged in chronological order, with the biographies being appropriately interspersed among them. In most instances, they follow the same order as the Provincial Year Book. An alphabetical list of Lodges is also provided in order to help locate a particular history.

In the contents pages, the biographies of the ProvGMs are indicated in red and those of the DepProvGMs are shown in blue. Other biographies are shown in green. Miscellaneous items appear in purple. A chronological list of the Provincial Executive Officers can be found on the next page.

The family trees are taken from the information provided on the Grand Lodge website. Likewise, the assigning of Mother (Sponsoring) and Daughter Lodges is based entirely on Grand Lodge records. The Sponsoring Lodge is the Lodge which formally signs the Petition, which then bears the signature of the Worshipful Master and Wardens of that particular Lodge. The Sponsoring Lodge is not necessarily the Lodge which provides the greatest number of Petitioners; indeed, in one history in this book, not a single Petitioner was a Member of the Sponsoring Lodge!

The abbreviations used for the various Masonic Ranks are those adopted by Grand Lodge in UGLE Masonic Year Books. There is one exception - Prov is used for an Active Provincial Rank or PProv for a Past Active Provincial Rank, whereas PPr is used for a non-Active Past Provincial Rank.

Provincial Grand Lodge of South Wales

Provincial Grand Masters

1727	Sir Edward Mansel, Bart.	1865	Theodore Mansel Talbot
1754	David Jones Gwynne	1876	Sir George Elliot, Bart, MP
1779	Sir Herbert Mackworth, Bart.	1894	Rt Hon John Allan, 1st Lord Llangattock
1794	Thomas Wyndham, MP	1913	Sir Charles L D Venables Llewelyn, Bart.
1814	Benjamin Hall, MP	1938	R P St John Charles
1817	Sir Christopher Cole, KCB, MP	1966	Rt Hon John Hussey Hamilton Vivian
1836	Sir John Josiah Guest, Bart, MP		4th Lord Swansea, OSM, CStJ, DL
1848	Edward John Hutchins	1999	Hywel Davies
1856	Charles Kemeys Kemeys-Tynte	2008	Captain Sir Norman Lloyd-Edwards, KCVO, GCStJ, RD*, RNR

Deputy Provincial Grand Masters

Circa 1765	Robert Jones III of Fonmon Castle	1915	Henry Pendrill Charles
1821	Christopher Hancorne	1925	Sir David William Evans
1831	William Shewen	1926	David John Jones
1833	Christopher Hancorne	1931	Edgar John Rutter
1840	Edward John Hutchins	1971	Harry Francis Stockwell
1848	Evan Morgan	1977	Geoffrey Malin Ashe, TD
1851	George Gwynne Bird	1992	Roy Keith Hopkin
1863	Theodore Mansel Talbot	1998	James Stuart Peters
1865	Edward James Morris	1999	Peter Frost
1876	Vacant	2007	Andew Lindsay Gretton
1877	Marmaduke Tennant	2011	Gareth Jones, OBE

Assistant Provincial Grand Masters

1945-1953	Charles Presgrave Palmer	1982-1993	Samuel Northway	1999-2004	Robert John Nettleship
1953-1956	Edgar William Lewis	1984-1998	James Stuart Peters	2004-2011	Geoffrey William Thomas
1953-1971	Harry Francis Stockwell	1987-1992	Roy Keith Hopkin	2007-2011	Gareth Jones, OBE
1956-1960	Russell Mabley	1992-1998	David Luther Protheroe	2007-2009	Rev Canon D Huw E Mosford
1960-1980	Harold Wilson	1993-1999	Peter Frost	2010-	H E Roy Woodward
1971-1976	Llewellyn George Bevan	1996-1999	Hywel Davies	2010-	David G Hackman
1976-1977	Geoffrey Malin Ashe, TD	1998-2007	Rev Norman Lea	2011-	Jeffrey Parry Thomas
1976-1984	Ronald Bowen Whittingham	1998-1999	John Taylor	2011-	Paul Raymond Marshall, OBE
1977-1987	Cuthbert Lionel Summers	1999-2007	Andrew Lindsay Gretton		
1980-1996	Ken Adams Morgan	1999-2010	Brian Eveleigh		

Provincial Grand Secretaries

1821	John Francis	1868	John James (Junior)	1904	George Whittington
1840	Roger Walker	1869	James Tregoning Nettel	1944	Harry F Stockwell
1848	John Ludford White	1870	Walter Whittington	1953	Aubrey M Burns
1851	Thomas Jones Dyke	1875	Edward C Phillips	1960	J Morgan James
1858	George Allen	1876	Vacant	1967	Malcolm H Thompson
1865	Walter Whittington	1877	Evan Jones	1990	James R Bevan
1866	John Felton	1880	John Jones		
1867	David Williams	1887	Walter Whittington		

Introduction

The Premier Grand Lodge of England, 'The Moderns', was founded on St John Baptist's Day, 24 June 1717, in London, when four Craft Lodges gathered at the 'Goose and Gridiron Ale-house' in St Paul's Church-yard in London and Constituted themselves a Grand Lodge.

In 1724, the Premier Grand Lodge began Warranting Lodges outside London with Lodge No.34 at Carmarthen being the first in Wales. Sir Edward Mansel, 2nd Bart of Trimsaran, near Burry Port, the Lodge's first Master, was appointed the first Provincial Grand Master of South Wales in 1727, making the Province one of the earliest to be formed. Tyrian Lodge, No.189 Haverfordwest was Warranted next, on 14 April 1741. Gradually new Lodges were Constituted across South Wales. The first Cardiff Lodge, Corinthian Lodge No.226 was Warranted in August 1754 closely followed in September by Lodge No.267, meeting at 'The Bear Hotel', Cowbridge.

Meanwhile, in London on 17 July 1751, at the 'Turk's Head Tavern', Greek Street, Soho, about eighty Freemasons, (mainly Irish) from six London Lodges formed themselves into a Grand Committee, for the establishment of a rival Grand Lodge. They could not accept the Ritual, which had been revised over several years by the Premier Grand Lodge, and decided to return to the 'Antient Charges'. They consequently became known as 'The Antients' and the Premier Grand Lodge as 'The Moderns'. Antient Lodges are also known as 'Atholl Lodges', after the Duke of Atholl, who became the first Grand Master.

In 1764, the first Antient Lodge was established in Brecon and by 1765, Antient Lodge, No.33 was operating at Bridgend. The Bridgend Warrant was transferred to Cardiff in 1808 to Constitute the present Glamorgan Lodge No.36.

Henry Somerset, 5th Duke of Beaufort became Grand Master of the Moderns in 1767. Two years later, the first Swansea Lodge, Beaufort Lodge No.433 was Warranted on 24 April 1767. The next important event was the Warranting of Knoll Lodge No.506, Neath, on 20 September 1777. This Lodge's Warrant was transferred to Swansea in 1800 to become today's Indefatigable Lodge No.237.

The majority of these early Lodges had a rather limited life and were Erased within a few years. By 1807 Freemasonry had almost completely died out in South Wales. The renaissance of Freemasonry can be attributed in the main to Benjamin Plummer, SGW of the Antient Grand Lodge. Plummer arrived in South Wales in 1807, to Constitute Ancient Britons' Lodge No.126 in Caerphilly. It was from this Lodge that Glamorgan Lodge No.36 evolved in 1808, followed by Loyal Cambrian Lodge No.110, Merthyr Tydfil, in 1810.

At the time of the Union of the Modern and Antient Grand Lodges in December 1813, to form the United Grand Lodge of England, the Province of South Wales consisted of five Antient Lodges (Ancient Britons', Glamorgan and Loyal Cambrian, already mentioned and 'Hwlffordd Lodge' No.81, Haverfordwest and 'Union Lodge' No.192 Carmarthen) and three Modern Lodges (Indefatigable, Swansea; Cambrian Lodge No.510 Brecon and St David's Lodge of Perfect Friendship No.631, Carmarthen). Of these eight Lodges, only three remain, namely Glamorgan, Loyal Cambrian and Indefatigable.

On 31 January 1821, a Warrant was granted for a Lodge in Neath, on the recommendation of the Provincial Grand Master, Sir Christopher Cole. This was Cambrian Lodge No.726, which was to play a significant role in the future development of the Province.

In 1848, the original Province of South Wales was divided into two Provinces - South Wales Eastern Division and South Wales Western Division, with just four Lodges in each Division. All but six of the Lodges which are now, or have been in this Province, are derived from these four Lodges. Within the Province, Glamorgan Lodge, Cardiff, heads a family tree of 102 Lodges; Cambrian Lodge, Neath, a family of 47 Lodges; Indefatigable Lodge, Swansea, a family of 15 Lodges and Loyal Cambrian Lodge, Merthyr

Tydfil, a family of 10 Lodges. The remaining 6 Lodges are headed by Brecknock Lodge No.651, Brecon, Warranted in 1856, a Daughter Lodge of St Peter's Lodge No. 476, Carmarthen, Province of South Wales Western Division. It should be added that Brecknock Lodge is the Mother Lodge of Lodges in other Provinces, mainly in North Wales and West Wales. One important exception is Loyal Hay Lodge No.2382; originally in this Province and Warranted in September 1890, it was transferred to the Province of Herefordshire in November 1920.

By the end of the 19th century, the Province totalled 23 Lodges, but by this time, one of the Lodges, St Quintin's Lodge No.1822 Cowbridge was inactive and was finally Erased from the Register of the UGLE in 1923. At the outbreak of the First World War, the total number of Lodges was 27, and during the war years a further 4 Lodges were Consecrated. At the outbreak of World War II, the Province had grown to 58 Lodges, with a further 12 Lodges being added during that War.

When Reginald Pendrill St John Charles became Provincial Grand Master in November 1938, he inherited a Province of 56 Lodges. On his resignation in 1966, a further 52 Lodges had been Consecrated, the vast majority of such ceremonies being conducted by him. During 1948, ten Lodges were Consecrated, a total for one year which had never been equalled, even under the prolific expansion of the Province under Lord Swansea. The latter was Provincial Grand Master from 1966 to 1999, during which time a further 68 Lodges were added to the Province, bringing the total to 176.

With RWBro Hywel Davies as Provincial Grand Master, two Day-light Lodges were formed, namely St Tydfil's Lodge No.9753, Merthyr Tydfil, in 2002 and Lodge of Contentment No.9763, Bridgend, Consecrated in 2003.

In 2008, the names of the two Provinces in South Wales were changed. The Province of South Wales Eastern Division became the Province of South Wales, and the Province of South Wales Western Division became the Province of West Wales.

Unfortunately, we have now entered a period of Lodges surrendering their Warrants. The first, since the Erasure of St Quintin's Lodge in 1923 was Shir Gâr Lodge No.7339, Erased in April 2005. Since then we have lost a further 6 Lodges – Sapphire Lodge No.5290 (2008); Lodge of Integrity No.6907 (2008); Lodge of Unity No.6030 (2009); Galen Lodge No.6366 (2010); Penlan Lodge No.6695 (2011) and St Canna Lodge No.6725 (2011). St Mildred Lodge No.5078 agreed to surrender its Warrant in September 2011, and it will be Erased in 2012, leaving the Province with 170 Lodges. The Province of South Wales remains one of the largest in England and Wales under the UGLE, ranking 15th in terms of the number of Lodges, out of a total of 46 Provinces.

WBro Peter M Davies, ProvJGW.

The Province of South Wales During the 18th Century

The Grand Lodge of England was founded on St John Baptist's Day, 24 June 1717, in London, when four Craft Lodges gathered at the 'Goose and Gridiron Ale-house' in St Paul's Churchyard in London and Constituted themselves as a Grand Lodge. During the early decades of the Grand Lodge, it was not the 'Grand Lodge of England,' neither in name nor in the minds of its Members. Rather, it limited its jurisdiction to Lodges in London and Westminster.

However, in 1724, the Premier Grand Lodge began Warranting Lodges outside London - Lodge No.28 was Warranted at Bath; No.29 at Bristol; No.31 at Chichester; Nos.32 and 33 at Chester and No.34 at the Bay Nag's Head & Star, Dark Gate, Carmarthen. Thus, the Carmarthen Lodge was at the forefront of the expansion of Freemasonry into the Provinces. This unnamed Lodge was Erased on 29 November 1754.

That Freemasonry should first emerge in Carmarthen might at first sight appear quite remarkable. However, in the early 18th century, Carmarthen was the most important town and port in South Wales. The person responsible for this development was the wealthy landowner, Sir Edward Mansel, 2nd Bart. of Trimsaran, near Burry Port, the Lodge's first Master. His father, also Edward Mansel, had been created 1st Baronet of Trimsaran on 22 February 1696 and on his death on 19 February 1719, his son assumed the title. The 2nd baronet was a Mason of some consequence in London, for, in 1723, he was Grand Steward and Junior Grand Warden in the same year; and in the following year Master of the Lodge of Antiquity, No. 1 (now No. 2) one of the four original Lodges of the Premier Grand Lodge; and also Senior Grand Warden.

Mansel was appointed the first Provincial Grand Master of South Wales in 1727, making the Province one of the earliest to be formed. In October 1753, he established the second Lodge in Carmarthen, No.240 at the Three Crowns, Notts Square. In 1767, the Lodge was named 'The Lodge of Perfect Friendship' (No.167), renamed 'Temple Lodge' No.132 in 1772; it was Erased on 5 February 1777. Previously, Lodge No.189 had been Warranted on 14 April 1741 at the 'Ship & Castle', High Street, Haverfordwest. As this town was another important port at that time, the Lodge was appropriately named 'Tyrian' Lodge No.95 in 1770, after the ancient Phoenician seaport of Tyre, 50 miles to the south of Beirut in SW Lebanon. It took as its symbol a Greek sailing ship with its customary bank of oars, a symbol still used today by 'Tyrian' Lodges. The only mention of this Lodge in Grand Lodge Minutes is an entry recording the receipt of the Constitution fee of two guineas. It was Erased from the Register on 23 April 1773.

Sir Edward Mansel died on 9 May 1754 and he was replaced as Provincial Grand Master on 15 May 1754 by David Jones Gwynne of Taliaris and Tregib, who the previous year had inherited the Taliaris and Tregib estates on the death of his father, Richard Jones of Tregib. Richard Jones was the great nephew of David Gwynne and he had inherited the Taliaris estate on the death of his uncle, on the condition that he adopted the name Gwynne. The old mansion of Taliaris is to be found four miles northeast of Llandeilo. David Jones Gwynne was born in 1726, educated at New College, Oxford and by 1754 was a very wealthy man and like his predecessor, Sir Edward Mansel, he owned considerable estates. The new Provincial Grand Master only made the occasional appearance in Grand Lodge and it would appear, from the historical correspondence preserved in Grand Lodge Library, that he left matters largely to his Deputy, John Evans, at Carmarthen.

John Evans was active in the Lodge of Perfect Friendship No.167, the second Lodge in Carmarthen. The first Lodge of 1724 by this time had lapsed, but was not Erased until the following year. This second Lodge regarded itself as a continuation of the original Lodge, even though it had taken a new Constitution and Lodge Number and considered itself to be the Provincial Grand Lodge of South Wales. His letter to Thomas French, Grand Secretary, dated 16 February 1769 states *we are by Virtue of a Deputation granted by the Marquess of Carnarvon, the Provincial Grand Lodge of South Wales and consequently obliged to relieve the Distressed Brethren in our Principality, which are very numerous and really a heavy burden on us, so we have nothing to do with your General Charity.'* (Henry, Marquess of Carnarvon became 2nd Duke of Chandos in 1744, and was Grand Master in 1738. His son, James, Marquess of Carnarvon became 3rd Duke of Chandos in 1771, and Grand Master 1754-1756.) This refusal to subscribe to the Grand Charity did not go down well with the Grand Secretary, nor did the claim to be a Provincial Grand Lodge. In consequence, on 19 April, Thomas French wrote to David Jones Gwynne, ProvGM- *'As the Brethren of No.167 seem to be ignorant of the Constitutions of Masonry as well as of the nature of a Provincial Grand Lodge, I am commanded by the Grand Master to request you to convince them of their mistake and to recommend the Book of Constitutions to their perusal. No private Lodge under the English Constitutions can assume the name of a Provincial Grand Lodge .... Lodges in the Province are to send or pay their liberal contributions to the General Fund of Charity.'*

John Evans continued as DepProvGM, but was soon again involved in another dispute with the Grand Secretary, when the Tyrian Lodge in Haverfordwest decided that if the Carmarthen Lodge had a DepProvGM, so should they. Bro Edwards of Johnstone was appointed as such and Bro Essex Jones became the Deputy to the Deputy! The Grand Secretary wrote once again to David Jones Gwynne, pointing out that in permitting these appointments he had exceeded his powers and warned him *'The Office of Provincial Grand Master is not for life'.*

The first two Provincial Grand Masters, Mansel and Gwynne had another important point in common; they were both Members of the Society of Sea Serjeants. The origins of the Society of Sea Serjeants are unknown, though it may have been a revival of a fraternal organisation dating from the War of the Roses. It came into existence as a Jacobite Club in about 1725, and its Members in their correspondence with one another subscribed themselves as 'brothers'. The officers consisted of a President, Secretary, Treasurer, Examiner, Chaplain and two Stewards. Its Membership, which was limited to 25, together with a number of probationers, consisted mainly of West Wales Squires, all of whom, as far as is known, were Tories. The Society met only once a year for its convivial gatherings. These lasted a week at one of the ports or tidal towns such as Tenby, Carmarthen, Cardigan or Haverfordwest, where Members indulged in such ostensibly innocent social entertainments as feasting, dancing, processions and water-parties, but their private meetings were conducted under the veil of secrecy. The Society's badge worn by Members showed a star (a popular emblem among Stuart sympathisers) with a dolphin in its centre, the latter perhaps being symbolic of Seaside Associations. Special wineglasses used at the gatherings carried a similar badge.

Nothing is known of the Society's anti-Hanoverian activities and there is no evidence of its participation in any Jacobite plots. On the other hand, some of its leading Members were avowed Stuart adherents. John Philipps of Picton Castle became its President in 1752. He was described by his cousin, Horace Walpole, as *'a notorious Jacobite',* and he had pledged his fidelity to the Pretender probably before the Society was established.

When Sir John Philipps unsuccessfully contested the Bristol constituency in 1754, he was accused by his opponents of dubious loyalty to the Crown, because of his Presidency of the Sea Serjeants. Such were the attacks upon him that he felt it necessary to issue a public statement denying that the Society had any seditious aims. *'The intent, indeed, of our annual meeting',* he declared, *'is to spend a week together in innocent mirth and recreation, as other gentlemen in England do at a horse-race, and for no disloyal purpose whatsoever that I know of, and I defy any person to charge us with anything of that nature'.* Doesn't that sound familiar Brethren? He was returned as MP for Petersfield in the same year; and later, until his death, represented Pembrokeshire in the House of Commons. The last known meeting of the Society of Sea Serjeants took place at Haverfordwest in 1763. Early in the year Sir John Philipps became one of George III's Privy Councillors, and died some eighteen months later.

The Welsh historian, J P Jenkins, in his article, 'Jacobites & Freemasons in Eighteenth Century Wales', published in the Welsh History Review in 1979, presents a strong case for the Society of Sea Serjeants to be the forerunner of the early Masonic Lodges. Wales, under George II, was one of the centres of Toryism and he claims that it was virtually impossible to distinguish between Jacobite Societies and Masonic Lodges, for both had common origins and a very similar Membership, and that under George III, Freemasonry inherited much of Tory ideology. Between 1714 and 1760, some of the main national leaders of the Tory party had their chief interests in Wales. For example, the Dukes of Beaufort, who hold the title of Lord of Gower and Kilvey and still own significant estates in eastern Gower. In particular, Henry Somerset, the 5th Duke, who had been Initiated into Freemasonry sometime prior to 1768 at the 'Horn' Tavern, London (now the 'Royal Somerset House and Inverness Lodge, No.4). He was the Worshipful Master of the 'Lodge of Friendship' (now No.6) in 1767, the same year that he became the Grand Master of the Premier Grand Lodge.

With the gradual demise of the Society of Sea Serjeants, new Masonic Lodges were emerging across South Wales. In August 1754, 'Corinthian Lodge' No.266 was Warranted to meet at the 'Red House', Cardiff, an inn on, or near, the site of the present Angel Hotel. The first Master of the Lodge was Dr Edward Saunders, who had been appointed Coroner to the County of Glamorgan at the Neath Quarter Sessions on the 11 July 1754. He was also a Lieutenant and a Doctor in the Glamorgan Militia. A more colourful Member was Captain Thomas Mathew of Llandaff, grandson of Admiral Thomas Mathew, whose stormy naval career had ended, perhaps unjustly, in a Court Martial. The Admiral built Llandaff Court, which is the main building of the present Llandaff Cathedral School. Captain Mathew was a noted figure in the grand society of Bath. In 1772, he fought a famous duel, near Covent Garden, with the Irish playwright, Richard Brinsley Sheridan. The duel was short and bloodless; however, honour had not been satisfied and a second duel was fought in August 1772, at Kingsdown, near Bath. Sheridan was seriously wounded and Mathew escaped in a post chaise. It is believed that the affair was the inspiration for Sheridan's famous comedy 'The Rivals'. Other Members of the Corinthian Lodge in 1765 included James Davies, Registrar of Llandaff and Robert Jones III of Fonmon Castle, Deputy Provincial Grand Master.

The first Cowbridge Lodge, No.267 was Warranted in September 1754 to meet at 'The Bear'. Its most important Member on the Register for 1770 was the above mentioned Robert Jones, DepProvGM. His father, Robert Jones II, had been a well-known Jacobite sympathiser. The family was friendly with the Dukes of Beaufort and also with John Wesley, who became a frequent visitor to the Castle. Robert Jones III, like Captain Mathew, who married Robert's sister on 9 November 1763, grew up to enjoy the life and society in London and Bath. In London he was a Member of the 'One Tun' Lodge in Noble Street and the 'Black Lion' in Jockey Field. He also attended Masonic taverns in London, like the 'Antwerp', the 'Turk's Head' and the 'Shakespeare'. The Grand Stewards' Lodge met at the Shakespeare's Head, Covent Garden, between 1750-1753, so it is most likely that this is one of the Lodges that he attended. His expenditure on amusements, recorded in his account books, includes visits to the theatre, buying raffle tickets, playing tennis, gambling at cards. He was also greatly involved in horse-racing. He spent considerable sums on the embellishment of Fonmon Castle, turning it into the fine eighteenth century house that it is today. In 1784, he fled to France to escape his creditors and in 1792, he was forced to sell some of his estate to pay off his debts. The Marquess of Bute was one such purchaser.

In 1770, the WM of the Cowbridge Lodge was John Edmondes. The Edmondes family of Cowbridge, St Hilary and Llandough were Attorneys and Estate Stewards of the Aubrey family of Llantrithyd. Colonel Thomas Edmondes of the 1st Regiment of Footguards was the younger son of Thomas Edmondes who had purchased the St Hilary (Beaupre) Estate in 1755. Col Thomas Edmondes was a Deputy-lieutenant of the county. He and his brother John (d. 1778), both lived at Llandough Castle as tenants of the Margam Estate. Robert Taynton, SW, was a Churchwarden and Bailiff of Cowbridge on three occasions. His family lived at Taynton House in Cowbridge. Edward Bates, JW, was a noted Doctor and a member of a well-known and respected family living at Cardiff; he was a boarder at Cowbridge Grammar School. In the History of the School by Iolo Davies, the author describes the treatment Dr Bates prescribed for smallpox consisting: - '*snails with cow's milk to be drunk early in the morning in bed and again in the evening*'. His trump card was '*the powder of dried vipers in his broth*' and despite this treatment, the patient survived!

By 1770, the Cowbridge Lodge was in difficulty with Grand Lodge for failing to deal with correspondence and not contributing to the cause of Charity. On 30 March, the Lodge Secretary, William Jones, wrote to William Heseltine, Grand Secretary as follows: '*We acknowledge the Receipt of your Letters and we have been very much to blame for not answering them. The reason was that our Lodge was very poor and in Debt. Our Deputy Provincial Grand Master of South Wales, Mr. Jones has made this Lodge a present of a Draught (sic) of Five Guineas, which we have thought proper to Remit to the Grand Fund of Charity, with our hearty wishes for the Support of Masonry. We have sent you a list of our Lodge in its present Situation, which we beg may be Registered. We hope to see our Lodge amongst the rest inserted in the next Committee of Charity.*'

Within a few years, the Cowbridge Lodge was once again in financial difficulties and, likewise, Corinthian Lodge, Cardiff. Both were Erased from the Register of Grand Lodge on 23 April 1775: '*for not contributing to the fund of Charity in one time and not having any reason for their neglect upon being in for that purpose*'.

Eighteen Lodges were Erased at the same Grand Lodge Meeting. Lodges at this time were mostly short lived and five years was their average life.

All the Lodges mentioned so far came under the jurisdiction of the Premier Grand Lodge of 1717. On 17 July 1751, at the 'Turk's Head Tavern', Greek Street, Soho, about eighty Freemasons (mainly Irish) from six London Lodges formed themselves into a Grand Committee for the establishment of a rival Grand Lodge - The 'Antient Grand Lodge'. They could not accept the Ritual, which had been revised over several years by the Premier Grand Lodge (which became known as 'The Moderns') and decided to return to the 'Antient Charges'.

On 27 December 1764, the Festival of St John the Evangelist, the first Antient Lodge, No.54 was Constituted at Brecon, meeting at the 'Sun Inn', Wheat Street. The Warrant of the Lodge had first been issued to a Lodge called St David's on the 14 June 1756, meeting at the 'Bear's Paw', London. This Lodge purchased for one guinea the dormant Warrant of Lodge No.12, and in consequence of No.54 being vacant, the Warrant was re-issued to the Brecon Lodge. Only one return of Members, consisting of 8 names, was sent to Grand Lodge. The Lodge lapsed soon afterwards. A second Lodge, No.337 (Modern) was formed the following year, meeting at 'The Bell Inn'. This Lodge only lasted four years and was Erased in 1769.

By 1765, Antient Lodge, No.33 was operating at Bridgend. The Antient or Atholl Grand Lodge had granted the original Warrant, No.33 on 15 March 1753 to a Lodge meeting at 'The Star & Garter', The Strand, London. According to Grand Lodge Minutes, this Lodge lapsed in 1755. The Warrant was re-issued in the early 1760s to a Lodge meeting in Bridgend. This was a common practice of the 'Antients', when, for a fee of typically one or two guineas, a Warrant of a lapsed Lodge could be purchased, the money being given to the 'Board of Charity'.

The first Grand Lodge Return of the Bridgend Lodge is dated 13 June 1765, and among the names listed were Richard Price, Michael & William Flew and Benjamin Coffin. It is likely that this Lodge had been established earlier, for part of the entry for 1

March 1765 in the Diaries (1762-1795) of William Thomas, Schoolmaster of Michaelston-super-Ely, near St Fagan's (published in 1995 by South Wales Record Society & South Glamorgan County Council Libraries & Arts Department), is as follows:

'The first of this month was held at the Bear in Cowbridge, the Society of the Free Masons, being in all about 24, and went to Cowbridge Church by two and two, in their white aprons, with their truels, hammers, and other Instruments as belong to Masonry, according to their rank in the fraternity, and had a sermon preached them by the Revd. Mr. John Williams of the Breach near Cowbridge, teacher now of the Free School in Cowbridge since Mr. Durel resigned. Here was several of Bridgend Lodge, as the two Flews etc., of Cowbridge Lodge, as Mr. Thomas Williams and Mr. Thomas Lewis, Lawyers, Mr. Morgans, Mr. Robert Taunton, Mr. Higgins of the Bear etc., of Cardiff's Lodge, Robert Jones Esqr., Dr. Edward Saunders as Master, and Esqr. Jones as Deputy Provincial Grand Master, also Captain Thomas Mathew of Llandaff, etc. A great crowd admiring and looking at the sight, being the like never before seen here'.

The Bridgend Grand Lodge Return for 4 November 1771 includes the name of Charles Bowen, owner of the Merthyr Mawr Estate. After his death in January 1787, his widow, Catherine married a Mr Richardson. She became involved in protracted litigation with her late husband's half-brothers and sister over the settlement of the Merthyr Mawr Estate (Case in Chancery1796-1804). Eventually the Estate was purchased by Sir John Nicholl, one of the Trustees. His son, also Sir John Nicholl, was MP for Cardiff (1832-1852) and was Initiated in Glamorgan Lodge on 19 August 1836.

The Rev Thomas Richards also appears on the same Lodge Return. Appointed Curate of Coychurch in 1742, he became Vicar of Eglwysilan, (near Caerphilly) in 1777. He collaborated with Dr John Richards, Rector of Coity in producing material for an English-Welsh Dictionary; he also revised and corrected an earlier Welsh-English Dictionary of William Evans (1771) and translated Dr. John Davies's Latin Grammar of 1621 into Welsh.

One of the earlier Members of the Lodge was John Lougher from the Parish of Pyle/Kenfig. He is listed in the book 'Bridgend 900', published by Bridgend & District Local History and Museum Society in 1993, as a Clock-maker (1780-1790) of Bridgend and also in Iorwerth Peate's book 'Clock & Watchmakers of Wales' published by National Museum of Wales in 1975.

On 25 October 1777, the Grand Secretary, James Jones issued the Bridgend Lodge with a replacement Warrant, assigned to Richard Price (WM), David Jones (SW) and Jenkin Williams (JW), the Lodge to meet at the 'Sign of the Bear' in the Town of Bridgend. The Bear Inn was situated on the corner of Cross Street and Elder Street, and part of that building can still be seen today, having been incorporated into the back of the present Wyndham Arms Hotel. It is not known why a replacement Warrant was issued.

It has been asserted that the WM Richard Price was Dr Price of 'Tynton', Llangeinor (North of Bridgend), the famous preacher, philosopher and mathematician, whose treatise on 'Reversionary Payments' for the 'Equitable Assurance Society' earned him the epithet 'Father of Life Assurance'. There is no concrete evidence to support this claim. However, Price was a close friend of Benjamin Franklin, who had been appointed Grand Master of the Provincial Grand Lodge of Pennsylvania in1734, in which year he published Anderson's 'Constitutions', thought to be the first Masonic Work published in America. Following the American War of Independence, which Price had supported in his sensational pamphlet 'Observations on the Nature of Civil Liberty', Franklin along with Arthur Lee and John Adams, invited Price, on behalf of Congress, to become a citizen of the United States, and to assist them in regulating the States' finances. Price had first met Franklin during the latter's stay in England from July 1757 until August 1763, during which time they both became members of the club of 'Honest Whigs'. During Franklin's next visit to London, which lasted from December 1764 until April 1775, a close and enduring friendship developed between the two men. They had many interests in common and frequently corresponded with one another. The late Dr David Oswald Thomas, Reader in Philosophy at Aberystwyth University, made the study of Richard Price his life's work. In 1977, he published the definitive study of Price, 'The Honest Mind', and this was followed by a three-volume edition of the complete correspondence, 'The Correspondence of Richard Price'. In all of Price's correspondence, there is no mention or discussion of Freemasonry. Dr Thomas stated that he had never come across any written evidence that Price was a Freemason, but he, Thomas, thought it very likely that he was - *'an argument from silence'*, as he put it.

There are, however, several family ties linking Price with the Bridgend Lodge. The local Doctor, Jenkin Williams, JW, was married to Catherine Morgan, the daughter of Dr Price's elder sister Sarah; William Flew (later SW and WM) had married Price's widowed younger sister Elizabeth, and Benjamin Coffin was the son of Price's half-sister Mary, married to Walter Coffin. Further, Price resided in London, was a person of great eminence, and he would have been well-placed to acquire a dormant London Lodge Warrant and arrange for its transfer to Bridgend, his home town, which he visited annually.

Soon after 1777, the Bridgend Lodge lapsed, the cause of which was reported by the then Junior Warden, D Willyams, in a letter, dated 25 October 1803 to the Grand Secretary in London.

'I have to inform you Sir - that I became a Member of Bridgend Lodge in '76. Soon afterwards, unfortunately and much to the Dishonour of Masonry, a misunderstanding took place amongst the leading Brothers and a total stagnation was the consequence. At that time Mr. Wm Flew was Master, Mr. Jenkin Williams Senior Warden and myself Jnr Warden.'

The Warrant was eventually transferred to Cardiff to Constitute Glamorgan Lodge No.33 on 4 Novembers 1808. The endorsement of the transfer to Cardiff is signed and dated on the back of the Warrant, 20 August 1808.

The Bridgend Lodge was the third Atholl Lodge to appear in South Wales. Previously, Lodge No.126 had been Warranted on 12 June 1764 to meet at 'The Green Dragon', Skinner Street, Newport. The Lodge lapsed soon afterwards and the Warrant was eventually reissued to a Lodge meeting at Caerphilly. In due course, the Caerphilly Lodge became known as 'Ancient Britons Lodge' No.126 and was Constituted on 16 December 1807.

The first Masonic Lodge to appear in Swansea was 'Beaufort Lodge' No.443, named in honour of Henry, 5th Duke of Beaufort, Grand Master of the Premier Grand Lodge. The Lodge had a Warrant of Constitution dated 24 April 1769. Details of this Lodge will be given separately.

In August 1775, David Jones Gwynne, ProvGM of South Wales died and he was buried on 18 August in Taliaris Chapel. His successor as Provincial Grand Master was Sir Herbert Mackworth, Bart of Gnoll Castle, Neath, but he wasn't appointed as such until 1779.

Herbert Mackworth of Gnoll Castle, only son of Herbert Mackworth, was born 1 January 1737, and married, in about 1761, Eliza, daughter of Robert Cotton Trefusis of Trefusis, Cornwall. He was Major of the Glamorgan Militia, 1761-1765, and Lieutenant-Colonel 1765 - 1791. Industrialist, Banker, and Agricultural Reformer, he was a Fellow of the Royal Society and a Vice-President of the Marine Society. Created a Baronet on 16 September 1776, he was also Deputy-Lieutenant of the County. He represented the Cardiff Boroughs in Parliament, 1766-1790, when he was forced to retire when John, Lord Mountstuart, heir to the Marquess of Bute, came of age and required the seat. Further biographical details are to found in the History of Gnoll Lodge No.506.

On 20 September 1777, the Warrant for the first Masonic Lodge at Neath was issued. This 'Modern Lodge' was 'Knoll Lodge' No.506, and it was in this Lodge that Sir Herbert Mackworth was Initiated in 1779, before taking up his duties as Provincial Grand Master. The Lodge is named after Sir Herbert's home, Knoll (Gnoll) House or Castle. In 1800, the Lodge was transferred to Swansea to become today's Indefatigable Lodge No.237. Further details of the history of this Lodge will also be given separately.

Freemasonry was to return to Cowbridge in 1787 with the issuing of a Warrant for a 'Modern' Lodge, No.496. Consecrated on

20 March 1787 by the new Provincial Grand Master, Sir Herbert Mackworth, it was named 'Mackworth Lodge' in his honour. Sir Herbert became Mayor of Cowbridge and Constable of the Castle of St Quintin in 1789 and was a Freeman of the Borough. Of the nine Founder Members, four had been Members of the previous Cowbridge Lodge. The location of the Lodge is unknown.

One of the most interesting of the Founders was the Junior Warden, the Rev Daniel Walters, son of the Vicar of Llandough, Cowbridge (Rev John Walters). Daniel Walters was a pupil of Cowbridge School and his diary of life at Llandough, the School and the Vale of Glamorgan in 1777/8 is in the National Library of Wales, Aberystwyth. Several pages of his schoolboy diary are included in Iolo Davies's History of Cowbridge Grammar School (Published by D Brown & Sons, Cowbridge, 1967). Walters left school in 1780 and became a Master at Norwich School and in January 1785, at the age of 23, he succeeded his brother John as Headmaster of Cowbridge School. He was a brilliant young poet, and was made a Freeman of Cowbridge in 1784. He contracted tuberculosis and died on the 14 August 1787 at the age of 25. His father composed an epitaph to his memory in eloquent and beautiful Latin, which is in the Chancel of Cowbridge Church.

The Lodge was short-lived and was Erased from the roll on 18 April 1792, shortly after the death of Sir Herbert Mackworth.

The final Lodge to appear in the Province in the 18th century was Cambrian Lodge No.542 at Brecon. This was a 'Modern' Lodge, Warranted on 1 August 1789 and meeting at the 'Swan Inn', Ship Street. The number of the Lodge was changed on three occasions. Having been allocated No. 542 in 1789, it was altered to 451 in 1792 and became 510 in 1814. Fortunately, the first Minute Book of the Cambrian Lodge has been preserved and it is worth recording verbatim part of the first Minute, to appreciate that the impressive Consecration Ceremonies of the present day were not performed in those early days.

October Brecon 1789

'At a meeting of free and accepted Masons at the Dwelling of Richard Hall, called the Swan Inn, Brecon, aforesaid Brother Theophilus Jones produced a Warrant under the Seal of the Right Worshipful Master, Sir Herbert Mackworth, Baronet, Provincial Grand Master for South Wales, countersigned by his Deputy Provincial Grand Master Richard Gough Esquire, and by Gabriel Jeffreys Esquire, his Provincial Grand Secretary, empowering him the said Theophilus Jones and several other Brethren to form themselves into a Lodge which Warrant being publicly read by Thomas Herbert - Brother William Jones Rt. Worshipful Master of the Beaufort Lodge at Swansea and acting upon this occasion as Provincial Grand Secretary by virtue of the said Warrant Invested the said Theophilus Jones with the badge of his office, whereupon the said Master chose Brother Samuel Jones to be his Senior Warden and Brother Thomas Powell to be his Junior Warden who accepted of the said offices.'

No. 542 Cambrian

The Lodge was opened in the first Degree in due form.

Present: Theophilus Jones, Right Worshipful Master. Samuel Jones, Wor. Senior Warden. Thomas Powell, Wor. Junior Warden. John Trees, Hugh Jones, John Lloyd, Morgan Jenkins, John Vale, Charles Price, Thomas Herbert, Joseph Hughes, William Vaughan. John Clark of the Holy Lodge of St John's.

The Right Wor. Master appointed Brother Thomas Powell to be Sec. of the said Lodge, which office he accepted of.

Thomas Bishop was proposed and seconded by Brother William Vaughan and Brother John Vale.

John Pierce was proposed and seconded by Brother John Trew and Brother Joseph Hughes.

Richard Hall was proposed and seconded by Brother William Vaughan and Brother Charles Price.

They were then Balloted for and unanimously approved.

The said T Bishop, J. Pierce and Richard Hall, were then regularly Initiated as Masons in the first Degree and paid their fees, that is to say, T. Bishop and J. Pierce the sum of £3.30 each and the said R. Hall only made as a Tyler being excused from payment save clothing.

The Lodge was then opened in the second Degree, and the said T. Bishop, J. Pierce and R. Hall were then passed to the 2nd Degree. The Lodge then chose Brother J. Pierce as Treasurer.

Four further Candidates were proposed and seconded namely, T.H. Powell, Thomas Williams, Charles Pritchard and Thomas Longfellow. Brother Charles Price then proposed that as the Lodge was now numerous an Emergency meeting would be called and so it would be expedient to Ballot for the Candidates that night, which was agreed and the four Candidates were unanimously approved.

The Lodge was afterwards closed until Tuesday the 24th of November.

Signed, 'Thomas Herbert'.

An Emergency Meeting was called prior to the next Regular meeting and was held on 4 November when Brothers Bishop, Pierce, and Hall were Raised. Seventeen Meetings were held in that first year, when 11 Candidates were Initiated and Passed and 10 Raised.

WBro Theophilus Jones was re-elected WM in 1790. Again, there did not appear to be a shortage of Candidates as 12 Meetings were held, when 6 Candidates were Initiated, 3 Passed and 5 Raised. Despite the large intake, attendances at Lodge Meetings were poor and this continued to be the case in the years ahead.

It was not surprising that Theophilus Jones continued to serve as WM until 1804, 15 years in all. He was only 30 years of age when he occupied the Chair in 1789. By profession he was a Solicitor, but better known as a Historian for his painstaking work in his 'History of Breconshire', considered to be one of the best of the Welsh County Histories. Throughout his 15 years as Master, 90 Meetings were held, of which 13 were adjourned due to *'insufficient Brethren being present'*. In all 41 Candidates were Initiated, 38 Passed and 32 Raised, many of whom came from as far afield as Birmingham, Oxford, Bristol, Evesham, Worcester, Merthyr, Hay and Aberdare.

There are no records of any Meetings being held between 1804 and 1813 and no further mention is made of Theophilus Jones, which is surprising as he did not pass to that GLA until 1812, when he was only 53 years of age. Afterwards, the Lodge went into serious decline and last met on 12 March 1819. It was finally Erased on 5 March 1828. (See also Benjamin Plummer.)

Sir Herbert Mackworth died at the age of 55 on 25 October 1791 from blood poisoning brought about by a thorn in his thumb. Thomas Wyndham, MP, of Dunraven Castle succeeded him as ProvGM in 1794, (Patent of Appointment dated 5 July 1794).His name appears on the Grand Lodge return of the Beaufort Lodge, by now No.292, for 1794. It states the he *was Made a Mason at the age of 30 on 18 December 1792'*. His family was related by marriage to the Jones family of Fonmon and his estate brought him an income of £10,000 pa. He spent a great deal of money on embellishing Dunraven Castle, where he was a popular and hospitable Squire, a keen sportsman and a model of benevolence. He was MP for Glamorgan from 1789 to 1814, thereby frustrating the Bute family's aspirations to impose their nominee on the county seat; however, his parliamentary career was far from distinguished, he was often absent from Parliament and his only reported speech was given in 1803. He died on 8 November 1814, almost one year after the signing of the Articles of Union between the Modern and Antient Grand Lodges to form the United Grand Lodge of England, which had taken place at Kensington Palace on 27 November 1813.

WBro Peter M Davies, ProvJGW, with grateful acknowledgement to WBro T O Haunch, MA, PDepGSuptWks, Grand Lodge Librarian and Curator of Museum, for his kind permission to refer to his 'Early Freemasonry in South Wales', a presentation given to Narberth Lodge No.2001, on 7 May 1982.

Beaufort Lodge No.443

Warranted : 24 April 1769

Met at the Star Tavern, Cross Street, Swansea. (1796)

Erased : 10 February 1809

The first Lodge to be established in Swansea was Beaufort Lodge No.443, with a Warrant of Constitution dated 24 April 1769, though it appears to have been operating unlawfully since 1768. It was named Beaufort Lodge in 1770, in honour of Henry Somerset, 5th Duke of Beaufort, who had become Grand Master of the Premier Grand Lodge two years earlier.

The Petition for a Warrant at Swansea appears not to have been properly vetted by Thomas French, the then Grand Secretary. Later in 1769, his successor, James Heseltine, described the late Grand Secretary's conduct as *'highly blameable'* in this respect, since two out of the four persons named in the Petition (and subsequently therefore on the Warrant) *'were not Masons, having only been made in a pretend Lodge, held at Bridge End near Swansea'*. This was an Antients' Lodge and its Members would not therefore be recognised as Regular Masons by the Premier Grand Lodge. So, to regularise the Beaufort Lodge, the DepProvGM, John Evans, went over to Swansea, and having first made the Irregular Brethren into 'Moderns', then Reconstituted the Lodge itself.*

In the correspondence about this affair between the Grand Secretary and Richard Lloyd, WM, the latter seems to be somewhat evasive in his replies, and it subsequently transpires why. He was one of the Irregular Masons who had to be 'remade' and what is more, he soon disappeared to Ireland, along with the Lodge Funds. The Lodge, not surprisingly, expelled him and for good reason - and in the words of the Secretary (Gabriel Jeffreys), declared him to be a *'Common Cowan'*.

Of the Regular Masons, one of the most senior was John Bevan, Esquire, who had been Initiated at the age of 21 in March 1742 at a Lodge meeting at the Crown & Anchor, Strand, London. Lanes Masonic Records shows that three Lodges were meeting at the Crown & Anchor, King Street, Seven Dials (which is near The Strand) in 1742. They were Lodge No.50, Warranted 1728 and Erased 28 April 1775; Lodge No. 148, Warranted 21 September 1737, ceased working in 180,1 and Lodge No. 166, Warranted 27 January 1739, now Royal Naval Lodge No.50.

Bevan, who by 1794, had become a JP, is shown on a Lodge Return as having been admitted into Beaufort Lodge on 2 October 1768, the year before the Warrant was issued! Two other Brethren are likewise shown as being admitted on that same day, thus casting further doubt on the legality of the opening of this Lodge in Swansea. They were William Jones, WM, Beaufort Lodge in 1786, Merchant, Initiated at the age of 24 in 1763; and Benjamin Jones, age 21, Merchant, residing at Swansea, *'made a Mason at Cowbridge in 1767'*. This must have been the first Cowbridge Lodge, meeting at the Bear, Cowbridge, between 1754 and 1775. Bevan is shown as *'gentleman'* on the Return of 27 October 1786 and living at White Rock, near Swansea.

The most significant Member of the Lodge was Gabriel Jeffreys. Initiated at the age of 24 on 18 September 1768, he too appears on the Lodge Return as being admitted into the Lodge on 2 October 1768.

The first official Master of the Lodge in 1769-1770 was the aforementioned John Bevan, who replaced the disgraced Richard Lloyd. However, the outstanding dues to the General Fund of Charity remained unpaid, and likewise the fee for the Warrant. John Evans, DepProvGM, writing form Carmarthen to James Heseltine, Grand Secretary, on 23 November 1769, begins '.. *expected the Swansea Lodge to have (according to repeated promises) sent their money here to remit you, for their Constitution, which they have not yet done, so you must write them a sharp letter.'*

Bevan was succeeded as Master by Gabriel Jeffreys in 1771. In 1770, as Senior Warden, Jeffreys effectively took full control of the Lodge. Gabriel Jeffreys belonged to a family of Bankers, Lawyers and Businessmen and he is described as 'Notary Public' on the Lodge return of 1780. He was an Alderman and Portreeve (Mayor) of Swansea in the 1780s and County Treasurer (discharged in1785) and in 1770 he was appointed the Deputy Steward of the Manor of Pennard. He was active in the development of the Docks and Canals, and one of the promoters of the construction of the Mumbles Railway, which in 1804 became the first passenger carrying railway in the world.

Early in 1770, when the Grand Secretary, James Heseltine reminded the Lodge that he was still awaiting the monies owed, Jeffreys immediately attempted to ingratiate himself with Heseltine by sending him three barrels of oysters. The Grand Secretary, in acknowledging them said they were '*very good.....and I am much obliged to you*' - but added that he still hadn't received the fees for the Warrant.*

During 1770, Jeffreys wrote several letters to the Grand Secretary, in the first of which, dated 11 January, he describes the state of the Lodge and requests that it be registered as 'Beaufort Lodge'. Then, on 28 April, he requests a supply of Jewels and Grand Lodge Certificates for four of the Members. On 12 May, he writes about his concern over an unrecorded payment made by the Lodge and explains that the first Master, Richard Lloyd has removed all the Lodge papers to his house and will not release them.

Exactly one week later, he writes again, this time about '*some masons very desirous of coming into our Lodge who were made at Bridgend near Cowbridge. I should be glad to know if they have distributed anything lately towards the General Fund of Charity. If not they shall not be admitted without It is by your orders/ I am not able to advise and leave it to your better Judgement in regards the Brethren having Certificates, being required in whatever lodge they shall go to If this is the case.'* The Bridgend Brethren, as mentioned previously, were Members of the Antient Grand Lodge, and were not strictly eligible for Membership of the Premier Grand Lodge, though there are several well known examples of Brethren belonging to both Grand Lodges. His letter goes on to mention the Cowbridge Lodge, which on 30 March 1770 had been able to clear its debts to the General Fund of Charity as a result of a donation of 5 guineas from Robert Jones III, DepProvGM. His letter continues ' *I think there is a reasonable case for refusing to admit them, but should take it a particular favour if you would hint to the Cowbridge Lodge, because of being at a certainty, and doing all I can for the good of the Craft and I am glad to find that W Jones Subscribed so handsomely for the Cowbridge Lodge, making no manner of Doubt but that we shall be able to do the same soon.'* It would, therefore, appear that Beaufort Lodge was still in arrears regarding payment to the General Fund of Charity.

Then Jeffreys organised a Masonic Extravaganza, with feasting and entertainment over three full days, from 27 - 30 June, to which Brethren from the Cowbridge Lodge were invited. There was ringing of church bells, firing of guns, an organist and singers providing musical entertainment and Brethren were accommodated in '*9 houses for 3 nights*'. The accounts run to several pages and are to be found in Grand Lodge Archives (Reference HC 6/J/10). Opulent Lodge Furniture was purchased, including such exotic items as gilt pomegranates and a sword so huge that no box could be found to transport it. Part of the accounts is given on the next page. The total cost for the three days came to £26 -17s -3d. Compared with the retail price index, this amount equates to over £3000 today. In terms of average annual earnings it equates to an income of about £38,000 pa. However viewed, these figures illustrate that the three days of festivities had cost a considerable amount of money.

During 1770, Gabriel Jeffreys communicated further with the Grand Secretary, sending him plans on 13 October for a Masonic Hall in Swansea, '*which will compare to any in England*', and intimating that Provincial Grand Lodge should be based at Swansea and not at Carmarthen. Also, in 1770, the Lodge number was changed to 378 on the Register. Reference to Jeffreys, PM and SW of Beaufort Lodge, is next to be found in the Grand Lodge Archives on a copy of the Certificate of Constitution of Knoll Lodge No.506 at Neath, which records that '*Gabriel Jeffreys, Master 'pro tempore' of the Beaufort Lodge Swansea did constitute and form them into a just and regular Lodge on the 14th October 1777.*'

In 1780, the Beaufort Lodge Number was once again changed, this time to 291, then to 292 the following year and finally to 244 in 1792. The meeting places of the Lodge are not fully documented. Lanes Masonic Records gives the 'Star Tavern', Cross Street, Swansea for 1796, the 'Mackworth Arms', Wind Street for 1797 and the 'Lamb Inn', High Street for 1801. There is evidence that Beaufort Lodge was meeting in the Mackworth Arms in 1787.

On 18 December 1792, Thomas Wyndham Esquire, MP, age 30, of Dunraven Castle was 'Made a Mason' in Beaufort Lodge. He was appointed Provincial Grand Master of South Wales on 5 July 1794 and remained as such until his death in 1814.

ACCOUNT

June 28	To 11 gentlemen at Breakfast, Tea & Coffee	0 - 7 - 4
	After church & before Dinner, Swansea & Cowbridge Gent.	
	To 3 Bottles of Punch, white wine, Brandy	0 - 12 - 4
	To 35 Gentlemen at Dinner in the Hall @ 2/6	4 - 7 - 6
	To 35 at Supper	1 - 3 - 4
	Liquor delivered to the Stewards in the Hall	
	20 Quarts of Porter	8 - 4
	22 Quarts of Ale	7 - 4
	2 Doz Wines	3 - 4 - 0
	4 Bottles of Lisbon at 2/-	8 - 0
	Spirits	
	7 Bottles of Brandy at 4/-	1 - 8 - 0
	4 .. of Rum at 4/-	16 - 0
		14 -16 -11
	Brought Forward	14 -16 -11
	2 Bottles	8 - 0
	6 Pounds Lump Sugar @ 10d	0 - 5 - 0
	2 Music Men - Dinner	0 - 4 - 0
	Quart Porter Quart Ale	0 - 2 - 0
	½Doz. Ale	0 - 0 - 6

John Byng, 5th Viscount Torrington, one of the most notable of English eighteenth-century diarists, described his travels on horseback in England and Wales during the summers of 1781 to 1794. In 1787, he undertook a tour of South Wales and his diary for Tuesday, 7 August, records: *'We pass'd over new bridge, and by many smoking works; and then over much bad pavement to our inn, in the High Street - Swansea, seems to be a place of trade and there is some idle bathing company. Swansea is a nasty town, and our inn, the Mackworth Arms, very dirty, and very dear. There was a Lodge of Free-masons at our inn to night; and we went up to see the Tyler, at their door, with his drawn sword; at our coming, he was (shame to say) asleep, and disarm'd; but on his awakening, I tipp'd him many signs, and he reeceiv'd others of acknowledgement; so, now, I feel myself as true a Mason, as was ever Don Quixote a knight!!!'*

Beaufort Lodge then went rapidly into decline and Jeffreys appears to lose all interest in its affairs. By 1800, the Lodge had practically ceased working, however, when George Bowen wanted to establish a new Lodge in Swansea, which was to become Indefatigable Lodge, the Grand Secretary suggested that he approach Jeffreys for the Beaufort Lodge Warrant. Jeffreys refused and in the early 1800s attempted to have this new Lodge banned by Grand Lodge, as will be described later in the histories of the Knoll and Indefatigable Lodges.

Beaufort Lodge was eventually Erased from the Register of Lodges on 10 February 1809.

* Early Freemasonry in South Wales, WBro Terence Osborne Haunch, MA, PAGSuptWks, Grand Lodge Librarian and Curator, Paper presented to Narberth Lodge No. 2002 in 1977

Compiled by WBro Peter Davies, ProvJGW.

Knoll Lodge
No.506

Warranted : 20 September 1777
Constituted : 14 October 1777
Met at the Angel Inn, Angel Street, Neath (1777)
Ship & Castle, The Parade, Neath (1784)
Renamed Gnoll Lodge No.412 in 1784
Lapsed about 1790

Knoll Lodge No.506, was Warranted by the Premier Grand Lodge of England on 20 September 1777, with the approval and support of the Members of Beaufort Lodge No.378, Swansea. The Grand Master of the 'Moderns' at that time was George Montague, Duke of Manchester. The Lodge originally met at the Angel Inn, Angel Street, Neath.

A Founder and the first WM of Knoll Lodge was John Bevan, Esquire, JP (1794) who had joined Beaufort Lodge on 2 October 1768, and became the WM the following year in 1769. He had been Initiated at the age of 21 in March 1742 at The Crown & Anchor, Strand, London. Lanes Masonic Records shows that three Lodges were meeting at the Crown & Anchor, King Street, Seven Dials (near The Strand) in 1742. They were Lodge No.50, Warranted 1728 and Erased 28 April 1775; Lodge No. 148, Warranted 21 September 1737, ceased working in 1801 and Lodge No. 166, Warranted 27 January 1739 and which is now Royal Naval Lodge No.50.

The first Senior Warden was Jeffrayson Holland, Gentleman, who had been Junior Warden of Beaufort Lodge in 1770. The first Junior Warden was William Jones, Merchant, of Swansea, who had been Initiated at the age of 24 in 1763 and had been WM of Beaufort Lodge in 1770. He became WM of Beaufort Lodge again in 1786. Also instrumental in the formation of the Knoll Lodge was the influential Swansea Notary, Gabriel Jeffreys (his biographical details are given in the History of Beaufort Lodge.) Jeffreys had succeeded the above mentioned John Bevan as WM of Beaufort Lodge in 1770.

The original Warrant has been lost, but there is a reference to Jeffreys, PM and SW of Beaufort Lodge, in the Grand Lodge Archives on a copy of the Certificate of Constitution of Knoll Lodge No.506 at Neath, recording that '*Gabriel Jeffreys, Master 'pro tempore' of the Beaufort Lodge Swansea did constitute and form them into a just and regular Lodge on the 14th October 1777.*'

The Lodge was originally named 'Knoll', meaning a small round hill or hillock. The first building in the area was situated on the circular mound at the western end of the hill known as 'Cefn Morfydd' to the north of the town of Neath. By the 17th century, a castle and country house had been built on the hillside, and from 1710 onwards it became 'Gnoll House,' the home of the Mackworth family.

The Lodge Number on the Grand Lodge Register was changed to 411 in 1770 and changed again to 412 in 1771 and by 1784 the name of the Lodge had also changed to become 'Gnoll'. On the Grand Lodge return of November 1786, the name is also spelt 'Gnoll'.

In 1779 /1780, Gnoll Lodge made history by sending from its funds a loan without interest, of at least £25, towards the extinguishing of a debt of £2000 on the Masonic Hall in London. In 1781, each Lodge which sent such a loan was presented with a medal known as the 'Freemasons' Hall Medal' and the WM of the Lodge had the distinction of wearing the Medal suspended from the arms of the Square upon the Master's Jewel. In 1783, every Subscribing Lodge was allowed to send an additional representative to Grand Lodge, besides the Master and Wardens, until the loan was repaid. The Medal bears a draped female figure standing by a Doric Column. Gnoll was one of only five Provincial Lodges contributing, the remainder were London Lodges. The original Medal has been lost; in fact only 8 Lodges have originals. Replicas were struck in 1880, and one such Medal was purchased by Indefatigable Lodge No.237, the successor of Gnoll Lodge.

Also in 1779, the wealthy industrialist, Sir Herbert Mackworth, was Initiated, Passed and Raised in Gnoll Lodge in a Ceremony restricted to people of high social eminence, known in those days as 'Passing the Chair'. Born on 1 Jan 1737, he was 42 years of age when he became a Freemason. On 3 February 1779, he attended Grand Lodge as ProvGM of South Wales, an Office he held until his death on 25 October 1791. In October 1779, he joined the Somerset House Lodge (now No.4), and in the following year became a Member of the London Lodge, (now No 108). He also joined the Lodge of Friendship (now No.6) and served as a Grand Steward for that Lodge. In 1782, he was appointed President of the Board of Grand Stewards and also joined the Grand Stewards Lodge (now the head of the list of Lodges without a number). At the Grand Lodge Festival of 1782, he was appointed Senior Grand Warden. Sir Herbert was a man of personal charm and wit. In addition to being a Member of Parliament, a Fellow of the Royal Society, Vice - President of the Marine Society, a Portreeve of the town of Neath, a Lieutenant Colonel of the Glamorgan Militia and a Deputy-Lieutenant of the County, he was created a Baronet in 1776.

The Lodge moved to the Ship and Castle Inn (now the Castle Hotel), The Parade, Neath, in 1782, where the landlord, William Meyrick, was a Lodge Member, and is shown on the Lodge Register as 'Master'. In 1786, the Inn was taken over by Charles Nott, father of Major General Sir William Nott, GCB, who in 1842 was in charge of the defense of Kandahar.

In the Archives of Grand Lodge Library, there is a letter (Ref. code: GBR 1991 HC 6/J/15), dated 5 November 1785 to William White, Grand Secretary from the Gnoll Lodge Secretary, Alexander Davis, forwarding Returns and Dues; asking for a copy of the Appendix to the Book of Constitutions; and enquiring whether the Lodge was entitled to hold a Royal Arch Chapter by virtue of its Constitution. Alexander Davis was a Surgeon in Neath, and had been Initiated at the age of 38 in 1782. This is an interesting question, as the holding of a Royal Arch Chapter was dear to the Ancients and not readily approved of by the Moderns. It was one of the major difficulties to be resolved between the two Grand Lodges before the Act of Union at the end of 1813.

Also, 1785 saw the Initiation in Gnoll Lodge of Sir Digby Mackworth, second son of Sir Herbert Mackworth, who in due course became the 3rd Baronet. Born 14 May 1766, and being a Lewis, he was Initiated at the age of 19, although he is entered in the Grand Lodge List as being twenty-two. In 1786, he is described as of the 'Royal Navy, Gibraltar' and was by then Provincial SW. He became Master of Gnoll Lodge in the same year as his Initiation and again in 1799. Sir Digby died on 2 May 1838.

The Lodge Return for 1786 includes 24 names, all of which were marked 'resigned' with the exception of eight Brethren. The Lodge was now beginning to go through a difficult period. It wasn't entirely doom and gloom at this time, for on 6

Indefatigable Lodge No.237

Warranted : 20 September 1777

Constituted : 14 October 1777

Meeting at the Masonic Hall, Swansea.

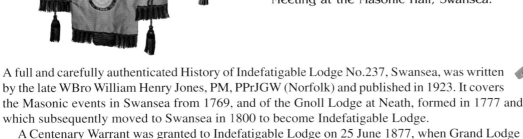

A full and carefully authenticated History of Indefatigable Lodge No.237, Swansea, was written by the late WBro William Henry Jones, PM, PPrJGW (Norfolk) and published in 1923. It covers the Masonic events in Swansea from 1769, and of the Gnoll Lodge at Neath, formed in 1777 and which subsequently moved to Swansea in 1800 to become Indefatigable Lodge.

A Centenary Warrant was granted to Indefatigable Lodge on 25 June 1877, when Grand Lodge accepted that the Lodge was a continuation of the original Lodge, Warranted at Neath on 20 September 1777. Likewise, a Bicentenary Warrant was granted in 1976, with effect from 20 September 1977. This makes Indefatigable Lodge the oldest existing Lodge in the Province. The fact that it has a higher Lodge number than Glamorgan Lodge No.36 and Loyal Cambrian Lodge No.110, is because the latter two Lodges were Antient Lodges, with lower Lodge numbers on the Register of the Antients, than Indefatigable, which was on the Register of the Moderns.

The events leading to the transfer of the Neath Lodge to Swansea have already been recounted in the previous section dealing with the History of the first Gnoll Lodge. The first Meeting of the Lodge at Swansea was held on 2 September 1800 and soon afterwards the name of the Lodge was changed to 'Indefatigable'. It is not known why the name was chosen, but it is in keeping with the tradition of naming Lodges after some outstanding characteristic of Freemasonry such as 'Perseverance'; 'Fidelity'; 'Fortitude'; 'Sincerity'; 'Endurance' etc.

As explained previously, Gabriel Jeffreys of the Beaufort Lodge was totally opposed to the transfer of the Lodge to Swansea. He continued to attack Indefatigable Lodge, as an entry in the Minute Book of April 1805 records: *'It being often times the pleasure and sport of the Officers of the Beaufort Lodge, and particularly Mr Gabriel Jeffreys to announce that the Indefatigable Lodge, No.333, had neither Constitution or Grant from the Grand Lodge, who (the Beaufort Lodge), through their own neglect and indolence suffered their own Lodge (once a respectable Lodge) to become dormant, and in order to put it out of their power for the future to deride the Brethren of the Indefatigable Lodge of the Imputation, our Rt. W. M. Bro Wm. Essery determined to write to the Grand Lodge for our Warrant of Confirmation'.* As the Lodge was working without being in possession of a Warrant of Constitution, it laid itself open to being styled a 'Clandestine Lodge', and the Members 'Clandestine Masons'. Gabriel Jeffreys, by his gibes, did the Lodge a distinct service in forcing them to regularise their procedure. This action was immediately successful, for Grand Lodge granted a Warrant of Confirmation on 8 May 1805. This document was to prove critical in Grand Lodge granting Indefatigable Lodge a Centenary Warrant in 1877.

The earliest Minute Book possessed by the Lodge commences with the St John's Day Festival on 27 December, 1804. After the demise of Beaufort Lodge (Erased 10 February 1809), Indefatigable Lodge assumed the title 'United Indefatigable and Beaufort Lodge' but this was never regularised at Grand Lodge and after several changes of mind it was finally decided in 1848 that the style should in future be 'Indefatigable Lodge', in accordance with the Grand Lodge Registry.

Between the Consecration at the Angel Inn at Neath in 1777, and the Lodge having its own Masonic Hall in 1871, the Lodge moved no fewer than twenty times, using twelve different meeting places. The first meeting place in Swansea was the Plume of Feathers Inn but by 1804 the Lodge was meeting at the Fountain Inn on the Quay. The Lodge then went on to meet at the Tiger Inn, Mackworth Arms Hotel, Crown and Anchor, Cambrian Hotel, Bush Inn, the Assembly Rooms, Cameron Arms, Cambrian Coffee House, and Mrs Young's house, using the drawing room and an adjoining room.

The reasons for the numerous moves were various: disputes with Landlords, size of meeting rooms or arguments over the terms of the lease, to name but a few. At a Provincial Grand Lodge Meeting at the Mackworth Arms in December 1816, the Lodge was inconvenienced by the family of the landlord passing through the Lodge room to bed. While at the Cameron Arms, there was a breach of confidence when the landlady learned matters confidential to the Lodge. At another venue, a Brother stated that he would procure the use of comfortable seats instead of benches and in 1855 it was resolved that proper seats be provided at a cost of 12 guineas. In the same year £9 was voted for the purchase of a sideboard for the use of the Lodge. It is a very handsome piece of furniture, bearing the then Lodge number 288. It is now in the Lounge of the present Masonic Hall, St Helens Road, Swansea.

Due to the unsatisfactory situation of continually moving meeting places, it was proposed in 1860 that a building fund be established with the aim of providing Indefatigable Lodge with its own Meeting Room. On 23 October 1860, £100 was deposited with the Glamorganshire Bank for that purpose. Regular transfers into the building fund then took place, and just over ten years later, on 10 May 1871 a contract for building a 'Freemasons' Lodge' was entered into between Thomas White (of the Strand), Builder, and ten Brethren of the Lodge, at a contract price of £710. Bro Thomas Davies was the Architect.

On 6 July 1871, the Provincial Grand Master, RWBro Theodore Mansel Talbot, was able to lay the Foundation Stone of the Indefatigable Lodge's own Masonic Hall in Caer Street, Swansea. The Ceremony took place in the presence of a very large gathering of Brethren from all parts of South Wales and beyond.

Although the weather was unfavourable, the principal streets of the town were gaily decorated with flags and streamers. The event like all others in connection with Freemasonry at that time was looked forward to with much interest, not only by Members of the Craft, but also by the public at large.

The ProvGM had called a Special Meeting of the Provincial Grand Lodge at the Mackworth Hotel, at which were present a large representation of this Province, and all the Provincial Grand Officers of Monmouthshire, excepting the ProvGM who was unavoidably absent. Provincial Grand Lodge having been opened in due form, a procession was formed under the direction of the ProvGDC, assisted by several Brethren of the Indefatigable Lodge as Stewards. The Brethren paraded from the Mackworth Hotel to the site of the Masonic Hall, their number including Members of the following Lodges; Talbot No.1323; Bute No.960; Afan No.833; St David's No.679; Brecknock No.651; Cambrian No.364; Indefatigable No.237; Loyal Cambrian No.110 and Glamorgan No.36.

Following these Brethren were the Architect with Plans, the Builder with Trowel on a cushion, the Grand Secretary, the Ewer with wine borne by Bro Thomas Powell, PM, PPrGDC; Ewer with oil borne by Bro T Nettell, PM; the PG Officers, of whom the Grand Superintendent of Works carried the Plate bearing the Inscription; the Grand Treasurer bore a Phial with coins etc; the Corinthian Light borne by Bro Peter Holway, Indefatigable Lodge; the Ionic Light by Bro Simon Goldberg and the Mallet by Bro W T Canton. The Provincial Grand Master was attended by WBro E J Morris DepProvGM.

Platforms had been erected around the space in which the Ceremony was to be performed, and a large number of ladies occupied seats thereon. The band of the Royal Glamorgan Artillery Militia played a selection of music; Bro the Rev J D Davies (of Llanmadoc), ProvGChap, offered prayers, and Bro Tulloch, WM of Indefatigable Lodge read the Inscription on the Plate to be affixed to the Foundation Stone, which read as follows:

'On the 6th day of July AD 1871, and in the thirty-fifth year of the reign of Her Majesty Queen Victoria, the foundation stone of this Lodge for the use and occupation of the members of the Indefatigable Lodge, No.237, Swansea, was laid in accordance with ancient custom, and with Masonic rites, by Theodore Mansel Talbot, of Margam Park, Taibach, Esquire, Right Worshipful Provincial Grand Master of Freemasons of South Wales Eastern Division'.

THOMAS DAVIES, Architect.	*THOMAS WHITE, Builder.*
LAWRENCE TULLOCH, W.M.	
GEORGE BRADFORD, S.W.	*WALTER EDGAR BROWN, J.W.*

In the cavity of the stone were deposited various coins of the present reign, a copy of 'The Cambrian' newspaper, a copy of the 'Freemasons' Magazine', The By-laws of the Provincial Grand Lodge and of the Indefatigable Lodge, a copy of the programme of the proceedings, and a parchment on which was written a summary of the History of the Lodge, as well as a list of the Brethren who had filled the Office of Worshipful Master of the Lodge between the years 1804 and 1871. Following the laying of the Upper Stone in accordance with ancient custom, the Provincial Chaplin pronounced the Benediction, and the procession reformed in the same order and returned to the Lodge Room, where the Provincial Grand Lodge was closed.

There then followed a dinner for 150 Brethren, with Bro L Tulloch, WM of Indefatigable Lodge presiding. A dinner was simultaneously given to the workmen engaged upon the new Hall, at the Nelson Hotel. The New Masonic Hall was Dedicated on 2 January 1872.

The Indefatigable Lodge Minutes of 13 September 1864 refer to a Provincial Lodge of Emergency to be held at Neath, under the presidency of the Deputy Provincial Grand Master, Bro T Mansel Talbot, for promoting uniformity of working in the Province. Each Lodge had been urged to send three PMs able and willing to devote themselves to the work of reform. On a vote, Bros E J Morris, J G Hall and W Cox represented the Indefatigable Lodge. It was not until 20 years later in 1884 that the Deputy PGM, WBro Marmaduke Tennant decreed that Lodges in the Province should use the 'Oxford Working'. At the earlier period there were no complete printed Rituals (although 'Exposures' abounded) and Lodges were anxious to secure uniformity. A Lodge Minute of 10 June 1862 states *'Resolved that the Lodge will subscribe fairly and proportionately with the Chapter and Lodges of Aberavon and Neath towards travelling expenses of Bro S B Wilson in the event of his accepting an invitation to visit the locality for the purpose of affording instruction to the Brethren'.*

A notable Jewel of the Indefatigable Lodge is the Freemasons' Hall Medal, which is appended to the Worshipful Master's Collar. The Lodge has the distinction of being one of only five Provincial Lodges, and twelve London Lodges, that are entitled to wear this particular Jewel. The Jewel was issued to Gnoll Lodge in 1781 in acknowledgement of a liberal contribution (minimum of £25), towards clearing the debt of £2000 outstanding on the cost of the first Freemasons' Hall, Dedicated on 23 May 1776. The original Freemasons' Hall Jewel was lost; however, in 1880 Replicas were struck. The Replica gives the Lodge's new name and number, and was first worn on 10 November 1879. A full description of the Master's Collar and this Jewel is given at each Installation Ceremony.

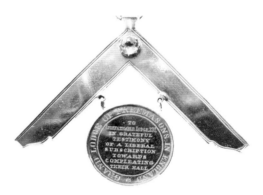

Freemasons' Hall Jewel (Front)　　　　　　　**Freemasons' Hall Jewel (Back)**

During the Lodge's long and interesting history, there have been many distinguished Brethren who have been Past Masters. Limited space allows only a few to be mentioned briefly.

Daniel Harris, Master in 1814 is worthy of note as he was the last to be referred to as RWM – 'Right Worshipful Master', the style WM was first used on 25 October of that year and has been employed ever since.

Starling Benson, WM in 1834, was a gentleman of much influence in Swansea. A distinguished Scientist, he became Mayor in 1843 and was a JP, an Alderman for Swansea & Glamorgan, Chairman of the Swansea Harbour Trust 1856 and of the Swansea Vale Railway. Later in life, he lived at Fairy-Hill, Gower, where, in 1879, he was fatally injured by falling into a quarry.

James Griffith Hall, Master in 1850, was for many years House Surgeon to the Swansea Infirmary, and Surgeon to HM Gaol. His death occurred on 27 May 1901, having served the Lodge for 56 years. His name is given to the Swansea Lodge of Freemasons No.3161, Consecrated in 1906. He was also an Honorary Member of Cambrian Lodge, Neath.

William Cox, Master in 1861, was the Governor of the 'House of Correction' at Swansea, and sometimes described in the Register as 'Gaoler'. A Lewis, he was Initiated on 23 October 1849. His Father, also named William, was also Governor of the 'House of Industry', which was later styled the 'House of Correction'. The long association of Father and Son with Swansea Prison led to its being popularly known as 'Cox's Farm'.

Stammers H Alabaster, Initiated into Indefatigable Lodge in 1908, became Master in 1922. He was a Dentist by profession, being one of the first properly qualified Dental Surgeons in Swansea. He was greatly admired for his knowledge of all things Masonic. He was the acknowledged doyen of Swansea Masons, having served the Lodge as Director of Ceremonies for over fifty years, and Preceptor of LOI for almost as long. He was a Founder Member of Penrice, Corinthian, and The Lord Swansea Lodges, and also a Member of the Lodge of Benevolence. He was equally assiduous in his work for Royal Arch Masonry, having been Exalted into the Virtue and Hope Chapter No.237 in 1913. He was First Principal in 1928, and in 1971-2 he was the Founder and First Principal of the Corinthian Chapter No.4971. At the time of his death in 1974, he was the longest serving Grand Lodge and Supreme Grand Chapter Officer in the Province.

Finally, George Challenger, who was born in 1908, Initiated into the Lodge in 1951 and attained the Chair in 1964. He was the grandson of George Challenger, Initiated in 1899, and the son of Volant Winford Challenger, who was Initiated in 1930 and became WM in 1944. George Challenger's son, David Winford Challenger, was Initiated in 1970, with both father and grandfather participating in the Ceremony. He became WM in 1989.

As well as having many outside interests, WBro George Challenger was an exceptionally active Freemason. In 1966, he became the President of the Swansea Masonic Study Circle, and in the same year became the 'permanent' Secretary of the Lodge, prior to which it had been a progressive Office. During his year as Master, he invited all the Masters of Centenary Lodges in both Eastern and Western Divisions to the September Meeting of the Lodge. In the period prior to 1977 (the Bicentenary Year of the Lodge), George was exceptionally busy liaising with Provincial Grand Lodge regarding the granting of the Lodge's Bicentenary Warrant, in the compiling of the Lodge history, and in organising, in a most exemplary manner, the arrangements for the many events to celebrate the Bicentenary. For his contribution to Freemasonry in Swansea in general and in particular his outstanding contribution to the Bicentenary celebrations; he was appointed PGStB in 1980. He was at one time Secretary of The Lord Swansea Lodge, which he relinquished on becoming Master of that Lodge in 1986. He was also active in the Virtue and Hope Chapter No.237. As the unofficial Lodge Historian and Archivist, one of his greatest contributions was in producing the Bicentenary Brochure in 1977, covering the period 1923-1977, and thus bringing the history of the Lodge up to date. Small in stature, but large in heart, he was always ready and willing to help and encourage the younger Brethren. WBro George Challenger had, like Stammers Alabaster before him, become the doyen of Swansea Masons, and when in 2007, in his 99th year he was promoted to PAGDC, it was met with much acclaim throughout the Province. WBro George was sadly lamented when he was called to the Grand Lodge Above just three weeks after his 100th birthday in April 2008.

In 1922, there were only six Lodges working in Swansea, namely, Indefatigable; Talbot No.1323; Caradoc No.1573; Dr James Griffith Hall No.3161; Beaufort No.3834 and Penrice No.4172. Both Dr James Griffith Hall and Penrice Lodges were Sponsored by Indefatigable Lodge; and Talbot Lodge Sponsored Caradoc Lodge, who in turn Sponsored Beaufort Lodge. Due to the small number of Lodges working in Swansea at that time, it was inevitable that Indefatigable Lodge would be closely involved with the formation of many of those Lodges. Indeed, many Indefatigable Brethren were Founder Members of all those Lodges. It is interesting to note, however, that the total Masonic Membership in those six Lodges was approximately the same as it is today, when there are now 23 Regular Lodges meeting (excluding the Lord Swansea Installed Masters' Lodge). Indefatigable Lodge went on to Sponsor Corinthian Lodge No.4917; West Glamorgan Lodge No.5291, Glantawe Lodge No.5378 and R P St John Charles Lodge No.6466.

As early as 1886, the Brethren had begun to complain of the unsuitability of the Masonic Hall at Caer Street. In 1907, an adjoining property was purchased, with a view to redesigning the buildings, of which no details are known. However, in February 1919, a committee was formed to represent the Lodge in discussions with the other Swansea Lodges with reference to new Lodge buildings. With the growing requirement of Freemasonry in Swansea, the futility of developing the present site was fully recognised. In October 1922, with the enterprise and foresight of a few Past Masters and Officers of the Lodge, guided by Stammers H Alabaster, WM, and Bro Trevor Evans (who introduced the property) the house and grounds known as Brunswick House, St Helens Road, were purchased.

The Old Masonic Hall at Caer Street, showing the Organ and Organ Loft.

The Lodge has had a number of Banners, which have either been lost or severely worn over the years. The present Banner dates from December 1921, and was presented by WBro Herbert George Davies (WM 1897) to celebrate the 25th Anniversary of his Election to the Chair of the Lodge. The Banner was Dedicated by WBro Henry Pendrill Charles, DepProvGM. The Banner may be described as follows: First Quarter - Arms of the Premier Grand Lodge of 1717 (Moderns), which were three Castles, Chevron, and Compasses, and were really the Arms of the Masons' Guild of the City of London from the earliest times. Second Quarter - The Tower and the Shield, containing the osprey and fish, are from the ancient Swansea Seal; introduced in order to localise the Arms of the Lodge. Third Quarter - Four lions, *passant guardant*, are the Arms of Wales. Fourth Quarter - The Arms of the Antient Grand Lodge of 1751 (the Ancients), comprising the four principal Banners of the twelve tribes of Israel viz: the Lion (Judah), Ox (Ephraim), Man (Reuben) and Eagle (Dan). The first and fourth Quarters, when used in juxtaposition, denote the Union of the two Grand Lodges in December 1813.

37

The Foundation Stone-laying Ceremony for the New Masonic Hall took place in November 1923. WBro E Landers Thomas of Dr James Griffith Hall Lodge was Chairman of the committee and 400 persons were catered for at a cost of £40 at the Shaftsbury Hall. The year 1926 was to prove to be a momentous one - Bro Arthur Edward Thomas became Master of the Lodge, and later that year became the first Secretary of the new Swansea Masonic Hall Company. Arrangements were made for the Opening Ceremony of the New Temple, and it was confirmed that the Lodge would move from Caer Street to St Helen's Road.

On Wednesday 15 September 1926, a Service of Dedication was held at St Mary's Parish Church; following which the Brethren proceeded to the New Temple and assembled outside, whilst the Provincial Grand Master, RWBro C L D Venables Llewelyn, formally opened the Temple. When the Brethren were seated, and the Lodge opened in the Third Degree, the Provincial Grand Master was admitted. He was proffered the Gavel, and took control of the Dedication Ceremony, assisted by a full team of Provincial Officers. Following the Dedication Ceremony, a dinner was held in the Connaught Hall for 253 Brethren. The following day, Provincial Grand Lodge was held under the Banner of Indefatigable Lodge. The first Regular Lodge at the new premises, was held on 11 October 1926. It was proposed at this Meeting that the organ from the Caer Street Masonic Hall be presented to the Swansea Guardians for use at Tawe Lodge (the Workhouse), and that the organ loft remaining in Caer Street be presented to the Cambrian Lodge No.364, Neath.

Indefatigable Lodge, like so many others, was of course affected by the war. The ground floor of the Masonic Hall was requisitioned, initially by the R A and then for use by the American Army; there being a grill-gate barring access to the Temples. It was instructed that Meetings start early and be finished by nine o'clock. Festive Boards consisted mainly of sandwiches, with no speech-making following Toasts, except in the case of a newly Installed Master.

Bro H J Rees lost his life in an air raid on Swansea on 19 July 1940, and in December it was reported that Bro George Vincent W Davies RAF was a prisoner of war, (which he was for over two years and was mentioned in Dispatches). It is also known from the Minute Book of the period, that three Brethren lost sons on active service. WBro Keith Flynn, in his book, 'A Province at War', states that Indefatigable Lodge lost three Brethren on active service. However, no account is to be found in the Lodge Minutes of that period.

Eleven Members of the Lodge were on active service during the war years; whilst large numbers were in the Warden Service, including T C Prosser (President of the Welsh Rugby Union 1966-1967), who was awarded the BEM. Eleven Members are shown in the Home Guard, including R P St John Charles (an Honorary Member of the Lodge), who was a Captain. Some were in the Special Constabulary, six in the Fire Service, others served in the First Aid Service and on Fire Watching. On the night of 1-2 September 1940, the Old Masonic Hall at Caer Street, still owned by Indefatigable Lodge, was destroyed by an enemy air raid. The Sea Cadet Corps, who were using the building, lost all their equipment. The Hon. Secretary of the Sea Cadet Corps wrote to the Lodge expressing his regret at the loss of the building, but thanked the Lodge for having allowed them to use the old Masonic Hall rent free.

The Caer Street premises after the Air Raid on 1 September 1940

In 1944, Volant Winford Challenger, WM was asked to Initiate Mr Robert Edwin Odell aged 23, a Corporal in the American Army, who had been regularly Elected at Clarkston Lodge No.143, F & A M, Clarkston, Washington. The American soldier was Initiated in uniform, along with two other gentlemen. Bro Odell was subsequently Passed and Raised in his home Lodge. When they departed at the end of the war, one of the American soldiers presented his host Lodge with an American Apron of pure lamb skin, which was framed and hung in the Masonic Hall.

The ground floor of the Swansea Masonic Hall was de-requisitioned on 1 January 1946, allowing normal Masonic activities to resume. The War Damage Commission paid the Indefatigable Lodge, £2500 compensation for the damage to the old Masonic Hall at Caer Street, and the Local Authority £1500 to acquire the site.

Since the last recorded history of the Lodge was published in 1977 (Bicentenary Year), the Lodge has continued to be active in its support of both Masonic and non Masonic charitable giving. In 1986, £20,000 was donated to the Festival in support of the Royal Masonic Trust for Girls and Boys. In 1991, the Province held a 'Mini Festival' to support its own Provincial Benevolent Fund, when £10,500 was contributed to that Appeal. In 1999, £21,500 was donated to the Festival held in aid of the New Masonic Samaritan Fund, thus ensuring the Lodge achieved the 'Gold Standard' (through raising £300 per Member). A Jewel, in recognition of this achievement is now permanently appended to the Charity Steward's Collar. In 2010, the Lodge was able to contribute £33,150 to the Festival held in support of the Freemasons' Grand Charity, which represented £650 per Member. The Lodge supports annually the Provincial Benevolent Fund, the Provincial Samaritan Fund and the 'Friends' of the Albert Edward Prince of Wales Court. Indefatigable Lodge is the only Lodge in Swansea to have 100% membership of the 'Friends' of AEPWC, and all the Members of the Lodge are Governors of the Provincial Benevolent Fund. Support is also given on an annual basis to the Swansea Masonic Children's Party Fund, the Swansea Almoners Fund, and to 'Swansea Freemasons Feed the Homeless'. Emergency collections were made in Lodge in October 2001 to support our Brethren in New York affected by 11 September 'Twin Towers' attack, when £250 was raised. In January 2005, £400 was raised to help the victims of the Asian Tsunami Flood Disaster. In the field of non-Masonic charitable giving, worthy local causes are supported annually, and on the occasion of the 225th Anniversary in 2002, the Lodge contributed £2,900 to eight worthy causes, whose representatives were presented with cheques at a community evening held at the Swansea Masonic Hall, as part of 'Freemasonry in the Community Year'.

In 2002, the Lodge celebrated its 225th Anniversary with a re-enactment of a Ceremony circa 1813, followed by a dinner, when 135 Brethren in the presence of RWBro Hywel Davies, ProvGM, enjoyed a most convivial evening. Two other Lodges also celebrated their 225th Anniversaries that year, The York Lodge No.235 and The Lodge of the Nine Muses No.236. A visit was made to the Lodge of the Nine Muses, in London. This was to be followed with a visit to the York Lodge, but at that time, the York Lodge was in dispute with the Provincial Grand Master, and we were advised by our Provincial Grand Secretary not to attend, as it would cause embarrassment to our Provincial Grand Master. Indefatigable Lodge did, however, receive a framed photograph of the Queen from the Brethren of the York Lodge to mark the occasion; this is now displayed in the Swansea Masonic Hall.

Official visits are made annually to the Prince of Wales Lodge No.671, Llanelli, in the Western Province; to the Gnoll Lodge No.5057, Neath and to R P St John Charles Lodge No. 6466, Swansea. Over recent years a link has been established with Tenby Lodge No.1177, resulting in regular exchange visits.

To commemorate the 250th Anniversary of Grand Lodge, all the Lodges were invited to subscribe the equivalent of £1 per Member. Those that did so, including Indefatigable Lodge, were given a Commemorative Medallion which is fastened to the apex of the Master's Collar. It bears the Arms of the City Company of the 'Hole Crafte and Fellowship of Masons' which was granted in 1472 and adopted by the Premier Grand Lodge (Moderns) when it was founded in 1717. Those Arms, which span 500 years, were incorporated in the Coat of Arms of the United Grand Lodge at the Union in 1813.

Grand Lodge 250th Anniversary Jewel   **Grand Lodge 275th Anniversary Jewel**

Much of the furniture and portraits in Swansea's Masonic Hall are owned by Indefatigable Lodge. One item which has an interesting story attached to it is the Tyler's Sword, displayed in the glass cabinet on the first floor. This Sword was presented to the Lodge by Bro Mathias of Pembrokeshire in 1805, who had petitioned the Worshipful Master and Wardens to become a Lodge Member. The Sword had been taken from a Frenchman in the act of chopping down a native of Fishguard during the attempted French Invasion at Fishguard in 1797.

The history of the Order of the Holy Royal Arch in the Province of South Wales will be for future Historians; however, it would do a disservice to the Royal Arch Order, and to Indefatigable Lodge, if the early beginnings of that Order were not mentioned. As early as 1770 the old Beaufort Lodge made enquiries with the Grand Secretary about the granting of a Royal Arch Warrant, and in 1771 a Warrant was granted for Chapter No.10 to meet at 'The Sign of the Falcon' in Swansea. It is unclear if this Chapter ever met or was Constituted. The Indefatigable Lodge made overtures soon after it was established in Swansea, and Virtue & Hope Chapter No.176 was Constituted on 14 July 1812; but it met infrequently and irregularly. The present Warrant, dated 7 November 1821, was later granted, but again continuity of working could not be established up to 1851. Supreme Grand Chapter acknowledged continuity of working from 1851 and consequently a Centenary Warrant was granted in 1951. The Virtue & Hope Chapter intends celebrating the 200th Anniversary of its first beginnings in 2012.

Compiled by WBro Peter A Richards, PAGDC.

Ancient Britons' Lodge No.126

Constituted : 16 December 1807

Met at the Boar's Head, Caerphilly.

Erased : 5 March 1828

At the beginning of the 19th century, Freemasonry had almost collapsed in the Province of South Wales. In 1800, the failing Knoll Lodge had been transferred from Neath to Swansea, to become Indefatigable Lodge, which had got off to a hesitant start. The Beaufort Lodge, also in Swansea was in terminal decline and the only other active Lodge was Cambrian Lodge No.451, Brecon, which was also experiencing difficulties. The turning point in the fortunes of Freemasonry in South Wales was the Constituting of the Ancient Britons' Lodge No.126 at Caerphilly, on 16 December 1807. It is strange that Caerphilly and not Cardiff should have been chosen for this new Lodge. Thomas Ridd's Trade Directory for Caerphilly in 1813 describes Caerphilly thus:

'Caerphilly has lately increased from an obscure village to a well-built little town; and the respectable appearance of its two inns may be in a great measure dated from the great increase of the visitants to the castle.

At Caerphilly there are two manufactories for flannel shawls, and spinning machines are kept at each for the accommodation of those who send wool to be spun into yarn for knitting stockings &c.

Caerphilly weekly market is on Thursdays – Fairs April 5, June 6, July 19, August 25, October 9 and November 16. ....etc.

The conveyance from London, Bristol &c to this town is by way of Cardiff, from which it is distant seven miles, and where a messenger attends three times a week, for the letters &c. for Caerphilly and its neighbourhood. The town contains about 90 houses and 300 inhabitants.'

During 1807, the requisite number of seven Freemasons wrote to Thomas Harper, Deputy Grand Master of the Antient Grand Lodge, applying for Warrant No.126, originally issued on 12 June 1764 to a Lodge meeting at 'The Green Dragon', Skinner Street, Newport, Monmouthshire, to be transferred to Caerphilly, so that a Lodge may be held in the house of John Williams, the nominated first Worshipful Master of the new Lodge. The letter explained that the Warrant had been lost for several years, but had now been found by a former Member residing at Caerphilly. One of the signatories was Jacob Nicholas, the first Master of the Newport Lodge, and another was John Owen, a former Member of the same Lodge.

The Petition is reproduced below:

To Right Worshipful Deputy Grand Master of Antiant Masons

We whoes Names are hereunder written and Subscribed antient Free Masons the surviving members of Lodge 126 are Jacob Nicholas, the first Master of Said Lodge and John Owens and was granted at Newport in the year 1776 and the Warrant was lost for several years and found by a member Residing at Carfilly.

That your petitioners having Intrest of the antient Craft very much at hart most humbly pray that the said Warrant be Renewed or Indors'd and granted to your petitioners duly Registered persuant to the Statute in that case made and provided to be heald at the house of Mr. John Williams, Carfilly Glamorganshire.

That should the prayers of this our petition be granted we promis a Strict Conformaly to all the rules and Regulations of the Grand Lodge as they shall from time to time be comunicated to us and shall as in duly Bound Ever pray.

Benjamin Plummer

1771 - 1820

Senior Grand Warden - Antient Grand Lodge

Past Senior Grand Warden - United Grand Lodge of England, (1813)

Superintendent Grand Commander - Knights Templars for Wales, (1813)

Benjamin Plummer was born at Shepton Mallet, Somerset, on 10 October 1771 and was Initiated into Freemasonry in the Royal Athelston Lodge No.10, London, on 4 June 1798. This Atholl Lodge still exists today as Lodge No.19. Plummer was Master of this Lodge in 1803 and in 1804, and was variously appointed Grand Sword Bearer, Grand Junior Warden and Grand Senior Warden (27 December 1805) of the Atholl Grand Lodge.

In the Grand Lodge Minutes of 3 June 1807: *'It was moved by Brother Ronalds, PM of Lodge No. 10 and seconded by Bro. Stoneham, PM of the same Lodge That a Gold Medal should be presented to our R.W. Brother Benj^m Plummer Past Senior Grand Warden for his upright and steady attention to the duties of his office in Grand Lodge, after some debate thereon and the question thereupon put passed in the Negative.'*

The next Minutes of 2 September 1807 record: *'Upon reading the minutes of the Grand Lodge of 3rd June last was moved and seconded that the same be confirmed except so much thereof as relates to the motion respecting Benj^m Plummer.*

It was thereupon moved by Bro. James Ronalds of Lodge No. 10 and seconded by Bro. Joseph Stoneham of the same Lodge, that the said Minute be rescinded which passed in the affirmative.

It was afterwards moved and seconded by the above named Brothers That the R.W. Bro. Benj^m Plummer Past Senior Grand Warden be presented with a Gold Medal as a token of the esteem and respect of the Grand Lodge for his constant attendance in discharge of his duties of the several offices which he had served with great credit to himself and integrity to the Craft.

After due consideration the question was whereupon put and carried by a majority of the Grand Lodge present.'

Plummer was a Member of the Antients' Committee for Masonic Union and is known to have attended a Meeting with the 'Moderns' Committee for Masonic Union held at Freemasons' Tavern on 30 April 1811 (Ref GBR 1911 HV 12/A/27) and at the 'Crown & Anchor Tavern' Strand, London on 13 December 1811(Ref GBR 1911 HV 12/A/41). After the Union in 1814, he became Past Grand Senior Warden of the United Grand Lodge of England.

Benjamin Plummer was also a Member of the Royal Naval Lodge No. 57, London (Now No. 59) and of two 'French Prisoners of War' Lodges - 'Paix Desiree', Wincanton, Somerset, in 1810 and 'Les Enfants de Mars et Neptune', Abergavenny, in 1813. Exalted a Royal Arch Mason in 1799; in 1813 he was made Superintendent Grand Commander of Knights Templars for Wales; Grand Expert for England under H.R.H. The Duke of Kent, and a Member of the Baldwyn Encampment at Bristol. He is described on one of his certificates as a Commercial Agent. He also acted (on behalf of Thomas & Edward Harper) as an agent for Masonic Regalia. The accounts for 1815 of the old 'Philanthropic Lodge', Abergavenny show 'paid to Bro. Plummer for Belts (collars or aprons?) £14 . This would account for his connection with so many Lodges in different parts of the country. He was a frequent visitor to Glamorgan Lodge and Loyal Cambrian Lodge, Merthyr, often occupying the 'Chair' and taking part in the work of the evening.

Following the Constituting of Glamorgan Lodge on 4 November 1808, the next Antient Lodge to be formed was Royal Cambrian Lodge No. 135, meeting at the 'Parrot Inn', High Street, Newport. Warrant No.135 was originally issued on 13 January 1765 to a Lodge meeting in Sheerness. It ceased working soon afterwards and the Warrant was transferred to Newport on 11 August 1809.

Judging from some of his later correspondence with the Grand Secretary, Plummer was probably present at the Constitution of this Lodge on 24 November 1809. (This Lodge ceased meeting in July 1823 and was Erased on 1 December 1839.)

The Constitution of Loyal Cambrian Lodge, Merthyr, followed on 7 August 1810, details of which have already been given in the history of The Ancient Britons' Lodge No.126, Caerphilly.

In October 1810, the Moderns issued a Warrant for St David's Lodge of Perfect Friendship No.623, which first met at the 'King's Arms', Priory St, Carmarthen. The Lodge moved in 1812 to the Old Ivy Bush, King's Street. A few months later, on 9 July 1811, the Antients issued a Warrant for a Lodge at Carmarthen. This was Union Lodge No.158, Constituted on 15 July at the Old Ivy Bush Inn. It transferred to the 'White Lion', Queen Street, in 1812, at the time the Moderns moved into the Ivy Bush! These two Carmarthen Lodges had a great deal in common -no fewer than thirty Members in fact! When WBro Terry Haunch (Grand Lodge Librarian & Curator of Museum) compared the Membership Registers of the two Grand Lodges, he found that of the fifty-four names in Lodge of Perfect Friendship between 1810 and 1811, thirty were duplicated in the Antients Register under Union Lodge. Terry goes on to explain that there was purely a practical reason for being a Member under both Constitutions. St David's Lodge of Perfect Friendship, being under the Premier Grand Lodge could not as a Lodge work the Royal Arch Degree, and so in order to do so, as they wished, they applied for an Antients Warrant under which they could. There were not enough Antient Masons in Carmarthen to form such a Lodge. William Couling, WM, and William Moss, SW of the Moderns, who were to become WM and SW respectively of the new Lodge, and neither being Antients, went to Royal Cambrian Lodge, Newport to be 'remade' Antient Masons. On 1 April 1811, a resolution was passed in Royal Cambrian Lodge, *'that two Candidates from Carmarthen, under the sanction of His Royal Highness the Prince of Wales* (Grand Master of the Moderns*), be admitted members of this Lodge, and they were afterwards admitted to the first, second and third Degrees.'*

There is a great deal of correspondence in Grand Lodge archives regarding Union Lodge and Benjamin Plummer's involvement with it. On 14 September 1811, William Couling, WM, wrote to William Moss, SW, instructing him to travel to Tenby, with the Lodge Tyler, bringing with them the Lodge Warrant and all the Regalia, in order to make several gentlemen Antient Masons. Other Lodge Members were to travel by boat to Tenby. This they did, where they opened a Meeting of Union Lodge and Initiated the Mayor, Town Clerk and two Aldermen into Antient Freemasonry. Also, two Modern Masons were remade Antients. They then proceeded to Pass and Raise all seven. Following the Meeting, all the Brethren celebrated in grand style and at great expense to the Lodge. The expenses included £10 for dinner, plus expenses for a copious supply of rum and ale and a box for the theatre. The whole affair was totally unacceptable to the Lodge Members who had not travelled to Tenby. William Couling consequently wrote a letter of resignation on 20 September 1811 to William Moss. On 5 November, Benjamin Plummer attended Union Lodge in the Old Ivy Bush Inn, and in his letter to Thomas Harper the next day, he writes that he found the Brethren *'thrown into great confusion from an irregular proceeding of the Master Wm Couling and others.'* ..... *'However I am happy to inform you also that by my interference the unwarranted proceedings of the late Master are annulled and unanimity prevails among them.'* Plummer, it turns out, had acted as WM and confiscated the Lodge Warrant and By-laws. This had caused great offence to some of the Lodge Members, and in a long letter, signed by William Moss and eight others, on 13 November 1811 to the Grand Lodge in London, they write in support of William Couling and disapprove most strongly of Plummer's actions *'Now we the Officers and Members of the said Lodge do declare that the said Benj^m Plummer has acted against our Will and Consent and without Consulting us and are of the opinion that he (not being a member of our Lodge has no right to take the Chair but may visit in like manner with others and he is usurping a power to himself for the which he had not authority.'*

Plummer, however, did have the support of 15 other Members of Union Lodge, who wrote to the Grand Secretary on 30 November 1811, deprecating what had happened at Tenby. *'That in consideration of the zeal and ability evinced and exerted on behalf of Masonry in general and our Lodge in particular by our highly respected and Right Worshipful Brother B Plummer, it is incumbent on us to render him the tribute of our grateful thanks and we accordingly request his acceptance of the same.*

This being done Right Worshipful Sir, we feel that we ought to go further in bearing testimony to the merits of Brother B Plummer by communicating, through you, to the Grand Lodge the eminent and essential services for which, as Masons, having the honour and prosperity of the Craft at heart, we stand indebted to that worthy Brother, and for which, the thanks of the Lodge were in due form presented to him on the above mentioned occasion.'

Also in1811, Plummer was instrumental in the formation of Hwlffordd Lodge No.59 at Haverfordwest. Writing from Brecon on 26 November he states:

I have a Petition from some worthy Brethren at Haverford West for a Warrant to hold a Lodge in a private House there and as such as I can with confidence recommend to the Grand Lodge and such request you'll further will reserve a Warrant of a low Number. They will not want any other Furniture than the Jewels, At first I have said you could supply them for £14 or Guineas – I expect to reach Home in abt 3 weeks & then will wait on you with particulars – I remain Dear Sir

A Warrant of low number was indeed allocated to the Haverfordwest Lodge No.59 and dated 23 January 1812. Warrant No.59 had originally been issued on 23 December 1756 to a Lodge meeting at the 'White Hart', Porters Street, Newport Market, London. This Lodge lapsed in about 1770. The Haverfordwest Lodge was Constituted in a 'Private Room' on 18 March 1812, with Plummer, acting by Deputation as Deputy Grand Master. Details of the Ceremony are given at the end of this section. (The Lodge was Erased on 5 March 1828.)

Plummer's visits were not confined to Antient Lodges, for the Minutes of Indefatigable Lodge No. 237, Swansea (Moderns) for 9 March 1811, record: *'Lodge of Emergency convened for the purpose of initiating Mr. William Edwards and Mr. Charles Styring, recommended and proposed by Bro. Sir Benjamin Plummer of the Royal Naval Lodge, London, Superintendent Grand Commander of the United Templars of Jerusalem, etc., for the Principality of Wales, under the Patronage of His Royal Highness the Duke of Kent.'* It is also interesting to note that Plummer, a visitor, is proposing Candidates for Initiation in the Lodge. Note also, we have an example of an 'Antient' Mason attending a 'Modern' Lodge. It was not uncommon for Brethren to be Members of Lodges under the jurisdiction of both Grand Lodges. John Bird, first Secretary of Glamorgan Lodge (previously mentioned in the history of Ancient Britons' Lodge), was Initiated in Indefatigable Lodge, Swansea on 10 November 1809, having first being Made an Antient Freemason in Caerphilly in June 1808.

On 1 December 1809, Bird wrote to Indefatigable Lodge, offering to assist them in holding a Royal Arch Chapter. As explained earlier, The Royal Arch Degree was not permitted by the Moderns, and the Antients' insistence in maintaining it was a major obstacle, which impeded the union of the two Grand Lodges for many years. Needless to say, nothing came of Bird's offer.

Hiram Lodge No.160, meeting at the 'Red Lion Inn', Commercial Street, Pontypool, and Warranted on 13 June 1812, was the seventh Ancient Lodge in South Wales to be Constituted by Plummer. Warrant 160 had already been recycled before being granted to Pontypool. First issued on 22 March 1769 to a Lodge in Norwich, the Warrant was renewed on 3 September 1787. In September 1791, Stewards' Lodge recommended it to be cancelled for irregularities. It was restored of all its former privileges in March 1792, but then 'apostatized' (Joined the Moderns) and the Warrant was eventually cancelled on 5 June 1793. On 5 June 1802, Warrant 160 was issued to a Lodge in Peterborough. There are no entries in the Register after 1802 and thereabouts the Lodge appears to have elapsed. The Ancients certainly made good use of their early Warrants. Hiram Lodge was Erased in 1830.

Benjamin Plummer was held in great esteem by many Brethren in South East Wales and Monmouthshire, evidence of which is provided by a report in 'The Cambrian' of Saturday, 22 October 1814:

'On Monday last a meeting took place at the Boar's-Head-inn, Caerphilly, of the W. Master and Wardens of the Masonic Lodge, No.150, of that place; Lodge No.175 at Merthyr Tydvil, and Lodge No.195 at Pontypool, together with many other Masonic members, for the purpose of presenting the R.W. Brother Benjamin Plummer, P.S.G.W. with a pair of very handsome silver pint goblets, as a token of the high respect in which he is generally held by the Free-masons in the Principality, and the members of the above-mentioned Lodges in particular.The same were presented by Bro Edward Gregory, WM of the Merthyr Tydvil Lodge, in a very appropriate address, and the R. W. Bro. Expressed himself gratefully sensible of the flattering honour conferred upon him. The day was spent with conviviality, and the performance of John Jones on the harp, added much to the harmony of the assembly.'

When Thomas Wyndam, ProvGM of South Wales, died in November 1814, Plummer wrote from Andover on 21 November to Edward Harper, Grand Secretary, requesting his name be forwarded to the Grand Master as a possible candidate for ProvGM of the Principality *'I find by the Newspaper we have lost our Provincial Grand Master of So. Wales – Windham Esqr. Member of Parliament for the County of Glamorgan and altho he was not known to the Brethren of the Principality or ever attended them – there was an excuse that I can make for him for before I was in the habit of visiting the Country there were but two Lodges in it and that was the one at Brecon which was in a manner dormant and the other at Swansea not much better and in a very low state and since I established the other Seven Lodges our late P.G. Master had been much afflicted with the Gout and looseness that we could not expect him to attend them.*

I wish you to give me your opinion in your next Letter whether you think it would meet H. R. Highness, our Grand Master's pleasure to give me the appointment of P. G. Master for the Principality until you can find some Nobleman or Gentleman of Consequence and eligible, as at present I do not know of any one and you must be assured I know the Country pretty well being in the practise of spending 6 months of each year among them. You must know my views in this and my sincerity to support the welfare of our Society.'

A fortnight later, Plummer writes again to Edward Harper, this time from Wells. The letter is dated 6 December:

'Your Favor the 26th Inst. I duly received to Wincanton. I am obliged by their contents. I hope by this time you are properly recovered from your Indisposition and had an opportunity of communicating with His R. Highness upon the subject of the Petition for a Warrant from my Friends at Abergavenny – also that of P. G. Master for The Principality of S. Wales. If it meets the pleasure of our Grand Master to grant the Warrant petitioned for, it will then be the third Lodge of my establishing in the County of Monmouth and as there was not a Lodge in this County before nor any P.G. Master and it should please His R. Highness to appoint one for the county of Monmouth, I should be proud to receive that appointment should he consider extent of the Principality exceed my capacity – I have engaged to attend the Brethren of Lodge 537 Shepton Mallet Wednesday evening for the purpose of passing some of them to the 2nd & raising some to the 3rd Degree. I will make enquiry respecting the Lodge No 49 late at Bath and inform you in my next ......'

Plummer wrote again to the Grand Secretary on 17 December 1814, this time from Gloucester:

'I particularly wish to know of the Petition for a Warrant or Dispensation to hold a Lodge at the Town of Abergavenny Monmouthshire is granted as the Brethren (Petitioners) were very desirous of being so favoured to open The Lodge on St John's Day next. It this is granted I will be glad you send me it with a Set of Jewels by The Glocester Mail Coach on Monday evening addressed to me at The Grey Hound Inn Abergavenny ....'

The Lodge in question was Philanthropic Lodge No.658, which, indeed, had its Petition granted on 27 December 1814 (St John's Day). The Lodge was the first Daughter Lodge of Loyal Cambrian Lodge, Merthyr, and was Constituted, by Dispensation, at the King's Head, Cross St, on 12 June 1815 with Benjamin Plummer acting as Grand Master, assisted by WBro F C Husenbeth, DepProvGM of Bristol. Plummer and Husenbeth were both present again at the Philanthropic Lodge for the Installation Meeting on Monday, 12 June 1817. Also present were Bro J Mathias, PM Haverfordwest Lodge and Bro Edward Gregory, WM Merthyr Lodge. The last return to Grand Lodge was sent in 1819. During the four years of active work, 8 Members were Initiated and the Lodge was Erased from the Register on 5 March 1828.

Later, in the same letter we have:

'You did not notice my intimation respecting the Provincial for the Principality of So. Wales or the County of Monmouth, of the two I should prefer the county of Monmouth as I at present have the honor of being the Superintendent for the Principality of the Order of the Knight Templars – '

In the end, Plummer was unsuccessful in becoming Provincial Grand Master of South Wales or of Monmouthshire. Towards the end of 1814, Benjamin Hall, MP was appointed for South Wales and Colonel Henry Harnage, appointed on 30 January 1801, remained ProvGM for Monmouthshire until his death in 1826.

The following year, Plummer was in Swansea and in a letter (GBR 1911 HC6/J/31) to Edward Harper, (Grand Secretary), dated 27 May 1815, the extent of his activities in promoting Freemasonry is revealed together with an indication that all is not going well with the 'Union' of the two Grand Lodges:

It is with unfeigned regret, I have to inform you, that the various country Lodges I am in the habit of visiting, three times in each year, throughout the Provinces of Somerset, Wilts., Glo'cester & Monmouth, and those of South Wales, are much disappointed since the Union of the Two Grand Lodges, expecting a regular quarterly communication, such as they heretofore have been used to receive, and at this time four Quarters are past, without any information; The ancient Lodges, in particular, finding themselves this neglected, feel disposed to retract from the Union and remain independent of any Grand Lodges, until they are satisfied that Business of the same, will be conducted according to the ancient Customs - - -'

'I trust you will be aware of the necessity of my addressing you on this Subject, being a constant visitor of all the Lodges throughout my Journey, and particularly in the Province where my endeavours to revive the ancient Order, during a period of about nine years, have been attended with no inconsiderable Success. At the commencement of my exertions, there were but two Lodges, one of them in this Town, which was very thinly attended, and the other at Brecon in a dormant state., since which I have opened eighth other Lodges, and made upwards of two hundred Masons, who look to me for information, as often as I visit their Lodge;

I beg of you to make known these observations to the Grand Lodge on Wednesday next prior to the new Laws being confirmed, in the hope it may have the desired effect...'

Plummer's last recorded visit to South Wales was to the Cambrian Lodge No.510, at Brecon on 12 March 1819. This Lodge had been in serious difficulty for many years. Only 10 Members attended the Installation Meeting of 16 August 1813, when WBro Thomas Mayberry was Installed as Master. He continued in Office for the next three years, but attendances were very poor. On 18 March 1816, the Lodge was simply opened and closed. No further meetings were held until 12 March 1819, the reason being *'The WM not having summoned us to attend since 12 March 1816, the Brethren availed themselves of the kind assistance of Bro Benjamin Plummer and convened the present Meeting for the purpose of electing new Officers, supporting the regularity of the Lodge and continuing our respectful correspondence with Grand Lodge'.* Bro Plummer, at the request of the Brethren, occupied the Chair. It was opened in the First Degree, and Brethren were Elected and Invested in their respective Offices *'from this day to St John's Day in December next; -*

WM pro tem – B. Plummer, W.M.'

This was the last Meeting held by Cambrian Lodge and the Lodge was Erased on 5 March 1828.

The part played by Plummer- the Provincial Grand Master we never had, deserves to be better known. It should be explained, however, that the Antient Grand Lodge never had a system of Provincial Grand Masters, and their existence was only accepted by the Antients, sometimes reluctantly, after the Union. Glamorgan Lodge ignored the existence of the Provincial Grand Master of South Wales for twelve years after the Union, to the exasperation of the Provincial Grand Secretary, WBro John Francis of Indefatigable Lodge. Writing from Swansea to the Grand Secretaries in London (for a number of years after the Union there were two Grand Secretaries) he states: *'I am directed by the P.G.M. for South Wales, Sir C. Cole, M.P. to inform you that since he has had the superintendence of this province, he has not been able to get the W. Master of the Glamorgan Lodge No.50 to attend to any of the many Summons's sent to him, nor have they in any shape answered one of my Letters.*

It will of course rest with G. Lodge to determine wether (sic) *they are within his Jurisdiction, and if so, to issue orders accordingly.'*

Unfortunately, there is no record of the reply to this letter.

The Office of Provincial Grand Master was first introduced by the Moderns with the appointment of Sir Francis Columbine for Chester in 1725. Wales had the distinction of the next two appointments, with Captain Hugh Warburton for Cheshire and North Wales in 1727, and in the same year, Sir Edward Mansel for South Wales. The appointment of a Provincial Grand Master did not necessarily imply the existence of a Provincial Grand Lodge. The appointment was often regarded as 'an honour conferred'. In the case of North Wales, there was no Lodge until Lodge No.194, meeting at 'The Angel & Crown', was established at Dolgelly in September 1743, and not until the 1760s did others come into existence.

So what finally became of Benjamin Plummer? There is no further correspondence in the archives of Grand Lodge after May 1815 and his attendance at Cambrian Lodge, Brecon on 12 March 1819, is the last record we have of him. In the Burial Records of St Giles Church, Cripplegate, London, a Benjamin Plummer, born 1772, age at death 48, address at time of death: Jewin Crescent; burial on 27 June 1820. This could be our Benjamin Plummer.

Compiled by WBro Peter M Davies, ProvJGW.

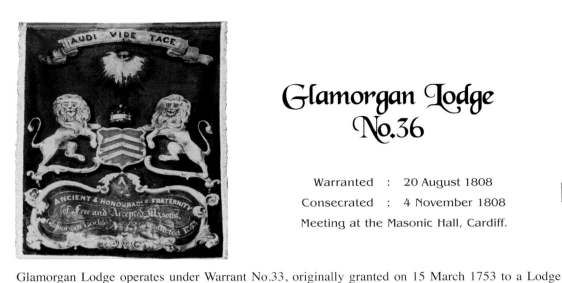

Glamorgan Lodge No.36

Warranted : 20 August 1808

Consecrated : 4 November 1808

Meeting at the Masonic Hall, Cardiff.

Glamorgan Lodge operates under Warrant No.33, originally granted on 15 March 1753 to a Lodge meeting at 'The Star & Garter', The Strand, London. According to Grand Lodge Minutes, this Lodge lapsed in 1755 and the Warrant was re-issued in the early 1760s to a Lodge meeting in Bridgend. Information regarding the Bridgend Lodge may be found in 'The History of the Province in the 18th Century'. On 25 October 1777, the Grand Secretary, James Jones, issued a replacement Warrant to the Bridgend Lodge. On the back of this Warrant is an endorsement, transferring the Warrant to Cardiff, signed by Thomas Harper, DepGM; Benjamin Plummer, PSGW and Robert Leslie, GSec, on 20 August 1808. Further details may be found in the history of Ancient Britons' Lodge No.126, which may be regarded as the Mother Lodge of Glamorgan Lodge.

The new Cardiff Lodge was 'Constituted' at a 'Grand Lodge', held by Dispensation, at the Cardiff Arms Hotel, at 11 am on Friday, 4 November 1808. The Dispensation permitted Benjamin Plummer to act as Grand Master for a period of 3 hours, with John Williams, first WM of the Ancient Britons' Lodge No.126, acting as DepGM; John Wood Senior of Lodge No.33, Bridgend, as SGW; John Wood Junior, of Lodge No.126, Caerphilly, as JGW; John Bird Senior of Lodge No.126, Caerphilly, as GSec; John Bird Junior of Lodge No.126, Caerphilly, as GTreas; and Robert Hillier of Lodge No.126, Caerphilly, as Grand Pursuivant. The exact form of the ceremony was not recorded; however, it was most probably similar to the Constitution of Hwlffordd Lodge No.59, Haverfordwest, on 18 March 1812, the details of which are to be found in Grand Lodge Archives. Using these records, it is possible to reconstruct the Ceremony, which would have commenced with the reading of the Dispensation. Then: ' *The following Brothers having been recommended to the Grand Lodge as Proper Persons to preside as Principal Officers of the said lodge were presented to our Right Worshipful Brother Benjamin Plummer for that purpose and were then examined by Bro. Williams as to their abilities for filling the said offices, viz. Bror. John Wood Senr, Worshipful Master; Bror. John Wood Junr, Senior Warden; Bror. John Thackwell, Junior Warden. And the Report of Brother Williams to Brother Benjamin Plummer of their being highly qualified and satisfactory, they were accordingly installed and received the usual honours on that occasion together with our Brother John Bird Senr, as Secretary to serve from this day until Saint John's Day the Baptist 1809.* ' Note that the next Installation was to be held on '*Saint John's Day the Baptist 1809*'. This is in accordance with the Warrant, which states: '*Such Installation to be upon (or near) every St John's Day during the continuance of this Lodge for ever.*' The Saint's Day is 24 June, and Glamorgan Lodge has always held its Installations on or near that day. Biographical details of John Wood Senior and John Bird Senior are to be found in the previous chapter. John Thackwell, first JW, was a Clock and Watchmaker. Around 1825, he made a fine bracket-clock in a mahogany and rosewood case with brass inlay for the 2nd Marquess of Bute. It is now displayed in the 'withdrawing room' of St Fagans Castle. John Thackwell was WM of Glamorgan Lodge for a total of three years, 1810-1811 and 1818-1820. Towards the end of his life he moved to Gloucester. He is recorded in the Lodge Minutes of 9 June 1828 as being from Royal Sussex Lodge No.69, Bath. John Thackwell died in Gloucester on 31 December 1830 at the great age of 90 years!

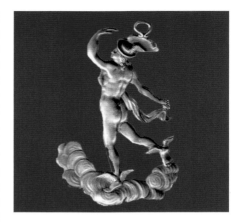

Thomas Harper Deacon's Jewel

A few days after the Constitution of Glamorgan Lodge, at the Glamorgan Quarter Sessions held on 12 November, John Wood Junior and John Bird registered the Lodge with the Clerk of Peace, as required by the 'Unlawful Societies Act' of 1799. The Clerk of Peace at the time was John Wood Senior! He and his son were prominent lawyers in Cardiff and held many of the key offices of Cardiff Corporation and the County of Glamorgan. For many years they acted as legal advisers to the 1st Marquess of Bute, until they were dismissed in 1817, after accusations of mismanagement of Corporation affairs.

In his letter to the Grand Secretary, dated Cardiff 18 June 1810, Benjamin Plummer, wrote: *'It is requested by this Lodge No.33 Cardiff that they may be favoured by Grand Lodge to name their Lodge called the Glamorgan Lodge, which if complied with please insert in your Books & on The Certificates – '*. Thus the name 'Glamorgan Lodge' dates from 1810. There was a move the following year to style the Lodge 'Royal Glamorgan Lodge', but this was not pursued.

Thomas Harper IPM's Jewel

On 7 September 1809, Wyndham Lewis of Llanishen House was Initiated into the Lodge. A Magistrate, Deputy Lieutenant for Glamorgan, Major of the Glamorgan Militia, MP for Cardiff 1820-1826, and for Aldeburgh, Suffolk, 1827-1830, he became Lodge Treasurer in 1811. He was MP for Maidstone, Kent, from 1835 until his death on 28 August 1838. Exactly one year later, his widow, Mary Ann, married Benjamin Disraeli, who became Prime Minister in 1868 and 1874-1880. A great favourite of Queen Victoria, Disraeli was created Lord Beaconsfield in 1876.

Friday, 9 August 1811 was a most momentous day for Glamorgan Lodge. A Lodge of Emergency was held to receive the Most Worshipful Deputy Grand Master of England, RWBro Thomas Harper. At the Emergency Meeting, the Brethren received *'Brotherly instruction from the R.W.D.G. Master'*. The following Monday, 12 August 1811, Thomas Harper went on to visit the Loyal Cambrian Lodge No.144 (now No.110), Merthyr Tydfil. Thomas Harper was also a Masonic Jeweller, and Glamorgan Lodge has a number of silver hall-marked Jewels bearing his maker's mark 'TH'. They date from 1808/09 and have been in continuous use since that time.

Joseph Davis, Timber & Iron Merchant, was Installed as Worshipful Master on 27 December 1811. He had been Initiated on 1 December 1808. His Atholl Grand Lodge Certificate, dated 28 June 1810, is in the possession of the Lodge. Note that it is printed in English and Latin.

Following the formation of the United Grand Lodge at the end of 1813, Glamorgan Lodge met on 6 January 1814 when *'The resolutions of the Especial Grand Lodge of free and accepted Masons of England of the 8th November last were read and highly approved of. The articles of Union between the two Grand Lodges of England were also read and approved Unanimously.'* As a consequence of the Union, Lodges were re-numbered and 'Antient' Glamorgan Lodge No.33 became No.50 on the Register of the United Grand Lodge of England.

For the first 47 years, Glamorgan Lodge met in the Cardiff Arms Hotel. The Arms of the old town of Cardiff were featured above the portico on the front of the building, and they became incorporated in the design of the Glamorgan Lodge Banners. The Arms consist of a red shield bearing three yellow chevronels, supported by two lions. The design is identical to the Arms of Cardiff as illustrated on John Speed's 1610 map of 'Cardyfe'. The earliest Lodge Banner, to be seen to the left and above the Master's Chair in the Duke of Connaught Temple, Cardiff, dates from around 1857. It bears the Lodge No.43, which was the Lodge's number from 1833 to 1863 (illustrated on the title page). The second Banner, to the right of the first Banner, was presented by the WM and Officers at the Centenary Meeting on 4 November 1908.

The Atholl Grand Lodge Certificate of Joseph Davis, dated 28 June 1810

While at the Cardiff Arms, various furnishings were acquired. In the Minutes of 8 February 1820: *'Ordered that 3 chairs might be procured under the direction of the W. Master and not to exceed Five Guineas Each and a platform be provided and one for each chair.'* The Accounts Ledger shows that the cost was £17.13.0 (£17. 65p) with a further charge in February 1821 for freight of chairs 6/9d (30.75p). These chairs, together with other items of furniture were sold to the Cardiff Masonic Hall Company in 1897 for £20 of Shares in the Company. They are now to be seen in the foyer of Cardiff Masonic Hall. The Lodge continued to meet at the Cardiff Arms Hotel until June 1855, when it moved to its own premises at No. 4 Church Street.

Lord James Patrick Herbert Stuart, brother of John Crichton-Stuart, 2nd Marquess of Bute, became a Joining Member of the Lodge on 7 June 1821, and remained as such until the 1840s. He was MP for Cardiff, 1818-1820 and 1826-1832; MP for Ayr Burghs, 1834-1852; and Lord Lieutenant of Buteshire, 1848-1859. When, on 14 April 1856, it was announced that Edward John Hutchins had resigned as ProvGM, the Minutes record that Bro Alexander Bassett, WM, 1856-1857, *'proposed that Lord James Stuart be applied to accept the vacant office and ultimately the Secretary was requested to write to that Noble Brother.'* Nothing came of this suggestion and, it was next agreed on 12 January 1857: *'That a memorial be addressed to the Worshipful G.M. in*

The Cardiff Arms Hotel

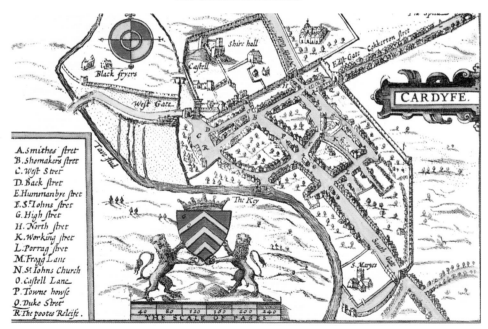

John Speed's Map of 'Cardyfe', 1610

56

reference to the appointment of the Provincial G.M. for South Wales, praying that the vacancy may be filled and recommending Capt. Tynte of Cefn Mably to the Office. The memorial as prepared was then read and agreed to and signed by the Brethren of the Lodge.'

On 22 June 1821, Edward Priest Richards was Installed as WM, and continued as such for two years. Born in 1792, the son of John Richards of Plasnewydd and Llandaff Court and his second wife Elizabeth Priest, he was a member of Cardiff's leading gentry family, and was to become the most powerful citizen of Cardiff. He was Under-sheriff of Glamorgan, 1817; Alderman of Cardiff, 1818; County Treasurer, 1825; Solicitor of Cardiff Corporation 1833, Town Clerk of Cardiff, 1836-1857. His nephew, Edward Priest Richards Junior, of Plasnewydd, was Initiated into the Lodge on 7 June 1852. The Minutes of 1852 go on to record: *'The Brethren afterwards sat down to an excellent supper provided at the sole expense of the newly initiated Brother'.*

Master's Chair circa 1820

E P Richards Junior was extremely wealthy and could well afford to meet the cost of the supper. He went on to be Passed on 10 February 1853, but there is no record of him being Raised. On 5 February 1856, he married Harriet Georgina Tyler, the eldest daughter of Vice-Admiral Sir George Tyler, MP, of Cottrell Park, former Governor of St Vincent (1833-1846). Sadly, the marriage was to end all too soon in tragic circumstances. On the afternoon of Tuesday, 12 November 1856, Edward was returning to Plasnewydd on horseback, when riding along Plwcca Lane (now City Road) and a few hundred yards from home, his horse was startled by an approaching scavenger's cart. He was thrown from his horse and fell heavily on the back of his head. He was carried unconscious into Plasnewydd and died later that evening. The following June 1857, his daughter, Harriet Diana Arabella was born. She married Alfred Donald Mackintosh (1851-1938) of Moy Hall, Inverness-shire, the 28th Chief of Clan Mackintosh and 29th Chief of Clan Chattan. Much of the Roath area of Cardiff formed a part of her estate, and street names like Mackintosh Place, Inverness Place, Strathnairn Street, Arran Street, Argyle Street, Keppoch Street show the Scottish Mackintosh connection. Arabella Street, Diana Street, Harriet Street are named after her and other streets in the area are named after her children (Donald, Diana, Alfred and Angus).

The Atholl Lodges did not have Provincial Grand Masters. After the Union, Glamorgan Lodge for many years ignored all communications from the ProvGM of South Wales. On the 8 January 1823, John Francis, ProvGSec, wrote to the Grand Secretaries in London thus: *'I am directed by the P.G.M. for South Wales, Sir C. Cole, M.P. to inform you that since he has had the superintendence of this province, he has not been able to get the W. Master of the Glamorgan Lodge No. 50 to attend to any of the many Summons's sent to him, nor have they in any shape answered one of my letters. It will of course rest with the G. Lodge to determine wether (sic) they are within his Jurisdiction, and if so, to issue orders accordingly.'*

Unfortunately there is no record of any reply to this letter. The first mention of the ProvGM in Glamorgan Lodge Minutes concerns a Lodge of Emergency on 11 August 1825: *'The W.M. with his Officers & Brothers have determined to meet the P.G.M. at Carmarthen on the 16th Inst.'* The occasion was the laying of the Foundation Stone of the monument to Sir Thomas Picton, who had been killed at the Battle of Waterloo. The Stone was laid by Lady Dynevor, assisted by the Provincial Grand Master and his Officers. There was a Grand Masonic Procession, which included the ProvGM of Hampshire, the Lord Lieutenants of Pembrokeshire, Carmarthenshire and Cardiganshire, the Corporation of Carmarthen and numerous clergy. Glamorgan Lodge was at the head of the procession of Provincial Lodges and at the banquet afterwards it was the first Lodge to be Toasted as *'Royal*

Glamorgan Lodge'.

During 1826, the Lodge sponsored its first pupil at the Royal Cumberland Freemasons' School (now the Royal Masonic Institution for Girls). This was Sibyl Eliza Lewis, daughter of the late W H Lewis, a Draper of Cardiff, who had been Initiated into the Lodge on 8 October 1819. Sibyl Eliza, bearing the same names as her mother, had been born on 20 June 1817 and the family lived at Marshfield, near Newport. She was admitted to the School on 19 October 1826 and the school records show that the Lodge sponsoring the Petition was Lodge No.50 (Glamorgan). She remained in the School until 19 July 1832, when the register finally states that she was *'delivered to the care of Mr. Scott, 20 Salisbury Street, Stroud, Watchmaker, by desire of her mother.'*

Returning to E P Richards Senior; his Clerk and Assistant County Treasurer, John Lloyd, was Initiated into Glamorgan Lodge on 26 March 1827. John Lloyd, who by profession was an Accountant, is unique in the history of the Lodge in that he served as WM for a total of 9 years; firstly, 1833-1835; then 1840-1844 and finally 1848-1851. He also served as Lodge Treasurer for a total of 17 years, covering the periods 1828-1831, 1835-1840, 1844-1848 and 1851-1856. In 1850, he was appointed Borough Treasurer. John Lloyd died on 8 September 1865 at the age of 68, and was interred in the family vault in St John's Church, Cardiff.

There are several instances of Sea Captains being proposed, Balloted and Initiated on the same night, just before setting sail from Cardiff. For example, Captain F Burns of Sunduland (Sunderland) was proposed, Balloted and Initiated on 8 January 1827 and Passed on 22 January 1827 - *'On account of going to Sea'*. Years later, at a Lodge meeting on 11 December 1874, a letter was read from the Almoner of the Birmingham Lodges asking for assistance for Bro Burns *'who was initiated in Glamorgan Lodge and had been deprived of his eyesight for three years past'*. This practice of Initiating Sea Captains became even more common later in the century, with the establishment of the Bute Lodge in the Docks.

A number Glamorgan Lodge Brethren were involved with shipping and its associated industries. One of the earliest of the Cardiff shipbuilding yards was that of Joseph Davis (WM in 1811) on the banks of the River Taff, off St Mary Street. Richard Tredwen, WM, 1827-1828; 1835-1837 and 1844 -1845; opened the first dry-dock in 1829 and he built a number of vessels there from 1830 onwards. Tredwen was Elected a Joining Member of the Lodge on 4 July 1816. His Mother Lodge was Brunswick Lodge No.260 (now No.159), Plymouth Dock (now Devonport), Devon. He resigned from the Lodge shortly before his death on 3 June 1857 at the age of 66 and was interred in Adamsdown Burial Ground. In the 1850s, his company was still building small boats and, after his death, the business was taken over by his nephews, John and Thomas Hodge. Thomas Hodge was Initiated into Glamorgan Lodge on 2 November 1844 and was WM, 1851-1852. In the Cardiff Directory of 1873, Thomas Hodge is listed *'Ship Builder &c, Dry Dock, East Wharf.'* Thomas Hodge died in February 1905.

On 3 June 1831, over a week of disorder and rioting broke out in Merthyr Tydfil, which led to the arrest of a 23 year-old miner by the name of Richard Lewis, better known as Dic Penderyn. Further details of the incident are given in the next chapter on the History of Loyal Cambrian Lodge No.110, Merthyr Tydfil. At his trial in Cardiff, Dic Penderyn was sentenced to the gallows, but, WBro John Bateman Woods, WM of Glamorgan Lodge, 1823-1825, Governor of Cardiff Prison, had great difficulty in finding someone to perform the execution. About twelve o'clock on the night previous to the execution, a man offered his services and was accepted. The gallows were erected in front of the Old County Gaol, which stood on the site of the present Cardiff Market (a blue plaque marks the spot in High Street.) Executions at that time were public spectacles and a crowd of 500 people assembled to witness the event at 8.00 am on 13 August 1831. His corpse was handed over to his widow and conveyed on a cart to his hometown, Aberavon. His grave is to be found in St Mary's churchyard. John Bateman Woods resigned from the Lodge in 1857. He died at the age of 86 years, on 27 January 1872 and was interred at Llandaff Cathedral.

At a Lodge Meeting on 14 January 1833, a communication was read from Grand Lodge informing the Brethren that *'several Lodges having been erased, the number of this Lodge upon the Register of Grand Lodge will be No. 43.'*

The last Meeting of the Lodge at the Cardiff Arms Hotel was on 11 June 1855, when Robert Langley was Installed as WM. Robert Langley was instrumental in the formation of St John's Chapter No.36, Warranted 7 November 1855, and Langley Mark

Lodge No.8, Warranted 15 June 1859. His biographical details are given separately in this book. The first Meeting at the new premises, 4 Church Street, was on Tuesday, 17 July, when one Brother was Initiated and five Brethren were Raised.

The Minutes of 1 April 1835, record the first occasion that the Lodge was involved in the public ceremony of laying a Foundation Stone: *'It was moved by Brother William Bird seconded by Brother Dempsey that the Lodge assist in the important Ceremony of laying the Foundation Stone of the Glamorgan & Monmouthshire Infirmary which was Resolved unanimously. Resolved - That application be made by the W.M. to the Deputy Provincial Grand Master and the W.M., Members of the Swansea, Merthyr and Neath Lodges to assist us on the occasion.'* The Foundation Stone was laid on Thursday, 9 April 1835. The Brethren met in the Lodge Room at the Cardiff Arms Hotel, when the Lodge was opened in the First Degree. They then walked in procession in full Regalia to the Town Hall, where they *'were joined by Members of the Building Committee, among whom we observed Daniel Jones, Esq., of Llantwit, the Principal benefactor of the Institution and John Nicholl, Esq., M.P., &c. &c., and then proceeded, in the same order in which they set out, to the site of the future Building. High-street, at the period, presented a most charming appearance, the windows of the different houses being crowded with elegant dressed females, and Duke Street, Crockherbtown, and the whole of the line of the procession, being equally attractive. On their arrival, a short prayer was given by the Chaplain (the Rev. Mr. Evans), and the following Anthem to the tune of "Rule Britannia", sung by the assembled multitude: …'* J. Nicholl, MP, was Sir John Nicholl of the Merthyr Mawr Estate, MP for Cardiff, 1832-1852; Lord of the Treasury 1833; Judge Advocate General & Privy Councillor, 1841. He must have been very impressed with the Freemasons present and with Glamorgan Lodge in particular, for the following year, on Friday, 12 August 1836, a Lodge of Emergency was held and all that is recorded in the Minutes is the following: *'A Letter having been received by Brother Lloyd from John Nicholl, Esq., M.P. expressing a wish to become Initiated into the Sublime Mysteries of a Mason, he was immediately proposed by Brother Lloyd and seconded by Brother W. Bird, Balloted for and unanimously elected.'* John Nicholl was Initiated on the 19 August and Passed on 23 September 1836. There is no record of him being Raised.

On Wednesday, 8 July 1840, the Lodge was involved in the Laying of the Foundation Stone of St Mary's Church, Bute Street. The Minutes for 8 July are as follows: *'Lodge opened in First Degree. The Lodge then proceeded to the Spot selected in St. Mary's Parish after attending Divine Service, and performed the usual accustomed honours to the pleasure of the Craft and amid the hearty good wishes of the assembled thousands - Returned to Lodge and closed. The Brethren dined at 5 and harmony and good nature smiled on every Countenance.'* The original St Mary's Church was in St Mary Street, on the site later occupied by the Prince of Wales Theatre, now a Weatherspoon's pub. In 1607, St Mary's was seriously damaged by floods and, by 1678, it was roofless and abandoned.

On Monday, 17 April 1854, the Lodge was involved in laying yet another Foundation Stone. This time it was for the new Parish Church of St John the Evangelist in Canton. *'At 3.00 pm a procession was formed at the Union Workhouse (later St David's Hospital) and walked to the site of the new building, an open field, the property of and presented by John Homfray, Esq, of Penlline Castle. At the head of the procession was the 'Glamorgan Lodge of Freemasons' two and two, etc.'* The Foundation Stone was laid by Rt Rev Alfred Ollivant, Bishop of Llandaff. Seventy-three years later, a special service was held at the church, attended by numerous Brethren of Glamorgan Lodge. In the Lodge Minutes it is recorded that: *'On Palm Sunday the 10 April 1927 the brethren of the Cardiff and district Lodges visited the Canton Parish Church to take part in the Special Service at 3 p.m. when the Rector Bro. John Thomas, P.P.G. Chaplain delivered a Masonic address to the brethren. The Worshipful Master of the Glamorgan Lodge W. Bro. Thomas McGowan Hole read the 1st Lesson, the second being read by Mr. W. P. James, High Bailiff, son of the late W. Bro. James, who in the year 1854 was the W. Master of the Glamorgan Lodge.'*

On 11 December 1855, the Lodge was presented with the Insignia of the late Sir Christopher Cole Bart, ProvGM, by the eminent antiquarian, Rev John Montgomery Traherne, of 'Coedriglan', St Hilary. An executor of Cole's will and a Member of Glamorgan Lodge (Initiated 4 September 1821), Traherne was married to Charlotte Louisa, the third daughter of Thomas Mansel Talbot

(Cole's step-daughter). For many years the Insignia was displayed in a glass case in the various Lodge Rooms and, in June 1972, it was placed on loan to the Grand Lodge Museum, Great Queen Street, London.

Cole was succeeded as ProvGM by Sir Josiah John Guest, who had been Initiated into Glamorgan Lodge on 5 April 1810, Passed on 7 August 1821 and finally Raised on 20 October 1836, just before his appointment as ProvGM for South Wales on 10 November 1836! His Installation as ProvGM was not held until Tuesday, 18 August 1840. This took place at Swansea and 15 Brethren of Glamorgan Lodge travelled in the Steam Packet 'Superb' in order to attend the Meeting, returning in a like manner to Cardiff the following day!

Sir J J Guest was succeeded by Col Charles Kemeys Kemeys-Tynte of Cefn Mably as ProvGM, who was Installed as such at a Provincial Grand Lodge held at Cardiff on 6 August 1857, under the Banner of Glamorgan Lodge. At his own request, he became a Subscribing Member of Glamorgan Lodge on 11 May of that year, and he continued as such for the remaining 34 years of his life. On 9 November 1857, John Caborn, the ProvGM's Butler was Initiated into the Lodge. Apparently, at this time, it was not unusual to Initiate the personal servants of distinguished Brethren. It enabled the 'personage' to enjoy the attention of his servant at the dinner following a Lodge Meeting as well as at home! John Caborn resigned from the Lodge in 1866. On a visit to the Lodge on 11 June 1860, the ProvGM thanked the Lodge warmly for his reception and alluded to the compliment paid him in placing his Coat of Arms in the Lodge Room, concluding by *'hoping that those who may also bear that shield in future may long be associated with the Glamorgan Lodge No.43'*. This Lodge Room was on an upper floor in the new Royal Arcade (the first of Cardiff's arcades), St Mary Street, and the Lodge held its first Meeting there on 11 July 1859. The Arcade's architect, Peter Price, was a Member of the Lodge.

Tynte Coat of Arms

The Consecration of Glamorgan's first Daughter Lodge, Bute Lodge No.1262, was held on 30 June 1863, with all but one of the Consecrating Officers being Members or Joining Members of Glamorgan Lodge. The Brethren had finally agreed to sign the Petition for the new Lodge in their Meeting on 8 April 1863, following five months of bitter disagreement and the final intervention of Col Tynte, ProvGM. Further details are given in the history of Bute Lodge, later in this book. Soon afterwards, Grand Lodge announced that Lodges had been re-numbered and in future Glamorgan Lodge would be No.36 and Bute Lodge No.960 on the Register of UGLE. From this time, the relationship between the two Lodges was extremely cordial and at a Regular Meeting of Bute Lodge on 15 December 1863, the WM of Glamorgan Lodge, WBro John Grierson, was Elected an Honorary Member of the Lodge. For many years afterwards, the WM of Glamorgan Lodge became an Honorary Member of Bute Lodge.

On 10 November 1863, a young Barrister, Gwilym Williams of Miskin, was Initiated into Glamorgan Lodge in the presence of RWBro Charles Kemeys Kemeys-Tynte, ProvGM. This event was to lead to a scandal involving the Lodge and the ProvGM, as Gwilym Williams had been Initiated previously in St David's Lodge No.679, Aberdare. Details of the events are included later in this book in the biographical profile of the ProvGM. Gwilym Williams did not become a Member of Glamorgan Lodge, but continued to be a Member of St David's Lodge and, in 1875, he was one of twelve Petitioners for Merlin Lodge No.1578, Pontypridd. He was to have a distinguished career as Judge in South Wales, and his statue, by William Goscombe John, is to be seen in front of the Law Courts, Cathays Park, Cardiff.

On 14 June 1864, David Roberts, an Accountant with the Taff Vale Railway Company, was Installed as WM and was Installed as such again on 26 June the following year. Initiated at the age of 26 on 6 December 1856, he was to remain a Member of the Lodge for over 50 years. In Province, he was first appointed ProvGReg in 1858, and in 1866 he became ProvJGW. In 1866, he established his own accountancy firm, which was to become one of the largest and most successful in South Wales. His two sons, Arthur Herbert Roberts, WM, 1889-1890, and David Robertson Roberts, WM, 1892-1893, joined him in the partnership. On 14 October

1892, Arthur Herbert Roberts presented Glamorgan Lodge with a Master's silver Chain and Collar to commemorate his brother's year as WM, which is still worn by the current WM. David Robertson Roberts died in October 1897 in Jerusalem, at the age of 57, leaving a widow and seven children. A third brother, Alfred Lewis Roberts, was Installed as WM on 27 June 1894, and again on 28 June 1900. He died at the age of 45 in February 1903.

On 24 June 1869, Col Edward Stock Hill was Installed as WM. Born in Bristol in 1834, he was a son of Charles Hill, owner of the City Line of steamers trading from Bristol. He was Initiated into Glamorgan Lodge on 13 December 1864, soon after his arrival in Cardiff, when he and his brother, Charles, acquired the Dry Dock formerly belonging to S & J Batchelor and soon established a very successful shipbuilding business (Hills' Dry Dock, Cardiff). In 1869, he became Vice-chairman of the Cardiff Chamber of Commerce and President in 1871 and 1873; President of the Chamber of Shipping of the UK, 1881; President of the Associated Chambers of Commerce, 1888-1891; Hill was also the Founder of Cardiff Shipowners' Association and first President, 1875-1881, and the representative on Lloyd's Register. He was appointed High Sheriff of Glamorgan in 1885. In 1866, he acquired Rookwood in Llandaff, where he built a grand house in the early English Gothic style (now Rookwood Hospital). In 1860, he joined the Glamorgan Artillery and in recognition of his services, was made a CB in 1881 and KCB in 1892. Whilst in London, he frequently attended Grand Lodge and became well acquainted with the leaders of the Masonic world. In Province, he was first appointed ProvGSwdB, 1866; ProvGReg , 1869; and promoted to ProvJGW, 1870. Following the death of Sir Pryce Pryce, Bart, ProvGM, Mark Master Masons for South Wales, 1881-1895, he was Invested as his successor, a position he held from 1899 until his death on Wednesday, 17 December 1902.

On 9 April 1875, Glamorgan Lodge agreed to the formation of a Joint Lodge Committee with Bute Lodge to find new Lodge premises. Final plans for a new Lodge Room in Working Street were accepted at the Meeting on 30 May 1876 and the first Meeting of Glamorgan Lodge in Working Street was held on 12 January 1877. At that Meeting, Edwin Seward and George Thomas were Initiated. Edwin Seward was the architect of the Coal Exchange, Mount Stuart Square, opened by Col Sir Edward Stock Hill, PM, on 1 February 1886. George Thomas was also an Architect and, by 1890, he was the Managing Director of the Barry Dock Town Syndicate and the Barry Land Company. On 11 September 1890, he was Installed as the first WM of Barry Lodge, No.2357, the third Daughter Lodge of Glamorgan Lodge. The second Daughter Lodge was Windsor Lodge No.1754, Penarth, Consecrated on 15 July 1878. The WM and Wardens of Glamorgan Lodge signed the Petition for that Lodge on 8 March 1878.

Dominick McGettrick Watson, Brewer & Maltster of the Cambrian Brewery, Quay Street, Cardiff, was Installed as WM on 25 June 1877. His father, George Watson, had started the Cambrian Brewery in Womanby Street, Cardiff, in 1848.

Masonic Hall, Working Street, Cardiff. 1876

Following his father's death in 1866, the business was run under 'Mrs. Watson & Son' and, finally, 'Dominick Watson' from 1875 until 1882, when the Brewery was sold to Samuel Arthur Brain and his uncle Joseph Benjamin Brain. Thus was founded 'S A Brain & Co, Cardiff'. Watson was appointed ProvGStwd in 1870, promoted to ProvGDC in 1879, and appointed ProvJGW in 1880.

On 12 January 1893, a Deputation of Brethren from the Bute Lodge was received, requesting support for a Petition for Tennant Lodge No.1992. WBro George Thomas proposed that the following endorsement to the Petition of the promoters be adopted and signed: *'We, the W.M., Wardens and Brethren of the Glamorgan Lodge No. 36, in open Lodge assembled, do hereby recommend to the Most Worshipful Grand Master, H.R.H. the Prince of Wales, for his favourable consideration the prayer of the within petition and humbly request it may be granted.'* In February 1893, it was agreed that should the Warrant for Tennant Lodge be granted, the new Lodge should be offered the use of the Masonic Hall at a rent of £30 pa, inclusive of furniture, gas and cleaning. Then, on 14 April 1893 it was agreed: *'That this Lodge, acting in conjunction*

Duke of Connaught Temple, 1895

with Bute and Tennant Lodges, sanction the purchase, by the Site Committee, of the premises selected by them for a Masonic Hall (viz. Guildford Street Chapel) for the sum of £4,500, and that this Lodge authorise the payment, out of the Lodge Funds, of a proportionate amount of the sum required to be deposited.' Tennant Lodge was Consecrated on 10 October 1893 at the Masonic Hall, Working Street. In 1894, the Masonic Hall Company was floated and, finally, on 26 September 1895, the new Temple was Consecrated under the Banner of Glamorgan Lodge, with Lord Llangattock, ProvGM, in attendance.

Shortly afterwards, it was agreed to present the Lodge's Masonic Emblem of the Pelican to the Caer-Daf Chapter No.118, Sovereign Princes - Rose Croix of HRDM, on the condition that it be renovated and hung in the new Masonic Temple. This was duly done, and it is to be seen in the central panel of the balcony of the Duke of Connaught Temple.

On 10 May 1895, it was agreed unanimously to support the Petition for a new Lodge to be called 'Prince Llewellyn Lodge' (Glamorgan Lodge's fourth Daughter Lodge) and *'the W.M. and Wardens to sign the same'*.

By December 1906, the decision to form a Past Masters' Lodge in Cardiff had been taken. The Minutes for 12 April 1907 record: *'The Secretary read a communication dated the 25th March 1907 from W.Bro. T. Rodway Hunt respecting the P.Ms.' Lodge relating to the terms of Membership thereof. Proposed by the W.M. and seconded by W.Bro. S. J. Hopkins that the Petition for the formation of a P.Ms.' Lodge be approved and signed and forwarded from the Glamorgan Lodge.'* Thus, Hendre Lodge No.3250 became Glamorgan Lodge's fifth Daughter Lodge.

The first attempt to obtain a Centenary Warrant and Jewel goes back as far as 1865

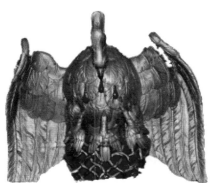

The Caer-Daf Pelican.

and, over the years, other unsuccessful attempts were made. Eventually, the application was granted in 1908 and the Centenary of the Lodge was celebrated on 4 November 1908, exactly 100 years to the day after the Lodge was Constituted at the Cardiff Arms Hotel. The Lodge was opened in due form with solemn prayer at 4. 35 pm. Among the distinguished visitors were RWBro the Lord Llangattock, ProvGM; WBro Marmaduke Tennant, DepProvGM; WBro Lord Kensington, SGW, England; and WBro Charles R Lyne, PDepProvGM, Monmouthshire. The Centenary Warrant from Grand Lodge was read by the Lodge Registrar, WBro Arthur Griffith Poyer Lewis, PM Prince Llewellyn Lodge, PGD, England, who also delivered a very interesting address on the history of the Lodge. The WM and his Officers presented a new Banner to the Lodge. After the Ceremony, 212 Brethren dined at the Park Hotel.

The Centenary Invitation Card

The Centenary Master was WBro Tom Wallace. Initiated on 8 June 1877, he was first Installed as WM on 24 June 1884. Elected Treasurer in November 1885 and in 1886, he was once more Elected Treasurer in 1896, an Office he was to hold until 1906, when he became JW for the second time, thus enabling him to occupy the Chair in the Centenary Year. In 1885, he was also appointed ProvJGD. He was re-appointed Lodge Treasurer in 1909 and continued as such until 1927, when on 24 June he was Installed WM for the third time. In Province, he rose to the Rank of ProvSGW in 1898 and was Installed WM of Hendre Lodge in 1917. He became a JGD of UGLE in 1909 and, from 1928 until his death in 1930, he was Grand Superintendent of Royal Arch Masons, Province of South Wales (Eastern Division). Unfortunately, his deteriorating health prevented him from attending Lodge for the last two years of his life.

On the afternoon of Saturday, 15 May 1909, a special meeting was held at the Cardiff Temple in Dr Tom Wallace's honour. Most of the Brethren attended accompanied by their wives, daughters and sisters and a Dispensation was granted permitting the Brethren to wear their Masonic Clothing and Jewels. The meeting opened with a hymn followed by a musical programme. During the proceedings, WBro Harry Cousins, WM, 1881-1882, Registrar of the Cardiff & Barry County Courts, presented Dr Tom Wallace with a silver salver and five silver fruit dishes. In making the presentation, Harry Cousins said '*he was delighted that Mrs. Wallace and some of her Daughters were there to see and know how highly W. Bro. Wallace is esteemed by the Brethren of the Lodge and asked him to accept the gift, not for its intrinsic value, but as the earnestly sincere expression of their satisfaction with the manner in which he had so worthily maintained the honour and dignity of the old Lodge.*' Almost 37 years later, on 8 February 1946, the WM reported the receipt of the generous gift to the Lodge by WBro Col John Wallace, OBE, of the silver pieces presented to his father, Dr Tom Wallace. Every year, at Installation, the silver is displayed at the Festive Board.

On 28 June 1914, just four days after the Installation of David Evan Roberts, Archduke Franz Ferdinand of Austria-Hungary was assassinated in Sarajevo by a Serbian activist, an event that led to the outbreak of WWI. David Evan Roberts, a Consulting Engineer, was born in Merthyr Tydfil, where his father was the manager of the old Plymouth Ironworks. Educated at Christ College Brecon, he trained initially at the Rhymney Ironworks before eventually becoming the Chief Engineer at the Dowlais Works. For nearly 50 years he was in private practice, dealing primarily with iron and steel matters, and his business took him to all parts of the world. He resided at 9, Museum Place, Cardiff, a convenient location for one who was a member of the Court of Governors of that institution and its treasurer for the last ten years of his life. He was also a member of the Court of Governors of the National Library of Wales, Aberystwyth. David Roberts was Initiated into Freemasonry in Glamorgan Lodge at the age of 38 on 12 January 1906. Installed as WM on 24 June 1914, he served as Lodge Treasurer 1931-1959. He was appointed ProvSGW, 1924; First Principal of St John's Chapter No.36, 1928; PAGSoj, in Supreme Grand Chapter, 1929; Grand Superintendent of Royal Arch Masons, Eastern Division of South Wales, 1931-1950; and SGD of UGLE, 1932. He had a tremendous love for Glamorgan Lodge and was one of its greatest benefactors. Among his gifts to the Lodge was a bound volume of Summonses and papers for the years 1917-1922, as a 'Substitute Minute Book' for the one lost in the fire at the premises of Messrs Collett & Whitefield on Tuesday, 23 February 1926. According to the 'Western Mail': *'One of the greatest fires in the history of Cardiff, involving damage estimated at £60,000, occurred on Tuesday night, and was still raging early this Wednesday morning. The fire took place in the large triangular block of buildings between Custom House-street, on the south, New- street, on the north and west, and Hope-street, on the east.'* Amazingly, with the exception of that one Minute Book, the Lodge is still in possession of all its Minute Books, covering the period from 4 November 1808 to the present day! On the 11 February 1938, the Brethren congratulated him on his election as President of the Institute of Mechanical Engineers. He was also a member of the Institution of Civil Engineers, the Institution of Electrical Engineers and an Honorary Member of the South Wales Institute of Engineers, having been President in 1922. A Freeman of the City of London and a Liveryman of the Worshipful Company of Blacksmiths, he was about to become the 'Prime Master' at the time of his death on 21 July 1950, at the age of 83.

WBro John Wallace, son of Dr Tom Wallace, was Initiated on 11 November 1904 and was Installed as WM on 24 June 1916. Educated at the University of Oxford, like his father, he was a medical man. In the Army during WWI, he rose to the rank of Colonel and was awarded the OBE. After the First World War, he worked for the Ministry of Pensions, London. He became PM of three London Lodges - Gihon Lodge No.49, Burton Court Lodge No.3864, and Old Rugbeian Lodge No.3551 and, in 1939; he was appointed AGDC of UGLE. Col Wallace was Elected an Honorary Member of Glamorgan Lodge on 9 January 1948 and, in 1951, he was promoted to the Rank of PGD of UGLE.

During WWI, four Lodge Members made the Supreme Sacrifice. WBro Alfred Hayward Howard, WM, 1904-1905, was a Bank Cashier. By 1910, he was working for the Metropolitan Bank in Haverfordwest. A Captain of the 4th Battalion the Welch Regiment, he was killed in action in the Dardanelles in August 1915. John Lewis Williams, Initiated at 30 years of age on 13 December 1912, was a Coal Exporter from Whitchurch, Cardiff. A Captain in the Welch Regiment from the outbreak of the war, he was killed on 1 July 1917. Frederick William Gibbon, Chartered Accountant from Penarth, was Initiated into the Lodge at the age of 27 on 16 June 1916. A Lieutenant with the Northumberland Fusiliers, he was killed on 25 August 1918. Sidney Archer Wilkes, MA, an Assistant Schoolmaster from Whitchurch, Cardiff, Initiated at 34 years of age on 10 December 1915, served as a Lieutenant with the Black Watch, and was also killed in August 1918.

Four Members of Glamorgan Lodge are known to have been awarded the MC. Bro Capt Harold James Brown, Initiated at the age of 23 on 13 December 1918, died on 10 January 1919. Bro Norris Langfield Flower, Bank Cashier, 28 years of age when Initiated on 12 December 1921. WBro Claude Luther Pendlebury, Chartered Surveyor, 32 years of age when Initiated on 13 May 1927. In 1937, he became WM of Lodge of Felicity No.5336, Plymouth. WBro Tom Wallace, Solicitor and nephew of WBro Dr Thomas Wallace, Installed as WM of Glamorgan Lodge on 24 June 1939, served in 7th Battalion Welsh Cyclists in WWI. He was wounded three times and awarded the MC for gallantry in the field. Vice-President in 1951 and President in 1953 of the Cardiff City Law Society, he was the senior partner in the firm of William Bradley & Wallace, Solicitors, Cowbridge Road, Cardiff.

On 8 March 1918, the eminent Welshman, Sir Frederick John Alban, was Initiated into Glamorgan Lodge. He became Grand Treasurer of UGLE in 1944 and later Inspector General Rose Croix for the District of South Wales & Monmouthshire, 1951-1963. His biographical details are given separately, later in this book. Although he was never an Officer in the Lodge, he remained a Member until ill health caused him to resign on 8 November 1963. He died on 2nd May 1965 in his 83rd year.

During 1920, plans were developed for the formation of a sixth Daughter Lodge, to be called 'Kibbor Lodge'. The driving force behind the scheme was the distinguished Past Master WBro Arthur Llewellyn Hopkins, WM, 1901-1903, who was to become the first WM of the Lodge. (See history of Kibbor Lodge for further details.) The Warrant for Kibbor Lodge No.4364 was eventually signed on 2 November 1921, the delay apparently due to the fact that the Founders wished to have the numbers '43' (Glamorgan Lodge's Number, 1833-1863) and '36' incorporated in the new Lodge Number, thus resulting in a wait until No.4364 became available! The first twelve WMs of Kibbor Lodge were all from Glamorgan Lodge - this really was a Daughter Lodge!

On Wednesday, 8 November 1922, Glamorgan Lodge was honoured with the presence of Arthur Oliver Villiers Russell, 2nd Baron Ampthill, Pro Grand Master. The Meeting, held on a Wednesday by Dispensation, was attended by 174 Brethren but, unfortunately, RWBro Charles L D Venables Llewelyn, Bart, ProvGM, and WBro Henry Pendrill Charles, DepProvGM, were unable to be present because of serious illness. During the Meeting, Mr Frederick William Pepperell, Schoolmaster, age 53 years, was Initiated. The Minutes record: *'At the completion of the ceremony, the Most Worshipful the Pro Grand Master congratulated the candidate, Bro. Pepperell in felicitous terms, and commended the Worshipful Master and the Lodge on the dignified manner in which the ceremony had been conducted. Finally the Pro Grand Master delivered an exhaustive and illuminating address on matters relating to Freemasonry, which was much appreciated by the Brethren.'*

At a Meeting of Provincial Grand Lodge, held at Swansea on 27 June 1928, RWBro Col Sir Charles D Venables Llewelyn, ProvGM, during his customary address to the Brethren, announced that all Masons should refrain from visiting Glamorgan and Kibbor Lodges, until they conformed in certain matters of Ritual with the rest of the Province. Further, no Members of those two Lodges were to be appointed to Provincial Office. Full details of this dispute are to be found in the ProvGM's biographical account given later in this book. One of the major points at issue concerned Glamorgan Lodge's Installation Ceremony. The Lodge performs the extended workings of a Board of Installed Masters, as practised by Antient Freemasons. Glamorgan Lodge was ostracized from the Province for a period of three years. Ultimately, the ProvGM conceded Glamorgan Lodge's right to perform the Ceremony. Only Loyal Cambrian Lodge No.110, Merthyr, another Antient Lodge, performs a similar Ceremony in Wales.

During 1928, the Lodge commissioned the Canadian Artist, Parker Hagarty (1859-1934) to paint a portrait in oils of WBro Dr Tom Wallace Senior. The portrait shows Dr Wallace in his Regalia as Grand Superintendent of Royal Arch Masons of South Wales (Eastern Division). Not being in sufficiently good health to attend Lodge, the painting was presented to Dr Wallace at an informal Lodge Meeting held at his home on 27 May 1929. Dr Wallace presented his portrait to the Lodge and, at one time, it was displayed in the Duke of Connaught Temple. The painting disappeared for several years and was eventually discovered by WBro Peter Davies, Secretary, in 2004, in the roof space above the anteroom of the Edgar Rutter Temple. The portrait was in very poor condition and it was expertly restored by WBro David Jenner, PM Hiraeth Lodge No.8834, Cardiff. The portrait now hangs in the Glamorgan Room at Cardiff Masonic Hall.

On Election Night, 13 May 1932, WBro Col John Wallace, OBE, at the request of the WM (John Summers) addressed the Brethren, and after making a brief reference to his late father's great interest and affection for Glamorgan Lodge (Dr Tom Wallace Senior), asked the Lodge to accept from him what he considered to be one of his most cherished possessions, namely his late father's Past Masters Jewel with two bars, he having been three times Master of the Lodge. The Jewel is now worn by the IPM, being permanently attached to the IPM's Collar. It is one of the Lodge's most treasured possessions. At that

Dr Tom Wallace Senior

Election Meeting, Daniel James Arthur Brown, Registrar of University College of South Wales & Monmouthshire, Cardiff, became Master Elect and was duly Installed as WM on 24 June 1932.

On 8 December 1933, WBro D J A Brown led a Deputation of thirty-five Founder Brethren of the Lodge, requesting support for the Petition of the proposed Universities Lodge No.5461. The Petition was then laid on the Tracing Board, and was duly signed by the WM and the two Wardens. The Consecration of Universities Lodge, Glamorgan Lodge's seventh Daughter Lodge, took place at the Masonic Temple, Cardiff, on Monday, 30 April 1934. WBro D J A Brown was Installed as the first Worshipful Master.

On 24 June 1937, Dr Thomas Wallace Junior, nephew of Dr Thomas Wallace Senior, was Installed as WM. Born in Northern Ireland in 1892, he served with the Irish Fusiliers, 1914-1917, and with the RAMC, 1918-1919. Following demobilisation, he came to Cardiff in 1919 as a Medical Practitioner in practice with his uncle at 224, Newport Road. In 1950, he was the President of the Cardiff Medical Society. He was also the Medical Officer at Cardiff Prison and was often called as a witness in criminal trials. Dr Wallace was a skilful rugby player, both as a three-quarter and later a full-back and he had played for Queen's University, Belfast, and for Ulster, 1911-1914. He was selected to play for Ireland when International Rugby was resumed in 1920. During that first season, he played in the three Internationals against England, Scotland and Wales. Later, he played for Cardiff and was the Captain for the 1922-1923 season, the first Irish International to achieve this honour! In Province, Dr Wallace was appointed PPrAGDC in 1944. He died on 9 September 1954 at the relatively young age of 62. Unfortunately, he did not live to see his son, Dr John Shannon Wallace Initiated in the Lodge on 9 November 1956. John Wallace was Installed as WM on 24 June 1969. Unfortunately, he also died at the relatively young age of 58 on 6 November 1985.

There is no record of any Member of the Lodge being killed on active service during WWII, though several Brethren lost their sons. The first bereavement was announced in Lodge on 11 October 1940. This was the death of a son of Bro Sir Herbert Merrett, Coal Exporter, who became President of the British Coal Exporters, 1946-1949, and had been Initiated into Glamorgan Lodge on 14 January 1916 at the age of 28. In March 1943, it was announced that Bro Lieut-Col Robert Henry Humphries had recently been officially posted 'missing'. His safe return was announced on 12 October 1945. He had been a prisoner of war in the hands of the Japanese, in the notorious Changi Prison Camp, Singapore, along with WBro HH Judge John C Rutter, son of WBro Edgar John Rutter, DepProvGM. Humphries attended Lodge on 9 November 1945, when he was welcomed on his return and Invested with the Collar of Senior Deacon. In October 1947, he was appointed Welfare Adviser to the Post Office in Wales. He was awarded the Territorial Decoration in 1948, appointed Deputy Lieutenant of the County in October 1951 and made an Honorary Colonel of his Regiment (Royal Artillery) in December 1951. He became WM of the Lodge on St John's Day 1950. At the February Meeting in 1943, the WM referred to the recent death, whilst on active service, of Mr Ray Hutchinson, a son of Bro Thomas Lancaster Hutchinson, District Engineer. Tragedy was to strike again, for on 13 October 1944, the WM announced the death of a second son of Bro Hutchinson. At the October 1944 Meeting, the WM referred to the loss suffered by Bro Florio Vincent Care, whose son had been killed whilst on active service.

At the Installation of Cuthbert Lionel Summers on St John's Day 1965, RWBro R P St John Charles, ProvGM, and WBros Harry F Stockwell and Harold Wilson, AProvGMs, were present. The 96 visitors included the WM and two PMs from Old Tauntonian Lodge No.5735, London, a Lodge associated with Cuthbert's former school, Taunton School, Somerset. His blood brother WBro Morlais James Summers, who had been Installed as WM on 24 June 1951, presented Cuthbert for Installation. Cuthbert was born in Cardiff on 8 March 1915 and was 33 years of age when his father, WBro John Summers, WM, 1931-1932, Initiated him on 12 November 1948. On leaving school, he was apprenticed to a company of wholesale clothiers, travelling the valleys of South Wales. In the 1930s, Cuthbert started 'Glamtax', the first taxi service in Cardiff, with a fleet of chauffeur driven maroon coloured 'Austin 12s'. The Company started with 12 cars and, by 1939, there were 150 cars with branches in Swansea, Newport and Birmingham. With the outbreak of WWII, Cuthbert was initially turned down for military service because of partial blindness in his right eye. Determined to serve, he memorized the medical eye chart and entered the Royal Army Services Corps! Commissioned into the Indian Army, he commanded a field supply depot in Assam on the North West Frontier. After the War, he rejoined Glamtax as General Manager. Following the death of his father, John, in 1949, he joined his brother, Morlais, in the family firm of Funeral Directors. In 1952, the two brothers purchased the historic house 'Roath Court', Newport Road, Cardiff, which, interestingly, had been the home of John Wood Senior, the first WM of Glamorgan Lodge. Cuthbert also enjoyed a very distinguished Masonic career. In 1971, he was appointed Acting ProvJGW and, in 1972, he became a Grand Officer with the Rank of PAGDC. In 1975, he became the Lodge Charity Steward, an Office he was to occupy for very many years. Appointed AProvGM in 1977, he continued as such until 1987. When the Lodge celebrated its 175th Anniversary in 1983, he had the honour of being Installed WM for the second time on 17 June of that year. His Installation required a Dispensation from Province, for at the time he was also WM of Lodge of Benevolence No.7305. Cuthbert Lionel Summers died on 11 May 1997 and many representatives of the Masonic Lodges of the Province attended his funeral service at Llandaff Cathedral on Friday, 16 May.

St John's Wort

The last Past Master of the Lodge to become a Grand Officer was WBro Lewis Kenneth Mark Loyns, who was appointed to the Rank of PGStB in March 1993. A Schoolmaster by profession, he taught at Gladstone Junior School, Whitchurch Road, Cardiff. He had commenced his Masonic career in the Far East, where he was a Member of Centenary Lodge No.7629 (WM 1958), Singapore and Aden Lodge No.7652 (Erased), Singapore, under the English Constitution. He became a Joining Member of Glamorgan Lodge on 13 October 1972 and, in 1977, he was Installed as WM of Discovery Lodge No.8601, Cardiff. In 1981, he was appointed ProvJGD and, a few years later, he was promoted to PPrJGW. On 24 June 1986 he was Installed as WM of Glamorgan Lodge. Sadly, he died at the age of 70, on the 3 October 1993, just a few months after being Invested PGStB, and never had the pleasure of attending Glamorgan Lodge in his Grand Lodge Regalia. Ladies were invited to attend the Festive Board following the Lodge Meeting on 10 March 1995. Kenneth's widow, Mrs Betty Loyns, was present together with Ken's blood brother, WBro Charles Leslie Loyns, PM Discovery Lodge. That evening, WBro Charles presented a silver quaich to the Lodge on behalf of the family and in memory of his late brother, Kenneth. The quaich is displayed every year at the Annual Installation Festival on St John's Day, when most appropriately it is filled with St John's Wort *(Hypericum perforatum)*, which always comes into flower around 24th June!

On Saturday, 15 March 2003, the Lodge celebrated the 250th Anniversary of the issuing, by the Antient Grand Lodge, of Warrant No.33, Glamorgan Lodge's original Lodge number. The Meeting, held by Dispensation, was attended by RWBro Hywel Davies, ProvGM; VWBro Peter Frost, DepProvGM; WBros Andrew Gretton, Brian Eveleigh, Robert Nettleship, AProvGMs; and VWBro Captain Norman Lloyd-Edwards, President of the New Samaritan Fund. Also present were representatives from the Association of Atholl Lodges, who during the proceedings presented an Atholl Gavel to the Lodge in commemoration of their visit. During the Meeting, WBro Peter Burkhardt, who was Initiated into the Lodge on 14 November 1980 and Installed as WM on 22 June 1990, provided the funds for the conservation of the re-issued Warrant No.33, dated 25 October 1777, read aloud the wording on that Warrant. Two historical presentations involving numerous Lodge Brethren were given: 18th Century Freemasonry in South Wales' and 'The Bridgend / Glamorgan Lodge 1765-1808'. These had been preceded by an address from WBro Paul Gardner, Secretary of the Association of Atholl Lodges, on 'The History of The Atholl Grand Lodge'. Bro Hugh Bennett presented the Lodge with a Tyler's Sword. (Hugh was Initiated into the Lodge on 13 November 1998, Installed as WM on 24 June 2005, and appointed ProvGPurs in 2011. On 23 March 2011, he was Installed as WM of Caradoc Lodge No.1573.) WBro David Murphy, Charity Steward, (Initiated into the Lodge on 8 December 1978 and Installed as WM on 24 June 1995.) on behalf of the Lodge, presented a cheque for 1000 guineas (£1050) to the ProvGM for the Provincial Samaritan Fund - Eastern Division of South Wales, and a second cheque for 1000 guineas to VWBro Peter Frost, DepProvGM, for the Friends of Albert Edward Prince of Wales Court,

Porthcawl. At the conclusion of the Ceremony, all Brethren were presented with a commemorative booklet, written by WBro Peter Davies, Secretary. At the Celebratory Banquet that evening, the ProvGM unexpectedly announced that he had decided to honour Glamorgan Lodge by appointing WBros Alastair Meikle, WM, and Peter Davies, to the Rank of PPrSGD. WBro Peter Davies had been Initiated into London Welsh Lodge No.2867 on 2 December 1983, joined Glamorgan Lodge on 13 October 1995, and was Installed as WM on 24 June 2000. In 2011, he was appointed Provincial Junior Grand WardenIn 2011, he was appointed Provincial Junior Grand Warden. As a consequence of the Warrant Anniversary Meeting, WBro Ray Sheppard, Atholl Historian, produced a beautifully illustrated Glamorgan Lodge family tree. He presented it to Glamorgan Lodge at the Regular Meeting held on 12 December 2003, and it is now displayed opposite the entrance to the Duke of Connaught Temple, at the Masonic Hall, Cardiff.

The Bicentenary Processional Banner

To mark the Bicentenary year (2008-2009), WBro Peter Burkhardt presented a Processional Banner to the Lodge. WBro Peter was at the time WM of Victoria Lodge No.IV, Dublin, Irish Constitution. The Dedication Ceremony was held on Friday, 4 March 2008, and was conducted by RWBro Hywel Davies, ProvGM, who was accompanied by his team of Provincial Grand Officers. The Banner had been made by RWBro Peter Marsh, PProvGM of Gloucestershire, who was present at the Ceremony.

The Bicentenary celebrations commenced on Sunday, 2 November 2008, when the Brethren, family and friends attended Solemn Mass at St German's Church, Adamsdown. Following the Service, a family luncheon was held in the Church Hall. The Bicentenary Lodge Meeting was held on Tuesday, 4 November, at the Cardiff Masonic Hall. The Lodge was opened at 5.35 pm, before which RWBro Thomas Caplin, PDepGDC, escorted RWBro Douglas Grey, DepGM of the Grand Lodge of Ireland, into the Temple. The domestic business having been completed, RWBro Captain Sir Norman Lloyd Edwards, ProvGM; accompanied by VWBro Andrew L Gretton, DepProvGM; WBros Brian Eveleigh; Geoffrey Thomas; Gareth Jones, OBE, AProvGMs; WBro Rev Alistair Swinford, ProvGChap; WBro James Bevan, ProvGSec and the customary full team of Acting Provincial Officers were admitted. RWBro Peter Geoffrey Lowndes, DepGM, (ProGM Elect), accompanied by VWBro Nigel Brown, GSec; VW Bro Thomas Caplin; RWBro Rev Malcolm Lane, ProvGM of Monmouthshire; and WBro Rev Canon Huw Mosford, PAGChap, AProvGM, were escorted into the Temple, and received with applause from the assembled Brethren. During the Ceremony, WBro David Murphy, Charity Steward, and Peter Davies, Secretary, presented a short historical account of the Lodge; the Grand Secretary read aloud the Bicentenary Warrant and the Provincial Grand Chaplain gave an Oration. The Charity Steward gave his report and informed the ProvGM that Glamorgan Lodge would pledge a minimum of £21,000 to the 2010 Festival. The Lodge was closed as 6.46 pm and, as the Brethren retired, Bro Robert Nicholls, Organist, played the Hallelujah Chorus, just as had been done at the conclusion of the Centenary Meeting on 4 November 1908. The Charity Collection of £418 was donated to the Provincial Benevolent Fund.

During the Lodge's existence, Members have included two Provincial Grand Masters, one Assistant Provincial Grand Master, a Grand Treasurer, three Grand Superintendents, five Provincial Grand Treasurers, three Provincial Grand Masters of Mark Masons, an Inspector General Rose Croix, three Lords and thirteen Knights of the Realm, Five MPs, one of whom was the brother of the Second Marquess of Bute, ten Mayors of Cardiff and four holders of the Military Cross. The Lodge is also proud that it is the head of a Provincial family tree of 102 Lodges.

Compiled by WBro Peter M Davies, ProvJGW, Secretary.

Loyal Cambrian Lodge No.110

Warranted   :   20 June 1810
Consecrated   :   7 August 1810
Meeting at the Masonic Hall, Merthyr Tydfil.

Loyal Cambrian Lodge was founded in 1810 by 10 Members of Ancient Britons' Lodge No.126, Caerphilly, who were mainly residents of Merthyr Tydfil. They were William Edwards, Solicitor, Merthyr; Fred Walters, Merthyr; William Williams, Merchant, Dowlais; Thomas Llewellyn, Sergt 1st Foot Guards; Thomas Lewis, Accompt (Accountant), Merthyr; John Morgan, Puddler, Penydarren Works; John Bryan, Brewer, Merthyr; John Treharne, Innkeeper, Dowlais Inn; William Lewis, Accompt, Cwmgarloch; and James Edwards, Plumber and Glazier, Merthyr.

The Warrant for Lodge No.144, Merthyr, was issued on 20 June 1810, on the authority of John Murray, 4th Duke of Atholl, Grand Master of the 'Antient and Honourable Fraternity of Free and Accepted Masons according to the old Constitutions'. The original Warrant, No.144, had been issued, probably in 1768, to a Lodge meeting at the King's Head, Strand, London. The Lodge lapsed in the course of a few years, and its Warrant was cancelled on 7 June 1775. On the margin of the present Warrant there is a note stating: *'This Warrant is registered in Grand Lodge, Vol. 6, Letter F, June, 1768 - Signed, Edward Harper, Deputy Grand Secretary'*. This refers to the registration of the original Warrant, issued to the London Lodge, and not to the present parchment, which was only issued, as already stated, on 20 June 1810, at the usual fee of two guineas (£2. 10p).

The Atholl Lodges were, almost without exception, known by their Warrant Numbers and not by a distinctive title or name. Loyal Cambrian was known as 'the Lodge at Merthyr Tydfil' and as 'No.144' in Grand Lodge. The name Loyal Cambrian appears for the first time in the Minutes in 1834, but it was not registered at UGLE until 1837.

Loyal Cambrian Lodge was Constituted on 7 August 1810 at the Castle Inn, Merthyr Tydfil. Bro William Williams was nominated to be the first WM but, for some reason did not take up that position. The WM of the Caerphilly Lodge, Bro Benjamin Thomas, was authorised in the absence of the GM or his Deputy, to act as GM for 3 hours, in order to *'Congregate, Install and Constitute the Petitioners'*. He was assisted by William Leyshon, JW, of Caerphilly Lodge; William Richard, JW, of Glamorgan Lodge No.33 (now No.36); and John Williams, the first WM of Caerphilly Lodge. Bro Thomas Richardson, Agent, Penydarren Iron Works was Installed as Primus Master. He had only been registered as a Master Mason in GL on 26 July 1810, just 15 days prior to his Installation as WM. This was only possible under the Ancients' Regulations on the formation of a new Lodge in a district where a suitably qualified Brother could not be found. The previously mentioned William Edwards, Solicitor, and William Williams, were

Invested as SW and JW respectively. Of the visiting Brethren, 3 were from Lodge No.33 (Glamorgan), 7 from No.126 (Caerphilly) and one from No.135 (Newport). Seven Candidates were proposed.

In August 1811 a Lodge of Emergency was held to receive the RWBro Thomas Harper, DepGM. On this occasion '*Mr. Hugh Barker was proposed and seconded, and in consideration of his being a sojourner, was Balloted for and unanimously accepted, and by a Dispensation from the Right Worshipful Brother Harper, was admitted to the Degree of an Entered Apprentice*'. A sojourner was a temporary resident, such as a commercial traveller, and the granting of a Dispensation in Open Lodge for the admission of a sojourner was unique. RWBro Thomas Harper was DepGM of the Ancient or Atholl Grand Lodge from 1801 to 1813 and was a Manufacturing Jeweller in the Strand, London. The old silver Officers' Collar Jewels were supplied by him and they bear his 'TH' mark. These Jewels are now displayed in a case on the wall to the left of the JW's Chair.

At a Meeting in 1812, two French Brethren were present - Bro Francis Julien, Lodge Grand Oriente de France, and Bro Antonie Ellioy, Lodge L'Orient, Rochfort. They were probably Members of the French Prisoners Lodge, 'Les Enfants de Mars et Neptune', Abergavenny.

When, in 1813, the United Grand Lodge of England was formed, the Lodge became No.175 and with 'the closing up' of Lodge numbers in 1832 it became 127. Then, in August 1863, when the last revision took place, the present number, 110, was allotted.

In 1814, the Installation Festival, which had hitherto been held on 24 June, the Festival of St John the Baptist, was transferred to 27 December, the Festival of St John the Evangelist. The reason for the change was that

Thomas Harper Jewels

the Brethren wished to commemorate the Union between Ancient and Modern Masons on that day. This date was regularly observed until 1872, when it was changed to the first Thursday in January, '*the convenience of the Members was considered of more importance than a commemorative Festival*'. In the 1990s, this was changed to the second Saturday in January, apparently for the same reason.

During 1814, Loyal Cambrian recommended the Petition for Philanthropic Lodge No.658, Abergavenny. Seven of the ten Petitioners were from Loyal Cambrian Lodge; the other three were from Hiram Lodge No.195, Pontypool. Philanthropic Lodge can, therefore, be claimed as the first Daughter Lodge of Loyal Cambrian Lodge. The Warrant was granted on 27 December 1814 and the new Lodge Constituted at the King's Head, Abergavenny, on 12 June 1815. The Lodge was Erased from the Register of UGLE on 5 March 1828.

In December 1827, the Lodge moved to the Bush Inn, High Street, Merthyr Tydfil. The reason for the move might have been because Bro Thomas Davies, a Joining Member, from Indefatigable Lodge No.427, Swansea, was the proprietor. This was to be the meeting place of the Lodge until, in 1881, the Lodge moved to the Masonic Hall in Lower High Street, Merthyr.

The Minute Book records that in June 1831: '*The Lodge was not held on this night on account of the disturbed state of the town, occasioned by a tumultuous assembly who paraded the place and committed several outrages*'. These riots, arising from labour disputes, were the third and most serious which have ever occurred. The first riot was in 1800, when the Penydarren

Company's shop in High Street, Merthyr, was ransacked. This disturbance was quelled with the arrival of the Cardiff Volunteer Cavalry. Two of the ringleaders were tried at Cardiff, found guilty and executed. The second riot in 1816 passed off without serious result. The 1831 riot was the most memorable and tragic. It was brought about by the resistance of the workmen to a reduction in their wages, which Richard Crawshay, the great Ironmaster of Cyfarthfa, felt compelled to make on account of the *'depression in trade'*. A strike followed and many shops in Merthyr and Aberdare were ransacked and pillaged. The situation was so serious that the authorities summoned the military from Brecon. On the morning of 2 June, a Company of the 93rd Highlanders arrived and were posted outside the Castle Hotel. A large crowd assembled and, encouraged by the fiery orations of the ringleaders, the mob attacked the soldiers, who, in self defence, opened fire, with the result that 15 were killed and a large number wounded. Several soldiers were also seriously injured. Two of the ring leaders, Richard Lewis, better known as 'Dic Penderyn' and Lewis Lewis 'Lewsyn yr Heliwr'-'Lewis the Huntsman', were afterwards arrested and tried at Cardiff Assizes, found guilty and sentenced to death. Lewis was reprieved and had his sentence commuted to transportation, but Dic Penderyn suffered the most extreme penalty of the law. He was publicly executed at Cardiff goal at 8 o'clock on Saturday, 13 August 1831.

On the death of Sir Christopher Cole, KCB, ProvGM, in 1836, Bro Sir Josiah John Guest of Dowlais was appointed ProvGM, but was not Installed as such until 18 August 1840. Five days earlier, on 13 August 1840, Sir Josiah John Guest

Sir Josiah John Guest's Regalia

had been Installed as Worshipful Master of Loyal Cambrian Lodge. He had only joined the Lodge in the July of 1840! A full account of his background and achievements is contained in a separate profile in this book. In 1899, Lord Llangattock, ProvGM, presented the Lodge with Sir J J Guest's Regalia, mounted in a walnut case. It is now displayed on the wall of the Temple, above the Secretary's desk.

The Festival of St John the Baptist in 1842 is of special interest, because it was the last occasion that Bro Edward Lewis Richards attended before leaving for Flintshire, having been appointed the first County Court Judge for the District. In token of his leaving, he presented the Lodge with the loving cup, which is still highly prized by the Brethren. At Installations it was filled with Madeira wine and passed around for every Brother to drink to the success of the Lodge. For many years, the late Bro David Rees Lewis related the history of the cup before passing it around, and at his own Installation in 1878, he ordered it to be passed around a second time, requesting the Brethren to drink to the memory of the donor. Just before his death, he had the cup *'mounted in silver for its better preservation'* and suitably inscribed at a cost of eight guineas. Bro A I Freedman carried out the work, from a design by Bro James Fraser. Due to the rapid increase in Membership and certain time constraints, this practice was then discontinued but reintroduced some years ago, to the great satisfaction of the Members.

At a Meeting in 1843, there was an innovation for which there is no apparent explanation. After a Third Degree Ceremony, *'a Past Master's Degree' was conferred on 7 Brethren'* after the Lodge had been opened in the Fourth (PMs) Degree. It seems for several years the Degree of a Past Master was often conferred on Brethren, the last entry relating to this practice appears in 1855. It is evident that it was also the practice under Scottish, Irish and American Constitutions to confer the Degree of PM on Candidates as a qualifying Degree for Holy Royal Arch, such as was necessary in English Freemasonry prior to the Union of the two Grand Lodges.

On the resignation of his uncle, Bro Sir John Josiah Guest, Bro Edward John Hutchins became ProvGM. Initiated into Loyal Cambrian Lodge in 1831, he had been Installed as WM the following year and again in 1873. His rapid rise in Freemasonry led to him being made DepProvGM in 1836. Accordingly, he has a separate profile included in this book.

With Membership in decline, the first Initiation for four years took place in 1849, but Mr Frederick Smith, Commercial Traveller, who had been Balloted for successfully nine months previously, had his Election declared *'null and void'*, being then under the age of 21, *'but was on this date accepted and Initiated'*. This was the turning point in the prosperity of the Lodge.

In the autumn of 1849, the ProvGM was invited to hold PGL at Merthyr. A letter from the ProvGSec expressed regret that this would not be possible, owing to the prevalence of cholera, which now gripped the town. This reply did not satisfy the Brethren and the ProvGSec was informed that, in the opinion of the Lodge, the Provincial Meeting might conveniently be called in the month of December. The communication had the desired effect and the Meeting was held on 13 December.

Bro Thomas Jones Dyke was born at Merthyr on 16 September 1816. Apprenticed at the age of 15, to Messrs David Davies & Sons, Surgeons, Cyfarthfa Works, he afterwards attended Granger's School of Anatomy, and Guy's and St Thomas's Hospitals, London, for a period of about 3 years. He qualified as a Surgeon in 1838 and, in January 1839, began to practise in the town. He was Merthyr's first Medical Officer of Health, a post he held for over

Dr Thomas Jones Dyke

fifty years *'with the very greatest ability'*. It was directly due to his able reports on the unhealthiness of towns that the first steps were taken to provide reservoirs, waterworks and drainage for the district. He became High Constable of Caerphilly Higher in 1876. He was Initiated into the Lodge in 1839, becoming WM in 1842, 1847 and 1854 and was also Lodge Secretary on three occasions, for a total of twelve years. When the Warrant to Constitute Loyal Cambrian Lodge's second Daughter Lodge, St David's No.679 at Aberdare, was granted in 1856, Bro Dyke was nominated to be the first WM.

In December 1861, William Thomas Lewis was one of seven Initiated into the Lodge. Bro Lewis was probably one of the most eminent of all the illustrious men who have been Members of Loyal Cambrian Lodge. At just 12 years of age, he was apprenticed in the Plymouth Engineering Shops. At the age of 20 he was appointed Junior Engineer and four years later, resident Engineer and Chief Assistant to the Mineral Agent. He was involved in the construction of Cardiff's East Dock, the Rhymney Railway and in developing the mineral resources of Aberdare and Rhondda Valleys. His rise was so rapid that in less than 20 years he was Managing Director. His invaluable service to the community was recognised when a Knighthood was conferred on him in 1885, and then a Baronetcy in 1886. He served on several Royal Commissions and was High Sheriff and Deputy Lieutenant of Brecknockshire. He was again the recipient of Royal Favour following the opening of the dock at Cardiff in 1907, being decorated by King Edward VIII, with the Badge of 'Knight of the Royal Victorian Order'. He laid the foundation stone of Merthyr General Hospital in 1887, where he had played a large part in its funding and building. Among his gifts to the town are two beautiful stained glass memorial windows in St David's Church. He was again recognised by King

William Thomas Lewis
Lord Merthyr

George V in 1911 by his elevation to the peerage. In recognition of his many services and gifts to the town, his statue in bronze was unveiled in the grounds of Merthyr Tydfil General Hospital in 1900. At the closure of that hospital, the statue was transferred to a site inside the gateway of St Tydfil's Hospital. Another bronze statue of him was placed, by public subscription, at the entrance to Aberdare Park in 1912.

A Petition for a new Lodge at Treharris, to be known as Fforest Lodge No.2606, was presented in July 1896 and it was unanimously supported. The Lodge was Consecrated on 28 October when Bro George Frederick Harris, PM, Loyal Cambrian Lodge, was Installed as its Primus Master, the Founder Members all being Brethren of Loyal Cambrian Lodge. Initiated in September 1879, and Installed as WM in 1887, Bro Harris was a reputable artist, having exhibited at the Royal Academy. Several PMs' portraits which once adorned the Lodge banqueting hall were from his brush. He attained the office of PPGSW and was the grandfather of the renowned Artist and Television Presenter, Rolf Harris. Further details are to be found later in the history of Fforest Lodge.

Colonel David Rees Lewis

Merlin Lodge No.1578, Pontypridd, was Warranted on 23 October 1875. The Sponsoring Lodges, named in order on the Petition are Bute Lodge No.960, Glamorgan Lodge No.36, St David's Lodge No.679 and Loyal Cambrian Lodge. Bute Lodge, being first named and providing two of the 12 Petitioners, is the Mother Lodge. None of the Petitioners were from Loyal Cambrian Lodge.

Bro David Rees Lewis, Solicitor, Initiated in 1872, was another influential Lodge Member, and his Installation in 1878 proved to be another turning point in the prosperity of the Lodge. He applied himself to the task of reviving interest in Freemasonry, carefully instructing the Brethren in all the Workings. During that year, he Initiated nine candidates and was again WM in 1890 when he Initiated 17 Candidates. When Prince Llewellyn Lodge was Constituted in Cardiff in 1896, Bro Lewis was its first WM. He was also a Founder Member of Fforest Lodge and, in 1906, was Master of that Lodge. David Rees Lewis Chapter No.110, Merthyr, is named after him and he was its Founder First Principal.

In 1878, WBro David Rees Lewis, WM, Initiated Col John James Jones, his partner in the legal practice of 'Lewis and Jones'. Bro J J Jones was to become as influential as WBro D R Lewis, both in Freemasonry and public life. He became a JP in 1898 and Deputy Lieutenant of the County of Brecknockshire in 1914. He was Installed as WM of the Lodge in 1886 by WBro D R Lewis.

WBro David Rees Lewis was also foremost in planning a new Masonic Hall and club, which was agreed upon in 1880 and also in forming a Joint Stock Company for that purpose. A site was procured at Lower High Street and, at a Special Meeting of PGL, on 6 September 1881, the Foundation Stone was laid. The DepProvGM, WBro Marmaduke Tennant (due to the ill health of the ProvGM), with his team were escorted by the Brethren and proceeded in procession through the town to the site of the new Masonic Hall, (now the Merthyr Tydfil Conservative Club) where the Corner Stone was laid. The first meeting of the Lodge took place in the new premises on 4 May 1882. The new premises were let to the Brethren at £40 per annum, but it was soon found that while the Lodge Room provided ample accommodation, the ante-rooms were too small to meet the requirements of the increased Membership.

In 1892, WBro E B Nash, WM, urged on the Brethren the necessity of taking steps to provide suitable Lodge premises. Several schemes were proposed over the next 17 years, but it was not until the autumn of 1909 that the present site in Pontmorlais was secured. The annual Meeting of the Provincial Grand Lodge was held at Merthyr on Thursday, 22 September 1910, for transacting the business of PGL, and for the purposes of laying the Foundation Stone of the New Temple and taking part in the Centenary Celebrations of Loyal Cambrian Lodge. The Drill Hall was hired for the occasion, the old Lodge premises being too small to

Laying the Foundation Stone of the first Masonic Hall on 6 September 1881

accommodate the large assemblage of Brethren. The Lodge Meetings were held in the lesser hall, the large hall being reserved for the banquet. WBro George Whittington, ProvGSec, read the inscription on the Stone as follows: *'1810 - 1910. This stone was laid on the 22nd September, 1910, by Wor. Bro. Marmaduke Tennant, Deputy Prov. Grand Master, Eastern Division, South Wales, and Past Grand A.D.C. of England. To commemorate the Centenary of the Loyal Cambrian Lodge of Freemasons, No. 110.'*

The new Temple was Dedicated on 4 January 1912, with the Ceremony again being performed by WBro Marmaduke Tennant, the ProvGM being too unwell to attend. Boisterous weather conditions prevented any outside proceedings. The WM presented the DepProvGM with a golden key, inviting him to declare the building open. The Brethren followed in procession up to the main corridor, where the Lodge key was used by Bro Col John James Jones to open the Lodge Room.

Bro David Alfred Thomas became MP for Merthyr Tydfil in 1888, only a year after being Initiated into the Lodge. He went on to become a Government Minister under Lloyd George, and later was ennobled as Viscount Rhondda. He presented the Lodge with the large handsome oak WM's Chair, carved in the Ionic order, with fluted columns, and having a shield carved with the Masonic and Welsh emblems. The Chair was designed by Bro George Frederick Harris. A similar Chair was also presented to St David's Lodge, Aberdare. In May 1917, WBro the Lord Rhondda was appointed to the distinguished Office of SW in UGLE. Sadly, he died at the age of 62, the following year, on 3 July 1918. The Dowager Viscountess Rhondda was received in September 1919, when the WM presented her with a Past Senior Grand Warden's Jewel. She confided that it was something he had looked forward to receiving with great pride and, in return, presented the Lodge with a portrait of her late husband in full Masonic Regalia. A profile of Viscount Rhonda is included separately in this book.

Another presentation was made in 1906 by WBro David Rees Lewis, PM, on behalf of his sisters. It was a magnificent silk Banner, of their own design and handiwork and denoting the Martyrdom of St

Tydfil, with the words *'Mae Yma Goleuni'*, which means *'Here is Light'*. A year later, at the Installation Ceremony of Bro James Fraser on 3 January 1907, WBro Thomas Nibloe, IPM, presented the Lodge with two magnificent Wardens' Chairs, which were specially designed and made from fumed oak by Messrs Kenning & Sons, London. The SW's Chair is of the Doric order, with plain columns, and the JW's Chair is of the Corinthian order, with fluted and reeded columns. The engraved silver plates for the Chairs were presented by WBro A I Freedman (WM 1908).

David Alfred Thomas
Viscount Rhondda

Those Brethren who were then serving their King and Country, especially those who were on active service in the Dardanelles, were referred to in 1915, with a strong expression of hope that they may return home safe and sound. A Notice of Motion *'That a Roll of Honour be prepared of the Members of the Loyal Cambrian Lodge now on active service'* was duly passed and it is now mounted in the Lodge Room. Under the careful eye of WBro Ernest Thomas Gwyther Barnes, it is customary for the Brethren to place a poppy spray beneath the board and also to lay a wreath at the Cenotaph on Armistice Sunday. WBro Gwyther has been a member of the local branch of the Royal British Legion for over 20 years and was Chairman of their Poppy Appeal in 2007 and 2008. In raising the substantial sum of £19,000 in both years, the branch achieved the highest per capita collection in the UK with considerable help from the very willing Freemasons of Merthyr, several of whom are also members and who even lent a hand in coin counting.

WBro James Fraser, author of 'The Illustrated History of the Loyal Cambrian Lodge No.110', covering the period from 1810 to 1914, published his book in 1916. He dedicated the book to the Centenary Master, WBro John James Jones, and presented him with a copy. WBro James Fraser also presented a cheque from the proceeds of the sale of the book to the Lodge Treasurer.

A Petition for another Daughter Lodge, North Glamorgan Lodge No.4055, was granted on 14 January 1920. Then, just two years later, WBro John Morgan, PPrSGW, was heartily congratulated on being Elected WM of Hendre Lodge No.3250. Likewise, in 1924, WBro J Richards, Chaplain, was congratulated on his appointment as Rural Dean and Bro J Griffiths Evans, ADC, on being appointed Headmaster of Queen's Road School, Merthyr Tydfil. At the very next Meeting Bro Henry Seymour Berry was congratulated upon his appointment as High Sheriff of Brecon, and WBro D W Evans on being Invested as Grand Senior Deacon in UGLE. In the same year WBro James Fraser donated a canopy for the Master's Chair, and WBro F A Phillips was elected Mayor for the County Borough of Merthyr Tydfil. In addition, Bro Rev J Richards Pugh, BA, Chaplain, was preferred into a Canonry of the Cathedral Church of Llandaff.

The Master's Chair
Presented by Viscount Rhondda

Bro John Mathias Berry, JP, Initiated into the Lodge in September 1889, was well known for his contribution to the community by way of his active involvement in issues of Local Government. However, it was his three sons who became more noteworthy. His eldest, Henry Seymour Berry (born 1877), began working life as a teacher, but after a short time, became a partner in his father's Estate Agency. He went on to estate management for D A Thomas (Lord Rhondda) and, in but a few years, became a Director of no fewer than 66 companies. His Masonic career began in 1918, when he was Initiated into Loyal Cambrian Lodge. He was created First Baron Buckland of Bwlch in 1927 after becoming Chairman of Guest, Keen and Nettlefolds. Sadly, he died in 1928, age 50, after a fall from a horse. The second son, William Ewart Berry (born 1879), followed a journalist's path, from reporting for his local newspaper, the 'Merthyr Tydfil Times' to Fleet Street, where he started a new periodical, 'Advertising World'. He invited his younger brother, James Gomer Berry (born 1883), to join him in a partnership which lasted 35 years. Together, they first acquired the 'The Sunday Times' in 1915 and then founded Allied Newspapers (later Kemsley Newspapers) in 1924, which gave birth to the 'Daily Telegraph'. They also acquired St Clement's Press, the 'Financial Times', the 'Western Mail', 'South Wales Echo' and other national and local newspapers. William Ewart Berry became the first Viscount Camrose in 1929. James Gomer Berry became Viscount Kemsley of Dropmore in 1938.

In the early 1930s, WBro W W Jones, PPSGW, achieved 60 years in Freemasonry and was made an Honorary Member, and WBro T A Goodwin, IPM, was appointed Chief Constable of Merthyr Tydfil.

In 1938, Bro Val Baker presented an inscribed Inner Guard's Sword and a Tyler's Sword to the Lodge. In 1940, RWBro R P St John Charles, ProvGM, and WBro Edgar J Rutter, DepProvGM, were present when the former presented Bro W H Jones with a carbon portrait of himself and an inscribed silver goblet, in celebration of his 87th birthday and fifty years service as Tyler of the Lodge.

Sadly, in March 1941, the homes of both WBro J Stuart Gray and Bro Harvey Owen were damaged during heavy bombing raids in Cardiff, although there is no record of any injuries being sustained by their families. In September, an organ was presented by Bro George William Webley and six months afterwards, WBro W J Canton was Invested as PGReg in UGLE.

RWBro R P St John Charles, ProvGM, was admitted in September 1945 after the business had been concluded. He accepted the Gavel and Provincial Officers took up their Offices. Mr Onward Ernest Honey was admitted and duly Initiated, after which the ProvGM Invested the Candidate with the Distinguishing Badge of an Entered Apprentice. The DepProvGM delivered the Charity Charge and also the Ancient Charge of the First Degree. To this day, there has been no explanation as to why the Ceremony was carried out by the ProvGM.

Bro Thomas Stanley Thomas, a Master Baker of Lodge St Margaret's Hope No.1184, Rosyth, Scottish Constitution, was welcomed as a Joining Member in 1946. A former PE Instructor, he became a Businessman of some repute, the founder of Thomas' (later Peter's) Pies. In 1960, he was elected Barker of the Variety Club of Great Britain, was awarded the MBE in 1984 and was made a Freeman of the Borough in 1992. He became a member of the Order of St John of Jerusalem in 1996.

In 1951, the Lodge was requested to Pass and Raise Bro John Edward Cameron Machen, EA of Old Masonians Lodge No.2700, London. Subsequently, Bro John became a valued Member of the Lodge.

WBro James Fraser was presented with a portrait of himself in 1952, in recognition of his many services to the Lodge. Initiated in 1895, Installed as WM in 1907, he was Chairman of the Committee set up to build the new Temple, of which he was the principal architect.

Bro E Jones, Rector of Penderyn was appointed Canon Residential of Brecon Cathedral in April 1954. In June 1955, WBro James Fraser occupied the Chair of King Solomon to mark his 60th Anniversary in Freemasonry, when Bro Ernest Thomas Gwyther Barnes and Bro Austen George Watkeys were Passed to the Second Degree.

In May 1956, WBro Reginald Freedman, District and County Registrar, was congratulated on being appointed Deputy Lieutenant of Glamorgan. At the same Meeting, Mr Norman Lloyd-Edwards, the son of Lodge Member Evan Stanley Edwards, Dentist, was Initiated.

James Fraser

He became ProvGM of South Wales in 2008 and has a separate profile in this book.

The 150th Anniversary Celebration of the Lodge was in June 1960, when WBro W J Canton took the Gavel to conduct the Ceremony. He explained that WBro James Fraser had intended to take the Chair but due to his declining health, was only able to act as IPM. However, the occasion marked his 65th Anniversary in Freemasonry. Nine PMs were called upon to occupy the various Offices and the Ceremony was carried out in a manner in keeping with this great occasion. It was followed by the presentation of a PMs Commemoration Board by Bro Ron Baker.

In January 1961, the Heavy Setting Maul was presented to the Lodge which had been used by WBro Marmaduke Tennant, DepProvGM, 1877-1915, in laying the Foundation Stone of the Merthyr Temple. WBro H Clive Bevan presented the Lodge with a set of Third Degree Working Tools in 1962, mentioning that the Tools had belonged to his father. In 1963, WBro Clive presented an Organ to the Lodge, saying he hoped that it would be an appropriate Memorial to WBro James Fraser, who had recently passed away. He explained that its purchase had only been possible through the Brethren's generosity to his Memorial Fund.

A Petition for another Daughter Lodge in Merthyr was signed in Open Lodge on 2 April 1964. The Warrant for Aelwyd Lodge No.7982 was granted on 29 April and the Lodge was Consecrated on 2 June 1964. Past Master, WBro Col Reginald Freedman, PPGSwdB, was the Primus Master. He was duly honoured in Grand Lodge in 1965.

The disaster at Aberfan was referred to in November 1966, particularly the loss suffered by Bro Norman Jennings, by the death of his sister. Six Brethren of Daughter Lodge, Fforest Lodge, had lost children in the disaster. No Festive Board was held on that occasion.

The Petitioners for a proposed new Lodge, led by WBro Gerald Williams, were received in June 1973. Once again the Petition received unanimous support and, subsequently, WBro Gerald became the Founder Master of Luminary Lodge No.8530, Consecrated on 13 November 1973.

WBro Kenneth Adams Morgan, PGStdB, AProvGM, became an Honorary Member in November 1981. In 1982, WBro Stephen Archibald Bates presented a Victorian Heavy Setting Maul to the Lodge as a mark of thanks for the way in which he had been received as a Joining Member. The gift was in memory of his late father, Bro Archibald Alfred Bates, of Tyndall Lodge No.1363, Downend, Gloucestershire, and his uncle, WBro Richard Bertram Bates, PPGW, of Caradoc Lodge No.1573, Swansea.

The Lodge Banner restoration was completed in June 1984 and a sum equivalent to the cost was donated to the Royal Masonic Hospital, linked with the name and memory of WBro Baden Longmore. This was at the specific request of the wives of WBros W Thomas J Jones and Ken Harris, who had spent much time in returning the Banner to its former glory. It was subsequently agreed that its rededication would be on the Lodge's 175th Anniversary Celebration, held in May 1985. VWBro Geoffrey M Ashe, TD, PGSwdB, DepProvGM, was the Dedicating Officer and his team included WBro W H Walsh, SW; WBro Richard W Dicker, JW; WBro Ken Adams Morgan, Chap; and WBro Cdr Roy K Hopkin, DC. WBro Brian Clifford, WM, had the honour of carrying the Banner and, with the assembled escort, processing it around the Temple and placing it at the right of the WM's Chair. The DepProvGM accepted the Banner and talked on the history of Banners through the ages. The Banner was then Dedicated, followed by most appropriate thoughts and words from WBro Ken Adams Morgan. A 160 year old edition of the John Brown Bible, of Scottish origin, was afterwards presented to the Lodge by WBro Gordon Cooper.

In June 1990, WBro H Clive Bevan was asked to deliver a short Eulogy after the death of WBro H Lingard Collins, PPSGW, who had almost completed 50 years in the Craft. He was a Member of many Lodges and his services to Freemasonry in general and to Loyal Cambrian in particular were incalculable. He had a deep love of Freemasonry, often speaking his mind, but all for the good. WBro Clive achieved fifty years in Freemasonry in 1996 and, as a token of the Lodge's high esteem for its Senior PM, he was presented with two Stuart crystal vases.

VWBro Peter Frost, DepProvGM, visited the Lodge especially to present Masonic Veterans' Certificates to WBro H Clive Bevan, PPSGW, and WBro Derek Budden, PPGSwdB, in February 2004. The 50th Anniversary of WBro Ernest Thomas Gwyther

Barnes's Initiation was later celebrated in October 2004, when he was also presented with a ProvGM's Certificate.

After the sad loss of Bro Derek Budden in January 2005, WBro H Clive Bevan recounted his career, firstly in the RAF, where he distinguished himself as a Lancaster Bomber Pilot and afterwards in the Midland Bank. WBro Stephen Archibald Bates was presented with his Veteran's Certificate in June 2005.

A most memorable occasion for the Lodge occurred in May 2005, when RWBro Hywel Davies, ProvGM, accompanied by RWBro Captain Norman Lloyd-Edwards, Chairman of the New Masonic Samaritan Fund, and by the Deputy and the AProvGMs joined the Brethren. After due formalities, Captain Norman Lloyd-Edwards gave a delightful and entertaining talk on his role as Lord Lieutenant of South Glamorgan. Afterwards, the ProvGM said that it was his very pleasant duty to present a certificate to RWBro Captain Norman Lloyd-Edwards to mark his 50 years as a Freemason.

In November 2006, RWBro Captain Sir Norman Lloyd-Edwards was warmly welcomed as a Re-joining Member of Loyal Cambrian Lodge. In 2008, he became ProvGM of the Province and a separate profile of him is included in this history book. His Re-joining had a revitalising effect on the Lodge. Whereas its fortunes had been merely of a mundane nature, other Joining Members, Candidates and visitors all abounded and, after he was invited to become the Bicentenary Master, the effect was more emphasised. Attendances reached record levels and the Lodge's Celebrations on reaching its 200th year were hugely successful. Double Ceremonies have since become the norm and the practice of First and Second Degree Ceremonies on the same evening has returned.

The Lodge's Bicentenary was celebrated on Wednesday, 22 September 2010, exactly 100 years to the day after the Lodge's Centenary Celebration, held on Thursday, 22 September 1910. The Meeting was held at the Rhydycar Leisure Centre, Merthyr Tydfil. Among the distinguished guests were MWBro Peter G Lowndes, Pro Grand Master, VWBro C Nigel R Brown, Grand Secretary and VWBro Thomas J Caplin, Deputy Grand Director of Ceremonies.

Compiled by WBro Richard Drake-Fyler, PPrJGD.

Centenary Procession Passing the Castle Hotel, where the Lodge was formed in 1810

78

Benjamin Hall, MP
1778 - 1817

Provincial Grand Master of South Wales
1814 - 1817

Benjamin Hall, the elder son of Rev Benjamin Hall, DD, Chancellor of Llandaff, 1796-1825, was born on 29 September 1778. He was educated at Westminster School, London, and Christ Church, Oxford, obtaining his BA in 1798 and MA in 1801. He joined Lincoln's Inn and was called to the Bar in 1801. In the same year, on 16 December, he married Charlotte, the younger daughter of Richard Crawshay of Cyfartha, who brought him a dowry of £40,000! His father-in-law made him a partner in the Rhymney Iron Works, which he purchased in 1803, and Benjamin, now a Barrister, carried out most of the legal transactions. Richard Crawshay also presented him with the Abercarn estate in 1808, and made him residuary legatee and executor of his will. Crawshay died in 1810, and by his will, thanks to the supposed incapacity for business of his brother-in-law, William Crawshay, Benjamin received three-eighths share in the Rhymney works, with the Union works, covering 1,112 acres of mines, quarries, houses and land. In 1816, however, he sold out to William Crawshay for £90,000. The previous year, he had acquired Hensol Castle for £45,500, which was reported in 'The Cambrian', (a weekly newspaper published in Swansea) on Saturday, 7 January 1815:

'We are glad to hear that Benjamin Hall, Esq. (the Representative of this county) has purchased the Hensol House Estate, formerly the magnificent seat and favourite residence of the last William Earl Talbot, who it is said, expended £60,000 in improving and beautifying this much-admired place.'

Benjamin Hall was MP for Totnes, 1806-1812, and Westbury, 1812-1814. He was elected member for Glamorgan on 28 November 1814, and remained as such until his early death in 1817. His predecessor as MP for Glamorgan was Thomas Wyndham of Dunraven Castle, Southerndown, who also preceded him as Provincial Grand Master of South Wales. Benjamin Hall's importance in the history of Wales lies in the fact that he was the first great industrialist to enter the political field in Wales, in opposition to the interests of the landed gentry.

His Masonic career began at exactly the same time as his appointment as MP for Glamorgan. The Articles of Union between the Modern or Premier Grand Lodge and the Antient or Atholl Grand Lodge had been signed at Kensington Palace, on 25 November 1813. The celebration of the reunion of the Ancient Freemasons of England took place, with great solemnity, at Freemasons' Hall on St John's Day (St John Evangelist), 27 December 1813. Glamorgan Lodge (Atholl Lodge No.33) Minutes

Benjamin Hall

for 6 January 1814 record: *'The resolutions of the Especial Grand Lodge of free and accepted Masons of England of the 8th November last were read and highly approved of. The articles of Union between the two Grand Lodges of England were also read and approved of Unanimously.'*

On 8 February 1814, Glamorgan Lodge met for the first time as Lodge No.50 under the United Grand Lodge of England, and it was during this first year in the history of the United Grand Lodge of England that Benjamin Hall was appointed ProvGM, following the death of Thomas Wyndham on 8 November 1814. It would seem that at the time of his appointment he was hardly a Freemason! The Minutes of a Lodge of Emergency of Indefatigable Lodge, (then No.427), Swansea, held on 8 December 1814 record:

'Bro. D. Long proposed Benjn Hall, of Abercarn, in the County of Monmouth, Esq., M.P. for the County of Glamorgan, to become a Mason if found worthy. Duly seconded, Balloted for and approved, and initiated and passed the same evening, and a proposal was approved that he shd be raised on the 10th inst.'

This was done and, Bro Hall, in accordance with the custom of the Lodge, paid the tavern bill for the Lodge of Emergency, which amounted to £7 12s 0d (£7.60p). On 16 December (six days after his Raising), the Lodge met again and it was Minuted that Bro B Hall, already Provincial Grand Master, became a Member of Indefatigable Lodge.

It appears that the manner in which he applied himself to the concerns of the Province did not meet with the approval of the Brethren of Indefatigable Lodge, for appended to their Minutes of St John's Day, (St John Baptist) 24 June 1817, there is the record:

'At a numerous and respectable Meeting of the members of this Lodge it was resolved unanimously that the Rt W. Provincial G.M. has neglected his duties as a P.G.M., and this Lodge in particular, and that a copy of this resolution be sent him forthwith by this Lodge accordingly. By order of the W.M., Officers and Brethren of the Lodge. Geo. Hazell, Secty Pro Temp.'

Whether or not Benjamin Hall received the resolution is not known, for on 31 July 1817 he died, his death being reported in 'The Cambrian' of Saturday 9 August:

'We record with extreme regret the death of our justly respected County Member, Benjamin Hall, Esq. Hensol Castle; the fatal event which has deprived Glamorganshire of his valuable service, took place at his home in London yesterday se'n-night; and has excited the most poignant grief in the breasts of his amiable family and all his numerous friends.'

The following Saturday, 16 August, 'The Cambrian' referred to his funeral:

'The remains of our much-regretted Member B. Hall, Esq. were interred on Wednesday at Llandaff, attended by nearly all the gentlemen residing within a circuit of 20 miles, and a great concourse of other persons, whose unaffected expressions of sorrow for his loss, afforded the best tribute of his worth.'

Subsequently, a memorial was erected at Llandaff Cathedral, which was in the form of a classical marble bier on a large pedestal and bearing the following inscription:

'In a vault near this place are deposited the remains of Benjamin Hall Esqr of Hensol Castle, Member of Parliament for the County, who died xxxj July MDCCCxvij aged xxxix. To record the high sense they entertained of his industry talents and integrity and as a tribute due to the man whose life was sacrificed to the zealous discharge of his public duties this monument was erected by a considerable body of the nobility, clergy, gentry and freeholders of the County of Glamorgan.'

Sadly, the monument was destroyed during the air-raid on Cardiff on the evening of 2 January 1941, when a bomb exploded alongside the Cathedral, causing considerable damage.

Benjamin Hall was succeeded by Sir Christopher Cole, not only as Provincial Grand Master of South Wales, but also as MP for

Glamorgan, just as Benjamin Hall had succeeded Thomas Wyndham.

On 8 November 1802, Benjamin Hall's son, also named Benjamin, was born. He too became an MP, initially for the Monmouth Boroughs, 1831-1837, and subsequently Marylebone. He was created baronet in 1838 and in July 1855 became Commissioner for Works. The great clock tower of the Houses of Parliament, which was erected during his period of office, was on that account called 'Big Ben'. He was raised to the peerage on 29 June 1859, taking the title of 'Baron Llanover of Llanover and Abercarn'. His importance in the history of Wales is entirely overshadowed by his wife, Augusta Waddington, Lady Llanover. Her many involvements in Welsh life included the endowment of two Calvinistic Methodist churches, Capel Rhyd-y-meirch and Abercarn, where services were to be conducted in Welsh (but with a liturgy based on the Book of Common Prayer). She was patron of the Welsh Manuscripts Society and of Llandovery College. She acquired the manuscripts of Edward Williams (Iolo Morganwg), which her grandson, Sir Ivor Caradoc Herbert, Baron Treowen (1917) presented to the National Library of Wales, Aberystwyth. Lady Llanover survived her husband by over twenty-eight years and died on 17 January 1896.

References: 'History of Parliament, The House of Commons', 1754 - 1790, Volume II – Members, Secker & Warburg for HMSO, 1986; 'The Dictionary of Welsh Biography down to 1940', Published under the Auspices of the Honourable Society of Cymmrodorion, London, 1959; 'History of the Indefatigable Lodge No.237', William Henry Jones, Spurrell, Carmarthen, 1923; 'Cardiff Records - Monuments in Llandaff Cathedral', Cardiff Central Library.

WBro Peter M Davies, ProvJGW.

Sir Christopher Cole, KCB, MP
1770 - 1836

Provincial Grand Master of South Wales
1817 - 1836

Christopher Cole, the youngest of six sons of Humphrey Cole, gentleman, of Marazion, Cornwall, was born on 10 June 1770. He entered the navy in 1780, before he was quite ten years old, on board the 'Royal Oak', 74, of which his second brother was chaplain. Cole had a distinguished naval career, Midshipman RN 1780; Lieutenant 1793; Commander 1800; Captain 1802. He commanded the yacht 'Royal Sovereign' in 1828, finally becoming Colonel of Marines in 1830, an office he held until his death. He was described as *'pleasant, with unaffected and naval manners'*. He served with distinction in every theatre of the war against France, but particularity in the Far East; his conquest of the Banda Isles from the Dutch in August 1810 was praised in Parliament by Prime Minister Perceval as *'an exploit to be classed with the boldest darings in the days of chivalry'*. He gave up active service in 1814.

On 29 May 1812, the honour of Knighthood was conferred upon him, and in the same year he was awarded an honorary degree of DCL from the University of Oxford. At the extension of the Order of the Bath on 2 January 1815, he became a Knight Commander.

Sir Christopher married on 28 April 1815, his 'old flame', Lady Mary Lucy Fox Strangways, daughter of Henry Thomas, 2nd Earl of Ilchester. She was the widow of Thomas Mansel Talbot (died 1813) of Margam and Penrice, Glamorganshire. The estate was in trust for its young heir, Christopher Talbot, and this was the direct cause of Cole's entry into Parliament. On the death of the county Member, and Provincial Grand Master of South Wales, Benjamin Hall, in 1817, there was no obvious contender to succeed him, and the leading interests, frightened by the appearance of the opportunist John Edwards, appealed to Cole to save the day for respectability. John Edwards was an Attorney, and in 1800 he had purchased the Rheola Estate, Neath, which had been part of the Gnoll Estate. Sir Christopher Cole, 'The conqueror of Banda', as he was styled, obliged and was returned unopposed. At this first election he had said *'I am not rich, but I am rich enough to be independent; and it is my chief pride, that whatever I do posses has never cost a poor man a tear, nor my country a farthing'*. At the ensuing election, however, his supporters were divided and, rather than fight the wealthy Edwards, he withdrew. His friends raised a fund to enable him to fight Edwards in 1820, and after a severe contest was successful. He was re-elected, without opposition in 1826, but his parliamentary career was not particularly distinguished and he did not speak in the House before 1820.

Sir Christopher Cole

He was described as *'a big man with a generous character to match'*. He could inspire affection in a wide range of people, from his ship's crew to his young step-family. His muddled and anecdotal debating manner in the House contrasted with a bluff style in his private correspondence. His great interest was in naval matters, and whenever these came up in the House, Cole could be depended upon to speak. He was humane in an age when this was rare in a seaman, and he voted for the abolition of flogging in the armed forces. In 1830, he withdrew from Parliament to make way for his stepson, Christopher Talbot, as his critics had always predicted he would.

Sir Christopher's involvement in Freemasonry began in 1817, when he was Initiated in Indefatigable Lodge (then No.427), Swansea. The History of the Lodge records the following:

'On the 23rd October, 1817 (Bro. C. Hancorne, still W.M.) Sir Christopher Cole, K.C.B was proposed by the W.M., seconded by Bro. D. Long, to be made a Mason, was Balloted for, and being unanimously approved, came forward properly prepared and initiated into the first Degree. 'Owing to an urgent circumstance', he was passed to the second Degree, and the Tracing-board was explained in the two Degrees. Then because of 'the particular urgency of the circumstances', he was forthwith also raised to the sublime Degree of a Master Mason, and the Tracing-board of the Degree explained to him.'

'The exact date of his appointment as ProvGM is not clear. The 'Freemasons' Quarterly Review', 1836, page 339, states *'By the calendar of 1817, it appears he was then appointed Provincial Grand Master of South Wales'* and in the Minutes of Indefatigable Lodge for 1817 we have:

'At a Lodge on St John's Day, held on the 29th December, Bro. Sir Christopher Cole, now Prov. G.M., occupied the Chair.' A rebuke, however, from Indefatigable Lodge awaited the Provincial Grand Master, for on 12 September 1820: *'Bror. Gwynne proposed that a letter be written to the P.G.M. referring him to that part of the Constitution, which requires that a Provl Lodge be held once in each year. Seconded by Bro. Morris.'*

A Provincial Grand Lodge was held the following year, when Sir Christopher Cole was Installed as ProvGM. The intention of holding the Lodge was advertised in 'The Cambrian' on Saturday, 23 June 1821:

'Great preparations are making to render the Masonic Festival advertised for the 5th of next month, the grandest spectacle of the kind ever witnessed here, and a very numerous attendance of the Brethren is confidently expected. The jewels, banners, dresses &c., we understand, will be of the most superb description and the procession to and from our Public Rooms, and to Church, will be correspondingly brilliant. After opening the Lodge in the morning, Sir C. Cole, M.P. for Glamorganshire, will be installed Provincial Grand Master for South Wales, by C.K.K. Tynte, Esq., P.G.M. for Somersetshire. The Craft will then attend Divine Service, and afterwards dine together. The Bath Harmonic Society will contribute their able vocal exertions on the occasion, and the excellent band of the Royal Glamorgan Militia is engaged. We hear that the evening will conclude with a splendid display of fire-works.'

On St John's Day in December 1832, a letter from Sir C Cole was read out in Indefatigable Lodge, announcing his intention of resigning as ProvGM. This, however, was not carried out, and Cole continued as ProvGM. He again announced his intention of resigning in 1836, and resigned as a Subscribing Member of Indefatigable Lodge in the July, probably on account of his impending retirement. The Lodge prevailed on him to rescind his resignation, and on 9 August a letter was read in Open Lodge, announcing Cole's intention of resuming office as ProvGM. Unfortunately, shortly afterwards, he died on 24 August 1836. His funeral was reported in 'The Cambrian' of 3 September 1836:

Funeral of Sir Christopher Cole, K.C.B. – The remains of this much lamented gentleman arrived at Swansea from Lanelay, on Wednesday evening last; and as a mark of sincere respect towards the deceased, all the shops in the lines of streets through which the procession had to pass, were completely closed. The body remained at the Mackworth-Arms during the night, and about seven o'clock on the following morning was conveyed to Penrice Church, where the burial took place in a spot selected by the deceased when living, amid that deep and heart-felt regret which ever accompanied the last solemn rites paid to departed worth. The funeral was private but imposing, and consisted of:

Four Mutes,
A Board of Plumes,
Two – Assistant mutes, with wands,
Undertaker.
The Hearse, drawn by Six Horses
Followed by Ten Under – Bearers, carrying Truncheons.
Three Mourning Coaches, drawn by Four Horses,
Containing the Gentlemen Members of the Family

Sir Christopher Cole's Masonic Insignia was presented to Glamorgan Lodge (then No.43) in 1855, by the antiquary, the Reverend John Montgomery Traherne, FRS, FSA, an executor of the will and a Member of Glamorgan Lodge. Traherne had married, on 23 April 1830, Charlotte Louisa, the third daughter of Thomas Mansel Talbot, Cole's stepdaughter. The Insignia consists of an Apron, Collar and Gauntlets plus two Jewels:

(i)   Provincial Grand Master's Collar Jewel by Thomas Harper, (gold), London 1816;

(ii) Gold Jewel by Thomas Harper, Fleet Street, London,
      Front inscription: 'Si talia jungere possis sit tibi scire satis' AL 5821 AD 1821;
      Back inscription: ' Deo rege fratrieu honor fidelitas benevolentia'.

For many years the insignia was displayed in Glamorgan Lodge's Masonic Hall, at No. 4 Church Street, Cardiff. On 15 June 1972, the late WBro Morlais Summers, PM Glamorgan Lodge No.36, placed it on loan in the Grand Lodge Museum, Freemasons' Hall, London.

References: 'History of Parliament. The House of Commons', Volume III - Members A -F. by R. G. Thorne, published by Secker & Warburg, 1986; 'History of the Indefatigable Lodge, No. 237', William Henry Jones, Spurrell, Carmarthen 1923; 'Glamorgan Members During The Reform Bill Period', Enid Ball, 'Morgannwg', Vol. X, 1966.

WBro Peter M Davies, ProvJGW.

Cambrian Lodge No.364

Warranted : 31 January 1821

Consecrated : 24 June 1823

Meeting at the Masonic Temple, Neath.

The Constitution of Knoll Lodge No.506, on 20 September 1777, is the first record of Freemasonry in Neath. The Lodge number was changed to 333 in 1792, at about which time the Lodge lapsed, probably in consequence of the death of Sir Herbert Mackworth in October 1791. The Lodge was transferred in 1800 to Swansea, where it became known as 'Indefatigable Lodge No.333'. The history of the old Knoll Lodge, Neath, and Indefatigable Lodge, Swansea, appears earlier in this book. After Knoll Lodge lapsed, there appears to be nothing of Masonic interest in Neath until 1820, when the Foundation Stone of the Town Hall was laid on 31 May, with full Masonic Ceremony by the Brethren of Indefatigable Lodge and Beaufort Lodge No.443 of Swansea, assisted by the Royal Arch Masons and Knights Templar of Swansea. This event, carried out in public in full Masonic Regalia, stimulated Masonic interest to such an extent that, five months later, a Petition is recorded in Indefatigable Lodge Minutes, *'approved and signed at Lodge for a Lodge at Neath to be called the Cambrian Lodge'*. The Petition, still filed at Grand Lodge, was recommended by Sir Christopher Cole, ProvGM for South Wales, and endorsed *'Granted'* with date D27, 1820, and signature of Augustus Frederick, Duke of Sussex, GM. On the outside is a note as follows: *'Dispensation, dated 31st January 1821, sent 2/2'* (presumably 2 February 1821). The Warrant is thus dated 31 January 1821. The Principal Officers named on the Warrant are: Rowland Pritchard, WM; Samuel Phillips Cohen, SW; and John Webb, JW. Rowland Pritchard was WM, 1821, 1822, 1824, 1825 and 1827. Samuel P Cohen became WM in 1823. On 25 January 1821, a meeting was held at the White Hart Inn to arrange for the opening of a Lodge in Neath. At that meeting, it was resolved: *'that the Brethren present do return their thanks to Brother Rees Jeffries for his willingness in giving up the furniture and jewels, the property of the late Gnoll Lodge.'* Rees Jeffreys was Secretary of Gnoll Lodge in 1788, and strongly objected to the transfer of Gnoll Lodge to Swansea in 1800.

The first Regular Lodge Meeting was held on 1 February 1821, at the White Hart Inn, Cattle Street, Neath, and the Minutes are still in existence. It is interesting to note that there is no mention of an Installation until the following December. The first Lodge was held the day following the date on the Warrant, which was probably signed and issued some time later, as *'Doyle'* who signs as DepGM, was General Sir John Doyle, KCB, DepGM, 1822-1824.

At a Lodge held on 20 March 1821, it was resolved to purchase from Bro Thomas Harper, of Temple Bar, London, a Master's, Past Master's and the two Deacons' Jewels, in addition to a Square and Compasses, all engraved, 'Cambrian Lodge No.726', this being the original Lodge number. All these are still used in the Lodge, except the Master's, the present one being of a much later date, bearing the hall-mark for 1873-1874. The original Jewels bear the maker's initial, 'TH', for Thomas Harper, who was Deputy Grand Master of the Atholl Grand Lodge, from 1801 until the Union of the two Grand Lodges at the end of 1813.

It was intended that the Lodge be Consecrated by Sir Christopher Cole, and the WM Installed, on St John's Day, 27 December 1821, at the then new Town Hall. Although the Provincial Grand Lodge Meeting was held, the Consecration Ceremony could not take place, as the Warrant had not been received. Cambrian Lodge was at this time working under a Dispensation, which is practically a copy of the Warrant. There is no record of the actual date of Consecration, but in the first Minute Book, there is an account for 4 February 1823: *'Carriage of Warrant, 3s/7d'* and also for a *'Frame for Warrant'*. It would therefore appear that the Lodge was Consecrated some time after this date in 1823, probably on St John's Day, June 24, as Consecrations generally were carried out at this time either on St John Baptist's Day in June, or St John the Evangelist's Day in December. From the Minutes of the Meeting on 24 June 1823, it is apparent that something special happened, and it is possible, if not probable, that this was the Consecration Ceremony. There is mention of a Special Anthem composed for the Meeting; this is probably the Consecration Anthem, a copy of which is still preserved in the Lodge.

On 1 November 1825, the Lodge met for the first time at the Eagle Inn, where it continued until 1831, when it was removed to the Castle Inn, but became dormant in December 1833. The Lodge restarted in June 1843, at the New Rooms of the Castle Hotel. The enumeration of the Lodge was changed from 726 to 472 in 1832; which it remained until, in 1863, it was given its present number of 364.

The present Masonic Hall was built between 1847 and 1848. WBro Matthew Whittington was the WM when the Hall was officially opened on 6 June 1848. In an article in the Cambrian Newspaper of 9 June 1848, the Hall is described as *'the only Hall especially devoted to the use of the Order in the Principality'*. The Consecration of the Hall took place on 8 August 1848, during a Meeting of Provincial Grand Lodge, when RWBro E J Hutchins was Installed as the first ProvGM for the Eastern Division of South Wales. Prior to that date the whole of South Wales was one Province.

The following year was a quiet one for the Lodge, due no doubt to the great cholera epidemic, which claimed WBro Matthew Whittington, IPM, at the age of 42, as one of its victims. He was buried in the churchyard of St Thomas's Church, Neath, on 9 August 1849. The connection of his family with Cambrian Lodge is unique. His son, Walter Philip Whittington, born in 1834, was the Postmaster of Neath, and a Printer & Stationer. Initiated in Cambrian Lodge, he became WM in 1864, 1865, 1879 and 1890. He was Provincial Grand Secretary, 1865-1866; 1870-1875, and 1887-1903. In December 1873, the Lodge presented him with an illuminated Address and a Past Master's Jewel. A Mr Kennington was commissioned to paint his portrait, which was subscribed for by the Brethren of Cambrian Lodge, and presented to him on 1 December 1891. The portrait was presented to the Lodge in 1920, by the widow of his eldest son, WBro Matthew William Whittington. Walter Whittington was presented with a service of silver, at a Meeting of Provincial Grand Lodge, held at Pontypridd on 24 September 1903. Sadly, he died a few weeks later on 2 October 1903, at the age of 69. VWBro Marmaduke Tennant, DepProvGM, wrote to all the Lodges on 3 November, asking them to go into Masonic mourning for three months, *'to mark the great loss sustained by the death of the late Bro W Whittington'*.

Matthew William Whittington was born in 1858, and established a successful business in Neath as an Auctioneer, Accountant

& Valuer, and Tramway Manager. Initiated into Cambrian Lodge, he became WM in 1895. On the death of his father, he became Lodge Treasurer, and held that Office until his death in 1920. He died at the relatively young age of 62, and was buried on 4 March 1920.

George G Whittington, born in 1866, joined his father in the Printing & Stationery Business. Initiated into Cambrian Lodge on 4 June 1895 by his eldest brother WBro George Whittington, WM, he became WM in 1903.

At the time of his Initiation, his father, Walter, was ProvSGW. Following his father's death at the end of 1903, George succeeded him as ProvGSec in 1904, and held that Office for forty years, until 1944. He became Grand Officer in 1916 with the Rank of PAGDC. In 1919, George has the honour of being Installed WM of Hendre Lodge No.3250 and the following year he had the privilege of Installing RWBro Sir Charles L D Venables Llewelyn, Bart, ProvGM, as his successor in the Chair of that Lodge. Also, in 1920, on the death of his brother, Matthew, he succeeded him as Treasurer of Cambrian Lodge. George died at the age of 88 in 1954. He had been a Freemason for 59 years.

Cambrian Lodge Sponsored its first Daughter Lodge, Afan Lodge No.833 in 1860. The new Lodge was issued with a Warrant on 29 September and Consecrated on 8 November 1860. When Afan Lodge celebrated its Centenary in January 1960, the Brethren of Cambrian Lodge were very proud to be involved, particularly as they had only recently discovered that Cambrian Lodge had been the Sponsoring Lodge, and not Indefatigable Lodge, Swansea, as had been previously believed.

In 1868, approval was granted for a Royal Arch Chapter to be attached to the Lodge, and named St David's Chapter. Consecrated on 9 June 1870, it ceased working towards the end of 1897. It would take a further 55 years before the Lodge would once again have it own Chapter. On 21 November 1951, it was agreed that the Lodge should Sponsor a new Royal Arch Chapter, and Cambrian Chapter No.364 was duly Consecrated at Neath on 19 September 1952.

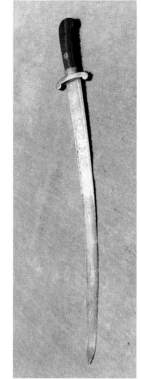

A Company of Brethren was formed in 1870 to take over the Hall. The total raised was £560 in £10 shares, out of which the Hall was purchased for £315 and the rest spent on alterations. The present dais was added in 1874, the Lodge was re-decorated and further shares issued, taking the capital value to £725. In 1901, a committee was appointed to consider purchasing part or whole of the British School property adjacent to the Masonic Hall, which was shortly to be put up for auction. In September, the purchase of the large room immediately behind the Lodge and also a small plot to the North was made for the sum of £325. Alterations and additions to the Lodge were made for the sum of £414, which was raised by a mortgage.

Also in 1870, Cambrian Lodge Sponsored its second Daughter Lodge, Talbot Lodge No.1323, Swansea. The Petition was signed in May, the Warrant issued on 20 June and the Lodge was Consecrated on 8 December 1870.

Sir Digby Mackworth, WM Gnoll Lodge, 1785 and 1799, had presented a Tyler's Sword to the old Gnoll Lodge. In 1878, his great grandson, Sir Arthur Mackworth, presented the Sword to Cambrian Lodge. It is now used at Installations and bears the inscription on the hilt, *'The gift of Digby Mackworth Esq. to the Gnoll Lodge No.412'*.

In January 1893 William Hopkins, WM, vacated the Chair due to illness and, shortly afterwards, expired in an ante-room. The Minutes record his vacating the Chair but not his death. The next entry records *'a list of Brethren at the funeral of our late Wor. Master'*.

Provincial Grand Lodge was again held at the Lodge on 27 September 1900, when WBro Henry Pendrill Charles, WM, was appointed ProvSGW. The only other Cambrian Lodge Brother holding Provincial Office that year was WBro Walter Whittington, ProvGSec. WBro Henry Pendrill Charles was again Installed as WM in March 1911. A Dispensation was granted from Grand Lodge for the purpose, as he was currently WM of Hendre Lodge No.3250. At the Installation in March 1914, WBro Henry Pendrill Charles was present as Acting DepProvGM. In February 1915, a letter was read from the ProvGSec, acquainting the Lodge that the ProvGM had appointed WBro H P Charles as his Deputy, from 11 February last.

On 10 July 1905, at a meeting of the Committee appointed to revise the By-laws, it was decided to alter the date of Lodge Meetings from the first to the third Tuesdays. In June 1912, it was resolved that no Regular Lodges be held during the months of July and August. The Cambrian Lodge of Instruction was formed in January 1913, later to become the Neath Lodge of Instruction. This LOI continues to work on the fourth Tuesday of the month.

At the Installation Meeting of 20 March 1906, the Past Masters' Tablet was presented to the Lodge. It was unveiled by VWBro Marmaduke Tennant, DepProvGM.

In May 1912, a vote of sympathy was passed for Bro R T Leyson on the loss of his son, Bro R W N Leyson, by the foundering of the 'Titanic'. Bro Leyson had only been Raised at an Emergency Lodge in March, just before sailing, and his body was identified by a Ritual which had been presented to him in Lodge at his Raising.

A Centenary Lodge was held on 1 February 1921, when VWBro Henry Pendrill Charles, DepProvGM, was Elected an Honorary Member. Owing to the dormant period, 1833-1843, Grand Lodge refused to issue a Centenary Warrant and Jewel.

Thanks of the Lodge were given to WBro T H Ingleton in June 1923 for generously defraying the cost of presenting every Member of the Lodge with a copy of the 'History of Cambrian Lodge', written by Bro Glen A Taylor.

The Lodge was opened and then adjourned on 16 March 1925, for the Brethren to attend the funeral of the late DepProvGM, Henry Pendrill Charles. The Lodge was ordered to go into mourning for three months.

In November 1926, the WM was authorised to arrange the removal from Swansea of the Organ Loft and Stairs, a gift to the Lodge from the Brethren of Indefatigable Lodge. The Organ Loft is still in situ in the Neath Temple.

The Petition for a third Daughter Lodge, Gnoll Lodge No.5057, Neath, was signed by the Principal Officers in May 1928. The Lodge was Consecrated on 1 August 1928 at the Gwyn Hall, Neath and WBro J Wesley Evans, PM, was Installed as the Primus Master. Cambrian Lodge loaned a carpet and furniture for the Ceremony.

In 1929, a new organ was built and paid for by the Brethren. WBro D J James, DepProvGM, Dedicated the new organ on 16 September 1930.

WBro Reginald Pendrill of RP St John Charles Lodge was congratulated on 27 March 1934 on his elevation to the Rank of PAGReg, in Grand Lodge.

At a meeting held on 25 April 1934, alterations to the Lodge premises were discussed. The proposed scheme was to build a large dining hall over the existing kitchens, with the ground floor being divided into cloakrooms and assembly rooms. Subsequently, at a joint meeting of Cambrian and Gnoll Lodges, the latter generously agreed to be responsible for half of the £1,500 cost and half of the existing £1,000 mortgage. The dining hall was first used on the occasion of the Installation of WBro W J S Taylor, on 26 March 1935.

WBro Edgar J Rutter, PGD, DepProvGM, was Elected an Honorary Member on 10 May 1937. The following year, he presented a new Past Masters' Board to the Lodge, which he unveiled on 22 March 1938. He was suitably thanked by WBro A J L Taylor, WM, on behalf of the Members of Cambrian Lodge.

A communication was received from Grand Lodge on 15 November 1938, announcing the appointment of WBro Reginald Pendrill St John Charles, PAGReg, as ProvGM of the Province, in succession to RWBro Sir Charles L D Venables Llewelyn, who had retired. The appointment gave particular pleasure to the Brethren, as WBro Charles was an Initiate of the Lodge, and SW at the time of the appointment. He was Installed as ProvGM at a Meeting of Provincial Grand Lodge, held in Cardiff on 2 February 1939. A few weeks later, he was Installed WM of Cambrian Lodge, on 28 March 1939.

A Deputation to Sponsor a new Lodge, Lodge of St Illtyd No.6078, was received on 16 January 1945. The Petition was duly signed, and Cambrian Lodge's fourth Daughter Lodge was Consecrated on 4 May 1945. WBro Charles Presgrave Palmer, PM, was Installed as Primus Master and on 15 May, it was announced that he had been appointed the Province's first AProvGM. Charles P Palmer was a Railway Contractor, born in Neath in 1875. His father, George, born in 1826 in Kingscliffe, Northants, was also a Railway Contractor. An Initate of Cambrian Lodge, he was Installed WM in 1896. Charles Presgrave was also Initiated into Cambrian Lodge, and was Installed WM in 1915 and again in 1916. In February 1916, he presented a Worhsipful Master's Chain and Collar to the Lodge. He was a Founder and first DC of Gnoll Lodge in 1928. He became a Grand Officer in May1931 with the Rank of PAGDC and was promoted to PJGD in May 1946. In 1939, he was Installed as WM of Hendre Lodge. He died in January 1953 at the age of 77, and the ProvGM ordered Masonic mourning until 30 March 1953. His son Frederick, born in 1907, was also Initated in Cambrian Lodge and was Installed as WM in 1945.

On 20 April 1948, letters were read from WBro Edgar J Rutter, DepProvGM, and VWBro Sydney A White, Grand Secretary, stating that Grand Lodge now recognised that Cambrian Lodge had continuity of working from 1843 to 1943, and could apply for a Centenary Warrant.The refusal of Grand Lodge to issue a Centenary Warrant in 1921, because the Lodge was dormant between 1833 and 1941, has already been mentioned. Then, also in 1948, the Lodge was informed that Grand Lodge was prepared to investigate the whole question further. As a result of the researches of Grand Lodge Librarian, WBro J Heron-Lepper, PGD, the Brethren were pleased to learn that the MW His Grace The Duke of Devonshire, KG, Grand Master, was pleased to grant a Centenary Warrant dating as from 31 January 1821. The Centenary Warrant was officially presented to the Lodge at an Emergency Meeting on 29 November 1949, by WBro J Heron-Lepper, representing the Grand Master, in the presence of RWBro R P St John Charles, ProvGM. The history of the Lodge was narrated by several of the Brethren, and the occasion suitably commemorated.

The Masonic Hall, Neath

On 19 April 1960, the question of obtaining Centenary Jewels was raised. The Centenary Jewel was exhibited on 20 December and a charge of £1 - 15s - 8d (£1. 78p) requested from Brethren wishing to acquire one. It was agreed that 150 Centenary Jewels be purchased, so that the Lodge would have a surplus for future Members. Every Brother is now presented with a Centenary Jewel as part of his Raising Ceremony.

In 1967, a contribution was made to an appeal on behalf of the Royal College of Surgeons, in commemoration of the 250th Anniversary of the Founding of Grand Lodge. A Commemorative Jewel marking this event is attached to the Lodge Charity Steward's Collar.

The 150th Anniversary of the Lodge was celebrated on 16 March 1971. This was also the Installation Meeting when, in the presence of RWBro the Rt Hon the Lord Swansea, DL, ProvGM, WBro James Binnie Thomson became WM.

On 19 November 1991, the Lodge Committee investigated the transferring of the ownership of the building for the good of Freemasonry in Neath. At this meeting, WBro T W Trott presented the Lodge with two books on the history of the Lodge, one dealing with the period 1821 to 1921, and the other, 1921 to 1940. These are presented to the incoming Master at his Installation.

The 175th Anniversary of the Lodge was celebrated at the Installation of WBro Roger Burnett Evans as WM, on 19 March 1996. To mark the occasion, the Past Masters presented new silver Square and Compasses to the Lodge. During the year, a third history of the Lodge was produced by Bro Keith Tucker, covering the period 1949 to 1996. All three histories are now presented to the incoming WM at his Installation.

On 16 September 1999, WBro Royston Blackwell, WM, was invited, as WM of one of the six Senior Lodges in the Province, to be in the Escort Party at the Investiture of the new ProvGM, RWBro Hywel Davies.

In January 2000, the Brethren of Cambrian Lodge were Balloted on the matter of sharing ownership of the building with the other Neath Lodges. The result was overwhelmingly in favour of sharing. By September, it was reported that the process of transfer was progressing well with a completion date of 1 January 2003 in view. On 19 November 2002, the transfer of ownership of the building and chattels to the new Association of Neath Freemasons was passed in Open Lodge. On 17 May 2005, the Deeds of the Masonic Hall were presented by Cambrian Lodge to the Chairman of the Neath Association of Freemasons, WBro Clive Evans, in the presence of RWBro Hywel Davies, ProvGM. At this Meeting, the ProvGM unveiled a commemorative plaque to mark this most historic occasion in the history of Cambrian Lodge in particular, and Neath Freemasonry in general.

Neath Temple Lamp

Working under Dispensation from Provincial Grand Lodge, A Ceremony of Dedication of the New Organ was performed on Monday 16 December 2002.

On 20 March 2007, the Lodge was again honoured with the presence of RWBro Hywel Davies, at the Installation of WBro Alwyn Richard Lewis as WM. At this Ceremony, the ProvGM was presented with the first Commemorative Jewel of the 2010 Festival. The presentation was made by WBro Andrew Gretton, AProvGM, President of the Festival.

On 24 July 2009, WBro Edward David Richards Coombs, WM, as Master of one of the six senior Lodges in the Province, was invited to be in the Escort Party at the Investiture of the new ProvGM, RWBro Captain Sir Norman Lloyd-Edwards. The Lodge was honoured with the presence of the new ProvGM at the Proclamation of WBro D J Watkins as WM for a successive year, at the Installation Meeting on 16 March 2010. The previous WM to serve for two successive years was WBro Charles Presgrave Palmer in 1915 and 1916.

Compiled by WBro Roger B Evans, PProvAGDC, Secretary, with additions from WBro Peter M Davies, ProvJGW.

Christopher Hancorne
1759 – 1842
Deputy Provincial Grand Master
1821–1831 & 1833–1836

Christopher Hancorne was of a well-known Swansea family. He was Captain in HM Service and fought in the Peninsular War (see below). In 1820, he was appointed Captain of the Royal Glamorgan Militia.

On 26 November 1816, he joined Indefatigable Lodge and on 10 June 1817, as SW of the Lodge, he was unanimously Elected Master (the period of Office being only six months at that time.) He was Elected Master for a second time in 1817, and again in 1821 and 1831 (a period of twelve months on these other occasions.)

Benjamin Hall, ProvGM, died on 31 July 1817 and shortly afterwards Sir Christopher Cole was appointed his successor. There was, however, a problem with the appointment; Sir Christopher was not a Freemason! At a Meeting of Indefatigable Lodge on 23 October 1817, WBro Christopher Hancorne, WM, proposed that Sir Christopher *'be made a Mason'*. The proposition was seconded and unanimously approved, and at that Meeting, Sir Christopher was Initiated, Passed and Raised, *'because of the particular urgency of the circumstances'*. It was not until 5 July 1821, that a Provincial Grand Lodge was eventually held at Swansea to Install the Provincial Grand Master, and only then, following a rebuke from Indefatigable Lodge to Sir Christopher, referring *'to that part of the Constitution which requires that a Provincial Lodge be held once in each year'*. At that PGL Meeting, Christopher Hancorne was appointed Deputy Provincial Grand Master. He retained that Office until 1831, when he was succeeded by William Shewen, PM Indefatigable Lodge.

William Shewen died on 25 March 1833, and in April, the Brethren of Indefatigable Lodge recommended to Sir Christopher Cole that he should re-appoint Christopher Hancorne as his Deputy, which he did.

In July 1836, Christopher Cole resigned as a Subscribing Member of Indefatigable Lodge, having previously announced his intention of resigning as Provincial Grand Master later that year. In July, Sir John Nicholl, of Merthyr Mawr, MP for Cardiff (1832-1852), wrote to Christopher Hancorne, DepProvGM, stating *'that he would be happy to be Elected Provincial Grand Master'*. The letter was read out in Indefatigabe Lodge, and a decision of this letter was deferred to a Lodge of Emergency, when Christopher Hancorne mysteriously resigned as a Subscribing Member of the Lodge. Interestingly, Sir John Nicholl was not a Freemason, but at about the same time, he had written to Glamorgan Lodge, expressing *'a wish to become Initiated into the Sublime Mysteries of a Mason'*. He was duly Initiated into Glamorgan Lodge on 19 August and Passed on 23 September 1836. There is no record of him being Raised – presumably because his ambition of becoming Provincial Grand Master of South Wales was not to be realised.

The Brethren of Indefatigable Lodge were much perturbed by information which they possessed, but which is not fully revealed in the Lodge Minutes, but regret was expressed that Bro Hancorne had not acquainted the Lodge with the matters which had passed between Sir Christopher Cole and himself as to the former's resignation. Shortly afterwards, on 24 August 1836, Sir Christopher Cole died.

At a Meeting of Indefatigable Lodge on 25 January 1842, , there was a *'letter read from the Revd Mr Phelps, Clergyman of Cowbridge, stating that Brother Christopher Hancorne had died in very distressed circumstances, and soliciting a contribution from this Lodge to pay the Funeral Expenses, etc.'*. A generous donation was forwarded to the widow. The death was also reported on 29 January in the 'Cambrian':

'Lately at an advanced age, sincerely regretted, Captain Christopher Hancorne, brother of the late Rev Thomas Hancorne, Vicar of Newcastle in this county. The deceased officer served during the whole of the Peninsular War; was present at the taking of Ciudad Rodrigo and the second siege of Badajoz.'

Christopher Hancorne was buried at St Illtyd's Church, Newcastle, Bridgend, on 24 January 1842. He was 82 years of age. Notes:

The Siege of Ciudad Rodrigo began on the night of 8 January 1812, when 450 men from the Light Division seized the French redoubt on the Grand Teson.

In the Battle of Badajoz (16 March - 6 April 1812) an Anglo-Portuguese army under the Duke of Wellington, besieged Badajoz, Spain and forced the surrender of the French garrison. The siege was one of the bloodiest in the Napoleonic Wars and was considered a costly victory by the British, with some 3,000 Allied soldiers killed in a few short hours of intense fighting as the siege drew to an end, and as many as 4,000 allied Spanish civilians, including many women and children, massacred by the allied troops after the battle.

The second British siege of Badajoz of 19 May-17 June 1811 was little more successful than the first siege, which had only lasted for one week before Marshal Beresford had been forced to lift the siege and move south to block Marshal Soult's first relief attack at Albuera. In the aftermath of that battle, Wellington had arrived in the south, and had taken personal command in Estremadura. Most of the army that had fought at Albuera remained in the south of Estremadura, under the command of Rowland Hill, watching the French, while Wellington directed the second attack on Badajoz.

WBro Peter M Davies, ProvJGW.

William Shewen
1764 – 1833
Deputy Provincial Grand Master
1831 – 1833

The only record we have of William Shewen is to be found in 'History of Indefatigable Lodge No.237', by William Henry Jones, PPGJW, Norfolk, published in 1923.

On St John's Day, 1814, 'Col Shewins' is named as a visiting Brother, and afterwards *favoured the Company with an excellent Masonic Song.* He became a Joining Member in 1815. He was Colonel of Volunteers, and he lived at Bellevue, near the Grammar School on Mount Pleasant. He was an ardent sportsman and supporter of the Swansea races; and *it was the delight of the townspeople to see him tool his pair of spanking greys in his smart carriage up the stiff hill from the Washing-lake to Bellevue.* William Shewen was Master of Indefatigable Lodge 1824-1826. The Provincial Grand Master, RWBro Sir Christopher Cole, Elected him to be his Deputy in 1831, which Office he continued to hold until his death in 1833.

His death, at the age of 68, on Monday, 25 March 1833, was reported in the 'Cambrian' on 30 March. The death of his widow, Maria, at the age of 74 on 18 August 1838, was also reported in the 'Cambrian'.

WBro Peter M Davies, ProvJGW.

Sir Josiah John Guest, Bart, MP
1785 - 1852

Provincial Grand Master of South Wales
1836 - 1848

Sir Josiah John Guest was born at Dowlais on 2 February 1785, the son of Thomas Guest (died 28 February 1807 and buried at St Tydfil's Church, Merthyr) and Jemima, daughter of T Phillips of Shifnal, Shropshire. He was educated at Bridgenorth and Monmouth Grammar Schools. His grandfather, John Guest (died 25 November 1787), had come to Dowlais from Broseley in Shropshire, where he had been a Brewer, Farmer and Coal-dealer. He had been appointed the Manager of the furnace on 30 April 1767, when he was 45 years of age. In 1786, John Guest was succeeded in the management of the business by his son, Thomas Guest, and his son-in-law, William Taitt, who had married his daughter Sarah. Taitt was the first Treasurer of Glamorgan Lodge (then No.33), Cardiff, and in 1808, he resided at 19, St Mary Street, Cardiff. By 1801, there were only three partners in the Dowlais Ironworks - William Taitt (eight shares), Thomas Guest (2 shares) and William Lewis (six shares). The directing and commanding personality was William Taitt, who was in charge of selling all iron made at Dowlais, and directing policy at Dowlais. He was, apparently, a very rude and dictatorial figure.

Sir Josiah John Guest

In 1807, Thomas Guest died, and the management of the works became the responsibility of his son, Josiah John Guest, together with Alexander Kirkwood, a nephew of William Taitt. Kirkwood died in 1814, leaving Josiah John Guest in sole charge. In 1815, William Taitt died, leaving his share of the business to his nephew, Josiah John Guest. In 1843, Dowlais received its first order from Russia for 30,000 tons of rails, followed by a further order for 12,000 tons and then in 1844 a colossal order for 50,000 tons of rails – the largest order of that type ever placed! At the close of 1844, with seventeen furnaces averaging 90 - 96 tons each week of the year, the ironworks was almost at its peak. The Dowlais Works in 1845 employed 7,300 men, women and children and covered an area of forty acres, ten acres of which were occupied by different buildings. In July 1851, Sir John realised his life-long ambition by becoming the sole proprietor of the Dowlais Iron Company.

Josiah John Guest first married on 11 March 1817 an Irish Lady, Miss Maria Elizabeth Ranken, third daughter of William Ranken, but she and her baby died in childbirth the following January, and were buried at Llandaff. It was during the period of this marriage that he built Dowlais House - a large Georgian Mansion with a fine stone portico.

In 1823, Josiah John Guest opened a Bank in Cardiff, with a branch in Merthyr, and issued promissory notes to the value of £1. The bank thrived until 1825 when, in an era of commercial disasters, it was closed.

J J Guest was a fairly religious man, of Wesleyan persuasion by birth, but Anglican because of business. In 1827, he built St John's Church, Dowlais, at a cost of £3,000. He also gave generously to many local chapels. In 1829, he created a Mechanics' Institute in Dowlais, for the benefit of his men, where weekly lectures were delivered. While the lectures covered philosophical and general subjects, they were in the main concerned with mineralogy and metallurgy.

In 1833, he married for the second time, Lady Charlotte Elizabeth Bertie, the only daughter of Albemarle Bertie, ninth Earl of Lindsey, and she bore him ten children. When in 1839, a second Ironworks was built, it was named 'Ifor Works', after their eldest son Ifor Bertie.

In 1846, Sir John purchased Lord De Manley's house at Canford, near Wimborne, Dorset, for £335,000, and commissioned Sir Charles Barry (Architect of the Houses of Parliament) to remodel it for him and Lady Charlotte as a home for their retirement. The House is now the site of the independent co-educational school, 'Canford School', founded in 1923.

On 21 June 1836, an Act of Parliament was passed for the building of the Taff Railway from Merthyr to Cardiff. The original capital was £300,000 in £100 shares. Two main shareholders were Josiah John Guest and his brother, Thomas Revel Guest. The Engineer was Isambard Kingdom Brunel, Engineer of the Great Western Railway. The Taff Railway was opened to Abercynon (Navigation House) in October 1840, and to Merthyr in 1841, and Sir J J Guest was the first chairman of the Company.

Sir John, during his lifetime, held many social, business and academic titles among which were: High Sheriff of Glamorgan, 1818; Fellow of the Geological Society, 1830; Fellow of the Royal Society, 1834; Vice-President of the Cambrian Society and an Associate of the Institution of Civil Engineers. At the coronation of Queen Victoria in July 1838, Josiah John Guest was made a baronet in the Honours List.

His involvement in politics began in 1826, when, on 26 June, he was elected the Member of Parliament for Honiton, Devon, a seat that he held until 23 April 1831. On 1 March 1831, Lord John Russell moved the first reading of the Reform Bill and in his several attempts to get the Bill through Parliament, he received great support from Josiah John Gust. Following several defeats, the Bill was eventually passed on 4 June 1831. The first Parliament under the Reform Bill assembled on 29 January 1833 and J J Guest went there as the first member for the newly created Borough of Merthyr, Aberdare and Vaynor – a seat he held up to the time of his death.

Josiah John Guest first became involved in Freemasonry on 1 March 1810, when he was proposed as a Candidate for Initiation in Glamorgan Lodge. He was duly initiated on 5 April of that year, but not Passed until 7 April 1821; and a further 15 years were to elapse before he was Raised! Glamorgan Lodge Minutes for 20 October 1836 read as follows:

'A Letter having been received from Brother J J Guest wishing to be raised to the sublime Degree of a Master Mason he having been duly initiated in the 2 first Degrees in this Lodge –

Brother Guest was afterwards raised to the Degree of Master Mason'

The Provincial Grand Master, Sir Christopher Cole, had died while still in Office, on 26 August 1836 and it would appear, from Guest's request to Glamorgan Lodge (then No.43) to be Raised, that he was already lined up to succeed Cole as ProvGM. This, of course, was unknown to the Brethren of Indefatigable Lodge (then No.288), Swansea, who were intent on getting their candidate, Henry, Duke of Beaufort, appointed as ProvGM. In the Minutes of Indefatigable Lodge we have:

'At a Lodge of Emergency on 20th September 1836, the Duke was Balloted for as a candidate for Freemasonry. He was

unanimously approved and duly initiated, passed and raised by Brother Bird. At the same meeting the Duke acceded to the brethren's wishes that he should allow himself to be nominated P.G.M. for South Wales.'

In the event, their address was unsuccessful for on 10 November 1836, the Grand Secretaries wrote to the Masters of the South Wales Lodges as follows:

We have to acquaint you that the most Worshipful Grand Master has been pleased to appoint Josiah John Guest, Esq., M.P. of Dowlais House, Merthyr Tydfil, Provincial Grand Master for South Wales, to whom, therefore, you will in future address all your communications relating to the Craft, excepting the returns of your Lodge. Applications for Certificates and other matters specially directed by the Book of Constitutions, and which are to be forwarded to us jointly as Grand Secretaries.

–With fraternal regards, we remain, your obedient Servants and Brethren,

WILLIAM H. WHITE, EDWARD HARPER, G. Secs.'

Sir J J Guest had in fact accepted the appointment of ProvGM of South Wales in a letter, dated 23 October 1836 to W H White, Grand Secretary. In the letter, he emphasises that his names were *'Josiah John Guest - not Joshua'*

In 1836, a movement had been inaugurated by the Lodges and Brethren of England to present HRH the Duke of Sussex with a suitable token, in appreciation of his services on the completion of 25 years as head of the English Craft. One of Guest's earliest duties as ProvGM was to write to the Lodges in his Province for a subscription towards this 'token,' and in the Minutes of Glamorgan Lodge, dated 8 January 1838 we have:

'A Letter having been received from J.J. Guest P.G.M. at the instance of Lord John Churchill W. Dep. G.M. requesting a return of the subscriptions from this Lodge in aid of the proposed Masonic Offering to the M W Grand M – and requesting to be furnished with a List of Officers and Members of this Lodge.

Proposed by Brother Wm. Bird and Seconded by Brother Mark Marks, and resolved unanimously that the Sum of Three Guineas be subscribed for the above laudable purpose.'

The presentation took the form of a service of plate, weighing over 1800 oz and was presented to HRH on 24 January 1838. The plate was afterwards presented, in 1845, to United Grand Lodge by the Duchess of Inverness.

While J J Guest had been appointed ProvGM in 1836, he was not Installed as such until 18 August 1840. On 28 January 1840, WBro Matthew Moggridge, WM of Indefatigable Lodge adopted the following course:

'Movd by Br Gutch, Secondd by Br Harris, that the Secty be requested to address a Letter to Sir Jh Guest, and respectfully solicit to name a day when it would be convenient for him to be installed W.P.G.M.'

This letter had the desired effect, for in Indefatigable Lodge Minutes we have:

'Movd by Br Bird, Secondd by Br T. Morgan, that the thanks of this Lodge be given to the W.M. for the zeal he has evinced in successfully calling the attention of the P.G.M. to the state of the Craft in the principality, and in prevailing on the distinguished Brother to exercise the duties of his high and important office.'

On 3 August 1840, the Provincial Grand Master wrote to the Worshipful Masters of the Province as follows:

'W. Master

You are hereby summoned with your officers to attend the Provincial Grand Master at Swansea on Tuesday, the 18th inst., at 10 o'clock a.m., either in person of by deputy, in order to furthering his Installation and to bring with you your Warrant, Books, Papers and Accounts, and also a list of all members who may be in arrears of payment, that the same may be inspected in order to ascertain the progress of the Craft and to enable the Provincial Grand Master to report to Grand Lodge accordingly.

Be so good as to inform me as early as possible the number that is likely to attend from your Lodge, to enable the Grand

Officers to make out the regular form of procession.

I am, W. Master,

Yours fraternally,

J. John Guest,

P.G.M. of S. Wales'

The Installation took place at Swansea on Tuesday, 18 August 1840. It was held at the Cameron Arms, which had recently become the meeting place of Indefatigable Lodge. The occasion was reported in the 'Cambrian' on Saturday 22 August, part of which is given below:

'On Tuesday last, a large and highly-respectable assemblage of Masonic Brethren from various Lodges in the Principality, met at the Lodge-house, the Cameron Arms, in this town, in compliance with the summons of the Provincial Grand Master for South Wales, Sir J. J. Guest, Bart., M.P., who was then and there to be installed; which imposing and interesting ceremony took place about eleven o'clock, A.M. The Provincial Grand Master then nominated his Provincial Officers, and having addressed them on various Masonic subjects, the Brethren, about 150 in number, were formed into Procession, in the order following, and walked to St. Mary's Church, preceded, flanked, and followed by the detachment of the 45th Regiment, now stationed at Swansea. We should here observe that the streets through which the procession had to pass, were literally crammed with spectators, and every window from which a glance could be caught of the Brethren, were filled with ladies and well-dressed and respectable individuals; and the procession evidently afforded all much gratification and delight. ....

The morning service at St Mary's Church was performed by the Provincial Grand Chaplain, the Rev. Wm. Hewson, D.D., Vicar, who afterwards delivered one of the most beautiful and effective discourses we ever heard in the course of our experience, from the 17th verse of the 2d chapter of the 1st Epistle General of St Peter – 'Love the Brotherhood, fear God, and honour the King.' ....

The procession then returned from church in the same order to the Lodge-room, where, after the closing of the Lodge, they separated until the hour of the festival, six o'clock; when they sat down, about 100 in number, in full Masonic costume, to an excellent dinner, which did much credit to the taste and management of the hostess, the Provincial Grand Master presiding, and the Deputy Provincial as Vice. The cloth being removed, "Non nobis domini," was sung ....Amongst the various toasts given, the following were most prominent, and drunk with much acclamation, attended by the usual Masonic honours:

'The Queen – the daughter of a Mason, and the Patroness of our Order.'

'His Royal Highness the Duke of Sussex, Grand Master of England.'

'The Provincial Grand Master,' with reiterated applause.

etcetera

The memory of the late Provincial Grand Master, Sir. C. Cole, on referring to whose amiable virtues in public and private life, the Provincial Grand Chaplain spoke most feelingly and eloquently.

'Lady Charlotte Guest,' with the most enthusiastic applause.'

Five days earlier, on 13 August 1840, Sir Josiah John Guest had been Installed as Worshipful Master of Loyal Cambrian Lodge, Merthyr Tydfil, and his name is displayed on the Board of Past Masters at the Masonic Hall in Merthyr. He had only joined the Merthyr Lodge in the July of 1840! An account of his Installation, given in 'The Illustrated History of the Loyal Cambrian Lodge', by James Fraser makes interesting reading:

'A Lodge of Emergency was again held on August 13th, when on the proposition of Bro. Rhys Davies, Mr. Thomas Shepherd

was initiated in the First Degree. The Secretary, Bro. White, afterwards read a communication from the Most Worshipful Grand Master, H.R.H., the Duke of Sussex, respecting mourning to be worn by the Craft on the decease of the lamented Pro Grand Master, the Earl of Durham. On this occasion Bro. Sir Josiah John Guest was present, and towards the close of the meeting "the Secretary read the charges on command of P.M. Bro. Hopkins, Worshipful Master pro tem, to the Right Wor. Prov. Grand Master, Sir Josiah John Guest, Bart., M.P., who was afterwards duly installed into the Chair as Worshipful Master, and regularly saluted as such by the whole of the Brethren, with Masonic Honours by Bro. Hopkins......'

James Fraser then writes – *'No information is given in the minutes as to the object of installing the Prov. Grand Master as Worshipful Master of the Lodge. The emergency meeting appears to have been called to initiate Bro. Shepherd, and the only inference that can be drawn from the account of the proceedings is that the Brethren desired to honour the Provincial Grand Master by installing him as Worshipful Master.'*

The following year, the next Provincial Grand Lodge was held at Carmarthen in order to Constitute the new St Peter's Lodge No.699 (now No.476). An announcement was placed in the Cambrian on Saturday, 11 September 1841:

'The Worshipful Master Elect and Brethren of St. Peter's Lodge at Carmarthen, beg to announce to the various Lodges throughout the Principality, and to their MASONIC BRETHREN generally, that the PROVINCIAL GRAND MASTER, Sir J. J. GUEST, Bart., M.P., had kindly signified his intention of honouring them with his presence at the OPENING of the NEW LODGE at the IVY BUSH HOTEL, which is fixed for TUESDAY the 14th of SEPTEMBER inst., on which occasion the company and assistance of those Brethren who can conveniently attend will be most highly esteemed.'

However, from the report in the Cambrian on Saturday, 18 September we have:

'The installation of the Worshipful Master and Officers of St. David's Lodge of Freemasons at Carmarthen, took place on Tuesday last, at the Lodge-room, Ivy Bush Hotel, by Brother Hutchins, Deputy Pro Grand Master for South Wales, assisted by Officers of the Provincial Grand Lodge and a numerous body of visiting brethren.'

The report mistakenly referred to St David's Lodge instead of St Peter's; but what is important, however, is the fact that Sir Josiah John Guest did not attend. He did attend the Provincial Grand Lodge the following year, which was held on Wednesday 23rd February in Cardiff under the banner of Glamorgan Lodge. The meeting was reported in the Cambrian on Saturday, 5 March 1842:

'PROVINCIAL GRAND LODGE OF FREEMASONS FOR SOUTH WALES. - The Right Worshipful Provincial Grand Master (Sir John Guest, Bart., M.P.) having summoned his Provincial Grand Officers and the Worshipful Masters and Officers of the various Lodges in the Province of South Wales, to hold a Provincial Grand Lodge at Cardiff, on Wednesday, the 23d. ult., the same was attended by the following Provincial Grand Officers, Worshipful Masters, and officers of Lodges: - Brothers Sir John Guest, Bart., M.P., R.W.P.G.M.; E.J. Hutchins, D.P.G.M.; Capt. Thos. Morgan, R.N., S.W.; C.B. Mansfield, J.W.; C.H. Smith, S.D.; F.D. Michael, P.G.M. of C.; R. Walker, P. G. Sec.; R. Tredwen, P.G.J.G.; Joshua Jones, P.G.T.; W.M. and Officers of Cardiff Lodge; W.M. and Officers of Swansea Lodge, No. 288; W.M. and Officers of Carmarthen Lodge, No. 699. The Provincial Grand Lodge having been opened in due form, and other Masonic business having been disposed of, the D.P.G.M. proposed, after an eloquent speech, which Brother C.H. Smith, Esq., seconded, that the following dutiful loyal Address be adopted, and be presented to Her Majesty, upon the joyous occasion of the Birth of the Prince of Wales.'

'We the Right Worshipful Master and Brothers of the Provincial Grand Lodge of Free and Accepted Masons of South Wales, beg to approach your Majesty, and to offer our dutiful and heartfelt congratulations on the auspicious Birth of a Prince and Heir to your dominions. We earnestly pray, that the Great Architect of the Universe may prolong your Majesty's life, to be a

blessing to your Majesty's devoted and loyal people, and to dispose the heart of the young Prince, that as he grows in years, he may imitate wisdom and virtue, and emulate the bright example set before him by his Royal Mother.'

Albert Edward, Prince of Wales, the eldest son of Queen Victoria, was born on 9 November 1841. He was Initiated in St John's Lodge, Stockholm, by the King of Sweden on 21 December 1868. He became Grand Master in 1874. On his accession to the Throne as King Edward VII in 1901, he assumed the title 'Protector of the Craft', and was succeeded as Grand Master by HRH, Arthur, Duke of Connaught and Strathearn, Grand Master 1901-1939.

During the 1840s, Sir Josiah John Guest's health was gradually declining and Lady Guest was informed that he was suffering from an incurable disease. He resigned as ProvGM on 3 August 1848 and his successor as ProvGM was Edward John Hutchins, PM of Loyal Cambrian Lodge, Merthyr.

**HRH Edward, Prince of Wales
Grand Master**

On 26 November 1852, after an illness which had grown progressively worse over the years, Sir John Guest died aged 67 years. He left immense wealth to his widow and family, not only the Dowlais Iron Company, but also large estates at Canford Manor, Wimborne, Dorset; and Sully, Glamorgan, together with mines in the Forest of Dean.

On his death, Lady Guest said *'He was born in Dowlais, he lived in Dowlais and he shall be buried in Dowlais'*. When he was buried on Saturday, 14 December, not a place of business was open, even the market stayed closed until the evening. He was laid to rest at the Dowlais Parish Church, and mourned by one and all of Dowlais. An account of his funeral was reported in the 'Cardiff & Merthyr Guardian' of Saturday, 11 December 1852:

'Early on Saturday morning, the body was deposited in the receptacle prepared for it, the innermost coffin – mahogany – having been made in the Dowlais Works. The next was of lead, the production of Mr. Robert Sims, Ironmonger, of Merthyr; while the third and outside one was formed of oak, and was, similarly to the first coffin, the production of the carpenters in the late Sir John Guest's employ. This was covered with rich black cloth, studded with the same sombre coloured nails; the handles and furniture being massive and beautifully gilt. On the lid was a pure silver plate, upon which the armorial bearings of the deceased baronet, together with the Motto 'Ferro non Gladio', -as likewise the following inscription, were exquisitely engraven: -

Sir JOSIAH JOHN GUEST,
Twenty Years M. P., for the Borough of Merthyr
Tydfil:
Born at Dowlais, 2d February, 1785
Died at Dowlais, 26th, November, 1852.

The corpse having been placed in the coffin, it was conveyed from up-stairs into a large room on the ground floor of Dowlais house. The hatchment was then placed at the head, and the coffin covered with a black pall, fringed with white silk, having the escutcheons of the late Sir John Guest worked in gold on white satin affixed, three on each side. The public were then admitted into this room, and during the two hours it remained open, members of the most respectable inhabitants availed themselves the considerate kindness of Lady Charlotte.

At about half-past twelve o'clock the mournful cortege left Dowlais house, proceeding little distance down High-street, then turning into Market-street, through Union-street, to the Church.'

Part of his Obituary in the 'Cardiff & Merthyr Guardian' of Saturday, 4 December 1852 is as follows:

'He was a man of great mental capacities –a good mathematician, and a thorough man of business, - not without taste for the refinement of literature. He was a man of generous impulses; but performance did not always wait on promise. As a politician he was not consistent: he began his career as an ultra-liberal; and we well recollect seeing ' VOTE BY BALLOT ' floating in the breeze, at the last contested election, upon the Dowlais flags; but he concluded his career as a Whig and a general supporter of Lord JOHN RUSSELL. As a Member of Parliament, Sir JOHN GUEST, while health permitted, was not inattentive to his political duties. He was not given much to oratory, and seldom spoke in the House; but he was something better than a fluent speaker, - he was a clear-headed man. He served frequently upon important committees, generally voted upon the great questions of the day, and, upon the whole, did his work fairly.'

In 1855, Lady Charlotte Guest married Charles Schreiber, MP, at one time tutor to her eldest son Ifor Bertie Guest. With her marriage, Lady Charlotte retired from business and an active part of Dowlais life. Ifor Bertie was created Lord Wimborne in 1880.

In 1897, Sir Josiah John Guest's Provincial Chain of Office and Regalia were presented to the Province by his son, the RWBro the Hon Montague Guest, ProvGM of Dorset, to commemorate the 60th Anniversary of Queen Victoria's reign. On the occasion of the Provincial Grand Lodge at Merthyr on 28 September 1899, RWBro Lord Llangattock, ProvGM, presented the Regalia and Chain, handsomely mounted in a walnut case, to Loyal Cambrian Lodge.

References
'The Dictionary of Welsh Biography down to 1940', Published under the Auspices of the Honourable Society of Cymmrodorion, London 1959.
'Notable Welshmen' by the Rev T Mardy Rees, London 1908.
'The History of the Dowlais Iron Works 1759-1970', John A Owen, The Starling Press, 1977.
'The Illustrated History of the Loyal Cambrian Lodge', James Fraser, Published Merthyr 1914.
'History of the Indefatigable Lodge', William Henry Jones, Spurrell, Carmarthen 1923.
'Grand Lodge 1717-1967', University of Oxford Press, 1967.

WBro Peter M Davies, ProvJGW.

Edward John Hutchins, MP
1809 ~ 1876

Provincial Grand Master of South Wales Eastern Division
1848 ~ 1856

Following the resignation of Sir Josiah John Guest as ProvGM of South Wales in 1848, little time was lost in appointing his successor. The Patent appointing his nephew, Edward John Hutchins, ProvGM for the new Province of South Wales Eastern Division, was signed on 30 June 1848.

Edward John Hutchins was born on 27 December 1809; the son of Edward Hutchins of Briton Ferry and Sarah Guest, sister of Sir Josiah John Guest, and was educated at Charterhouse and St John's College, Cambridge. He was married in Ireland in 1838 to Isabel Clara, daughter of the Chevalier Don Juan de Bernaben, of Alicante, Spain, and to mark the occasion, the Brethren of Loyal Cambrian Lodge (then No.127), Merthyr Tydfil, *'resolved to send him a congratulatory address.'* His early career involved him with his uncle, Sir J J Guest, in the organisation of the Dowlais Iron Works. In due course, he acquired two shares in the Company, which he eventually sold in July 1851 to his uncle for £58,000, thus making Guest the sole owner of the Works. In the same year, Hutchins became the Chairman of the Rhymney Iron Works, a position he held until his resignation in 1875.

Some indication of his personality may be gained from the following extract, taken from 'The History of the Iron, Steel, Tinplate, and other Trades of Wales', by Charles Wilkins and published in 1903:

'He had been given a good insight into ironmaking at Dowlais, and though not so practically competent as his uncle, who could cut a ton of coal, or puddle, or roll a rail with anyone, he was untiring in the acquisition of knowledge. Kindly disposed, he yet had a leaven of the autocrat in his composition; and, being somewhat spoiled by the extreme deference of workmen, given unstintedly to the employers, he could not brook the assertion of independent minds.

One illustration of his virtues is quite worth recording. It was in the days when Mr. B. R. Jones was manager of the blast furnaces at Rhymney, and Mr. Hutchins, coming there on one occasion, said to him. 'I see you have increased the make; but mind, keep the quality!' Rhymney Ironworks had a good character for its iron, and Mr. Hutchins, like many of the old-fashioned ironmasters, knew that this was of the first importance.'

Edward John Hutchins, MP

In addition to his involvement with the iron industry, Hutchins was a director of the South-Western Railway, a Magistrate and Deputy-lieutenant for Glamorganshire, and a Magistrate for Brecon and Monmouthshire. He also had political aspirations. A Liberal, in favour of the Ballot and opposed to all State endowments of religion, having converted to Roman Catholicism at an early age, he was returned by the Roman Catholic vote as one of the members for Marylebone and Hampstead, in the first School Board for London. He sat first as an MP for Penryn and Falmouth from January 1840 until the general election of 1841, when he unsuccessfully contested Southampton; and although his opponents were subsequently unseated on petition, he did not obtain the seat. He was unsuccessful once again in July 1847 when he attempted to become the member for Poole. Finally, he was returned for Lymington in April 1850, a seat which he held until his retirement from Parliament in 1857.

Hutchins first became involved in Freemasonry in 1831, when on 3 February, he was Initiated in Loyal Cambrian Lodge (then No.175), Merthyr Tydfil. He was Passed on 3 March 1831 and Raised and Installed as WM of Loyal Cambrian Lodge (then No.127) on 20 December 1832. He was re-elected Master of the Lodge the following year on 27 December 1833. During this period, he was Masonically superior to his uncle, Sir J J Guest, who was not Raised until 20 October 1836 – the same day as the Patent appointing him ProvGM of South Wales was signed! When Guest was eventually Installed as ProvGM at Swansea on Tuesday, 18 August 1840, he Invested Edward John Hutchins as his Deputy, a position he was to hold until his own appointment, on 30 June 1848, as ProvGM of South Wales Eastern Division. There was little delay on this occasion before the Installation, which took place on Tuesday, 8 August 1848 in the new Masonic Hall at Neath. This was a particularly important day in the history of the Province, for it not only marked the commencement of the Eastern Division of South Wales, but after the Installation of the ProvGM, there followed the Consecration of the Masonic Hall by the new ProvGM. The Hall was built by John Townsend, Contractor, to designs of Egbert Moxham, Architect, for the Cambrian Lodge (then No.473), Neath. It was opened with entertainment, on 6 June 1848, the WM, WBro Matthew Whittington, being in the Chair. In the report of this entertainment in the 'The Cambrian', of 9 June, it was described as *'the only Hall specially devoted to the use of the Order in the Principality'*.

A report of the Provincial Grand Lodge proceedings was published in the 'Cardiff & Merthyr Guardian' on Saturday, 12 August:

NEATH –on Tuesday morning last our town was much enlivened by the appearance of various vehicles, conveying members of the Masonic Order to witness the installation of the P.G. Master, and the dedication of our new Masonic Hall. At eleven o'clock the Grand Lodge was opened and W.P.G.M. was installed. After that ceremony the brethren, to the number of eighty, or upwards, formed a procession, attended Divine service in our parish Church. Prayers were read by the Rev. Walter Griffiths, and a sermon was preached by the P.G. Chaplain, the Rev. D. Jeffreys. Afterwards the procession re-formed, and walked to the hall, preceded by a band of music. The members of the Grand Lodge especially attracted the admiration of the assembled crowds, by the splendour of their dress and decorations. The Grand Lodge having been formed, the ceremony of dedication ensued; and admirable addresses were delivered by the W.P.G. Master, the D.P.G. Master of Bristol, and the P.G..M of Ceremonies, Mr. Michael, of Swansea. In the evening, the brethren sat down to a sumptuous dinner provided for the occasion by Mr. Savours, of the Castle Hotel. The weather proved propitious throughout, and added much to the gratification of the numerous parties that had come together from considerable distances to witness the consecration of the first building in the Principality to the purposes of Masonry. All appeared highly gratified; and after a very pleasant and agreeable meeting, the party broke up early, in order to allow the brethren to return to their respective homes.

During the Ceremony, Cambrian Lodge was particularly honoured by the appointment of a number of Lodge Members to Provincial Office as follows: Bro David Jeffreys, ProvGChap; Bro G Evans Aubrey, ProvGTreas; Bro John Jones, ProvJGD; Bro Frederick Ashmead, PProvGOrg, and Bro William Dossan, ProvGTyler.

The first annual Provincial Grand Lodge under Edward John Hutchins was held under the Banner of Glamorgan Lodge (then

No.43) at the Cardiff Arms Hotel on Thursday, 17 October 1850. For this event, Glamorgan Lodge was particularly grateful to Loyal Cambrian Lodge at Merthyr for the loan of some of their Lodge furniture. There was the usual public procession in 'full Masonic costume' to St John's Church, when a sermon was preached by the Provincial Grand Chaplain, the Rev D Jeffreys. There was, however, some discontent at the banquet in the evening, where it was reported in the 'Cardiff & Merthyr Guardian': *'A deal of confusion occurred, not only as regards the quality of the wine, but also to the supply of this item and we feel bound to say that in both the arrangements were very defective'*!

The following year, Provincial Grand Lodge was held on Thursday, 24 July at Swansea, under the Banner of Indefatigable Lodge (then No.288). In the report of the 'Cardiff & Merthyr Guardian on Saturday, 26 July 1851, is the first reference to ladies being admitted to a part of the proceedings!

'On the motion of the Grand Master, the Grand Director of Ceremonies was requested to introduce the Ladies, and the Lodge was honoured by the company of the fairest of Swansea ladies, proverbial as the good town is for fair dames.

Brother William Donne Bushell[1] addressed them humorously and eloquently; and, at some length, expatiated on the benefit of Freemasonry, urging the Ladies at all times to choose Freemasons for husbands.

Dr. Bird[2], also, at the request of the Grand Master, addressed the ladies, and 'God save the Queen,' having been sung by the brethren, led by Brother W. Bowen, the Ladies retired, much gratified by the attention shown them.'

On 1 October 1852, a Provincial Grand Lodge was held in Neath under the Banner of Cambrian Lodge. In the report of this event in 'The Cambrian' of 8 October 1852, there is another reference to *the ladies being admitted and seated in the neat little gallery attached to the Hall.'* This gallery was situated at the West end of the Temple, and was removed during the alterations carried out in 1870.

Edward John Hutchins continued to preside at the annual Meetings of Provincial Grand Lodge: 30 August 1853 at Merthyr Tydfil (Loyal Cambrian Lodge); 15 August 1854 at Cardiff (Glamorgan Lodge) and finally 2 August 1855 at Swansea (Indefatigable Lodge). He resigned as ProvGM in 1856 (his resignation was announced in Glamorgan Lodge on 14 April) and he was succeeded by Colonel Charles Kemeys-Tynte of Cefn Mably. He died, *'after a lingering illness',* at Hastings, on 11 February 1876 and an Obituary was published in the 'Western Mail' on Monday, 21 February 1876.

Notes:

[1] William Donne Bushell: Member of Royal Sussex Lodge of Hospitality No.221 (now No.187), Bristol, PDepProvGM, for Bristol (1847); Managing Director Taff Vale Railway Company; Treasurer of The Cardiff Infirmary; Joining member of Glamorgan Lodge (2 March 1852).

[2] Dr Bird: George Gwynne Bird, WM Indefatigable Lodge, Swansea, 1832, 1845 and 1848, DepProvGM, South Wales Eastern Division 1851-1863.

References

 'Who's Who of British Members of Parliament', Volume I, 1832-1885, Harvester Press 1976

'The History of the Dowlais Iron Works 1759 –1970', John A Owen, The Starling   Press, 1977

'The History of the Iron, Steel, Tinplate, and other Trades of Wales,' Charles Wilkins, FG.S, Published & Printed by Joseph Williams, Merthyr Tydfil, 1903

'The Illustrated History of the Loyal Cambrian Lodge', James Fraser, Published Merthyr 1914.

'History of the Indefatigable Lodge', William Henry Jones, Spurrell, Carmarthen 1923

'Cambrian Lodge, No. 364, 1821 - 1921', Bro Glen A Taylor.

WBro Peter M Davies, ProvJGW.

Evan Morgan
1794 - 1877

Deputy Provincial Grand Master
1848 - 1852

Evan Morgan was born at Swansea in March 1794. He embarked on a military career, joining the army in 1812. He served under Wellington in the Rocket Troop Royal Horse Artillery during the final months of the Peninsular War from 13 October 1813 until the end of the War. The War ended with the Battle of Toulouse on 10 April 1814, which resulted in Napoleon's abdication and a Battle Medal for Evan Morgan. Evan then embarked from Bordeaux for North America and served in the army on the Niagara Frontier. In 1834, he was appointed to the Rank of Second Captain and finally retired from the Army in 1844. The previous year, his brother, Captain Thomas Morgan RN, who had served under Nelson in the Battle of Trafalgar, died.

In July 1836, Evan Morgan married Sarah Catharina Chesshyre, daughter of Rear Admiral John Chesshyre. Sarah, who was born in Canterbury, was 15 years younger than Evan. In 1841, her parents were living at Mount Pleasant, Swansea. John Chesshyre was promoted to Vice Admiral of the Blue in August 1840 and Vice Admiral of the White in December 1841. He died at the age of 85 in March 1843.

Also in 1836, Evan was Initiated into Indefatigable Lodge and 10 years later, in 1846, he became Master of the Lodge. In 1845, he had been made a Magistrate and in the Local Government Elections of 1847, he was elected a councillor for the St Helen's Ward, Swansea.

Because of his failing health, the Provincial Grand Master, Sir Josiah John Guest resigned in 1848. His successor was his nephew, Edward John Hutchins, who had also been his Deputy Provincial Grand Master. Hutchins was Installed on Tuesday, 8 August 1848 at a Meeting of Provincial Grand Lodge, held in the new Masonic Temple at Neath, under the Banner of Cambrian Lodge. At that Meeting, Evan Morgan was Installed as the first Deputy Provincial Grand Master of the newly created Province of the Eastern Division of South Wales.

Evan's wife Sarah died on 5 April 1850 at the age of 41. She had, during her time in Swansea, taken a keen interest in the education of the local children and had been the Treasurer of York Place Church School. Her funeral was held at St Mary's Church on 11 April and the ladies and children of the School attended the service.

Evan Morgan relinquished his Office as Deputy Provincial Grand Master in 1852, when he was succeeded by George Gwynne Bird, who had been WM of Indefatigable Lodge in 1832 and again in 1845, thus being Evan Morgan's IPM.

In 1853, Russian troops advanced into Romania, then part of the Turkish Ottoman Empire, and in 1854, an alliance of Britain, France and Turkey declared war on Russia - the start of the Crimea War. This led in Britain to the formation of local Militia, and in Swansea in 1854, Evan Morgan was appointed Lieutenant Colonel of the Royal Glamorgan Artillery Militia.

On 24 February 1857, Evan Morgan married Maria Rodney Winthrop in Taunton. His new wife was the daughter of another

Rear Admiral, Rear Admiral Robert Winthrop! From his two marriages, Evan is known to have had three sons and two daughters. The sons all embarked on military careers.

One son, Jeffrey Llewelyn Morgan of the Royal Engineers, predeceased his father. As a young officer, he fought under Sir Robert Napier (later Lord Napier of Magdala) at the Battle of Magdala, capital of Abyssinia (Ethiopia) overthrowing Emperor Tewodros II. Sadly, the young officer died - '*succumbing to the fatigues he underwent*'. A Memorial Tablet on the north wall of the chancel in St Mary's Church, Swansea, recounts the tale of his services and early death.

His other two sons were Captain Thomas Llewelyn Morgan of the Royal Artillery and Lieutenant William Morgan of the Royal Engineers, both of whom served with distinction in India.

Evan had another brother, who also had a distinguished military career. This was General John Morgan, who died at the age of 84 in April 1869. His funeral service was also held at St Mary's, Swansea, and he is buried there in the family vault.

Evan Morgan, JP, DL, died after a long illness on Wednesday, 3 October 1877 at the age of 83. His Obituary, in the 'Cambrian' stated that '*he was widely known and respected as one of the oldest residents of the town*'. He had died at his residence, St Helen's, Swansea. His funeral took place on Tuesday, 9 October and he, too, was interred in the family vault in the churchyard of the Parish Church of St Mary's.

WBro Peter M Davies, ProvJGW.

Dr George Gwynne Bird
1803 ~ 1863

Deputy Provincial Grand Master.
1851 ~ 1863

 George Gwynne Bird was born in Crickhowell, Breconshire on 1 January 1803, the son of George Gwynne Bird, MD, and Elizabeth Priest. He was the eldest of 10 children. His parents had married on 23 April 1802 at St James's, Paddington. His father was born on 19 August 1779, at Drybridge House (Grade II listed), 51 St Martin's Street Hereford, came from a long line of Gwynnes, who had lived in Herefordshire since Norman times.

   The young George Bird was educated at Madley School, Hereford, and Monmouth School, before becoming apprenticed to his father at the age of 16, when he gained experience in the treatment of accidents in the iron works. At the age of 20 he became a student at St Bartholomew's Hospital, London, where his father had also studied, and in 1823 received his Diploma (LSA - Licentiate of the Society of Apothecaries). On 11 January 1824, he became a member of the Royal College of Surgeons (MRCS). After qualifying in London, he returned to Crickhowell, where he assisted his father for a few years, before taking up the appointment of Surgeon at Swansea Infirmary. Located in St Helens Road, the Infirmary had been founded as a Dispensary in 1814, and became an Infirmary in 1817. It was closed in 1968. Having practised as a Surgeon for 14 years, he resigned and was appointed Physician and subsequently Consulting Physician. He had obtained his LRCP (Licentiate of the Royal College of Physicians) in 1839. Dr Bird was also Medical Officer to the Swansea Gaol and House of Correction. On 11 April 1850, he was appointed a Fellow of the Royal College of Surgeons (FRCS). He was elected a Permanent Vice-President of the British Medical Association in 1861.

   On 31 May 1828, George married a Mrs Jeffreys, the widow of William J Jeffreys of Swansea. The marriage took place at Hay. Within a few years of his marriage, George had been Initiated into Indefatigable Lodge, Swansea and became Worshipful Master of the Lodge for the first time in 1832. In April 1841, the Cambrian reported the death of Harriet Bird, the wife of Dr Bird of Swansea. George married secondly Mary Padley and their engagement was announced in the Cambrian on 18 December 1841. Mary was the daughter of Sylvanus Padley, Harbourmaster and businessman of Swansea. There were two children from this second marriage; a son, George Gwynne, born in 1845 and a daughter, Mary Bessie born in 1847.

   Dr Bird became involved in local politics, became an Alderman and was Mayor of the Borough of Swansea 1842 - 1843. In November 1844, he was made a Magistrate, and the following year he was once again Worshipful Master of Indefatigable Lodge. He became WM of the Lodge for the third time in 1848. Three years later, at a Meeting of Provincial Grand Lodge, held at Swansea on Thursday, 24 July 1851, WBro George Gwynne Bird was Installed Deputy Provincial Grand Master of the Province. A report

Dr George Gwynne Bird

of the Meeting was published in the Cambrian on the Saturday:

'In obedience to the command of the Right Worshipful Provincial Grand Master of Eastern Division of the Province of South Wales, E. J. Hutchins, Esq., M.P., the grand lodge assembled in the Lodge-room of the Indefatigable Lodge, Swansea, yesterday (Thursday). There was a large number of brethren belonging to the lodges attached to the Province – Cardiff, Merthyr, Neath &c. – and several visiting brethren from other provinces. The business of the day was commenced by Brother Thos. Hodges, W.M., and Officers of the Glamorgan Lodge, Cardiff (No. 43) opening the Lodge, as the senior lodge in the province.

On the introduction of the Right Worshipful Grand Master and the Officers of the Grand Lodge, which was opened in ancient and solemn form, the minutes of the last Grand Lodge being read and confirmed and other routine business being disposed of, the grand Master requested that excellent mason, the Right Worshipful Brother William Donne Bushell, to install Brother George Gwynne Bird, M.D., as Deputy Provincial Grand Master of the Province: - Brother Bushell being assisted in the Ceremonies by the Provincial Grand Director of Ceremonies, Brother F. W. Michael and the whole of the brethren present.'

(Thomas Hodges, Ship-Builder of Cardiff, had been Installed WM Glamorgan Lodge on 24 June 1851. William Donne Bushell was Deputy Provincial Grand Master of Bristol (1847) and joined Glamorgan Lodge on 2 March 1852. He was the Deputy Chairman of the Taff Vale Railway Company.)

The account later continues: '*..... a subscription was made to the poor of the parish and £5, 14s. 6d. was subscribed Brother Dr. Bird. Deputy Provincial Grand Master, with Brother Owen Gethin Williams, Past Grand Superintendent of Works, Mayor of Swansea, was required to call upon Mr. Squire, and present the same in the name of the brethren.'* ....

(WBro Owen Gethin Williams, WM of Indefatigable Lodge, 1852-1854, originally from Ferryside, was a Surgeon in Swansea and Mayor 1850-1851.)

And '*On the motion of the Grand Master, the grand Director of Ceremonies was requested to introduce the Ladies, and the Lodge was honoured by the company of the fairest of Swansea ladies, proverbial as the good town is for fair dames.*

Brother William Donne Bushell addressed them humorously and eloquently: and, at some length, expatiated on the benefit of Freemasonry, urging the Ladies at all times to choose Freemasons for husbands.

Dr. Bird also, at the request of the Grand Master, addressed the Ladies, and "God save the Queen," having been sung by the brethren, led by Brother W. Bowen, the Ladies retired, much gratified by the attention shown them.'

In February 1856, George Bird was presented with a portrait of himself, painted by R Jeffreys Lewis of Swansea. The fund was originated by the inhabitants of the town, but was completed by the Members of Indefatigable Lodge. At the presentation, WBro George Augustus Munro, WM, requested that the portrait should be hung in the Lodge Room, to which George Bird assented, '*because amongst his brother masons he had spent much of his leisure time in peace, harmony, and retirement.*' The portrait (illustrated) is to be found above the staircase at Swansea Masonic Hall.

Dr George Gwynne Bird died after a short but severe illness at his home, 9 Dynevor Place, Swansea, on Sunday, 2 August 1863. He was a widower of 60 years of age. Living with him were two unmarried daughters, Mary Jane, age 22, from his first marriage and Mary Bessie, age 14, from his second marriage. For a few years before his death, he had been afflicted with total blindness, but continued to pursue his professional duties up to the period of his last illness. He had also continued as Deputy Provincial Grand Master up to the time of his death. Interestingly, his father died on 25 May 1863 at Bowmanville, Ontario, having emigrated to Canada in 1833, where he became a noted Naturalist.

Dr George Gwynne Bird

WBro Peter M Davies, ProvJGW.

Brecknock Lodge No.651

Warranted : 4 May 1855

Consecrated : 28 July 1855

Meeting at the Masonic Hall, Brecon.

A Petition dated October 1854 for a Warrant to Constitute a new Lodge in Brecon was presented by eleven Members of St Peter's Lodge No.699, (now No.476), Carmarthen. St Peter's Lodge had been Warranted on 26 April 1841 on the recommendation of Sir Josiah John Guest, ProvGM. The Petition for Brecknock Lodge nominated Bro Frederick Bolingbroke Ribbans of Carmarthen to be the first Master; Bro Col Lloyd Vaughan Watkins, MP, of Penoyre, Brecon, to be the first SW; and Bro Capt John Peter Parland of Woodlands, Hay, to be the first JW. Ribbans, a graduate of Corpus Christi College, Cambridge, was Headmaster of Queen Elizabeth's Grammar School, Carmarthen, and had become WM of St Peter's Lodge in 1845. In 1856, he was instrumental in establishing the Prince of Wales Lodge No.671, Llanelli, and was again the first Master of the Lodge. He was Elected the first Honorary Member of Brecknock Lodge in 1856 and, in 1857, he served as ProvSGW of the Province of South Wales Western Division. Following his retirement in 1857, he returned to England, and settled at Windsor.

The Warrant of Brecknock Lodge was issued on 14 May 1855 and the first summons read: *'Sir & Bro, I beg to inform you that the Brecknock Lodge of Freemasons will be opened on Saturday the 28 July 1855 at the Castle Hotel, Brecon, when your assistance will be esteemed.'* The original number of Brecknock (the old name for Brecon) Lodge, which is still evident on the Volume of the Sacred Law was No.936, but in November 1863 it was changed to its present number of 651.

In 1855, the Ceremony of Consecration was much simpler than the Ceremony of today. The Lodge was opened and the Warrant read and approved, then the ProvGM's Dispensation was read, Constituting the Meeting. The WM, F B Ribbans, Invested his Officers and the Lodge was closed. The duties of the Tyler were *'to keep furniture and Jewels in a proper manner; lay out the Lodge, and deliver summonses in Brecon, for which he would receive 2/6.'* (12½p)

At the second Meeting of the Lodge, the Founders agreed that the annual subscription would be set at one guinea, payable half-yearly, and Initiation fees at three guineas (at today's prices £250). The Brethren were informed that the next Provincial Grand Lodge Meeting would be held in Brecon on Friday, 4 August 1858, with RWBro Charles Kemeys Kemeys-Tynte, ProvGM, presiding.

Freemasonry appears to have been far more open at this time, as in March 1863, the Brethren joined a public procession, by Dispensation from the ProvGM, to the Priory Church. They joined in a full Choral Service *'to participate in the Patriotic Demonstration, being the marriage of HRH The Prince of Wales.'* Attendances at Lodge Meetings were giving cause for concern, however, so fines were introduced. The Senior and Junior Deacons were each fined 2/6, *'their excuses for non attendances not being accepted.'*

Bro J D Perrott was first Installed as Master in December 1864 and occupied the Chair for two years. He played an important role in the formation of the first Daughter Lodge, Aberystwyth Lodge No.1072, and became its first WM. Twelve Brecknock Members signed the Petition, there being insufficient Masons in Aberystwyth to do so, and on 30 November 1865, Aberystwyth Lodge was Consecrated.

1866 was an unusual year because two Installations were held. Firstly, in January, WBro J D Perrott was Installed by the RW ProvGM, Theodore Mansel Talbot, when the Brethren witnessed for the first time the *'Grand Spectacle'* of his entrance into the Temple. To mark the occasion, a Masonic Ball was held at the Castle Hotel where dignitaries of the town attended. The second Installation was in December with Bro Evan Jones having been Elected as WM. However, it was announced that *'Bro Evan Jones was too ill to attend, but as the Brethren had been summoned for the purpose of Installation, he proposed that the Ceremony be carried out at his home.'* The WM and two PMs then proceeded to Bro Evan's residence where the Ceremony was performed. Upon their return to the Lodge, the Officers were Invested and the Lodge closed.

In 1866, the Castle Hotel, Brecon, offered the Lodge a spacious room detached from the Hotel, which the Members gratefully accepted as a Meeting place. This was Dedicated on 14 June 1866 as the new Freemasons' Hall by the ProvGM, in the presence of 60 Brethren. The tenancy expired in 1896, when the Castle Hotel gave the Lodge 'notice to quit'. Rooms were found at Ruperra House, 1 Glamorgan Street, Brecon and the first Lodge Meeting was held there in January 1897. Ruperra House was Grade II listed in December 1976.

The Lodge first hosted a Meeting of PGL on 18 July 1867. It was held at the Town Hall. The start was delayed to allow Aberystwyth Lodge Brethren sufficient time to travel to Brecon in order to witness the Investiture of Officers. In all, 120 Brethren were present. The next occasion that PGL was held under the Banner of Brecknock Lodge was on 13 June 1878. The Meeting was held once again at the Town Hall and WBro Marmaduke Tennant, DepProvGM, presided.

An advertisement was placed in the Brecon County Times in 1868 requesting all Brethren to attend Lodge Meetings, after concern had been expressed about absences. For the next three years, the Chair was occupied by WBro F Broughton, a Dispensation having been obtained for his third year. A further Dispensation was granted so that his son, who was under 21 years of age, could be Initiated into the Lodge.

In 1875, Bro Edward C Phillips was Installed as WM and, while in the Chair, he was appointed ProvGSec, an Office he held for just one year. On 28 April 1875, he and five other Lodge Brethren attended the Royal Albert Hall for the Installation of HRH The Prince of Wales, KG, as Grand Master.

On 29 April 1879, Loyal Wye Lodge No.1807, the second Daughter Lodge of Brecknock Lodge, was Consecrated at the Lion Hotel, Builth Wells. The Primus Master was WBro Herbert Charles Ingram Rich, Installed WM of Brecknock Lodge in 1868. The third Daughter Lodge, Loyal Hay Lodge No.2382, was Consecrated at Hay on Wye on 25 November 1890, by WBro Marmaduke Tennant. There were 12 Petitioners, of whom 9 were Members of Brecknock Lodge. The Primus Master was Brecon Solicitor, WBro John Tudor, who had been Installed as WM of Brecknock Lodge in January 1888. While Master of Brecknock Lodge, a Dispensation was granted to hold a *'special dancing party'* on 19 December 1888 at the Castle Hotel, Brecon, and permitting Masonic Jewels and clothing to be worn.

Having obtained the permission of the DepProvGM in 1891, the Brethren agreed to incorporate the Brecon Borough Coat of Arms with its Motto *'Canmol dy Fro a Thrig Yno'*, which may be translated *'Praise thy Land and Dwell Therein'*. The central part of the Coat of Arms also appears on the PM's Jewel.

In 1896, the RWBro the Rt Hon John Allan, the Lord Llangattock, ProvGM and VWBro Marmaduke Tennant, DepProvGM, attended the Installation of Bro T A R Littledale. At the end of his year in Office, he presented a silver Square, still in use, inscribed as follows *'Presented to the Brecknock Lodge No.651 by Bro Littledale, WM, to mark the sixtieth year of Her Majesty Queen Victoria's glorious reign and as a memento of a pleasant sojourn in the Lodge, June 1897'*.

A Special Meeting was held in April 1902 to welcome two Brethren who had returned safely from the Boar War. Then, in October 1905, congratulations were sent to a Joining Member, Bro Alderman Vaughan Morgan, upon his election as Lord Mayor of London and inviting him to attend the Lodge during his year of office. Sir Walter Vaughan Morgan, Lord Mayor of London in 1906, attended a Meeting at the County Hall Chambers in September 1906, accompanied by his nephew and Chaplain, Bro Rev Hornby Steer, and Bro Sir George Smallman, Alderman and Sheriff of London. Walter Vaughan Morgan (1831 - 1919) with his brother, Major William Vaughan Morgan (1826 - 1892) and four other brothers, were the founders in 1881 of the now international Morgan Crucibles Company plc.

The year 1909 must have been a memorable one for WBro J Meredith (WM 1890), as he proposed his four sons into Freemasonry. Three were Initiated in April and one at the Meeting in June. In September, all four were Passed and the Minute reads, *'there were eight Candidates to be Passed that evening, the WM arranging that he would take four at a time'*. WBro Meredith's four sons were Raised by their father in the December.

Bro John Evans, who had served as Tyler for 28 years, passed to the Grand Lodge Above in June 1909. The Brethren attended his funeral, walking in procession to the house, with the Assistant Secretary carrying the Tyler's Sword and Emblems, which were placed on the coffin. After the service, the Brethren walked around the grave dropping sprigs of Acacia upon the coffin.

The Minutes of the Installation Meeting of October 1914 read, *'The Acting WM WBro W. J. Nott presided and explained that owing to the outbreak of the War WBro David Jones the WM was unable to be present but that he would continue in office until a successor had been Installed in his stead.'* However, a Dispensation was obtained in 1915 permitting the Election of WBro David Jones *'in his absence'* as he was at the time serving in the Armed Forces. At the Installation in October 1916, WBro Nott was able to congratulate WBro David on his safe return from India, and WBro Jones thanked the Brethren for having Elected him WM in his absence. Throughout the War, Meetings were held regularly, no Meeting appears to have been adjourned, and 9 Candidates were Initiated, 8 Passed and 5 Raised. An Instruction had been received from Grand Lodge that *'Members who had not paid their fees whilst on active service were not to be prejudiced'*.

WBro W J Nott, who had been Installed as WM in 1892, and had acted as WM for three years during WWI, was Elected WM in 1919. The ProvGM and the DepProvGM attended his Installation, and during his year as Master, 12 Meetings were held, when 18 Candidates were Initiated, 11 Passed and 4 Raised.

Over the next few years, the prime objective was to find more suitable premises. Several properties were inspected, and finally agreement was reached to purchase for £110, land at Cerrigcochion Road, the site of the present Masonic Temple. The Foundation Stone was laid by RWBro Sir Charles L D Venables Llewelyn, Bart, ProvGM, on 25 January 1928, prior to which a musical Service was held at Brecon Cathedral. WBro T A R Littledale informed the Lodge that the sum of £500, shown on the accounts as a loan from him towards the new Building, should be considered as a gift. He was thanked by the Brethren for his generosity. Generosity it certainly was, £500 in 1929 would be worth almost £24,000 today.

Due to the withdrawal of the SW in 1936, the Brethren Elected WBro T A R Littledale, WM, 1896-1897, as Master. He had been made an Honorary Member in 1926, which he had to relinquish to become a Subscribing Member in order to take Office.

Regular Meetings were held during WWII, and there is no record of any Lodge being cancelled or adjourned. There was certainly no shortage of Candidates, 41 were Initiated, 33 Passed and 33 Raised. During 1941, a father and son, Mr R Gittins, aged 59, and Mr W

Gittins, aged 29, were Initiated. Twin brothers, Gerald and Garnet Morris, were also Initiated. Bro Garnet served in the RAF during the War and was awarded the DFC. Unfortunately, he was killed in a flying accident in Canada. In his book 'Province at War' WBro Keith Flynn, OBE, recounts the following incident: '*In the winter of 1943 five Brethren from a Swansea Lodge having come into possession of a car and some petrol coupons decided despite the blackout to visit a Lodge some distance away beyond the intervening hills. The journey was apparently of a nightmare quality and eventually they arrived unexpected, tired, hungry and anxious. From the outset their reception was anything but Brotherly. Indeed it had been described as hostile and throughout the proceedings both in and out of the Temple they suffered, much to their dismay, the coldest of shoulders. It was some months later that putting two and two together they learned that they had been mistaken for food Inspectors and one can only conjecture that things were not all that they should have been in that particular quarter at that time.*' Unfortunately, the Lodge they visited was Brecknock, but diplomatically, this was not mentioned.

In 1953, the DepProvGM, RWBro Edgar J Rutter, OSM, PGW, was invited to occupy the Chair for the 1955 Centenary Celebrations. It was first necessary for him to relinquish his Honorary Membership and, in October 1953, he became a Joining Member. A Special Dispensation had to be obtained, as RWBro Edgar Rutter would still be occupying the Chair of Worcestershire Installed Masters' Lodge No.6889, at the time of his Installation. The Installation Ceremony was held on 29 September 1954 and was performed by WBro Edgar W Lewis, AProvGM. All the Officers Invested that year were PMs of the Lodge, apart from the Chaplain, Assistant Organist and Stewards. While Master, the DepProvGM performed all but one of the Ceremonies.

The Centenary Meeting was held at the Guild Hall, Brecon, on 28 July 1955, with the DepProvGM in the Chair, and in the presence of 235 Brethren. The chief guest was VWBro J Howell Evans, MA, MD, MCh, OSM, PDepProvGM, Middlesex. His Worship the Mayor of Brecon, Bro Col D L Jones, TD, JP, extended a Civic welcome to the Lodge upon its Centenary. The Warrant was read, the Meeting adjourned, and the Brethren walked in procession, accompanied by the Mayor and Corporation, to Brecon Cathedral for a service led by the Very Rev William Edward Jones, MA, Dean. WBro Rev Canon Arthur Dyfrig James, Head Master of Christ College, Brecon, gave an excellent Address. On returning to the Lodge, the Meeting was resumed, the Centenary Warrant was presented and read, and Centenary Jewels were presented to all Members. The presentation of an embroidered blue and gold cushion was made by Brecknock Lodge No.6369, London, which is still in use today. The Members adjourned to Dering Lines Army Camp for an excellent banquet. Then at Bro T Walters's Installation in 1956, Bro Col D L Jones, TD, as Mayor of Brecon, presented a plaque to commemorate the Centenary of the Lodge.

WBro Kingsford Sydney Fawkes, PPrGW, celebrated his Golden Jubilee in Freemasonry in 1960. Initiated into Lebanon Lodge No.34, Langdon, North Dakota, USA, he joined Brecknock Lodge in 1910 and was Installed as WM in 1926. Another Joining Member, who was to become a most distinguished Freemason, was Bro Islwyn Evans. He was Initiated into Cartref Lodge No.5572, Cardiff on 21 April 1947 and joined Brecknock Lodge in 1950.  Installed as WM of the Lodge in 1964, he obtained his first Grand Lodge Collar as PGStB in 1978 and in the Province was promoted to ProvSGW in 1987. In 1989, he was promoted in Grand Lodge to PAGDC. He celebrated his Golden Jubilee in Freemasonry in April 1997, receiving his Veteran's Certificate from Honorary Member, VWBro Cdr Roy K Hopkin, RN, DepProvGM. In 2000, he was again promoted in Grand Lodge to the Rank of PJGD.

In March 1968, Brethren from the Loventium Mark Lodge No.1287, Aberaeron, presented three inscribed oak Gavels, for the use of the WM and Wardens, which remain in use today. They were given in gratitude for the gift of the Mark Regalia and furniture, which Brecknock Lodge had allowed to be removed to Aberaeron, on the demise of the former Brychan Mark Lodge, Brecon, in 1882. Also, in 1968, a Petition was presented by

WBro Tom Walters, who had been Installed as WM in 1956, for the formation of a fourth Daughter Lodge, Vivian Lodge No.8267. This Lodge was Consecrated at the Masonic Hall, Brecon, on the 10 March 1969, when WBro Tom Walters was Installed as Primus Master. In 1970, WBro Tom became the first PM to become a Grand Officer, when he was Invested with the Rank of PGStB. He had the honour to represent the ProvGM, RWBro the Rt Hon the Lord Swansea, at the Installation of Bro Gwyn Herbert as WM of Brecknock Lodge in 1970. Further biographical details of WBro Tom are given in the history of Vivian Lodge, later in this book.

At the Installation of Bro Aneurin Rees, Headmaster of Brecon High School, in the presence of the ProvGM, a Petition was presented to form a new Royal Arch Chapter in Brecon. Brecknock Chapter No.651 was Warranted on 10 November 1971. The Brethren of Brecknock Lodge agreed to a sum of £150 being donated to the new Chapter. WBro Aneurin Rees subsequently became a Grand Officer in 1985.

Another Petition was presented to the WM and Brethren in 1974 for the formation of the fifth Daughter Lodge, Aberhonddu Lodge No.8588, which was duly Consecrated on 18 October 1974. The Primus Master was WBro Foster Ball, Installed as WM of Brecknock Lodge in 1966.

In 1984, a gold PM's Jewel was presented to the Lodge by the family of the late WBro D Hughes Morgan, who had been Installed as WM in 1907. The Jewel is always worn by the IPM. Also in 1984, the Brethren agreed to relinquish ownership of the Masonic Hall and vest it in an Association of Lodges and Chapters. An Association of Brecon Freemasons was formed in 1985, its first AGM being held in September, when WBro Islwyn Evans became the first Chairman.

The Bicentenary of recorded Freemasonry in Brecon was celebrated at Brecon High School on 20 October 1989. This was in reference to Cambrian Lodge No.542, meeting at the Swan Inn, Ship Street, Brecon, which had been Warranted on 1 August 1789, but Erased on 5 March 1828. The banquet was graced by the presence of RWBro the Rt Hon the Lord Swansea, ProvGM, and VWBro Geoffrey M Ashe, TD, DepProvGM. Also present were RWBros Col Myrddin Jones, OBE, TD, DL, ProvGM of Monmouthsire; A S C Blench, ProvGM of Herefordshire; Sir Maynor Jennor, KStJ, TD; WBro Major General Morgan Llewellyn, OBE; WBro Graham Rees, DepProvGM of Monmouthshire and WBro B G Lambert, DepProvGM of Herefordshire. Members of all the Brecon Lodges and Lodges in Builth Wells, Llandrindod Wells, Hay, Aberystwyth, Carmarthen, Merthyr, Aberdare and Abergavenny were present. Prior to the banquet, the Rt Hon the Lord Swansea unveiled a plaque in the Masonic Hall to commemorate the event.

ASSOCIATION OF BRECON FREEMASONS
TO COMMEMORATE THE BI-CENTENARY
OF RECORDED FREEMASONRY IN BRECON
1789-1989
UNVEILED BY
THE PROVINCIAL GRAND MASTER
RW BRO THE RT HON THE LORD SWANSEA DL

A number of Brethren became Honorary Members in 1990; RWBro the Rt Hon the Lord Swansea, VWBro Geoffrey Malin Ashe, WBro Malcolm Thompson, WBro Richard Griffiths, (WM in 1957 and 1958) and WBro L J Hoggarth, (WM in 1963). The following year, Bro Gerald Morris and Bro Percy Schilling became Masonic Veterans and, in 1992, WBro Richard Griffiths, WBro David Harpur and later that year Bro Col Ted Edwards, CVO, OBE, TD, also completed 50 years in Freemasonry.

The presence of woodworm was discovered in some of the Temple furnishings in 1991, resulting in the replacement of the three pedestals. A new Secretary's desk was donated by the future ProvGM, WBro Hywel Davies. At the Installation of Bro T R Eirian Jones in 1993, WBro Brian Matthews, PM Windsor Lodge, Penarth, presented an electric organ on behalf of his mother, the widow of late WBro Albert Matthews, for use by all Brecon Lodges. It was replaced in 2004 by the present organ, which was funded from a legacy in memory of Bro Caradoc Evans.

On his retirement as AProvGM in 1996, WBro Ken Adams Morgan was presented with a painting of Brecon. He was Elected an Honorary Member of the Lodge in October and, in 1997, he was awarded the OBE.

On 26 June 1996, a celebration dinner was held at Bishops Meadow Restaurant, Hay Road, Brecon, to mark the appointment of WBro Hywel Davies as AProvGM. Brethren from all the Brecon and surrounding Lodges were in attendance. In September, Bro

Anthony Edwards, the son of the late Bro Col Ted Edwards, unveiled a plaque to the memory of his father, whose bequest had funded the purchase of a new Lodge carpet.

In 1997, WBro Bill Rees and Bro Mike Oxnard received the OBE and MBE respectively, and were suitably congratulated. The same year, WBro Hywel Davies was promoted to PSGD in Grand Lodge. The two Ballot Boxes, which he had presented to the Lodge, were used for the first time at the Installation of Bro W S John Swain in September 1997. Unfortunately, the SW, Bro John Morris, had to resign due to ill health and consequently in September the following year, WBro John Swain was Proclaimed WM. This was only the second time since 1916 for a Brother to occupy the Chair for two consecutive years.

RWBro Hywel Davies was Invested as ProvGM at the Royal Welsh Showground, Builth Wells, on 16 September 1999. Brethren of Brecknock Lodge were present in goodly numbers to support him, and WBro John Swain, WM, had the honour of being one of the escort party. At the October Meeting, the new ProvGM was Elected an Honorary Member of the Lodge.

A bequest, in memory of Bro Meurig Jones, was used to purchase Masonic implements for the Inner Guard. These are mounted inside the door of the Temple. At his Installation in September 2003, Bro Peter Cooper presented alms plates to the Lodge. WBro Gwynne Clark, who was retiring after ten years as DC, was presented with a decanter and glasses, inscribed with the Lodge Logo, by the newly Installed Master. Sadly, WBro Peter passed away in June 2004, before completing his year. In his short period as Master, he raised over £2000 for charity. Also in 2003, Bro P G Davies became a Masonic Veteran and to mark the occasion he was presented with his Veteran's Certificate and suitably inscribed drinking glasses.

The appointment of Lodge Member, WBro Des Preece, as the new ProvJGW was announced in April 2005. He had been Installed as WM in 1995. On 28 July 2005, 112 Brethren attended an Emergency Meeting in the presence of RWBro Hywel Davies, ProvGM, his Wardens, Officers and four AProvGMs, to celebrate the 150th Anniversary of the Lodge. Present were representatives from Brecknock Lodge's Mother Lodge, its five Daughter Lodges, and its four Granddaughter Lodges. After a short address by the ProvGM, the Secretary, WBro David J Davies, read a copy of the Petition and the ProvGSec read the Warrant. A plaque to commemorate the 150th Anniversary was presented by WBro Gwynne Clark (Installed WM in 1990) to WBro Robin Harris, Chairman of the Association of Brecon Freemasons. Afterwards, at a celebratory Festive Board, the Brethren were presented with a copy of a booklet on the history of the Lodge by WBro Islwyn Evans together with a glass engraved with the Lodge Insignia.

At Bro Richard J Ackroyd's Installation in September 2005, WBro Des C Preece, ProvJGW, represented the ProvGM. In gratitude for his service as Lodge Secretary for over twelve years, WBro David J Davies was presented with an inscribed painting and, in October, WBro Mark Morgan, PM Aberhonddu Lodge, Mayor of Brecon, presented a plaque on behalf of the Town Council, to commemorate the Lodge's 150th Anniversary. WBro Islwyn Evans, PJGD, was Elected an Honorary Member in November, a very fitting honour to a worthy Mason, who had contributed much to the development of Freemasonry in Mid-Wales. Sadly, having served Freemasonry so well for 62 years, he passed away in the summer of 2009, but he will be fondly remembered and his influence will be lasting.

In 2007, WBro Des Preece was warmly congratulated on two occasions; firstly, on receiving Grand Lodge honours and being Invested as PAGDC, and secondly, on being awarded the MBE. Then, in April 2008, Lodge Secretary, WBro T R Eirian Jones, received congratulations upon his appointment as the AProvGM for the Provincial Grand Lodge of Mark Master Masons of South Wales.

Compiled by WBro T R Eirian Jones, PPrJGW, with due acknowledgement for information extracted from
'A Brief History of 200 years of Recorded Freemasonry' and
'Brecknock Lodge, the 150 years', by the late WBro Islwyn Evans, PJGD.

Robert Francis Langley
1821 - 1892

Founder First Principal
St John's Chapter No.36

Robert Francis Langley was born in Cardiff in 1821, the son of Captain John Langley, who had moved to Cardiff from Swansea in about 1793 to serve as Captain and Paymaster in The Royal Glamorgan Militia. Robert qualified as a Solicitor and in 1862 was appointed Registrar to Cardiff County Court, an Office he held until his death in 1892. In 1854, he married Rosa Lydia Price, who originally came from Bromley in Kent. The marriage took place in Greenwich, London and they lived initially at 'The Elms', Penarth. Their son, Alfred Francis Langley was born in 1858, and he followed his father into the legal profession, completing his articles with Messrs Ingledew, Ince & Vachell, Cardiff. He subsequently worked with his father and officiated as joint Registrar. The family now lived at 1 St Andrew's Place, Cardiff.

Langley was Initiated into Glamorgan Lodge on 17 May, Passed on 19 November and Raised on 12 December 1852 and became Worshipful Master of the Lodge on 11 June 1855. During Langley's year as Master there were no fewer than 27 Initiations! On 17 July 1855 one person was Initiated, one Passed and five Raised, and on 11 February 1856 six Brethren were Passed! On 26 February 1856, Langley Initiated the Barrister and wealthy landowner John Whitlock Nicholl-Carne (1817-1889) of Dimlands Castle, near Cowbridge.

On 10 September 1855, Langley proposed that a Royal Arch Chapter should be established and attached to Glamorgan Lodge. His proposal was passed unanimously, though at the time Langley was not a Royal Arch Mason! No time was lost; he was Exalted the following day in the Beaufort Chapter No.120 (Now No.103), Bristol. The Petitioners for the new Chapter were all Members of the Bristol Chapter and with one exception were Members of Glamorgan Lodge. The St John's Chapter was Consecrated on 30 January 1856 and Langley was named on the Charter as the Founder First Principal, even though by that date he had only been a Royal Arch Mason for a little more than four months! Langley became First Principal of the Chapter again in 1866 and Second Principal in 1868.

In July 1858, Langley was once again Installed WM of the Lodge. Shortly afterwards the Brethren decided to present him with a silver salver, to mark the high esteem in which he was held. Consequently, a Lodge of Emergency was held on Monday, 27 January 1857, and the Minutes record:

'The lodge was called for the purpose of presenting to Bro. R.F. Langley P.M. a testimonial consisting of a Silver Salver with Masonic Emblems, and a gold P.M. Jewel which had been subscribed for by the brethren of this lodge.

Several letters on this subject were read and the brethren adjourned to a banquet at the Cardiff Arms, which was presided over by Bro. Col. C. K. Kemeys Tynte Prov. G.M. who in grateful and eloquent terms presented the testimonial.

Bro. Langley in a feeling and truly Masonic address thanked the brethren for the compliment paid him, and expressed the pleasure he felt in seeing the prosperity of the Glamorgan Lodge No. 43 and that he should at all times be ready to further that prosperity, and the good of Freemasonry in general.

Several Masonic and other toasts were given and the evening was spent in perfect harmony.'

The salver, made by E & J Barnard, hall-marked London 1858, is circular in shape and stands on three scroll feet and was supplied to C. Taylor & Son in January 1859 at a cost of £27 plus 1s 6d for a fitted box. It has a moulded scroll strap-work border and the edge is engraved with scrollwork and Masonic emblems - the Square and Compasses with the letter G.; the Square, Level and Plumbline; the 24 Inch Gauge, Gavel and Chisel; and a Past Master's Jewel. There are four central panels containing figures representing 'Faith, Hope & Charity', 'Justice & Prudence', 'Temperance & Fortitude' and a scene from the parable 'The Good Samaritan', together with the following inscription:

'Presented to Brother Robert Langley PM by the Officers and Brethren of The Glamorgan Lodge No. 43 as a token of Fraternal regard and in acknowledgement of the valuable services rendered by him to the cause of Freemasonry, January 1859.'

Over 100 years later, the silver salver came up for auction at Sotheby's on 26 October 1971. A few weeks earlier, WBro A R Hewitt, PAGDC, Librarian & Curator of the Grand Lodge Library & Museum, London, wrote to the Secretary of Glamorgan Lodge about the impending sale and stated:

'It is a handsome piece and one which I should like to see in the Grand Lodge Museum. At the moment I have not been able to get an idea of the price it is likely to reach; it might well be in the region of £200.

I think you ought to know of the sale in case your lodge would be interested in acquiring it. Will you please let me know as soon as possible because if the price is not too high then Grand Lodge would be interested in purchasing it, but I should add that I have not yet had authority to enter the market.'

Glamorgan Lodge decided to contribute £50 towards the purchase of the salver, which was acquired for Grand Lodge Museum at a purchase price of £135. Later, WBro Hewitt wrote to the Lodge:

'I was delighted to learn that Glamorgan Lodge has agreed to contribute the sum of £50 towards the cost of the purchase of the Langley Salver. It is indeed a most generous gesture and one which I can assure you is greatly appreciated. The acquisition of the salver will be duly recorded as a joint purchase by your Lodge and the Grand Lodge.'

Returning to Robert Langley, it should be added that he played an important part in the formation of the first Mark Masons Lodge in South Wales, Langley Lodge No.28, Consecrated on 15 June 1859 and named in his honour. On 13 May 1859, Langley and five other Members of Glamorgan Lodge went to Bristol, where they were Advanced in Canynges T I, Mark Masons Lodge, which at that time was under the jurisdiction of the Grand Lodge of Scotland. Langley Lodge was the second Daughter Lodge of Canynges, and at the time of the Consecration is was No.16 on the Scottish Register. The English Grand Lodge of Mark Master Masons had been founded in 1856, but it was not until 1869 that Langley Lodge applied to join the English Grand Lodge. A Warrant of confirmation was issued later that year, when Langley Lodge became No.28 on the English Register.

In Provincial Grand Lodge, Langley was appointed Grand Registrar in 1857, Junior Grand Warden in 1859 and Senior Grand Warden in 1861. He was Installed WM of Glamorgan Lodge for a third time on 25 June 1866.

Robert Francis Langley died at his country residence in Llanishen on Tuesday, 28 June 1892 at the age of 71. Almost a year earlier, he had suffered a paralytic stroke, which deprived him of speech for some time and prevented him from returning to work.

According to his Obituary in 'The South Wales Echo' on 29 June, Langley claimed that he could trace his ancestry back to Geoffrey de Langley, a Knight who distinguished himself in the Third Crusade.

WBro Peter M Davies, ProvJGW.

St David's Lodge No.679

Warranted : 6 May 1856
Consecrated : 18 June 1856
Meeting at the Masonic Hall, Aberdare.

St David's Lodge was, in the main, formed by several Members of Loyal Cambrian Lodge No.127 (now No.110)) Merthyr, who had developed business and professional interests in Aberdare and often spent the night in the town. Among these were Thomas Jones Dyke, Medical Officer of Health for Merthyr; Thomas Davies Jnr, Bank Manager; and Rees Hopkin Rhys, a gentleman, who, although Initiated into Loyal Cambrian Lodge, lived at Llwydcoed, Aberdare.

On 18 June 1856, a group of fourteen Masonic Brethren, including those already mentioned, met at the Queen's Hotel in Aberdare, a site now occupied by Burton Menswear. Ten of these were Brethren from Loyal Cambrian Lodge, one from Cambrian Lodge No.472 (now No.364), Neath, two from St George Lodge No.333, Glasgow, and one from Silurian Lodge No.693 (now No.471), Newport.

It is recorded that *'The Lodge was opened in the first degree under the Presidency of Bro. Robert Jones, WM Loyal Cambrian Lodge 127 Merthyr Tydfil, Bro. George Roach PM 127 and Bro, J W Russell, PM 127 officiating as Junior and Senior Wardens'*. Thomas Jones Dyke then formerly presented Bro Robert Jones with the Warrant dated 16 May 1856 which was *'given under the Seal of the United Grand Lodge of England granting certain Brethren the right to hold a Regular Lodge at Aberdare'*. The Warrant continues *'know ye that we by the authority of the United Grand Lodge of England, vested in us for that purpose, and at the humble Petition of our Right Truly and Well Beloved Brethren, Thomas Jones Dyke, Thomas Davies Junr., Rees H. Rhys..............etc, DO HEREBY CONSTITUTE the said Brethren into a Lodge of Free and Accepted Masons under the Title of Denomination of ....No. 979...........ST. DAVID'S LODGE.'* An intriguing and interesting feature of the Warrant is that the Lodge was incorrectly described as being in North Wales (although this wasn't noticed until January 1857). WBro Dyke was then Installed as the first Worshipful Master of St David's Lodge, and subsequently Invested Bros Thomas Davies and Rees Hopkin Rhys as Senior and Junior Wardens respectively.

Immediately after the Installation Ceremony, a Ballot was taken for nineteen gentlemen who had been proposed and accepted as being worthy to be made Masons. This large number was certainly evidence of the need for a Masonic Lodge in Aberdare. Fourteen of those proposed, who had been within call, were admitted in groups and Initiated into Freemasonry, the Ceremony being conducted only twice. The first Initiate, James Gawn, became the first Secretary of the Lodge on that day and at the next

Meeting, Bro T B Powell was Elected as the first Treasurer, a post he held for well over a quarter of a century.

The Queen's Hotel, where the early Meetings had been held, closed in 1857 and the Provincial Grand Master authorised that the Lodge could move to the Black Lion Hotel in April 1858. The Warrant stated that the Lodge would meet on the third Wednesday in each month. However, in the early days, Meetings would commonly be postponed for two or three days or even a week, so Emergency Lodges were fairly frequent. The time of day at which Meetings commenced also varied greatly, but the amount of work carried out was not curtailed. For the first quarter of a century, very often two Degrees would be performed on the same evening, together with explanations of both Tracing Boards. The records show that at some Festivals, a Ballot would be taken for two Candidates, who would then be Initiated before the Installation Ceremony was proceeded with.

In 1860, St David's Lodge entertained Provincial Grand Lodge at Aberdare, when the chief business was the adoption of the report of the Committee on Masonic Charities.

Remarkably, from January 1862 to January 1864, St David's Lodge closed and, when it resumed, the Brethren were informed that the Lodge number had been changed. Henceforth it was to be No.679 and not 979 as previously recorded in the Roll of Lodges. The change was due to the number of Lodges that had lapsed and become defunct, and so we must assume that 'gaps' were closed. Since that time, Freemasonry in general having grown, no further adjustments have had to be made. However, the Lodge went through another crisis between 1865 and 1869, when again no Meetings were held. It was only the diligence of WBro William Morris in paying the Grand Lodge dues during that time, which saved it from complete extinction. He also had the foresight to forward the Warrant to Provincial Grand Lodge for safe keeping, during that period when St David's Lodge was 'in abeyance'.

The only reason for decline appeared to be the lack of experienced Brethren to go forward, the first WM having apparently 'retired into the background'. The two Masters who were responsible for the Lodge throughout these critical years had progressed from Inner Guard to the Wardens' Chairs in just one step. As a result, the next decade became one of consolidation, with Masonic labour steadily increasing, often with two or sometimes three Ceremonies being performed on the same evening. One example of this was in June 1874, when a Ballot was held, after which one Brother was Raised, another Passed, and two successful Candidates were Initiated.

In 1874, two Brethren 'of high standing and rank,' WBro Sir George Elliot, Bart, MP, and his son-in-law, WBro J C Parkinson, DepProvGM for Middlesex, were accepted as Joining Members. Both were connected with the rapidly expanding coal industry in the Welsh valleys. The latter became WM of St David's Lodge in March 1874. Just two months later he became 'Acting Junior Grand Deacon of England' and, despite his many honours and the heavy demand on his time, he presided over six Ceremonies during his year, when no less than eleven Candidates were Initiated. Not many Lodges have had as their ruling Master, a Brother who was at the same time the DepProvGM and an Acting Junior Grand Deacon. This was a privilege enjoyed by St David's Lodge in that year.

The Lodge archives and records have revealed an extract from an Italian newspaper, L'Opinione, printed in Rome, dated 31 October 1876 under the heading 'HONOUR SHOWN TO A WELSH FREEMASON'. Translated, excerpts read: *'On the evening of Saturday, 28th October the Freemasons of Rome were specially assembled in the Temple Grande Oriente d'Italia – one of the largest Halls in Europe – to welcome Mr. J.C. Parkinson late W. M. of the Aberdare Lodge and one of the greatest Freemasonical dignatories in Great Britain and to present him with an address showing the great esteem he is held in by the Freemasons of Italy, and as a remembrance of his visit to this part of the World.............. The Grand Master of Italy, The Hon. Georgio Tamio, in a most eloquent speech, presented the Address, which was engraved and painted in the most elegant and costly manner.*

The presentation was followed by repeated applause from all present. Mr Parkinson, who was visibly affected by his reception in expressing his thanks, spoke with such eloquence of the duties of Freemasonry and touched on its origin and present state. .... He also hailed with pleasure, the establishment of the New Grand Lodge in Rome, the ancient capital of the world............

The speech by Mr. Parkinson lasted one hour and was applauded to the echo............ Other Masons then spoke at length and all made mention of speeches that had been made in England by Mr. Parkinson in defence of Freemasonry as practised in Italy and at a late hour the meeting ended. This was the most splendid reunion the Roman Lodge has held since it was established.'

It was a truly great honour when WBro Sir George Elliot, Bart, MP, was Installed as Provincial Grand Master at Aberdare in April 1877. Although the account of his Installation occupies twenty three pages in the Minute Book, it fails to state where the event was held. It is thought to have been held at the Temperance Hall - now the Palladium Cinema. The banquet was held afterwards at the Old Market Hall - a site since occupied by the Cowbridge Inn and latterly the Market Tavern. Details of the Installation are given in Sir George's biographical details, later in this book.

In 1877, the search began in earnest to find a suitable site on which to build a Masonic Hall. One was found in Canon Street and purchased in 1878 for approximately £370. The Provincial Grand Master, Sir George Elliot, laid the Foundation Stone on 9 October 1879 and on 14 July 1880, the Lodge met for the last time at the Black Lion Hotel.

The first Meeting at Canon Street was on 11 August 1880 with St David's Lodge starting life there substantially in debt, a debt which took nearly twenty years to repay. There were many reasons for it having taken so long, one being the disturbing feature of a large number of resignations, many involving prominent Brethren who had helped to strengthen the Lodge only a few years earlier. Candidates nominated by those Brethren were unsuccessful and both Proposers and Seconders subsequently resigned.

In September 1883, an Emergency Meeting of Provincial Grand Lodge was held at the British Schools, Cardiff Road, Aberaman, under the Banner of St David's Lodge. Sir George Elliot officiated and he was supported by, RWBro Marmaduke Tennant, DepProvGM. WBro Evan Jones (Surgeon - WM 1871) acted as ProvJGW. Also present were WBro J C Parkinson, Junior Grand Deacon of England, PM St David's Lodge, and RWBro George William Elliot, MP, Senior Grand Warden for the Province of the West Riding of Yorkshire. Representing St David's Lodge was WBro F R Howell (WM) accompanied by his Wardens, numerous PMs and Brethren. After the Lodge was opened, Sir George explained that he was in Aberdare to open the new church of St Mary of Antioch, which was nearby and which he had built in memory of his wife and daughter. A cordial invitation was offered to the Brethren to accompany him to the Service and afterwards a luncheon at Aberaman House.

The Lodge has benefited from many presentations over the years and, between 1892 and 1898, various items of furniture and other artefacts were donated. The Worshipful Master's Chair by the executors of the late WBro Watkin Jones Thomas; the Senior Warden's Chair by WBro Evan Jones, Surgeon; the Junior Warden's Chair by WBro Thomas Phillips; the Senior Deacon's Chair by Bro John Williams, the Senior Deacon in Office; and the Junior Deacon's Chair by Bro David Hughes, the Junior Deacon in Office. Other chairs on the dais were presented by WBros Charles Botting, S T Jolliffe, Thomas Rees, Lewis N Williams and James

A piece of rock from King Solomon's Mines

Thorney; and the Working Tools were given by WBro W D Phillips and Bros T Rhys and T E Morgan. A set of Ivory Gavels were presented by Bro F W Mander, which are used today. In 1880, Bro Edwin Gregor presented the Lodge with a set of Tracing Boards to commemorate the opening of the Aberdare Masonic Hall. Then, in 1883, the wife of WBro Evan Thomas, Ironmonger, presented the Lodge with a handsome Loving Cup. All the Officers' Chairs and most of these artefacts remain a very significant part of the Lodge furniture.

In 1884, Bro D A Thomas (later Lord Rhondda) presented the Lodge with a copy of Gould's 'History of Freemasonry'. Another interesting gift was received by the Lodge in 1898 from Bro T E Morgan, namely a piece of rock cut from King Solomon's Mines, Aqaba, Jordan. It is now mounted in a glass case and represents the Rough Ashlar.

A framed photograph of WBro Thomas Jones Dyke, the first WM, was presented by Loyal Cambrian Lodge in 1914. Then, in 1921, WBro W D Phillips presented a sword which his late father, WBro Thomas Phillips (WM 1880) had worn and used as a Colonel in the Volunteer Force during the Boer War. WBro Gaunt presented those Emblems of Mortality, the Skull and Cross Bones, in 1925, and these are also still in use. In 1928, a portrait was presented of the Brother who had possibly been the most generous, WBro W D Phillips, in his Regalia of ProvSGW. Also, the Rt Hon Sybil, Viscountess Rhondda, presented the Lodge with a portrait of her late brother, the Lord Rhondda. Then in 1931, the relatives of the late WBro Frank Hodges presented the Lodge with his Jewels and Regalia together with the Grand Lodge Certificate of his father, Bro William Hodges, who had been among the first Initiates in 1856. Bro J D Williams presented a wireless licence and loud speaker *'for use within the dining hall'*, in 1932.

During The Great War, 1914-1918, Bro D A Thomas survived the sinking of the SS Lusitania, which was torpedoed in 1915. The very next year, he was raised to the Peerage as Lord Rhondda and, in 1917, he became Senior Warden of Grand Lodge. Bro W H Roberts was killed in action at the Front. In the same year, news also arrived that Bro Major R D Williams had been awarded the Distinguished Service Order.

St David's Lodge was always to the fore in supporting charity. There are very many recorded instances of its private and local philanthropic work. Between 1924 and 1938, the years of the great depression, the Lodge contributions and subscriptions towards the Benevolent Fund and Home Charities amounted to well over £500. Aberdare, of course, was at the heart of that depression, Parliament describing it as *'an economic cemetery'*. Allowing that there was the burden of a mortgage as well as the upkeep of the building, the donations represented a great deal of hard work and sacrifice. As a result of its contributions, the Lodge was notified that it was entitled to become a Vice-President of the Benevolent Institution.

On behalf of the Master, Officers and Brethren of St David's Lodge, Aberdare, WBro Edgar J Rutter, DepProvGM, presented a set of Gavels to RWBro HRH The Duke of York, KG, ProvGM, Middlesex, to commemorate his Consecration of the Middlesex St David's Lodge No.5460. His Royal Highness in turn formerly presented the gift to Middlesex St David's Lodge. A communication received and dated December 1934 concerned a Resolution that *'the Master for the time being of St David's Lodge, Aberdare, be and is hereby Elected as an Honorary Member of Middlesex St David's Lodge.'* St David's Lodge, Aberdare, suitably reciprocated in February 1935.

Installation Festival Banquets and Ladies' Nights were by now held at the Memorial Hall and during a Ladies Night in 1934, a message of congratulations was sent to Their Royal Highnesses the Duke and Duchess of Kent who had been married that day. A telegram of thanks was received in return *'trusting that all were spending an enjoyable evening'*. In less than five years His Royal Highness was to become the Grand Master of the United Grand Lodge of England.

Immediately following the Second World War, it was evident that the numbers attending Lodge would be substantially increasing and that the accommodation at Canon Street would be inadequate. It had been some 50 years previously that Brethren living in Mountain Ash had Petitioned in vain for a new Lodge in their home town. It was now felt that Aberdare Masonic Hall would be an ideal venue at which to start a new Lodge, chiefly for Mountain Ash Brethren.

So it was in June 1946, the Lodge received a Deputation designated the 'Aberpennar Lodge Committee', led by WBro Shad C Lewis, WM of St David's Lodge in 1933. A Petition was presented on behalf of the proposed new Lodge which was accepted and agreed unanimously. Within three months, news was received that the Petition had been duly approved, and Aberpennar Lodge No. 6354 was Consecrated on Tuesday, 29 October 1946 by RWBro R P St John Charles, ProvGM, their first Master being WBro Shad C Lewis. He was Installed in the Chair of King Solomon by RWBro Edgar J Rutter, DepProvGM. St David's Lodge presented the new Lodge with a Volume of the Sacred Law, and with Officers' Collars. The Masonic Hall was put *'unreservedly at the disposal of Aberpennar Lodge for all Masonic purposes'* and *'no rent will be charged for the first year'*. Relationships between the two Lodges flourished and it is enough to say that Mother and Daughter Lodges have, as it were, lived amicably under the same roof ever since.

It was nearly ten years later that extensive works were carried out in the Temple to increase accommodation and to strengthen supports to the floor. It was enlarged sufficiently to accommodate 112 Brethren and on special occasions, with extra chairs provided, accommodation for 140. All the work was carried out in a few months in order to have everything prepared for the Centenary of St David's Lodge in the summer of 1956.

However, it had been in June 1953 that a letter from the Deputy Provincial Grand Master intimated that the question of a Centenary Jewel was being investigated and that no difficulty was envisaged, but in the spring of 1956, to the disappointment of the Brethren, it was learnt that Grand Lodge could not grant a Centenary Warrant. Although Founding had been proved in 1856 and it had fully paid its dues during those one hundred years, *'there had been interruption in the work in the early years'*. Regrettably, it was not until 1969 that the Centenary could be celebrated, and a service of celebration was held at St Elvan's Church, Aberdare, on Sunday, 23 November 1969.

At an Emergency Meeting in November 1969, the Deputy Provincial Grand Master presented the Centenary Warrant to the WM, WBro Thomas J Tucker, at the same time decorating him with the Centenary Jewel. Thus we had, as Bro Rev Ivor Parry, ProvGChap said, *'arrived at the end of the beginning'*.

The second Daughter Lodge, Afon Dâr Lodge No.8829, was formed by Members of both St David's and Aberpennar Lodges and its Warrant was issued on 8 February 1978, the Consecration following on 22 May 1978. Its first Master was WBro Henry E Sturge, who was Installed in the Chair of King Solomon by VWBro Geoffrey M Ashe, DepProvGM.

In 1980, St David's Lodge was presented with a carved Past Masters' Board by Miss Jean McCormack in memory of her late father ,WBro A C McCormack, WM in 1927. Later, in 1988, new Tracing Boards and Tools were presented to the Lodge in memory of WBro Maldwyn E Jones, JP, PPGW, PAGDC, WM in 1953. In his public life, he had been High Constable of Miskin Higher for two consecutive years, the office ceasing to exist in 1969.

In 1990, WBro Brynley Rees, WM in 1966, had been given the task of publishing Bro Rev Ivor Parry's History of St David's Lodge entitled 'These Hundred Years'. A week before he died, he was still concerned that he had failed in his task because his copy of the manuscript had been lost. WBros Stuart Evans and Gareth Gait promised to find the lost history, which they did, but it was not published until 1997.

WBro Stuart L Evans and his father Bro Leslie J Evans, a stalwart of the Lodge as Chief Steward, presented an Apron Cushion embroidered with the Lodge Emblem to the Lodge in 1999. At the Installation of the new ProvGM, RWBro Hywel Davies in 1999, Masters of both St David's and Aberpennar Lodges were delegated to form part of his escort.

The Lodge Committee sought ideas for a new Banner as the condition of the old one had deteriorated over the years. After some months, during which the College of Arms refused several designs submitted, the final Banner design was agreed and manufactured. It was Dedicated on 13 September 2000.

In common with most Lodges, the last few years have seen a steady decline in attendance and, sadly, 2006 marked the first year since WWII that St David's Lodge failed to Initiate a Candidate at the April Meeting.

The 150th Anniversary of the Consecration of the Lodge was held on 10 May 2006 at which the ProvGM, RWBro Hywel Davies, unveiled a commemorative plaque. He was in turn presented with a suitably inscribed Masonic Bible to mark the occasion.

Compiled by WBro Graham D Hobson, PPrGSuptWks.
(Some information obtained from: 'These Hundred Years'
by Bro Rev R Ivor Parry MA, PPrGChap and other sources.)

Charles Kemeys Kemeys-Tynte

1822 – 1891

Provincial Grand Master of South Wales Eastern Division
1857 – 1865

When the resignation of Edward John Hutchins, ProvGM, was announced in Glamorgan Lodge No.43, on 14 April 1856, the Lodge Secretary proposed that *'Captain Tynte of Cefn Mably be respectfully recommended to the Grand Master for the Office of PROVGM'*. An amendment was, however, passed that *'Lord James Stuart should be applied to accept the vacant office and ultimately the Secretary was requested to write to that Noble Broth*er'. Lord James Stuart was the younger brother of the Second Marquess of Bute and he had joined Glamorgan Lodge in June 1821, but nothing came of this proposal. At the same time, the Brethren of Indefatigable Lodge No.288, Swansea, were once again urging the appointment of Henry, Duke of Beaufort, and *'Bro. M. Moggridge, P.M., was deputed to wait on the Duke to ascertain his disposition in the matter; but he had to report that his interview did not meet with the success that might have been anticipated.'* (The Lodge had previously attempted to have the Duke appointed ProvGM in 1836, when Sir Josiah John Guest was ultimately appointed.) When Glamorgan Lodge met on 12 January 1857, it

The Tynte Coat of Arms

was passed *'That a memorial be addressed to the Worshipful Grand Master in reference to the appointment of the Provincial Grand Master of South Wales, praying that the vacancy may be filled and recommending Captain Tynte of Cefn Mably to the Office. The memorial as prepared was then read and agreed to and signed by the brethren of the Lodge.'* Twelve days later, on 24 January, the Patent appointing Captain Charles Kemeys Kemeys-Tynte of Cefn Mably as Provincial Grand Master was signed.

The ancestry of the Kemeys-Tynte family is quite complicated; however, a brief account will be given. The Kemeys family lived at Cefn Mably in the parish of Michaelston-y-Fedw on the eastern side of Cardiff from the 15th century. The family gained in prominence over following generations, providing Sheriffs of Glamorgan in the 16th & 17th centuries and later Members of Parliament. During the Civil War, Sir Nicholas Kemeys, a staunch Royalist, was created a Baronet in 1642, but was killed defending Chepstow Castle in 1648. Succeeding Baronets added to the estate through marriage and improved their Cefn Mably House. Charles, the 4th Baronet died without issue in 1735 and the title became extinct. The Estate passed to his widowed sister Jane, who had married the Reverend Sir John Tynte, 2nd Baronet, of Halswell, Somerset and Rector of Goathurst (died 1710), and then in turn to their three sons - Sir Halswell Tynte, 3rd Baronet, 15 November 1705 - 12 November 1730, MP for Bridgwater, 1727-1730; Sir John Tynte, 4th Baronet, 27 March 1707 - 15 August 1740; and finally, the youngest son Sir Charles Kemeys Tynte, 5th Baronet, 19 May 1710 - 25 August 1785, MP for Monmouth, 1745-1747, and Somerset, 1747-1774. Sir Charles was the first Tynte to be associated with Somerset Freemasonry, and was Initiated in 1767 at a Lodge meeting in the Bear Inn, Bath, now the Royal Cumberland Lodge No.41. He died without children in 1774, whereupon the Baronetcy became extinct. The estate passed to his niece, Jane Hassell, whose second husband, Colonel John Johnson, took the name Kemeys -Tynte, by royal licence, granted on 28 October 1785. The Colonel died in 1806, and when Jane died on 29 January 1824, their son, Colonel Charles Kemeys Kemeys-Tynte of Halswell and Cefn Mably (born 29 May 1778), the grandfather of our Provincial Grand Master, succeeded to the estates.

Grandfather Charles married on 25 April 1798, Anne Lewis, the widow of Thomas Lewis of St Pierre, (now the Marriott St Pierre Hotel & Country Club) and daughter of Rev Thomas Leyson of Bassaleg, Monmouthshire. He was MP for Bridgewater, 1820-1837, and a Colonel of the West Somerset Yeomanry. He was Initiated into Lodge of Perpetual Friendship No.135, Bridgwater, Province of Somersetshire, in 1817. Only three years later, on Friday, 30 September 1820, he was

Cefn Mably

Installed Provincial Grand Master of Somerset. The Ceremony took place in the Guildhall, Bath, where all the Lodges in the County were officially represented and several Members from Wiltshire and Gloucestershire also attended. He was Installed as WM of Lodge of Perpetual Friendship in 1836. Twenty-six years later, on Friday, 27 March 1846, he was unanimously Elected Grand Master of the Ancient and Honourable Order of Masonic Knights Templar, in succession to his late Royal Highness, the Duke of Sussex. On his death, on 22 November 1860, his son Charles John Kemeys-Tynte (born 9 April 1800 at Halswell Manor, Goathurst) inherited the Cefn Mably and Halswell estates.

Charles John Kemeys-Tynte, father of our ProvGM, was appointed Colonel of the Royal Glamorgan Light Infantry on 4 January 1849 and was MP for West Somerset, 1832-1837, and Bridgewater, 1847 - 1865. He was Initiated into Lodge of Perpetual Friendship a few months after his father, in 1817, by the Provincial Grand Master, RWBro Arthur Chichester. In 1831, he was appointed Provincial Grand Master of Monmouthshire; however, at the beginning of 1847, the Board of General purposes had become very concerned that as yet he had not been Installed as such. In his letter, to the Grand Secretary from Cefn Mably, dated 2 February 1847, he wrote: '*In regard to the Board considering it their duty to bring to the notice of the M.W.G.M. the fact of my not having been Installed, although appointed to the Office as far back as 1831. I beg to observe that at the Period of my appointment there and for many years afterwards was no lodge at work in the province and by the advice of His late Royal Highness the then Grand Master, I took no steps whatsoever to force the renewal of Masonry upon the Province. I was afterwards abroad for some years, and upon my return I and two Lodges in my Province appointed a period for my Installation, which was twice postponed from the circumstances of my father, the Provincial Grand Master of Somerset, having been seriously ill at the time, as he was to have officiated at my Installation. I should add that previous to that another domestic calamity prevented my Installation.*'

In his letter, he goes on to offer his resignation as ProvGM, should The Board of General Purposes find his conduct in the matter unsatisfactory. The only two Lodges in the Province of Monmouthshire at this time were Loyal Monmouth Lodge No.671, Warranted 21 December 1838; and Silurian Lodge No.693, Newport, Warranted 3 August 1840. It may appear strange to appoint a ProvGM in 1831, when there are no Lodges in the Province! This was not unusual; however, the appointment to such an Office was regarded as being 'an honour conferred'. Further, the appointment of a ProvGM did not necessarily imply the formation of a Provincial Grand Lodge, which was sometimes formed several years after the appointment of a ProvGM. In the end, Charles John Kemeys-Tynte's Installation took place at a Lodge of Emergency of Silurian Lodge on 30 June 1847. The Brethren of that Lodge assembled in force and were accompanied by visiting Brethren from Loyal Monmouth Lodge, the different Bristol, Bath, Bridgewater and Highbridge Lodges and also Glamorgan Lodge, Cardiff. The Past Deputy Provincial Grand Master for Bristol, WBro William Donne Bushell, acting for the Provincial Grand Master of Bristol, presided, supported by his Officers. (William Done Bushell became a Joining Member of Glamorgan Lodge on 2 March 1852, around the time that he was appointed Managing Director of the Taff Vale Railway Company.) The Brethren of the Bristol Grand Lodge had commenced the Ceremony at 1.00 pm and afterwards all the Brethren proceeded in a grand procession to the Town Hall, where a *'sumptuous dinner'* was prepared for them by Bro S T Hallen, of the Westgate Hotel. Eight years later, on 29 August 1855, Colonel Charles Kemeys-Tynte, ProvGM Monmouthshire, presided over the laying of the Foundation Stone of Silurian Lodge's Masonic Hall, which remains the centre of Freemasonry in Newport to this day.

Charles John Kemeys-Tynte's first marriage, (18 July 1820) was to Elizabeth, the daughter of Thomas Swinnerton of Butterton Hall, Staffs. Their first son and heir and our future Provincial Grand Master, was born to them at Shaftsbury, on 16 March 1822. A second son, Millborne Kemeys-Tynte was born in 1823. He became a Lieutenant of the 4th Royal Irish Dragoon Guards, but was killed at the age of 22 as a result of a fall from his horse, on 10 March 1845. The Cambrian Newspaper, published in Swansea, on 30 August 1845 reported: *'We are rejoiced to find that the fine old mansion of Cefnmably is once more about to be permanently occupied by a son of that ancient house, Charles John Kemeys Tynte, Esq., who with his amicable wife and family now inhabit the seat of their ancestors.'* It would appear that the Cefn Mably residence had been neglected for several years, in favour of the family seat, Halswell Manor, at Goathurst, Somerset. In the same year, on 10 October, The Cambrian reported: *'Charles Kemeys Kemeys-Tynte, Esq., of Cefnmably, eldest son of Charles John Kemeys Tynte, Esq., and grandson of Colonel Tynte, had been promoted to a troop in the 11th Light Dragoons.'* The Census of 1841 shows that he was already an officer at the age of 15 and was stationed at the Hounslow Cavalry Barracks at Heston, West London. In due course, he became a Captain with the 11th Hussars and later with the Grenadier Guards. Subsequently, he was appointed Honorary Colonel Third Battalion Prince Albert's Somersetshire Light Infantry.

When Glamorgan Lodge met on 13 April 1857, a letter from the Grand Secretary, dated 10 March 1857, was read, informing the Brethren of the appointment of (Captain) Charles Kemeys Kemeys-Tynte to the Office of Provincial Grand Master for the Eastern Division of South Wales. At that same Meeting, the Lodge Secretary also read a letter from C K Kemeys-Tynte, stating his wish to become a Subscribing Member of the Lodge. He was then duly proposed and seconded and at the next Meeting, on 11 May, Kemeys-Tynte was Elected as such. His Installation as Provincial Grand Master followed soon afterwards. The Ceremony took place at the Town-hall, Cardiff, on Thursday, 6 August 1857 and Glamorgan Lodge was charged with making the arrangements. Adverts for the meeting of the Provincial Grand Lodge were placed in the Cambrian and published on 17, 24 and 31 July. On 31 July, Indefatigable Lodge also advertised the Meeting and informed the Brethren in Swansea that arrangements had been made for them to leave Swansea for Cardiff by the 8 am train. The 'Cardiff & Merthyr Guardian', published on Saturday, 8 August, gave a full account of the Meeting, part of which is given below.

'A grand demonstration of the Provincial Grand Lodge of South Wales (Eastern Division) took place in the Town Hall, Cardiff, on Thursday last. The brethren who numbered upwards of 200, represented the following Lodges: - St. David's, Aberdare; Brecknock, Brecon; Cambrian, Neath; Indefatigable, Swansea; Loyal Cambrian, Merthyr; Glamorgan, Cardiff. There were besides visiting brethren from Newport, amongst whom were the Mayor (Charles Lyne, Esq.,); ....A considerable

number of gentlemen were also present from Bristol, Gloucester, Hereford, Bath, Taunton, London, &c. Not the least interesting feature of the meeting, exemplifying the true force of the mystic tie of the brotherhood, was the attendance of the veteran Colonel Tynte, of Haswell Court. (The new P.G.M's. grandfather)

The Lodge having been duly constituted, the R.W. Brother F. Beadon, Past Junior Grand Warden of England installed the R.W. Brother C.R. Kemeys Tynte, of Cefn Mably, Provincial Grand Master for the Eastern Division of South Wales – the installation having been performed according to the usual ceremony of the ancient Order.

The business of the Lodge having been performed, the brethren walked in procession to St. John's Church in the following order:

Visiting Brethren.

St. David's Lodge, Aberdare.
Brecknock Lodge, Brecon.
Cambrian Lodge, Neath.
Indefatigable Lodge, Swansea.
Loyal Cambrian Lodge, Merthyr.
Glamorgan Lodge, Cardiff.
Officers of other Provincial Grand Lodges.
Provincial Grand Lodge.
Tyler, with Sword.
Organist and Superintendent of Works.
Director of Ceremonies.
Senior and Junior Deacons.
Secretary and Registrar.
Treasurer.
Three Great Lights borne by a Master Mason.
Chaplain.
Senior and Junior Wardens.
Deputy Provincial Grand Master.
Installing Grand Master.
Banner of the Provincial Grand Master.
Provincial Grand Master.
Two Stewards with Gilt Wands.
Pursuivant with Sword of State.

Crowds of people lined the streets as the procession moved towards St John's, various orders of the brotherhood earned in foreign lands, which several gentlemen bore on their breasts, attracting much attention. The Order having reached the church, the central pews were mainly occupied by the brethren, while the side seats and galleries were allotted to the public, most of whom were ladies.

The Sacred Services were conducted by the Rev. Mr. Stacey; after which the Rev. Mr. Harris of Merthyr, Provincial Chaplain to the Eastern Division of the Order in South Wales delivered a very edifying discourse from Prov., xviii., 24: "A man that hath friends must show himself friendly: and there is a Friend that sticketh closer than a brother." The religious services over, the brethren retired from the church and separated at the Town Hall.

At six o' clock between 250 members of the various Lodges who assisted in the solemnities of the day banqueted at the Cardiff Arms Hotel. The Provincial Grand Master presided.

The usual loyal and constitutional toasts having been dedicated with brimful bumpers, the harmony of the evening was prolonged till a late hour with toast, song and sentiment; and the brethren separated rejoicing in the fact of having truly participated in "the light" of Freemasonry.'

On 9 August 1857, just three days after Charles Kemeys-Tynte's Installation, the death of his infant daughter occurred at the age of 3 years and 8 months.

Kemeys-Tynte's first visit to Glamorgan Lodge, was on 19 October 1857, when it was proposed and seconded that his Butler, John Caborn should be Initiated into Freemasonry. John Caborn was duly Initiated on 9 November 1857, Passed on 10 October 1859 and Raised on 8 September 1863. Apparently, at this time, it was not unusual to Initiate the personal servants of distinguished Brethren. It enabled the 'personage' to enjoy the attention of his servant at the dinner following a Lodge Meeting as well as at home! The Census of 1861 shows that Caborn was married, 50 years of age and had been born in Horncastle, Lincolnshire. He resigned from the Lodge in 1866, probably on the termination of his employment as Butler at Cefn Mably.

When Kemeys-Tynte became ProvGM in 1857, the Province consisted of just the six Lodges listed in the above report of his Installation. Two of these had only recently come into existence, namely Brecknock Lodge (then No.936), Warranted 14 March 1855, and St David's Lodge (then No.979), Aberdare, Warranted 16 May 1856. During his Provincial Grand Mastership, two further Lodges were added to the Province. The first of these was Afan Lodge (then No.1135), Port Talbot, a Daughter Lodge of Cambrian Lodge (then No.472), Neath, Warranted on 29 September 1860. The second Lodge was Bute Lodge (then No.1262), Cardiff, Warranted 13 April 1863, the formation of which proved initially to be a rather controversial affair. (See histories of Glamorgan and Bute Lodges.)

In a letter dated 6 July 1863, Grand Lodge informed Lodges of the decision to close up the gaps in the numeration of Lodges on the Register, and that Glamorgan Lodge would change from 43 to 36; Loyal Cambrian Lodge from 127 to 110; Indefatigable Lodge from 288 to 237; Cambrian Lodge from 472 to 364; Brecknock Lodge from 936 to 651; St. David's Lodge from 979 to 679; Afan Lodge from 1135 to 833, and Bute Lodge from 1262 to 960. This was the second and last change in the numeration of Lodges since the formation of the United Grand Lodge of England at the end of 1813. The previous change had taken place in 1833.

Later in 1863, the ProvGM became involved in a 'Masonic Scandal', which commenced on 13 October during a visit to Glamorgan Lodge. He came to witness the Initiation of Gwilym Williams, aged 24, of Miskin, Llantrisant, Barrister-at-law. His father was David Williams, originally of Ynyscynon, Aberdare, who had become an immensely wealthy colliery owner and had some years earlier purchased the Miskin Manor Estate (now the Miskin Manor Country Hotel). Young Gwilym had just inherited the estate on the death of his father in the February of that year, and being newly qualified, had recently taken up an appointment as a Barrister of the Inner Temple. He and his family would have been well known to Charles Kemeys-Tynte, who no doubt was eager to see him being Initiated. Just before the ProvGM was admitted, Bro James Gawn, who had been WM of St David's Lodge, Aberdare, (17 March 1859 - 28 March 1861) and who had joined Glamorgan Lodge in January 1859, got up and announced to the Brethren that he had previously Initiated Gwilym Williams in the Aberdare Lodge two years earlier! (St David's Lodge records show that the Initiation took place on 16 October 1861.) The Senior Deacon then appeared between the Pillars and announced that *'the candidate declared himself to him a Brother.'* After some discussion the WM decided to proceed with the Ceremony, at which point several Past Masters left the Lodge in protest. The ProvGM was then admitted and the Initiation Ceremony took place. The following month, a full report of the Ceremony and the controversy surrounding it was published on 10 November in the 'Freemasons' Magazine' (published in Fleet Street, London, 1856-1871, initially as a monthly journal, it became a weekly publication from January 1858). Worse was to follow. A second article was published in the Magazine on 21 November, which was severely critical of what had occurred, and with even the ProvGM coming in for severe criticism. The final paragraph of the article is given below:

'It is not for us to say what course will be pursed by the Masonic authorities, but we have no hesitation in asserting that Bro. Charles Kemeys Tynte ought at once to be relieved of the duties of Provincial Grand Master, which he evidently does not understand, and that the W.M. of the Glamorgan Lodge, the officers who assisted him in the ceremony, and, indeed, every brother who sanctioned the scandalous proceedings by his presence should be suspended from all Masonic privileges until they can be brought to a better understanding of their obligations, and have made a sufficient apology to the Craft through Grand Lodge for their conduct. Had the brethren generally followed the example of their oldest member and retired, the lodge would have been dissolved, and the Master prevented from enacting a ceremony which we feel cannot properly be treated as a farce, but must be visited with severity as a grave Masonic offence, to prove to other brethren that our ceremonies are not to be lightly dealt with, and that Freemasonry is not to be made a mere plaything for the frivolous and unreflecting members of the Craft.'

Glamorgan Lodge met in Emergency on 25 November to discuss the affair. A letter from a Joining Member, Frederick Ware, was read, in which he stated that while he was not the correspondent, he had vouched to the Editors of the Freemasons' Magazine for the accuracy of the events as described, claiming that he was the *recognised reporter to the Magazine, by authority of the R. W. Prov. G. M.* Among several resolutions passed that evening was the following:

'That this Lodge express to the R. W. P. G. M. the deep regret it feels that his name should have been used in the report in the Freemasons' Magazine; and that it considers the subsequent article a scandalous and most unjustifiable attack upon him, and this lodge begs to offer him its sympathy, and assurance of profound respect.'

A copy of the Minutes of that Meeting was sent to the ProvGM. The Lodge met again on 8 December, when a reply from the ProvGM was discussed. In his letter he stated:

'Bro. Ware laboured under a grievous misapprehension when he stated in his letter to you of the 24 inst., that he was the recognised reporter to the magazine by authority of the R.W. ProvGM

I must distinctly and emphatically state that I never gave him that authority.' ....

The letter concludes:

'I must request you to convey my grateful and cordial thanks to the Brethren for the spirit in which it is couched, and let them be assured that while I have their support, I care nothing for the remarks of the Editor of the Freemasons' Magazine, whose aim appears rather to create dissension than to promote harmony and good will among the brethren of our ancient order.'

The dispute raged on for fifteen months, with more correspondence being published in the Freemasons' Magazine. Glamorgan Lodge failed to find who the original correspondent was, but it seems that in all probability it was Frederick Ware. He, however, denied responsibility. Grand Lodge did not become involved and no disciplinary action was taken. By January 1865, it was decided that it was in everyone's best interest that the matter should be brought to a close. In January 1866, Frederick Ware became involved in another acrimonious dispute, which culminated in his expulsion from Glamorgan Lodge on the 26th March of that year. There is, however, a somewhat amusing sequel to these events. The Glamorgan Lodge Minutes of 10 December 1869 contain the following:

'Bro. John Williams (PM Bute Lodge) briefly called to the remembrance of the W M., certain unpleasant matters which took place in this Lodge three or four years ago, which resulted in the expulsion of Bro. Frederick Ware. He stated that Bro. Ware was desirous of expressing his regret for the part he bore in those occurrences, and that he was then in the ante room awaiting permission of the W.M. to enter the Lodge for that purpose.

Permission having been given, Bro. Ware entered the Lodge and offered an explanation, and expressed his regrets for what had taken place, with which the brethren expressed themselves satisfied.'

- and the reason for this apparent 'change of heart'? On 30 December 1869, Bro Ware was to be Installed as WM of Bute Lodge, by which time it had become customary to make the Worshipful Master of Glamorgan Lodge an Honorary Member of Bute Lodge!

But what of the Initiate involved in the 'scandal'? At a Glamorgan Lodge Meeting on Tuesday, 12 January 1864, it was agreed that the fee of £5.5.0 paid for the Initiation of Bro Gwilym Williams should be refunded. He never became a Member of the Lodge. Gwilym Williams went on to enjoy a successful legal career. Following an appeal in the House of Commons for bilingual Judges, he was appointed by the Home Secretary as Stipendiary Magistrate for Pontypridd and the Rhondda in 1872. It was said of him at this time that he was *'a terror to malefactors'*. In 1884, he was appointed a Judge of the county courts, mid-Wales circuit and then in 1885, he was promoted to Judge of the county courts of Glamorgan, a post which he held until his death on 25 March 1906. He was also chairman of the Glamorgan Quarter Sessions from 3 July 1894 until his death. His statue by William Goscombe John stands in front of the Law Courts, Cathays Park, Cardiff.

In June 1864, Charles Kemeys Kemeys-Tynte's wife, Mary Sophia, died at the age of 39. She was the daughter of the Rev George Frome of Puncknoll, Dorset, and they had been married on 2 November 1848. In the June of 1865, Kemeys-Tynte's resignation as Provincial Grand Master was announced to the Brethren. He had been the ProvGM for just over eight years. Following his resignation, he more or less withdrew from public life. During his lifetime, his appointments included being Deputy Lieutenant for Monmouthshire and for Somerset, Honorary Colonel of the Somersetshire Militia and, in 1881, a Magistrate for Glamorgan. In 1873, he married Hannah, the widow of a Mr Lewis. She died two years later and then in 1879, he married for the third time Elizabeth, the eldest daughter of Ironmaster Richard Fothergill III (1822-1903). Fothergill had owned the Abernant Ironworks, Aberdare and had also acquired the Plymouth Works at Merthyr Tydfil. He was MP for Aberdare and Merthyr from 1868 until 1880, when he retired to Norton, near Tenby. Interestingly, Kemeys-Tynte was the same age as his new father-in-law, and Elizabeth was 29 years of age at the time of their marriage!

Colonel Charles John Kemeys-Tynte died on 16 September 1882, and the Cefn Mably Estate then passed on to his son, Charles Kemeys Kemeys-Tynte. He in turn died at Cefn Mably on Saturday, 10 January 1891. His death was sudden and unexpected, though he had been suffering severely from bronchitis for some time. A full account of his funeral was published in the 'Cardiff Times & South Wales Weekly News' on Saturday 17th January, some extracts from which are given below:

'Amid widespread manifestations of deep regret and genuine respect the mortal remains of the late Colonel Charles Kemeys-Tynte, of Cefn Mably, whose lamented death occurred so suddenly on Saturday last, were laid in their last resting-place in the yard of Michaelston-y-Fedw Church on Thursday morning. By special direction of the deceased gentleman the mournful ceremony was throughout as quiet and simple as it could possibly be, every endeavour being made to avoid an imposing procession and an elaborate performance of the last sacred rites. Though the funeral was essentially a private one, it was only to be expected that a large number of the late Colonel's friends, and his more immediate neighbours at Cefn Mably, as well as his tenants and employees, would desire to show their regard for one so deservedly esteemed on account of his numerous excellent qualities, by following his remains to the grave. The informal procession, therefore, in which the body was borne from the residence of the deceased to the parish church was representative of all classes in Cefn Mably, St. Mellons, and the surrounding parishes. There were no carriages, and no hearse was used, the corpse being carried by successive bearers the entire distance. Punctually at eleven, the cortege started from the house in the following order: Tenants of the Cefn Mably Estate and servants of the deceased, to the number of about 80, farmers and tradesmen of the district; the coffin covered with wreaths and crosses of white flowers, the chief mourners and relatives and friends of the deceased; the domestic servants of Cefn Mably. Mrs. and Miss Kemeys-Tynte were unable to attend the funeral. The chief mourner was Mr. Halswell Kemeys-Tynte,

eldest son of the late gentleman, and there was also present Mr. Charles Kemeys-Tynte and Mr. Eustace Kemeys-Tynte, grandsons of the deceased;.........

The internment took place in the family vault, which is a little to the south-west of the church.

The coffin, which was of polished oak, was perfectly plain with plain brass handles and studs. On the brass plate was the engraved inscription:

CHARLES KEMEYS KEMEYS-TYNTE,

January 10th, 1891.

Aged 68

From the church to the grave the corpse was preceded by Mr. Rose, the faithful and constant servant of the late Colonel, who bore in his hand a handsome cross of white flowers and evergreens, which he placed with the others on the coffin. The melancholy task of lowering the remains into their final resting place was performed by six of the deceased's old retainers, namely, Samuel Joyce, William Rees, John James, Daniel James, William Samuel, and James Weston. The same party, it may be mentioned, had previously conveyed the coffin from the library at Cefn Mably out on to the bier. At the graveside the concluding portion of the burial was read by the Rev J W Evans.'

His eldest son, Captain Halswell Milbourne Kemeys-Tynte (born 1852), succeeded to the estates and he died on 18 February 1899. He in turn was succeeded by his son, Charles Theodore Halswell Kemeys-Tynte (born 18 September 1876). The abeyance of the Barony of Wharton, with which a branch of the family had been connected, was terminated in his favour by writ of summons to Parliament on 15 February 1916, in consequence of which he became the 8th Baron Wharton. Philip, 6th Baron Wharton had been created Duke of Wharton on 20 January 1715. On 17 January 1722, he was Invested and Installed as Grand Master of the Premier Grand Lodge (The Moderns) in succession to the Duke of Montague. A most controversial character, he only occupied the Office for one year! Further, he supported the Jacobite cause, resulting in him becoming outlawed by Parliament in 1728, whereupon he fled to Spain and retired to the Cistercian Monastery of St Bernard, near Tarragona. He died there on 31 May 1731, aged thirty-two, when all his honours became extinct. In 1844, Colonel Charles Kemeys-Tynte laid claim to the Barony, but erroneously, the Committee of Privileges of the House of Lords ruled against him. Further, the Committee ruled that the title had passed to the Duke of Wharton's sister Jane (7th Baron) and that on her death it had fallen into abeyance.

It is interesting to note that RWBro Charles Kemeys Kemeys-Tynte, ProvGM, could trace his family connections with high Office in Freemasonry over a number of generations. This long association with Freemasonry in general, the Province of Somerset, and Bridgwater in particular, was finally recognised on 9 September 1964 with the Warranting of Tynte Lodge No.7994, meeting at Bridgwater. In 1915, the family of Kemeys-Tynte was able to revert to the Barony of Wharton and it was Charles John Halswell Kemeys-Tynte, 9th Baron Wharton (1908-1969), who readily gave his permission to use the family name for Tynte Lodge and to the reproduction of their Arms for the Lodge Banner and Past Master's Jewel.

WBro Peter M Davies, ProvJGW.

Afan Lodge No.833

Warranted : 29 September 1860

Consecrated : 10 January 1861

Meeting at the Masonic Hall, Port Talbot.

Afan Lodge was formed by Brethren who were Members of various Lodges throughout the areas of Western Glamorganshire, notably Indefatigable Lodge No.237, Swansea; Cambrian Lodge No.364, Neath; and Prince of Wales Lodge No.671, Llanelly. Cambrian Lodge is the head of a family of 47 Lodges, and Afan Lodge is the first of its 4 Daughter Lodges. Records show that five meetings took place during the late 1850s, to establish a new Lodge at Aberavon, Port Talbot, and, as recorded in an entry in the cash book, dated 1 November 1860, Grand Lodge was paid £6-12s-6d (£6. 60.5p) for the Warrant. From this, it is obvious that Meetings were held prior to those recorded in the attendance book.

The Warrant was granted to Afan Lodge under the hand of the MWBro Thomas Dundas, 2nd Earl of Zetland, Grand Master, 1844-1870. Dated 29 September 1860, it Constituted eight Brethren as a Lodge of Free and Accepted Masons to meet at The Walnut Tree Hotel, Aberavon, on the first and third Thursday of every month during the winter, and the first Thursday during the summer months. Records show that while Afan Lodge initially met in the Walnut Tree Hotel, it later moved to various venues throughout the town. They included the Victoria Institute in Station Road; the Prince of Wales Inn, above Bro Abel Jones's Shop, opposite the Municipal Buildings; the Public Hall - all in Aberavon; and The Grand Hotel, Port Talbot.

The first WM of Afan Lodge was WBro Theodore Mansel Talbot of Margam. He later

The Walnut Tree Hotel, Port Talbot

became Deputy Provincial Grand Master of South Wales Eastern Division in 1863 and was Provincial Grand Master from 1865 until his death in 1876. His biographical details are given separately in this book. In addition to Theodore Mansel Talbot, the Founders of Afan Lodge were: William Llewellyn Powell, Merchant of Taibach, Port Talbot, WM of Cambrian Lodge in 1851; George Newman, Inn Keeper of Cwmafan, Indefatigable Lodge; David Jenkins, Ships' Broker of Church Street, Aberavon, Indefatigable Lodge; David Longdon, Brewer of Avonside House, Aberavon, Cambrian Lodge; William E Chalindor, GWR Superintendent of Aberavon, Prince of Wales Lodge; Richard Gillet, Accountant of Cwmafan, Cambrian Lodge; and John Jones, Inn Keeper, Walnut Tree Hotel, Aberavon, Cambrian Lodge.

The Grand Hotel, Port Talbot

Theodore Mansel Talbot's Installation took place at The National Schools, Aberavon, on 10 January 1861. The Lodge is fortunate to still have in its possession a Bible, embossed 'Afan Lodge No.1135'; Silver Square and Compasses, also marked with the original Lodge Number 1135, and a mahogany box of Working Tools, with a plate inscribed *'Presented to the Afan Lodge No. 1135 by Theodore Mansel Talbot. First Worshipful Master 1860';* and three ebony and ivory Gavels. In fact, all of these items were presented to the Lodge by the first WM, including a set of Officers' Collar Jewels, also marked No.1135. Theodore Mansel Talbot served as WM for two years and, on 3 February 1863, he Installed his successor, Bro William Powell, SW, as Master for the ensuing year. During the course of the evening, WBro T M Talbot was presented with a Past Master's Jewel, and an Illuminated Address, autographed by the 38 Officers and Brethren. These two objects are well preserved and are exhibited in the museum case in the lounge of the present Masonic Hall. His full Masonic Regalia as ProvGM and Grand Superintendent of South Wales ED is also on display.

Another important day in the history of Afan Lodge was Thursday, 20 February 1863, when Provincial Grand Lodge met at Aberavon under the Banner of Afan Lodge No.1135. Soon afterwards, UGLE renumbered the Lodges on the Register, and Afan Lodge became No.833.

On 15 August 1872, Provincial Grand Lodge met under the Banner of Afan Lodge No.833. On this occasion, the first WM, now RWBro Theodore Mansel Talbot, ProvGM, laid the Foundation Stone of the Masonic Public Hall. An extract from the 'Western Mail', dated 23 August 1872 recorded:

During proceedings of Provincial Grand Lodge, a procession was formed, and all the Brethren proceeded to the site of the new Building in Water Street Aberavon, at the rear of the Walnut Tree Hotel. The procession was headed by the band of the Ninth Glamorganshire Rifle Volunteers.

On arriving at the site of the building, the Brethren at the head of the Procession halted and opened right and left facing inwards so as to leave room for the RW Provincial Grand Master to pass up the centre of the avenue thus formed. He was preceded by his Standard Bearer and Sword Bearer, the DepProvGM, Provincial Grand Lodge Officers and Brethren following in succession from the rear.

The Band commenced playing a selection from the Creation 'Marvelous Works' and the Ceremony of laying the stone commenced. A prayer was offered up by the Prov Grand Chaplain and the inscription on the Plate was read by the WM of Afan Lodge as follows: -

This Foundation Stone of the Masonic and Public Hall, Aberavon, was laid with Masonic Honours on Thursday, August 15 1872, by Theodore Mansel Talbot, Esq, RW Provincial Grand Master of the Province of South Wales (ED) at a Provincial Grand Lodge meeting held under the Banner of Afan Lodge No. 833, Aberavon, Edward Daniel WM, Edward Jones SW, Rev D Parker Morgan, JW, Architect Rees Roderick, Builder John Davies.

The ProvGTreasurer having by command of the RWPGM deposited in the cavity various coins of the present reign, copies of local newspapers, By-laws of the Provincial Grand Lodge and of Afan Lodge 833, a list of present Officers of Afan Lodge and the copy of the programme; the cement was laid on the stone with the Trowel presented for the purpose, and the upper stone was let down slowly, solemn music being played.

The stone being properly placed the RWPGM proved it was properly adjusted by the Plumb Rule delivered by the ProvJGW, by the Level delivered to him by the Prov SGW, and by the Square delivered to him by the DepPGM. The Mallet was handed to him, and he gave the stone three knocks. The RtWorPGM then delivered to the builder the several instruments for his use. The plans of the building were presented by the ProvGSuptWks and the RWPGM having approved of them delivered them to the Architect for his guidance.

Three Brethren then approached. Bro John Jones PPGSec bore a Cornucopia with Corn; a second, Bro Edward Daniel PPGJD carried a Silver Ewer with Wine and a third, Bro David Longdon PPGDC bore a Silver Ewer with Oil. They each presented their vessels in order to the RWPGM who, after pouring their contents upon the stone, declared it properly laid according to Masonic Law and ancient custom. The ProvG Chaplain then pronounced the Benidiction, the band played the National Anthem and the procession reformed in the same order and returned to the Lodge-room when Provincial Grand Lodge was closed.

The silver trowel used had an ivory handle and bore the following inscription: 'Presented to Theodore Mansel Talbot, Esq RWPGM of the South Wales Eastern Division by the members of Afan Lodge of Freemasons 833 on the occasion of his laying the foundation stone of the new Masonic Public Hall, Thursday, August 15 1872.'

At 4 o'clock the Brethren sat down to dinner in a large marquee erected in the Forge Field, presided over by the RWPGM. The dinner was substantial, abundant and well laid out, being provided by Bro Jones of the Walnut Tree Hotel and gave satisfaction to the large number assembled.

Afan Lodge used the Masonic Public Hall for its Meetings, and no doubt retired to the Walnut Tree Hotel for the Festive Board. It continued to produce Freemasons of considerable distinction and high standing, and foremost amongst these was Marmaduke Tennant of Cae Hir, Aberavon. Initiated in Afan Lodge on 2 April 1863, his advancement in Freemasonry was rapid, and he was Installed as WM in 1871 and 1875. When Theodore Mansel Talbot, ProvGM, died in 1876, his successor, WBro Sir George Elliot, appointed Marmaduke Tennant as DepProvGM. He created great interest in Masonic Charities and was responsible for setting up the Educational Fund for orphans of Freemasons in this Province. He was also instrumental in creating a fund for the relief of widows of deceased Masons, 'The Victoria Fund', during the year Queen Victoria celebrated her Golden Jubilee. He was held in such high esteem that, on two occasions he was presented with Illuminated Addresses, and also a purse of 200 gold sovereigns at the Glamorgan Lodge Festival on St John's Day, 1889. On his death, the Provincial Grand Lodge perpetuated his memory by installing a beautiful stained glass window in St Mary's Church, Aberavon. The Commemorative Tablet was unveiled by WBro Henry Pendrill Charles, DepProvGM, during Divine Service on Sunday, 28 January 1917. Marmaduke Tennant's portrait was presented to Afan Lodge by his son, Bro Ernest Theodore Tennant. Further biographical details appear separately in this book.

A significant milestone in the history of Afan Lodge was achieved with the completion of its own purpose-built Masonic Temple. Work on the new Temple had commenced in July 1907, on land leased from the Margam Estate, and was completed in September 1909. On Thursday, 21 October 1909, the new building accommodated its first Installation Ceremony, to coincide with the official opening of the Afan Masonic Temple. Brethren attending included WBro Marmaduke Tennant, DepProvGM, accompanied by Provincial Officers, and numerous distinguished Brethren, including the WMs of almost all the Lodges in the Province. The new WM was WBro D J Arnallt Jones, JP, MD, DPH, Medical Officer of Health for Aberavon. He had practised at Aberavon since 1884 and joined Afan Lodge in 1898. After the Ceremony, the Brethren repaired to the Grand Hotel where a banquet was held.

The Wardens' Chairs were presented to the Lodge on 5 May 1910, in memory of WBro T W Jenkins, PAGStB. The Director of Ceremonies' Chair was donated to Afan Lodge by Initiates of WBro T Llewellyn David during his year in Office, 1914-1915. The two great Pillars in the Temple were subscribed for by the Brethren of the Lodge as a token of their affection and high regard for WBro Marmaduke Tennant, and they were presented to the Lodge in 1914.

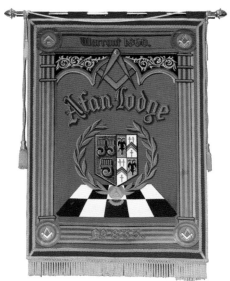

The original Afan Lodge Banner was presented on 5 February 1914, by WBro Humphrey Jones, WM. The original Banner is now in need of serious attention, and contact has been made with the Archive section at The National Library of Wales to carry out restoration. The next Afan Banner was created by the late WBro Vivian Knowles, and presented to the Lodge in 1987. The Arms depicted on the Banner and Past Master's Jewel are those of the old Aberavon Corporation, and are the reverse of those on the head of the ancient Borough Mace , one of only twelve 15th century Maces in the country. The dexter half, consisting of three rests or clarions, are those generally attributed to Robert Consul, and his son, William, Earl of Gloucester, Lord of Glamorgan, 1147-1183, who gave considerable gifts to Margam Abbey. The sinister half has been quartered: 1 & 4 - a double headed eagle, displayed; attributed to some of Earl William's descendants; 2 & 3 - three chevrons between three crosses pommes - fitchees. The three chevrons were borne by all the descendants of Iestyn ap Gwrgan, and undoubtedly have reference to the conferring of the original franchise to the old Borough by Caradog ap Iestyn (1079-1148). This family were the Lords of Afan at the time of the Norman conquest of Glamorgan, following which, the only Welsh Lordship having access to the sea, was that of Afan.

**The Banner created by
WBro Vivian Knowles in 1987**

During WWI, Bro Hugh Forbes was killed in action and Bro Glyn Howell was lost at sea. WBro Captain David Jenkins, MC, was awarded the Military Cross *'for gallantry'*. There were three casualties during WWII; Bro Captain Thomas Jones was killed in action at sea; Bro Thomas P Evans, Mercantile Marine, was also lost at sea, and likewise, Bro Thomas H David, RN. WBro Major Ivor Barkley John, MC, TD, JP, was awarded the Military Cross *'for gallantry in the face of the enemy'*. Bro Charles Pollard was Chief Engineer of the Merchant Vessel, San Demetrio. On 5 November 1940, the tanker San Demetrio was travelling in convoy, carrying gasoline destined for Avonmouth, when it was attacked in mid-Atlantic by the German pocket battleship, Admiral Scheer. Badly hit and on fire, the ship was abandoned, but a few days later, Bro Charles Pollard re-boarded the ship and managed to save her. He was awarded the OBE for *'his gallant exploit in the salvage of his ship'*. In 1943, the story was made into a film 'San Demetrio London', and starred Robert Beatty amongst its cast. While in Neath, many Brethren of the American Forces were regular visitors to Afan Lodge. In February 1940, a letter was received from the Ministry of Supply, stating that under their powers, the Masonic Hall would be requisitioned in the event of an emergency during the period of hostilities. A second letter dated 5 March 1942, was received from the Ministry, requesting to store extra supplies of emergency rations in the Masonic Building. On 5 March 1941, permission was granted to the Municipal Authority to erect an air raid shelter on the waste ground adjacent to the Masonic Building, while a few weeks later, on 27 March, the Festive Board had to be abandoned because of an air raid. The Lodge Committee agreed to recompense the Steward for his loss.

Afan Lodge has five Daughter Lodges. The first was Ogmore Lodge No1752, Warranted on 24 April 1878. It would be almost 53 years before the Sponsoring of the second Daughter Lodge, Margam Abbey Lodge No.5257, Warranted on 4 February 1931. WBro William Nicholas Howells, PM Afan Lodge was the Primus Master. The IPM and two Wardens were also Members of the Lodge. One of the Founders was WBro Ivor Vaughan John, PGSuptWks, who subsequently became a Founder and Primus Master of Baglan Lodge No.6079, Afan Lodge's third Daughter Lodge. This Lodge was Warranted on 7 March 1945. Three Afan Lodge Members, who were Founders of the fourth Daughter Lodge, Ynys Lodge No.8274, became Grand Officers. They were, WBros Morlais Davies, PAGDC; Dr Arthur E Jones, PAGDC; and Edgar M Abraham, PGStdB, who became Primus Master, when the Lodge was Consecrated on 25 April 1969.

In October 1953, for the first time in the history of the Province, RWBro R P St John Charles, ProvGM, appointed two Assistant Provincial Grand Masters. One was WBro Edgar W Lewis, PAGDC, AProvGM, 1953-1956, Afan Lodge, and the other was WBro Harry F Stockwell, Penarth Lodge No.4113.

The Lodge celebrated its centenary on 10 January 1961. A Service of Devotion and Thanksgiving was held at St Mary's Church, Aberavon, at 3.00 pm. RWBro R P St John Charles, ProvGM, supported by a large number of Provincial and Grand Officers, accompanied WBro William Arthur Thompson, WM, at the Service. WBro Rev W S Pontin, ProvGChap, Rector of Radyr, gave the Address and the ProvGM read the Lesson. After the Service, Brethren proceeded to the Temple where tea was served. The Lodge was opened at 5.00 pm, and the ProvGM, accompanied by VWBro. Edgar J Rutter, DepProvGM and a full Provincial team was received. The Lodge Secretary read the Warrant issued by Grand Lodge on 29 September, 1860; and VWBro Edgar J Rutter read the Centenary Warrant. At the conclusion of the Ceremony, the Brethren proceeded to the Dining Hall, where Bro James Alford, Club Steward, had prepared a sumptuous repast. The ProvGM had recently celebrated his 82nd birthday on 6 January, and when proposing the Toast to Afan Lodge, he was in reminiscent mood, recalling his many visits, and friends he had made in the Lodge who had done so much to promote its welfare. The cost of printing 'A History of The Afan Lodge', was defrayed by WBro Ivor Barclay John, MC, TD, JP, in memory of his father and grandfather, both of whom had been Masters of the Lodge on two occasions.

During the early 1980s, many organisations in Port Talbot made exchange visits with their opposite number in Heilbronn, Germany. A member of the local organising committee happened to be a Member of Afan Lodge, and he arranged for two Freemasons of the German exchange party to attend a Lodge Meeting. This subsequently resulted in a partnership between Zum Brunnen Des Heils Lodge No.367 and Afan Lodge. Despite the language barrier, many successful exchanges were organised between the two Lodges. Heilbronn Lodge shares its building with an American 'Forget-me-Not Lodge'. One of many visits to Heilbronn happened to coincid with a NATO exercise, when the Brethren and their ladies were confronted by a Tyler in full Battle Dress, and Masonic Regalia, 'armed' with a 'walkie-talkie', which constantly interrupted the proceedings! Many presentations took place and gifts were exchanged, notably a magnificent print from Heilbronn, now displayed in the bar, together with Commemorative Jewels which are displayed in the museum cases. Although official visits have now ceased, individual exchanges continue on a personal basis.

Afan Lodge has been well represented in local politics, with 10 Brethren having been Mayors of the Borough. Bro B Edward Howe, MA, the local Coroner, was the father of the Rt Hon Sir Geoffrey Howe, MP, PC, later Lord Howe of Aberavon. Bro Sir William Jenkins, MP, OBE, MP for Neath, 1922- 1944, was also a Lodge Member. In sport, three Members have been President of WRU: WBro W R Thomas, MBE, JP, President, 1954-1955; Bro Hywel Thomas, TD, LLB, Solicitor and Clerk to Port Talbot Justices, President, 1976-1977; and Bro Alun Gruffydd Thomas, President, 1985-1986. The latter was a rugby union centre, who played international rugby for Wales between 1952 and 1955. At club level he represented Cardiff, Swansea and Llanelly. In 1955, he toured with the British Lions and managed the team 19 years later on the 1974 tour of South Africa.

WBro G Vivian Knowles, PPrJGW, was a Photographer, whose talents were well known throughout the Province of South Wales. The photographs that adorn Afan Masonic Temple are the result of his skills. WBro 'Viv' took over the position of Lodge Preceptor in 1973, and without changing the Ritual, endeavoured to make the Ceremonies more enjoyable for the Brethren. In 1985, he began the tradition of presenting Masonic Lectures to enable Brethren to increase their Masonic knowledge. He also directed a presentation of the 1825 American Initiation Ritual. WBro Viv was Preceptor for 18 years and, in 1992, he was succeeded by WBro T Gerwyn Davies who, for the following 14 years, maintained the standards and traditions set by his predecessor. WBro Gerwyn was Installed WM in 1987.

WBro R Alistair Hopper, Installed WM in 1984, is one of the most senior Members of the Lodge. He became a Grand Officer in 2003, with the Rank of PGStdB. Past Master Members of Afan Lodge, also honoured by Grand Lodge are WBro Dr Leonard I Trott, PAGDC; and WBro J R Spender, PAGReg.

The original Lodge organ, costing £10 when purchased in 1898, was replaced in 1930 by a new one at a cost of £80. In July 1960, the organ was overhauled and an electric blower added at a cost of £100. In 2004, a new organ was donated to the Lodge, through the generosity of WBro Michael Couch, PPrJGW, Organist, Installed WM in 1992. The organ Dedication Ceremony was carried out by WBro Rev Norman Lea, PDepGChap, AProvGM. WBro Michael has also been instrumental in providing replacement organs for other Lodges, including those at Bridgend, Pontyclun and Porthcawl.

Afan Lodge celebrated its 150th Anniversary in 2011. The Anniversary Year commenced in December 2010, with a Dedication of the new Lodge Banner, (a picture of which is shown at the heading of this history), in the presence of WBro Gareth Jones, OBE, PSGD, AProvGM, the Banner being carried into the Temple by WBro Clive Brynley Davies, WM, accompanied by his escort party. WBro Gareth Jones explained that the design of the Banner was also related to the insignia of the ancient mace of the Borough of Aberavon, which was attributed to the Earl of Gloucester, Lord of Glamorgan, 1147-1183, who gave considerable gifts to the nearby Abbey at Margam. The Banner was Dedicated by WBro Gareth Jones, and WBro Rev Alastair Swinford, ProvGChap, gave the Dedication Prayer.

The Lodge celebrated its 150th Anniversay in January 2011 and every Brother who attended the celebrations was presented with a commemorative clock, hand-crafted by WBro Ken Davies, MMStwd of Baglan Lodge No.6079. Bro Ken also made the superb hardwood timepiece, presented to RWBro Capt Sir Norman Lloyd-Edwards, ProvGM, during the evening.

Compiled by WBro T Gerwyn Davies, PPrJGW.

Bute Lodge No.960

Warranted : 13 April 1863

Consecrated : 30 June 1863

Meeting at the Masonic Hall, Cardiff.

The middle of the Nineteenth Century was a period of unprecedented growth. Britain acquired vast tracts of Africa; Queen Victoria was created Empress of India and the British carved out a global Empire upon which the sun would never set. The Empire was founded on the power of the Royal Navy. The Navy was powered by Welsh steam coal exported from Cardiff Docks, the biggest coal port in the world, where captains of industry rubbed shoulders with captains of ships, and where the world's first million pound cheque was written and signed.

Freemasonry, imbued with the spirit of the Age, was also growing. In 1856, certain Brethren of Glamorgan Lodge No.36, the only Masonic Lodge in Cardiff, felt that for the sake of convenience, a new Lodge should be set up to meet in the vicinity of the Bute Docks to facilitate the ease with which Members, whose business was connected with the sea, could attend Meetings. The suggestion was rejected by a majority of the Lodge, then meeting in Church Street, but they declared their intention to do all in their power to meet the discontented Brethren from the lower end of the town. The discontent, however, continued and in December 1862 there were renewed calls from a substantial minority for a new Lodge to be formed to meet at the Docks. These calls were led by WBro John Charles Thorp, a Joining Member of Glamorgan Lodge and PM Alfred Lodge No.340 (Oxford). A towering figure in the history of Bute Lodge; his Memorial '... *praying that the sanction of this Lodge be given to the formation of a new Lodge at the Docks*' also failed. A majority of Glamorgan Lodge Brethren considered the wording of the Memorial to be ' ... *objectionable and contrary to the spirit of Masonry - and several Brethren whose names were attached thereto being in arrear in their subscription to the Lodge - Bro Gaskell proposed and W.M. seconded - That the petition stand till next Lo. Night and that Bro. Thorp be requested to amend the same - and to intimate to those Brethren whose subscriptions are in arrear to this Lodge, that they must pay the same before their names can be received - carried nem. con.*'. Strength of feeling was running high. In January 1863, the Petition was amended and WBro Thorp again proposed ' ... *That the sanction of the Officers and Brethren of this Lodge be given to the formation of a New Lodge at the Docks.*' This amendment was also narrowly defeated.

There is a tide in the affairs of men which, taken at the flood, leads on to fortune. Momentum was with WBro Thorp and he was not to be denied. He and his allies attended a meeting at Silurian Lodge (Newport) in February 1863 and asked them to back him in an approach to the ProvGM, Col Kemeys-Tynte. The Brethren of Silurian Lodge consented, and their recommendation was, it seems, instrumental in gaining the approval of the ProvGM. He informed the Brethren of Glamorgan Lodge of his intention to approach the Grand Master and asked them to support him in proposing the formation of a new Lodge in Cardiff to meet at the Docks. The direction of the prevailing wind was correctly ascertained by Glamorgan Lodge and at a Lodge of Emergency, held on 8 April, they unanimously supported the proposal. The Petition then was signed by 16 Glamorgan Members including the WM, Wardens and Secretary and 3 Brethren from Silurian Lodge. Four other Lodges were represented among the signatories. Thus Glamorgan Lodge became the Mother Lodge.

The Petition was successful and the GM, the Earl of Zetland, signed the charter on 13 April 1863. Bute was to become the eighth Lodge in the Province, one of only two in Cardiff. The Lodge was originally given the number 1262, (the number on the Warrant) but a week after the Consecration Ceremony, the Lodge was informed that Grand Lodge had decided to close the gaps on the Register and Bute was now Lodge No.960. At this time, it was also decided to adopt the Arms of the Marquess of Bute, and meet in the vicinity of Cardiff Docks. If Geometry is established as the basis of our Art, it was Geography that was the basis for the establishment of Bute Lodge.

WBro Thorp thanked the Brethren of Glamorgan Lodge and asked to borrow the harmonium for the Consecration Ceremony. This incident has been the subject of a long-standing joke between the two Lodges. The return of the harmonium was never mentioned in the Minutes of Glamorgan Lodge, and Bute Lodge Brethren are to this day light- heartedly reminded by Glamorgan Lodge Brethren that they are still awaiting its return.

Bute Lodge was Consecrated on 30 June 1863 in the Consulate Chambers at Bute Docks. The Consecrating Officers included WBro Bryant, PPSGW of the Royal Clarence Lodge No.68 (Bristol) in the Chair, as both the ProvGM and his Deputy could not attend. WBro Thorp was duly Installed the Primus Master of Bute Lodge. The Board of Installed Masters was dispensed with as Thorp was a PM Alfred Lodge No.340. The Master then thanked the Consecrating Officers, and the independent spirit of the Lodge was affirmed when he rather pointedly proposed '... *a special vote of thanks be given to the visiting Brethren from Newport who came forward in so truly a Masonic manner in assisting us to procure our warrant and were the first to sign our Petition to the Grand Lodge.*' A procession was then formed to St Mary's Church and after the Oration, a collection was raised for the Cardiff Infirmary. The Bute Lodge later honoured WBro Bryant by making him a Life Member in September 1863.

From 1863 to 1876, Bute Lodge met at the Consulate Chambers. Bridges were built with Glamorgan Lodge when their WM WBro John Grierson was Elected an Honorary Member of the Lodge, beginning a Fraternal trend that was to last many years. The Lodge quickly settled down to work, Regular Meetings taking place every two weeks with Lodges of Emergency a common occurrence. The overwhelming majority of Members having some connection to the sea, there was frequently a nautical flavour to proceedings. Many Candidates being foreign seamen, there was often a need for interpreters; and the Lodge owed a debt of gratitude to Brethren fluent in French, German, Italian and Finnish. The Minute Books record that Bros Morteo, Weichert, Bellisario, Strina, Larsen and Emery were particularly helpful. The Bute Lodge's independence of spirit again raised its head in the case of Bro Larsen. Having thanked him for his translation services, the Lodge blackballed him when he later attempted to join! The Minute Books record the practice of blackballing as a frequent occurrence and Ceremonies being delayed or postponed. On one occasion, a Candidate refused to sign the Declaration and was forced to retire. A Ceremony was suspended because a visiting Brother arrived armed with a dagger. This was Jan Jonker, a Pawnbroker in Bute Street and a Member of Glamorgan Lodge. At the next Regular Meeting of the Lodge, Jonker was Balloted for as a Joining Member and, perhaps not surprisingly, he was blackballed ... twice! On the Wedding Day of the Marquess of Bute, the Lodge cancelled a Ceremony as a mark of respect and deference, but that independence of spirit became manifest when he requested the Lodge cease to bear his name and no longer use his Coat of Arms. The latter request was complied with but the former was declined, the Lodge declaring it to be '*inconvenient*'. The nautical theme continued with the Lodge making a substantial donation toward the cost of buying and equipping a lifeboat. Indeed, to this day the Lodge makes an annual donation to the RNLI. Absent Brethren were remembered during the Festive Board by singing the Seaman's Hymn, together with a Toast as near to the hour of ten as possible. A custom still honoured today.

Those early years at the Consulate Chambers were dominated by WBro Thorp, the first Master of the Lodge, who continued in the Chair for 18 months. His record as WM is near legendary. He five times worked all 3 Degrees; twenty times worked 2 Degrees and twenty four times worked 1 Degree. He Initiated seventy six Candidates in 18 months and in one meeting in

September 1863, ten Brethren were Passed. He also gave a lecture on the First and Second Degree Tracing Boards in what the Minute Book describes as *'an excellent and highly interesting lecture on the 3rd degree'*. He sat on the PGL Committee to look into uniformity of Ritual and given his connections with Oxford, our first WM is widely credited with introducing the Oxford Ritual to the Lodge and possibly to the Province. In 1868, he returned his Jewel, intimating that he would no longer attend Masonic Meetings. That Jewel is now worn with pride by each IPM. In the 147 years of Bute Lodge's existence, his achievements have never been equalled, let alone surpassed.

From 1877 to 1895, the Lodge met at 9, Working Street, Cardiff. At this point, there appears to be some disquiet about the number of Candidates requiring translation services, although no resolutions were passed, and the number of blackballing incidents continued to concern the Past Masters. The Lodge continued its close relationship with Glamorgan Lodge. In 1875, the Lodge Petitioned for its first Daughter Lodge, Merlin Lodge No.1578, Pontypridd. A Petition, in conjunction with Glamorgan Lodge for Windsor Lodge No.1754, Penarth, followed in 1878. The Petition for Tennant Lodge No. 1992 was signed in January 1883, also with the support of Glamorgan Lodge, and it became the third Lodge in Cardiff. At this time it was resolved to form a Chapter and The Sir George Elliot Chapter No.960 was Consecrated in 1888 and attached to Bute Lodge. The Lodge celebrated its 25th Anniversary on 3 April 1888 with the purchase of a new Bible, a set of Collars and Jewels for the Officers, and a presentation of an Ivory Gavel to the WM, WBro J Radley. A banquet was also held at the Angel Hotel. Two years later (1890), the Lodge, in conjunction with Glamorgan Lodge and Windsor Lodge, supported the Petition for Barry Lodge No.2357. In November of that year, a Joint Committee with Glamorgan Lodge and Tennant Lodge was established to look into the possibility of buying a new Masonic Hall. The proposed move to new premises was approved and £4,500 was allocated to buy the chapel at Guildford Street.

The new Temple was officially opened at Guildford Street on 26 September 1895 with a meeting of PGL. Bute Lodge's first Ceremony took place on Tuesday, 1 October 1895 with WBro H C Ensor in the Chair. The Minute Books of this period record that the Lodge expelled 50 Brethren for being 3 years or more in arrears; a letter being read from Granite Lodge No.1328 asking Bute Lodge to subscribe to a guarantee fund to secure the conviction of *'the murderer of Bro Alexander Willis'*; and support for Llangattock Lodge in a Petition for another new Cardiff Lodge - Loyal Commercial Lodge No.2720. The new building, meanwhile, needed maintenance. Thirty guineas were given towards the cost of internal renovations to the Temple and a total of £100 for the purchase of a new organ. In 1910, a hundred guineas were presented to WBro T Matthews, PM, for 38 years of valuable and continual service to the Lodge. The Brethren also raised over £40 towards the £66 cost of a Memorial to WBro G Bedford who had been WM in 1896.

The Lodge celebrated its Golden Jubilee on 1 July 1913 by working a Ceremony of Initiation with four Candidates in front of 170 Brethren. Every Member of the Lodge wore a Jubilee Medal especially designed for the occasion. An Ivory Gavel was presented to the WM, WBro I Vaughan Evans and a banquet held at the Royal Hotel. The attendance included 21 PMs and 154 Members and guests, including the WMs of Glamorgan and Silurian Lodges. An important guest was Bro Joseph Milner, the only surviving Founder Member of the Lodge. It was decided at this time to compile a short history of the first 50 years, a task later completed by WBro I Vaughan Evans. This was a busy time. Caerdydd Lodge No.3959 became the latest Daughter Lodge (1919), the first Ladies' Night was held and the Lodge took a prominent part in the last public procession of Masons in Cardiff (March 1926). The Brethren assembled at the Temple and proceeded in morning dress, black ties, white gloves and the majority in top hats to Bethany Chapel for the funeral service of DepProvGM Sir David W Evans. In 1936, the Minutes record the adoption of a new Lodge Badge *'designed with the view to drawing attention to the early connection of the Bute Lodge with the town of Cardiff, more especially that part which is known as the Bute Dock. The antlers are taken from the Bute Arms which are represented on the Lodge Banner. The mural crown, ostrich feathers and leek are taken from the coat of Arms of Cardiff, the shield and crown of which was adopted by the Lodge in 1895'*. The Lodge Charter was also embellished at this time. Busy times indeed, but dark clouds were gathering on the horizon.

At this point it is proper to mention Lodge activities during both World Wars. The majority of Brethren served in the Merchant Fleets, as you would expect, but Brethren also served with distinction in the Army, Navy and RAF. There were others also who served in Home Guard units and some Brethren who joined in the post-war period had served their country as Bevin Boys. In the Great War, Lodge activities included setting up committees to make regular hospital visits, contributing £742 to War Charities and £75 to the Memorial Tablet in the Hall. During WWII, Lodge activities were affected by air-raids, but Meetings continued and were a great comfort to Brethren, especially in the dark days before 1942. Several Brethren of the Lodge suffered injury and great privations during both wars, especially at sea. Bro Trevor Holbrook and Bro Hurman Thomas both made the Supreme Sacrifice.

The post war years saw a return to normality; two more Daughter Lodges, Amity No.5823 and St Canna No.6725 were Consecrated, and the Brethren were kept busy. In 1963, the Lodge was a hundred years old. Divine Service was celebrated at the Church of St John the Baptist and attended by five hundred people. WBro W Walsh, WM, summoned the Brethren to the Centenary Meeting, with several Provincial luminaries in attendance. An Ivory Gavel was presented to the WM who, in turn, presented Province with a cheque for £500 toward the 1967 Festival. There were over two hundred Brethren at the subsequent banquet. The Lodge produced another short history, researched and written by WBro T Wyndham Richards, chronicling a century of work in Freemasonry.

The distinguishing characteristic of a Freemason's heart is Charity. It would be quite impossible to give even an estimate of the amounts distributed by the Lodge throughout its history. In 1899, the Bute Lodge Charity Association was founded to make quarterly contributions toward Masonic Charities. It has been the heart of the Lodge. Several Brethren have given sterling service, among them WBro H Crabtree, and more recently WBro R Dicker.

Bute Lodge has long been known for the quality of its Ritual. This is due to the zeal of the Masters and the quality of the LOIs. As early as 1870, at the Town Hall and in the presence of the ProvGM and his Officers, the Lodge worked seven sections of the 1st Degree Lectures to great acclaim. To maintain the high standards, WBro David Hopkins, the only WM to have served two complete successive terms, instituted reforms. He rebuked Brethren for whispering in Ceremonies, retiring when Candidates were being prepared and railed against plurality of Candidates and the over-use of blackballing. He was a strong supporter of LOI, the first of which was held in 1863. During the closing years of the 19th Century, a Joint LOI was in progress with Glamorgan Lodge and this continued until 1897, when the two Lodges went their separate ways. Since that year, the Bute LOI has been held on the second Tuesday of each month. WBro W Ferrier being the first long serving President, he was succeeded by WBro I V Evans. This proud tradition has been continued since the 1963 centenary by other distinguished presidents, WBro H Walsh and WBro P Bennett.

No history of the Lodge would be complete without reference to the Bute Reading Circle. Its origins, like those of the Craft itself are lost in the mists of time, but there were certainly Meetings, however sporadic, in the twilight years of the Victorian Age. The first recorded Meetings appear in 1923 with regular Minutes surviving since 1931. The Reading Circle exists to explore the meaning of Masonry and to promote a deeper understanding of the Order by encouraging debate and contributing to the daily advancement in Masonic knowledge. The intention was always to stimulate scholarly debate for the thinking Mason. Many eminent Masons throughout the history of the Province have attended Meetings or presented papers. Subjects discussed have included *Symbolism in the Temple, Role of the Almoner, The Knights Templar, The Bible and Masonry, Masonic Music, The Hiram Key, Secrecy and Freemasonry.* Exchange visits have been held with Study Circles in Penarth and Swansea. Distinguished Presidents include WBros F Fisher, T R Hughes, J Aitken, G Brown and more recently S A Woodberry.

Time has moved on since the Lodge Centenary Celebrations and more chapters have been added to the story. Bute Lodge has been a part of the fabric of Masonic life in this Province for nearly one hundred and fifty years. Under the supervision of nine Provincial Grand Masters, the Lodge has proclaimed its unswerving allegiance to the sacred dictates of Truth, Honour and Virtue.

Compiled by WBro Stephen Attwell, PM.

Theodore Mansel Talbot
1839 - 1876

Deputy Provincial Grand Master
1863 - 1865
Provincial Grand Master of South Wales
1865 - 1876

The Mansel Talbots were descendants of the Mansel family of Margam, Penrice and Oxwich, and the Talbot family of Lacock Abbey, Wiltshire. The Mansels, of Norman descent, arrived at Oxwich, Gower, circa 1300. When Margam Abbey was dissolved in 1537, its lands were bought by Sir Rice Mansel of Oxwich. In 1611, James I created the Baronetcy of Margam. When the fourth and last Baron Mansel, Bussy Mansel, died without a male heir in 1750, the title became extinct and the estates passed through marriage to the Reverend Thomas Talbot of Lacock Abbey.

Theodore Mansel Talbot was born on 7 July 1839, the son of Sir Christopher Rice Mansel Talbot (1803-1890) and Lady Charlotte, the second daughter of the 1st Earl of Glengall. Theodore's grandfather, Sir Thomas Mansel Talbot, had died in 1813, leaving his estate in trust for his nine year-old son, Christopher. Two years later, Theodore's grandmother, Lady Lucy Strangways, married Sir Christopher Cole, Provincial Grand Master of South Wales, 1817-1836.

Theodore's father, Christopher Mansel Talbot, affectionately known as 'Kit' to his family and friends, was MP for Glamorganshire, 1830-1885. He was returned for the Mid-Division of the County in 1885, and sat as a Liberal Unionist from 1886 until his death in January 1890. For many years, he was also the Lord-Lieutenant of the County. An extremely wealthy man, he amassed a considerable fortune, mainly through shrewd investments in railway stock, estimated at three million pounds at the time of his death. When the 'Returns of Owners of Land' were made in 1873, he held nearly 34,000 acres of land, which yielded an annual rental of £44,000. He was responsible for building Margam Castle. Construction of the Castle commenced in 1830 and the main building was completed by 1840. When the English Copper Miners' Company built the first dock near Aberavon, 1835-1836, the directors recognised the co-operation he had accorded them by naming the new port after him - hence the new town of Port Talbot was born. In addition, he was a brilliant mathematician, obtaining a first class honours degree at Oriel College, Oxford, in 1824. He went on to write the standard work on 'The Law of Curvatures' and, in 1831, was elected a Fellow of the Royal Society.

Theodore Mansel Talbot

Theodore, a sickly child, was educated at home by private tutors under the supervision of his father. Like his father, he read mathematics at Christ Church, Oxford, obtaining a second-class degree in 1860. Subsequently, he devoted himself to the Volunteer movement and gained the admiration of all ranks for his competence and skill with the rifle. He eventually became the Lieutenant-Colonel of the 1st Glamorgan Administrative Battalion. He also did great service in promoting the interests of the County's Agricultural Society and for a time farmed Hall Farm, North Cornelly, on his own. Fox hunting was another great passion and having first led the Ledbury hounds, he was determined to re-establish the sport at home. To that end, he restocked the Vale with hundreds of foxes and built kennels and stables on the Talbot estate at Llandough! He also took an active interest in the game of Bando, a crude kind of hockey, which was played twice a week on the Margam sands.

Life changed profoundly for Theodore when, in 1869, he entered St Columba's Church Haggerston during the London Mission, at which Father Arthur Stanton was preaching. Theodore approached Fr Stanton after the service and reportedly said, *'Here I am. What can I do?'* - to which Fr Stanton responded, *'Come to St Alban's and help us there'*. At St Alban's Church, Holborn, London, one of the centres of the Anglo-Catholic revival, Theodore found his true vocation working with the Vicar, Fr Mackonochie and his Curate Fr Stanton, who was destined to become his life-long friend. Disappearing from society, he was to spend his time in the slums of Holborn, where he would nurse sick children, carry the dead to burial, stand in as a godfather at street children's baptisms and teach in Sunday Schools. Meanwhile, when back on the family estates, Theodore promoted the restoration of neglected churches and the appointment of Anglo-Catholic clergy. As a consequence, the Abbey Church at Margam became a centre of Catholic Faith and teaching, subsequently leading, much to Theodore's disgust, to disputes with Bishop Ollivant, Bishop of Llandaff. A successful attempt was made at Margam to improve Church Music in the Llandaff Diocese, *'and choirs in the parishes were taught by the late Mr. Richard Seaton, under whom in the Abbey itself Gregorian chants and hymns were sung with a devotion and beauty which fitted its ancient tradition'*. Theodore Talbot also conceived the idea of restoring the abbey and establishing a training school for the Welsh Clergy there, but the project was never realised owing to his early tragic death. Inherently humble, selfless, and devout, Theodore Talbot has been described as one of the most saint-like characters of his generation.

Theodore's involvement in Freemasonry began during his student days in Oxford, when he was Initiated in Apollo University Lodge No.460 (now No.357) and shortly afterwards, in 1857, he became a Joining Member of Indefatigable Lodge No.288 (now No.237), Swansea. Two years later, in 1859, he became a Joining Member of Cambrian Lodge No.472, Neath (now No.364). He became an Honorary Member of that Lodge in July 1870, being Provincial Grand Master of the Province by that time. On 29 September 1860, a Warrant was issued for a new Lodge, Afan Lodge No.1135 (now No.833) at Aberavon, which was the first of the Port Talbot Lodges. The Petition for this new Lodge was signed by the Bethren of Cambrian Lodge, Neath. The Lodge was Consecrated on 10 January 1861, and Theodore Mansel Talbot was Installed as the first Worshipful Master. For the first two years, Afan Lodge met at the Walnut Tree Hotel, High Street, Aberavon.

Further Masonic advancement was to come in 1863 when Theodore Mansel Talbot was appointed Deputy Provincial Grand Master of the Province. In the history of Indefatigable Lodge, it is claimed that the appointment *'was largely due to the influence of the Brethren of the Indefatigable Lodge'*. The Provincial Grand Master, Charles Kemeys Kemeys-Tynte, writing to the Lodge on 14 September 1863 stated: *'I felt when I offered him the high post that in so doing I was materially strengthening the interests of the Craft in this large and important Province'*. The new DepProvGM, writing to Indefatigable Lodge on 11 October, remarked that *'I cannot feel that the expressed wishes of the Indefatigable Lodge on the subject weighed greatly with the R.W. the P.G.M. in his choice.'*

In September 1864, Theodore Mansel Talbot, DepProvGM, laid the Foundation Stone of St David's Church, Neath, *'with Masonic Ceremony'*. A full report of the Ceremony is given in the 'Swansea & Glamorgan Herald', of 28 September, and included is the following inscription on the plate of the Foundation Stone: *'The Foundation Stone of this Church, dedicated to St. David, was laid on Thursday, the 22nd day of September, A.D. 1864, on land presented by Howel Gwyn, Esq., of Duffryn, by Theodore Mansel Talbot, Esq., Deputy Provincial Grand Master of the Order of Freemasons, assisted by Mrs. Gwyn.'*

When The Provincial Grand Master, Charles Kemeys Kemeys-Tynte announced his resignation in 1865, the Brethren of Glamorgan Lodge No.36 called a Lodge of Emergency on 16 June to vote on an Address to the MW Grand Master, *'praying him to appoint Bro T M Talbot to the vacant Office of P.G.M.'* However, since the issuing of the Summons, the appointment of

Theodore Mansel Talbot as the next ProvGM had been made, consequently the Brethren of Glamorgan Lodge resolved '*That the members of this Lodge desire to express to the R.W. Bro. Theodore Mansel Talbot their sincere gratification at the M.W. the Grand Master having been pleased to appoint him to the Office of Provincial Grand Master for the Eastern Division of South Wales. They feel assured that the zeal, energy and eminent Masonic Monuments so prominently displayed by him whilst acting as Deputy Provincial Grand Master will cause his appointment to be hailed with heartfelt pleasure by all the Brethren throughout the Province.*'

The Patent appointing Theodore Mansel Talbot as ProvGM had been signed on 13 June 1865 and his Installation was held later in the year, on Thursday, 28 September in Cardiff. An account of the proceedings appeared the following day in the 'Cardiff & Merthyr Guardian':

Yesterday (Thursday) a Provincial Grand Lodge was held in the Assembly-room at the Townhall, which was elegantly fitted up with regalia connected with a lodge. The proceedings of the day excited a great deal of interest, and hundreds of persons waited at the corners of the streets to witness the procession. At 12 o'clock a very large number of the masons of the eastern division of the province of South Wales assembled in the Town-hall. The Grand Master, Theodore Mansel Talbot, Esq., who had been appointed Grand Master on the resignation of Colonel Tynte, was formally installed in that office. The lodge business occupied the members till three o'clock, when they formed in procession and, headed by the Glamorgan Militia band, under the leadership of Mr. G. F. Davis, marched to St. John's Church, where special Divine Service was held. The church was crowded with visitors. The Rev. J. D. Davies preached a most excellent sermon from 133rd Psalm, 1st and 2nd verses. It was, as might be judged from the text, an address to the members, and both the text and the tenor of the sermon, were most appropriate for the occasion. On the conclusion, the members again formed in order, and, preceded by the Militia band, marched to the Stuart Hall, near the Hayes Bridge, where a most sumptuous repast was provided by Mr. Cousins, of the Angel. Nearly 300 members were present. The streets through which the procession passed, and various other parts of the town, were gaily decorated with flags for the occasion.

(Note: The Stuart Hall, built in the Hayes in 1865, seems, among its other functions, to have been given over to theatrical productions, but by 1894, it had been acquired by the Salvation Army. It was demolished in 1965.)

During Theodore's tenure of Office as ProvGM, three new Lodges appeared in the Province. The first, honouring the ProvGM by carrying the family name, was Talbot Lodge No.1323, Swansea. The Mother Lodge was Cambrian Lodge, Neath, but Brethren from Indefatigable Lodge also signed the Petition. The Warrant was issued on 20 June 1870 and the Consecration took place on 8 December of that year, the Lodge meeting in the Masonic Rooms of the Mackworth Hotel, Swansea. These were a suite of rooms, added to the Mackworth Arms Hotel by the landlord for the purpose of Talbot Lodge. WBro Edward John Morris, DepProvGM, was the first Master of the Lodge, and at his Installation there were 125 Brethren present from all parts of the Province.

The following year, another significant event in Swansea Freemasonry occurred with the laying of the Foundation Stone for a Masonic Hall in Caer Street for Indefatigable Lodge. The Stone was laid by Theodore Mansel Talbot on 6 July 1871. Details are given in the history of Indefatigable Lodge, earlier in this book.

The former Stuart Hall in the Hayes

In 1875, Petitions were signed by Brethren of Indefatigable Lodge for a new Lodge at Swansea, and by Brethren of Bute Lodge for a new Lodge at Pontypridd. The Warrant for Caradoc Lodge No.1573, meeting at the New Masonic Hall, Caer Street, was signed on 8 October 1875. The Lodge was Consecrated by the ProvGM on 17 February 1876. The Warrant for Merlin Lodge No.1578, Pontypridd, was signed on 23 October 1875 and the Lodge was Consecrated on 27 April 1876. Unfortunately, due to illness, the ProvGM was unable to attend the Ceremony, which was performed instead by WBro Edward J Morris, DepProvGM.

Freemasonry in the Province under the guidance of Theodore Mansel Talbot was going from strength to strength, when on 18 June 1876, a great tragedy occurred in the sudden death of the ProvGM. Many speculated that the cause of his death was due to injuries sustained from falls when foxhunting, for he was well known for being a reckless rider to hounds. An account of what had occurred was given in the 'Western Mail' on Tuesday, 20 June:

'There is an impression that the late Mr. Theodore M. Talbot met with an accident in the hunting field quite recently, but this is a mistake. It is true that many months ago he fell from his horse in the hunting field, when the bones of his arm were fractured; but he apparently recovered from the effects of the fall and was subsequently as well as ever. The symptoms which unfortunately terminated fatally, first made their appearance while he was hunting at Miskin, accompanied by Mr. Gwilym Williams, to whom he complained that he was suffering great pain between the shoulders, and the impression at the time was that he was suffering from an attack of rheumatism. He was at Miskin a fortnight, still suffering severely and was advised to bathe the painful part with warm water, which appeared to give him relief. He became better, and visited Mr. Stacey at Llandough Castle. Thence he went to Buxton, where he became worse, and the medical gentlemen who were in attendance at the time of his death were sent for, and they treated him for an abscess on the spine. He went from Buxton to his father's London residence, where he died.'

(Notes: Gwilym Williams was Judge Gwilym Williams of Miskin Manor who, in 1863, had been involved in a 'Masonic Scandal', when he underwent a second Initiation in Glamorgan Lodge, having previously been Initiated in St David's Lodge, Aberdare – see biographical details of Charles Kemeys Kemeys-Tynte, ProvGM, given earlier in the book. Mr Francis Edmund Stacey of Llandough Castle was the brother of Rev John Thomas Cyril Stacey, Member of Glamorgan Lodge and a son of Rev Thomas Stacey, curate of St John's Church, Cardiff.)

Notice of his death also appeared in the 'Western Mail' the same day:

'Mr. Theodore Mansel Talbot, the heir of Margam, died yesterday morning at the town residence of his father, the member for Glamorgan, of a spinal infection, caused by a fall from his horse. He was the Provincial Grand Master of the Freemasons of South Wales, and was very active in Church matters. He was attended in his last illness by Sir William Jenner and Sir James Paget, but their professional skill proved unavailing.' (Sir William Jenner had attended Prince Albert, when he died from typhoid on 14 December 1861.)

On Saturday, June 24 the 'Western Mail' carried a brief account of the funeral:

'The funeral of the much-esteemed and lamented Theodore Mansel Talbot took place at Margam, on Friday. The remains of the deceased gentleman were conveyed from London by a special train, and were met at the station by a large body of tenantry, notwithstanding that it had been arranged that the funeral should be conducted in the most private manner possible. Lord Ilchester, Lord Stanhope, and the Rev. Arthur Stanton were amongst those present. Immediately after the ceremony, Mr. C. R. M. Talbot, the father of the deceased, left Margam for his town residence, where his daughter lies in a precarious state.'

Theodore Mansel Talbot was interred in the Talbot Chapel of the Abbey Church Margam. Theodore's magnificent tomb is the most striking feature of the Chapel and it is a copy of the 13th century tomb of Archbishop Walter de Gray in York Minster. The marble recumbent effigy of Theodore lies under a Gothic canopy of elaborate design, supported by eight slender columns with foliate capitals. The effigy is reputed to bear a faithful likeness to Theodore Talbot. Mural tablets near the tomb commemorate his father, Christopher Rice Mansel Talbot (1803-1890), and his sisters Olivia and Emily Charlotte, the last of the Margam Talbots.

Theodore Mansel Talbot's successor as ProvGM was Sir George Elliot. At his Installation in Aberdare on 4 April 1877, no reference was made to his predecessor. Many Brethren felt very strongly about this oversight – *'that to allow a brother who had governed them for 11 years, so just, so kind, and excellent a chief, to go to his last home without one word of regret or one syllable of gratitude appearing in the archives of the Province, in which he had ruled so well, would be out of harmony with the feelings of its members, a lasting discredit to the Provincial Grand Lodge, and but a poor encouragement to those who might come after'*. These words were spoken by WBro Col Sir Edward Stock Hill, PProvGW, WM of Glamorgan Lodge, 1869-1870, (ProvGM Mark Master Masons of South Wales, 1899-1904) at a Provincial Grand Lodge of Emergency, held as *'the result of a numerous and very influential requisition to the Provincial Grand Master, asking him to call a P.G. Lodge of Emergency to afford an opportunity of repairing the grave omission'*. The Meeting, held under the Banner of Glamorgan Lodge in their new Masonic Hall, 14 Working Street, Cardiff, took place on Thursday, 30

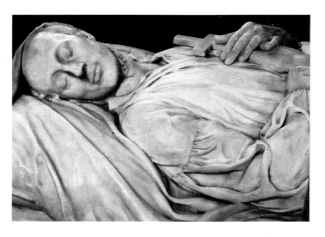

The effigy of Theodore Mansel Talbot

August 1877, in the presence of Sir George Elliot, when the following resolution, proposed by WBro E S Hill, was passed:

'That the Brethren of the Province of South Wales, Eastern Division, with grateful recollection of the very eminent services rendered to Masonry by the late R.W. Bro. Theodore Mansel Talbot, during the 11 years he held the distinguished office of Provincial Grand Master – an office the duties of which he performed with untiring zeal, with dignity worthy of the Craft, and with urbanity endearing him to the Brethren – desire formally to record their high appreciation of his services, and their profound regret at the irreparable loss they have sustained by his early death'.

It was also agreed that a copy of the Resolution be sent to Mr C R M Talbot, Lord-Lieutenant of the County. Following the closure of the Provincial Grand Lodge, a banquet was held at the Royal Hotel, Cardiff, presided over by Sir George Elliot.

After the death of Christopher Rice Mansel Talbot, the estate passed to Miss Emily Charlotte. Like her brother, she had deeply rooted religious convictions and an unbounded philanthropy. Among her very many benefactions, the churches of St Theodore, St Agnes, St John (Pontrhydyfen) and St Tydfil (Bryn) came into being between 1897 and 1913. St Theodore's Church, built between 1895 and 1897 and consecrated in 1898, was erected to the memory of Theodore and Olivia Talbot and the cost of £25,000 was entirely met by Miss Talbot. The foundation of St Michael's Theological College, Llandaff (formerly at Aberdare) was due to Miss Olivia Talbot, (1842-1894); after her death in 1894, it continued to receive the unstinted support of her sister, Emily Charlotte.

References:

'Who's Who in Welsh History', Deborah C Fisher, Published by Christopher Davies 1997. ISBN 0.7154.07317]
'Margam Abbey', by A Leslie Evans, 2nd Edition, published by the Port Talbot Historical Society, 1996
'History of the Indefatigable Lodge, No. 237', William Henry Jones, Spurrell, Carmarthen 1923;
'Cambrian Lodge, No. 364, 1821 - 1921', Br. Glen A Taylor, published in 1949
Lane's Masonic Records 1717-1894
'Cardiff & Merthyr Guardian', 29 September 1865
'Western Mail', 20 & 26 June 1876, 30 August 1877

WBro Peter M Davies, ProvJGW.

Edward James Morris
1839 ~ 1917

Deputy Provincial Grand Master
1865-1876

Edward James Morris, the son of Thomas and Ann Morris, was born in Shoreditch, London in 1830. By 1851, his mother was widowed and Edward still lived with her and his sister Elizabeth at 19 St Olave, Old Jewry, London. He was now employed as a Stockbroker's Clerk in the City. Shortly afterwards, he moved to Swansea, where he was employed as an Accountant with Messrs Richardson & Sons, Copper-ore Merchants, Copper Ore Wharfs, Tyrllandwr.

He was Initiated into Indefatigable Lodge No.237 in 1856 and became Worshipful Master in 1860. Also in 1860, he married Sarah Jane Jeffrey, from Temple Mead, Bristol and the following year their first son Edward Edmond Morris was born. The young family were now living at 53 Brunswick Street, Swansea.

In 1864, he was once again Installed Worshipful Master of Indefatigable Lodge. Towards the close of this second term, a testimonial of the Lodge's admiration of his work was presented to him in the form of a gold Past Master's Jewel adorned with a brilliant, a silver vase of Egyptian design, and an Illuminated Address. Indefatigable Lodge possesses 3 cabinets containing a large number of the Jewels and the clothing belonging to him, as well as the Illuminated Warrant of his appointment as Deputy Provincial Grand Master in 1865.

Theodore Mansel Talbot, his predecessor as DepProvGM, had been Installed Provincial Grand Master of the Eastern Division of South Wales at a Meeting of Provincial Grand Lodge, held at the Stuart Hall, Cardiff, on 28 September 1865. It was at that Meeting that Edward James Morris was Invested as his Deputy.

When Talbot Lodge No.1323 was Consecrated on 8 December 1870, Edward J Morris was Installed the first Worshipful Master.

By 1871, Edward J Morris was living at 11 Heathfield Street, Swansea, which was to be his home for more than 20 years. He now had seven children, 2 sons and five daughters. Around this time he became the Actuary for the Swansea Savings Bank.

In 1872, Talbot Chapter was Consecrated, when Edward J Morris, a Founder, became the first Z. On 4 September 1872, he was Elected an Honorary Member of Cambrian Lodge No.364, Neath. Two years later he became the first Master of Talbot Mark Lodge No.179.

The tragic death of Theodore Mansel Talbot, ProvGM, at the age of 37, on 18 June 1876, led to the appointment of Sir George Elliot as the next Provincial Grand Master. At his Installation at Aberdare on 4 April 1877, no reference was made to his predecessor. Many Brethren were dismayed that no tribute had been made and subsequently petitioned Sir George Elliot to hold a Provincial Grand Lodge of Emergency to rectify the matter. Further, Edward J Morris had resigned his Office as Deputy at the end of December 1876 and had not been re-appointed by the New Provincial Grand Master.

At the PGL of Emergency, held at the Masonic Hall, Working Street, Cardiff, under the Banner of Glamorgan Lodge, on 30 August 1877, two resolutions were passed. The first was the tribute to Theodore Mansel Talbot (see biographical details). The second resolution, proposed by Bro Charles Bath, PPGW, Indefatigable Lodge was as follows: *'That this Provincial Grand Lodge desires to record its grateful acknowledgements of the eminent services rendered to the province by the Worshipful Brother Edward James Morris, Junior Grand Deacon of England, during the long period he filled the office of Deputy Provincial Grand Master, and to which the present high position held by the province is due, and its regret at the loss which the province has sustained through his withdrawal from active Masonic life.'*

The resolution was seconded by Bro Alexander Bassett, JP, PM Glamorgan Lodge and supported by Walter Whittington, PM Cambrian Lodge (Provincial Grand Secretary 1870-1875) and other Brethren, and on being put to the Meeting was carried nem con. It was also agreed that a copy of this second resolution be sent to WBro Edward J Morris.

Thus, unfortunately, Edward J Morris's involvement with Freemasonry came to an end. He continued to live in Swansea until his death at the age of 87 in 1917.

WBro Peter M Davies, ProvJGW.

Talbot Lodge No.1323

Warranted : 20 June 1870

Consecrated : 8 December 1870

Meeting at the Masonic Hall, Swansea.

In 1805, there were but two Swansea Lodges in existence namely, Beaufort Lodge No.244, Erased in 1809 and Indefatigable Lodge No.237, which was originally Knoll Lodge No.506 of Neath, transferred to Swansea in 1800. From 1809 to 1870, Indefatigable remained the only Lodge in Swansea.

WBro Edward Morris, DepProvGM, who had been Installed WM of Indefatigable Lodge in 1860, with other Past Masters and Members of Indefatigable Lodge, requested Cambrian Lodge No.364, Neath, to Sponsor a new Lodge in Swansea, to be known as 'Talbot Lodge'. The Lodge is named after RWBro Theodore Mansel Talbot, ProvGM, 1865-1876. He became a Joining Member of Indefatigable Lodge in 1857, a Joining Member of Cambrian Lodge in 1859, and an Honorary Member of Cambrian Lodge in July 1870. The Petition for the new Lodge was duly signed by the WM and Wardens of Cambrian Lodge in May 1870. The Warrant was granted on 20 June 1870, with WBro E J Morris, WM Designate; WBro Charles Bath, PPSGW, WM Indefatigable Lodge 1866, 1867, SW Designate; and WBro George Browne Brock, PPJGW, WM Indefatigable Lodge 1869, JW Designate. All the Founders were Members of Indefatigable Lodge, including Bro Henry Simons, who became Tyler. The Founders did not pay a Founders' fee, with the exception of three Founders; they paid 5 guineas, consisting of a Joining fee of 1 guinea, Subscription for 1871 of 2 guineas, and a further 2 guineas for the purchase of the Jewel of their Office. (1 guinea is equivalent to £1. 5p)

Talbot Lodge No.1323 was Consecrated in the Masonic Rooms, Wind Street, Swansea, on 8 December 1870, in a Ceremony conducted by RWBro Theodore Mansel Talbot. The Masonic Rooms were leased from, and were part of, the Mackworth Arms Hotel. The first Minute Book of Talbot Lodge records in full the Ceremony of Consecration and Dedication. The Lodge was opened in the First Degree by WBro Clement S B Gardiner, ProvGTreas, WM of Cambrian Lodge, assisted by Past Masters of Cambrian Lodge, who occupied the Officers' Chairs. The ProvGM accompanied by WBro Edward James Morris, DepProvGM, and attended by Officers of Provincial Grand Lodge, entered in procession, being marshalled by WBro John Jones-Hewson, ProvGDC. The ProvGM, having taken the Chair, appointed WBro James Griffith Hall, ProvSGW, Installed WM of Indefatigable Lodge in 1850, and WBro Edward Stock Hill, ProvJGW, Installed WM of Glamorgan Lodge No.36 in 1869, as Wardens pro tempore. The Master Designate, WBro Edward James Morris, on behalf of the Members of Talbot Lodge requested the ProvGM to Consecrate and Dedicate the Lodge in conformity with ancient custom. The ProvGM then read the Petition and Warrant. The ProvGChap read the portion of scripture appointed for the occasion, after which the Brethren sang the anthem, 'Hail Universal Lord'. Whilst the elements of the Consecration were carried out the Brethren sang an anthem from the 133rd Psalm. The ProvGM having reached the East, the vessel containing corn was presented to him, and he sprinkled the Lodge with corn, whilst the Chaplain read Psalm LXXII v16. The second circuit having been made, the chalice of wine was presented to the ProvGM, who sprinkled the Lodge with wine, the Chaplain reading Numbers XV v 7. After the third circuit a vessel containing oil was presented to the ProvGM, who then anointed the Lodge with oil, the Chaplain reading Exodus XXX v 25 and 26. The ProvGChap offered up the Consecration prayer. Finally. salt was presented to the ProvGM, who seasoned the Lodge therewith and the Chaplain read Leviticus II v 13. The ProvGM declared the Lodge Consecrated and Dedicated in conformity with usual custom, and the Ceremony concluded with the anthem, 'Hail Masonry Divine'. Contrary to present day procedure, the Consecration Ceremony was conducted in the First Degree. On the completion of this Ceremony, the ProvGDC presented the Master Designate to the ProvGM. The Master Designate in turn presented his Wardens. The ProvGM then requested the Talbot Brethren present to signify their approval of the Officers named in the Warrant of Constitution. This done, the Lodge was opened in the Second Degree, and Bro Edward J Morris, being presented to the ProvGM as Master Designate, took the usual Obligation and Invested his Officers .

WBro Charles Bath, SW, was Mayor of Swansea, 1863-1864 and WBro George Browne Brock, JP, JW, was Mayor of Swansea, 1876-1878. Bro Rev Charles Tebbotts Heartley, ProvGChap, Head of Mount Pleasant Grammar School, Swansea, was Lodge Chaplain. The first Treasurer, Bro Samuel B Power, was a Ship-owner, who joined with Mr T P Richards to form Richards, Power & Co Ltd. They owned 14 sailing ships. Bro Power was a generous patron of the YMCA. A very religious man, he was a Church Warden of St Mary's Church and, being a Ship-owner, took a keen interest in St Nicholas Church, the Sailors' Church, in Gloucester Place. WBro William Cox, PProvGTreas, first Secretary, was Installed WM of Indefatigable Lodge in 1861. A most humane Governor of Swansea Gaol, then known as 'The House of Correction', he was known for doing all he could for the prisoners under his care. For several years, he was Deputy Governor to his father, whom he succeeded in 1849. The long association between father and son in Swansea Prison led it to being nicknamed, 'Cox's Farm'. WBro Dr James Griffith Hall, PPSGW, Installed WM of Indefatigable Lodge in 1850, was DC. House-surgeon at Swansea Infirmary and Surgeon to Swansea Gaol, his name is given to Dr James Griffith Hall Lodge No.3161, Consecrated on 19 July 1906. Bro Richard Aubrey Essery, SD, was Town Clerk of Swansea. WBro George Allen, PProvGSec, Installed WM of Indefatigable Lodge in 1863, was Lodge Organist. A musician of considerable ability, he was, by profession, the Cashier at the Glamorgan Bank, Swansea. Bro Howell Walter Williams, IG, was a Newspaper Proprietor and Editor of the 'Cambrian', the weekly paper that served Swansea for nearly a century.

Founder Member WBro Dr Owen Gethin Williams, WM of Indefatigable Lodge in 1852, was a leading Surgeon of great stature as well as a prominent Town Councillor who, when Mayor, 1850-1851, presented a drinking fountain to the town. He also presented five hundred books to the Free Library and a bell for the Town Crier.

Francis David Michael, who signed the Petition but did not become a Subscribing Member, was Installed WM of Indefatigable Lodge in 1819. His grandfather, David Michael, born in Germany in 1727, founded the Jewish Colony in Wales in 1749. In 1768, he persuaded Swansea Council to grant a plot of land at Baptist Well for the Jewish Cemetery. His two sons, Levi and Jacob, founded the first Synagogue in the town. Francis, the son of Levi, was Initiated in Haverfordwest in 1814 and completed his Second and Third Degrees in Indefatigable Lodge. He was a wonderful Ritualist and ProvGDC for many years. He was held in high esteem in Masonic circles in Swansea and Neath. In 1852, Lodges in both towns commissioned C H Toplis, the Swansea Artist, to paint his portrait in oils. This portrait hung in the Swansea Masonic Hall until 2000, when it was taken down along with many others, to be kept in the West Glamorgan Archives. Two of his second cousins, William Henry Michael and James Michael, were Initiated together in Talbot Lodge on 7 February 1872. William Henry was admitted to the MRCS and LSA. In 1843, he acted as Honorary Medical Officer for Swansea, became a Town Councillor, and Mayor in 1857. He founded the Ragged School in 1857 and inherited a considerable fortune from his uncle Michael John Michael. He left Swansea for London in 1864, in which year the Middle Temple called him to the Bar. He became a QC in 1874.

WBro Edward J Morris, the first WM of Talbot Lodge, was also a Founder and first Z of Talbot Chapter No.1323, Warranted 7

Road Ironmonger business of WBro R B Bates was totally destroyed. Lodge Meetings continued without attendances being markedly affected, although Festive Boards were restricted. The threat of air raids caused Meetings to be held at 2.30 pm on Saturday afternoons by the end of 1940 and in the winter of 1941. At the close of the Regular Meeting of 7 May 1945, Brethren were advised that a Declaration would be made by the Prime Minister, the Rt Hon Winston Churchill, at 3.00 pm on 8 May 1945, stating that the war in Europe was at an end.

From the outset, Caradoc Lodge was able to attract Brethren of some substance. The first WM, WBro John Rogers, PPrGSwdB, proved to be a most distinguished Freemason and a prime mover in the formation of Talbot Chapter No.1323. At his funeral in Danygraig Cemetery on 22 April 1914, Brethren were instructed to wear white gloves. The first SW, Bro James Livingston, was a well-known coal exporter and American Consul, in addition to serving as Mayor of Swansea. Other Caradoc Brethren who also served as Mayors of Swansea include WBro Thomas Arthur Merrells, WBro Thomas Taliesin Corker, WBro David Davies, and WBro William Daniel Rees (killed in an air raid on 21 February 1941). An early Member who came to prominence was WBro Rev Thomas Walters, DD, Vicar of Llansamlet. He was Initiated on 2 April 1877 and Raised on 2 July 1877, immediately Invested as Lodge Chaplain, becoming ProvGChap in May 1880. He served as WM of Caradoc Lodge in 1882, gaining eminence for his support of three bi-lingual Churches at Llansamlet, Glais and Ystradgynlais. Walters Road, Llansamlet, is named in his memory. In April 1880, he proposed the Rt Hon the Earl of Jersey, a Member of Apollo University Lodge No.357, Oxford, as a Joining Member. The Earl of Jersey remained a Caradoc Lodge Member until June 1912. Although a number of letters of apology for non attendance are recorded, there is no evidence of him being in attendance throughout this period.

Caradoc Lodge has two Daughter Lodges, both in Swansea, namely, Beaufort Lodge No.3834, Warranted on 11 January 1918; and Sketty Hall Lodge No.8752, Warranted on 8 December 1976. Caradoc Lodge also played a significant part in the formation of Dr James Griffiths Hall Lodge No.3161, Warranted on 3 April 1906. Of the 23 Petitioners for that Lodge, 13 were Members of Caradoc Lodge. The Petition was recommended and signed by the WM and Wardens of Indefatigable Lodge, thereby making it the Sponsoring Lodge, even though only 4 Petitioners were Members of that Lodge.

There is only one recorded instance of the Brethren of Caradoc Lodge appearing in public in full Regalia. This was following the Installation of Rev Thomas Walters, DD, in 1882, when, by Dispensation from the ProvGM, the Brethren formed a procession from Caer Street to St Mary's Church for a service. The Offering on this occasion was for a new East window in the Church, though sadly it was later destroyed in the air raid of 1941. Following the service, Brethren returned to the Lodge for the closing and then to the Cameron Hotel for the Festive Board.

Full Masonic Regalia was also worn by Dispensation from WBro Marmaduke Tennant, DepProvGM, on 22 October 1885, at a Ball held at the Albert Hall, Swansea, though the WM was charged *'to ensure that no tickets are sold to the public openly and indiscriminately'*. No further details are recorded, but in November 1911, at a Regular Lodge Meeting, the WM invited the Brethren *'to discuss the desirability of holding a Ladies' Evening under the Banner of Caradoc Lodge to take the form of a Banquet, Concert, Dance and Card Party.'*

Differing points of view between individual Lodges and Provincial Grand Lodge are rare, but such an occasion occurred in September 1921, when Caradoc Brethren agreed to advise PGL that it would not participate in a plan to form a Masonic Library and Museum in Cardiff. Members were of the opinion that books and objects of interest relating to Swansea should remain in the town.

Records for 1927 show that the Master was to present WBro E R Jones, PPSGW, *'a purse of gold to commemorate his Golden Wedding.'* A 'purse of gold' had also been presented in 1908 to WBro Charles David Richards, *'for services rendered.'* He had been Installed as WM in 1896.

A Meeting of Provincial Grand Lodge, under the Banner of Caradoc Lodge, was held in Swansea on 19 June 1930, with RWBro Sir Charles L D Venables Llewelyn, Bart, ProvGM, presiding.

The effect of the Depression on the economy of South Wales is illustrated by the following event. In 1930, United Grand Lodge proposed an increase in the per capita charge from sixpence per annum to sixpence per quarter. The Brethren, meeting on 3 November 1930, resolved to inform Provincial Grand Lodge that *'due to the distressing conditions at that time in South Wales, it was not an appropriate time for such an increase'*. Despite the obvious poverty in the area at that time, the meeting was attended by 91 Caradoc Brethren and 55 visiting Brethren. Provincial Grand Lodge was also mindful of resisting the increase. The WM stated that he intended to travel to London to be present at a meeting of United Grand Lodge in December 1930, when the matter was to be considered. He invited the Past Masters and Wardens also to attend and support Provincial Grand Lodge in voicing opposition to the proposal.

The Lodge Insignia consists of a shield incorporating the Square and Compasses, surmounting a trefoil, presumed to represent the three Principal Officers, the whole enclosed in a circle inscribed with the Lodge name, number and town of origin, Swansea.

The Lodge Banner bears the above Insignia design between the two great pillars, on which are placed the celestial and terrestrial globes, the pillars being supported by the Level and Plumb Rule and five-pointed star respectively, the whole surmounted by the 'All Seeing Eye'. The Lodge has no Motto.

It was recorded that on 7 November 1881, *'thanks for the presentation to the Lodge of a handsome Banner'* by WBro WC Jones, WM, were made. The Banner remained in continual use for over ninety years, with renovations made in 1954, by the wife of Bro Daniel. A gift of a replacement Banner (illustrated) was made in March 1972 by a Brother, who wished to remain anonymous. The original Banner was incorporated in the new Banner as a liner.

It is interesting to record that in August 1900, the Proprietor of the Cameron Arms in Swansea requested permission to display the Caradoc Coat of Arms to help decorate the hall of the Hotel. The request was refused.

Returning to more recent times, in 1978, a contribution was made toward the cost of a memorial window in St Luke's Church, Swansea, in memory of Rev Bro Tom Walters, who had served as Lodge Chaplain.

In April of the following year, a Past Masters' Meeting debated the possible extension to the Masonic building in Swansea. The proposal receiving a mixed response and, what was thought to be a high cost venture, did not proceed further. By the end of 1986, a request had been made to the Grand Charity to set up a Relief Chest for Caradoc Lodge, which was granted.

In March 1994, approximately £16000 was transferred from the Lodge charity chest to honour the pledge given to the 1999 Festival Appeal. As a result of this effort, the Lodge received a Silver Award, in the form of a 'permanent Jewel' to be attached to the Charity Steward's Collar, in recognition of the support given by Members of the Lodge to the 'Samaritan Fund Appeal'.

In 2000, Bro Kevin Lloyd, JW, made and presented a set of wooden Gavels to the Lodge for the use of the WM and Wardens at the Festive Board. This was in response to a proposal by RWBro Hywel Davies, ProvGM, that Gavels should be used at the Festive Board.

Due to rising costs, the Treasurer proposed at the June Meeting in 2002 that the Lodge should cease meeting in June. This was agreed by the Brethren and permission having been granted by the ProvGM, was put into effect.

It would be remiss not to record the remarkable courage of WBro Bill Estcourt and his determination to be Installed in the Chair of King Solomon. Bill suffered from cancer and, during his progression through the Lodge, his attendance was often interrupted by spells in hospital for treatment. He was eventually Installed in March 2005, well aware that his condition was terminal. Unfortunately, by the April Meeting he had to return to hospital for further treatment and was not to return to the Lodge. During the summer recess he passed to the Grand Lodge Above. WBro Barry C Smith acted as Master for the remainder of the Masonic year.

WBro Bernard Jones stepped down as Secretary in 2007, after 18 years' service to the Lodge. Three years later, in October 2010, the Lodge received a cheque for £1000, from the estate of WBro Francis Hemp, who had passed to the Grand Lodge Above in 2009.

Compiled by WBro Bernard J Jones, PPrSGW,
with later additions by WBro Barry C Smith, ProvGStwd.

Merlin Lodge No.1578

Warranted : 23 October 1875

Consecrated : 27 April 1876

Meeting at the Masonic Hall, Pontypridd.

The Minutes of Glamorgan Lodge No.36, for 9 July 1875 state: *'Brothers Price (E. J. Price) and Cousins presented a Petition to Grand Lodge praying for the grant of a Charter for a new Lodge at Pontypridd to be called the 'Merlin Lodge' and soliciting our recommendation. The W.M. (Sigmund Weichert), while answering Bros. Price and Cousins in the name of the Lodge, and as well as for himself, that their request will be cheerfully granted, begged them, on their return to Pontypridd, to convey to our Brethren, that this Lodge will be at all times most happy to give them every practical assistance they may need, and expatiating on the excellence of Freemasonry, its universality and cosmopolitan character, and finally its beneficial influence, assured the applicants that the object they have in view is worthy of the trouble they have already taken, and is encouragement to still further exertion.*

It was then proposed by the W.M. and seconded by Bro. Frederick Cowderoy Hill, I.P.M. that the petition be duly signed. – Carried unanimously.'

The Petition was also supported by Loyal Cambrian Lodge No.110, St David's Lodge No.679, and Bute Lodge No.960. Grand Lodge records show Bute Lodge as the Mother Lodge.

The Warrant was granted on 23 October 1875, and the Consecration Ceremony took place at the New Inn, Taff Street, Pontypridd, on 27 April 1876, attended by WBro Edward James Morris, DepProvGM, and his Officers. RWBro Theodore Mansel Talbot, ProvGM South Wales ED was too ill to attend. The silver vessels used in the Consecration Ceremony were loaned by the DepProvGM and the WM of Talbot Lodge No.1323.

The First Master was Bro John Edward Price, who remained a faithful Member for the remainder of his life. Following the Consecration, 18 gentlemen were proposed as Candidates, of whom the most notable were Mr Lewis Gordon Lennox, and Francis Richard Crawshay and Tudor Crawshay. The remainder were Surgeons, Solicitors, Chemists, and a Lieutenant in the Militia.

Lewis Lennox, of 'Brown, Lennox & Co Ltd', Chain and Anchor Manufacturers of Pontypridd, was Initiated on 4 May 1876. The Firm had been making chains for the Royal Navy since 1808. Closely associated with the famous Engineer, Isambard Kingdom

Brunel, they provided cables for the 'Great Eastern' (1856), the 'Mauretania' (1906) and the 'Aquitanaia' (1908). They claim to have manufactured the 'world's strongest chain' in 1929. Though he never took an active Office. Lewis Lennox was a Regular Member of the Lodge.

Bros Thomas Richard and Tudor Crawshay were also Initiated on 4 May 1876, along with 15 other Candidates! The Crawshays were well known Industrialists and Land-owners, involved in coal mining and, with Mr. Homfray, the construction of the Glamorgan Canal. Exercising great influence in the area, they lived at Forest House, which later became the 'Treforest School of Mines', 'Glamorgan Polytechnic' and is now the site of the 'University of Glamorgan'. They were greatly influenced by Dr. William Price, a Druid, and as a result they built a Druidic circle in the grounds of the house. It is noted that they were not very regular attendees at Lodge Meetings.

Bro Gwilym Williams presented the Lodge with a silver Square and Compass, and Bro William Williams the Volume of the Sacred Law. Both gifts are still in use today.

The first Regular Lodge was held on Monday, 4 May 1876, which was preceded by a banquet at 5.00 pm. Tickets were priced at 7 shillings and 6 pence (37½p) to include desert and waiters. The Lodge was opened at 7.40 pm and was attended by the DepProvGM, who suggested that as there were 18 Candidates for Ballot, that they be Balloted for by the WM and that '*the result of the Ballot be the opinion of the Lodge'!* It was unanimously resolved that his suggestion be accepted. The Special Dispensation of the ProvGM that '*more than 5 gentlemen be Initiated*' was read to the Lodge, and duly entered into the Minutes.

An Initiation Ceremony was performed three times that evening, with some 200 Brethren present, including visitors. The Initiation fee was 6 guineas (£6.30p). The Lodge was Closed at 11.00 pm with special arrangements being made for special trains to Cardiff, Merthyr and Aberdare, with the Cardiff train timed to meet the Night Train to the West!

At the 1876 September Meeting, which opened at 8.00 pm, 6 candidates were Passed to the Second Degree. It was intended to Initiate a Mr William Cooper Penn immediately following the Passing Ceremony, but the WM decided that owing to the lateness of the hour, the Initiation Ceremony would be deferred to a later date, although the first presentation of the 1st Degree Tracing Board was given. At the next Regular Meeting, Mr Penn was duly Initiated, and then Passed to the Second Degree along with 7 other Brethren! At this Meeting the Lodge fees were increased to 10 Guineas (£10.50p).

The WM announced that he was '*grieved to learn that some of the younger Members had displayed considerable indiscretion in talking about Lodge matters and subjects too closely connected with the Craft for speech in public*'. He went on to say that had he known their names he would have remonstrated with them in private. He also pointed out the relevant sections of the Book of Constitutions relating to this. He stated that he had serious concerns regarding the different *workings* in the Province, and suggested that a qualified Preceptor be appointed in order to perambulate the Province in order to learn, and subsequently produce a harmonious method of working a Ceremony, especially with regard to the Third Degree. Bro S D Hunter (SD) undertook this task, and although there does not appear to be any written record of his researches he did say that '*he was not impressed with the way in which ceremonies were performed!*' In June 1877 the first LOI was held.

During this period, Bro William H Llewellyn, an Engineer and a partner with the firm, Llewellyn and Cubitt, at Pentre, Rhondda, while walking from Ogmore Valley to the Rhondda, fell to his death over a wall at the Parc Colliery, Cwmparc. A sum of 3 guineas (£3.30p) was voted in favour of a fountain to be erected in Pentre, Rhondda, to his memory. The site, adjacent to St Peter's Church, is still visible, although the fountain itself has long since disappeared.

On 28 April 1879, St Quintin's Lodge No.1822, Cowbridge, was Warranted. The new Lodge was jointly Sponsored by Merlin Lodge, together with Glamorgan Lodge No.36, St. David's Lodge No.679 and Loyal Cambrian Lodge No.110. By 1895, this Lodge had become dormant and it was finally Erased from the Register of UGLE on 5 September 1923.

In November 1882, WBro Richard Male, WM, presented a suitably engraved Loving Cup to the Lodge. The Cup used to be displayed at every Installation Meeting, and at the end of the formal proceedings it was filled with either whisky or sherry and passed around the tables for Brethren to partake. This practice, however, was discontinued some years ago on hygiene grounds.

On his Installation in 1884, Bro Henry Naunton Davies presented the Lodge with a Banner, which depicts Merlin in a seated position. Merlin is a legendary figure, best known as the wizard in the Arthurian Legend. The standard depiction of the character first appears in Geoffrey of Monmouth's '*Historia Regum Britanniae*', written circa1136. Later authors have Merlin serving as King Arthur's advisor, until he is bewitched and imprisoned by the Lady of the Lake. The Banner does not have a Motto, but it does bear the name of its benefactor. It was under this Banner that Provincial Grand Lodge held its Meeting at the New Inn, on 24 July 1885,which was presided over by RWBro Sir George Elliot, Bart, MP, ProvGM South Wales ED. This was at a time when Provincial Grand Lodge had no regular Meeting place but was held at different Lodges throughout the Province.

On 26 June 1885, an agreement was entered into regarding the purchase of a parcel of land adjoining the County Court, Courthouse Street, Pontypridd, as a site for a Masonic Hall, at a price of £175.00. £500 was borrowed from the Pontypridd Self Help Society towards the construction of the Masonic Hall. A silver Trowel was presented to RWBro Sir George Elliot, on having laid the Foundation Stone of the new Masonic Hall on a previous occasion, but that stone, recording that event, is not now visible in the fabric of the building.

The following year, the WM announced that on 6 May, Sir George Elliot, accompanied by WBro Col Shadwell Clarke, GSec, and other distinguished visitors, would be visiting the town. It was decided to meet the distinguished visitors at the railway station and present an Address to the GSec accordingly. When the WM, accompanied by a number of Officers, attended the station RWBro the Earl of Limerick, ProvGM of Bristol, together with Col Shadwell H Clarke, Sir George Elliot, Col Somerville Burney, PJW, and J C Parkinson, PGD, alighted, they were presented with a long Address. Unfortunately, the commitment of the party did not enable them to partake of the full welcome that would have been accorded them. The Earl of Limerick, accompanied by the Countess of Limerick, did, however, visit the Masonic Hall, when the GSec stated that '*he had seldom seen a structure so* which depicts Merlin in a seated position. Merlin is a legendary figure, best known as the <u>wizard</u> in the <u>Arthurian Legend</u>. The standard depiction of the character first appears in <u>Geoffrey of Monmouth</u>'s '<u>*Historia Regum Britanniae*</u>', written circa1136. Later authors have Merlin serve as King Arthur's advisor, until he is bewitched and imprisoned by the <u>Lady of the Lake</u>. The Banner does not have a Motto, but it does bear the name of its benefactor. It was under this Banner that Provincial Grand Lodge held its Meeting at the New Inn, on 24 July 1885,which was presided over by RWBro Sir George Elliot, Bart, MP, ProvGM South Wales ED. This was at a time when Provincial Grand Lodge had no regular Meeting place but was held at different Lodges throughout the Province.

On 26 June 1885, an agreement was entered into regarding the purchase of a parcel of land adjoining the County Court, Courthouse Street, Pontypridd, as a site for a Masonic Hall, at a price of £175.00. £500 was borrowed from the Pontypridd Self help Society towards the construction of the Masonic Hall. A silver Trowel was presented to RWBro Sir George Elliot, on having laid the Foundation Stone of the new Masonic Hall on a previous occasion, but that stone, recording that event, is not now visible in the fabric of the building.

The following year, the WM announced that on 6 May, Sir George Elliot, accompanied by WBro Colonel Shadwell Clarke, GSec, and other distinguished visitors would be visiting the town. It was decided to meet the distinguished visitors at the railway station and present an address to the GSec accordingly. When the WM, accompanied by a number of Officers, attended the station RWBro the Earl of Limerick, ProvGM of Bristol, together with Colonel Shadwell H Clarke, Sir George Elliot, Colonel

Somerville Burney, PJW, and J C Parkinson, PGD alighted, they were presented with a long Address. Unfortunately, the commitment of the party did not enable them to partake of the full welcome that would have been accorded them. The Earl of Limerick, accompanied by the Countess of Limerick, did, however, visit the Masonic Hall, when the GSec stated that '*he had seldom seen a structure so admirably suited its purpose*'.

To commemorate the visit the following Brethren were Elected as Honorary Members of the Lodge – RWBro Sir George Elliot, The RWBro The Earl of Limerick, VWBro Colonel Shadwell H Clarke, GSec, WBro Colonel Omerville Burney PGD, and WBro I C Parkinson, PGD.

At the following Lodge Meeting, it was resolved that no more than 5 Brethren of the Lodge should attend the Jubilee celebrations of Queen Victoria at the Royal Albert Hall.

The first Meeting at the new Masonic Hall was held on 26 May, 1887. On 28 July 1887, WBros E H Howard and Stephen Lewis, presented the Lodge with the gift of two Pillars, which are still in use today.

WBro H Naunton Davies, PProvGR proposed, and Bro W M Davies seconded, that Mr William Abraham, MP and first President of the South Wales Miners' Federation, should become a Member of the Lodge. He was duly Initiated on 12 December 1882. Born on 14 June 1842, at Cwmafan, he was better known by his Bardic name 'Mabon'. His burly appearance and powerful voice were features which made him well known and effective as a conductor of eisteddfodau. Endowed with a good tenor voice, he would often sing to the audiences. A devout Christian, he spent much time as a Lay Preacher.

In 1885, he was the first South Wales miners' representative to be elected a Member of Parliament. Initially he represented the Rhondda Division, and then from 1918 to the time of his death in 1922, he was the representative for Rhondda West. He is especially remembered in the Valleys for his introduction of *Mabon's Monday,* operative from 1892 to 1898, when South Wales miners did not work on the first Monday of each month. This was a scheme to limit coal output in order to maintain wages, and it also gave opportunities for holding miners' meetings.

In March 1891 a sum of '*not more than £20 was voted for the purchase of a stove to heat the Lodge rooms, and a safe*'. The safe is still in use today.

On 12 August 1892, there was a mining disaster at the Great Western Colliery, Trehafod, in which 58 miners were killed. A sum of 15 guineas (£15.75) was donated in aid of the Relief Fund.

When, in 1896, it became known that the MWBro, HRH The Prince of Wales, GM, would be passing through Pontypridd, it was resolved that '*steps be taken for him to accept an Address from the Lodge*'.

Lodge subscription fees were increased to 2 guineas for Members in March 1897, but to only 1 guinea for Past Masters!

In January 1900, WBro Richard Male, WM, asked to be relieved of his duties, having been appointed to command one of the contingents delegated for service in the Boer War. As a consequence, a fund was set up for the relief of distressed Brethren in South Africa, also for the Welsh Hospital in South Africa. It was during this year that the first Ladies' Evening was held.

There is no record of any Lodge Brother being killed during the Great War of 1914-1918, but in 1915, the son of Bro J P Williams, and in 1916, the son of WBro D McGregor, were killed in action. Following the death of Bro Williams's son, a sum of 10 guineas was voted by the Lodge to assist distressed Brethren confined in internment camps in enemy territories. Bro Clive Price, the son of the first WM, who had been Initiated into the Lodge, was now serving in East Africa. It was resolved that Harmony Lodge No.3084, Nairobi, Kenya (English Constitution), be authorised to complete his Degree Ceremonies. Arrangements were made by cablegram, but there is no record of these Ceremonies being performed.

A Notice of Motion was given on 20 March 1919, '*that a new Lodge be formed to be called Rhondda Lodge, No3979, with*

Merlin Brethren only to be Founders'. The Warrant was duly granted on 22 July 1919. On 5 November 1924, a Warrant was issued to Hen Bont Lodge No.4691, and once again, Merlin Lodge was the Sponsoring Lodge.

On 9 September 1939, following Emergency Orders from HM Government, all Masonic activities were suspended until further notice. This was only a temporary ban and the Lodge was re-opened the following month.

In 1941 Bro E E Morris presented a carved panel to the Lodge, and he also carried out repairs to the WM's Chair. Following the death of Bro Morris, a £50 legacy was made to the Merlin Lodge Charity by the Mr Johnny Morris, OBE, the well known Welsh Television Presenter. Born in Newport, Monmouthshire on 20 June 1916, he was mostly associated with BBC children's programmes on the topic of zoology, most notably the programme 'Animal Magic'.

By special Dispensation, on 19 June 1969, the late WBro David T Lewis Initiated his three sons, David Meiron, Dilwyn Idris, and John Hywel Lewis. They were Invested by WBro Harry Stockwell, AProvGM. Bros John and Dilwyn Lewis became Masters in 1985 and 1998 respectively, with WBro John Lewis becoming Master for the second time in 2005. Due to ill health, Bro Meiron Lewis could not progress, and eventually he resigned from the Lodge. Mrs Elizabeth Lewis, widow of WBro David Lewis, presented the Lodge with a magnificent complete set of Working Tools in her husband's memory.

On 17 October 1907, Mr John Davies, a Schoolmaster in the Pontypridd Intermediate School, and later the Pontypridd Grammar School, was Initiated into the Lodge. On 17 October, 1971, WBro Davies passed to the Grand Lodge Above at the great age of 102!

A Celebration Service to mark the Centenary of the Lodge was held at St Matthews Church, Trallwyn, Pontypridd, on 27 April 1976. During the Service, the Centenary Warrant was presented to the Lodge by RWBro the Lord Swansea, ProvGM, South Wales ED.

On 20 October 1981, Pontypridd Lodge No.9001was Consecrated at the Pontypridd Temple, by Lord Swansea. Although the Petitioning Brethren were from Merlin Lodge No.1578, Rhondda Lodge No.3979, Hen Bont Lodge No.4691, Craig yr Hesg Lodge No.6724, Ystradyfodwg Lodge No.7638 and Newton Lodge No.8261 the Petition was signed by the Worshipful Master and Wardens of Merlin Lodge, thus making Merlin the Sponsoring Lodge.

The Lodge Membership at the beginning of 2011 stands at 62 Brethren. WBro T R Clayton, PPrJGW, is the senior Past Master. Initiated on 16 February 1956 and Master in 1967, he is now a Masonic Veteran.

Compiled by WBro A T Higgs, PPJGW,
with a special tribute for their contributions to the late WBro John Burgess, PPrGD, and WBro T R Clayton, PPrJGW.

Sir George Elliot, Bart, MP
1815 - 1893

Provincial Grand Master of South Wales Eastern Division
1877 - 1893

Sir George Elliot was probably the most exceptional of the Provincial Grand Masters, - a self-made man who began his life in the most humble of circumstances.

He was born in relative poverty at Gateshead on 18 March 1815, the son of Ralph Elliot, a pitman at Penshaw Colliery in County Durham. He left school at the age of nine and commenced work at Whitefield Colliery as a trapper boy. (A boy stationed to open and shut a trap-door for the passage of trams in a coalmine.) From his wages of half-a-crown (12½p), he saved whatever he could in order to educate himself at night school. By the age of seventeen, he had obtained a fair proficiency in mathematics and he continued his studies in surveying and mining engineering. Such was his determination that, by the age of twenty, he was appointed a deputy-overman (deputy foreman) in the colliery and, in 1837, aged twenty-two, an overman. His next appointment was that of under-viewer at Belmont Colliery, then viewer (inspector) at Wearmouth Colliery and eventually the chief viewer at Lord Londonderry's Rainton Collieries. By 1844, at the age of twenty-nine, he was the manager at Wearmouth, which at that time was the deepest mine in Britain.

At the age of twenty-six, he had already become the part-proprietor of a colliery. Later, he acquired interests in Usworth and North Biddick Collieiries and then in 1864 he became the sole owner of the Whitefield Colliery, which he acquired from the Londonderry family and where he had commenced work as a trapper boy! In due course, he was to acquire mining interests in Staffordshire, South Wales and Nova Scotia.

Sir George's association with South Wales commenced in 1864, when he bought collieries belonging to Thomas Powell, Esq, thus establishing the well-known 'Powell Duffryn Steam Coal Company'. His residence in Aberdare was Aberaman House. In 1875, he was involved in the funding of the Alexandra Docks at Newport. He thus became a Director of the Alexandra Dock Company and at the time of his death in 1893, he was the Chairman of the Company. He was also a JP for Glamorganshire and a Deputy-Lieutenant of Monmouthshire.

Sir George Elliot was in the forefront of experiments in mining technology and safety, and unlike many of his colleagues, he supported the establishment of a Mines Inspectorate. In 1852, he helped found the Institute of Mining Engineers, becoming its President, 1868-1869.

Sir George Elliot, Bart

Previously, in the early 1850s, he had become associated with wire rope manufacturing, going into partnership with Richard Glass, when they took over the rope manufacturer Kuper & Co, at Morden Wharf, East Greenwich. The business was renamed 'Glass, Elliot & Company' and eventually had its head office at Great George Street, Westminster. When submerged cables (submarine cables) for telegraph purposes were introduced, the Company manufactured and laid the first Atlantic cable, between Ireland and Newfoundland (completed in 1866) for which purpose they purchased cheaply Brunel's steamship 'The Great Eastern' in 1864! Each mile of cable weighed 8 tons - such was the scale of the operation.

Sir George Elliot first became involved in politics in 1868, when he sat as a Conservative MP for Durham North from December 1868 to February 1874. He was re-elected there in June 1874, but was defeated in 1880, re-elected in 1881, and continued to hold the seat until the dissolution of Parliament in 1885. In December 1885, he unsuccessfully contested Durham South East. He returned to Parliament in 1886 as the MP for Monmouth, a seat that he held until his defeat in 1892.

During his parliamentary career, he became a great favourite of Prime Minister, Benjamin Disraeli (later Lord Beaconsfield), who created him a baronet in 1874. Following his Knighthood, Disraeli sent Sir George out to Egypt to act as a financial adviser to the Khedive. ('Khedive' - the title granted by the Turkish Sultan to his Egyptian Viceroy in 1867.) He was instrumental in persuading Disraeli to acquire, on behalf of Britain, a major share holding in the Suez Canal, thus ensuring that Britain held control of the profitable new sea-route to India.

During his stay in Egypt, Sir George Elliot became involved in building the Port of Alexandria. He also acquired a collection of antiquities, amongst which was the mummy of an Egyptian princess, which was obtained from the Luxor region. Later in life, Sir George spent much of his time at his grand house on the Royal Crescent in Whitby, a place which was becoming increasingly popular with tourists. In the

George (Geordie) Elliot
Spy cartoon from 'Vanity Fair'

summer of 1890, one such tourist was the theatrical manager and novelist Bram Stoker, who took up residence in the Royal Crescent and where he began work on his most famous novel 'Dracula'. Stoker's lesser-known work, 'The Jewel of the Seven Stars', has as its central character, the mummy of an Egyptian princess, brought back to life by a group of scholarly gentlemen in a remote coastal location. It therefore seems likely that Sir George's mummified princess had some bearing on Stoker's vivid imagination! The mummy is now in the ownership of the Hull Museums.

Sir George Elliot's involvement in Freemasonry in South Wales began in December 1873, when he and his son-in-law, WBro John C Parkinson (married Sir George's daughter Alice Ann in 1867), DepProvGM for Middlesex, visited St David's Lodge No.679, Aberdare. They were proposed as Joining Members of the Lodge and were accepted the following January. At the election held in the next month, WBro William Morris (the oldest Member of the Lodge) proposed that WBro Parkinson be invited to occupy the Master's Chair for the ensuing year and it was carried unanimously. A letter inviting WBro John Parkinson to accept the Chair was signed by twenty Brethren and part of its contents is as follows:

'..... *Knowing the distinguished position you hold in the Craft as P.M. Universal Lodge, London No. 181; P.M. Bard of Avon Lodge, No. 778, Hampton Court; and of the Prince of Wales' Lodge No. 259, London; D.P.G.M. for Middlesex, and a member of the Board of General Purposes, we have unanimously elected you to take the Chair of this Lodge for the ensuing year; trusting your other numerous engagements will not prevent your acceptance of the appointment .... And we pledge ourselves individual'*

In his reply Parkinson wrote: ' *...... Having submitted the requisition to my Provincial Grand Master, Colonel Burdett, and consulted some of the authorities of the Grand Lodge of England, it is with much pleasure I accept the position of Master of the St. David's Lodge, No. 679, counting with confidence upon the diligent co-operation and support of the Members of the Lodge during my term of office.*

Although my duties call me to South Wales for a portion of every month, you are aware that I reside chiefly in the immediate neighbourhood of London; and it is proper to add that my engagements are too numerous and heavy to make it probable that I shall be able to attend every meeting. I shall however, strive to be with you as frequently as is reasonably practical; and it will afford me sincere gratification to discharge the various duties your kindness has imposed upon me.....'

On 5 March 1874, WBro J C Parkinson was duly Installed Master of St David's Lodge, the Ceremony being performed by WBro Frederick Ware of Bute Lodge No.960, Cardiff. Two months later, he became Junior Grand Deacon of England, and was Invested with his Collar by the Marquis of Ripon. Despite his numerous commitments, he remained true to the promise he had given to the Brethren of St David's Lodge. He presided at six ceremonies in all during his year of Office; and during that year eleven Candidates were Initiated. When his year of Office came to an end, the Brethren of the Lodge presented him with a Commemorative Jewel as a mark of their appreciation. The Jewel was specially designed by Sir Alfred Woods, the Garter King at Arms, and cost £25. 11s. 6d, (£25. 57½p) which sum was collected by subscription from among the Members. WBro Parkinson responded with a generous donation to the Lodge funds.

On 18 July 1876, the untimely death of the Provincial Grand Master, Theodore Mansel Talbot of Margam, occurred - just a few weeks before his 37th birthday. He had been Provincial Grand Master since 1865. It was not until 13 December 1876, that the Patent appointing Sir George Elliot as the new Provincial Grand Master was signed by the Grand Master, HRH the Prince of Wales, and the Lodges in the Province were informed of the appointment by the Grand Secretary, John Hervey, in the New Year. The Western Mail later reported that the '*unusual delay* ' in making the appointment '*has been due to a natural anxiety on the part of His Royal Highness the Prince of Wales to select the fittest man for the responsibility.*' The Brethren of St David's Lodge were delighted with the news and immediately wrote a letter of congratulation to Sir George Elliot. In his reply to their letter, Sir George intimated that he would like to be Installed as ProvGM at Aberdare, under the Banner of St David's Lodge.

Events now moved rapidly and on Wednesday, 4 April 1877, Sir George Elliot was duly Installed at Aberdare. An account of the proceedings was given in the Western Mail the following day:

'*The opening of Grand Lodge was performed by Brother Aeneas McIntyre, Q.C., Grand Registrar of England, who was accompanied from London by Brother Thomas Fenn, who had been instructed by Brother Sir Albert Woods, Garter-King-at-Arms, with the superintendence of the ceremony of installation, Brother J. Moncton, president of the Masonic Board of General Purposes, and Brother Colonel Francis Burdett, P.G.M. for Middlesex, in connection with whom, it may be stated; both Brother Parkinson, and subsequently Sir George Elliot filled the position of Deputy.*

The ceremony took place in the Temperance-hall, which was fitted up as a lodge-room. The interior of the spacious structure was so transformed in appearance, that those who have seen it under ordinary circumstances would certainly have not recognised it in its altered condition. At one end, upon the platform, which was draped with crimson and purple cloth, fringed with gold, was placed the throne, encircled by a zone of imitation marble, surmounted by a crown. Banners and bannerettes were tastefully arranged at various points, and the open spaces of the platform at each end were filled with flowering plants and shrubs from the floor to the ceiling. Imitation marble pillars graced the walls all round the interior, and the gallery was covered with crimson drapery. The windows were draped with blue and chocolate coloured drapery, looped up with orange coloured rosettes. The body of the lodge, as was also the platform about the throne, was carpeted throughout, along the front of the platform being placed a row of shrubs, the whole having a very striking effect.

At twelve o'clock the brethren began to assemble in large numbers. The rain came down heavily, yet; notwithstanding the unfavourable state of the weather, a concourse of spectators had gathered together round the Temperance-hall, and at various points throughout the town. The Boot Hotel, the Black Lion, and other places were profusely decorated with flags, and streamers were thrown across the streets in several places, wanting nothing but fine weather to give the town a holiday appearance. The bells of St. Elvan's rang a merry peal of welcome as the various railways brought their crowds of visitors from all parts of the province, together with many from the adjoining and some distant provinces. There was great excitement in the vicinity of the Temperance-hall, where the crush was considerable.'

The Provincial Grand Lodge was opened at 1.30 pm with solemn prayer. The Patent of Office was read, then the Provincial Grand Master Elect entered the Lodge, escorted by the ruling Masters of the eleven Lodges in his Province; and the RWBro Sir George Elliot was duly Installed Provincial Grand Master. During the proceedings, the Provincial Grand Lodge voted 110 guineas for various Masonic Charities. A Collection by the Deacons realised £20. 9s. 8d (£20. 48p), which was given in aid of St Elvan's Church, Aberdare, where the Brethren had attended Divine Service at the close of the Lodge.

From the description given in the Western Mail, it is evident that the occasion was a lavish affair and cost the astonishing sum of £220. The Brethren of St David's Lodge resolved to meet their financial obligation by using the balance in their Lodge Funds, by holding a sale of the materials used for decorations etc., and by circularising the Brethren for subscriptions to meet the debit balance. However, their fears were put completely to rest by a magnificent gift of £160 from Sir George Elliot himself. Neighbouring Lodges also gave valuable assistance, particularly the new Merlin Lodge No.1578, Pontypridd, which lent its handsome new furnishings; and Indefatigable Lodge No.237, Swansea, which gave the use of its Lodge Room carpet.

A scheme to build a Masonic Hall in Aberdare had been initiated in June 1874, but it was not until the middle of 1879 that the plans were nearing completion. In October 1879, it was learnt that the Provincial Grand Master would be at Aberdare in connection with a Royal Commission then in session. Hurried preparations were made for him to lay the Foundation Stone of the new building. Unfortunately, there was no time to invite Provincial Grand Officers, so no Provincial Grand Lodge was held to mark the occasion. It was decided that Sir George Elliot should lay the Foundation Stone *'unofficially'* with the Brethren proceeding to the site without their Regalia. On Thursday, 9 October 1879, twenty two Brethren of St David's Lodge, with seventeen visitors, some from as far north as Anglesey and Durham, attended an Emergency Lodge at the Black Lion Hotel, after which the Foundation Stone was laid in Canon Street with a silver trowel presented to Sir George by the Brethren. The first meeting of the Lodge in its new premises was held on 11 August 1880.

In 1836, Sir George had married Margaret, daughter of George Green, Esq, of Rainton, Houghton-le-Spring. Lady Elliot died in the January of 1881, and on 29 January, Glamorgan Lodge, No.36, wrote a letter of sympathy to Sir George Elliot *'on account of the heavy bereavement sustained by you and your family in the recent death of Lady Elliot; and we trust that the Great Architect of the Universe may grant you his solace and support in this your heavy troubles.*

The Right Worshipful Brother Coln. Kemeys Tynte P.P.G.M. expresses a special wish to join in this vote of sympathy.'

(Colonel Tynte, ProvGM, 1857-1865, was a Member of Glamorgan Lodge.)

On 29 September 1883, Sir George Elliot was present at an Emergency Meeting of the Provincial Grand Lodge, held at the British Schools, Cardiff Road, Aberaman, under the Banner of St David's Lodge. Also present were WBro Marmaduke Tennant, DepProvGM; WBro John C Parkinson, Grand Deacon of England (Sir George's son-in-law and PM St David's Lodge); and Sir George's son, RWBro George William Elliot, ProvSGW, West Riding of Yorkshire. The Lodge was opened with solemn prayer at 1.00 pm. Sir George explained that he was in Aberdare to open the new nearby Church (St Mary of Antioch), which he had built in memory of his late wife and daughter. He gave a cordial invitation to the Brethren to accompany him to the Service and afterwards to luncheon at Aberaman House. The DepProvGM expressed the sympathetic regards and the thanks of the Lodge, which was then closed. The inscription on the Memorial Stone at the Church reads as follows:

THIS CHURCH WAS ERECTED BY SIR GEORGE ELLIOT, BART, M.P.

AND DEDICATED TO THE GLORY OF GOD

AND IN MEMORY OF HIS BELOVED WIFE MARGARET

AND THEIR DAUGHTER ELIZABETH.

29th September 1883

The following month, on Wednesday, 10 October, Sir George Elliot was present at the Masonic Temple, Working Street, Cardiff for the Consecration of Tennant Lodge, No.1992. He was accompanied by his Deputy, WBro Marmaduke Tennant, in whose honour the Lodge was named, together with the ProvGM of Monmouthshire, RWBro Charles Lyne and his Deputy, WBro Geoffrey Homfray. Sir George invited WBro Marmaduke Tennant to carry out the Ceremony of Consecration, after which a Consecration Banquet was held at the Royal Hotel, Cardiff.

Perhaps the highlight of Sir George Elliot's Provincial Grand Mastership was the visit of HRH the Prince of Wales to Swansea on Tuesday, 18 October 1881, when he received a Loyal Address from the Freemasons of this and surrounding Provinces. The Prince was accompanied by the Princess Alexandra, and the following day he opened the Prince of Wales Dock, Swansea. An abridged account of the visit of 18 October, published in the Western Mail, is given below:

'Before 11 o'clock everything was in order, the Masonic stand being occupied by upwards of 1000 true and loyal Masons, whose bright and varied regalia glistened in the sunshine. With them were a large number of ladies the whole company sitting expectantly listening to the music of the Choral Society, interspersed with selections splendidly rendered by the brass band. Seated at the top of the wide steps leading to the centre of the pavilion was Sir George Elliot, Bart., M.P., the Provincial Grand Master, and among the other officers present were Mr. Tennant, D.P.G.M and Mr. George Elliot, M.P. (son of Sir George Elliot), the Senior Grand Warden of the North and East Ridings of Yorkshire. From Monmouthshire Division: - General Lyne, P.G.M. Monmouthshire, Captain S. G. Homfray, D.P.G.M ,……. Sir Pryce Pryce, Gogerddan, P. Prov. Grand Master of Western Division. The grandstand, occupied by the strong number of Freemasons, was beautifully draped with flags, streamers, and wreaths, and roses hung along the front. The decoration of the splendid Masonic Arch, through which the procession had to pass, was not finished until late on Monday night, but now it shone resplendent in the sun, with the words "Deo Regi Frateribus, Honor, Fidelitas, Benevolentia," forming a circle on each side of the simple but expressive welcome "Hail Grand Master."

Just as the Dragoon guards entered the arch they struck up "The March of the Men of Harlech", and as they moved off and the Royal carriage came up, the Choral Society commenced singing "God Bless the Prince of Wales". The moment the voices of the singers ceased there went up cheer after cheer, all standing bareheaded.

A few yards further on the carriage stopped again, as Sir George Elliot descended the steps from the dais to present
THE FREEMASONS' ADDRESS
This was taken as read.

The Prince of Wales said 'Thank you very much. This is my answer,' and handed to Sir George the following written address:
'To the Freemasons of South Wales – I thank you with the warmest feelings of fraternal friendship for your address, and for your expressions of loyal brotherhood towards me as your Grand Master. It is especially gratifying to me to be so welcomed by a body of Welshmen belonging to the Order with whom I am so intimately connected, and in whose prosperity and welfare I take so deep an interest. I can assure you that I am very sensible of the distinction I enjoy of being able to bear the name of a country, which like your Principality, boasts of associations and ancient traditions of so varied and interesting a character, and which has always been so conspicuous for the loyalty of its inhabitants. I will not fail to convey to the Princess of Wales all the kind words which you have used referring to herself. We have both experienced great pleasure in the opportunity which has been afforded us to become acquainted with the inhabitants of this part of Wales, and trust that further opportunity will be given to

us to renew our visit.'

The occasion was marked by a Masonic Ball, held in the evening at the Music-hall (later the Albert Hall), which was a pronounced success. The visit proved to be a rather expensive affair and Provincial Grand Lodge appealed to the fifteen Lodges of the Province for contributions from Lodge Funds *'towards liquidating the debt incurred in receiving the Grand Master.'*

On 3 May 1886, Sir George Elliot laid the Foundation Stone of the new Masonic Hall for Merlin Lodge No.1578, Pontypridd. Further details are given in Merlin Lodge history. Also in 1886, Sir George Elliot, entirely at his own expense, founded the Elliot Home for Seamen, in Temple Street, Newport, together with the attached Church for Seamen.

Sir George Elliot, together with the Marquess of Tweeddale and other Brethren, were Founders of Telegraph Cable Lodge No.2470, Warranted on 18 February 1893. The Lodge met initially at the 'Ship and Turtle Tavern', Leadenhall Street, London. It now meets at Mark Masons' Hall, 86 St James's Street, London. Later that year, Sir George Elliot died on 23 December 1893. In his Obituary in 'The Times' it was stated:

*'**Sir George Elliot**, Bart., died at his residence, 17, Portland-place, at 3 o'clock on Saturday afternoon. His family were in town, but only a servant was in the room when he breathed his last. Sir George caught a chill while at Cardiff with **Lord Salisbury** a few weeks ago, and his death is attributed to acute pneumonia and complications.'*

He was buried on 28 December in the family vault in the hillside cemetery at Houghton-le-Spring. His son, RWBro George William Elliot (13 May 1844 - 15 November 1895) died within two years of his father, on 15 November 1895. He was MP for Northallerton, 1874 -1885; and for Richmond, Yorkshire, 1886-1895. The name Elliot lives on in South Wales with Elliot's Town in the Rhymney Valley and in the Province with 'Sir George Elliot Chapter, No. 960', in Cardiff. The Warrant for this Chapter was granted on 3 August 1887 and it was Consecrated at the Masonic Hall, Working Street, Cardiff on Tuesday, 29 January 1888 (The Masonic Hall, Guildford Crescent was officially opened on 11 October 1895.) There are no records in the Minutes of Sir George ever attending the Chapter.

Sir George Elliot's character is best summed up with two quotations from his biographical sketch, published in 'Vanity Fair' on 29 November 1879, where it was stated that *'among his companions he was known as "Geordie" – a name which has stood by him to this day:'* And: *'Sir George is a very keen man of business; he is simple, unaffected, and cordial, yet without any pretension, so that his manners are good and his companionship is as pleasant as for those who desire to inform themselves it is profitable. He takes perhaps too great an interest in Egypt, but when he is in England few men are more congenially welcomed by those who know him.'*

References

Who's Who of British Members of Parliament", Volume II, 1886 - 1918, published by Harvest Press, Sussex, 1978
Who's Who in Welsh History", Deborah C. Fisher, Published by Christopher Davies 1997. ISBN 0. 7154. 07317
'These Hundred Years' (1856 - 1956) - A History of St David's Lodge, No. 679, Aberdare'. By Bro Rev R Ivor Parry, PPG Chaplain. First Published in 1997.
Vanity Fair, November 29, 1879 - STATESMEN. No. 317 - 'Geordie'.
Hull City Council

Compiled by WBro Peter M Davies, ProvJGW.

Marmaduke Tennant, PAGDC
1838 - 1915

Deputy Provincial Grand Master
1877 - 1915

Marmaduke Tennant was born in 1838 at Castle Bytham, South Lincolnshire, where his father, Rev William Tennant was the Vicar of the Church of St James' in the village. He was the youngest member of the family, which consisted of five sons and a daughter. At the age of 23, Marmaduke was living with his unmarried 33 year-old brother Edmund, an Attorney and Advocate, at Wheatley Cottage, Hanley, Stoke-upon-Trent. His widowed mother and an unmarried sister had also moved to live with Edmund. Marmaduke was now an Articled Clerk.

Shortly afterwards, he moved to Aberavaon as a qualified Solicitor and in 1863 was appointed Town Clerk of Aberavon. Early in 1864, he married Sarah, the only daughter of Mr Charles Decimus Matthews of Chipping Camden. Sarah had been born in the same year as Marmaduke. They had eight children, six daughters and two sons. Two daughters predeceased him, firstly in January 1894 and secondly in March 1910. The youngest member of the family was Ernest Theodore, born in 1882, who was to follow his father into the legal profession, and by 1911, at the age of 29, he was practising independently as a Solicitor in Aberavon and later became Deputy Town-clerk to his father.

His eldest son, Alfred Marmaduke, born in 1872, went on to hold a senior Government Appointment in Egypt. During the First World War, WBro John Wallace, former Captain in the Royal Army Medical Corps, WM Glamorgan Lodge (1916) reported to the Lodge, in October 1916, that while he was in the Hospital at Alexandria, he had *'received a visit from Bro. Tennant, the son of the late Deputy Provincial Grand Master, Marmaduke Tennant'*.

Marmaduke Tennant was Initiated into the Afan Lodge No.833, Port Talbot on 2 April 1863. His first Provincial appointment, only four years later, was that of Grand Registrar (1867). He was Installed Worshipful Master of Afan Lodge in 1871 and the following year he served as Provincial Senior Grand Warden. He was WM of Afan Lodge once again in 1875. On 4 April 1877, Sir George Elliot, Bart, MP, was Installed as Provincial Grand Master of South Wales (Eastern Division) at a Provincial Grand Lodge held in Aberdare. Two months later, 'The Cardiff Times &

Marmaduke Tennant

South Wales Weekly News', published on Saturday, 12 June 1877 printed the following: *'We learn from reliable authority that Sir George Elliot, yesterday, made an offer to Mr Marmaduke Tennant of Afan Lodge No.833 to become Deputy Provincial Grand Master of the eastern division of South Wales. It is not yet known whether Mr Tennant will accept the post, but there can be little doubt that should he do so, he would be one of the most popular officers in the principality in connection with Masonry, being well-known and highly respected for his social and moral qualities.'*

Having accepted the post, Marmaduke Tennant was soon thrown in at the 'deep end', by having to Consecrate several new Lodges, in the absence of the Provincial Grand Master. The first of these was Ogmore Lodge No.1752, on 2 July 1878. This was followed a few days later by the Consecration of Windsor Lodge No.1754 on 2 July 1878. The following year, on 29 April 1879, he Consecrated Loyal Wye Lodge No.1807 and just over four years later, on 26 July 1883, he Consecrated their new Masonic Hall in Builth Wells. Barry Lodge No.2357 was also Consecrated by him on 11 September 1890, followed later that year by the Consecration of Loyal Hay Lodge No.2382 on 25 November. Loyal Hay Lodge was part of the Province of South Wales (ED) at the time but it was transferred to the Province of Herefordshire on 25 November 1920.

In his role as DepProvGM, Marmaduke Tennant must have attended almost every Consecration Ceremony in the Province. When accompanying the Provincial Grand Master, he would normally be the Installing Master. There was one important exception – the Consecration of Tennant Lodge No.1992 in Cardiff, which was named in his honour. The Lodge was Consecrated on 10 October 1883, in the presence of Sir George Elliot, ProvGM and RWBro Charles Lyne, ProvGM (Monmouthshire) and WBro Geoffrey Homfray, DepProvGM (Monmouthshire). On this occasion, Sir George invited WBro Marmaduke Tennant to perform the Consecration Ceremony. He became an Honorary Member of Tennant Lodge in January 1885 and for the remainder of his life he only missed two Installation Meetings of that Lodge.

He was once again honoured by the Brethren of Tennant Lodge with the Warranting of Marmaduke Tennant Chapter No.1992 on 2 May 1894. He had been Exalted in the St. David's Chapter No.364, Neath and appointed Grand Superintendent on the creation of the Provincial Grand Chapter of South Wales (Eastern Division) in 1886. He held that Office until his death on 24 January 1915.

On the occasion of his silver wedding in 1889, the Brethren of the Province decided to mark their great esteem for the Deputy Provincial Grand Master by raising a fund in order to make a presentation to him. Brethren were invited to make individual donations of not more than one guinea. The presentation to Marmaduke Tennant, consisting of an Illuminated Address and a purse containing 200 gold sovereigns, was duly made at a Provincial Grand Lodge, held at the Town Hall, Cardiff on 24 June 1889. That date being St. John's Day, it was also the Installation of the WM of Glamorgan Lodge, Arthur Herbert Roberts. The Provincial Grand Lodge was opened at 12.30 pm with Sir George Elliot, ProvGM, presiding. A Provincial Grand Banquet was held at 6.00 pm that evening at the Park Hotel.

On 1 January 1894, 'The Craftsman', a Monthly Masonic Journal and Review devoted to the Interests of Freemasonry in Wales and the Border Counties, was first published under the patronage of the Provincial Grand Masters and Deputies of the Provinces of South Wales, Eastern Division & Western Division, Monmouthshire and North Wales. It was published from 283, Cowbridge Road, Cardiff, and was produced for a period of eight years. The cost was 3 pence per issue or 3/6d annually (17.5p). The second issue, February 1894, carried an interview with the DepProvGM, part of which is given below:

When did you first join the Brotherhood?

'I am not able just now to refer to my Certificate, but I think I was Initiated in 1863.'

In 1867 I occupied the Chair for the first time. Since then, and previously to my accepting the Office of Dep. Prov. Grand Master, I have been Elected to the Chair four times, so that I have since my Initiation presided over my Mother Lodge for five years.'

<u>Was Freemasonry flourishing locally in those days?</u>

'At the time I speak of, Freemasonry was young in the Provinces. The late Colonel Kemeys Tynte was Provincial Grand Master, and the late Bro. Theodore Mansel Talbot was his Deputy. The Ceremonies in the several Lodges were performed by a few of the more expert Craftsmen; indeed, some of the Masters were very glad to pay an old and well-known Brother in those days to attend Lodge and work the ceremonies rather than take the trouble to do so themselves.'

<u>Can you call to mind any interesting incidents connected with Welsh Freemasonry in the past?</u>

'At the time mentioned as at present there was great unanimity and good feeling throughout the Province. 'The Indefatigable Lodge' at Swansea, which at that time held its meetings in the old Assembly Rooms, 'The Cambrian Lodge', at Neath and 'The Afan Lodge' at Aberavon, might almost be considered as one Lodge, so frequently were they interchanging visits, and annually they had a joint picnic.'

Marmaduke Tennant celebrated 25 years as Deputy Provincial Grand Master in 1902. The Brethren of the Province decided to mark the occasion by making another presentation to him. This was carried out at a Meeting of Provincial Grand Lodge, held in Cardiff on 25 September 1902. A few days later he sent the following letter of thanks to the various Lodges in the Province:

29 September 1902

'I cannot allow any more time to pass by without writing to thank you & the Brethren of your Lodge for the very generous manner in which you & they have subscribed to the testimonial which was presented to me at Cardiff on Thursday last. I really did not realize the value until after my return home when I unpacked the magnificent service of plate, which is admired not only by my wife & myself but by those of my friends who have seen it.

The album is also as I expressed in Lodge a real work of art & is much admired.

I really do not know how I can repay the Brethren of the Province for all their kindness of which I feel unworthy.

My wife also desires to thank the Brethren for their thoughtfulness of her in presenting to her a very handsome Dressing Case, which she much admires and appreciates.

As I cannot thank the Brethren individually will you kindly ask your Secretary to read this at your next meeting.'

In December 1907, the Brethren of Glamorgan Lodge sent Marmaduke Tennant a letter of congratulations 'upon the attainment of his 70th Birthday.' He replied as follows:

'Pray tender to the Brethren of Glamorgan Lodge my sincere thanks for their congratulations on my attaining the age of 3 score years and ten – I have indeed every reason to be thankful to TGAOTU for the good health I have and I am enjoying and thus enabling me to attend to my professional and Masonic duties.'

During the last twelve months of his life, he had been in failing health, and spent most of that time in his appropriately named second home, 'Afan Lodge', Llangammarch Wells, Breconshire. Still employed as Town-clerk of Aberavon, his professional duties were carried out by his younger son, Ernest.

On Sunday, 24 January 1915, Marmaduke Tennant died at the age of 77. The Death Notice appeared in the 'Western Mail' on Tuesday, 26 January:

'TENNANT – Jan 24th at Cae Hir, Aberavon, Marmaduke Tennant, Town-clerk of Aberavon, D.P.G.M. E. Div. S. Wales. No flowers because of the sorrows of warfare. Funeral Thursday, at 2.30 p.m. Gentlemen only. Friends will please meet at Aberavon parish church at that hour. The internment will take place afterwards at Baglan'.

At the time of his death he was described as the 'oldest Town Clerk in the United Kingdom'. The funeral service was held at

St Mary's Church, Aberavon on the Thursday. Prior to the service, the Mayor, Aldermen, Councillors, Officials of the Borough and County Justices of the Peace assembled in the Town-hall Square and marched in procession to the Church. Freemasons, all wearing sprigs of acacia and representing every Lodge throughout Wales, assembled in the Masonic Temple and they too processed to the Church. Later the Province subscribed for a stained glass window to be erected in St Mary's Church in his memory.

It was decided that the Cardiff Freemasons should be invited to subscribe to a fund in order to place a Memorial Tablet in the Duke of Connaught Temple, Cardiff. The bronze Tablet was unveiled on St John's Day 1915, by WBro Henry Pendrill Charles, who had recently succeeded Marmaduke Tennant as Deputy Provincial Grand Master. Being St John's Day, it was also the Installation Meeting of Glamorgan Lodge. The wording on the Memorial is shown below.

IN MEMORIAM
MARMADUKE TENNANT, P.A.G.D.C. ENG.
DEP. PROV. GRAND MASTER OF THE EASTERN DIVISION
OF SOUTH WALES
WHO DIED 24 JAN. 1915
AND WHO FOR THIRTHY-EIGHT YEARS ABLY
AND ASSIDUOUSLY LABOURED
FOR THE WELFARE OF THE CRAFT
THIS TABLET WAS PLACED HERE BY THE
FREEMASONS OF CARDIFF
AS A TOKEN OF THEIR
LOVE AND APPRECIATION
UNVEILED
SAINT JOHN'S DAY 1915

The Commemorative Window in St Mary's Church, Aberavon

Compiled by WBro Peter M Davies, ProvJGW.

166

Ogmore Lodge No.1752

Warranted : 24 April 1878

Consecrated : 2 July 1878

Meeting at the Masonic Hall, Bridgend.

HRH Albert Edward, Prince of Wales, MWGM, granted the Warrant for Ogmore Lodge on 24 April 1878. Prior to the Consecration of the Lodge, two recorded meetings were held at the Wyndham Arms Hotel, Bridgend. The first, on 22 May 1878, when WBro John Sim Wooley was nominated Master Designate, and the second, on 22 June 1878. It is obvious that there must have been several meetings before these dates. The Sponsoring Lodge was Afan Lodge No.833, and ten of the Founders were Members of that Lodge. Their names are recorded in Ogmore Lodge Record Book of Members, which is still in use today. They were: Bros Oliver J Brook, SW; George Pennington, JW; William Podmore, Treasurer; John Hemming, Secretary; John Howell, SD; John Bennett, JD; Capt M T Tozer, DC; I H Thomas, IG; and R Burnell, Tyler. With the exception of WBro John Wooley and Bro W Podmore, they were all Members of Afan Lodge. The first WM, John Sim Wooley, was Initiated into St Teilo Lodge No.695, Llandeilo, (Erased in 1868). He became a Member of Indefatigable Lodge No.237 in 1863, was its WM in 1877, and appointed ProvGDC in 1878. A Commercial Traveller by profession, he travelled widely and performed Ceremonies in Lodges that he visited.

Before proceeding further, it is worth noting that Bridgend Lodge No.33 was meeting in the town of Bridgend from 1765 to 1777. No return of Members was sent to Grand Lodge (Antients) by this Lodge after 1774, and the Lodge subsequently lapsed. Glamorgan Lodge No.36, meeting in Cardiff, now works under the Warrant re-issued to Bridgend Lodge No.33 in 1777.

The Consecration of Ogmore Lodge took place on 2 July 1878, at the Wyndham Arms Hotel, Bridgend. The Lodge was opened in due form by WBro W T Canton, ProvGTreas, a Member of Indefatigable Lodge, assisted by Officers and Members of his Lodge. The DepProvGM, WBro Marmaduke Tennant, and Officers of Provincial Grand Lodge entered the Lodge and took up their respective places. Provincial Grand Lodge was then opened in the customary manner. WBro Mathew Wayne Morgan, ProvGSuptWks, of Merlin Lodge No.1578, requested the Consecration of Ogmore Lodge on behalf of the Petitioners. The ProvGReg read the Warrant of Constitution and WBro Marmaduke Tennant Consecrated the Lodge according to Antient Custom, in a solemn and impressive manner. The WM Designate was then introduced for the benefit of Installation. The Ceremony was duly carried out and the first Officers were Invested. Twelve gentlemen were then proposed as Candidates for Initiation.

Between 1876 and 1900, a period of 24 years, 160 Members are recorded in the Register. In the Millennium year of 1900, Bro James Pratt McGual was Installed as Master. (It is interesting to note that the Installation took place in the month of July, whereas currently the traditional month is October). James McGual was the 139th Member, who was Initiated on 2 February 1896. His Grand Lodge Certificate, No.1079, was presented to him on 26 April 1897.

At the Regular Lodge Meeting held on 26 October 1885, WBro John Blandy Jenkins and Bro L Beha proposed '*a Masonic Hall be built for the use of Ogmore Lodge, and a committee be formed*'. No further reference is recorded about this project until 9 April 1886, when a sub-committee was formed to negotiate terms for the purchase of the Ogmore Club premises. On 28 June 1886, the proposal was dropped. However, a scheme was launched to raise funds to build a hall. At this stage there was £100.00 available in Lodge funds and Members promised to take shares to the value of £300. Some plans had been prepared, which included three sets of offices. The estimated cost for the erection of the building was £800. It was hoped that the offices would produce an income of £36 per annum. It was suggested that capital for the building could be raised either by forming a limited company, or by issuing debentures; alternatively, a mortgage advance could be obtained.

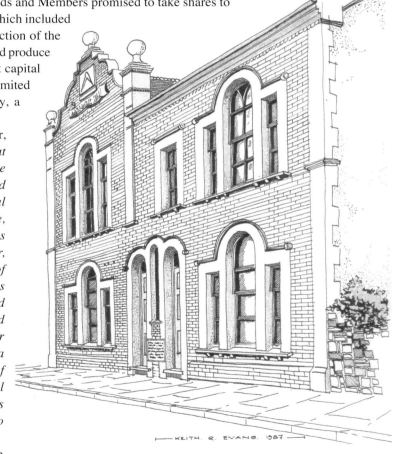

The Minutes of the Lodge held on 25 October, 1886, record the following: '*Bro Boles reported that he had seen Lord Dunraven with reference to a site for the Masonic Hall and that his Lordship expressed his willingness to grant a site near the National Provincial Bank, free of charge during his lifetime, at the same time making the suggestion that shops should be built under the Lodge room. However, Marmaduke Tennant called attention to the terms of His Lordship's offer, viz. that the gift of the site was for his lifetime, and suggested some provision should be made by the Lodge for the future. He proposed insurance on His Lordship's life to provide for payment of ground rent after his death. However a problem occurred in connection with the raising of funds. The committee recommended that the capital Sum of £2000 should be raised by issuing 400 shares at £5 each which were to be issued exclusively to Members of the Lodge.*'

During the next twelve months, it appears from the Minutes concerning the building that meetings

Old Masonic Hall, Adare Street, by WBro Keith Robert Evans

were of a turbulent nature. On 25 June 1888, Bro Randall was instructed to wind up the company. In March 1890, the company was finally wound up, and the monies subscribed by the shareholders were returned.

On 6 January 1891, a new building committee was formed. At the February Lodge Meeting, progress was reported and, from this point, events proceeded rapidly. The committee was empowered to raise funds in order to erect a building and the sum of £100 was voted from Lodge funds. How the remainder of the necessary capital was to be obtained is not recorded. The first indication emerges with a printed account headed 'Ogmore Lodge (New Hall) Building Account', attached to the Minutes and approved at a meeting held on 24 July 1893. The capital was raised by Members making repayable contributions to the value of £722 @ 5% interest per annum. A further appeal was made on 14 June, 1892, when Bro Boles made a gift of £50. It was suggested that a mortgage advance be raised on the security of the building, to cover any deficiency. According to the Minutes of the Regular Lodge held on 22 June, 1891, *'it was resolved that the details of laying the Memorial Stone (Foundation Stone) of the Masonic Hall be left to the committee.'*

On 28 July 1891, WBro Marmaduke Tennant presided at a Meeting of Provincial Grand Lodge. At the conclusion of business, and with new Provincial Officers appointed, the Lodge was adjourned. The Brethren then formed in procession, and headed by the Tondu Brass Band, proceeded to the site of the new Masonic Hall in Adare Street. There, Marmaduke Tennant laid the Foundation Stone according to ancient custom, assisted by Officers of Provincial Grand Lodge. He was presented with a Silver Trowel and an Ivory Mallet to mark this historical event. The Trowel was subsequently returned to Ogmore Lodge by Bro Neville Walsh and formally presented to the Lodge on 16 November 1958, by WBro Edgar Abrahams of Afan Lodge. It is now on display in the new Temple at Coychurch Road. Also displayed in the new Masonic Hall is a pen and ink drawing by WBro Keith Robert Evans, PPrJGW, of the Old Masonic Hall, Adare Street, which was demolished in 1968, as part of the town re-development. WBro Keith Robert Evans was Installed as WM of Penybont Lodge No.6743, in 1988. He presented his drawing to the new Masonic Hall in 1987, and a copy was also presented to WBro Ronald Whittingham (see below), to mark his 50 years as a Freemason.

Ogmore Lodge has ten Daughter Lodges: Llynfi No.2965, Consecrated 28 July 1903; Venables Llewelyn Lodge No.3756, Consecrated 3 June 1916; Trisant No.4154, Consecrated 12 November 1920; Llangeinor No.4194, Consecrated 27 April 1921; St Quentin's No.4778, Consecrated 16 December 1925; Morganwg No.5084, Consecrated 7 January 1929; Penybont No.6743, Consecrated 22 October 1948; Glanogwr No.8508, Consecrated 11 June 1973; Adare No.9247, Consecrated 6 November 1987; and United Services No.9605, Consecrated 19 February 1996.

One of the most distinguished Members of the Lodge was WBro Ronald Bowen Whittingham. Initiated in Ogmore Lodge in 1936, he was Installed as WM in 1953, and became Treasurer in 1955. He was a Founder Member of Penybont Lodge No.6743, Consecrated on 22 October 1948, and became Master in 1951. A former pupil of Queen's College, Taunton, he was a Founder Member of Queen's College Taunton Lodge No.6988, Province of Somerset. This Lodge was Consecrated on 8 July 1950, and WBro Ronald Whittingham was Installed as WM in 1958. During WWII, he had served in the RAF and, subsequently, he became a Joining Member of Royal Air Force Lodge No.7335, Metropolitan Grand Lodge of London. The Lodge, Founded by a group of serving Royal Air Force Officers to provide a central Masonic base for Officers who might be posted anywhere in the world, was Warranted on 3 February 1954. The Lodge caters exclusively for serving and retired Officers of the Royal Air Force, including Auxiliaries and Reserves, and the Royal Flying Corps. In Province, WBro Ronald Whittingham served as ProvGDC, 1957-1958, and, in 1960, he was appointed ProvSGW. First appointed a Grand Officer in 1963, with the Rank of PAGReg, he was promoted in 1976 to PJGD. Also, in 1976, he was appointed AProvGM, in which capacity he served until 1984. In 1971, he had the honour of being Installed as WM of Lodge of Benevolence No.7305, and likewise, in 1979, he was Installed as WM of Hendre Lodge No.3250.

Ronald Bowen Whittingham was born on 24 March 1909, and he passed to the Grand Lodge Above, at the age of 86, in April 1995.

Mention should also be made of WBro Alfred James Worts, PPrJGW, Installed WM in 1966, who served as Lodge Secretary in both the old and new Temples, until his passing, at the age of 84, to the Grand Lodge Above in 1991. He was one of the negotiators of the sale of the Masonic Hall in Adare Street, and was involved in the design of the new Masonic Hall, Coychurch Road, Bridgend.

WBro Cyril William Shickle was Initiated into the Scottish Constitution and became a Joining Member of Ogmore Lodge on 25 April 1960. In 1973, he was Installed as Master. He became a Grand Officer in 1986, with the Rank of PGStB and, in 1997, he was promoted to PAGDC. He celebrated his Golden Anniversary in the English Constitution on 25 April 2010, having previously celebrated that Anniversary in the Scottish Constitution. WBro Cyril is the Lodge's longest serving Grand Officer.

The senior PM of the Lodge, WBro Stanley Bernard Roberts, was Installed as Master in 1970. He became a Grand Officer in 1987, with the Rank of PAGDC. WBro Stanley was the ProvGM of the Mark Degree in the Province of South Wales from 1983 to 1991.

The Lodge's most recent Grand Officer, WBro Colin E Mogg, served as Treasurer for some 21 years. He was Provincial Grand Registrar from 2004 to 2007, and was Installed WM of the Lodge in 2007. WBro Colin was appointed a Grand Officer in 2006, with the Rank of PAGDC.

Following on from 'Freemasonry in the Community', in 2000, Ogmore Lodge, together with Glanogwr Lodge, formed the Bridgend Masonic Golf Society in May 2001. WBro Ralph Jones, PPrDepGReg, Installed WM of Glanogwr Lodge in 2000, is the Founder Secretary; and WBro Phillip Aubrey, PProvSGD, Installed WM of Ogmore Lodge in 2000, is the Founder Captain and Treasurer. The Society holds an annual 'Open Golf Tournament' at Pyle and Kenfig Golf Club. The Inaugural Open Golf Tournament was held on 3 August 2002, and since then over £31,000 has been raised in support of local charities and the 2010 Festival. The Society has approximately 50 members and, on 10 May 2011, a special dinner, hosted by the President, RWBro Hywel Davies, PProvGM, was held to mark the Society's 10th Anniversary.

From the Consecration of the Lodge in 1878 to its Centenary in 1978, there have been 894 Members. The Centenary Master was WBro Jack Reeves, PPrJGW, who was Initiated on 23 November 1964. Jack was Installed as Master in October 1977 and presided over the Centenary celebrations on 3 July 1978. The Millennium WM, WBro Phillip A Aubrey, was Initiated on 6 December 1991. He is the Secretary of Ogmore Lodge, and was appointed to the active Rank of ProvSGD in June 2006.

Having celebrated its Centenary in 1978, the Lodge looks forward to celebrating its 150th Anniversary in April 2028.

Compiled by WBro Phillip Aubrey, PProvSGD, Secretary.

Windsor Lodge No.1754

Warranted : 24 April 1878

Consecrated : 15 July 1878

Meeting at the Masonic Hall, Penarth.

In 1853, Lady Mary Windsor Clive, who was living with her family in St Fagans Castle, acting on the advice of her estate manager, Mr John Maughan, purchased the Manor of Penarth which had previously been leased by the Plymouth Estate from the Dean and Chapter of Bristol. It was also on the advice of Mr Maughan that she decided to build a Dock at Penarth at a cost of two million pounds. The creation of the Dock drew many important and influential people into contact with Baroness Windsor and her advisers, none more so than Mr James Hurman the Superintendent of the Taff Vale Railway Company, and Mr Robert Forrest, who in 1874, at the age of 29 was appointed the Estate Agent for Baroness Windsor. Amongst his many responsibilities to the Plymouth Estate was the creation of Penarth as a town.

James Hurman and Robert Forrest were Freemasons. James Hurman was a Past Master of Bute Lodge No.960 and a Joining Member of Glamorgan Lodge No.36 and Merlin Lodge No.1578. Robert Forrest was a Master Mason, Initiated into a Scottish Lodge. They both played an important part in the formation of Windsor Lodge. James Hurman was the first Master and Robert Forrest the first Senior Warden.

It was from the Earl of Plymouth's family name, Windsor-Clive, that Windsor Lodge took its name. The Lodge Crest, which appears on the Lodge Banners and the Past Master's Jewel, is based on the Coat of Arms of the Earls of Plymouth. It is described thus: 1st and 4th quarters are silver, on a black bar three mullets (stars) in gold. 2nd and 3rd quarters are red with an 'X' shaped cross in silver. In the angles of the cross, twelve crosses, three in each angle. The Motto: *'Je me fie en Dieu'* translates *'I trust in God'*.

A Petition had been presented to Glamorgan Lodge No.36 on 27 November 1865, requesting support for the formation of a Masonic Lodge at Penarth. WBro Robert Francis Langley proposed and WBro Frederick A Ware seconded the proposition in support of the Petition, which was unanimously passed and signed by several Brethren. Although the details of why the Petition was eventually abandoned are not known, it is recorded that WBros Langley and Ware were later in dispute, the latter having accused Langley of Masonic touting. The dispute ultimately led to the expulsion of Ware from Glamorgan Lodge.

Further, it is possible the matter was not pursued because the Founder Members of the proposed new Lodge were mainly located in Cardiff, and travelling to Penarth prior to 1878 was mainly by horse-drawn transport, chain ferry across Penarth Dock, or by the boat ferry from Cardiff Dock to Penarth beach where, as Penarth Pier was not built until 1894, the passengers had to land by man-handled landing stages or on a purpose built landing stage at Penarth Dock. Neither ideal, as the route into the town from Penarth Dock or Penarth beach was via a steep road. Consequently, it was no coincidence that the Consecration of Windsor Lodge in 1878 took place when the railway was being extended from Penarth Dock to the town centre.

James Hurman

Robert Forrest

A second Petition was raised in 1878, and WBro James Hurman, to ensure its success, visited in five days of March 1878, Glamorgan Lodge No.36, Bute Lodge No.960, Loyal Cambrian Lodge No.110, St David's Lodge No.679 and Merlin Lodge No.1578, soliciting and receiving the full support of each Lodge. The Petition was submitted to United Grand Lodge, but being undated it was refused, as it did not comply with the official requirements. A further Petition, dated 15 April 1878, was submitted and accepted and the Warrant for the new Lodge was signed on 24 April 1878.

In 1868, the Taff Vale Railway Company built the Penarth Hotel, which overlooked the Penarth headland. It was at this Hotel that the Windsor Lodge Consecration took place on 15 July 1878. This was to be the first of five locations where Lodge Meetings were to be held. A report of the Consecration Ceremony was fully documented in the South Wales Daily News on 16 July 1878 and in the Western Mail on 18 July 1878. In attendance were the Deputy Provincial Grand Master, VWBro Marmaduke Tennant and his four Acting Officers, the Deputy Provincial Grand Master and the Past Provincial Grand Director of Ceremonies of Monmouthshire, plus representatives from 16 Lodges. Of the 12 Officers Invested, seven were not Members of the Lodge, but they became Joining Members at the next Regular Lodge Meeting.

The Penarth Hotel

Mr Francis Sydney Newman Johnson, age 27, has the distinction of being the first Candidate of Windsor Lodge to be Initiated, together with Mr George Cooper, a Shipbuilder, age 35, Mr Harry Snell, an Architect, age 29, and Mr Amos Jenkins, a Drill Instructor, age 41, who soon afterwards became Tyler.

In December 1878, Bro David Hopkins proposed, and Bro Dominick Watson seconded, the proposition for the Lodge to empower the Officers to sign a Petition for a Lodge to be formed at Cowbridge. This was St Quintin's Lodge No.1822, which was ultimately recommended by Bute Lodge No.960, Merlin Lodge No.1578, Windsor Lodge, and the Provincial Grand Master of South Wales ED, Sir George Elliot. The Petition was sent on 15 March 1879, approved on 28 April 1879, and the Lodge was Consecrated on 21 August 1879. Unfortunately, St Quentin's Lodge was only active for just over two years and was Erased form the Register of UGLE on 5 September 1923. It does, however, have the distinction of being the first of Windsor Lodge's Daughter Lodges.

Windsor Lodge, in conjunction with Glamorgan and Bute Lodges, were the Sponsoring Lodges for Barry Lodge No.2357, which received its Warrant in April 1890. Since then, Windsor has been the sole Mother Lodge of six Daughter Lodges, namely Penarth Lodge No.4113 (Warranted 11 May 1920); Sapphire Lodge No.5290 (Warranted 5 August 1931 and Erased December 2008); Dinas Powis Lodge No.5997 (Warranted 2 August 1944); Clive Lodge No.6973 (Warranted 1 March 1950); Services Lodge No.7139 (Warranted 13 November 1951) and Owain Glyndwr Lodge No.8015 (Warranted 10 February 1965).

The first Election for Master of Windsor Lodge was held on the 3 October 1879. The names of four Brethren were put forward for Election: WBro James Hurman, WM; Bro Robert Forrest, SW; Bro John Guthrie, JW and WBro David Hopkins (PM Bute Lodge), who regularly attended Meetings, and when the occasion arose also stood in as Master, or Senior Warden. The result of the Ballot was David Hopkins, 15 votes, Robert Forrest, 4 votes. This is the only time, in the history of Windsor Lodge that the Senior Warden has failed to be Elected Master.

The non-election of Robert Forrest is not surprising, as he had only attended 3 out of a possible 12 Lodge Meetings. Indeed, he very rarely attended the Lodge after the Election and resigned his Membership on 8 January 1892. His absence had been due to his many commitments. In addition to his duties as the Estate Agent for the Plymouth Estates, he also looked after the interests of Lord Romilly and his co-owners, the Estate of Mr Jenner at Wenvoe Castle, the Vachell Estate, with its important properties in Cardiff, and the Ham Estate at Llantwit Major. These Estates covered an area of between 60,000 to 70,000 acres, comprising all classes of property - dock, railway, town, industrial and agricultural.

Windsor Lodge continued to meet at the Penarth Hotel for approximately 15 months until November 1879, when it relocated to a new meeting place in Windsor Road, Penarth, in rooms above a chemist shop, referred to as the 'New Lodge Rooms'. Many highlights of the early history of Windsor Lodge took place there, during the ten years that the Lodge remained at those premises.

In November 1883, WBro Francis Pinney Adey, on the day of his Installation as Master, presented the Lodge with a Banner, which remained in use until 3 October 2003, when the Lodge was presented with a replacement Banner as part of Windsor Lodge's 125th Anniversary Celebration. This Banner was Consecrated by the Provincial Grand Master RWBro Hywel Davies. The original Banner is now exhibited in a purpose built, hermetically sealed, perspex box, hung in the stairwell of the Penarth Masonic Hall.

The Windsor Lodge of Instruction was formed in January 1879, and in May 1887 the Lodge's associated Royal Arch Chapter, Tennant No.1754 was Warranted in Penarth.

Financial difficulties arose in mid 1889 and the Treasurer, WBro William David John was ordered to pay all monies into a recently opened bank account. There is no record or explanation why the order was given. It certainly had a massive effect on the Lodge, for WBro John, the owner of the premises where the Lodge held its meetings, gave the Lodge peremptory notice to quit the building. The Lodge, after receiving Provincial Dispensation, held an Emergency Meeting at the Lansdowne Hotel, Plymouth Road, Penarth, which was under the ownership or management of WBro Francis Pinney Adey. It was agreed at this Meeting that the Lodge would continue to meet at the Lansdowne Hotel until such time as the situation could be resolved. On 6 April 1894, William David John was excluded from the Lodge for being five years in arrears.

In 1891, it was resolved to consider the expediency of building new premises for the Lodge. This culminated in forming the Windsor Masonic Hall Company, to raise the necessary finances to fund the project. A site was found and the first purpose built Masonic Hall in Penarth was constructed, conveniently, alongside Penarth Railway Station, in Station Approach, Penarth, by Mr Frederick Speed. The property consisted of a ground floor and first floor, the ground floor being occupied by a Brewery Off-licence. The Hall is now the property of the Penarth British Legion. The original pillars, presented by the first Junior Warden, WBro John Guthrie, which stood on the floor of the Temple at Station Approach, now stand either side of the entrance of the Grand Temple, at the Masonic Hall, Stanwell Road.

John Guthrie

It is recorded that in 1900, a Norwegian seaman was washed ashore onto Penarth beach. The Membership of the Lodge at that time included twelve Norwegian Brethren, amongst whom was Bro Carl Frederick Hansen, a Shipbroker, who was also the Norwegian Consul in Cardiff. He was called upon to make the funeral arrangements for the deceased. Amongst the effects found on the seaman was a small locket, battered and somewhat the worse for wear, containing Masonic Symbols. Bro Hansen arranged for the locket to be mounted in a gold square, attached to the Worshipful Master's Collar and suitably inscribed, where it remains to this day.

In 1916, WBro Albert James Nurton was invited by the Provincial Grand Master to compile the first Provincial Year Book. At the time, there were only thirty Lodges in the Province, covering thirteen centres, with five of them meeting at Cardiff. He continued with this task for sixteen years and, in 1929, he became the first Grand Officer of the Lodge, when he was awarded the Rank of Assistant Grand Director of Ceremonies. The same year he had the dual honour of being conferred with the Rank of Grand Standard Bearer in Supreme Grand Chapter.

With the end of the First World War in 1919, the Brethren of Windsor Lodge subscribed towards the purchase of a 'Peace Chair' to commemorate the end of hostilities. The Chair, still in use today as the Master's Chair, was presented on behalf of the Brethren by The Deputy Provincial Grand Master, WBro H P Charles, and was Dedicated by Bro Rev Gwilym Francis, Past Provincial Grand Chaplain, who delivered an impressive Oration.

During the thirty-four years that Windsor Lodge remained at the premises in Station Approach, Penarth Lodge No.4113 and Stability Mark Lodge No.758 were Consecrated.

The Pillars and Senior Warden's Chair - Temple - Station Approach

They, with Windsor Lodge, at that time had an average Membership of 250 and together with the Membership of Tennant Chapter, would have found the one storey building somewhat crowded. This may have been the reason why Windsor Lodge reduced its Regular Lodge Meetings from twelve to ten, holding Emergency Meetings as and when required. Not that this made much difference to the recruitment of Candidates. WBro Max Wideman, Master of Windsor Lodge, 1918-1919, holds the record, with ten Regular Lodge Meetings and twenty-five Emergency Meetings, during which time, twenty-nine Brethren were Initiated and eleven became Joining Members.

In 1919, Windsor Lodge appointed three Trustees; WBros W H Maton, a local Jeweller; R Guy, a local Pork Butcher and William Lougher Yorath. The latter was a remarkable man. A Solicitor by profession, he was Deputy

The Temple at Station Approach

Lord Mayor of Cardiff in 1905 and served as the Coroner for Cardiff from 1907 to 1924. He was also the head of the Cardiff Finance Committee; President of the Incorporated Law Society (Cardiff Branch); President of the Cardiff Agricultural Society and a Justice of the Peace. He was the first Secretary of Glamorgan Cricket Club and played for them in 1888 and 1889 against Surrey at the Oval and at Cardiff, and against the MCC at Lords, Cardiff, and Swansea. He was also the Honorary Solicitor and a Founder of Cardiff Golf Club, and a Founder of Radyr Golf Club.

Following a Notice of Motion to secure larger premises, passed on 5 December 1924, a site became available on playing fields, at Stanwell Road, Penarth. The Architects appointed to design and oversee the building work were Bro Edmund Charles Morgan Wilmott, Initiated into Windsor Lodge in January 1915 and Bro Thomas Edgar Smith, Initiated into the Lodge in September 1920. They were also the Architects for Swansea Masonic Hall, Caerphilly Masonic Hall, and Llandough Hospital, and were among a short list of ten in connection with the design of Freemasons' Hall, London.

The work began in 1927 with the cutting of the first sod by 87 year old WBro Frederick George (Daddy) Hodges, the Senior Past Master, and the building was completed in 1928. The magnificent domed ceiling of the Grand Temple, the larger of the two Temples in the building, decorated with stars and planets, was designed by Mr Dan Jones, FRAS. It is said to be an accurate representation of the Northern Heavens in September. The builders were Messrs Tucker Bros, Broadway, Roath, Cardiff and the final cost of the work was between £10,000 and £11,000.

The opening of the Masonic Hall coincided with the Windsor Lodge Jubilee, which is commemorated by the stained glass window fitted above the Junior Warden's Chair.

The Jubilee Window

175

The first loss to the Lodge due to enemy action during the Second World War was that of Bro John Murray, a Master Mariner. In total, seven Members of the Windsor Lodge were killed during the war. Their names are recorded on a Memorial Plaque at the Masonic Hall. Out of an average Membership of one hundred & fifty, no less than one hundred and twenty Brethren joined the various branches of the Armed Forces, the Civil Defence Service and other work of national importance. Four of the Brethren received decorations. The ground floor of the Masonic Hall was requisitioned by the Air Ministry as a recruitment centre and stores until 1945. Nevertheless, Windsor Lodge met on a regular basis, although the Festive Board was severely restricted, due to rationing. Whilst bombs were dropped within fifty yards of the Hall, the building suffered no damage. At a special function held at the Masonic Hall in 1948, Bro William (Billy) Boyle presented a cheque to the Deputy Provincial Grand Master, RWBro Edger J Rutter, and the Assistant Provincial Grand Master, WBro Charles P Palmer, in final payment on the mortgage.

In 1954, the original American organ in the Grand Temple, now relocated in the Lesser Temple, was replaced by a pipe organ built by Mr Vernon Gill, proprietor of Cardiff Organ Works. It was formerly fitted in a small church at the entrance to Cardiff Docks, said to be used as a Seaman's Mission and purchased for £1,600. Due to the poor acoustics of the Temple, only five percent of the original pipe organ was installed. Following the completion of the work, a Dedication Ceremony was held. Amongst those present were all the Masters and Past Masters meeting at Penarth, the Chaplains of Windsor and Dinas Powis Lodges, who performed the Dedication Ceremony and Bro Donald W Bate, ARCO, Organist of Bute Lodge, who gave an organ recital. Vernon Gill later became a Member and Organist of the Windsor Lodge and the Tennant Chapter.

At the Installation Meeting in 1956, RWBro R P St John Charles and RWBro Edgar J Rutter were once again in attendance, together with WBro Harry F Stockwell, AProvGM, Wardens and Officers of Provincial Grand Lodge, and occupied the Officers' Chairs. The ProvGM, from the Master's Chair, announced the resignation, through ill health, of WBro Edgar W Lewis as AProvGM and proceeded to Invest his successor WBro Russell Mabley. The Ceremony completed, the Provincial Grand Master returned the Gavel and the domestic Ceremony of Installation proceeded.

The twenty five year's service of WBro R P St John Charles as Provincial Grand Master was celebrated at a Meeting of Windsor Lodge in 1963. The ProvGM was himself present, together with RWBro Edgar J Rutter and WBros Harry Stockwell and Harold Wilson, AProvGMs, and a full complement of Provincial Grand Officers. The Deputy Provincial Grand Master referred to the high esteem in which the ProvGM was held and announced that all 150 Lodges in the Province had contributed towards a Presentation Fund of 1,000 guineas. He further explained that he was expected to make the presentation, but instead called upon two Entered Apprentices, Bros Brinley Jones and Derek Strong to perform this duty, which was done under his guidance.

The Centenary Celebration Meeting was held on 20 October 1978 in the presence of RWBro the Lord Swansea, ProvGM; VWBro Geoffrey Ashe, DepProvGM; three Assistant Provincial Grand Masters, the Provincial Grand Wardens, and other Officers of Grand Lodge and Provincial Grand Lodge. A total of 181 Brethren signed the Register. The Centenary Warrant was presented by the ProvGM to WBro Ralph Wynne Evans, WM of Windsor Lodge. The Provincial Grand Chaplain, WBro Elfed Jones, delivered an impressive Oration. WBro Jolliffe James Dyer presented the ProvGM with a cheque for one thousand guineas, as the first instalment of the Windsor Lodge Centenary Covenant and announced that a further £150.00 would be donated annually from Lodge Funds, for the next seven years. Before closing the Lodge, the Master announced that the charity door collection would be donated to the Royal Masonic Hospital. The Meeting closed at 7.30 pm, following which the Brethren assembled in the Windsor Room to witness WBro John Arthur Mc'Beth unveil the Windsor Lodge Past Masters' Board, which he had constructed and presented to the Lodge. Mc'Beth, a Master Joiner, also made all Past Masters' Boards on display in the Windsor Room, at Penarth and supplied and fitted the Bar at Penarth, which he donated free of charge to the Masonic Hall Company. He also made various Masonic items for the Lodges and Chapters meeting at Penarth.

At the Installation Meeting held on 3 November 1978, five Australian Brethren from Lodge Windsor No.770, were admitted into the Lodge. After receiving permission from the WM, the Master of Lodge Windsor, WBro Reay together with the other four Members of his group lined up in front of the WM, with the senior Member in the North East and the junior Member in the South East. The junior Member passed a small storage box, a parchment scroll and finally an Australian Director of Ceremonies' Mace, down the line to WBro Reay, who presented each of the items to the Worshipful Master and gave a full description of their history and origin. The Worshipful Master reciprocated by presenting WBro Reay with a leather-bound Bible. He also presented WBro Reay with a china loving cup, at the Festive Board.

The Director of Ceremonies' Mace is made out of polished fossilised wood, decorated with opals, sapphires and other precious gems found in various parts of New South Wales and set in sterling silver. The wooden box containing the Mace was made out of 'Black Butt', a native hardwood, by Sergeant Ron Riley of the Royal Australian Air Force, an Entered Apprentice of Lodge Windsor. The artwork on the Parchment Scroll was carried out by Ros Blackburn, the daughter of a Member of Lodge Windsor. During Regular Lodge Meetings, the Mace is carried into the Lodge by the Director of Ceremonies, placed in a purpose made open box, hung on the side of the Director of Ceremonies' Chair, where it remains until the business of the Lodge has been completed, before being carried out of the Lodge in the retiring procession.

In April 1981, a copper copy of the Parchment Scroll bearing the name 'Windsor' was framed and given to WBro James Leho, who had written to every Lodge with the name 'Windsor', prior to the Lodge's Centenary Celebration in 1989. It was only through his efforts that the presentation of the Mace had taken place. The framed copper copy is exhibited in the Tyler's corridor at the Penarth Masonic Hall.

The 4 May 1979 marked the sad death of WBro Francis Clifford (Cliff) John, Lodge Almoner. A man of great integrity, who in addition to working quietly in the background for the benefit of dependents of Windsor Lodge was the instigator, Founder Member and motivating force in the formation of the Penarth Good Neighbours Club in November 1976. Its first meeting was held on 6 January 1977.

An 'Open Day' was organised at the Penarth Masonic Hall for Sunday 22 June 2002, by WBro William Barratt of Wings Lodge No.8651. A visual exhibition on 'The Progress of Freemasonry in Penarth', supported by maps and photographs, was presented by WBro Arthur J Nurse (Windsor Lodge). The Open Day was a great success and attracted in excess of 50 visitors, one of whom became a Member of Windsor Lodge.

The DC's Mace

Friday, 3 October 2003, marked a very important day in the history of Windsor Lodge. Not only was it the 125th Anniversary of the Lodge, but also the Dedication of a replacement Lodge Banner. The Dedication Ceremony was conducted by RWBro Hywel Davies, ProvGM, and his Officers.

Compiled by WBro Arthur J Nurse, PPrJGW.

Loyal Wye Lodge No.1807

Warranted : 4 February 1879

Consecrated : 29 April 1879

Meeting at the Masonic Hall, Builth Wells.

Loyal Wye Lodge No.1807 was one of 47 Lodges Consecrated in 1879. Many of these Lodges have ceased to exist but, Loyal Wye Lodge has flourished and in 2011, celebrates 132 years of Freemasonry in Builth Wells.

The Petition for the formation of the new Lodge was Sponsored by Brecknock Lodge No.651 and was suitably rewarded by the granting of a Warrant, on 4 February 1879. The Warrant is displayed in the Temple, Builth Wells, to the right of the WM's Chair.

At a Meeting of Brecknock Lodge on 7 April 1879, it was announced that the new Lodge, Brecknock Lodge's second Daughter Lodge, would be Consecrated at the Lion Hotel, Builth Wells, on 29 April 1879. The Minutes of Brecknock Lodge also record that a letter had been received from Bro Benjamin Davies, who was to become the first Secretary of Loyal Wye Lodge, asking for the loan of the Brecknock Lodge furniture for the Consecration Ceremony. Officiating at the Consecration Ceremony was WBro Marmaduke Tennant, DepProvGM, of the Province of South Wales Eastern Division. WBro Thos Butcher, WM of Brecknock Lodge, assisted by his Officers, opened the Lodge in due form. The DepProvGM was announced, whereupon he assumed the Chair and proceeded to open Provincial Grand Lodge. The Charter having been read, WBro Marmaduke Tennant duly Consecrated the Lodge in conformity with ancient custom. After Provincial Grand Lodge was closed, WBro Herbert Charles Ingram Rich, PPrGSuptWks, was Installed as the first WM. He had been Installed as WM of Brecknock Lodge in 1868. He then proceeded to Invest his Officers, with Bro A Gwynne Vaughan as SW, and Bro J W Coulthard as JW.

Subsequent Lodge Meetings appear to have been held at the Masonic Rooms, the Lion Hotel, Builth Wells, but within a short time moves were afoot to erect, or

WBro Herbert Charles Ingram Rich, first Worshipful Master of the Loyal Wye Lodge, 1879 -1881

otherwise obtain, permanent and exclusive premises in which to meet. During the planning stages, meetings were held at various venues to thrash out the detail, but little progress appears to have been made. However, in February 1883, Bro Rev Wm Williams informed the Brethren that he had purchased two cottages in Market Street, Builth Wells, and offered to lease the said properties to Loyal Wye Lodge for £20 per annum. At the Regular Meeting of the Lodge the following month, the offer was fully discussed, agreed, and ratified, by all the Members present.

On 26 July 1883, the New Masonic Hall was duly Consecrated by WBro Marmaduke Tennant, DepProvGM. At this Meeting, Bro William Price was first Installed into the Chair of King Solomon and, after he had appointed and Invested his Officers he, on behalf of Loyal Wye Lodge, requested the DepProvGM to Consecrate the new Lodge Room *in due form*. This he proceeded to do, the elements of Consecration being carried out by WBros. H C I Rich, A Gwynne Vaughan, J A Whittle and the WM. Most unusually, according to the Minutes, it was afterwards that the ProvGM, RWBro Sir George Elliot, Bart, MP, was announced and was duly received and greeted by the Brethren. He addressed the Lodge on the religious influences of Freemasonry and then the ProvGChap delivered an Oration on Freemasonry and its history. The ProvGM went on to present a PM's Jewel to Bro Wm Williams, PM, PPGChap, on behalf of

The Masonic Hall, Builth Wells

Loyal Wye Lodge, *'for his invaluable services to Freemasonry'*. After the Lodge had been closed, the Brethren formed in procession and marched to the Assembly Rooms, afterwards known as the 'Kino' Cinema, and today as the Wyeside Arts Centre. This was the second time in four years that Provincial Grand Lodge had been held in Builth Wells, the first time being the Consecration of the Lodge.

The furniture used at the Consecration had been borrowed from Brecknock Lodge. Loyal Wye Lodge soon became self-sufficient in this regard, following generous donations from various Members. The Lodge Pillars were acquired as the result of the efforts of the Senior Deacon, Bro William Price, in 1881. They are still in their original positions, adjacent to the entrance to the Temple and in front of the SW's Chair. Another unusual feature is the clock, situated above the SW's Chair, which bears a brass plate stating that it was presented to the Lodge in 1883, by WBro William Price, WM. The Temple boasts all 'The Virtues', which adorn the walls in the south, west and north. These were donated by Bro Herring in 1886. At the time, these were said *'to augment the gift* (the Banner) *donated by Miss Thomas'* a few years earlier.

Miss Thomas, of 'The Castle', donated the Banner in 1883. It bears the Lodge number '1807', below which is depicted a bull, above the word 'BUALLT'. The name 'Builth', in Welsh 'Buallt' or perhaps 'Buellt', is older than the town to which it now refers. Buallt/Buellt originally applied to the Cantref or Hundred, an area defined within the old administrative system. The Cantref is the area of land between the Rivers Wye and Tywi and north of a line roughly drawn between Erwood and Llanwrtyd, covering an area of some 174 square miles. It has long been thought that the name of this Cantref, later the town, came from the Welsh words 'Bu' and 'Allt' and therefore could be translated as 'The Wild Ox of the Wooded Slope' or 'Cow Pasture'. Across the bottom of the Banner is the Lodge's Welsh Motto: *'Fyddlon Hyd Angau',* which translates as *'Faithful unto Death'.*

The Lodge Crest

The Lodge went from strength to strength during the ensuing years, although finance was a continuing problem. Membership increased quite sharply, with 25 Initiations and the addition of two Joining Members between 1879 and 1881. The pattern continued, albeit to a lesser degree, in the years that followed. The Masonic Lodge building was purchased in 1907 from the beneficiaries of the late Bro Rev Wm Williams, for the sum of £400.

In 1908, many PMs were instrumental in raising a Petition for the formation of a new Lodge in Llandrindod Wells. This was Ithon Lodge No.3320, Loyal Wye's Daughter Lodge, Consecrated on 25 September 1908.

In 1910, the Lodge Elected RWBro the Rt Hon John Allan Rolls, 1st Lord Llangattock, ProvGM, as an Honorary Member. It is also very interesting to note that two former ProvGMs of the Province were also natives of, and resided in, Builth Wells or in close proximity.

Lt Col Sir Charles Leyshon Dillwyn-Venables-Llewelyn, 2nd Baronet of Llysdinam, held the Office of ProvGM between 1913 and 1938 and lived at Llysdinam House, Newbridge-on-Wye, Brecknockshire. He was made an Honorary Member of the Lodge in 1921, along with the DepProvGM, Henry Pendrill Charles.

The Rt Hon John Hussey Hamilton Vivian, 4th Baron Swansea, OSM, CStJ, DL, held the Office of ProvGM between 1966 and 1999. A native of the area, he owned Caer Beris Manor, Builth Wells, which had been purchased by his father in 1923. The estate was broken up in the 1970s, and the historic Manor House, which is grade 2 listed, is now a Country House Hotel and Restaurant.

The Worshipful Master's Chain was purchased in 1929 to mark the Lodge's Golden Jubilee. It bears a suitable inscription which is quite unobtrusive, so as not to take away its full effect.

During WWII, an association sprang up with Brethren of Old Bromsgrovian Lodge No.5743. The Lodge meets at Bromsgrove School with Membership, in the main, being drawn from its Staff and Old Boys. During the War, many pupils were evacuated from this Midlands town and continued their education at Llanwrtyd Wells, some 14 miles west of Builth Wells. As many of the Staff were Freemasons and, in order to continue their Masonic careers, they held their separate Lodge Meetings at Builth Wells Masonic Hall. Thus, this association gained strength, and regular visits are still made between the two Lodges.

On the momentous occasion of the Lodge Centenary, which took place on Monday, 30 April 1979, the Lodge Room was full to its capacity of 108. The Lodge was opened in the First Degree and the ProvGM, RWBro the Rt Hon the Lord Swansea, DL, accompanied by his Provincial Officers and Grand Lodge Officers, was admitted, welcomed and suitably received. After the Assistant Secretary, WBro Owen R Evans read the Lodge Warrant, the Secretary, WBro Harold J Bicknell, read the Minutes of the first Regular Lodge Meeting held on 29 April 1879. WBro Tudor Hopkins, PPGD, then gave a résumé of the history of the Lodge that he had compiled and with the printing made possible by the generosity of WBro Elmer E F Sayce, every Brother of the Lodge was issued with a copy. Later in the proceedings, a copy was presented to the ProvGM and a copy given to all the Provincial Officers present. The ProvGSec read the Centenary Warrant, which was then presented to the Lodge by the RWBro the Lord Swansea. In a speech, befitting the occasion, the WM also presented the ProvGM with a sherry decanter that had been cut and suitably inscribed by a young Builth craftsman, Mr David Williams. The Lodge was then closed in due form and with solemn prayer, the Brethren retiring from labour to refreshment to the supper room. Afterwards, a banquet was enjoyed at the Greyhound Hotel, Builth Wells, bringing to a close a very happy and enjoyable day.

'Dandelion Dead' was the title of a British TV mini-series produced in 1994. It told the true story of Herbert Rowse Armstrong, a practising solicitor in the provincial town of Hay-on-Wye, who, in May 1922, was convicted and hanged for the murder of his wife and the attempted murder of a fellow solicitor and business rival, Mr Oswald Martin.

Herbert Rowse Armstrong

The title of the film was derived from the fact that Armstrong used arsenic to carry out the evil deed, his excuse being that he bought it to kill dandelions in his garden. Most of the filming took place in and around Hay-on-Wye, but one section was filmed in Builth Wells. As Armstrong was a PM of Loyal Hay Lodge No.2382, now in the Province of Herefordshire, part of the plot centred on his Masonic career, with the requirement to film a small part of the Ceremony of opening a Lodge. The Loyal Hay Lodge Temple has an up-to-date décor and was unsuitable for this period drama, therefore arrangements, with suitable permissions granted, were made to use the Loyal Wye Lodge Temple, with its original décor and furniture. However, only Brethren of Loyal Hay Lodge featured in the filming. Further details of the Armstrong murder case are to be found later in this book, in the early history of Loyal Hay Lodge, which originally was in the Province of South Wales Eastern Division.

The piano, situated in the supper room, has replaced the one purchased more than fifty years earlier, and was presented to the Lodge by Mrs Bradley in memory of her late husband, WBro George L Bradley, PPGW. For many years, he was Lodge Organist. His accompaniment to various types of 'musical honours' at the Festive Board will never be forgotten. Their son, WBro Colin Bradley, is a senior and most respected Past Master, who is maintaining the family tradition.

It is very satisfying to register that interest in Freemasonry at Builth Wells continues unabated, and Fraternal visits continue with Brecknock and Ithon Lodges, the Mother and Daughter Lodges, as well as with Old Bromsgrovian Lodge.

Compiled from 'The first 100 years' by WBro Tudor Hopkins, PPrGD, by WBro W Malcolm Taylor, PPrGReg, with assistance from WBro W R Nicholas, PPrSGW.

The Temple in the West - Builth Wells

The annual subscription was set at £1.50. Lodges of Instruction were held twice monthly, sometimes three a month, and in June 1880, four Lodges of Instruction and one Regular Lodge Meeting were held. Lodge suppers were held quarterly in the Bear Hotel. As a Logo, the Lodge adopted the Crest of the former Cowbridge Borough Council in use until 1888. It depicts a cow, crossing from left to right, a three arch bridge.

The first Regular Meeting of the Lodge after the Consecration was held on 5 September 1879, when Mr Morgan Morgan, Boot and Shoemaker, was Initiated.

In 1880, WBro John Jones, PPGReg, PM Merlin Lodge, and a Cardiff Solicitor, who had opened the Lodge for the Consecration Meeting, became a Joining Member. In October of the following year, he succeeded WBro Titus Lewis to become the second WM of the Lodge.

It appears that the Lodge worked well for over ten years. The last Annual Return was received by Grand Lodge at the end of 1891 and the final registration of Candidates was in April 1892. In due course, the Grand Secretary wrote to the Lodge, which resulted in a reply, dated 13 February 1895, from Bro Sidney Gibson, Secretary, stating: *'that the Lodge had almost ceased to exist and owing to the non-attendance of members the meetings could not be held. On very many nights not more than three or perhaps four with the Tyler would attend. As a result it was thought desirable to adjourn for a time. Since then those that did not attend and take an interest in the Lodge are either dead or left the town.'* He further stated that, since the Consecration of the Lodge, no Almoner had been appointed and he (the Secretary) had paid out of his own pocket several pounds towards distressed Bethren and he could not see his way clear to pay the quarterly dues as well. The Lodge lapsed, then in 1909, the Provincial Grand Secretary raised the matter, finally writing to the Grand Secretary stating that he had been in correspondence with a Brother of the Cowbridge Lodge, who was unable to find the Lodge Charter. The first St Quintin's Lodge Charter was never found, despite extensive enquiries locally made by several Founders of St Quentin's Lodge No.4778, Consecrated on Friday, 30 October 1925. (Note the different spellings *Quintin's* and *Quentin's*).

No trace of further correspondence exists and the Lodge was Erased from the Register of Grand Lodge on 5 September 1923.

The loss of interest in St Quintin's Lodge may be attributable to the demise of WBro Titus Lewis. He retired as a Commercial Agent for S & J Watts, Manchester in 1887, with a good pension. A few weeks later, while staying with family in Llanstephan, he passed away in the early hours of Saturday, 10 September 1897. The Western Mail, of 12 September, published a fulsome Obitiuary, which included the following:

'The immediate cause of Mr Lewis's death was a serious attack of bronchitis, but his constitution had been seriously affected by blood poisoning arising from the bite of a rat some ten years ago, since which time Mr Lewis had never enjoyed such vigorous health as he did before.'

Compiled by WBro Peter M Davies, ProvJGW, with partial references from
'Freemasonry in Cowbridge, 1754 to 2000', by the late WBro Hubert Thomas, PPrJGW.

Tennant Lodge No.1992

Warranted : 20 February 1883

Consecrated : 10 October 1883

Meeting at the Masonic Hall, Cardiff.

On 21 December 1882, a Meeting was held in the Royal Hotel, Cardiff, for *'the purpose of considering the desirability of forming a new Lodge of Freemasons in Cardiff'*. Twenty-two Brethren attended - the WM and nineteen Brethren of Bute Lodge No.960, Bute Lodge being the Sponsoring Lodge, and a Brother from each of Glamorgan Lodge No.36 and Windsor Lodge No.1754. The meeting made the following decisions: the Lodge would be called 'Tennant Lodge' after the DepProvGM, WBro Marmaduke Tennant; the joining fee would be 1 guinea (£1. 05p); fees of honour would be - WM 1 guinea, the Wardens 10s 6d (52.5p) each, other Officers 5 shillings (25p) each. The Initiation fee was to be 7 guineas (£7. 35p) and the annual subscription 25 shillings (£1. 25p). The Lodge Meetings were arranged to be held on the second Thursday of every month at 7.30 pm.

The reason for forming the Lodge has been lost in the mists of time but it is known that many of the early Members were of seafaring origins. Some indication of this lies in the fact that at the December 1905 Meeting, the hymn, 'Eternal Father, Strong to Save', was sung prior to the closing of the Lodge and, in June 1906, three of the four Candidates were Merchant Mariners. It is not recorded why the Lodge Insignia was so chosen. The Latin Motto *'Vis Recte Vivere'* means *'To Live by the Law'* or *'Do you wish to live rightly?'*

A second meeting was held on 17 January 1883, when it was announced that arrangements had been made with the Joint Lodge Committee (consisting of Members of Glamorgan and Bute Lodges) to use the Masonic Hall, Working Street, Cardiff, at a rental of £30 per annum. It was announced that the DepProvGM ,WBro Marmaduke Tennant wished *'to thank the Lodge for the Honour of connecting his name therewith and that he had great pleasure in being thus associated with the new Lodge'*. Also, Brother Tarnish agreed to purchase the various articles required by the new Lodge at a discount, and was given permission to display them in his shop window prior to the Consecration!

On Wednesday, 10 October 1883, Tennant Lodge was Consecrated in the Masonic Temple, Working Street, Cardiff. RWBro Sir George Elliot,ProvGM, accompanied by the DepProvGM and the ProvGM for Monmouthshire, RWBro Col Charles Lyne, and his Deputy, WBro Captain Samuel George Homfray, were present. Sir George Elliot invited WBro Marmaduke Tennant to carry out the Ceremony of Consecration. The Minutes record *'The Lodge was then Consecrated according to the Ceremonies proper and usual on the occasion but not proper to be written'*. There were 28 Founder Members, 25 from Bute Lodge, 1 from Glamorgan, Lodge, 1 from Windsor Lodge and 1 from Silurian Lodge No.471, Newport. The Consecration Banquet was held at the Royal Hotel, Cardiff.

The first Regular Meeting of the Lodge was held on 8 November 1883, when Mr Joseph Henry Jones, a Solicitor of Duke Street, Cardiff, became the first Initiate of the Lodge. At the same Meeting, Bro Francis Pinney Adey, Master Elect of Windsor Lodge, became the first Joining Member. A call from labour to refreshment was made on the conclusion of the Initiation Ceremony and it is recorded *'that a most enjoyable half hour was spent by the Brethren in social and fraternal intercourse, the health of the WM, the WM Elect of the Windsor Lodge, and the newly initiated Brother having been proposed and received with acclamation'*.

At the January 1884 Meeting, WBro Marmaduke Tennant was made an Honorary Member of the Lodge. During the Meeting in May of that same year, he presented the Lodge with a photograph of himself indicating *'that as you now have my portrait my absence will be less felt as you will now have my shadow if not substance'*.

In March 1893, following numerous complaints regarding the poor condition of the Masonic Hall in Working Street, it was proposed that a Committee, representing Glamorgan, Bute and Tennant Lodges, look into the purchase of the Guildford Street Chapel and School for use as the new Masonic Hall. The following month, the Brethren of these three Lodges agreed to the purchase at a cost of £4,500.

A proposal was passed in January 1894 to form a Royal Arch Chapter to be associated with Tennant Lodge. St John's Chapter No.36 and Sir George Elliot Chapter No.960 gave the proposal their full support. It was decided to name the new Chapter 'Marmaduke Tennant' as Windsor Lodge, Penarth, had previously been granted a Charter in the name of 'Tennant Chapter'. The new Charter was granted on 2 May 1894.

A Festive Board at the completion of a Lodge Meeting was held for the first time in March 1894. Mr George Bull, an Organist, was Initiated at the April Meeting of the same year and was subsequently appointed PPrGOrg. He is the composer of the tune 'Hendre', which is used in the opening hymn.

Tennant Lodge's second Daughter Lodge, Llangattock Lodge No.2547, was Consecrated on 27 March 1895. Duke of York Lodge No.2453, had previously been Sponsored by Tennant Lodge in conjunction with Glamorgan Lodge, and Warranted on 21 November 1892, but was not Consecrated until 26 September 1915. The reason for the delay is explained in the history of Duke of York Lodge, in this book. A third Daughter Lodge was to follow with the Warranting of Cardiff Exchange Lodge No.3775, on 20 June 1916. The Petition had been formally signed in Open Lodge at the March Meeting.

On 10 January 1895, five members of Tennant Lodge were included in the Joint Lodge Committee running the Cardiff Masonic Hall. Representatives from Duke of York Lodge had previously joined the Committee, and later that year, representatives from Llangattock Lodge and Prince Llewellyn Lodge No.2570 were also included. The Cardiff Masonic Hall Committee was eventually dissolved in January 1910, and the running of the Cardiff Masonic Hall was vested in a Board of Directors of the newly formed 'Cardiff Masonic Hall Company'. WBro Thomas Matthews, WM, announced at the April 1895 Meeting that he was going to present one of the Wardens' Chairs for the new Masonic Hall, and encouraged others to follow his example. The last Lodge Meeting held at Working Street was on 12 September and the new Temple at Guildford Crescent was opened on 26 September 1895.

In May 1910, WBro William Lloyd, WM, and two Past Masters presented a Worshipful Master's Collar, of two rows of silver chains, between which are shields, bearing the names of the Past Masters. This Collar is still worn by the WM.

WBro Marmaduke Tennant died on 24 January 1915. He had been the DepProvGM for 38 eventful years. On 9 September of the same year a Mr Edgar Rutter was Initiated into the Lodge and so began one of the most illustrious Masonic careers in the history of this Province.

During WWI, it is interesting to note that Masonic Passports were issued to Brethren serving in the Armed Services. A copy of the one issued by WBro E R Paterson, WM, to Bro Arthur Morgan of Tennant Lodge is illustrated on the next page.

A Memorial to those Cardiff Brethren who made the Supreme Sacrifice in the Great War can be seen at the entrance to the Edgar Rutter Temple in Cardiff. The Memorial is inscribed with these words: *'TO THE EVER CHERISHED MEMORY OF THOSE MEMBERS OF THE CARDIFF LODGES WHO GAVE THEIR LIVES FOR THE CAUSE OF JUSTICE AND FREEDOM IN THE GREAT WAR 1914 - 1918. THIS TABLET IS GRATEFULLY ERECTED BY THEIR MASONIC BRETHREN.'* The Tennant Brethren were: D C Andrews, MM; S Gronhaug, MM; L H H Harris, MM; W G Pearn, MM; O T Thomas, MM; and G A Turner, EA. *'THEIR NAME LIVETH FOR EVERMORE'*.

During 1919, it was quite common for three Ceremonies to be worked in Lodges of Emergency and three such Meetings were held between the March and April Meetings of that year. The Notice for a Lodge of Emergency held in November cited 12 Candidates for Initiation, 15 for Passing and 3 for Raising and, in April 1920, 11 Candidates for Initiation, 8 for Passing and 10 for Raising were listed. The only way to cope with these numbers was by having frequent Lodges of Emergency. In the years 1919 to 1920, in addition to the ten Regular Lodges, there were 34 Lodges of Emergency!

In June 1925, a Petition was made by several Brethren to form the fourth Daughter Lodge, Carmel Lodge No.4774, which was Warranted on 2 September 1925. It was announced at this Meeting that Provincial Grand Lodge would be meeting under the Banner of Tennant Lodge at the Cardiff Masonic Temple, on 21 September 1925. A letter received from the ProvGSec stated that prior to that Meeting, the last recorded instance of the Provincial Grand Lodge meeting under a private Lodge Banner was on 24 July 1884, when it was held at the New Inn, Pontypridd, under the Banner of Merlin Lodge No.1578. In July 1934, Provincial Grand Lodge was again held under the Banner of Tennant Lodge when 335 Brethren were in attendance.

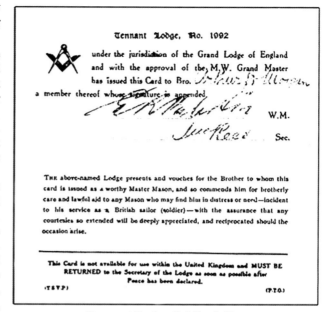

Tennant Lodge Soldier's Pass issued to Bro Arthur Morgan

The 50th Anniversary of the Meeting of the Lodge was held in October 1933, but does not appear to have been marked with any special function. A letter was read from WBro Edgar Rutter, DepProvGM, apologising for his absence, and explaining that he was attending the Installation of Loyal Wye Lodge. He congratulated the Lodge on attaining its Jubilee and stated that it was the largest Lodge in the Province, adding: *'Apart from wealth, the name you have established, the deeds you have achieved and the part you have sustained in the Masonic Life of our Province precludes you from taking a second place among our Lodges. See to it that you keep your first place'*. It was noted that he did return in time to join in the celebrations at the Festive Board. In November 1934, WBro Edgar Rutter was Installed as Master of Tennant Lodge. The ProvJGW presented him for Installation.

By 1936, it became established practice for the SW to deliver the Charge to the Initiate and present the Working Tools to the Fellow Craft, with the JW delivering the Charge to the Fellow Craft and presenting the Working Tools to the Initiate.

The Installation Meeting in November 1941 was the first occasion for a son to follow his father's footsteps to the Chair of King Solomon. WBro Douglas Ashton was Installed exactly ten years after his father, WBro Archibald Ashton.

In common with all the Lodges in South Wales the war years took their toll; in October, the death was reported of Bro Roy Pendle, who was killed while on active service with the RAF over Germany. In September 1945, the congratulations of the Lodge were sent to WBro Edgar Rutter in response to the news of the release of his son Bro John Rutter from a Japanese POW camp.

In 1946, the congratulations of the Lodge were also conveyed to WBro Edgar Rutter on his recent Investiture with the Order of Service to Masonry. The Investiture afforded Edgar Rutter the Rank of Very Worshipful Brother, a fitting accolade for such a charismatic Freemason. The Order is limited to 12 holders, confers no precedence on them, but entitles them to place the letters OSM after their names, preceding the initials of any other Masonic Rank they may hold. The Order is a neck decoration in the form of a Garter blue ribbon from which hangs the Jewel of the Order.

At the September Meeting in 1947, the Lodge representative on the catering committee reported that, as a result of a directive from the Ministry of Food, only one hundred meals per Lodge could be served because of food shortages and rationing! On the subject of rationing, there was a period when white gloves were not worn, but at the December Meeting of 1951, an instruction from UGLE was received stating that all Brethren were to wear white gloves from 1 January 1952. During this same year, the WM of the Lodge was congratulated on his 22nd year in Freemasonry, an indication of how long it took a Brother to reach the Chair of King Solomon during this era!

In 1954, Lodges of Emergency were held to Pass and Raise Bro Roy Keith Hopkin, who had been serving with the Royal Navy in Korea, thus, following his father, WBro 'Bill' Hopkin into the Lodge. In 1957, the Master Elect, Bro Edmund J Jones, was presented for Installation by his son, Bro Kenneth E Jones. He later Invested his blood brother, Albert Jones, as Senior Warden. WBro J T W Rowles was congratulated at the September Meeting in 1958 on reaching his Masonic Veteran status of 50 years Membership in the Craft. WBro Rowles then resumed the Traditional History, gave the lecture on the Third Degree Tracing Board and followed by explaining the Further Signs! In 1959, the death was reported of the Treasurer, WBro W James Smart, PProvSGW. He had given the Lodge 13 years service in this important role. Also in this year, Bro Fred W Fuse, the Lodge Organist, was appointed DepProvGOrg, and the Lodge presented him with his Regalia to mark this special occasion.

Moving into the 1960s, congratulations were in order when the Lodge Chaplain, WBro George E Serjent, celebrated his 90th birthday in February 1962. September 1965 was the 50th Anniversary of Edgar Rutter's Initiation into Tennant Lodge. To mark this very special occasion, WBro Harold Lloyd, WM, Invited RWBro Edgar Rutter to work the Initiation Ceremony, with the Provincial Officers. The AProvGM, WBro Harry Stockwell, delivered the Charity Charge. Mr Gwyndraeth Davies Thomas, the Initiate, must have been most impressed by the Ceremony on what was a most important night in the history of the Lodge. At the conclusion of the evening, a presentation of cut glass was made to RWBro Edgar Rutter from the Members of the Lodge. There were present, in addition to the DepProvGM, five Brethren with more than 50 years service to Freemasonry, including Bro H F Baker, a Co-Initiate with RWBro Edgar Rutter. In December 1965, the ProvGM resigned and RWBro Edgar Rutter became DepProvGM-in-Charge.

On 24 October 1966, the WM and a number of Brethren attended the Installation of RWBro the Rt Hon the Lord Swansea, DL, JGW, as ProvGM, at Sophia Gardens. At the March Meeting of this same year, the WM and the Brethren of the Lodge were delighted to receive the news that WBro A E Lemmer was appointed PGStB in United Grand Lodge.

At the Installation Festival in November 1967, the Master Elect, Bro Kenneth E Jones, was presented for Installation by his blood brother, Bro Bernard Jones. His father, WBro Edmund J Jones later gave the Address to his son. WBro J T W Rowles, senior PM, celebrated his 60th year in Freemasonry. In order to mark this auspicious occasion, he was invited to work a Third Degree Ceremony. RWBro Edgar Rutter visited the Lodge to add his congratulations to WBro Rowles. Sadly, WBro Rowles passed away in 1969, after a long and selfless service to Freemasonry.

Bro David Harries, SW, presented alms plates inscribed with the Lodge name and number at the December Meeting of 1969. Dr David Harries gave tremendous service to the Lodge and was a highly respected GP in the Heath area of Cardiff. He was later to become the Primus Master of Ymlaen Lodge No.8419. He had the distinction of being one of the first former pupils of Cathays High School to qualify in Medicine, and is fondly remembered by those Members of Ymlaen Lodge who had the privilege of knowing him.

The Annual Festival in 1970 was the last occasion that RWBro Edgar J Rutter attended Tennant Lodge. The following year, WBro Harry H Stadon, Installed as WM in 1939, reached the 50 years in Freemasonry milestone. Harry was presented with an Illuminated Address to mark this special occasion at the March Meeting in 1971. A Past Master's Jewel that had been presented to WBro A Maurice Bailey in 1899 was found among records in the basement of The Cardiff Masonic Hall in December 1976.

Sadly, at the April Meeting in 1978, the death was reported of the President of the Lodge of Instruction, WBro William 'Bill' Hopkin, PPrJGW, the father of WBro Roy. WBro Albert E Lemmer, ProvGStB, stepped in to act as President for the remainder of the year. At the May Meeting, a Certificate was presented to Bro F W Fuse, PProvDepGOrg, to commemorate his having achieved 50 years in Freemasonry and 37 years as Lodge Organist. Bro Fuse was Elected an Honorary Member of Tennant Lodge at the

October Meeting. Prior to the Installation Meeting in November, a scroll was presented to WBro Albert E Lemmer, to mark his 50 years in Freemasonry.

The death of WBro Rev Francis Rees, PPrJGW, was announced at the Meeting in January 1979. Although not a Past Master of Tennant Lodge, he had acted as Lodge Chaplain for many years, and was Chaplain at the time of his death. At the Annual Investiture of United Grand Lodge in April, WBro Albert E Lemmer was appointed PAGDC; while at the April Lodge Meeting, the death was reported of Bro E F W (Bob) Allsop. He had acted as Organist for many years at the Lodge of Instruction, and in later years despite very poor eyesight, had acted as Lodge Tyler. He wrote the words of the song sung at Tennant Lodge Festivals. The year ended on a happier note, for at the December Meeting, a scroll was presented to WBro H K (Bert) Myers on his attaining 50 years in Freemasonry within Tennant Lodge.

The 1980s opened with the 1,000th Regular Meeting of the Lodge, which was held on 10 January 1980. In June 1981, WBro RK Hopkin, RN, PPrJGW, was appointed ProvGDC and in 1982 he was promoted to ProvAGDC. Thus Roy followed in the footsteps of WBro George E. Serjent, Master of Tennant Lodge in 1925, who had also held similar Offices in the Province and Grand Lodge. A separate biographical profile of WBro Roy Hopkin appears later in this history book. In November 1982, the 100th Master of Tennant Lodge, WBro Dr David Hugh Evans was Installed. WBro Roy Hopkin was given the task of compiling a history for the Centenary Meeting to be held in October 1983. The foreword in the booklet, written by WBro Huw, described the task given to Roy as a labour of love! In May 1983, the Three Principals and 20 Companions of Marmaduke Tennant Chapter paid an official visit to the Lodge. To commemorate the Centenary, the Royal Arch Chapter presented a Senior and Junior Warden's Apron bearing the Badge of a Warden and the name and number of the Lodge. The Ladies' Festival had been held in March at Cardiff City Hall, where over two hundred enjoyed an excellent meal and an evening of dancing and celebration. The Centenary Meeting of Tennant Lodge was held on 13 October 1983, at the Masonic Hall, Cardiff.

On 9 April 1992, VWBro Roy Hopkin celebrated 40 years in Masonry. He was appointed DepProvGM in October 1992. On 12 May 1994 the Marmaduke Tennant Chapter celebrated its Centenary and the IPM, WM and the Wardens of Tennant Lodge donated a large Bible to the Chapter. WBro Phillip Humphreys donated a suitably engraved Staff, crafted by WBro Leslie Jeanes.

By 1999, the Lodge was in some difficulties because of falling Membership, a shortage of Candidates and poor attendance. This was in stark contrast to the Lodge returns for the year ending 31 December 1945, which indicated that Membership stood at 425, by far the largest Lodge in the Province at that time. However, since 2002, thanks to great efforts by Past Masters, seven new Members have been Initiated, five Past Masters and one Brother have become Joining Members and two Past Masters of the Lodge have re-joined. Thus it is felt that the Lodge has turned the corner and is now well on the way to recovery.

The April Meeting of 2002 was particularly eventful for the Members of Tennant Lodge, when two of their number who had been Initiated together on 10 April 1953, celebrated 50 years of continuous Membership of the Lodge. They were VWBro Roy Hopkin, PGSwdB, DepProvGM, and Bro John Lavery. WBro David Protheroe, PAProvGM, read the Agenda and Minutes of the Meeting held in 1952 and then presented the Certificates to commemorate their combined 100 years in Freemasonry. A very large number of guests was in attendance and the Members of the Lodge presented both Brethren with suitable mementos to mark their lengthy and happy association with Tennant Lodge.

At the December Meeting of 2003, WBro John Humphreys, PM, donated a complete set of Officers' Collars to the Lodge in memory of his beloved wife, Peggy, and in recognition of the support and encouragement he had received during her long illness. These Collars replaced many which belonged to a set donated in 1913.

WBro Ken Jones, PPrSGW, celebrated his 50 years of continuous Membership of Tennant Lodge in the Meeting of December 2006. The Ladies of Members of the Lodge and many other honoured guests attended the Festive Board and WBro Ken was duly presented with his 50 years in Freemasonry Certificate.

Compiled by VWBro Roy K Hopkin, RN, PDepProvGM,
with further additions by WBro Ken E Gummery, PPrJGW.

Barry Lodge No.2357

Warranted : 15 April 1890

Consecrated : 11 September 1890

Meeting at the Masonic Hall, Barry.

The history of Barry Lodge is closely associated with that of the town and docks. In the 1880s, the Trustees of the Marquis of Bute exercised a monopoly over the coal trade in South Wales with docks at Cardiff and Penarth. David Davies ('Davies the Ocean') and a number of fellow Rhondda colliery owners came together to solve the problem of congestion on the Taff Vale Railway and at Cardiff's Bute Docks. They promoted the construction of a railway from the coalfield to a new dock facility at Barry which, in 1881, consisted of the three small villages of Cadoxton-juxta-Barry, Merthyr Dyfan and Barry, with a combined population of only 478 residents. Despite fierce opposition from the Bute faction, the dock opened on 18 July 1889.

The first Managing Director of the Barry Dock Town Syndicate and the Barry Land Company was WBro George Thomas. He had been Initiated into Freemasonry in Glamorgan Lodge No.36 on 12 January 1877 and was Installed Worshipful Master of the Lodge on 26 June 1882. The Minutes of Glamorgan Lodge for 8 November 1889 record that WBro George Thomas appeared before the Brethren to ask the support of the Lodge in the formation of a new Lodge at Barry, when it was unanimously agreed *'That the Glamorgan Lodge authorise the WM and Wardens to sign the Petition for a Warrant of Constitution for the Barry Lodge.'* Bute Lodge No.960 and Windsor Lodge No.1754 also supported the Petition.

The Petition was successful, and on Thursday 11 September 1890 the Consecration of Barry Lodge took place at the Dunraven Hall, opposite Cadoxton Railway Station, Vere Street, Cadoxton-juxta-Barry, at precisely twelve noon.

The Consecrating Officer was the DepProvGM, Marmaduke Tennant and WBro George Thomas, PPrGSuptWks was Installed as the Primus Master. The Ceremony was followed at 5.00 pm by a banquet, held at the Picnic Hall, Royal Hotel, Cadoxton, at a cost of 6s/6d (32.5p) per head, exclusive of wine.

Of the seventeen Founder Members, three Lodges, namely: Glamorgan, Bute and Windsor, truly formed the nucleus of the newly formed Barry Lodge. Their names are shown on the original Petition, the cost of which was the then princely sum of £12.12s.6d.

Within ten years, the decision was taken to move the Lodge from the Royal Hotel, Cadoxton, to rooms 15, 16, and 17, situated on the second floor of the Barry Hotel, Barry. These rooms had been prepared for the exclusive use of Barry Lodge. Rooms 16 and 17 were converted into one large room at the expense of the hotel owners. The rent payable by the Lodge by equal quarterly payments was £30.00 per annum, the agreement to run from June 1900, with coal and gas included in the rent. One of the main reasons for the proposed move was that the number of Brethren in the Lodge had risen from 17 Founder Members in 1890 to 120 Brethren in 1900.

In 1904, with the lease of the Lodge Rooms at the Barry Hotel due to expire in June 1905, the Lodge Committee considered a letter from W H Hancock & Co Ltd, the owners of the Barry Hotel, that they were prepared to renew the lease for three years, subject to the rental being increased from £30 to £50 per annum. After a lengthy discussion, the full renewal of the lease was rejected and a sub-committee was formed for the purpose of building a Masonic Hall. In January 1905, it was agreed to accept the offer from Hancock's, of a 999 year lease, at a ground rent of £10 per annum with an option to purchase, for a plot of land adjacent to the Barry Hotel. A Trust Company was then formed, Bro J A Owen was appointed as Architect and after further meetings, it was agreed to accept the tender from Mr W T Morgan of Cardiff for the building of the Masonic Hall at a cost of £2,625. 1s. 0d. The Lodge eventually purchased the land in 1924.

The Installation Meeting of 1905 should have been held on 10 October, but the Secretary was instructed to apply for a Dispensation to alter the date to 16 October, to coincide with the laying of the Foundation Stone of the new Masonic Hall. He also sought permission for the wearing of Masonic Jewels and Regalia outside the building during the Ceremony, which was performed by the Provincial Grand Master, The Lord Llangattock, assisted by the DepProvGM, WBro Marmaduke Tennant. A very full and comprehensive account of the day's activities was reported, not only in the Lodge Minutes, but also in the 'Barry Dock News', the local newspaper. The Meeting itself was a great success with some 236 persons attending. The last Regular Meeting of The Lodge at the Barry Hotel was on 13 March 1906.

Barry Lodge has always held a close association with those who go down to the seas in ships. At the Election Night Meeting in 1905, it is recorded in the Minutes that the WM congratulated Bro C W Vine on his being *'Up and about again and able to attend the Lodge after his severe illness in endeavouring to save a person from drowning on Barry Island.'* The Minutes of 13 February 1906 record: *'The Worshipful Master stated that he had received notification that a Brother of The Barry Lodge, Bro C T Pratt, had lost his life by drowning in an attempt to save his ship by swimming ashore with a line. He was swept back because of the rough sea and was stunned against the stern of the vessel. His body was not recovered.'*

At the Meeting on 8 April 1919, it was agreed that Barry Lodge should Sponsor the formation of a new Lodge in Barry. The following month, on 13 May, a Deputation, led by WBros Arthur Llewellyn Hopkins, PM Glamorgan Lodge No.36, (WM Designate); George Wareham, PM (SW Designate) and Bro E R Hinchcliffe (JW Designate) was received and the Petition for the first Daughter Lodge, Vale of Glamorgan Lodge No.3977 was duly signed.

Also during 1919, it was decided that it was necessary to purchase a new organ. It was proposed that the organ be presented to the Lodge as a 'Peace Offering' marking the end of the First World War. In September, WBro George Wareham asked the WM to accept the newly installed organ, which had been purchased on the guarantee of about forty Brethren. Then, on 14 October, WBro William Graham, PM, PPrAGSec, presented a Banner to the Lodge, also as a 'Peace Offering'.

The Temple organ was pumped manually until 1932, when Bro George White of Whites Shows, Barry Island, presented an electric motor for the purpose of working the bellows. He also presented a Volume of the Sacred Law to the Lodge.

The organ remained in use until 2004, when a substantial amount of money was required for its repair. An 'Organ Appeal' was launched, and many Brethren and Lodges contributed. Unfortunately, the engineer's report was so disappointing that it was decided to forego the restoration and all monies were returned, with grateful thanks to the subscribers. Nevertheless, it was decided to keep the beautiful façade and pipe layout. The problem with the organ was finally resolved when a new electronic organ was very generously donated by WBro E T Wood, PPrSGW ('Ted' Wood), Past Master of Vale of Glamorgan Lodge, *'To celebrate over 55 years in Freemasonry'* in November 2000.

WBro George Wareham was the first Initiate of the Lodge to become a Grand Lodge Officer, when in 1927 he was Invested with the Collar of PAGDC of the United Grand Lodge of England. This Honour was soon followed by that of PGStB in Supreme Grand Chapter. In total, 10 Brethren have become Grand Officers in the Craft.

The Ship's Bell

On 13 April 1938, the FSI Committee agreed that an engraved plate, suitably inscribed, be affixed to the Ship's Bell which had been presented to Barry Lodge by Captain George Matthew Hudson of the Merchant Navy. It was further agreed that *The Bell shall be struck at all After-meetings of the Lodge*. Ever since, it has been the custom for Barry Lodge to place the Ship's Bell in front of the Worshipful Master's seat at the high table. At or near 22.00 hours, during the Festive Board, it is customary to drink a Toast to all 'Absent Brethren', and to strike four bells on the Ship's Bell.

Whenever a new Initiate joins Barry Lodge the following 'History of the Ship's Bell', as recounted by the late Bro George Hudson, Master Mariner, is delivered.

'In 1936 I was lying in the port of Abu Zenima in the Sinai Peninsula with Mount Sinai in the distance. One morning when ashore on ship's business, I watched the British Manager of the firm for whom I was taking a cargo, as he cast a cover for a valve on one of the locomotives. When he tested the casting for cracks it emitted a beautiful bell-like sound and I intimated to him that I would like a Bell of the same metal.

When he found out the use to which the Bell would be put, he gladly undertook the task, and put twenty-one pounds of Bell Metal into the casting.   He then made himself known as a Past Master of a Lodge in Bedford.

The Bell finally came to rest in The Barry Lodge in July 1938.'

In December 2002, the Bell was completely stripped, cleaned and polished by WBro Don Oliver, himself a past member of the Merchant Navy, and a Member of Penarth Lodge No.4113.

At its Meeting on 8 June 1939, the FSI Committee considered the question of celebrating appropriately the coming Jubilee Year of Barry Lodge, and agreed that the event should be suitably marked. It was proposed that the celebration should be held, by Special Dispensation, on the 11 September 1940.   However, at 11.15 am on 3 September the Prime Minister, Mr Neville Chamberlain, broadcast from Downing Street the announcement that Great Britain was at war with Germany.

The effect of the War was quickly brought home to the Lodge when, at the December 1939 Meeting, it was announced that the Master of the SS 'Trevanian', recently reported as not having reached port and, therefore, presumed lost at sea, was a Member of Barry Lodge, namely Bro J A Edwards. Thankfully, at the January Meeting, news was reported of Bro J A Edwards who, whilst his ship had, indeed, been sunk by enemy action, was himself safe and looking forward to returning to his home port of Barry. Barry Docks lost more Merchant Seamen in the Second World War than any other seaport of comparable size in Britain. Because of the conditions then pertaining and after consultation with the DepProvGM, the proposed celebration of the Fiftieth Anniversary of the Lodge was abandoned.

Many Lodge Meetings received reports of Brethren being killed, missing in action or taken prisoner. Sometimes, a happier note was sounded when a Brother presumed lost was reported to be alive and well, albeit a Prisoner of War. In all, eight Brethren made the Supreme Sacrifice and three were severely disabled. Amongst these reports to the Lodge, there were those of congratulations being extended to Bro C A Gentles, Master Mariner who had received the honour of the OBE and Lloyd's Medal for sinking an enemy submarine; Bro J Lewis, Master Mariner, awarded the OBE and Soviet Star; Bro Gordon L Bastian, Chief Engineer, awarded the MBE, the Albert Medal and the Lloyd's Medal for saving life when his ship was torpedoed; Bro W G Rogers for Distinguished Conduct at Sea; Bro J R Woods, BEM, and also to Bro James A Edwards, who had received the Lloyd's Medal for Distinguished Conduct at Sea in connection with the 'Graf Spee' incident in the Battle of the River Plate.

At a Regular Lodge held on 10 February 1948, it was agreed to Sponsor the formation of a New Lodge, to be named 'Old

Barrians Lodge', which was intended as a Schools' Lodge, exclusively for Old Barrians and Staff of Barry County School. The Petition was presented on 9 March by WBro JW Lennox (WM Designate) and duly signed. The Warrant for Barry Lodge's second Daughter Lodge was granted on 5 May 1948.

In 1960, it was pointed out that some Lodges were charging for drinks at the Festive Board, and others might wish to do so. It was further pointed out that this was illegal and could only be legalised by the possession of a licence. Consequently, proposed rules for a licensed dining club were presented, but there was a considerable divergence of opinion between those who did not desire to be associated with any licensed club, and those who felt that Members should automatically become members of the club. After considerable discussion, a resolution was placed before the Meeting that the Trust Committee proceed with arrangements for obtaining a licence, and that draft rules for the club be circulated.

At a Meeting of Barry Lodge Committee on 24 April 1979, at the request of the Lodge Secretary, WBro T Bishop raised the matter of the Tyler's Toast. It appears that at a Meeting of the Lodge of Instruction, a Member from another Barry Lodge stated that the phrase *'And in the Air'* should not be included in the Toast. At a Committee Meeting some years previously, it had been decided and approved that Barry Lodge should keep to its traditional Toast out of consideration for members of the Royal Air Force and Airline Pilots. The matter was discussed once again at the Committee Meeting held on 12 June, and it was confirmed that Barry Lodge would retain the phrase '*And in the Air*'.

The Meeting of the 10 January 1984 was not only the first of the New Year, but one of the most memorable occasions in the history of the Lodge. The Lodge having been opened, and visiting Brethren admitted, the ProvGM, the Rt Hon the Lord Swansea, DL, entered the Lodge, escorted by the ProvGDC and Provincial Grand Lodge Officers. The arrival of the Most Worshipful Pro Grand Master, the Rt Hon Lord Cornwallis, OBE, DL, was then announced. The Pro Grand Master then entered the Lodge, escorted by the Grand DC, VWBro Phillip Ashley Mann, TD, the Deputy Grand Secretary, WBro John Geoffrey Ross Guy and WBro G Holtam, PGStB, the Mandated Officer of Barry Lodge. The Worshipful Master welcomed the Pro Grand Master and proffered the Gavel, which was returned with thanks. He was then greeted under the direction of the Grand DC. An Initiation Ceremony then followed, and in the Centennial History of Barry Lodge it is recorded: *'The entire ceremony was complimentary to the Barry Lodge No. 2357.'*

In reporting cases of illness at the Regular Lodge Meeting on the 11 May 1982, it was mentioned that the son of Bro E T Williams was a survivor of HMS Sheffield, which was sunk off The Falklands, and although he suffered from shock and concussion, he was now improving in health.

The Centenary of the Lodge was celebrated by Special Dispensation on Friday, 28 September 1990 at the Masonic Temple, Barry. Whilst the Lodge was disappointed that due to unforeseen circumstances, Lord Swansea was unable to attend, the Lodge was honoured by the presence of VWBro Geoffrey M Ashe, DepProvGM. Among the distinguished guests were WBro Cdr Roy K Hopkin, AProvGM; WBro J S Peters, AProvGM; and WBro C L Summers, PAProvGM. The DepProvGM, accompanied by Officers of Grand Lodge and Provincial Grand Lodge, having been admitted, Mr John Strain was Initiated into the Mysteries and Privileges of Ancient Freemasonry. Following the Initiation Ceremony, the Secretary was requested to read the Warrant of the Lodge, granted on 15 April 1890 and also the Minutes of the Consecration of the Lodge, held on the 11 September, 1890. During the Meeting, a Presentation Case containing a complete set of Working Tools was presented to the Lodge by the Worshipful Master, WBro Owen Gibbon. Also, the Worshipful Master presented the DepProvGM with a cheque for £2,357.00 as a contribution to the Provincial Benevolent Fund and the 1991 South Wales Eastern Division Festival.

The Petition for the third Daughter Lodge, Loyal Sportsman Lodge No.9197 was signed on 11 March 1986. The Deputation was led by WBro Ronald Winston Boon, PPrSGD, PM Old Barrians Lodge No.6671 (WM Designate); WBro David Samuel Davies, PPrAGStdB, PM Barry Lodge (SW Designate) and WBro Gordon John Watkins, WM Old Barrians Lodge (JW Designate). The Warrant was granted on 1 May 1986.

In 1993, another landmark was achieved with the 1,000th Meeting of the Lodge, when the Worshipful Master was delighted and honoured to welcome the ProvGM to both the Meeting and the Festive Board which followed.

Grateful thanks and appreciation must be made to the late WBro Leonard Norman Albert Davies, CStJ, MA, MBIM, PPrGStdB (Shropshire) of Idsall Lodge No.7133, Shifnal and PM Barry Lodge, for his outstanding contribution to the History of Barry Lodge, as the author of 'The Centennial History of the Barry Lodge No. 2357, 1890-1990'.

Before closing this account of the Lodge, two more names must be mentioned, those of WBro Raymond Blake Teagle, TD, PPrSGW, who was Chairman of the Barry Masonic Hall Trust Company , 1971-2001; and WBro Alan Ford Thomas, PPrJGW, Lodge Secretary who, in October 1998, resigned after thirteen years of devoted service to the Lodge. Recently, Bro 'AFT' has not enjoyed the best of health, and it was only fitting that at the April 2007 Regular Lodge Meeting, the Ballot proved unanimously in favour of him being made an Honorary Member of the Lodge.

Compiled by Trevor Thompson, PPrGReg, Secretary.

The Temple in the West - Barry

Loyal Hay Lodge No.2382

Warranted : 17 September 1890

Consecrated : 25 November 1890

Meeting at the Masonic Hall, Hay-on-Wye.

As a border town, the history and development of Hay on Wye has always been influenced by its geographical remoteness. The railway line from Hereford was not available until 1863 and motor coach services were not introduced until the early 1930s. In modern times, it is much to its credit that it has the reputation of being the centre of the national second hand book trade and for its annual Festival of the Literary Arts.

The early discussions about the formation of a new Lodge in Hay on Wye began on 31 July 1890, when 11 prospective Founders met at the Wine Vaults. They were Members of The Brecknock Lodge No.651, meeting in Brecon, and in due course they Petitioned Grand Lodge for a Warrant of Constitution. It had been suggested to name the new Lodge '*Wyeside*', but at a further meeting on 7 August, it was unanimously agreed to adopt the name '*Loyal Hay Lodge*'. During this meeting, the local Doctor, Bro Hinks, announced that he would present Skull and Crossbones to the Lodge, which the Lodge still possesses.

The Warrant of Constitution was signed on 17 September 1890 and the Consecration Ceremony took place on 25 November, when WBro John Tudor, a Brecon Solicitor and Past Master of Brecknock Lodge, became the first Worshipful Master. At this inaugural meeting, two Joining Members were Elected and four Candidates were proposed and seconded.

The new Lodge first met in the old Town Hall, above the Butter Market, having taken the premises on a five year lease, but where they were to remain for some 18 years. In November 1908, the Lodge was offered, and accepted, a 21 year lease at a rental of £7.00 per annum, at new and better premises at Bank Chambers, above the United Counties Bank in Broad Street. This Bank had been formed from an amalgamation of various Banks in 1907 and became Barclays Bank in 1917. The Lodge remained at these premises for the next 65 years.

Two names of Worshipful Masters from the first quarter of the 20th Century have become immortalised within the Lodge. WBro C E Tunnard Moore founded the Herefordshire Masonic Golfing Competition, and is widely remembered for his charitable work and for presenting the cup, which is competed for each year by the Lodges. Loyal Hay Lodge continues to provide the miniature cups which are retained by the winners, and presented by the Provincial Grand Master at the Annual Meeting of the Herefordshire Masonic Charity Association in June.

On a more infamous note, WBro H Rowse Armstrong, the notorious 'Hay Poisoner', and whose presence in a group photograph hanging within the Lodge room, attracts much interest from visitors to Loyal Hay. In October 1913, Brother Major Herbert Rowse Armstrong, TD, MA, a local Solicitor, and local Clerk to the Magistrates of Hay was Installed as Worshipful Master. He was a loyal, regular and attentive Member of the Lodge in which he served for some years as Director of Ceremonies. On 31 December 1921, however, he gained public notoriety when he was arrested and charged with unlawfully administering arsenic with intent to murder a fellow solicitor and Freemason, Oswald Norman Martin. The police cell in which he was kept is still known today as *'Armstrong's Cell'*. His wife had died on 22 February 1921, and her body was subsequently exhumed for clinical examination, the outcome of which resulted in WBro Armstrong also being charged for her murder, by arsenic poisoning. He was tried at Hereford Assizes, found guilty and was sentenced to be hanged, which was carried out at Gloucester Gaol. The detail and circumstances have been well publicised in several books and films and at the time of its hearing in 1922, became a classic and sensational murder case. At the time, he was the only British Solicitor to have been hanged for murder. There is a wide body of well informed people today who consider he was wrongly sentenced and that the evidence against him was largely circumstantial. Masonically, he must stand alone as being the proposer of a Candidate for Initiation, whilst he himself was under arrest for the attempted murder of Bro Martin, who happened to be the Candidate's seconder.

Poor and unreliable communication within Wales proved a difficulty and, in 1920, the Lodge applied to be transferred from the Province of South Wales Eastern Division to Herefordshire. The respective Provincial Grand Masters having given their consent, Grand Lodge authorised the transfer in a letter dated 25 November 1920. Brother Harry Morris was the first Master to be Installed under the Herefordshire jurisdiction. This move enabled Members to attend more easily Provincial Grand Lodge Meetings, and to a large extent overcame the difficulty often experienced by Members in travelling to and from Hay on Wye, when visiting other Lodges.

On 17 January 2000, the Deputy Provincial Grand Master of Herefordshire, WBro E Beasey, JP, accompanied by Officers of Provincial Grand Lodge attended the Lodge in order to dedicate the new Hay Masonic Temple and the new Lodge Banner. Among the distinguished guests were RWBro A S C Blench, Past ProvGM for Herefordshire; RWBro P A Marsh, ProvGM for Gloucestershire and RWBro Hywel Davies, ProvGM for South Wales Eastern Division, together with their respective Deputies. Work to enlarge the original building had been in hand for several years and was almost complete. It was an achievement brought about by the co-operation and dedication of the Members, who could well be proud and pleased with the result. In Dedicating the Banner, reference was made to RWBro Peter Marsh who had made it. The Worshipful Master expressed the appreciation of the Lodge and thanked Peter for such a splendid result.

The Banner design includes an illustration of the Gateway to the ruined portion of Hay Castle as seen from the Memorial Square in Castle Street. This structure is almost directly opposite the old Butter Market, where the Lodge originally met. The Motto is, *'In Haia Salus'*, which translates as *'There is Safety in Hay'*. This translation is not intended to reflect the sort of safety that might be felt when sheltering behind the fortified walls of a castle. The Latin word, *'Salus'*, may be interpreted to mean *'health'*, as in being morally, spiritually or mentally sound as in well being, safety, deliverance and being wholesome. It may also be construed as *'Salutary'* (salutaris) as in greeting, good wishes, respect and courteous recognition. A visitor to Loyal Hay Lodge, having regard to all these inherent qualities which are evident in the Fraternity, and having experienced the warmth of friendship and hospitality of the Brethren, will take his leave feeling that he has experienced a little of each. Not the least of his impressions will be that in their company he was always safe from harm.

(Adapted from 'A History of Craft Freemasonry in Herefordshire 1727-2000', by Alwyn D Williams, published by the Provincial Grand Lodge of Herefordshire.)

Compiled by WBro Peter M Davies, ProvJGW,

Duke of York Lodge No.2453

Warranted : 21 November 1892
Consecrated : 26 September 1895
Meeting at the Masonic Hall, Cardiff.

September 26 1895 marks an historic Masonic landmark in Cardiff Freemasonry, for on that day the new Masonic Temple, Guildford Crescent, Cardiff was officially opened and immediately followed by the Consecration of Duke of York Lodge. The Ceremonies were conducted by RWBro Lord Llangattock, ProvGM, assisted by WBro Marmaduke Tennant, DepProvGM. The Sponsoring Lodge was Tennant Lodge No.1992 in conjunction with Glamorgan Lodge No.36, though 9 of the 12 Petitioners were Members of Bute Lodge No.960.

Whilst Duke of York Lodge was Warranted on 21 November 1892, the Consecration was delayed for almost three years, due to difficulties in obtaining permission from HRH the Duke of York, to use his Royal Title. The death of the Provincial Grand Master, Sir George Elliot, on 23 December 1893, also played a part in this delay. The Lodge was finally Consecrated on 26 September 1895.

It may be noted that Llangatock Lodge No.2547, with a later Warrant, dated 18 January 1895, was Consecrated on 27 March 1895, before Duke of York Lodge. A further explanation of this apparent anomaly is given in the following correspondence:

'The Craftsman   April 1901

To the Editor of the Craftsman

Dear Sir,

In your current issue, under the heading 'Craflets' appears the following: - Wor. Bro Marmaduke Tennant mentioned the singular fact that the 'Duke of York Lodge' was named after Royalty who was not a Freemason. To avoid any misunderstanding, may I be permitted to point out that on the formation of the Lodge, the Grand Secretary declined to place the Petition before the Grand Master until His Royal highness, the Duke of York had given direct permission to use the title, and only on production of the written permit did the Grand Secretary present the Petition for signature. The name 'Duke of York' was not used or appropriated haphazard (ly), but was obtained with difficulty. Being personally responsible for so designation of the Lodge, I do not wish anyone to imagine that the founders of the 'Duke of York' Lodge appropriated the title without paying

that need of courtesy which is due to our Royal House.
Yours fraternally, Steffano Vorzopollo, PM, PPGW, Cardiff, March 13th, 1901.'

At first sight, it appears strange that the Founders should choose the name 'Duke of York' for their new Lodge, particularly when he was not a Freemason. While the Founders were planning the formation of the new Lodge, on 24 May 1892, Queen Victoria announced that she was creating her grandson, Prince George Frederick Ernest Albert, Duke of York. The title had not been used since the death of Queen Victoria's uncle, Prince Frederick, in January 1827. Further, the new Duke of York was the second son of the MW the Grand Master, HRH Edward Prince of Wales. The first son, Prince Albert Victor, had died a few months earlier, leaving Prince George second in line to the throne. These events would have been headline news at the time.

With the death of Queen Victoria in 1901, the Prince of Wales became King Edward VII and, consequently, had to relinquish his position as Grand Master. Following his death in 1910, the Duke of York became King George V. The illustrated portrait of King George V hangs in the Mansion House, Cardiff. It was painted by WBro George Frederick Harris, grandfather of the Australian Artist and Entertainer, Rolf Harris. WBro George was an Initiate of Loyal Cambrian Lodge No.110, Merthyr, and was the Primus Master of Fforest Lodge No.2606, Treharris, Consecrated on 26 October 1896.

The first Master of Duke of York Lodge was WBro Charles Edwin Dovey, PProvJGW, who had been Installed WM of Bute Lodge No.960 in 1891. Separate biographical details of WBro Charles Dovey, PProvJGW, are given

HM King George V

elsewhere in this book. The Installing Master was WBro Marmaduke Tennant. Both the ProvGM and the DepProv GM were afterwards made Honorary Members of Duke of York Lodge, on a show of hands.

A description of part of the Installation Ceremony was give in 'The Craftsman', Volume II, October 1895, as follows: *'The Lodge was opened in the Third Degree. The DepProvGM and six Past Masters, afterwards adjourned for the purpose of holding a Board of Installed Masters, when the WM Designate was tested as to his knowledge of the secrets of an Installed Master. On the return of the DepProvGM , the RWProvGM ascertained and was assured by the DepProvGM that the WM Designate was well skilled in the science of Freemasonry. The WM was afterwards placed in the Chair of KS by the RWProvGM and after being saluted as WM, closed the Lodge in the Third Degree, and then in the Second. The newly-elected WM appointed and Invested his Officers as follows: ......'*

IPM: WBro William Charles Peace, PPSGW, WM of Bute Lodge in 1884; SW: WBro James Radley, PPGDC, WM of Bute Lodge in 1888; JW: WBro Charles Carey Thomas, PPGDC, WM of Bute Lodge in 1889; Secretary: WBro William Best Ferrier, PPGReg, WM of Bute Lodge in 1892; Treasurer: WBro John Thomas Hogg, PPGTreas, WM of Tennant Lodge in 1892; and DC: WBro John Munday, PPJGW, WM of Bute Lodge in 1887.

Following the Ceremonies, upwards of 250 Brethren dined at the banquet held at the Assembly Rooms of the Town Hall (in St

Mary Street), served by Bro W G Hunt, of the Queen's Hotel, Westgate Streeet, Cardiff.

Charles Dovey was to be the first of many famous Masters of Duke of York Lodge - all of whose signatures may be found on a unique roll of Past Masters in the ante room of the Lord Swansea Temple.

Included amongst the names of Past Masters can be found WBro S M Wilkinson, PPrGW, (WM in 1904) and WBro R H Seel, PPrGW, (WM in 1907) well known Cardiff Auctioneers and Estate Agents. Between them, they served the Lodge as Treasurers from 1917 to the early 1950s. The noted Masonic Ritualist and Historian, WBro Rev J Sansam Iles, PPrGChap, was Master in 1932 and still President of the Lodge of Instruction in 1951. WBro T John Evans, OBE, PPrGD, an Oxford scholar and Chief Inspector of Schools in Wales, was Master in 1941.

The two World Wars saw Brethren from Duke of York Lodge giving their lives whilst serving in HM Forces. Three Brethren died in World War I and seven, including a civilian, in WWII.

WBro W J Foster, MC, PPrGW, affectionately known as 'Tiny Foster', was the Master in 1934, and later became Secretary, holding the Office for eleven years. During WWI, he was decorated with the Military Cross, as was WBro Douglas Worgan, MC, PPrGD, who was Master in 1963. WBro R J Hedley, PPrGW, served as Treasurer from 1953 to 1964; he and WBro 'Tiny Foster' were a formidable pair. On 21 March 1950, WBro R J Hedley occupied the Chair to Initiate his son John, who held an executive position with the railway in Southern Rhodesia, and became Master of Msasa Lodge No.6802 (Erased in 2003) in that country and later held the Rank of PDistGStdB, (Rhodesia - now Zimbabwe).

WBro Edward James Smith, PGStdB, the Master of the Lodge in 1959 ,was also a Past Master of Hendre Lodge No.3250, the Lodge of Unity No.6030 and Installed as the first Master of St Cecilia Lodge No.8748, on 1 March 1977. In addition to being Organist of Duke of York Lodge, he was Organist of several other Lodges and also conducted the Guildford Singers. This octet sang the anthems at the Consecration Ceremonies of approximately thirty-five Lodges. He also conducted the Rumney and St Mellons British Legion Choir, which was honoured to perform at the Festival of Remembrance at the Royal Albert Hall, London, in 1961.Further biographical details are to be found in the history of St Cecilia Lodge.

During the first hundred years, four Past Masters of the Lodge were appointed Grand Officers, namely, C E Dovey, W C Jolliffe, PGStdB, E J Smith and Roland Parker, PAGDC.

WBro Roland was Charity Steward of the Lodge for sixteen years, and has held the Office of Chaplain for many years. He is also active in other Degrees, being a Supreme Grand Chapter Officer and served as Intendant General of the Red Cross of Constantine for South Wales and Monmouthshire from 1983 to 1991.

For many years, each Lodge was responsible for supplying its own drinks at the Festive Board. During that time, WBros Ernest James, PPrGD, (WM in 1961) and Stanley M Kendal, PPrSGW, (WM in 1962) were Transport Managers of Hancock's and Brains Breweries respectively. The Duke of York Brethren drank Hancock's and Brains beers on alternate years, and much mirth was derived over the merits and strengths of the different brews!

Seven Brethren have occupied the Master's Chair for two years: H C Bolter, 1940/41; R E Takel, PPrJGW, 1965/66; Frank Parsons, PPrJGW, 1973 and 1988; M I Swetman, PPrJGD, 1990/1991; John Beasley, PPrSGD,1992 and 2008; Alan Gardener, PAGSupWks, 1997/1998; and R A Willett, PProvGStwd, 2004/2005.

Famous people who were Members of the Lodge include the Sculptor, Bro Sir William Gascombe John, RA, and Bro Meurig Evans. The former, who was a brother of the Artists Gwen and Augustus John, designed the Lodge's Past Master's Jewel. This design was based on a ducal crown and the white rose of York. Sir William's works include an equestrian figure of Edward VII in Liverpool; Viscount Wolseley, Horse Guards Parade; and Prince Christian Victor at Windsor. He was also responsible for the memorial to Sir Arthur Sullivan in St Paul's Cathedral as well as for many of the fine statues that can be seen in Cardiff City Hall, including one of St David. Numerous examples of his work are to be found in the National Museum of Wales, Cardiff. Bro Meurig Evans achieved fame as a Judge on the North Wales circuit.

WBro E J Hobbs, PPrJGW, served as Lodge Secretary from 1967 to 1979. At the Regualr Meeting on 17 January 1984, he occupied the Chair in celebration of his thirty years as a Past Master of the Lodge. In recognition of his many years' service to the Lodge, he was made an Honorary Member, as were E J Smith and A V Jones, PPrAGDC, the latter travelling regularly from Devon in his retirement, to play the organ at Lodge Meetings.

The Hill family has played a prominent part in Duke of York Lodge during the last forty years. WBro Harry Hill, PPrGStdB, was proposed into the Lodge by his brother-in-law, WBro Herbert G Vodden, PPrGStdB, and Initiated on 17 February 1953. In 1967, he was Installed as Master, during which year he presented the Lodge Banner in memory of his dear wife. The Banner was Dedicated by WBro Harry F Stockwell, DepProvGM. WBro Alfred Ivor Hill, PPrGOrg, was Initiated on 18 May 1954, having been proposed by his blood brother WBro Harry Hill. Alfred was appointed Lodge Organist in 1955 and Installed as Master in 1970. In 1976, he was appointed ProvGOrg. WBro Vivian Hill, PPrJGW, was Initiated on 20 December 1960, having been proposed and seconded by his father, WBro Harry Hill, and his uncle, WBro Alfred Hill, respectively. Vivian was Installed as Master in 1974, and in 1979 he became Secretary of the Lodge, and continued to serve in this position until 1997. In 1980, he was appointed ProvAGDC and promoted to PPrJGW in 1986. He was also a Founder Member of Croeso Lodge No.8377. Last, but not least, WBro David Roy Hill, PPrAGDC, Harry Hill's son and Vivian's brother, was Initiated into the Lodge in 1968. Roy subsequently became a Founder Member of Ystrad Mynach Lodge No.8567 and became its Master in 1979.

Bro T J Gwynne Williams, PPrGStwd, better known as 'Gwynne the Bank', was Initiated in 1969 and took over the position of Treasurer from WBro Reginald Pickett, PPrAGReg, PPrGW, (Mon), in October 1981 until 1997. In recognition of his good work in Freemasonry, he was made a PPrGStwd in June 1986. This was a singular honour for both Gwynne and the Lodge, as he was the first Member of the Lodge to gain Provincial Rank, without being Installed in the Master's Chair. In 1991, Bro Desmond Harding was similarly honoured.

At one time, to build up the strength of the Lodge, the Masters had a strenuous time performing two and three Ceremonies on the same evening. One older Member recalls being one of five Initiates, one of nine for his Passing and one of ten for his Raising! One Lodge was closed at 10.20 pm and, on another occasion, after working a Second Degree, a Third Degree Ceremony was begun at 10.00 pm, when two actors visiting Cardiff, (described as 'Theatricals'), were Initiated.

WBro J Beasley, Charity Steward since 1994 and President of the Lodge of Instruction since 1998 was promoted to PPrSGD in 2002. WBro A Gardener, Treasurer, 1999-2003, and Secretary since 2003, became the fifth Member of the Lodge to become a Grand Officer, with the Rank of PAGSuptWks.

Looking back over the years, Duke of York Lodge has been served well by so many Brethren, too numerous to mention. It is to those un-named Brethren, together with those already named, that we give thanks for such devoted service over the last hundred and sixteen years.

Compiled by WBro Robert E Gill and WBro Alan Gardener, PAGSuptWks.

John Allan Rolls, Lord Llangattock
1837 - 1912
Provincial Grand Master of South Wales Eastern Division
1894 - 1912

Sir George Elliot, ProvGM of South Wales Eastern Division, died on 23 December 1893 and the Patent appointing John Allan Rolls (Lord Llangattock) as his successor was signed on 20 April 1894.

John Allan Rolls was born on 19 February 1837, the son of John Etherington Welch Rolls (1807-1870) and Elizabeth Mary Long, a granddaughter of William Carnegie, 7th Earl of Northesk. He was educated at Eton and Christchurch, Oxford, and went on to gain the Rank of Captain in the service of the Royal Gloucestershire Hussars. He married in 1868, Georgiana Marcia, the youngest daughter of Sir Charles MacLean, Bart. They had four children - three sons and a daughter. Lady Llangattock, during the last 30 years of her life (she died in 1923), developed a great interest in the life of Lord Nelson, who had made a brief visit to Monmouth in 1802, and had been given the Freedom of the Borough. She assembled a large collection of Nelson memorabilia, which she bequeathed to Monmouth, and the original Nelson Museum opened in the town in 1924.

Lord Llangattock's involvement in Freemasonry commenced on 5 April 1859, when he was Initiated in Loyal Monmouth Lodge No.457. He was Passed on 25 October of that same year, Raised on 9 November 1860 and Installed Worshipful Master of Loyal Monmouth Lodge on 1 March 1864. The previous year, his father had been appointed the Provincial Grand Master of Monmouthshire (Date of Patent: 4 March 1863) in succession to Charles John Kemeys Tynte of Cefn Mabley, the father of Charles Kemeys Kemeys-Tynte, ProvGM of South Wales Eastern Division. History was about to repeat itself!

In August 1881, John Allan Rolls was appointed Past Grand Junior Warden of the United Grand Lodge of England. An even greater honour was bestowed upon him the following year, when,

John Allan Rolls, Lord Llangattock

the Chairmanship of Lord Llangattock. Loyal Commercial Lodge's Installation banquet was held four weeks later on 22 October.

Loyal Cambrian Lodge, Merthyr Tydfil, hosted the Provincial Grand Lodge the following year on 28 September 1899. Lord Llangattock, who was present, had previously been given the Masonic Regalia of the late Sir John Guest (ProvGM and PM Loyal Cambrian Lodge), and he decided that these relics should be placed in the care of the Loyal Cambrian Lodge. These were duly presented and placed in a case provided at his Lordship's own expense.

Two further Lodges were added to the Province over the next few years. Llynfi Lodge No.2965, Maesteg, was Consecrated on 28 July 1903 at a Ceremony held in the Mission Hall of St David's Church, Maesteg. This was followed by the Consecration of Dr James Griffith Hall Lodge, No.3161, Swansea, on 19 July 1906. The DepProvGM, Marmaduke Tennant, was the Officiating Officer on both occasions.

On 19 February 1907, Lord Llangattock celebrated his 70th birthday and, in consequence, the DepProvGM wrote the following letter to the Lodges in the Province:

'My dear Sir & Wor. Bro.,

Proposed Presentation to the Rt. Wor. Prov. G. Master

It has occurred to me that Lord Llangattock having presided over this province so efficiently since the year 1894 and His Lordship having now attained the allotted age of three score and ten this would be a fitting opportunity of showing our appreciation of those services in some tangible form.

Provincial Banner presented by Lord Llangattock

As you are aware the Prov. G. Master had been a regular attendant at the Meetings of Provincial Grand Lodge and has taken a lively interest in all matters appertaining to the welfare of the Province. His Lordship has also not only subscribed liberally to the several Masonic Charities, but he has presided at the Festivals of the Royal Masonic Institution and the Royal Masonic Institution for Girls and he had promised to preside at the Festival of the Royal Masonic Institution for Boys in 1908.

I shall be glad if you will bring this matter before the Brethren of your Lodge at their next meeting and let me know whether the suggestion meets with their approval.

The form of Presentation must of course for the present be decided after obtaining the consent of the Prov. G. Master to accept a presentation and after ascertaining his views of the matter, but it had been suggested that the amount to be divided amongst the several Lodges of the Province would not exceed £250.

Your early reply will oblige.

Yours faithfully and fraternally,

M. Tennant'

In due course, the Brethren of the Province decided to present the Provincial Grand Master with a marble bust of his Lordship. The presentation was made at a Provincial Grand Lodge, held at Cardiff on 24 January 1908, which was also the occasion of the Consecration of the Province's first Past Masters' Lodge, Hendre Lodge No.3250. A cast of the original bust used to occupy a prominent position in the Duke of Connaught Temple, Cardiff.

The decision to form a Past Masters' Lodge had been taken in December 1906 and a committee was formed to implement the decision. It was resolved that the Lodge should be named after Lord Llangattock's Monmouthshire home, 'The Hendre' (Welsh for a 'winter dwelling'). The Consecration was conducted by VWBro Sir Edward Letchworth, Grand Secretary, after which Lord Llangattock was Installed as the first WM. During the proceedings, Marmaduke Tennant, the first SW of Hendre Lodge presented the WM with the marble bust, which had been executed by the famous sculptor, Sir William Goscombe John, RA. Copies of the bust were later given to the various Masonic Halls of the Province.

Marble Bust of Lord Llangattock

'The Hendre', Lord Llangattock's former home, is now 'The Rolls of Monmouth Golf Club'. Built of stone and brick in the Norman and Tudor styles, it was visited by many famous people, including the Duke and Duchess of York, personal friends of Lord Llangattock, who later became King George V and Queen Mary. It was also the venue for several Lodge picnics, which were to become a feature of Lord Llangattock's period as ProvGM. One such instance was reported in 'The Craftsman':

'On the cordial invitation of the R. W. Provincial Grand Master, Bro. Lord Llangattock, the first picnic of the Llangattock Lodge (No. 2547), Cardiff will be held at the Hendre, Monmouth, on July 29th 1896. (The picnic in fact took place on Wednesday, 24 July 1896.) *A party of 60 ladies and gentlemen arrived at the Hendre at 12.30 p.m. and luncheon was served at 1.00 p.m. After formal toasts, followed by photographs the Mansion was viewed. Then followed organ and piano recitals, tea at 4.30 p.m. and departure at 7.15 p.m. The party arrived back in Cardiff at 10.00 p.m.'*

Returning to 1908, Provincial Grand Lodge was held that year on 25 September at the Albert Hall, Llandrindod Wells. This was also the occasion of the Consecration of Ithon Lodge No.3320, which was performed in the presence of Lord Llangattock, the Ceremony being conducted by VWBro Sir Edward Letchworth, Grand Secretary. The Province now consisted of 27 Lodges and was to remain at this number until the appointment of Charles Dillwyn Venables-Llewelyn as ProvGM and the Consecration, on 3 June 1916, of the Lodge named in his honour.

On 12 July 1910, Lord Llangattock suffered the tragic loss of his youngest son, the Hon Charles Stewart Rolls, at the age of 32. He was the co-founder, with Frederick Henry Royce, of the world famous firm 'Rolls - Royce'. In 1903, Rolls had entered an automobile sales venture in London selling expensive French cars, when, one day, a friend introduced him to F H Royce, who was just beginning to build quality automobiles. The following year they agreed that Royce would build cars and Rolls would sell them, thus 'Rolls - Royce' was born! Earlier in 1910, Charles Rolls had acquired fame when he became the first man to fly non-stop across the English Channel both ways. A few months later he was killed when his French-built Wright bi-plane broke up in mid-air while flying over Bournemouth. Although he came down from only 20 feet, he cracked his skull – thus becoming Britain's first aircraft fatality.

Just over two years later, on 23 September 1912, Lord Llangattock died at the age of 75. Glamorgan Lodge sent a letter of sympathy to Lady Llangattock and in December a letter was read from her, asking Glamorgan Lodge *'to accept a framed portrait of the late Lord Llangattock as a memento of the high position he occupied in Freemasonry in the Division.'* The following year, Provincial Grand Lodge decided that the Memorial to Lord Llangattock should take the form of an extension to the 'Home Charities'.

His first son, Major John McLean Rolls, succeeded his father to become the 2nd Lord Llangattock. He died at the age of 46, four years later, on 31st October 1916, at Boulogne, from wounds received a few days earlier at the Battle of the Somme. With his death his title became extinct.

The middle son, the Hon. Henry Allan Rolls, had died, unmarried, at the age of 44, only a few months earlier, on 26 June 1916.

Compiled byWBro Peter M Davies, ProvJGW.

Llangattock Lodge No.2547

Warranted : 18 January 1895

Consecrated : 27 March 1895

Meeting at the Masonic Hall, Cardiff.

In 1895, there were only 3 Lodges working in Cardiff, namely Glamorgan Lodge No.36, Constituted in 1808; Bute Lodge No.960, Consecrated in 1863 and Tennant Lodge No.1992, Consecrated in 1883. Duke of York Lodge No.2453, although Warranted on 21 November 1892, was not Consecrated until 26 September 1895. With Cardiff expanding rapidly as a commercial centre, there was general agreement that there was a need for the formation of another Lodge in the Town. The records do not show that the prospective Membership was to be focused on any one section of the community.

At the Founding Brethren were all Members of Tennant Lodge and they met at the Park Hotel on Friday, 30 November 1894 in order to pursue the matter. They included WBros Thomas Matthews, PPrSGW, who had been WM of Bute Lodge in 1880 and of Tennant Lodge in 1884; W E Miles, PPrGReg, WM Tennant Lodge, 1890-1892. The general agreement to form a new Lodge having been taken, it was agreed that a Petition be prepared for presentation to Tennant Lodge at their next Regular Meeting. The meeting then discussed the name of the new Lodge and Bro Charles Jones proposed *'That, providing that our RW Provincial Grand Master, Lord Llangattock would grant his permission, the Lodge be named, Llangattock Lodge'*. The appropriate letter was sent to his Lordship, and in due course his consent was received. It was further agreed that the Founder Brethren should pay a fee of £2.10.00 (£2.50) each.

At the second meeting held on Saturday, 8 December, at 42, Queen Street, 15 Brethren attended, and the Founder's Fee was increased to £3.3.0 (£3.15) and the following Officers Designate were appointed:

WBro Thomas Mathews, WM; WBro John Shaw, IPM; WBro W E Miles, SW; Bro Charles Jones, JW and Bro Samuel Jones, Secretary.

A third meeting of the Founder Brethren took place on Saturday, 12 January 1895, at which WBro Marmaduke Tennant, DepProvGM, proposed that Duke of York Lodge No.2453 and Llangattock Lodge, be Consecrated on the same day. This was rejected as it was felt that each Ceremony should be separate and distinct.

The Warrant for Llangattock Lodge No.2547 was signed a few days later on 18 January 1895 and the Consecration took place at the old Masonic Hall, Working Street, Cardiff, on Wednesday, 27 March 1895. The Ceremony was performed by the RWBro Rt Hon John Allan, Lord Llangattock, ProvGM, assisted by WBro Marmaduke Tennant, DepProvGM, and other Officers of Provincial Grand Lodge. Among those present were representatives from every Lodge in the Province, bar two.

Lord Llangattock presented the new Lodge with its Banner, bearing his Arms and Motto *'Celeritas et Veritas'* (Promptness and Truth). This Banner was displayed in the Temple for many years before losing its colour. It was carefully copied and replaced under the guidance and generosity of WBro Ronald Warry. The new Banner was Dedicated by Lord Swansea, ProvGM, in October 1978, but unfortunately, due to ill health, Ronald Warry was unable to be present.

The last Meeting at the Old Temple in Working Street was held on 4 September 1895. The new Temple at Guildford Crescent was Dedicated by Lord Llangattock on Thursday, 26 September 1895. This was immediately followed by the Consecration of Duke of York Lodge No. 2453. The following evening, by Special Dispensation, the first Regular Lodge Meeting of Llangattock Lodge was held in the new Temple.

On 28 April 1898, a Petition was presented and signed for the formation of a Commercial Traveller's Lodge. The Petition was also signed by Bute Lodge and the Warrant was granted on 28 June 1898, and Loyal Commercial Lodge No.2720 became Llangattock's first Daughter Lodge in conjunction with Bute Lodge. Three further Daughter Lodges were to follow. The Petition for Henry Pendrill Charles Lodge No.3769 was signed on 28 February 1916 and it was subsequently Warranted on 19 April 1916. Likewise, the Petition for Gwalia Lodge No.4213 was signed on 21 May 1920 and Warranted on 13 December 1920. The final Daughter Lodge, Cambrensis Lodge No.6608, was granted its Warrant on 4 February 1948.

An important Initiation took place on 28 January 1901, that of David John Jones. In 1923, he was the first Lodge Member to be appointed a Grand Officer, with the Rank of PAGDC. He became Deputy Provincial Grand Master in April 1926, but sadly, he was not to be in Office for very long, for he died five years later on 27 April 1931. At the time of his death he held the Rank of PGD and the Brethren of the Province erected a bronze tablet to his memory in the Duke of Connaught Temple, Cardiff.

Following extensive alterations to the Masonic Hall, Cardiff, Llangattock Lodge held its Installation Banquet there for the first time on 23 March 1914.

The First World War period, 1914-1918, saw many Members giving active service in many branches of the armed forces, and five of them made the 'Supreme Sacrifice', namely WBro J Nicholas, Bros S Bower, R Chissel, J N Jutson and T H Roberts.

Mention must be made of Bro John Elisha Grimshaw, VC, who was Initiated in Llangattock Lodge on 24 September 1928. Born on 20 January 1893 at Abram, near Wigan, Lancashire, he was employed as a carpenter at Cross & Tetley's Collieries in the Wigan coalfield. He was enlisted into the 1st Battalion Lancashire Fusiliers in June 1912, when he was 19 years old. He was first posted to India, and by the time of the Lancashire Landings at Gallipoli on 25 April 1915, he was a Lance-Corporal signaller, whose role was to maintain contact between the HQ on board HMS Euryalus and the Units on the ground. During furious fighting on the beach, his Company was reduced to 4 Officers and 83 men. Grimshaw's pack and water bottle were riddled by bullets, and his cap badge was smashed by a bullet, but by a miracle he was unharmed. He had remained calm and cheerful throughout the ordeal and frequently braved intense close range enemy fire to get his signals through.

Although 6 men, including Grimshaw, were nominated for the Victoria Cross, the rules at that time did not allow for this to happen and only 3 were awarded, with Grimshaw receiving the Distinguished Conduct Medal. Following furious questions in the Houses of Parliament as to why bureaucracy should be more important than bravery, the rules were changed and all the nominated 6 were eventually awarded the VC. The Citation reads:

'On 25 April 1915 west of Cape Helles, Gallipoli, Turkey three companies and the Headquarters of the 1st Battalion, Lancashire Fusiliers, when landing on West Beach, were met by very deadly fire from hidden machine-guns which caused a large number of casualties. The survivors, however, rushed up and cut the wire entanglements notwithstanding the terrific fire from the enemy and after overcoming supreme difficulties the cliffs were gained and the position maintained.'

Following active service, he became a Recruiting Officer in Cardiff, and resigned from the Lodge in 1934, on moving back to his home area of Lancashire. He spent his last days at Twickenham, where he died on 20 July 1980.

Other Brethren of note include three Lord Mayors of Cardiff, namely Bro Sir Charles William Melhuish (1931); Bro James

Griffiths (1942) and Bro George James Ferguson (1946). While during the Second World War, four Brethren made the 'Supreme Sacrifice', namely A F Newman, R G C Robbins, C H Warren and I L Williams.

Tribute must be paid here to WBro Herbert H Harrison, PPrGW, PAGDC, whose extensive notes on the formation and background of Llangattock Lodge's first fifty years form the précis for this part of the Lodge history.

The Lodge Summons for December 1963 included the following:

'To Ballot for Mr Douglas Allenby Gardner; Mr Ronald Warry, Mr George Morgan Jones and to Initiate Mr John Frederick Valentine Curtis Stinchcome.' They all became Worshipful Masters of the Lodge - D A Gardner in 1976, J F Stinchcome in 1977, R Warry in 1978 and G M Jones in 1979. Could this be a Masonic record?

The Three Miniature Carvings

In 1977, a Fraternal Visit was arranged through the good offices of Bro Frederick Edgar Court and his brother-in-law, Bro John Jenkins, with Orpheus Lodge No.7697, Downend, Bristol, in the Province of Gloucester. These Fraternal exchanges are still active. Fred Court was Installed WM of the Lodge in March 1984, but sadly died during his year in Office.

In recent years, Brethren attended the Consecration of Scaldis Lodge No.295 (Under the Grand Orient of the Netherlands) in Goes, SW Netherlands. The Lodge is named after the river 'Scaldis', which runs through Goes. This visit came about through a long acquaintanceship that WBro Celfyn Lewis had enjoyed with WBro Walter Uythoven. The latter, together with other Dutch Brethren, visited Llangattock Lodge on 24 March 2003, and to commemorate the visit, Walter Uythoven and Bro Karel Van de Beck of Lodge 'Der Opgaande Ster' No.276 (The Lodge of the Ascending Star) presented the Lodge with three miniature carvings. These are copies of carvings to be found on a flying buttress of St John's Cathedral at s-Hertogenbosch (Den Bosch), the capital of Noord-Brabant, the largest Province of the Netherlands. The original carvings are about one metre high and face up the buttress towards the Cathedral, giving the appearance of performing the duties of an EA, FC and MM (note the Working Tools). The miniature copies are on display in a cabinet in the foyer of Cardiff Masonic Hall.

In keeping up the international connections of the Lodge, a letter was received in 1952 from Bro E J Lacey, now residing at Fort Jamison, Northern Rhodesia, enclosing a copy of the *'Order of Service for the Consecration and Installation Ceremonies of the Lodge of Fort Jamison No.1467'* (Scottish Constitution), at which meeting he was to be Installed WM on 10 May 1952.

In a Lodge with such a long history, it is inevitable that some Brethren will have attained the status of Masonic Veterans; amongst those honoured were WBro Evan S Palmer, Bro Jim Hall, WBro William Albert John Adams, BEM; WBro David T G Harris, MBE, PPrJGD, and more recently WBro Celfyn H Lewis, who in March 2010 was made an Honorary Member of the Lodge.

Further honours are recorded for WBro Tom Holley, MBE (1985) and WBro John D Allen who, in 1988, was honoured with the CBE, and a Knighthood in 1995.

Treasured possessions include a silver salver bearing the signatures of the Founders, a loving cup and two silver candlesticks, which, together with a presentation Gavel and Block (given by Orpheus Lodge No.7679), form an impressive display at the Festive Board. The Tyler's Sword is the one used by WBro D A Gardiner, who also presented the new Collar for the WM, complete with silver discs for the traditional engraving of the names of future Worshipful Masters. Also, amongst our treasures is a superbly bound copy of the V O S L with full Masonic References, presented in 1981 by the Brethren of Carrolton Lodge No.1400 Texas, USA. It is also inscribed with the names of the Officers at that time.

Compiled by Celfyn Harman Lewis, PPrJGW.

David Alfred Thomas, Viscount Rhondda
1856 ~ 1918

Senior Grand Warden
1917 ~ 1918

David Alfred Thomas, First Viscount Rhondda, was born on 26 March 1856. He was the son of Samuel Thomas, a coal owner of Ysgubor-wen, Aberdare, and his second wife, Rachel, the daughter of Morgan Joseph, a Mining Engineer of Merthyr Tydfil. They had seventeen children, of whom David Alfred Thomas was the fifteenth! The family spoke Welsh until David's mother employed an English nurse to teach her children English. The family attended the Calfaria Welsh Baptist Chapel but moved to the English Baptist Chapel, Carmel, in 1859, to improve their English language skills.

Thomas was educated at Manila Hall, Dr Hudson's School, Clifton, Bristol, before going up to Cambridge University. Originally he had a place at Jesus College on a scholarship but he was unable to accept this, suffering an attack of typhoid fever contracted in Clermont-Ferrand, France. However, he obtained a scholarship to Gonville and Caius College, Cambridge University, to study Mathematics. Although his health remained poor, he became a member of the University rowing and boxing teams. With the death of his father on 24 April 1879, he left University before completing his studies but, nevertheless, obtained his BA in 1880. He was awarded an MA in 1883 and was made an Honorary Fellow in 1919.

Although raised as a Baptist and later a Congregationalist, he was never baptised into either church. He became a strong swimmer and rescued a boy who fell through the ice on Hirwaun Pond, Aberdare, in 1881, for which he received an award from the Humane Society. He was baptised as an Anglican at St Andrew's Church, St Andrew's Major, near Barry, in 1882, and shortly before marrying Sybil Margaret, the daughter of George Augustus Haig of Pen Ithon, Radnorshire, on 27 June 1882. Their only child, a daughter Margaret, was born in 1883.

He started work at the sales department of the Cambrian Collieries, later moving to Clydach Vale where he gained experience in mine management. He worked in a Stockbroker's Office in Cornhill, London in 1882, returning to manage the Cambrian Collieries after the death of the Manager, Mr Osborne Riches. After he inherited his father's business in 1879, he converted the company from private ownership to a limited liability concern in order to expand. During the coal strike of 1898, he refused to side with the coal-owners' organisation and in consequence the Cambrian Collieries continued to work through the strike. When he was involved in a strike at the Ely Pit, Penygraig, in 1910, his attempts to break the strike precipitated the Tonypandy Riots in which one miner died and nearly eighty policemen and over five hundred citizens were injured.

He leased Llanwern House, Newport, Monmouthshire, in 1887, later purchasing it in 1900. Just before his death, he purchased Pencoed, the neighbouring estate, as a gift to his daughter.

He was elected as Liberal Member of Parliament for Merthyr Tydfil in 1888,

David Alfred Thomas
Viscount Rhondda

representing the seat until 1910, when he stepped down in order to fight the marginal seat of Cardiff, which he held for just one year. He served as President of the South Wales Liberal Federation from 1894-1897. When he was not offered a ministerial post following the 1906 General Election, he spent more time on his business affairs than politics and, in 1908, he formed the Cambrian Combine of Coal Mines, with a capital of £2 million. He also purchased coal bearing land in North America before returning to politics and serving as David Lloyd George's (Prime Minister of Great Britain, 1916-1922) emissary to the United States, for which he was created Baron Rhondda in January 1916 and Viscount Rhondda in June 1918.

During WWI, following a visit to America in 1915, and accompanied by his daughter, he departed New York on 1 May, bound for Liverpool aboard the RMS Lusitania. Unknown to the passengers, but probably no secret to the Germans, almost all her hidden cargo consisted of munitions and contraband destined for the British war effort. On May 7 the ship neared the coast of Ireland. At 2:10 in the afternoon a torpedo fired by the German submarine U 20 slammed into her side. A mysterious second explosion ripped the liner apart. Within 18 minutes the giant ship slipped beneath the sea. Of the 1,924 people aboard there were only 805 survivors, including Viscount Rhondda and his daughter, Margaret.

The following year he was appointed a Privy Counsellor, President of the Local Government Board in 1916 and, in June 1917, Minister of Food Control. Thus D A Thomas returned to his first love – politics – and the unbending individualist proved himself an outstanding success as the architect of a great socialist experiment – food rationing, during the latter part of WWI.

His involvement in Freemasonry commenced with his Initiation into Loyal Cambrian Lodge No.110, Merthyr Tydfil, on 5 September 1889, where he was Passed on 3 October, and Raised on 5 December the same year. He was Installed as WM on 3 January 1883. The magnificent large oak Master's Chair was presented by him to the Lodge. Carved with fluted columns in the Ionic Order, and having a shield carved with Masonic and Welsh emblems, the Chair was designed by Bro George Frederick Harris, grandfather of the Artist and Entertainer, Rolf Harris. Viscount Rhondda presented a similar Master's Chair to St David's Lodge No.679, Aberdare, and became a Joining Member of that Lodge in 1890. He was also a Founder of Hendre Lodge No.3250, Cardiff, in 1908, and Cardiff Exchange Lodge No.3775 in 1917. He served as Provincial Assistant Grand Director of Ceremonies for South Wales (Eastern Division) in 1895. He was appointed Senior Grand Warden by the United Grand Lodge of England in 1917. In Ancient and Accepted Rite he became a Member of Caer-daf Chapter No.118, Cardiff. He supported the Masonic charities and became Vice-Patron of the three Masonic Institutions. He was also a subscriber to the Freemasons' War Hospital and Masonic Nursing Home and served as Vice-President of the South Wales Eastern Division Home Charities.

A lifetime of strenuous labour took a great toll on his health and, in April 1918, he offered his resignation to Prime Minister, Lloyd George, which initially was declined. His health continued to deteriorate and he died at the age of 62 of heart failure at his home, Llanwern, Monmouthsire, on 3 July 1918. Tributes to his work and to the public loss sustained by his death were paid in both Houses of Parliament. He bequeathed £20,000 to Gonville and Caius College Cambridge, to provide 'Rhondda Scholarships'. He was cremated at Golders Green Crematorium, London, and his ashes were returned to Wales. On his death, the title Viscount Rhondda became extinct but, having a female heir, he had insisted with Lloyd George, on accepting the title that by 'Special Remainder' the King would permit his daughter to become a Peeress in her own right. Further, the title could pass down through the female line. Margaret Mackworth, 2nd Viscountess Rhondda (1883 - 1958), divorced her husband in 1922 and, as there were no children from the marriage, on her death that title also became extinct.

In the Dictionary of Welsh Biography, Professor Brinley Thomas, PhD, wrote:

'Viscount Rhondda had a boyish zest for life and a remarkable capacity for managing men. His enthusiasm knew no bounds: a passion for bird-nesting which he acquired as a boy at Ysgubor-wen remained with him all his life. Apart from his towering influence on the development of the South Wales coalfield, he was not absorbed in the national life of Wales. He was a true Victorian individualist for whom life was a tournament offering glittering prizes to the enterprising. He will be chiefly remembered for his masterly administration of Great Britain's food supply in the darkest year of the First World War.'

References: Library & Museum of Freemasonry, United Grand Lodge of England;
Dictionary of Welsh Biography Down to 1940, John Edward Lloyd and R T Jenkins.

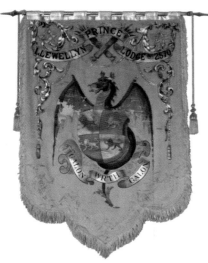

Prince Llewellyn Lodge No. 2570

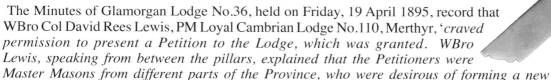

Warranted : 25 June 1895

Consecrated : 16 January 1896

Meeting at the Masonic Hall, Cardiff.

The Minutes of Glamorgan Lodge No.36, held on Friday, 19 April 1895, record that WBro Col David Rees Lewis, PM Loyal Cambrian Lodge No.110, Merthyr, '*craved permission to present a Petition to the Lodge, which was granted. WBro Lewis, speaking from between the pillars, explained that the Petitioners were Master Masons from different parts of the Province, who were desirous of forming a new Lodge, to be called the 'Prince Llewellyn' Lodge. The Petitioners intended to hold their meetings periodically at Cardiff and they decided upon asking the support of the Glamorgan Lodge, as it was the most ancient Lodge in the Province. WBro Lewis concluded by an earnest appeal to the WM and Brethren that they would be pleased to accede to the request of those whom he represented and assist them in obtaining a Warrant from the Grand Lodge of England. The Petition was then presented to and received by the WM.*

The WM addressing Bro Lewis stated 'that he had no doubt that the Lodge would be pleased to render him the assistance he desired, but as the Petition had come upon him rather as a surprise, he would like to consult a Board of Past Masters, which would be meeting on the following Tuesday, before laying the Petition before the Lodge for its acceptance. The next meeting of the Lodge would be on 10 May, and the Brethren would then decide whether their approval should be testified.' Bro Lewis thanked the WM for his courtesy and promised to attend at the next Meeting to learn the decision of the Lodge'.

The Worshipful Master and Wardens of Glamorgan Lodge signed the Petition on 10 May and thereby Prince Llewellyn Lodge became Glamorgan's fourth Daughter Lodge.

Of the twenty-one Founders, eleven were Solicitors, five were Surgeons, and three were Barristers-at-Law, one a Physician and one an Ophthalmic Surgeon. They came from various parts of the Province, including The Mumbles, Swansea, Penarth, Porth, Merthyr Tydfil and of course Cardiff. Twelve were Members of Glamorgan Lodge.

The Primus Master, WBro Col David Rees Lewis, Solicitor and Magistrates' Clerk, came from Plas Penydarren, Merthyr Tydfil. He had the honour of having the David Rees Lewis Chapter No.110 bear his name.

The first IPM, WBro Dr Henry Naunton Davies, who resided at Glyn Rhondda House, Porth, was honoured by the naming of the Naunton Davies Chapter No.1578.

Yet another Founder, Dr J G Hall, is commemorated by the naming of the Dr James Griffith Hall Lodge No.3161 and the Dr Hall Chapter No.3161. After his death, in 1901, his relatives presented a Memorial Bowl for competition among Members of Prince Llewellyn Lodge and St John's Chapter. It was decided that the competition should be at golf and the bowl be known as the James Hall Bowl. Each year, the winner was presented with a miniature, the cost being shared between the Lodge and the Chapter. The only record of the competition in the Minutes record that in April 1939 and 1940, a sum not exceeding £2-2s-0d was voted as the Lodge share of the cost.

In November 1896, the VWBro The Right Rev Richard Lewis, Lord Bishop of Llandaff, Grand Chaplain, Apollo Lodge No.357, Oxford University, became a Joining Member and was the first Chaplain of the Lodge. He continued in that Office for many years. His son, Arthur Griffith Poyner Lewis, Barrister-at-Law, also Initiated in Apollo Lodge and a Joining Member of Glamorgan Lodge (1877), was a Founder Member of Prince Llewellyn Lodge and WM, 1897-1899. The Arthur Lewis Mark Lodge No.585 is named after him.

Sir William Thomas Lewis, Bart, Loyal Cambrian Lodge No.110, joined the Lodge in November 1896, while WBro Col Sir Edward Stock Hill, KCB, MP, WM Glamorgan Lodge, 1869-1870, joined in April 1899.

Another Founder Member of note was the Solicitor, WBro Thomas Rodway Hunt, who had joined Glamorgan Lodge in 1891. Having been WM of Talbot Lodge No.1323, 1892-1893, he became WM of Prince Llewellyn Lodge in 1899. He played an important role in the formation of Hendre Lodge No.3250 and became the 5th WM of that Lodge in 1912.

It is not known why 'Prince Llewellyn' was selected as the name of the Lodge. It is clear, however, that the Lodge was named after Llewelyn ap Gruffydd who lived from 1236-1282 and was formally acknowledged to be Prince of Wales by Henry III, by the terms of the Treaty of Montgomery in 1267. The Arms of Llewelyn ap Gruffydd, later assumed by Owain Glyndwr, when he proclaimed himself Prince of Wales in 1402, are displayed on the Lodge Banner, and consist of 'Quarterly Or and Gules, Four Lions, Passant, Guardant, Counter-changed'. They are charged on a shield, which is borne in a dragon 'displayed'. The name and number of the Lodge appear in the ribbon above, supported by two leeks 'in saltire'. Thus, the Lodge's heraldic achievement features not only the Arms of our country but also its Badge, the Dragon and its Emblem, the Leek. Underneath appears the Lodge Motto *'Calon wrth Galon'*, (*'Heart with Heart'*) and signifies that feeling not only towards each other but also towards all Freemasons in general. The Banner was presented by Col David Rees Lewis in March 1896.

The Lodge was Consecrated on Thursday, 16 January 1896, following a Meeting of the Provincial Grand Lodge, held in the Duke of Connaught Temple, Cardiff. The Consecrating Officer was the RWBro the Lord Llangattock, ProvGM, who was assisted by his Officers. The Installing Master was VWBro Marmaduke Tennant, DepProvGM. The large and distinguished company included VWBro Lt-Col Charles Robert Lyne, DepProvGM, Monmouthshire, VWBro John Thornhill Morland, DepProvGM in charge of Berkshire, the Officers of Provincial Grand Lodge, thirteen of the Founders and a large number of Brethren, representing all the Lodges in the Province. After the Ceremony, the Brethren of Prince Llewellyn Lodge held a banquet at the Whitehall Rooms, Park Hotel, Cardiff.

The Jewels of Rank worn by the Lodge Officers are all solid silver and were presented to the Lodge by the original holders of the Offices, and whose names are engraved thereon. The exceptions are those of the Inner Guard, which cannot be found and has been replaced by a modern Jewel, and the Jewel of the Charity Steward, which was presented by WBro Martin S Hoskins in memory of his father, WBro Reginald J Hoskins. In 1907, WBro Herbert Cook presented the avel used by the Worshipful Master; in 1908 WBro Cornelius Griffiths that used by the Senior Warden and in 1909, WBro Mitchell Stevens that used by the Junior Warden. The cabinet of Working Tools was presented by WBro R A Richards in 1918. A Heavy Setting Maul was presented by WBro Peter Thomas.

In November 1903, the WM, WBro Tatham Thompson, objected to the scheme for the proposed re-decoration of the Masonic premises in Cardiff, on the grounds that it was *'lacking in taste'* and also drew attention to the fact that Prince Llewellyn Lodge was not represented on the Joint Lodge Committee. The Secretary was instructed to write in protest to the Committee; then in January 1904, the Committee resolved that *'every Worshipful Master for the time being of a Craft Lodge meeting at the Masonic Temple, shall be a Member of the Joint Lodge Committee by virtue of his Office'*.

Again, it was WBro Tatham Thompson, who in 1906, solicited subscriptions from the Brethren for the new Organ Fund. Unfortunately, the appeal did not produce a sufficiently large enough sum for the purpose, with the result that a further appeal had to be made. This appeal was put to the Brethren by WBro Herbert Cook, the then Master. On this occasion, Bro George Henry Cole, FRCO, Organist, Professor of Music, gave the one and only Organ Recital during a Meeting of the Lodge.

During the First World War, twenty-five Candidates were Initiated into the Lodge. All the Candidates were Passed and Raised in the Lodge except Bro Kenneth B Jones, Initiated on 21 March 1918, but Passed in April 1921 and Raised on 18 May, 1921, in Storey Point Lodge No.313, New York, at the request of Prince Llewellyn Lodge. The Initiates included three Medical Officers from the 2nd Welsh War Hospital at Whitchurch and a further Candidate from the Whitchurch War Hospital was Initiated on 21 November 1919. Col William Daniel Arthur, RAMC was also an Initiate but his unit is not recorded.

At the January meeting in 1921, a resolution was passed that the Worshipful Master and the ten senior Past Masters should meet to consider whether it was desirable to revise the Membership qualifications. No further reference to Membership qualifications appears in the Minutes. Then in April 1925, the Lodge appointed an Investigation Committee consisting of the Worshipful Master, three Founders and the Secretary. Since then, membership of the Lodge has been open to any acceptable candidate, without any restrictive qualifications.

A few Brethren of note include VWBro Sir David William Evans, one of the Lodge's first Initiates (June 1896), who became DepProvGM in 1925. His biographical details are recorded elsewhere in this book. He was also a Welsh Rugby International as was Bro Wilfred Wooller who was capped 18 times for Wales. A sportsman par excellence he captained Glamorgan County Cricket Club for more than a decade, played soccer briefly for Cardiff City and represented Wales at squash.

Arthur Leopold Nind Tomson, an Insurance Manager, Initiated in 1919, became Worshipful Master in 1931 and Provincial Grand Treasurer in 1937. David Bernard Morgan, a Director of the Departmental Store in the Hayes, was Initiated in October 1923 and became Worshipful Master in 1936. He later did much to organise the Jubilee of the Lodge and compiled the Historical Notes at that time. Evan Llewellyn Roberts, owner of the outfitting store in Queen Street was Initiated in October 1928 and later became Secretary. He became Worshipful Master in 1946, after returning from war service, and later became Treasurer.

Finally, mention must also be made of Bro Geoffrey Malin Ashe, who was Initiated into the Lodge on 16 October 1947. In 1976, he was appointed AProvGM and the following year he was appointed Deputy Provincial Grand Master, an Office he was to occupy until 1992. His biographical details are also included elsewhere in this book.

In 1938, Bro Herbert Frederick Reeman presented a Challenge Cup for competition at Golf among Lodge Members. It was decided this should be known as the 'Prince Llewellyn Cup'. The first competition took place at Radyr Golf Club in September 1938. There are records that the two competitions were held in 1938 and 1939. The competition for the Prince Llewellyn Cup still takes place. Herbert Reeman was a Chartered Mechanical Engineer, Initiated in October 1931; he became Secretary in 1940 and Worshipful Master in 1942 and 1943.

On 17 November 1938, WBro G J Morley Peel, PM Graveney Lodge No. 5285, Staines, Middlesex, led a Deputation proposing to form a new Lodge of Emulation in Cardiff and seeking the recommendation of the Brethren of Prince Llewellyn Lodge. The Petition was supported and the recommendation signed by the Master, WBro Richard P Care and the Wardens Bro F R Fifoot and Bro Gwilym A Thomas. Richard Penberthy Care, a Ship Owner, was Initiated in October 1925. Frank Ronald Fifoot was an Insurance Broker and became Worshipful Master in 1939. The new Lodge, Cartref Lodge No. 5772 was Consecrated on 18 January 1940. Prior to the Consecration, the Provincial Grand Lodge was opened in the Third Degree by Officers of Prince Llewellyn Lodge.

The first wartime Meeting was held on Saturday, 21 October 1939. The Summons to attend the meeting was issued by the Assistant Secretary, Bro Bernard F Mattey, in the absence of the Secretary, Bro Evan Llewellyn Roberts, who was on active service. Bro Rev D J Lane Griffiths, Junior Deacon was similarly absent. Ten Members and three visitors were present.

At the Meeting on Thursday, 16 November 1944, it was decided that the Worshipful Master for the time being of the Prince Llewelyn Lodge No.4596 (Wallasey) be an Honorary Member of the Lodge. This honour was reciprocated by the Wallasey Lodge.

The first Meeting after the cessation of hostilities in Europe was held on Thursday, 17 May 1945. WBro Charles W Lewis, WM, thought it fitting that the Brethren should give thanks for their deliverance and preservation. He also spoke of Brethren who were serving with the Armed Forces and of the great loss the Lodge had suffered when the late Bro Griffith Williams was killed, while serving as an Officer in the Royal Air Force. Bro Griffith Williams was a Steward of the Lodge and a Barrister of great ability on the South Wales Circuit. The Lodge suffered another loss when Bro Joseph Cotterill died on War Service in India. Bro Cotterill, a Civil Engineer, was aged 22 when he was Initiated by his father WBro H W B Cotterill in March 1939 and had served from the commencement of the war.

The Jubilee was celebrated at the 377th Meeting of the Lodge on Thursday, 17 January 1946. RWBro St John Charles, ProvGM, and VWBro Edgar J Rutter, DepProvGM, were present. The Minutes of the Consecration Meeting were read by the Secretary, Bro J Halifax Smith. WBro D Bernard Morgan read extracts from the Jubilee History Notes and copies were given to all the Brethren present. WBro A L N Thomson, PPrGTreas, Treasurer of the Lodge, presented a cheque for 100 guineas to the DepProvGM, as a donation to the Royal Masonic Hospital.

At the Installation Meeting in April 1948, visitors were admitted in the Third Degree, a practice which continued into the 1950s. Then, at the Installation Meeting of 19 April 1951, WBro Llewellyn Francis of Observer Lodge No.6015 presented a Petition for the formation of a new Lodge, to be known as the 'South Wales Jurists' Lodge'. The Lodge supported the Petition, which was signed and handed to WBro Llewellyn Francis, SW Designate, in the absence of the Master Designate, WBro Judge Owen Temple Morris KC, PGD, a Past Master of Prince Llewellyn Lodge. The South Wales Jurists' Lodge, No.7092, was Consecrated at the Cardiff Masonic Temple by the RWBro R P St John Charles, JP, ProvGM, on 4 June 1951 and Judge Owen Temple Morris was Installed Founder Master.

The 75th Anniversary of the Lodge in January 1971 was celebrated on a low key, as had been usual, with the exception of the Jubilee Celebrations. The Summons to the Meeting on 21 January 1971 was headed: *'The Lodge celebrates its 75th Anniversary this year, having been consecrated on Thursday, 16 January 1896'*. The Minutes of the Meeting make no mention of the Anniversary. The summons to the Meeting on 18 March 1971 bore a similar heading, but the agenda included; *'To receive a brief address on the 75th Anniversary of the Lodge'*. WBro Vivian Care gave the Brethren a résumé of the history of the Lodge during the past 75 years. The Lodge celebrated Vivian Care's completion of fifty years in Freemasonry at the Meeting on 18 May 1978, which was attended by WBro Geoffrey Malin Ashe, DepProvGM.

In May 1979, it was announced that WBro Michael Roberts, MP had been appointed Under Secretary of State for Wales. This was followed by sadness in March 1983, when it was announced that Michael Roberts had collapsed and died at the Despatch Box in the House of Commons. Michael Roberts was the first Headmaster of the Bishop of Llandaff Church in Wales High School.

The Lodge celebrated its Centenary on 18 January 1996 with WBro Paul Drew in the Chair. The Provincial Grand Master, the Right Honourable the Lord Swansea, DL, and many of his Officers were in attendance. WBro Richard Edwards gave a lecture on 'the First Hundred Years'. Worshipful Bro Martin Hoskins read the Minutes of the first Regular Meeting of the Lodge. A donation of £4,000 was made to the Masonic Benevolent Fund 1999 Festival. Later the Brethren attended a Centenary Banquet, where they were presented with a Firing Glass and a copy of the Lodge History to commemorate the occasion.

Compiled by WBro David Philip Edwards, PPrSGD, and WBro Richard Owen Watcyn Edwards, PPrJGW, Chaplain.

Fforest Lodge
No.2606

Warranted : 27 March 1896

Consecrated : 28 October 1896

Meeting at the Masonic Hall, Treharris.

On 29 March 1895, a meeting took place in the Commercial Hotel, Treharris. During this meeting, it was suggested and unanimously agreed that Bros D E Jones and M P Morris contact WBro Col David Rees Lewis, PM Loyal Cambrian Lodge No.110, with a view to the formation and subsequent naming of a new Lodge. It was agreed that the First Officers were to be appointed in order of Seniority of Rank, the one exception being that of WBro Col David Rees Lewis, who declined the Worshipful Master's role in favour of WBro George Frederick Harris. The reason for this late change of plan has been lost in the mists of time. The Petitioners' list shows David Rees Lewis's signature to have been crossed out and George's name added alongside. It is interesting to note that George Harris was the grandfather of the popular Australian artist and entertainer, Rolf Harris.

In August, September and October of 1895, further meetings were held. It was agreed that the new Lodge would be known as *'Fforest Lodge'*, named from the location of these meetings, at the Fforest Farm area. Other meetings were held in the Ocean Colliery office, a coffee tavern and the Bank Room in the Public Hall, Treharris. It was decided that the Lodge Initiation fee would be £7 10s 0d. The cost of £10 0s 0d for the Warrant was to be met by the Founder Members, and not as a charge on the Lodge. The cost of furniture and fittings was met by a loan of £50 from Bro M P Morris, at an interest rate of 5%.

The task of Sponsoring the new Lodge was willingly undertaken by Loyal Cambrian Lodge, and as a result of undertaking this responsibility, a very close affinity has existed between the two Lodges ever since. The Lodge was Consecrated on 28 October 1896, and the event was fully reported in the Merthyr Express. The following is an extract from that report. *'On Wednesday night the Provincial Grand Lodge of South Wales (Eastern Division) foregathered at the Public Hall, Treharris, for the purpose of Consecrating the new Fforest Lodge No.2606 and of installing WBro GF Harris, Past Master No.110 as Worshipful Master. The Ceremony was announced to be conducted by the Rt Hon Lord Llangattock who, accompanied by WBros Marmaduke Tennant, JT Wordsworth, Chaplain, and Bro J H Taylor arrived in Merthyr by the 9.30pm train. They were met at the station by WBro GF Harris who accompanied them to Quakers Yard by the next train. Here the carriage of Bro W Jenkins of the Ocean Colliery awaited them, and they were driven to Bargoed House.'*

The Primus Master, George Frederick Harris (1856-1924), made his living as a Photographer and Portrait Painter in Merthyr Tydfil. He painted the portrait of King George V, which now hangs in the Mansion House in Cardiff. In 1920, he sold three of his paintings to fund his family's emigration to Australia, where they first settled in Perth, Western Australia, later moving to the outskirts of Sydney. The portrait overleaf is believed to be a self-portrait and was painted after 1910. George is shown wearing the Centenary Jewel of Loyal Cambrian Lodge, which had been Warranted on 20 June 1810. This portrait was repaired and restored by

WBro G H G Hooper of Loyal Cambrian Lodge and presented to Fforest Lodge in 1981. It now hangs in pride of place outside the entrance to the Lodge Room in Treharris.

The first Lodge Meetings were held in a room over a chemist shop on the square in Treharris, known as Thomas' Assembly Rooms. Eventually the Lodge moved into the Bank Room in the Public Hall, Treharris.

Fforest Lodge proved to be, and still is, such a popular Lodge that on many occasions more Brethren attended than could be comfortably accommodated, consequently urgent consideration was given to search for larger premises. At a Lodge Meeting on 14 January 1909, it was resolved that a Committee be formed to investigate the possibility of finding a satisfactory solution to this rather pressing matter. Full plenary powers were given by the Brethren for the Committee to select a design of a suitable building and to transact all business required to attain this objective. Mr R D Dowdeswell, Cardiff, prepared the building designs, in the style of the Georgian period.

The Committee set about their task with alacrity and dedication and on 9 June 1910, a major milestone in the History of the Lodge took place, for it was on this day that the Foundation Stone of the new building was finally laid on the Williams Terrace site. A Special Meeting was held in the Public Hall, Treharris, following which a large Procession of Members formed in front of the Public Hall and marched to St Mathias Church where a Freemasons Service was held. The Members then processed to the site of the new hall for the Ceremony of laying the Foundation Stone. WBro Marmaduke Tennant, ProvGDC, duly carried out the Ceremony in accordance with Masonic custom and tradition. It was reported that the whole affair was attractive and picturesque, the gathering numbering over two hundred Brethren, who were attired in full Masonic regalia. The Brethren then returned to the Public Hall to attend the banquet.

WBro George F Harris

Procession from St Mathias Church

The photograph shows the procession from St Mathias Church on 9 June 1910 to witness the laying of the Foundation Stone of the new Masonic Temple, Williams Terrace. The bearded Marmaduke Tennant may be seen turning his head towards the photographer, and George Harris, the Primus Master of Fforest Lodge, is situated just to his left in the foreground of the picture (circled).

On 11 May 1911, RWBro the Lord Llangattock, ProvGM; WBro Marmaduke Tennant, DepProvGM; and Provincial Grand Officers, conducted the Ceremony of Opening and Dedicating the New Temple, for which purpose Lord Llangattock was presented with a gold key. In appreciation of the enormous amount of time and effort that WBro D Myrddin Williams had devoted to the project, he was afforded the honour of opening the first Lodge Meeting in the new Temple. He then returned the Gavel to WBro J P Gibbon, WM, who occupied the Chair of King Solomon to receive the ProvGM, his Deputy and the remainder of the Provincial Grand Officers. The Minute Book records that: *'The ProvGM addressed the Brethren on the motive of the Meeting and the ProvGChap gave the Opening Prayer, Bro Dowdeswell delivered the Tools etc., which had been entrusted to his care at the laying of the Foundation Stone. On behalf of the Lodge, Bro John Morgan then presented a Past Secretary's Jewel to WBro Myrddin Williams, and Bro T W Jenkins presented the Lodge with a very handsome Banner, to mark his appreciation of the advance of Freemasonry.'* The Contractors were Mr H Davies, Bargoed, and Mr John Sutherland, Abercynon, and the estimated cost of the building was £1,000.

On 8 June 1911, Lord Llangattock gifted the Fforest Lodge Brethren £25, in appreciation of the interest shown in Freemasonry. On the same date, WBro George Fredrick Harris, the first WM, was Elected the first Honorary Member of the Lodge.

In 1912, Bro W Lewis received congratulations from the Lodge on the occasion of his Election to the Office of Mayor and Chief Magistrate of the Borough of Merthyr Tydfil. The Brethren of the Lodge attended the Mayor's Procession at St Mathias Church, Treharris, on 17 November 1912.

Seven years later, another milestone in the History of the Lodge was reached, when on 13 November 1919, just nine momentous years from the Laying of the Foundation Stone by Marmaduke Tennant, a loan for the building of the Temple was repaid to the Provincial Benevolent Fund. In 1921, it is recorded the Silver Jubilee of the Lodge was held and was suitably marked by the presentation to the Lodge of a Worshipful Master's Collar *'heavily mounted with silver chain'*. The DepProvGM, WBro Henry Pendrill St John Charles made the presentation.

WBro John Morgan attained Grand Rank in 1926, and at the Lodge's Annual Festival in the same year, the DepProvGM, WBro David John Jones, presented him with his portrait, in full Masonic Regalia, painted in oils. He was considered *'as a very valuable asset to Fforest Lodge, and the one Freemason, who had improved Fforest Lodge, by raising its status in the eyes of the Province to a position equal to any other.'*

The Temple in 1911

Five years later, on 10 December 1931, at the 35th Anniversary of the Lodge, the DepProvGM, WBro Edgar John Rutter, presented WBro John Morgan with a Bar to be added to his PM's Jewel, in recognition of his services as Acting Master of the Lodge during that year. It is believed that this is the only instance of a Bar being awarded to a Master of Fforest Lodge.

At the Lodge Meeting held on 13 June 1946, a Petition was presented by WBro W Eli Gough, Master Designate, supported by the Wardens Designate and Founder Members, praying that Fforest Lodge should Sponsor a new Lodge, to be known as 'Themis Lodge'. ('Themis' was the Greek Goddess of Justice). Unanimous approval was given to the Petition, and Themis Lodge No.6355 was Consecrated at the Masonic Temple, Cardiff, on 7 October 1946. Thus, the Golden Jubilee of Fforest Lodge was complimented and completed with the birth of a Daughter Lodge.

The years following WWII were heralded in with adverse circumstances, with the imposition of food rationing and other shortages, which resulted from the prevailing severe economic conditions. During the extreme winter weather and extraordinary snow fall of February 1947, Fforest Lodge's heating system failed, and a Ceremony was performed with Regalia being worn on top of overcoats!

Perhaps in anticipation of slowly improving circumstances and with the approaching Diamond Jubilee year of 1956, a new set of Collars and Cuffs were purchased. There were several important events during this sixtieth year, one of which was the establishment of reciprocal visits with North Glamorgan Lodge No.4055. On 1 February 1956, the WM had written: *'With my Officers, I have accepted an Invitation to Conduct a Ceremony at our Sister Lodge, the North Glamorgan and the WM WBro Jesse Roberts extends a warm welcome to as many of the Fforest Brethren as would find it convenient to attend. This Inter-Lodge event, to be held on 27 February, has been conceived as to foster a closer relationship between the two Lodges and we hope to reciprocate the Honour at an early date.'*

There was indeed a reciprocation of this offer, for on 2 May it is recorded: *'The Ceremony was conducted by the WM of the North Glamorgan Lodge, WBro Jesse Roberts, assisted by his Officers, in a dignified and sincere manner. There would appear to be a consensus of opinion that this idea of inter-lodge courtesy has taken root and can result in naught but good for all concerned.'*

WBro D Roger Jones wisely decided to produce a journal during his year. It was in fact a collection of monthly bulletins and requests for information of any sickness amongst the Brethren. It was the forerunner to the present day Lodge Summons. The journal records that the freehold of the Temple had been acquired, following negotiations over a period of four years and involving all kinds of complications attendant upon the existence of two separate leases. The consequence of this development was such as to induce the comment, *'We may now consider improving our Premises and bring it more in line with what one would appreciate in a Masonic Meeting place.'* Examination of the Minute books reveals that there were several occasions during the years 1948, 1950 and 1951, when inspections, reports and repairs were required regarding the fabric of the building. By1954, such was the condition of the building, that a special meeting of the Trustees decided to increase the annual subscriptions for the purpose of funding improvement and for the purchase of the said freehold.

The Festival Year for Masonic Girls and Boys was in 1957, when the Lodge had pleasure in recording that one of its own Brethren had been appointed as one of two, to supervise the Festival Campaign. Incidentally, it was the same Brother who had ten years previously been responsible for writing and compiling the Golden Jubilee Booklet, namely, WBro J Vaughan Harries PPrGW, PAGSuptWks, and Fforest Lodge Home Charity Representative.

In April 1960, a Special Dispensation was granted for the Lodge to hold its Regular Meetings at the Merthyr Temple, in order that repairs and improvements could be carried out on the Treharis Temple. The work being completed, Meetings were resumed at Treharris on 8 September 1960. During the whole of this period it was 'business as usual', and the Lodge continued Initiating Candidates. In 1970, RWBro the Lord Swansea, ProvGM, visited Fforest Lodge and actively involved himself in an Initiation Ceremony by delivering the Charity Charge to Bros J D N Thomas and D G R Morgan.

An opportunity arose to purchase freehold land at the rear of the Lodge building, and thoughts were focused on extending the premises to provide kitchen and bar facilities. The NCB was the freeholder, and negotiations to acquire the land commenced in 1971 and were completed in the following year. The estimate to carry out such work made it necessary to postpone such plans, until sufficient funds became available. At this time, the Lodge donated a windbreak of Cypress Leylandii trees to the Albert Edward Prince of Wales Court, Porthcawl, for their bowling green. In 1976, the Lodge felt justifiably proud of its Charity Steward WBro George Roy Watkins, who worked tirelessly to manage, what was then, a large contribution of £11,000 to the Festival of that year.

On 27 April 1978, a Warrant was granted to WBros E Williams, Tom L Wilson and J M Williams, to hold Holy Royal Arch Chapter Meetings at the Fforest Temple. This Warrant is now displayed on the South East wall of the Temple. Unlike any of the other Warrants, this one was specially treated so that it could not be damaged by damp / water etc. The cost was paid for by Comp Douglas John Davies, Founder Assistant Scribe E.

In this same year, it was decided at the Officers' Meeting, to commence the extension to the premises. Full planning permission was obtained and suitably qualified Fforest Lodge Brethren took responsibility for the project. However, woodworm was discovered in some of the joists and rolled steel joists had to be installed to replace the affected parts. A party of Members worked heroically to repair these defects, and afterwards continued with the planned extension of the kitchen and bar areas.

In 1980, Lord Swansea outlined a scheme to promote closer contact between Lodges and the Province. It was thus that WBro Les Jeans became the Mandated Grand Officer and, in 1982, he accepted Honorary Membership of the Lodge. He continued as Mandated Officer until WBro Elwyn Williams attained Grand Rank in 1990. Until this time, the Offices of Director of Ceremonies and Secretary had been progressive Ranks, but it was Lord Swansea's wish that these Offices should become permanent. However, in order to maintain continuity with administrative matters, it was not until the Installation Meeting in December 1987, that this was implemented. Thus in 1987, WBro Alun Jehu was appointed DC, and continued to serve in that role for 17 years.

WBro Viv A Telling was appointed to the Office of Secretary and remained in that post until 1997.

In 1981, a generous gift of a portrait in oils of the distinguished Primus Master, WBro George Frederick Harris, was received from our Mother Lodge, Loyal Cambrian Lodge, Merthyr. This gift further underlined the close links that have always existed between the two Lodges.

By 1988, the condition of the building was again in doubt, when the presence of dry rot was reported at a Lodge Officers Meeting. Work on the front exterior of the building revealed the severity of the problem. In essence, the whole fabric of the building had to be replaced, and whilst this was happening, the Lodge again obtained Special Dispensation to hold its Meetings at Merthyr Tydfil. WBro John R Rees, C Eng, led the restoration team and WBro D Hubert Davies was responsible for recording details of donations received from the Brethren, together with details of invoices and the payment of bills etc. The Fforest Lodge building was closed for normal business between July 1988 and April 1989. Normal Lodge would never have been resumed had it not been for those Lodge Members who willingly gave of themselves and their time in order to repair and replace most of the building, and those who worked so effectively to raise the necessary funds. One such individual was Home Charity Representative WBro Elwyn Williams, PAGDC, who deserves particular mention. He was Initiated in March 1950, became WM in 1964, and attained Grand Rank in 1990. As a successor to the Mandated Officer, WBro Les Jeans, WBro Elwyn served the Lodge for 42 years, until his passing in April 1992.

A year later, discussions were held under the Banner of the United Orders of Knights Templar and Knights of Malta to form a Preceptory at the Fforest Temple. WBro David H Withers made all the relevant applictions, which resulted in the issue of a Warrant on 4 June 1993, for Fforest Preceptory No.582. Just two years later, WBro D Gwilym Edwards received Grand Lodge Honours, being Invested as PGStB. His celebrations heralded the start of the Centenary Year, and then in December 1995, WBro R L Hughes Installed his successor WBro Ivor Pike. It was destined to become a landmark year in the History of the Lodge, with the additional Ruby Anniversary Celebration of the Reciprocal Visits with North Glamorgan Lodge.

At the June 1995 Meeting, there was a special presentation of cut glass whisky glasses, a decanter and a suitably inscribed wooden tray to WBro Ken Adams Morgan, AProvGM, to mark his recent retirement. Ken responded by saying *'The Fforest Lodge was the first Lodge I visited after being Initiated in June 1946, and it is true to say that as a result I have always felt a close affinity to the Fforest Lodge throughout my Masonic life.'* WBro Ken Adams Morgan was an Honorary Member of the Lodge.

Special Dispensation was granted to hold the Centenary Meeting on 30 October 1996. Due to the restricted seating capacity of the Lodge Room, some Members would unfortunately be unable to attend! The Centenary Jewels were ordered and the Agenda was set for this most important Meeting. RWBro the Lord Swansea, ProvGM, and a full supporting Provincial Team were received in due form. WBro E M Howells, PPrAGDC, read a brief version of 'The First One Hundred Years of Fforest Lodge, No.2606'. The Secretary, WBro Viv A Telling, PPrGReg, read out the Warrant of the Lodge. WBro James R Bevan, PAGDC, ProvGSec, read the Centenary Warrant and the ProvGM presented the Centenary Jewels to the Lodge. The WM reciprocated by presenting a Centenary Jewel to the ProvGM, who was then asked if he would unveil the Centenary Commemorative Plaque. The Lodge Charity Steward, WBro David G Edwards, PGStB, presented a donation to the ProvGM as a contribution to his next Festival List. The ProvGChap, WBro Rev N Lea, then delivered an Oration.

The Brethren then retired to the dining hall for the banquet. During the Toasts, the WM paid tribute to the ProvGM, who responded by Proposing a Toast to Fforest Lodge. A surprise last minute presentation of a miners lamp to the ProvGM was made by WBro Terence Arthur Rowe. A cake was then produced, which Lord Swansea was invited to cut, a slice of which was taken with him as he was chauffeured back to Cardiff in order to board the train for London.

Since the Centenary Year, the Lodge has Dedicated a new Banner, the original Banner having disintegrated over time. The new Banner was beautifully crafted in acrylic paint by WBro Sid Robling of Yr Efail Lodge No.9502, Pontyclun. The Dedication Ceremony took place on 12 October 2000, during which the DepProvGM, VWBro Peter Frost addressed the Brethren.

Compiled by WBros Ivor B Pike, PPrJGD and Viv A Telling, PAGDC with acknowledgements to WBros J Vaughan Harris, PPGW, PAGSuptWks, and WBro Mansel Howells.

Loyal Commercial Lodge No.2720

Warranted : 14 June 1898

Constituted : 22 September 1898

Meeting at the Masonic Hall, Cardiff.

Towards the end of the 19th century, Brethren mainly from Llangattock, Bute and Tennant Lodges in Cardiff found it difficult to attend their Lodges, because their work/business took them away during the week. (All Lodges in the Province met on Monday to Friday at that time). This prompted them to form a Saturday Lodge and on 6 April 1898, the first recorded meeting was held at the Park Hotel, Cardiff to discuss the project and to make preliminary arrangements for the Lodge's formation.

There were 24 Petitioners, of whom ten were Commercial Travellers, the remainder consisting of Accountants, Solicitors, Tailors, a Chemist, a Music Teacher, a Merchant, an Iron-founder, an Insurance Inspector, a Boot-maker, and a Clerk in Holy Orders. It was resolved that the Petition would be presented by the WM, SW and JW Designate (see below) first at Llangattock Lodge on 25 April, and afterwards at Bute Lodge on 10 May 1898. These two Lodges are therefore the Joint Sponsoring Lodges.

It appears there was great difficulty in deciding a name for the Lodge. Marmaduke Tennant, DepProvGM, wished them to adopt the Warrant of the then almost defunct Talbot Lodge. The Brethren had other ideas and insisted on a new name. After many attempts, they finally decided on 'Loyal Commercial', the DepProvGM conceding with the remark *'Commercial Gentlemen are Men of Honour'*.

The Principal Officers Designate were WBro William James Jenkins, Worshipful Master, a PM from Gloucester who was also PM Tennant and Bute Lodges; WBro Henry Y White, Senior Warden, PM Llangattock and Bute Lodges, and Brother Albert Gardner, Junior Warden, a Steward of Bute Lodge. WBro Henry White withdrew his nomination after the issue of the Warrant, and the Lodge had to seek Dispensation from Grand Lodge to have the name WBro Charles Jones substituted. This can be seen by the post-script to the Warrant.

The Consecration of the Lodge was reported in 'The Craftsman', a Masonic Magazine, published in Cardiff towards the end of the 19th century: *'Consecration of the Loyal Commercial Lodge took place on 22nd September 1898. Lord Llangattock was present and Marmaduke Tennant was in attendance. The consecration followed the meeting of the P.G.L. in Cardiff. The banquet was held at the Park Hotel under the chairmanship of Lord Llangattock. The first W.M. was William James Jenkins, P. P. G. Standard Bearer of Gloucestershire.'*

The Consecration Banquet was not held until the following month, and this was reported in the next edition of 'The Craftsman':
The Installation Banquet & Concert of Loyal Commercial Lodge was held the following month on the 22nd October in the Lesser Park Hall, under the supervision of Bro. Evans, Manager of the Park Hotel. D.P.G.M. Marmaduke Tennant was present. The ceremony in the Temple, Guildford Crescent, was the initiation of Bros. Thomas, Dobbs and Howells. The concert included an orchestra of 26 performers under their conductor T. E. Aylward. They 'played selections in grand style'. The 'Goodwillie Singers' gave some excellent glees. The soloists included Madame Emily Francis, Miss Marion Isaacs and Miss Miriam Jones. Madame Clara Novello Davies (The Mother of Ivor Novello) *presided at the pianoforte, and her charming presence and skilful accompaniment added much to the success of the gathering.'*

The Lodge fees were initially set at £2.2.0 and were inclusive of the annual banquet. The Badge and Banner were designed by Henry White. The Lodge Motto *'Hic Et Ubique'* means *'Here and everywhere'*, which was considered to be appropriate for Commercial Travellers. From the beginning, it was not unusual to have Double Ceremonies and multiple Candidates. In January 1899, 4 Entered Apprentices were to be Passed and 5 Candidates were to be Initiated.

The first Initiate to attain the Chair of King Solomon was Lewis Lougher, who had been Initiated into the Lodge in December 1898. He was Installed as such in 1905. That same year, he was also appointed Provincial Grand Registrar. In 1921, he became Provincial Senior Grand Warden and five years later he was appointed Senior Grand Deacon of UGLE. Lewis Lougher was a Founder of Hendre, Caerdydd, Amethyst and St Quentin's Lodges. Educated in Cardiff Secondary School and Cardiff Technical College, he was first apprenticed to Corn Merchants, but soon entered the Shipping Business, establishing in 1910, the Shipping Company 'Lewis Lougher and Co., Ltd', with a fleet of ships in Bute Docks. He became Chairman of a large number of Shipping Companies in Cardiff, Penarth and Barry, Chairman of the Federation of Bristol Channel Shipowners in 1919 and Chairman of the Cardiff Chamber of Trade. He was a member of Glamorgan County Council, 1922-1949, MP (Conservative) for Cardiff East, 1922-1923, and for Cardiff Central, 1924-1929. A JP for Glamorganshire and High Sheriff in 1931, he received a Knighthood in 1929. He contributed generously to all kinds of organisations and philanthropic causes, including the Masonic Institutions, and in 1923 he donated the magnificent sum of £10,000 to the Cardiff Infirmary. A bachelor, he lived for a long time in the mansion 'Danybryn', Heol Isaf, Radyr (now the Leonard Cheshire Disability Home), but in about 1939, he and his unmarried sister Charlotte Lougher moved to live nearby in Northlands, Radyr, where he died on 28 August 1955.

February 1910 saw the first official visit to Dr. James Griffith Hall Lodge No.3161, Swansea, followed in the April by a return visit form the Swansea Brethren. These annual exchange visits remain unbroken through two Great Wars and a typhoid epidemic!

In September 1913, Sergeant-Major Charles Burley Ward, a Physical Training Instructor of 6 Soberton Avenue, Whitchurch, Cardiff was Initiated. Although this entry meant very little at the time, a most interesting story developed in the 1980s. He was a 22 year old Private serving in the 2nd Battalion, King's Own Yorkshire Light Infantry, during the Boer War, when the following deed took place, for which he was awarded the VC:

Citation London Gazette 28 Sept 1900 *'On 26th June 1900 at Lindley, a piquet of the Yorkshire Light Infantry was surrounded on 3 sides by about 500 Boers at close quarters. The two officers were wounded and all but six of the men killed or wounded. Pt. Ward then volunteered to take a message asking for reinforcements to the signalling station about 150 yards in the rear of the post. His offer was at first refused owing to the practical certainty of him being shot, but on his insisting, he was allowed to go. He got across untouched through a storm of shots from each flank and, having delivered his message, he voluntarily returned from a place of absolute safety and re crossed the fire swept ground to assure his C.O. that the message had been sent. On this occasion he was severely wounded. But for this gallant action the post would certainly have been captured.'*

of PAGDC. In 2005, he was appointed Provincial Senior Grand Warden, one of the few Brethren to have served actively as Junior and Senior Provincial Grand Wardens. In 2009, Peter was promoted in Grand Lodge to PJGD.

At the end of 1979, the Lodge decided to take part in the formation of the 'Family Lodges', meeting in Cardiff; with Llangattock Lodge No.2547 as Mother Lodge of Loyal Commercial Lodge and Gwalia Lodge No.4213; and Amethyst Lodge No.4026 and Preswylfa Lodge No.5792 as Daughter Lodges of Loyal Commercial Lodge and Gwalia Lodge respectively. Amethyst Lodge declined to take part, but the Brethren of the other Lodges agreed to support each other by visiting at least once a year.

The February Meeting of 1980 was designated to honour WBro Harold Wilson's 50th Anniversary of joining the Lodge. As a mark of respect, the Lodge was visited by the Rt Hon the Lord Swansea, DL, ProvGM, VWBro Geoffrey Malin Ashe, TD, PGStB, DepProvGM, and WBro Cuthbert L Summers, PGSD, AProvGM, together with 77 distinguished guests from around the Province and from adjoining Provinces. WBro Robert Harvey, WM, invited WBro Harold Wilson, to occupy the Chair, and perform the Second Degree Ceremony. He was ably assisted by VWBro Geoffrey Ashe, who presented the Tools of the Degree; WBro Cuthbert Summers who delivered the Charge, and RWBro the Rt. Hon the Lord Swansea, who explained the Tracing Board; making this a truly unique occasion.

For 85 years from its inception, the Lodge had maintained a book containing the Installation Ceremony which was passed on to each successive WM. In 1983, it was decided this historic document was too important to be held by individual WMs and it was resolved that in future the book would be kept in the Lodge 'safe' to be duly signed by each consecutive WM immediately after Installation.

In 1991, WBro Peter Gough reported that he had found the first Past Master's Jewel in a Jeweller's in Cowbridge, and had bought it to present to the Lodge. He also reported that through the good offices of Prince Llewellyn Lodge, the original Inner Guard Jewel had been returned, and in future it would replace the substitute worn on the IG's Collar. It was decided that the first PM Jewel inscribed *'Primo WBro W J Jenkins 1898'* should be presented together with a new PM Jewel each year. The new Jewel was to be worn at Masonic Functions outside the Lodge, while the original one only when on duty in the Lodge.

In February 1998, Lodge Meetings were reduced to 4 per year. On 28 November 1998, the Lodge Celebrated its Centenary, which was attended by RWBro the Lord Swansea, ProvGM, who presented the Centenary Warrant to WBro Royston E Lewis, WM, who in turn presented Lord Swansea with a cheque for £2720.

Justin Peter Christian Gough, the younger son of WBro Peter Gough, was Initiated by his father on 16 February 2002. The following year, on Saturday, 22 February, WBro Peter was afforded the privilege of Raising his son. He was assisted in the Ceremony by WBro Geoffrey W Thomas, AProvGM, acting as DC; VWBro Cdr Roy Hopkin, PDepProvGM ,who delivered the Charge; WBro Robert Nettleship, AProvGM, who presented the Working Tools of the Degree and a number of Past Masters of the Lodge.

The Centenary visit to Dr James Griffith Hall Lodge, Swansea, took place in March 2009. It was celebrated by the exchange of Silver Loving Cups and a Loving Cup Ceremony was held at the Festive Board. These proceedings were repeated in April 2009 at Cardiff, when RWBro Capt Sir Norman Lloyd-Edwards, KCVO, GCStJ, RD*, RNR, ProvGM, was in attendance.

Compiled by WBro David R Findlay, PPrSGD,
from the Centenary Booklet by WBro Kenneth L Chapman, PPrGD.

Llynfi Lodge No. 2965

Warranted : 17 April 1903

Consecrated : 28 July 1903

Meeting at the Masonic Hall, Maesteg.

Llynfi Lodge is so named after the river which runs through the valley. The name, 'Llynfi', is taken from the Welsh word 'Llyfnwy', which means smooth waters, and conjures up a picture of tranquil scenery in this broad valley, prior to industrialisation. During the years 1890 to 1925, the Llynfi Valley gained a worldwide reputation as a producer of Admiralty-grade steam coal, high quality coking coal and what was regarded as the best house coal in South Wales. By the early 1920s, there were over 7,000 miners at work in the valley.

Llynfi Lodge No.2965 is the Daughter Lodge of Ogmore Lodge No.1752. At the time, Ogmore Lodge met at the Masonic Temple, Adare Street, Bridgend and, in 1902, some twenty-three Members of Ogmore Lodge lived in Maesteg and its surrounding area. These twenty-three Brethren decided to form a Lodge of their own. They were obviously influenced by the lack of transport, and of course the time committed to the working day. They felt that they could make greater strides in their own town, rather than spend time and effort in travelling the eight miles to and from Bridgend to attend Lodge Meetings, and other commitments associated with Ogmore Lodge. It appears that their proposal met with great opposition, but the Maesteg Brethren were united in their endeavours. There were nine Petitioners for the formation of Llynfi Lodge, namely: Thomas Bainbridge Boucher, Jonah Phillip Gibbon, Paul Hughes Watkins, Samuel Sampson Harries, Robert Seales, Isaac Jenkins Thomas, William Isaac, William Henry Llewellyn and Walter Kirkby.

A Charter of the Lodge or Warrant of Constitution was granted on 17 April 1903, and the Consecration of the Lodge took place on 28 July 1903. As Maesteg had no Masonic Temple, the Mission Hall of St David's Church was used to conduct the Ceremony. The organisation of the Consecration Ceremony revolved around the train timetables on the day. In order for the dignitaries, who had been invited to attend, to enjoy both the Consecration Ceremony and the Festive Board, proceedings had to be completed before the last train left the valley in the evening.

The Provincial Grand Master, RWBro the Rt Hon John Allan, 1st Lord Llangattock, was unable to attend the Consecration Ceremony, which was conducted instead by WBro Marmaduke Tennant, DepProvGM, who also Installed Thomas Bainbridge Boucher into the Chair of King Solomon. The WM Invested Bro Jonah Phillip Gibbon, SW; Bro Paul Hughes Watkins, JW, and the rest of the team of Officers. After the Consecration Ceremony, the Brethren, having had permission to appear clothed in Masonic Regalia in a public place, walked to the Star Hotel, Commercial Street, Maesteg, for the Festive Board. On 1 August 1903, the Neath Gazette' reported that one hundred Freemasons, drawn from various parts of the Province, had Consecrated a new Lodge in Maesteg. Also, that the people of Maesteg had lined Talbot Street to witness the colourful procession from the Mission Hall to the Star Hotel.

The first Regular Meeting of the Lodge took place on 14 October 1903, whereupon twelve Candidates, who had been proposed in open Lodge at the Consecration Ceremony, were duly Balloted for, and Initiated into the mysteries and privileges of Ancient Freemasonry.

For the first two years, Llynfi Lodge met at the Star Hotel in Commercial Street but, due to increasing Membership, a new Lodge building was constructed on a site adjoining the White Lion (later to become Woolworths Stores) at a cost of £655.00. It included an extra room for the Festive Board, which also meant that an annual Ladies' Festival could now be held.

The By-laws of the Lodge which were written in 1903, and re-confirmed on 11 March 1924, are largely those still in existence today.

As Llynfi Lodge flourished, it was becoming obvious that a bigger and better building was necessary to meet the present needs of the Brethren. After much discussion, in 1922, a Management Committee was formed to find a suitable site for a replacement Temple. Several sites were looked at, and finally the present site of 9-12, Castle Street, was agreed.

The colourful Ceremony of cutting the first sod was performed on 22 May 1924, under the command of WBro J W Cooper, WM. WBro Paul Watkins addressed the WM from the East before cutting the first sod. Bro B T Harris, SW, cut the sod in the West; Bro T Jones, JW, cut the sod in the South; and WBro Dr Walter Kirkby cut the sod in the North. The DC was WBro Alfred Nicholls. The records show that the Secretary, WBro David Thomas, read the Deed of Covenant; the WM addressed the Brethren; and the Chaplain, Bro Albert Edward Lockyer, offered Prayer.

The Foundation Stone was laid by RWBro C L D Venables Llewelyn, ProvGM, on 25 June 1924. He was accompanied by the WM, WBro J W Cooper. A second Foundation Stone was laid by WBro Henry Pendrill Charles, DepProvGM. The Provincial Grand Treasurer, WBro J Edgar Lewis, deposited a phial containing coins of the realm into the wall cavity. The Provincial Registrar, WBro J Percy Mountjoy, deposited a second phial into the cavity containing a parchment, which described the history of the Lodge, together with a current newspaper and many documents pertaining to that era. On addressing the Brethren, the WM stated that *'these deposits will make interesting reading in the far distant future where they will reveal some of the aspects of our lives at this time'*. The vessels containing corn, wine, oil, and salt were carried by WBros Dr Walter Kirkby, H Morgan, T J Bell, D Thomas, and A King-Davies, respectively. The Architect, Bro E J E Moore, presented the plans of the proposed building to the ProvGM.

Wednesday, 25 June 1924, was certainly a unique occasion in the history of the Lodge and for the town of Maesteg, and one that is unlikely to be repeated. Approximately two hundred Brethren had special Dispensation to walk in procession, clothed in Masonic Regalia, from the White Lion in Commercial Street, through Talbot Street, and on to the new Temple at Castle Street. This event created great interest for the people of Maesteg, who gathered in large numbers to witness the event. The procession was followed by a short ceremony.

Although Lodges were already holding Meetings in the new Temple, the Official Opening did not take place until 13 May 1925. WBro Sir David W Evans, DepProvGM, officiated at the Opening Ceremony. The door to the Temple was opened by WBro J J Harris with the aid of a gold key, which had been presented to him by the builder, Bro W J Lewis. Bro Lewis also presented the tools of his trade, which along with the gold key are still on display at the entrance to the Temple.

There are no records of any of the Brethren who served their Country in WWI. However, this Lodge was firmly established by the start of WWII. Many of the younger Brethren were called up for active service, several of the older Brethren volunteered for the Home Defence Service, and others were Bevin Boys, producing coal to keep industry going to aid the war effort. At this time, 103 Lodge Members were actively involved in the defence of their Country. Twenty were in the Army, one in the Royal Navy, one in the Merchant Navy, twenty-three in the Royal Air Force, twelve were Policemen, and forty-six were members of the Home Defence Service. W Bro A M Davies, Secretary, was pleased to confirm to the Provincial Grand Secretary at the end of the conflict, that no Llynfi Lodge Member had made the Supreme Sacrifice while defending his country.

The highest ranking Officer among the Brethren was WBro Oswald Herbert Lucas, PJGD. He joined the Territorial Army in March 1939 and was embodied into the Regular Army in September 1939. He was evacuated from Dunkirk in 1940 and commissioned into the Indian Army, having won a Sam Browne Belt for being an 'A' Cadet. He spent the 1941/1942 years in Burma, where he was in command of a Company of Sikhs. When he was de-mobbed in 1945, he had attained the rank of Lieutenant Colonel. WBro Oswald Lucas was Installed WM in 1968.

WBro Lynworth Rees Lewis, PPrSGW, joined the Army in 1939. When war was declared, he was posted to the Shropshire Light Infantry as a Pay Clerk. Promoted to Corporal, then Vice Sergeant, he was recommended for a Commission in 1941. He was promoted to 2nd Lieutenant, seconded to the Indian army and posted to South Africa. His secondment to the Indian Army ended in 1942. Promoted to the rank of Captain, he was posted to Burma, where he remained until the conclusion of hostilities. On his return to London, he played a large part in organising the VE Day celebrations. At this time, he was promoted to the rank of Major, becoming the youngest Major in the British Army.

Another Brother of note is WBro Glyndwr Morgan, PPrJGD. WBro Glyn enlisted in 1945, at the age of 17. After his basic training, he was posted to Germany for the 'clean-up' operation, and was involved in the Berlin Air Lift, and the repatriation of Jewish people to Israel. At the conclusion of the clean-up, Glyn was sent to serve as a Sergeant in the Army Air Corps, where his specialty was training personnel in the dispatch of large containers by parachute from Dakota Aircraft. It was during one of these training missions that Glyn became the subject of Court Martial Proceedings, for falling out of the Aircraft at 10,000 feet. Five of the eight containers had been successfully dispatched, but during the unloading of the sixth, Glyn's foot became entangled in a loose static line which caught on the container as it was being ejected, dragging him out of the aircraft. He was caught in the slip stream and dragged along the fuselage, where he stayed until his colleagues could drag him back on board. His injuries were only slight, and included bruising, grazes, and shock. His Commanding Officer recommended no further action at the Court Martial. WBro Glyn was de-mobbed in 1948, but was recalled under the Z Reservist Regulations, when the Korean War broke out. Glyn was offered a Commission and attained the rank of Lieutenant. He was finally de-mobbed in 1953.

One of the Lodge's treasured possessions is its Banner. The original Banner was presented to the Lodge by WBro Paul H Watkins in memory of his dear wife, Jane. The Banner had its design painted onto silk, but due to the ravages of time, the delicate fabric disintegrated. Fortunately, the Lodge has been presented with a new Banner by the late WBro Colin John Goodwin Davies. The new Banner design has been kept as closely as possible to the original, and the methods of needlework employed include appliqué and gold work. This Banner took many months of hard work to complete, and the Lodge is greatly indebted to Mrs Mary Davies, wife of WBro C J G Davies, who accepted the challenge. The finished product is a credit to her, and beholds her position as a Senior Lecturer in Textile Arts at the University of Wales. A typical colliery scene is depicted on the Banner, in recognition of the prominent part played by the coal mining industry in the development of the Llynfi Valley. The Banner was Dedicated by

WBro Geoffrey Malin Ashe, TD, in September 1978, at the 75th Anniversary celebration of the Lodge.

Two further Lodges have been born out of Llynfi Lodge. In 1948, Llynfi Lodge Sponsored Maesteg Lodge No.6805, Warranted on 1 December 1948 and Consecrated on 31 January 1949. One of the Founder Members of Maesteg Lodge is still alive today, in the person of WBro Thomas King-Davies. WBro Tom is still a Member of Llynfi Lodge as well as being a Past Master of Maesteg Lodge. In 1978, Llangynwyd Lodge No.8854 was Sponsored by Maesteg Lodge, and it is consequently a Granddaughter Lodge of Llynfi Lodge. WBro Tom King-Davies was a Founder Member, and the first Worshipful Master of the Lodge.

Being a long established Lodge, it is inevitable that some traditions have become firmly entrenched in our Masonic lives. Of these traditions some are as old as the Lodge itself and some are more recent. Among the long established traditions are the Annual Ladies' Festival, dating back to 1904; the singing of the Master's song at every Installation Festival; the singing of the Entered Apprentice's song, whenever possible at every Initiation; and the Hymn to absent Brethren followed by the Welsh National Anthem, at every Festive Board.

Two of the more recent traditions are jointly shared with the two other Lodges in Maesteg. Firstly, the Annual Church Service, which takes place in the month of May at Llangynwyd Church. The Masters of each Lodge read a portion from the scriptures, and a Minister, with Masonic connections, is asked to deliver the sermon. Secondly, since 1998, a Christmas Party for children with special needs from within the Llynfi Valley has been funded jointly by the three Lodges. There has been an average attendance of seventy children plus, if necessary, their carers. The primary entertainment is provided by Ms Vickie Evans, a Puppeteer ably assisted by Coco the Clown, in the person of WBro William David Wanklyn, PPrDepGDC, WM 2000 and 2009. The finale is the appearance of Father Christmas bearing a sack full of presents; the joy on those children's faces is a sight to behold.

The Centenary of the Lodge was celebrated in 2003. A Committee was formed to oversee the arrangements for this special occasion and comprised WBros Colin John Goodwin Davies, WM 1974; David Adams Treharne, PGStB, WM 1977; James Vaughan Harries, PPrGSuptWks, WM 1975; Colyn Chadwick Bennett, PPrJGW, WM 1982, Chaplain; Siriol Williams, PPrJGW, WM 1988; Peter Hamley, PPrGSwdB, WM 1998, Secretary; Brian Michael Kelly, PPrAGDC, WM 2001; and Richard Williams-Jones, PPrAGDC, WM 2002. The week of celebrations began on Sunday, 14 September with a Church Service at St Cynwyd's Church, Llangynwyd, followed by Sunday lunch at the Masonic Hall, Maesteg. On Wednesday, 17 September, an Emergency Meeting was held, by special Dispensation, to celebrate one hundred years of Llynfi Lodge. RWBro Hywel Davies, ProvGM, and many of the Provincial Executive were in attendance. Charity is a subject close to every Freemason's heart, and the Brethren of Llynfi Lodge are noted for their generosity. So much so that at the Centenary Meeting, WBro Peter Hamley, Secretary, on behalf of the Lodge, presented a cheque for £2,965 to the ProvGM. The amount, in pounds, was equivalent to the Lodge's Number on the Register of UGLE. The ProvGM congratulated the Brethren for their generosity, and immediately invited the Lodge Charity Steward, WBro Bryan Treharne Morgan, to receive the cheque and to deposit it in the Lodge's Charity Chest for the 2010 Charity Festival. The final event of the week-long celebrations was the Annual Ladies' Festival, hosted by WBro Richard Williams-Jones, WM, and his good lady wife, Jacqueline.

The Lodge continues to have a strong tradition, with eighty-six Brethren playing an active part in the life of Llynfi Freemasonry, assisted by a large number of subscribing Past Masters of wide-ranging Provincial Ranks, boding well for continued success.

Compiled by WBro Peter Hamley, JP, PProvGSwdB, Secretary.

Dr James Griffith Hall Lodge No.3161

Warranted : 3 April 1906
Consecrated : 19 July 1906
Meeting at the Masonic Hall, Swansea.

At the beginning of the 20th century there were three Lodges meeting at the Masonic Temple in Caer Street, Swansea. They were Indefatigable Lodge No.237, Talbot Lodge No.1323 and Caradoc Lodge No.1573, which met on Monday or Wednesday nights.

There were numerous professional and commercial Brethren who found it difficult or impossible to attend these Lodges during the week. This was sufficient reason for the Founding of a new Lodge which would meet on a Saturday night, thereby providing the opportunity for those who spent much of the week away from the area and their homes to attend Lodge Meetings.

The name of the proposed new Lodge, 'Dr James Griffith Hall Lodge', was suggested by WBro Marmaduke Tennant, PAGDC, DepProvGM. It is named after the distinguished surgeon and zealous Mason who was born in 1814, the year of the Battle of Waterloo. The son of James Hall, the Harbour Master and Corporation Treasurer, he trained at Guy's Hospital, London. His reputation as a caring doctor was well known. In fact, during 1851, he made 1,380 house visits. On 18 August 1840, he was appointed House Surgeon to the Swansea Infirmary, where he served in various capacities for over 50 years, during which time he was appointed a local magistrate. A Member of Indefatigable Lodge, he was Installed WM of the Lodge in 1850. In August 1890, he was presented with an Illuminated Address by the Committee of Management of Swansea Hospital in recognition of his 50 years uninterrupted service. This Illuminated Address is displayed in the Lounge of the Swansea Masonic Hall, and is printed at the end of this history. In 1890, when the Hospital adopted the newMotto: *'Pity and Need make all flesh Kin'*, the man depicted with the words was Dr Hall. He attended Indefatigable Lodge on the evening of 11 February 1895, which marked the 50th Anniversary of his Initiation into the Lodge. An Honorary Member of Cambrian Lodge No.364, Neath, WBro Dr James Griffith Hall died on 27 May 1901 and was buried at Danygraig Cemetery, Swansea. He left £500 towards a new operating theatre at Swansea Hospital. People made mention of his help of poorer people, and his readiness to give time and money – he was *'genial and straightforward'*.

There were twenty-three Petitioners, of whom thirteen were Members of Caradoc Lodge. The Petition, however, was recommended and signed by WBro Abraham Lyons, WM, and the Wardens of Indefatigable Lodge, thereby making it the Sponsoring or Mother Lodge, even though only 4 Petitioners were Members of that Lodge. Two Petitioners were Members of Talbot Lodge No.1323; with one Petitioner a Member of both Indefatigable and Talbot Lodges; and with one Petitioner from Cambrian Lodge No.364; Albert Edward Prince of Wales Lodge No.1429, Newport; and Holden Lodge No.2946, London. WBro William John Treharne, PM Caradoc Lodge, PPGReg, Solicitor, Swansea, was WM Designate. WBro Thomas William Thomas, PM Albert Edward Prince of Wales Lodge, PPGStB Monmouthsire, Timber Merchant, Swansea, was SW Designate. WBro David Gladstone Davies, IPM Talbot Lodge, PPGSwdB, Veterinary Surgeon, Swansea, was JW Designate.

The Lodge was Consecrated in the Swansea Masonic Temple on 19 July 1906, by WBro Marmaduke Tennant, due to the unavoidable absence of the Provincial Grand Master, Lord Llangattock. The Ceremony was held under the new Lodge Banner, with its Motto *'In Deo Confidamus' - 'In God we Trust'*. WBro William John Treharne was duly Installed as Primus Master. At the conclusion of the Ceremony, the Festive Board was held at the Metropole Hotel, Wind Street, Swansea.

In the early years of the Lodge, there was at least one Initiate, sometimes two, but as the years passed, so the number of Initiation Ceremonies increased. The largest increase occurred after WWII, when up to nine Candidates were Initiated during the Masonic Year. A large number of these were Commercial Travellers, who had spent most of the week away from their homes and families.

Charity was of great importance to the Lodge, and within four months of its Consecration, the first donation was sent to the Royal Masonic Institution for Boys.

In 1910, WBro E L Thomas, the Master of the Lodge, together with WBro H J Walliker, Master of Loyal Commercial Lodge No.2720, Cardiff, were instrumental in initiating the interchange of visits between the two Lodges. In March 2009, the two Lodges celebrated 100 years of uninterrupted visits, despite transport difficulties during the two World Wars and the outbreak of foot and mouth disease in the early 1960s. To celebrate this unique occasion, both Lodges exchanged Loving Cups, which are used by the two Lodges at specially arranged Ceremonies.

In 1927, Dr Hall Chapter No.3161 was Founded. For many years, this was a 'closed' Chapter, but has recently accepted Members from other Lodges. Indeed, the first non-Dr James Griffith Hall Lodge Member was Installed as First Principal in January 2008.

In September 1947, Dr James Griffith Hall Lodge Sponsored the Foundation of Lodge of St Cenydd, No.6567. In 1982, it Sponsored the Foundation of another new Lodge, Clyne Lodge No.9049. A number of Past Masters were Founder Members of this second Daughter Lodge. Annual exchange visits have since taken place with St Cenydd Lodge and Clyne Lodge.

For many years, the Lodge held a Ladies' Night in February each year which, due to the large Lodge Membership, was restricted to Lodge Members and their wives, and even then it was on a 'first come, first served' basis. Some 20 years ago, it was decided to combine the Ladies' Night with the December Meeting, and to invite Brethren and their wives from other Swansea Lodges. It has now become a tradition for the Lodge to hold its Candlelight Ceremony, followed by carol singing, on the third Saturday in December. Dr James Griffith Hall Lodge is unique in Swansea, as being the only Lodge to perform this Ceremony. The Ceremony of the Candles was conducted for many years by the Chaplain, the late WBro Vernon Probert, and after his demise it has been conducted by his successor as Chaplain, WBro E L Thomas. The carol singing has been conducted by WBro Geraint Morgan for many years. Thanks to their assistance and the popularity of the Ceremony, there are regularly between 120 and 150 in attendance on this night.

On Saturday, 21 October 2006, 120 Brethren were in attendance when the Lodge celebrated its Centenary in the presence of the

Provincial Grand Master, RWBro Hywel Davies and his Provincial team. The Master, WBro I R Lewis Jones, welcomed the RW Provincial Grand Master to Dr James Griffith Hall Lodge, and it was considered a great honour for the Brethren of the Lodge to receive their Centenary Jewel from the Provincial Grand Master. Later in the evening, all enjoyed a sumptuous feast and everyone who attended had an excellent evening.

Text of Illuminated Address, presented to Dr James Griffith Hall by the Committee of Management of Swansea Hospital:

'*Dr James Griffith Hall Esq,*
Honorary Consulting Surgeon,
Swansea Hospital.

Dear Sir,
On the 18th day of August 1840 you were appointed House Surgeon to the Swansea Infirmary and from that day to this, have faithfully served the Institution in the several offices of House Surgeon, Visiting Surgeon and Consulting Surgeon without interruption.
The Committee of Management desire to avail themselves of this, the 50th Anniversary of your appointment, to convey to you their keen sincere and heartfelt congratulations: and at the same time to express their deep appreciation of the skill, attention and kindness invariably displayed by you in the discharge of your onerous and important duties, and the very valuable services rendered by you to the sick and suffering extending over a period of no less than half a century, an incident unparalleled in the history of the Institution. During that time you have not only won but retained the regard and esteem of all with whom you have been brought in contact, especially the poorer classes to whom your name has become a household word.
'An arm of aid to the meek,
A friendly hand to the friendless,
But whose echo is endless:
The world is wide. These things are small,
They may be nothing, but then are all.'
In conclusion the Committee very earnestly hope that in the enjoyment of the health and every needful blessing you may yet be spared to see many happy returns of this Anniversary, and that the remembrance of a lifetime spent in alleviating the suffering of humanity may shed a halo over your declining years, and at the close impart to you that calm and peace which passeth all understanding and which the world can neither give nor take away.
Brethren in sunshine will reunite the kind.

Swansea Hospital, August 18th 1890'

Compiled by WBro A Jones, PPrSGD.

Hendre Lodge
No.3250

Warranted	:	30 July 1907
Consecrated	:	24 January 1908

Meeting at the Masonic Hall, Cardiff.

'Hendre Lodge was established primarily so that Masters and Past Masters throughout the Province of South Wales Eastern Division could meet and establish new friendships, ensuring Freemasonry, through an exchange of ideas, prospered under their leadership'.

The decision to form a Past Masters' Lodge in Cardiff had been taken on 14 December 1906, when it was decided that WBros George Clarry, WM Glamorgan Lodge No.36 (1893), ProvSGW (1897); Arthur Llewellyn Hopkins, WM 36 (1901) ProvSGW (1910) and WM Hendre Lodge (1921) and Thomas Farrance, WM 36 (1906) ProvGReg (1907) be appointed to serve on a committee to implement the decision. The Secretary of the Committee was the Solicitor, WBro Tom Rodway Hunt, ProvSGW (1901), WM of Talbot Lodge No.1323, Swansea (1892), WM Prince Llewellyn Lodge No.2570 (1899) and a Joining Member of Glamorgan Lodge (10 July 1891). He was the guiding light leading up to the formation of Hendre Lodge and beyond, being the Founder Secretary and WM in 1912. The recommending or Sponsoring Lodge was Glamorgan Lodge No.36, thus Hendre Lodge was to become Glamorgan Lodge's fifth Daughter Lodge.

On 25 March 1907, Rodway Hunt wrote to all the Lodges in the Province, informing them that it had been resolved to form a Past Masters' Lodge, to be called 'Hendre Lodge' to meet at the Masonic Temple, Cardiff on the 4th Thursday in January, April and October. In his letter, Rodway Hunt emphasised *'to make the movement the success it deserves, we are desirous of starting with a large number of Petitioners and Founders'*. The Founders' fee, including Jewel, would be £2.2.0 and the annual subscription £1.1.0 (inclusive of suppers, but not wine). He further stated that RWBro Lord Llangattock, ProvGM, was nominated as WM Designate; VWBro Marmaduke Tennant, DepProvGM as SW Designate and WBro Arthur Griffith Poyer Lewis, WM of Prince Llewellyn Lodge (1897), WM Narberth Lodge No.2001 (1898), ProvSGW (1902), PGD (1905), as JW Designate. The latter was a Barrister-at-Law, Registrar of the Diocese of Llandaff (1885), Recorder of Carmarthen (1890), DepProvGM of Mark Masons, 1899-1909, and the son of WBro Rt Rev Richard Poyer Lewis, Bishop of Llandaff, 1883-1905, GChap (1896). Bishop Lewis died in May 1909.

The response was remarkable, 162 Past Masters signed the Petition, and at the Consecration a further 69 became Joining Members. The Warrant for Hendre Lodge No.3250 was signed on 30 July 1907, on which the following seven Petitioner's names are displayed: The Rt Hon John Allan Rolls, Baron Llangattock, Marmaduke Tennant, PAGDC, Arthur Griffith Poyer Lewis, PGD, Tom Rodway Hunt, George Clarry, Charles Edwin Dovey and David Rees Lewis.

Some other well known Founders were: Henry Pendrill Charles PPSGW, PM Cambrian Lodge No.364, Neath SD Designate; H

B Crouch, PPrGStdB (Somerset), PM Pilgrims Lodge No.772 Glastonbury, Somerset, (Designer of the Founder's Jewel); Charles Edwin Dovey, PProvSGW, PM Bute Lodge No.960, Kennard Lodge No.1258, Monmouthshire, Duke of York Lodge No.2453, Treasurer Designate; The Rt Hon Lord Glantawe, PProvJGW, PM Talbot Lodge No.1323; Charles Robert Lyne, PGD, DepProvGM Monmouthshire, PM Silurian Lodge No.471 and Charles Lyne, Installed Masters' Lodge No.2964, Monmouthshire.

A large number of Masons from this Province and surrounding Provinces gathered at the Masonic Hall, Cardiff, at 3.30 pm on Friday, 24 January 1908 to witness the Consecration of Hendre Lodge No.3250. The name 'Hendre' means 'Winter Dwelling' and was the home of Hendre Lodge's first Master, Lord Llangattock. Situated near Monmouth, golfers know the estate as the prestigious Rolls of Monmouth Golf Club. (The ProvGM's third son, the Hon Charles Stewart Rolls together with Sir Frederick Henry Royce founded Rolls-Royce Ltd. Charles died tragically in a plane crash near Bournemouth in 1910 at the young age of 32.)

The Consecration Ceremony was conducted by VWBro Sir Edward Letchworth, FSA, Grand Secretary, assisted by WBro Lieutenant-Colonel Charles R Lyne, PM, PGD, DepProvGM (Mon), as SW, and WBro Fred Phillips, PGD, DepProvGM (Mon), as JW. During the proceedings, RWBro the Hon and Very Reverend Dean of Hereford, PGChap, ProvGM (Herefordshire), as Chaplain, delivered an address on 'The Nature and Principles of the Institution', after which Lord Llangattock was Installed as the first WM.

During the proceedings, Marmaduke Tennant, SW, presented the new WM with a life-size white marble bust of himself, the work of the famous sculptor Goscombe John, which had been subscribed for by the twenty-four Lodges of the Province. In the course of his acknowledgement, the WM stated that *'he considered the bust to be a wonderful work by a wonderful man'*, humorously adding that *'the likeness was so exact that he did not know which was the more like, himself or the bust'*.

A Consecrating Officer's Jewel was presented to Sir Edward Letchworth, who during his period as Grand Secretary (1892 - 1917), Consecrated over 400 Lodges and Chapters, more than any previous Grand Officer. Jewels were also presented to the WM and Founders of the Lodge. The Jewels, designed by Henry Bryon Crouch of Cardiff, are of sterling silver, manufactured in Birmingham, and are full of Masonic significance.

The basis is the gold Pythagorean Star (five points) representing the five points of Masonic Fellowship, and golden, as golden light represents the warmth of Brotherhood and Charity. On an escutcheon in the centre is an enamelled painted view of 'The Hendre', the seat of Lord Llangattock, and beneath, on an enamelled ribbon, the name and number of the Lodge, from which the Past Master's Emblem descends. The upper part of the Star is linked by means of elaborate scroll-work to the lower ribbon mount, which has upon it three silver plumes, being the crest of the Prince of Wales and his motto *'Ich Dien'* (*'I Serve'*). The lower bar of the ribbon suspender, with foliated ends, is enamelled 'South Wales Eastern Division'. The upper ribbon mount represents the Arts of Freemasonry. Between the finials of the circle is an elaborate trophy, the upper portion being heart shaped, representing Fidelity, and bearing a Shield, containing the Crest of the Barons Llangattock, being a Knight's Helmet in blue enamel, sitting on a Baron's Coronet in red and white enamel and with white and black enamel plumes. Above the Helmet is a straight forearm with enamel detailing and holding a scroll of parchment. Partially framing the crest is a Banner infilled with white enamel and with text reading *'Celeritas et Veritas'* (*'Swiftness and Truth'*). In the lower division are crossed Leeks, while the two side divisions bear the Arms of South Wales and the Red Lion (the Arms of the Princely State of Powys). This trophy is completed with a light blue enamelled ribbon with Celtic decoration. The ribbon is dark blue, and the entire Jewel, the designer ventures to think, is a very worthy representation of the district represented by Hendre Lodge.

In the evening an extensive banquet was held at the Park Hotel and a programme of music was presented by 'The Llandaff Cathedral Quartet', consisting of Bros C J White, Harold Green, W O Balcombe and Harry Miller.

At the Election Meeting on 27 October 1910, the Ladies were invited to attend after the closing of the Lodge. They were entertained to an Organ Recital by WBro Westlake Morgan, PGOrg, UGLE. This is the only occasion that the Ladies have been entertained by the Lodge.

At the April Meeting in 1915, following the death of RWBro Lord Llangattock, WBro Henry Pendrill Charles moved that *'a Sum of thirty guineas be voted from the Lodge Funds to the Masonic Educational and Widows Fund, in memory of the late Provincial Grand Master'.*

Between 1921 and 1926, the October Meetings of the Lodge were held in Swansea. (The Province's second Past Masters' Lodge, Lord Swansea Lodge No.8364, was not Warranted until 9 December 1970.)

At the January meeting in 1933, WBro Edgar John Rutter, DepProvGM, was Installed WM in the Lodge's 25th Anniversary year.

The Lodge Meeting of May 1934 was held by Dispensation at Wood Street Congregational Church, Cardiff. This was the occasion of a presentation to RWBro Lt-Col Venables Llewelyn, Bart, to commemorate the 21st Anniversary of his Installation as ProvGM of SWED. RWBro the Rt Hon Lord Ampthill, Pro Grand Master, attended the Ceremony and a banquet was held afterwards in Cardiff City Hall. Approximately 1100 Brethren assembled to celebrate this event and a full report appeared in the 'Western Mail' on 31 May 1934.

In October 1940, WBro Rev Howell Elvet Lewis, MA, DD, LlD, PM Dewi Sant Lodge No.4728, PAGChap and Archdruid of Wales, 1924-1928, whose Bardic name was 'Elfed', became an Honorary Member of the Lodge. On this occasion, a fraternal visit was received from RWBro the Rt Hon the Earl of Derby, Provincial Grand Master of the Eastern Division of Lancashire.

On 6 March 1946, the Warrant for Beehive Lodge No.6265, Hendre's first Daughter Lodge, was signed.

During the Second World War, on the night of 2 January 1941, Cardiff underwent a severe aerial bombardment; 95 homes were totally destroyed, 233 so badly damaged that demolition was the only alternative and another 426 houses were uninhabitable until repairs were made. A bomb fell alongside Llandaff Cathedral and only Coventry Cathedral, among British Cathedrals suffered greater damage. In 1949, an appeal was launched for the restoration of the Cathedral, which was supported by all the Lodges in the Province, under the encouragement of Edgar John Rutter. At the October Meeting (1949), it was agreed that the Lodge should enter into a covenant to pay from the Lodge Funds, one hundred and fifty guineas, over a period of seven years, to the Llandaff Cathedral Restoration Fund.

In April 1952, a Deputation led by VWBro Edgar John Rutter was received, requesting Hendre Lodge's support for a Petition to form a new Lodge to be known as 'High View' (The Name of E J Rutter's home in Cyncoed, Cardiff). This name was subsequently changed to 'Grand Design' and later to 'Edgar Rutter'. Thus Edgar Rutter Lodge No.7196 became Hendre Lodge's second Daughter Lodge.

The Golden Jubilee Meeting of the Lodge was held in January 1958. During the ceremony, Edgar J Rutter gave a presentation on the first 50 years of the Lodge's existence. Reference was made to the banquet menu which followed the Consecration in 1908 and to the presence of WBro James Fraser, who was Installed WM of Loyal Cambrian Lodge No.110 on 3 January 1907. Edgar Rutter also referred to the close association of the ProvGMs, DepProvGMs and Provincial Grand Secretaries with the Lodge since its inception, all of whom had been Masters of Hendre Lodge. He expressed his hope for the future, that it would be the same as had prevailed for the past fifty years and he invited the Brethren present to join with him in singing 'O God, our help in Ages Past'. WBro Harry F Stockwell, AProvGM, proposed a vote of thanks to the DepProvGM, *'who had kept the Lodge going and alive'*, which was carried with acclamation.

In April 1971, WBro His Honour John Cleverdon Rutter (Edgar John Rutter's son) was Installed WM. A few months later, on 23 June 1971, Edgar Rutter died and a tribute was paid to him by Lord Swansea, ProvGM, at the October Meeting. At the time of his passing, he was the Senior Past Master. Likewise, his son John was the Senior Past Master of Hendre Lodge at the time of his passing on 14 May 2009, at the age of 89. A splendid raconteur with a keen dry wit, he was the regular proposer of the Toast to the visitors. His ongoing sagas took up where they left off at the previous Meeting and were keenly awaited by all present.

The number of Lodge Meetings was reduced from three to two on the proposition of VWBro Harry Stockwell, DepProvGM, in January 1974. The April Meeting was abandoned and the Installation Meeting was transferred to the October.

WBro J Stuart Peters, AProvGM, should have been Installed WM in October 1997, but because he had recently undergone a hip replacement operation, an Emergency Meeting for his Installation was arranged instead at the Masonic Hall, Swansea, on 24 November 1997. Unfortunately, he was still unable to be present, his hip replacement having become dislocated, and WBro John I Brown continued for another year as WM, under Rule 108b, Book of Constitutions. VWBro J Stuart Peters, by now DepProvGM, became WM of Hendre Lodge the following year, in October 1998.

In January 2002, VWBro Norman Lloyd-Edwards, President of the New Masonic Samaritan Fund, gave a lecture about the 'The New Masonic Samaritan Fund'. Little did the Brethren think that in 2008, Captain Sir Norman Lloyd-Edwards would be the Provincial Grand Master of South Wales.

At a Provincial Grand Lodge Committee Meeting on Friday, 4 May 2007, RWBro Hywel Davies, ProvGM announced that he would be appointing WBro Andrew Lindsey Gretton his Deputy Provincial Grand Master at the Provincial Grand Lodge Meeting on Monday, 25 June 2007. WBro Andrew was Installed as such on Thursday, 25 October 2007 and he was WM of Hendre Lodge, when the Lodge Centenary was celebrated on Thursday, 24 January 2008. The Centenary Celebrations were attended by RWBro David Kenneth Williamson, AGM.

Whilst researching the Lodge's records for its Centenary Celebrations, the Secretary, WBro Kelvin L Jones, ProvJGW, realised that a Lodge Banner had never been acquired. Consequently, a Banner was designed, manufactured and eventually Dedicated by Captain Sir Norman Lloyd-Edwards, on Wednesday, 21 January 2009. The design of the Banner is based on the five-star emblem of the Past Master's Jewel, within which is contained a representation of 'The Hendre', the home of Lord Llangattock.

At the Lodge Meeting on Thursday, 28 January 2010, WBro Sidney Cameron Richards, PPrJGW, PM Llangattock Lodge No.2547 was Elected to the Chair of King Solomon. Unfortunately, just a few days previously he had been admitted into hospital and consequently he was unable to be present at his Election. Tragically, he died in hospital just three weeks later. Had he been Installed in October as planned, he would have been the first Master of Hendre Lodge, since the outbreak of the Second World War, not to have already been an Officer of the United Grand Lodge of England.

In consequence of the untimely death of WBro Sidney Richards, PPrJGW, an Emergency Meeting of the Lodge took place by Dispensation on Tuesday, 20 April 2010 in order to Elect a Worshipful Master for the ensuing year. WBro Bernard Edward Smith, PPrJGW, a Past Master of Caerdydd Lodge No.3959, was Elected and his Installation took place on Thursday, 28 October 2010. It was the first time for a Provincial Officer to attain the Chair of King Solomon within Hendre Lodge since 1931, when WBro Willoughby Davies Hodges, PPrSGW, a Past Master of Merlin Lodge No.1578, became the Master.

At the Lodge Meeting on Thursday, 27 January 2011, RWBro Capt Sir Norman Lloyd-Edwards, KCVO, GCStJ, RD*, RNR, ProvGM was Elected to succeed WBro Bernard Smith as the next WM of Hendre Lodge. The Installation Ceremony will be held on Thursday, 27 October 2011.

Throughout the Lodge's History, the Prestonian Lecture had been delivered officially on several occasions (and sometimes unofficially). The table below lists all such lectures.

1928	WBro John Stokes, MD, PGD	'Masonic Teachers of the 18th Century' (Contemporaries of William Preston)
1931	WBro Rev W W Covey-Crump	'Mediaeval Master Masons and their Secrets'.
1934	WBro F Fighiera, PGD, WM and Secretary, Jubilee Masters' Lodge No.2712, London	'The Art, Craft, Science or Mystery of Masonry'
1947	WBro G Y Johnson, PAGDC	'A short biography of William Preston and an account of his early Masonic career'
1949	WBro Fred L Pick	'The Deluge' (An examination of early Masonic and other legends relating to the Antediluvian Pillars, the Ark and the Tower of Babel)

1950	WBro Ivor Grantham, OBE	'Lodges of Instruction-their Origin and Development'
1951	WBro H W Chetwin	'Variation in Masonic Ceremonial' Lecture delivered by WBro J Heron Lepper, PGD, Grand Lodge Librarian
1952	WBro Bernard E Jones, PAGDC	'Free in Freemason and the Idea of Freedom through Six Centuries'
1965	WBro Edward Newton, LGR, Assistant Librarian UGLE	'Brethren Who Made Masonic History'
1971	VWBro The Rev Canon Richard Tydeman	'Master and Master Masons-A theory of the Third Degree'
1992	VWBro The Rev Dr Michael Morgan, ProvGChap	'Masonry Pure and Applied'
1994	WBro M L Brodsky	'English Freemasonry in Europe 1717-1918' (An unofficial Presentation of the Prestonian Lecture)
1997	WBro John Goodchild	'Freemasons and the Friendly Societies' (An unofficial Presentation of the Prestonian Lecture)

As mentioned previously, the majority of the Lodge's Past Masters have been Grand Officers and no attempt has been made to give their biographical profiles in this account. In most cases, further details may be found in the histories of their other Lodges and to assist the reader, a comprehensive list is given below.

<u>Hendre Past Masters 1908 - 2010</u>

1908	RWBro The Lord Llangattock, ProvGM, PM 457
1909	WBro Marmaduke Tennant, DepProvGM, PM 833
1910	WBro Charles Edwin Dovey, PM 960; 1258; 2453
1911	WBro Henry Pendrill Charles, DepProvGM, PM 364;1323
1912	WBro Thomas Rodway Hunt, PM 2570
1913	WBro Sir John James Jones, PM 110
1914	WBro Henry Simons, PM 237
1915	WBro Tom Evans, PM 1992; 2720
1916	WBro William Roberts Davies, PM 1578
1917	WBro Thomas Wallace, PM 36 (Grand Superintendent 1928 - 1930)
1918	WBro William Lougher Yorath, PM 1754
1919	WBro George Whittington, PM 364
1920	RWBro Lt Col Charles L D Venables Llewellyn, ProvGM, PM 3320
1921	WBro Arthur Llewellyn Hopkins, PM 36; 3977; 4364
1922	WBro John Morgan, PM 110
1923	WBro James Barclay, PM 1323
1924	WBro Thomas George Dew, PM 2720
1925	WBro Richard Prichard, PM 2570
1926	WBro Sir David William Evans, DepProvGM, PM 2570; 4026
1927	WBro David John Jones, DepProvGM, 2547; 4213
1928	WBro Charles John Tazewell, PM 1573

1929	WBro George Wareham, PM 2357
1930	WBro William David Phillips, PM 1578
1931	WBro Willoughby Davies Hodges, PM 1578
1932	WBro Edmund Landers Thomas, PM 3161
1933	VWBro Edgar John Rutter, DepProvGM, PM 651; 1992; 3775; 5567; 5793;7196; 7305
1934	VWBro Edgar John Rutter, DepProvGM, PM 651; 1992; 3775; 5567; 5793; 7196; 7305
1935	WBro Richard Albert Richards, PM 2570; 3775
1936	WBro George Hagley, PM 36
1937	WBro Rees Williams, PM 3161
1938	WBro Sir Lewis Lougher, PM 2720
1939	WBro Charles Presgrave Palmer, AProvGM, PM 364
1940	WBro Reginald Pendrill St John Charles, ProvGM, PM 365; 3756
1941	WBro John Gibson, PM 2547
1942	WBro Edgar William Lewis, AProvGM, PM 833; 3756; 4778
1943	WBro David Evan Roberts, PM 36 (Grand Superintendent 1931 - 1950)
1944	WBro Griffith Jenkins, PM 2357; 3977
1945	WBro John McGregor, PM 1752
1946	WBro John Percy Mountjoy, PM 36; 4364
1947	VWBro Sir Frederick J Alban, 36; PM 4521; GTreas
1948	WBro Thomas John, PM 2720
1949	WBro Walter G Bishop, PM 1754
1950	WBro W J Canton, PM 110
1951	VWBro Harry Francis Stockwell, DepProvGM, PM 4113; 5793; 6015; 7196; 8364
1952	WBro David Thomas, PM 2965; 5084; 6805
1953	WBro Gerald Tudor, PM 4113
1954	WBro Lt. Col G J Morley Peel, PM 3327; 5160; 5285; 5772
1955	WBro Edgar W Young, PM 4113; 5290; 7139
1956	WBro Arthur W Shenton, PM 5997
1957	WBro Aubrey M Burns, ProvGSec, PM 3775
1958	WBro Henry Gethin Lewis, PM 2570; 4778; 4790; 7194
1959	WBro Rhys Morgan, PM 679
1960	WBro Richard T McGregor, PM 3959
1961	WBro Russell Mabley, AProvGM, PM 3756; 7305
1962	WBro Gwilym A Thomas, PM 2570
1963	WBro Hadyn Shaw, PM 4364; 7194
1964	WBro J Morgan James, ProvGTreas, PM 5772
1965	WBro Harry F Frost, PM 2547
1966	WBro Harold Wilson, APGM, PM 2720; 7196; 8364
1967	WBro Rev W E Mathias-Williams, PM 6695
1968	WBro Trevor B Phillips, PM 3959; 7353
1969	RWBro the Rt Hon the Lord Swansea, ProvGM, PM 1827
1970	WBro Arthur E Randall Edmunds, PM 7194

1971	WBro HH Judge John Cleverdon Rutter, PM 5793; 7196
1972	WBro Llewellyn G Bevan, AProvGM, PM 8364
1973	WBro Dudley E Morse, PM 5997
1974	WBro A E Lemmer, PM 1992
1975	WBro Malcolm Hays Thompson, ProvGSec, PM 3834; 7196
1976	WBro H Gethin Davies, PM 3769
1977	WBro G M Campbell, PM 7638
1978	WBro Gordon L P Elias, PM 6265; 8524
1979	WBro Ronald Bowen Whittingham, AProvGM, PM 1752; 7196
1980	WBro E J Smith, PM 2453:6030; 8748
1981	WBro Leslie H Jeans, PM 7196
1982	WBro Geoffrey Malin Ashe, DepProvGM, PM 7196: 8364
1983	WBro Windsor T Roper, PM 4364
1984	WBro Cuthbert Lionel Summers, AProvGM, PM 36; 7196; 7305; 8364
1985	WBro L G J Hamber, PM 3977; 8358
1986	WBro William H Walsh, PM 960
1987	WBro Samuel Northway, AProvGM, PM 6700; 7305; 8289; 8533
1988	WBro Ken Adams Morgan, AProvGM, PM 4055; 7196; 7982; 8364
1989	WBro E Haydn Lloyd, PM 5830
1990	WBro William G Cornfield, PM 8015
1991	WBro Richard W Dicker, PM 960
1992	WBro Thomas King-Davies, PM 6805
1993	VWBro Cdr Roy K Hopkin, DepProvGM, PM 1992
1994	WBro Ronald Moon, PM 5084
1995	WBro Stanley M Mortimer, PM 6299
1996	WBro John I Brown, PM 3775;8934
1997	WBro John I Brown, PM 3775;8934
1998	VWBro J Stuart Peters, DepProvGM, PM 6626; 7196; 8364
1999	WBro John D Hann, PM 6030; 8748
2000	RWBro Hywel Davies, ProvGM, PM 6354; 7305; 8364
2001	WBro Alvern M M Hart, PM 6299
2002	WBro Keith B Lockyer, PM 6805
2003	VWBro Peter Frost, DepProvGM, PM 3959
2004	WBro Melvin D M Thomas, PM 6299
2005	WBro James R Bevan, ProvGSec, PM 6729
2006	WBro W Graham Lloyd, PM 5084
2007	VWBro Andrew L Gretton, DepProvGM, PM 6015; 8512
2008	WBro S W Jeffrey Clarke, PM 5857
2009	WBro S Colin Best, PM 8024
2010	WBro Bernard E Smith, PM 3959

**Hendre Lodge
Founder's Jewel**

Compiled by WBro Kelvin L Jones, PAGDC, ProvDepGReg, Secretary.

Ithon Lodge No.3320

Warranted : 4 July 1908

Consecrated : 25 September 1908

Meeting at the Masonic Hall, Llandrindod Wells.

The Petition for the formation of the Lodge was submitted on 25 May 1908, having been recommended for a favourable consideration by the Master, Wardens and Officers of Loyal Wye Lodge No.1807, in the neighbouring town of Builth Wells. The Warrant of the Lodge was duly issued on 4 July 1908. Of the 20 who had appended their names to the Petition, 13 Brethren were Members of Loyal Wye Lodge.

Ithon Lodge was Consecrated at the Annual Meeting of the Provincial Grand Lodge of South Wales Eastern Division on 25 September 1908, which took place at the Albert Hall, Llandrindod Wells, in the presence of RWBro the Lord Llangattock, ProvGM, the Ceremony being conducted by VWBro Sir Edward Letchworth, Grand Secretary. Also present were RWBro the Hon and Very Rev James Wentworth Leigh, DD, ProvGM, Herefordshire, and Dean of Hereford Cathedral; WBro Marmaduke Tennant, DepProvGM; WBro Col Charles R Lyne, PGD, PDepProvGM, Monmouthshire, together with 71 Past Masters and 49 Master Masons representing 52 Lodges. At the time of its Consecration, Ithon Lodge was the 25th active Lodge in the Province. There were 26 Lodges, but St Quintin's Lodge No.1822, Cowbridge, had not met for over 15 years, and was eventually Erased from the Register on 5 September 1923. With the Grand Secretary occupying the Chair of King Solomon, WBro Marmaduke Tennant was invited to act as SW, and WBro Col Lyne as JW. The Warrant of the new Lodge was read, *'and the Officers named thereon were approved by the brethren in Masonic Form'*. During the customary Ceremony, the Warrant and Tracing Boards were paraded around the Lodge a total of four times. Then, the Primus Master of Ithon Lodge, WBro J H Tutton, PPGPurs, was duly Installed as WM, with Bro Grafton Sprague, Arrow Lodge No.2240, Headbrook, Kington, Hereford, Invested as SW, and Bro Penry C Jones, Loyal Wye Lodge, as JW. The remainder of the Founder Officers were Invested and they proceeded to conduct the first Meeting of Ithon Lodge, at which four Brethren were proposed as Joining Members and six names submitted as Candidates.

For almost the next 26 years, subsequent Meetings of the Lodge were held at the former Gwalia Hotel, 1-2 High Street, Llandrindod Wells. The Lodge eventually purchased a former private school at Park Terrace, which was converted into the present Masonic Hall. The building was opened and Dedicated by RWBro C L D Venables Llewelyn, ProvGM, on 22 March 1934.

The Lodge Banner was presented and Dedicated at the very first Installation Meeting at the Park Hall, Gwalia Hotel, on 26 November 1909, to the outgoing Master, WBro J H Tutton, by Bro E Powell Careless, first Initiate, on behalf of all the Brethren Initiated by WBro Tutton during that first year. WBro Tutton, in turn, asked the incoming WM, WBro A Grafton Sprague, to receive it as a gift from himself to the Lodge. This is duly acknowledged and recorded at the foot of the Banner.

The motif on the Banner depicts the Greek Goddess Hygeia with a snake entwined around her upraised left arm, striking a rock from which flows a stream. The falls are thought to refer to the various spa waters for which the town was famous. Hygeia was the Greek Goddess of Health and Well-being who, along with her father Asclepius, the God of Medicine, feature as dedicatees in the Hippocratic Oath. She is usually depicted with an entwined snake, a symbol of healing. Her name is the root of the word 'hygiene'.

In April 1913, Bro Lt Col Charles Leyshon Dillwyn Venables Llewelyn, of Llysdinam, Newbridge on Wye, a Member of Athlumney Lodge No.3245, was proposed as a Joining Member of Ithon Lodge, and was warmly welcomed as such at the Lodge Meeting held on 22 May 1913. On 27 October of that year, he was Installed at the Albert Hall, Swansea, as Provincial Grand Master for the Province of South Wales Eastern Division. Following his

Opening the new Masonic Hall 22 March 1934

Installation, he was Invested SW of the Lodge in November 1913, and was subsequently Installed as WM on 26 November 1914. His appointment to the Office of ProvGM certainly boosted the status and fame of the newly formed Ithon Lodge, and cemented a very special relationship. Upon his retirement as ProvGM in 1938, he returned to live in the family home at Llysdinam. He died on 24 June 1951 and was interred in the churchyard of All Saints' Church, Newbridge on Wye. His name appears on the family plaque alongside the church organ.

An illuminated scroll containing the names of Lodge Members who had served during WWI was presented to the Lodge by Bro Frank Edwards in 1921. Of the six Brethren recorded, one stands out : 'Bro. C.L.V. Llewelyn (P.G.M.) - Lt.Col. - Glamorgan Yeomanry'

On 12 May 1922, the Consecration of Dinam Lodge No.4521 took place in Ithon Lodge's new building. The Lodge was Founded by the Medical Staff and Officers of King Edward VII Welsh National Memorial Association. Initially, it met mainly at Ithon Lodge premises, until moving permanently to its current home in Penarth in June 1979. The Installation Festival was held in the Rock Hotel, Llandrindod Wells, in 1928 and, also in 1928, a Regular Meeting was held in Cardiff Masonic Hall. Indeed the pattern of changing locations for its Meetings continued until 1964, although invariably the Installation Festivals were held in Llandrindod Wells. It was not until 1964 that the venue for their Meetings was changed formally to Penarth. The Master and Secretary of Ithon Lodge were Elected as Honorary Members of the new Lodge and in October 1978 the Brethren of Dinam Lodge presented a new Bible to Ithon Lodge in recognition and thanks for the services rendered by the Lodge Members to Masonry during the 55 years' history of the Lodge. The new Bible was first used in December of that year, and is still used at Installation Meetings. It is very interesting that Dinam Lodge requested that their Installation Meeting be held at the Ithon Lodge Temple in 1981, indicating perhaps that they still look back fondly on their past links with Llandrindod Wells.

After long and distinguished service to the Lodge, WBro J Morgan James, who was Initiated in September 1922, was appointed as ProvGSec in 1960, an Office he held until 1967. He was made an Honorary Member of the Lodge in 1973, on the completion of 50 years in Freemasonry.

Strong links are maintained with the Mother Lodge, Loyal Wye Lodge and Grandmother Lodge, Brecknock Lodge No.651, in addition to the other Brecon Lodges, Vivian Lodge No.8267, Aberhonddu Lodge No.8588, and likewise, Loyal Hay Lodge No.2382, now in the Province of Herefordshire. Similarly, links are maintained with Arrow Lodge Herefordshire, Mother Lodge of Bro A G

Sprague, first SW, and his blood brother, Bro J Grafton Sprague, Treasurer until 1926.

In addition, Ithon Lodge maintains extremely good relationships with the neighbouring Lodges of Cedewain Lodge No.1594, Newtown; St Idloes Lodge No.1582, Llanidloes; Powis Lodge No.7355, Welshpool, all in the Province of North Wales; and Teme Lodge No.4267, Knighton, Shropshire. The close association the Lodge enjoys with the neighbouring Provinces was demonstrated at the Installation of WBro Ernie Beaumont in 2009, when he commenced his second term in the Chair of King Solomon, when RWBro Hywel Davies, ProvGM, was present, together with RWBro Rodney Smallwood, ProvGM of Herefordshire, and RWBro J B Lloyd, ProvGM of South Wales Western Division.

During the first ten years, Membership grew from 22 to 38. The first year of 1908-1909 was particularly impressive, with 18 Initiates and 1 Joining Member. However, the largest yearly increase was in 1920, when there were 18 Initiates and 4 Joining Members. Lodges of Emergency were a regular feature, for example in April 1920, there was a double Initiation Ceremony immediately followed by a double Second Degree Ceremony. Then, in the post WWII years, the numbers increased even further to 122 by 1951. Regrettably, the numbers since then have declined and, at the beginning of 2011, there are 51 Members.

No less than twelve Brethren have served 50 years in Freemasonry. These Masonic Veterans include PMs of the Lodge and Joining Members and they are WBro Austin Jenkins (Initiated 1919), WBro F J Edwards (1920), Bro J M Griffith (1920), W Bro J Morgan James (1923), WBro V Dilwyn Jones (1923), WBro L A Robertson (1933), WBro D Edgar Morgan (1946), WBro W Vernon Jones (1947), WBro K W Griffiths (1949), WBro J Rudge (1949), Bro Lt Col Evans, WBro Colin James and WBro Don Graham. The last three Brethren continue to be active Members of the Lodge. WBro L A Robertson became a Joining Member in 1984. He was Initiated with his younger brother by their father, who was WM of Cornerstone Lodge No.4941, London, and working in Great Queen Street at the time. He went on to complete 70 years in Freemasonry, which he celebrated in 2003.

In 1996, it became necessary to replace the central heating boiler and, in so doing, problems were encountered in fitting the internal chimney flue. Eventually the obstacle was found to be a bird's nest, no less than 10 ft long in size, situated between the second and third floors. It must have caused problems previously, as when it was removed so was a flue-brush and rods!

In 2008, on the precise Anniversary of its Consecration, the Lodge celebrated its Centenary at the Conference Centre, Llandrindod Wells. The recently Invested ProvGM, RWBro Captain Sir Norman Lloyd-Edwards, KCVO, GCStJ, RD*, RNR, was in attendance and presented the WM, WBro Keith W Harvey, with the Centenary Warrant. He also presented the Brethren of the Lodge with their respective Centenary Jewels. The Lodge Secretary, WBro Viv Lloyd, PPrAGDC, gave a précis of the history of the Lodge, and all those present received a book on the history of the Lodge. Just prior to the Centenary Meeting, a Founder's Jewel which had been presented to Bro Charles Selwyn, first Secretary, in September 1908, was returned to the Lodge by WBro and Mrs D Marlow. It had been given to them by Mrs Marlow's mother, whom Bro Selwyn had known for many years. Mrs Marlow senior taught the author, WBro Viv Lloyd, mathematics at Cyfarthfa Grammar School, Merthyr Tydfil, in the early 1940s. WBro David N Marlow is a PM of Harlequins Lodge No.5793, Cardiff.

The ProvGM, RWBro Captain Sir Norman Lloyd-Edwards, presented the Centenary Warrant to the WM, WBro Keith Harvey, at the Centenary Meeting.

Ithon Lodge's final claim to fame is that it is not only the northernmost Lodge in the Province but also, very probably, the highest, since the Temple is situated on the third floor of the building! Visitors all comment on this fact, but it does not deter them from coming time and time again. Although like most Lodges, numbers have decreased, the Lodge still enjoys attendances of 90 or more at Installations. This necessitates the Ceremonies being held elsewhere in the area, and has been a continuing feature since the Lodge was first formed, thereby demonstrating the warmth and friendship that emanates from the Lodge Members.

Compiled by WBro Viv Lloyd, PPrJGW.

The required declaration is always included in Glamorgan Lodge's Installation Ceremony. In some Lodges, the Ceremony had been known as the 'Past Masters Degree', hence the need for the final part of the declaration.

The 21st Anniversary of the appointment of Charles L D Venables Llewelyn as ProvGM was celebrated in the Province in 1934. It was decided to mark the occasion by presenting him with an Illuminated Address and Register of Freemasons, signed by every Member of all the Lodges in the Province. This is now on display at the Masonic Hall, Guildford Crescent, Cardiff.

In 1935, a Petition for the formation of Penllergaer Lodge No.5567 was Sponsored by Corinthian Lodge No.4917, Swansea. Brethren from Indefatigable Lodge No.237; Talbot Lodge No.1323; Beaufort Lodge No.3834 and Caradoc Lodge No.1573 were also included among the 40 Founder Members. The Warrant of the Lodge was signed on 7 August 1935, and the Consecration Ceremony took place at The Masonic Hall, St Helen's Road, Swansea on 24 September of that year, bringing the number of Swansea Lodges to ten. The Ceremony of Consecration was carried out by the ProvGM, who then Installed WBro Edgar J Rutter, DepProvGM, as the first Master of the Lodge. This was the final Lodge to be Consecrated during Charles D L Venables Llewelyn's tenure as ProvGM.

The Penllergaer Lodge is named after the ProvGM's ancestral home, which he inherited in 1927 on the death of his father, Sir John Talbot Dillwyn Llewelyn. The Estate boasted a very fine Victorian landscape which had been laid out by the PovGM's grandfather, John Dillwyn Llewelyn, who among other things was a nationally important figure in horticulture. The ProvGM chose to reside at his seat, Llysdinam, Newbridge on Wye, near to Llandrindod Wells. The Penllergaer Mansion was run with a diminished staff under the superintendence of the Butler, Robert Charles Richards and, in 1936, the ProvGM auctioned the contents of the house. The Mansion, requisitioned during WWII and occupied by American Troops, was badly vandalised. After the War, the house and immediate grounds were leased to the Bible College of Wales and, in 1961, the house was blown up in an exercise by the Territorial Army. Part of the Estate was eventually acquired by Glamorgan County Council, and Council Offices now occupy the site of the former mansion. The important landscape partially survives and, in 2000, the Penllergaer Trust was formed to save what remained from falling into further dereliction. Restoration is now continuing with the aid of Heritage Lottery Funding.

Charles Venables Llewelyn resigned as Provincial Grand Master in 1938, having served for a period of 25 years. He died at his home at Llysdinam, Newbridge-on-Wye, on Sunday, 24 June 1951. On the Friday of that week, he would have celebrated his 81st birthday. His son, Sir Charles Michael Dillwyn Venables-Llewelyn, who was not a Freemason, succeeded him to the title of 3rd Baronet of Llysdinam.

In the 1960s, Charles Michael was instrumental in establishing the local county Wildlife Trust. To bring long term financial stability to the core of the Llysdinam Estate, he established the Llysdinam Charitable Trust, with educational objectives centred around the land peripheral to Llysdinam House. In 1970, the Llysdinam Field Centre was opened by Sir Michael, which is run by the School of Biosciences at Cardiff University. He died on 15 March 1976, aged 76, and was succeeded by his son, Sir John Michael Dillwyn Venables Llewelyn, 4th Baronet.

Compiled by WBro Peter M Davies, ProvJGW.

Henry Pendrill Charles
1850 - 1925
Deputy Provincial Grand Master
1915 - 1925

Henry Pendrill Charles was born in June 1850, the son of Pendrill Charles, an Ironmonger and Grocer in Neath, and his wife Ann Jones, from Llandeilo, Carmarthenshire. Sadly, Henry's mother, Ann, died in December 1857, when he was only six years of age. His father remarried in 1868. His second wife, Alice Catherine née Williams, from Aberdare, was 19 years his junior. The young Henry was now an Articled Clerk and by 1871, a qualified Solicitor. In September 1875, he married Elizabeth Wearne, daughter of James Kempthorne, Attorney-at-Law, of Orchard Street, Neath, originally from St Ives, Cornwall. Four years later, their second son, Reginald Pendrill St John Charles was born, and destined to become Provincial Grand Master of the Province.

Henry was to immerse himself in local politics. He first became Mayor of Neath in 1878 and again in 1889, 1901 and 1916. His other appointments included Alderman; Chairman of the School Board, Neath; Chairman of Glamorgan County Council 1892-1895; a Justice of the Peace for the County of Glamorgan and Borough of Neath; Chairman of the Local War Tribunal Committee and Chairman of the War Pensions Committee. In addition, he was a Member of the Llandaff Diocesan Board of Finance and of the Governing Body of the Church in Wales.

The year 1900 was to prove to be most memorable and eventful. An Initiate of Cambrian Lodge No.364, Neath, Henry was first Installed as Worshipful Master of the Lodge on Tuesday, 13 March 1900. The event was unique inasmuch that the Master Elect was also Mayor of Neath and the Registrar of the Neath County Court. The ProvGM, Lord Llangattock, and his Deputy, Marmaduke Tennant, attended and 120 Brethren dined at the Festival Banquet held in the Castle Hotel.

On 20 September 1900, Henry Pendrill Charles was made the

Henry Pendrill Charles

first Freeman of the Ancient Borough of Neath. Over 300 people attended the banquet held in the evening, when he was presented with an oil painting of himself, and Mrs. Charles was given a magnificent silver tea and coffee service. This was also the occasion of their Silver Wedding Anniversary.

One week later, at Provincial Grand Lodge held in Neath on Thursday, 27 September, Henry was Invested Provincial Senior Grand Warden of the Province.

He was Installed Worshipful Master of Cambrian Lodge for the second time in 1911. A Special Dispensation had to be obtained, for at the time he was the fourth Worshipful Master of Hendre Lodge No.3250. In 1913, he became a Grand Officer with the rank of Past Assistant Grand Registrar.

The Deputy Provincial Grand Master, Marmaduke Tennant died on 24 January 1915 and on 11 February Henry Pendrill Charles was appointed to succeed him. Tragedy struck in March the following year, when his wife, Elizabeth died at the age of 65. Letters of condolence were sent from the Lodges in the Province.

The year 1916 was not all gloom and doom. On Saturday, 3 June, the Venables Llewelyn Lodge No.3756 was Consecrated and Henry Pendrill Charles was Installed as the first Worshipful Master. Then, on 23 August a new Lodge was Consecrated in Caerphilly and named in honour of the Deputy Provincial Grand Master - Henry Pendrill Charles Lodge No.3769. Sir Charles Venables Llewelyn, ProvGM, was unable to attend on account of his military duties, so it was, therefore, very appropriate that the Consecrating Officer was none other than Henry Pendrill Charles.

The following year, and for the same reason, the Deputy Provincial Grand Master was again the Consecrating Officer for Cardiff Exchange Lodge No.3775, which took place on Wednesday, 17 January 1917.

One of his last major public duties was the laying of a Foundation Stone of the new Masonic Hall in Maesteg. On Wednesday, 25 June 1924, approximately 200 Brethren, clothed in Masonic Regalia (by Special Dispensation), paraded publicly in procession from the old Masonic Temple in Commercial Street to the site of the present Temple, where the Foundation Stone was laid by RWBro Sir Charles Venables Llewelyn, ProvGM. VWBro Henry Pendrill Charles, DepProvGM, laid a second stone.

His death on 11 March 1925 was announced in the 'Western Mail' on Friday, 13 March: *'CHARLES – on the 11 inst. Henry Pendrill Charles, of Westfield, Neath, D.L., J.P., Deputy Provincial Grand Master Province of South Wales (Eastern Division) in his 75th year. Masonic funeral, Monday, 16 March, leaving Westfield at 2.30 for Cadoxton-juxta-Neath. No flowers, at his special request. He wished that all monies intended to be spent on flowers should be given to the Home Charities.'*

An account of his funeral appeared in the 'Western Mail' on Tuesday, 17 March, part of which is reproduced below: *'Masonic circles were well represented at the funeral at Neath on Monday of Mr. H. Pendrill Charles, for many years a prominent Freemason and Deputy Provincial Grand Master of South Wales (Eastern Division). Mr. Charles was registrar of the county-court, four times mayor of Neath, its first freeman, and a borough and county magistrate.*

The remains had been removed from London, where he died, to his residence, Westfield, Neath, and the burial took place at the Cadoxton Parish Church. Representatives of a large number of public bodies attended, and the vast concourse was an eloquent tribute to the esteem in which the general public held Mr. Charles.

The surplice clergy who officiated at the funeral were the Rev. Gwilym Francis, MA, rector of Neath and Masonic Chaplain, who conducted the impressive funeral rites of that body; the Rev. J. D. James, Vicar of Cadoxton, the Rev. T Bowen and the Rev. J C K Buckley, a nephew of the late Mr. Charles.

The mourners were Mr. Reginald P. St. John Charles (son), Mrs. Frank Gaskell (daughter), Mr. Rhys P. Charles (brother), Mr. A P Charles (brother), Mr. T K Godsell (nephew)...... Mr. Frank Charles, Registrar of the Swansea County-court (brother), was unable to attend owing to illness.

All along the route, from the house to Cadoxton, were groups of sympathetic onlookers, and the pupils of the county schools were lined outside as the cortege passed. The burial was in the family vault at the west side of the church, and on the coffin was a sheaf of primroses.

The cortege was headed by a body of the borough policemen under the chief-constable, Capt. Rawlings, and Inspector Michael, and a number of the Glamorgan Constabulary in charge of Superintendent Davies.

Following were: Mayor of Neath (Councilor Richard Jenkins), attended by the town-clerk (Mr. A E I Curtis) ......

Among the Freemasons who attended were:- Col. Venables Llewelyn, PGM. ....'

It was decided that Brethren of the Province should be invited to subscribe to a Memorial to the late DepProvGM. In September 1925, WBro George Whittington, ProvGSec, wrote to all the Lodges, and the main points of his letter are recorded below:

'*The Provincial Memorial Committee has met, and has come to the following unanimous decisions: -*

That the Memorial to the late Worshipful Deputy Provincial Grand Master, Wor. Bro. HENRY PENDRILL CHARLES, take the form of: -

(a) *An Organ at a cost of not more that £1,200 to be erected in the new Masonic Temple at Swansea.*

(b) *That a tablet suitably inscribed, together with a Framed Photograph of the late Wor. Bro. Deputy Provincial Grand Master, be supplied to every Lodge Room in the Province.*

(c) *That the Lodges in the Province be asked to subscribe towards the Memorial, and*

(d) *That a sum of at least 200 guineas be voted from the funds of Provincial Grand Lodge towards this object.*

It was suggested that I should communicate with each Master, inviting him to confer with the Treasurer of his Lodge as to what support would be likely to be given to the proposal by his Lodge. We hope to raise over £1,400.'

WBro Peter M Davies, ProvJGW.

Charles Edwin Dovey
1853 - 1927
Grand Superintendent of South Wales Eastern Division
1915 - 1927

Charles Edwin Dovey was born in Pontypool on 20 July 1853, the second of three sons of William Dovey, Schoolmaster, and his wife. Mary, Schoolmistress, both of whom were from Middlesex. There was also an older sister, Jane Maria Elisabeth, who was born in Aberdeen and who also became a Schoolmistress. In 1871, the family was living in Crane Street, Pontypool, and Charles, now 17 years of age, was employed as a Railway Clerk. Charles, Frederick and their sister Jane never married and, in 1901, all three were living together at 58 Cathedral Road, Cardiff.

Charles Edwin Dovey

Charles and his older brother Frederick both qualified as Chartered Accountants and, in 1887, he became a partner in the firm 'W C Clarke & Dovey', 31 Queen Street, Cardiff. His several appointments included City Auditor; Director of the Cardiff Gas Company; JP for Cardiff; Governor of the University College of South Wales & Monmouthshire; Vice-President of Cardiff Infirmary; Secretary of South Wales Merchants Protection Association; Secretary of the Mercantile Accident & Guarantee Insurance Company; Secretary / Liquidator for the National Bank of Wales Ltd and People's Warden of St John's Church, Cardiff.

Charles Dovey was a Lewis, his father being a Past Master of Kennard Lodge No.1258, Pontypool, and Provincial Grand Registrar of Monmouthshire. Charles was Initiated into that Lodge in 1875 and became Worshipful Master in 1904. He moved to Cardiff in July 1874, became a Joining Member of Bute Lodge No.960 in 1875 and was appointed Lodge Secretary in 1888. He became Worshipful Master of Bute Lodge in December 1890 and during his year in the Chair of King Solomon there were 20 Regular Meetings, 5 Lodges of Emergency and 25 were Initiated. During his year as Master, he presented the Lodge with a Bible. He became a Joining Member of Glamorgan Lodge No.36 on 9 October 1891. Also in 1891, he was a Founder Member of the Caer-Daf Rose Croix Chapter and of the Royal Ark Mariners attached to the Langley Lodge of Mark Masons. In 1891, he was appointed Provincial Grand Director of Ceremonies and was Provincial Junior Grand Warden 1893-1894. He became a life governor of the Benevolent Institution of the Royal Masonic Institution for Boys, of the Royal Masonic Institution for Girls and of the Masonic Educational and Widows' Fund. Charles Dovey was appointed chairman of the

250

committee responsible for the arrangements for the Installation of the RW Provincial Grand Master, RWBro the Lord Llangattock, in September 1894 and received the highest praise from the Pro Grand Master, the Rt Hon the Earl of Lathom, who attended the Ceremony.

The following year, Duke of York Lodge No.2453 was Consecrated on Thursday, 26 September 1895. This Ceremony immediately followed a Meeting of Provincial Grand Lodge in the presence of Lord Llangattock, ProvGM, which had been assembled for the formal opening of the new Cardiff Temple at Guildford Crescent. WBro Charles E Dovey, PProvJGW, was Installed as the first Worshipful Master of the new Lodge. Dovey was also a Founder Member of Loyal Commercial Lodge No.2720 (Warrant 14 June 1898).

On 20 December 1898, the Presidents and Vice-Presidents of the Cardiff Lodges of Instruction met at the Masonic Temple, Cardiff. The Meeting had been called by WBro Demetrius Steffano Varzopollo, PM Bute Lodge and President of Loyal Commercial Lodge of Instruction. The object of the meeting was '*to bring the whole of the Lodges to the same line of thought of working*'. Charles Dovey attended the meeting in his capacity as President of Duke of York Lodge of Instruction.

The Dovey Bowls Cup

Dovey became Chairman of the Board of Directors of Cardiff Masonic Hall Company in 1902 and was very involved in extending the premises and in acquiring the organ for the Duke of Connaught Temple. In 1907, he was appointed Provincial Senior Grand Warden. In the same year he was a Founder Member of Hendre Lodge No.3250 and his name appears among those of the seven Petitioners cited on the Warrant, dated 10 July 1907. He succeeded WBro Marmaduke Tennant, DepProvGM, as Master of Hendre Lodge in 1910. In 1911, he presented Bute Lodge with a photographic portrait of himself and a Jewel in commemoration of his appointment as Past Grand Deacon of the United Grand Lodge of England.

In 1915, he was appointed Grand Superintendent of Royal Arch Masonry, South Wales (Eastern Division). He had been the First Principal of Sir George Elliot Chapter No.960 in 1895; Provincial Grand Haggai in 1904 and Past Grand Sojourner in Supreme Grand Chapter in 1911. Dovey Chapter No.2720, attached to Loyal Commercial Lodge and Warranted on 2 August 1922, was named after him.

Charles Dovey was also a Member of Langley Mark Lodge No.28. In 1909, he became Most Worshipful Sovereign of Caer-Daf Rose Croix Chapter No.118, Cardiff, (Warranted in 1891) and had the 31^0 conferred upon him by the Supreme Grand Council in 1915.

He was a Founder of Amethyst Lodge No.4026 and he is the fifth Petitioner named on the Lodge's Warrant, dated 5 November 1919.

In 1922, Charles Edwin Dovey presented a solid silver loving cup to be competed for by the bowlers of the Cardiff Masonic Lodges. Glamorgan Lodge entered a team for the competition, and having been successful in two rounds, took part in the final. This was held on Cardiff Green, Sophia Gardens, on the 25 August. The Loyal Commercial Lodge team beat the Glamorgan Team in the final game!

Charles Edwin Dovey died in Cardiff at the age of 74 on Thursday, 1 September 1927.

WBro Peter M Davies, ProvJGW.

Venables Llewelyn Lodge No.3756

Warranted : 20 July 1915

Consecrated : 3 June 1916

Meeting at the Masonic Hall, Porthcawl.

Despite the ever-darkening clouds of war, a number of Brethren met in the Porthcawl Hotel on 16 January 1914, to consider the formation of a Lodge in Porthcawl. A further five preliminary meetings were held over the next eighteen months; a Warrant was granted on 20 July 1915 and Venables Llewelyn Lodge No.3756 was Consecrated on Saturday, 3 June 1916 by the ProvGM of Monmouthshire, RWBro Frederick Phillips. The ProvGM of the Province of South Wales (Eastern Division), RWBro Col Sir Charles L D Venables Llewelyn, from whom the Lodge takes its name, was unable to be present, as he was serving in France with his Regiment, the Glamorgan Yeomanry. There were 36 Founders, mainly from the Mother Lodge, Ogmore No.1752 and Windsor Lodge No.1754. WBro Henry Pendrill Charles, PAGSwdB, DepProvGM, was Installed as the first Master, with WBro John Phillip Cadogan, ProvGSwdB, as SW; and WBro Albert John Gear Evans, ProvJGD, as JW.

It is reported that the Lodge was formed at the behest of a number of local businessmen, and Brethren from the Cardiff and Penarth area, who were Members of the Porthcawl Golf Club (now the Royal Porthcawl Golf Club). These Brethren regularly stayed in Porthcawl over the weekends to play golf, hence the choice of Saturday as Lodge night. The following were the Founders whose names appear on the Charter: Henry Pendrill Charles, Talbot Lodge No.1323; John Phillip Cadogan, Windsor Lodge No.1754; Albert John Gear Evans, Ogmore Lodge No.1752; Frederick Vaughan Cleves, Windsor Lodge; William Charles Mole, Bute Lodge, No.960; Arthur James Boyle, Ogmore Lodge; Frederick William Nicholls, Ogmore Lodge; Henry Thomas Beeche Comley, Ogmore Lodge.

Of the 36 Founders, 20 were residents of Porthcawl; the other 16 were spread far and wide; Manchester being the most northerly and easterly point, Penarth the most southerly and Milford Haven the most westerly. They were from a variety of professions and occupations. Nineteen of the Founders remained Members until their death, fourteen resigned, and surprisingly, three were excluded.

The Lodge was privileged by the ProvGM agreeing to grant the use of his family name. Col Sir Charles Leyshon Dillwyn Venables-Llewelyn, 2nd Baronet, CB, TD, DL, of Llysdinam, Newbridge-on-Wye, Radnorshire, was Initiated into Athlumney Lodge, No.3245, London, on 18 October 1912. He was Passed on 9 December 1912 and whilst a Fellow Craft he was designated ProvGM, in succession to the Rt Hon the Lord Llangattock. Sir Charles was Raised on 27 March 1913, and Installed as ProvGM the same year by his uncle, Sir Michael Hicks-Beach, 9th Baronet PC, DCL, LLB, MP. The Ceremony took place at the Albert Hall,

Swansea. Sir Michael Hicks-Beach was subsequently created 1st Viscount St Aldwyn, and later, in 1915, he was granted an Earldom.

At the first Regular Meeting on Saturday, 1 July 1916, four sons of Members were Initiated, the senior being Bro Reginald Vaughan Cleeves, a RNVR Lieutenant, who was killed in action in 1917, before he had the opportunity of progressing further. Five Brethren became Joining Members, including the Master's son, Bro Reginald Pendrill St John Charles, who served as Master in 1922 and 1929, and was ProvGM from 1938 to 1966. The first Assistant Secretary, WBro Edgar W Lewis, served as AProvGM, 1953 - 1956.

The Lodge had purchased for £1,200 the former Congregational Chapel on New Road, for use as a Masonic Temple. Several Founder Members presented various items of furniture, etc., some of which is in use in the new Masonic Temple, built on the site in 1965. The Master and Wardens' Chairs and Pedestals were presented respectively by WBro Henry Pendrill Charles, WBro John Phillip Cadogan and Bro Richard Edwin Jones. The Tracing Boards and Table were presented by Bros F Vaughan Cleeves, William C Mole, Edgar W Lewis, William Samuel John Bray and Frederick William Nicholls.

In its early days, the Lodge met on the first Saturday of every month, but over a period of time the number of Meetings has been reduced to eight, with Installation being held in October.

In WWI two Members were lost. The plaque on the Obligation Pedestal, Dedicated on 4 June 1921 states:

'TO THE GLORY OF GOD, AND IN MEMORY OF TWO BRETHREN OF THIS LODGE, WHO MADE THE SUPREME SACRIFICE FOR KING AND COUNTRY DURING THE GREAT WAR 1914 - 1918. BRO JENS CHRISTIAN JENSEN, CAPTAIN MERCANTILE MARINE, A FOUNDER OF THIS LODGE, PRESUMED LOST AT SEA THROUGH ENEMY ACTION, AUGUST 25/26 1917. BRO REGINALD VAUGHAN CLEEVES, SUB LIEUTENANT R. N. V. R., KILLED IN ACTION AT CAVRELLE, FRANCE, ST GEORGE'S DAY 1917.'

The ProvGM, RWBro Reginald P St J Charles, asserted many times, that when he returned from WW1, in which he served as a Lieutenant in the Royal Gunners Battalion, he would not have progressed to the Chair of King Solomon had it not been for WBro Edgar W Lewis, WM in 1920. It was his influence and persuasion which ultimately encouraged him to progress. He became WM in 1922 and again in 1929.

Due to the misplacement of one of the early Minute Books, an accurate recording of the early events of the Lodge cannot be reported but it is important to mention that the Lodge Banner was presented to the Lodge by the ProvGM, RWBro Charles Leyshon Dillwyn Venables-Llewelyn, after whom the Lodge was named.

Some Brethren said that the first Meetings of the Lodge were held at the Porthcawl Hotel, others say that this was where the Brethren held the Festive Board. WBro Donald C B Comley recalled that, in the early days there was no dining room, and the Brethren stood around a table in the old Chapel Vestry and partook of tea and sandwiches, and occasionally a glass of beer. In 1922, WBro Henry Studt, a Founder and well known Amusement Caterer, presented the Lodge with a corrugated iron building for use as a dining room, together with a wooden structure with less than 8ft by 5ft of floor space, for use as a kitchen. The dining room was officially opened by the DepProvGM, WBro Henry Pendrill Charles, on 1 April 1922. To mark the occasion, WBro Studt presented WBro Charles with a gilt key. Subsequently, RWBro Reginald P St J Charles donated the key to Venables Llewelyn Lodge for safekeeping, and as a reminder of WBro H P Studt's generosity. The key is currently in the hands of Mrs Nena Holmes, the great-great-granddaughter of WBro Henry Studt. In those days a two course meal was served by the Tyler, Bro William H C Heaven, assisted by his wife. Bill did the carving at the end of the table and the Lodge Stewards did all the serving. The charge for the meal was 2/6 (12½p) per head. Drinks were dispensed by the Chief Steward, who did his best to limit everyone to one drink only - and to shut the cupboard promptly at the Tyler's Toast.

Throughout the years, Venables Llewelyn Lodge appears to have pursued its quiet path. Its reputation for good fellowship and hospitality was ever bright, with annual exchange visits with Windsor Lodge, No.1754, Penarth, and Silurian Lodge, No.471, Newport. The problems of catering in no way diminished the quality and excellence of the repast during WW11, and later, when rationing was still in place. Neither was the Lodge lacking in the number of visitors, who were kind enough to share in the pleasures of the work in the Temple. Lodge folklore recalls, with amusement, an occasion when the visiting Brethren were greater in number than anticipated, and many Members were served with fish and chips from a nearby shop. As usual, however, the Stewards, who dined before the Brethren, had an excellent meal, which included a bottle of beer and a tot of whisky for the top table. It was the tradition at that time to hold the Installation Festive Board at either the Esplanade Hotel or the Porthcawl Hotel, this practice ended in 1968.

During WWII, many American Servicemen were stationed in Porthcawl, prior to the invasion of France. Amongst them was the 107th Field Artillery Battalion (28th Infantry Division). Numerous Brethren, from some fourteen different Grand Lodges in the USA, visited the Lodge in 1944.

In 1956, Provincial Grand Lodge started using the Grand Pavilion, Porthcawl, for the Annual Meeting. The Lodge became involved in setting up the hall, and in providing Members for Tyling duties, under the guidance of WBro Russell Mabley, AProvGM, who was appointed as such in 1956. Initially, the squared carpet, candlesticks and other furniture were borrowed from St Quentin's Lodge, No.4778, Cowbridge, but this duty was later devolved to Venables Llewelyn Lodge. In 1960, the ProvGM, who had twice served as Master, presented a new squared carpet to the Lodge, with the understanding that it would be made available for the Annual Meetings of Provincial Grand Lodge. A plaque affixed to the Secretary's desk reads *'To commemorate the presentation of a new squared carpet on the 4th of June 1960 by the ProvGM Rt WBro R P St John Charles, J.P. in memory of his father WBro H P Charles, First Master Venables Llewelyn Lodge No.3756.'*

The original Temple in the converted Congregational Church served the Lodge well for some thirty plus years, but in 1956/57, the rapidly decaying fabric of the Temple became a concern. The walls were frequently streaming with moisture, the paint flaking off the walls, the squared carpet was constantly damp, and from a health point of view the building was a hazard. Ventilators were installed, in an attempt to correct the inherent dampness, but this was not facing up to the real problems, namely that the whole structure was in an advanced state of general decay. Consideration was given to building an inner skin and concreting the floor of the Temple, but after this work, the Lodge would still possess a Temple heading towards total decay. It was ultimately agreed to employ expert opinion to report on the fabric and structure of the building. Williamson and Partners carried out the survey, and later confirmed that the building had passed a point where it could be effectively and economically repaired. Messrs Williamsons recommended Copthalls Ltd, a London based firm of property developers, and the committee and Members eventually agreed to sell the whole site to them for £12,000, on the agreement that the Lodge could build a Temple on part of the site, and pay a peppercorn rent for 999 years.

WBro G Morgan Joseph, who was Chairman of the Building Sub-committee, occupied the Chair of King Solomon in the old Temple for the last time in June 1963. On 16 June 1963, a meeting of the Members was held in the old dining room, when the Williamson proposals were agreed. Messrs. Williamson and Partners were confirmed as Architects and Messrs Joseph, Evans and Helyar were awarded the building contract. Letters were sent to Members appealing for loans and donations, and the Provincial Benevolent Fund was approached for a loan towards the total estimated cost of £20,000.

The Secretary, WBro C B Brian Richards, successfully negotiated with Glamorgan County Council Education Committee for the Lodge to hold its Meetings at Nottage Junior School, Suffolk Place, (where Bro David W Jenkins was Headmaster), while the new Masonic Hall was under construction. Bro David M Jones, of Porthcawl Furnishings Ltd, very generously provided storage for the Lodge furnishings, which had to be collected from the furniture repository on the Saturday morning of a Lodge Meeting and returned on the Sunday. Let history know that although this was a makeshift arrangement, the excellent School Assembly Hall, with its apron stage and tiered steps, provided a setting of great dignity, and nothing was lost from the Ceremonies. During this period, committee meetings were held either at the Porthcawl Hotel or at 1 Victoria Avenue, the home of WBro Luther Protheroe. He had been Initiated into the Lodge in 1943, Installed as WM in 1955, and became a Grand Officer with the Rank of PAGSuptWks, in 1978. Lodges of Instruction were held at the Porthcawl Hotel. Festive Boards were held in various Porthcawl hotels, but the Porthcawl Hotel and the Brentwood Hotel were most frequently used. The last Lodge Meeting at Nottage Junior School was held on 5 June 1965. WBro Jack Musson, Installed as Master in October 1963, was the only Master to occupy the Chair in premises not owned by the Lodge.

Despite a national shortage of bricks, the building was completed on time. The new Temple was Dedicated on Monday, 27 September 1965 by RWBro Reginald P St John Charles, ProvGM, assisted by RWBro Edgar J Rutter, DepProvGM, and WBros Harry F Stockwell and Harold Wilson, AProvGMs. During the Ceremony, WBro Rev F Kenneth Brunsdon, ProvGChap, emphasised that if the threefold duty of every Mason - *'towards God, his neighbour and himself'* - was realised by every Founder of the Lodge, the future of Masonry in Porthcawl would be assured. No doubt, the Founders would have been pleased to see today 6 Craft Lodges; 3 Royal Arch Chapters and 7 other Orders meeting in Porthcawl, with the new Temple serving the Masonic needs of some 350 Brethren.

In March 1964, WBro Luther Protheroe presented the Lodge with a unique plate, made from the wings of tropical butterflies on which is depicted the letter 'G', and which he had brought from South America. The plate is now affixed in the centre of the ceiling of the Temple.

The first Ceremony in the new Temple was held on Saturday, 2 October 1965, when WBro Benjamin K Michaelson, WM, Installed WBro Donald C B Comley, PProvJGW, as Master. WBro Comley had been Master in 1938, and had been chosen as Master to celebrate the Golden Jubilee of the Lodge. It was not until May 1967 that the dining room was used for the first time for the Festive Board. In addition to the assistance of many Members of the Lodge, particular mention must be made of WBros George W Helyar, John C Ireland, G Morgan Joseph, Luther Protheroe and C B Brian Richards, for their contribution in providing such a magnificent Masonic Hall for Porthcawl Freemasons.

In December 1965, the Lodge's senior and most respected Past Master, RWBro Reginald P St J Charles, who was the first Joining Member and had served as Master on two occasions, announced his retirement as ProvGM, at the age of 87. He was succeeded by RWBro Lord Swansea in 1966. It is interesting to note that whilst RWBro Charles rarely missed a Meeting of the Lodge during his period as ProvGM, RWBro the Rt Hon the Lord Swansea, ProvGM, 1966-1999, never visited the Lodge.

Until the end of 1965, Venables Llewelyn Lodge was the only Lodge working in Porthcawl. With some 170 Members, progression to the Chair tended to be slow, and coupled with long waiting lists of gentlemen wishing to become Freemasons, it was felt that more Lodges were required. The Petition for the first Daughter Lodge, Lodge of Sker No.8924, was signed in Open Lodge on 2 January 1965, and the new Lodge was duly Consecrated on 9 November 1965. The first Master was WBro John C Ireland, Treasurer of Venables Llewelyn Lodge. Two further Daughter Lodges followed, Newton Lodge, No.8261, Consecrated on 24 January 1969; and Kenfig Lodge, No.8289, Consecrated on 20 June 1969. WBro Lloyd was a Founder and first SW of Kenfig Lodge.

It was thought that the establishment of additional Lodges in Porthcawl would have an adverse effect on numbers applying to become Masons in Venables Llewelyn Lodge. This proved to be wrong with the Membership peaking at 206 in 1980. The Lodge then adopted a policy of reducing numbers. By 1990, there had been a reduction of 24 to 182; by 2000 it was down by a further 46 to 136 and by 2010, the Membership stood at 105 - still one of the highest in the Province.

The 50th Anniversary of the Consecration of the Lodge was celebrated on Saturday, 4 June 1966, in the presence of RWBro Reginald P St J Charles, RWBro Edgar J Rutter, and other distinguished Brethren. A Ceremony of Passing was worked by the

Master, WBro Donald C B Comley, PProvJGW, assisted by WBro Llewellyn G Bevan, ProvSGW, and WBro John Powdrill, ProvJGW, as Wardens; WBro W Clay Davies, ProvGDC, and WBro Leslie H Jeans, ProvAGDC, as Deacons; and WBro Luther Protheroe, ProvAGDC, as Inner Guard. RWBro Edgar Rutter addressed the Lodge on the subject of its Consecration. The following year, the Lodge was placed in Masonic Mourning for a period of three months on the sad news of the passing to the Grand Lodge Above of RWBro Reginald P St J Charles, on 9 December 1967.

The ownership and management of the new Masonic Hall had been vested in Venables Llewelyn Lodge and its trustees. In order to ensure the smooth running of affairs and to give the new Lodges a say in the management, it was decided to form a limited company. The Porthcawl Masonic Hall Co Ltd was incorporated on 3 January 1968. The Lodge elected WBros Donald C B Comley and G Morgan Joseph to serve with the Master as Directors of the Company, for three years, two years and one year respectively. WBro Donald Comley was elected Chairman and WBro John C Ireland, Company Secretary. WBro Joseph succeeded WBro Comley as Chairman.

After 1921, Members of the Lodge who wished to become Royal Arch Masons sought Exaltation in Atholl Chapter, No.1752, Bridgend. On 3 February 1968, Venables Llewelyn Lodge was Petitioned to form its own Chapter. Venables Llewelyn Chapter No.3756 was duly Consecrated on 14 June 1968, with first cousins, WBros Donald Comley, PAGDC, PZ Atholl Chapter, and Kenneth G Dare, PZ Barry Chapter, No.2357, both PMs Venables Llewelyn Lodge, as First and Second Grand Principals respectively,

In connection with the proposed financing of the new Temple and the proposed Consecration of Lodge of Sker, WBro C B Brian Richards, Secretary of Venables Llewelyn Lodge, in the company of WBro Luther Protheroe, visited the Deputy ProvGM in Cardiff. During this visit, it came to light that the RMBI was looking for a suitable site to build a Residential Home in South Wales. Arising from informal meetings with Porthcawl UDC and various ground landlords, four sites were inspected and recommendations made to WBro Squadron Leader D Alun Lloyd, Secretary, RMBI. The Penylan Avenue site was eventually chosen. The Foundation Stone of the Albert Edward Prince of Wales Court was laid on 21 September 1970 and the Court was formally opened on 24 September 1973. Venables Llewelyn Lodge is proud to record the part it played in establishing a Residential Home in Porthcawl. In December 1973, an association known as the 'Friends of the Albert Edward Prince of Wales Court' was formed and WBro John C Ireland, PAGDC, Treasurer of Venables Llewelyn Lodge, was Elected the first Secretary/Treasurer. He had been honoured with the Rank of PAGDC in 1971, when he was presented with the Regalia which the Lodge had presented to WBro Russell Mabley in 1955.

The following Past Masters of Venables Llewelyn Lodge attained high Office: RWBro Reginald P St J Charles, JP, ProvGM, 1938-1966; VWBro Henry Pendrill Charles, DepProvGM, 1915-1925; WBro Edgar W Lewis, AProvGM, 1953-1956; and WBro Russell Mabley, AProvGM, 1956-1960.

The Venables Llewelyn Lodge has continued to work, hopefully, as the Founders intended. Over the years certain idiosyncrasies have developed, believed to be unique to the Lodge. For example, since 1974, the Secretary reads excerpts from the corresponding Meeting of fifty years earlier; the National Anthem is not sung in the Temple, but precedes the Loyal Toast at the Festive Board; and the Brethren sing to the health of the Worshipful Master at every Meeting.

Compiled by WBro Brian B Comley, PJGD.

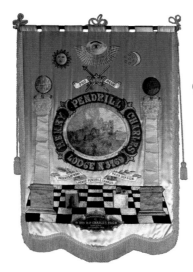

Henry Pendrill Charles Lodge No.3769

Warranted : 11 April 1916

Consecrated : 23 August 1916

Meeting at the Masonic Hall, Caerphilly.

Henry Pendrill Charles Lodge was formed and Consecrated in 1916, during the dark days of the First World War, and much credit is due to the fifty-five Founders who persevered in its formation, in spite of innumerable difficulties. There had been a Lodge in Caerphilly previously, namely the Ancient Britons' Lodge No.126, but this Lodge had been Erased from the Register of Grand Lodge on 28 March 1828, and many Freemasons living in the Caerphilly area felt that it was high time for a town of the importance of Caerphilly, to once again have a Lodge of its own. It is of interest to note that in St Martin's churchyard there is a tombstone to the memory of the first Worshipful Master of the Ancient Britons' Lodge, WBro John Williams. The stone (illustrated on page 45) is engraved with many Masonic emblems, and for many years the maintenance of the stone was undertaken by Henry Pendrill Charles Lodge.

The Lodge was granted its Warrant on 11 April 1916 and Consecrated on Wednesday, 23 August 1916 at the Higher Elementary School, Crescent Road, Caerphilly.

Sir Charles Venables Llewelyn, Bart, ProvGM, was unable to attend on account of his military duties, but it was very appropriate that the Consecrating Officer was WBro Henry Pendrill Charles, DepProvGM, after whom the Lodge is named. The Sponsoring Lodge was Llangattock No.2547, and the Members of that Lodge played a very significant part in the musical content of the Consecration Ceremony, with Llangattock Lodge Glee Party giving an excellent rendering of Mendelssohn's 'Festal Greeting', and Bro Carston of the Llangattock Glee Party rendering the solo 'Be thou faithful unto Death'.

The Consecration Ceremony was carried out according to ancient custom and established form, and concluded with the Patriarchal Blessing by the Consecrating Officer and the singing of the Hymn 'O God of Love, O King of Peace'. WBro Henry Pendrill Charles then called upon the Installing Master, WBro David John Jones, IPM of Llangattock Lodge, and a Founder of this Lodge, to perform the Ceremony of Installing WBro Sidney Williams as the first WM of the Lodge.

WBro Henry Pendrill Charles then addressed the WM on the 'Government of the Lodge', and presented him with a beautifully worked Banner, as his gift to the Lodge. The WM thanked him for the Banner, and presented him and his Officers with Founder Jewels. Ten Candidates for Initiation were then proposed. The Brethren retired to the Clive Arms Hotel for Dinner.

The Lodge Banner, which was refurbished in 1965, still hangs in the Caerphilly Temple, and is now framed and behind glass, by courtesy of the Newman family (WBro David Newman, WM in 1966). The Banner includes many well known symbols of Freemasonry and is dominated by a depiction of the famous leaning tower of Caerphilly Castle. The Lodge Motto, also on the Banner, is: *'Pro Rege'* (For the King), and is the Motto of the Pendrill family, whose permission was granted for it to be adopted by Henry Pendrill Charles Lodge.

The second Regular Lodge Meeting was held at the Clive Arms Hotel, Caerphilly, on 4 October 1916. A large room on the first floor in the west wing of the Clive Arms Hotel had been beautifully furnished and equipped for Masonic Ceremonies. The furnishings of the Lodge Room cost slightly more than one hundred pounds. Some of the items of furniture, among them the Tracing Boards, which cost £5.5.0 (£5.25), were made to order, and are still in use today. At this Meeting, a Ballot was taken for the ten Candidates proposed on 25 August, which proved successful. The first five Candidates, namely Messrs T F Howells, T E Williams, Owen Jones, E M Bevan and E T Griffiths were then Initiated in due form.

The Clive Arms was to remain the home of the Henry Pendrill Charles Lodge until 1931, a period of fifteen years. During that time, 157 Brethren were Initiated, 25 of whom were Initiated in the first year; a remarkable achievement.

Although the Lodge was comfortably accommodated in the Clive Arms Hotel, the Brethren always felt that a Masonic Temple of their own should be built, as soon as they could find a suitable site and raise sufficient money to cover the cost. In October 1917, a Temple Building Fund was set up for this purpose. At the Regular Meeting of the Lodge in October, Bro Charles Jones and Bro Thomas Coggins donated a plot of land in North View Terrace, Caerphilly, free and unconditionally, for the purpose of building a Masonic Temple. However, in 1924, this land was returned to the donors, it being rather inconveniently situated and too small for the intended buildings. Next, in October 1925, an agreement was made with the Plymouth Estates Ltd, to lease for 99 years a building plot at the corner of St Fagans Street and Crescent Road, with the intention of building a Temple on the site, as soon sufficient funds were available. Unfortunately, in the Summer of 1929, the Caerphilly Urban District Council, under the Town Planning Act, demanded the reservation of a strip of land on the site. It was considered that, with the curtailment of the site, it would not be in the best interest of the Lodge to erect a Temple there, and it was decided to surrender the Agreement and the Lease. Elim Church now occupies this site.

Late in 1929, Underwood Villa and Gardens came up for sale. It was considered an ideal site for a Masonic Temple, being in a secluded position, in one of the best residential parts of Caerphilly, having ample accommodation for cars and being in close proximity to the Bus and Railway Station. With the Building Fund now having reached the figure of £3090, it was decided to proceed with the purchase, and in 1930, Underwood Villa became the property of the Trustees of Henry Pendrill Charles Lodge. The work of converting Underwood Villa into a Masonic Centre was undertaken by A J Rossiter at a cost of £3,872, in a timescale of nine months. The Architect was Bro J T Jenkins and the Clerk of Works was Bro Lewis Williams

On 25 September 1930, a Special Meeting of the Lodge was held, attended by WBro D J Jones, DepProvGM, and Officers of Provincial Grand Lodge. The Lodge was 'called off 'and the Brethren adjourned to the site of the new Temple in Underwood. When the Brethren arrived at the site, they put on their Regalia for the Ceremony of Laying the Foundation Stone. The DepProvGM, assisted by Officers of Provincial Grand Lodge, laid the Foundation Stone so as to cover a cavity in the wall, in which a small casket had been placed. It contained currency of the realm - a pound note, a ten shilling note, a half a crown, a florin, a shilling, a sixpence, a threepenny piece, a penny, a halfpenny and a farthing. Four inscribed Commemorative Stones were then laid by WBro Oscar G Bush, WM; WBro Sidney Williams, on behalf of the Lodge Trustees; WBro W Gladstone Rees, Chairman of the Building Committee; and Bro Christopher Preece Howells, in memory of his father, Bro T F Howells, a former member of the Building Committee. This last stone was laid because the Lodge had decided that anyone who wished to lay a stone could do so, by donating £25 to the Building Fund.

The last Lodge Meeting at the Clive Arms Hotel was held on 2 September 1931. The Lodge furniture and all other Masonic paraphernalia required in the new Temple in Underwood were taken there in readiness for the Dedication Ceremony. Some new furniture was purchased and it is interesting to note that the cost of a dais chair was £5.75 and the cost of a chair for general seating in the Temple was 5s 3d (approximately 26p).

The new Masonic Temple at Caerphilly was Dedicated on 16 September 1931 by Sir Charles L D Venables Llewelyn, ProvGM, assisted by WBro Edgar J Rutter, DepProvGM, and Officers of Provincial Grand Lodge. The Dedication Ceremony was preceded by a Religious Service at Van Road Congregational Church, Caerphilly, conducted by Bro Rev J F Jones, ProvGChap, assisted by the Rev E Pryce Jones, Lodge Chaplain. After the Service, the Brethren retired to the new Temple, where the Brethren (99 Lodge Members and 107 visitors) assembled to see the DepProvGM open the front door of the Masonic Building with a suitably inscribed key, which was afterwards presented to WBro George J Davies, WM. A replica of this key is incorporated into the Founders' Jewel. The Brethren then entered the building and proceeded upstairs to witness the opening of the door of the Temple by the ProvGM. The Brethren of Henry Pendrill Charles Lodge then entered the Temple, and the WM and his Officers opened the Lodge in the Three Degrees. Visiting Brethren were then admitted and the ProvGM, accompanied by the DepProvGM, Grand Lodge Officers and Provincial Grand Lodge Officers entered the Lodge, and Dedicated the Temple in accordance with ancient rights and established custom. Later, the Brethren assembled in the Banqueting Hall for the Festive Board, after which there was entertainment in the form of speeches and songs. One song, 'Open ye the Gates of the Temple', most appropriate for the occasion, was beautifully sung by Mrs Rossiter.

On 1 September 1937, the Lodge celebrated its 21st Anniversary. This coming of age occasion was honoured by the presence of WBro Reginald Pendrill St John Charles, ProvGM, 1938-1966, the son of WBro Henry Pendrill Charles, whose honoured name the Lodge bears. The Minutes of the Consecration Ceremony and the Installation of the first Master were read. The Lodge Founders assembled in the centre of the Lodge, and were addressed in an appropriate manner by WBro Charles. Finally, Bro C L Taylor presented the Lodge with a set of ebony Gavels with ivory handles, and Bro Ivor Davies presented the Lodge with a bookcase.

On Sunday, 3 September 1939, the Prime Minister, Mr Neville Chamberlain, broadcast that Britain was at war with Germany. At a Meeting of the Lodge Finance and Standing Committee on 4 September 1939, it was decided that there should be no Festive Board after Lodge Meetings for the time being. Then, at the Finance Committee Meeting on 19 August 1940, a letter was read from the Welsh Board of Health, requisitioning the Masonic Hall as an Annexe to Caerphilly Miners' Hospital. The Welsh Board of Health took full use of the whole of the ground floor and one room on the first floor, together with the grounds outside. The Board took possession in October 1940; the Dining Hall was transformed into a Hospital ward containing forty beds and the kitchen was used for preparing meals for the Hospital staff and patients. The Brethren had to be content with light refreshments, served in the Marshalling Room upstairs, after closing the Lodge. The Welsh Hospital Board relinquished its tenancy, and the Annexe was closed at the end of November 1945, after a busy period of five years. It is of interest to note that during those War years, at the request of Grand Lodge, a number of American soldiers stationed in the area were Passed and Raised. These ceremonies were carried out in Lodges of Emergency convened for the purpose. As a result, a close link was formed between Henry Pendrill Charles Lodge and certain Lodges in the United States, which existed for some years afterwards.

The Lodge met regularly and preformed its functions throughout the War period. The six WMs who were Installed during the period that the building was requisitioned were: Edward Savage, 1939-1940); Walter P Cole, 1940-1941); Archie Bundy, 1941-1942; Earnest Coleman, 1942-1943; Philip C King, 1943-1944; and H W Gethin Davies, 1944-1945. They were deprived of the opportunity of entertaining their own Brethren at the customary Installation Festive Board. So, the six of them decided to have a joint celebration of their Installations, by holding a Ladies' Festival on the evening of 22 January 1947. After a Reception in the Temple, hosted by WBro Thomas J Davies, WM, and Mrs Davies, and a short Service, all returned to the Dining Hall for entertainment.

Since the Consecration of the Lodge in 1916, a Harmonium had been in use to provide musical accompaniment in the Temple. When plans were drawn for the new Temple in Underwood, space was allocated for the building of an organ loft to accommodate, when funds allowed, a pipe organ. WBro Hubert Gatehouse, Lodge Member and Organist of St Martin's Church, Caerphilly, discovered that there was a suitable pipe organ for sale in a Chapel in Newport, which he was authorised to purchase on behalf of the Lodge. The organ has six ranks of pipes with two manuals, a pedal keyboard with the usual couplers, and an electric blower. It was made by Banfield of Birmingham circa 1900. The total cost of the organ and its installation was £238.50.

A Lodge of Emergency was convened on 13 February 1961 to Dedicate the newly installed organ. The Ceremony was performed by RWBro Edgar Rutter, who addressed the Brethren, and stated *that it was right and proper to have music in the Lodge, because it enhanced the Harmony that should always exist among Brethren of the Craft'*. WBro Rev W E Mathias-Williams, ProvGChap read the prayers, and WBro Hubert Gatehouse played two voluntaries on the organ 'Salut d'Amour' by Sir Edward Elgar and 'Postlude in D Minor' by Selmer Müller.

The Lodge celebrated its Golden Jubilee on 8 September 1966, when WBro David Newman was the WM. The Festival Celebration was attended by RWBro Edgar J Rutter, DepProvGM. The WM read the Minutes of the Consecration Ceremony held on 23 August 1916. WBro W R Barker read extracts from the history of the Lodge, compiled by the late WBro Gladstone Rees, and WBro Phillip King presented the DepProvGM with a cheque for £500, as a special donation from the Brethren of the Lodge to the Royal Institution for Boys 1967 Festival. WBro D J Davies, the senior PM, delivered a short address and the Celebration concluded with the WM, WBro David Newman, presenting a Commemorative Bar to be added to the Founders' Jewel to the only surviving Founder Member, Bro W F Rowland.

There was no special celebration of the 75th Anniversary of the Lodge in 1991, but on the occasion of the 90th Anniversary, the Worshipful Master, WBro Gareth Stagg, was presented with a suitably inscribed fruit bowl, and all the Brethren of the Lodge received inscribed whisky glasses.

The Lodge has Sponsored the formation of four new Lodges, namely, Gelligaer Lodge No.6298, Consecrated 8 July 1946; Lodge of St Ilan No.6624, Consecrated 30 April 1948; Associated Engineers Lodge No.7303, Consecrated 18 September 1953; and Ancient Britons' Lodge No.9672, Consecrated 30 March 1999. The Lodge also supported the formation of Henry Pendrill Charles Chapter No.3769, Caerphilly, which was Warranted on 12 February 1964.

It is worth mentioning that the Lodge has two close links with the Provincial Executive. Firstly, the Lodge is proud to be named after WBro Henry Pendrill Charles, who was DepProvGM from 1915 to 1925. Secondly, WBro David John Jones, who was a Founder Member of the Lodge, the first Installing Master, President of the Lodge of Instruction for many years, and a Trustee of the Lodge, held the Office of DepProvGM from 1926 to 1931.

When the Lodge was Consecrated in 1916, it was decided that it would hold ten Regular Meetings a year. This number has been maintained throughout its existence, and up to the time of writing it has Initiated seven hundred and fifty two Candidates, a clear indication of how strong the Lodge has been throughout the years. The Lodge looks forward to celebrating its 100th Anniversary in 2016.

This history was compiled by WBro Colin Howell. WBro Colin was Initiated into the Lodge in 1961, and was Installed as WM in 1972. He was a Founder member of Ancient Britons' Lodge No. 9672 in 1998. In Province, he was appointed PPrGD in 1978 and promoted to PPrJGW in 1990. In Royal Arch Masonry he was Exalted in Henry Pendrill Charles Chapter No.3769 in 1966, and was Installed as First Principal in 1991. He became a Joining member of Hendre Chapter No. 3250 in 1995. In Provincial Grand Chapter, he was appointed Provincial Assistant Grand Director of Ceremonies in 1995 and appointed Provincial Director of Ceremonies in 1998. In Supreme Grand Chapter, he was appointed Past Grand Standard Bearer in 1998. He also served as Deputy Grand Superintendent, 2004-2010.

Compiled by WBro Colin Howell, PGStB, with grateful acknowledgement to WBro R I Jones, PPrJGW, and the late WBros W Gladstone Rees, PPrSGW, and T J Williams, PPrAGDC.

Cardiff Exchange Lodge No. 3775

Warranted : 20 June 1916

Consecrated : 17 January 1917

Meeting at the Masonic Hall, Cardiff.

The Petition for Cardiff Exchange Lodge was signed by the Worshipful Master and Wardens of Tennant Lodge No.1992 at the Regular Lodge Meeting on 9 March 1916, thus Cardiff Exchange Lodge became a Daughter Lodge of Tennant Lodge. The first meeting of the Founder Members was held on Wednesday, 16 February 1916 in the Chamber of Commerce Room at the Cardiff Exchange Building, Mount Stuart Square. The Founders decided that the Lodge would meet 9 times each year on the second Wednesday of the month, with no Meetings during June, July and August. The annual subscription was set at 2 guineas, which surprisingly remained unaltered until 1953, when it was raised to 3 guineas. It was also decided that the Lodge Motto would be *'Spectemur Agendo'* (*'By your deeds shall you be known'* or *'Let us be judged by our acts'*.) It comes originally from Book XIII of Ovid's Metamorphoses, where it is attributed to the hero, Ajax.

The WM Designate was Frederick Henry Hathaway, a Colliery Sales Manager of Cardiff, who had been Initiated in Windsor Lodge No.1754 in 1894. On 30 May 1916, WBro Hathaway wrote in support of the new Lodge to WBro Henry Pendrill Charles, DepProvGM, as follows:

'I would like to be kindly permitted to say that I, and other Founders of the proposed Lodge in question have observed that the Cardiff Lodges now existent are from their heavy point of membership becoming – so we have considered – a little over-crowded and for that reason and the other, that the population of our city has, of recent years, become very largely increased, not only by the ordinary means, but by a considerable influx of those necessary to carry on the business of this active port, A new Lodge, consequently would receive, very easily that support which is needful to its sure and solid establishment.'

Cardiff Exchange Lodge was originally formed with the express purpose of creating a Lodge whose Members were restricted to Principals or Associated Members of the Cardiff Coal and Shipping Exchange, hence the name of the Lodge. There is a clause in the original By-laws stating this fact, and when they were sent for approval to Provincial Grand Lodge, concern was expressed at such exclusivity. It appears that the Lodge ignored Province's concerns and doubts. This situation continued until March 1925, when this clause was finally rescinded. Its removal had previously been proposed by the then Master, WBro Edgar John Rutter in 1924. Nevertheless, it still appeared to carry some weight as late as 1953, when one of the current senior Past Masters, WBro

F G Richardson, PPrSGW, was interviewed for selection, and had to prove a connection with the Cardiff Docks. He in fact worked in the Petroleum Industry.

The Election of the Worshipful Master Designate was not without controversy. At an early meeting of the Founders, WBro Hathaway and WBro David Alfred Thomas, PPrAGDC, (created Baron Rhondda in 1916 and Viscount Rhondda in 1918) were proposed and seconded as Worshipful Master Designate, with Hathaway winning by the narrowest of margins of 17 votes to 16. Lord Rhondda was the owner of the Cambrian Collieries and resided at Llanwern House, Newport, Monmouthshire. He had been Initiated in Loyal Cambrian Lodge No.110 in 1889.

Other names were afterwards added to the Petition, about 50 in all. They included 10 Coal Exporters; 4 Ship-owners; 2 Colliery Sales Managers; 3 Shipbrokers, all of whom were in business in Cardiff Docks. Amongst them was the previously mentioned Edgar John Rutter, (the future DepProvGM) MM of Tennant Lodge No.1992, who at the time was a Coal Salesman of 1 Princes Street, Cardiff. The failure of Lord Rhondda to win the nomination resulted in 9 Brethren withdrawing their names from the Petition. They included seven Members of Glamorgan Lodge No.36, Trevor Stanley Jones, MM, Prince Llewellyn Lodge No.2570 and Lewis Lougher, PPGReg, PM Loyal Commercial Lodge No.2720. The latter was a Ship-owner and chairman of a large number of shipping companies in Cardiff, Penarth and Barry. He became Chairman of the Federation of Bristol Channel Ship-owners in 1919 and was honoured with a Knighthood in 1929.

Henry Pendrill Charles, DepProvGM, had to write to Sir Edward Letchworth, Grand Secretary, on 25 May, informing him of the withdrawal of names from the Petition. Further, he explained that of the 41 remaining Petitioners, 33 approved of the choice of the three Principal Officers Designate and 8 disapproved, but that nevertheless, the Petition had the full support of RWBro Sir Charles L D Venables Llewelyn, Bart, ProvGM. The Warrant was granted on 20 June 1916.

The SW Designate was Arthur Jones, a Coal Contractor from Penarth. Initiated in Tennant Lodge, he had been WM of the Lodge, 1914-1915. The JW Designate was James Colvin Watson, a Marine Insurance Secretary, of Victoria Road, Penarth. A Master Mason, he had been Initiated in St John's Lodge No.1712, Newcastle-upon-Tyne, Northumberland, in 1897.

The Consecration took place at Cardiff Masonic Hall on Wednesday, 17 January 1917, the Consecrating Officer being the Deputy Provincial Grand Master, WBro Henry Pendrill Charles. Also present were 24 Founder Members and 136 guests. The Lodge Banner was presented to the Lodge anonymously and the identity of the donor remains unknown.

At the first Regular Meeting of the Lodge, 25 Candidates were Balloted and 5 were Initiated. This was not a 'one off' situation. Several Emergency Meetings had to be held and at one of them 15 Candidates were Passed and 7 were Raised. A total of 23 Ceremonies were held in that first year! During this time, men were being called up to serve in the Armed Forces and the Lodge was keen that they should begin their Masonic careers before leaving to fight in the First World War – hence the need for so many Ceremonies. Later, United Grand Lodge ruled that no more than two Candidates were permitted to participate in any one Ceremony and by 1923 the number of Lodge Meetings had been greatly reduced.

Lord Rhondda died from pneumonia at the age of 62 on the morning of Wednesday, 3 July 1918, a year after the Lodge's Consecration. He had been MP for Merthyr Tydfil from 1888 until the January General Election of 1910. He then became MP for Cardiff until the General Election of December 1910, when he left politics. Returning to politics in 1916, he became a Privy Councillor and Lloyd George appointed him his Emissary to the United States.

In 1920, the then IPM, WBro J Colvin Watson, presented a Master's Apron to the Lodge for the Installation of the fourth Worshipful Master, WBro J Sidney Rees. Since then, this Apron has been passed on to successive Masters, all of whom have signed the back of the Apron.

The first official visit of the Brethren of Canynges Lodge No.1388, Bristol, took place in 1928. For this visit, Special Dispensation was granted to move the meeting date to a Saturday for the convenience of the 24 visiting Brethren from Bristol. Such Fraternal

Visits were to become a tradition, but had to be halted during the Second World War and were not resumed until 1949. In recent years, these visits have not been held so regularly. In 1951, WBro Edgar Rutter, who was then Deputy Provincial Grand Master, presented the Lodge with a Volume of the Sacred Law, which he instructed should be signed by each new Candidate on his Initiation. This practice continues to this day.

Since 1970, it has been the custom of the Lodge to present the Past Master's Jewel at the Festive Board. This was also done in 1968, when the Jewel was presented by WBro John I Brown to Edgar J Rutter. This was during the Lodge's Golden Jubilee, when the Lodge's most notable Founder Member, Edgar J Rutter, was the Worshipful Master for the second time. The Lodge also presented Edgar Rutter with a silver loving cup to mark his career as Deputy Provincial Grand Master. The Cup is kept on display at the Masonic Hall, Cardiff, and is used at the Festive Board at every Installation Meeting.

Edgar Rutter Loving Cup

Mention has already been made of the most notable Founder Member of the Lodge, VWBro Edgar John Rutter (DepProvGM 1931 - 1971). Another Member of note was WBro Lewen Littledyke, the Lodge's first Masonic Veteran The current most senior Past Master, WBro A N Lawrence, PPrSGW, is a third generation Member of the Lodge. Initiated on 14 November 1950, he was Installed Master of the Lodge in 1963. He was closely followed by WBro John I Brown, Initiated 15 November 1951, WM in 1963, and appointed a Grand Officer in 1985 with the Rank of PAGDC. He had the honour of being WM of Hendre Lodge No.3250 for two consecutive years, 1996-1998. The late Bro R L Pugh was another Masonic Veteran. Initiated on 20 May 1963, he Passed to the Grand Lodge Above in 2009. WBro F G Richardson, PPrSGW, Initiated in 1961 and WM in 1972, was the first Candidate to be presented with that well known pamphlet 'What every candidate should know'.

Two Members deserve mention for their services to the Lodge. The longest serving Treasurer was WBro H L Hodge who carried out this task for twenty years. The late WBro Colin Evans served as Lodge Secretary for many years. He produced a concise history of the Lodge and without his legacy a large part of this account would not have been possible.

The universality of Freemasonry was demonstrated during the Second World War, when in 1942 Captain R Seaborne was Initiated. He subsequently completed his Third Degree in 1943 in Capetown, South Africa, whilst on active service. Three Brethren of the Lodge, all Master Mariners paid the Supreme Sacrifice during this time, namely T G Dyer, T Morley and J Parke, as did the sons of three of the Brethren.

In more recent years, Brethren who have been offered an Active Provincial Rank have been WBro J E Evans, appointed Provincial Grand Sword Bearer in 1995 and WBro R R Morgan, appointed a Provincial Grand Steward in 2007.

Cardiff Exchange Lodge has been the Sponsoring Lodge of three Daughter Lodges; Howardian Lodge No.5317, Consecrated 18 November 1931; Juventus Lodge No.8105, Consecrated 6 May 1966 and Lodge of Concord No.8418, Consecrated 18 March 1972. It should also be noted that in 1943, Howardian Lodge passed a resolution, stating that the present and all succeeding Masters of Cardiff Exchange Lodge should by made Honorary Members of Howardian Lodge.

The Brethren are now looking forward to celebrating the Centenary of the Lodge in 2016.

Compiled by WBro Mark A James, PPrAGDC, Secretary.

Beaufort Lodge No.3834

Warranted : 11 January 1918
Consecrated : 9 May 1918
Meeting at the Masonic Hall, Swansea.

No history of this Lodge can be written without first mentioning the 'old' Beaufort Lodge No.443 which was Constituted on 24 April 1769. The present Beaufort Lodge takes its name from this, the first Masonic Lodge in Swansea.

The original Beaufort Lodge was on the Register of the Premier Grand Lodge of England, known as the 'Moderns'. It was named after the Fifth Duke of Beaufort who, at that time, was Grand Master of the 'Moderns', 1769-1771, and as such, issued and signed the Warrant. The Dukes of Beaufort have, for some centuries, been closely connected with Swansea, being Lords of Gower and large landowners in the district.

The original Warrant hung for a number of years alongside the Warrant of the present Beaufort Lodge, issued nearly 150 years later. The Warrant number of the old Lodge was changed to 378 in 1770, to 291 in 1780, and to 292 in 1781. On the new list of 1792, the number was again altered to 244, which it remained until the Lodge was Erased from the Grand Lodge List on 10 February 1809. Details of the first Beaufort Lodge are to be found near the beginning of this book.

When the present Beaufort Lodge was formed, the Province of South Wales Eastern Division comprised 30 Lodges, four of which operated in Swansea. They were: Indefatigable Lodge No.237, Talbot Lodge No.1323, Caradoc Lodge No.1573 and Dr James Griffith Hall Lodge No.3161. The Provincial Year Book shows 28 Lodges, but in 1918, there were 30 Lodges. St Quintin's Lodge No.1882, Cowbridge, though dormant, was not Erased until 5 September 1923 and Loyal Hay Lodge No.2382 was not transferred to the Province of Hereford until 25 November 1920.

The first meeting of the Founders of the Lodge was held at the old Masonic Hall in Caer Street on 20 September 1917, which 19 Brethren attended. Subsequent Meetings were held in the Exchange Buildings, the Cameron Hotel and 12 Fisher Street. It is interesting to note that the Founder's fee was five guineas, inclusive of the cost of the Jewel; the Initiation fee was ten guineas (£10. 50p); and the annual subscription, one pound eleven shillings and six pence (£1. 57½p), payable half yearly in advance.

Caradoc Lodge agreed to be the Sponsoring Lodge. The Warrant is dated 11 January 1918, but the Grand Secretary wrote that the Petition would be granted, subject to the withdrawal from the list of Founders of the names of nine Brethren, who were not Master Masons of three years standing. These Brethren afterwards became Joining Members of the Lodge.

RWBro Charles L D Venables Llewellyn, ProvGM, was away on active service, and in such circumstances, WBro Henry Pendrill

Charles, DepProvGM would be expected to perform the Consecration Ceremony. Grand Lodge, however, did not deem this to be appropriate, because the DepProvGM, was the Master Designate. It was resolved that the Grand Secretary, VWBro P Colville Smith, MA, be invited to undertake the duties of Consecrating Officer, to which he agreed. The Consecration Ceremony was held at the Albert Hall, Swansea, on 9 May 1918. Amongst the names in the Attendance Book at the Consecration Meeting, was one R P St John Charles, MM, of Cambrian Lodge No.364, who was to become Provincial Grand Master in 1938.

In 1924, Beaufort Lodge was one of the 6 Founder Lodges responsible for the acquisition of the premises in St Helen's Road, Swansea, with a view to providing a full and complete venue for the use of Swansea Freemasons. The first Chairman of the Swansea Masonic Hall Co Ltd was the Lodge Treasurer, WBro C J Tazewell, who held the Office until his death in 1933. It should be added that the present Chairman is also a Member of Beaufort Lodge, namely WBro Francis Langford, who has held the Office since 1999.

The first Regular Meeting of the Lodge was held on 13 June 1918, when a Ballot was held for nine Joining Members and eight Candidates for Initiation. On that evening, two of the eight Candidates were Initiated. Between June and December 1918, eight Meetings were held at which fifteen Candidates were Initiated and there were fourteen Joining Members.

The Lodge Insignia includes a view of Swansea Castle at a very early date, (see illustration) and the Motto, in Latin: *'Fiat Lux'* translates as *'Let there be light'*. The meaning of the symbols on the Banner is not on record and so is open to conjecture.

With the outbreak of hostilities in September 1939, the Meeting scheduled for that month was cancelled, which is the first recorded mention of the Second World War in the Minutes. A number of Meetings of the Lodge were cancelled or re-arranged in 1940, and as a result of the 'blackout restrictions', Meetings in the winter of 1940/41 were held in the afternoon, usually starting at 2.30 pm. With the coming of summer, the Meetings reverted to a 6.30 pm start. No dinner was held following the April 1941 Installation, because of the emergency orders and the strict rationing measures which had been introduced.

The Lodge Members and their families who died or were reported missing are recorded as follows:

1940 June	Bro G Gender's son reported missing on active service.
1941 January	Bro Hedley Jones reported missing on active service.
1941 March	WBro W D Rees and his wife killed as a result of enemy action.
1941 May	Bro Hedley Jones (reported missing in January) now confirmed as a prisoner of war.
1942 June	WBro F R Conybear's son reported missing from an operational flight over enemy territory. In September 1942, official confirmation was received that his son had been killed on active service.
1942 September	Bro D Lewis's brother was reported missing, his ship having been torpedoed.
1943 January	Bro A H Rice's son killed on active service in the Middle East.

On a brighter note, Bro Hedley Jones, who had been a POW since May 1941, was Passed to the Second Degree in May 1945, and Bro P C A Griffin, who was Initiated on 12 June 1941, was Passed and Raised in Loyal Lodge No.3719, Freetown, Sierra Leone, in April and June 1942 respectively. Beaufort Lodge was informed of his Passing and Raising by letter from the Secretary of Loyal Lodge.

It is interesting that during this period, the Lodge held 8 Emergency Meetings, which were necessary due to the large number of applications for Membership. In 1940, 5 applications for Membership were received; there were 8 in 1941, 7 in 1942, 6 in 1943 and 9 in 1945. It is also apparent from the Minutes, that despite the restrictions in force, the number of Brethren and visitors attending each Meeting remained high. Indeed, visiting Brethren travelled great distances to attend Meetings, particularly the Installation Meetings.

Other than the original Founders, every Master has been an Initiate of the Lodge, with only four exceptions, all of whom were

Joining Members. Nine Initiates have been honoured by Grand Lodge, as has one Joining Member. In its 93 years' history, there have been only four sons who have followed their fathers as Master of the Lodge. They are: WBro Malcolm Thompson in 1962, WBro Keith Ferguson in 1982, WBro Francis Langford in 1984 and WBro Philip Radford in 1994. WBro Anthony Robbins, son of WBro Leslie Robbins, who was Lodge Treasurer for almost two decades, became Master in 1987. WBro Leslie was Master of Lodge of Progress No.7928 in 1978.

Probably the best known and a most respected Member of the Lodge was WBro Malcolm Hayes Thompson, PPSGW, PSGD, who, as a Merchant Navy Radio Officer was proposed, Balloted for, and Initiated at an Emergency Lodge, held under Rule 160 Book of Constitutions, on 14 September 1948. He was Passed on 9 June 1949, and Raised to the Sublime Degree of a Master Mason on 10 November 1949. WBro Malcolm Thompson went on to be WM in 1962. In 1967, he was appointed Provincial Grand Secretary in the Craft and Holy Royal Arch and served in both capacities until 1990. In 1991, he became Provincial Grand Master of Mark Master Masons, and held that Office until 1996. Sadly, he passed to the Grand Lodge Above in 2004; his presence and advice are still greatly missed.

Other Brethren who have made significant contributions to the Provincial Executive in the Craft, Royal Arch and Mark Master Masons include: in the Craft: WBro Rev Canon Huw Mosford, AProvGM, 2007-2009; in the Holy Royal Arch: WBro Francis T A Langford, Third Provincial Grand Principal in 1973; his son, WBro Francis Langford, Third Provincial Grand Principal, 2005 - 2007, Provincial Grand Treasurer since 2009; in the Mark Degree: WBro Wilfred K Jones, Provincial Grand Secretary, 1982 - 84, Provincial Grand Treasurer, 1984-1995; WBro Francis Langford, Provincial Grand Treasurer, 1995-2002, and WBro Keith B Ferguson, Provincial Grand Treasurer since 2002.

Finally, WBro Peter Griffin, PAGDC, a Farmer, who was Initiated into Beaufort Lodge on 12 June 1941 and was Installed as Master in 1957, was a Founder Member of 3 Lodges: Lodge of Progress No.7928; The Lord Swansea Lodge No.8364, of which he was Master in 1988; and South Wales Eastern Division Provincial Grand Stewards Lodge No.8900. In 1984, WBro Peter attained his ultimate rank in Craft Masonry, when he was appointed PAGDC in UGLE. In 2010, he celebrated 69 years in Beaufort Lodge and 53 years since being Installed in the Chair of King Solomon. Sadly, WBro Peter passed to the Grand Lodge Above in January 2011. He was 94 years of age.

In 2001, the Lodge secured its first Initiate through the internet, when a Mr Leighton Lloyd made contact with Provincial Office and through a series of connections, joined the Lodge. He became Worshipful Master in 2010.

Compiled by WBro Frank Langford, PGStB.

Caerdydd Lodge No.3959

Warranted   :   7 May 1919

Consecrated :   21 November 1919

Meeting at the Masonic Hall, Cardiff.

Caerdydd Lodge is the third Daughter Lodge of Bute Lodge No.960. The Petition for a new Lodge to be formed in Cardiff, and named Caerdydd (Welsh for Cardiff) was signed by the WM, Wardens and eligible Brethren of Bute Lodge on 1 April 1919. A total of 64 Brethren signed the Petition. At this time, Bute Lodge had a Membership in excess of 300 Brethren, a long waiting list for new Members, and Emergency Meetings were regularly held to Pass and Raise Candidates. It was, therefore, evident that there was a need for a new Lodge in Cardiff.

The situation had been exacerbated two years earlier, when on 26 May 1917, Grand Lodge had issued the following edict: *'No Lodge shall initiate or confer any one Degree on more than two Candidates on the same day unless by Dispensation from the Grand Master or the Provincial or District Grand Master'*. This communication was reported to the Brethren of Bute Lodge on 4 September 1917, and thus, for a Lodge which regularly Initiated, Passed or Raised more than two Candidates on the same evening, the edict must have given rise to some consternation!

When the Founders first met on 18 March 1919, the name 'Caerdydd' was adopted and it was agreed that the position of Worshipful Master Designate be offered to WBro Charles Edwin Dovey, PGD, who was given a short time to consider his decision. Failing his acceptance, the Office would be offered to WBro Charles H Dean, PPrGTreas, who ultimately became the Primus Master of the new Lodge and Dovey became the first IPM. (A profile on Dovey is given elsewhere in this book.)

Further meetings of the Founders were to take place between April and November 1919. The design of the Banner and the Crest were approved and it was agreed that WBro C E Dovey and WBro T Richardson (WM of Bute Lodge) be made Honorary Life Members of Caerdydd Lodge, in recognition of their services in helping to Found the Lodge.

Additionally, such was the enthusiasm of the Founders that Bro Walter Empsall presented the Lodge with a case of Working Tools; the Music sub-committee compiled the musical service and presented the Lodge with one hundred copies; and thirteen Founders joined the Worshipful Master (Designate) in sharing the cost of £35 for the manufacture of the Lodge Banner.

The Lodge Minutes give no indication as to how the Founders chose the design of the Crest. However, when compared with the Cardiff City Coat of Arms, it can be seen that there is a great similarity between the two. Both Crests consist of a Tudor rose and three ostrich feathers supported by a tilting helmet. The supporters of each shield are a Welsh goat (an ancient emblem of the mountains of Wales) and a hippocamp or sea-horse (representing the Severn and the Port of Cardiff). The Caerdydd Lodge Motto is *'Sola Nobilitas Virtus'* meaning *'Virtue Alone is Noble'*.

On 21 November 1919, and in the presence of 52 Founders and 108 visiting Brethren, the Lodge was Consecrated by RWBro Charles Leyshon Dillwyn Venables Llewelyn, ProvGM, assisted by WBro Henry Pendrill Charles, PAGReg, DepProvGM, as SW; and WBro Charles Dovey, as JW. The DepProvGM later occupied the Chair as Installing Master, and during the remainder of the evening's business, the WM proposed his son, Mr Herbert Victor Dean (age 22) as the first Initiate of the Lodge; three Brethren were proposed for Joining Membership; and fourteen gentlemen were proposed as fit and proper persons for Membership of the Lodge. The evening concluded with the WM announcing that the Founders had unanimously Elected WBros Dovey and Richardson Honorary Life Members of Caerdydd Lodge. Ten years after the Consecration of the Lodge, on 15 November 1929 and in the presence of the DepProvGM, the first Initiate, Herbert Victor Dean was Installed as Worshipful Master.

Having had a successful year as Senior Warden, during which he stood in as Master on two occasions, WBro T J Major decided not to put his name forward for Election as Master. However, he requested the Brethren to give their unanimous support to the Junior Warden, Bro W J Le Neve Rice, who, consequently, was duly Elected. At his Installation on 19 November 1920, the DepProvGM was unavoidably delayed and WBro Dovey acted as the Executive Officer. WBro Charles eventually arrived in time to address the Master, and later he had the unique pleasure of presenting the Lodge's first Past Master's Jewel to the Installing Master, WBro C H Dean.

On two occasions in the 1920s, Emergency Meetings were called to Ballot for and, if accepted, Initiate Candidates who would shortly be leaving this Country to reside abroad. The first of these instances occurred on 14 August 1922, for Mr William Russell, and the second occurred on 18 August 1924, for Mr Arthur Humphrey Jones. Subsequently Bro Russell was Passed and Raised in the Lodge prior to leaving for Zambesi, South Africa, whereas Bro Jones was only Passed. His Raising took place at the Lodge of Harmony, No.1411, Valparaiso, Chile, on 14 April 1927. It is pleasing to note that both these Brethren maintained their connection with Caerdydd Lodge for many years.

In 1920, following the suggestion of WBro C L Richardson, 'The Caerdydd Association', an association to support various Masonic Charities, was formed. In 1924, the Brethren went on to form the Caerdydd Benevolent Fund, the purpose of which was to relieve *'distressed Brethren of the Lodge'*, as well as *'necessitous widows and children of deceased Brethren of the Lodge'*. It is a testament to the Brethren who supported these initiatives that the Caerdydd Association and Benevolent Fund are still in existence today. As a token of appreciation for the charitable work undertaken by WBro Sam Thomas for Masonic Charities during the 1920s, the Provincial Grand Charity Steward, WBro Trevor Evans, presented him with the Grand Lodge Charity Jewel, at the Installation Festival held on 15 November 1929.

During the 1920s, Installation Ceremonies attracted quite a gathering, usually in excess of 200 Brethren. The record attendance occurred at the Installation of Bro Percy Edward Thomas, OBE, on 19 November 1926, for the Minutes show that 21 Officers, 7 Past Masters, 81 Members and 121 visitors were present: a total of 230 Brethren! Percy Thomas, an Architect by profession, was a Founder Member of the Lodge. During the 1920s and 1930s, he was a recognised authority on the planning and design of public buildings. In 1935, he was elected President of the Royal Institute of British Architects, and in 1939, was awarded its Royal Gold Medal. In 1943, he was elected President of the RIBA for a second time. Such were his talents that in 1942 when the Ministry of Production was set up, he was appointed Regional Director and Chairman for the Welsh Region, a post he held throughout the existence of the Ministry. He later became the first Member of Caerdydd Lodge to receive a Knighthood.

On 15 June 1928, WBro Woodcock, PM Godalming Lodge No.3811, Surrey, supported by several other Brethren, presented a Petition for a Warrant to hold a new Lodge to be named 'St Mildred Lodge'. The Brethren of Caerdydd voted in favour of the Petition, which was forwarded to United Grand Lodge, and the Warrant was duly issued on 8 November 1928. Thus, St Mildred Lodge No.5078 became Caerdydd's first Daughter Lodge.

The 1930s began with both the Senior and Junior Wardens declaring that they would not be seeking election as Master. Consequently, the Primus Master, WBro Charles Dean, PPGW, agreed to occupy the Chair for the second time. Then in 1933, he became the first Member of the Lodge to become a Grand Officer, with the Rank of PAGDC. The Minutes record that when presenting him with his Regalia on behalf of the Lodge, WBro Edgar John Rutter, PGD, DepProvGM, '*admirably expressed the sentiments of the brethren and the great honour which the Lodge had received through WBro Dean's well merited conferment*'.

The next Grand Lodge preferment was to be in 1939, when on 17 March, the Worshipful Master announced that WBro Sam Thomas had also been honoured with the Rank of PAGDC. The DepProvGM once again had the pleasure of presenting him with his new Regalia.

During WWII, one very young Brother, Arthur John Peter Watts, made the Supreme Sacrifice, while serving with the Royal Air Force, and Bro Edward Thomas Mitchell sustained a very severe disablement, while serving with the Royal Artillery. While it is not possible to give the complete record of the services rendered to their Country by all the Brethren of the Lodge, it is known that at least 19 served in the Armed Forces; 18 with the Home Guard; 26 were involved with Civil Defence Services and 5 with the National Fire Service. Furthermore, the Lodge is proud to record that His Majesty, The King, was graciously pleased to confer the following honours: WBro Sir Percy E Thomas, a Knighthood; WBro George A Bainbridge, The Kings Police & Fire Service Medal; Bro William Phillips, an MBE; Bro Cyril J Salmon, an OBE; Bro Islwyn Roberts, The British Empire Medal. Also, Bro J C Howley was mentioned in Dispatches, Normandy, 6 June 1945 and Bro J M Ford was awarded the Medaille Populaire Francaise, by the French Government, for services rendered to French Nationals during the War.

The Lodge Crest

Finally, mention must be made of Bro Cyril Salmon, who was Initiated into the Lodge in April 1933, at the age of 21. At that time, his profession was listed as Assistant to the Cardiff City Treasurer. During the 1930s, he became a Career Serviceman in HM Forces and, in 1937, the Minutes record that he was '*warmly welcomed*' into the Lodge following his recent return from service abroad. In February 1944, the Secretary sent him a congratulatory letter on his recent promotion to Group Captain in the RAF and, again in January 1945, when he was appointed OBE in the New Years Honours. He resigned from the Lodge in

**The City of Cardiff
Coat of Arms**

September 1967. By then, he had achieved a distinguished military career attaining the Rank of Air Vice-Marshall as well as being further honoured by the Queen with the award of Companion of the Bath (CB). In January 1968, The WM was pleased to inform the Brethren that Bro Salmon had received a Knighthood in the New Year's Honours.

In September 1946, WBro Sam Hague presented a Petition for the formation of a new Lodge to be known as 'Galen Lodge'. The Warrant was issued on 1 October 1946, and in February 1947 the Worshipful Master, WBro H G Yardly, informed the Brethren that he, together with WBro J W Butler, IPM, and Bro H Coles, SW, who had acted as Sponsors at the formation of this second 'Daughter Lodge', had been Elected Honorary Members of Galen Lodge No.6366.

The decade concluded with yet another preferment in Grand Lodge for one of the Lodge's Brethren. This time the honour was bestowed on WBro Robert T McGregor who was appointed PGStB for the many services he had rendered to Freemasonry.

Bro McGregor was Installed as the sixth Master of the Lodge on 21 November 1924 and during his year in Office he Initiated sixteen Candidates into the Lodge. On his vacating the Chair of King Solomon, and as a memento of their Initiation, the same Brethren presented him with a silver plated pillar lamp in the Corinthian style with each of their names inscribed over the four facets at the base of the pillar. Some 42 years later, and by which time he had celebrated 50 years in Freemasonry, Bro McGregor presented the lamp to the Cardiff Masonic Hall Company, where to this day, it adorns the Secretary's Desk in the Duke of Connaught Temple.

One of the foremost Brethren who made an outstanding contribution to the running of the Lodge was Bro Leslie Whitehead. Bro Whitehead was Initiated in 1953, became Master in 1969, and throughout the 80s and part of the 90s served as Treasurer. Indeed, he was held in such high esteem that WBro W H Batstone, BEM, congratulated him in Open Lodge for all his hard work as Treasurer and stated that he formed the backbone of the Lodge both in and out of Meetings. In October 1996, he was Elected to serve as Master once again but, unfortunately, health problems forced him to stand down and another Election had to be held at the November Meeting. Sadly, WBro Whitehead died a month before achieving his 50 years in Freemasonry but, happily, the memory of him remains with those who were fortunate to know him and who still fondly refer to him today.

The Corinthian Pillar Lamp

In April 1960, the Lodge was again honoured with the preferment in Grand Lodge of WBro Trevor B Phillips to the Rank of AGDC. Attendances at Installation Festivals in the 1960s were still excellent. This is borne out by an amusing anecdote which WBro Theodore Evans still relates today: *'that having become a Master Mason, a Brother is entitled to sit anywhere in the Lodge with the exception of the Officers' Chairs or the dais'*. However, at the Installation in November 1961, so full was the Temple that when the Brethren were instructed to be seated there was one Master Mason who found himself with nowhere to sit! Fortunately for him, RWBro Edgar Rutter, OSM,PGW, DepProvGM, was the Presiding Officer and the rules were relaxed, with the Brother finding himself sitting in close proximity to the DepProvGM on the dais!

The Minutes of the Lodge Meeting held on 16 March 1962 also record an occurrence where Edgar Rutter, together with the Provincial Senior and Junior Grand Wardens, visited the Lodge. No special reason is given for the visit, but the Minutes state that he and his Wardens occupied the Master's and Wardens' Chairs respectively. Edgar Rutter then countersigned the Minutes and presided over the first part of the proceedings, in which Bro Alan H Williams of Old Goreans Lodge, No.7193 became a Joining Member. It is pleasing to note that, in 2011, Bro Williams is still an active Member of the Lodge and has served as an auditor for many years.

The year 1962 is also significant, insomuch that on 18 April, a 28-year-old Detective Constable by the name of Peter Frost was proposed for Membership of the Lodge. Bro Frost was Initiated on 21 September 1962, became WM in 1974 and again, 25 years later, in 1999, taking the Lodge into the new Millennium. Bro Frost, a profile of whom is given separately elsewhere in this book, went on to serve both as an Assistant and Deputy Provincial Grand Master. His services to the Province culminated in 2007, when he received sustained applause at the Meeting of Provincial Grand Lodge, having given 15 years continuous service to the Province. As a tribute to his devotion to Freemasonry, and especially the Caerdydd Lodge, the Brethren Elected him to Honorary Membership on 18 November 2005.

The 1960s were undoubtedly eventful times as regards Masonic Veterans, for WBros G A Bainbridge, R T McGregor, T B Phillips and Sir Percy Thomas each completed 50 years in the Craft. Additionally, Bro N D Warr had the distinction of celebrating his 60th Anniversary in Freemasonry on 15 October 1965.

In 1967, WBro Lt-Col Arthur J Lennox was awarded the OBE in the New Year's Honours. Bro Lennox, whose occupation is listed in the Members' Register as a 'Master Fruit Salesman', was Initiated into the Lodge in 1943 at the age of 40. The Minutes of the meeting held in October 1956 indicate that he was promoted to Deputy Commandant of the Glamorgan Army Cadet Force. In 1958, Bro Lennox became Master of the Lodge. Obviously, he was a very active Mason, for the Lodge Minutes of 1968 refer to the fact that the WM congratulated him on his recent nomination to the Office of Grand Treasurer of the Grand Lodge of Mark Masons. In September 1974, he was again congratulated on his appointment as Inspector General (Designate) of the Masonic and Military Order of the Red Cross of Constantine. His Masonic career did not end there, for in March 1977, he was appointed as Great Sword Bearer in the Knights Templar Great Priory, and in 1978, he was Invested DepProvGM of the Provincial Grand Lodge of South Wales Mark Masons. Finally, in May 1983, the Brethren of Caerdydd Elected him to Honorary Membership of the Lodge in recognition of the services he had rendered over many years.

The 1970s also saw two Brethren of the Lodge receive Honours of a different nature – the one in Grand Lodge and the other in the Civil List. WBro Percy Vivian Thomas was appointed to the Rank of PGStB, and WBro Harold Batstone received the BEM.

It is true to say that since its inception, the Lodge has been synonymous with the names of some of the most prominent Freemasons in the Province of South Wales and, indeed, in the Craft as a whole and other Degrees. However, what is not widely known is the fact that one Brother of the Caerdydd Lodge rose to the Rank of RWBro by virtue of him becoming 'Land Grand Master of the British Freemasons in Germany'. The Brother concerned was Bro Major W D J Heath-Smith, who was Initiated into Caerdydd Lodge in 1956. Bro Heath-Smith, also a Career Serviceman, served with the British Army of the Rhine after WW II. There are a few references to him throughout the Minutes in the 1970s, but the final reference to him appeared in the Minutes dated 19 December 1986, when WBro Leslie Whitehead informed the Brethren of the Lodge that the Quarterly Communication from UGL stated: *'that amongst the Distinguished Brethren there were three members of the Grand Lodge of British Freemasons in Germany'*. One of those mentioned was none other than WBro Major W D J Heath-Smith, PSGD, Past Grand Master of the British Freemasons in Germany.

In October 1983, the first instance of a Grand Lodge Officer being mandated to the Lodge, under Rule 124 of the Book of Constitutions, occurred with the appointment of WBro R C Hilton, PAGDC. WBro Leslie H S Jeans, PJGD, followed him in February 1985, and remained in that capacity until WBro Peter Frost attained Grand Rank in 1993. In October 2003, because of his Provincial commitments, VWBro Frost appointed WBro Vivian A Telling, PAGDC, to serve as Mandated Officer to the Lodge in order to assist the Lodge during his absences. Bro Telling subsequently became a Joining Member of the Lodge in October 2007, and has served the Lodge as Secretary since April 2008.

In April 1986, the Lodge Chaplain, WBro Frank Garwood, celebrated 50 years in Freemasonry. He was followed, in the early 1990s, by Bro Thomas Forse. It appears that longevity is a feature of the Lodge, for Membership of this exclusive society continues today, with WBros Robert Meyrick and Theodore Evans and Bros Ivor Thomas and Alan Williams adding their names to the list of Masonic Veterans.

The year 1996 also proved to be an eventful one for the Lodge, with WBro D S Borthwick, WM, Initiating his three sons, by Dispensation, at the Lodge Meeting held on 15 March 1996. He subsequently Passed and Raised his three sons, again by Dispensation, during his year as Master.

Over many years, Caerdydd Lodge has been a great supporter of Masonic Charities. It is, therefore, no surprise that the Charity Steward, WBro C J Clifford, was able to inform the Brethren that the Lodge had achieved the Gold Medal Target for the 1999 Festival. On behalf of the Lodge, WBro Clifford received the Gold Medallion at a presentation Ceremony held at Hendre Lodge in January 1999.

Before ending this narrative, mention must be made of one other Lodge Member, namely, WBro Bernard Smith, PPrJGW, Installed as WM in 1979 and in 1996. In October 2010, he had the distinction of becoming the first WM of Hendre Lodge No.3250, since 1931, to hold that Office without being a Grand Officer.

Since the 75th Anniversary in November 1994, the Lodge has, sadly, been in decline. However, the Brethren who remain are hopeful that they can now bring about a change in its fortunes, and look forward to celebrating the Lodge's Centenary in 2019.

Compiled by WBro Vivian A Telling, PAGDC, and WBro Alf Townsend, PPrSGD.

Vale of Glamorgan Lodge No.3977

Warranted : 22 July 1919

Consecrated : 23 October 1919

Meeting at the Masonic Hall, Barry.

In the period following the Great War, demobilisation resulted in many men returning home after absences of up to four years. This increase in the male population, in conjunction with the prevalent changes in social attitudes, resulted in a broadening appeal of the Craft. Barry Lodge No.2357 was by this time well established, and recognised the need for a new Lodge in the town of Barry to cope with the increasing numbers of prospective Candidates, and to facilitate their progress to the Chair.

Consequently, at a regular meeting of Barry Lodge, held on 8 April 1919, WBro George Wareham PPrJGW, a Past Master of the Lodge, put forward a proposal, seconded by WBro Rees Phillips, that steps be taken to form a new Lodge in Barry. The motion was adopted with enthusiasm by the Brethren present, and the WM, WBro John Robert Woods, was empowered to proceed in the matter.

The 39 Founders comprised Members of the following Lodges: Barry Lodge No.2357 (29); Glamorgan Lodge No.36 (5); Tennant Lodge No.1992 (2); Bute Lodge No.960 (1); Llynfi Lodge No.2965 (1); and Silurian Lodge No.471, Newport (1).

A meeting of the Founders was held on 25 April 1919, when the first order of business was to select the Principal Officers Designate. After some discussion, WBro A L Hopkins, PGD (Eng), WBro George Wareham, PPrJGW, and Bro Edward Robert Hinchsliff, were Elected as the Founder Worshipful Master, Senior and Junior Wardens respectively.

Arthur Llewellyn Hopkins was a Colliery Agent, residing at 19 The Walk, Cardiff, and also at Sutton House, Southerndown. Initiated in Glamorgan Lodge on 8 November 1895, he was Installed WM on 21 June 1901 and remained in the Chair for two years. In 1902, he was appointed ProvGTreas and in 1910 he became ProvSGW. He was later appointed a Grand Officer with the Rank of PGD. Installed, WM of Hendre Lodge No.3250 in 1921, he was also the Primus Master of Kibbor Lodge No.4364, Consecrated on 14 February 1922 and a Founder Member of Amethyst Lodge No.4026. He died, age 63, at Sutton House on 17 August 1924.

George Wareham, PPrSGW, was born in Southampton and worked as a Clerk at the Dry Docks, Barry. Initiated in Barry Lodge in 1897, he became WM of the Lodge in 1904. He became a Grand Officer on 12 April 1927, when he was appointed PAGDC. He became a Masonic Veteran and died at the age of 82 in 1949.

Edward Robert Hinchsliff arrived in Barry from Crewe in 1900, taking up the post of Deputy Town Surveyor. After serving as a Major in the army during WWI, in 1925 he was appointed Surveyor and, in 1939, he became the first Borough Engineer. He was also Barry's Architect, Civil Engineer and Valuer. He was the Designer and Architect of The Barry Memorial Hall and Cenotaph, probably his most outstanding achievement. The Memorial Hall was opened in 1932 and the first Annual Meeting of Provincial Grand Lodge was held there on 29 June 1981. The Hall has continued to be the venue for PGL ever since. The original layout and development of the lake at the Knap and Barry Island, together with the Central Estate, were also his responsibility. Edward Hinchsliff died in 1940 at the relatively early age of 63.

The next item on the agenda was the selection of a name for the new Lodge. This involved lengthy discussion, ultimately leading to WBro Wareham's proposition, seconded by Bro Hinchsliff, that the name of the new Lodge be 'Vale of Glamorgan'. All the Brethren present agreed that no better name could be found for the Lodge, and the proposition was carried unanimously.

Before matters could progress, there remained one item unresolved, namely the selection of a suitable Lodge Crest. WBro W M Davies and Bro P T Rendell agreed to search for an emblem worthy of the new Lodge, and shortly afterwards, they set off on the latter's motor cycle combination to scour the Vale for inspiration. After visiting many local places of interest, they arrived at Beaupre Castle. Situated approximately a mile South West of St Hilary, in the Vale of Glamorgan, Beaupre Castle comprised a medieval manor house complex dating from circa 1300 AD, which had been extensively renovated and remodelled in the sixteenth century. It was at this time that its most striking feature had been added, namely the outer gatehouse with its three-storeyed porch. It is worthy of note that this

The Founders at Beaupre Castle Porch in 1919

arched porchway (or entrance), with its pseudo-classical decorative surround, is flanked on each side by three pairs of pillars, modelled after those three noble orders in architecture, namely the Doric, Ionic and Corinthian. A more appropriate emblem could not be imagined, so the Brethren hastened back to report to the Founders' Committee that a most suitable emblem had been found. The 'Beaupre Porch' was immediately adopted as the Lodge Crest, and its image was incorporated into the Founders' Jewels. The emblem also features prominently on the Past Masters' Jewels. It is reproduced on the Lodge Summons, and forms the central feature of the Lodge Banner.

At a Regular Meeting of Barry Lodge, held on 13 May 1919, WBro A L Hopkins, WM Designate, accompanied by WBro George Wareham, SW Designate, and Bro E R Hinchsliff, JW Designate, made an eloquent appeal to the WM and Brethren for their sanction to start a new Lodge to be named 'Vale of Glamorgan' Lodge. The WM, in supporting the application, proposed that the Petition be recommended, which was seconded by Bro Griffith Jenkins, SW, and carried unanimously. The Petition was then signed by WBro John Robert Woods, WM, and his Wardens.

The Lodge was Consecrated at the Masonic Hall, Barry, at 2:45 pm on Thursday, 23 October 1919, with RWBro Henry Pendrill Charles, PAGReg, DepProvGM, acting as Worshipful Master; RWBro C L D Venables Llewelyn, ProvGM, acting as SW; and WBro C E Dovey acting as JW. These Worshipful Brethren were supported by Grand Lodge and Provincial Grand Lodge Officers, Ruling Masters, Past Masters and Brethren, numbering in all, approximately one hundred and fifty. The Consecration Ceremony was an impressive and colourful occasion and was only the second time such an occasion had been arranged, the first being that of the Barry Lodge almost thirty years earlier. At the close of the Ceremony, the Founders were called to gather in the centre of the Lodge and attend to the reading of the Warrant. Following the Consecration, a board of Installed Masters was opened and WBro A L Hopkins was Installed as the first Master, and addressed by the ProvGM. The Officers were Invested, and a committee was formed to formulate By-laws for the Lodge. After much consideration the By-laws were presented to the Lodge and adopted on 28 January 1920.

Shortly after the Consecration, one of the first social activities of the Lodge was arranged by the WM, WBro A L Hopkins, in the form of a visit to Beaupre Castle. This was attended by thirty-three Brethren who were photographed in front of the porchway.

The Lodge quickly established a high standard of Ritual that has been maintained to the present day.

One of the Founders of the Lodge was Sir William Graham. Originally from Jarrow, Newcastle-on-Tyne, in 1891, he was appointed Assistant Manager of Messrs C H Bailey Ltd, Tyne Engine Works, of Newport and Barry. Some years later, he became a joint Partner with Mrs C H Bailey, and they purchased the Cardiff Junction Dry Dock and Engineering Company, Ltd, and the Tubal Cain Foundry, Tyndall Street, Cardiff. His elder son, William Hedley Graham became the Lodge's first Initiate in October 1919. As Captain William Hedley Graham, he had served with distinction during WWI, and was awarded the Military Cross. He became Master of the Lodge in 1929.

The Lodge at one time boasted its own Glee Party, consisting of up to eighteen Brethren, under the baton of Bro David John Thomas, the Lodge Organist. He was the first conductor of the Barry Male Voice Choir, founded in 1902, and remained as such until his death in 1940. The Lodge Glee Party regularly entertained at the Festive Boards, not only of Vale of Glamorgan Lodge, but also, by invitation, those of several Cardiff Lodges.

The original Banner was embroidered by the wife of WBro E G Dobson, which he presented to the Lodge in 1937. This Banner continued to grace the Barry Temple until around 1990, by which time its condition had deteriorated to such an extent, that if steps had not been taken to protect it, it would have fallen to pieces. At a meeting of the Lodge committee, it was decided that as soon as a replacement could be acquired, the Banner should be protected in a suitably sealed display case. WBro Akram Baig, PAGDC, immediately offered to donate a new Banner to the Lodge and arranged for a replica of the original Banner to be made. The new Banner is currently to be found in the Barry Temple, whilst the original can be seen in its display case in the ante-room.

During the 1940s and 1950s, Membership continued to grow steadily. An interesting point to note is that following the Initiation of the fifth and sixth brothers of the Redrup family by WBro Edgar John Rutter, OSM, DepProvGM, in 1949, the Lodge could boast of having a father and six sons as Members (enough to form their own Lodge). All went on to become active in the Craft and Holy Royal Arch. WBro E J 'Ted' Redrup, PPrGReg, the second longest serving Member, was Initiated on 23 May 1949, Installed WM in 1962, and is now a Masonic Veteran, still regularly attending the Lodge.

The tradition of entertaining was evident again in the 1950s/60s when the Ted Wood Dance Band would provide the music and entertainment at many Ladies' Festivals. WBro E H 'Ted' Wood, PPrSGW, the longest serving Member of the Lodge, was Initiated on 22 March 1944 and was Installed as Master in 1955. An accomplished musician, he has, in addition to serving Vale of Glamorgan Lodge well for many years as Organist, added harmony to two Lodges, two Chapters and three Rose Croix Chapters.

On Wednesday, 22 October 1969, the Lodge celebrated its 50th Anniversary with a visit to Beaupre Castle arranged by the WM, WBro L W Smith. WBro M B Edwards, PPrGD, acted as guide and provided a tour of the Castle and lecture on its history, after which twenty four Officers of the Lodge were photographed in front of the Porch.

The Brethren then returned to the Masonic Hall to attend a Regular Lodge Meeting at 5 pm during which a lecture entitled 'The Porchway to King Solomon's Temple', was presented by WBro Rev F J Rees, PPrGChap. In 1994, a further visit to Beaupre was arranged by the Worshipful Master, WBro John Cripps, PPrGSwdB, to mark the 75th Anniversary of the Lodge. Twenty four Members of the Lodge attended a very pleasant lunch in a local hostelry, before strolling across the fields to the Castle for the now traditional photograph.

By the end of WWII, the number of Lodges in the Province had grown substantially, whilst in Barry there remained only two. The increased interest in the Craft once again led to a situation where, in order to cope with the increasing numbers of prospective Candidates, and to facilitate their progress to the Chair, a new Lodge was needed At a meeting of the Finance Standing and Scrutinising Committee of the Lodge held on 29 November 1945, WBro Griffith Jenkins proposed and WBro F J Watts seconded that '*Vale of Glamorgan Lodge take the initiative in forming a new Lodge in Barry*'. Matters were progressed and on 1 May 1946 the Warrant for Porthkerry Lodge No.6299 was issued. The Founder Members of the new Lodge comprised twenty Brethren from Vale of Glamorgan Lodge, eight from Barry Lodge, and one Brother from Gwalia Lodge.

In more recent times, two further Lodges have been Sponsored by Vale of Glamorgan Lodge, namely Breaksea Lodge No.8358, Consecrated 1 April 1971, and Lodge of Round Table No.9549, Consecrated 3 June 1994.

Among the Past Masters of the Lodge, WBros Norman Bullock and Akram Baig have been appointed to Grand Rank. WBro Norman Bullock was Initiated into the Lodge 28 October 1953 and was Installed as Master in 1964 and again in 2003. He was appointed PAGDC in 1993. WBro Akram Baig was Initiated into the Lodge in 1981 and was Installed as Master in 1990. He was appointed PAGDC in 2000.

Compiled by WBro Anthony W Seymour, PPGSwdB.

Barry Temple - viewed from the Master's Chair

Rhondda Lodge No.3979

Warranted : 22 July 1919

Consecrated : 30 September 1919

Meeting at the Masonic Hall, Pontypridd.

At the turn of the last century, there was only one Masonic Lodge in the Pontypridd area, Merlin Lodge No.1578. The Membership was approximately 200, with a long waiting list of applicants. Officers felt that the Lodge was getting too big and did not afford the opportunity for Brethren to take Office within a reasonable time. It was, therefore, considered appropriate to establish a new Lodge. About 40 Members expressed their willingness to become Founder Members. A meeting was subsequently held at the New Inn, Pontypridd, to discuss the formation of this new Lodge and the Merlin Lodge agreed to accept the responsibility of Sponsoring the new Lodge. The Brethren were unanimous in inviting WBro John Davies to become their first Master.

The Petition was then read out in open Lodge, the three Principal Officers Designate were called by name, and they, along with all the other Founder Members, remained standing whilst the Petition was being read. The Petition was sent to, and approved by, both Provincial and United Grand Lodge. This approval resulted in Rhondda Lodge No.3979 being formed.

On 22 July 1919, a Warrant or Charter of Constitution was issued to the Lodge. A meeting was promptly held by the Founder Members and Bro Ludo Morgan was appointed Acting Secretary, later to become the Lodge's first Secretary. On 1 September 1919, he sent out the first notification of the forthcoming Lodge Consecration. The Ceremony took place at 2.30 pm on Tuesday, 30 September 1919, at the Congregational Hall, Gelliwastad Road, Pontypridd. The Consecrating Officer was WBro Henry P Charles, PAGReg, DepProvGM. He was assisted by WBro Arthur Llewellyn Hopkins, PGD, former Provincial Grand Treasurer, PM Glamorgan Lodge, as Senior Warden and WBro Charles Edwin Dovey, PGD, Provincial Grand Superintendent, as Junior Warden. The Director of Ceremonies was WBro Charles Presgrave Palmer, who later was to become the first Assistant Provincial Grand Master, 1945-1953. There were 94 Brethren in attendance. The first Master, WBro John Davies, PPrAGPurs was then Installed and WBros Morgan E Williams and Edgar E Arnott were Invested as Senior and Junior Wardens respectively. WBro Rev William Lewis, PPrGChap, also a Founder Member, was appointed Chaplain.

At the next Meeting, on 23 October 1919, the Senior Warden, WBro M E Williams, proposed and WBro J Davies, WM, seconded that a vote of thanks be tendered to the Officers and Brethren of the Merlin Lodge No.1578, for their kindness in lending their furniture, tools, carpets etc, for the Consecration Ceremony. It was also agreed to forward a letter to the members of the

Congregational Hall thanking them for their kindness in lending the Hall, free of charge, for the Ceremony.

The Membership in 1919 was 31. Numbers continued to increase, reaching a high of 212 in 1971. Today (2011), the Lodge has 69 Subscribing Members. Unfortunately, the records do not show what Members paid for their joining subscription fees in 1919; however, by 1924 it is known that the fee was £4-4-0. It currently stands at £165-00.

The Lodge Banner was unveiled at a Regular Meeting held at the Masonic Temple, Courthouse Street, Pontypridd, on Thursday, 22 April 1920. The Lodge was opened in due form and with solemn prayer, WBro John Davies occupying the chair and assisted by his Regular Officers. The Minutes of the last Regular and Emergency Lodges were duly read and confirmed. The Lodge was then opened in the 2nd Degree, and the Candidate, Bro William Griffiths was Passed. The Lodge was Closed in the Second Degree and resumed in the First Degree. The WM called upon WBro W R Davies to unveil the Banner, which had been presented to the Lodge by Bro Alfred Orchard (the first DC). On doing so, he referred to the beautiful design of the Banner and also, to the donor, mentioning a few of his many good qualities.

In those early years, the Rhondda Valleys were world famous for their production and export of coal, and it is likely that the majority of Founders had some connection with the coal mining industry. Therefore, it is probable that they wished to commemorate the name that serves the two valleys, Rhondda Fawr (Large) and Rhondda Fach (Small). The word Rhondda is derived from "Roddneu", which means 'bubbling stream'.

The Motto chosen by the Officers of the Lodge is *'Gwell Angu na Chywilydd'* which translates as *'Death before Dishonour'*.

Since the Consecration Ceremony, all subsequent Meetings have been held in the Masonic Temple, Courthouse Street, Pontypridd. Though, on Friday, 21 January 1944, it was proposed by WBro Thomas Williams that Rhondda Lodge be moved to an alternative location in the Rhondda Valley. This proposal was put on hold *'until a suitable building becomes available at a later date'*. No such site was ever found. Besides Rhondda Lodge, six other Lodges meet at the Masonic Temple, in Pontypridd.

The outbreak of War in September 1939 affected many facets of Masonry. Rhondda Lodge suffered inconvenience due to the whole of the ground floor being requisitioned. This comprised the cloakrooms, dining hall, kitchen and toilets. However, the ante-rooms upstairs were not affected and, therefore, the average attendance of the Brethren was maintained during those troubled times.

On 4 September 1939, the Installation Ceremony was cancelled in consequence of a letter received from Grand Lodge stating that *'in view of the National Emergency all Meetings are to be suspended'*. On 28 September, further notification was received informing the Lodge that Meetings should be resumed, but *'the Master had to act with proper regards to the National Emergency'*. The Installation Ceremony was then held on the 12 October. It started at 6.10 pm and finished at 7.15 pm with no Festive Board, which was suspended for a period of three months.

Over 100 Lodge Members served their Country during the war years. Amongst them were: Bro A D Griffiths, a Major, who served in North Africa, Italy, Yugoslavia and Austria and Bro D W Rees, who was also a Major, and served in North Africa, Sicily and Italy. Also, WBro A M Robertson, who was a Surgeon in charge of the Mobile Ambulances, a Lecturer in First Aid, a Surgeon in the Surgical Unit in Merthyr General hospital, and Deputy Chairman of the National Service Medical Board.

After the cessation of hostilities, Members returned from the forces, whilst others joined, thereby increasing the Lodge Membership from 155 to 206. As with many Lodges, the composition and opulence of its Members have changed over the years. Many Members were principals of their own firms and could arrange to leave their employment at times of their choosing. This is no longer the case; consequently, some years ago, the time for Regular Lodge was moved from 6.00 pm to 6.30 pm to accommodate those Brethren who could not leave work so early.

A unique event took place in Rhondda Lodge on 18 January 1948, when three blood brothers, instead of the customary two, were Initiated into the Lodge. Following the Special Dispensation agreed by the ProvGSec on the 17 December 1947, Kenneth Brittian Jefferies, Lewin David Jefferies and Michael Clifford Jefferies were Initiated on 8 January, Passed on 13 May and Raised on 11 November 1948.

The concept of forming a Daughter Lodge was considered as early as 1944 and it was agreed that Rhondda Lodge should be the Sponsoring Lodge for a new Lodge at Pontypridd, namely Craig yr Hesg Lodge No.6724. This Lodge was Consecrated on 18 October 1948.

Ten years later, on 19 December 1958, WBro W J C Jefferies proposed that a Committee should be elected to proceed with the necessary formalities for the formation of a second Daughter Lodge at Pontypridd. WBro Frederick G Hutchings was the catalyst for the formation of this Lodge. He was elected as Chairman, together with 14 Founder Members, 3 of whom were his sons, Leighton, Derek and Grenville. Frederick Hutchings had been Initiated into Rhondda Lodge in 1925 and Installed as Master in 1939. In Province, he had been appointed PPrJGD in 1946 and promoted to Junior Grand Warden in 1960. He became a Grand Officer in 1963 with the Rank of PAGDC.

On 4 March 1959, a Warrant or Charter of Constitution was issued and Ystradyfodwg Lodge No.7638 was finally established. The Lodge was Consecrated on the second Saturday in May 1959 and WBro Frederick G Hutchings was inevitably Installed as Primus Master. The Lodge's first Ceremony took place on the second Saturday in September 1959.

In September 1992, Sebastian Schiermann enrolled as an Engineering student in the Polytechnic of Wales. He had left Hanover, Germany, after being Initiated into the Schwarzor Bar Lodge No.79, on the 21 March 1992. He was Passed on the 11 February, Raised on the 13 May 1993 into the Rhondda Lodge, at the request of the Grand Secretary of the Grand Lodge of Germany, and with permission of the Grand Secretary of the United Grand Lodge of England, (under Rule 173 of the Book of Constitutions). Details of his Passing and Raising were sent to United Grand Lodge of England for forwarding to the Grand Lodge of Germany, in order that a German Grand Lodge Certificate could be raised and issued to him. He then became a Joining Member of the Lodge on 14 October 1993.

At the time of his Raising, Bro Schiermann's father, a Past Master in Hanover, visited and presented the Lodge with a Past Master's Jewel of the Schwarzor Bar Lodge, which was gratefully accepted on behalf of the Lodge by WBro Thomas William Condon, WM. WBro Tom has since been promoted to PPrJGW.

The Lodge was very proud to have had as one of its Members, the late WBro Percy Frank Hooper. An Electrical Contractor by profession, he was Initiated into Rhondda Lodge in 1974 and was Installed as Master in 1985. He was a Founder Member of Pontypridd Lodge, No.9001 in 1981, and became Master of that Lodge in 1990 and again in 2006. He was also a Founder Member of Saint Catherine's Lodge, No.9503. In 1997, WBro Percy attained his ultimate rank in Craft Masonry, when he was appointed PGStB in the United Grand Lodge of England. Sadly, he passed to the Grand Lodge Above on 4 January 2011 at the age of 70. Unknown to the Brethren he had been seriously ill for some time.

Mention should also be made of WBro Phillip Collin Weatherall, WM in 1991, who was promoted to ProvGSE in Royal Arch in 2005 and PGStB in Supreme Grand Chapter in 2006.

During recent times, Rhondda Lodge has continued to thrive with a full programme of social events, to which the ladies are always invited. These include fish and chip suppers, quiz nights and the ever popular week-ends away. Ladies' Festivals are always well attended, just like the first one held in 1940. The proceeds of that evening amounted to the healthy sum of £2-18-0 and were donated to the Glamorgan County Welfare and Comforts Fund.

Rhondda Lodge is continuing to flourish. The following extract from Rev G H Llewellyn's letter of resignation, dated 18 July 1939, echoes the thoughts of our Members today: *'It has been my privilege to visit several Lodges in the Midlands, but I have not found one so full of true Masonic Brotherliness, with a happy and helpful fellowship, that prevails in the Rhondda Lodge.'*

Compiled by Michael James Smith, PPrJGD.

Amethyst Lodge
No.4026

Warranted : 5 November 1919

Consecrated : 5 March 1920

Meeting at the Masonic Hall, Cardiff.

In May 1919, thirty Brethren met at the Masonic Temple, Cardiff to consider the formation of a new Lodge. WBro David William Evans, PM Prince Llewellyn Lodge No.2570 was unanimously elected to preside and it was resolved that a new Lodge be formed. It would meet on the first Friday in the month and it would be a Teetotal Lodge to demonstrate that Brethren could thoroughly enjoy themselves without the recourse to alcohol. It was further resolved that the name of the Lodge would be 'Amethyst' and WBro David Evans was appointed Master Designate.

David Evans had been Initiated at the age of 28 at the Third Regular Meeting of Prince Llewellyn Lodge on Thursday, 18 June 1896 and became WM of that Lodge in 1905. He was the first Director and Legal Adviser to the King Edward VII Welsh National Memorial Association for the Prevention and Treatment of Tuberculosis. His distinguished professional career was rewarded with a Knighthood in the King's Birthday Honours of June 1925, and later that year RW Provincial Grand Master, Sir Charles L D Venables Llewelyn, Bart, appointed him as his Deputy Provincial Grand Master, on the death of VWBro Henry Pendrill Charles.

The Brethren next met on 9 February 1920, when the Master Designate reported that he had received the Charter (Dated 5 November 1919) from Grand Lodge and it was resolved that the Consecration Ceremony and the Installation of the Master Designate would be held on 5 March 1920 and that dark morning dress would be worn.

The Sponsoring Lodge was Loyal Commercial Lodge No. 2720. There were 57 Founder Members of whom 10 were Past Masters of Loyal Commercial. Among the Founders were three Grand Officers, namely WBro Charles Edwin Dovey, PGD (Eng), PM Bute Lodge No.960 and a Founder Member of Loyal Commercial Lodge; WBro Arthur Llewellyn Hopkins, PGD (Eng), PM Glamorgan Lodge No. 36 (Appointed Provincial Grand Treasurer in 1902) and WBro Thomas Wallace, MD, PGD (Eng), PM Glamorgan Lodge and PM Hendre Lodge No.3250, Grand Superintendent, 1928-1930.

The Consecration Ceremony was performed on Friday, 5 March 1920 by RWBro Lt-Col Sir Charles L D Venables Llewelyn, ProvGM. He was assisted by WBros Charles Edwin Dovey as SW; Arthur Llewellyn Hopkins as JW; VWBros W P Besley, PGChap (Eng) as Chaplain and J S Granville Grenfell, GDC (Eng) as DC and WBro George Clarry, PAGDC (Eng), PM Glamorgan Lodge as IG. Following the Consecration, the Installation of WBro David W Evans, PProvJGD, Worshipful Master Designate was performed by WBro P Colville Smith, Grand Secretary (Sir Philip Colville Smith, Grand Secretary, 1917-1937, Knighted in 1925). WBro Arthur John Howell, PM Loyal Commercial Lodge, PPJGD, was Invested as Senior Warden and WBro James Ingram Rees, PM Windsor Lodge, PPrGStB, as Junior Warden.

The following year, on 27, 28 and 29 January 1921, David Evans, WM worked all Three Degrees himself, when six were Initiated, six Passed and six Raised. He was WM for two successive years. Then, at the Regular Lodge Meeting on 6 January 1922, he gave notice that a Deputation would attend the next Regular Meeting to ask for the support of Amethyst Lodge for a Petition for a new Lodge (Dinam Lodge). At that next Meeting, as Worshipful Master Designate of the new Lodge, he led the Petitioners and, in consequence, Dinam Lodge became the first Daughter Lodge of Amethyst Lodge. It is interesting to note that the Consecration of Dinam Lodge on 12 May 1923 was also performed by the Provincial Grand Master, Sir Charles L D Venables Llewelyn; the DC was again VWBro J S Granville Grenfell, Grand Director of Ceremonies and that WBro David W Evans was once again Installed in the Chair of King Solomon by the Grand Secretary, Philip Colville Smith.

Also, at the Regular Meeting of 6 January 1922, it was agreed that the WM should send a letter to Gwalia Lodge No.4213, informing them that 3 Brethren of Amethyst Lodge had been elected to form a committee to consider the formation of a Royal Arch Chapter and inviting Gwalia Lodge to elect 3 Members to serve on this committee. Amethyst Chapter No. 2026 was duly Warranted on 7 May 1924 and the close association between the two Lodges continues to this day.

Sadly, WBro Sir David William Evans, DepProvGM, died on 17 March 1926 at the age of 59. His extensive obituary in the Western Mail on Thursday, 18 March 1926 referred to him as *'one of the leading Freemasons in the Principality'* and said of his widow *'Lady Evans has achieved some success as a writer of fiction under the pseudonym of 'Amethyst,' and it is an interesting fact that out of compliment to her, one of the Cardiff Lodges of Freemasons was given this name'*.

The comradeship of the Lodge was never warmer than during the dark years of the Second World War, 1939-1945, and the able leadership of the Masters and Officers during this period will be long remembered. Good news spontaneously called forth the singing of the Doxology (a hymn or verse in Christian liturgy glorifying God), and bad news concerning so many of our Brethren at sea was eased as we sang the hymn 'For those in peril on the sea'. Lodge Regular Meetings were held in July, August and September in lieu of November, December and January, and Festive Boards were curtailed and visitations limited. Regulations concerning the wearing of morning dress and white gloves were relaxed for obvious reasons. Grand Lodge appealed *'for the surrender by the Brethren of their Masonic Jewels to be melted down and the proceeds presented to the Treasury as a Masonic gift towards the Country's urgent needs'*. The Amethyst War Savings Group was formed and received loyal support.

Three Captains, Bros D Emlyn Powell, Ernest Fear and David George Evans were reported lost at sea because of enemy action. Bro S Raymond Heal died in South Africa and Bro O T Jones experienced a grim period as a prisoner of war in Germany. For *'conspicuous bravery at sea'* three captains were awarded the OBE viz. Bros Owen Thomas Jones, William Royal Thomas and C J B Cornwell. At the end of the War, the Lodge sent a 'Thanksgiving Gift' of one hundred guineas to the Royal Masonic Hospital. The names of the Brethren who died due to enemy action in WWII, are recorded on a Memorial Plaque in the Cardiff Masonic Hall. In total, 29 Brethren served in His Majesty's Forces during this period. Since World War II, a further 12 Brethren have served in HM's Armed Forces.

The 1940s saw the emergence of three further Daughter Lodges; the first of which was Emerald Lodge No.5907, with a Warrant dated 1 September 1943. The first WM of this Lodge was WBro George Jones, PPrSGD, PM Amethyst and Dinam Lodges. This was soon followed by Fidelity Lodge No.6112, Warranted on 2 May 1945. On 6 May 1949, the WM of Amethyst Lodge, WBro Alban J Rees signed the Petition for Lodge of Integrity No.6907. The Petition was also signed by Bros L J Thomas, SW, and Reginald J Crews, JW, and the Warrant was issued on 27 July 1949. Unfortunately, this Lodge became unviable and was Erased from the Register of the UGLE in December 2008.

In 1947, two blood brothers, one from Amethyst Lodge and the other a Member of Lodge of Friendship No.6169 (Province of Monmouthshire) arranged Fraternal Visits between the two Lodges and it is pleasing to report that such visits are still continuing.

Early in 1952, Brethren from several Cardiff Lodges were considering the formation of yet another Cardiff Lodge and WBro Edgar Harries, WM of Amethyst Lodge, indicated that the Lodge was prepared to be the Sponsoring Lodge. Thus, Môr Hafren Lodge No.7294, with its Warrant issued on 7 May 1952, became the fifth and final Daughter Lodge of Amethyst Lodge. In addition to the five Daughter Lodges, Amethyst has four Granddaughter Lodges, namely: Penlan Lodge No.6695, Crystal Lodge No.8713, City of Cardiff Lodge No.7528, and Tudor Lodge No.8886.

The Golden Jubilee of the Lodge was celebrated on Friday, 6 March 1970, when WBro Tudor Smith was WM with Bro Trevor

K Dewey, SW and Bro John E Lewis, JW. On this occasion, the WM, Past Masters and Officers entered the Lodge led by the youngest and oldest Brethren carrying the Lodge Banner. The Lodge having been opened by the WM, the Past Masters of the Lodge carried out the Third Degree Ceremony, when Bros Brian F McCarthy and Kenneth G Griffiths were Raised. WBro William J Thomas occupied the Master's Chair and WBros W B Hughes and I R Lamb occupied the Senior and Junior Wardens' Chairs respectively. Following the conclusion of the Third Degree Ceremony, WBro Rev D Hopkin Morgan presented a history of the Lodge. To mark this important landmark, the sum of £200 was placed in a special account, known as 'The Amethyst Lodge Golden Jubilee Trust Account', with the capital and income of the account *to be applied in support of such Masonic Charities as the Lodge may, from time to time, direct'*. A copy of the Celebration Brochure was presented to all present and sufficient copies were printed to enable future Members of the Lodge to be presented with one.

In 1984, Mrs S Hughes (wife of WBro Bryn Hughes) presented the Lodge with a set of silver Working Tools in memory of her husband's many happy times spent in Amethyst Lodge. On Friday, 2 March 1990, WBros Brian F McCarthy and Kenneth G Griffiths presented the Lodge with a set of silver Square and Compasses, to mark the 20th Anniversary of their being Raised (6 March 1970, The Golden Jubilee Celebration Night).

The 75th Anniversary of the Lodge was celebrated on Friday, 3 March 1995, when WBro Jeff Williams, PPrGStB was Worshipful Master, with WBro Brian W Hithersay, PM Haven of Peace Lodge No. 8857, London, Senior Warden and WBro Keith Pearson, PM, Junior Warden. The format of the Ceremony was identical to that of the Golden Jubilee Celebration held in 1970, with Past Masters occupying all the Offices and Bros Peter C Stenstrom (Passed 5 December 1993) and John A Hughes (Passed 6 May 1994) were raised to the Sublime Degree of a Master Mason. This part of the Ceremony was conducted with WBro Robert R Harry, PPrAGDC occupying the Chair of King Solomon and WBros Brian F McCarthy, PPrJGD and Kenneth G Griffiths occupying the Senior and Junior Warden's Chairs respectively. WBro Roger Pearce Invested each newly Raised Brother with the Distinguishing Badge of a Master Mason.

During the Lodge's 91 years existence, a number of Brethren became, or are Masonic Veterans. They include: WBro Charles Langmaid, PAGDC, an eminent Neurosurgeon based at the Cardiff Royal Infirmary, who was Initiated by his father WBro Sidney Langmaid, PPrGD on 1 December 1939. WBro Charles died in 1997. His son, Bro Paul Langmaid, is a Member of the Lodge. Bro Reginald Molineaux, who was employed as a Civil Servant on Accounts, was Initiated on 1 March 1940. Bro Ernest G Evans, a GPO Telephone Supervisor, Initiated on the 15 July 1942, completed 50 years in Freemasonry in July 1992. Bro William Thomas Pearce (Bill), Initiated on 29 June 1945, is the only Amethyst Mason to achieve over 60 years in Freemasonry. After being discharged from the RAF in 1947 as a Warrant Officer, Bill joined the South Wales Electricity Board in 1948 and qualified as a Chartered Secretary. Sadly, Bill died on Friday, 29 April 2011, at the age of 87. He had almost completed 66 years in Freemasonry. He was the father of the present Secretary, WBro Roger Pearce, PPrGSwdB. WBro Phillip I Mabin, a Joining Member and PM Lodge Malaya No.5213, London, was Initiated on 27 June 1949. At the time he was a Lieutenant in the Corps of Royal Electrical and Mechanical Engineers. WBro Philip is still a Member of the Lodge. WBro Stanley Rundle, PPrAGReg, an Electrical Wholesale Manager, was Initiated on 2 January 1948. Bro Samuel R Lewis, was Initiated on 2 March 1951. WBro Eric Lewis, PPrAGDC, Pharmacist, was Initiated on 4 January 1957 and is still a Member of the Lodge. WBro Robert R Harry, PPrJGW, who was WM in 1973 and again in 2000, was Initiated on 1 April 1960. Born in Toronto, Canada, he and his family moved to the UK in 1939. He was the Welsh Piano Accordion Champion on six occasions and was also a soloist in the BBC National Orchestra of Wales. WBro Robert is still a Member of the Lodge.

While several Brethren, in common with other Lodges, have gained distinction in other Degrees of Freemasonry, mention should be made of WBro David G Edwards, who is Inspector General of the Supreme Council 33° (District of South Wales & Monmouthshire) and WBro Walter Hammond, who was Deputy District Grand Master of Royal & Select Masters, 2002-2004, and Substitute Provincial Grand Master of The Royal Order of Scotland, 2002-2004. Most recently, WBro Keith Pearson, PPrGSwdB, was appointed Deputy District Grand Master in the Order of Royal and Select Masters, South Wales, in December 2009 and re-appointed as such in December 2010.

Compiled by WBro Brian F McCarthy, PPrJGW and WBro David G Edwards, PAGDC.

North Glamorgan Lodge No.4055

Warranted : 14 January 1920

Consecrated : 22 July 1920

Meeting at the Masonic Hall, Merthyr Tydfil.

In the early part of the 20th century, detailed discussions took place in Loyal Cambrian Lodge No.110 about the possibility of forming a Daughter Lodge in Merthyr Tydfil. On 6 November 1919, three Worshipful Brethren, W R Harris, John Morgan and Alexander Duncan, with a Petition signed by 17 PMs and 16 Brethren, appeared before a Committee of the Loyal Cambrian Lodge, requesting formal approval for the presentation of that Petition to the Provincial Grand Master. After some discussion, the Petition was duly approved, signed by the WM, Senior and Junior Wardens, and forwarded to Provincial Grand Lodge for approval.

On 5 February 1920, the WM and Brethren of Loyal Cambrian Lodge were informed that the Charter for a new Lodge, named North Glamorgan and numbered 4055, had been issued. The name had been chosen in view of its relative situation in the old County of Glamorgan and the remains of Morlais Castle, from which the Lodge Crest is derived. The Castle was built in 1270 by Earl Gilbert de Claire, the Earl of Gloucester and the Lord of Glamorgan, as an outpost of the main stronghold at Caerphilly, where he had built a massive Castle. Morlais Castle's main function was to provide early warning of any attacks from the North. Legend has it that there are many secret passages and secret entrances, one at the trench or moat surrounding the Castle, another from the crypt – the only room which is preserved. A third entrance is reputed to have been situated on the rocky, tree-covered banks of the Taf Fechan. The crypt was situated beneath the main tower, and a good example of 13th century architecture, had a long flight of stone steps leading to an arched doorway and a central pillar, which is depicted in the Lodge Crest, supporting the grained roof of twelve arches.

The Consecration Ceremony took place on 22 July 1920, presided over by RWBro C L D Venables Llewelyn, ProvGM, and WBro Henry Pendrill Charles, DepProvGM, Installed WBro Simon Sandbrook, PPrJGW, PM Loyal Cambrian Lodge, as the first Master of the Lodge. WBro W R Harris, PPrSGW, also PM Loyal Cambrian Lodge, was Invested as IPM. The Lodge worked in very close affinity with Loyal Cambrian Lodge until January 1932, when North Glamorgan set up its own Lodge of Instruction and became independent of its Mother Lodge. Lodge Membership increased to over 100 by the end of WWII. Interestingly, at that time there was a suggestion that an age limit should be set at 50 to encourage 'younger' applicants. There was a condition attached to this proposal, that the WM should be allowed to propose two Candidates during his year. There is no record that this motion was ever adopted but growth continued so that in June 1967 there were 150 Members. The figure has declined over more recent years in common with the national trend.

Some of our more distinguished Members are covered later, but it is certainly worthy of note that Bro Seymour Berry became High Sheriff of Brecon and Bro Julian Pode, later to become Sir Julian Pode, a Director of one of 'the big four' banks, and of Steel Company of Wales / British Steel fame, became High Sheriff of the County of Glamorgan in 1947.

Rather uncommonly, visitations between North Glamorgan and Loyal Cambrian Lodges had begun formally, but only at Installation Ceremonies, and were restricted to the WM and his Wardens. Happily, that practice ceased and it is now open to all Members who wish to attend either Regular or Installation Meetings.

The Mother Lodge, being the owner of the Lodge premises, initially charged an annual 'rental' of a guinea per Member, and from 1958 the rental gradually increased with inflation. Fees are now paid to the Joint Management Committee which controls the administration of the Masonic Temple. All the Merthyr Lodges are now represented on this Committee.

With the formation of other Lodges in Merthyr, a happy relationship has always existed. Indeed, in January 1956, when WBro Jesse Roberts was WM of North Glamorgan Lodge and WBro Robert Jones was WM of Fforest Lodge No.2606 in Treharris, they instigated a Fraternal arrangement whereby North Glamorgan Lodge would perform a 2nd Degree Ceremony at Treharris Masonic Temple in May each year, and similarly Fforest Lodge would carry out a 2nd Degree Ceremony in Merthyr in March. This happy practice continues to this day and Fraternal visits have been expanded since, as in February 1982, Aelwyd Lodge No.7982 formally invited the WM and Brethren of North Glamorgan Lodge to join them at their Meeting the following month and North Glamorgan Lodge suitably reciprocated with Aelwyd Lodge visiting later that year. This exchange also continues to be enjoyed by the Brethren to the present day.

Although there is no record of the Dedication of a Lodge Banner, in 1966, at the recommendation of WBro Ken Adams Morgan, it was agreed that WBro D H Gwyn Davies would deal with its 'renovation'. The Banner, with St Tydfil representing Merthyr Tydfil, illustrates the crypt at Morlais Castle and a laurel wreath with the Motto *'Ofner Na Ofno Angau'*, the translation being *'Let Him Fear Who Fears Not Death'*. It was during a 'table meeting' between the Loyal Cambrian and North Glamorgan Lodges in January 1924 that it was agreed that the crypt depicted on the Lodge Banner should be represented on its Coat of Arms. This appeared on the next Lodge Summons and has done so ever since.

Many distinguished Brethren have passed through the Chair of North Glamorgan Lodge, and those that have subsequently been accorded the honour of appointments in Grand Lodge are as follows: in 1982, WBro Kenneth Adams Morgan as PGStB; followed in 1992, by WBro Gareth Whale as PAGDC; in 1996, WBro D Gerald Williams as PAGDC; and WBro William Porter Vaughan, a Joining Member, as PGStB; then in the year 2000, WBro Alan John Davies was appointed PGStB.

Three of our long serving Brethren have been presented with Diamond Jubilee Certificates. They are WBro Kenneth Adams Morgan in July 1996, WBro Howard Leighton Jones in September 2004 and WBro Dr Arthur G Jones in September 2006. WBro Howard being the Senior PM of the Lodge, joined Freemasonry during the War years, and an Emergency Meeting had to be arranged for his Initiation in August 1944. He was Passed in December 1944 and Raised in April 1945. He subsequently became WM in October 1962.

One of these names will be immediately recognised as a former AProvGM. WBro Ken Adams Morgan was born in Merthyr Tydfil on 13 April 1922. Having completed his education at Merthyr Tydfil County Grammar School, and at St Luke's College, Exeter, he joined the Army and was commissioned as a Captain in the 19th Signal Regiment, seeing active service during the Burma

Campaign. WBro Ken was Initiated into North Glamorgan Lodge on 24 June 1946 and was Installed as WM in 1958. WBro Ken had the distinction of being promoted in Grand Lodge to Acting Grand Senior Deacon in 1982. He was both liked and respected by all and was a most eloquent after-dinner speaker and was a Member of many Lodges and Chapters in the Province. He retired as AProvGM in June 1996, and prior to his death in April 1997 was also an Honorary Member of 70 Craft Lodges in the Province of South Wales (Eastern Division). He had a favourite and most appropriate saying, *'it is nice to be important, but it is far more important to be nice'*, and frequently used quotations such as *'if you are true to yourself, then you can be false to no man'* and *'it is better to reign sovereign in the hearts and affections of men, than to rule over their lives and fortunes'*, for which he will always be remembered.

WBro Gerald Williams will perhaps be remembered not only as a GLO of the Lodge but also as District Grand Master of the Royal and Select Masters of South Wales. He held this position for just a year before his untimely passing to the Grand Lodge Above. A retired school teacher, he was highly respected in the community in general and in Freemasonry in particular where he certainly made his mark. He was also a former Provincial Grand Supreme Ruler in the Order of the Secret Monitor, and was affectionately known as 'Gerald the gentleman'.

Thanks to an idea voiced in 1977 by WBro Derek Price Davies, North Glamorgan's own Chapter was Consecrated on 17 January 1978. Of those who took Office that day, three Brethren are affectionately remembered in addition to EComp Ken; they are EComps Jesse Roberts, Ken Bibby, and Reg Wilson.

To conclude on an unusual and lighter note, the Lodge was always honoured to welcome the former ProvGM, RWBro the Rt Hon the Lord Swansea, OSM, CStJ, DL, at its July Meeting, when it was the custom to conduct a Third Degree Ceremony. Over a period of over twenty years, he not only attended, but took the Chair whilst the Candidate had been allowed to *'leave the Lodge to restore himself to his former comforts'*. He then conducted the remainder of the Ceremony. During this period, it was likewise his custom to join WBro Ken Adams Morgan, and others, after the Festive Board, for a further repast at the local Conservative Club late into the night.

Compiled by WBro Christopher Sharp, PPrJGW.

Penarth Lodge No.4113

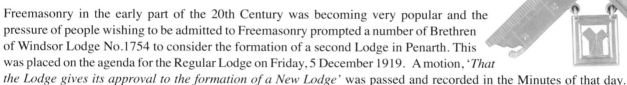

Warranted : 11 May 1920

Consecrated : 23 November 1920

Meeting at the Masonic Hall, Penarth.

Freemasonry in the early part of the 20th Century was becoming very popular and the pressure of people wishing to be admitted to Freemasonry prompted a number of Brethren of Windsor Lodge No.1754 to consider the formation of a second Lodge in Penarth. This was placed on the agenda for the Regular Lodge on Friday, 5 December 1919. A motion, '*That the Lodge gives its approval to the formation of a New Lodge*' was passed and recorded in the Minutes of that day.

The inaugural meeting took place at the Masonic Temple, Station Approach, Penarth, on Friday, 13 February 1920, with the purpose of deciding administrative matters. (note the old Masonic Temple is now the Penarth Branch of the Royal British Legion). That night, the new Lodge was born. Among the names suggested were 'Penarth', 'Kymin', 'Clive' and 'Connaught', but 'Penarth' was chosen. Enthusiasm was so great that it was passed that the number of Founders should not exceed 50. In fact, 41 Founders signed the Petition. Among these Founder Members were 5 Shipowners, 6 Master Mariners, 4 Consulting Engineers as well as 9 Shop-owners. WBro Richard Guy was chosen as WM Designate, WBro Albert Taylor as SW Designate, and WBro Albert James Nurton as JW Designate.

The Petition was duly presented to Windsor Lodge and the Warrant for Penarth Lodge No.4113 was granted on 14 May 1920.

The Town Coat of Arms was deemed appropriate for the Lodge Crest. Permission was sought from Penarth Urban District Council and approval was granted. The Lodge Crest not only bears the Town Coat of Arms but also a Dragon, a Ship and a Bear's Head. The Welsh Dragon needs no explanation; neither the Sailing Ship, as Penarth was a sea-port, but, controversy exists over the Bear's Head. A popular explanation is that the English translation of 'Penarth' is 'Bear's Head.' It is usual in Heraldry to use animals and objects, known as 'Charges', as pictorial representations of a name, in which case, this explanation makes sense. The Lodge Motto, in Welsh: '*Cynghori er Llesiant*', loosely translates as '*Counselling for Good or Betterment*'.

The Consecration Ceremony was held at the Baptist Church Schoolroom, Stanwell Road, on Tuesday, 23 November 1920, the Masonic Temple being considered too small for such an important occasion. RWBro C L D Venables Llewelyn, ProvGM, was in attendance, accompanied by WBro Henry Pendrill Charles, PAGReg, AProvGM, as SW; WBro Thomas Wallace, PGD, as JW; Bro Rev Gwilym Francis as Chaplain, and a full team of Provincial Officers. A Board of Installed Masters was then formed and WBro

Richard Guy was Installed as the first WM. There were 150 Brethren in attendance and so the decision not to hold the Ceremony in the Masonic Temple, Station Road, proved correct.

Two Lewises were Initiated at the first Regular Meeting in December, Wilfred James Guy, son of the first WM and Kenneth Lougher Yorath, son of a PM Founder. The Ceremony being conducted by the WM up to and including the Obligation, and from there on by WBro W L Yorath, who also gave the Charity Charge and the Ancient Charge. During the proceedings, it was announced that WBros Arthur Jones, Frank Morgan and F Pardoe Williams had presented Wardens' Chairs; Bro H O King had presented the set of Working Tools, and the Lodge Banner had been presented by the WM, WBro Richard Guy. The Collars were donated by the individual Officers. The wear and tear of time has necessitated that the Banner be restored and the Collars replaced.

The first death among the Brethren was reported on 16 March 1921, when it was announced that WBro Arthur Jones, Founder and one of the donors of the Wardens' Chairs, had passed to the Grand Lodge Above. According to the Minutes, a sum of 15 guineas was voted from Lodge funds for a memorial to this departed Brother, but there is no record of the nature of the memorial.

Bro William Hodgeson, affectionately known as 'Daddy Hodgeson', was appointed Organist on 25 January 1921, the day of his Initiation. He held this Office for almost 18 years, until he was made an Honorary Member on 27 September 1938, 'for faithful service'. He was succeeded by Bro Lancelot D Bailey, who remained the Lodge Organist until September 1996. Penarth Lodge has a just claim to what must be a record for the least number of Organists and the longest serving Organist; only two in 73 years, with Lancelot Bailey holding the Office for 56 years. WBro John R Paley has been the Lodge Organist for the last twelve years. Is this another record in the making?

Among those Balloted for on 26 April 1921, were Mr Gerald Tudor, later to be appointed as the Cardiff Coroner and Mr Henry Francis Stockwell, who was to become DepProvGM in 1971 (his biographical details are given separately in this book). Gerald Tudor was Initiated that day, and Harry Stockwell was Initiated on 14 June 1921. Between November 1920 and June 1921, 16 Members were Initiated and 9 Joining Members were admitted, increasing the Lodge Membership to 66 Brethren.

On 25 September 1928, Brethren of Windsor and Penarth Lodges, accompanied by a goodly number of Brethren from other Lodges, marched with all due Ceremony and Banners flying, from Station Approach to their new home at Stanwell Road, where they held their first Regular Meeting in the New Temple. The retiring WM, WBro Frederick S Francis, Installed *'that great little man'*, WBro Louis Fifoot. The story goes, that when Louis, who was under five foot in height, received a certain telephone call, the caller was heard to ask, *'is that Fivefoot?'*; after which, he became known as *'that great little man'*.

A stained glass window was purchased in 1929 at a cost of £14. 3s. 0d and is still situated on the south side of the Temple. In November 1931, the 100th Regular Meeting was held, which coincided with the Lodge's 10th Anniversary.

On Friday 8 March 1934, the three Penarth Lodges, Windsor, Penarth and Sapphire (Consecrated in 1931), were hosts to the Prestonian Lecture. At the combined Meeting, they welcomed many notable Masonic personalities, including the Prestonian Lecturer, WBro F C C M Fighiera, PGD, who delivered a lecture entitled, *'The Responsibility of a Lodge to its Candidates'*.

The War Years, 1939 - 1945, made Lodge Meetings difficult. The Installation of WBro D T Roderick was postponed from September to October 1939. For several years, the Hall was used both as classrooms for boys from Penarth Grammar School and as an office for the RAF. Penarth was bombed several times, and very severely on the 3 March 1941, with 6 civilian fatalities. Fortunately, there was no damage to the Hall. Among the civilian casualties were Mr and Mrs A E Matthews, the parents of WBro A Sidney Matthews of Penarth Lodge, who was Initiated in 1952.

During this period, Penarth Lodge met on the fourth Saturday of the month at 2.30 pm. But, despite these difficulties, 17 Emergency Lodges were held and 50 Members Initiated.

Dispensation was obtained for the Meeting on 28 April 1942, to allow WBro Gerald Tudor to Initiate his son, Pilot Officer Gerald

Leslie Tudor, who was just 20 years of age. He was subsequently Passed and Raised, but sadly, on 21 August 1942, 14 days after being Raised, he was killed in action. A list of all those lost during WWII can be found in the Lodge History Book. Two years later, WBro Gerald presented the Lodge with three ivory Gavels, in memory of his son. These Gavels are regarded as treasured possessions and were used at every Regular Lodge until 1987, when it was decided, that because of their value, their use should be restricted to Installation Ceremonies.

The Silver Jubilee of the Lodge was celebrated on 27 November 1945, and on this occasion no visitors were allowed. WBro George Moon gave a short résumé of the Lodge History but, unfortunately, this content cannot be found.

The War was over and society was rejoicing, which may have influenced Bro Ivor Jones to present the Lodge with two carved collection plates, both still in use today. Also, still in use is the velvet cushion, presented in 1985 by Bro Harry Williams, beautifully embroidered by his wife with gold Square and Compasses.

Not many Brethren reach the age of 102, but this was the distinction that singled out WBro Arthur Brown. He was Initiated into the Lodge at the age of 33, became Master in 1936, moved to Essex in the 1970s, and when offered Honorary Membership in the 1980s, he promptly refused!

By 1931, there had been 37 Emergency Meetings; there were 94 Members by 1937 and Membership peaked at 121 in 1960. The large increase in Membership after WWII was probably due to ex-servicemen seeking the male camaraderie they had been accustomed to during their military service. Thereafter, numbers declined steadily to 93 in 1990. Since then, there has been a more rapid reduction in Membership to only 31 Members in 2011.

Prior to 1961, when the ground lease was purchased from the Earl of Plymouth, a clause in the lease prevented alcohol being sold on the premises. Further, the Masonic Hall Company did not have a licence to sell alcohol. This problem was overcome by the Chief Steward purchasing a quantity of beer for consumption at the Festive Board, and increasing the cost of the meal. This arrangement satisfied the Custom and Excise Officers who were Members of the Lodge! This made the proceedings rather abstemious and festivities usually concluded by 9.15 pm, giving Members time to visit the British Legion, which closed at 10.00 pm. At Installations and Ladies' Festivals, the WM arranged for an outside licensee to organise a bar upstairs, serving spirits as well as beer.

For many years, up to and including the 1960s, it was the custom for the WM to wear White Tie and Tails and the ladies full length evening gowns at Ladies' Festivals. The SW would present the First Lady with a bouquet, on behalf of the Officers and then all would assemble at the Tracing Board, to be greeted by the WM and his Lady. A short Service was then held, followed by an address from the WM. The Ceremony ended with a suitable musical rendition, and then the assembled company repaired to the dining room. At an appropriate time, dancing would commence, and for those who wished, there were also whist tables. Brethren served a buffet around 10 .00 pm and carriages were at 1. 00 am.

The Penarth Lodge pays tribute to the Charity Stewards and to the Ladies, who are to be applauded for raising large amounts of money on these occasions and at other social events throughout the years.

Compiled by WBro Robert W Lee, PAGDC.

Trisant Lodge No.4154

Warranted : 13 July 1920

Consecrated : 12 November 1920

Meeting at the Masonic Hall, Pontyclun.

Trisant means *'Three Saints'*, the Lodge being named after the three Saints of the village of Llantrisant, namely Illtyd, Dyfodwg (or Tyfodwg) and Gwynno.

The Lodge was Sponsored by Ogmore Lodge No.1752 and thirteen of the fifteen Founders were Members of that Lodge. The Lodge was Consecrated on 12 November 1920, the Ceremony taking place at the Institute Hall, Pontyclun (now the Pontyclun Athletic Club) at 2.30 pm. RWBro Charles L D Venables Llewelyn, Bart, ProvGM, South Wales ED, assisted by his Officers, conducted the Ceremony.

At 3.45 pm, a Board of Installed Masters was formed and WBro Henry Pendrill Charles, DepProvGM, Installed WBro H C Sloman, PM Ogmore Lodge, as the first Master.

The first Regular Meeting was held at the Ivor Arms, Brynsadler, on 2 December 1920, when Mr Edward Thomas Davies and Mr David Rees Llewellyn were Initiated into the Craft.

During the formative years of the Lodge, the opportunity for Dispensations for holding additional Lodge Meetings was frequently taken. In 1921, for example, ten Regular Meetings and fourteen Emergency Meetings were held, when a total of 26 Candidates were Initiated, 20 were Passed, and 19 Raised. In 1922, there were 16 Emergency Meetings, and in 1923 there were 15, with this pattern continuing until 1932, when 14 Emergency Meetings were held.

A Notice of Motion, dated 20 March, 1925 stated *'That an application be made to the RWProvGM for the permanent removal of the Trisant Lodge No.4154, under the Grand Lodge of England from the Masonic Hall, Ivor Arms, Brynsadler to the National School, Pontyclun'*. Lodge Meetings continued to be held at the Ivor Arms until 30 September 1925.

A sum of money amounting to almost £170 was paid to convert these premises into adequate facilities suitable for a Masonic Hall, and an annual rent of £50 was agreed. WBro Sir David William Evans, DepProvGM, who was presented with a golden key by WBro T Ajax Lewis, opened this converted schoolroom on 1 October 1925.

On 11 February 1927, a Ladies' Festival held at the Bear Inn, Cowbridge, began with a Whist Drive from 6.30 pm to 9.00 pm, followed by dinner until 10.00 pm, with dancing until 2.00 am. Tickets were 10s/6d (52½p) single, and 1 guinea (£1.05p) double.

On 2 January 1928, the Pillars presented to the Lodge by Bro James Tallboy were Dedicated by WBro David John Jones,

DepProvGM, and Consecrated by WBro A E Turtlee, ProvGChap.

In December that same year, the Lodge Banner, bearing the Arms of the town of Llantrisant, was presented to the Lodge by the first Secretary, Bro Thomas Jenkins.

Some years previously, a number of Lodge Members had felt that their own purpose-built premises were required, and discussions regarding this were instigated. The first meeting of the Building Committee took place on 2 February 1923, when Bro Gomer Morgan informed them, that following a meeting with the Agent to the Bute Estate, he had obtained an option of purchasing a site opposite the Pontyclun War Memorial at a cost of 2d (approx 1p) per square yard. Bro Morgan was instructed to prepare preliminary drawings for the proposed new Masonic Hall.

By 9 May 1923, the Bute Estate was prepared to sell the plot of land, and Bro Morgan was instructed to go ahead with firm plans for a Masonic Hall large enough to accommodate 250 Members. In the meantime, WBro S A Tucker, WM, reported that he had been offered Hope Chapel, Pontyclun, as a Masonic Hall. The Secretary was instructed to write to Hope Chapel offering the sum of £2,300 for the building. On 27 July 1923, the representatives of Hope Chapel declined the offer.

Two further sites were offered for consideration, and Bro Morgan submitted plans for a proposed new Temple and Dining Hall at an estimated cost of £3,100. After some correspondence with Provincial Grand Lodge, it was agreed that the new Temple and Dining Hall would be erected at the earliest possible date, on the site near the Pontyclun War Memorial, at an inclusive cost of £4,000, in accordance with draft plans submitted to the Building Committee.

It was not until 10 March 1930 that the next move took place, when a sub-committee was elected, and on 6 November 1930, four Brethren were appointed as the first Trustees of the Masonic Temple, Pontyclun.

At 2.30 pm on Wednesday, 3 June 1931, the Officers and Brethren of the Lodge, supported by Officers of United Grand Lodge and Provincial Grand Lodge, Present and Past, Ruling Masters, Wardens and Visiting Brethren of the Province, assembled for the Ceremony of Laying the Foundation Stone of the new building. The Laying of the Foundation Stone and the Dedication Ceremony were carried out in a most impressive manner by RWBro Sir Charles L D Venables Llewelyn, assisted by Officers of Grand Lodge and Provincial Grand Lodge. Exactly six months later, on Thursday, 3 December 1931, the Brethren assembled in the main entrance of the new Masonic Building for the Opening Ceremony. This Ceremony was performed by WBro Edgar J Rutter, DepProvGM.

The first Ladies' Festival in the new building took place on 11 October 1932.

When war was declared on 3 September 1939, all Masonic Meetings were temporarily suspended, in accordance with instructions from Grand Lodge. However, in October, with certain restrictions, the suspension was lifted and the Lodge went through a period when Meetings took place on Saturday afternoons. These restrictions applied particularly to Installations. Naturally, visitors were few, with many Brethren serving in the armed forces.

During the 1940s, there was some return to normality, although the customary intake of Candidates slowed up for a while. On 2 April 1942, Mr Melfin Hughes was Initiated. He

Laying the Foundation Stone of Trisant Lodge Masonic Hall

289

was the nephew of Bro John Hughes, 1873-1932, composer of the hymn tune 'Cwm Rhondda'. To mark the occasion, 'Guide Me O Thou Great Jehovah' was sung to the tune 'Cwm Rhondda'.

In 1944, the ProvGM requested that hospitality be given to members of the American Armed Forces, while stationed here, who were Freemasons.

There were cases of kin of Brethren being taken prisoners of war. The son of WBro Webb Stokes (Secretary) escaped from captivity. He lived in terrible conditions in the Italian mountains for seven months, before being recaptured!

On 8 May 1945, Victory in Europe was announced. In June, Sergeant Ieuan Hughes, the WM's son, received General Montgomery's Certificate for Gallantry and Devotion to Duty.

The Silver Jubilee of the Lodge was celebrated on Thursday, 12 July 1945. There were 48 visitors, including RWBro R P St John Charles, WBro Edgar J Rutter and WBro Harry F Stockwell, ProvGSec. The ProvGM conducted an Initiation Ceremony. While at the 1946 December Meeting, 88 Members and 58 visitors were present, making a total of 146 Brethren. The war was certainly over for Trisant Lodge!

By 1980, three sets of blood brothers, and three sets of fathers and sons had attained the Chair of King Solomon.

When Trisant Lodge was formed, the annual subscription was 3 guineas (£3.15), which represented an average weekly wage at that time. This was not increased until 1950, when it became 4 guineas (£4.20). Thus, for the first thirty years of its existence the Lodge fees remained unchanged.

The Masonic Hall - Pontyclun

On 9 March 1948, WBro H H Phillips suggested that a Lodge Motto should appear beneath the Lodge Crest. The first Lodge Summons, with the Motto: *'Goreu Golud - Golud Calon'*, meaning *'Best Health - Best Heart'*, was printed in May of that year.

In 1969, an organ fund was set up. Trisant Lodge and Talygarn Lodge No.7216 both contributed £150 and the organ was finally purchased in 1974.

A Maintenance Committee was formed in 1975. Over the years, volunteers from all the Lodges meeting at the Pontyclun Temple have performed sterling work in keeping the building up to standard. The maintenance costs have been met largely through social events organised by this Committee.

Compiled by WBro Ken Pontin, PPrGStB.

Penrice Lodge No.4172

Warranted : 1 September 1920

Consecrated : 10 December 1920

Meeting at the Masonic Hall, Swansea.

When Bro Thomas Oakley Walters was Installed Worshipful Master of Indefatigable Lodge No.237 on 12 January 1920, the Lodge consisted of 230 Members. Although Beaufort Lodge No.3834 had only been Warranted two years previously, the need for yet another new Lodge at Swansea was clearly evident, the proposal of which was commended to the Indefatigable Brethren at the aforementioned Installation. Indefatigable Lodge immediately agreed to be the Sponsoring Lodge and meetings were held to bring the proposal to fruition.

At a Meeting held on 12 April 1920, it was announced that WBro Lord Blythswood, who had recently inherited Penrice Castle and Estates, had agreed to be the first Worshipful Master. Captain the Rt Hon Archibald Douglas Campbell, 4th Baron Blythswood, MVO, was at the time Junior Grand Warden of Scotland. He became Senior Grand Warden of Scotland the following year and, in 1922, he became Provincial Grand Master of the Province of Renfrewshire East. Initiated at the age of 21 in Lodge Ancient Stirling No.30 in 1891, he had become a Master Mason on 18 December 1901. (This Lodge, dating from 1599, is very much older than the Grand Lodge of Scotland.) He was also a Member of Lodge Prince of Wales No.426, Renfrew, outside Glasgow, where the family home, Blythswood House (demolished in 1935) was situated. In December 1926, he was installed as Grand Master of the Grand Lodge of Scotland, and continued as such until his death at the age of 59, on 14 November 1929.

The name of the Lodge 'Penrice' clearly comes from Lord Blythewood's recently inherited Penrice Castle Estate. There is, however, an earlier association with Penrice Castle and Freemasonry. The Mansion was built in the 1770s, near the ruined Norman Castle, for Mansel Talbot, the grandfather of Theodore Mansel Talbot, ProvGM, 1865-1876. It had also been the residence of Sir Christopher Cole, ProvGM, 1817-1836.

The Petition for Penrice Lodge was signed by Thomas Oakley Thomas, WM, and his Wardens at a Regular Meeting of Indefatigable Lodge on 14 June 1920. All the Petitioners were Members of Indefatigable Lodge, with the exception of Lord Blythswood. The Charter was signed on 1 September 1920 and Penrice Lodge was to become the sixth Lodge in Swansea.

The WM Designate was also a Member of Household Brigade Lodge No.2614, meeting at 10 Duke Street, St James's, London. A Military Lodge, with Membership restricted to the Guards Brigade, Lord Blythswood had been WM in 1918. He had signed the

Proposal Form and Declaration as the Seconder for HRH Prince Edward, Duke of Windsor, to be Initiated into Household Brigade Lodge on 2 May 1919. The Duke became Provincial Grand Master of Surrey in 1924 and in that same year, Lord Blythswood became Senior Grand Warden of UGLE. The Proposal Form, a treasured possession of Penrice Lodge, was donated to the Lodge by Lord Blythswood.

The SW Designate was WBro David John Davies, Grocer and Director of the Morriston Tinplate Works, who had been WM of Indefatigable Lodge in 1911. He became the second WM of Penrice Lodge in 1921, when he was Mayor Elect of Swansea. According to Bro T Mainwaring Hughes, (WM in 1933) in his definitive book on Swansea Mayors, D J Davies was the uncrowned King of Morriston. With his two neighbours, David Mathews and Edward Harris, they were a formidable trio who exercised great influence on Swansea affairs.

The JW Designate was Wilfred James Phelps, Merchant of Uplands, Swansea, who had been WM of Indefatigable Lodge in 1917.

On 29 September 1920, Lord Blythswood wrote to Bro Trevor Evans, Secretary *pro tempore* as follows: '*Dear Bro Trevor Evans,*
I full approve of the Blythswood Coat of Arms being used on the Banner of the new Penrice Lodge.

Yours faithfully & fraternally,
Blythswood'

Penrice Castle

The following day, Trevor Evans wrote to WBro George Whittington, PAGDC, Provincial Grand Secretary: '*I now enclose the design for the intended Coat of Arms of the Penrice Lodge together with a letter from Lord Blythswood giving his approval and consent for the use of the Blythswood Coat of Arms.*

The Arms are, on the left, of the ancient family of Penres or Penrice of the Norman Period and on the right, of Lord Blythswood, the present owner and intending first Worshipful Master of the new Lodge.'

Thus, the Lodge adopted the Family Crest of Lord Blythswood with the Motto: '*Quae Serata Secura*', which translates as '*Things locked up are safe*', displayed on the Lodge Banner.

The Lodge was Consecrated at the Patti Pavilion, Swansea, on 10 December 1920. The Consecrating Officers were RWBro Sir Charles L D Venables Llewelyn, Bart, ProvGM, assisted by WBro Henry Pendrill Charles, PAGReg, DepProvGM, as SW; WBro Tom Wallace, PGD, PProvSGW, PM Glamorgan Lodge No.36, as JW; Bro Rev Gwilym Francis as Chaplain; WBro George Whittington, PAGDC, ProvGSec, as DC; WBro Charles Prescott Palmer, PProvGDC, as ADC and WBro J Broad Excell, PAGDC, as IG. Following the Consecration, Lord Blythswood should have been Installed WM by WBro Lt-General Sir Francis Lloyd, PJGW, but was Installed instead by WBro Henry Pendrill Charles. The IPM was WBro Joshua Broad Excell, PAGDC, a highly regarded PM Indefatigable Lodge, who had first been WM in 1904 and again in 1915. The first Treasurer was WBro James Dadford Rawlings, Solicitor and WM Indefatigable Lodge in 1916. Bro Trevor Evans was the first Secretary. Following the Ceremony, the

Brethren enjoyed a seven course banquet for which they paid the sum of 10/6p (55p).

The first Initiate of Penrice Lodge was Rev Harrington Clare Lee, who later became Archbishop of Melbourne, Australia. On his death in 1929, the Lodge went into mourning for one month. Another Cleric, Rev Cecil W Wilson, Vicar of St Mary's Church, Swansea, Worshipful Master in 1926, had been Padre to the Forces during the First World War and later became Bishop of Bradford. It was said that if one wanted to become a Mayor of Swansea or a Bishop, one should join Penrice Lodge.

In 1922, Trevor Evans, (first Secretary), who was an Estate Agent, was authorised by the Worshipful Master of Indefatigable Lodge, WBro Stammers Alabaster to purchase Brunswick House in St Helen's Road for the sum of £4,000.00 for a new Masonic Temple. The Members of Indefatigable Lodge stood as security and the property was purchased by Indefatigable Lodge. The other 5 Lodges (including Penrice Lodge) fitted out the premises which we enjoy today. The first floor Major and Minor Temples and Committee Rooms, the ground floor Connaught Hall, refectory and kitchens were erected in the gardens of the former Brunswick House.

In 1925, Penrice Lodge, in conjunction with London Welsh Lodge No.2867, Sponsored Dewi Sant Lodge No.4728, London. Sadly, this Lodge was Erased from the Register of UGLE in June 2002. The Warrant was returned to Grand Lodge in order that Dewi Sant Lodge could amalgamate with Gwalia Lodge No.7893, London. In consequence of the amalgamation, Gwalia Lodge was renamed 'Dewi Sant a Gwalia Lodge' No.7893. Brethren of Penrice and Dewi Sant a Gwalia Lodges have a reciprocal arrangement of Honorary Membership.

When WBro James Dadford Rawlings, Founder Member and Treasurer, died in 1926, he was accorded a full Masonic Funeral. The Lodge has a copy of this Funeral Service, which includes the prayers, address and details on how to conduct such a Funeral and accord 'Grand Honours'. Also in 1926, on St Andrew's Day (30 November) Lord Blythswood was Invested as Grand Master Mason of the Grand Lodge of Scotland, a position he was to occupy until his death, at the age of 59, on 14 November 1929. The Lodge has in its possession a photograph of Lord Blythswood in his full Masonic Regalia. It is displayed in Swansea Masonic Hall alongside portraits of other distinguished Freemasons of Swansea.

In 1932, Indefatigable Lodge Sponsored Glantawe Lodge No.5378, Consecrated on 31 October 1932, and a number of Penrice Brethren were Founder Members.

During the Second World War, 'Utility' Master Mason Aprons were produced with no metal tassels. Such an Apron was presented to Bro Travers Howells in December 1944, and it is now displayed in a cabinet on the first floor crush-landing at Swansea Masonic Hall. In 1946, for donating a sum of 100 guineas, Penrice Lodge became a Patron of the Royal Masonic Hospital

The 50th Anniversary of the Founding of the Lodge was celebrated at the Installation Meeting on 23 November 1970. The Rt Hon the Lord Swansea, ProvGM, was in attendance and he invited the Lodge to Sponsor a new Installed Masters Lodge in Swansea, to be named 'The Lord Swansea Lodge' No.8364. The Petition was duly signed by WBro Hal Jones, WM, together with Bro Peter Beynon, SW, and Bro Meidrym Howells, JW. The Lord Swansea Lodge was Consecrated on 2 February 1971.

On 18 April 1994, a new Lodge Banner was Dedicated and during the Ceremony the Lodge was informed that the authorisation for the original Banner could not be found, only correspondence relating to its design and purchase. It was, therefore, assumed that the original authorisation had been lost in the mists of time. The Dedicating Officers were VWBro Cdr Roy Hopkin, RN, DepProvGM, Bro Rev Norman Lea, AProvGChap, and WBro Andrew L Gretton, DepProvGDC.

In 1995, eight Members of the Lodge, together with Brethren of other Lodges, supported the Petition for, and were Founder Members of, Meridian Lodge No.9603. The Sponsoring Lodge was Lodge of Sincerity No.8531 and the new Lodge was Consecrated on 23 February 1996.

Compiled by WBro T O Murphy, PPrSGW, and WBro D Gerwyn Harris, PPrJGW.

Llangeinor Lodge No.4194

Warranted : 3 November 1920

Consecrated : 27 April 1921

Meeting at the Masonic Hall, Bridgend.

There appears to be no particular reason for the formation of Llangeinor Lodge other than that the Ogmore Lodge No.1752 was the only Lodge meeting in the town of Bridgend. It can be seen from their records that the rate of entry into that Lodge indicated that the demand for Membership was considerable. Even after the Consecration of Llangeinor Lodge, from the large number of Initiates involved in both Lodges, records show that this high rate of demand continued for several years. It can, therefore, be concluded that there was sufficient interest in the Craft to adequately support two Lodges in the town of Bridgend in order to serve local areas and, in particular, the Ogmore and Garw Valleys.

It had previously been decided at the Founders' Meeting that the Lodge would meet nine times a year, on the first Wednesday of the month, October to June inclusive. The Election Meeting would be in April with the Installation Meeting in May.

The Mother Lodge was Ogmore Lodge No.1752. The first Worshipful Master was WBro George J Cunningham, PM Ogmore Lodge. Eighteen Members of Ogmore Lodge were Founder Members and seventy-three Brethren from that Lodge attended the Consecration.

Llangeinor Lodge received its Warrant on 3 November 1920. The Consecration took place at the Nolton Institute in Bridgend on 27 April 1921 presided over by the Deputy Provincial Grand Master VWBro Henry Pendrill Charles. Altogether, 133 Brethren attended the Consecration Ceremony comprising of 6 in the Provincial team, 5 Grand Lodge Officers, 5 Provincial Grand Lodge Officers, 5 Past Masters, 6 Ruling Masters, 102 Master Masons and 4 Fellow Craft Freemasons. Six gentlemen's names were proposed as fit and proper persons to be made Freemasons.

The name of the Lodge is derived from the small village of Llangeinor in the Garw Valley. Its English translation is the Church of St Ceinor or St Ceinwyr.

The Lodge Banner and Coat of Arms are those of Col John Blandy Jenkins, DL, JP, of Llanharan House in Mid- Glamorgan. He was WM of Abbey Lodge No.945, Abingdon, Berkshire, in 1869. He served as Sheriff of Berkshire and Chairman of Glamorgan County Council from 1895 to 1915. On 16 December 1878, he became a Joining Member of Ogmore Lodge and was Master for 2 years, from 1884 to 1886 and held the rank of PPrSGW. His connections with the Ogmore and Garw Valleys, as well as the Mother Lodge, appear to have prompted the use of his family Coat of Arms on the Lodge Banner. It is understood that this was to involve the residents of the two valleys. The two Mottos: *'Ex Urna Resurgam'* meaning *'from the urn we will resurrect'* is for the Blandy Family and *'Fe Dal Am Daro'* meaning *'he will pay for striking'* (hitting), is for the Jenkins Family. It is said that each Motto is particularly apt for each family. The description of the Banner is as follows: on the Coat of Arms the Funeral Urns emitting flames were the Arms of the Blandy family, and are shown on quarters 1 and 4. The Cockerels, described as 'game' or 'fighting cocks', came from the Arms of the Jenkins family, and are shown in quarters 2 and 3, being those of the mother's family. The Lion has no significance other than to display the Funeral Urn in its paws. The Mantling around the Shield is merely decoration, and colouring should reflect the main colours of the Arms. The Banner was presented to the Lodge by WBro Dapho L Powell, a local Solicitor, at the sixth Meeting held at the Nolton Institute on 2 November 1921. The Banner was unveiled by VWBro Henry Pendrill Charles, DepProvGM and Dedicated by WBro T B Bevan, ProvGChap. This Banner was extensively refurbished by WBro John E R Hughes in 1986 because it was beginning to disintegrate; and as it was being moved to the new premises, it was felt wise to extend its life for a few more years.

The first Initiation took place at the second Meeting of the Lodge on 12 May 1921; the first Passing at the fourth Meeting on 6 July 1921 and the first Raising at the eighth Meeting held on 14 December 1921. For the first twenty years of the existence of the Lodge, an average of about ten Candidates were Initiated each year, all in Double Ceremonies. This often involved Emergency Meetings to cope with the demand. This rate of Initiations continued over the next thirty years, all taking place at Double Ceremonies.

Founder's Jewel

During the years leading up to 1934, there were some difficulties experienced with the accommodation available to the Bridgend Lodges and the Ogmore Lodge undertook the considerable task of providing the new Temple in Adare Street. During this rebuilding programme, Llangeinor Lodge, by Dispensation, then met over a period of twelve months at the Cafe Royal in Wyndham Street, Bridgend, the Porthcawl Masonic Hall, and the Masonic Hall at Maesteg, before finally returning to the new Temple in Adare Street in April 1934. As with the other Lodges in Bridgend, Llangeinor Lodge moved to the new Temple at Coychurch Road in 1986.

There are no details recorded of any difficulties affecting the Lodge during the Second World War, other than on two occasions, when Members of the Royal Air Force were granted special leave by their Commanding Officers to attend their Passing Ceremonies. They were, however, expected to return to their base immediately following the Ceremony and not allowed to attend the Festive Board.

The 75th Anniversary of the Lodge was celebrated on 3 January 1996. Those in attendance included WBros W J Stuart Peters, PSGD, AProvGM; David L Protheroe, PSGD, AProvGM; Samuel Northway, PSGD, AProvGM and WBro Kenneth R Roberts, ProvAGDC, Officers of United Grand Lodge and Provincial Grand Lodge together with Brethren of lower Ranks, who were present in abundance. This Anniversary coincided with the 50th year of Membership of the Lodge of WBro Deighton (Deri) R Edwards,

PPrJGW (later PPrSGW), who occupied the Chair of King Solomon for the evening. He addressed the Lodge, outlining his memories of Freemasonry and of Llangeinor Lodge in particular. WBro J Stuart Peters gave a short address on the organisation of Provincial Grand Lodge, while WBro David L Protheroe outlined the progress towards the 1999 Festival. The Lodge proceedings were completed by WBro John E R Hughes, PPrAGDC, who spoke about the history of the Lodge, particularly the Banner, which he had studied in detail.

In Llangeinor Lodge, 'Absent Brethren' is sung as near to 9.30 pm as possible, the Welsh National Anthem is always sung at the close of the Festive Board and the Officers of the Lodge form a choir dressed in Father Christmas outfits to lead and direct the carols at the December Lodge Meeting. However, it should be added that since the Consecration of Llangeinor Lodge, it has been a custom that at the Election Night and Installation Meetings of Ogmore and Llangeinor Lodges, the Senior Wardens and Worshipful Masters respectfully respond on behalf of the visitors. The same arrangement exists between Llangeinor and Ewenny Lodges.

The Llangeinor Ladies section has now been in being for over thirty years, organising various events and in so doing have raised thousands of pounds towards the different charities.

No particular fraternal visits are associated with the Lodge except for the usual ones involving the Worshipful Master at Installation Meetings and the Wardens at Election Nights. In this, the Lodge has arrangements with fifteen other Lodges. Various Members of the Lodge have made visits to Lodges overseas in Gibraltar, Hong Kong and Malaysia.

In due course, Founder Members became Honorary Members of the Lodge and in the case of WBro Dapho L Powell, he was the only one to become a Grand Officer. He was a continuing Member of Ogmore Lodge at the time. In its 90 years' history, there has been no Grand Lodge appointment solely attributable to Llangeinor Lodge.

In total, six late Members, Initiated in Llangeinor Lodge, each served in excess of 50 years Membership in the Lodge. They were WBros John E R Griffiths, David L Evans, Herbert J Davies and Deri R Edwards and Bros Henley H Jenkins and Ron J Stanford. Deri Edwards, PPrSGW completed 63 years as a Member of the Lodge before his death in July 2009. It should be added that his father became a Member of the Lodge in 1925 and between them they totalled 84 years continual service. WBro Alan William Hines became a Masonic veteran with 50 years service on 5 March 2008, after becoming an Honorary Member on 7 March 2007. He was presented at home with his Certificate by WBro James R Bevan, ProvGSec. Many Lodge Members, including his Initiating Master, WBro Deri Edwards, were present to congratulate him and witness the unique event before his death in June 2010. On 1 March 2011, WBro Graham Berridge completed 50 years as a Member of the Lodge, closely followed on 20 May 2011 by a Joining Past Master, WBro Brian K Long.

At the Lodge Meeting in February 2000, WBro Peter R Vincent, WM, PPrSGD, congratulated the Director of Ceremonies, WBro Brian A Smith, on being invested with the OBE, by by Her Majesty the Queen, for services to the Royal Mint.

On the 18 Jan 2009, after 9 months in Office, WBro Alan Griffiths, WM, passed to the Grand Lodge Above following a heart attack at the age of 58. February Festive Boards are now an austere remembrance and reflection of that event.

In February 2010, the Lodge participated with the BBC in the making of 'Meet the Masons' for the television programme 'Week In Week Out'. This was done with the approval of United Grand Lodge, and through a request from the Provincial Grand Secretary, WBro James Bevan and Provincial Grand Registrar, WBro Martyn Daley. On Wednesday, 3 February, three quarters of an hour before the Lodge was to open, the producer and film crew arrived in order to record the entrance of the WM and Officers into the Temple. The remainder of the programme would include interviews with various Brethren in the Province and a representative from Grand Lodge. There were three rehearsals of the entrance, some being used in the final programme, which gave the appearance of an empty Lodge. The final entrance was recorded; the Master gavelled and asked the Brethren to assist him to open the Lodge. At this point the television producer and film crew left with the Provincial Grand Secretary, after the latter had thanked the Brethren for agreeing to participate at only 4 days notice. The programme was broadcast on BBC Wales on Tuesday, 2 March 2010.

In 1972, Llangeinor Lodge Sponsored a Daughter Lodge, Ewenny Lodge No.8485. Ewenny Lodge received its Warrant on 13 September 1972, the Consecration being held on 2 March 1973. Four Members of Llangeinor Lodge were Founder Members, with its first Secretary being WBro H J Davies, PPrSGW of Llangeinor Lodge. In 2002, the Lodge also Sponsored Llangeinor Chapter No.4194. This Chapter received its Warrant on 13 November 2002 and was Consecrated on 12 April 2003, with seven Members of Llangeinor Lodge being Founder Members. The Chapter is aimed at research and lectures to improve the knowledge and understanding of the Royal Arch in general.

The Lodge began its long history at the Nolton Institute in Bridgend, then at the Adare Street Temple, before finally moving with the other Lodges to Coychurch Road in 1986. At present, the Lodge meets seven times a year, the January and June meetings being dispensed with. This is as a result of fewer Candidates now being available, but hopes are still held that one day the Lodge will revert to the original nine meetings. To date, the Lodge has Initiated 533 Candidates.

The authors are grateful to the late WBro Roy Jones, PPrJGD, for his precise statistical records, and the late WBro John E R Hughes, PPrAGDC, for his detailed Lodge and Banner History.

Compiled by WBros Roy Hart, PPrJGW; Brian A Smith, OBE, PPrJGD; and Peter R Vincent, PPrSGD.

The Temple in the West - Bridgend

Gwalia Lodge
No.4213

Warranted :   13 December 1920

Consecrated :   25 February 1921

Meeting at the Masonic Hall, Cardiff.

The Genesis of the Gwalia Lodge occurred in the Masonic Year of 1919-1920 ,when 6 new Lodges were formed and Consecrated, making a total of 40 Lodges in the Province of South Wales – Eastern Division. The Provincial Grand Master was RWBro Sir Charles L D Venables Llewelyn, Bart, and the Deputy Provincial Grand Master was WBro Henry Pendrill Charles.Eleven Lodges met at Cardiff and the Membership of the senior Lodges was so large as to cause concern in the Province. Glamorgan Lodge No.36 had 310 Members, Bute Lodge No.960 had 322 Members, Tennant Lodge No.1992 had 437 Members and Llangattock Lodge No.2547 had 285 Members.

It was this concern that prompted the Worshipful Master and Past Masters to summon, by circular, all Members of Llangattock Lodge to a Meeting, to be held at the Masonic Hall, Guildford Crescent, Cardiff, at 8.00 pm on 17 November 1919, to discuss the formation of a new Lodge. At that Meeting, it was proposed and carried unanimously that the IPM of Llangattock Lodge, WBro Edward Hurford, should chair the Meeting. The chairman stated that in the opinion of the Members, the time had come to form a new Lodge, with the object of facilitating the work and *'bringing in useful Members who are at present unable to join Llangattock Lodge, and to give all Master Masons on opportunity of Office, if they so desire'* . A free and full discussion ensued and it was proposed, seconded, and unanimously agreed , that the Lodge be formed and that all Founder Members should be Members of Llangattock Lodge. In the meantime, every Member of Llangattock Lodge was circulated, and 40 Members agreed to become Founder Members and sign the Petition.

The 40 Members that had agreed to sign the Petition were summoned to a Meeting of the Founders , held at Guildford Crescent, Cardiff, on 16 April 1920. WBro Edward Hurford took the chair. After discussion, the 34 eligible Members signed the Petition for the new Lodge. Members with less than 3 years as Master Masons in the Craft were not eligible to sign.

It was resolved that the name of the Lodge would be 'Gwalia Lodge', (the very old name for Wales and very popular in Victorian times). WBro David John Jones should be the first Worshipful Master. He had been WM of Llangattock Lodge in 1915 and was appointed ProvGChStwd in 1920. It was also resolved that Bro Fred Brown be appointed SW, Bro Thomas George, JW and Bro Charles Mill, Secretary. The Lodge was to meet on the 4th Friday of September to June. The Founders' fee was to be 7 guineas, (£7. 35p.), to include a Founder's Jewel and first year's subscription; annual subscriptions to be 2 guineas, (£2.10p), and the Initiation fee to be 20 guineas, (£21.00). WBro George P Venables was to be appointed Treasurer; the Past Masters, who were also

Founders, Senior and Junior Wardens and the Secretary, were to form the Finance and Standing Committee.

The Petition, signed by the Founder Members at the meeting, was sent to the Provincial Grand Master, accompanied by a hand written letter from Charles Mill, Secretary (pro tempore), dated 14 June 1920. It outlined the reasons for wishing to form a new Lodge : *'The Membership of Llangattock Lodge had become so large that Brethren who were anxious for Office were precluded from attaining such Rank due to the number of suitable candidates for Office.'* There were 28 Candidates accepted for Initiation before the recently Installed Master had commenced his year in Office and this list had a tendency to increase rather than diminish. The Petition was successful and matters progressed to begin forming the new Lodge.

An Emergency Meeting of the Founder Members was called for 31 January 1921, the reason being that the Charter of the Lodge was ready for delivery and to do so required payment of the fees forthwith. The costs were as follows: the Warrant £10.10.0 (£10.50p); 34 Petitioners at 2/6 (12½p) each, £4.5.0 (£4.25p); Book of Proposal Forms, 4/6 (22½p). The total came to £14.19.6, (£14.97½p).

It was requested that Friday, 25 February 1921, be nominated as the date of the Consecration. It was resolved that the Lodge Motto would be: *'Gwna Dda'* - *'Do Good'*, and that the Officers so appointed should present their Collars as a gift to the Lodge. The first meeting of the Finance and Standing Committee was held on 15 February 1921 (10 days before the Consecration Ceremony).

Arrangements for the Consecration (vessels, incense, corn oil, wine and salt) were completed and it was decided that the colours of the Banner should be the same as those of the Founders' Jewel. The Master Designate was to receive 40 guineas (£42.00) for expenses. Brother T G Gardener was to be appointed Tyler, and two cupboards for the Regalia were to be hired from the Masonic Hall Company.

The second Meeting was held on 23 February 1921, (2 days before Consecration), when 5 Candidates were approved for proposal in Open Lodge on 25 February.

At the Consecration of the Lodge, there were present, 37 Founder Members, 6 Members of United Grand Lodge, 42 Members of Provincial Grand Lodge and 122 vsitors.

The first Regular meeting of Gwalia Lodge was held on 24 March 1921, when the By-laws of the Lodge, having been approved by the Provincial Grand Secretary, were accepted by the Lodge and signed by the Worshipful Master and Wardens. It was agreed that the Annual Installation Festival would be held on the 4th Friday in May of each year.

At the Regular Meeting on 23 September 1921, a gift of the Lodge Banner was made to the Lodge by WBro David John Jones, WM. It was unveiled by WBro Sidney Williams, of Henry Pendrill Charles Lodge No.3769, who had assisted in its design, (reputed to be Caernarvon Castle with Snowdonia in the background). The Banner was made by Miss Spencer, of the Welsh School of Arts, Park Place, Cardiff. The Banner now hangs in the North East corner of the Duke of Connaught Temple, Cardiff. The Lodge possesses a second Banner, which is used for Regular Meetings. It was made by Mrs Doris Brookes, wife of WBro Ivor Brookes, Installed WM in 1975. During the fist year of the Lodge's existence, there were 55 Lodge Meetings: 12 Regular Meetings, 37 Emergency Meetings and 6 Lodges of Instruction. 52 Candidates were Initiated, 52 Passed and 52 Raised !

It is worth noting that during the first year, the Lodge made a Charity donation of 400 guineas (£420.00) to the Royal Masonic Institute for Girls, - 2 guineas (£2.10) per Member, the equivalent of one year's subscription.

The first Master, WBro David John Jones, a Building Contractor, of 50 Oakfield Street, Cardiff, PM Llangattock Lodge, was promoted to ProvGSuptWks in 1919, ProvGChStwd in 1920, ProvSGW in 1922 and PAGDC of UGLE in 1923. In 1926, he was promoted to

The Second Banner

DepProvGM, a position he held until his death in 1931 There is a commemorative plaque in the north-east corner of the Duke of Connaught Temple (beneath the original Banner) which reads:

'In Memoriam of WBro D J Jones, PG.D, Deputy PG.M, Eastern Division of South Wales, who died April 27th 1931.
This tablet was erected by the Freemasons of the Province.'

Gwalia Lodge went on to receive two further promotions to United Grand Lodge: in 1931, WBro George P Venables (Founder Treasurer), and in 1989, WBro Edward J Forse.

Membership of the Lodge peaked around 1963, when there were 212 Members on the Register.

There was a close tie between the Lodge and Tennant Lodge No.1992, Amethyst Lodge No.4026, Loyal Commercial Lodge No.2720, Llangattock Lodge No.2547 and Preswylfa Lodge No.5792, when these Lodges would support each other at Installation Meetings under the guise of 'Family Nights'; this ceased in the early 1980s.

At the Regular Meeting on 27 January 1922, a letter was received from WBro D W Evans of Amethyst Lodge, stating that three Brethren of Amethyst Lodge had been elected to form a committee, to consider the formation of a Royal Arch Chapter and inviting Gwalia Lodge to elect three Members to serve on this committee. The Chapter was duly formed in 1924 and the association remains to the present time.

In 1938, the Membership of Gwalia Lodge exceeded 200 and the concerns of the Brethren were the same as those which led to the formation of Gwalia Lodge in 1921. Consequently, Preswylfa Lodge No.5792 became a Daughter Lodge of Gwalia Lodge. The name 'Preswylfa' may be translated as 'Home', 'Abode', or 'Dwelling Place'.

During the next 88 years, (up to 2009), Gwalia Lodge has Initiated a total of 576 Brethren. The most prolific years were during the 1920s, when 172 were admitted, (in addition to the 52 Candidates in the first year), and 1943 to 1947, when 60 Brethren were Initiated.

In 1997, the Lodge received a small legacy from a Canadian gentleman, Mr Norman Forbes, whose father, Bro. Peter Forbes is recorded as being Initiated on 6 April 1921, (the first Emergency Meeting following the First Regular Meeting on 24 March 1921). At those first two Meetings, 4 were Initiated on the Regular and 4 on the Emergency Meeting. Regrettably, Bro Peter Forbes died before he could attain Office. His son, Norman Forbes, was educated at the Masonic School for Boys. Later, he emigrated to Canada, where he remained until his death in 1996. In appreciation of his education, he left a legacy to Gwalia Lodge. Some of the money was used to replace the Lodge's ageing Regalia (Collars, Working Tools, etc.), which had become well worn by this time, and some was used to commission a commemorative plaque, in remembrance of the fallen Brethren of the Cardiff Lodges, who made the Supreme Sacrifice during the Second World War, 1939 - 1945.

The plaque was presented to the Cardiff Masonic Hall Company Limited at a suitable ceremonial presentation in October 1998. It is now situated in the foyer, to the right of the entrance to the Edgar Rutter Temple. The plaque reads:

'In memory of Brethren of Cardiff Lodges
Who made the Supreme Sacrifice
During the second World War 1939 - 1945'

Listed are the names of 28 Brethren from 10 Cardiff Lodges. Beneath the Plaque is a brass plate: *'This memorial has been donated by Gwalia Lodge No.4213, thanks to a bequest by Mr Norman Forbes, in recognition of his education at the Royal Masonic School, October 1998.'*

It is with some irony that at the time of writing this history of the Lodge, the Worshipful Master of 2007, WBro Christopher Lloyd Weatherill is the grandson of one of the Founder Members of the Lodge, namely WBro Llewellyn Pugh, who was Installed as Master in May 1927, some 79 years before his grandson attained that privilege.

Compiled by WBro Dwyfor Lynn Jones, PPrSGD,
Treasurer & Charity Steward.

Kibbor Lodge
No.4364

Warranted   :   2 November 1921

Consecrated   :   14 February 1922

Meeting at the Masonic Hall, Cardiff.

During 1920, plans were developed by Brethren of Glamorgan Lodge No.36 for the formation of a new Daughter Lodge. The first suggestion of forming a new Lodge was back in 1917, when a letter, dated 2 November, was circulated by the Lodge Secretary, Frank Harry Llewellyn, inviting Brethren to attend a meeting on 13 November to discuss the matter. The driving force behind the scheme was the distinguished Past Master WBro Arthur Llewellyn Hopkins, WM, 1901-1903. Nothing appears to have happened for the next few years, then on 20 May 1920, Hopkins wrote to WBro David Evan Roberts to persuade him to take the Collar of Senior Warden, and requesting his view on the possibility of William Benjamin Francis as Junior Warden. Francis, who was been born in London in 1853, was a Solicitor with the firm of 'R S Thomas & Francis'. He became a Joining Member of Glamorgan Lodge (8 November 1895), from St David's Lodge No.384, Bangor, North Wales. Francis became the first Junior Warden of Kibbor Lodge and the second WM in 1923. In 1925, he became Lord Mayor of Cardiff and he presented the Lodge with a Bible to commemorate his year of Office. In Province, he attained the rank of Provincial Senior Grand Deacon.

Two other Lodge Members became Lord Mayors of Cardiff, namely Bro William Charles, 1929-1930, and Bro George Llewellyn Ferrier, 1954-1955.

In a second letter to David Evan Roberts on the 11 June, Hopkins states that Frank Llewellyn had accepted the Collar of SW of the new Lodge and the letter goes on to suggest who should occupy some of the other Offices. In the end, Frank Llewellyn did not become SW Designate. That honour went to WBro Frank Munn, a Metal Dealer, who had been WM of Glamorgan Lodge, 1917-1918, and appointed Provincial SGD in 1921. He resigned from Kibbor Lodge in March 1924, and so never occupied the Chair.

Among the business printed on the Glamorgan Lodge Summons for the Installation of Frank Harry Llewellyn on 24 June 1920, was the following: *'To consider and, if approved, support a Petition for a Warrant for a new Lodge, to be called the Kibbor Lodge, to meet at the Masonic Temple, Cardiff.'*

Presumably this was done, for this item does not appear on any other Summons. The Warrant for the Kibbor Lodge was eventually signed on the 2 November 1921, the delay apparently due to the fact that the Founders wished to have the numbers 43 (Glamorgan Lodge's Number, 1833-1863) and 36 (the Lodge Number since 1863) incorporated in the new Lodge Number, thus resulting in a wait until No.4364 became available!

Kibbor Lodge was Consecrated in the Duke of Connaught Temple, Cardiff, on 14 February 1922 by RWBro Sir Charles Venables Llewelyn, ProvGM, accompanied by WBro Henry Pendrill Charles, PAGReg, DepProvGM, acting as PrSGW, and WBro Charles Edwin Dovey (Grand Superintendent), acting as PrJGW. A total of 155 Brethren from 35 Lodges in the Province were present in the Temple. Following the Consecration Ceremony, WBro Arthur Llewellyn Hopkins was Installed as Primus Master and WBros Munn and Francis were appointed as Senior and Junior Wardens respectively. WBro Dr Thomas Wallace, PJGD, PM Glamorgan Lodge, Grand Superintendent, 1928-1930, was appointed Acting IPM.

Arthur L Hopkins, a Coal Exporter, was Initiated into Glamorgan Lodge on 8 November 1895 at the age of 34. He occupied the Chair of the Lodge for two consecutive years, 1901-1903. Appointed Provincial Grand Treasurer in 1902 and Provincial Senior Grand Warden in 1910, he was a Founder Member of Hendre Lodge No.3250 and WM 1921-1922; Founder and Primus Master of Vale of Glamorgan Lodge No.3977; and a Founder Member of Amethyst Lodge No.4026.

The first Secretary, Bro George Bowen Hughes, was a Schoolmaster, (Initiated in Glamorgan Lodge in January 1907); he became the third Worshipful Master of Kibbor Lodge. He was awarded the OBE for his services to Education.

In selecting a name for the new Lodge, the Founders wished to associate it in some way with the name of the Mother Lodge, 'Glamorgan'. The name 'Kibbor' is derived from the manor of 'Kibbor' (Cibwr). The district (Commote) of Kibbor lies entirely east of the Taff and comprises all the area between the rivers Taff and Rhymney south of Senghenydd, with the northern boundary coinciding with the northern boundaries of Llanedeyrn, Lisvane and Llanishen. At Thornhill, it follows the course of the Brunant southwards through the parish of Whitchurch and joins the river Taff at Llandaff and Whitchurch. The name 'Kibbor' was felt to be an appropriate name for the new Lodge, it being a part of Glamorgan consisting of Cardiff and its environs.

Many a visitor and Mandated Officer have been confused by the idiosyncrasies of the Kibbor Lodge Ritual, most of which are from Glamorgan Lodge. The differences are as follows: -

1   The lights at the Worshipful Master and Wardens' Pedestals are 'on' prior to the 'opening' and left 'on' until the Lodge has been vacated.
2   The 'Knocks' for a report consist of a single 'knock'
3   The 'Knocks' for an 'alarm' consists of the 'knocks of the Degree'
4   The Senior Warden delivers all the 'Charges'
5   The Junior Warden explains the 'Tools' in each Degree
6   The Master Elect is Invested with his 'Collar' and 'Badge' of his Office in the South East Corner of the Temple prior to his being 'placed in the Chair of King Solomon
7   The Master is saluted with the salutation of a 'Master in the Chair' whilst the Lodge is formally 'opened' as an 'Installed Board'
8   At the 'closing of the Lodge' the Master does the three 'risings' without halting or pausing and at the end he turns to the Secretary and asks for the reports from Grand Lodge, Provincial Grand Lodge, etcetera.

The Lodge Insignia consist of a Red Dragon of Wales Rampant surmounted on a grassy hill, holding the banner of the Welsh Princes proudly aloft, together with the flowering Leek. The Lodge Motto: *'Audi, Vide, Tace'* meaning *'Hear, See, Be Silent'*, is taken from the Roman Proverb *'Audi, vide, tace; si vis vivere in pace.'* (*'Listen, see, be silent; if you wish to live in peace'*). It is also the Motto of Glamorgan Lodge and was adopted by the United Grand Lodge of England on its Coat of Arms in 1815.

The Lodge is fortunate in still retaining the original Jewels attached to the Officers' Collars, which were donated by the respective Officers at the Consecration Ceremony. The Lodge Tools together with the Master's and Wardens' Gavels were donated by WBro Denis J Field, WM, 1963-1964, in memory of his Brother F J Field.

During the first 15 months of its existence, Kibbor Lodge was under the superintendence of Arthur Llewellyn Hopkins, at the end of which time the Lodge had 45 Members, 15 of whom were Initiates and 7 were Joining Members. Unfortunately for Kibbor Lodge, Hopkins died at the age of 63 on 17 August 1924, at his home, Sutton House, Southerndown. As a mark of respect, the Lodge was placed in Masonic Mourning for three months. His Obituary in the 'Western Mail' described him thus:

'Possessing a quiet manner, he was very much beloved because of his sincerity, and very often matters where differences were likely to exist, were referred to him for judgement, while his advice was very largely sought after in matters of procedure. It is doubtful whether any other brother had been more interested in the province. It was his only hobby, and his devotion to it brought him into great prominence and several distinguished positions in the Craft. He was always active in rendering important help where needed, and he was one of the most trustworthy exponents of the principles of the Craft'

At the October Meeting in 1924, it was agreed that the Kibbor Brethren would join with those of Glamorgan Lodge to establish a 'Memorial' to WBro A L Hopkins. The Memorial consisted of his portrait in oils, a box of Working Tools and a Bible. Since its Dedication on 8 January 1926, the Bible, suitably inscribed, has been used for every Glamorgan Lodge Meeting.

The first LOI was held in the small Temple at the Cardiff Masonic Hall on 28 September 1926 and in attendance were three Past Masters, twenty Brethren and three visitors, under the superintendence of the Worshipful Master, WBro Reuben Pugsley and the LOI President, WBro John Percy Mountjoy. The first business was to authorise a letter of thanks to Glamorgan Lodge for its support and use of the LOI facilities.

Reuben Pugsley, later Sir Reuben Pugsley, OBE, JP, was the South Western Manager for Messrs J A Rank (Millers) and a Founder of the Cardiff Business Club in 1912. He was Initiated in Glamorgan Lodge in April 1914. John Percy Mountjoy, OBE, WM, 1925-1926, was a Chartered Accountant and had been WM of Glamorgan Lodge, 1919-1920. On 11 October 1955, the WM congratulated him on his 50 years in Freemasonry. He was the Lodge Treasurer at this time. It should be added that the first 12 Worshipful Masters of Kibbor Lodge all originated from Glamorgan Lodge.

At the Provincial Grand Lodge Meeting in Swansea on 27 June 1928, RWBro Sir Charles Venables-Llewelyn, ProvGM, publicly denounced Glamorgan and Kibbor Lodges for failing to conform to practices established throughout the Province. Points at issue included the positioning of the Wardens' Columns and Ashlars, precedence afforded to Ruling Masters over Non-Executive Provincial Officers, the opening of a Board of Installed Masters and in the case of Glamorgan Lodge, the Workings of the Installation Ceremony. Kibbor met on 9 April 1929 to debate the Lodge's response. One view was that Province was being dictatorial and the Brethren wished to retain their traditional methods of working, others argued that there should be conformity across the Province and that they would be following guidelines issued by Grand Lodge in 1916. The debate was followed by a vote 'that the Lodge follow the guidelines issued by Provincial Grand Lodge,' with 17 Brethren in favour and 7 against. (Glamorgan Lodge did not concede and an Appeal was sent to Grand Lodge in February 1931. At the PGL in Penarth on 31 July 1931, the ProvGM declared the dispute with Glamorgan Lodge *'over'*.)

The first Annual Ladies' Night was held at the Masonic Hall Cardiff on 26 February 1932. It was very successful and well attended, although there is no mention of wines being served and there was a strict 'No Dancing' restriction in the terms of hire of the Hall. The following year, the event was held at the Masonic Hall, Penarth, on 20 January, where dancing was permitted.

When war was declared in September 1939, the WM was Brother Hadyn Shaw (Installed May 1939). He encountered difficulties

Yr Hen Bont Lodge No.4691

Warranted   :   3 November 1924
Consecrated   :   7 May 1925
Meeting at the Masonic Hall, Pontypridd.

The Lodge takes its name 'Yr Hen Bont' (The Old Bridge) from the famous stone bridge built in 1750 by William Edwards of Eglwysilan. The bridge was considered to be one of the great achievements of the time and when it was built it was the longest single spanning bridge in the world. It was very important in the development of Pontypridd as a commercial centre. Prior to the opening of the bridge, the communications between the Rhondda Valleys and those of the Cynon and Merthyr Valleys were very difficult, with traders and others having to travel many miles either to the north or to the south. This bridge, at the confluence of the rivers at Pontypridd, revolutionised life in the area and resulted in Pontypridd becoming the unofficial capital of the South Wales valleys.

Following the end of the First World War in 1918, there was a growing demand for Membership of the Craft and this resulted in the formation of many Lodges. During the period from the end of the First World War to the end of the 1920s, 21 Craft Lodges were formed in the South Wales Eastern Division. Such was the reason behind the formation of Hen Bont Lodge.

In 1924, a sub-committee was formed by Merlin Lodge No.1578 to consider forming a Daughter Lodge. This was expertly and thoroughly done under the chairmanship of WBro W R Davies, with WBro W H Todd as Secretary. This committee decided that Merlin Lodge, should Sponsor the Petition for a new Lodge at Pontypridd under the proposed name of 'Yr Hen Bont'. The Petition is worded as follows:

'To the Most Worshipful the Grand Master of the United Fraternity of Ancient, Free and Accepted Masons of England.

We, the undersigned, being regularly registered Master Masons mentioned against our respective names having the prosperity of the Craft at heart, are anxious to exert our best endeavours to promote and diffuse the genuine principles of the art; and, for the conveniency of our respective dwellings and other good reasons, we are desirous of forming a new Lodge, to be named THE HEN BONT LODGE.

In consequence of this desire, we pray for a Warrant of Constitution, empowering us to meet as a regular Lodge at the Masonic Temple, Pontypridd on the second Monday of each month (August excepted), and there to discharge the duties of Masonry, in the constitutional manner, according to the forms of the Order and the Laws of Grand Lodge; and we have nominated and do recommend that Brother William Roberts Davies, who has served the Office of Warden in a regular Lodge to be the first Master; Brother John Griffith Jones to be the first Senior Warden; and Brother John Colenso Jones to be the first Junior Warden of the said Lodge.

Should the prayer of this Petition be granted, we promise strict obedience to the commands of The Grand Master and the laws and regulations of Grand Lodge.

William R Davies Lodge No.1578 (Solicitor); J Griffith Jones No.1578 (Accountant); J Colenso Jones No.1578 (Solicitor); William Phillips No.1578 (Rating Officer); E Parry Thomas No.1578 (Auctioneer); Oliver Davies No.1578 (Chemist); E Morgan Phillips No.1578 (Master Butcher); R Edgar Arnott No.1578 (Bank Manager); William H Todd No.1578 (School Master); Tom Jeremy No.1578 (Provision Merchant).'

The Warrant was granted on 5 November 1924, and the Consecration Ceremony took place on 7 May 1925 in the Masonic Hall, Pontypridd, conducted by Sir Charles L D Venables Llewelyn, ProvGM.

The Installation Ceremony immediately followed the Consecration.The First Master was WBro W R Davies, with WBro John Griffith Jones as SW and WBro J Colenso Jones as JW.

The first Candidates proposed for Membership of the Lodge were George Sinclair Ross, Walter Trevor Lewis, Rev Illtyd Jones and Owen Robert Jones.

The first 25 years witnessed a rapid growth of the Lodge. There was an inflow of Candidates to swell the 35 Founder Members to 206 Members by the end of 1949. This demand for Membership had to be met by holding Emergency Lodge Meetings as well as the 11 Regular Lodge Meetings each year. In the first year, there were 19 Lodge Meetings (11 Regular and 8 Emergency) of which 5 were Double Ceremonies. This made a total of 24 separate Ceremonies, all of which had two Candidates. The following year was not a great deal less busy with 16 Lodge Meetings and 3 Double Ceremonies. During the first ten years, there were no less than 156 Lodge Meetings with a total of 177 Ceremonies being performed.

The number of Regular Lodge Meetings had been set at 11 per year (August being the only month without a Meeting). This continued until 1942, when the Lodge changed to its now familiar 10 Meetings per year. (The second Monday of each month except July and August).

In 1931, Hen Bont Lodge was very proud when WBro Colenso Jones, PM, was awarded the Grand Lodge rank of PAGDC. This was the first Grand Lodge Rank to be awarded to a Member of the Lodge; though the first Master of the Lodge, WBro William R Davies had received Grand Rank whilst in Merlin Lodge.

The Installation Ceremony of April 1939 was the first occasion, since the Consecration of the Lodge some 14 years earlier, that an Initiate of the Lodge, Bro John P Maddox, became Master. Since that time, with only four exceptions, every Master has been an Initiate of the Lodge. The four exceptions were WBro Sydney Brooks in 1964, WBro Theo Picton in 1968, WBro Owen Morris in 1970, and WBro David Williams in 2004.

With the onset of World War II on 3 September 1939, the United Grand Lodge of England cancelled all Lodge Meetings due that month. This meant that the Regular Lodge Meeting planned for 9 September would not occur. This would appear to be one of only two occasions that the Lodge has not met as planned. The other was on 12 January 1982, when the Meeting had to be abandoned due to very heavy snowfalls that had occurred during the previous few days. No Meetings were held in September 1974, June 1975 and September 1975. This was because Meetings were being poorly attended and it was decided to discontinue them for a trial period. However, attendance grew again and the Meetings returned to their now familiar 10 per year.

At the commencement of the War, several Brethren of the Lodge left to serve in HM Forces. They served their country with distinction during the conflict and some, unfortunately, were taken Prisoners of War. Happily, after the hostilities, all returned home and became active Members of the Lodge. Most of the other Brethren who did not serve in the Forces became members of the Home Guard, Special Constabulary, or became Air Raid Wardens, Firemen, etc.

In the early years of the War, the number of Members attending Lodge was reduced and the number of visiting Brethren virtually non-existent. During the latter years of the War, however, this trend seems to have been reversed and between November 1943 and September 1945, there were 13 Emergency Meetings, 6 of which were Double Ceremonies. This influx of new Members stems from the fact that many servicemen were returning from the war with fraternal friendships gained during the conflict, and looked forward to maintaining these friendships with the Freemasons they had met.

The Lodge progressed steadily during the war years and prospered with a large Membership, even though the Festive Boards were very austere, sometimes consisting only of a sandwich and a beer taken in the committee room. The dining hall had been commandeered for use as a hospital.

During the war years, another change was to manifest itself. Due to the requirements to have coupons to purchase clothing, Grand Lodge allowed the wearing of dark lounge suits instead of formal dress suits. This ruling has never been rescinded and the customary dress in Lodge is now lounge suits, with the Officers wearing formal dress suits, though this is only customary and not a mandatory requirement of the Lodge.

With the cessation of hostilities, servicemen began to return to civilian life and those who were Brethren again attended Lodge. With Membership of around 200 and many more now attending, seating at the Festive Board became difficult. Some Brethren were unable to dine, as all the available seats had been taken. This situation was not conducive to harmony and it was felt that another Lodge was needed to meet this demand. This was very similar to the situation after the First World War, which resulted in Hen Bont Lodge being formed in 1925.

In 1949, an attempt was made to form a LOI, but there was no general support for the idea. The Brethren who were intent on forming the LOI did not abandon their ideas, and through their persistence another application for a LOI was made two years later, which was successful.

Hen Bont Lodge continued to prosper throughout the 50s, 60s and 70s and waiting lists of three years were not exceptional. The Lodge of Instruction continued to play its part in the life of the Lodge, as it does today.

Monday, 13 November 1950 witnessed the Initiation of Mr Peter Lane, a 25-year-old student in Mechanical and Electrical Engineering. He was born the year the Lodge was formed, was Worshipful Master in 1972 and has the Rank of PPrSGW. He is now 87 years of age and still an active Member of the Lodge. In November 2010, he celebrated 60 years in Freemasonry. He is also a Past Master and Founder Member of Cwm Rhondda Lodge.

It was in October 1952 that the first mention of a Ladies' Evening appears in the Lodge Minutes, though other sources indicate that these occurred from a very early time. They have become an integral part of the life of the Lodge. Ladies' Evenings took place in the dining room of the Pontypridd Temple, but with the demand for this event being in excess of the seating capacity of the dining room, the Ladies' Evenings have been held at other venues throughout the locality. Social Evenings are also held each year.

On 11 October 1954, Mr Henry James Mars was Initiated into the Lodge. In 1971, he attained the Chair of King Solomon and was the first Initiate to become a Grand Lodge Officer in 1985. Harry, as all affectionately know him, has given many years of faithful service to this and other Lodges within the Temple. His enthusiasm, guidance and approachability are models for others to follow. Whenever there is a query on some Masonic matter in Lodge, the usual answer is to '*Ask Harry!*'

The last Initiation Ceremony of the 1970s took place on the 8 October 1979 when two gentlemen were Initiated into the Lodge. These Co-initiates were WBro Ken Cook, PPrJGW, the current Treasurer and Bro Graham Mundy, who were Initiated into Freemasonry by the then Master, WBro Desmond Barnett.

The first Initiation Ceremony of the 1980s was on 14 January 1980, when WBro Phillip Wayman was Initiated into the Craft. He has the unique distinction of being the only Master to have held Lodge Meetings outside the Pontypridd Temple. Lord Swansea, ProvGM, granted Dispensation for the Lodge Meetings of 9 January 1989 and 13 February 1989 to be held in the Aberdare Temple. This was due to structural repair work that had to be carried out on the Pontypridd Temple. Other Lodges from the Pontypridd Masonic Hall also held their Meetings at Aberdare during this period.

The 1990s started in fine form with Candidates on the waiting list and the Lodge having six Initiates each year. However, by the end of the decade, the number of Candidates was dwindling with only four Initiates and no waiting list.

The social side of the Lodge has thrived over the last two decades with well-supported Ladies' Festivals being held in February or March each year. The number of social events has also increased from one to two each year in June and November, both of which well patronised, and many thousands of pounds have been raised for charity. The Brethren have been instrumental in organising and supporting several other social and charitable events. Among these is the Good Neighbours Club, which was founded by the determination and effort of WBro Peter Lane and meets on a monthly basis. Another event is the Children's Christmas Party, held for disabled or disadvantaged children in the locality.

For the first twenty-two years, the Merlin Lodge Musical Service Book was used. In 1947, Bro John Powell, a well-respected Organist of the Lodge, compiled the Lodge's own Musical Service Book. This book has recently been reprinted.

Mention must be made of Bro Graham Mundy, the Lodge's longest serving Tyler, 1982-2007. He was also the Tyler for three other Craft Lodges meeting in the Pontypridd Temple, namely Ystradyfodwg, Pontypridd, and Saint Catherine's. He was also Tyler for the Arthur Lewis Mark Lodge No.585 but, sadly, ill health forced him to relinquish his duties in 2007.

On 5 June 1996, WBro Desmond Barnett was Installed as ProvGM of Mark Master Masons, and the following year, he became the second Initiate of Hen Bont Lodge to receive Grand Lodge Honours, being Invested with the Rank of PAGDC. WBro Desmond is a Founder Member of Pontypridd Lodge No.9001, Saint Catherine's Lodge No.9503, Keystone Lodge No.8289, and Cwm Rhondda Lodge No.9692. He also holds Grand Rank in both Mark and Royal Ark Mariners. He retired as ProvGM of the Mark Degree in 2007.

On 15 March 1999, Cwm Rhondda Lodge No.9692 was Consecrated. This Lodge was Sponsored by Hen Bont Lodge and is the first Lodge to meet in the Rhondda Valley. The Primus Master was WBro Desmond Barnett.

Since the Lodge was formed, only one Brother has been Master more than once. This happened when WBro David Morgan occupied the Chair for the two consecutive years from 2002 to 2004.

On Thursday, 6 May 2010, at an Emergency Meeting of Proscenium Lodge No.9095, WBro Wayne Buffet Warlow, PPrJGW, presented the 2010 Prestonian Lecture, 'Music in Masonry and Beyond'. This was one of four official deliveries of the lecture. He is only the second Prestonian Lecturer to be appointed from the Province, the first being WBro Keith Flynn, OBE, PJGD. WBro Wayne was Initiated in Hen Bont Lodge in 1967 and was Installed as WM in 2005. A Founder Member and first JW of Proscenium Lodge, he was Master in 1984. He is a Joining Member of Royal Rose Lodge No.2565, London, and was Master in 2007 and 2008. In Province, he was promoted to PPrJGW and, in April 2011, he was Invested as a Grand Officer with the appropriate Rank of Past Grand Organist. WBro Wayne is a Member of numerous side Degrees. In 2006, he was Installed as the first Chief Adept of Societas Rosicruciana in Anglia in the newly formed Province of South Wales.

Compiled by WBro R John Edmunds, PProvSGD.

Sir David William Evans
1866 - 1926

Deputy Provincial Grand Master
1925 - 26

David William Evans was born in Dowlais on 4 November 1866, the son of Thomas Evans originally from Rhymney. At the time of David's birth, his father had become a well-established Grocer and a keen musician in Dowlais, and from whom he inherited a love of music which remained with him all his life. For the first few years of his life, David's family lived in Mary Ann Street, but later moved to 2 Cross Morlais Street, Dowlais. In his early teens, David attended Pengam Grammar School for Boys, Gelligaer (Lewis School, Pengam), where he was one of 13 boarders. Admitted to Llandovery College on 24 January 1882, he then went up to Jesus College Oxford to study Law, matriculating in 1885. While at Oxford, he played in the University Rugby team as a forward in 1887 and 1888, but Cambridge won on each occasion. He captained Cardiff in rugby, 1891-1892, and played for Wales against Ireland and Scotland in 1889 and against England and Ireland in 1890 and 1891.

He qualified as a Solicitor in 1893 and practised in Cardiff, initially at St Mary's Chambers. In 1913, he was appointed as Director and Legal Advisor of the King Edward VII National Memorial Association for the Prevention and Treatment of Tuberculosis. Welsh speaking, he was interested in all things pertaining to Wales, particularly matters of health, education, and music. He was a member of the Council of the Cardiff Royal Infirmary, the Prince of Wales' Hospital, the Nursing Association, the National Eisteddfod Association, the National Council of Music and the Ministry of Health Consultative Council (Wales). He was also involved with the Church and Musical Festivals of Gymanfa Ganu and was Chairman of the Cardiff Music Festival in 1902, 1904 and 1907.

In 1896, he married Clara Gertrude, one of five daughters of Rees Jones, JP, Colliery Manager of 17 Newport Road, Cardiff. The young couple also lived in Newport Road, initially at 169 and later at 199. They had two sons and two daughters. His wife, Clara became well known as a writer of fiction under the pen-name 'Amethyst'.

In recognition of his tremendous contribution to so many aspects of Welsh life, he was Knighted in 1925. The London Gazette, of 3 June 1925, carried the following announcement: *'The King had been graciously pleased, on the occasion of His Majesty's Birthday, to signify his intention of conferring the*

Sir David William Evans

honour of Knighthood on the following: David William Evans, Esq, Advisor of the Welsh National Memorial Association, for public services to Wales.' Interestingly, also listed in the Gazette as being similarly honoured: *'Philip Colville Smith, Esq, CV, Grand Secretary of the United Grand Lodge of English Freemasons.'*

He was Initiated into Freemasonry at the third Regular Meeting of the recently Consecrated Prince Llewelyn Lodge No.2570 on Thursday, 18 June 1896. He became WM of the Lodge in 1905. On 8 December 1905 he became a Joining Member of Glamorgan Lodge and was made an Honorary Member of the Lodge on St John's Day 1925.

WBro David Evans, PProvJGD, was a Founder Member and Primus Master of Amethyst Lodge No.4026. Following the Consecration of the Lodge on 5 March 1920 by RWBro Lt-Col Sir Charles L D Venables Llewelyn, Bart, ProvGM, he was Installed in the Chair of King Solomon by WBro Philip Colville Smith, Grand Secretary, 1917-1937. The following year, on 27, 28 and 29 January 1921, David Evans, WM worked all three Degrees himself, when six were Initiated, six Passed and six Raised. He was WM for two successive years.

It was during his second year as WM that he led a Petition to Amethyst Lodge in support of their first Daughter Lodge, Dinam Lodge No.4251. The Consecration of Dinam Lodge on 12 May 1923 was also performed by the Provincial Grand Master, Sir Charles L D Venables Llewelyn and WBro David W Evans, Primus WM, was once again Installed in the Chair of the new Lodge by the Grand Secretary, Philip Colville Smith.

In 1925, not only did he receive his Knighthood, but later that year, the RW Provincial Grand Master, Sir Charles L D Venables Llewelyn, appointed him as his Deputy Provincial Grand Master, on the death of VWBro Henry Pendrill Charles. Towards the end of the year, he was suffering from a serious heart complaint, and he was obliged to absent himself from his office. A fortnight before Christmas he entered a nursing home and went to the South of France for the New Year, returning in the middle of February. He then attended to business in London for a few days, and was able to be Installed as WM of Hendre Lodge No.3250, but was compelled to take to his bed immediately afterwards. He died at Cardiff on 17 March 1926, at the age of 59.

Following his death, Provincial Grand Lodge determined that Lodges should be invited to subscribe to a Memorial to the late Deputy Provincial Grand Master. The subscription was sufficient to enable a new Light Department for the treatment of cases of lupus and surgical tuberculosis by ultra violet rays, to be installed at the Glan Ely Hospital, near Cardiff in his memory. Sir David's Masonic Jewels are exhibited in the Cardiff Masonic Hall and his photograph is displayed in the Masonic Hall, Port Talbot.

His Obituary in 'The Times' on Thursday, 18 March stated *'The keenness and energy he displayed as the organizing head of the national fight against tuberculosis unquestionably had far-reaching effects on the health of the Principality.'*

WBro Peter M Davies, ProvJGW.

Carmel Lodge No.4774

Warranted : 23 September 1925

Consecrated : 17 December 1925

Meeting at the Masonic Hall, Cardiff.

On 11 June 1925, at a Regular Meeting of Tennant Lodge No.1992, a Petition for a new Lodge, to be called Carmel Lodge, was signed by Arthur Henry Morgan, WM Tennant Lodge and SW Designate of Carmel Lodge; George E Serjent, SW Tennant Lodge, WM, 1925-1926, and William H Smale, JW Tennant Lodge, WM, 1926-1927.

The WM Designate was WBro George Gray, an Initiate and PM Tennant Lodge, WM, 1904-1905, who was also the Tennant Lodge Treasurer. By profession, he was a Secretary/Clerk and resided at Park End, Tydraw Road, Cardiff. In a letter, dated 8 July 1925, he wrote in support of the Petition to the Grand Secretary as follows: '*In asking you to grant a Charter for this proposed new Lodge, we feel a Lodge such as this is intended to be, is greatly needed in Cardiff, it is to be a Jewish Lodge as its name would indicate, (not necessarily exclusive), but, a Lodge where the Jew, who is worthy, may be proposed and if accepted Initiated into our Order. We have a community of Jews in Cardiff, numbering several hundreds, but very few indeed are allowed to be Members of Cardiff Lodges, this brief outline will shew you the need for the proposed Carmel Lodge.*'

WBro Arthur Henry Morgan was the Senior Warden Designate. Initiated in Tennant Lodge and Raised in 1908, Installed WM of Tennant Lodge in 1924, he was a Clerk residing at 329 Newport Road, Cardiff.

In total, there were 54 Petitioners, and while no less than 33 were Past Masters and Brethren of Tennant Lodge, several other Lodges were represented, including most of the Cardiff Lodges. WBro Lewis Lionel Fine, JW Designate, a Merchant residing at 40 Newport Road, Cardiff, had been Initiated in St David's Lodge No. 2226, Rhymney (Province of Monmouthshire); Raised in1887, he was a PM St David's Lodge. Another Petitioner, Isaac Fine, an Outfitter, residing at 67 Penylan Road, Cardiff, was also an Initiate of St David's Lodge, Rhymney. Other Petitioners included: Lewis Joseph, a Hat & Cap Merchant of Howard Gardens, Cardiff, and Clement Stone, a Fine Art Dealer of Newport Road, Cardiff, both Initiates of Lodge of Israel No. 205, London; while Myer Zeidman, Master Tailor; 117 Queen Street, Cardiff, had been Initiated in Lodge of Israel No.1474, Birmingham, and Israel Abrahams, Master Tailor of 25 Talbot Street, Cardiff, had been Initiated in Egyptian Lodge No.27, London. It is interesting, perhaps, to note that one of the Founders rejoiced in the name of Brother River Jordan!

The Warrant for Carmel Lodge No.4774 was signed on 2 September 1925. The name 'Carmel' is Hebrew in origin and its meaning is 'fruitful place' or 'park'. The Past Master's Jewel and Lodge Banner depicts the scene from Mount Carmel in Israel, which is often snow covered and provides water for Northern Israel. The Lodge Motto: '*Cor Unum, Via Una*', translates as '*One Heart, One way*'.

There are several references to Carmel in the Bible. Carmel is mentioned as a city of Judah (1 Samuel 15:12 and 55 and also in Joshua 15:12 and 55). It is mentioned as the place where Saul erects a monument after the expedition against the Amelekites (1 Samuel 15:12) and Carmel's pasturelands were once the home of David's wise wife, Abigail, and her first husband, the wealthy but foolish Nabal (1 Samuel 25).

Tennant Lodge Centenary Festival Booklet records that on 17 December 1925, a Special Lodge of Emergency was held for the purpose of Consecrating Carmel Lodge. The WM, WBro Serjent, said, prior to the opening of the Lodge, that it was a special occasion for the Province and invited the following Brethren to occupy the Officers' Chairs.

WM	WBro J Gibson	WM Llangattock Lodge No.2547
IPM	WBro G Serjent	WM Tennant Lodge No.1992
SW	WBro W W Hopkins	IPM Duke of York Lodge No.2453
JW	WBro T L McBride	WM Prince Llewellyn Lodge No.2570
Chaplain	Bro F W Rees	Chaplain Tennant Lodge No.1992
DC	WBro W H Parker	DC Tennant Lodge No.1992
SD	WBro F W Glossop	IPM Loyal Commercial Lodge No.2720
JD	WBro R T McGregor	IPM Caerdydd Lodge No.3959
Organist	Bro G Bull	Organist Tennant Lodge No.1992
IG	WBro C Scoble	WM Amethyst Lodge No.4026

The Lodge was opened in the three Degrees and RWBro Sir Charles L D Venables Llewelyn, ProvGM; WBro Sir David William Evans, DepProvGM; Provincial Grand Wardens and other Provincial Grand Officers were admitted. The Minutes then record that Carmel Lodge was Consecrated. No other details were given, though it would have been customary for the ProvGM to Consecrate the Lodge and for the DepProvGM to act as Installing Master. During the first year of the Lodge's existence there were 26 Initiations, 18 Passings and 12 Raisings.

One disappointed Mason was WBro S Cecil Berg, PPrGD, then a Master Mason. Having been Initiated in India, he was one of the intended Founders of the Lodge. Despite being the possessor of two Grand Lodge Certificates, a misunderstanding at Grand Lodge deprived him of the honour of appearing on the Roll of Founders; but, he was present, and, must be regarded as a Founder in equity if not in law.

A somewhat more liberal view seems to have prevailed at the Festive Board in those far-off days, for at the Consecration Banquet, harmony was provided not only by Bro Morris Cohen but by a lady singer as well. The late Mrs Leah Jessel, then Leah Stone, an aunt of a future Worshipful Master, WBro Dennis Cantor recited – believe it or not – 'The Shooting of Dan McGrew'. A warning, perhaps, of the somewhat more awful fate in store for Acting Officers at those ordeals 'by fire' known as Carmel Lodges of Instruction.

No Lodge can have preserved the memory of its first Officers, and cherished that memory, more closely than Carmel Lodge. Throughout the years, aspiring Officers have been told of the almost legendary standards of perfection set out and demanded by WBro George Gray, the first Master; by WBro George Edward Serjent the first Secretary; and, later, by WBro Alfred Joseph, a

Masonic student and interpreter par excellence, who subsequently Founded the Daughter Lodge of Carmel, namely the Friendship and Justice Lodge No.5830.

Although it has always been known as 'the Jewish Lodge' of the Province, the original intention was never to restrict membership to Jewish Brethren alone. That would have been contrary to one of the basic tenets of Freemasonry. It was originally hoped to have a 50/50 split in the Membership. The custom of Initiating one Jewish applicant and one non-Jewish applicant led to the Jewish Brother standing 'and head shall be covered', and the other kneeling at the Volume of the Sacred Law. This is because Jewish people are not meant to kneel at prayer except on the Day of Atonement in the Synagogue. For the greater part of its history, the tradition of Initiating Jew and Gentile side-by-side has been jealously guarded and the Lodge now has representatives of the three great faiths, Christianity, Judaism and Islam.

One of the main reasons for establishing Carmel Lodge was to enable Jewish Brethren to dine while observing their dietary laws. Consequently, the Brethren commissioned the manufacture of a large quantity of crockery and cutlery to enable them to maintain their Kosher traditions at the Festive Board. At that time, all of the food preparation was inspected by the local Clergy, and religious traditions forbade Brethren from dining from other crockery. Since then, not only have the religious requirements relaxed, but the proportion of Jewish Brethren in the Lodge has reduced markedly. The cutlery was used for many years by the Cardiff Masonic Hall Company, and the last pieces of the crockery, amounting to some 200 items were donated in 2003 to the Cardiff Action for Single Homeless.

WBro Cecil Rapport was a distinguished and influential Member of the Lodge. Initiated into Carmel Lodge in November 1936, he became Worshipful Master in 1952, when he had the unique privilege of Initiating his father. For a number of years he was the Lodge Treasurer. He was a Founder Member of City of Cardiff Lodge No.7528, and became the First Master following the Consecration Ceremony on 25 June 1957. Also, in 1957, he served as Provincial Senior Grand Deacon, and was promoted in 1960 to PPrJGW. Appointed Provincial Junior Grand Warden in 1973, two years later he became a Grand Officer with the rank of PAGDC. Honoured with the MBE and subsequently the CBE and KStJ, he was later promoted in Grand Lodge to PJGD. Cecil Rapport also played a great role in civic affairs. He was Deputy Lord Mayor of Cardiff, 1970-1971, and High Sheriff of South Glamorgan, 1984-1985. In the days when Cardiff Masonic Hall served lunches, Cecil Rapport dined there every weekday with his Secretary, and was always seen sporting a carnation in his buttonhole.

During WWII, Cecil Rapport was a Staff Sergeant with the Welsh Regiment, 1940-1946. Several Brethren served with distinction during the War. They include Bro A B Rivlin - Squadron Leader RAF (Mentioned in Despatches); Bro Walter Cyril Makepeace, Royal Naval Reserve, Lt Salvage Section. 1939-1945, awarded the Burma & Atlantic Defence Medal; WBro L Weinhard, Deputy Controller, Royal Observer Corps-Awarded the Defence Medal; Bro Alfred A Edwards, Group Leader, Awarded the Defence Medal; WBro Col T H Fligelstone, Royal Army Ordnance Corps, Awarded the Military Medal; Bro Israel Jacob Froedman, Lieutenant, 1939-1945, awarded Star of Africa, France, and Germany and the Burma and Pacific Defence Medals. One Member, Bro K Reynolds, made the Supreme Sacrifice.

On 10 January 1940, a Deputation of Founders, led by WBros Alfred J Joseph and Ernie H Rees, was received at a Regular Meeting of the Lodge and the Petition for Friendship & Justice Lodge was heartily approved by the Brethren and duly endorsed by WBro Sam S Stone, WM; Bro Sol H Joseph, SW and Bro Abe Zeidman, JW. The Warrant was granted on 6 March 1940, thus Friendship & Justice Lodge No.5830 became Carmel's Daughter Lodge. Two years later, on 6 May 1942, the Charter for Friendship & Justice Chapter No. 5830 was signed. This Chapter was formed to serve Brethren from both Carmel and Friendship & Justice Lodges.

On 6 February 1952, King George VI died in his sleep at Sandringham House. The Installation was held exactly one week later, on Wednesday, 13 February, and in consequence of the King's death, no Installation Banquet was held. The Worshipful Master Installed that evening was WBro Cecil H Rapport. The remainder of his year of Office was one valued for remarkably fine Meetings and contributions to charity. He had the distinction of Initiating his father, the late Bro M A Rapport, then 70 years of age, into Carmel Lodge.

In 1975, the Lodge's 50th Anniversary year, WBro Dennis Cantor, PPrSGW, was Installed as Master. A businessman, who always believed that whatever you put into life, you will get out of it, fully immersed himself in Freemasonry. He was a Founder of Carmel's Granddaughter Lodge - Lodge of Enterprise No.8757, Consecrated on 7 March 1977. He became Master of that Lodge in 1989. While Master of Carmel Lodge, it was his remit to collate a history of Carmel's first 50 years, which he did with gusto. Sadly, he passed to the Grand Lodge Above in 2007, just six months before his son, Ross was Installed Master of the Lodge (February 2008). This record was thought to have been lost; however, in March 2011 Ross discovered his father's history in the LOI Minute Book dating from 1926. In that account, there is a reference to WBro Henry Barnett, PPrGD, as follows:

'Respected and loved by every brother of Carmel Lodge, W Bro Henry J Barnett is now the sole remaining Founder Member. An initiate of the Silurian Lodge No.471, Henry received his Stewards Collar on the evening of the Consecration and for 50 years has held Office in Carmel Lodge; a remarkable achievement. Master of the Lodge in 1937, he is the senior Past Master of the Lodge and his experience and wisdom have done much to ensure that Carmel Lodge always moves 'within the established landmarks'. The Lodge Chaplain for many years, and, now in his 80s, he remains a constant inspiration to his Brethren and long may he continue to guide and perfect the transactions of Carmel Lodge.'

Dennis Cantor also recalls another senior Member and Masonic Veteran of Carmel Lodge, WBro Fred W Gilbert, PPrAGSuptWks thus: *'Initiated in the Henry B Loch Lodge No.2383, Kimberley, South Africa (Erased) on 27 February 1906, this remarkable Mason is now 94 years young and still an active and enthusiastic Past Master with a keen and unerring eye for Ritualistic misdemeanours. He is the senior 'veteran' in the Province.*

WBro 'Fred' is one of a remarkable Masonic family being one of six brothers all of whom were Members of the Craft, not to mention three fathers-in-law also Masons. His son, WBro Frank M Gilbert, ProvAGDC and the Director of Ceremonies of the Lodge was Installed as Master of the Carmel Lodge in 1970, with his father participating in the Installation Ceremony.

Another son Bro Arthur Gilbert was Initiated into the Lodge in 1943 and the third generation of the family is now represented by Bro David Gilbert.

WBro Fred W Gilbert served as Master of the Lodge in 1955 and remained in Office in 1956 following the death of the Master Elect.'

In a Letter dated 19 April 1983, WBro Anthony Blasebalk, MPS (SW at the time, Installed WM 1984, and now PPrJGW), wrote to the Assistant Librarian at United Grand Lodge enquiring whether there were any other Lodges named 'Carmel': *'I should like to find out so that I might invite the WM or SW to visit our Lodge in the near future, possibly on Election Night or at Installation.'* In reply, two days later, John M Hamill [1] wrote: *'The only other Lodge in the U.K. with the same name as yours is No. 7835 and the Secretary is R Myers, 47 Clairville, Lulworth Road, Southport, Merseyside, PR8 2BG. I hope this information will enable you to contact your 'twin' Lodge.'* Consequently, in 1984, Anthony Blasebalk, WM, and his late father-in-law, WBro Leslie Kaye visited Carmel Lodge, Liverpool, where they were royally entertained.

[1] - VWBro John M Hamill, PGSwdB, is currently the Director of Special Projects at Grand Lodge and is researching the history in preparation for the Tercentenary Celebrations in 2017.

Also in 1984, Anthony Blasebalk Initiated Rabbi Leonard Book, the acting Rabbi of the Cardiff Jewish Orthodox Community. Two Masons were invited from all the Cardiff Lodges and around 250 Brethren were present in the Temple to witness the Ceremony. Leonard Book is now the Rabbi of St Anne's Hebrew Congregation in Lancashire and he is still an active Freemason.

Until October 1987, MWBro Max Seligman, CBE, Grand Master of the State of Israel, was an Honorary Member and, in 1964, he participated at the Ladies' Festival by proposing the health of the Ladies. Max Seligman, a Lawyer from Tel Aviv, defended Jewish Underground Fighters before the British Military Courts in Palestine. He played an important role in the formation of the State of Israel in 1948, and he was also instrumental in Founding the Grand Lodge of Israel. He was also the first Chairman of the Israel and British Commonwealth Association, founded in 1951; its principal aims being to encourage, develop and extend social, cultural and economic relations between Israel, Britain and the Commonwealth.

Another foremost and respected Member is WBro Martin Bernstein, PProvJGW. Martin was Initiated into Carmel Lodge on 11 October 1967, during what can only be called Carmel's 'golden age'. He was Master of the Lodge in 1978 and in 1998. It was said of him that after being Initiated, Passed and Raised, within twelve months he could recite every Charge, knew the Ritual of every Office and the explanation of the Tracing Boards in the Three Degrees. A great Ritualist, in life he is an ordinary man, but to Carmel Lodge and to Freemasonry in general, he is a giant. He is now an Honorary Member of the Lodge.

For many years, Carmel Lodge has run a Widows' Fund, known as 'The Major Louis Charles Widows' Fund', which ensures that the widows of deceased Lodge Members receive a cheque each Christmas time, to show they are not forgotten. This Fund, named after Major Louis Charles Cohen, ADC, a Major on active service during WWII, is almost self-supporting from interest received from investments.

Finally, mention should be made of Bro Sol Stone, Initiated into Carmel Lodge on 9 March 1966. He was not a great Ritualist and never went through the Chair of King Solomon. He was, however, a world class table tennis player. Not only the first Jew to represent his country at table tennis, he was the first Welshman to reach the final of the World Table Tennis Championships, held in Hungary in 1925.

Regretfully, as with other Lodges, Membership has dropped from over 180 to the present level of 30 (2011). It is immensely important that a Lodge founded on a diversity of faiths by Brethren of those faiths, should survive and survive well.

Compiled by WBro Peter M Davies, ProvJGW, PM Glamorgan Lodge No.36,
with extracts from the 50th Anniversary Record by the late WBro Dennis Cantor, PPrSGW,
compiled by WBro Ross Cantor, PPrAGDC, PM.

St Quentin's Lodge No. 4778

Warranted : 2 September 1925
Consecrated : 16 December 1925
Meeting at the Town Hall, Cowbridge.

The commitment and dedication of Cowbridge based Freemasons differs greatly in many respects from those of their counterparts in the majority of the Province. In this 'Ancient Borough', meetings are held in the historic Town Hall and refreshments are taken at the Bear Hotel, the old coaching inn in the centre of the Town. All Masonic furniture, including carpet, pedestals, chairs and other sundry items for use by several differing Orders, are stored neatly and compactly in a tiny storeroom, accessed by means of a small staircase at the side of the Town Hall stage. Lodges are set up by the help of willing volunteers from those fit and able Brethren; likewise, when the Meeting is over, the same items have to be stored and locked away. Thus it has been since the early days, and so it continues today.

St Quentin's Lodge was Sponsored by Ogmore Lodge No.1752, and the WM of that Lodge occupied the Chair of King Solomon for preliminary purposes. There were 65 Founder Members present. Ogmore Lodge provided 18 Founders; Trisant Lodge No.4154, 11; Bute Lodge No.960, 7; Glamorgan Lodge No.36, 4; Afan Lodge No.5257, 2; Merlin Lodge No 1578, 1, and Loyal Commercial No.2720, 2.

It is interesting to note that some of the Lodges that took an active part in the formation of the earlier St Quintin's Lodge No.1822 also provided Founders for St Quintin's Lodge No.4778. The former St Quintin's Lodge (note the different spelling of the name) in Cowbridge was Sponsored by Merlin Lodge No.1578, in conjunction with Glamorgan Lodge No.36, St David's Lodge No.679 and Loyal Cambrian Lodge No.110. The Lodge was Warranted on 28 April and Consecrated on 21 August 1879. By the early 1900s it had lapsed and it was finally Erased from the Register of UGLE in 1923.

When St Quentin's Lodge was formed, Meetings were held in January, March, April, May, September, October, November and December. Installations were held in January. Initiation fees were 25 guineas (£26. 25p) and annual subscriptions were 2 guineas (£2. 10p). These fees remained unchanged until 1965.

The Consecration took place at the Town Hall, Cowbridge, on the 16 December 1925, and was carried out by the ProvGM, the RWBro Sir Charles Venables Llewelyn, Bart, with VWBro Sir Philip Colville Smith, CVO, Grand Secretary, acting as SW with other Grand Lodge Officers assisting. Following the Consecration Ceremony, the Grand Secretary Installed WBro Sir David W Evans,

PGD (Eng), DepProvGM, as the first WM, with WBro R P St John Charles, as JW. Over 200 Masons attended and 121 Founders and visitors sat down to a banquet at the Duke of Wellington Hotel. Dinner tickets were 10 shillings (50p).

Sir David Evans had been appointed Deputy Provincial Grand Master in 1925 and WM of Hendre Lodge in the same year. Also in 1925, he was honoured with a Knighthood, having been the Director and Legal Advisor to the King Edward VII Welsh National Memorial Association, which had been set up to deal with the high incidence of tuberculosis in Wales. In addition, he sat on numerous committees and bodies dealing with health matters in Wales. About this time, he became ill and he and his wife spent some time in the South of France, with the hope that a complete rest from his many activities would aid his recovery. It was initially proposed that the Consecration would be held on 30 October 1925, but it is likely that Sir David's ill-health made it necessary to defer the Ceremony to 16 December. Sadly, Sir David did not complete his year as WM. Having conducted the Ceremony of Initiation of Thomas Thomas of Stallcourt House, and Vivian S Gwyn on the 13 February 1926, he died suddenly on the 17 March.

The Minutes for the Lodge Meeting on 3 April 1926 contained a vote of condolence with the family of Sir David, and the Lodge went into mourning for three months. The Minutes include a beautifully worded and sincere tribute made by Bro Henry Gethin Lewis, SW. The Minutes also record the feelings of the Brethren on the death of the first Worshipful Master. WBro Sir Lewis Lougher, MP, proposed a vote of condolence with Lady Evans and her family. He referred to Sir David's contribution to Masonry and his work as Legal Advisor to the King Edward VII Welsh National Memorial Association. Bro Henry Gethin Lewis Senior, SW, seconded the motion. He referred to the friendship between their families. WBro J S Longdon, the Lodge Chaplain made the final tribute. He stated that their friendship extended over 40 years. As boys they had met at the annual rugby contests between Brecon and Llandovery Colleges. Their school friendship developed at Jesus College, Oxford, where they were both undergraduates. The vote of condolence was passed in silence, all Brethren standing.

The death of the WM so soon after the Lodge's Consecration was a great blow. There was, however, a wealth of talent and experience among the Past Masters and there was full support from the Province. Lewis Lougher, IPM, now took charge of the Lodge. He was an industrialist and a politician, a member of Glamorgan County Council from 1922 to 1949, a member and chairman of Cardiff Rural Council, and MP (Conservative) for Cardiff East, 1922-1923, and for Cardiff Central, 1924-1929. He was JP for Glamorganshire, High Sheriff in 1931, and he received a Knighthood in 1929.

There was a heavy workload with many double Ceremonies being performed. Lodges of Emergency were deemed necessary to deal with the demand for Membership. The Ogmore and Trisant Lodges helped out by placing their Temples at the disposal of the Lodge.

The Grand Secretary returned to St Quentin's Lodge in 1926 and 1930. In 1926, he took the Chair for an Initiation Ceremony, gave the Charity Charge, presented the Working Tools and delivered the Charge after Initiation. In 1930, he Installed Bro Henry Gethin Lewis Junior as Master. Henry, Initiated into Prince Llewellyn Lodge No.2570, was a Founder Member and the first JD of St Quentin's Lodge. For several years afterwards he occupied the SW's Chair at the Installation Ceremony, and addressed the Wardens, until poor health prevented his attendance at Lodge. On one occasion, during his term as Master, Henry asked the Secretary, WBro T J Yorweth to take the Chair, whilst he played the organ in the absence of the Organist. He was one of the 'characters' of the Lodge, DC for several years; an excellent exponent of the Ritual, which he delivered with great dignity. He had a happy disposition and was universally liked. It should also be mentioned that he had been a prisoner of war during the hostilities of WWI, 1914-1918.

The University of Wales invested WBro Henry Gethin Lewis, Senior, the first SW, with the Honorary Degree of Doctor of Civil Law. His brother Ivor was WM in 1938. Unfortunately, he was killed in a car accident in the same year. 1938 was a sad year for the

Lodge. In addition to the death of the WM, two young and fairly active Past Masters died suddenly; WBro T R Thomas, WM 1933; and WBro W McAdam, WM 1936. Five of the Lewis family were Members, three as Past Masters and all great supporters of the Lodge. This family made the biggest contribution in the early years to the life of St Quentin's Lodge.

The Brother who made the greatest individual contribution was WBro Edgar W Lewis, PProvGTreas, (no relation to the above Lewis family). He was the first DC of the Lodge and he could take any Office at a moment's notice. He was the second AProvGM to be appointed in this Province.

Although St Quentin's was referred to as 'The Farmers' Lodge, the active Founders were prominent Cardiff businessmen. Bro T R Thomas (father of WBro Hubert Thomas, Lodge Historian, who compiled the Lodge history from which this account is taken) was the only farmer to hold an active office. He was also the first farmer to be Installed as WM in 1933. It was at his Installation Dinner at the Bear Hotel that the Farmers' Song, composed by WBro C J O Evans, was sung for the first time. In modern times the song is sung on the evening of Initiation. The Candidate's Toast is given, his health drunk, and then the Brethren form at one end of the dining room and welcome the new Member in song.

The Lodge Song

1. *In old St Quentin's Lodge doth shine*
      The Light of Masonry
   For with the Tools we emulate
      The sons of husbandry
   The Square our scythe, the Rule our spade
      To achieve the Grand Design,
   So we plough and sow and reap and mow
      Just like a farmer's boy.

2. *The Ancient Landmarks we observe*
      Our hearts we do not spare:
   Upon the Level we all meet
      And part upon the Square
   So that is why we loudly cry
      And sing with might and main:
   We plough and sow and reap and mow
      Just like a farmer's boy.

In 1926, Bro Thomas of Stallcourt House, Llanblethian, one of the first Initiates of St Quentin's Lodge donated an area of land at Westgate, Cowbridge, opposite the Police Station, for the purpose of erecting a Masonic Hall in memory of Sir David W. Evans. Mr. Cowper, a London architect, prepared plans and Bro Vivian S Gwyn carried out the conveyancing of the land. Bro Gwyn was a fellow Initiate of Bro Thomas. Three sets of plans were prepared with estimates of the cost. For some reason the proposal did not go forward, perhaps due to the Depression, which started about this time. The Lodge retained the land until the 1940s, when it was sold by public auction for approximately £300. This sum formed the basis of the Lodge Building Fund. A substantial sum of money has been raised by the Cowbridge Brethren over the years. Optimism has been high, whenever a suitable property or site has appeared on the market, but time after time hopes have been dashed.

The Motto of St Quentin's Lodge is *'Awn Rhagom'*, meaning *'Let us go forward'*. The Arms of the Borough of Cowbridge, granted to the new Corporation on 7 April 1888, were adopted by the Lodge and shows a shield divided by a chevron, the lower part of which depicts a cow crossing a three-arch bridge from right to left. The Crest consists of a cow, also facing right, holding in its mouth an ear of corn.

Bro Wybert Thomas, Founder Member, made the oak pedestal which houses the Tracing Boards, from a piece of old oak removed from Cowbridge Church roof, during major works carried out in the early 1920s. One of the alms dishes in current use was made from a piece of timber salvaged from the Guildhall, London, after it was destroyed by bombing on 29 December 1940. The Wardens' Columns were first used by St Quintin's Lodge in 1879. When that Lodge ceased to meet, Bro Tom Morgan, owner of the Cowbridge Brewery and the Dunraven Hotel, Bridgend, gave these Columns to Venables Llewelyn Lodge, Porthcawl, probably when that Lodge was formed in 1915. When St Quentin's Lodge was formed in 1925, new furniture was purchased, including new Wardens' Columns. At a Meeting of St Quentin's Lodge, held on the 8 May 1926, a Deputation from the Venables Llewelyn Lodge was received. They returned the old Wardens' Columns from the 1879 Lodge. In return, St Quentin's Lodge presented the newly purchased Columns to the WM of Venables Llewelyn Lodge.

During WWII, the Lodge met without interruption, and was fortunate not to lose any Members through enemy action. Lodge numbers were swelled through the visits of American servicemen stationed locally. Their generosity ensured that the Festive Board was always well supplied.

The Lodge's first Daughter Lodge, Industria Cambrensis No.6700, was Consecrated on 4 October 1949. A second Daughter Lodge, Y Bont Faen Lodge No.8533 was Consecrated on 4 December 1973.

From the early days, when three of its first five Masters were Knights of the Realm and Grand Lodge Officers, St Quentin's has been recognised for the quality of its Members. In recent time, there have been five Members who have been appointed Grand Officers. WBro Keith Tod Browning, a Joining Member, DepProvGM of the Mark Degree in the Province of South Wales, 1990 - 1995, was appointed PAGDC in 1990. David A Tilley, who gave such great energy to the Office of Provincial Almoner, was Initiated into the Lodge in 1970 and Installed as Master in 1984 and 2002. In Province, he was appointed PPrAGDC in 1989 and promoted to Provincial Grand Almoner in 1998 and PPrJGW in 1999. He became a Grand Officer in 2001, with the Rank of PAGDC. WBro Sidney J Robling, Secretary of Y Dalaith Magazine, was Initiated into the Lodge in 1981, and Installed as Master in 1992 and 2010. He was appointed PAGDC in 2007. WBro John A Roberts, a Joining Member, became Treasurer of the Masonic Benevolent Fund (SWED), and was appointed PAGDC in 2004; and Laurence Owen, a Joining Member, was appointed PAGDC in 1997. Another Past Master of note was WBro Ken Muir, OBE, PPrSGW, who became WM in 1966. Commissioned and holding the rank of Major during WWII, his recognition (a Military OBE) was awarded for saving the life of a fellow Officer. He also gained a Degree from the Open University at the age of 83.

The current Master, WBro Roger A E Andrews, is a renowned sculptor, who produced a magnificent statue of Bro Sir Tasker Watkins, VC, for the Welsh Rugby Union. Sir Tasker Watkins, was Initiated into South Wales Jurists' Lodge No.7092 in 1951, and progressed to the Office of SW, before his resignation in 1961. His statue now stands at the entrance to the Millennium Stadium in Cardiff.

Compiled by WBro S J Robling, PAGDC, from a history written by the late WBro Hubert Thomas, PPrSGW.

David John Jones
1866 - 1931

Deputy Provincial Grand Master
1926 - 1931

David John Jones was born in Dowlais in 1866. The family lived at 5 Cross Ivor Street, where his father, Enoch, was a Greengrocer at the time of David's birth, later he became a Commission Agent. At the age of 15, David became a Clerk and soon afterwards was an Apprentice Mason at the Dowlais Iron Works. In the summer of 1893, he married Jane Hughes, of Briton Ferry and in 1898, their son David John Jones was born. The latter changed his name to David Ioan-Jones, no doubt to distinguish himself from his father, and was appointed Assistant Surgeon at Cardiff Royal Infirmary in 1932, remaining there until his retirement as Senior Surgeon in 1963. (He died 27 June 1967). Following the death of his first wife, David John Jones later married her younger spinster sister Elizabeth, who for many years had been a Nursing Sister at the Cardiff Royal Infirmary. During WWI, she had been Assistant Matron of the 3rd Western General Hospital, a Military General Hospital at Cardiff. David Jones Senior was also a prominent member of the Finance Committee of the CRI, and in addition took an active part on the Committee of the Welsh National School of Medicine.

In 1889, the family moved to Cardiff and for many years resided at 57 Moreland Road, Splott. David John Jones was now engaged in the building of the Dowlais Works at the East Moors, and in 1895, he was appointed Masonry Contractor for these Works, an appointment he held until his retirement in 1923. During that period he built or re-built the whole of the blast furnaces at the Dowlais Works, Cardiff, and was also responsible for their maintenance.

A life-long Congregationalist, he was, in his early years in Cardiff, a member of the Ebenezer Welsh Church, and later joined the Bethlehem Welsh Congregational Church, Splott, where he was deacon and for 25 years precentor and choirmaster, and in the latter capacity conducted a number of oratorios and cantatas. He was also an original member of the Cardiff Male Voice Choir and of the Cardiff Harmonic Society, and was for a number of years chairman of the respective committees of those bodies and deputy-conductor. He had also been a member of the Cardiff Festival Choirs in 1902 and 1904.

He successfully contested the Splott Ward for the Liberals in the 1925 Council Election, and held that position until his retirement from the Council in 1928.

He was a keen devotee of bowls. On two occasions he captained the Cardiff Bowling Club, was a former member of the Welsh International Bowling Team and President of the Welsh Bowling Association.

His Masonic career commenced on 28 January 1901, when he was Initiated in Tennant Lodge No.1992. He became a Joining Member of Llangattock Lodge No.2547 and its Worshipful Master in 1915. Following the Consecration of Henry Pendrill

David John Jones

Charles Lodge No.3769 on 23 August 1916, by the ProvGM, Henry Pendrill Charles, he was called upon to perform the Ceremony of Installing the first Worshipful Master, Bro Sidney Williams. David Jones was a Founder of the Lodge.

Promoted to Provincial Grand Superintendent of Works in 1919, the following year he became Provincial Grand Charity Steward and as Founder of the first Home Charity Festival, he was responsible for collecting the record sum of more than £14,500. Then, for the Charity Festival in connection with the Masonic School for Girls, he raised no less than £20,000. These were regarded as considerable sums of money at that time. His success as Provincial Grand Charity Steward was rewarded in 1922, when he became Provincial Senior Grand Warden and the following year he became a Grand Officer of the United Grand Lodge of England as Past Assistant Grand Director of Ceremonies.

David Jones was a Founder and the first Worshipful Master of Gwalia Lodge No.4213, which was Consecrated on 25 February 1921. Later that year he presented his new Lodge with a Banner.

On 10 April 1926, Sir Charles Venables Llewelyn, ProvGM, appointed him his Deputy. When Morganwg Lodge No.5084 was Consecrated on 7 January 1929, at the Town Hall, Bridgend, David J Jones, Founder Member, was Installed as the first Worshipful Master by the Grand Secretary, Sir Percy Colville Smith.

David John Jones died at the age of 65, on 27 April 1931. His Masonic Funeral on Friday, 1 May was extensively reported in the Western Mail the following day.

'*Prominent Members of the Masonic Order from all parts of South Wales, together with representatives of the religious, civic and social life of the city, attended in large numbers the funeral of ex-Councilor David John Jones, the Deputy Provincial Grand Master for the Eastern Division of South Wales. Freemasons, Deacons of Bethlehem Welsh Congregational Church and late contractor to the Dowlais Iron Works, East Moors, whose death occurred at his residence, 50 Oakfield-street, Roath on Tuesday, after a long illness.*

The cortège was half-a-mile long, and many thousands lined the streets leading to the Cardiff Cemetery.

The officiating minister was Revd D R Jones, MA of Moorland-road Congregational Church, Weston-super-Mare, former minister of Bethlehem Church, assisted by the Revd W D Evans, BA, the present pastor. The Masonic Rites at the graveside were performed by the Revd F R Williams, Provincial Grand Chaplain (Vicar of Tonna), the Revd Gwilym Francis, Past Provincial Grand Chaplain (Rector of Neath), the Revd David J Thomas, Past Provincial Grand Chaplain (Rector of Canton), and the Revd Canon F W Rees, Vicar of St. Catherine's, Canton, Past Provincial Grand Chaplain.

The cortège was marshalled by Provincial Grand Directors of Ceremonies Charles Scoble, John Gibson, Edgar Rutter and Sam Thomas, and there were also present: Messrs. Colenao Jones (Provincial SGW), Harry Baker (Provincial JGW) ....

The principal mourners were: - Mrs. D J Jones (widow); Mr. D Ioan-Jones (son); Sir William James Thomas, Bart, JP, DL[1] and Lady Thomas; .... Sir William Diamond, KBE[2]; Sir T P Thomas (Dinas Powis)[3]. Sir Charles Venables Llewelyn, ProvGM was absent through illness.'

Practically every Lodge in the Province was represented, each by several Brethren, and all Lodges sent floral tributes. Well over 250 Freemasons' names are listed.

Towards the end of 1931, the Lodges of the Province were invited to contribute towards a Memorial to the late DepProvGM.

In due course, a bronze plaque was placed in the Duke of Connaught Temple, Cardiff. The inscription is illustrated on the right.

IN MEMORY OF
WOR. BRO. D. J. JONES,
P.G.D.
DEPUTY PROVINCIAL
GRAND MASTER
EASTERN DIVISION
OF SOUTH WALES
WHO DIED APRIL 27TH
1931
THIS TABLET WAS ERECTED
BY THE FREEMASONS
OF THE PROVINCE

[1] The Thomas Baronetcy of Ynyshir in the County of Glamorgan, was created in the Baronetage of the UK on 10 May 1919 for the Coalowner and philanthropist William James Thomas, benefactor of the Welsh National Medical School.

[2] Sir William Diamond was Chairman of CRI.

[3] Sir T P Thomas (Dinas Powis) was involved with the Welsh Bowling Association and represented Wales in 1912.

WBro Peter M Davies, ProvJGW.

Corinthian Lodge
No.4917

Warranted : 6 June 1927

Consecrated : 22 June 1927

Meeting at the Masonic Hall, Swansea.

The sentiments which inspired the making and acceptance of the suggestion that Corinthian Lodge be formed had a touch of originality. They were two-fold and yet synonymous. The first was the natural desire to further promote the growth and strength of Freemasonry and, the second was to afford to men of outstanding ability and high repute, opportunities to make more prominent and tangible contributions to the activities of our beloved Craft. They had been unable to avail themselves of this opportunity earlier in their lives, because of the extreme pressure of their professional work, and other important activities. All those who subscribed to this view were convinced, from their own experiences, that the example, influence and personality of the men who would constitute the Founder Members, would be of so fine and permanent a character, as to ensure the establishment and continuance of a Lodge, worthy of the hall-mark of Masonic standards and traditions.

WBro W Arthur Davies presided and Bro Frank Randell acted as Secretary at meetings held on 29 January and 12 February 1927.

The subjects appertaining to the formation of a new Lodge, such as the Sponsoring Lodge, Regalia, Banner, By-laws, design of Founders' Jewels, and annual subscriptions were discussed and important decisions were made. There was a general wish that the first Officers should present their respective Collars to the Lodge.

Many names were suggested for the new Lodge, among them being 'Corinthian', 'Connaught', 'Abertawe', 'Glantawe', 'Ffynone', 'Morganwg', 'Glanmor', 'Brunswick', 'Singleton' and 'Clyne'.

After a full discussion and a vote having been taken, the name, 'Corinthian', was chosen.

Invaluable assistance was given by Bro Grant Murray of the Swansea School of Art in the designing of the Lodge Banner, and by a Miss Hall in the making of it. Great care was taken in the choice of the Motto, which was to appear on the Banner and in this important matter the Founders enjoyed the benefit of the advice and guidance of the Rev R S Rogers, a renowned Minister of Religion and a notable Welsh classical scholar. The Motto chosen was: *'Y Llaw a Rydd a Gynnull'*, meaning, *'The Hand that Gives, will Gather'*.

The Founders invited Indefatigable Lodge No.237 to Sponsor the formation of Corinthian Lodge. WBro A E Thomas, the first IPM of Corinthian Lodge, made the arrangements necessary for WBro W Arthur Davies and Bro Frank Randell to attend the Regular Meeting of Indefatigable Lodge on 14 February 1927, to formally request Indefatigable Lodge's support for the Petition.

It was decided that the Regular Meetings of the Lodge would be held on the first Thursday of every month, excepting for the vacation months of July, August and September. In March 1989, the Lodge resolved not to meet in January and June. The number of Founders was intended to be between twenty and thirty-six, the Brethren being drawn from many of the Swansea Lodges.

A letter from WBro George Whittington, ProvGSec, was read at a meeting on 19 May 1927, in which it was stated that the Most Worshipful the Grand Master had been pleased to accede to the Petition and that the new Lodge was No.4917 and named Corinthian. The Meeting was informed also that Grand Lodge had approved the design of the Founders' Jewel and that the DepProvGM had arranged for the Consecration Ceremony to be held at 3.30 pm on 22 June 1927. The Committee appointed to make arrangements for the banquet to follow the Consecration Ceremony was composed of WBros Trevor Evans and Stammers Alabaster, and Bros F W Randell, William Molyneaux, A Jarrett and H O Davies. The musical arrangements were made by WBro H P Pool. With great agreement and enthusiasm, WBro W Arthur Davies was chosen as the first WM, on the proposition of Bro Edward Harris, seconded by Bro Frank Randell. WBro Arthur Davies accepted the honour and promised to do all in his power to promote the good of Freemasonry and of Corinthian Lodge. WBro Trevor Evans proposed and Bro Randell seconded that Bro Edward Harris be the First SW. The Officers of Corinthian Lodge were then chosen from the list of Founders.

Arrangements were made for the Ceremony to be held on 22 June 1927 at the Masonic Temple Swansea. This was the very first Consecration of a Lodge in the new Temple, which was only Consecrated in January 1927. RWBro Sir Charles L D Venables Llewelyn, Bart, ProvGM, was in attendance, supported by many distinguished Brethren. The Lodge was opened in the Three Degrees by the Worshipful Masters of the six Swansea Lodges. The Consecrating Officers, led by the ProvGM, entered the Lodge and took up their Offices. The ProvGM addressed the Meeting and the Chaplain, Canon Cecil Wilson, gave the opening prayer. The DC greeted the ProvGM, and the Founders and Brethren were announced in proper Masonic form. The Warrant from the Grand Lodge of England was read by the ProvGSec and approved by the Brethren. The Chaplain delivered a scholarly and deeply impressive oration on the nature and principles of the order. He gave the Dedication prayer for which the Brethren gathered round facing East. The Consecrating Officer pronounced the introduction. The Ceremony of Consecration was performed in the traditional manner, the Consecrating Officer accompanied by the Acting Wardens, four times sprinkling corn, the symbol of plenty; wine, the symbol of cheerfulness; oil, the symbol of peace and unanimity; and salt, the symbol of fidelity and friendship. The Chaplain pronounced the Patriarchal Benediction. The Consecrating Ceremony being complete, thereupon the Chair was occupied by the Deputy ProvGM.

The First Regular Meeting of Corinthian Lodge No.4917 was held on Thursday, October 6 1927. Ballots for many Joining Members and many proposed Initiates were taken collectively. It was resolved that the Consecrating Officers be Elected Honorary Members of the Lodge, and that £100 be sent to the Swansea Masonic Hall Company and a tenancy be applied for. John Owen Smith, a Lewis, and Arthur Matthew O'Brien, were duly Initiated into Freemasonry, and Bro J H Bateman delivered the Charge in a most impressive manner.

Meetings continued throughout WWII and, in spite of the difficulties, attendances were good and enthusiasm was unimpaired. It was recognised that it was everybody's War, and almost every Brother performed some duty which contributed to the ultimate victory. The names of the Brethren who served their country are chronicled in the Minute Book. It is realised that this list is incomplete, but it reminds us that the Lodge remembered its duty to its town and country.

Corinthian Lodge in due course was honoured to Sponsor the formation of Penllergaer Lodge No.5567, Warranted on 7 August 1935.

The Lodge has been blessed with a goodly number of Grand Officers including: WBro Edward Harris, WBro Stammers Henry Alabaster, WBro David Thomas, WBro Leonard Daniel Matthews, WBro Aubrey Macnamara, WBro Winston T Trott, WBro Paul Raymond Clement, WBro Charles W Penny and WBro Roy Woodward.

WBro Paul Raymond Clement was Initiated in Corinthian Lodge in 1978 and was Installed WM in 1989. He is a Joining Member of Lodge of Progress No. 7928 and Lord Swansea Lodge No.8364. A Grand Officer, he was appointed DepGOrg in 1993, GOrg in 2000 and promoted to PJGD in 2005. In the Mark Degree, he was Advanced in Neath Mark Lodge No.1125 in 1993; appointed DepProvGM of Mark Masons of South Wales, 1996-2008; and since 2008, he has been the ProvGM. He is also involved in a number of other Degrees.

In 2002, the Lodge celebrated its 75th Anniversary, and to mark the occasion a new Banner was Dedicated. It is not clear from the archives of the Lodge whether or not the original Banner was Dedicated, either as part of the Consecration Ceremony, or at a subsequent Meeting. Time had inevitably taken its toll on the original Banner, and the new Banner is a faithful reproduction. The name Corinthian Lodge is emblazoned across the Banner, against a blue background, with the Lodge No.4917, and Swansea, included. Two Corinthian Pillars are a prominent and imposing feature, as is the Blazing Star on which the 'All Seeing Eye' is set, and finally included is the Lodge Motto: *'Y Llaw a Rydd a Gynnull'*. The Dedication Ceremony was undertaken by VWBro Peter Frost, DepProvGM, assisted by eight Provincial Grand Officers.

In November 2009, WBro Roy Woodward was appointed an Assistant Provincial Grand Master and Installed at Swansea's Penllergaer Lodge in January 2010. WBro Roy was Initiated into Corinthian Lodge in 1981, and Installed as WM in 1992. He became a Member of Lord Swansea Lodge in 1994, and acted as Director of Ceremonies for four years, and became a Joining Member of The Lodge of Benevolence No.7305, and Dewi Sant Lodge No.9067 in 2007. In Provincial Grand Lodge, WBro Woodward was appointed PPrJGD in 1997 and promoted to ProvJGW in 2004. In UGLE, he was appointed PAGDC in 2006 and promoted to PSGD in 2010. WBro Roy was exalted into Corinthian Chapter No.4917 Swansea in 1982, becoming First Principal in 1997, and subsequently a Joining Member of Chapter of Progress No.7928, Hendre Chapter No.3250, a Founder Member of Meridian Chapter No.9603, and Founder Member of Lord Swansea Chapter. Administratively in the Province, he was Executive Chairman of the South Wales Provincial Magazine Committee from 2005 to 2010, and appointed as a Liaison Officer in the West Area Committee of the Province's 2010 Festival Appeal in support of The Freemasons' Grand Charity. In 2010, following his appointment as AProvGM, he succeeded WBro Brian Eveleigh, PAProvGM, as the head of the Provincial Communications Committee.

This history is based on the work of WBro Stammers Henry Alabaster, Installed WM Indefatigable Lodge in 1922, with additional material provided by WBro Phillip J Morris, PPrGReg, Installed WM Corinthian Lodge in 1995.

Compiled by WBro Roger D Gale, PProvSGD and Roy Woodward, PSGD, AProvGM.

Gnoll Lodge No.5057

Warranted : 1 August 1928

Consecrated : 29 October 1928

Meeting at the Masonic Hall, Neath.

Freemasonry began in Neath on 20 September 1777, with the issuing of a Warrant for Knoll Lodge No.506 by the Premier Grand Lodge of England. In 1784, the Lodge was entered on the Grand Lodge Register as 'Gnoll', and it remained as such until its transfer to Swansea in 1800, when it became 'Indefatigable Lodge No.333'. The history of the first Gnoll Lodge is given at the beginning of this book. Early in 1779, Sir Herbert Mackworth of Knoll Castle, later to become known as Gnoll House, from which the Lodge name was taken, was Initiated, Passed and Raised into Knoll Lodge in a Ceremony restricted to *'people of high social eminence'*, known in those days as 'passing the Chair'. On 3 February 1779, he was attending Grand Lodge as ProvGM of South Wales, an Office he held until his demise in 1791. Sir Herbert Mackworth was the son of Herbert Mackworth, and a grandson of Sir Humphrey Mackworth, who is credited with developing Neath as an industrial town, having developed coal mines on the Gnoll Estate, together with a copper smelting works at Melincryddan and several other ventures.

For almost the first quarter of the 19th century, there was not a Masonic Lodge in Neath, until the Consecration of Cambrian Lodge (then No.726) on 24 June 1823. A number of artefacts, originally belonging to the first Gnoll Lodge, were subsequently presented to Cambrian Lodge. They are among the treasured possessions to be found at the Neath Masonic Hall, and their details may be found in the history of Cambrian Lodge No.364, earlier in this book. For the next 105 years, Freemasonry in Neath was in the capable hands of Cambrian Lodge, which flourished to such an extent that by late 1927, the Neath Brethren were of the opinion that a new Lodge of Freemasons should be formed under the Sponsorship of Cambrian Lodge. Of the thirty-seven Founder Members, thirty-two were Brethren of Cambrian Lodge. The other five Founders were Members of Indefatigable Lodge No.237, with whom Gnoll Lodge also maintains close ties. On 6 June 1928, receipt of the Petition was acknowledged by UGLE and the Warrant for Gnoll Lodge No.5057 was signed on 1 August 1928, by Command of MWBro HRH the Duke of Connaught and Strathern, GM, and signed by Lord Cornwallis, Deputy Grand Master. The Lodge is proud to bear the name of one of the earliest Masonic Lodges in South Wales. The historical and geographical connections with Neath make 'Gnoll' a most appropriate choice of name. This is further empathised in the design of the Lodge Banner, Insignia and PM's Jewel, where Gnoll House, the former home of Sir Herbert Mackworth is depicted. The Banner and Insignia also bear the Lodge Motto: *'Bid Ben Bid Bont'*, meaning *'To be the Head be a Bridge'*.

The present Gnoll Lodge was Consecrated at the Gwyn Hall, Neath, on Monday, 29 October 1928, by RWBro Sir Charles L D Venables Llewelyn Bart, ProvGM. He was assisted by WBro Edgar Lewis, ProvSGW, as SW; WBro R A Richards, ProvJGW, as JW; together with a team of distinguished Provincial Brethren. The first Officers Invested were led by WBro J Wesley Evans, a local Businessman, and all were prominent members of the local community, indeed a goodly proportion were already distinguished Brethren.

The first Meeting of Gnoll Lodge, after the Consecration, was held only nine days later, on 6 November 1928, and was almost entirely devoted to dealing with propositions. Three Joining Members were proposed: Bros Glanmore Lloyd, T T Lloyd and Gomer Richards and such was the number of Candidates seeking Initiation into the Lodge, that several Emergency Meetings were necessary, in addition to the ten planned Regular Meetings per year. Presentations to the Lodge at that first Meeting were greeted with grateful thanks. Firstly, a VSL was presented by WBro George Ball, PPrGSwdB, who was afterwards appointed the first IPM. Next, the Square and Compasses were presented by WBro William A Leyshon, and afterwards, the Third Degree Working Tools were presented by WBro Morgan H Daniel.

A number of notable occurrences took place during WWII, when quite a number of Brethren served in the Armed Forces. Shortly after the outbreak of war, an Emergency Meeting was held to Initiate Bro J G Lloyd, who was only 19 years of age. He left for active service only a few weeks afterwards. Records show that there was an exceptional workload; for example, in 1944,

Carved Crest in case on the Organ Loft

there were 5 Emergency Meetings in addition to the usual 10, with 6 Candidates being Initiated, no less than 9 Second Degree Ceremonies and 9 Third Degree Ceremonies. It is also very sadly recorded that *'Bro B Jones of Bridgend and Bro D R Jones of Llanelli both lost sons who were serving in the Armed Forces'*. Another Minute records that Bro Tim Taylor had received serious injuries from a phosphorous bomb dropped on the town during an air raid. Bro Gwyn Phillips became a prisoner of war under the Japanese, after the fall of Singapore. The family had no news of his health or welfare, until, in October 1945, they were informed that Allied troops had liberated the camp, giving rise to hope that he may be one of the ones to be repatriated. However, the grim news to reach the family and the Lodge was that he had died under tragic circumstances whilst a prisoner. With hostilities at an end, a Thanksgiving Service was held by the Lodge in October 1945 at St Thomas's Church, Neath, *'commemorating Victory over the enemy'*. The Collection, in aid of the Royal Masonic Hospital, raised £15. 15s. 0d (£15. 75p). Gnoll Lodge, together with the other Lodges in Neath and Port Talbot, continue to maintain a close relationship with St Thomas's Church. A Carol Service is held there every Christmas as well as 'Summer Evenings', which are held in conjunction with Gnoll Chapter of the Holy Royal Arch.

Gnoll Lodge is proud of both its antecedents as well as its more recent history. In 1978, it celebrated its 50th year, which was suitably marked with the publication of a history book compiled by WBro W Alcwyn Griffith, Gnoll Lodge No.5057 - Golden Jubilee, 1928-1978. In 1988, the Lodge hosted a splendid lunch to mark its 60th year, when Members, their families and widows of the Lodge, were all presented with a commemorative tumbler. Since its Consecration in 1928, seventy-five Brethren have had the distinction and honour of being Installed as Worshipful Master. Only three have occupied the Chair of King Solomon on more than one occasion. They are WBro R Anthony Shorney, Installed in 1980 and 1991, the late WBro D Hedley Williams in 1962 and 1992 and WBro Jim Wolsey in 1987 and 1998.

The Lodge has had eight Treasurers, the longest serving being the late WBro D Hedley Williams. Only seven Brethren have occupied the Office of Secretary, the longest serving being the late WBro Trevor Matthews, MBE, JP. The Lodge decided in 1964 that the Office of DC should be progressive, but this only continued until 1968. The Lodge has had eight permanent DCs, the longest serving being the late WBro Jack Mill, MBE, a stickler for perfection, who is remembered with affection. There is no doubt that the quality of the Ceremonial work is due to the dedication of these Brethren, who have carried out their duties with both humour and expertise. WBro Philip Burton, the present DC also ensures that those high standards continue to be achieved.

The longest serving Charity Steward was the late Bro Joe Copp, whose name is engraved on the Charity Steward's Jewel, which he donated to the Lodge. In his time, he held the record for Festival Donations, with £10,500 being donated by Lodge Members to the RMBI Festival of 1976. The Lodge's contribution to the 1986 Festival was amongst the best, and like the other Festivals, the Lodge was very well represented. The late WBro Danny Davies, who was Charity Steward for the 1999 Festival, was to exceed that figure and to earn the Lodge the Gold Medal, now attached to the Charity Steward's Collar. Lodge Members donated £21,540, more than double the sum raised in 1976, and from a much smaller Membership. The present Charity Steward, WBro Jim Wolsey, continues to maintain the standards set by his predecessors and, under his direction the Lodge raised a grand total of £37,000 towards the 2010 Festival.

The Lodge has provided many illustrious Acting and Past Officers of Provincial Grand Lodge. Founder Member and first DC, WBro Charles Presgrave Palmer was appointed AProvGM in 1945 and held that Office until 1953. He had been Installed as WM in his Mother Lodge, Cambrian, in 1915 and remained a Subscribing Member of Gnoll Lodge until his demise.

Six Members have been honoured in United Grand Lodge, commencing with the late WBro Charles Palmer. He was followed by WBro William Johns, Installed WM in 1934, and then WBro D Hedley Williams, who received Grand Lodge honours in 1984, and was promoted to PJGD in 1994. WBro George Owen, Initiated in 1945 was Invested with the Rank of PAGDC in 1987. WBro Jeffrey Parry Thomas, Installed as WM in1986, was appointed PAGDC in 1999 and became ProvGChStwd in 2005. In 2009, he became ProvSGW and, in February 2011, he was the first Initiate of Gnoll Lodge to be accorded the honour of being Invested as AProvGM. WBro J Andrew McCutcheon was appointed PGStB in 2002. He was also appointed Provincial Third Grand Principal in 2008 and, two years later, Provincial Second Grand Principal. He is very well known and respected throughout the Province, particularly for his willingness to stand in for absent Organists. Andrew is the latest in a long line of distinguished Brethren bearing the name McCutcheon, who have served the Lodge and Freemasonry in Neath over many generations. Andrew was instrumental in acquiring, installing and dedicating an electric organ in the Neath Temple.

In July 1995, the Lodge held a special dinner to mark the 50th Anniversary of the cessation of hostilities in Europe of WWII. For the occasion, ration books had to be produced and coupons taken. Suitable after dinner entertainment was provided by the Ladies' section and, by courtesy of ENSA, the Melincryddan Choir, all of whom were dressed in uniform. This illustrates the imagination and fund-raising abilities of the Brethren.

A number of celebrations were held to mark the new Millennium. January 2000 was heralded with the presentation of a Master's Collar with a new silver chain, on which the names of every Master since 1929 are recorded. The Melincryddan Male Voice Choir sang, as usual, at the Festive Board following the March Meeting, making it a truly memorable occasion in celebration of St David's Day. Music has always featured prominently and the Lodge is fortunate to have the Briton Ferry Brass Band accompanying the carols at the Christmas Meeting. These are always sung with the greatest enthusiasm. In July, a unique and remarkable evening was arranged on American Independence Day. In his travels, WBro Jeff Thomas has made many Masonic friends in North America. His invitation to a friend in Boston resulted in four Brethren from Boston 2 District of the Grand Lodge of Massachusetts making a visit to Neath especially to join in the Lodge's celebrations, and to demonstrate a portion of the Massachusetts Working of the Second Degree Ceremony. Such was the interest stimulated that 138 visitors attended the Lodge Meeting to relish the occasion when, despite their jet-lag, the visitors conducted two demonstrations during the evening.

The highlight of the 'Freemasonry in the Community' initiative in 2002 was the donation of a Renault Scenic car to the Alzhiemer's Society at their Tonna Hospital base. This was just another example of the close relationship and cooperation between the Neath and Port Talbot Lodges which, by their considerable fund raising efforts, made this magnificent gift possible. The vehicle was presented on the Lodges' behalf by RWBro Hywel Davies, ProvGM, at the hospital, in the presence of the local Welsh Assembly Government Members for Neath and Port Talbot.

Gnoll Lodge has enjoyed a vibrant social calendar, particularly during the last forty years. In addition to those occasions already highlighted, it has been customary to enjoy harmony during the Festive Board and to enjoy Ladies' Festivals at the Cimla Court Hotel, the Glyn Clydach Hotel, Afan Lido, the Gwyn Hall and other prestigious venues. There have been Sunday lunches as well as summer excursions to various locations around the Province and beyond. For over thirty years, Brethren have organised a bus trip to attend Provincial Grand Lodge at Barry, followed by a dinner at the Masons' Arms at Bryncethin. Visits have also been arranged to Freemasons' Hall, London, to Brecon and Llandaff Cathedrals, as well as to the Investitures of Provincial Grand Masters, RWBro Hywel Davies and RWBro Captain Sir Norman Lloyd-Edwards. On each occasion, a suitable repast had been enjoyed on the return journey. Many of these events were organised by WBros Dewi Williams and Bill Grove, whose infectious enthusiasm guaranteed their success.

In addition to annual Fraternal visits to Indefatigable Lodge, visits are also made to Cambrian Lodge, Lodge of St Illtyd No.6078 and Lodge of St Theodore No.8536. The latter visits were encouraged by the late WBro Ron Edwards, a Founder Member of Lodge of St Theodore.

As this history is being compiled, the Lodge has fifty-eight Members, twenty five of whom are PMs and three Honorary Members. It is not possible to credit all the Brethren who have, and indeed continue to contribute to the success of Gnoll Lodge. It is perhaps enough to say that without their tremendous support and enthusiasm, the Lodge would not be the happy and thriving one that it remains today.

Compiled by WBro Jeffrey Parry Thomas, PAGDC, AProvGM,
and WBro R Anthony Shorney, PPrGSuptWks.

St Mildred Lodge No.5078

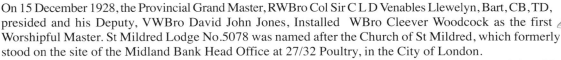

Warranted : 7 November 1928

Consecrated : 15 December 1928

Meeting at the Masonic Hall, Cardiff.

On 15 December 1928, the Provincial Grand Master, RWBro Col Sir C L D Venables Llewelyn, Bart, CB, TD, presided and his Deputy, VWBro David John Jones, Installed WBro Cleever Woodcock as the first Worshipful Master. St Mildred Lodge No.5078 was named after the Church of St Mildred, which formerly stood on the site of the Midland Bank Head Office at 27/32 Poultry, in the City of London.

The Sponsoring Lodge was Caerdydd Lodge No.3939 and initially St Mildred Lodge was a 'closed Lodge', open only to members of the staff of Midland Bank Ltd, as it was known at the time. In 1995, the Lodge became an 'open' Lodge and has subsequently become a 'daylight' Lodge in more recent times.

The Banner of the Lodge represents its origins, and shows the Arms of the City of London, of the City of Birmingham (where the Midland Bank originated) and the Church of St Mildred as it appeared prior to its demolition around 1870. The PM's Jewel also carries the image of the Church as its centrepiece.

A book published in 1872 entitled 'Milbourn's History of St Mildred's Church, London', by Thomas Milbourn, the late Honorary Secretary to the London and Middlesex Archaeological Society, gives a detailed history of St Mildred's Church. It is interesting to read how the Church had been endowed, although the endowments were lastly used for charitable purposes within the City of London.

As early as 1902, at the annual Sports Meeting of the Midland Bank, a Brother named W H Hillman commented on the advantages to the younger members of the staff of the Bank of such social gatherings. He suggested that the formation of a Masonic Lodge, closely allied to the Bank, would do much to promote friendly and happy relations among the older and younger men, as well as inspire them with the aims and ideals upon which the Craft is founded. The suggestion met with a ready acceptance from Bro Edward Holden (afterwards Sir Edward Holden, Bart) the then Managing Director of The London City and Midland Bank Ltd. Immediate steps were taken to put the suggestion into effect and to form what was to be the second 'Banking' Lodge. That new Lodge was to bear his name. The first such Lodge affiliated to a Bank was Bee Hive Lodge No.2809 (Lloyds Bank) London, founded in 1900.

It must be remembered that when the Holden Lodge No.2946 was formed, the 20th century was still in its infancy and in the midst of significant national events such as the death of Queen Victoria and the ending of the South African War.

Holden Lodge became successful in attracting many Initiates and Joining Members from the Bank. It was not unknown for there to be 200 attending a Lodge Meeting. The success of this Lodge was followed by the creation of 'Sister Lodges' in the Provinces and on 6 October 1928, Vis Unita Lodge No.5041 was Consecrated in Manchester; closely followed by St Mildred Lodge, Cardiff, on 15 December 1928; Cambrensis Lodge No.5523, Wrexham, in 1935; Fortior Lodge No.6172, Birmingham, in 1945; and Broad Acres Lodge No.7012, Leeds, in 1950.

The 'family' of Lodges emanating from Holden Lodge has a real significance in the history of St Mildred Lodge as the Brethren were always very keen to support them as well as Cambrensis Lodge in attending their Meetings. A most notable supporter of both Lodges at the time was RWBro Edgar J Rutter, DepProvGM, SW (Eastern Division). Sadly, Cambrensis Lodge handed in its Warrant in 2004.

When St Mildred Lodge was Consecrated, it met 5 times a year in Cardiff with an additional meeting in Swansea for the benefit of the Members living in West Wales. Unfortunately, the Swansea Meetings were discontinued in the early 1970s.

Since those early beginnings, over 300 Brethren were either Initiated or became Joining Members. It became 'open' in the mid 1990s and it was a great joy to all the Brethren when Bro David Hill, the first non Midland Bank/HSBC staff member to join the Lodge attained the Chair of King Solomon, becoming WM in 2003. Since WBro David was Initiated, there have been many Initiates who have had no connection with the Bank. It must also be recognised that the Membership of the Lodge is spread over a wide geographic area. This has been the situation since the early days and perhaps even moreso in recent times.

Fortunately, the War years seem to have had little effect on the workings of the Lodge. A minor inconvenience was, however, recorded in that the presentation of PM's Jewels had to be *postponed until such time as they could be obtained.* At Installations, menu cards, rather than include an actual menu, were annotated *'Lord Woolton controls our food and the Cardiff Masonic Catering Committee will do their best under the circumstances'*. Seventeen Brethren were called to arms and with no casualties reported, the sole reminder of hostilities in the records is a copy of a letter sent to two Brethren of a Sister Lodge who, having been transferred from Head Office in London to Bath, with their safety in mind, had been 'bombed out' of their lodgings, but were reported safe and well.

Reference has already been made to the family of Lodges, all related to that certain financial institution and particularly the close relationship between St Mildred and Holden Lodges, resulting through the years in very many of the 300 plus Members also having been Members of Holden Lodge.

The late WBro Martin Lewis, whilst a District Staff Superintendent in the Midland Bank based in Shrewsbury, was Master of Cambrensis Lodge. He was transferred to South Wales and became the Master of St Mildred Lodge in 1977. It is believed that he was the first Brother to have been Master of two of the Bank Lodges, although there have been others since.

It has been the custom that the Masters of each of the 'Sister Lodges' participate at the Installation Festival of each Lodge by taking the Wardens' Chairs. It is a tradition much valued by the Brethren of all the 'Bank' Lodges and it is the intention to continue this practice. In common with St Mildred Lodge, all the 'Sister Lodges' are now 'open'. The principles and tenets of the Craft are truly practised in these Meetings when experiences, news and important events are shared, and fraternal relationships renewed.

It is appropriate to recognise the contribution which has been made by many PMs of the Lodge. WBro Arthur Francis Thomas (WM 1944) was a Member from the time the Lodge was Consecrated until his death. Another long serving Member was WBro Arthur Lloyd Thomas, who was Initiated in 1950. The considerable work of WBro Ben Francis Bennett, a Joining Member at the Consecration (WM 1931) is also appreciated. He was adept at encouraging Members of the Craft living in West Wales to come to Cardiff to support the Lodge. WBro Thomas Edgar Davies was Initiated in 1930, became WM in 1948 and was promoted to Grand Rank on the recommendation of the Province of Monmouthshire. He is remembered for his insistence on well presented Ceremonies. He did much to maintain the high standards of work in the Lodge around that time.

St Mildred Lodge is proud to have been the Sponsoring Lodge in the formation of Croeso Lodge No.8377, whose Warrant was issued on 10 February 1971.

Her Majesty the Queen has honoured a number of Lodge Brethren for services to local communities. Most recently, the late WBro Iori Phillips was awarded the MBE for services to the St John's Ambulance Service and he was also created a Knight of the Order.

Of the other senior PMs who have made outstanding contributions, particular mention should be made of WBro Tudor Davies

(WM 1964), who served as Treasurer and Chaplain for many years. He celebrated 50 years in Masonry in 2002, and must be acknowledged as having been a tower of strength to numerous Brethren. He provided wise counsel, help, understanding and guidance towards the success of the Lodge, especially in more difficult times. WBro Hugh L Clatworthy, WM 1981 and 1982, became Lodge Secretary after serving as IPM and still holds that Office. In more formative years, WBro T Edgar Davies and WBro R T Evans, JP, both Grand Officers, assisted in making the Lodge a success. More recently, WBro Walter Hammond, PAGDC, and WBro Bryan Tansley, PGStB, the latter being the first Honorary Member proposed in recent times – he was accorded this honour in recognition of the help he gave over a long period, even before being appointed Mandated Officer. He was always on hand and able to fill a vacant Office or to deliver a piece of Ritual at short notice. WBro John A Roberts, PAGDC, a distinguished PM of the Lodge has also held Office with great distinction as Treasurer of the Masonic Benevolent Fund of South Wales. As Chief Executive of the Northern Bank in Northern Ireland, his signature appeared on their Bank Notes for some years.

On the 11 March 1978, Holden Lodge celebrated its 75th Anniversary and this coincided with the 50th Anniversaries of Vis Unita Lodge and St Mildred Lodge. Brethren travelled to London to join in the celebrations in No 1 Lodge Room at Freemasons' Hall, London. There were 200 Brethren present, including the Grand Secretary RWBro J W Stubbs, PJGW. It was a very memorable occasion for all who attended. Likewise, many Brethren from the Lodge attended the Centenary Meeting of Holden Lodge on 4 March 2003, when there were some 150 Masons present.

The Lodge was honoured on 28 January 1980 with a visit from the ProvGM, RWBro the Rt Hon the Lord Swansea, DL, when he delivered the Second Degree Tracing Board, using the full version in the Emulation Ritual. It was a memorable Ceremony for Bro Garry Prankerd and Bro Laurence Payne, who were the Candidates that evening.

St Mildred Lodge Brethren have consistently been very generous in their support of Masonic Charities as well as non-Masonic Charities. The Brethren owe a debt of gratitude to Charity Stewards who have all worked very hard in raising funds. It is pleasing to acknowledge that the Lodge has always met its target for Provincial Festivals.

The declining trend in Membership had its effect on the Lodge with attendances resulting in an average of only 10 Brethren supporting Meetings. The PMs tried a number of initiatives in an attempt to attract both Initiates and Joining Members, but were not overly successful. A point was reached where the Officers of the Lodge were being 'recycled' on a regular basis with many Brethren occupying the Chair of King Solomon as many as three times. The PMs recognised that this was not a desirable situation and carried out an in depth analysis of past initiatives – their success or otherwise – and an honest appraisal of what was not successful. The subsequent report was discussed fully with the Provincial Executive, whose support and co-operation is gratefully acknowledged. At the time, great assistance was given by WBro Kelvin Jones, Secretary of Proscenium Lodge No.9059. With his help, eight new Joining Members added valuable experience and expertise to the Lodge.

Later, it was recommended that St Mildred become a 'daylight' Lodge, meeting just twice a year instead of four times. This was considered more appropriate, because travelling difficulties would be largely overcome with no night driving or travelling on public transport necessary. The Resolution was approved in the customary manner, and it was agreed that the Lodge would meet in March and September (Installation Meeting).

Sadly, this proved to be a temporary solution, and by the beginning of 2011, it was evident that the Lodge was no longer viable. The final Meeting of the Lodge was held by Special Dispensation at midday on Thursday 1 September 2011, with WBro David Hackman, AProvGM, in attendance. The WM had a hospital appointment, the two Wardens were on holiday, and only 9 Lodge Members were present. Amongst the 16 or so visitors was a PM of Fortior Lodge. During a short and dignified Ceremony, the Members unanimously agreed to surrender the Lodge Warrant. Various Lodge artefacts were presented to Fortior Lodge, to be displayed at the Masonic Centre, Handsworth, Birmingham, and to be used at future Fortior Lodge Installation Meetings. Finally, it was agreed to make donations to a number of specified local charities.

Compiled by WBro Ian J Knight, PPrSGW, SLGR, and WBro Hugh L Clatworthy, PPrJGW,
with assistance from WBro Tudor Davies, PPrGJW, on the War years.

Morganwg Lodge No. 5084

Warranted : 7 November 1928

Consecrated : 7 January 1929

Meeting at the Masonic Hall, Bridgend.

The formation of Morganwg Lodge can be attributed mainly to the efforts of John Davies, who was, at that time, Superintendent of Police in Bridgend. He had been Initiated into Caradoc Lodge No.1573 in 1916, and was a Founder Member and first Almoner of St Quentin's Lodge No.4778, following its Consecration in 1925. Whilst Junior Warden of that Lodge, he had the idea of forming a Lodge whose Membership would be confined to employees of Glamorgan County Council. WBro Dapho Powell, WM Ogmore Lodge No.1752, promised his support, and the Petition for Morganwg Lodge was signed by him and his Wardens. Thus, Ogmore Lodge became the Sponsoring Lodge and the Warrant was issued on 7 November 1928.

Dapho L Powell, a Barrister-at-Law, was also a Founder Member. He was well liked by all his contemporaries and affectionately known as the 'Briefless Barrister', for he was always found to be available for Masonic functions and other worthy occasions. He became the third WM of Morganwg Lodge in 1932 and was appointed a Grand Officer in 1951.

The Founder Members contained a preponderance of Police Officers, Headmasters and Schoolmasters, with a smattering of employees from the nearby Glamorgan County Mental Hospitals consisting of Angelton Hospital (renamed Glanrhyd) and Parc Hospital. For some years afterwards the 'County employees only' rule was maintained, but this has changed over the years to a more general Membership.

The WM Designate was Founder Member WBro David John Jones, DepProvGM. Sir Charles Venables Llewelyn, ProvGM, had appointed him his Deputy on 10 April 1926. Separate biographical details are given elsewhere in this book.

Morganwg Lodge was Consecrated in the Town Hall, Bridgend, on Monday, 7 January 1929, by Sir Charles Venables Llewelyn. The Installing Master was VWBro Sir Percy Colville Smith, CVO, PGD, Grand Secretary, who duly Installed WBro David John Jones as the first WM, who then Invested Bros John Davies and David Thomas as his Wardens. Besides the Founder Members, there were 155 visiting Brethren present to witness the Ceremonies. Following the Installation Ceremony, the names of five Candidates for Initiation were put forward, one of whom, Joseph Jones, became the first Initiate of the Lodge. He was then a Police Inspector and later became the Chief Constable of Glamorgan. Before the Lodge was closed, the WM presented Founders' Jewels to the Consecrating Officers. The Brethren then proceeded to the Dunraven Hotel, Bridgend, where a banquet was held, for which they paid half a guinea (52.5 pence).

In November 1929, the Brethren Balloted for Bro John Davies as Master Elect and he was Installed as the first Elected Master in January 1930. The following year he was Elected Treasurer, and he held that Office until his death in 1937. In January 1931, Bro David Thomas was Installed as Master.

Founder Member, William C May, Initiated in Ogmore Lodge, was Installed as Master in 1934. He was Superintendent of Police in Bridgend from 1937 to 1945. He became Lodge Treasurer in 1938 and served in that Office for 23 years. During WWII, he had the heavy responsibility of supervising the policing of the largest geographical division of Bridgend and the Vale, containing the Aerodromes at St Athan, Llandow and Stormy Down, together with a long coastal strip, the Royal Arsenal factory and the Island Farm German Prison Camp. His diaries at that time contain fascinating entries of wartime activities.

During the 1930s, the Lodge found no shortage of Candidates and regularly held Emergency Lodge Meetings to cope with the 'problem'. When the Lodge was Consecrated, the Lodge By-laws provided for six Meetings each year, from January (Installation) to March, May, October and November. However, by 1947, a decision was taken to increase the number of Meetings to eight, with additional Meetings in the months of April and June. Even so, for very many years afterwards, double Ceremonies had to be held, with the WM in the Chair for a Second Degree Ceremony, followed by the Past Masters taking charge for a Third Degree Ceremony.

Founder Member and popular Headmaster, Bro Thomas Jones, was Installed as Master in 1939. He became Preceptor of the Lodge soon after leaving the Chair, and kept a strict watch on the correct use of the Ritual.

February 1939 saw the first indication of war with the Initiation of a Candidate described as an ARP Officer (Air Raid Precautions Officer). Between 1939 and 1945, Regular Meetings continued to be held but attendance became very limited, with Members on military service, and Police Officers on regular standby, together with travelling restrictions and food rationing. The Minute Book records in 1945 that 72 members (out of 75 in 1942) were enrolled in Police or Civil Defence duties, but that no loss of life occurred. The dress regulations at that time specified that 'Uniforms could be worn', but this was rescinded by 1950.

Harold S Williams, a Weights and Measures Inspector, had been Initiated into the Lodge in 1931 and was Installed as Master in January 1940. At all Ladies' Festivals he would be the first on the dance floor with his wife.

During the 1950s, large numbers of Candidates were admitted, resulting in a continuation of double Ceremonies. In 1952, Ogmore Lodge, who owned the Bridgend Temple, requested a rental increase. This led to the formation of the Bridgend Joint Lodges Consultative Committee, composed of two representatives from each of the Craft Lodges using the Temple, the forerunner of the present Joint Management Committee.

The Silver Jubilee year of the Lodge was celebrated in 1954, with the ProvGM attending the January Installation Meeting, accompanied by his Provincial Grand Officers and a host of important visitors. WBro Jacob Jones gave an account of the history of the Lodge. The Ceremonies for the rest of the year were carried out mainly by the Past Masters. In October, the Secretary, WBro Walter Bucquet, asked to be relieved of his duties at the end of the year. He died in 1960, and his widow became the Lodge's first resident in the Albert Edward Prince of Wales Court, Porthcawl.

When WBro Telfer McGuiness was Installed as Master in January 1961, he notified the Brethren that, as a Schoolmaster, he would find it difficult to leave the classroom to attend the funeral of a Brother who died during his year of Office. The Brethren took careful note of this, and all managed to survive for that year!

Ronald Moon, who was Installed as Master in 1963 had been Initiated into the Lodge in 1943. He served during WWII with the

National Fire Service, and later became Deputy Chief Fire Officer for the County of Glamorgan. A Member of many Lodges and Degrees, he was Secretary for 10 years and a very successful Charity Steward for several years. He was appointed a Grand Officer in 1981. In 1994, he had the honour of being Installed as Master of Hendre Lodge No.3250.

The Lodge Crest is loosely based on the Coat of Arms of Glamorgan, the shield bearing the three red chevrons from Arms of the de Clare family. The Lodge Banner also has the shield as the main feature, and it was presented in 1964 by WBro G Elwyn Lloyd, during his year as Master. The Lodge Motto: *'Malais Na Ddwg'*, may be loosely translated as *'Evil to None'*. The Banner was Dedicated in November 1964 by WBro Harry Stockwell, AProvGM.

 Bro Frank Knights, who had been Initiated into the Lodge in 1955, when he was a young Bank Clerk, became Master in January 1968. He held active Office in the Lodge for 38 years, during which time he served as Treasurer for 25 years. He was Elected an Honorary Member of the Lodge and subsequently wrote the Lodge history, covering the period, 1929-2002. In Province, he was finally promoted to PPrSGW.

During 1968, approaches had been made by property developers to purchase the Bridgend Temple, then owned by Ogmore Lodge. Progress was very slow but, by 1986, the new Temple was complete. Ogmore Lodge generously offered joint ownership of the new building to the Bridgend Craft Lodges through the formation of a Charitable Trust. This was organised by WBro Ron Whittingham of Ogmore Lodge, a Grand Lodge Officer and a Solicitor. The Foundation Stone was laid by RWBro the Rt Hon the Lord Swansea, ProvGM, in 1984 and he performed the Consecration Ceremony in 1986. At the October Meeting in the new Temple, WBro Frank Knights recounted the history of Freemasonry in Bridgend and gave details of the building of the new Temple.

On four occasions, Masters of the Lodge had the pleasure of Initiating their sons, one of whom was WBro Elwyn Lloyd (WM in 1964). WBro William Graham Lloyd was Initiated in 1972 and was Installed Master in January 1984. He became a joining Member of Y Bont Faen Lodge No.8533 in 1973 and was Installed Master of that Lodge in 1979. In Provincial Grand Lodge, he was appointed ProvSGD in 1985, and promoted to ProvJGW in 1993. He is a Founder Member and Trustee of Cowbridge Masonic Lodges Charitable Trust and Masonic Hall Committee. He was appointed a Grand Officer in 2000, with the Rank of PAGDC. In 2006, he had the honour of being Installed WM of Hendre lodge No.3250. In 2008, he was promoted to PJGD, and is the current Mandated Grand Officer of Morganwg Lodge.

WBro Martyn L Daley, JP, was Initiated into the Lodge in 1992 and Installed as Master in January 2003. He joined Hendre Lodge No.3250 in 2003, and served as Junior Warden in 2006. Martyn is a Founder Member of Lodge of Contentment No. 9763, which was Warranted on 11 September 2002. In Provincial Grand Lodge, he was appointed ProvAGSec in October 2001, promoted to ProvAGReg in 2003, to ProvDepGReg in 2005 and to ProvGReg in 2007, the Office which he still holds. One of three Trustees of the Province, he has been a representative of the Province on the Rulers' Forum Group 4, since its formation. He has been the Provincial Information Officer and Secretary of the Provincial Communications Management Committee, and he is currently the Hon Secretary of the Masonic Benevolent Fund (South Wales - Eastern Division). He established the Provincial Website in1995. Appointed a Grand Officer in 2008, he holds the Rank of PGStB.

Morganwg Lodge has one Daughter Lodge, namely Keystone Lodge No.9521, which was Warranted on 9 June 1993 and Consecrated on 3 December 1993.

Compiled by WBro Frank Knights, PPrSGW.

Margam Abbey Lodge No.5257
A Hall Stone Lodge

Warranted : 4 February 1931

Consecrated : 8 September 1931

Meeting at the Masonic Hall, Port Talbot.

Margam Abbey Lodge is the first Daughter Lodge of Afan Lodge No.833, but it took almost seven years, from the time that the new Lodge was first discussed, to its Consecration. At a Regular Meeting of Afan Lodge, on 4 December 1924, WBro W N Howell, Treasurer, on behalf of a number of Brethren, reported that it was their desire to form a new Lodge, and asked Afan Lodge to Sponsor the same. On the Proposition of Bro Pryce Jones, IG, seconded by WBro Capt Humphrey Jones, it was resolved to support the Petition. The proposed new Lodge encountered some stormy weather, and nothing further seems to have been done until 11 April, 1930, when the proposed new Lodge was discussed at an Afan Lodge Finance Committee meeting. The Finance Committee next met on 8 May 1930, when Bro George Crisp, ASec, called the attention of WBro W J Samuel, WM, to the Minute of 4 December 1924. It was then resolved that the Brethren of Afan Lodge should be recommended to support the formation of a new Lodge. On the Notice of an Emergency Lodge, dated 12 May, 1930, it was stated that: *'Brethren desirous of becoming Founder Members of the new Lodge should hand their names to the Secretary.'* In the Minutes of the Regular Lodge held on 5 June 1930, reference was again made to the Minute of 4 December 1924. It was not until the Regular Lodge Meeting of 4 December 1930, on the proposition of WBro I Vaughan John, WM, seconded by Bro George Crisp, SW, that it was resolved *'that this the Afan Lodge No.833 on the Register of the United Grand Lodge of England recommend the grant of a Charter for the proposed new Lodge at Port Talbot.'* The Petition was finally signed on 1 January 1931 by WBro Ivor Vaughan John, WM; Bro George Crisp, SW; and Bro Andrew Scott, JW.

There were twenty-three Founders, seven of whom were Past Masters. All were Members of Afan Lodge, with the exception of Bros Henry James, Ogmore Lodge No.1752 and Frank Seymour Francis, Windsor Lodge No.1754.

The name of the Lodge is obviously derived from the ancient Abbey in Margam, but unfortunately the reason for the choice of name is unknown. There is, however, a strong Masonic link with the Abbey. At the east end of the north aisle is the so-called Talbot Chapel, containing tombs and memorials to some of the members of the Mansel Talbot family. The most striking is the magnificent tomb erected to the memory of Theodore Mansel Talbot, DepProvGM, 1863-1865, and ProvGM, 1865-1876. His biographical details are given separately, earlier in this book. Further, his widowed grandmother had married Sir Christopher Cole,

MP, who was ProvGM of South Wales, 1817-1836. The Lodge Insignia is based on the ruins of the Abbey's magnificent polygonal Chapter House. Built circa 1200, externally it has twelve sides, while internally it is circular. It is regarded as almost unique in Cistercian architecture, and is considered to be an excellent example of pure Early English work. The Chapter House is one of the oldest in Britain. When the Abbey was taken over by Sir Rice Mansel, the Chapter House was allowed to fall into decay, and was used by the Mansels to store coal and to brew beer. The building was restored to its present condition in 1951.

The Warrant for Margam Abbey Lodge No.5257 was signed on 4 February 1931 and the Lodge was Consecrated by RWBro Sir Charles L D Venables Llewelyn, Bart,

The Chapter House, Margam Abbey

ProvGM, on 8 September 1931, assisted by the Provincial Grand Officers, which included WBro Edgar J Rutter, PPrGDC, DepProvGM; WBro Percy Mountjoy, OBE, ProvSGW; WBro Sam Thomas, ProvJGW; WBro J Francis Jones, ProvGChap; WBro George Whittington, PAGDC, ProvGSec; and WBro K J Pugsley, JP, ProvDepGDC. The Ceremony was held at Afan Lodge's Masonic Temple, Port Talbot. The Ceremony of Installation was performed by WBro Edgar J Rutter, PPrGDC, DepProvGM, assisted by WBro Cleaver Woodcock, PrSGD (Surrey), PM St Mildred Lodge No.5078, Cardiff, and WBro D G Wade-Evans, WM of St Mildred Lodge. The ProvGM presented WBro William Nicholas Howell, PProvGTreas, WM Designate, for the benefit of Installation, and later addressed the Worshipful Master, after which the following principal Officers were Invested: WBro John Benjamin Jones, PPrGStB, IPM; Bro James Brinley Jenkins, SW; Bro Benjamin Edward Howe, JW; WBro Thomas Gibb, PProvDepGDC, Chaplain; WBro Thomas William Jenkins, PrGDC, Treasurer; and WBro Norman Edward Mackie, PPrAGSec, Secretary.

In June 1919, Grand Lodge held an Especial Meeting at the Royal Albert Hall to celebrate peace to the world after the Great War. The Grand Master, The Duke of Connaught, expressed a wish that a memorial be erected as a fitting honour to the many Brethren who made the Supreme Sacrifice during the four years of hostilities. Such a memorial would be a new central home to accommodate the continued growth of Freemasonry, to be erected *'in this Metropolis of the Empire dedicated to the Most High and worthy of the great traditions of the United Grand Lodge of England'*. 'The Masonic Million Memorial Fund' was then launched, and all Brethren in the English Constitution were encouraged to contribute the one million pounds necessary to build and furnish the new 'Masonic Peace Memorial' in Great Queen Street, which was eventually opened 14 years later in 1933. Contributions from Brethren and Lodges at home and overseas were to be recognised by the presentation of a commemorative Jewel, to be called the 'Hall Stone Jewel'. The Jewel is in the form of a cross, symbolising sacrifice, and on the sides are inscribed the dates 1914-1918, four years in which that sacrifice was made. In the centre, is a winged figure representing peace, supporting a Temple. The medal is suspended by the Square and Compasses, two of the great emblematical lights in Freemasonry. The Jewels awarded to Lodges were of gilt-

The Hall Stone Jewel

finished silver, appended to a light blue collaret, and are worn by Masters of Lodges that contributed an average of 10 guineas (£10. 50p) per Member. These Lodges have their names and numbers inscribed on the marble wall panels in the vestibule at Freemasons' Hall. Margam Abbey Lodge is extremely proud that it is one of only three 'Hall Stone Lodges' in the Province of South Wales. The other two are Howardian Lodge No.5317, Cardiff, and Glantawe Lodge No.5378, Swansea.

Records of service during WWII were recorded by A W Whatley, Secretary. No Member of the Lodge lost his life through enemy action, or suffered any serious injury. Meetings were held regularly throughout the period, were well attended, and the Lodge did not suffer any loss of property.

At a Lodge committee meeting held on Tuesday 15 May 1973, the Secretary reported that he had supplied WBro Gordon J Toms, Secretary Designate of a proposed new Lodge, with Clearance Certificates and other relevant information regarding the Brethren who were proposing to become Founders. A Deputation was received from WBro A Lyn Jenkins, WM Designate, stating that the majority of the proposed Founders were Members of Margam Abbey Lodge, and requesting that Margam Abbey Lodge be the Sponsoring Lodge. It was with great pleasure that WBro W L Stow proposed, and WBro H E Williams seconded, that the request be granted. The Committee unanimously agreed to the proposal. The Warrant for the Lodge of Saint Theodore No.8536, was granted on 12 September 1973, and the Daughter Lodge was Consecrated on 10 December 1975. WBro A Lyn Jenkins was duly Installed as the first WM. The choice of name for the Daughter Lodge is yet a further link with the Mansel Talbot family of Margam and Margam Abbey. The Church of St Theodore, Port Talbot, consecrated on 5 August 1897, was built entirely at the expense of Miss Emily Charlotte Mansel Talbot, in memory of her brother, the previously mentioned former ProvGM, Theodore Mansel Talbot, and her younger sister Olivia, who had died in 1894. The architect chosen for the design was the famous John Loughborough Pearson, RA, who had previously been responsible for restoration work on Westminster Abbey, and was the architect of Truro Cathedral. St Theodore's Church became the Parish Church of Port Talbot on 15 June 1901.

Several Brethren of Margam Abbey Lodge have held high positions in the local authority: Town Clerks, Borough Chief Engineers, Mayors, Aldermen, Councillors, Justices of the Peace etc; and also high Acting Rank in the Province. Two AProvGMs became Joining Members, WBro Edgar W Lewis and WBro Harry F Stockwell. WBro T R C Raikes, JP, PPrJGW, was awarded the OBE in 1960 for his work in Ghana. In 1997, he received the Certificate of Service to Masonry from the District Grand Master of the Grand Lodge of Sierra Leone and the Gambia. A number of Worshipful Brethren have occupied the Chair of King Solomon on more than one occasion. The late WBro Llewelyn Owen was WM in 1979. He became WM again in 2001, stepping in when the late Noel W Williams was unable to progress. WBro Noel finally became Master in 2008 but, sadly, died just a few months into his Mastership.

The Lodge celebrated its 75th Anniversary in 2006. The occasion was commemorated in December 2007, when the Lodge purchased a Bible Fall and Anniversary Aprons for the WM, SW and JW, to be worn at Regular Meetings of Margam Abbey Lodge.

Compiled by WBro David Williams, PPrGSwdB, Secretary.

Edgar John Rutter, OSM, PGW
1892 ~ 1971

Deputy Provincial Grand Master
1931 ~ 1971

Edgar John Rutter was born in 1892, the son of William Rutter of Cardiff, a Shipowner's Accountant and Alice Caroline née Honey, daughter of John C Honey, 'Bible Christian Minister', from Devon.

Edgar's grandparents, Isaac and Sarah Ann, had moved to Cardiff when in their early twenties. Isaac, age 23, was a Baker from Trowbridge, Wiltshire and his wife, Sarah Ann, age 24, came from Leominster, Herefordshire. In 1851, they were married and lodging at 18 Caroline Street, Cardiff. The family were to establish a Bakery Business in Cardiff.

In 1916, Edgar married Nellie Parker, a young typist from Cardiff. Her mother, Rhoda Parker, was the first woman member of Cardiff City Council and its first female magistrate. On 5 June 1918, their first son, Frank William Eden Rutter was born. Educated at the Welsh National School of Medicine, Cardiff, and Westminster Hospital Medical School, London, he became Chairman, Health Committee, Cardiff Rural District Council, 1960-1962. He soon afterwards emigrated to Auckland, New Zealand, where he had a distinguished medical career. Appointed CBE in 1981 and KBE in 1986, Professor Sir Frank William Eden Rutter died at the age of 84 on 28 October 2002.

The second son of the marriage, John Cleverdon Rutter, was born on 18 September 1919. Awarded a scholarship to read Law at Exeter University, his studies were interrupted by the outbreak of war, and he joined the 77th Regiment Royal Artillery, serving as a Second Lieutenant. Posted to the Far East in 1942, his regiment was diverted to Java after the fall of Singapore. Captured by the Japanese, he was held prisoner, first in Java and then in Changi for a total of three and a half years. After demobilisation, he resumed studying at Keble College, Oxford, before moving to London to study for his Masters. Graduating in 1948, John Rutter was called to the Bar by Lincoln's Inn that same year, joining the Wales and Chester Circuit. Later he built a formidable civil law practice from his Chambers in Park Place, Cardiff. In 1972, he became one of the first of the new style resident judges for the City of Cardiff after the Courts Act of 1971, and was promoted to senior circuit judge in 1990. His Honour WBro Judge John Rutter was a highly respected Freemason in Cardiff. He regularly proposed the Toast to the visitors at Hendre Lodge Festive Board, an eagerly anticipated event, which was always regarded as one of the great highlights of the evening. He died on 14 May 2009, aged 89.

Edgar John Rutter was Initiated at the age of 23 in Tennant Lodge No.1992 on 9 September 1915. He was Passed on 12 October and Raised on 9 November 1915. He did not become Worshipful Master of the Lodge until 1934. Instead, two years

Edgar John Rutter

later, he became a Founder Member of Cardiff Exchange Lodge No.3775, which was Consecrated 17 January 1917. This Lodge was originally formed with the express purpose of creating a Lodge whose Members were restricted to Principals or Associated Members of the Cardiff Coal and Shipping Exchange, the business in which Edgar Rutter was now employed. In 1924 Edgar Rutter was Installed Worshipful Master of this new Lodge. Four years later, at Provincial Grand Lodge on 30 June 1928, he received his first Provincial Appointment as Provincial Grand Director of Ceremonies. Only three years later, at Provincial Grand Lodge, held on 30 July 1931, he was Installed Deputy Provincial Grand Master by Sir Charles Venables Llewelyn, ProvGM, an Office he was to occupy for the next forty years.

In the latter part of 1927, his first wife, Nellie died and the following year he married her younger sister Jessie Anne Parker, four years Nellie's junior. At the time, such a marriage, while permitted by State Law was against the Church's Canon Law. Edgar Rutter had been a very active Churchwarden at St Saviour's Church, Splott Road, Cardiff, but the Church's opposition to his second marriage resulted in him transferring all his huge energies into Freemasonry. In 1930, their son Gerald Annersley Rutter was born. All three sons, Frank and John from the first marriage and Gerald from the second, were to become Founder Members of the future Edgar Rutter Lodge.

Edgar Rutter had been a pupil at Howard Gardens High School for Boys, which in 1970 became the co-educational Howardian High School. It was natural, therefore, that he should be an enthusiastic Founder Member and WM Designate of the first School's Lodge in the Province. Howardian Lodge No.5317 was Consecrated on 18 November 1931, when Edgar John Rutter was duly Installed as the first WM. He was re-elected WM in 1932. In October of the following year, he was elected to the Board of Management of The Royal Masonic Institution for Boys. Later he became Chairman.

Also in 1932, he was nominated by the MW the Grand Master, HRH the Duke of Connaught and Strathearn, to a vacancy on the Board of General Purposes and was elected to the Board in 1933, an appointment he was to retain for the remainder of his life. He served on all six Committees of the Board and in later years did invaluable work as Chairman of the Overseas Relations Committee, an Office which took him to many Provinces around the world. He was elected Vice-President of the Board of General Purposes on three occasions (1936, 1944 and 1971), the first person to hold this important position three times, and was Vice-President at the time of his death in 1971. He was to play an important role in the 250th Anniversary Celebrations of the United Grand Lodge of England on 27 June 1967. The occasion was marked by an Especial Grand Lodge, held at the Royal Albert Hall, when HRH 2nd Duke of Kent was Installed as Grand Master by the 11th Earl of Scarborough, Pro Grand Master.

In April 1932, Edgar Rutter became a Joining Member of Hendre Lodge No.3250 and was Installed Worshipful Master of the Lodge in the January of the following year. He was WM for two consecutive years, 1933-1935. In 1933 he was again honoured by Grand Lodge, when he was appointed Acting Junior Grand Deacon. Also in 1933, he was responsible for opening 'an Office for Masonic Business at 7, Guildford Street, Cardiff', which was to be the Provincial Office until the move to 128 Newport Road on 27 March 2006.

A Special Dispensation had to be sought from Grand Lodge in November 1934, to enable him to be Installed as WM of his Mother Lodge, Tennant Lodge, as he was currently the WM of Hendre Lodge.

Also in 1934, he was a Founder Member of Middlesex St David's Lodge No.5460 and became WM of that Lodge in 1936.

During 1935, he became involved in the Founding of Penllergaer Lodge No.5567, Swansea, named after the estate of the then Provincial Grand Master, Sir Charles Leyshon Dillwyn Venables Llewelyn. The ProvGM Consecrated the Lodge on 24 September 1935, and once again Edgar John Rutter was Installed the first WM of another new Lodge in the Province.

On 3 March 1939, he became a Joining Member of Vale Royal Lodge No.4775, Tarporley, Cheshire, but resigned from that Lodge on 31 December 1946.

A second School's Lodge and first Daughter Lodge of Howardian Lodge, Harlequins Lodge No.5793, for former pupils of Cardiff High School for Boys, was established in 1939. The Province now had a new Provincial Grand Master, RWBro R P St John Charles, who was supposed to Consecrate the Lodge on 15 May 1939. He was unable to be present due to illness, and his Deputy

Provincial Grand Master, Edgar J Rutter, performed the Ceremony in his stead. On 8 May 1944, Edgar Rutter became a Joining Member of Harlequins Lodge and in 1946 he was appointed Lodge Secretary, a position he was to hold until May 1952, when he became WM of the Lodge. Strong family ties were developed; his two sons, Frank William Eden Rutter and John Cleverdon Rutter had been educated at Cardiff High School and both were Initiated into the Lodge. Frank Rutter was Initiated at the age of 21 on Monday, 13 November 1939. He, together with Wilfred James Pallot, were the Lodge's first Initiates. John Rutter was Initiated at the age of 21 on Thursday, 2 January 1941, during an air-raid on Cardiff by 111 German planes. There was no Festive Board that night! Both became Worshipful Masters of the Lodge, Frank in 1948 and John in 1949.

It was most appropriate, therefore, that when the Federation of School Lodges was formed in 1947, Edgar Rutter was elected the first President. He remained as President until 1956, when he became the first Honorary Patron.

On 9 October 1942, Edgar Rutter was Installed Primus Master of Lodge of Three Pillars No.5857 and in July 1945, he became a Joining Member of The Bard of Avon Lodge No.778, Middlesex, becoming WM of that Lodge in 1952. He Joined Middlesex Masters Lodge No.3420 on 30 January 1947 and was WM of the Lodge in 1955. A Founder and Primus Master of Old Masonians Lodge No.6762, Staffordshire, on 28 January 1949, he resigned from the Lodge in January 1955. He also joined Worcestershire Installed Masters' Lodge No.6889 in October 1950 and became WM in 1953.

In 1946, when the MW the Grand Master, the Earl of Harwood created the Order of Service to Masonry, Edgar John Rutter was one of the first recipients and at the time of his death was its senior member. The following year, the Board of Benevolence was re-constituted and he was elected one of the Provincial representatives. He remained on the Board for the rest of his life, being re-elected on the expiration of every four-year term. Next, in 1951, as one of the special appointments to mark the Installation of the Earl of Scarborough as Grand Master, he was promoted to the Rank of Past Junior Grand Warden. In consequence of this promotion, WBro Harry F Stockwell, ProvGSec, wrote on 7 September 1951 to all the Lodges in the Province:

'You will be pleased to know that our Deputy Provincial Grand Master was honoured yesterday with promotion from the rank of Past Grand Deacon to PAST GRAND WARDEN.

From now on his title, for printing on Lodge notices and on Toast lists, will be:

R.W. Bro. EDGAR J. RUTTER, O.S.M., P.G.W.

Deputy Provincial Grand Master

and he will, of course, be entitled to a salute of seven.'

In 1952, RWBro Edgar J Rutter reached the age of 60 and had completed 21 years as Deputy Provincial Grand Master. To mark the occasion, his friends and relatives considered that it was fitting to Found a Lodge named after him, in token of his highly distinguished Masonic career. Although fully supportive of the founding of the new Lodge, Edgar Rutter was not willing for it to bear his name and, furthermore, it was against the policy of Grand Lodge for a Lodge to be named after a living Member of the Craft. Initially, the name '*Highview*' was proposed, that being the name of his home at 56 Lake Road East, Roath Park, Cardiff. This, however, did not meet with the approval of Grand Lodge and the name on the Petition was changed to '*Grand Design*'. Grand Design Lodge No.7196 was Consecrated on 23 June 1952, with RWBro Edgar Rutter as first Master. Several years later, Grand Lodge was once again requested to change the name of the Lodge, this time with the Deputy Provincial Grand Master's approval, and on 13 March 1968, it became 'Edgar Rutter Lodge' No.7196.

On 21 September 1953, Edgar Rutter Consecrated Lodge of Benevolence No.7305 in the Duke of Connaught Temple, Cardiff and then went on to Install RWBro R P St John Charles, ProvGM as the first WM. The ProvGM remained in the Chair for three years. This new Lodge was the first Daughter Lodge of Edgar Rutter Lodge. At the new Lodge's first Regular Meeting in May 1954, Edgar Rutter became the first Joining Member and in 1956, he became the second WM of the Lodge, serving as such for a period of two years. The Installing Officer on this occasion was the Assistant Grand Master RWBro Sir Allan Adair, Bt, CB, DSO, MC, DL, who was present to give Grand Lodge's recognition of RWBro Edgar Rutter's Silver Jubilee as Deputy Provincial Grand

Master of the Province. Previously, in 1954, he had been Installed Worshipful Master of Brecknock Lodge No.651, during that Lodge's Centenary year. This required a Special Dispensation from Grand Lodge, for at the time he was also WM of Worcestershire Installed Masters' Lodge No.6889.

In December 1963, Edgar Rutter became a Founder Member of Ben Marsh Lodge No.7938, Dudley, also in the Province of Worcestershire. The final Masonic Lodge he joined, at the end of March 1964, was Lodge of Progress No.7928, Swansea, which had been Consecrated on 30 September 1963.

On 9 September 1965, Edgar Rutter completed 50 years in Freemasonry and he received congratulatory addresses from many Lodges in the Province. On the 10 December, Lodges were informed of the resignation of the Provincial Grand Master by WBro J Morgan James, ProvGSec:

'I am directed to advise you, though with sincere regret, that RWBro Reginald P St John Charles has, because of advancing years and declining health, resigned from the positions of Provincial Grand Master of the Craft, and Grand Superintendent of the Royal Arch, in this Province, and the Grand Master, with equal regret, has accepted these resignations.

RWBro Edgar J Rutter is now Deputy Provincial Grand Master-in-charge, and Provincial Grand H-in charge of the Craft and Royal Arch respectively.'

In March 1966, the Provincial Grand Secretary wrote to announce the appointment of *'RWBro The Rt Hon the Lord Swansea, SGW, to the position of Provincial Grand Master of South Wales, ED and the appointment of RWBro Edgar J, Rutter, OSM, PGW, to be Deputy Provincial Grand Master.'*

In 1967, Edgar Rutter was Installed for the second time WM of Cardiff Exchange Lodge, on the occasion of the Lodge's Golden Jubilee. That same year he was also honoured by becoming WM of Jubilee Masters Lodge No.2712, London. He had joined this prestigious Lodge in 1958, which has its origins in the Especial Communication of Grand Lodge, held at the Royal Albert Hall on 14 June 1897, presided over by the Prince of Wales in his capacity as Grand Master, to mark the Diamond Jubilee of Queen Victoria. A committee had been formed to arrange a dinner on 22 June 1897, which only the Masters of London Lodges were eligible to attend. Some of the Brethren present at the dinner decided that they wished to form a new Lodge to commemorate the occasion.

This account would not be complete without mention of Edgar Rutter's involvement in the Holy Royal Arch. This is summarised briefly as follows:

Exalted in Marmaduke Tennant Chapter No.1992 on 9 October 1922, MEZ 1934, he resigned 28 January 1952. Promoted PAG Sojourner in 1935, he went on to be a Founder of Middlesex St David's Chapter No.5460, 17 May 1938 becoming MEZ in 1939. Founder and first MEZ of Howardian Chapter No.5317, 28 February 1942, he was promoted to PGSN in 1951. He became 2nd Grand Principal of South Wales ED in 1963 and in 1966 Grand Superintendent, an Office he was to hold until his death in 1971, when he was succeeded by Harry F Stockwell.

Edgar John Rutter died at the age of 79 on 23 June 1971 at Rookwood Hospital. A private funeral was held on Friday, 25 June at Roath Court Funeral Home, followed by cremation at Thornhill. Several weeks later, a Memorial Service was held at Holy Trinity Church, Kingsway, London, on Wednesday, 8 September.

There can be no doubt that Edgar John Rutter was one of the most distinguished Freemasons that the Province has ever produced. His achievements are second to none. Forty years as Deputy Provincial Grand Master is a record that will never be surpassed, though almost equalled by Marmaduke Tennant, who served as such for 38 years. Not only did he further the cause of Freemasonry in South Wales with great distinction, but in addition he gained the tremendous respect and admiration of the Rulers of the Craft and his services to Freemasonry were also recognised and appreciated in Provinces overseas.

WBro Peter M Davies, ProvJGW.

Sapphire Lodge
No.5290

Warranted : 5 August 1931

Consecrated : 21 October 1931

Erased : 10 December 2008

Met at the Masonic Hall, Cardiff.

There were originally 51 Founder Members or Petitioners, 13 of whom were Past Masters. They were mainly from Windsor Lodge No.1754, (Sapphire's Mother Lodge), but after the Petition had been received by the Grand Secretary, one Petitioner wished to have his name removed from the Petition. This was Bro Sydney James Morris of Windsor Lodge – an Engineer Salesman of 40 Canada Road, Cardiff. The Petition was signed by the WM, SW and JW of Windsor Lodge on 10 April 1931.

The reason for the formation of this Lodge was that Masons had to travel long distances to attend Lodge, so decided to set up a Lodge for non-drinkers, known as a teetotal or dry Lodge. This ensured that they caught their train home in a state of sobriety and did not miss their stops through falling asleep. The name 'Sapphire' was chosen, because at that time all teetotal Lodges were named after gemstones. The letter of the WM Designate in support of the Petition stated: *'This is to be a Lodge to operate on temperance lines.'*

The first Master was Edgar Walter Young, a Shoe Retailer, of Stafford House, Victoria Road, Penarth. He was Initiated into Windsor Lodge on 3 January 1914 and was a PM Penarth Lodge No.4113.

The SW Designate was Samuel Owen Carter, a Department Manager of Powell Duffryn Steam Coal Co Ltd. He was Initiated in Windsor Lodge and Raised on 5 April 1919. The JW Designate was Paul Fairweather, a Shipbroker and Underwriter of Pencisely Road, Cardiff. Initiated in Cardiff Exchange Lodge No.3775 and Raised 16 October 1914; he was also a Member of Lodge No.14, Calais.

The first Candidate, Initiated on 18 November 1931 was Joseph James Pring, a Clerk.

A School Master, Thomas George Thomas, was Initiated on 15 March 1944. He resigned on 6 December 1965, in order to pursue a political career and went on to become the Speaker of The House of Commons, retiring with the title Viscount Tonypandy.

On 21 November 1973, two Baptist Ministers were Initiated on the same evening. This brought the number of Ministers in the Lodge up to four, none of whom occupied the Chair of King Solomon.

There were so many Members who were connected to the Coal Industry and the NUM that it was once referred to as *'The Coal Board Lodge'*.

In 1986, the Lodge Membership partook of the well known bottled alcoholic beverage, 'Double Diamond', for the first time.

This appropriately followed a Ceremony to Initiate a father and son with the surname Diamond; thus, celebrating a 'Double Diamond' that evening! In 1991, to celebrate the Diamond Anniversary of the Lodge, the younger Bro Diamond attained the Chair of King Solomon, allowing the Brethren to enjoy another 'Double Diamond'. WBro Bob Diamond remained in the Chair for two years and the following year he Installed his father, Viv, and yes, a further 'Double Diamond'! In the light of all these 'Double Diamonds', it was decided by the Members, in 2001, to change the By-laws, to allow the Lodge to have alcoholic beverages at the Festive Board. Sadly, this did not increase the Membership or the number of visitors.

Sapphire Lodge Jewels and Regalia

The last Candidate was Initiated on 20 February 2002, but resigned on 4 March 2005. Unfortunately, due to a lack of Candidates, the Lodge numbers gradually fell and it was close to being closed, with a Membership of 17, only nine of whom were active Members.

WBro Romeo Tambini was the last Worshipful Master of the Lodge. He had progressed through the various Offices after his Initiation and the Past Masters decided that to enable him to attain the Chair of King Solomon, they would fill all the other Offices, assisted by two Honorary Members and regular visitors. Without the efforts and willingness of those Brethren, the Lodge would have closed at an earlier date. Having seen their efforts come to fruition, it was reluctantly decided to hand in the Warrant and the final Regular Meeting was held on Wednesday, 17 September 2008.

On 28 October 2010, at the Hendre Lodge No.3250, a long standing Member and PM Sapphire Lodge, WBro Rosslyn Leyshon, PPrJGW, was presented with his Masonic Veteran Certificate, by RWBro Captain Sir Norman Lloyd-Edwards, ProvGM. In the Supreme Order of Holy Royal Arch Masons, Province of South Wales, E Comp Rosslyn Leyshon, PAGSoj, PPrGJ, was Installed as Third Grand Principal, 2003-2005, and in 2008, he was Installed as First Principal of Hendre Chapter No.3250.

The Lodge will not be forgotten, for there is a stained glass window in the Penarth Temple with the Lodge Crest. A Commemorative Display Cabinet housing various Sapphire Lodge Artefacts and Masonic Jewels can be seen on the first floor of the Penarth Masonic Hall. The Brethren of Sapphire Lodge did not resign from Freemasonry but became Joining Members of Lodges closer to their home addresses.

Compiled by Robert B Diamond, PPrSGD.

Sapphire Lodge Window

West Glamorgan Lodge No.5291

Warranted : 5 August 1931

Consecrated : 17 November 1931

Meeting at the Masonic Hall, Swansea.

On Thursday, 30 April 1931, WBro H Ivor Routley, Past Master of Penrice Lodge No.4172, convened a Meeting at the Masonic Hall, St Helen's Road, Swansea, to consider the desirability of forming a Temperance Lodge. A total of fourteen Brethren attended this Meeting, when it was decided to go ahead to form such a Lodge. During the Meeting several names were suggested for the new Lodge, including 'Abertawe', 'Doric' and 'Mirador'. However, no agreement could be reached on this matter, and it was left in abeyance. WBro D Emlyn Rees was nominated as Secretary Designate, and it was further agreed that the third Tuesday would be the most suitable night on which to meet.

On 15 May 1931, a further Meeting resolved that the name of the Lodge would be 'Gore Lodge', to commemorate the 250th Anniversary of the Founding of the Swansea Grammar School by Bishop Gore. The Meeting was also informed that Indefatigable Lodge No.237, would, at its Meeting on 8 June 1931, support the Petition for the new Lodge, and that it would also draft its By-laws. It was further agreed that all the Founders had to be Members of Lodges meeting in Swansea. Many of the Founders were residents in the Manselton area of Swansea, and had a common interest in being employed by the old Swansea Borough Council, thus pre-empting by 40 years, what became West Glamorgan County Council. Several councillors of differing political persuasions were Members, but nevertheless, they enjoyed the harmonious Meetings. Other Founder Members came from the predecessors of Social Services and the Local Hospital Board.

At a Meeting on Friday, 5 June 1931 the desirability of changing the previously suggested name was considered and eventually a proposal by WBro W Arthur Davies that the name 'West Glamorgan Lodge' should be adopted was unanimously accepted.

On Tuesday, 25 June 1931, the Secretary Designate reported that Grand Lodge had granted the Petition and that the Lodge number would be 5291. The Consecration Ceremony would take place on Tuesday, 17 November 1931. Bro Ivor Saunders had designed a Lodge Banner, and this was accepted pending approval by Grand Lodge. In the meantime the Secretary Designate went ahead and purchased all the necessary Lodge Regalia and Jewels. The Founder's fee was £7.7s.0d (£7.35), which included the cost of the Founder's Jewel. Each Founder was also responsible for six tickets for the Consecration Ceremony!

On Wednesday, 30 September 1931, word was received that Grand Lodge disapproved of the Banner design, and immediate steps were taken to amend it. On 14 October 1931, an amended Banner design was shown to the meeting and the quotation from Messrs Kenning for a 3 foot by 2 foot Banner was accepted. The Lodge Banner bears the Lodge Crest, which is circular in design, with a Castle Keep in the centre and a Welsh Dragon immediately below the Keep. The circle is bordered with the Welsh Emblems of Daffodils and Leeks. The whole is surmounted by a Golden Eagle. The Banner was presented to the Lodge by Bro John Sydenham Richards in 1931. The Lodge has a Motto: *'What I Spent - I Had, What I Saved - I Lost, What I Gave - I Have'*, but it does not appear on the Banner.

Bro Andrew Mattey offered to provide an appropriate Grace, set to music, for use at the Festive Board, and Bro Peacock offered a soda fountain for the use of the Lodge! This last item conjures up some amazing pictures to an imaginative mind. It is understood that this most unusual gift was later presented to the YMCA, as had been suggested on 12 January 1932.

The Lodge was Consecrated on 17 November 1931, with two hundred Brethren present, including twenty five Founder Members. The Ceremony was performed by RWBro C L D Venables Llewelyn, ProvGM, assisted by his Deputy, WBro Edgar Rutter. The Dedication Prayer was given by WBro Rev W T Harvard, ProvGChap, of Indefatigable Lodge, who later became Bishop of Saint Asaph.

The first Master was WBro David Emlyn Rees, who had Colliery interests in Gwaun-Cae-Gurwen, near Neath. Sadly, he passed away in April 1932, during his year as Master. In his memory, the Lodge always provides a vase of pink carnations at the Installation Festive Board. The second Master, WBro Edwin Davies, was Installed by WBro Edgar Rutter, DepProvGM. He was a Solicitor, whose son was Initiated into West Glamorgan Lodge and was Treasurer for many years. The family were involved with Oakleigh House School, which still flourishes as a Co-educational Preparatory School in Swansea.

The first DC, WBro William Arthur Davies, PM of both Talbot Lodge No.1323 and Corinthian Lodge No.4917, was another prominent Solicitor in Swansea. He was a gifted speaker and Ritualist and a leading member of Walter Road, Congregational Church. The first Chaplain was Rev Watkin Davies, PM Caradoc Lodge No.1573. Another Cleric, Rev W J Thomas, MA, Vicar of St Catherine's Church, Gorseinon, PM and Chaplain of Indefatigable Lodge, was the first JW. Bro H J Routley, brother of Ivor Routley, PM Penrice Lodge No.4172, and who convened the original organising meeting, was the first Treasurer and Almoner.

At its first Regular Meeting on 15 December 1931 two Candidates were Initiated, and three Brethren became Joining Members.

The fourth Master was Arthur Lloyd, another Solicitor, who was the Lloyd in 'Beor Wilson Lloyd', one of the foremost Legal Practices in Swansea and one of the oldest in Wales. He had been the first Secretary, and having been at the preliminary meetings before the Lodge's Consecration, he may rightly be considered the 'Father of the Lodge'. His son, WBro John Lloyd, became a Grand Lodge Officer, and Chairman of the Swansea Masonic Hall Company. His grandson, Richard, is a Past Master of Tuscan Lodge No.7267, which is a Daughter Lodge of West Glamorgan Lodge.

Also meriting mention is WBro David Ivor Saunders, who was the Borough Estate Agent, 1925-1954. He made an immense contribution to the town. He bought, on behalf of the Corporation, the Singleton Estate from the Vivian family (Lord Swansea's Estate), and the 800 acres of Sketty Park from Sir Robert Armine Morris, which led to the Westward Housing developments in Swansea. David Ivor Saunders acquired all the blitzed properties in Swansea, but before that, in 1935, as secretary of the Basque Refugee Movement, he turned Sketty Park House into a hostel and school for some 120 children fleeing from General Franco's Army in Spain. He was a well known historian of Swansea and a sought-after lecturer on the town.

WBro Edward Roe Brown was Installed as Master in 1937. He was an architect who saw service in Egypt in WWI and served on the Board of Management on the old Swansea General Hospital. In WWII, he joined the Ministry of Works in the design of explosive factories, finally becoming Regional Engineer for Wales. He was the first Master of the Lodge of Endurance in Cardiff in 1948, and was a Founder and first Master of the Daughter Lodge, Tuscan, but sadly passed away before taking Office.

On 6 December 1944, 25 Brethren from West Glamorgan Lodge, Glantawe Lodge No.5378, and Penllergaer Lodge No.5567, met to discuss the formation of a new Lodge to serve the Swansea Valley. The Lodge was to be named 'Dyffryn Tawe Lodge'. Amongst those Brethren were WBros Aneurin Rees and W E G Roberts, who were instrumental in West Glamorgan Lodge Sponsoring the new Lodge. The Petition was signed at the December Meeting in 1944. Dyffryn Tawe Lodge No.6056 was duly Consecrated on 15 March 1945 and WBro Aneurin Rees, PPrGOrg, was Installed as its first Master.

Due to the large Membership, it was suggested by certain Brethren that a second Daughter Lodge, with the same temperance morality, be formed. Hence, on the 4 March 1953, Tuscan Lodge was Warranted. A close relationship has been maintained between the Lodges, with annual visits being very important events in the calendar. However, Tuscan Lodge amended its By-laws several years ago, to allow alcoholic drinks at the Festive Board.

Two Members, who had suffered during WWII, went on to become Masters of the Lodge. Arwyn Lewis, who was Installed in 1964, was disabled after losing a leg. He was a brilliant Ritualist and served as Preceptor for 25 years. An Engineer at the Mond Nickel Works in Clydach, he introduced several senior employees to the Lodge. The other was Tom Coles, who became a prominent Swansea Freemason. As a young employee of the 'Western Mail', he, together with two colleagues, became prisoners of war under the Japanese. He suffered from his incarceration for the remainder of his life: he was secretary of the Far East Prisoner of War Association and his half yearly news letters are deposited in the Imperial War Museum.

In 1971, the Lodge set up a Welfare Committee, whereby each Lodge Member and widow was allocated to a Welfare Committee Member, who had the responsibility of maintaining contact and alleviating distress. This has proven to be very successful and has been a model for other Lodges to emulate.

A newsletter is published every year and distributed to all interested parties. It gives news of promotions, bereavements or any other relevant information and it has proved to be very successful.

West Glamorgan Lodge was one of the first Lodges in Wales to be placed on the internet. This gave the Lodge a wide arena and it is receiving communications from Brethren throughout the world. The Lodge also pioneered the principle of mentoring many years ago, by volunteering a Past Master to be close to a young Officer, as he progressed through the various Offices. This proved to be a great confidence builder and gave the Office holder an insight into the more senior workings of the Lodge, and the Craft in general.

A Lodge Church Service is celebrated annually. The ladies of the Lodge assist and it is always well attended. The Offerings are donated for the benefit of the Church. Many visits were made to Ystradfellte Church in the Brecon Beacons, when WBro Denis Thomas, Grand Chaplain, was the incumbent. On his promotion to Dukinfield, Manchester, the Lodge visited Sketty United Reform Church for many years. Later, visits were arranged to St Augustine's Church, Brynmill, and now to St Gabriel's Church in Brynmill.

Compiled by WBro Richard J Evans, PPrJGW.

Howardian Lodge No.5317 A Hall Stone Lodge

Warranted : 4 November 1931

Consecrated : 18 November 1931

Meeting at the Masonic Hall, Cardiff.

Howard Gardens High School for Boys was established in 1885. In 1970, the Boys' and Girls' Schools merged, to become Howardian High School, but as a result of a major school reorganisation in 1990 the school ceased to exist. 'The History of Howard Gardens School' contains the following extract: *'although in no way on the initiative of the Old Howardian Association the Howardian Lodge of Freemasons was Consecrated in November 1931. The formation of the Lodge was mainly due to the efforts of VWBro Edgar J Rutter who had devoted much of his life to this field of activity.'*

The Petition for the formation of the Lodge was signed in 1931 by 32 Brethren, including nine Past Masters. It was submitted in August and was suitably recommended by the ProvGM, RWBro Sir Charles Venables Llewelyn. The Sponsoring Lodge was Cardiff Exchange Lodge No.3775. WBro Edgar was the DepProvGM at the time and became the first Worshipful Master of Howardian Lodge. In his letter to Grand Lodge supporting the Petition he stated *'the chief motive is to give an opportunity of closer association between old and young 'Old Boys', present and former members of staff, as well as any other Brethren interested in the welfare of the School. A Lodge of Freemasons named 'Howardian' would do much to keep old school fellows in touch with each other and at the same time provide them with an incentive to be of service to the community and one another.'*

The Warrant was granted on 4 November 1931 and the Consecration Ceremony was held on 18 November 1931. WBro Edgar was duly Installed in the Chair of King Solomon, with WBro Dr Llewellyn Woosnam being Invested as SW and WBro George Hughes as JW. WBro Herbert G Daniel (PM 1944) was Invested as Secretary and was actively involved until his death, as was WBro Walter Parker, both Masters who, together with other Masters and Old Boys of the School, were among the Founders.

In September 1933, the Lodge, together with two other Lodges in the Province, Margam Abbey Lodge No.5237 and Glantawe Lodge No.5378, were each presented with the Hall Stone Jewel, celebrating the completion of Freemasons' Hall, London. The transference of the Jewel from Master to Master each year always serves to remind Brethren to *'put service before self'*; it also provides visible evidence that the Lodge has discharged its obligation to the Fraternity. *'It is the Grand Master's command that this Jewel be worn on all Masonic occasions and at the After Proceedings and will ever adorn the Master of the Lodge until time with us shall be no more.'* Furthermore, ever since that time the three Hall Stone Lodges have exchanged annual visits, when the ruling Masters take the Wardens' Chairs in the host Lodge.

Unfortunately, during an air raid on Cardiff in March 1941, which severely damaged the School, the residence of the Lodge Secretary, Bro C H Mould, was destroyed and his family tragically killed. The Lodge books were buried in the debris and the first

Minute Book and Lodge Register were never recovered. Regular Meetings were held throughout WWII without incident, but naturally attendances were affected by the number of Brethren serving in the armed forces, home guard and civil defence. Two Members of the Lodge made the Supreme Sacrifice and 35 carried out some form of war service.

Howardian Lodge was the first Schools' Lodge to be formed in South Wales Eastern Division. Since then six more Schools' Lodges have been formed and each Lodge holds an annual Schools' Night. At the Festive Board, much light hearted banter is made during responses by the visitors about the relative educational quality of the respective Schools, their former pupils and the consequent differences between the Lodges.

VWBro Edgar Rutter was also to become the First Principal of Howardian Chapter after it was granted its Warrant in 1942. The Chapter and indeed the Lodge were extremely honoured when he became Grand Superintendent, 1966-1971. WBro Leslie H Jeans was later to become Deputy Grand Superintendent, 1975-1998. Another Brother to make a considerable contribution, not only to the Lodge and to the Craft, but also to Royal Arch Masonry, was WBro Anthony (Tony) Ough, now the Senior subscribing Past Principal. He became Batham Lecturer in Royal Arch in 1991 (the equivalent of the Prestonian Lecturer in the Craft) and also a regular and very popular lecturer in the Craft, being constantly in demand on a slightly more informal basis within the Province.

Both during and after the war, many distinguished Masters and Old Boys joined the Lodge, including three Headmasters. Between 1960 and 1990, the Lodge prospered and Membership was as high as 140, drawing in particular from the BBC and the Police Service. However, in common with many other Lodges, Membership began to decline. Only one Member of the Lodge was an Old Boy when this history was compiled, that being WBro Trevor Saunders, 1938-1943.

As a result of falling numbers, since 1998, PMs have had to take the Chair for a second and even a third time, notably the late WBro Leslie H Jeans, WBro C William (Bill) Laskey, WBro Christopher M L Davies, WBro Paul Graham and WBro Frederick (Fred) J Poole.

Fortunes then reversed, for in 2007 WBro Phillip Poole, son of WBro Fred Poole, progressed to the Chair through the Ranks, and Brethren have since been ready to follow on through all the active Offices. WBro David Ellis, who had advanced to JW but had delayed further progression, agreed to serve as WM and was duly Installed in the Chair in 2008. In the same year, the Lodge was fortunate in being able to welcome as a Joining Member, Bro Lennard Davies, who had progressed to SW in a London Lodge and was then duly Elected as Master Elect shortly afterwards. He was Installed in the Chair of Howardian Lodge in 2009. He served for very many years in the Armed Forces, completing his service as RSM and afterwards, as a member of the Queen's Bodyguard. He organised private visits to Windsor Castle for the annual Order of the Garter Ceremony, and to the Tower of London for the Ceremony of the Keys.

Although the School no longer exists, and new Members come from many walks of life, the Lodge continues to retain the high standards set by the Founder Members, both in its Ceremonies and Masonic traditions. The standards of Ritual in what could be called the 'boom time' (1960s), had been further enhanced with the help and encouragement of WBro Les Jeans while acting as both Preceptor and DC, and similarly by WBro Bill Laskey, who succeeded him and served the Lodge for 13 years in that capacity. During this whole period, the 'competitive edge' between the Schools' Lodges was certainly 'sharpened' a little more and also served to add to the feelings expressed at the Festive Board. We are also grateful to WBro Clinton A Cook, long serving Secretary of the Lodge, who is responsible for producing a full set of Ceremonies strictly in accordance with those principles and traditions which will remain as a guide for future Members.

The 75th Anniversary of the Lodge was celebrated in style on 2 November 2006 with a distinguished guest in attendance, VWBro Peter Frost, DepProvGM. He proposed the Toast to the Lodge, during which he pointed out many of the highlights in its history, he drew attention to the influence and example set by certain PMs, mentioning WBro Les Jeans as well as WBro Keith Tod Browning, who were both accorded Grand Lodge Honours. In total, the Lodge is proud that no less than eight Brethren were accorded this honour. VWBro Peter concluded by expressing total confidence in the future of the Lodge.

However, more recently with Membership in Freemasonry in general again suffering, it is as well to remember that our Lodge Banner which incorporates the School Badge is inscribed with the School Motto: *'Labor Omnia Vincit'* which translated means *'Labour Overcomes All Things'*.

Compiled by WBro Trevor C Saunders, PPrSGW.

Glantawe Lodge No.5378
A Hall Stone Lodge

Warranted   :   22 June 1932

Consecrated :   31 October 1932

Meeting at the Masonic Hall, Swansea.

Glantawe Lodge was Sponsored by Indefatigable Lodge No. 237. There were 30 Petitioners, including 9 Past Masters, and the Petition was signed by the WM and Wardens of Indefatigable Lodge at a Regular Lodge Meeting on 9 May 1932. A letter in support of the Petition, dated 20 May, was sent to the ProvGM and ultimately to Grand Lodge, stating: *'This title had been selected by the Brethren as being to some extent descriptive of the area from which it is proposed to draw a large proportion of the Membership, namely the Swansea Valley and the thickly populated districts within a radius of 10/12 mile from the centre of the Borough of Swansea.*

All the Petitioners either reside, or have business connections in this area, and it is of interest to note that at least twelve are intimately connected educationally, industrially or commercially, with metallurgical interests, which are so important to the well-being of the Borough and Port of Swansea.

We are of the opinion that the eight Lodges at present existing in Swansea are unable to cope adequately with the needs of this district with its population of something like 200,000.' The Warrant was duly signed on 22 June 1932.

Among the Founders and early Initiates of Glantawe Lodge were a number of Steelworks' Owners and Managers, and from this influence the Lodge was sometimes referred to as 'the Metallurgists' Lodge'. The WM Designate was WBro David John Davies PGD, PPrSGW. He was Installed WM of Indefatigable Lodge in 1911 and of Penrice Lodge No.4172 in 1922. 'DJ', as he was known to his friends, was a Magistrate, a Councillor and Alderman of the County Borough of Swansea, and was Mayor in 1922. Born in Morriston, he was a Provision Merchant, and became Managing Director and Chairman of the Upper Forest and Worcester Steel and Tinplate Works in Morriston, of which his father was the owner. He was a deacon and father figure in Tabernacle Welsh Independent Chapel, and was a founder member of Morriston Golf Club.

Glantawe Lodge was Consecrated by RWBro Sir Charles L D Venables Llewelyn, Bart, ProvGM, assisted by the Provincial Grand Wardens and other Provincial Grand Lodge Officers, on Monday, 31 October 1932. Following the Consecration Ceremony, WBro Edgar J Rutter, DepProvGM, Installed WBro David John Davies, PGD, WM Designate, as the first WM of the Lodge. WBro Joseph Sidney Davies, Initiated in Dr James Griffith Hall Lodge No.3161, PM Corinthian Lodge No.4917, was Invested as SW. Professionally, he was a Steel & Tinplate Manufacturer in Morriston, Swansea. Bro Charles Alfred Edwards, Initiated in Dr James

Griffith Hall Lodge, Principal of University College, Swansea, was Invested as JW. Dr Charles Alfred Edwards, DSc, 1882-1960, was an eminent Metallurgist. In 1920, he became Head of the Department of Metallurgy and Vice-Principal at the newly established University College of Swansea. Appointed Principal in 1927, he was elected a Fellow of the Royal Society (FRS) in 1930. A kindly and dignified person, he was capable of inspiring enthusiasm and lasting friendship, and his loss was felt by many when he died on March 29, 1960.

The Installation Banquet in 1936, was a sumptuous affair, and carried a charge of 6 shillings (or 30 pence in today's currency!). The annual subscription was three guineas (£3. 15p)!

The Founder Members included Head Teachers, Doctors and Consultants, Ministers of Religion, an Auctioneer, a Painter and Decorator, a Haulage Contractor, a Stockbroker, a Commercial Traveller, a Farmer, a Haberdasher, and so on. Over the years, the Membership has further diversified, and the Lodge now draws on Membership from all walks of life and all parts of Swansea and its environs.

The name of the Lodge, 'Glantawe', literally translated means 'bank of the river Tawe', the major river running through the Swansea Valley to the sea, along the banks of which were many 'ancient and modern' factories and industries. However, the name 'Glantawe' was adopted by the Lodge, not only because of its geographical location, but also from the legendary WBro John Jones Jenkins, first Baron Glantawe.

John Jones Jenkins was born in Clydach in the Swansea Valley on 10 May 1835, and as a boy, following in his father's footsteps, he earned his living by working in the Upper Forest Tinplate Works, Morriston. Here he obtained practical knowledge and experience of the trade in which he was destined to be so eminent. At 23 years of age, he was appointed Outdoor Manager of the works, and during that time did much to improve the lot of the workers, including inaugurating singing classes and establishing a library. In later years, Morriston was to become notable for activities in the Workers' Education Association, where highly intelligent and literate men, denied the benefit of extended formal education, none the less honed their literary and political skills and attitudes. In 1855, John Jones Jenkins was elected to Swansea Town Council, and was Mayor of the town three times, in 1869, 1879 and 1880. In 1870, a new Masonic Lodge, Talbot Lodge No.1323, was Consecrated in the Wind Street Masonic Hall, and the first Initiate was John Jones Jenkins. In 1875, he was Installed as Master of the Lodge, and in the same year was appointed ProvJGW. He was the MP for Carmarthen Borough from 1882 to 1886, and 1895 to 1900. In the course of a very full and active life, including being High Sheriff of Glamorgan, he was Knighted in 1880 by HRH The Prince of Wales (later King Edward VII), on the occasion of the opening of the Prince of Wales Dock in Swansea. He received the Honorary Freedom of Swansea in 1885. He was president and founding member of the Langland Bay Golf Club, and officially opened the club on 10 September 1904, by driving off from the first tee. He was created Baron Glantawe on 18 July 1906. He took the title 'Lord Glantawe' after the locality in which he was brought up, and adopted a Coat of Arms and a family Motto *'Perseverance'*. He died two months after his eightieth birthday, on 27 July 1915. He was interred in Oystermouth cemetery, and in Oystermouth church are two stained glass windows, one to his memory and one to that of his wife.

On adoption of the name 'Glantawe Lodge', the Founders determined that the Lodge Motto should also be *'Persverance'*. The Lodge Banner was designed by the son of one of the Founders, WBro Ivor Griffiths, PPrGReg, under the guidance of the Swansea Art School in Alexandra Road, Swansea. The design consists essentially of Lord Glantawe's Coat of Arms, together with his Motto. A breast badge bearing this design was issued to all Founder Members, and is an integral element of the Past Master's Jewel.

From the Minutes of the early 1930s, each Meeting tended to attract some 35 to 40 Members, and anything from 5 to 25 visitors. As Freemasonry expanded rapidly in Swansea, a number of Daughter Lodges were established. One reason was that as Lodges became larger there was little hope of promotion to the Chair of King Solomon, surely an ambition of most dedicated Brethren, while the creation of smaller Daughter Lodges enhanced that opportunity.

Glantawe Lodge has the distinction of being the youngest of the three Hall Stone Lodges in the Province, the other two being Margam Abbey Lodge No.5257 and Howardian Lodge No.5317. Each year there are reciprocal visits between the three Lodges, meeting respectively in the Masonic Temples in Swansea, Port Talbot and Cardiff. The title 'Hall Stone Lodge' was awarded to those Lodges contributing an average of 10 guineas per member to the Masonic Million Memorial Fund, instigated by the Most Worshipful the Grand Master, HRH the Duke of Connaught and Strathearn in 1919 to embark on the building of a new headquarters for the English Craft as a memorial to the many Brethren who had given their lives during the 1914-1918 war. Each Hall Stone Lodge was presented with a medal, the Hall Stone Jewel, in gold on a light blue collarette, to be worn by successive Masters of the Lodge.

A notable link between the early years of the Lodge and the more recent past is the involvement in the Lodge of the late WBro F A Henshall, PAGDC. The Minutes indicate that WBro Henshall was Initiated into the Lodge on 8 February 1933, Passed on 5 April, and Raised on 7 June of the same year, the first full year of the Lodge's existence. WBro Henshall was an early DC of the Lodge and was Installed in the Chair of King Solomon in 1944. He took up that Office again exactly 50 years later, during 1994-1995, a quite remarkable achievement. WBro Henshall is well remembered and respected by many current Members of the Lodge.

Glantawe Lodge has two Daughter Lodges, Old Goreans Lodge No.7193, Warranted on 7 May 1952, and Singleton Lodge No.8399, Warranted on 8 September 1971. The Lodge also has an associated Royal Arch Chapter, Glantawe Chapter No.5378, Warranted 13 November 1968.

Of late, the Lodge has been reduced in Membership, a not uncommon phenomenon among Lodges. From a high point of a number in excess of 120 Members in the 1960s, Membership as of December 2009 was 29. However, the Lodge remains viable and effective, and is noted locally for the high quality of its Ritual, and for the friendliness among the Brethren and visitors alike.

The Lodge is fortunate in having a wealth of experience in its Provincial Officers, and in its three Grand Officers. WBro Michael John Hoare, PJGD, was Initiated in Glantawe Lodge in 1965 and Installed as WM in 1977. A Founder Member of Lodge of Sincerity No.1973, he was Installed as WM in 1991. In Province, he was appointed ProvSGD in 1983 and was subsequently promoted to PPrSGW. He became a Grand Officer in 1993 with the Rank of PAGDC and was promoted in 2001 to PJGD. In Royal Arch Masonry, he was Exalted in Virtue and Hope Chapter No.237 in 1968 and was Deputy Grand Superintendent of the Province, 1999 - 2004. In Grand Chapter, he was first appointed PGStB in 1993 and promoted to PGSwdB in 2000. WBro E Geoffrey Jenkins, Installed as WM in 1986 and again in 1998, became a Grand Officer in 2001, with the Rank of PGStB. WBro Christopher I Lewis was Initiated in Glantawe Lodge in 1987, Installed as WM in 1992, 2004 and 2005, and has served as Lodge Organist since 2007. In Provincial Grand Lodge, he was appointed ProvGOrg in 1998, and promoted to ProvGSwdB in 2004. He became a Grand Officer with the Rank of DepGOrg in 2010. The Lodge suffered a sad loss some years ago when the long serving Secretary, WBro J Hywel Williams, PPrSGW, was called to the Grand Lodge Above on 19 October 2005, after over 30 years in Office. He had been Installed as WM in 1973.

In 2007, Glantawe Lodge celebrated its 75th Anniversary.

Compiled by K L Jones, PPrGSwdB.

Universities Lodge No.5461

Warranted : 7 February 1934

Consecrated : 30 April 1934

Meeting at the Masonic Hall, Cardiff.

The prime mover in the formation of the Lodge and its first Worshipful Master was WBro Daniel James Arthur Brown, who for 23 years was Registrar of the University College of South Wales and Monmouthshire (now, Cardiff University) which had been founded by Royal Charter in 1883.

A native of West Lulworth, Dorset, and privately educated, D J A Brown came to Cardiff in 1889, when he was 18 years old. He began working for the University College in 1895 as an assistant to the Registrar and became Deputy Registrar in 1911. Appointed Registrar in 1913, in succession to Sir Percy E Watkins (who had resigned to become Assistant Secretary at the Welsh Board of Health and in 1925, Permanent Secretary at the Welsh Department of Education), he continued as such until his retirement at the age of 65 in September 1936. Sir Percy Watkins described him as a man of *'the highest integrity and efficiency'*. Brown was the co-author with Dr Trow of 'A Short History of the University College of South Wales and Monmouthshire', published in 1933 to mark the Jubilee of the College, 1883-1933, and which is still regarded as a most valuable account of the first fifty years of the College's existence. His distinguished services to Welsh education were recognised by the University of Wales, who honoured him with the degree of MA in 1933.

Daniel James Arthur Brown, who had been Initiated in Glamorgan Lodge No.36 on the 30 November 1917 was WM Designate. He had been Installed Worshipful Master, as is the custom of Glamorgan Lodge, on St John's Day (24 June) 1932. The SW Designate, Bro Lambert Rogers, RND, was an Australian, who had served in the Royal Navy during the First World War. He was a prominent surgeon and consultant at the Cardiff Royal Infirmary. The JW Designate, Bro David Evans, was Professor of Music at University College, Cardiff. A very popular teacher, he was known affectionately as 'Dai Solfa'. They in turn became the second and third WMs of the Lodge.

The names of the Founders are recorded in the By-laws of Universities Lodge. They consisted of two College Registrars, two Professors, seven Lecturers, seven members of the Medical Profession, three members of the College Court of Governors, two Directors of Education, four Headmasters, five Assistant Schoolmasters, one Barrister, one Solicitor and one Dentist. Among them were Archie Blyton, Headmaster, and Ewart Lewis, French Master at Canton High School. Also, there were Edwin Drew,

Registrar of University College Swansea; J Morgan Lloyd, who succeeded WBro David Evans as Professor of Music at Cardiff; Roy Jones, Professor of Metallurgy at Cardiff, and Louis Thomas, who succeeded D J A Brown as Registrar of University College, Cardiff. All became WMs of Universities Lodge.

On 8 December 1933, WBro Arthur Brown led a Deputation of 35 Founder Brethren to Glamorgan Lodge. The reasons in support of the application were fully explained by the Deputation and in the Glamorgan Lodge Minutes, it is recorded that it was unanimously resolved:

'That the Glamorgan Lodge, No. 36, having made full enquiry and being satisfied that the reasons given for the foundation of the proposed "Universities" Lodge, Cardiff, are adequate, recommend the Petition of the Founders to the favourable consideration of The Most Worshipful The Grand Master, and: -

That the Worshipful Master and Wardens of the Glamorgan Lodge be authorised to sign the Petition.'

The Petition was then laid on the Tracing Board, and was duly signed by the Worshipful Master and the Senior and Junior Wardens. (The Warrant for the new Lodge was signed on 7 February 1934.)

That same evening, the following poem was presented to DJA Brown:

Province of South Wales - Eastern Division
Glamorgan Lodge No.36
TO
WBro D J A Brown, M.A.
Registrar of University College, Cardiff

Dear Brother! In Aquarius's Sign
The Sun was at your birth,
"TRUTH SEEKER" you will ever be,
and make for moral worth.
E'er balancing the Wrong by Right
E'er measuring false by true
You'll weigh fore'er in Truth's pure Scale
Whate'er you say or do.

True Education hath long claimed
The magic of your love
T'will be your great delight and pride
Wherever you may rove
To keep the budding youthful mind
E'er fashioned unto good
To all that manhood truly serves
And makes for Brotherhood.

May Truth, Relief, Fidelity
For ever be your guard
The "Square", "The Level", "Compass" too
O'er you keep watch and ward
Long may you live! And, when you leave,
To tread the heights above
GRAND LODGE above close tyle you safe
In God's pure, lasting love.

8 December 1933   (YSTWYTH)
                                      PM Loyal Cambrian Lodge No.110

The author of the poem could be R E James, who was WM of Loyal Cambrian Lodge, 1924-1925. 'YSTWYTH' is clearly a Bardic Name.

Previously, at a Meeting of the Founders held on 15 November 1933, it was decided that the Founder's Fee should be £5. 5. 0, to provide Collars at around £2 each and other necessary equipment; also that the Lodge Jewel should have a lighthouse incorporated in its design.

The draft By-laws were discussed at a Meeting on 19 January 1934. It was decided that the Regular Meeting of the Lodge shall be held on the fourth Wednesday in January, February, April and October, and on the second Saturday in May, June and December, and that held in June being the Annual Meeting at which the Installation of the Master-Elect shall take place; that the Initiation Fee shall be 15 guineas, Joining Fee shall be 3 guineas, and the Re-admission Fee be 1 guinea; the annual subscription, which is payable in advance on 1 June, shall be 2 guineas. The other By-laws are the ones applying to all Lodges, but as Universities Lodge is what is called a 'Closed Lodge', there is a preamble, which indicates who are eligible to become Members of the Lodge.   The complete By-Laws were duly adopted at the First Regular Meeting held on 12 May, 1934, confirmed at the Regular Meeting held on 6 June, 1934 and approved on 7 July, 1934 by the Provincial Grand Master and the Most Worshipful Grand Master.

The Consecration of the Lodge was performed at the Masonic Temple, Cardiff, on Monday, 30 April 1934 by RWBro Sir Charles L D Venables Llewelyn, Bart, ProvGM, assisted by his Provincial Officers.

The Installation of WBro D J A Brown, WM Designate, was performed by WBro Edgar J Rutter, DepProvGM. The Consecrating Officers were made Honorary Members of the Lodge, as is the usual custom, and each presented with a Founder's Jewel. (At that time the cost of the Jewel was £6). The Ceremonies were followed by a 'Consecration & Installation' Dinner. The menu consisted of hors d'oeuvres, thick ox-tail soup, fillets of sole, roast chicken with vegetables, peach melba, and coffee; the charge being 7/ 6d (37½p).

Sadly, just over three years later, on Monday, 13 September 1937, WBro D J A Brown died after a short illness. He was 66 years of age and had been retired for just twelve months.

The first Regular Meeting of the Lodge was held on 12 May 1934, when two members of the Medical Profession, M D Arwyn and Ernest H Evans, sons of Bro David Evans, JW, were Initiated. At the same Meeting, four Joining Members were admitted. One of these was Bro L J D Richardson, who had been very active in the preliminary Meetings of the Founders, and wished to be a Founder, but was precluded from being so, as he was not registered under the English Constitution, being a Member of a Lodge in Dublin. As he was Head of the Department of Latin, he was asked to produce a Motto in Latin, bearing in mind that a lighthouse had already been adopted in the design for the Lodge Jewel. He produced '*Una Lux Consociat*' which, to quote his own words, means '*The one light brings us together in Comradeship*'.

The Lodge suffered a severe loss on 10 January 1939 with the sudden passing of WBro W Ewart Lewis, WM. At the time, the Lodge had only a small number of Worshipful Brethren and many of the Founding Past Masters had either died or resigned. WBro Edgar J Rutter, who was always kindly disposed to the Lodge, performed the Ceremonies for the remainder of the year.

In May 1942, WBro Sydney Thomas, PM St David's Lodge No.2226, Rhymney, Province of Monmouthshire, took over as Treasurer. He found that the accounts were in a somewhat 'mixed state', corrections were necessary and there were some outstanding charges. He introduced a more professional method of 'book-keeping'. A crisis in Lodge affairs was averted by the tactful handling of the matter by WBro Garforth Mortimer, WM. At the time, the Board of Trade informed Grand Lodge that the manufacture of Jewels was to be suspended, as all metal, now in short supply, was required for the War effort. The Treasurer then laid aside the sum of £10 each year for the purchase of Past Master Jewels, when they next became available, which wasn't until 1951 The Lodge finances were now in such a condition, that £100 was Invested in the Cardiff Masonic Hall Company in 1945, and £100 was donated to the Royal Masonic Institution for Girls. WBro Sydney Thomas resigned as Treasurer in 1957, after 15 years of outstanding service.

Before the War, it had been the Lodge's original intention for Lodge Meetings to take place in turn at Cardiff, Aberystwyth, Bangor and Swansea, the locations of the four constituent Colleges of the University of Wales. This arrangement was never implemented.

In May 1948, the Lodge received a Deputation of Brethren connected with the Ministry of Works, who were Petitioners for a new Lodge to be named 'Lodge of Endurance' No.6729. The Warrant for this Lodge was signed two months later, on 28 July 1948.

A similar Deputation was received in December 1953. This Petition was signed by WBro G G Hammett, WM; Bro T J Salmon, SW and Bro Wyndham Richards, JW and resulted in the formation of Shir Gâr Lodge No.7339. The WM Designate was WBro David Evan James Davies, Secretary of Universities Lodge; the SW and JW Designate were the Past Masters WBro Gwilym Emrys Harries and David Owen Jones. Shir Gâr Lodge was Warranted on 3 March 1954, but sadly decided to surrender its Warrant and was Erased in September 2005.

Yet another Deputation was received in November 1954, resulting in the formation of the third Daughter Lodge, Llanilltud Fawr Lodge No.8644, Porthcawl, Warranted on 12 February 1955. This Lodge was formed primarily for Brethren in the Education Profession, and so it was most appropriate that Universities Lodge should be the Sponsoring Lodge. One of the Petitioners was Past Master, WBro David E Thomas, CBE.

In 1974, John Taylor was Initiated in the Lodge and he was Installed as Master in 1986. A Founder Member of Sir Francis Drake Lodge No.9008, he became the second Master in 1983. In 1988, he was appointed Senior Provincial Grand Deacon and became the first Provincial Grand Almoner in 1992. He served for many years as Assistant Secretary of the Provincial Masonic Benevolent Fund. Exalted in Edgar Rutter Chapter No.7196 in 1979, he was First Principal in 1989. In Provincial Grand Chapter, he was appointed ProvAGDC in 1992, Scribe E in 1993, when he was also the Consecrating Officer of Adare Chapter No.9247. In 1998, he was Invested Assistant Provincial Grand Master, but one year later he relinquished the Office on becoming Most Excellent Grand Superintendent of the Province, an Office he held until 2009. In Grand Lodge, he was appointed PAGDC (1994), PSGD (1999) and PDepGSwdB (2000). He is now VWBro John Taylor, having been promoted to PGSwdB in 2004.

The Lodge Banner was Dedicated on 25 April 1980. The Ceremony was presided over by WBro Harold Wilson, PSGD, AProvGM, assisted by WBro L G J Hamber, PAGDC, as SW; WBro Haydn Lloyd as JW; WBro Rev Canon T K Brunsden, PAGChap, Chaplain; WBro A Whitehurst, Pursuivant and WBro Frank Newbury, PAGDC, Director of Ceremonies. The Banner was paraded around the Temple by WBro Ronald E Lindsay, WM, escorted by his Officers.

The Banner had been made by Betty Harris, the wife of the then Lodge Secretary, WBro Ken Gwyther-Harris, from drawings made by their daughter. The Banner had been presented to the Lodge by the Secretary, on condition that a donation was made to Masonic Charities. During the Banner Dedication Ceremony, the Brethren received a lecture entitled 'The Interior of a Mason's Lodge; its History and Representation' delivered by Ken Gwyther-Harris.

At the beginning of 2005, Grand Lodge set up 'The Universities Scheme Group', which set as its objective *'To establish and/ or enhance arrangements and opportunities for undergraduates and other university members to enjoy and join Freemasonry'*. A discussion document was prepared in 2008, which was subsequently considered by the Lodge Committee. Later, Lodge Members were approached and it was finally decided that the Lodge should join the scheme. On Saturday, 30 May 2009, UGLE held a Universities Scheme Conference and General Meeting at Freemasons' Hall, Manchester, which was attended by WBro Gareth Andrews, WM, prior to Universities Lodge undertaking to Initiate its first undergraduate under the scheme.

This was Mr Eugen Chirovici, a student reading Economics at Cardiff University, the son of the Grand Master of Romania, MWBro Eugen Chirovici. He was Initiated on 23 October 2009 by WBro John Phillips, WM, with important contributions from distinguished visitors, including RWBro David Williamson, AGM, who delivered a flawless rendition of the First Degree charge. This followed a moving moment when the MW Grand Master of Romania, who had travelled to Cardiff to witness his son's Initiation, Invested him with the Distinguishing Badge of an Entered Apprentice Freemason. RWBro Captain Sir Norman Lloyd-Edwards, ProvGM, and VWBro Andrew Gretton, DepProvGM, were present to welcome the distinguished Brethren from UGLE and Romania. MWBro Eugen Chirovici was accompanied by three very senior Brethren from the Grand Lodge of Romania. The Assistant Grand Master was escorted by WBro Nicholas G I Bosanquet, PDepGDC, the Liaison Officer for the Universities Scheme in Wales and the West, and RWBro David Williamson, who had originally met the Grand Master of Romania when visiting Romania shortly after UGLE's recognition of that Grand Lodge. It was on that occasion that the Grand Master had suggested that his son be Initiated under the English Constitution, and the Universities Scheme immediately came into its own, with Universities Lodge providing the ideal setting and opportunity to complete the plan. At the conclusion of the Ceremony, WBro Edward Lord, LGR, Chairman of the Universities Scheme, gave an excellent presentation on progress within the scheme to date to the 67 Brethren present.

Adapted from a text by WBro Sam Evans, PPrGW (WM 1947) and WBro Tom Evans, PPGD, WM 1958.
Compiled by WBro C B Pearce, PPrGSwdB, Secretary
and WBro Peter M Davies, ProvJGW, PM Glamorgan Lodge No.36.

Penllergaer Lodge No.5567

Warranted   :   7 August 1935

Consecrated   :   24 September 1935

Meeting at the Masonic Hall, Swansea.

A Petition for the formation of Penllergaer Lodge was Sponsored by Corinthian Lodge No.4917. Brethren from Indefatigable Lodge No.237, Talbot Lodge No.1323, Caradoc Lodge No.1573 and Beaufort Lodge No.3834, are also numbered among the 40 Founder Members. The Warrant of the Lodge was signed on 7 August 1935, and the Consecration Ceremony took place at The Masonic Hall, St Helen's Road, Swansea, on 24 September 1935, bringing the total number of Swansea Craft Lodges to ten.

The Lodge derives its name from the estate of Sir Charles Leyshon Dillwyn Venables Llewelyn, who was at that time Provincial Grand Master of the Province of South Wales Eastern Division. The Ceremony of Consecration was carried out by the ProvGM, who also Installed WBro Edgar John Rutter, PGD, DepProvGM, as the first Master of Penllergaer Lodge.

Among the distinguished Founder Members was Sir William J Firth, a prominent Industrialist and Chairman of the Richard Thomas & Co. Steel Company, who was instrumental in the rescue of the threatened steel works at Ebbw Vale in the early 1930s. He generously donated the Banner, which was presented to the Lodge at the first Regular Meeting in November 1935. The motif of the Banner is derived from the armorial escutcheon of Sir Charles L D V Llewelyn and is in the form of a quartered shield. The first and fourth quarters are taken from the Arms of the Llewelyn family, being: argent, goutte de poix, three chevronels gules, in base a lamb passant proper. The second and third quarters, belonging to the Dillwyn Family, are: gules on a chevron nebulee argent, five trefoils slipped of the first. On an escutcheon of pretence are hands joined in prayer. The Motto: *'Ofna Gywilydd'*, is a Welsh translation of the Latin inscription on the original escutcheon and is translated as *'Fear Shame'*. The design of the escutcheon represents the conjoint interests of agriculture and industry, which characterised the Swansea area from the 18th century.

Many of the Founder Members were generous in their support. The Master's Apron was donated by Bro Moses Thomas; the three Gavels by Bro J Ackland; the Square and Compasses by Bro Mansel Glasbrook and the Poingard by Bro Sydney Williams. Probably the most generous gift was the stained glass window, now in the reception area of the Swansea Masonic Hall, which is a depiction of the Lodge Crest. The Donor was WBro John Gibson, PGSD, and the window was Dedicated at a Ceremony held on 8 January 1938, by WBro Iles Sampson, ProvGChap.

The first two Joining Members of the Lodge were Herbert E Davies, LLB, and Rhodri Harris. WBro Rhodri Harris, PPrGW, was

Installed WM in 1946. He first became a Grand Officer in 1961 with the Rank of PAGReg and was promoted in 1975 to PJGD. In 1946, he donated the Past Masters' Board to the Lodge.

The Membership in the early years was drawn from the ranks of professional and business men with Doctors, Lawyers and Managers comprising the majority, but from the 1950s, a blurring of the class divisions and increasing prosperity permitted a wider diversity of occupations. Further, an improvement in transport arrangements saw recruitment from a wider area. Both of these factors combined to enrich the perspective of the Lodge and to increase the numbers. By 1970, Penllergaer Lodge had become the largest progressive Lodge in Swansea, a status which it continues to hold.

The upheaval of WWII receives only a sparse mention in the Minutes, but the May Meeting in 1945 coincided with the official celebrations marking victory in Europe. This, being the second Tuesday of the month, the Lodge met as normal to perform a Second Degree Ceremony with two Candidates. However, Bro Secretary was sufficiently moved to record : '*A day destined to become memorable in the history of the world and of mankind. A day officially designated VE Day, when the forces of Germany capitulated and Europe was liberated from its bondage by the freedom loving nations*'. The loyalty of the Membership was demonstrated by the turn out, only two Officers were absent and in total 25 Brethren and 11 visitors were present. The Ceremony was a quick one. The Lodge opened at 6.30 pm and closed at 7.30 pm, and included a Ballot for 4 Candidates, one of whom was rejected.

The Golden Jubilee of the Lodge was celebrated at an extraordinary Lodge Meeting in September 1985, presided over by WBro Geoffrey Ashe, DepProvGM. Among the honoured guests that evening was WBro Judge John Rutter, the son of WBro Edgar Rutter, Founder Member and first Master of the Lodge.

In 1989, a group of Lodge ladies formed 'Merched y Felin', which held monthly meetings coinciding with Regular Lodge Meetings, and organised lectures and social events of a wide and various character. Sadly, after twenty very successful years, time took its toll of the membership and it was wound up in May 2010. During this time and, due in no small measure to the energetic leadership of Mrs Nansi Kent, MBE, the group raised more than £15,000, which was donated to local Charities.

The original Banner succumbed to the ravages of time and, by 1997, it was agreed that a new Banner should be commissioned as an exact copy. There was no record of the maker of the first Banner but, fortunately, the original drawings, by Miss Eunice N Hall, of Pontardulais, were discovered in the Lodge archives. South Wales Regalia, of Swansea, produced a replica Banner, which was Dedicated by WBro J Stuart Peters, DepProvGM, on Tuesday, 9 June 1998. Coincidentally, this occasion was the precise 59th Anniversary of the Emergency Meeting in 1939, when RWBro Reginald Pendrill St John Charles presided. It was the first and only occasion that a Provincial Grand Lodge Meeting had been held under the Banner of Penllergaer Lodge. However, in February 2010, Penllergaer Lodge was selected to host the Meeting of Provincial Grand Lodge at which RWBro Captain Sir Norman Lloyd-Edwards, ProvGM, Invested WBro Roy Woodward as APGM, an occasion fraught by extreme weather conditions.

Two Ruling Masters have been called to the Grand Lodge Above during their year in Office. Undoubtedly, the most poignant was the demise of WBro Tom Phillips, who was Installed in 1993. Such was WBro Tom's popularity that, at his Installation, the Temple was crowded with no less than 178 Brethren. WBro Ken Adams-Morgan, AProvGM, was the Executive Officer. He expressed his delight with the proceedings, and made certain that an account of the Installation was published in the Provincial Magazine, 'The Guildford Gazette'. However, what promised to be a very successful year was not to be. As was customary at that time, WBro Tom accompanied the Secretary, WBro Bernard Davies, in setting out the Temple for the first Ceremony of the new session. Before leaving, they both signed the Lodge Register. During the afternoon, WBro Tom suffered a severe heart

Penllergare House, Llangyfelach - Built by John Dillwyn Llewelyn, circa 1836

attack and passed away. WBro Tom's commitment to the Lodge was shared fully by his wife Jean, and she insisted that the Ladies' Festival for that year should continue as planned. Escorted by their son, who was also a Brother, she presided over a very successful evening, and that is exactly what WBro Tom would have wanted.

The senior Past Master of the Lodge is WBro Leonard I Trott. Initiated in Penllergaer Lodge on 12 June 1956, he is a Masonic Veteran, with 55 years of service to the Craft. Installed as WM of the Lodge in 1984, he was appointed PPrGReg in 1960 and promoted to ProvJGW in 1993. He first became a Grand Officer in 1995, with the Rank of PAGDC, and in 2011, he was promoted to PJGD. Dr Leonard Trott is also a Joining Member of Old Goreans Lodge No. 7193 and was Installed as WM of that Lodge in 1987.

The Lodge has earned a reputation for the quality of artistes at social functions. It was not uncommon for applications for tickets to be rejected due to the limitations of the Connaught Hall. The success of these functions has enabled the Lodge to make substantial contributions to non-Masonic charities as well as fully supporting the several Masonic Charity Festivals. These local charities have benefited by £2000 each year for the last ten years and the Lodge is committed to continuing this level of support.

Compiled by WBro D Elwyn Davies, PPrJGD

Reginald Pendrill St John Charles
1879 ~ 1967

Provincial Grand Master of South Wales Eastern Division
1938 ~ 1966

Reginald Pendrill St John Charles was born in March 1879, the son of Henry Pendrill Charles, DepProvGM of South Wales Eastern Division, 1915-1925, and Elizabeth Wearne Kempthorne, daughter of James Kempthorne, Attorney-at-law, Neath. His father was a Solicitor, whom he followed into the legal profession, and by 1901, at the age of 22, he was an Articled Clerk, lodging at 40 Burlington Road, Paddington, London. After qualifying as a Solicitor, he eventually succeeded his father by becoming Registrar of the Neath County Court. During the First World War, he served as a Lieutenant with the Royal Artillery.

He married Edith Ermyntrude Sutton on 16 April 1914, daughter of Herbert Selwood Sutton of Glynleiros, Neath. Messrs Thomas S Sutton and Sons where the proprietors of a tin smelting business at the Millands Works, Gas Works Road, Neath, and the Pontycaron Works, Skewen. R P St John Charles was Initiated into Cambrian Lodge No.364, Neath, in May 1915. He became a Joining Member of Venables Llewelyn Lodge, No.3756, at the first Regular Meeting of the Lodge on Saturday, 1 July 1916. His father had been Installed the first WM of that Lodge the previous month, on Saturday, 3 June 1916, and he in turn became WM of the Lodge in 1922 and again in 1929.

When Charles Venables Llewelyn resigned as Provincial Grand Master in 1938, the MW HRH Arthur, Duke of Connaught and Strathearn, Grand Master, appointed Reginald Pendrill St John Charles, PAGReg as his successor, the Patent of Appointment being signed on 2 November 1938. On 15 November, the appointment was announced to the Brethren of Cambrian Lodge, who decided that the sincere congratulations of the Lodge should be conveyed personally to the new Provincial Grand Master by the WM, WBro A J Lawson Taylor. At the time, RP St John Charles was the Senior Warden of Cambrian Lodge.

On Thursday, 2 February 1939, WBro Charles was Installed as ProvGM at Cardiff, by the MWBro, the Pro Grand Master, the Rt Hon the Earl of Harewood, KG. Provincial Grand Lodge was opened at 2.30 pm and an account of the

Reginald Pendrill St John Charles

365

arrangements for the day was given in the 'Cardiff Times' on Saturday, 4 February as follows:

Earl of Harewood

Visits Cardiff

'In his capacity of Most Worshipful Pro Grand Master of English Freemasonry, the Right Hon. The Earl of Harewood visited Cardiff on Thursday to install Mr. Reginald Pendrill St. John Charles of Porthcawl into the office of Provincial Grand Master of South Wales (Eastern Division) in succession to Sir Charles Venables-Llewelyn, Bart., who resigned the office in July of last year after 25 years service.

The Earl arrived in Cardiff from London before noon and was accompanied by prominent officers of the Grand Lodge of England, including the Deputy Grand Master (General Sir Francis Davies), The Senior Grand Warden (the Right Hon. Viscount de Vesci), the Grand Chaplain (the Rev. the Right Hon. Lord Blythswood), the Grand Secretary (Mr. Sydney A. White), the Grand Directors of Ceremonies (Messrs. Philip Bull and Cecil Cumberlege), and the Grand Tyler (Major Boyd, M.C.)

They were met at the station by Mr. Edgar Rutter, who has acted as deputy to Sir Venables-Llewelyn since 1931, and he conducted the party to the City-hall, where they were received by the Lord Mayor and Lady Mayoress (Alderman and Mrs. W. G. Howell).

Following the reception in the Lord Mayor's Parlour, nearly 500 Brethren were entertained to luncheon in the City-hall.

The Installation Ceremony, attended by 1,800 Brethren took place at the Wood-street Congregational Church, after which the London guests were entertained by the Lord Mayor to tea.'

The Wood Street Congregational Church had been the venue for the Installation of Lord Llangattock as Provincial Grand Master on 8 September 1894. The building was demolished in the late 1960s and the present Southgate House was built on the site in 1973.

On 28 March 1939, the new ProvGM was Installed Master of Cambrian Lodge. Four weeks later, on Saturday, 29 April, he officiated at the Consecration of Preswylfa Lodge No.5792, Cardiff. This was to be the first of 52 Lodges, Consecrated during his 28 years as ProvGM. Unfortunately, illness prevented him from being present at the Consecration of Harlequins Lodge No.5793 a fortnight later on 15 May, and the DepProvGM, Edgar J Rutter, officiated in his stead. The usual format for these Ceremonies was for the ProvGM to conduct the Consecration part of the proceedings, followed by the DepProvGM who performed the Installation of the Primus Master.

By the end of 1944, the Province consisted of 64 Lodges and, on 15 May 1945 the appointment of WBro Charles Presgrave Palmer, PAGDC, PM Cambrian Lodge and Hendre Lodge No.3250, as the first Assistant Provincial Grand Master of the Province, was announced. The year 1945 had commenced with the Consecration of two Lodges, Observer Lodge No.6015 on 11 January and Lodge of Unity No.6030 the following day, both Ceremonies being conducted by the ProvGM. Four more Lodges were Consecrated during that year and, in 1946, a further six Lodges were added to the Province. The ProvGM officiated at all of them.

In February 1947, Indefatigable Lodge No.237 agreed to Sponsor a new Lodge in Swansea, to be called 'R P St John Charles Lodge', in honour of the ProvGM. Warrant No.6466 for this Lodge was signed on 5 March 1947 and the Lodge was Consecrated by the ProvGM on Monday, 9 June 1947. R P St John Charles took a very keen interest in his new Lodge, and Brethren were invited to visit him and Mrs Charles at their home in Porthcawl. These visits developed into annual events eagerly anticipated by those privileged to attend. It also became customary for the ProvGM to record a message for the Lodge, to be played at a future meeting. A tape-recorder was used for this purpose, but unfortunately these recordings have been lost.

During 1948, a further ten Lodges were Consecrated, a total for one year which had never been equalled, even under the prolific expansion of the Province under Lord Swansea. Further, the ProvGM conducted all the Ceremonies. Of the ten Consecrations, three were held in April (Cambrensis Lodge No.6608; Ionic Lodge No.6626 and Lodge of St Ilan No.6624, on 5, 24, and 30 April respectively) and four in October (Industria Cambrensis Lodge No.6700, Craig Yr Hesg Lodge No.6724, Penybont Lodge No.6743 and Lodge of Endurance No.6729, on 4, 18, 22 and 30 October respectively).

The expansion of the Province continued at a gentler pace for the remainder of R P St John Charles's tenure as Provincial Grand Master. By the end of 1952, the Province consisted of 97 Lodges and so in 1953 two Assistant Provincial Grand Masters were appointed. One was Edgar William Lewis, an Initiate of Afan Lodge No.833, who had been WM of Venables Llewelyn Lodge in 1921, and where he had had a great influence on the early Masonic career of the ProvGM. The other was Henry Francis Stockwell, who had been Initiated in Penarth Lodge No.4113 on 14 June 1921. Both Brethren, like the ProvGM, were Past Masters of Hendre Lodge No.3250. (The ProvGM was WM in 1940; E W Lewis in 1942 and H F Stockwell in 1951.)

R P St John Charles celebrated his Golden Jubilee in Freemasonry on 18 May 1965 by attending, most appropriately, his Mother Lodge, Cambrian Lodge, Neath, where he witnessed a Double Initiation Ceremony.

On Monday, 27 September 1965, he Dedicated the new Temple in Porthcawl, assisted by his Deputy, Edgar J Rutter. This was to be almost his last official engagement. Finally, on 9 November 1965, he performed his last Consecration Ceremony, that of Lodge of Sker No.8024, which brought the number of Lodges in the Province to a total of 108. During his 28 years in charge, he had almost doubled the size of the Province.

Then, on 10 December 1965, the Brethren were informed that because of advancing years and declining health, RWBro Reginald Pendrill St John Charles was resigning from the positions of ProvGM of the Craft and Grand Superintendent of the Royal Arch (he had been appointed to the latter Office in 1951). Edgar J Rutter was then appointed 'Deputy Provincial Grand Master-in-charge'. The appointment of the Rt Hon the Lord Swansea, SGW, as the new Provincial Grand Master, was announced in March 1966.

Exactly two years later, on 11 December 1967, the Provincial Grand Secretary wrote informing the Lodges of the death of RWBro R P St John Charles, Past Provincial Grand Master, and instructed that '*Masonic Mourning was to be observed until 31 March 1968, with the exception of Installations, which are Festival occasions.*'

The announcement of his death, in his 89th year, appeared in the Western Mail on 11 December:

CHARLES – *on December 9, 1967, in Cheltenham, Reginald Pendrill St John, J.P. of 10 West Drive, Porthcawl, Glam. Dearly loved father of Tim. Cremation private. No letters please.*
No obituary was published in that newspaper.

Compiled by WBro Peter M Davies, ProvJGW.

Cartref Lodge
No.5772

Warranted : 7 December 1938

Consecrated : 18 January 1939

Meeting at the Masonic Hall, Cardiff.

The Lodge was formed by professional people working in and around Cardiff, many of whom were in the Insurance Business, operating out of London. There were fifteen Founder Members; among them, WBro Lt Colonel George John Morley Peel, MBE, TD, WM Designate; Bro Lewis Christmas Simons, SW Designate; and Bro Robert Keeling Williams, JW Designate.

WBro Lt Col G J Morley Peel was Initiated in Queen Mary's Lodge No.3327, London in 1921, and became Master of the Lodge in 1940. He was a Founder Member of Graveney Lodge No.5285, Staines, Middlesex, in 1931 and was Installed Master in 1935. In 1936, he joined Assurance Lodge No.5160, London, and became Master of this Lodge in 1948. He was also a Member of the prestigious Jubilee Masters Lodge No.2712, London. (RWBro Edgar J Rutter, DepProvGM, joined Jubilee Masters Lodge in 1958 and was Master of the Lodge in 1967.) In 1946, WBro Morley Peel was appointed Provincial Grand Sword Bearer and, in 1949, he was appointed Deputy Grand Sword Bearer of the United Grand Lodge of England.

The Founders decided that as many of them were accustomed to Emulation Working, they would adopt Emulation for the Lodge Ritual. They were assisted in conveying this Ritual to the new Lodge by Brethren from Prince Llewellyn Lodge No.2570, which was the Sponsoring lodge. It was also decided that the new Lodge would be named 'Cartref', the Welsh for 'Home', the Lodge thus becoming a home for Freemasons residing in the Principality.

The Lodge being formed at the onset of the Second World War and with the inevitable forthcoming involvement of many Brethren in active service, it was deemed appropriate to include a representation of the Welsh National War Memorial in the design of the Lodge Insignia. The Memorial, situated in Alexandra Gardens, Cathays Park, Cardiff, was designed by Sir Ninian Comper and unveiled in June 1928 by the Prince of Wales. It commemorates the servicemen who died during the First World War. In 1949, a plaque was added to commemorate those who died during the Second World War.

The Memorial takes the form of a circular colonnade surrounding a sunken court. At the centre of the court is a group of bronze sculptures by Alfred Bertram Pegram, arranged around a stone pylon. Around the base, stand three figures, a soldier, a sailor and an airman, holding wreaths aloft; they represent the three services. On the top is a bronze nude figure of the winged Archangel Michael, representing victory.

Cartref Lodge was Consecrated on Wednesday, 18 January 1939 at the Masonic Temple, Cardiff, by WBro Edgar John Rutter, PGD, DepProvGM, and his team of Provincial Officers. Among the 123 Brethren attending the Ceremony was WBro Reginald Pendrill St John Charles, PGReg, ProvGM Designate, who at the conclusion of the Consecration Ceremony, presented Lt Colonel George John Morley Peel, WM Designate, for the benefit of Installation. The Installation Ceremony was conducted by WBro H

G Lewis, WM, and Officers of Prince Llewellyn Lodge. The newly Installed Master was addressed by WBro Edgar J Rutter, who then presented the Lodge with an inscribed copy of the Volume of the Sacred Law, on which WBro Morley Peel had taken his Obligation. WBro Edgar J Rutter also presented the WM with the Lodge Warrant, Book of Constitutions and a leather case for the preservation of the Warrant. Bro Lewis Christmas Simons was Invested as SW and Bro Robert Keeling Williams as JW. The Chaplain, Bro H J Powell, was Invested the following month, on 23 February 1939. It was then proposed by the WM that the Consecrating team be made Honorary Members, and this was unanimously approved by the Members. The charity collection realised the grand amount of £5.10s.0d, which was donated to the Samaritan Fund for the Royal Masonic Hospital.

Lodge Meetings are held on the fourth Thursday in the months of January, February, March, April, October and November. The Installation Meeting is held in February. WBro G J Morley Peel was proclaimed Master for a second year by WBro Edgar J Rutter at the Installation Meeting on 22 February 1940. At that Meeting, the DepProvGM was Elected a Joining Member of the Lodge and the WM Invested him as his IPM. It was not unusual for Brethren to either remain in the Chair for a successive year or to be Installed Master again a few years later. WBro Leonard Charles Burt, PPrJGW, is the only Brother, thus far, to have been WM of the Lodge three times.

A goodly number of Brethren of the Lodge served their country during WWII, including 5 in the Army, 3 in the Royal Navy and 2 in the Royal Air Force. Because they were often called at short notice, it was sometimes necessary to request Emergency Meetings to accommodate them. They were often proposed, Balloted and Initiated at the same Meeting, under Rule 160, Book of Constitutions.

The WM was happy to report in October 1946 that no Lodge Members were lost, disabled or killed in consequence of the War. The only inconvenience suffered by the Lodge was due to the enemy night air raids, which prompted a change of Regular Lodge Meetings from Thursday evenings to Saturday afternoons.

On 30 August 1947, the ProvGM decreed the following: *'the Lodge dress code for Members at Meetings should be morning or dark lounge suits with white collars and black ties and that he is ever mindful of clothes rationing, purchase tax and other matters.'* The first mention of 'white gloves' appears on the Summons for February 1952. This was for the Installation Meeting of WBro Frederick Edward Constant, who had been Initiated on 28 March 1946. It is interesting to note that the annual subscription at the time was 5 shillings (25 pence) and that the Lodge set aside the princely sum of £12 for the hire of the small Temple for the Lodge of Instruction.

On 24 March 1977, Item No. 5 on the Lodge Business was to receive a Deputation of Petitioners, for the formation of a Royal Arch Chapter to be attached to Cartref Lodge, and to take any necessary action. The Brethren agreed to support the Petition and it was signed by WBro G Board, IPM and Bros P L Botfield, SW, and W H Lawrence, JW. The Warrant for Cartref Chapter No.5772 was granted on 28 April 1977.

Bro Paul Leonard Botfield, SW, was Initiated into Cartref Lodge in March 1970 and was Installed as Worshipful Master on 23 February 1978. He is a Founder Member of Tudor Lodge No.8886, which was Consecrated on 2 July 1979 and was Installed as Master in September 1994. In the Province, he was appointed Provincial Junior Grand Deacon in 1984 and promoted to PPrJGW in 1990. He first became a Grand Officer in 1997 with the Rank of PGStB and was promoted to PAGDC in 2006. In the Province of South Wales and Monmouthshire, he is currently Provincial Grand Supreme Ruler of the Order of the Secret Monitor and Provincial Grand Summus of the Ancient and Masonic Order of the Scarlet Cord, which are the equivalent of Provincial Grand Master in the Craft. WBro Paul Botfield is also a member of the Committee of Management of the Masonic Benevolent Fund (Eastern Division of South Wales).

Sir Francis Drake Lodge No.9008 is Cartref Lodge's only Daughter Lodge. The Lodge's Warrant was signed on 10 June 1981.

The Lodge Banner, bearing the Lodge Insignia design of the Welsh National War Memorial, was Dedicated, by Dispensation, on Saturday, 24 June 1995. The Motto on the Banner is: *'A Elli Gwna'*, which when translated means *'Those who can, do'*. The Dedicating Officer was WBro David L Protheroe, PSGD, AProvGM.

Apart from the Emulation Ritual, a custom of Cartref Lodge, regularly commented upon, is the Firing of all Toasts, including the Loyal Toast, at the Festive Board. This frequently results in mayhem for the visitors.

Compiled by WBro C L Evans, PPrGSwdB.

Preswylfa Lodge No. 5792

Warranted : 2 March 1939

Consecrated : 29 April 1939

Meeting at theMasonic Hall, Cardiff

In 1920, Llangattock Lodge No.2547 had 285 Members, many of whom would never be able to occupy the Chair of King Solomon. It was this concern that prompted the Worshipful Master and Past Masters to call for the Founding of a new Lodge. The new Lodge was named Gwalia Lodge No.4213. By 1936, the average Membership of Gwalia Lodge exceeded 250 and it took a Brother some 18-20 years to reach the Master's Chair. Consequently, in 1938, the Brethren of Gwalia Lodge decided to Sponsor a Petition for a new Lodge - Preswylfa Lodge No.5792.

The fifteen Founder Members were from six Lodges in the Province, two of whom were Past Masters. The nucleus of the new Lodge was the nine Brethen of Gwalia Lodge No.4213, and it was agreed that 'Gwalia Working' would form the basis of the Preswylfa Ritual.

Of the other Founder Members, two came from Bute Lodge No.960, one from Tennant Lodge No.1992, one from Amethyst Lodge No.4026, one from Afan Lodge No.833, and one from Loyal Commercial Lodge No.2720. More will be said of these Brethen later, but it is first necessary to say a few words on the matters leading up to the Consecration of the Lodge.

No one can recall why the name 'Preswylfa' was chosen, but it is of course possible that a Welsh name was selected because both the Mother Lodge, 'Gwalia Lodge' and the Grandmother Lodge, Llangattock Lodge also had Welsh names. The name translated means 'Home', 'Abode'; or 'Dwelling Place', which is a most appropriate choice for a Masonic Lodge. It is sometimes translated as 'Spiritual Home', but,this is not a strict translation of the word.

Information exists, however, regarding the design of the Lodge Crest, which appears on the Lodge Banner, on the Founders' and Past Masters' Jewels, and on the Lodge Summons. Attached to the Minutes of the Second Regular Lodge Meeting, dated Friday, 1 September 1939, is a letter from the first Lord Davies of Llandinam, who for many years had been actively associated with the League of Nations. In 1939, he commissioned the building of the Temple of Peace in Cathays Park, Cardiff. Part of his letter reads: *'I was pleased to hear that your Installation went successfully and that the 'Device' of the Temple of Peace has been adopted for the Jewel and Banner of the Lodge.'* This 'Device', as shown on the Lodge Banner, consists of four pillars, representing the four large pillars, which are the main feature of the Temple of Peace, Cardiff. The Founder Members, being children of their time could well have wished to symbolically link the ideals of the Temple of Peace to their own new Lodge, though a Masonic Temple only has two pillars. The Temple of Peace in Cardiff was built from marble donated by the various Member countries of the League of Nations and one feels that the Founder Members knew of this and associated it with the worldwide connections of Freemasonry. The Lodge Crest was completed by adding the Lodge name 'Preswylfa' above the four pillars, and above that again, the Dove of Peace with an olive branch in its beak. Below the pillars is the word 'Tangnefedd', which translated means 'Peace of Mind' or 'Serenity of Spirit'. The Lodge honoured Lord Davies for his kindness by making him an Honorary Founder Member on 6 October 1939. It is of interest to note that he was also a Member of Prince Llewellyn Lodge No.2570, St Mildred Lodge No.5078 and Dinam Lodge No.4521.

The Lodge was Consecrated on Saturday, 29 April 1939, the Ceremony being performed by the RWBro R P St John Charles, PAGReg, ProvGM, at the Masonic Temple, Cardiff. He was ably assisted by: WBro T L Jenkins, ProvSGW; WBro E Claude Jones, ProvJGW; Bro the Rev L C Simmonds, ProvGChap; WBro George Whittingham, ProvGSec; and WBro J Brindley Jenkins, ProvGDC.

Following the Consecration Ceremony, WBro A C J White, PPGD, was Installed as the first WM by VWBro Edgar J Rutter, PGD, DepProvGM. The Address to the Master was delivered by RWBro R H B Parnall, PGD, ProvGM of Monmouthsire. All the Consecrating Officers, together with the Deputy Provincial Grand Master, were made Honorary Members of the Lodge.

Of the fifteen Founder Members who took Office that evening, all but two eventually became Worshipful Masters of the Lodge. The first Worshipful Master was WBro A C J White, PPGD, a Paint and Glass Merchant, who had been WM of Gwalia Lodge No.4213 in 1932. The first Senior Warden was Bro George Bull, PPGOrg, Professor of Music. A Member of Tennant Lodge No.1992, he had been Initiated into Loyal Commercial Lodge No.2720 at the end of the 19th century. The first Junior Warden was WBro Sydney Hearn, a Corn Merchant, who had been WM of Gwalia Lodge in 1936. The following were also appointed to Office that evening: Treasurer: Bro W H Davies, Principal of a Commercial School, Member of Amethyst Lodge No.4026; Secretary: Bro C.E. Howells, Insurance Manager, Member of Gwalia Lodge; DC: Bro A McTaggart-Short, Company Director, Member of Bute Lodge No.960. No appointments were made for the Offices of Chaplain, ADC, Almoner, Organist, Assistant Secretary, Tyler, and of course IPM; these Offices were filled over the years, as the necessity arose.

It is unfortunate that the register of those attending the Consecration is no longer available. The first cash Book shows, inter alia, that a Founder Member's fee was 10 guineas (£10.50), and that the total monies received for the Consecration Supper amounted to £37. 8. 0d (£37.40). From records available, it would seem that in 1939, the average cost of a meal for a Regular Lodge Meetings was 3/- (15p) and the cost of the Consecration dinner was approximately 4/3d (21p). The Supper consisted of: brown Windsor soup, fillet of sole mornay, roast Surrey chicken and bacon, new potatoes and peas, fruit salad and ice-cream, and coffee. This was a repast of grand proportions, and chicken, not being battery produced, was expensive. Approximately 200 Brethen were present that night. The evening's Toast list was similar to that currently used, except that the Loyal Toast was to 'The King and the Craft'.

The original Lodge By-laws, which were approved on 6 February 1940, contained amongst other things: Initiation Fee - 20 gns (£21.00); Joining Fee - 6 gns, (£6-30); and annual subscription - 3 gns, (£3.15), inclusive of meals for all Regular Lodge Meetings.

At the first Regular Lodge Meeting, held on 2 May 1939, the first Initiates were two blood brothers, Arthur Stephen Scourfield and John Harries Scourfield. Eventualy, they were Installed as WM of the Lodge, Arthur Stephen in 1952 and John Harries in

1953.

During the war years, and for some years following, many Brethen who had joined HM Forces, were unable to attend Regular Lodge Meetings. Lodges of Emergency became necessary to enable such Brethen to complete their Three Degrees. No business, other than the particular Ceremony could be performed, and the Summons had to state clearly the reason for the Emergency Meeting, which required the approval of the Provincial Grand Master. WBro Reginald Parfit, the 22nd Master, was Initiated at a Lodge of Emergency, held on 6 March 1943. The Lodge summons stated: *To ballot for and, if elected, to Initiate as a matter of urgency Mr. Charles Reginald Parfit, a lieutenant in H.M. Forces proceeding overseas.'* There are still Lodge Members who came into Masonry at such Meetings. Indeed, the 50th Master, WBro Trevor Lawrence was Initiated, Passed and Raised at such Meetings of Emergency. The War seems to have claimed the life of only one Member, Bro L J Rodd , who died at sea. No mention is made of whether he was serving with the Royal or the Merchant Navy.

Scrutiny of the Lodge Minutes make very interesting reading. In 1942, the longest recorded Meeting was held, which consisted of a Lodge of Emergency to Pass a Brother, followed almost immediately by a Regular Lodge Meeting to Raise another. Business commenced at 6.15 pm and ended at 9.35 pm. The record for the Meeting with the greatest number of visitors was at the Installation of WBro D W Jenkins, the 5th Master, in September 1943, when 218 Brethen were present, by far the highest number ever to attend a Lodge Meeting. In 1950, the Installation Meeting had to be postponed, becaue Bro R E Lawrence, Master Elect had suffered a serious heart attack. A First Degree ceremony was performed instead. Bro Lawrence was Installed at the following Meeting in October but, unfortunately, his illness did not allow him to complete any of the Ceremonies during his year in Office. On 14 March 1952, there appeared a footnote on the Lodge Summons stating: *'The Worshipful Master requests, following a Grand Lodge recommendation, that white gloves be worn by all Brethen.'* Prior to that date, only Lodge Officers wore white gloves.

The first milestone was the Lodge's 21st Anniversary, when WBro Lionel J Mee was the Master. During his year in Office, the first fraternal visits between Preswylfa Lodge and Casnewydd Lodge No.6779, Newport, took place. These visits are now part of the annual Masonic Calendar of both Lodges.

On 14 February 1969, the Lodge was honoured with a visit from RWBro the Rt Hon the Lord Swansea, DL, ProvGM.

During a Pastmasters' Third Degree Ceremony in October 1974, WBro John Scourfield, who had then been acting as Junior Warden, suddenly collapsed and died. He passed away only a few minutes after he had given the prayer *'Endue them with such fortitude that in the hour of trial they fail not, but passing safely under Thy protection through the valley of the shadow of death they may finally arise from the tomb of transgression, to shine as the stars for ever more.'*

On the 8 April 1983, at a Lodge Committee Meeting, WBro H D Barnes, the 31st Master, suffered a fatal heart attack. His house had always been open to all aspiring young Masons. The help and encouragement he gave to younger Brethen was a tremendous asset, both to them and to the Lodge.

In 1980,the first Provincial Liaison Officers were appointed to assist individual Lodges. Preswylfa Lodge was particularly fortunate in its appointee, WBro Cuthbert Banham, MBE, PGStdB.

The Lodge Banner was Dedicated on 10 April 1987 by WBro Cuthbert L Summers, AProvGM, ably assisted by WBro L Jeans, PProvSGW; WBro P Gough, PProvJGW; WBro Rev E H Brown, ProvGChap; and WBro M Thomas, ProvGPurs. The imposing floor work was under the direction of WBro Cdr Roy K Hopkin, RN, ProvGDC.

The Lodge was fortunate to have as its first Senior Warden a very distinguished musician,WBro G Bull, PProvGOrg. This quite extraordinary man was originally Initiated into Loyal Commercial Lodge No.2720 on 10 May 1894. He must have been around 70 years of age when he became the second Master of Preswylfa Lodge in 1940. He was a Professor of Music and a Fellow o£ the Royal College of Organists. He was very quickly recognised by Province and given the Rank of PProvGOrg, many years before becoming a Worshipful Brother. He wrote the music for the opening hymn 'Hendre', named after the Past Masters' Lodge of the same name. This tune is virtually unique to Cardiff Lodges and is rarely, if ever, heard outside, although the words of course are very well known throughout Freemasonry. He was also the Organist for many other Lodges in the Province, and arranged

The Loving Cup, Decanters and Candlesticks laid out for the Ceremony

many of their musical services. The other musician to leave his mark on the music of the Lodge was WBro Wilf Goddard, who composed the words of the Visitor's Song, which is sung to the tune 'All through the Night'.

A Loving Cup Ceremony has been a feature of the Festive Board for many years. The Loving Cup, together with decanters, were presented to the Lodge by WBro A McTaggart-Short. He also wrote the words for the Ceremony, which is used to welcome the Initiates. This Ceremony is normally held in October, and only following a First Degree Ceremony. It symbolises the coming together of the new and old Members of the Lodge, i.e. the newest Initiate and the Founder Members, so that at each such Ceremony, a new link is added to the Preswylfa chain. The words engraved on the loving Cup are: *'Heddwch a Tangnefedd - Peace and Tranquillity'*. The Cup stands on a plinth, on which the names of all the Past Masters of the Lodge are engraved.

Preswylfa Lodge had one Daughter Lodge, Lodge of Unity No. 6030, Warranted on 6 December 1944. Sadly, this Lodge was Erased from the Register of UGLE on 11 March 2009.

Compiled by WBro Christopher Ribton, PPrJGD.

WBro Granville S Angell, MEd, BSc, BA, whose topic was 'The Victoria Cross - Freemasons' Band of Brothers'. The Charity that benefited from the £1,440 proceeds of the evening was 'VC Grave Concern', which looks after the restoration and maintenance of the neglected graves of holder's of the VC who were Freemasons. Among the Honoured Guests were, RWBro Hywel Davies, ProvGM; VWBro Peter Frost, PGSwdB, DepProvGM; WBro Rev Norman Lea, PDepGChap; the four APGMs and a full Provincial Team. Holy Royal Arch was represented by VWBro John Taylor, MEGSupt. Also present were the President of NMSF, RWBro Capt Norman Lloyd-Edwards, PGJW; VWBro Graham Rees, PGSwdB, PDepProvGM, Monmouthsire; and the Chairman of the Lodge Organising Committee, WBro John I Davies, CBE, PAGDC. The School Lodge Masters in attendance were: WBro John Lawrence, Nioba Lodge; WBro Fred Poole, Howardian Lodge; WBro Gareth Parsons, Ymlaen Lodge; WBro Richard Witcombe, Old Cantonians Lodge; and WBro Robert E Thorne, PPrJGD, Old Monktonians Lodge. Representing the Federation of School Lodges were WBro Fred Fox, Chairman, WBro Peter Whittingham, IPC, WBro E D Humphries, and WBro H S Craig, Joint Secretaries, plus 185 Members from 67 different Lodges of the Province of South Wales.

Each School Lodge holds an annual 'Schools' Night', to which Members of other School Lodges are particularly invited to be present. The Festive Board is an opportunity to renew old School rivalries, and woe betides any Officer whose performance in the Ceremony is not up to scratch! The Lodge also holds 'Family Nights', when Members of Mother and Daughter Lodges are welcomed.

The Lodge's two silver cups are treasured possessions which are displayed at the Installation Festive Board and on special occasions, the inscriptions on them are shown below.

PRESENTED TO
THE HARLEQUINS LODGE
No. 5793
ON ITS FIRST BIRTHDAY 15TH May 1940
By Wor. Bro. R. P. Care
THE FIRST MASTER
OF
RWBro EDGAR J. RUTTER
PGW OSM
THE 14th MASTER
MAY 1952

PRESENTED TO
THE HARLEQUINS LODGE No5793
By W.Bro. R.P. Care PPGW PAGDC
THE FIRST MASTER
TO COMMEMORATE THE TWENTY ONE YEARS
AS DEPUTY PROV.G.M.

Documentation of the Lodge's most distinguished Brethren must be headed by RWBro Edgar John Rutter, DepProvGM, who joined Harlequins Lodge on 8 May 1944 and was Installed as WM in May 1952. His sons, Frank William Eden Rutter and John Cleverdon Rutter, were also Members of the Lodge, and both subsequently became distinguished in their chosen professions. Frank Rutter was Initiated at the age of 21 on Monday, 13 November 1939. He, together with Wilfred James Pallot, were the Lodge's first Initiates. John Rutter was Initiated at the age of 21 on Thursday, 2 January 1941, during an air-raid on Cardiff by 111 German planes. There was no Festive Board that night, and consequently no Toasts to the Initiate! Both became Worshipful Masters of the Lodge, Frank in 1948 and John in 1949.

Dr Frank William Eden Rutter PProvGW, studied Medicine at Westminster Hospital in London and later joined the Royal Army Medical Corps during WWII and was present at the D-Day landings in France, maintaining a front-line field medical service for casualties. He emigrated to New Zealand in 1963, but his journey was interrupted when the liner, Canberra, in which he was travelling with his wife Mary, six daughters, two dogs and a cat, caught fire in the Mediterranean, and they completed their journey by air. He became a GP in Papatoetoe, now a suburb of Auckland, but interested himself in the wider applications of the profession and was elected Chairman of the Auckland Hospital Board in 1974. He was responsible for the establishment of a 'super-clinic' in South Auckland. He was widely considered as an astute politician and a man of remarkably wide and varied interests, including dog-breeding and flying. He was made a CBE in 1981, and was Knighted in 1986 for his services to Hospital Boards.

WBro HH Judge John Cleverdon Rutter, PProvGW, PGD, was well known to Masons in this and other Provinces, not only for his services to the Legal Profession and Freemasonry, but also as an after-dinner speaker par-excellence. He was a Founder of Grand Design Lodge, renamed Edgar Rutter Lodge No.7196, and became WM in 1966. In 1951, he became a Founder and first IPM of South Wales Jurists' Lodge No.7092. He was also a Member of Hendre Lodge No.3250, where he served as Junior Warden and a Member of Apollo University Lodge No.357, Oxford. A Consecrating Officer of Aelwyd Lodge No.7982, he was made an Honorary Member of the Lodge. WBro HH Judge John served as ProvGStwd in 1955, PProvGD in 1956 and ProvSGW in 1963. Further biographical details of the Rutter family may be found in the chapter on Edgar John Rutter, earlier in the book.

Judge Owen Temple-Morris, QC, PSGD, WM of Prince Llewellyn Lodge No.2570 in 1934, became a Joining Member in 1945.

Another milestone in the History of the Lodge occurred on 14 March 1983, when the Lodge met to mark the 70th Anniversary of the Initiation of WBro Harry Caulfield-Giles. Item 10 of the Lodge Minutes record:

'The Lodge then paid tribute to our P M Harry Caulfield-Giles. Our beloved Harry entered Freemasonry in 1913 into Llangattock Lodge No.2547 and has been actively connected with Freemasonry ever since, except for the war years. Bro. Harry joined on 14 January1952 and was Elected Master of the Harlequins Lodge in 1964, and attended each meeting without fail except for the past year on account of his age; WBro Harry is now in his 94th year. His presence at this Lodge meeting only goes to show how keen he is on Freemasonry. He has made a special effort to attend, and his effort has been greatly appreciated by all the Brethren. The WM paid tribute to WBro Harry and presented him with an engraved cigar cutter, cigars and a scroll. VWBro Geoffrey Ashe on behalf of Grand Lodge, Lord Swansea, and members of Provincial Grand Lodge then added his tribute. WBro B. Chedzey of Llangattock Lodge No.2547 also paid his respects.'

WBro Glyn Winter, WM 1967-1968, played on the wing for Cardiff RFC, while WBro Clifford Evans, WM 1969-1970 obtained a half-blue swimming for Cambridge against Oxford, as well as playing rugby football for Cardiff.

WBro Peter D Williams, OBE, TD, DL, born 22 July 1922, Initiated on the 14 January 1952, Installed as WM in 1962, appointed Aide-de-Camp to HM The Queen in 1976, completed over 50 years in Freemasonry before his death in 2007.

WBro Wg Cdr John Irfon Davies CBE, PAGDC, was the first PM to be made a Grand Lodge Officer since RWBro Edgar Rutter. A Joining Member in 1977 from Hugh De Pudsey Lodge No.4490, Durham, and the Royal Air Force Lodge No.7335,

London, he received the MBE (Military) in 1963, for inverting V Force from High to Low Level and the CBE for Services to Wales, particularly the NHS, in 1998. In Provincial Grand Lodge, he was appointed ProvJGD in 1988 and PAGDC in Grand Lodge in 2001. In 2010, he was Founder IPM of Welsh Installed Masters' Lodge No.9857, London. WBro John was also honoured by being appointed ProvSGW in 2010. He has had a long and distinguished career in Mark Masonry, culminating in his appointment as Grand Junior Warden in 2009, thus becoming a Very Worshipful Brother.

WBro Gareth Jones, OBE (for Services to the Welsh Assembly Government), was subsequently appointed Registrar of Companies for England and Wales and Chief Executive of Companies House. He was Initiated with his blood brother, WBro Peter Jones, on 13 February 1984, and Installed as WM on 10 May 1993. In Provincial Grand Lodge, he was appointed ProvGSwdB in 1999. Promoted to ProvGDC in 2004, he received his first appointment in Grand Lodge in 2005 as PAGDC and was appointed AProvGM in 2007. Further biographical details are given separately in the book.

Over two hundred Brethren attended the Lodge on Monday 14 March 2011 to witness a very special Meeting when, after the Lodge was opened in due form, the ProvGM, RWBro Captain Sir Norman Lloyd-Edwards entered in procession, with a full team of Active Provincial Officers. He accepted the Gavel from WBro Peter Jones, PProvJGW, Acting WM, and announced that his purpose was to Invest WBro Gareth Jones, OBE, PAGDC, as Deputy Provincial Grand Master and WBro Paul Raymond Marshall as Assistant Provincial Grand Master. WBro Dennis Tucker, ProvDepGDC, Installed as WM in 1994, was accorded the honour of acting as DC. It was indeed an impressive Ceremony conducted with both precision and dignity which made it an even more memorable event, not only for Harlequins Lodge, but for the Province of South Wales.

The Lodge is very proud of its two Daughter Lodges. Firstly, Observer Lodge No.6015, Consecrated on 11 January 1945. Its name is unique in Freemasonry, and is the only Lodge of its kind in the world. Special Dispensation had to be obtained from Grand Lodge to use the name. The Founders belonged to No.25 Observer Corps, which later became the Royal Observer Corps. The Lodge was the brainchild of WBro Harry Stockwell, ProvGSec, who was the First Master. Secondly, Llanfair Lodge No.7353 comprising Freemasons who were members of Glamorgan Wanderers Rugby Football Club, was Consecrated on 28 September 1954. Harlequins Lodge was the Sponsoring Lodge, in that the Petition was signed by the WM and Wardens of that Lodge, though only one Member of Harlequins Lodge was a Founder Member, namely Bro E J Joseph Evans. Harlequins Lodge, however, provided one of the Consecrating Officers, WBro Vivian Care, ProvDepGDC, as ADC.

Finally, mention must be made of the School Song or Songs, of which there were at least five! The earliest School Song was sung in Latin. A later English version, perhaps more pertinent to the present day, is given below. The Lodge does not inflict this song on the other School Lodges, as is so often the case, on other School Nights.

Where Severn's mouth falls open wide, far-steaming ships on every tide:
Here stands our City, and our School, our boast this motto, our prayer this rule:
'On t'wards the light that rims the East, avoid the dark, escape the beast,
Where strongly breaks the morning beam, we seek new glory and the dream,
We seek new glory and the dream'.

Compiled by WBro Frederick Fox, PGStB, WM 1978 and 1987,
and WBro Martin C Richardson, ProvSGD, WM 2002, Secretary.

Lodge of Amity No.5823

Warranted   :   1 November 1939

Consecrated   :   29 February 1940

Meeting at the Masonic Hall, Cardiff.

The movement leading to the formation of the Lodge of Amity commenced in 1938. Six members of Bute Lodge No.960, decided that in view of the size of the Membership and the remote chance of Brethren achieving Office, a new Lodge should be formed. This driving force of six Brethren consisted of David Richards (WM 1941), Lewis Richards (WM 1942), Herbert E Gowen (WM 1943), Thomas M Dyer (WM 1944), William J Creemer (WM 1945), and David G Williams. The first five all became Masters of Amity Lodge and were Installed as such in the years indicated. WBro David G Williams had been Installed as Master of Bute Lodge in 1936.

At a Regular Meeting of Bute Lodge on 2 May 1939, with WBro John Allison, WM in the Chair, it was agreed that Bute Lodge would be the Sponsoring Lodge.

A number of preparatory meetings were held at Park Grove, Cardiff, the office of the organising Secretary, Bro Herbert Gowen. WBro William M Bryant, who had been Installed as Master of Bute Lodge in 1933, was invited to attend one of these meetings and was invited to become the first Master of the Lodge of Amity. This he duly accepted.

A Petition was raised and presented to the Most Worshipful Grand Master in the proper form and Lodge of Amity was accorded the Lodge Number 5823 on the Register of the United Grand Lodge of England. This new Lodge was given guidance and direction by VWBro E J Rutter, DepProvGM.

The Charter from the United Grand Lodge of England was received and signed 'Harewood', Pro Grand Master, and was supported by the MW the Grand Master, MWBro HRH George Edward Alexander Edmund, 1st Duke of Kent, who had recently been Installed as Grand Master at Olympia, on 19 July 1939. The greetings included reference to 9 Meetings, each to be held on the third Thursday of the month at the Masonic Temple, Guildford Crescent, Cardiff, in the County of Glamorgan, with the exception of June, July and August. It also documented that Bro David Richards be the Senior Warden and Lewis Richards the Junior Warden.

The Lodge was Consecrated on 29 February 1940, under the Banner of its Mother Lodge, Bute Lodge. The Consecrating Officer was RWBro R P St John Charles, PAGReg, ProvGM, assisted by VWBro Edgar J Rutter, PSGD, DepProvGM. The

Consecrating Officers were made Honorary Members and presented with Founders' Jewels to mark the occasion. The Installation of the Master was undertaken by the DepProvGM. Well over two hundred guests attended the Festive Board.

In late 1940, due to enemy action, Meetings were moved temporarily to Saturdays, to allow Brethren a greater degree of safety in their travelling to and from the Temple. They reverted to Thursdays towards the end of 1945.

The Lodge name 'Amity', meaning 'Friendship', comes from the Latin 'amicus' meaning 'friend'. The Founders considered that the aim of the Lodge, should by its name, imply that very quality.

WBro David G Williams designed the Lodge Badge. It consists of the name and number in a scroll, superimposed on open Compasses, with a smaller scroll below it bearing the Lodge Motto: *'Facta Non Verba'* meaning *'Deeds not Words'*. The pendant Compasses and Square are fully embraced by a wreath of fruit and flowers.

As the Lodge Founders considered friendliness, happiness and peace crucial to the Lodge's being, Toasts are never fired, with the exception of the Tyler's Toast, which is silent. Another Lodge tradition occurs in the Initiation Ceremony, where the Worshipful Master presents the Candidate with a pair of white gloves, and upon his Raising, he is presented with a copy of the Oxford Workings.

The Brethren of Bute Lodge presented the Officers' Regalia. Bro James Davies gave a set of Hymn Books and Bro A A Brooks the oak offertory plates. WBro William Fiddler, MBE, presented the Lodge with a Ballot Box and the Volume of the Sacred Law was presented by WBro C Manley. In 1990, WBro Michael Stringer presented the Lodge with a Banner, to mark its 50th Anniversary.

At the Lodge's inception, there were 22 Members; Membership rose steadily until 1961, when it reached 95. In 1971, the Lodge Sponsored the formation of the Lodge of Harmony No.8414. This Lodge was formed for the principal purpose of helping Brethren, advanced in years, to achieve the Chair of King Solomon. It was Consecrated on 5 May 1972.

At the Master's Installation in 1974, WBro David Harding recalls that there were 186 Brethren present. The Chief Steward recruited 20 volunteer Stewards in order to accommodate the high numbers. WBro Harold Wilson, AProvGM, was in attendance. Since then, WBro David Harding has been invited to sing the Master's Song at many Lodges, and is accompanied at Lodge of Amity's Installation by WBro Terrence Noonan.

WBro Bill Aslett, one of the senior Worshipful Brethren, served with distinction in the Royal Navy during the Second World War. Amongst his voyages were the bombardment of Sicily, supporting the Russian convoy and operations in Iceland. He was awarded the Italian Star, Atlantic Star and the Burma Star as Campaign Medals. After military service, WBro Bill joined the Police Force in Cyprus and was commended on several occasions. One of these was for *'initiative and a display of personal courage'*, during rioting in the Troodos district of Cyprus. WBro Bill returned to South Wales and re-joined the Cardiff City Police Force and achieved the Rank of Chief Inspector in 1973. He was Initiated into Freemasonry in Malta on 17 March 1954. He became a Masonic Veteran in 2004 and has the Rank of PPrJGW.

WBro John Sydenham, PPrGReg, another senior Past Master received his Masonic Veteran Certificate in 2005. He was Initiated on 20 October 1955 and was Installed Master of Lodge of Amity in 1976.

Bro Richie Evans took part in the second wave of D-Day Normandy Landings and received the 1939- 45 Star, France & Germany Star and a Defence Medal. More recently, Bro Richie became a member of the Normandy Veterans Association.

WBro Alan Lee, PPrJGW, WM in 1982, served in the Welsh Regiment. He was posted to Maindy Barracks in November 1939, and in 1941 he qualified as a Physical Training Instructor. Following a posting to HMS Westcliffe in Essex, he then joined the 8th Parachute Regiment. He took part in the D-Day Normandy Landings, returning home in August, before being sent to the Ardennes in December 1944, where he saw action in the Battle of the Bulge. In January 1945, Alan was in the last big airborne drop over the Rhine before being made a Sergeant in the field on 24 March 1945. Unfortunately, on 1 April, WBro Alan took on a half-track vehicle sporting cannon shell and lost a leg.

A Lodge of Instruction was formed in the Lodge's first year and a great many Worshipful Brethren and Brethren have given valuable service. The first President of LOI was WBro John Allison, followed by many distinguished Members of the Lodge. Without the support and guidance we have received from these Worshipful Brethren and their respective Vice-Presidents, the Ceremonies would have suffered and many traditions would have been lost. We will be eternally grateful to them.

During 1999, WBro Percy Hooper, PGStB, became the Lodge's Mandated Officer. A tradition evolved whereby Brethren of the Lodge visited his Lodge, Rhondda Lodge No.3979, for the December Meeting. In 2006, WBro Percy welcomed 26 Brethren to his Lodge. Sadly, WBro Percy Hooper died at the age of 70, on 4 January 2011.

In 2007, the Installed Worshipful Master, WBro Robert John Manfield, aged 41, became the second youngest Brother in the Lodge's History to occupy the Chair. The youngest was WBro Paul Sydenham, who did so at the age of 34 years. WBro John Manfield was Initiated in December 1990 by WBro Paul Sydenham. Upon reaching the Chair, in March 1999, John Initiated his blood brother, Robert Manfield, at the April Meeting. In October of that year, he Initiated his son Robert. The following year, as IPM, he witnessed the Initiation of his stepson, Bro Peter Wright.

Apart from the first Master, WBro William M Bryant, WBro John is the only Master to repeat his year in the Chair. In 2007, all four members of the same family held office thus: WBro Robert John Manfield, WM; WBro Robert Manfield, IPM; WBro A John Manfield, DC and Bro Peter Wright, ASec.

Compiled by Bro Peter John Wright.

WWI Memorial, Cardiff Masonic Hall

Friendship & Justice Lodge No. 5830

Warranted : 6 March 1940

Consecrated : 30 April 1940

Meeting at the Masonic Hall, Cardiff.

At the onset of the Second World War and at the end of 1939, there were 20 Masonic Lodges meeting in Cardiff. Lodge of Amity No.5823, although Warranted, was not Consecrated until 29 February 1940, bringing the total number to 21 Lodges. The established Lodges each had a Membership well into three figures, and many potential Candidates for the Craft and young Masons were faced with a lengthy waiting period for admission or promotion. To address this problem, several Brethren from Tennant Lodge No.1992 and Carmel Lodge No.4774, came together to form the nucleus of Founders for a new Lodge, whose objectives were to provide an opportunity for a number of keen Brethren, of several years standing, to take a more active part in Freemasonry. This formed the basis of a Petition presented to the Worshipful Master and Brethren of Carmel Lodge on 10 January, 1940. The Deputation of Founders was led by WBros Alfred J Joseph and Ernie H Rees. The Petition was heartily approved by the Brethren and duly endorsed by WBro Sam S Stone,WM, Bro Sol H Joseph , SW, Bro Abe Zeidman , JW. On 28 February 1940, the Petition received the approval of RWBro R P St John Charles, PAGReg, ProvGM.

There were 14 Founder Members, of whom five were from Tennant Lodge and five from Carmel Lodge. They included: WBro Alfred J Joseph, PPrGD, PM Carmel Lodge, WM Designate; WBro Ernest H Rees, PM Carmel Lodge, SW Designate; Bro William Stephens, MM of Tennant Lodge, JW Designate; Bro Charles William Burston, MM of Tennant Lodge, Treasurer Designate; Bro Christopher Howard Bulman, MM of Tennant Lodge, Secretary Designate; and Bro Lewis Jacobs, MM of Carmel Lodge, DC Designate.

The Warrant was granted on 6 March 1940 and the Consecration Cermony took place at the Masonic Hall, Guildford Crescent, Cardiff, on Wednesday, 30 April, 1940. The Ceremony was performed by the RW Provincial Grand Master, assisted by WBro Edgar J Rutter, PGD, DepProvGM, as Installing Master; WBro George Whittington, PGD, ProvGSec; WBro Frederick J Alban, CBE, PSGW, as SW; and WBro W Johns, ProvJGW.

The First Regular Lodge was held on Wednesday, 22 May 1940. Dark or Service Dress was the dress code, which continued as such until 1956.

The Lodge Ritual was more or less identical to the Ritual practised in the two main Founder Lodges. It was desired to create a Lodge in which Brethren of all denominations could work in love and harmony. The title 'Friendship & Justice' was therefore considered very appropriate. The Lodge Emblem, consisting of embracing hands supporting the scales of justice, overlaid on the Square and Compasses, was devised to symbolise the Founders' hopes and intentions.

A Bible was presented to the Lodge by Bro L Weisbard, ASec, on 30 April 1940. Printed in Hebrew and in English, it reflects the make-up of the Lodge Membership. On 23 October 1940, the WM and Brethren of Carmel Lodge presented the Lodge with a Master's Collar and a set of Gauntlets for the WM and the Wardens. A Bannerette was presented to the Lodge by WBro Reuben Fligelstone, PPrGStwd, on 27 November 1940.

Initially, seven Regular Lodge Meetings were held on the fourth Wednesday of January, February, March, April, May, October and November. Such, however, was the demand for Membership, that these Regular Meetings were soon overtaken by a considerable number of Emergency Meetings. This was mainly due to members of HM Forces who, due to service requirements, were unable to attend Regular Lodge Meetings. Records of Meetings for the years 1939 to 1945, indicate that the Membership rose very rapidly to a total of 80 Members, comprising 14 Founders, 15 Joining Members and 51 Initiates. It was not unusual for a Lodge Summons to announce *'To Raise one or two'* of seven qualified Brethren or, as on another occasion *,'to present ten Grand Lodge Certificates'*.

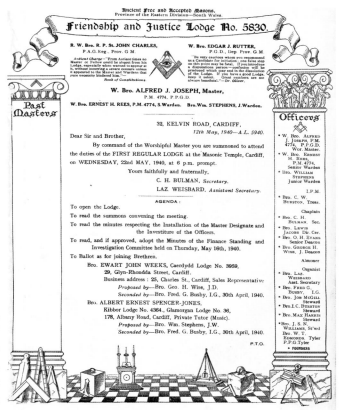

First Regular Lodge Summons

In 1941, a total of 22 Ceremonies were performed, which included 12 Initiations. One notable Meeting, held in March 1942, lasted from 3.00 pm to 7.40 pm - nearly five hours. It included one Brother Raised to the Third Degree, two Brethen Passed to the Second Degree, a discussion and proposal to form a Friendship & Justice Chapter of Royal Arch Masonry, two Candidates Initiated, and the Dedication of the Lodge Banner by WBro Edgar J Rutter, DepProvGM.

The Lodge Banner was presented by Bros Harry and Abe Sherman, in memory of their blood brother, Jack, who had been the third Candidate Initiated into the Lodge in October 1940, and who had died in April 1941.

On 28 January 1942, a gift of three candlesticks was received from Mrs C W Burston, in memory of her late husband, Bro Charles Burston, Treasurer. They were formally presented on her behalf by her son, Bro I C Burston. They were placed on the family Bible, and received by WBro E H Rees, PPrSGD, WM. Candles were placed in them and afterwards lit by Bro I C Burston, and positioned on the pedestals of the three 'Lesser Lights' in Freemasonry.

Shortly after the Consecration, the Brethren thought that there should be a Royal Arch Chapter attached to the Lodge, providing the Members of Friendship & Justice Lodge and Carmel Lodge with their own home for Royal Arch Masonry. Friendship

& Justice Chapter No.5839 was duly Warranted on 6 May 1942.

Following the end of the War, it was the practice to present suitably inscribed Ritual Books to returning Brethren in recognition of their war service, and to express the pleasure of the Members on their safe return.

Lodge Membership peaked at 126 in the mid-sixties, making it necessary to increase the number of Regular Meetings to eight. However, in the 1970s, with an increase in the number of Lodges meeting in Cardiif, greater use of the Temples was required, and the number of Regular Meetings was reduced to seven.

The 250th Regular Meeting of the Lodge was held on Wednsday, 22 October 1969 , when WBro H Freedman, WM, welcomed RWBro the Rt Hon the Lord Swansea, DL, ProvGM, who was visiting the Lodge for the first time, and who participated in the Ceremony of Raising two Brethren to the Sublime Degree of a Master Mason. At the 374th Regular Meeting in 2001, the Lodge was again honoured with the presence of RWBro Hywel Davies, ProvGM, accompanied by his Officers and Officers of United Grand Lodge.

From the beginning, the Lodge has always played a full part in support of all Masonic appeals and charities. During its first fifty years, it contributed to the Provincial Festivals held in 1944, 1955, 1967, 1976 and 1986, when the total sums donated were: Royal Masonic Benevolent Institution, £9,460.00; Royal Masonic Institution for Girls, £2,000.00; Royal Masonic Institution for Boys, £3,663.00, and the Masonic Trust for Girls and Boys, £13,000.00.

To mark the 50th Anniversary of the Lodge, donations were made to: The Provincial Grand Master's 1991 Festival for the South Wales (Eastern Division) Provincial Benevolent Fund, Cardiff Masonic Hall Rebuilding Fund, George Thomas (Hospice) Trust, St John Ambulance Brigade (South Glamorgan), Llandough Hospital Appeal, Velindre Hospital Cancer Research Fund, and Cardiff Home for Aged Jews. In 1987, the Lodge established its own Charitable Fund or 'Charity Chest', under a scheme sponsored by the Grand Charity.

Over the years, the Lodge has been blessed with several distinguished Brethren. WBro Leonard Roy Evans, PPrSGW, was Initiated into the Lodge on 22 October 1952. He was Installed WM in 1965. In October 1975, he became Founder Chaplain of Wings Lodge No.8651, an Office he held until he was Installled WM of that Lodge in 2000. At the Regular Lodge Meeting of Friendship & Justice Lodge, held in October 2002, WBro Len was presented with his Masonic Veteran's Certificate, marking his 50 years in the Craft. Sadly, WBro Len passed to the Grand Lodge Above on 29 January 2011. He was 97 years of age.

The late WBro Hadyn Lloyd, PJGD, was born in Whitchurch, Cardiff, in 1923. Too young to be called up for the Services during WWII, and being in a reserved occupation, he joined the St John's Ambulance as a messenger, riding his motorcycle throughout the Cardiff air-raids. He was Initiated into Friendship & Justice Lodge on 20 March 1948 and is the first and only Initiate of the Lodge to have been appointed a Grand Officer. This was only one of his many appointments. In the Craft, he held the position of ProvGPurs,ProvGOrg, and ProvSGW. He was the Consecrating Officer of over 22 Lodges. He also received high office in Royal Arch Masonry, Mark Masonry and several of the side Degrees. In United Grand Lodge, he was appointed Past PAGDC in 1982 and promoted to PAJGD in 1991. He was a Member or an Honorary Member of more than 80 Lodges. His was a very remarkable and illustrious Masonic record. He was truly a Ruler in the Craft, who *'lived respected and died regretted'*.

This Lodge history had been compiled from extracts taken from an Eulogy given on 25 January 1995 by WBro A Moorcraft, PPrSGW, and from 'Fifty Years of the Friendship & Justice Lodge', by the late WBro B Silver, PProvGPurs, in co-operation with WBro A Unger, PProvJGD.

Compiled by WBro A M Hardy, PPrAGDC.

Lodge of Three Pillars No.5857

Warranted : 2 september 1942

Consecrated : 9 October 1942

Meeting at the Masonic Hall, Cardiff.

In early 1942, there were only 22 Lodges meeting in Cardiff. Even though the number of Lodges was fewer, the Membership of these older Lodges was much greater than today. As a result there was never any shortage of Candidates and, in order to cope with the influx of Initiates, Lodges of Emergency were regularly held. A number of Brethren, however, were unhappy about the situation, and a phrase in common currency at the time was *'It is easy enough putting men into Freemasonry, but quite another thing putting Freemasonry into men'*. But what could be done about it? An idea emerged that a new Lodge, not attached to any older Lodges should be formed. A Lodge that would restrict its intake of Candidates to about two a year and a Lodge that would curtail Toasts and responses at the Festive Board (but retaining the Loyal Toast) was mooted. This would enable the time saved to be utilised to invite an expert Brother to speak on some interesting and perhaps unusual aspect of Freemasonry, thereby ensuring the *'daily advancement in Masonic knowledge'* by the Brethren, especially the younger Brethren.

The idea took form and came into being in the middle of WWII, with the Consecration of Lodge of Three Pillars, on 9 October 1942 by RWBro R P St John Charles, ProvGM. He was assisted by WBro Samuel Jones, PPrGW, acting as SW, in the absence of WBro David Rees, ProvSGW; WBro Gerald Tudor, PPrGW, as JW; and WBro Rev J Humphries, ProvGChap, as Chaplain. At the conclusion of the Ceremony, the ProvGM vacated the Chair in favour of WBro Edgar W Lewis, PAGDC, PPrGW, WM of Hendre Lodge No.3250, who Installed the Master Designate, WBro Edgar J Rutter, PGD, DepProvGM as WM. He then appointed and Invested the first Officers of the Lodge with WBro W Gilbert as SW, WBro R G Vercette as JW, and WBro R E Ward as IPM.

WBro Edgar John Rutter became the DepProvGM in 1931, an Office he held for 40 years with great distinction, until his death in 1971 at the age of 79. He was Initiated into Tennant Lodge No.1992 and was appointed to the Rank of PGJW in 1951 as one of the special appointments to mark the Installation of the Earl of Scarbrough as Grand Master. He also had the Order of Service to Masonry conferred on him, and was the senior holder at the time of his death. Further biographical details are included separately, earlier in this book.

The Consecrating Officers, together with WBro Samuel Jones, were Elected as Honorary Members. WBro Albert E Lemmer, WM of Tennant Lodge, the Sponsoring Lodge, was Elected an Honorary Member.

Sir Frederick John Alban
1882 - 1965

Grand Treasurer
Inspector General Rose Croix,
District of South Wales & Monmouthshire
1951 - 1963

Frederick John Alban was born on 11 January 1882, at Abergavenny, Monmouthshire. His mother, Jane Hannah née Williams died on 28 September 1884 and his father, David, died on 2 January 1891. He was brought up by a maiden aunt, Miss Mary Ann Williams, a Tailoress, at 56 Lower Monk Street, Abergavenny, until he was 16 years old. He attended the National School at Abergavenny until the age of 12, when he had to leave because of the increase in the weekly school fee to 6d (2½ p). He obtained a junior post with Spicketts Solicitors, Pontypridd, where he gained proficiency in shorthand and typing. At the age of 17 he was appointed Clerical Assistant to the Local Board of Guardians and three years later he became an Accountant to the Urban District Council. He went on to further his studies as an Accountant and in 1909 he won the gold medal of the Society of Incorporated Accountants and Auditors and became a Fellow of the Institute of Chartered Accountants.

In the summer of 1906, Frederick John married Alice Emily Watkins at Crickhowell. His young bride, from Ewyas Harold, Herefordshire, was working as a Milliner for Ebenezer Davies, Draper, High Street, Crickhowell. Following the marriage, they first lived at 5 Mackintosh Road, Pontypridd. They were to have four sons and two daughters. Two of the sons and both daughters qualified in medicine, and the other sons in their father's profession. (See History of Dinam Lodge No.4521.)

For two years (1910-1912) Frederick was the Accountant to the United Water Board of Pontypridd and Rhondda after which he became Deputy Accountant, Welsh National Insurance Commissioners (1912-1916) and Consulting Accountant and Registrar, Taf Fechan Water Supply Board. In 1916, he was appointed Secretary and Controller of the 'King Edward VII Memorial Association', which had been established by David Davies (later Lord Davies of Llandinam) and his sisters, Margaret and Gwendoline, to commemorate King Edward VII and to combat

Sir Frederick John Alban, CBE

tuberculosis in Wales. In the 1920s he established, with Ernest Norman Lamb, the firm of Alban & Lamb Chartered Accountants of Cardiff and Newport.

He became a Freemason on 8 March 1918, when he was Initiated into Glamorgan Lodge. He was Passed on 3 May and Raised on 31 May 1918. Though never an Officer in Glamorgan Lodge, he was a Founder Member and the second WM of Dinam Lodge No.4521, Penarth (Consecrated 12 May 1923 at Llandrindod Wells). The Lodge is named after David Davies, MP (see above), who was from 'Plas Dinam' in the village of Llandinam, Montgomeryshire, an early Joining Member of the new Lodge. Provincial honours followed in 1929, when he received the Rank of PPrGReg.

A Founder Member of Sapphire Lodge No.5290 in 1931, he also became a Member of Amethyst Lodge No.4026. He was the Consecrating Officer for Lodge of Amity No.5823 (29 February 1940) and for Friendship and Justice Lodge No.5830 (30 April 1940) and was made an Honorary Member of both Lodges. In 1939, he was appointed Provincial Senior Grand Warden.

Exalted in St John's Chapter No.36, he was a Founder of Amethyst Chapter No.4026 and its First Principal in 1928. He became Provincial Registrar in 1929, Scribe E in 1939 and Grand Treasurer in Supreme Grand Chapter in 1944.

In January 1932, he was made a Commander of the British Empire. In Grand Lodge he was appointed PSGW in 1939, and five years later (1944) he became Grand Treasurer of the United Grand Lodge of England, which afforded him the title of VWBro. In the summer of 1945, HM King George VI honoured him with a Knighthood. Next, in 1947, he was Installed Worshipful Master of Hendre Lodge No.3250. Also in 1947, he became President of the Society of Incorporated Accountants. The University of Wales awarded him the honorary degree of LLD in 1956.

Frederick Alban's interest in Freemasonry was not just confined to the Craft and Chapter. He was Advanced in Stability Mark Lodge No.758 and became its Master in 1935. He was Provincial Registrar in 1936 and Senior Warden in 1938. For three years (1947 - 1950), he was the Deputy Provincial Grand Master of Mark Master Masons of South Wales. This was followed by the appointment of Inspector General Rose Croix for the District of South Wales & Monmouthshire (1951-1963). Throughout this time he had remained a Subscribing Member of Glamorgan Lodge, but on 8 November 1963, his resignation from the Lodge, due to ill health, was accepted with regret. He died in his 83rd year, on 2 May 1965. At a Glamorgan Lodge Meeting, held on 12 November 1965, a donation of a new set of Officers' Collars was gratefully received from the late VWBro Sir Frederick Alban.

With the Warranting, on 4 December 1975, of Sir Frederick Alban Mark Lodge No.1455, meeting at Swansea, the name of this most distinguished and remarkable Freemason lives on in the Province.

WBro Peter M Davies, ProvJGW.

Doric Lodge No.5968

Warranted : 20 May 1944

Consecrated : 12 June 1944

Meeting at the Masonic Hall, Swansea.

The first entry in the Minutes is dated 20 March 1944, recording the first Founders' meeting, under the Chairmanship of VWBro Edgar J Rutter, DepProvGM. The stated reasons for applying for a Warrant were that the ten existing Swansea Lodges had lengthy waiting lists and, as the Second World War was drawing to a close, a flood of applications from demobilised Servicemen returning to civilian life was anticipated. Furthermore, owing to the large number of Members in the Lodges, with up to 190, or even 200 in some, Brethren could see but a remote opportunity of making progress towards the Chair of King Solomon. This was supported by the presence of twenty-four Brethren at the meeting, who were desirous of Petitioning for a new Lodge in Swansea.

The meeting appointed WBro Francis W Randell as Master-Elect and, at his suggestion, his Mother Lodge, Talbot Lodge No.1323, was requested to support the Petition for a Charter. Thus, Talbot Lodge became the Mother Lodge of Doric Lodge. Indeed, WBro R T Hughes, WM of Talbot Lodge, became a Founder Member and Lodge Organist, an Office he held for more than 20 years.

The reasons for Founding the Lodge did not, of course, only apply to Doric. By 1950, four further Lodges had been Consecrated, namely, Dyffryn Tawe Lodge No.6056, R P St John Charles Lodge No.6466, Lodge of St Cenydd No.6567 and Ionic Lodge No.6626. As a result, the number of Masons in Swansea increased from 1,335 in 1943 to 1,854 in 1950, almost a forty percent increase. However, waiting lists of up to three years for prospective Candidates persisted for at least a further twenty years.

The Founders' second meeting considered the proposed name of the Lodge. The following names were considered: 'Doric', 'Connaught', 'Abertawe', 'Ffynnone', 'Glanmor', 'Brunswick', 'Singleton' and 'Clyne'. After discussion, the name 'Doric' was unanimously decided upon. The Founders went on to discuss fees and the following were agreed: annual fee - 3 guineas; Joining fee - 5 guineas; Initiation fee - 25 guineas. (1 guinea is £1. 5p) The very considerable sum required for Initiation was taking advantage of the imbalance between supply and demand, and was intended to place Lodge finances on a sound footing. It was further agreed that Lodge dress should be dark suit or service dress.

The third Founders' meeting decided on the design of the Lodge Banner. The design consists of a sun-burst, containing the 'All Seeing Eye', between a pair of Doric columns. In the centre is the well-known illustration of Euclid's 47th Proposition, otherwise known as Pythagoras's Theorem. Also included in the design is the Lodge Motto: *'Goreu Defawd Daioni'*, which translates as *'Goodness is the best of ideas'*.

On the matter of Regalia, owing to the conditions of war, it was almost impossible to obtain Collars, Aprons, Working Tools etc, and thus it was agreed that, as soon as possible, each Officer should present his Collar to the Lodge. The Minutes continued to record the placing of orders for Regalia until late 1947.

The Consecration of the Lodge took place in the Masonic Temple, St Helen's Road, Swansea, on 12 June 1944. The Consecration Ceremony was conducted by RWBro R P St John Charles, ProvGM, and the Installing Master was VWBro Edgar J Rutter, DepProvGM. The Attendance Book records the presence of 23 Founder Members, 8 Grand Officers, 29 Provincial Grand Lodge Officers, and 102 Ruling Masters, Past Masters and Brethren.

By the end of 1944, the Lodge had Initiated six Candidates and had a total Membership of thirty-two. Until 1973, at least six Candidates were Initiated each year. Numbers peaked at 129 in 1973. In the early years, Emergency Meetings were held to Initiate, Pass and Raise Candidates from the substantial waiting list. It was commonplace for Candidates to be on a waiting list for three years, even as late as 1966. The Minutes record several discussions about whether or not to close the waiting list. The sense of frustration in some quarters can be felt in the Notice of Motion of 1948 to the effect that *'membership be limited to 100, that Candidates be Initiated in twos until the Lodge attained sixty Members, then singly thereafter, and that the Worshipful Master may select from the waiting list which Candidates he wishes to Initiate.'* These proposals were withdrawn, following the intervention of WBro Harry F Stockwell, ProvGSec. It was also common practice to conduct two Ceremonies at one Meeting, 'calling- off' for refreshments in between Ceremonies.

There was a special entry in the Minutes, dated August 1946, which may have been a copy of a report to Provincial Grand Lodge, as follows: *'Each of the Founder Members gave service to the war effort either in the Home Guard, Civil Defence, Special Constabulary, Bomb Reconnaissance, First Aid, or National Fire Service. WBro C H Sanders, first JW, was awarded the MBE for services as Telegraph Superintendent during air raids on Swansea. WBro W T G Cross received the Police Long Service Medal and Bar. Bro A Bassett founded the first Mechanical Transport Platoon in Swansea.'*

From 1973, sadly, the number of resignations began to increase and exceeded the number being Initiated. The reasons are not referred to in the Minutes, but are not hard to find. These were the days of high rates of inflation, reflecting the economic realities of the nation. This can be seen in the rate of increase in annual fees, from £10 in 1974 to £18 in 1975 and £28 in 1980. It was also at about this time when it was first necessary for a Past Master to go back into the Chair. By the 1990s, this became common practice, in contrast with those days when access to the Chair of King Solomon was seen as a remote possibility, and a reason for the Lodge's foundation.

Of more recent origin is the annual official fraternal visit with Lodge of Sincerity No.8531, which takes place in January, with its reciprocal visit in April. This arrangement, which has been in place since 1999, initially on an informal basis, owes its origins to personal friendships between some of the Brethren.

A number of Lodge Brethren have progressed to Masonic distinction. The Founder Worshipful Master, Wardens and Senior Deacon were all appointed to Grand Rank. Since that time, further Brethren have been so honoured, as follows: WBro F W Randell, PAGDC, in 1946; WBro T L Jenkins, PAGDC, in 1947; WBro C H Sanders, PAGDC, in 1958; WBro W Porter, PAGDC, in 1962 and later promoted to PJGD; and WBro R F Cope, PAGDC, in 1999.

In 2007, the Lodge had 45 Members and enjoyed a mini-resurgence in its fortunes, with five Initiates in 2006-2007.

Compiled by WBro Roy Hewson, PPrGSuptWks, WM 1997 and 2006.

Dinas Powis Lodge No.5997

Warranted : 2 August 1944

Consecrated : 13 September 1944

Meeting at the Masonic Hall, Penarth.

Dinas Powis Lodge is the third Daughter Lodge of Windsor Lodge No.1754. It was founded as the result of discussions and subsequent agreement amongst Masonic Brethren living in the Dinas Powis area, who also had business connections or worked in Cardiff, and more particularly at Cardiff Docks.

More than 200 Brethren attended the Consecration Meeting, held at the Masonic Temple, Stanwell Road, Penarth, on Wednesday, 13 September 1944. RWBro R P St John Charles, ProvGM, was the Consecrating Officer, assisted by his Provincial Grand Lodge Officers. Also present were 140 visiting Brethren and the 57 Brethren who had signed the Petition requesting the formation of Dinas Powis Lodge.

It was not possible to hold a Consecration Banquet (as had been hoped) in the Plymouth Rooms of the Penarth Masonic Hall. The function room and kitchen had been commandeered by the Government as a Mess Room for American Forces stationed at Penarth Docks. Instead, light refreshments were served in the Connaught Room, now the Provincial Room, on the first floor. It was the last year of WWII, and many difficulties had to be overcome. Blackout restrictions were still strictly enforced, and food and petrol were rationed. This had an effect on mobility and on the extent to which the 'After Proceedings' could properly be a 'Festive Board'.

The first Master of the Lodge was WBro Arthur Wesley Shenton of Dinas Powis, PM Sapphire Lodge No.5290, and Chief Accountant of the Powell Dyffryn Steam and Coal Co Ltd, Cardiff. The first Senior Warden was WBro Albert Brockington, JP, of Wellwood Drive, Dinas Powis, PM Penarth Lodge No.4113, and Proprietor of Brockington's Gentleman's Outfitters and Tailors, Windsor Road, Penarth. The first Junior Warden was WBro Albert Griffiths, of Murch Road, Dinas Powis, PM Sapphire Lodge, and Manager of the Pearl Assurance, Cardiff. He was also Choir Master of St Peter's Church, Dinas Powis. The first Treasurer was Bro Frank E Perry of 'Chantrys', St Andrews Road, Dinas Powis, a Partner in Care Lines Ltd, Ship Owners, Cardiff Docks. He became the third Master of the Lodge in 1946.

The first Initiates were Mr Gerald Ongley and Mr Kenneth Glyn Jones. During the first year, eight Emergency Meetings were held. In those early days, Initiates consisted entirely of Dinas Powis businessmen and tradesmen as well as some professional residents of the village. WBro Arthur Shenton encouraged many of the staff of Powell Dyffryn and its subsidiary companies to join, and it was from this early connection with that Company, that the Lodge acquired the sobriquet, still often referred to today, of 'Dinas Powis Lodge DPPD', namely, 'Dinas Powis Powell Dyffryn'.

Mr Heurtley Newman (NUT) Rees, the Headmaster of the Church in Wales School, Dinas Powis, was Initiated in April 1945 by his blood brother, WBro J C C Rees, the first Lodge Secretary. In 1955, Bro Heurtley Newman was the first Initiate of the Lodge to become WM.

At a meeting of the Lodge Committee in 1952, it was decided that the Brethren should wear dinner jackets when attending Regular Lodge Meetings and that the wearing of dinner jackets would be obligatory for all Officers of the Lodge.

In 1954, WBro Arthur Shenton very deservedly received Grand Lodge Honours, with the Rank of PAGDC. He was the first Lodge Member to become a Grand Officer. It was not only a great personal honour, but a delight for all in Dinas Powis Lodge. The Lodge's next Grand Officer was WBro Dudley E Morse who, in 1967, was appointed PAGSuptWks, and later promoted to PJGD. He became a Masonic Veteran in 1977.

In April 1966, 32 Members and guests of the Lodge, led by the Master, the late WBro E W (Peter) Jones, flew from Rhoose airport to Guernsey, where they enjoyed a two night stay in the Royal Hotel, St Peter Port. At the invitation of the Master of St Martin's Lodge No.4142, Province of Guernsey and Alderney, the Brethren of Dinas Powis Lodge performed a First Degree Demonstration Ceremony in Oxford Working.

WBro Albert Griffiths, the first Junior Warden, completed 50 years as a Member of the Craft in 1967. Likewise, two years later, the Primus Master, WBro Arthur Shenton, also completed his 50 years service in the Craft.

The Lodge originally held eight Regular Meetings each year, but in1968 it was decided to reduce the number of Meetings to seven. The May Meeting was discontinued and the Lodge now meets on the second Wednesday in the months of October to April.

In 1982, Dinas Powis Lodge Sponsored a new Lodge to be known as 'Wenvoe Lodge No.9038', to meet at the Masonic Temple, Barry. Wenvoe Lodge was Warranted on 10 March 1982 and close ties have been maintained with this Daughter Lodge ever since.

Dinas Powis Lodge has a very creditable record for contributing to Charity. The Lodge became a Grand Patron of the Royal Masonic Hospital, and many Lodge Members proudly wore the Hospital Jewel.

Within the present Membership, there are Brethren whose Mother Lodges are in Ireland, Scotland, Hong Kong, Sri Lanka (Ceylon) and South Africa.

Amongst the PMs who should be mentioned is the late WBro Ronald McFarlane, PPrAGDC, who was Installed as WM in 1977. He served in the Royal Air Force during World War II. WBro Ron, an aircrew member, was shot down during combat, but, happily, he survived the ordeal and as a result was 'Mentioned in Despatches'. The late WBro Edward Coles was a Joining Past Master from Grant Lodge No.2862, Colombo, Sri Lanka (formerly Ceylon), who for many years was a Pilot for the Port of Colombo. WBro Edward originally joined a Lodge under the Scottish Constitution in Sierra Leone and he completed over 60 years in Freemasonry. In 1998, the late WBro Gwilym Pate, PPrSGW, WM in 1961 and again in 1965, was another Member who completed 50 years Membership of the Craft. For many years, he was the Lodge Preceptor and a mentor to many of the younger Brethren. WBros McFarlane, Coles and Pate were all granted Honorary Membership of Dinas Powis Lodge, in recognition of their many achievements.

Currently, the Lodge has two Masonic Veterans. Firstly, Bro P H Evans, who was Initiated on 13 February 1957, and secondly, WBro Ian B Munn, PPrJGW, who was Initiated on 10 November 1952. The latter was Installed WM in 1987, and again in 1999, and is still very active, having been Lodge Preceptor for many years.

Compiled by WBro Ian Munn, PPrJGW.

Observer Lodge
No.6015

Warranted : 1 November 1944

Consecrated : 11 January 1945

Meeting at the Masonic Hall, Cardiff.

During the Second World, the local section of the Royal Observer Corps became a very efficient unit and, with the spirited confidence engendered, led to a strong camaraderie amongst its members. In February 1944, it was felt that the friendship formed should be continued after the War ended, and to this end it was suggested that a new Masonic Lodge be formed to consolidate those friendships. This resulted in an informal meeting of proposed Founders and Joining Members, which was held in the Masonic Hall, Cardiff and presided over by WBro Harry Stockwell. The outcome was the formation of the Observer Lodge No.6015, which was Warranted on 1 November 1944. It was originally intended to use the title 'Lodge of Observers', but this was not accepted and the singular version 'Observer Lodge' was adopted and became unique, as no other Lodge was formed from the vast numbers of Members of the Royal Observer Corps in the country.

The Sponsoring Lodge was Harlequins Lodge No.5793, which loaned its Regalia for the Consecration Ceremony, held in Cardiff on 11 January 1945. The Consecrating Officer was RWBro RP St John Charles, ProvGM, accompanied by 39 Grand and Provincial Grand Officers. Also present were 30 Founder and Joining Members, 16 visiting Masters and 93 Brethren – a grand total of 179.

The first Master was WBro Harry Francis Stockwell, who had been appointed Provincial Grand Secretary in 1944. He held that Office until 1953, when he was appointed Assistant Provincial Grand Master and finally Deputy Provincial Grand Master in 1971. His biographical details are included elsewhere in this book. The first Initiate was WBro Joe Williams, a Member of the Observer Corps.

In the 65 years the Lodge has been in existence, there have been 214 Candidates for Initiation. The first Secretary of the Lodge, WBro Cliff Hawkes, took considerable trouble to collect and keep all the documentation relating to the Lodge, even for the months prior to the Consecration. Not only did he preserve it for posterity, but on the occasion of the Lodge's one hundredth Meeting in September 1960, he presented the documents and up to date Minute Books to the then Worshipful Master, WBro John Hall. Cliff Hawkes was known to the Brethren as 'Bish', probably because he had the appearance of one high up in the

Church, and, following this theme, it is perhaps relevant to say that those records have been kept religiously ever since.

Unfortunately, the initial connection between Observer Lodge and the Royal Observer Corps has passed into history, with the disbanding of the Corps in September 1991. However, several former Corps Members attended the Installation Meeting in February 1992 and presented the Lodge with a plaque, embellished with the Corps' Logo. This is displayed at every Lodge Meeting, together with a statue of an 'Observer' also presented by the same former Members in February 2001.

In early 1973, a very prominent Cardiff Solicitor, the late Julius Hermer, who became Lord Mayor of Cardiff, 1987-1988, requested that Observer Lodge support a Petition for a new Lodge in Cardiff. This was granted and Observer Lodge became the Mother Lodge of Dinas Llandaf Lodge No.8512, which was Warranted on 14 March 1973.

The ages of Candidates throughout the Lodge's existence have been remarkably similar, the average being around the thirty-five mark. Their occupations are somewhat varied - at one time they were Publicans, Policemen, Post Office Workmen and more recently Firemen. Overall the list shows a wide selection of occupations from Managing Directors to Professional Sportsmen. From soccer: Bro Cyril Henry Spiers, Manager of Cardiff City, 1939-1946 and 1947-1954; and from cricket: WBro Jim Pleass, Glamorgan County Cricket Club, a member of the Glamorgan team that won the County Title for the first time in 1948.

Throughout the years, there have been many eminent Masons within the Lodge, none more so than the previously mentioned VWBro Harry Francis Stockwell. Most recently, VWBro Andrew Lindsey Gretton, who has served in every Office, became the ninth Observer Lodge Secretary and was appointed Deputy Provincial Grand Master of South Wales in 2007.

The Lodge originally met four times a year on the second Thursday of the month in February (Installation), May, October and December (Election Night). Within a few years, the Lodge Meetings became so popular that it was necessary to increase the number of Meetings to seven. More recently, it has become increasingly difficult to find a suitable number of Candidates for Initiation and the number of annual Lodge Meetings has reverted to four. The Lodge is now in the throes of altering the By-laws in order to become a quality Dining Lodge, and thereby requiring an increase in subscriptions.

While we go forward with much hope and enthusiasm on an exciting and expanding path, we remember those wonderful Brethren of the Royal Observer Corps who had the foresight and integrity to form a fine legacy of Masonic history.

Compiled by WBro Colin Raybould, PPrJGW, Secretary,
with grateful thanks to WBro JE Pleass, PPrJGW.

Lodge of Unity No.6030

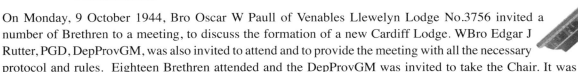

Warranted : 6 December 1944

Consecrated : 12 January 1945

Erased : 11 March 2009

Met at the Masonic Hall, Cardiff.

On Monday, 9 October 1944, Bro Oscar W Paull of Venables Llewelyn Lodge No.3756 invited a number of Brethren to a meeting, to discuss the formation of a new Cardiff Lodge. WBro Edgar J Rutter, PGD, DepProvGM, was also invited to attend and to provide the meeting with all the necessary protocol and rules. Eighteen Brethren attended and the DepProvGM was invited to take the Chair. It was agreed that a new Lodge should be formed and that WBro A Charles White, PPrJGW, would be the first Worshipful Master. He thanked the Brethren for placing their confidence in him and he then took the Chair for the remainder of the meeting. WBro Charles White was a Founder Member of Preswylfa Lodge No.5792 and was Installed as the Lodge's first WM in1939. Consequently, it was decided to approach Preswylfa Lodge to be the Sponsoring Lodge. WBro John C Taylor was appointed SW Designate and Bro Oscar Paull, JW Designate. The first Secretary was Bro Charles Carpenter and WBro D W Jenkins, MC, was the first IPM. The Treasurer Designate was Bro George Flook, a Coal Exporter, who had been Initiated in Glamorgan Lodge No.36 on 13 June 1917. He became WM of Lodge of Unity in 1952 and, in 1954, he received his first Provincial appointment of PPrAGReg. In 1956, he was appointed ProvGReg, an Office he was to hold for several years. He was further promoted in Province to PPrJGW in 1960 and, in 1963, he became a Grand Officer, with the Rank of PGStB.

At a further meeting , held on 19 October, the WM Designate expressed the hope that *'unity'* should prevail among the Members, and this was to be the motivating factor that inspired the name 'Lodge of Unity' for the new Lodge. A Latin inscription, meaning *'Each for One and One for Each'*, was chosen as the Lodge Motto.

In the latter part of 1944, the guinea was still a coin of the realm and Founders' fees were set at 7 guineas, to include the first year's subscription; annual fees were set at 3 guineas; joining fee plus first year's subscription would be 7 guineas; and the Initiation fee together with the first year's subscription was set at 20 guineas.

There were 183 Brethren present to witness the Consecration of Lodge of Unity No.6030, which, followed by the Installation Ceremony, took place at the Masonic Temple, Guildford Crescent, Cardiff, at 2.30 pm on Friday, 12 January 1945. The Consecrating Officer was RWBro R P St John Charles, JP, ProvGM, South Wales, Eastern Division, accompanied by a team of Provincial Officers. The first Master, Charles White, was Installed by WBro Edgar J Rutter, PJGD, DepProvGM.

The first Regular Meeting of the Lodge took place on Wednesday, 14 February 1945, and the agenda included to Ballot for: Mr George Alexander Flook (a Lewis – son of George Flook) age 23 years, Civil Engineer; Mr Colin Vivian Miles, age 36 years, Incorporated Account; and Mr Arnold Gwynne Davies, age 43 years, Insurance Agent; and then to Initiate (if accepted) Mr George Alexander Flook and/or Mr Colin Vivian Miles.

There is no indication in the Lodge records regarding the design on the Lodge Banner, but it may be assumed that it is intended to represent 'World Brotherhood' by having the Globe at its centre. The Two Pillars were a very important part of King Solomon's Temple and the lily-work over the Globe denotes whiteness and peace. The rows of pomegranates, from the exuberance of their seeds, denote plenty. The Motto on the Banner is *'With One Consent'*, but it is similar in meaning to the original thought of *'Each for One and One for Each'*. This Banner design and Motto first appeared on the Lodge Summons in October 1948. The original Banner was replaced in 1967. The new Banner was hand embroidered at a cost of 100 guineas.

On 13 January 1949, the Lodge Summons reported that WBro A Charles White, the first WM of Lodge of Unity, had been called to the Grand Lodge Above and in tribute to this highly respected Brother, the Lodge observed a three month period of Masonic mourning.

It was during the early years that two Brethren of note were Initiated, WBro Reginald H Addis, PPrGD, and WM in 1959; and WBro John D Hann. WBro John Hann was Initiated into Lodge of Unity on 9 October 1946 and, in 1960, he was Installed WM of the Lodge. Eventually, in 1992, he became a Grand Officer with the Rank of PAGDC, and appointed Mandated Officer of the Lodge. These Brethren served the Lodge for nigh on 60 years until their deaths.

The initial years saw a high demand for Membership, with Emergency Meetings being called to cope with the intake. Membership of the Lodge grew steadily from its 25 Founders to its peak Membership of 130, 1969-1971.

Throughout its existence, the Lodge has been blessed by long serving Treasurers, most of whom were Initiated into Lodge of Unity. Examples include WBros Glyn Phillips, E James Smith and Clive Lisk. WBro Clive Lisk, PPrSGW, was Initiated on 21 May 1954, and was Installed WM of the Lodge in 1970.

Initially, the Office of Secretary was progressive, but eventually it became a permanent Office. The Lodge is very grateful to such Brethren as the late WBro Sidney Thane, PPrGD, Installed WM in 1961, WBro Gwilym Evans, John D L Baskerville, WM in 1972, and Maurice Warman, PPrJGW, Installed WM in 1982 and 1992; all of whom served the Lodge in a commendable manner for many years. Mention should also be made of WBro F W Siddall, PPrJGW, a Joining Member from Duke of York Lodge No.2453, who had been Initiated on 21 May 1946, and became a Masonic Veteran.

Sadly, the latter part of the 20th century brought with it a general decline in Membership and, by 2007, Lodge of Unity had been reduced to 26 Members. Finally, with a further decline in Membership, the Lodge regretfully decided to surrender its Warrant. This was done at the last meeting of the Lodge, held on 13 November 2008. It was Erased from the Roll of Grand Lodge on 11 March 2009.

Compiled by WBro David M Allen, PPrGSuptWks.

Dyffryn Tawe Lodge No.6056

Warranted : 7 February 1945

Consecrated : 15 March 1945

Meeting at the Masonic Hall, Swansea.

An initial meeting was held on 6 December 1944, when twenty-five Brethren of West Glamorgan Lodge No.5291, Glantawe Lodge No.5378, and Penllergaer Lodge No.5567, met at the Masonic Hall, St Helen's Road, Swansea, to discuss a proposed new Lodge to serve, in the first instance, the Swansea / Tawe Valley, and also to be essentially Welsh in character.

The proposed new Lodge was to be named the 'Dyffryn Tawe Lodge'. It was agreed that the West Glamorgan Lodge would be asked to Sponsor the new Lodge and, in accordance with Rule 116 of the Book of Constitutions, the proposal appeared in the West Glamorgan Lodge Summons for the Regular Meeting of 19 December 1944. Further, it was agreed that the Founder's fee and Initial Joining Members fee would be 7 guineas, such fee to include the annual subscription for the first year. The annual subscription was set at 4 guineas, and the annual subscription for Country Members at 3 guineas, such Members to reside outside the radius of 30 miles of Swansea. It was also decided at this meeting that Bro W M Richards be Elected Treasurer. He was to hold that Office for 30 years, 1945-1975; a record very difficult to surpass. A MM when Dyffryn Tawe Lodge was Consecrated, he had been Initiated into Lodge of Grand Design No.7196 (now Edgar Rutter Lodge) and was Installed WM of that Lodge in 1954.

A further Meeting of the Founders was held on 13 February 1945. WBro Aneurin Rees informed the meeting that he had received a communication from WBro Edgar J Rutter, DepProvGM, informing him that a Warrant had been granted to Dyffryn Tawe Lodge and that the Lodge Number would be 6056. A third Founders' meeting was held at the Masonic Hall, Swansea, on Tuesday, 27 February 1945, when it was agreed that WBro E D Jones, Bro C B Jones and Bro W J Davies would produce a design for a Lodge Banner, based on the Lodge Badge as designed by WBro E D Jones. Finally, it was also agreed that the first four Candidates for Initiation would be: William Llewellyn Watkins, Assistant Labour Officer; Rowe Harding, Barrister-at-law; Frank Gwynne Evans (a Lewis), Pharmacist; and William Wayne, Grocer. Two of them subsequently became Masters of the Lodge. Frank Gwynne Evans was Installed as WM in 1956 and attained the Rank of PPrGD; and William Wayne was Installed as WM in 1957 and attained the Rank of PPrGW.

Dyffryn Tawe Lodge was Consecrated at the Masonic Temple, Swansea, on Thursday, 15 March 1945 by RWBro R P St John Charles, JP, ProvGM. He was assisted by WBro Vaughan John, ProvSGW; WBro John Summers, ProvJGW; and Rev Canon Dr J

Gwyn Davies, ProvGChap. The Installing Master was WBro Edgar J Rutter, PGD, DepProvGM. Following the Consecration Ceremony, the DepProvGM Installed WBro Aneurin Rees, PProvGOrg, PM West Glamorgan Lodge, as the first Master. WBro Evan Daniel Jones, WM of Corinthian Lodge No.4917, was appointed IPM. WBro Alfred W Jenkins, PM Wimbledon Lodge No.3160, Surrey (Erased 2008) was Invested as SW. Bro Rev Oswald R Davies, Chaplain of West Glamorgan Lodge was Invested as JW. WBro Evan A Davies, PM Talbot Lodge No.1323 was the first DC, with WBro William P Lewis, PM Dr James Griffith Hall Lodge No.3161 as ADC. Bro W Glynn Miles was the first Secretary and became WM in 1948. WBro S G Simmons, PProvGTyler, was the first Lodge Tyler, and held that Office from 1945 until 1969.

WBro Aneurin Rees held 14 Meetings during his year in Office; nine Regular Meetings in which Brethren were Initiated and Raised, and five Emergency Meetings in which Candidates were Passed to the Second Degree. At the Regular Meeting in September 1945, the Lodge received a visit from the ProvGM, and a number of the Provincial Officers who had assisted at the Consecration Ceremony. The ProvGM accepted the Gavel and appointed his accompanying Provincial Grand Officers to be Acting Wardens, Deacons and Inner Guard. They then conducted a First Degree Ceremony in which Mr William Thomas Harris and Mr Ivor Arthur Davies were Initiated. The First Degree Charge was given by WBro Edgar J Rutter, DepProvGM.

The Lodge Badge and Banner were designed by the first IPM, WBro Evan Daniel Jones. WBro Jones was Architect to the Pontardawe Rural District Council and, at that time, Pontardawe was regarded as the 'Valley Capital'. Translated into English, 'Pontardawe' means 'Bridge on the Tawe', hence the bridge and the river on the Badge and Banner. Also included is an impression of the Temple at Jerusalem, Masonic Square and Compasses and the leeks to represent Wales, all on a sky blue background. The Lodge Motto: *'Gwna dda ni waeth i bwy'*, may be translated as *'Do good to all, no matter who'*. The Banner was presented in 1953 by three blood brothers, WBros David and Gwylfa Francis and Bro Clifford Francis. After being displayed at every Lodge Meeting for nearly 40 years, the original Banner became very fragile and was replaced with a Banner of identical design in March 1992. The new Banner was Dedicated by VWBro Geoffrey Malin Ashe, TD, PGSwdB, DepProvGM.

It is interesting to note that in the very early years of the Lodge, the Office of Secretary was progressive, the current Secretary moving to Junior Warden and eventually to Worshipful Master. This practice continued until 1949 when Bro W J Davies was appointed Secretary. He held the Office for three years, 1949-1952, during one of which (1950), he was also WM of the Penllergaer Lodge. In 1952, the Office of Secretary took on a more permanent nature, with WBro D Hood Williams, Secretary, 1952-1966.

WBro Aneurin Rees, PGOrg, was the first of four Members of the Lodge to become a Grand Officer, the others being: W Bro J Elwyn Watkins, PAGDC, Installed WM in 1949, and DC from 1958 until 1972; WBro T H C Quick, PGStB, Installed WM in 1965; and WBro B G Hardwidge, PAGDC, Installed WM in 1977.

Every newly Raised Brother of Dyffryn Tawe Lodge is encouraged to join a Royal Arch Chapter. Until 1983, these Brethren had to join a Chapter attached to another Lodge, principally Glantawe Chapter No.5378, although some Members joined other Chapters, such as Doric Chapter No.5968, and Talbot Chapter No.1323. For many years, the Brethren had deemed it desirable to form a Dyffryn Tawe Royal Arch Chapter. Consequently, on the Lodge Summons for 17 September 1982, the following notice appeared: *'To receive an application from the proposed Founders for a Royal Arch Chapter to be attached to the Dyffryn Tawe Lodge No.6056 and, if approved to resolve that the Master and Wardens sign the Petition for the new Chapter and to confirm any acts necessary to further the Petition.'* The Petition was duly signed on Monday, 28 February 1983. The new Chapter was Consecrated by the Most Excellent Grand Superintendent, the Rt Hon the Lord Swansea. EComp T H C Quick, PPrGSN, was Installed as 1st Principal; EComp D H Rees, PPrGStB, was Installed as 2nd Principal; and EComp B G Hardwidge, PPrAGDC, was Installed as 3rd Principal.

Compiled by WBro J H Davies, WBro E H Michael, PPrJGD, and the late WBro B Quick PPrGReg.

Lodge of St Iltyd
No.6078

Warranted : 7 March 1945
Consecrated : 4 May 1945
Meeting at the Masonic Hall, Neath.

The Lodge of Saint Illtyd No.6078 was formed in 1945. There were 34 Petitioners, 16 of whom were Members of Cambrian Lodge No.364, Neath and 15 were Members of Gnoll Lodge No.5057, Neath. The three other Petitioners were from Afan Lodge No.833, Port Talbot; St David's Lodge No.679, Aberdare; and Tennant Lodge No.1992, Cardiff. A Deputation requesting support for the Petition was received at a Regular Meeting of Cambrian Lodge on 16 January 1945, which was duly signed by the WM and Wardens, thus Cambrian Lodge became the Sponsoring Lodge.

WBro Charles Presgrave Palmer, WM Designate, wrote in support of the Petition on 17 February 1945, to the ProvGM, RWBro R P St John Charles, as follows:

'I have pleasure in submitting for your approval and through your good offices, that of The Most Worshipful The Grand Master, a petition for the formation of a new Lodge at Neath to be named 'The Lodge of St. Illtyd'.

It is seriously felt that the two existing Lodges have so large a membership that they offer little opportunity for the progress of Brethren to the Chair, and many enthusiastic young Masons are debarred for many years from achieving their ambition.

The petitioners feel that the formation of his new Lodge will enable them, and others who follow, to fulfil their ambition of being in office and attaining the Chair of the Lodge within a reasonable time, and we therefore pray that you will give this petition your favourable consideration.'

The ProvGM's recommendation was obtained, the Warrant was signed on 7 March 1945, and the Ceremony of Consecration held on 4 May of that year. The success of Freemasonry in Neath ensured that a third Lodge could be readily established. Following the agreement to form an Association of Neath Freemasons in 2005, the three Lodges in the town now share ownership of the first purpose-built Masonic Hall in Wales.

Prior to the building of the present Temple and Hall, the Neath Lodges had met in a variety of premises in and around the town. The building of the present Masonic property first began in 1847, primarily through the dedication of WBro Nicholas B Evans, Brickworks' owner and Steamship Constructor. It was Consecrated in 1848. The Architect, of what is believed to be the first purpose-built Masonic Temple in Wales, was Egbert Moxham of Neath, 1822-1864. The original Lodge building was smaller than that used today, with the Festive Board being held in the body of the Lodge Temple, following the Ceremony. Over the years, the Brethren of Neath Lodges have obtained several distinctive items that grace the Temple and Lodge rooms, including the very distinctive Victorian lamp in the foyer; the organ loft, which was a gift from Indefatigable Lodge No.237; (illustrated on next page), and an original Tracing Board, a rare and irreplaceable item, that is now preserved for posterity and displayed mounted on the south-west wall.

During the reign of Queen Victoria, the Tyler, once employed by the Neath Lodges, was accommodated in the building next door (now shop premises); and the present dais was constructed. By 1863, gas lighting was installed, and by 1870, a 'Company of Brethren' was formed and the Freehold purchased. In 1905, the Tyler's tenancy was replaced by a £10 yearly fee.

A kitchen was provided at the rear of the building, utilising a former school yard; electric lighting was fitted in 1916, and additional space obtained by purchasing the adjoining British

The Organ Loft donated by Indefatigable Lodge

Schools for Girls and Infants' premises. This allowed for more expansion and, eventually, a two storey building was completed by 1934. The dining hall was located on the upper floor and the ground floor altered to provide classrooms and meeting rooms, with the kitchen remaining at the rear. Another distinctive feature is the ornamental fireplace behind the Secretary's desk within the Temple.

Externally, the Lodge building is now listed as an historic building by Cadw ('Cadw' is the Welsh for 'To Keep', and is the historic environment service of the Welsh Assembly Government, which is responsible for conserving, protecting, and presenting the built heritage of Wales.) It is situated in the heart of the town, in the now pedestrianised Queen Street, and presents two courses of white stone within the dressed stone frontage, forming pillars some forty feet high, topped by carvings of Masonic symbols and the 'All Seeing Eye'.

The Lodge Insignia features the original Church of St Illtyd, first built in the Norman period, on the southern bank of the River Neath at Tonna, just outside the town. The Church underwent major structural improvements in 1867, additional work in 1875, and further work to date to keep it as a valued and regular place of worship. The Lodge Jewel and Banner bear the Latin Lodge Motto: *'In Omnibus Caritas'*, the most apt translation being *'Charity in All Things'*.

The Lodge Consecration Ceremony took place at 3.30 pm on Friday, 4 May 1945. RWBro R P St John Charles, PAGReg, ProvGM, South Wales Eastern Division, conducted the Ceremony, assisted by WBro Edgar J Rutter, PGD, DepProvGM, and the Provincial team, which included WBro W Abraham (known by his Bardic name 'Mabon'). The Primus Master was WBro Charles Presgrave Palmer, PPrGW, PAGDC, PM Cambrian Lodge No.364 and Hendre Lodge No.3250, who was also announced as being the new AProvGM for the Province. The Collars for the Incoming Officers were kindly loaned for the occasion by the Brethren of Cambrian Lodge. Bro John Henry Bowen, ASec of Gnoll Lodge No.5057, Company Director, residing in Skewen, was Invested as SW. Bro Edgar Price, Cambrian Lodge, Police Sergeant, residing at the County Police Office, Neath, was Invested as JW. The annual subscription was set at 3 guineas (£3. 15p), the Initiate's fee at 20 guineas (£21).

The first Lodge Meeting was held on 22 May 1945, with WBro J M Davies, Installed WM of Cambrian Lodge in 1940, acting as WM. He was appointed ProvJGW in 1948. The two Initiates for the evening were Mr John Gordon Lloyd and Mr John

Raymond Evans, who became the first Masonic Veteran of the Lodge. In December 1952, WBro Wynn Jones, one of the Founder Members, presented the Lodge with a framed photograph of St Illtyd's Church. This image of the Church is the one that now appears on Lodge Jewels and it is also used in the Lodge Insignia on Lodge documents.

In February 1953, WBro C P Palmer, WM, passed away. Also in 1953, WBro E Courtney Trott, who had been Installed as WM in 1952, became the first IPM to wear the new PM's Collar, inscribed with the names of his predecessors, which had been presented by WBro George Whittington, ProvGSec, 1904-1944. In 1955, the Tyler's Sword was presented by WBro Oswald James.

50th Anniversary Commemorative Tankards and Plate

The Church of Saint Illtyd, from which the Lodge takes its name and image, is believed to date from the Norman period, and to have been improved in the 14th century. At the time of the Renaissance, the Church was plundered in the name of King Edward, although until the entry in Parish Records of 1882 there was little documentation, despite work of restoration and extension being reportedly underway in 1858, and a drawing of 1867 showing the Church without a roof. Distinctive features of the present Church include bells from the 15th and 17th centuries, a Norman font of 12th century origin, and a triple-deck pulpit, the only one known in the Diocese of Llandaff, and possibly even in the Province.

The Lodge reached its 50th Anniversary in 1995, and during that year a series of celebratory events were held, which included a Golden Jubilee Dinner and a Commemorative Service at St Illtyd's Church, Tonna, Neath. A new Master's Apron was presented by WBro John Thomas (WM in 1987), new Hymn Books were presented by WBro Keith M Davies (WM in 1978) and a specially embroidered cushion for the Volume of the Sacred Law, featuring the Insignia of the Lodge, was presented by WBro Edwin J Wearne (WM in 1993). A commemorative porcelain plate and tankards were commissioned for distribution amongst Lodge Members, together with a leather-bound commemorative book compiled by the then Bro Roger D Gale, detailing the history of the Lodge since its formation.

In that Golden Jubilee year, the Lodge received a set of firing glasses from Cambrian Lodge, and these are used by the WM and his Wardens to drink the traditional whisky Toast. The Lodge was also presented with a fine ceremonial Gavel by the Brethren of Gnoll Lodge, Neath, and in later years a boxed set of Square and Compasses presented by WBro Roger D Gale, (WM in 2002), in memory of his late grandfather William H Gale (WM in 1960) and his late father, Les G Gale. WBro Roger followed them into Lodge of Saint Illtyd as a Lewis, and is the only third generation Mason in Neath.

Lodge of St Illtyd enjoys a close affinity with the other Neath Lodges, along with many others in the Province, particularly Baglan Lodge No.6079, Port Talbot, which is traditionally regarded as the 'Sister Lodge', although this is not technically the case. Both Lodges were Warranted on 7 March 1945, with Baglan Lodge, a Daughter Lodge of Afan Lodge No.833, being Consecrated 3 weeks earlier, on 19 April 1945.

In 2010, WBro Rhys L Thomas, who had been Installed as WM in 1998, was the first Master to take that Office for the second time since the formation of Lodge of Saint Illtyd in 1945.

Compiled by WBro Roger Gale, PPrSGD.

Baglan Lodge No.6079

Warranted : 7 March 1945

Consecrated : 19 April 1945

Meeting at the Masonic Hall, Port Talbot.

In order to enable the Brethren of Afan and Margam Abbey Lodges to have the opportunity to take Office, and increase their interest in Freemasonry, it was decided to form another Lodge in Port Talbot. This initiative was enthusiastically supported by Members of both the aforementioned Lodges.

At a Regular Meeting of Afan Lodge No.833, on 4 January 1945, the Petition for the proposed new 'Baglan' Lodge was submitted by WBro Ivor V John, PrSGW, WBro Andrew Scott, PPrSGW, and Bro Gwyn Saunders. The Petition was signed by WBro James Clee, WM; Bro J Reg Webster, SW; and Bro Alfred Lewis, JW; on behalf of Afan Lodge. Masonically speaking, Baglan Lodge is one of twins. Lodge of St Illtyd No.6078, Neath, was Consecrated the day before Baglan Lodge, and both Lodges were Warranted on 7 March 1945. Reciprocal official visits between the two Lodges have been held annually since their Consecrations.

Baglan Lodge No.6079 was Consecrated on 19 April 1945, by RWBro R P St John Charles, ProvGM. The Installing Master was VWBro Edgar J Rutter, PGD, DepProvGM. WBro Ivor Vaughan John was Installed as the first WM, and he Invested WBro Andrew Scott as SW and Bro Gwyn Saunders as JW. The remaining Officers were appointed, and consisted of Brethren well known in the area.

The Lodge Logo, which appears on the Banner and Past Master's Jewel, depicts St Catharine's Church, Baglan, with its clock tower and the golden weather-cock on top of the spire. The spire is easily visible from the M4 motorway, between junctions 41 and 42. The Church, dedicated to St Catharine of Alexandria, is grade I listed, and is the gift of Mr and Mrs Griffith Llewellyn of Baglan Hall (demolished 1958). The foundation stone was laid on 26 June 1875 and the Church was consecrated by Dr Ollivant, Bishop of Llandaff, on 7 March 1882. Constructed at a cost of over £17,000, the Church is an excellent example of Victorian Gothic in the early Decorated style of the late fourteenth century, built according to the plans of John Pritchard, the Diocesan Architect.

In the early days, Lodge Members paid for their meals and visitors came free. Visitors and Members then had a whisky 'on the house'. Since its Consecration, the Lodge has had sixty-two Masters, each only serving one year. No Past Master has had to go into the Chair of King Solomon for a second time. The Lodge has had fathers and sons as Masters. WBro Brinley D Beynon was Installed WM in 1974, and his sons, Bruce M Beynon in 1988, and Adrian B Beynon in 1993. WBro Tom Phillips, Installed WM in 1965 and Barry J Phillips in 1987; WBro Godfrey V Bendall became WM in 1975 and John Llewellyn Bendall in 1996; and the late WBro John Chappell, WM in 1990, his son, Christopher Chappell became WM in April 2010.

The Founder Secretary of the Lodge was WBro Brinley Jenkins. WBro Gordon J Toms served as Secretary from 1958 to 1964,

every Installation Meeting of the Lodge, except on very rare occasions, when he was away from Cardiff.

WBro W H Davies, the first Master, was the Principal of Davies Commercial College, Keppoch Street, Cardiff, which he ran with his daughter, Phyllis. She married WBro D Gerwyn Thomas, PPrGSW. who was the first Senior Deacon of the Lodge. Initiated on 8 March 1940, he became Master of Lodge of Fidelity in 1951. He was active in the Lodge, working as Chaplain, until a nasty fall in 2003. In fact, at the age of 90, he was seen up a ladder painting the bargeboards of his house. Mrs Mary Davies, wife of WBro W H Davies, the first Master of the Lodge, had two brothers – WBro J Charles Price, PAGDC, who was the first Senior Warden of the Lodge and the second Master. Later he became Editor of the Provincial Masonic Year Book. Her second brother was WBro Alcwyn Price, who became Master of the Lodge in 1960.

It was open to any Founder to submit a drawing for the Lodge Crest and two did so. It posed an awkward decision for the Founders, but the problem was removed from the sphere of personalities and a decision arrived at on the basis of 'Masonic' versus 'Heraldic'. The 'Masonic' Crest was the inspiration of the late WBro Ernest Davies. A truly splendid 'Heraldic' drawing had been submitted by the late WBro Cecil Oakes. He proved to be a magnanimous loser, when the final vote was unanimous for the 'Masonic' design.

The resulting Crest was beautifully executed by a Birmingham Jeweller, and, ultimately, it found its way onto the Founders' Jewels, the Master's Collar, the Past Master's Jewel and, as a motif for the Lodge Banner. The Banner was presented to the Lodge by WBro Arthur McTaggart Short, Founder and first Chaplain, who regrettably resigned in 1951, due to pressure of his many commitments. Several suggestions were made for a Motto and that finally accepted was the one submitted by WBro Ronald V Davies: *'Fide et Fiducia'* - *'By faith and Confidence'*. It was considered to go well with the name of the Lodge and to fit well into the outline of the Crest.

Launching a Lodge in 1945 posed many problems. Not the least of these was the matter of supplies, the provision of Lodge 'furniture', Jewels and the like. So many things and materials were in short supply or virtually non-existent. Rations and quotas abounded. The Founders turned to WBro Elfed Davies to overcome some of their difficulties. At that time, he was a buyer for a large warehouse in Cardiff and in that capacity he was at least 'mobile', in that he toured and scoured the country in the search of supplies for his firm. He could therefore keep an eye open for what the Lodge required. There was ribbon for the Collars, metal for the Chain on the Master's Collar and Badges on the Officers' Collars, and lambskin to make Aprons. A manufacturer was found in Birmingham to execute the work. All this labour required twenty odd journeys to Birmingham and cost the Lodge not a penny. Perhaps it may be added that the lambskins, all fourteen of them, were discovered at a tannery in Leicester and it required much pleading to secure them!!

The first Initiate was to have been WBro Alcwyn Price. He was the first Candidate but there was a technical hitch at the last moment and WBro Alcwyn Price had to drop a place. Nevertheless, he was the first Initiate of the Lodge to reach the Chair.

The first Initiate was Bro Horace Field, an accomplished and highly qualified Musician. It was hoped he would have remained as Lodge Organist, but after a while he decided he wanted to 'progress' and ultimately reached the Office of Senior Deacon, at which point, in 1955, he resigned due to the pressure of his professional duties.

In February 1947, WBro W H Price was Initiated. He became Master in 1962 and subsequently served five years as Preceptor of the Lodge of Instruction. He had been a Sergeant Major in the Army during the First World War and ran the Lodge of Instruction that same way, but with compassion. He was highly respected and expected a very high standard of Ritual from the Brethren. He was renowned for his many interesting sayings at the Festive Board.

During 1957, Lodge of Fidelity agreed to Sponsor The City of Cardiff Lodge No.7528, which was Consecrated on 25 June 1957.

In 1984, WBro Reginald Lukins was the first Joining Member of the Lodge to reach the Master's Chair. In the late 1980s, the Lodge ran into trouble, having had no Candidate for three years. WBro Lukins again took the Master's Chair in 1988 and also in 1991. Although fighting cancer during the last year, he never missed a single Meeting or a Lodge of Instruction.

The Lodge now experienced great difficulties, as there were not enough Officers to fill the posts. WBro Tom Hogg was both Director of Ceremonies and Treasurer, which he carried out extremely well. Bro Charles Beddous, a very keen Member of the Lodge, was now sick and housebound, but listed as Senior Deacon. At the time, visitors would arrive, be given a Ritual Book, and asked to fill an empty Office.

WBro Ian Munn, Dinas Powis Lodge No.5997 and the late WBro John Morgan, Tudor Lodge No.8886, both brilliant Ritualists and regular visitors, worked at every Meeting and took every Office in the Lodge, except Worshipful Master and Steward. Both later became Honorary Members.

Mention must be made here of WBro Tony Ough, PGStB, whose many lectures never failed to bring interest to the Meetings. He is also an Honorary Member of the Lodge.

By 1998, there were very few Members; there was no money in the Charity Account; and there was talk of the Lodge surrendering its Warrant. Fortunately, two blood brothers, WBros Michael and George Asprou, had the sense and initiative to persuade WBro Dr Akram Baig to join the Lodge. He was Balloted as a Joining Member in 1998, when WBro George Asprou was Installed in the Chair of King Solomon. WBro George appointed WBro Akram as his Senior Warden and WBro Akram succeeded him as WM of the Lodge in 1999.

A new era for the Lodge had now begun; the Lodge started to get Initiates and Joining Members, and the Lodge began to prosper. The Lodge's Charity Account blossomed due to the many social functions WBro Akram organised, several with the active support of his wife Joan at their home and garden. The Lodge fought back against all the odds and attained a Gold Jewel for the 1999 Festival.

WBro Dr Akram Baig received Grand Lodge Honours in 2000 and was appointed the Lodge's Mandated Officer. Due to his unstinting energy and great enthusiasm, he transformed the Lodge into the vibrant, professional and successful entity any visitor would witness today. He proposed WBro Nicholas Gough Martin as a Joining Member, who became the Secretary of the Lodge. His tireless work, not only for this Lodge but generally for the Craft, was rewarded with Grand Lodge Honours of PAGDC in 2009. WBro Akram also brought in as Joining Members WBro Michael Briscombe, WBro Alan Evans, WBro Wayne Boyland, WBro Ceri Bevan, WBro Trevor Thompson and WBro Alistair Shave-Cox, all of whom have made significant contributions to the Lodge's recovery.

A continuing influx of Candidates, mainly from the medical profession, has seen a growth in Lodge Membership, comprising Orthopaedic Surgeons, ENT and Eye Surgeons, an Anaesthetist, a Cardiologist, General Medical Practitioners and other professional Brethren, who tend to be relatively young, and who take great pride in the Ritual.

WBro Dr Baig and his wife Joan open their house to Brethren every Sunday morning in order for them to practise Ritual and learn about the Craft. The results manifest themselves in superb Ceremonies and firm friendships. Junior Brethren now perform set pieces of Ritual soon after their Initiation and every encouragement is given to these young Brethren from the start.

For the last ten years, the Lodge has performed 2 double Ceremonies at every Meeting, except at Installation. Its Charity Account continues to flourish, with the Lodge proud of the fact that over £1,000 per Member was donated to the 2010 Festival.

Success breeds success and there is now a significant waiting list for Candidates wishing to join, whilst Members and visitors alike continue to enjoy the Meetings and several annual social events.

Compiled by the late WBro Terry Laurie, PPrJGW.

Beehive Lodge
No.6265

Warranted   :   6 March 1946

Consecrated   :   27 April 1946

Meeting at the Masonic Hall, Cardiff.

Beehive Lodge was born from an idea of following the example of the two existing Lloyds Bank Lodges, Bee Hive Lodge No.2809, which was Consecrated in London on 14 June 1900, and Black Horse of Lombard Street Lodge No.4155, London, Consecrated on 20 November 1920. In those early days of the 20th century, the Members of those Lodges comprised not only senior management, management and staff of the Bank, but also Directors, some of whom became very influential within Freemasonry. These included the Earl of Scarborough, who was Grand Master from 1951 to 1967.

Naturally, a close relationship developed between those early Lloyds Bank Lodges and other Bank Lodges which were Consecrated during that period. Amongst the foremost of these were Holden Lodge No.2946, associated with Midland Bank, and Consecrated on 12 June 1903; National Westminster Lodge No.3647, Consecrated on 8 April 1913; St Christopher's Lodge No.4170, Consecrated on 30 October 1920 ; and Porta Episcopi Lodge No.5708, Consecrated on 29 January 1938; these last two Lodges being Bank of England Lodges. Holden Lodge was Erased in June 2010, and National Westminster Lodge amalgamated with Peace and Goodwill Lodge No.5801, London, in September 2002.

Bee Hive Lodge was formed on the initiative of the then Chairman of Capital and Counties Bank, along with two fellow Directors, who were all Members of Lodge of Loyalty No.1533, Marlborough, Province of Wiltshire. Among the Founders were Members of Parliament, a Right Worshipful Brother and the Most Honourable Marquess of Ailesbury. Although Membership had steadily increased from 100 to around 130, WWI intervened to delay further progress but, subsequently, numbers again rose, and it was during this time that Capital and Counties merged with Lloyds Bank.

Lloyds Bank had its origins in Birmingham and was most prominent in the Midlands and the North East, but Capital and Counties was strongest across the South, particularly in South Wales. However, it was the growth in Membership that necessitated the formation of the Black Horse of Lombard Street Lodge in 1920. The choice of title seems perfectly obvious to those with any Banking background, but there had been very serious debate about it, with a goodly number of Founders favouring the 'Richard Vassar-Smith Lodge', as it was he, Sir Richard Vassar-Smith, a long serving Director who had led the way. He became Chairman of Lloyds Bank and also of Port Talbot Steelworks.

However, there was already a Vassar-Smith Lodge No.2994, Lydney, in the Province of Gloucestershire, which had been named after him, so a similarly named Lodge would not be allowed. It may be of interest to note that he created a Charitable Fund for Widows and Orphans of Bank employees which is still in existence. He became the Primus Master of Black Horse of Lombard Street Lodge, being Installed by the Grand Secretary VWBro Philip Colville Smith. Among those assisting him were the ProvGM of Warwickshire, RWBro Col W F Wyley, a Director of the Bank, as SW; RWBro E E Cooper, Lord Mayor of London, as JW; and VWBro J S Granville Grenfell (of the Banking dynasty) as DC. Sir John Ferguson, who shortly afterwards became Grand Treasurer, acted as IPM.

After WWII, both Lodges became Hall Stone Lodges for their contribution towards the building of Freemasons' Hall and, with interest still growing in Freemasonry, they continued to flourish. Encouraged by this trend, some of the Management and staff of Lloyds Bank in South Wales, who were already Freemasons, had the idea of following their example, and set about forming their own Lodge. There were meetings in November 1945 and January 1946, following which 30 would-be Founders signed the Petition. All were staff of Lloyds Bank and from as far afield as the Midlands and West Wales.

It was decided that the name should be 'Beehive', as opposed to 'Bee Hive', and Sponsorship was sought from Hendre Lodge No.3250. The Petition was duly endorsed and RWBro R P St John Charles, ProvGM, performed the Consecration Ceremony on 27 April 1946. There was strong representation from the other two Bank Lodges, the attendance being just over 200, of which 147 were visiting Brethren. The Master Designate, WBro Charles W Jones, PProvGTreas, (Manager of the Aberdare Branch and PM St David's Lodge No.679) was presented by the ProvGM and duly Installed by VWBro Edgar J Rutter, OSM, PGD, DepProvGM. The Acting Officers included WBro Harry F Stockwell, PAGDC, acting as Secretary. Afterwards, the Master Invested Bro R M Wignall as SW, and Bro Ron Pinney as JW, along with the rest of his Officers. Bro Ron, WM in 1948, was later to become influential both within the Lodge and in the Bank, where he served as Manager of the St Mary Street, Cardiff Branch, for many years.

RWBro R P St John Charles, VWBro Edgar J Rutter and the Worshipful Masters of Bee Hive and Black Horse of Lombard Street Lodges were all Elected as Honorary Members. The actual wording in the Election of the latter being *the WM for the time being of the Bee Hive Lodge No.2809 and the Black Horse of Lombard Street Lodge No.4155*.

Both Bee Hive and Beehive Lodges take their name from the earliest symbol of Lloyds Bank, although it actually dates back at least to the 1720s, as the 'distinguishing mark' of thrift and industry, naturally associated with savings and banking institutions. There was reference to the beehive insignia in relation to Lloyds Bank in the Birmingham Gazette in 1765. When the Lombard Street headquarters of the Bank was purchased, the hanging sign on both sides of the building bore a beehive, with the year 1677 below. This was adopted by the Bank as its insignia until it was challenged by the Midland Bank in the 1960s, when the date was removed, only because Lloyds was unable to prove that it had anything to do with its origins. Then, in quite a short period of time, it gave way to the black horse, the 'Dark Horse' having been the name of the staff magazine for numerous years. The Bank's signage, its cheque books and letterheads had to be changed, but the sign together with the date still survives on some of the stonework and fascias, and the Bank's Official Seal incorporated a beehive until 1982.

It was, therefore, quite natural for the Founders to have adopted the Beehive (technically called a 'skep') with the date 1677 above for its Crest and Banner, on which it is surmounted by the Welsh Dragon. Bee hives are commonly depicted symbols in Freemasonry as they represent humility, as well as the importance of a strong team-based work ethic. It also symbolises the practice of secrecy, as only the busy bees know what takes place within the hive. The bee hive (skep) is also depicted on the front of every Freemason's Collar at the lower centre of the 'V' immediately above the Jewel, in allusion to the desirable attributes mentioned above.

It had been agreed that PM Founders would not seek advancement, so that younger Members would be given ample opportunity of progressing to the Chair of King Solomon. Applications for Membership were numerous after the Consecration, and Emergency Meetings were quite common during the first five years. In 1948, the increase in numbers led to Lodge Meetings being increased from four to six. Membership peaked in 1962 at just over a hundred, and it was at this time that it was particularly noted that *'Brethren travelled from far and wide to attend our Saturday Meetings'*.

In 1951, the Brethren were invited to join the other two Bank Lodges at Grand Lodge, for what was set to become a regular five-yearly Meeting of all three Lodges. It was the idea of the Most Worshipful Grand Master, the Rt Hon The Earl of Scarborough, a Director of the Bank, that a meeting *'to attract all Freemasons on the Board and on the staff'*, would benefit greatly and add to the *esprit de corps*, which the Bank always strongly promoted. It was held on 5 July 1951 at Freemasons' Hall, under the Banner of Bee Hive Lodge, whose Master at the time was WBro Robert H G Marshall. Some 224 Brethren attended that Meeting and afterwards dined at the Connaught Rooms. Miss Grace Nevern, soprano, accompanied by Bro Stanley Mole, entertained them, but the entertainment does not appear to have been repeated at subsequent Meetings. The business of the Meeting was to read a short history of all three Lodges.

It was the specific wish of the Grand Master that such Meetings be held every five years. In 1956, under the Banner of Black Horse of Lombard Street Lodge, the second Meeting was held, also with the MWGM in attendance, with a paper being delivered by the ProvGM for Middlesex. In 1961, the combined Meeting witnessed the Dedication of the Black Horse of Lombard Street's Banner, which was carried out by the ProvGM for Norfolk, in the presence once more of the MWGM. The Joint Meeting was similarly honoured in 1966, when another Director of the Bank was present, RWBro the Hon the Lord Kenyon, ProvGM for North Wales, who, with the DepProvGM, RWBro Major General Sir Allan Adair, regularly attended Meetings up until 1987. In that year, RWBro Norman Victor Watkins, a retired Lloyds Bank Manager and Member of Black Horse of Lombard Street Lodge, attended and, by then, had become ProvGM for Gloucestershire. He was central in overseeing Black Horse of Lombard Street Lodge's move from London to Downend, Bristol, in 1992, following the Bank's Head Office move to that city. The five-yearly Meetings were held at Freemasons' Hall or Mark Masons' Hall until 22 June 1996, when Beehive Lodge No.6265 hosted the Meeting at Cardiff Masonic Hall.

With WBro Ian Dodd in the Chair, the Lodge hosted not only Members of the other two Lodges, but also a large number of visiting Brethren from across the Province. All present heard the Prestonian Lecturer, WBro Keith Flynn OBE, give a most comprehensive talk on 'Freemasonry in the War'. WBro Keith had been Initiated into Beehive Lodge in March 1961 and pursued his Masonic career mainly in Dinas Llandaff Lodge No.8512 where he was a Founder Member. He received Grand Lodge Honours as PAGDC in 1994 and was Promoted to PJGD in 2002. He published his first book under the title of his Prestonian Lecture and another entitled 'Behind the Wire', a few years later.

In preparation for this event, Brethren had decided that it was due time the Lodge had an appropriate Banner. All the work was sponsored by a very fondly remembered WBro Carlton Johnson, WM in 1991. It was Dedicated by VWBro Cdr Roy K Hopkin, RN, PGSwdB, DepProvGM, supported by WBro Rev Norman Lea, PAGChap, ProvGChap, along with WBro D Gerald Williams, PGStB, ProvSGW; WBro Keith B Lockyer, ProvJGW; WBro Arthur O'Neil, ProvSGD; and WBro Selwyn G J Craze, PProvGStwd. WBro Bill Lloyd, WM 1994, had the honour of presenting the Banner for Dedication. It was a grand affair and the festivities continued afterwards at an hotel in St Mary Street. The new Banner was naturally prominently on display at the Golden Jubilee Celebrations, and now hangs proudly in the Duke of Connaught Temple.

Then, in 2000, it was Bee Hive Lodge's turn to Celebrate, this being its Centenary year, it was decided that it should be marked with a combined Lodge Meeting. As by this time the merger of Lloyds Bank with the Trustee Savings Bank was well under way, it was also decided to contact Lodge of Prudence No.8946, which had been formed for the benefit of TSB staff. It was Consecrated in Stamford, Province of Northamptonshire & Huntington on 25 October 1980 and it is empowered to hold Meetings under

Dispensation in other Provinces and, indeed has done so in Temples as far apart as Manchester and Jersey. Contact was made with the Lodge Secretary, and it was extremely pleasing to see many Members of that Lodge present at the festivities. This marked the first occasion that the Combined Meeting comprised four Bank Lodges. Again, a large number of Masonic dignitaries attended, among them RWBro Peter Marsh, ProvGM for Gloucestershire, who had been a Cheltenham & Gloucestershire Building Society Executive and had a very tangible association with Lloyds Bank as just after his retirement, the Society had been embraced by the Bank. Over 140 Brethren attended and it is certain that the Earl of Scarborough would have been delighted that his initiative was still being well supported some 50 years later. Continuing the tradition, in 2006, the Meeting took place at Downend, under the Banner of the Black Horse of Lombard Street Lodge.

On 11 June 2011, marking the 60th Anniversary of the Joint Meetings, Beehive had the very great pleasure of hosting the Five Yearly Meeting again when, in the presence of RWBro Captain Sir Norman Lloyd-Edwards, ProvGM, WBro Kevin Hearne gave a talk entitled 'Banking on Freemasonry' and for the very first time WBro Paul Constable, WM of Lodge of Prudence added to the proceedings by giving a short Lecture on the History of his Lodge. At the same Meeting, the ProvGM presented Certificates to WBros G Eddie Jones, Keith T Flynn and Robert T Davies who all celebrated 50 years in Freemasonry.

Society has undergone significant changes over the last two decades particularly and these have impacted on Freemasonry in general and the Bank Lodges in particular. Candidates have been much more difficult to come by because of constraint in the public sector, and also with the more general changes in working patterns and increasing pressures on family life. Although Bee Hive and Black Horse of Lombard Street Lodges became 'open' much earlier, it was in 1998 that Beehive Lodge had to make the tough decision to follow suit, although initially only to the wider financial sector. Within the Bank there had already been substantial change with a much smaller and younger proportion of male staff. Relationships within the network have also changed and today Freemasonry is far less prevalent and understood amongst the Directors and executive staff. Selectivity and retention are the bywords for today.

At this stage in the history of Beehive Lodge, it is fitting that we recognise and pay tribute to those Members who have made their mark within the Order and have helped to shape the character of the Lodge and indeed its workings and customs.

The first Grand Officer was WBro Col Gordon L P Elias, who was the Primus Master and the driving force behind the formation of the Daughter Lodge, Cape St Vincent Lodge No.8524, Consecrated on 17 September 1973. He was appointed PAGDC in 1970, in recognition of his influence and work, not only within Beehive Lodge where he had been Treasurer for 18 years, but throughout the Province. He was subsequently appointed Provincial Senior Grand Warden in 1978. He was also Treasurer of the Lodge of Benevolence No.7305 for a period of 5 years.

Mandated Officers have included such stalwarts as WBro Cecil Rapport and WBro E Wyndham Powell. To mention real personalities among the list of PMs would require a book apart, but among those we would wish to include is WBro Idris J Williams, WM in 1958, number one Cashier in Lloyds, High Street Branch, Cardiff , who overcame a serious stammer to perform Masonic Ritual extremely well. It was he, together with his Wardens, Bro John Roberts and Bro Cliff Taylor, who presented the Lodge with its Gauntlets. WBro Ben Williams (WM 1963) who went on to become a General Manager of the Bank in the 1980s and WBro Gruffydd John Morgan (WM 1967), PPSGW, affectionately known as '*the general*', who became an Instructor at the Staff College in Surrey and continued his Masonic career in Southampton. It was in Southampton that the MWGM, the Earl of Scarborough suggested another Bank Lodge could be established. On this occasion, however, there seems to have been a lack of sufficient support, and the idea had to be dropped.

Two PMs stood out in another way in the late 1970s and 1980s, WBro G Eddie Jones, WM in 1971, PProvSGW, Treasurer for 21 years, and WBro Mike Thomas, PPrJGW, WM in1980, who unofficially acted as Preceptors to the Lodge in the days when practices were held either in Bank premises or in local hostelries. WBro Mike's wife, Brenda, worked in Provincial Office and was a real stalwart during the days when WBro Malcolm J Thompson was ProvGSec. Lodge Gavels were commissioned in memory of the late WBros G John Morgan and Mike Thomas.

WBro Michael George Jones (Mike), WM 1973, PPrJGW, one of three brothers who all left their mark on Freemasonry, went on to be Founder SW of Afon Dâr Lodge No.8829, in February 1978. WBro Brian E Langley, WM 1986, served the Lodge for 12 years as DC. He is principally known throughout the Province for taking charge and guiding the Provincial Magazine, 'Y Dalaith', formerly known as 'The Guildford Gazette', into more productive and prosperous times. He also succeeded VWBro Roy K Hopkin, RN, PGSwdB, PDepProvGM, as Chairman of the Cardiff based Charity 'Masonic Feed the Homeless', and, in 2005, was accorded Grand Rank being appointed as PGStB. Mirroring WBro Gordon's appointment in 1978, WBro Brian was Invested as Senior Warden of the Province in 2011. The Lodge DC's wand commemorates Brian's huge contribution to Beehive Lodge. His Co-initiate in 1976 was WBro Martyn Ridge, WM 1984, PPrGReg, who has been Lodge Organist for well over twenty years.

As active Members within the Province and indeed for their outstanding contribution to Beehive Lodge, WBro John M Steward, WM in 1992, PPrGSwdB; and WBro Kevin Hearne, WM in 1993, PPrDepGDC, will perhaps be best known as ProvAGDC and ProvGStwd respectively, WBro Kevin having served the Lodge as DC for over twelve years. Another talented and outstanding PM is WBro William (Bill) L Lloyd, WM in 1994, PPrJGD. Firstly, as a Joining Member, he achieved the Chair in Bee Hive Lodge in 1991, was WM in Black Horse of Lombard Street Lodge in 1993 and was then Installed in the following year in the Chair of his Mother Lodge, Beehive Lodge, Cardiff. WBro Bill has been accorded London Grand Rank.

It is, perhaps a little unusual for a regular visitor to be Elected an Honorary Member, but the late WBro Peter Madsen (PM Gwalia Lodge No.4213) having not missed a single Meeting over a period of 20 years was accorded that honour in 1996, and in the following year he presented the Lodge with mahogany based cushions for the presentation of the Working Tools and Aprons.

It was only at the beginning of the 1990s that Beehive Lodge felt that their original 'utility' Officers' Collars had come to the end of the road and a new set was ordered. The original Collars were shorter than the regular length and exactly an inch narrower, but they had certainly served the Lodge well.

Within living memory it has always been the practice to invite the WM and Wardens of not only our Sister Bank Lodges, but also other Bank Lodges in the Province, for example St Mildred Lodge No.5078 and Celtic Eagle Lodge No.9132 to our Installations. Insofar as the Lloyds Bank Lodges are concerned, this has been reciprocated with Beehive's WM being invited to take one of the Wardens' Chairs for the actual Installation Ceremony.

A practice developed in relatively recent years, and becoming a tradition, is the delivery of a Past Masters' Third Degree Ceremony once a year. Retention being as important as selective recruitment, it is now customary to invite up to 20 PMs to occupy Offices and perform Ritual mostly in unaccustomed Offices and positions. Adding interest for visitors and Members alike, it stimulates mature Brethren and ensures healthy attendances.

Beehive has always been an extremely friendly Lodge, where democratic discussion has always led to unanimity and harmony within the Lodge.

Compiled by WBro William L Lloyd, PPrJGD, LGR,
and WBro Brian E Langley, PGStB, ProvSGW.

Gelligaer Lodge No.6298

Warranted   :   1 May 1946

Consecrated   :   8 July 1946

Meeting at the Masonic Hall, Bargoed.

The Lodge was formed between 1945 and 1946 by Brethren who thought that a Lodge was required to serve the northern reaches of the Rhymney Valley. At that time, the Rhymney Valley was a very busy place and the only Lodges nearby were St David's Lodge No.2226, Rhymney, in the Province of Monmouthshire, and Henry Pendrill Charles Lodge No.3769 at Caerphilly, in the Province of South Wales. The latter became the Sponsoring Lodge; however, many of the Founders came from both of these Lodges.

The man responsible for setting up the Lodge was WBro Stanley Jacob Vowel Hood, PPrGW, who became the Primus Master, and was the father of the late WBro John Basil Hood, PAGDC. An Accountant by profession, he ran a well known accountancy business in Bargoed.

There were twenty-seven Founder Members, and the Lodge was Consecrated at the Masonic Temple, Princes Avenue, Caerphilly, on Monday, 8 July 1946 by RWBro R P St John Charles, ProvGM South Wales Eastern Division, assisted by his Provincial Officers. The Installing Master was VWBro Edgar Rutter, OSM, PGD, DepProvGM.

The Lodge name is derived from the historical village and Borough of Gelligaer. The Lodge Crest shows the clock tower of the ancient Parish Church of St Catwg, Gelligaer. The Lodge Motto is: 'Brawdgarwch' ('Brotherly Love'). The Lodge Banner was made from a sketch drawn by Bro Percy Ford, from which WBro Redvers England produced a full size drawing, which was used to make the actual Banner. The drawing, showing St Catwg's Church tower, was sent to a ladies' home run by Nuns in West Wales where the Banner was constructed and embroidered. RWBro Edgar Rutter Dedicated the Banner in the Lodge Room at Calfaria Chapel in 1961. It now hangs above the Master's Chair in the Lodge's current home at Trinity Masonic Centre, Bargoed.

The early Lodge Meetings were held in the Central Hall of the Methodist Chapel Assembly Rooms in Bargoed. Before the Lodge could be opened, the Lodge furniture etc. had to be set up, and later dismantled at the close of the Lodge by the Brethren, who then stored everything safely in a secure cupboard.

The Lodge's second home was the Vestry of Calfaria Chapel, using the same procedure as had been employed at the previous meeting place. This room was so small that attendance was restricted to a maximum of twenty Brethren. During this period, the Festive Board was held at the nearby Hanbury Hotel, where the landlord, WBro B Burgess gave them a warm welcome. Since the Consecration, however, the Installation Meetings and subsequent Festive Board have been held at the Masonic Temple, Caerphilly.

When Calfaria Chapel and the Royal Hotel were demolished in 1966 to make way for a new supermarket, the Lodge was effectively left without a home. Henry Pendrill Charles Lodge No.3769 then kindly invited Gelligaer Lodge to hold its Regular Meetings at the Caerphilly Masonic Temple. The offer was gratefully accepted and the Lodge met there for the next five years.

In due course, enquiries were made to find suitable premises to convert into a Masonic Temple. In 1970, Trinity Chapel at Bargoed became available. A decision was made to purchase the building, the Brethren agreeing to take on what was a very large commitment at that time. A local builder converted the building, with the Brethren undertaking certain other aspects of the work, thus giving Gelligaer Lodge its own permanent home.

RWBro the Rt Hon the Lord Swansea, ProvGM and his team of Officers Consecrated the new Temple in 1971. The first Worshipful Master to preside in the new premises was WBro Colin J James. Initiated in 1959, and Worshipful Master in 1971, he is now one of the Masonic veterans of the Lodge. During 200-2002, the Lodge rooms underwent a major renovation and modernising programme, consisting of a new committee room, toilets, kitchen, and a tastefully decorated function suite. Working to a very tight schedule, the work was completed in time for its Official Opening by RWBro Hywel Davies, ProvGM on Friday, 6 September 2002. The building is entirely self-contained and accommodates Ystrad Mynach Lodge No.8567, Gelligaer Holy Royal Arch Chapter No.6298, The Trinity Mark Lodge No.1845, and various charitable organisations.

St Catwg's Church, Gelligaer

The Lodge is very proud of its two United Grand Lodge Officers, namely WBros Brian Eveleigh, PSGD, and Victor G Watkins, PAGSuptWks, who were both Initiated into the Lodge and give such sterling service.

WBro Brian Eveleigh, PSGD, was Initiated into the Gelligaer Lodge in 1977 and became Worshipful Master in 1987. First appointed Provincial Senior Grand Deacon in 1993, he was promoted to Provincial Junior Grand Warden in 1997. He became a Grand Officer of the United Grand Lodge of England in 1999, with the Rank of PAGDC. Later that year, he was appointed Assistant Provincial Grand Master, an Office he held until 31 December 2010. In 2000, he was promoted to Past Senior Grand Deacon. During his period as AProvGM he was the Executive Officer responsible for all aspects of communication, education and training throughout the Province. WBro Brian is active in a number of other Masonic orders, including Royal Arch, Rose Croix, Mark and Royal Ark Mariners. He is a Founder Member of St Catherine's Lodge No.9503, and Gelligaer Chapter No.6298. An Honours Graduate in Law, he was a Police Officer by profession, retiring in 1999 from his post of Divisional Commander at Merthyr Tydfil.

WBro Victor George Watkins was Initiated into Gelligaer Lodge in 1972 and became Worshipful Master in 1982. In 1988, he was appointed PPrJGD and promoted to PPrJGW in 2001. He became the Acting Provincial Senior Grand Warden in 2008. A Joining Member of Luminary Lodge No.8530 in 1999, he served as WM in 2001. WBro Victor became a Grand Officer in 2003, with the Rank of PAGSuptWks. Since 2005, he has been Chairman of Geoffrey Ash Court, Cowbridge. WBro Victor is a Member of a number of other Masonic orders, holding Acting Rank in Royal Arch, Mark, and the Order of the Secret Monitor. He is a Founder Member of St Tydfil's Lodge No.9753 and Luminary Chapter No.8530. An Electrician by profession, he worked in industry before establishing his own business. Since his retirement in 1995, he spends much of his time sitting as a Magistrate in Gwent, having been appointed a Justice of the Peace in 1997.

A distinguished Brother worthy of mention is WBro John Hood, the son of WBro Stanley Jacob Vowel Hood, PPrGW, the Primus Master of Gelligaer Lodge. He was the first Initiate of the Lodge on 14 April 1947, and was very proud of the fact that he was Initiated, Passed and Raised by his father. He was Installed as Worshipful Master in 1957. A Masonic Veteran of 64 years standing, he was also a Masonic Veteran of 54 years as a Worshipful Brother. He was appointed to United Grand Lodge in 1983 with the Rank of PGStB, and promoted to PAGDC in 1994. An Accountant by profession, he joined his father's business in Bargoed after completing his training in Cardiff, and remained in practice there until 2002 when, at the age of 80 years, he decided to retire. Interestingly, at one time he was the Treasurer in no less than 31 Lodges and Chapters! Sadly, WBro John B Hood, PAGDC, passed to the Grand Lodge Above on Friday, 1 July 2011.

At the time of writing (2011) the Lodge has four Brethren who are Masonic Veterans; Redvers C B England, PPrJGD, (PPrSGD, Bucks.), Initiated 11 January 1954; D Benjamin (Ben) Evans, PPrSGW, Initiated 10 October 1955; Peter H Smith, PPrGSwdB, Initiated 12 January 1959 and Colin H J James, PPrAGDC, (PPrSGW, Mon), Initiated 12 January 1959.

WBro Redvers England was Initiated in 1954 and became Worshipful Master in 1964. Interestingly, he and WBro Ben Evans were Raised together in 1957. He was appointed PPrJGD in 1970 and to PPrSGD in the Province of Buckinghamshire in 1985. A Draughtsman by profession, he became Chief Draughtsman for Coal Products (NCB), and it was he who produced the full size drawing used to make the Lodge Banner.

WBro Ben Evans was Initiated in 1955 and became Worshipful Master in 1966. Appointed PAGDC in 1971, he was promoted to PPrJGW in 1988 and to PPrSGW in 1990. He was Secretary of the Lodge for seventeen years, between 1983 and 2000. He is particularly well known locally for his contribution to the Royal Arch. He was the Founding Scribe Ezra of Gelligaer Chapter in 1988, a position he still holds 23years later!

WBros Colin James and Peter H Smith are Masonic 'twins', having been Initiated together in 1959. WBro Peter has two sons in the Lodge, one of whom, Bro Major Howard Smith, represented Great Britain as a member of the Four Man Bobsleigh team at the 1984 Winter Olympics held in Sarajevo.

Compiled by WBro Peter Smith, PPrGSwdB; WBro Vernon Perry, PM,
and WBro Brian Eveleigh, PSGD, PAProvGM.

Porthkerry Lodge No.6299

Warranted : 1 May 1946

Consecrated : 9 July 1946

Meeting at the Masonic Hall, Barry.

In common with more than half the Lodges in South Wales, Porthkerry Lodge is related to Glamorgan Lodge No.36, which in 2003, celebrated the 250th Anniversary of its original Warrant, which was granted in 1753. The family tree indicates that Barry Lodge No.2357 is the Daughter of Glamorgan Lodge, which in turn formed Vale of Glamorgan Lodge No.3977, Old Barrians Lodge No.6671 and Loyal Sportsman Lodge No.9197. Not only is Vale of Glamorgan Lodge the Mother Lodge of Porthkerry Lodge No.6299, but also of Breaksea Lodge No.8358 and Lodge of Round Table No.9549. Llantwit Major Lodge No.9241 is a Daughter Lodge of Porthkerry Lodge and consequently its relationship with Glamorgan Lodge is Great Granddaughter.

The Consecrating Officer on 9 July 1946 was RWBro R P St John Charles, JP, PAGReg, ProvGM. Among others, he was assisted by WBro Harry F Stockwell, PAGDC, ProvGSec. The Installing Officer was VWBro Edgar J Rutter, OSM, PGD, DepProvGM, who placed the Primus Master, WBro Griffith Jenkins, PPrGW, PGStB, PM Barry Lodge and PM Hendre Lodge No.3250, into the Chair of King Solomon. He then Invested WBro Francis James Watts, PM Vale of Glamorgan Lodge, PPrAGDC, as SW; WBro John William Lennox, PPrAGStB, PM Barry Lodge as JW. WBro Samuel Archibald Evans, PPrAGDC as IPM, with WBro John Richard Kempe Vickery, PPrGSuptWks as the Founder Chaplain, both PMs Vale of Glamorgan Lodge. Another Founder was Bro Charles Kenneth Brynmor Lennox, who was born in 1913 and is still alive as this history is being written.

The name 'Porthkerry' translated means 'Harbour of Kerry'. When it came to selecting a suitable name, the Founders had sought one that would somehow link the Vale of Glamorgan and the town of Barry with its thriving sea-going industry. They found that link in the railway which was used for transporting coal through the Vale of Glamorgan over the large stone viaduct just outside the village of Porthkerry.

Amongst the Founders of the Lodge were a goodly number of Brethren who had seen active service during WWII. This is reflected in the choice of Lodge Motto included in the Insignia: *'In Loco Isti Dabo Pacem'* which translates as *'In this place will I give peace'*. The central geometrical figure in the Insignia and on the Banner is a vesica piscis bearing a representation of Porthkerry Park, consisting of a green sward with trees spanned by a viaduct, being imperfect (as it is in the actual structure), and referring to the imperfection of man's hands. The Heavens are represented in the upper part of the figure, which also shows the 'All Seeing Eye' of the Great Architect of the Universe. The Figure rests upon a base taken from the Arms of the Borough of Barry, consisting of a representation of the waves of the sea and the pebble shore, to which has been added a ship, reproduced from the Crest of Barry Lodge. The whole refers to the Lodge's connection with the town of Barry and its seafaring activities. The encompassing ribbons are taken from the Crest of the Vale of Glamorgan Lodge and bears the Welsh Dragon in the upper part, with the Lodge number and name on the base. The waves and the pebble beach seem particularly apt, as we are led to believe that at one time the sea-shore was only yards from the Barry Hotel and adjacent to the Masonic Hall building.

The first thirty years of the Lodge's history were dominated by Brethren who really were truly stalwart supporters of Freemasonry who, together with many other PMs, encouraged new Members and ensured the Lodge ran very smoothly. The most prominent were WBro Trevor G Andrews, PPrJGW, Treasurer, and WBro David W Thomas, PPrJGW, Secretary. The President of the LOI during that period was WBro Trevor. He was a wonderful character and always maintained that the happiness of the Brethren was of paramount importance. He and many other PMs including WBros Evangelos Germanicos, Frederick A Flint, Charles John Morris, Edrick Hedley and, in more recent years, WBro Glyn T Evans have been Presidents of the LOI. WBro Glyn has been ably assisted by the Vice-Presidents, WBros Ian R Macdonald, Adrian Mizen, Leslie Davies and Malcolm Lucas who all strive to ensure this tradition is carried on.

The foundations laid by the Founders in promoting happiness and friendship have proved those original precepts to be absolutely right, leading to a steady growth in Membership, peaking in the mid 1970s at around 150. In those days the new Bindles Ballroom featured prominently in the Lodge's social activities, as many successful Ladies' Festivals were held there. Many other Masonic events were also held, not only at the Masonic Hall, but also at the Memorial Hall in Barry. These also did a great deal to promote the enjoyment side of Freemasonry and in turn encouraged other gentlemen to join and thus enjoy the camaraderie and friendship.

The Founders had made it a rule that all Officers of the Lodge should wear dinner suits. A polite letter from the Secretary, WBro Leslie Watts Thomas, PPrJGW, to the Brethren in 1971, served to remind them to adhere to this rule, which is still being observed. At that time, the cost of the meal at the Installation Festival was £1.25p.

In the early 1970s, WBro William Annand Reid, whose nickname was 'Jock' for obvious reasons, turned a lot of heads when he arrived at Lodge in tartan trews and short black Scottish dress jacket. He continued to do so for many years, and this colourful tradition was followed by other Brethren with Scottish connections. His son, WBro Duncan Andrew Reid, together with WBro Ian Robinson Macdonald are foremost in carrying on this tradition. Latterly, in conjunction with WBro David James Goodall of Beehive Lodge, Fraternal visits to Lodges in the Scottish Constitution have been organised, all of which have been well supported and thoroughly enjoyed by all who have taken part. At least one of the trips included a visit to Rosslyn Chapel, with the symbolism contained therein explained by a very experienced Scottish Mason. On another one of the visits, a South Wales Mason volunteered to be a 'token' Candidate in a purely Scottish Raising. Their Ceremony and floor work differing quite a lot from our own, he returned home rather battered and bruised, which necessitated some explanation to his wife and family!

With the approach of the 50th Anniversary, the Committee decided to have a Lodge Banner made and WBro George C F Wilson, PPrJGW, Secretary, with the assistance of WBro Alvern M M Hart, PJGD, produced a beautiful design, which was approved by the MW the Grand Master on 14 March 1994. One of the Brethren, Bro Ken Rogers, owner and Managing Director of Hyper-Value, using some of his numerous business connections, arranged for the Banner to be made and generously donated it to the Lodge. A formal Banner Dedication Ceremony was held on 27 January 1995, when the Dedicating Officer was WBro

Ken Adams Morgan, PSGD, AProvGM. The WM on that occasion was WBro Gareth Thomas Jones. The Banner proved to be somewhat larger than the Brethren had expected, and the story still prevails that it was designed and planned in imperial units (feet and inches) but that it was subsequently made using metric units (metres and centimetres).

Bro Ken Rogers also donated a limited edition of key-rings, each one being individually numbered, with a somewhat optimistic original production run of 500. The idea of presenting such a key-ring to each Member and Initiate carries on to this day. At the present rate of usage, the Lodge should have an ample supply for the next decade or so!

Approximately 18 months later, in October 1996, a Dinner was arranged to commemorate the 50th Anniversary of Porthkerry Lodge. The WM was WBro David Hopkin, PPrJGD, and the menu card for the evening records the names of all Members and Initiates of Porthkerry Lodge during the preceding 50 years, which numbered over 300 Brethren.

Highlights in the history of Porthkerry Lodge include the Initiations of sons by their fathers. WBro Trevor G Andrews, PPrGW, Installed as WM in 1951, Initiated his son, Brian Andrews, and both were present when Brian's son, Timothy B Andrews, was Initiated, thus three generations of one family were together in the Lodge. WBro Evangelos Germanacos, PPrJGW, Installed as WM in 1955, Initiated both his sons, Theodore and Andreas. More recently, WBro Robert Louis Ayres, PPrSGD, Installed as WM in 1977, Initiated, Passed and Raised his son, Bro Adam Ayres. An even more recent Member, Bro Karl Alexander Butler, was proposed into the Lodge by his father, Bro Derek Butler. It is a source of pleasure, hope and optimism for the future to see the sons of Masons, and thus much younger Brethren, join our Fraternal Organisation.

On 24 May 2002, at the 500th Meeting of the Lodge, WBro Ian Robinson Macdonald was Installed into the Chair of King Solomon, just cause for a double celebration and a suitable Festive Board. The names of all the original Officers at the Consecration in 1946 were listed on the Menu Cards alongside their counterparts of 2002.

The Barry Lodges, together with Llantwit Major Lodge, have a long established tradition of supporting each other. Consequently, Porthkerry Lodge is very fortunate in always being blessed with a goodly number of visiting Brethren of all Ranks at its Ceremonies. A number of Brethren who have moved away and, consequently, have been unable to attend Lodge regularly, have remained Subscribing Members. One such Brother was Bro Arthur Cuthbert Williams, Initiated on 23 November 1951. He had 56 years of unbroken service until, sadly, he passed away in March 2007. Also, WBro Frederick Graham Smith, PPrAGDC, who was Initiated into the Lodge on 28 November 1952, and was Installed as the 18th Master in May 1963, is still a Subscribing Member.

Very many Lodge Members have become Founders and active Members of other Lodges, Chapters and Degrees. Prominent among these are other local Lodges, Breaksea Lodge; Lodge of the Seven Seas No.8693, Wenvoe Lodge No.9038 and Loyal Sportsman Lodge.

The contribution made by the Lodge's Grand Lodge Officers in offering valued help and wise advice over many years is appreciated by all. The Lodge is very fortunate in having had five such Brethren recognised for their hard work. Three have passed to the Grand Lodge Above, namely, WBros Griffith Jenkins, PGStB; John W Lennox, PGStB; and more recently, Stanley Michael Mortimer, PAGDC, who passed away towards the end of 2006. WBro Stan together with WBros Alvern Myron Murray Hart, PJGD, Installed as WM in 1969, and Melvyn D M Thomas, PAGDC, Installed as WM in 1977, would be known and recognised all over the Province. For many years, Porthkerry Lodge was unique in having three Grand Officers concurrently attending Lodge Meetings.

A most moving and sincere tribute was paid to the late WBro Stan by VWBro Peter Frost, DepProvGM, on 23 February 2007, when he presented Stan's 50 year Masonic Veteran's Certificate to his son, WBro Jeffrey Mortimer. It was a very special occasion, necessarily tinged with sadness. WBro Stan had been Initiated on 24 November 1956, Installed as WM in 1964, and in 2006/7 was the First Principal of Hendre Chapter. He had been unable to be present on his actual 50th Anniversary in 2006, as he was attending the Chapter's Election Night. Other tributes and presentations were made at the Festive Board, where the atmosphere was one of joy, with each Brother having his own recollections of happy times in company with WBro Stan. Everyone who knew him will acknowledge the tremendous work he did to promote and support Masonry right across South Wales.

WBro Alvern Murray Hart, a great friend of WBro Stanley Mortimer, spent most of his professional career as an Engineer with BP Chemicals, (formerly the Distillers Company), Sully. He was Initiated into Porthkerry Lodge on 24 April 1961, and was presented with his Masonic Veteran's Certificate by VWBro Andrew Lindsay Gretton, DepProvGM, at a Regular Lodge Meeting on 25 April 2011. Later, at the Festive Board, WBro Peter B Evans, WM, presented WBro 'Al' with a crystal tantalus, on behalf of the Brethren of the Lodge. Al was a Founder of the Lodge of the Seven Seas and of Wenvoe Lodge, and an Honorary Member of several Lodges. A Joining Member of Hendre Lodge No.3250, he was Installed as WM in 2001. In Province, he was appointed ProvAGDC in 1975, promoted to ProvAGReg in 1983 and further promoted to PPrJGW in 1985. He first became a Grand Officer in 1988, with the Rank of PAGSuptWks and promoted to PJGD in 1999. He was also well known in the Province for his work over 18 years in the Provincial Office in Cardiff.

It is pleasing to be able to put on record that Porthkerry Lodge continues to thrive, with many younger, enthusiastic Masons ready to carry the Lodge forward into the 21st century with exactly the same aspirations, hope and commitment that the original Founders envisaged when the Lodge was formed over 60 years ago.

On a very interesting but rather sobering and perhaps chilling note, a goodly number of our departed Brethren have chosen the Porthkerry Churchyard as their final resting place. This has an excellent view of the Porthkerry viaduct shown on the Lodge Insignia and Banner and is a place of solitude and tranquillity. So Mote It Be.

Compiled by WBro Malcolm Lucas, PPrGSwdB,
with acknowledgements to WBro A M M Hart, PJGD;
WBro R L Ayres, PPSGD; and WBro D A Reid, PPrGSuptWks.

Aberpennar Lodge No.6354

Warranted : 7 August 1946
Consecrated : 29 October 1946
Meeting at the Masonic Hall, Aberdare.

In the very early years of the 20th century, Brethren residing in the Mountain Ash area first Petitioned for a Lodge to be formed to cater for their needs. Their request was denied on the grounds that St David's Lodge No.679, meeting at the Masonic Hall, Aberdare, was sufficient for this area of the Cynon Valley.

At the end of WWII, interest in Freemasonry was healthy and growing strongly. Attendances at St David's Lodge were excellent and with Membership growing steadily all the evidence pointed to the trend continuing, although accommodation both in the Temple and the dining room, was becoming a problem. The situation encouraged the Mountain Ash Brethren to press their cause for a second time. In June 1946, St David's Lodge received a Deputation, designated 'The Aberpennar Lodge Committee'. It was led by WBro Shadrach Charles Lewis, a well known Mountain Ash publican who had been WM of St David's Lodge in 1933. A Petition was presented on behalf of the proposed new Lodge which was unanimously agreed upon, accepted and signed by the WM, WBro Cyril Griffiths and his two Wardens, Bros D J Davies, Solicitor, and Idwal G Thomas, a local Businessman.

It had been decided that the new Lodge would be named 'Aberpennar', this being the Welsh name of the town of Mountain Ash. The 'Pennar' is the stream that runs down the hills to join the River Cynon at Mountain Ash. Reputedly, the English name came from the trees that dominated the surrounding woodlands, the 'mountain ash' or 'rowan' trees.

The Petitioners, and indeed the Members of St David's Lodge, were quite certain that Membership would be mainly for Brethren living in the environs of Mountain Ash. It was intended that the Lodge would meet at Aberdare Masonic Hall, thereby helping to alleviate the accommodation problems, easing the strain on St David's Brethren to attain Office, and at the same time, offering opportunities to Mountain Ash Brethren to fulfil their Masonic ambitions.

Later in the summer of that year, there was great joy and excitement when the United Grand Lodge of England granted a Warrant on 7 August 1946. . The Consecration of Aberpennar Lodge took place at Aberdare on Tuesday, 29 October 1946. The Consecrating Officer was RWBro R P St John Charles, JP, PAGReg, ProvGM, assisted by his Provincial team of Officers. Following the Consecration, WBro Shadrach Lewis was Installed as the first Worshipful Master by the Installing Master, VWBro Edgar J Rutter, OSM, PGD, DepProvGM. His Officers were duly appointed and Invested, and included members of the legal profession, businessmen, educationalists and local dignitaries, all from Mountain Ash and the surrounding district. The new Lodge then welcomed RWBro R P St John Charles, VWBro Edgar J Rutter, WBro Charles Palmer, AProvGM, and WBro Cyril Griffiths, WM of St David's Lodge and who had signed the Petition, when all were Elected as Honorary Members. The very first Joining Member was Bro David Elwyn Howells of Fforest Lodge No.2606, who was subsequently Installed as WM in 1953.

In its early years, Aberpennar Lodge was fortunate in having continual support and encouragement from its Mother Lodge. As well as guidance, many presentations were made by the Worshipful Masters, Officers and Brethren of St David's Lodge. These included the gift of a Volume of the Sacred Law, as well as suitably inscribed Officers' Collars from WBro Idwal G Thomas who was WM of St David's Lodge in 1948. A year later, Bro Ben Roderick, Organist, presented the Hymn Books, which are still in use today. Then, in 1951, when he was WM of St David's, WBro Herbert Davies gifted a set of Gauntlets to the Lodge.

The circumstances surrounding the origins of Aberpennar Lodge's Ballot Box, which was presented by Bro William Ivor Reginald Perryman in April 1951, deserve special mention. The story begins many years earlier. Just prior to the declaration of war in 1939, Bro Perryman had been working in South Devon, helping to demolish a tithe barn. During the course of the work, an oak beam bearing the Masonic symbol was removed. After some research it was concluded that the symbol had been carved in the 13th century by workers, possibly stone masons, engaged in the building of nearby Bovey Tracey Church. Bro Perryman procured a part of that beam and from it made the Ballot Box. Also in 1951, Members of Aberpennar Lodge were proud to present Jewels to both its Consecrating Officers and Founder Officers, this at a time when the Lodge was growing both in numbers and in stature.

The Lodge was honoured in June 1953, when WBro Shadrach Lewis received active Provincial Rank, becoming Provincial Junior Grand Warden, a just reward for a man who had played a major part in the formation of the Lodge.

In October 1954, Bro Ralph Ponting was the first Initiate of Aberpennar Lodge to be Installed as WM.

Three Brethren of the Lodge had the distinction of holding the Office of High Constable of Miskin Higher. They were Bro Edward Thomas, a Pharmacist in Mountain Ash; WBro John Morgan, a Mountain Ash Solicitor; and WBro Maldwyn Jones, an Aberdare Businessman. This was a very old Office, dating back at least to 1252. Until 1922, the High Constable had functions in relation to juries. Those went under the Juries Act 1922. His only remaining office was in connection with rates, for which purpose he was appointed at the annual meeting of the justices at petty sessions, when hearing rating appeals. In 1925, their jurisdiction to hear rating appeals was taken away from them. The custom of appointing a High Constable continued until 1969. The Office is now obsolete, there being no person or body of persons with power to appoint to that Office.

The Lodge Banner was Dedicated by WBro Harry F Stockwell, AProvGM, in 1965. The immense honour of carrying the Banner into the Lodge for the first time was accorded to WBro Harry E Sturge, PPrGW, Installed WM in 1957 and 1964.

The Rivers Dare and Cynon are depicted on the Banner, with the predominant colours being green and red, which correspond not only to our national colours, but also those of Mountain Ash Grammar School. In its early days, the School played an important part in the development and structure of Secondary Education.

The profile of the Lodge's most distinguished Member, RWBro Hywel Davies, who has brought particular honour and pride to the Lodge, appears later in this book. Having been Initiated into Freemasonry in Aberpennar Lodge, he became WM in 1979 and, quickly gaining the utmost respect within the Province, firstly became a Grand Officer and then an Assistant Provincial Grand Master, before succeeding RWBro the Rt Hon the Lord Swansea, DL, as ProvGM in June 1999. This was the peak of his Masonic career, and suitably marked the proudest and most notable time for the Lodge and all its Members. The Lodge was proud and happy to purchase his Undress Regalia, which was duly presented to him in September of that year.

The Aberpennar Lodge of Instruction was held on an informal basis in various local hostelries prior to 1955. However, from then onwards it became a formal and an 'official' LOI, held in the Masonic Temple. It has established a tradition which is, perhaps, unique, being totally self supporting and indeed, undertaking its own fund raising. Earliest records show 'subscriptions' per Member being as little as 15p, but they grew steadily with the times and a simple 'after proceedings' were introduced to add enjoyment as well as to swell the funds. The Minutes record a sum of £7.09 being handed over as the 'profit' or surplus, after a meal of faggots and peas. A 'joining fee' was added, and over the years this token fund raising has resulted in many gifts and presentations to the Lodge. It is a long list and includes Peterborough Booklets, given to every Initiate since 1999; an embroidered cushion to enhance the presentation and investment of the Apron to the Candidate; and an engraved set of Square and Compasses, presented on the Lodge's 50th Anniversary. Also presented has been a set of specially hand-crafted Wardens' Gavels and, perhaps the most outstanding, a portrait of RWBro Hywel Davies, commissioned to commemorate his appointment as Provincial Grand Master. It hangs in the Masonic Hall Dining Room at Aberdare. The Lodge is justly proud that an Initiate, a Brother and a Past Master chose to follow his Masonic career in this Lodge.

With regard to the LOI, Aberpennar Lodge has been extremely fortunate to have been able to rely on dedicated and outstanding Preceptors. Brethren, not yet eligible to progress, are encouraged not only to attend but to take part, and visitors have frequently been complimentary of those 'youngsters' who not only participate but acquit themselves well. WBro Gordon Davies Evans must be mentioned, not only as a long serving Preceptor and a Grand Lodge Officer, but also for what he has accomplished in other Degrees. WBro Gordon was Initiated into the Lodge in 1973, attained the Chair of King Solomon in 1985, and was appointed as ProvAGDC in 1990. After being promoted to PPGSwdB five years later, he was Invested with the Collar of PAGDC in Grand Lodge in 2002. He is a Member of many other Degrees and an Honorary Member of an Order in New Delhi.

There have been many memorable events for the Brethren of Aberpennar to enjoy over the years. No less than a Past Grand Master of the Grand Lodge of the State of New York, namely RWBro N Lloyd-Jones, who made a visit to a Regular Lodge Meeting in May 1963. He was visiting his family in Mountain Ash at the time, and in his response to the visitors' Toast, he expressed his delight in attending a Lodge of Masons from his home town of Mountain Ash. He was Elected an Honorary Member of the Lodge and maintained contact until his untimely death in August 1969. Then, in 1977, the Lodge was again honoured when, RWBro the Rt Hon the Lord Swansea ProvGM, attended the Installation of WBro Glyn Griffiths.

In celebrating its 50th Anniversary in 1996, the Lodge was led by WBro Frederick Dixon, WM. The Warrant and the Minutes of the first Meeting were read by the long serving Lodge Secretary, WBro Leslie Williams, and the Lodge Treasurer, WBro Elwyn Williams presented the Lodge with a boxed set of Square and Compasses, on behalf of the Aberpennar Lodge of Instruction. Presentations were also made to RWBro Hywel Davies, to mark his appointment as AProvGM in September 1996, and to WBro Gwyn Davies, upon his retirement as, and in appreciation of, his many years of service as Lodge Secretary. The presentations were a traditional Welsh miner's lamp for WBro Hywel and an inscribed Masonic Bible for WBro Gwyn. The whole evening was an extremely joyful occasion, demonstrating the continuing harmony of Aberpennar Lodge, with visitors and guests expressing their appreciation by offering their best wishes for the Lodge's future.

One of the most outstanding and proudest events in the Lodge's history was the Consecration of a Daughter Lodge, Afon Dâr Lodge No.8829, on 22 May 1978. The Installing Master was VWBro Geoffrey Malin Ashe, TD, DepProvGM, and the first WM was WBro Harry E Sturge, PM Aberpennar Lodge. WBro Glyndwr Griffiths was the Acting IPM. There is nothing stronger than the bond between mother and daughter, and that is true of the relationship that exists between Aberpennar Lodge and its Mother Lodge, St David's Lodge and Afon Dâr Lodge, its Daughter Lodge.

Aberpennar Lodge is justly proud of its history and of the Brethren, past and present, who have made it so varied and interesting. The Lodge aims to sustain the great Masonic traditions that its Members have evolved for over the six decades of its existence and looks forward to the continuance of Brotherhood and harmony in the years to come.

Compiled by Bro Gary G Marsh, JW, and WBro Gordon Davies Evans, PAGDC.

Themis Lodge
No. 6355

Warranted : 7 August 1946

Consecrated : 7 October 1946

Meeting at the Masonic Hall, Cardiff.

The Principal Brethren who had a vision of a Lodge Founded by Members whose everyday vocation was based on transport, were WBro W E Gough, PM Fforest Lodge No.2606, and his blood brother, Bro E Gough; WBro T W Forse, PM Caerdydd Lodge No.3959; WBro J H Watts, PM Vassar-Smith Lodge No.2994, Lydney, Gloucestershire; WBro T H Lovitt, PM Gwalia Lodge No.4213, and Bros R T Wynn, R C Evans, H Sampson, T J E Price and M Summers.

Early meetings were held at the Fforest Lodge in Treharris, and in the 'Wobbly Wheel', (to be explained later). As time elapsed, further Brethren with the requisite connection in transport, were invited to support the Petition for a new Lodge, Sponsored by the Worshipful Master and Brethren of Fforest Lodge. Themis Lodge, being a Daughter Lodge of Fforest Lodge, which is a part of Loyal Cambrian Lodge No.110 Family Tree, is the only Lodge meeting at Cardiff Masonic Hall which is not descended from Glamorgan Lodge No.36.

A major consideration of the Founders was a name and Emblem. One might have thought that St Christopher would have been suitable. At that time, the Road Haulage Industry was under threat of being nationalised by the Government, and as most of the Founders were involved with road transport, they considered this to be an intolerable injustice to their businesses. The wise decision made by the Founders, was to use the Goddess of Justice, 'Themis', as the Lodge Emblem and name, in the hope that justice would ultimately prevail. In time, their wishes were granted on de-nationalisation.

In Greek religion, Themis is the personification of Justice and the Goddess of Wisdom and Good Counsel, who presided over the assessments of Gods and Men and was the interpreter of God's will. According to some sources of Greek Mythology, she was the daughter of Uranus (Heaven), and Gaea (Earth) and was Zeus's second consort. Themis maintained good order and supervised the ceremonial. She was a giver of oracles, and the cult of Themis was widespread in Ancient Greece. She was often represented as a woman of sober appearance, carrying a pair of scales. A statue of Themis is to be seen on the dome of the Central Criminal Court London, holding the Sword and Scales of Justice.

Supported by Fforest Lodge, a Petition for Themis Lodge was submitted to RWBro R P St John Charles, JP, PAGReg, ProvGM, and subsequently to the Most Worshipful Grand Master.

The Lodge was Consecrated on the 7 October 1946, and by that date, twenty-six Founder Members had signed the Petition.

The first Regular Meeting was held on 29 October 1946, and the Meeting to celebrate the first fifty years of the Lodge was held by Dispensation, on 29 October 1996. At the first Regular Meeting, an additional nine Brethren became Joining Members, and a further four gentlemen were proposed as Candidates. By the time of the second Installation, the total Membership had grown to fifty one.

The Consecration of the Lodge took place during a period of austerity in the aftermath of WWI. Until 21 September 1948, it was permissible to wear Service Dress to Lodge Meetings and, due to food rationing, refreshments at the close of the Lodge were 'light', and consisted mainly of sandwiches and bottled beer.

The winter of 1947 was severe and, as a result of the weather conditions, the Emergency Meeting of 31 January 1948 had to be postponed until 12 February, with the Regular Meeting being held on 18 February. At the latter Meeting, the WM of Fforest Lodge presented Themis Lodge with a cabinet of Working Tools, in cleberation of the 'birth 'of the Daughter Lodge, and the 50th Anniversary of the Founding of the Mother Lodge.

The Lodge continued to prosper in its growth of Membership. It was not unusual in the early years for two separate Degree Ceremonies to be performed during one Meeting and by 1960, Lodge Membership had risen to one hundred and eight. Unfortunately, during the subsequent years, this has declined to the current Membership of forty-three.

In 1980, a new WM's Collar was donated to the Lodge by WBro L Prosser Rees; the bars attached to the Collar were contributed by the Past Masters. This Worshipful Brother also designed the Lodge Banner, which was donated by WBro T G Davies, who had joined the Lodge on 29 October 1946. WBro T G Davies was Installed WM of Themis Lodge in 1952. The Banner was Dedicated on 15 February 1983 by VW Brother Geoffrey M Ashe, TD, PGSwdB, DepProvGM.

In 1977, Duke of York Chapter No.2453 was Consecrated, with Themis Lodge being significantly involved in its formation. In preceeding years, friendships were formed as a consequence of the two Lodges meeting on the same Tuesday of the month. WBro R Parker, Duke of York Lodge, and WBro T A Harber, Themis Lodge, and others, met to discuss the formation of a new Chapter.

Due to the seniority of Duke of York Lodge, the name 'Duke of York Chapter No.2453', was accepted as the name. To date, fourteen Members of Themis Lodge have been Installed as first Principal of the Chapter.

Earlier in this history, mention was made of the 'Wobbly Wheel'. This was the affectionate name given to the air raid shelter at the rear of WBro R T Wynn's house in Lake Road East. It was the venue for some of the early meetings preceding the Consecration of the Lodge. Later, with a seating capacity for twelve Members, it was used for Lodges of Instructon and Lodges of Rehearsal, followed by an hour or two of conviviality.

During the Lodge's first sixty-one years, six Worshipful Masters have Initiated their sons: WBro R T Wynn Initiated N R Wynn in 1950; WBro E W Jones Initated M E Jones in 1960; WBro T T Nicholls Initiated J Nicholls in 1961; WBro Idris M Price Initiated Jeffrey W Price in 1974; WBro G Evans Initiated G G Evans in 1985; and WBro A H Moore Initiated A Moore and B G Jones in 1987.

The late W Bro T J E Price, MBE, PPrJGW, ' Eddie', as he was affectionately known to all, was the last surviving Founder Member of this Lodge. He was Initiated on 12 February 1943 into Preswylfa Lodge No.5792, and qualified as a Masonic Veteran. In 1954, he was Installed in the Chair of Themis Lodge. He was instrumental in proposing his blood brothers, the late WBro Idris Price and WBro Dilwyn Price into the Lodge. WBro Eddie was also a Past Master Founder of Discovery Lodge No.8601. He was one of the last surviving Founder Members of the Tenovus Charity. From small beginnings in Cardiff Royal Infirmary, this has progressed to a National Charity under Royal Patronage, with particular involvement in Cancer Research. Eddie had been an active member and Chairman of the Road Haulage Association and the Institute of Transport. In 1934, he was invited to join, and became a Member of the Worshipful Company of Car Men, a Livery Company in the City of London. He was also a past President of the Cardiff Rotary Club, and a Paul Harris Fellow, which is one of the highest awards in Rotary International. The Lodge is pleased and honoured that WBro Eddie was a Founder Member, and is greatly appreciative of his years of service to Freemasonry in general and to this Lodge in particular. The Brethren were delighted that they were able to enjoy his company at the 50th Anniversary of the Lodge, held on 29 October 1996.

Compiled by WBro J Colin Jones, PPrJGD, with acknowledgement to
WBro M E Jones, PPrJGW, who compiled the Lodge's History for the 50th Anniversary in October 1996.

Galen Lodge No.6366

Warranted : 1 October 1946
Consecrated : 31 October 1946
Erased : 8 December 2010
Met at the Masonic Hall, Cardiff.

In the 1940s, Pharmaceutical Companies employed qualified Pharmacists as their Representatives, and in the course of their normal business calls, they discovered that some of their number, and many of their customers, were Freemasons. It was from this basic knowledge that the idea grew to form a 'Lodge of Pharmacists'.

The Lodge is named after Galen, who was a physician to the Roman Emperor, Marcus Aurelius. He also practised in the Gladiator Schools and was a prolific writer (almost two hundred of his books have survived), and his influence was a dominating factor until the Renaissance. He was the first to recognise the need for using standard strengths in medicines, and standard preparations such as tinctures. Medicines prepared according to the formulae of Galen are known as *'galenicals'*. The term is used in modern day pharmacy to denote standard preparations containing one or several organic ingredients, as contrasted with pure chemical substances.

Caerdydd Lodge No.3959 was approached and agreed to become the Sponsor of the new Lodge. It was agreed that the Membership would consist entirely of Pharmacists, and it remained an *'exclusive'* Lodge until the 1950s.

The Warrant was granted on 1 October 1946, and the Lodge was Consecrated on Thursday, 31 October 1946 by RWBro R P St John Charles, JP, PAGReg, ProvGM South Wales ED. The Installing Master was VWBro Edgar J Rutter, OSM, PGD, DepProvGM. The first Master was WBro Samuel Hague PPrAGDC, PM Caerdydd Lodge. Bro C G Howell, Cartref Lodge No.5772 was a Founder, but he was absent through illness on this occasion. There were twenty Founders, of whom seventeen were Pharmacists and three Pharmaceutical Representatives.

The Lodge Motto: *'Spectemur Agendo'*, translates as *'By your deeds shall you be known'*.

At the November Meeting in 1946, seven Pharmacists and one Chemist's Assistant became Joining Members, and four gentlemen were Balloted for as Candidates, namely, David H Lewis, John EH Edwards, John R Jones, and Harold W Davies. The Ballot proved successful for all four, and as a result David H Lewis and John E H Edwards, WM 1959-1960, were duly Initiated.

In the past, a number of Emergency Meetings were found to be necessary, the last being held on 3 April 1947. The first Minute

Book did not contain details of the fare at the Festive Board. However, it must be remembered that in the early years of the Lodge, Great Britain was still in the iron grip of food rationing and, as a consequence, all Festive Boards would have been restricted accordingly. The first known menu card is dated Thursday, 7 May 1959 (an Installation Festival), and the menu was as follows : asparagus soup, salmon with Hollandaise sauce, new potatoes, peas, fruit ices, cheese and biscuits, coffee. An almost identical menu (but with no mention of Hollandaise sauce) was used for the Installation Festival on 5 May 1960, and again on 3 May 1962 (this time with Hollandaise sauce).

It was a Lodge tradition that the first WM's Jewel should be passed on to each succeeding Master. In addition, the IPM received his own PM's Jewel, his by right for completing the year as Master. The IPM, therefore, wore two PM's Jewels.

The Lodge Banner, which hangs in the Duke of Connaught Temple, Cardiff, displays the Arms of the Pharmaceutical Society of Great Britain. The Lodge considered it a singular honour to be granted permission by the Society to incorporate these Arms into the Banner. One of the 'supporters' of the Arms is a figure representing Galen.

In 1977, the Lodge became the Sponsoring Lodge for Lodge of St Martin No.8771, which meets at the Masonic Hall in Caerphilly. There exists a very strong bond of friendship between the two Lodges, and there has never been a Meeting of Lodge of St Martin where at least one Member of Galen Lodge has not been present.

This close bond was forged even closer on the night of Thursday, 15 January 1987. The winter weather had been particularly inclement that day, with snow falling in abundance in Cardiff and the northern valleys area. The mountain road between Caerphilly and Cardiff, however, had been cleared enough to allow vehicular traffic to pass, but parts of Cardiff and the far reaches of the valleys were still largely impassable. This meant that some Brethren of Galen Lodge were unable to attend Lodge that evening. Three Brethren residing in Caerphilly, throwing caution to the wind drove to Cardiff., and entered the Masonic Temple, to find that the total attendance of Galen Lodge to be six Members plus four visitors. The Brethren consisted of WBro Alfred Thomas, WM; Bro Denis J Woods (Lodge of St Martin) Acting SW; Bro Clive Nicholson, JW; WBro Francis C McAndrews, Chap; Bro Michael S Gallacher (Lodge of St Martin), Acting SD; Bro M R Morgan, JD; Bro R S Morgan, IG; WBro Bernard L Morris, Sec; WBro M Hinton (Cardiff Exchange Lodge), Acting IPM, and WBro K Morgan, ProvGTyler, as Tyler. Without the help of the visiting Brethren, the Lodge could not have been held in accordance with Ancient Custom that evening.

The WM duly opened the Lodge at 6.30 pm. WBro Francis McAndrews announced that the Lodge had won £500 in a prize draw, which news cheered everyone up immensely! The WM thanked everyone for their attendance and closed the Lodge in due form at 6.40 pm. There was a 100% attendance at the Festive Board, which was held in the Savoy, a nearby restaurant. The two Brethren from Lodge of St Martin have, subsequently, considered themselves as Honorary Senior Warden and Honorary Senior Deacon of Galen Lodge!

On Thursday, 1 April 2010, the Lodge held its last Regular Meeting, when the Warrant was to be finally surrendered. This sad and regrettable situation was due to the Lodge being unable to attract Candidates. The recycling of Past Masters was deemed counterproductive to the spirit of Freemasonry. It was attended by many distinguished Brethren, including WBro Geoffrey W Thomas, PSGD, ProvAGM, WBro Brian Eveleigh, PSGD, PAProvGM, and WBro S W J Clarke PAGDC, the Officer Mandated to the Lodge. Also present were Officers and Brethren of our Daughter Lodge, the Lodge of St Martin, plus the WM, SW and JW of Caerdydd Lodge, the Sponsoring Lodge, and regular visitors from Aberpennar Lodge No.6354.

During the Meeting, the WM, WBro Raymond K Rees, PPrJGD, paid tribute to the Officers and Brethren of Galen Lodge. WBro Denis J Woods, PPrJGW, Honorary Member and Tyler of the Lodge for many years, delivered the history of the Lodge.

The Lodge was finally closed in due form and in perfect harmony by WBro Roger Mitchell, PPrGSuptWks. When the Officers and Brethren retired from the Lodge, they were led by WBro Raymond Rees and WBro Roger Mitchell, proudly carrying the Warrant between them. The Warrant was subsequently returned to Grand Lodge.

At the Festive Board, tributes were paid by WBro Geoffrey Thomas and WBro Brian Eveleigh. WBro Raymond Rees presented the WM of Lodge of St Martin with the Galen Lodge Gavels. They had been made and presented by the late WBro Francis C McAndrews. The evening ended with all the Brethren forming a circle, with clasped hands, and singing Auld Lang Syne, to the accompaniment of WBro Brian Eveleigh on the piano. It was a sad and poignant moment.

On Friday, 8 June 2010, six former Galen Brethren became Joining Members of Lodge of St Martin. They were WBros Gareth T Lloyd, PPrJGD, Roger D Mitchell, PPrGSuptWks, David A Tomlins, PPrGReg and Bros Graham C Burston, Richard L G Pask and David G Williams.

The Lodge was finally Erased from the Register of Grand Lodge on 8 December 2010.

Compiled by WBro Denis J Woods, PPrJGW.

Cardiff Masonic Hall, 1895

R P St John Charles Lodge No.6466

Warranted : 5 March 1947

Consecrated : 7 June 1947

Meeting at the Masonic Hall, Swansea.

In the period closely following the end of World War II, there was a large increase in the number of men wishing to become Freemasons. So great was the surge of prospective Brethren that the existing Lodges were unable to accommodate them, unless they held Emergency Meetings for the purpose. This practice was not favoured by Provincial Grand Lodge, which preferred the formation of new Lodges to cope with the influx.

It was decided that a new Lodge would be formed to meet in Swansea and that it would bear the name of the Provincial Grand Master, RWBro R P St John Charles. Reginald Pendrill St John Charles was a Solicitor in Neath. His father, WBro Henry Pendrill Charles, also a Solicitor and eminent Freemason was Deputy Provincial Grand Master from 1915 to 1925. Henry had already given his name to Lodge No.3769, Consecrated in 1916 and meeting in Caerphilly. The naming of one Lodge after an eminent Mason and another after his equally eminent son, is a permanent reminder to us all of the invaluable contribution these Brethren made to the Craft.

Indefatigable Lodge No.247 readily gave its support to the establishment of the new Lodge, and the Worshipful Master and Wardens signed the Petition in February 1947. The Warrant was granted on the 5 March 1947. Indefatigable Lodge has been regarded as the 'Mother Lodge' ever since, and exchange Lodge visits are held regularly. The Consecration quickly followed in the Masonic Temple, Swansea on Monday, 9 June 1947. The Consecrating Officer was RWBro R P St John Charles, who led a team of twelve Consecrating Officers. The first Master of the Lodge, WBro Thomas Lewis Jenkins, OBE, PProvSGW, was Installed by the Deputy Provincial Grand Master, VWBro Edgar John Rutter.

WBro T L Jenkins was a Schoolmaster who also spent some time in the Civil Service. He had been Installed as WM of Indefatigable Lodge in 1931, and was a Founder Member and third WM of West Glamorgan Lodge No.5291, Consecrated on 17 November 1931. He was also a Founder Member and second WM of Doric Lodge No.5968, Consecrated on 12 June 1944. He was one of a group of Masons who visited Ireland, and later gave demonstrations of Irish Working. He had an exceptionally good delivery, and older Members spoke of his impressive rendering of the Ritual and of his polished well-delivered after-dinner speeches. He became a Grand Officer in 1931.

Following the Ceremony, a banquet was held in the Connaught Hall, attended by over 200 Freemasons. This was possible because the ground floor, which had been requisitioned by the War Department in 1941 for use by the newly arrived American Forces, had been derequisitioned in 1946.

R P St John Charles took a very keen interest in his new Lodge, helping with his wide experience and knowledge, to shape the early years. He came to Lodge Meetings, where he mingled with the Brethren irrespective of Rank, chatting in his affable and courteous manner. Some Brethren were invited to visit him and Mrs Charles at their home in Porthcawl. These visits developed into annual events, eagerly anticipated by those privileged to attend and greatly enjoyed by them. It became customary for the ProvGM to record a message for the Lodge, to be played at a future Meeting. A tape-recorder and a cine-camera were used for this purpose, equipment then at the fore-front of audio-visual technology. The equipment was provided by WBro Leslie M Rees and operated by Bro George Wallace Davies. Sadly, the tape recordings have gone astray but one of the silent cine-films is still available. Bro George Wallace Davies was the Deputy City Librarian, and made a very knowledgeable duo in the Lodge with Bro Ralph Wishart. Ralph owned a book shop near High Street Station, later re-located to Dilwyn Street. His fame spread nationwide, because there were very few undergraduates at Swansea University who were unaware, or had not made use of the expertise available from 'Ralph the Books'.

Always bearing in mind the need to live up to the name of RP St John Charles, the Lodge flourished for many years, Initiating a steady flow of six Candidates each year. In 1977, the peak year, there were 118 Members, but as in Freemasonry in general, numbers have declined and today Subscribing and Honorary Members total one third of that number.

Despite the reduction in numbers, the quality of the Lodge has been maintained and it is noted throughout the Province for producing Degree Ceremonies of impressive standard. The success is due to the hard, but hugely enjoyable work of the Lodge of Instruction, which took its present form as far back as 1955, when Reginald Watson, the third Master of the Lodge became Preceptor. His patient coaxing and coaching style of keeping everyone happy set a pattern, which has survived to the present day, and has been adopted by WBro Stuart Seabourne, the current Preceptor, with outstanding results.

No history of the R P St John Charles Lodge would be complete without reference to the charitable ethos of the Lodge. This is probably due to the foresight of the Founders, who selected as the Lodge Motto: *'Date et Dabitur Vobis'*, translated as *'Give and it shall be given to you'*. Support for local charities has in recent years been concentrated on fundraising at the Christmas Lodge Meeting. The Lodge provided a special wheelchair for the children's ward of a local hospital, and has made regular donations to the Air Ambulance, various local Hospitals and the PDSA.

The Lodge also has an unofficial Motto: *'No one needs a smile as much as he who has none to give'*. This embodies the spirit in which visitors are greeted, and ensures that the Lodge is always well supported by Members of other Lodges, who always seem to leave in a happy and contented frame of mind.

On 17 February 2011, the Lodge was honoured to host the Installation of WBro Jeffrey Parry Thomas as Assistant Provincial Grand Master. The meticulous planning of the occasion by Lodge Secretary, WBro J Colin Bunyan, was thrown into turmoil, when just as the procession was about to enter the Temple, the organ broke down. The day was saved by some of our younger Members, who having the strength of Samson, carried the electric organ from the Connaught Hall upstairs to the Temple, thereby allowing the Ceremony to proceed. This prompted RWBro Captain Sir Norman Lloyd-Edwards, ProvGM, who performed the Ceremony, to comment that this was the first time that he had witnessed an organ transplant in a Masonic Lodge.

Compiled by WBro Stuart Seabourne, PPrJGW.

Lodge of St Cenydd No.6567

Warranted	:	5 November 1947
Consecrated	:	6 December 1947

Meeting at the Masonic Hall, Swansea.

It had long been considered by many Members of the Craft in Swansea, that the missing years of those who had served in the Armed Forces should be addressed, and opportunities offered to those who wished to become Freemasons. With this in view, a meeting was convened on 7 August 1947, attended by WBros Ernest E Morgan, George Hider, WT Mainwaring Hughes, and T Leonard James.

WBro Edgar J Rutter, DepProvGM, had made an approach to WBro Ernest Morgan regarding the desirability of forming a new Lodge, as it had become obvious that owing to long waiting lists, applicants were unable to join existing Lodges.

A list of possible Founders was prepared and a meeting was arranged for them to meet the above four Brethren at the Masonic Hall, Swansea, on Tuesday, 19 August 1947. In the preamble of the Minutes of the meeting, it was decided that the name of the Lodge would be 'The Lodge of St Cenydd', because of the connection and affection which WBro Ernest Morgan had with the church of Llangennith in Gower. Further, his generous offer to prepare and submit to the next meeting, designs for a Banner and Past Master's Jewel, were accepted. It was also agreed that the Lodge Motto should be: *'None is free from anxiety but the good'*.

On 25 August 1947, a meeting was held at the Masonic Hall, Swansea, which was attended by WBro Edgar J Rutter. He suggested that Dr James Griffith Hall Lodge No.3161 be approached to Sponsor the new Lodge at their Meeting on 20 September 1947. It was then decided to have Regular Lodge Meetings on the first Friday of the months of January to June and September to December.

At a further meeting, held on 26 September 1947, WBro Ernest E Morgan informed those present that the Deputation of probable Founders attended Dr James Griffith Hall Lodge No.3161 on Saturday 20 September 1947, and a resolution supporting the Petition to form a new Lodge was carried unanimously. As arranged, the Petition was duly signed and delivered to the Deputy Provincial Grand Master. It was decided that the date of the Consecration would be 6 December 1947 and the first Regular Lodge Meeting be on Friday, 2 January 1948.

The Petition was subsequently approved by Grand Lodge and the Warrant for Lodge of St Cenydd No.6567 was signed on 5 November 1947.

The Consecrating Officer was RWBro R P St John Charles, JP, PAGReg, ProvGM, accompanied by his team of Provincial

Grand Officers, which included WBro Edwin Drew, ProvSGW, WBro G J Davies, ProvJGW, and WBro Harry F Stockwell, PAGDC, ProvGSec.

Thus, the Lodge was launched, and it is true to say that the solid foundations laid down by the Founders have been illustrated through the years by the high standard of the Ceremonies. Strict discipline has been the order of the day in the Temple, and light heartedness and much good humour reserved for the Festive Board.

The Lodge being Consecrated so soon after WWII, it became obvious that the Initiates would be younger than those Brethren already established in Freemasonry. This lent itself to a fresh approach and outlook, in keeping with the younger man's enthusiasm for a 'new experience'.

In due time, the Lodge of St Cenydd organised itself into a Lodge which established itself as one committed to the highest standards, as expected by the Oxford Ritual – tidy and efficient in its floor work in the Temple and concise and precise in the delivery of the Ritual.

On 7 May 1948, a letter was received from WBro Rhodri Harris, stating that the Feast of St Cenydd would be celebrated on 5 July 1948 and suggesting that the Lodge should consider attending Llangennith Church on that day. This was acted upon, and the Feast of St Cenydd has been celebrated annually by the Worshipful Master, Brethren and their ladies, at Morning Service, on the nearest Sunday to that date, ever since. As children were born to families of the Brethren, they in turn came along with their parents. After the Service, they enjoyed a picnic on the beach, and, if the weather was not inclement, swimming in the sea. Many long-standing friendships have been established by the informal but serious visit to the Church, on the Feast of St Cenydd. To record the close attachment that the Lodge has established with the Church at Llangennith, a presentation of a suitably inscribed Lectern Bible was made at one such Morning Service. Bro Robert James took it upon himself to clean and refurbish the Lych-gate at the Church, where now the full effect of the operative craftsman's art may be seen in splendid detail.

It is worthy of note that the close affinity between Dr James Griffith Hall Lodge and the Lodge of St Cenydd, as Mother and Daughter Lodges respectively, has resulted in an annual exchange of visits to each other's Lodges.

Lodge of St Cenydd celebrated its 50th Anniversary in December 1997 with an impressive guest list, headed by VWBro Cdr Roy K Hopkin, RN, DepProvGM, accompanied by WBro Peter Frost, AProvGM. At the Festive Board, a Toast was proposed by the senior Past Master Edgar Owen, who was also the author of a special commemorative booklet produced for the event. Cdr Hopkin complimented him *'on his achievement in producing such an excellent book, which he had enjoyed reading'*. In congratulating the Lodge on its 50 years, he reminded those present: *'We have a wonderful past and we have nothing to be ashamed of in our past. It is the youngsters coming into Freemasonry that will be the future. It is up to all of us to make sure we look after our future- our candidates should be cherished for the future'*.

RWBro the Lord Swansea, CStJ, DL, OSM, ProvGM wrote a foreword to the commemorative booklet as follows:

'It gives me great pleasure to congratulate the Lodge on reaching its fiftieth anniversary.

The years immediately following the end of the last World War were a period of great expectation in this Province and indeed in the whole Craft.

The Lodge of St Cenydd has in the last fifty years carved out a worthy niche for itself in the Province and has now laid a firm foundation for the next fifty years and more. I must also compliment WBro Edgar Owen on his enterprise in compiling the history of the Lodge. Notwithstanding his skill and scholarship, I fear that the likelihood of him and me seeing the Centenary of the Lodge is somewhat remote.

I wish the Lodge continued success and prosperity in the years to come and may it continue to set an example to younger Lodges'.

On 6 February 2003, the Brethren celebrated the 50th Anniversary of the Initiation into Freemasonry of WBro Tom Thomas,

to Sponsor. Consequently, the first Daughter Lodge, Danycoed Lodge No.8127 was Consecrated on 25 November 1996. Many talented and experienced Brethren from the Lodge of St Ilan became Officers in this new Lodge.

While the Lodge of St Ilan has celebrated many high points, its history has not been entirely without difficulty. In 1991, the appointed Lodge Auditors discovered that Lodge funds had been misappropriated, thus leaving the Lodge in debt and almost bankrupt. Under the leadership of WBro Gwynfryn George, investigating officers were appointed, namely WBro Arthur O'Neill and WBro Norman Hughes. In March 1992, they reported to the Lodge Committee that after some repayments and restitution had been made by the Treasurer, there remained a nett loss of over £11,000. The Committee approved their report into the financial affairs of the Lodge over the previous 5 years and thanked them for their perseverance. A new Treasurer, Bro John Seaton Elvet Davies, was soon appointed, and by September 1992, he was in a position to submit a draft report and statement of accounts for the two years to 31 May 1992. From that time, the Lodge began to recover and within a few short years had once again become strong, happy and financially sound.

The Lodge's second Daughter Lodge, Princes Lodge No.9036 was issued with its Warrant on 10 March 1982 and it was duly Consecrated on 4 June of that year.

The year 2006-2007 was noted as the '*Father and Son*' year, as the WM, WBro John Holloway, not only introduced his own son, Bro Lee Kristian John Holloway into Freemasonry, but he also Initiated a father and son, Bro Stephen David Walters and Bro Robert Stephen Walters, in a Joint Initiation Ceremony.

The 50th Anniversary has already passed and the Brethren are now looking forward with confidence to the Lodge's 75th birthday in 2023.

Compiled by WBro Arthur O'Neill, PPrJGW.

The Organ, Caerphilly Temple.

Ionic Lodge No.6626

Warranted : 4 February 1948

Consecrated : 24 April 1948

Meeting at the Masonic Hall, Swansea.

With the ending of WWII just a few years earlier, the Brethren of Talbot Lodge No.1323 announced on 19 November 1947, that a new Lodge, to be known as Ionic Lodge, was to be formed in Swansea. Exactly one month later, on 19 December 1947, the Worshipful Master and his Wardens signed the Petition for the new Lodge. The reason for the choice of name, 'Ionic', is not recorded, but, a sister Lodge, Doric Lodge No.5968, Warranted on 20 May 1944, had also been Sponsored by Talbot Lodge. Doric and Ionic are two of the three Greek classical orders of architecture, the third being Corinthian. All three are frequently used as names for Masonic Lodges, and their symbolic significance is explained in the Ritual. The Ionic column also represents HA, who by his skill and artistic talents beautified King Solomon's Temple at Jerusalem.

WBro Joseph William Faull Batley, PM Talbot Lodge, was WM Designate, with WBro Cyril Augustine Luce, PM Talbot Lodge, SW Designate, and Bro David Charles Jones, JW Designate. The Warrant of Constitution was given under the seal of United Grand Lodge on 4 February 1948. The Founders and first Officers came from a large area and a wide range of jobs and professions - Technical Sales Representatives, Colliers' Agent, Company Secretary, Surveyor, Painter/Decorator, Headmaster, Garage Proprietor, Insurance Agent, Architect, Banker and Sea-going Engineer.

Ionic Lodge was Consecrated 24 April 1948, at the Masonic Temple, St Helen's Road, Swansea. The Consecration Ceremony was conducted by RWBro R P St John Charles, JP, PAGReg, ProvGM, assisted by VWBro Edgar J Rutter, OSM, PGD, DepProvGM, and Officers of Provincial Grand Lodge. The DepProvGM duly Installed WBro William Batley as the first WM, WBro Cyril Luce was Invested as SW, and Bro Charles Jones as JW. The first Secretary was Bro T A J Phillips, who subsequently became Lodge Treasurer, 1963-1980, while WBro William Batley was Lodge Secretary, 1951-1974. He became a Grand Officer in 1956 with the Rank of PAGDC, and was promoted in 1967 to PJGD. Bro Llewellyn G Bevan, Founder Steward, was Initiated in Talbot Lodge and was Installed as WM of Ionic Lodge in 1982. A much loved Mason, he was AProvGM, 1971-1976. In Grand Lodge, he held the Rank of PSGD. He was also Deputy Grand Superintendant of the Provincial Grand Chapter of South Wales, 1971-1987.

Amongst the first Initiates into Ionic Lodge were WBro S Gwyn Williams, PPrSGW, the first Initiate to be Installed as WM in 1958, and WBro John Noakes, PPrJGW, Installed as WM in 1960. In 1998, they both became Masonic Veterans in the Craft. WBro Gwyn, a benefactor of the Lodge, sadly, passed away, soon after achieving veteran status.

The first Initiate was WBro Derek R Luce, a Lewis, the son of WBro Cyril Augustine Luce, first SW. WBro Derek was installed WM of Ionic Lodge in 1959, and he too became a Masonic Veteran in 1999.

The first Lodge Banner was presented by WBro Robert Ivor Edwards, Founder and first Treasurer, in October 1948. The design consists of a circular Greek shield showing the seven islands in the Ionean Sea, superimposed on which is a prominent broken Ionic Pillar, marking the death of HA. It was drawn and painted on linen by Bro Ernest E Morgan of Dr James Griffith Hall Lodge No.3161. This original Banner was replaced in 1975. The second Banner was a gift from WBro John A M Davies to mark his appreciation to Ionic Lodge for the manner in which it had kept in touch with his late aunt, the widow of his late uncle, WBro I G Hughes, PM. Following the sad death of WBro S Gwyn Williams, it was decided to use his bequest to the Lodge to purchase a new Banner, and on 7 November 2001, the latest Banner was Dedicated by VWBro Peter Frost, PGSwdB, DepProvGM. WBro Gwyn's generosity to the Lodge also extended to the purchase of a set of Working Tools and also to funding the printing of the handbook, produced to celebrate the first fifty years of Ionic Lodge. The Lodge Motto: *'Wisdom is better than Rubies'*, is also displayed on the Banner.

For many years, commencing in the early 1960s, the Lodge arranged an annual outing by pleasure steamer to Ilfracombe. The organiser in the early days was WBro Captain George Gunn, PPrGSuptWks. The organising later fell to the current Junior Warden, and the trips continued for nearly forty years.

In the early 1960s, it was decided that all Members were to wear dinner dress to Lodge Meetings. Also, in the 1960s, Ionic Lodge Sponsored its first Daughter Lodge, namely, Lodge of Progress No.7928, which was Warranted on 12 June 1963.

In June 1973, a Petition was presented to the Lodge to Sponsor a new Lodge to be known as Lodge of Sincerity, with WBro Dudley Roe, PPrGSuptWks, who had been Initiated in Ionic Lodge on 6 January 1954 and Installed as WM in 1965, as WM Designate. Thus, Lodge of Sincerity No.8531 became the second Daughter Lodge. WBro D R Brown is now (2011) the senior Past Master of Ionic Lodge, and he became a Masonic Veteran in 2004.

In June 1976, WBro Bill Batley presented a Petition for a new Royal Arch Chapter, Ionic Chapter, to be attached to the Lodge, with EComps J W F. Batley, L G Bevan and T A J. Phillips as First, Second and Third Principals respectively. The Charter for Ionic Chapter No.6626 was signed on 10 November 1976.

Also in 1976, Lord Swansea Lodge No.8364 encouraged the formation of a demonstration team to re-enact a Russian Initiation Ceremony, as described by Tolstoy in his novel, 'War and Peace'. Five Members of Ionic Lodge, WBros D R Brown, Lewis Rees, J Stuart Peters, Tom Phillips and Bro Brian Phillips, were numbered amongst the 20 strong team. They gave demonstrations in this and neighbouring Provinces, thereby raising money for several charitable purposes.

During its existence, the Lodge is proud to record that it had six Grand Officers. They are VWBro J Stuart Peters, PGSwdB; WBros J W F Batley, PJGD; Lewellyn G Bevan, PSGD; Lewis Rees, PAGDC; Dudley Roe Brown, PAGSuptWks (1997) and most recently, WBro John T J Davies, PAGSwdB (2009). WBro John Theophilus Davies was Initiated in Llanfair Lodge No.7353 in 1984 and became WM of that Lodge in 1992. He became a Joining Member of Ionic Lodge in 1991, and was Installed as WM in 1998. In Provincial Grand Lodge, he was appointed ProvGSwdB in 1998, and promoted to ProvJGW in 2007. He has been Provincial Grand Charity Steward since 2009.

The most distinguished Member of Ionic Lodge, however, is VWBro J Stuart Peters, who was Deputy Provincial Grand Master, 1998-1999. VW Bro Stuart Peters was Initiated into Ionic Lodge on 5 June 1957 and was Master in 1969 and again in 1993. His separate biographical details appear elsewhere in this book. He has been honoured by the Brethren of Ionic Lodge on two occasions. Firstly, in April 2000, to celebrate his many Masonic achievements and, secondly, in 2007, to mark his 50 years of service to Masonry.

On 6 May 1998, the Lodge celebrated its 50th Anniversary. WBro John Davies was WM with WBro D R Luce (first Initiate) as SW, and WBro S G Williams, as JW. The Provincial party was led by VWBro J Stuart Peters and included WBro Peter Frost, WBro Norman Lee and WBro John Taylor. During the Ceremony, WBro Brian Phillips, PPrJGW, Secretary, read out the Summons and Minutes of the Consecration and Installation Meeting held on 24 April 1948. WBro D A Morris, PPrJGW, Treasurer, gave a brief history of the Lodge, 1948-1998. The history was written by WBros D A Morris and George E Jowett, PPrAGDC, and all Brethren present were given a copy. Sadly, there were no surviving Founder Members, but from the Minutes, it was established that at the Consecration in 1948, two young Freemasons, Bros E J Williams and F Newbury had attended as guests. They were, therefore, invited and attended the 50th Anniversary Celebrations as special guests.

Compiled by WBro Brian R Phillips, PPrJGW, Secretary.

Old Barrians Lodge No.6671

Warranted : 5 May 1948

Consecrated : 8 May 1948

Meeting at the Masonic Hall, Barry.

The Petition to form the Lodge was submitted to RWBro R P St John Charles, JP, ProvGM, on 10 March 1948, with a view to strengthen the association between Members of the Craft in the town of Barry, who had been educated at Barry County School. The Mother Lodge was Barry Lodge No.2357, and most of the Founder Members came from that Lodge, which at that time had a Membership of 281. The other Founders were Members of Vale of Glamorgan Lodge No.3977. At a Meeting held on 14 April 1948, it was agreed that the Membership should be limited to ex-scholars and former members of staff of Barry County School. It was also agreed that the Barry County School song would be sung on the second perambulation, at the close of all Lodge Meetings.

A further meeting was held on 17 April 1948, when the following were agreed: the Lodge would meet four times a year in March (Installation), May, October and January with Lodges of Instruction in February, April, September and December; the fees were to be at Initiation 25 guineas, the annual subscription 1 guinea, joining fee 3 guineas, and the Founders' fee 5 guineas. At the same Meeting, it was also agreed to Initiate four Candidates in the first year and two per year subsequently, and that there would be a total of eleven Joining Members. The design of the Lodge Crest and the musical arrangements were also approved.

The Consecration of Old Barrians Lodge took place on 8 May 1948. The Consecrating Officer was RWBro R P St J Charles, JP, ProvGM, assisted by WBro Edwin Drew, ProvSGW, WBro George J Davies, ProvJGW, WBro Dr J Gwyn Davies, ProvGChap, WBro Harry F Stockwell, ProvGSec, and other Provincial Grand Officers. Also present was Bro L D Bailey, ProvGOrg, who was later appointed a Grand Officer. WBro J W Lennox was WM Designate, WBro Dr William Hughes was SW Designate, and WBro G C Hughes was JW Designate. The Installing Officer was VWBro Edgar Rutter, OSM, PGD, DepProvGM.

On Friday, 4 June 1948, framed copies of the Founders' photograph were presented to Major Edgar Jones and Mr E T Griffiths, the past and present Headmasters of Barry County School. It was decided to adopt the workings of Barry Lodge, with minor modifications. At a Meeting on 19 July 1948, it was agreed to give financial support to Barry Lodge for the purchase of a Tracing Board Table, to commemorate the Brethren of Barry who gave their lives in WWII. The Lodge By-laws were prepared by Bro Guy Sixsmith, a Cardiff Stipendiary Magistrate, and adopted by the Lodge at the first Meeting held on 1 October 1948. These By-laws were rewritten in 1991, based on the Grand Lodge Model.

At the end of WWII, many Members of Old Barrians Lodge, who were Marine Engineers etc. resumed their voyages, and Emergency Meetings were held to accommodate their Passing and Raising. In one Meeting, after radio contact had been made with his ship, Captain Cutler was brought into port from the Barry Roads on the Barry Pilot Cutter. He and Mr T R Taylor, a Marine Engineer, were Initiated together at 11.10 pm and the Lodge was closed at 00.20 am on Saturday, 11 February 1949. Forty of the brethren stayed for the complete Meeting. The Lodge had been opened at 7.10 pm on the Friday.

History was made on the night of the fourth Regular Meeting, held on 6 May 1949, when the DepProvGM, VWBro Edgar J Rutter, accompanied by his Officers, consented to perform the first Third Degree Ceremony of Old Barrians Lodge.

In 1951, the Lodge increased its Meetings to nine a year. On 7 March 1952, Bro Dr C K B Lennox was Installed into the Chair of King Solomon by his father, the first Master of the Lodge, WBro J W Lennox. WBro C K B Lennox became Organist and Treasurer of the Lodge and at the age of 93 years still attended Installations as the last surviving Founder Member of the Lodge.

In October 1952, invitations were extended to the Brethren of Schools Lodges in this Province and the Province of Monmouthshire. This established the principle of Schools' Nights, a tradition which is still practised.

In April 1957, the committee approved the design of a Lodge tie, to be worn by Lodge Members when attending other School Lodges. A Past Masters' Honours Board was approved in May 1980 and permission was granted by the Barry Masonic Hall Trust Company to site the Board in the foyer of the Temple. The Board was provided by WBro R D Boon and on it are recorded the names of all the Past Masters of the Lodge. On 9 January 1998, a three-drawer box of Working Tools was presented to the Lodge in memory of WBro A R Duff, PPrSGW, a Mason well known in Barry, who was for many years responsible for the Stewardship of Barry Masonic Hall.

WBro David A Westall was Initiated into Old Barrians in 1976. He became a Joining Member of Lodge of St Andrew No.8934 in 1983 and was first Installed as Master of that Lodge in 1986. He was again Installed Master of Lodge of St Andrew in 2005 and 2006. A Grand Officer, he was appointed PAGDC in 2004 and promoted to DepGSwdB in 2010. In Royal Arch Freemasonry, he was Exalted in Vale of Glamorgan Chapter No.3977 in 1987, appointed GStB in 2007 and Installed as ME Grand Superintendent of the Province of South Wales in 2009.

WBro Nicholas G Martin was Initiated into the Lodge in 1979 and was Installed as Master in 1989 and in 2000. A Joining Member of Greystone Border Lodge No.9449, Launceston, Province of Cornwall, he became WM of that Lodge in 2003. He is a Founder Member of Loyal Sportsman Lodge No.9197 and of Hafan Deg Lodge No.9520, and was Installed as Master of Hafan Deg Lodge in 2008. In Provincial Grand Lodge, he was appointed ProvSGD in 1995 and promoted to PPrJGW in 2001. He was appointed a Grand Officer in 2009 with the Rank of PAGDC.

Thanks to the generosity of WBro L J Hollinshead and his wife, Old Barrians Lodge was finally able to place its own Banner among those surrounding the Master's Chair. The Banner was Dedicated at an impressive Ceremony at the Regular Lodge Meeting held on Friday, 14 October 1994, by WBro David L Protheroe, PSGD, AProvGM, and his team of Officers. The Lodge Motto on the Banner is 'Goreu, Golud Goleuder', which translates as 'From Learning Comes Light'.

WBro George C Royle, RRC, TD, JP, joined Old Barrians Lodge in 1996. In Provincial Grand Lodge, he was appointed ProvGStwd in 2002, and promoted to ProvGSwdB in 2006. Also, in 2006, he was appointed Provincial Grand Almoner. He became a Grand Officer in 2008 with the Rank of PAGDC. WBro George Royle is the Right Worthy Grand Preceptor of the Commemorative Order of St Thomas of Acon, Province of South Wales.

The Lodge celebrated its 50th Anniversary in 1998 with WBro S F Pyecroft in the Chair. The 60th Anniversary was celebrated in 2008 with WBro S P Woodfin in the Chair. Since the Consecration, over 250 Masons have been Initiated into the Lodge.

Compiled by WBro B E James, PPrAGReg.

Penlan Lodge No.6695

Warranted	:	5 May 1948
Consecrated	:	29 September 1948
Erased	:	8 June 2011

Met at the Masonic Hall, Cardiff.

The ProvGM, RWBro R P St John Charles Consecrated Penlan Lodge on 29 September 1948 and the Sponsoring Lodge was Emerald Lodge No.5907. Penlan Lodge was formed by a group of Freemasons who were employed in the banking profession. The Founders were influenced in the choice of the Lodge name by one of their number, WBro Rev W E Mathias-Williams, PAGChap, JW Designate, a greatly respected Freemason and a well-known Baptist Minister in South Wales. He was Initiated in Henry Pendrill Charles Lodge No.3769 in 1944, and became the second Master of Penlan Lodge in 1950. He was also a Member and Past Chaplain of Hendre Lodge; served as ProvGChap and was appointed ProvSGW in 1958. Ten years later, in 1969, he became the South Wales Area Superintendent for the Baptist Church. The Lodge was named after the Hymn tune 'Penlan' written by David Jenkins, 1848-1915, which is sung to the Hymn tune 'In heavenly love abiding'. The Lodge opening hymn was also sung to the 'Penlan' tune. The Welsh word Penlan can be loosely translated as *'the top of the hill'* but a more accurate translation would be *'the top of the bank'*.

The Lodge Crest depicts a hill with the rising sun behind it, with the Lodge Motto: *'Lift up your heads'* written on the open pages of The Volume of the Sacred Law. The Lodge name and Motto can thus be seen as a combination of both: *'Lift up your heads towards the top of the hill'*. We are informed that Freemasonry is a progressive science, it is fitting as Freemasons that we should lift up our heads and view *'the top of the hill'* and by doing so, achieve higher ideals in life.

The events leading up to the Banner Dedication are unusual. Capt Walter Makepeace, who was the Tyler of Carmel Lodge No.4774, made it known that he would like WBro Ron Redwood to Initiate into Penlan Lodge his only living relative, his nephew, Donald George Mackenzie. Ron readily agreed to his request and Donald's Initiation into Penlan Lodge took place on 14 December 1965. Walter Makepeace later became a Joining Member of the Lodge. As time moved on and Walter Makepeace passed to the Grand Lodge Above, he left a substantial amount of money to his only beneficiary, Donald. Tragically, Bro Donald was killed in a traffic accident some years later. However, on the death of Donald's widow, the Lodge was left a portrait of him and the significant sum of £22,000 in her will. This money was used to benefit various charities over the years and also assisted the Lodge in defraying the cost of designing and purchasing the Lodge Banner. WBro Adrian Green, Member of The City of Cardiff Lodge No.7528, and a local artist of some distinction, designed the Banner. Mrs Graham Tagg, whose husband was a Member of

Three Pillars Lodge No.5857, kindly embroidered the Banner and also the Lodge's Presentation Cushion. The Banner Dedication Ceremony was held on 30 May 1997, the 49th Anniversary of the Warranting of the Lodge. WBro Hywel Davies, AProvGM, was the Dedicating Officer, and this was his first Ceremony as a recently appointed AProvGM. The Principal Officers of Penlan Lodge were WBro G Anthony Howell, PPrAGDC, WM; WBro Ron Redwood, PPrSGW, SW; and Bro Nicholas Mais, JW. The Penlan Banner is displayed in The Edgar Rutter Temple, which had been the Lodge's usual Lodge Room.

The 50th Anniversary of the Founding of the Lodge was marked by the commissioning of commemorative plates from Rumney Pottery. The design of the centrepiece of the plate is taken from the design of the Past Master's Jewel. It was beautifully produced by Rumney Potteries' owner, WBro Robert Giles, of the City of Cardiff Lodge. Copies of the plate were given to each Member of the Lodge and the original was placed in the display cabinet in the reception area of Cardiff Masonic Hall. Another was sent for display in the United Grand Lodge Museum in London.

A famous Brother of the Lodge was Bro Derek Tapscott, a former professional footballer and Wales international, who played for Arsenal and Cardiff City. Derek was Initiated, Passed and Raised in Penlan Lodge, but he did not progress to the Chair of King Solomon. Affectionately known to local football fans as 'Tappy', he started his career with Barry Town before being signed by Arsenal in September 1953, for a fee of £2,750. He made his first-team debut at Highbury in April 1954, scoring twice in a 3-0 win over Liverpool. Two days later, he was selected by Wales to face Austria, the first of fourteen appearances for his country. In five years with Arsenal, he scored 68 goals in 132 matches, before being transferred to Cardiff in September 1958 for £10,000. Derek stayed with Cardiff until the 1965 season, helping the Bluebirds to win promotion to the old Division One in 1960, when he finished top scorer with 21 league and cup goals.

Another well-respected Member of the Lodge was WBro Leonard Boyle who, in 1956 moved from Kent to Cardiff, to take up an appointment as General Manager of the Principality Building Society. By the time he retired in 1978, the Society's assets had increased from about £4 million to £100 million. During his career with the Principality Building Society, he was elected as the Welsh Societies' representative on the Building Societies Association and became chairman in 1973. The role required frequent and close co-operation with the Government. In 1974, he was the first Briton to be elected President of the Federation of European Building Societies and was awarded the CBE in 1977. Leonard also devoted a great deal of time and effort to the Boys' Brigade and was National Treasurer in the early 1980s.

Penlan Lodge has celebrated many family ties between its Members. On 14 March 2001, WBro Keith Hyde, WM, Initiated his cousin's two sons, Bros Phillip Alan Stansfield and Martin John Stansfield. Their father, Bro Alan Stansfield, a Member of Penlan Lodge, proposed his sons into Freemasonry and WBro Keith seconded both of them.

The two brothers continue the family Masonic tradition, their grandfather, WBro William Stansfield, having been a Member of Lodge of St John No.104, Stockport, Cheshire. Their great grandfather, Bro Albert Edward Hyde, was a Member of Cerealia Lodge No.3165, London. It is interesting to note that Cerealia Lodge was formed before the First World War by German Bakers in London. In ancient Roman religion, the 'Cerealia' was the major festival celebrated for the grain goddess Ceres, hence the name 'Cerealia'. At the commencement of hostilities in 1914, German Bakers were interned and, rather than see the Lodge closed, Bro Albert, the Senior Captain of the Essex Volunteer Regiment, along with other Army Officers, stepped in, thus ensuring the future of the Lodge. The Lodge is still in existence and meets at the Imperial Hotel, Russell Street, London.

During its existence, the Lodge had seen many fathers introduce their sons to Freemasonry. Strong family ties are good for Freemasonry in general and have been beneficial for Penlan Lodge in particular. The Willmott brothers are a case in point, each having served the Lodge loyally as Worshipful Masters. J Alan Willmott, PPrSGD, served as WM in 1986 and 1999, Dennis P

Willmott, PPrSGD, in 1988 and 2002, and D Brian Willmott, PPrSGD, in 1987.

By the beginning of 2009, it was evident that the Lodge was no longer viable. Membership had declined to 24 Brethren, and all Officers, with the exception of the IG and the only Steward, were all Past Masters. WBro Nicholas Mais, PPrAGDC had been Installed as WM on three occasions: 1998, 2006 and 2007. WBro Keith C Hyde, PPrJGW had occupied the Chair in 1983 and again in 2000. It is of interest to note that in May 2010, WBro Keith was Installed as the Rt Hon the Lord Mayor of Cardiff.

The Brethren of Penlan Lodge met for the last time on Tuesday, 8 December 2009. The following account is of the final Meeting of Penlan Lodge but it does little to convey the emotionally charged nature of the occasion. *'The evening began by WBro Ron Redwood taking the Chair of King Solomon, in his own inimitable style. The AProvGM, WBro Geoffrey W Thomas, was asked to present and explain the Grand Lodge Certificate to Bro Paul Ralph, who was only Raised the previous month. It was decided to present the Senior Past Master, WBro Ron Redwood, with the Master's Collar. This was a very special moment for both Ron and the Members of Penlan Lodge. The remaining Collars were given to the Brethren in Office. The Bible was given to WBro Dennis Willmott. WBro Keith Hyde received the Working Tools, for him to present to Keystone Lodge No.9521 Aberdare, where he is a Joining Member. The Brethren were invited to share their feelings about what the Lodge had meant to them. It now really felt that this was the final Meeting of Penlan Lodge. The Lodge was closed with great dignity, in due form, and for the final time, by the Senior Past Master, WBro Ron Redwood. The DC, WBro Stephen Hughes, then formed a procession by calling firstly on the AProvGM, WBro Geoffrey Thomas and the Lodge Mandated Officer, WBro David Edwards. The Senior and Junior Wardens were called next, followed by the Brethren in Rank order. WBro Ron Redwood and WBro Keith Hyde, being the Senior Past Masters present, were called on to carry the Lodge Warrant from the Temple. WBro G Anthony Howell, being Master of the Lodge when the Lodge Banner was Dedicated, was called on to carry the Lodge Banner. The WM then took his place in the procession and all of the Brethren followed in turn, for the final time, under the direction of the Director of Ceremonies.'*

Compiled by WBro Keith Hyde, PPrJGW, and WBro John Donovan, PPrSGD, with assistance from WBro Graham Wilcox, PPrGSwdB.

INDUSTRIA CAMBRENSIS
LODGE No. 6700

Industria Cambrensis Lodge No.6700

W.M. 1999 - 2000

Warranted : 2 June 1948

Consecrated : 4 October 1948

Meeting at the Town Hall, Cowbridge.

The historical account of Industria Cambrensis Lodge must necessarily start some years prior to its Consecration.

The Royal Ordnance Factory (ROF), Bridgend, or the 'Bridgend Arsenal', as it was known locally, functioned successfully until the end of WWII, when it became surplus to requirements. As it had its own water, gas and electricity producing plants, telephone, drainage systems and sixteen miles of rail track connected to the main lines, it was decided to establish a Trading Estate, to help provide employment for ex-service personnel and redundant war-workers. To this end, from early 1946, the ROF buildings were being converted for light industrial manufacturing use. South Wales Trading Estates Ltd, Treforest, established in 1937, had experience in converting buildings and inducing firms to occupy them, was appointed by the Government to implement the scheme. For this project to be successful, and to get a rapid start in providing employment, existing operating companies were required to occupy these buildings. This was achieved largely, though not entirely, by negotiating with going concerns functioning outside Wales.

Every company agreeing to transfer part, or all of its business to Bridgend, and other selected sites in Wales, had of necessity, to bring with it certain key personnel with the necessary professional and technical qualifications, as well as managerial experience. Many were Freemasons, and in some cases they had to spend at least two days away from business in order to attend their Mother Lodges.

A number of these Freemasons conferred together and decided to form their own local Lodge. The assistance of some prominent local Freemasons was solicited, resulting in the new Lodge being Sponsored by St Quentin's Lodge No.4778. A team of Founders was established, consisting of ten Subscribing Members from St Quentin's Lodge and 10 Brethren having industrial connections with Bridgend and district. It was decided to give the new Lodge the Latin name 'Industria Cambrensis', meaning 'Industry of Wales', and that the Lodge should meet in the Town Hall, Cowbridge. The Crest was designed to depict the then basic industries of South Wales, namely, coal, steel and tinplate. The Motto allied to the Crest *'Crescit, Fortuna, Merendo'*, was also appropriate, as its literal meaning is *'Grow, Enrich, Deserve'*.

Official application was made to Grand Lodge; the Warrant, dated 2 June 1948, was issued; and the Lodge was Consecrated at the Town Hall, Cowbridge, on Monday, 4 October 1948, by RWBro R P St John Charles, JP, PAGReg, ProvGM. The Installing Master was VWBro Edgar J Rutter, OSM, PGD, DepProvGM. Also present, was WBro Harry F Stockwell, PAGDC, ProvGSec. WBro Cyril James Oswald Evans, WM of St Quentin's Lodge in 1947, was Installed as Primus Master. Bro Eugene Brunning, CBE, Chairman of Wales and Monmouthshire Trading Estates Ltd, of The Cottage, St Hilary, Cowbridge, was Invested as SW. He was honoured with the CBE in January 1946, being the Regional Controller, Board of Trade for Wales. Bro George Inwood Payne, Owner/Managing Director Tuscan Motors Ltd, of The Rowans, Merthyr Mawr Road, Bridgend, was Invested as JW.

Among the Founders named on the Warrant are Sir Lewis Lougher, PGD, and Gilbert David Shepherd, MBE, PGD. Sir Lewis Lougher had been Initiated in Loyal Commercial Lodge No.2720, in December 1898, and was Installed WM of St Quentin's Lodge in 1926. His biographical details may be found in the history of Loyal Commercial Lodge. Gilbert D Shepherd was a Chartered Accountant, of Gilbert Shepherd, Owen & Co. In 1946, he was Vice-President of the Institute of Chartered Accountants of England and Wales, and was President 1947-1948. Also named are WBro Edgar William

Alms Dish presented by WBro Col Arthur B Walters

Lewis, PAGDC, Installed as WM of St Quentin's Lodge in 1934, who acted as the first IPM; and WBro Col Arthur Baraf Walters, PDepGSwdB, the first Lodge Chaplain. To commemorate his year as Founder Chaplain, he presented the Lodge with an alms dish, made of oak from Guildhall, London, which was destroyed by enemy action on 29 December 1940.

WBro Cyril James Oswald Evans, first WM, was well versed in the Ritual. He presented excellent ceremonies and ensured that every Candidate, on becoming a MM, would borrow his Ritual book to complete their own book, with initials only of missing words, thereby ensuring uniformity. He was also an historian and keen researcher in local history, and published in 1938, 'Glamorgan - Its History and Topography', which has been reprinted several times. His collection of Glamorgan Deeds, 1591-1857, is now in the National Library of Wales, Aberystwyth. WBro Edgar Lewis, first IPM, always brought Members back into line whenever they strayed from Masonic convention. Founder Member, WBro Wyndham Jones, first DC, was outstanding in conducting floor-work in the Temple, and also at the Festive Board, with his Toasts, quips and stories. He became WM in 1953, and was Lodge Secretary for many years. No Masonic work was too much for WBro Windsor Taylor Roper to tackle. He would undertake any Office at a moment's notice. One of the Joining Members at the first Regular Lodge Meeting, in January 1949, he immediately took Office as SD. He became WM in 1951 and rose to the Rank of PPrGW. He was DC for many years, and he left a distinctive mark on the quality of the Ceremonies, and on the procedure at the Festive Board.

Immediately following the Installation Ceremony, a Committee of Founders was formed, charged with drawing up the By-laws of the Lodge. It is interesting to note the following extracts from the first By-laws of 1948: *'Initiation fee - £25.00; Joining and re-Joining fee - £7.00; Lodge shall meet eight times per annum; Annual subscription - £4.00 (to include all dinners except the Installation Festival).'* These By-laws were approved by Grand Lodge on 25 March 1949. At the Regular Meeting in May 1949 they were amended, so that the Lodge met five times per annum as at present. Grand Lodge approval of the amendment is dated 5 October 1949. The salient points of the By-laws were unaltered and remained in force until a proposal to increase the fees to £5.00 per annum was approved on 26 October 1959. That was an increase of 25% after a period of 10 years. In 1968, fees rose to £6.00 pa, to include meals except at Installation.

The early Members made every effort to Initiate into the Lodge those Candidates who had attained success in their trade, profession or calling, either in or allied to, industry. This was necessary, not only to maintain industrial connections but also, as a young Lodge, every Candidate had to be deemed capable of progressing through all Lodge Offices to the best of his ability. The first Regular Lodge Meeting following the Consecration was held in January 1949, when five Joining Members were admitted, while during the first year, four Candidates were Initiated.

While every Member brings his own character to bear on the Lodge, the three Northway brothers, Samuel, William and Percy should certainly be mentioned. WBro Sam Northway, PSGD, was Initiated in Bute Lodge No.960 in 1953. In 1958, he became a Joining Member of Industria Cambrensis Lodge and was Installed as Master in 1964. He served as Secretary, 1968-1984. In 1973, he was the Organising Secretary and a Founder Member of Y Bont Faen Lodge No.8533. Appointed AProvGM, 1982-1993; he was WM of Hendre Lodge No.3250 in 1987. He was also appointed PAGSoj in Supreme Grand Chapter and was a Member of many other Orders. WBro William Job Northway, PJGD, was Initiated in Industria Cambrensis Lodge in 1959, and Installed as Master in 1968. He was the Charity Steward, 1976-1997. He is a Founder Member of Kenfig Lodge No.8289 and Y Bont Faen Lodge No.8533. He was appointed ProvAGDC in 1987. In Supreme Grand Chapter he was appointed GStB at the 1987 Investiture, and was ProvGDC, 1985-1995. He, like his Bro Sam, was a Member of many other Orders. WBro Percy Northway was Initiated in Kenfig Lodge. He became a Joining Member of Industria Cambrensis Lodge and was Installed WM in 1990. While Percy was not a Masonic giant like his brothers, he was an artist of local repute, specialising in landscapes and scenes derived from his own private thoughts.

WBro H Hedgecox, as Secretary for many years, went out of his way to ensure the success of Industria Cambrensis Lodge. He became WM in 1956. He was also a Member of St Quentin's Lodge and was Installed WM of that Lodge in 1965.

The annual Church Service was always a well-attended family occasion in those earlier days. Bro Leo Gill, a Lodge Member and landlord of the Duke of Wellington Hotel, Cowbridge, always provided 'never-to-be-forgotten' strawberry/cream teas after the Service. Although well provided for at the 'Duke' on these occasions, the Lodge Festive Board always took place at the Bear Hotel, Cowbridge.

Compiled by WBro Martyn Wake, PPrGSwdB, mainly from
the 50th Anniversary history by WBro Vivian Charles Warwick, PPrJGW.

Craig yr Hesg Lodge No.6724

Warranted : 28 July 1948

Consecrated : 18 October 1948

Meeting at the Masonic Hall, Pontypridd.

After the 1939-1945 war, life gradually began to return to normal as Brethren who had served in the armed forces returned home to resume their civilian life once again. Soon, several Members of Hen Bont Lodge No.4691, which had a Membership of about 200, began to make their feelings known. They considered the Lodge had too many Members, which did not allow Brethren the opportunity to achieve Office within the Lodge in a reasonable time. And so, the seeds were sown to form a new Lodge.

A meeting was held to discuss this project, and as a result some 30 Members expressed their willingness to become Founders of a new Lodge. The first major problem then manifested itself. There were so many Past Masters expressing a wish to go through 'The Chair' of the new Lodge that Provincial Grand Lodge announced that they would not support the new Lodge if it was going to be a Lodge of 'Past Masters'. This would defeat the whole concept of starting a new Lodge! It was finally agreed that the number of Past Masters would be limited to 3, whereupon a few disgruntled PMs withdrew their application to become Founder Members.

Early in 1948, WBro W I Williams presented a Petition to Rhondda Lodge No.3979 to form a new Lodge, which received the approval of the Lodge Members. The Petition was approved by both Provincial and Grand Lodges and arrangements were set in motion for a Consecration Ceremony.

Finding a suitable name for the new Lodge became the subject of some lengthy discussion, with such names as, 'The Graig-Graigwen', and 'Bryn Taff' being considered. The final choice, however, was 'Craig yr Hesg', being the rock upon which to build a foundation.

The Consecration Ceremony took place on Monday, 18 October 1948, and was carried out by RWBro R P St John Charles, JP, PAGReg, ProvGM, South Wales Eastern Division. The Installing Master was VWBro Edgar J Rutter, OSM, PGD, DepProvGM, and the first Master was WBro D Rees, PPrSGW, PAGReg. The first Initiates were Mr Isaac Thomas and Mr David Morgan Rees.

Food rationing was still in force, which greatly curtailed the extent of the Festive Board. Clothing coupons were also still being used and as a result an order was issued from Grand Lodge that Brethren could wear dark lounge suits instead of the more formal

Lodge of Endurance No.6729

Warranted : 28 July 1948
Consecrated : 30 October 1948
Meeting at the Masonic Hall, Cardiff.

In May 1948, Universities Lodge No.5461, received a Deputation of Civil Service Brethren connected with 'The Ministry of Works', who were Petitioners for a new Lodge to be named 'Lodge of Endurance' No.6729. The Petition was successful and the new Lodge was granted a Warrant on 28 July 1948.

Lodge of Endurance was Consecrated on Saturday, 30 October 1948, at 2.45 pm, in the Masonic Temple at Guildford Crescent, Cardiff. The Ceremony was conducted by RWBro R P St John Charles, JP, PAGR, ProvGM, South Wales, assisted by a team of 12 Officers. All Officers Designate were in attendance, together with 21 visitors. On completion of the Consecrating Ceremony, WBro Edgar J Rutter, DepProvGM, assumed the Chair of King Solomon and Installed the first WM, WBro Edward R Brown, who then appointed WBro H R H Ward as IPM, and Bros C F Fox and W F Kermode as SW and JW respectively. Little more is known of this first Meeting, as the original Minute Book was lost.

The Lodge seemed set for a good start when, at the Lodge Committee Meeting on Thursday, 14 April 1949, five Candidates for Initiation were proposed. Seeking to ensure good attendance at their Lodge of Instruction, the Committee decided to hold LOIs on the fourth Monday of every month jointly with Amethyst Lodge. The subscriptions were set at £3.3s.0d.(£3.15p) and as it was proving difficult to borrow Regalia and Lodge furniture such as Working Tools etc., the Lodge should endeavour to purchase its own. Concern was felt that some Brethren would find it hard to purchase white gloves, and with this in mind, they decided that white gloves should be worn only by those who could afford them.

The Lodge experienced its first serious hiccup in October 1951. Bro David Williams, WM Elect, was due to be Installed on the first Monday of November, but fell ill and was taken to hospital. WBro H R H Ward, a Founder Member and PM Leigh Lodge No.887, Birmingham, stepped into the breach and was Installed instead.

Throughout the 1950s, Membership of Lodge of Endurance continued to increase and at the Meeting in March 1956, a Second Degree Ceremony was performed, followed by a double Initiation Ceremony. By the end of the decade, Membership stood at over 64. Due to fire damage at the Cardiff Masonic Hall, the Lodge found it necessary to use local hotels for the Festive Board.

During this decade, it was the practice of the Lodge to hold 'Masonic Funerals', with 'Masonic Rites' conducted by eminent Members of the Lodge. This practice was abandoned when United Grand Lodge held its debate on the relationship between Masonry and Religion.

The end of the decade was occasioned by the passing of WBro Ted Brown, the first WM of the Lodge, and in January 1951, his son, WM of Ionic Lodge No.6626, Swansea, presented Lodge of Endurance with Musical Ritual Books in memory of his father.

In April 1956, the Lodge authorised 'token' payments of ten guineas toward the cost of suitable Grand Lodge Regalia for WBros John Taylor and J Batley, the first Brethren to attain the Grand Lodge Rank of PAGDC.

Another faithful and long serving Brother worthy of mention is Owen P Davies. He held the post of Almoner from 1957 to 1997, and only then reluctantly relinquished the Office, because of ill health.

The early 1960s saw the Lodge applying to the MW the Grand Master for Dispensation, to allow WBro John C Taylor to hold simultaneously the position of WM of Lodge of Benevolence No.7305 and Lodge of Endurance.

A peculiar situation arose towards the end of 1961. The Board of Managers of the Cardiff Masonic Hall Company appointed Mr Leslie Tudor as caretaker, on condition that he became a Member of the Craft. Lodge of Endurance was asked to Initiate him without a fee.

The Lodge continued to grow throughout the 1960s. By the end of 1969, there were 85 Members and the Lodge was holding 8 Regular Meetings and 9 LOIs per year.

With the introduction of decimal currency in 1971, prices started to rise; bar prices increased and subscriptions increased from £5.5s.0d. in 1969 to £8.50p in 1973.

In November 1975, the WM, WBro Bill Hamblin died whilst still in Office. Of historic significance to the Lodge was the subsequent presentation of a PM Jewel to his widow, Florence.

Lodge of Endurance can claim to be unique by the fact that not only is the ProvDepGSec, WBro John Weldon, PAGDC a Member, but so also is the ProvGSec, WBro James Richard Bevan, PJGD.

WBro Jim Bevan was Initiated into Lodge of Endurance in February 1978, and he attained the Chair of King Solomon in 1986. Prior to his Masonic career, WBro Jim was a Quantity Surveyor and South Wales Area Manager for a Chartered Surveying Practice. He is currently the longest serving ProvGSec in the United Grand Lodge of England, having been appointed as such in 1990. He is also a Member of the Committee of Management of the Royal Benevolent Institution, a Member of the Commission for Appeals Court of the UGLE as well as being Chairman of the Masonic Benevolent Fund of South Wales (1990 - 2005 Hon Sec) and Trustee of the Welsh Charitables RFC. If that is not enough; he is or has been a Member of five Craft Lodges, three Chapters, three Mark Mason Lodges, three RAM Lodges and two Chapters of the A&AR, actively serving and holding High Office in most, if not all. His attributes and commitments to Freemasonry are too numerous to mention, but he does like to relax with his not too strenuous hobbies of motor rallying and shooting.

WBro John Francis Weldon was Initiated into Lodge of Endurance in 1982 and Installed as Worshipful Master in 1991. In Provincial Grand Lodge, he was appointed ProvAGDC in 1997 and promoted to ProvDepGDC in 1999. He became the AProvGSec in 2002 and a Grand Officer with the Rank of PAGDC in 2005.

It is appropriate to mention here that the Lodge has been blessed with many worthy Brethren who served in various Offices for many years. One outstanding Brother was Owen Davies who, in 1975, was presented with a leather wallet for 21 years service, and again, in 1997, he was presented with a suitably inscribed radio-cassette player, to mark 40 years as Almoner of the

Lodge. Another worthy Brother was WBro Harold Ward, the Founder IPM, who received a presentation to mark 50 years in Freemasonry.

The Lodge had been borrowing certain items of Regalia for many years, particularly the Working Tools. That changed in February 1983, when the Social Committee gave a generous donation, augmented by personal donations from WBros D G Thomas, Jim Bevan, and Bro Jim Duggan. Bro Pat Martin had the Tools engraved with the Lodge Name and Number and WBro Arthur Petty presented the WM with a Setting Maul and stand.

Good Neighbour Lodge No.8378, Chislehurst, Province of West Kent, when visiting the Albert Edward Prince of Wales Court, Porthcawl, in April 1991, Passed Bro Mark Evans to the 2nd Degree. This occasion was attended by the Rt Hon the Lord Swansea, ProvGM, and other distinguished guests.

On Monday, 14 December 1998, the Lodge celebrated its 50th Anniversary. As part of the celebrations three special Aprons were acquired, to be worn by the Principal Officers and passed to their successors. Also a booklet, containing a brief history of the Lodge, was produced by WBros G Evans and E Davies.

WBro Colin Richards, PPrJGW (WM 1981) was made High Sheriff of the County of Glamorgan for the year 2000 and on 6 November 2000, WBro Dudley Brown, PAGSuptWks, son of the first WM, Edward R Brown, presented the Lodge with his father's PM's Jewel and Founder's Jewel.

On 5 November 2001, WBro Andrew Gretton presented WBro Don Wilson, PPrSGW, with his Certificate for fifty years in Freemasonry. For forty of those years, he was Charity Steward. He was also presented with a picture of HMS St David, on which he served with RWBro Captain Sir Norman Lloyd-Edwards, whilst in the RNVR.

WBro Don Wilson was made an Honorary Member in December 2006. On the same evening, WBro Owen Davies, PPrSGD, was presented with a Certificate for fifty years in Freemasonry and a photograph of himself in his Provincial Regalia. WBro Owen passed away in December 2002.

Sadly, the last of the Founder Members, WBro Cyril Fox, having served the Lodge admirably for over 39 years, passed to the Grand Lodge Above in 1997. Cyril was honoured with the OBE for services to Architecture.

Compiled by WBro Eric J Davies, PPrSGD, and WBro Arthur J Petty, PPrSGW.

Penybont Lodge No.6743

Warranted : 28 July 1948

Consecrated : 22 October 1948

Meeting at the Masonic Hall, Bridgend.

On 24 March, 1948, WBro R G Kyte, PPrGD, who had been Installed WM of Ogmore Lodge No.1752 in 1928 and 1929, convened a meeting at the Masonic Hall, Adare Street, Bridgend, (now redeveloped as a shopping area) for Brethren interested in forming a new Lodge. At this time there were three Craft Lodges in Bridgend: Ogmore Lodge No.1752, Consecrated 2 July 1878; Llangeinor Lodge No.4194, Consecrated 27 April 1921 and Morganwg Lodge No.5084, Consecrated 7 January 1929. Twelve Brethren, together with R G Kyte attended this initial meeting, when it was decided to form a new Lodge to be called 'Penybont Lodge'. It was agreed that six Lodge Meetings a year would be held, one of which would be a lecture on Masonic research. The Meetings were to be held in the months of September, October, November, March, April and May with the Installation Meeting being held in March. It was decided that the annual subscription should be 3 guineas (£3. 15p) and the Initiation fee £20.0.0d.

At the Founders' meeting held on Friday, 11 June 1948, WBro Harry Stockwell, ProvGSec, presided, and stated the Grand Lodge conditions for the formation of a new Lodge. At the time, Penybont Lodge was sixth in line for applying for a new Warrant.

On 28 June, 1948, R G Kyte, WM Designate; Bro T H Benson Evans, SW Designate; and Bro F J Little, JW Designate; presented the Petition for approval at a Regular Meeting of Ogmore Lodge. The Petition was duly signed by the WM and his Wardens, and Ogmore Lodge became the Sponsoring Lodge. Ogmore Lodge, the owner of the Masonic Hall, Adare Street, Bridgend, agreed that the new Lodge could have the use of the premises for six Meetings, together with Lodges of Instruction and Committee meetings at a rent of £45 per annum. The rental fee was to include heating, lighting and cleaning. (In 1952, the rent was increased to £52. 00 pa.)

At a Founders' meeting held on 13 August 1948, WBro R G Kyte informed them that Friday, 22 October 1948, had been designated as the date for the Consecration of the Lodge. Prior to the Consecration Ceremony, the WM Designate, at his own expense, entertained the Consecrating Officers to lunch at the Blue Bird Café, Bridgend. They included: RWBro St John Charles JP, ProvGM; VWBro Edgar J Rutter, DepProvGM; WBro Charles P Palmer, AProvGM; and WBro Harry F Stockwell, ProvGSec. There were seventy-six visiting Brethren at the Consecration Ceremony. The Festival Dinner was held at Bridgend Town Hall (now demolished, and the present site of the Post Office) at a cost of 15 shillings (75p) per head.

On 22 April, 1949, VWBro Edgar J Rutter presented a Bible to the Lodge as a personal gift; at the same Lodge Meeting he gave a lecture on 'Masonic Aprons'. The Lodge Ceremonial Cushion was presented by WBro R B Whittingham in February, 1953.

The Lodge Crest was designed by Bro R B Hardcastle, a Joining Member of the Lodge, and dates from November 1950. The Crest depicts the mediaeval bridge, from which Bridgend gets its name. The suggested Motto was: *'Deus Satis Est'* a close Latin for the Welsh *'Duw yw Digon'*, or in English *'God is sufficient'*. The Crest was first used on the Lodge Notice for the 1951 Annual Festival held on 16 March. By this time the Motto had been changed to *'Deus Sufficit Omnibus'*. A rough translation being *'God is sufficient or enough'*.

On Friday, 16 March, 1951, Bro Ronald Bowen Whittingham was Installed as Worshipful Master of Penybont Lodge. Initiated in Ogmore Lodge in 1936, he was a Founder Member and first SD of Penybont Lodge. He became an AProvGM of the Province, 1976-1984. Further biographical details may be found in the history of Ogmore Lodge.

In 1953, it was agreed at a Lodge Committee meeting that the Lodge should increase the number of Regular Meetings to seven and that the Annual Festival be moved to February. The Primus Master, WBro R G Kyte, was not present at that meeting, and wrote a letter in opposition to the changes, giving seven valid reasons to leave things as originally agreed by the Founders. The committee, however, voted in favour of the change.

At a Lodge Committee Meeting held on 7 May 1954, it was announced that WBro Aneurin Mitchell would present a Banner to the Lodge at the next Regular Meeting on 28 May. The Banner was given in memory of his son, Gerwyn, who had died suddenly in August 1952. The Banner was to have been Dedicated by the Lodge Chaplain, WBro Rev Arthur Vodden but, unfortunately, he was unable to be present. Instead, the Banner was Dedicated by Bro Rev Munro Cape, after it had been unfurled by RWBro St John Charles, ProvGM.

In 1980, a presentation set of Working Tools was purchased with a sum of money left to the Lodge by the widow of WBro Aneurin Mitchell and used for the first time at the Installation Meeting of February, 1981.

In 1982, the Founders of a proposed new Lodge formally asked the Master and Brethren of Penybont Lodge to support their Petition. The support was unanimously given, and Penybont Lodge became the Sponsoring Lodge of 'Dewi Sant Lodge No. 9067', which was Consecrated on 1 March 1983 (St David's Day). The new Lodge had hoped to be allowed to perform the Ritual in Welsh, and translations of the Three Degree Ceremonies had been carried out by WBro David R Walters, a Past Master of Penybont Lodge.

In May1986, the new Masonic Temple at Bridgend was opened and the old Temple in Adare Street was demolished to accommodate an area of shops. Penybont Lodge held the first Craft Meeting in the new Temple. WBro W D Jones was the Worshipful Master at the time; he later donated the Lodge Honours Board in memory of his late wife.

It is worth noting that the Penybont Lodge is unique in the annals of crime detection in South Wales, with three of its Past Masters being Fingerprint Experts. The Fingerprint Bureau of the former Glamorgan Constabulary, later to become the South Wales Police, was established by the late WBro Frederick Thomas Knipe, PPrSGW. Tom, as he was affectionately known, was also the first Fingerprint Expert in South Wales. The other two Members who served with Tom, and who also became Fingerprint Experts, were Bro Glyn Rogers and WBro David Moelwyn Llewellyn. All three became Senior Police Officers and served with distinction, giving evidence in many of the criminal trials held in South Wales.

In 1993, the Lodge Sponsored the formation of Hafan Deg Lodge No.9520, which was Consecrated on 23 November 1993.

On 16 October 1998, the 346th Regular Meeting of the Lodge was held, which was also the 50th Anniversary of the Lodge. At this Meeting, WBro J Stuart Peters, DepProvGM, entered the Lodge in procession, accompanied by WBro Norman Lea, AProvGM, together with Grand Officers and Officers of the Province. WBro Glyn G H Miller gave a résumé of the formation and history of the Lodge. WBro E E Jones was the Worshipful Master during this important episode in the Lodge's history.

The Lodge has continued in good health with a steady number of new Initiates and a Membership of 60 Brethren (2011). Bro Dr Donald John Thomas, MBE, is the longest serving Member of the Lodge.

Compiled by Bro Colin Evans, PPrGStwd.

Maesteg Lodge No.6805

Warranted : 1 December 1948

Consecrated : 31 January 1949

Meeting at the Masonic Hall, Maesteg.

Maesteg Lodge was Consecrated on 31 January 1949. The Mother Lodge was Llynfi Lodge No.2965 and the Grandmother Lodge was Ogmore Lodge No.1752. Until that date, Llynfi was the only Lodge in Maesteg, and its numbers had by then reached 200; consequently, some Members felt that it was time to form a second Lodge in the town. The driving force behind this initiative was WBro David Thomas, a local Primary School Headmaster, who had been Worshipful Master of Llynfi Lodge in 1926 and of Morganwg Lodge No.5084 in 1932; he was appointed an Officer of United Grand Lodge in 1946.

At the Consecration Ceremony, the Principal Consecrating Officer was the ProvGM, RWBro R P St John Charles, JP, assisted by nine other Officers, including WBro Harry F Stockwell, ProvGSec. Also in attendance were 21 Founder Members and 82 visiting Brethren.

It is interesting to note that WBro Tom King-Davies, was the first Organist; Bro Albert E Lockyer, grandfather of WBro Keith B Lockyer, (both now deceased) was the SW; Bro W Penry Thomas, Headmaster of Maesteg Grammar School, was the JW; and Bro Walter Gibbs, father of WBro David W Gibbs (deceased), was a Founder Steward.

For many years, Initiation into the Lodge was restricted to individuals residing or working in the Llynfi Valley, but this restriction was relaxed in 1979, when the Daughter Lodge, Llangynwyd Lodge No.8854, was Consecrated on 12 March 1979. Subsequently, a small band of Scottish Members from the Porthcawl area have strengthened the Membership of Maesteg Lodge with their commitment, enthusiasm, and willingness to accept responsibility.

The Badge or Crest of the Lodge has an interesting history: it is the Badge or Emblem of 'Y Tir Iarll' ('The Earl's Land') and it appears on the Banner and on every Master's Jewel. It depicts a burning castle on green fields. The Earl referred to was Robert Fitzhammon, Earl of Glamorgan, who built Castell Coch at Llangynwyd in the 11th century, shortly after the Norman Conquest. He shared out the lowlands of Glamorgan amongst his followers, but made sure that he kept the best ground for himself. This land lay between the rivers Afan and Ogmore. Castell Coch was one of the very few hill castles in Glamorgan. It failed to subdue the local Welsh, who joined Llewelyn the Great's forces, and made the monks of Margam pay tribute to them. Led by Llewelyn AP Gruffydd, the last Prince of Wales, they captured and demolished the castle during the occupancy of Earl Richard de Clare. It was rebuilt by 1263. Edmund Mortimer, 3rd Earl of March, was born at the castle in1351, and married Philippa, daughter of

Lionel, Duke of Clarence, who was a son of Edward III. It was during the occupancy of the castle by Phillippa that the famous garter episode occurred at the court of Edward III, which led to the institution of the Most Ancient and Honourable Order of the Garter. In 1316, men from Y Tir Iarll joined the revolt of Llewelyn Bren, who, with his brother Madog Fychan of Llangynwyd, was imprisoned in the Tower of London. Madog was ultimately released. Bren was brought to Cardiff, hanged, beheaded, quartered and buried at Greyfriars. It is, therefore, understandable that much local support was given to Owain Glyndwr's rebellion, when the Castle was captured and razed to the ground, leaving little trace of its former existence. Indeed, its existence was later disputed until archaeological excavations were carried out on land at Castell farm in 1906, which proved that the Castle had indeed existed. It is a remarkable story of part of the history of our area and shows how firm, unconquerable and resilient the men of Y Tir Iarll were – and, hopefully, still are!

The Lodge Banner, incorporating the Lodge Crest, was designed by WBro Gerwyn Thomas and was Dedicated at the Lodge Installation Meeting in 1986.

The 50th Anniversary of the Consecration of the Lodge was celebrated in 1999, when WBro Granville Howells was Worshipful Master. Of the Officers in that year, 14 are still Members, with 10 of them currently holding Office. The celebrations were held in January 1999, when Members received a commemorative plate to mark the occasion.

The Lodge is proud of its relationship with the widows of former Members. The Officers and wives entertain them to a special Christmas dinner at a local hostelry every December, and provide a Christmas gift. All the widows are well known to many of the Members, and are visited regularly.

Maesteg Lodge happily participates with Llynfi Lodge and Llangynwyd Lodge in organising a party for special needs children from schools in the Llynfi Valley. The party is held annually at the Masonic Hall, Maesteg, on the second Thursday in January.

The Members of Maesteg Lodge owe a great deal of gratitude to the three Grand Officers who have served the Lodge well in many different capacities. As stated earlier, WBro David Thomas was the Founder Master and, although his main Masonic efforts were in Llynfi Lodge prior to the formation of Maesteg Lodge, his contribution and influence during his eight years' Membership were immense.

WBro Tom King-Davies, a Solicitor by profession, was Worshipful Master of the Lodge in 1954. He was also Installed as WM of South Wales Jurists' Lodge No.7092 in 1972, the first Master of Llangynwyd Lodge in 1979, and of Hendre Lodge No.3250 in 1992. He became a Grand Officer with the Rank of PAGDC, in 1980, and was promoted to PJGD in 1990. His wise counsel and vast experience were greatly appreciated by all. For further biographical details, see the history of South Wales Jurists' Lodge, in this book.

WBro Keith Brill Lockyer, a local businessman, was Initiated in Maesteg Lodge in 1954, when WBro Tom King-Davies was Worshipful Master. He was Installed as WM in 1968, and appointed a Grand Officer with the Rank of PAGDC, in 1994, when he was the Provincial Education and Training Officer. A Founder Member of Llangynwyd Lodge, he was Installed as its WM in 1992, and in 2002, he was Installed WM of Hendre Lodge. WBro Keith was a Joining Member of Old Leysian Lodge No.4520, Cambridge, a Lodge for staff and former pupils of the Leys School, Cambridge. He was also a Joining Member of Lord Swansea Lodge No.8364 and of Llynfi Lodge. Keith held many Offices in Maesteg Lodge, including that of Charity Steward, all of which he fulfilled with great dignity. His death, in January 2006, was a great loss to the Lodge.

Maesteg Lodge has the reputation of being a friendly Lodge, and evidence of this is the eagerness of visiting Brethren to repeat their visits. The Lodge has been fortunate in always having Officers and Brethren prepared to make every effort to maintain and enhance the welfare of the Lodge.

Compiled by David J Brown, PPrGReg, Almoner and Home Charities Representative.

Lodge of Integrity No.6907

Warranted : 27 July 1949

Consecrated : 30 September 1949

Erased : 10 December 2008

Met at the Masonic Hall, Cardiff.

Early in 1949, a number of Brethren of Amethyst Lodge No.4026, met to discuss the possibility of forming a new Lodge, to accommodate the number of Brethren who were being transferred from Government departments in London to Cardiff and who were more at ease with Emulation Workings.

Following this meeting, a Petition was raised on 6 May 1949 by 15 Petitioners, 8 of whom were Civil Servants and which was signed by Members of Amethyst Lodge : Alban J Rees, Worshipful Master, I J Thomas, Senior Warden and R J Crews, Junior Warden. Unusually, of the 15 Petitioners, only one was a Past Master.

A letter in support of the Petition from Leonard Charles Parker, who was to be the Worshipful Master Designate states :

'The Lodge is to be formed for the benefit of Brethren who have been, or may be, transferred to the Cardiff area. There is a considerable increase in the population here and many of the local Lodges have very large membership lists. Moreover, the Petitioners are in the main, Inland Revenue Officials, who have been transferred to Cardiff and who are more accustomed to the Emulation Working, whereas the existing Lodges, with one exception, work the Oxford Ritual.'

The Officers Designate were: Worshipful Master, Leonard Charles Parker, a Civil Servant of Albany Road, Cardiff, Initiated in Palladian Lodge No.120, Hereford, PM St Thomas's Lodge No.142, London; Senior Warden, Frederick William Cory Hall, a Civil Servant of Gabalfa, Cardiff, Initiated in Trent Lodge No.4933, West Bridgford, Nottinghamshire, and Senior Deacon of Trent Lodge; Junior Warden, William Charles Henry Heal, a Civil Servant of Romilly Road, Cardiff, Initiated in King Edward Vll Lodge No.3252, Wigmore, East Kent and a Member of Amethyst Lodge.

The first Initiate of the Lodge, on 6 December 1950, was J Arthur Cowley, who became Master of the Lodge in 1960 and again in 2000. Arthur was born on 4 April 1916 and he is now a Masonic Veteran of almost 61 years. He was appointed Secretary of the Lodge in 1961, and remained in that Office for well over 15 years. In 1967, he became Charity Steward and was appointed Treasurer of the Masonic Benevolent Fund (Eastern Division of South Wales) in 1972, yet another Office he held for several years. In Province, he served as ProvGStwd in 1966, was promoted to PPrJGD in 1967 and to PPrJGW in 1969. WBro Arthur is a Grand Officer of many years standing, first appointed PGStB in 1976 and was promoted to PAGDC in 1984. In

1976, he also had the honour of being appointed SW of Hendre Lodge No. 3250 and Almoner of Lodge of Benevolence No.7305. Following the Consecration of Tudor Lodge No.8886, the Daughter Lodge of Lodge of Integrity, on 2 July 1979, Arthur was Installed as the Primus Master. In 1973, he was a Founder Member of Integrity Chapter of Royal Arch Masons No.6907. WBro Arthur is well known to Brethren in the Cardiff Lodges, as both he and his late wife, Doris, 'Dos' to all who knew her, were always involved in any remedial or new work required at the Masonic Hall, in Cardiff. Arthur served on the Board of the Cardiff Masonic Hall Co Ltd for over 50 years. During his time as a Director of the Company, Arthur was responsible for the organisation and building of the Ladies' Room and the refurbishment of the kitchen. Arthur had to resign from Lodge of Integrity in 2000, because of the illness of his wife, whom he nursed until her sad death on 4 May 2005. Now in his 96th year, Arthur is not in the best of health, and he resides in the Shire Hall Care Home, Dumballs Road, Cardiff.

Due to dwindling numbers, with Membership down to 20 Brethren, and with only 10 to 12 Members attending Lodge Meetings, it was reluctantly decided in 2008 that the Lodge would hand in its Warrant. The Lodge was Erased from the Register of the United Grand Lodge of England in December 2008.

Lodge of Integrity, despite its small number of Brethren, was a very proud Lodge. All the Members were always immaculately attired in evening dress and every Toast was followed with 'Masonic Fire,' with a firing glass. Anyone out of time was fined £1.00, and the proceeds given to Charity.

Compiled by WBro Don Jones, PProvSGD.

The Lord Swansea Temple, Cardiff

Clive Lodge
No.6973

Warranted : 1 March 1950

Consecrated : 28 April 1950

Meeting at the Masonic Hall, Penarth.

On 1 March 1950, a new Lodge appeared on the roll of the United Grand Lodge of England, namely Clive Lodge. It was Sponsored by Windsor Lodge No.1754, also of Penarth. It was from the Earl of Plymouth's family name, Windsor-Clive, that Windsor Lodge took its name (see history of Windsor Lodge for further details). It would therefore appear to be appropriate that a Daughter Lodge of Windsor Lodge, also meeting in Penarth, should adopt the other half of the Plymouth family name and be called 'Clive Lodge'. The 'Clive' part of the family name comes from the male line of the family. Robert George Windsor-Clive, created 1st Earl of Plymouth in 1905, was the great-great-grandson of 'Clive of India'.

Clive Lodge does not possess a Banner, but does have a Lodge Crest, illustrated above. The elephant, supporting the Masonic Symbols is also the 'supporter' in the Windsor-Clive Coat of Arms, and is from the Coat of Arms of Lord Clive of India. The other 'supporter' is of course the Welsh Dragon.

There were 28 Founder Members of Clive Lodge, of whom 5 were Past Masters. WBro D T Evans, PM Cedewain Lodge No.1594, Newton, Montgomeryshire, Province of North Wales, was the WM Designate. WBro Taliesin Williams, PM Sapphire Lodge No.5290, was appointed the IPM. WBro Bernard F Mattey, who had been Installed WM of Prince Llewellyn Lodge No.2570 in 1941, was Invested as the first DC. WBro John N Bull, Past Master of Cardiff Exchange Lodge No.3775, was appointed the first Treasurer, and WBro Reginald V Coles, who had been Installed WM of Windsor Lodge in 1948, was Invested as the first ADC.

Clive Lodge was Consecrated on Friday, 28 April 1950 at the Masonic Temple, Penarth, in the presence of RWBro R P St John Charles, JP, PAGReg, ProvGM, with VWBro Edgar J Rutter, OSM, PGD, DepProvGM, as Installing Master, assisted by nine Provincial Grand Lodge Officers. In total, 171 Brethren attended. Bro L D Bailey, who later held the Rank of PPrGOrg, was Invested as SW, and Bro D Moseley was Invested as JW.

The first two Initiates (in the early days, Candidates were always admitted two at a time) were Mr Cyril Thomas and Mr Victor Frederick Alexander Thorpe. During the 1950s, it was not unusual for the Lodge to hold double Ceremonies, a Second Degree Ceremony at 5.15 pm, usually followed by an Initiation Ceremony at 6.45 pm.

Mr Leonard Free was Initiated on the 21 November 1950 and later became the Lodge Organist, an Office which he served with great distinction for many years.

In Lodge, on the 19 February 1952, WBro Lancelot Bailey, WM, was saddened to report the death of MWBro His Majesty King George VI, PGM, and the Brethren were called to order as a mark of deep respect.

The brothers Grashoff, John Parsons and Frederick George, were Initiated on 16 October 1951. Sadly, Frederick died at an early age, but John went on to occupy the Chair in 1963.

On 18 May 1954, the Lodge was delighted to Initiate two Canadian gentlemen, Mr Harold Emmot Williams and Mr Walter Yeomans McKenzie, both Penarth residents. Each eventually became Worshipful Masters of the Lodge, Bro McKenzie in 1967 and Bro Williams in 1968.

On 17 October 1959, the Lodge 'came of age', when Bro Aubrey P Williams (the 5th Initiate) was the first Initiate to be Installed in the Chair of King Solomon.

In the 1950s and 1960s, the Lodge often had 4 or 6 candidates awaiting Initiation, with between 60 to 70 Brethren regularly attending the Lodge Meetings. Indeed, in the late 1960s, WBro Lancelot D Bailey announced that when the Lodge Membership reached 100, he intended to propose that the Lodge should Initiate just one Candidate at a time.

Clive Lodge Window, Penarth

During the Lodge's existence, the country has honoured three of the Brethren: WBro Harold Emmot Williams, PPrJGW, with an OBE; WBro Kenneth W Abraham, with the Queen's Police Medal (QPM) and Bro Richard C G Richings was awarded the George Medal (GM). Richard Charles George Richings (Richie) was born on 15 July 1913 in Canton, Cardiff. After leaving Severn Road School, Canton, at 14, he started work as an office boy for the Western Mail and Echo, before joining the Grenadier Guards. Later, he followed in his father's footsteps and joined the Glamorgan Police Force. When war broke out in 1939, Richie was one of the first to volunteer, and was recruited as a Military Policeman. For a brief time he was bodyguard to King George VI. When the war ended, he returned to the police, where he embarked on an illustrious career which saw him work his way up through the ranks to Chief Superintendent with the Bridgend Division, before retiring in 1973.

The highlight of Richie's career occurred at Tonyrefail in 1961, when he was based in Aberdare as an Inspector. After rugby-tackling a man armed with a double-barrelled shotgun to the floor, he stuck his finger in the trigger mechanism to stop the man firing the gun, injuring his finger in the process. These actions led to him being awarded the George Medal, second only to the George Cross, for bravery. He received the Medal at Buckingham Palace, accompanied by his family. Bro Richard Richings died at the age of 96, in the Albert Edward Prince of Wales Court, Porthcawl, on 7 December 2010.

The Lodge has three Masonic Veterans. Bro J R Henderson and WBro F C Beacon, PPrSGW, were Initiated together on 20 May 1952; WBro Beacon is the senior Past Master of the Lodge, having been Installed as Master in 1964. The third Veteran is Bro T C Bishop, who was Initiated into the Lodge on 20 May 1953.

In April 2000, the Lodge Members marked the Lodge's 50th Anniversary with a Celebration Dinner. Despite a gradual fall in Membership since then, the Lodge still managed to make a contribution of £25,000 towards the 2010 Festival. Clive Lodge is now on an upward curve of Membership, and it is hoped that by 2013, there will be a complete line up of Master Masons ready to progress through the various Offices.

Compiled by Bro Leslie Jones, Secretary.

South Wales Jurists' Lodge No.7092

Warranted   :   2 May 1951

Consecrated :   4 June 1951

Meeting at the Masonic Hall, Bridgend.

The South Wales Jurists' Lodge was formed six years after the cessation of the hostilities of the Second World War. There was still a war going on in Korea, petrol was 3/6d (17.5p) per gallon and Income Tax was raised in the Budget of 10 April 1951 to 9/6d in the pound (47.5p).

A Petition for the Lodge in the name of Jurists' Lodge was presented on Thursday, 19 April 1951, which was granted on 2 May, subject to the name being changed to South Wales Jurists' Lodge. The Sponsoring Lodge was Prince Llewellyn Lodge No.2570. The WM Designate was WBro HH Judge Owen Temple Morris, KC, PJGD, who had been Initiated in Prince Llewellyn Lodge on 21 February 1922 and was WM of that Lodge, 1934-1935. He had been appointed a Grand Officer with the Rank of PJGD in 1946. Judge Temple Morris also enjoyed a political career. He was Conservative MP for Cardiff East from 1931 to 1942.

The Lodge had been proposed as one for whom Membership would be restricted to qualified lawyers only, hence the name, whether they be Judges, Barristers or Solicitors. As long as Candidates were qualified in one of the two branches of Law, they would be eligible for Membership. This was, and has remained to this day, an unwritten restriction only: it has never been carried into the By-laws of the Lodge. The notion of 'opening up' the Lodge to non-lawyers has been suggested to, and debated by, the Members from time to time, but has always been overwhelmingly rejected.

The Consecration of the new Lodge took place at the Duke of Connaught Temple, Cardiff, on Monday, 4 June 1951. It was a hot summer's day and a total of one hundred and fifty Brethren attended. The newly appointed Secretary recorded in his personal diary: *'A wonderfully impressive ceremony, a brilliant supper, Speeches showered us with congratulations from everybody.'*

It is apparent from the Consecration Notice and Agenda, that all of the Acting Provincial Grand Officers took part in the Ceremony. HH WBro Judge Owen Temple-Morris, KC, PJGD, was Installed as first WM by the Deputy Provincial Grand Master, VWBro Edgar J Rutter, OSM, PGD, whose son, WBro John Rutter was appointed Acting IPM. In total, eighteen lawyers became Members of the South Wales Jurists' Lodge that day, including one County Court Judge (the first WM), a Stipendiary Magistrate (nowadays called District Judge) and five Barristers of which three later went on to become either County Court or

Circuit Judges. Additionally, there were eleven propositions for Joining Membership and two Candidates for Initiation, Mr Harry T C Lloyd, Clerk to the Cardiff Magistrates, and Mr Tasker Watkins, VC.

Bro Tasker Watkins, VC, progressed to the Rank of SW, before his resignation in 1961. Sir Tasker Watkins VC, CBE, PC, as he became, was born on 18 November 1918 at Nelson, near Caerphilly. Called to the Bar in 1948, he made a unique contribution to the administration of justice as the first Senior Presiding Judge for England and Wales, 1983-1991; Lord Justice of Appeal, 1980-1993; and Deputy Chief Justice of England, 1988-1993. He was Knighted in 1971. Before his legal career had even begun, he was awarded the Victoria Cross for his outstanding bravery and leadership during the campaign in Normandy. He won the decoration for two actions in one evening, during the Battle of the Falaise Gap in August 1944. He was prominent in the work of the British Legion as President for Wales for many years and as national Vice-President; and the Territorial Army Association. He guided the affairs of Glamorgan Wanderers throughout the postwar years, latterly as their president, and was, from its inception, Chairman of the Trustees of the Welsh Rugby Union Charitable Trust, formed to assist injured players. He was President of the Welsh Rugby Union from 1993-2004. He died at the age of 88 in September 1997. A bronze statue of Sir Tasker Watkins, VC, by WBro Roger Andrews, PPrAGReg, Secretary of Llantwit Major Lodge No.9241, was unveiled at the Millennium Stadium on Sunday, 15 November 2009.

**Statue of Sir Tasker Watkins, VC
by WBro Roger Andrews**

The third WM of the Lodge, Installed in 1953, was Judge Rowe Harding. WBro HH Judge W Rowe Harding, PJGD (1901-1991), was a Welsh and British Isles international rugby union wing, who played club rugby for Swansea. In 1926, he attended Cambridge University and played for Cambridge in a varsity match. He gained his first international cap against England on 20 January 1923, which Wales lost 7-3. He gained 17 caps in total, scoring five tries for his country and had the honour of captaining Wales on four occasions. Rowe Harding retired from rugby at the age of 28, when he was called to the Bar, and became a County Court Judge in 1953. Rowe Harding was Welsh Rugby Union Vice-President, 1953-1956, Chairman and President of Glamorgan County Cricket Club and President of Swansea Lawn Tennis and Squash Rackets Club. It appears from the Membership record that he resigned from the Lodge in February 1956. In the days before the passing of the Courts Act in 1971, the old County of Glamorgan was served by Courts of Assize and of Quarter Sessions. Assize, or High Court Judges visited the County three times each year, alternating between Cardiff and Swansea, visiting each twice in alternate years and the other town, (as Swansea then was), or city once. Meetings of the South Wales Jurists' Lodge were arranged to coincide with the holding of the Assizes on the dates when they sat, either in Cardiff or Swansea.

The first Regular Meeting was held at Swansea, coincident with the Assizes at which the ProvGM, his Deputy and Assistant were present. The ProvGM was thanked for presenting the Lodge with an inscribed Square and Compasses, as was his Deputy, who had made a presentation of an inscribed VSL. One of the visiting Brethren that night was WBro William Arthian Davies, a London Barrister, who was attending the Assizes. He subsequently became a Joining Member of the Lodge. The following year, on 1 October 1952, he was appointed a Justice of the Probate, Divorce and Admiralty Division of the High Court of England and Wales, and a few days later he was Knighted. He was transferred to the Queen's Bench Division on 3 April 1959, and on 9 January 1961, he was promoted to be a Lord Justice of Appeal in the Court of Appeal of England and Wales. Following that appointment, he was made a member of the Privy Council of the United Kingdom. At that first Regular Meeting, Bro E Onslow Powell, TD, became a Joining Member. He had been Initiated into Penybont Lodge No.6743 in April 1950. He was Installed as WM of South Wales Jurists' Lodge in 1959 and two years later he was Installed into the Chair of Penybont Lodge. He was appointed PPrDepGReg in 1964, and was promoted to PPrSGW in 1970. In 1975, he became a Grand Officer with the Rank of PGStB. He went on to make an important contribution to the Lodge, as later appears.

As the result of the peregrinations of the Lodge, it was not unusual during the 1950s and the early 1960s, for visiting High Court Judges to be guests at the Ceremonies. These included Sir George Malcolm Hilbery, 1883-1965, who for many years was chairman of the Board of Governors of the Royal Masonic Hospital, and Sir Seymour Edward Karminski, 1902-1974. Mr. Justice Karminski was the senior Judge of the Divorce Division for many years, and became Lord Justice of Appeal in 1969 and a member of the Privy Council.

By the September Meeting of 1965, the wanderings of the Lodge ceased, and it settled in its permanent home, Bridgend, where it has remained ever since. Not only that, but the nights of the Meetings were changed from Tuesdays to the fourth Friday, and the months were changed to January, May, September and November.

In February 1966, it was announced that the Province was to have a new ProvGM, RWBro the Rt Hon the Lord Swansea, DL. In April of that same year came the announcement that WBro John Rutter had been appointed to the Active Rank of JGD in United Grand Lodge. However, by the September Meeting of that year, WBro John Rutter had been appointed Stipendiary Magistrate for the City of Cardiff, and due to the increase in his commitments, decided that he had to resign from the Lodge.

On 14 January 1972, it was decided to move the May Meeting to April and the September Meeting to October.

In 1976, the Lodge celebrated its Silver Jubilee. At the Meeting held on Tuesday, 12 October, it was reported that WBro Ronald B Whittingham, then the Lodge Almoner, had been appointed AProvGM. WBro R B Whittingham (who never became WM of South Wales Jurists' Lodge) had been Initiated into Ogmore Lodge No.1752 in 1936, and Installed as WM of that Lodge in 1953. He had been the first Member of South Wales Jurists' Lodge to be appointed to Grand Rank (PAGReg) in 1963.

When WBro A V F Parker was Installed as Master in 1978, the Lodge was honoured by the presence of the ProvGM, accompanied by WBro R B Whittingham, AProvGM; the ProvSGW and ProvJGW, the ProvGDC and other Officers of Provincial Grand Lodge. That night, no fewer than ninety four guests attended. The AProvGM addressed the Master; the ProvSGW addressed the Wardens; and the ProvGM, the Brethren.

In 1980, Joining Member WBro Thomas King-Davies, PPrJGW, who was WM, 1972-1973, was appointed to the Grand Rank of PAGDC. At the time, he was SW of Hendre Lodge No.3250. He had been Initiated in Llynfi Lodge No.2985 on 7 April 1941. In 1954, he was Installed WM of Maesteg Lodge No.2985 and was Primus Master of Llangynwyd Lodge No.8854 in 1978. In Province, he was appointed ProvSGD in 1959 and promoted to PPrJGW in 1977. In 1990, he was promoted to PJGD in Grand Lodge. WBro Tom King-Davies died on 6 August 2009, at the age of 95. He had continued to attend the Lodge and participate actively almost to the

Services Lodge No.7139

Warranted : 13 November 1951

Consecrated : 29 January 1952

Meeting at the Masonic Hall, Penarth.

A Meeting was held on 21 June 1951 at 1900 hours, having been called by WBro Edgar W Young, PPrGW, PAGDC, PM Penarth Lodge No.4113 and of Sapphire Lodge No.5290. It was to consider the Founding of a new Lodge in Penarth, in the nature of a United Services Lodge.

One of the interesting topics of this early meeting was in fact the name of the proposed Lodge. The Chairman of the Meeting had ascertained that there were already a number of Services Lodges in Great Britain and it was agreed that a proposition would be made to the United Grand Lodge of England to sanction the same name for this new Lodge; there not being a similar name existing in the Province of South Wales Eastern Division. An approach was made to Windsor Lodge No.1754, Penarth, to recommend the Petition, and Windsor Lodge agreed to be the Sponsoring Lodge.

At a Meeting with the DepProvGM, VWBro Edgar J Rutter and the ProvGSec, WBro Harry F Stockwell, it was stated that the DepProvGM agreed that the name be 'The United Services Lodge', but to have an alternative 'The United Services Lodge of South Wales' available, should United Grand Lodge raise any objections.

A discussion took place concerning the Master's Collar. It was decided that the quotation of £38.10.6d was exorbitant at the present time, so it was decided to start with a plain blue Collar, as worn by other Officers of the Lodge. Officers' Gauntlets, priced at £6.0.0d per pair, were thought to be too expensive, and Provincial Grand Lodge was approached with a view of obtaining an easement in respect of Officers wearing Gauntlets. Confirmation was received that it was permissible for Gauntlets not be worn in the new Lodge. A further easement also applied in respect of the Penal Sign. To the present day in Services Lodge, when communicating the Penal Sign to an Entered Apprentice, he is instructed to extend the fingers and thumb of his right hand in the form of a square and bring it directly to the tip of his left shoulder and draw it sharply across his throat and return it to his side. This came about because Services Brethren felt that extending the right arm was too reminiscent of the Nazi Salute, which was still very fresh in the minds of Services Brethren.

The name of the proposed Lodge was still not clarified until a meeting on 20 September 1951, when a number of optional names were put forward. It was decided that the name be 'The United Services Lodge East Glamorgan' and this name was applied for to United Grand Lodge. Provincial Grand Lodge was informed that the Brethren were not willing to adopt the name of 'United

Services Lodge'. At a further meeting' on 30 October 1951, the name 'The Services Lodge' was finally agreed. The annual subscription was set at £4.4.0d and for Country Members it was £2.12.6d. Country Members were subscribing to the Lodge until the early 1970s, when it was agreed to drop the title 'Country Member' and to refer only to Joining Members or Re-joining Members.

It was decided that the Lodge Insignia would be a circle divided into quarters over a Square and Compasses held on either side by a Welsh Dragon; each quarter of the circle holding a Badge, representing each of the Armed Services. The Lodge Motto, in Latin, is: *'In Fides et Armis'* - *'In Faith and Arms'*.

The Warrant was issued on 13 November 1951. The Consecration of Services Lodge was held in the Masonic Temple, Penarth, on Tuesday, 29 January 1952. A total of twenty three Founder Members were present. The Consecration Team comprised RWBro St John Charles, JP, PAGReg, ProvGM, who was assisted by WBro Gwilym Thomas, ProvSGW; WBro Ivor Saunders, ProvJGW; Bro Rev C Davie, ProvGChap; and WBro Harry F Stockwell, PAGDC, ProvGSec.

Services Lodge was the Sponsoring Lodge for Wings Lodge No.8651, which was Warranted on 12 March 1975.

One Member worthy of mention is WBro Hugh Johns, PPrSGW. Initiated into Services Lodge in 1969, he was Installed in the Chair of King Solomon in 1976 and promoted to his ultimate Rank of PPrSGW in 2002. However, WBro

Services Lodge Window, Penarth

Hugh had an interesting connection with 'the Beautiful Game' and in particular the 1966 World Cup Final. Many will remember Kenneth Wolstenholme of the BBC saying: *'Some people are on the pitch...they think it's all over – it is now!'* But if you had been watching the final on ITV, you would have heard the velvet-voiced guardian of ITV's early football coverage, Hugh Johns, describe the closing seconds with these words *'Here's Hurst, he might make it three. He has! He has! So that's it. That is IT!'* Sadly, WBro Hugh died in 2007.

It is a long established custom of Services Lodge that Lodge Officers attending all Regular Meetings should wear uniform or dinner suit. Unfortunately, the wearing of his uniform by a Lodge Officer never took place until recently, when Bro Michael Rudall, as a Member of the Royal Marines Reserve, was Initiated. In January 2010, he was Installed as Worshipful Master of the Services Lodge with the distinction of being the first Master of the Lodge to wear uniform whilst in the Chair of King Solomon.

Compiled by WBro George Wilford, PPrJGW (Deceased) and WBro Gordon P Thomas, PPrAGReg.

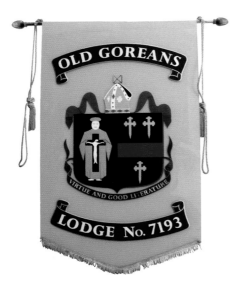

Old Goreans Lodge No.7193

Warranted : 7 May 1952

Consecrated : 5 June 1952

Meeting at the Masonic Hall, Swansea.

In 1951, a number of Brethren who had been pupils, or who were on the academic staff of Swansea Grammar School, held an informal meeting to discuss the formation of a Lodge. It was felt that the School, which had been founded by Bishop Hugh Gore in 1682, had contributed to Swansea and its environs more academic and economic benefits than all the other educational bodies put together. Some apprehension was felt that, with the phasing out of Grammar Schools as part of State Policy, the reputation and traditions of the School might be forgotten.

Despite an active Old Boys Association, the opinion was expressed that a greater degree of perpetuity would be achieved by the formation of a Masonic Lodge that would be closely linked to the School. This was unanimously accepted and it was decided to form a Lodge to be known as 'Old Goreans Lodge', that the Lodge should adopt the Coat of Arms of Bishop Gore and should also adopt his Motto: of *'Virtue and Good Literature'*.

A Deputation of proposed Founders of the new Lodge attended the Regular Lodge Meeting of Glantawe Lodge No.5378 held on Wednesday, 13 February 1952, when WBro G Alan Madel spoke in support of a Petition to form a new Lodge to be called 'Old Goreans Lodge'. The Brethren of Glantawe Lodge gave full support to the Petition and the Lodge Warrant was issued on 7 May 1952.

On 5 June 1952, the Consecration Ceremony was performed by RWBro R P St John Charles, JP, PAGReg, ProvGM. The Installation of the first Master, WBro G Alan Madel, was conducted by VWBro Edgar J Rutter, OSM, PGW, DepProvGM.

A Lodge of Instruction was formed, and the Preceptor was the DC, WBro R T W Cross, who held both Offices for fifteen years, until his Election as Master.

The Lodge worked happily and successfully, in the greatest of harmony, and the 25th Anniversary was celebrated by a dinner at the University College of Swansea, at which the ladies were guests of the Lodge.

The close association with the School, which commenced when the then Headmaster, WBro Ellis Lloyd became the second Worshipful Master, has continued, though Membership of the Lodge became unrestricted in the mid 1970s. Bro Leslie Evans became Headmaster in 1966.

The first Initiate of the Lodge, in December 1952, was WBro RM Glyn Thomas, who became Master in 1961. Another Initiate,

WBro Herbert T Morgan, became Master in 1966 and was elected Mayor of the City of Swansea in 1975. He also became a Freeman of the City of London. In 1982, Bro Paul Valerio had the distinction of being the first Lord Mayor of the newly-created City of Swansea. WBro Anthony Davies, who was Initiated by WBro Herbert Morgan at the 100th Regular Meeting of the Lodge in 1966, became Professor and Head of Physics at Swansea University, and in 2000 was appointed Pro-Vice-Chancellor of the University.

Since its Consecration, two of the Brethren, WBro Haydn Llewelyn and WBro Richard Savours, became Masonic veterans. Three Initiates, WBros Martin Glass, Michael Glass and Ken Rees were Lewises, and all became Masters of the Lodge.

Dilwyn Jenkins, WM in 1970, was behind the idea of a Lodge Banner, and he wanted something special

Opening of the Swansea Grammar School, 1853

and different. He, together with Trevor Wignall (WM 1988) and Joining Past Master, David Richard Morgans (same year pupils at Swansea Grammar School) researched documents and old photographs. Being an Architect, David Morgans was asked to produce some ideas and sketches, based on their research. A design, incorporating the Arms of Bishop Gore, together with the Lodge Motto, was agreed upon by the Past Masters. David then produced a full size coloured drawing, which was accepted by the Lodge. Trevor Lewis Signs Ltd, Llansamlet, Swansea, made an acrylic Banner from David's template. The Banner is maintenance free, but heavy. It is kept in a purpose made wooden case, with a glass front. It is believed to be the only Banner of its type in existence.

The Membership of the Federation of School Lodges has widened our horizons and increased our circle of friends. The Old Goreans Lodge has always attended the Annual Festivals and was invited to chair the 32nd Annual Festival in September 1979. The Lodge Meeting was held by Dispensation in the Hall of Bishop Gore School, when WBro Anthony J Davies was Worshipful Master, WBro Clifford Rose was Senior Warden and WBro John Booth, Junior Warden.

The Festival was attended by RWBro the Rt Hon the Lord Swansea, DL, ProvGM South Wales ED, accompanied by distinguished Brethren of this and other Provinces. The President of the Federation of School Lodges, WBro H T Seymour, FREconS, PGStB, LGR, PPrGW (Surrey) was also in attendance, accompanied by the Officers of the Federation.

Following the calling of the roll of Lodges present, Members of Swansea Lodge, No.8364, gave a demonstration of an early 19th century Russian Initiation Ceremony, based on the description in Book V of Tolstoy's 'War and Peace'. The Festive Board was held in the Great Hall of University of Wales, Swansea.

Just as the School has changed and adapted to meet the needs of today's society, so has the Lodge changed to meet altered circumstances. The opening of the Lodge has introduced new Members from a wide range of backgrounds and this has enriched our experience. Many of the Brethren still have links with the School and, in its workings and social activities, the Lodge continues to preserve and cherish those virtues that are exemplified by the life of Hugh Gore, which have set an example to succeeding generations for over three centuries.

Compiled by WBro Desmond Price, PPrSGW.

I cannot trace that;'Highview' is part of the address of any Provincial Grand Lodge Officer.'

On 8 May, the Grand Secretary wrote to Edgar Rutter as follows:

'The Petition for the above Lodge was considered by the Advisors to the MW Grand Master at their meeting yesterday, and the grant of a Warrant was recommended.

Regarding the name, however, the Grand Master has considered the reasons put forward by the Petitioners but feels that 'Highview' might well be taken to have reference to the name of a building or to some geographical prominence. I should be glad, therefore, if the Petitioners would submit some alternative title which would not be subject to such misinterpretation.

I also have to inform you, that in the special circumstances, the name of Bro. G A Rutter has been allowed to stand in this Petition.'

On 10 May, Edgar Rutter replied:

'I much regret that the name submitted lends itself to misinterpretation, which I quite agree if it is as one word; but the Founders intention was to have 'High View', and I am sorry that this was not made clear on the Petition. If 'High View' as two words is still deemed to be capable of misinterpretation as a Masonic phrase, the Founders would submit 'Grand Design' as an alternative, and they express the hope that one of these suggested titles will find favour, and that we may be allowed a number.

Finally, on 10 May, we have from the Grand Secretary:

Thank you for your letter of the 10th instant, submitting an alternative title for the new Lodge.

There would be no objection to 'Grand Design'. I think, probably, however that the Petitioners would prefer 'The Lodge of Grand Design' rather than 'Grand Design Lodge'. Perhaps you would let me know. The number of the Lodge will be 7196 and I will send you a formal notification on receiving your reply.'

Thus, Grand Design Lodge No.7196, with its Motto: *'First Things First'* was Warranted on 7 May 1952. The Lodge was Consecrated on 23 June 1952 by RWBro the Rt Hon the Lord Swansea, OSM, CStJ, DL, ProvGM, after which RWBro Edgar John Rutter was Installed as Primus Master. The first Senior Warden was WBro Rev Thomas Arthur Roberts, PPrGChap, of the Rectory, Neath. Initiated in Gnoll Lodge No.5057, Neath, in 1939, he was also a Member of Cambrian Lodge No.364, Neath. WBro William Matthew Richards, PPrGStdB, was Installed as JW. He was a Leather Merchant from Swansea and had been Initiated in Corinthian Lodge No.4917 in 1932. He was Treasurer of that Lodge and also a Member of Dyffryn Tawe Lodge No.6056, Swansea.

The 26 Founder Members were conscious of the fact that South Wales (Eastern Division) covered a considerable geographical area and one of the major aims of the new Lodge was to bring together Brethren from different parts of the Province. A further aspiration was to endeavour to act as a *'Lodge of Progress'*, to enable enthusiastic Brethren to take office when, for reasons of business, etc., they would otherwise find it difficult so to do. Additionally, contacts with the Cardiff Schools' Lodges were actively promoted.

Many eminent Masons within the Province have become Joining Members of the Lodge over the years in support of these aspirations, as well as a substantial number of Grand Officers. The following are particularly of note:

WBro HH Judge John Cleverdon Rutter, PJGD (Founder; WM 1966/67)

WBro Harold Wilson, AProvGM (Founder) (WM 1977/78)

VWBro Henry Francis Stockwell, DepProvGM (Founder; WM 1974/75)

WBro Ronald Bowen Whittingham, AProvGM (Joined 30 January 1962)

VWBro Geoffrey Malin Ashe, DepProvGM (Joined 1 July 1964, WM 1986/87)

WBro Llewellyn George Bevan, AProvGM (Joined 1 July 1964)

WBro Rev Thomas Kenneth Brunsdon, DepGSupt (RA) (Joined 3 January 1970)

WBro Leslie Herbert Jeans, DepGSupt (RA) (Joined 3 January 1970, WM 1994/95)

WBro Malcolm Hayes Thompson, ProvGSec (Joined 26 January 1972, WM 1998/99)

VWBro James Stuart Peters, DepProvGM (Joined 26 May 1983, WM 1999/2000)

WBro Cuthbert Lionel Summers, AProvGM (Joined 29 October 1983, WM 1999/2000)

WBro Kenneth Adams Morgan, AProvGM (Joined 30 January 1992, WM 1993/94)

WBro Robert John Nettleship, AProvGM (Joined 3 June 2000)

Indeed, until recent times, it was a custom of the Lodge that at least one Member of the Executive Team (viz. DepProvGM or AProvGM) was always a Subscribing Member. Currently, VWBro Peter Frost, PGSwdB, PDepProvGM and WBro Rev Norman Lea, PDepGChap, PAProvGM, are highly respected and enthusiastic Honorary Members of the Lodge.

In drawing up procedures for the new Lodge, the Founders were particularly keen to avoid verbosity and unnecessary ceremony, both of which they considered would detract from the meaning and performance of ceremonies. Visitors are admitted prior to the opening of the Lodge, with no procession into the Lodge. By tradition, the Lodge has always kept as closely as possible to the Oxford Ritual and subscribing Provincial and Grand Officers wear undress regalia at all Meetings including Installations. Minutes are noted for their brevity, whilst containing all necessary information. Speeches at the Festive Board are kept short and to the point, with no Master's or Initiate's song, and no response to the Toast to the visitors.

One of the prime aspirations of the Lodge was to draw both ends of the Province together. Thus, the aim was to recruit Members from all parts of the Province. This aspiration continues to be fully supported today. A further objective was to enable Provincial Stewards, Chaplains and less able Ritualists to pass through the Chair (not precluding able Ritualists, of course). The passage of time has seen other Lodges Consecrated to fulfil these particular objectives; Lodge of Progress No.7928, Consecrated 30 September 1963; South Wales Eastern Division, Provincial Grand Stewards' Lodge No.8900, Consecrated 2 November 1979 and South Wales Clerics' Lodge No.9298, Consecrated 7 April 1989.

In 1953, the Lodge Sponsored a rather special Daughter Lodge, Lodge of Benevolence No.7305. This Lodge of Grand Officers, Consecrated on 21 September 1953, is referred to elsewhere in this book.

In the years immediately following the Consecration, discussions continued to be held regarding the name of the Lodge and the desire of the Members to satisfy the original intention of the Founders. This culminated in a Petition to Grand Lodge for the name to be changed from 'Grand Design' to 'Edgar Rutter Lodge'. This time, both RWBro Edgar Rutter and Grand Lodge agreed to the change, which was approved on 13 March 1968. Henceforth, Lodge No.7196 bore the name of its Principal Founder. On Saturday, 30 March 1968, the Lodge met for the first time under its new name and received an Oration from its first Master, RWBro Edgar Rutter.

On 30 January 1968, the Lodge Sponsored the formation of Edgar Rutter Chapter No.7196, with Members of the Lodge as Founders. The Warrant for this Chapter was subsequently granted on 25 April of that year and the Chapter was Consecrated on 21 June 1968.

The Lodge meets four times in the year on the third Saturday of the month: September (Installation), January, March and May (Election night) and a further tradition has been to invite the Ladies to the Festive Board following the January Meeting.

Since 2009, there had been a concerted effort to encourage Members to increase their donations to charity. Though only a relatively small Lodge (36 Members in 2010), the Brethren made the substantial donation of £21,000 to the 2010 Festival. In addition, the Provincial Benevolent Fund and the Friends of AEPWC, Porthcawl, both received £2,250; and various South Wales

Charities, including Children's Therapy Centre, Wales (for children with Cerebral Palsy), Velindre Cancer Centre, Guide Dogs for the Blind and the Swansea Centre for Deaf People, have been supported.

In 2012, the Lodge will celebrate 60 years since its Consecration. During this period, there have been many Brethren to which the Lodge owes a great deal, not least RWBro J Edgar Rutter himself and his son, the late WBro HH Judge John Rutter, PJGD. Two Secretaries have served the Lodge well, viz. WBro Albert E Lemmer, PAGDC, who held Office continuously from 1958 to 1985 and WBro Malcolm H Thompson, PSGD, who was Secretary for a total of 13 years subsequent to his tenure as Provincial Grand Secretary. Another stalwart Member was WBro Lawrence D Bailey, PGStB, who was the Lodge Organist for a remarkable period of 45 years. The Lodge has had two long-serving Treasurers - WBro Harold F Strawford, who served for 16 years and WBro Robert W Lee, PAGDC, who occupied that Office with distinction from 1980 to 2000, whilst the longest serving Director of Ceremonies was WBro Jeffrey G Thomas, PPrGSwdB.

The last surviving Founder of the Lodge was WBro HH Judge John Rutter, PSGD, who sadly passed away aged 89 on 14 May 2009. He was Wales' most senior Lawyer. Further biographical details may be found in his father's biography, in this book. It is, however, interesting to add further details of his experiences whilst a Prisoner of War of the Japanese. The following extract is taken from WBro Keith Flynn's book 'Behind the Wire', published in August 1988:

'Lieutenant John Rutter, now His Honour John Rutter, was Initiated in Cardiff on 2 January, 1941, and on his Raising was presented with a book of Ritual. In December of that year his regiment was sent to Java, where they were captured by the Japanese in March, 1942. They were sent to a prison camp just outside Jakarta and John Rutter's Ritual was used by a group of some thirty Masons, mostly Australians, who met to discuss Masonic subjects and to rehearse ceremonies. While at this camp, the group met some four or five times in a disused hut in the early evening, and although they always made use of an outer guard, they were never interrupted. They also prepared a memorandum containing the signatures of the members of the group and on his return after release in 1945, John Rutter presented it to the Howardian Lodge in Cardiff in whose archives it now resides.

It was in this camp that a member of the RAF, a prisoner named Skinner constructed a wireless receiver on which they were able to receive all the current war news, which then spread throughout the camp, very carefully, by word of mouth. The prisoners were thus consistently better informed than their guards. The wireless was concealed in two water bottles, with spares in a third and, to complete the concealment each bottle had a false compartment in its top which contained a little water. This device always succeeded in preventing discovery whenever searches were made.

In September, 1943, John Rutter was sent to Singapore and at first to the prison camp at Changi. He travelled with Skinner and Wilf Wooller (WRU international) and each carried one of the water bottles containing the wireless parts. Later they were transferred to Changi Jail where the wireless was concealed in bed posts in one of the many grass huts outside the jail itself. As far as is known it was the only wireless in the whole of Changi and was never discovered.'

In 2011, the family of this most remarkable and dearly loved Brother commissioned a Lodge Banner in WBro John Rutter's memory. It is intended to hang the Banner above the Worshipful Master's Chair in the Edgar Rutter Temple. The Banner will be Dedicated by RWBro Captain Sir Norman Lloyd-Edwards, ProvGM, accompanied by his full team of Provincial Grand Officers, on Saturday, 21 January 2012. The Banner was designed by WBro Hugh Bradnum, a close friend of the family and WM of Edgar Rutter Lodge, 2006-2008. It is noteworthy that WBro Hugh is the only WM in the Lodge's history to have occupied the Chair twice. The design has an image of the Rutter family home 'Highview' in the centre, with the Lodge Motto: *'Firsts Things First'*, immediately below. The blue and yellow sections radiating outwards represent rays of light emanating from the upper windows of the house, emblematically recalling part of the Oration, delivered by RWBro Edgar John Rutter at the Consecration of the Lodge on Monday, 23 June 1952. Edgar Rutter's own words provide a fitting conclusion to this historical record.

'In my passing from, the general to the particular, I suggest that the younger of us might see visions, and the older dream dreams and I invite you all to take an imaginary journey to my home and to look out with me from my upper windows, depicted here on this Jewel (and new Banner) *. You will have your back to the East, as I have now, and you will have a full half circle's view from South to North. Come preferably when the sun is about to set and due South you will see the Bristol Channel - the Severn - 'Môr Hafren' which will have its special Masonic meaning for us on Wednesday* (Môr Hafren Lodge No.7194 was Consecrated two days later on 25 June 1952.) *Coming round toward the West, you will see the guiding lights of the Channel, you will see Penarth Head, with its Church and its Christian Message - further round you will see the new television pylon lit up by night, sending its message by picture and sound to those who may be able to see and hear. Due West, in the middle distance, the shattered spire of Llandaff Cathedral speaking of the ravages and wickedness and uselessness of war - in the far distance the setting sun with its message of a new tomorrow - the lights of vehicles on the main road, ascending and descending Tumble-down-Dick, and round towards the North-West, the Garth mountain, Castle Coch, the valley between – speaking of the works of nature, right round to due North, with the hills Cefn Onn and Caerphilly Mountain, partly sheltering Cardiff from the North winds.*

A semicircle of Grand Design - the works of God combining with the works of man; and near at hand on the still waters of the lake, the light of the setting sun and the long shadows of trees and buildings. And for our Lodge may we just reverse the process. Our immediate view, the light and shade of 26 Founders, Priests of the Church, whose lives are specially dedicated to God's service, Stewards of the Province, Organists, Tylers, businessmen, professional men, undergraduates - all combining in a Grand Design.'

Compiled by WBro Dr A P Wardle, PGStB, Former Lodge Secretary
and WBro D Gerald Rowbottom, PAGDC.

Edgar Rutter Temple, Cardiff

Talygarn Lodge No.7216

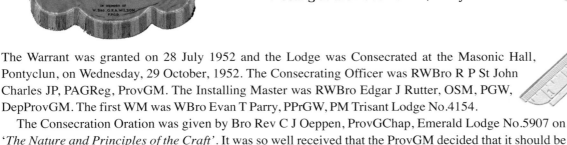

Warranted : 28 July 1952

Consecrated : 29 October 1952

Meeting at the Masonic Hall, Pontyclun.

The Warrant was granted on 28 July 1952 and the Lodge was Consecrated at the Masonic Hall, Pontyclun, on Wednesday, 29 October, 1952. The Consecrating Officer was RWBro R P St John Charles JP, PAGReg, ProvGM. The Installing Master was RWBro Edgar J Rutter, OSM, PGW, DepProvGM. The first WM was WBro Evan T Parry, PPrGW, PM Trisant Lodge No.4154.

The Consecration Oration was given by Bro Rev C J Oeppen, ProvGChap, Emerald Lodge No.5907 on 'The Nature and Principles of the Craft'. It was so well received that the ProvGM decided that it should be offered for sale throughout the Province, at a cost of one shilling (5p) per copy!

It is unfortunate that the first Minute Book of the Lodge has been lost, therefore an accurate account of the early years of the Lodge cannot be given.

The Lodge name is derived from the name of the local parish and the one-time Miners' Rehabilitation Hospital, Talygarn Manor and estate belonging to the Clarke family. George Thomas Clarke, 1809-1898, was an Engineer and an Antiquarian, who worked for Isambard Kingdom Brunel on the Great Western Railway. In 1852, he became a Trustee for the Dowlais Ironworks, effectively controlling the works until his death. He was deeply committed to improving the appalling living conditions of the town and was Chairman of the Board of Guardians of Merthyr Tydfil Poor Law Union, as well as the Local Board of Health.

In 1865, Clarke purchased Talygarn Manor, which at the time was in a very poor state. The house, greatly restored by Clarke, is now a Grade II listed building. It was sold by his grandson in 1923 to the South Wales Miners' Welfare Committee, when it became a Miners' Convalescent Home and later, in 1943, a Miners' Rehabilitation Centre. It was put up for sale in 2000 and it has recently been converted into a series of luxury homes.

The Lodge Banner was presented to the Lodge by Bro W Cyril Brown in memory of WBro G R A Wilson, PPGD. Bro Cyril was associated with 'Corona Soft Drinks', the firm created by William Thomas and William Evans, at their grocery store in Hannah Street, Porth, Rhondda. The Banner was Dedicated on Monday, 18 April 1966 by WBro Harry F Stockwell, PGD, AProvGM, assisted by Provincial Grand Officers, during which the hymn 'O God Our Help in Ages Past' was sung. The Banner bears the Motto: 'Try and Tryst' thus encouraging the Members to meet in harmony. The fleur-de-lis in the centre of the Banner is derived from the wrought iron gates of the Miners' Hospital.

Twenty- one years after the formation of the Lodge, Talygarn Chapter was Consecrated. The Ceremony was performed by the Grand Superintendent, EComp Harry F Stockwell, on Monday, 7 January 1974. At the time, Trisant and Talygarn were the only two Lodges meeting in Pontyclun.

On Monday, 21 October 2002, the Lodge celebrated its 50th Anniversary, which was also the occasion of the Annual Installation Festival. WBro Gilbert Martin was Installed for a second term. During the proceedings, he invited WBro Ken Proctor to give a speech in Commemoration of the 50th Anniversary. WBro Ken then read the Oration given by the ProvGChap on the occasion of the Consecration of the Lodge in October 1952. Afterwards, the WM, assisted by WBro Andrew L Gretton, AProvGM, and WBros Ken Proctor, Norman John and Norman Griffiths, Dedicated the Cushion to Talygarn Lodge and placed it beneath the VSL, on the pedestal in front of the WM's dais.

Talygarn Manor, Pontyclun

WBro David Kenneth Proctor was for a number of years the senior Past Master of the Lodge, until his resignation in 2010. He was Initiated in Royal Connaught Lodge No.3266 (Trinidad & Tobago) on 6 October 1954 and became a Joining Member of Talygarn Lodge in 1966. He became WM in 1974. He is a Founder Member of Miskin Lodge No.8625 and was Installed Master in 1987. He is also a Founder Member of Pontypridd Lodge No.9001. In 1989, he was appointed the Provincial Junior Grand Warden of the Province, and the following year he was Invested SW of Hendre Lodge No.3250. In Grand Lodge, he was first honoured with the Rank of PAGDC and promoted to PJGD in 2002. A Masonic Veteran, he will have been a Freemason for 57 years in October 2011.

The Lodge had two other Masonic Veterans, namely WBro J J Williams, PPrJGD, Initiated on 20 January 1958, and Bro J G Walker, Initiated on 15 June1959. Sadly, both have now passed to the Grand Lodge Above. Mention should also be made of WBro J J Roberts, who was WM in 1988 and who became a Grand Officer with the Rank of PGStB in 2003.

WBro David Lindsay Protheroe was Initiated into Talygarn Lodge on 21 June 1965, in the presence of RWBro R P St John Charles, ProvGM and WBro Harry Stockwell, AProvGM. The ProvGM was also present when he was Raised on 18 April 1966, immediately following the Banner Dedication Ceremony. WBro David Protheroe was the first Tyler of Newton Lodge No.8261, Consecrated 24 January 1969, and became Master of that Lodge in 1975. In Provincial Grand Lodge, he was promoted to ProvGDC in 1987 and appointed PAGDC in 1988. He was AProvGM, 1992-1998, and promoted to PSGD in 1993.

Compiled by WBro Alan Kaye (WM 2006)
assisted by WBro Peter M Davies, ProvJGW, PM Glamorgan Lodge No.36.

Tuscan Lodge No.7267

Warranted : 4 March 1953

Consecrated : 30 April 1953

Meeting at the Masonic Hall, Swansea.

Tuscan Lodge was one of the last Lodges in the Province to be Consecrated during the post-war boom, and owes its existence largely to the initiative of an inspirational figure, WBro Edward Roe Brown, who had already played a significant part in Masonic development in the Province during the 1930s and 1940s.

In 1931, WBro Brown had been a Founder Member of West Glamorgan Lodge No.5291, and subsequently became its Master. It was the only teetotal Lodge in Swansea and, with a Membership of over 100, Brethren had a long wait to reach the Chair of King Solomon. WBro Brown felt that another teetotal Lodge would help to relieve this backlog and, as a Quantity Surveyor, it was entirely in keeping that he chose the name, 'Tuscan', with a direct connection to Operative Masonry.

The Petition was granted on the 4 March 1953 and arrangements set in train for the Consecration of the Lodge on 30 April 1953. It was the fourth Swansea Lodge to be named after one of the five classical orders of architecture and the seventeenth Lodge in Swansea. WBro Brown had enlisted Brethren from a wide range of social, cultural and religious backgrounds. He was fortunate to obtain the services of the learned and meticulous WBro Evan Lloyd Griffiths as Director of Ceremonies. As Senior and Junior Wardens he selected Bros Arthur and Clifford Jones respectively, a father and son team from the Mother Lodge, West Glamorgan Lodge.

Although the Provincial Grand Master, RWBro R P St John Charles, intended to officiate at the Consecration, an illness prevented him from doing so. Consequently, RWBro Edgar Rutter, DepProvGM, officiated at the Consecration Ceremony and Installed WBro Brown as the first Master, in the presence of 167 Brethren.

At the September meeting, the Master invited WBro Arthur Lloyd of West Glamorgan Lodge to Initiate his son as the new Lodge's first Candidate. This Initiate, John A Lloyd, was himself Installed as Master in September 1960 and first became a Grand Officer in 1987, with the Rank of PAGDC, and was promoted in 1998 to PJGD.

The Lodge's first year was a sad one, however, for by October, the Master had become very ill and his death was announced at the November Meeting. It was also a distressing time for the new Initiate, for shortly after completing his Third Degree, his father died.

Despite such losses the new Lodge was undergoing an exciting period of development. Under the wise direction of such experienced Brethren as WBros David Davies, Harold Cooke and Evan Lloyd Griffiths, it quickly established itself. There was a healthy flow of Candidates, at least five a year for the first ten years, and this, coupled with a steady trickle of distinguished Joining Members, resulted in 46 Members subscribing by 1961.

As the Membership increased, there were proportionately fewer Brethren who had links with the Mother Lodge. It was, therefore, felt that an interchange of visits between the two Lodges should commence and, in 1963, WBro John James, WM, announced that he and his Officers would pay an official visit to West Glamorgan Lodge. The close affinity between the two Lodges was thus reinforced, and an annual exchange continues to this day, cementing an association which provides much mutual pleasure and pride.

In the two-year period, 1959-1961, the Lodge Initiated an outstanding group of Brethren. First, there was William Elwyn Lewis, who was Installed as Master in 1970, and eventually attained the Rank of PPrSGW. WBro Lewis was the Lodge Secretary for many years, as well as being Preceptor in the late 1980s. His contribution to the Lodge was enormous and, in many ways, he was 'Mr Tuscan Lodge'. It was to him that Brethren always turned for information and advice, and he never failed them. Unfortunately, WBro Lewis died shortly after his appointment as an Honorary Member, and just before he would have completed 40 years in the Craft.

Besides Initiating a number of distinguished Brethren, such as WBros Peter Glyn Williams and David Beynon, WBro John Lloyd himself became a Brother of great distinction. He was a PJGD of UGLE, Deputy Lieutenant of the County of Glamorgan, and awarded the OBE. He was, for many years, a Swansea Magistrate and Chairman of the Bench and served a considerable period as Chairman of the Masonic Hall Company Ltd, Swansea.

WBro P G Williams is the most senior Grand Officer, whose Masonic achievements have been immense. He was Installed as Master in 1971, and was Invested with his first Grand collar as PAGDC in 1987, and promoted to PSGD in 1995. Included in his many appointments in other Masonic degrees are PAGSoj in Supreme Grand Chapter and PGSW in the Grand Lodge of Mark Master Masons, in which order he subsequently became Grand Secretary. He is now an esteemed Honorary Member of Tuscan Lodge.

Father and son teams have contributed much during the past fifty years or so. As has been mentioned, a precedent was set at the Consecration when WBros Arthur and Clifford Jones were Invested as Founder Wardens. Initiated in West Glamorgan Lodge in 1946, WBro Clifford Jones was the senior Masonic Veteran. A Past Senior Grand Warden in Provincial Grand Lodge, he held Grand Rank in Royal Arch Masonry. WBros John and David Beynon were powerful personalities in the Lodge, and were Masters in 1968 and 1973 respectively. WBro John Beynon was Treasurer in the late 1970s and, as an accomplished Ritualist, WBro David Beynon contributed enormously to the operation of the Lodge in many roles during the 1980s and early 1990s.

Occasionally, it has been necessary for a Past Master to occupy the Chair of King Solomon for a second time. WBro John Lloyd was prevailed upon to do so in 1982, when there was a break in the natural progression, and claimed that he did a much better job the second time round. WBro David Beynon, WM in 1973, became WM again in 1991 and, by a strange twist of fate, Installed WBro William Floyd as his successor in 1974, and again in 1992. WBro Desmond Healin, the Master in 1985, was re-Installed in September 2007. In turn, WBro Gerald Mabbett, Master in 1999, was re-Installed in September 2008.

The Lodge has also been fortunate in having a number of well-known Brethren transferred to the area through their professional occupations. WBro Zeph Daniel moved from Bridgend's Morganwg Lodge No.5084 in 1961 and established himself as a popular Brother who was Installed as WM in 1977. The next year, WBro Haydn Osborne's profession as a Chartered Accountant brought him to Swansea and Tuscan Lodge, becoming Master in 1984. He was for a time Company Secretary of the Swansea Masonic Hall Company Ltd, of which he was also a prominent member of the Executive Committee, and Secretary of Lord Swansea Lodge No.8364. Interestingly, WBro Zeph Daniel Installed a third Joining Member, Bro Dr Antony Wardle, in 1978. His academic career had led him to Swansea in 1967, where he became a prominent member of the University and the Craft. A series of promotions within the Province culminated in 2004, when he became a Grand Officer with the Rank of PGStB.

In the early 1980s, the Lodge Membership reached a peak of over 100 Members and, as has already been touched upon, many of the Brethren who were progressing at that time, remain prominent Members of the Craft. 1987 stands out as a memorable year, for the Lodge was doubly honoured when WBros John Lloyd and Peter Williams both received their Grand Officers' Collars at the same ceremony in United Grand Lodge.

Mention must also be made, however, of the wider social life of the Lodge community. Ladies' Evenings had become well-established by the mid 1960s but, because of the teetotal tradition, such events were generally held in local hotels where the company were able to indulge in a glass of wine with the meal. It was only in 1999 that the Lodge unanimously approved the availability of alcoholic beverages at its Festive Boards. Many Brethren have played major roles in the organisation of such events. WBros William Floyd and Aubrey Varney distinguished themselves by their vigour and imaginative planning of Ladies' Festivals, car rallies and treasure hunts. More recently, the Lodge has been able to call upon the talents of WBros Gerald Mabbett, John Taylor and Geoffrey Thorburn, OBE, to organise the social activities, and WBros Kenneth Hutin and Harry Richards to lead musical events.

It is in the realm of music that the Lodge has been particularly fortunate in having talented Brethren, such as Bro George Armstrong and WBro Harry Richards to occupy the important Office of Organist. Although some Past Masters claim that they would not have attained the Chair of King Solomon had a voice test been involved, no one doubts the value of musical accompaniment at important stages in the ceremonies, and Tuscan's commitment to this practice is widely appreciated. Occasionally, the Lodge has been indebted to Organists of other Lodges, such as WBros David Cox and Michael Fenton, who have stepped into the breach at critical times.

No Lodge history would be complete without mention of its unsung work-horses, the Secretaries. Tuscan Lodge has been particularly well-served by three individuals, WBros F Hudson, W Lewis and A Wardle, who between them have occupied the Secretary's Office for 50 of the Lodge's 57 years. Furthermore, two Members deserve commendation for their efforts over the past 25 years, namely WBro Reginald Healing as Charity Steward and Preceptor, and WBro Bryan Allen as an outstanding Director of Ceremonies.

Compiled by WBro G G Thorburn, OBE, PPrJGD.

Associated Engineers Lodge No.7303

Warranted : 29 July 1953

Consecrated : 18 September 1953

Meeting at the Masonic Hall, Cardiff.

Brethren of Henry Pendrill Charles Lodge No.3769, recognising that there was an increasing number of Engineers amongst the Brethren, gave thought to the founding of a new Lodge to accommodate all the various branches of Engineering and its associated professions.

At a meeting, held on 30 April 1953, it was proposed that Henry Pendrill Charles Lodge should Sponsor a new Lodge. Over the next few months, names such as 'Underwood', 'St Martin's', 'Cefn Onn', 'Castle' and 'Ubique' were considered. 'Ubique' was the first choice, but was rejected on the advice of RWBro R P St Charles, ProvGM, as it is the Motto of the Royal Engineers. On 25 August 1953, after due deliberation, the name 'Associated Engineers' was adopted.

The Consecration of Associated Engineers Lodge No.7303 took place at The Masonic Temple, Caerphilly, on Friday, 18 September 1953. The Consecrating Officer was the Provincial Grand Master, assisted by WBro Bernard F Mattey, ProvSGW, acting as SW, and WBro Harry F Frost, ProvJGW, acting as JW. The Acting DC was WBro Harold Wilson, ProvGDC, and WBro Rev W E Mathias Williams acting as Chaplain. Following the Consecration, the DepProvGM, RWBro Edgar J Rutter, OSM, PGW, Installed WBro H J Starns as the first WM, and Bros G E Roberts and J Powdrill, MBE, as SW and JW respectively.

The Lodge Insignia or Crest was designed to include a hand holding a bolt of lightning, signifying Electrical Engineering; another hand holding a flaming torch, signifying Gas Engineering; a river signifying Water Engineering; and a road and a bridge signifying Civil, Municipal, Structural, and Highway Engineering. The design was approved on 18 December 1953. The Lodge Banner is augmented by a second Banner on which is inscribed a list of PMs. There is no Lodge Motto.

The Lodge meets five times a year, September, December, February, April and May, and attained a Membership of 43 by February 1957. Regretfully, by 2011 the number had fallen to 32. At the April Meeting, the Lodge holds its 'Old English Night', a night of social cordiality when the loving cup filled with mulled wine is passed from one to another. Actually, the Lodge has three Loving Cups which they regard as treasured possessions. In times gone by, Brethren would smoke clay pipes bought for charity; alas, the cost eventually outweighed the charitable donations.

The late WBro Rev W E Mathias Williams, ProvGChap, who officiated at the Consecration of the Lodge, wrote a special prayer

Provincial Grand Master in October 1966.

WBro Hywel Davies, who had become a Joining Member of the Lodge in June 1993, was Installed as Provincial Grand Master at Builth Wells on 16 September 1999. Hywel Davies was Installed as Master of the Lodge of Benevolence in October 2000.

WBro Captain Sir Norman Lloyd-Edwards, who had been Installed as Provincial Grand Master at Barry in July 2008 joined the Lodge in October of that year.

Meetings of the Lodge have been held by Dispensation in the Masonic Temples in Cardiff, Swansea, Porthcawl, Barry, Bridgend, Maesteg and Pontypridd, also at the Albert Edward Prince of Wales Court in Porthcawl and the Sophia Gardens Pavilion in Cardiff.

The Provincial Grand Tyler has always acted as Tyler of the Lodge and at Installations; the Provincial Grand Wardens act as Wardens until the appointment and Investiture of the new Wardens of the Lodge. Immediately following the Installed Board, it has been the custom to resume the Lodge in the First Degree; Proclaim the new Master for the first, second and third times; and to present him with the Working Tools of each Degree prior to presentation of the Charter and the Book of Constitutions, etc. A warning is given, usually by the Provincial Grand Master, that on no account is the shortened version of the Installation Ceremony peculiar to this Lodge to be used in any other Lodge.

The Past Master's Jewel depicts 'Benevolence' as an Almoner's bag bursting with ears of corn. In 1969, it was agreed that it be affixed to the IPM's Collar, for each successive holder to wear, and that the money which would have been expended on such a Jewel, would be given by the Lodge in the name of the IPM to a charity of his choice.

The Lodge of Benevolence has one Daughter Lodge, the South Wales Eastern Division Provincial Grand Stewards' Lodge, No.8900, the 150th Lodge in the Province. The Petition for its formation was presented by the Deputy Provincial Grand Master, VWBro Geoffrey M Ashe, PGSwdB, at a Regular Meeting of the Lodge in May 1979, and signed by the Provincial Grand Master, RWBro the Lord Swansea.

In Cardiff, on 3 July 1956, RWBro Edgar J Rutter, was Installed as the second Master by the Assistant Grand Master, RWBro Sir Allan Adair, Bt, CBE, DSO, MC, DL. RWBro Col Kelway, ProvGM for South Wales Western Division, acted as Senior Warden; The Hon W R S Bathurst, ProvGM for Gloucestershire, as Junior Warden; WBro Capt Gerald Tudor, OBE, PAGDC, as Chaplain; and WBro Lt-Co G J Morley Peel, PDepGSwdB, as Inner Guard. The Master Elect was presented by RWBro Charles, ProvGM; and, after the Installation and the Investiture of Officers, the Wardens, WBros Edgar W Lewis, PJGD, and Harry F Stockwell, PJGD, both Assistant Provincial Grand Masters, were addressed by WBro H E Clive, OBE, DepProvGM for Worcestershire; and the Brethren by Lt-Col. H A Mann, ProvGM for Surrey.

Some 300 Brethren had assembled in the Cardiff Temple for the occasion, and included representatives from the Provinces of Middlesex, Worcestershire, and Staffordshire; representatives of the Board of General Purposes and Benevolence, the Board of Management of the Royal Masonic Institution for Boys; Bro Lawson, Secretary and Governor of The Royal Masonic Hospital; the Chairman, Secretary and Treasurer of the Federation of School Lodges; Members of Middlesex St David's Lodge No.5460, the Master of the Old Masonians Lodge, No.2700; the ProvGM for Monmouthshire, RWBro Col Roderick Hill, DSO; VWBro Stanley Meacock and VWBro J Howell Evans, each holders of the OSM, three Deputy Provincial Grand Masters, three Assistant Provincial Grand Masters, and many other Grand Officers, Provincial Grand Officers and 80 Masters of Lodges in the Province. Full details of the many Lodges and organisations with which RWBro Edgar Rutter was associated are to be found in a separate biographical account, given earlier in this book.

At the Festive Board, held in the Assembly Room of the City Hall, the Master proposed the health of the Deputy Grand Master and the Assistant Grand Master, RWBro Sir Allan Adair, the latter in reply spoke of the pleasure it gave him to be in the Province and at the Lodge of Benevolence on this historic occasion. The health of the Provincial Grand Master was proposed by the Lord

Mayor of Cardiff, WBro D T Williams, OBE, DL. The Assistant Grand Master then proposed the health of the Master; bringing with him the congratulations of Grand Lodge and saying how privileged he felt to Install such a great stalwart of the Craft. The Toast of the Visiting Brethren was proposed by the Junior Warden, WBro Russell Mabley, JP, AProvGM, RWBro Col Roderick Hill, DSO, ProvGM for Monmouthshire, and WBro R B Mummery, the AProvGM of Staffordshire, responded.

Provincial history was made on 8 April 1959, when an Emergency Meeting of the Lodge was held by Dispensation of the MW, the Grand Master, at the Sophia Gardens Pavilion in Cardiff, for the purpose of commemorating the 21st year as Provincial Grand Master of RWBro R P St John Charles, JP. This, to date, has been the only visit of a Grand Master to the Province.

Some 1,200 Brethren were assembled when the Lodge was opened by the Master, WBro Harry F Stockwell, PGD, AProvGM. After the Provincial Grand Master was welcomed and saluted, the Most Worshipful Grand Master, the Rt Hon the Earl of Scarborough, KG, GCSI, CCIE, GCVO, TD, entered in procession, accompanied by five Provincial Grand Masters; the Grand Secretary; RWBro Col James W Stubbs; six Deputy Provincial Grand Masters; two Assistant Provincial Grand Masters and other distinguished Brethren. The Grand Master occupied the Chair and appointed RWBro Harry A Mann, ProvGM for Surrey, as Senior Warden; and RWBro Trevor G Kelway, ProvGM for South Wales Western Division, as Junior Warden. After the AProvGSec, WBro J W F Batley, PAGDC, had read the Illuminated Address in the presentation albums, they were presented to the Provincial Grand Master by the MW Grand Master, together with a cheque for £2,500. RWBro Charles suitably responded and the Grand Master vacated the Chair. The Master moved that the grateful thanks of the Lodge and of the whole Province be tendered to the MW the Grand Master for the honour of his presence.

The Lodge was closed and some 600 Brethren and guests then assembled at the City Hall for dinner. The Worshipful Master, WBro Harry F Stockwell, PGD, AProvGM, presided at the banquet and was supported on his right by the MW the Grand Master and the RW Provincial Grand Master. The Master proposed the Toast to the Grand Master, the Earl of Scarborough, referring to the fact that this was the first ever visit made to a Masonic function in the Province by a ruling Grand Master. In responding, the Grand Master stated that this meeting of the Lodge of Benevolence was probably the largest assembly of a private Lodge that he had ever attended. At the conclusion of his speech he went on to propose the health of the Provincial Grand Master and spoke of the pleasure it gave him to join with the Brethren of the Province in paying tribute to the work of RW Bro Charles for over twenty years and wished him many more years of health, happiness and leadership of the Province. In replying to the Toast, the Provincial Grand Master mentioned the wonderful inspiration the presence of the Grand Master had been, hoping that he would be spared for many years to rule over us. The Provincial Grand Master then proposed the health of the Master, WBro Harry Stockwell, who expressed thanks to the Deputy Provincial Grand Master, RWBro Edgar Rutter, for the tremendous work he had done in organising the day's functions and all those other Brethren who have assisted so nobly. After the Master had acknowledged his Toast, the Brethren were most delightfully entertained by the Royal Welsh Male Voice Party. The Deputy Provincial Grand Master then invited the whole company to drink to the health of all the guests from outside the Province. RWBro the Hon Mr Justice Arthan Davies acknowledged the Toast on behalf of all the guests.

At an Emergency Meeting on 21 September 1970, the Lodge was honoured by the presence of the MW Pro Grand Master, the Earl Cadogan, MC, DL, to hear an Address by the Secretary of the Royal Masonic Institution, WBro Sqn-Ldr D Alun Lloyd, PAGDC.

At the Installation Meeting held on 27 June 1977 at the RMBI, Albert Edward Prince of Wales Court, Porthcawl, the Past Deputy Grand Master, RWBro Major-General Sir Allan Adair, Bt, GCVO, CB, DO, MC, DL, occupied the Chair for the Installation of WBro Eric W Cule, PGStdB. Also present were the Grand Secretary, RWBro James W Stubbs, PJGW, and Grand Director of Ceremonies, WBro Allan F Ferris.

Lodge of Benevolence Past Masters 1953 - 2010

1953/55	R P St John Charles, ProvGM	1985	Leighton G Hutchings, PAGDC
1956/57	Edgar J Rutter, OSM, PGW, DepProvGM	1986	J Arthur Cowley, PAGDC.
1958	Harry F Stockwell, PGSuptWks, DepProvGM	1987	Bernard Rowe, PJGD
1959	Russell Mabley, PJGD, AProvGM	1988	F J Verdy Harverson, PJGD
1960	Harold F Strawford, PJGD	1989	Vernon G A Upton, GM, PJGD
1961	John C Taylor, PJGD	1990	Peter C A Griffin, PAGDC
1962	J William F Batley, PJGD	1991	J Stuart Peters, PGSwdB, DepProvGM
1963	J Vaughan Harris, PAGSuptWks	1992	Frank Newbury, PJGD
1964	Harold Wilson, PJGD, AProvGM	1993	William J Northway, PJGD
1965	Aubrey H Jenkins, PJGD	1994	Islwyn Evans, PJGD
1966	Rt Hon the Lord Swansea, ProvGM	1995	Roy Keith Hopkin, PGSwdB, DepProvGM
1967	David W Jones, PAGDC	1996	A Roy Shopland, PAGDC
1968	Sidney Essex Williams, PAGDC	1997	John B Hood, PAGDC
1969	Wilfred B Porter, PJGD	1998	Harry Mars, MBE, DL, PAGDC
1970	George E Gibbs, PJGD	1999	Walter Hammond, PAGDC
1971	Ronald B Whittingham, PSGD, AProvGM	2000	Hywel Davies, ProvGM
1972	Malcolm H Thompson, PJGD	2001	Julius H Hermer, PJGD
1973	Hubert L Jackson, PAGDC	2002	Donald L Lewis, OBE, PJGD
1974	Llewellyn G Bevan, PSGD, AProvGM	2003	Brian B Comley, PJGD
1975	Kenneth H Robinson, PAGDC	2004	Peter Gough, JP, PAGDC
1976	Lancelot D Bailey, PGStB	2005	Peter Frost, PGSwdB, DepProvGM
1977	Eric W Cule, PGStB	2006	D Kenneth Proctor, PJGD
1978	D T Roderick, PProvSGW	2007	Norman H. Bullock, PAGDC
1979	Geoffrey Malin Ashe, TD, PGSwdB, DepProvGM	2008	Desmond Barnett, PJGD
1980	Donald C B Comley, PAGDC	2009	Paul L Botfield, PAGDC
1981	Cecil H Rapport, CBE, KStJ, DL, PJGD	2010	Edward Wyndham Powell, PJGD
1982	Cuthbert Lionel Summers, PSGD, AProvGM	2011	Robert John Nettleship, SGD, PAProvGM
1983	Kenneth A Morgan, PSGD, AProvGM.		
1984	Samuel Northway, PSGD, AProvGM		

Compiled by Brian B Comley, PM, PPrSGW, PJGD.

Shir Gâr Lodge
No.7339

Warranted : 3 March 1954

Consecrated : 7 May 1954

Erased : 24 April 2005

Met at the Masonic Hall, Cardiff.

Although Shir Gâr Lodge was Erased from the Register of the United Grand Lodge of England on 24 April 2005, some 51 years and 4 months after its Consecration, it is only right that its history be included in this book as it was a Lodge with a real Welsh feeling and strong connections with the County of Sir Gâr - Carmarthenshire.

The principal Founders of the Lodge were Freemason members of the Cardiff & District Carmarthenshire Society, which was originally established by many Cardiff residents who were associated with the County of Carmarthen (Sir Gâr) by birth, descent, marriage or residence. The Society's aims and objectives were to enable its members to maintain contact with Carmarthenshire people in Cardiff and also to succour and give a warm welcome to those who had left their native County for the bright lights of Cardiff, for employment, university etc.

The first informal discussion took place around 1948, but it was some five years later, on 28 July 1953, that the first formal meeting took place, and when the decision to create a Lodge was taken. The leading light in all the proceedings was WBro David Evan James Davies, known to all as 'Jimmie', who was to become the Primus Master. He was a Barrister-at-law, a Past Master of St Marylebone Lodge No.1305, London, and a Joining Member and Secretary of Universities Lodge No.5461, Cardiff, the Lodge which agreed to Sponsor the Petition. There were 26 Petitioners.

As there was already a Carmarthenshire Lodge in existence in London, it was decided that the Lodge's name should be the Welsh translation 'Sir Gâr', or as an alternative, 'Maredunium', which was the ancient Roman name for the County. However, although 'Sir Gâr' was decided upon, it soon became 'Shir Gâr' to prevent the name of 'Sir Gâr' being mispronounced by non-Welsh speaking Brethren. The number 7339 was allocated by the United Grand Lodge of England and permission was sought and obtained from the City of Cardiff and the County of Carmarthen to use their Coats of Arms in the Lodge crest. Also included are appropriate Masonic Emblems. The Lodge Motto was: *'Teg Edrych Tuag Adref'*, which translated means *'it is pleasant to look homewards'*.

Shir Gâr Lodge became the 101st Lodge in the Province of South Wales, Eastern Division, when it was Consecrated on Friday,

7 May 1954, by RWBro Reginald Pendrill St John Charles, ProvGM, with his Consecrating team of Officers. Also present were RWBro Col G T Kelway, ProvGM of South Wales Western Division, and RWBro Col E Roderick Hill, ProvGM Monmouthshire, the 26 Founder Members and over 130 Brethren. VWBro Edgar John Rutter, DepProvGM, Installed WBro D E J Davies as Worshipful Master, who Invested his Wardens, WBro Gwilym Emrys Harries, PM Universities Lodge, as SW; and WBro David Owen Jones, PM Universities Lodge and an Initiate of Beaufort Lodge No.3834, Swansea, as JW. The WM was presented with two Bibles, a Welsh one by WBro William Evans and an English one by VWBro Edgar J Rutter. Ten Brethren were proposed as Joining Members and four Initiates were proposed, two of whom were Initiated at the first Regular Meeting on 25 June 1954. Thus, at the conclusion of that Meeting the Lodge had 38 Members.

Initially, Membership grew steadily to 55 by 1959, reached a peak of 87 in 1969 and stayed in the low 80s for several more years, but in the subsequent decade, decline set in. Membership had fallen to 35 in 1990, 29 at the Millennium and just 19 by 2003.

The Lodge took the greatest pride in its Ritual and floor work, where the standards were set by the first Preceptor of the LOI, WBro William Davies, who was a hard but fair task master. The many visitors always looked forward to the warm Welsh greeting they received, which often included singing around the piano at the Festive Board. The DC for many years, WBro Aubrey Jenkins, would conduct 'Sospan Fach' with great aplomb, and Bro Clayton Thatcher, the first Inner Guard, would entertain with his powerful and melodious baritone voice. Many years later, WBro John Steward, also a fine baritone, succeeded to this mantle and is well known in the Province and beyond through his singing of the Master's song.

The first Tyler, Bro Arthur James, was a retired soldier and a stickler for the correct procedure. However, his flamboyance when saluting the WM with his sword in military fashion caused many to fear execution if they stood too close. Apart from those already mentioned, WBro Aubrey Jenkins, who was a Founder, received Grand Lodge honours in 1960, when he was Invested as PJGD.

Later in the life of the Lodge, WBro William John Llewellyn (Bill) Thomas, became a Joining Member. He proved to be a tower of strength for many years with his wise advice and excellent Ceremonial. First Installed as WM in 1979, the twenty fifth year of the Lodge, he was Installed as WM again in 1983 and 1996. WBro Ainsley Morgan, a Joining Member from Universities Lodge, Cardiff, in 1967, Installed as WM in 1976, was Lodge Secretary, 1978-1981, DC, 1982-2005 and Almoner, 2000-2005.

WBro John Martin Steward, Initiated in 1987, was Installed as WM in 1994, and again in 1998. He was also Secretary, 2001-2005. In Ceremonial, he was extremely versatile and in the final Ceremony in January 2005, he acted as Secretary, Chaplain and DC as well as delivering parts of the Ritual.

Over the years, the Lodge had Members who were distinguished in other ways. Bro W Clement was Secretary of the Welsh Rugby Union; Bro W Linford Rees was Professor of Psychiatry, Past President of the Royal College of Psychiatrists, President of the British Medical Association, and the father of the actress, Angharad Rees. Last, but not least, Bro Ryan Davies was a TV personality and popular Welsh entertainer of the 1960s and 1970s. He made his name on Welsh language television shows such as the sitcom 'Fo a Fe' and 'Ryan a Ronnie', in which he appeared with Ronnie Williams. They were the first comedians ever to make TV series in Welsh and English, and were thought of fondly as the Welsh answer to Morecambe and Wise.

By June 2007, all the Founder Members had passed to the Grand Lodge Above. Only one Brother now survives from those early days of the Lodge, namely WBro D Gerwyn Thomas, PPrSGW, who was one of the first ten Joining Members, having himself been Initiated as long ago as 8 March 1940. He had the distinction of serving the Lodge as Chaplain for 30 years, and was regarded as the 'Father' of the Lodge and one of its longest serving Members.

WBro Edward Wyndham Powell, PJGD, a first Initiate, and WM in 1964, passed to the Grand Lodge Above on 19 June 2011. He was 81 years old. A Stockbroker by profession, WBro Wyndham was Initiated into Shir Gâr Lodge on 25 June 1954. Wyndham became a Joining Member of the Striguil Lodge, No. 2186, Province of Monmouthshire, in 1973 and remained a Member up to the time of his death. In 1995, WBro Wyndham was honoured by appointment as PGStB in the United Grand Lodge of England and he was promoted to his ultimate Rank of PJGD in 2003. On his first appointment to Grand Rank, he joined Lodge of Benevolence No 7305, and was the Worshipful Master of that Lodge at the time of his sad passing. He used his considerable professional talents and expertise for the benefit of the Province's Masonic Benevolent Fund (Eastern Division of South Wales, a Registered Charity primarily devoted to the welfare of Brethren of the Province and their dependents). He oversaw the investments, the income from which contributes the lion's share of the money disbursed by the charity each year. During his time at the helm, the value of the fund multiplied several times over and at the end of 2010, stood at over £2.3 million. In recognition of his magnificent efforts, in May 2011, WBro Wyndham was made an Honorary Vice-President of the Charity, a distinction conferred only once previously in the 100+ year history of the Fund.

Under Local Government reorganisation in 1974, the Counties of Carmarthen, Cardigan and Pembroke were amalgamated to form the new County of Dyfed, and the Lodge changed its Membership requirements accordingly. Unfortunately, this did not prove particularly successful and resulted, a few years later, in the Lodge becoming 'open', but this dilution of the original objects was felt by many to cause the Lodge to lose its way, and fortunes changed. Over the ensuing years, many efforts were made to sustain and increase the Membership once more, but it all proved to no avail. With continually falling numbers, the Lodge reluctantly determined in 2005 to return its Warrant, bringing to an end over half a century of history.

Many of the Members were already Members of other Lodges, and so have continued in the Fraternity, while most of the remainder have now joined other Lodges, most notably Oriel Lodge No.9023.

Compiled by WBro J M Steward, PPrGSwdB, assisted by the late WBro E Wyndham Powell, PJGD.

Llanfair Lodge No. 7353

Warranted : 2 June 1954

Consecrated : 28 September 1954

Meeting at the Masonic Hall, Cardiff.

Early in 1954, a number of Freemasons, all of whom were Members of the Glamorgan Wanderers Rugby Club, decided to form a new Lodge for Brethren who had a common interest in Rugby. At that time, the Club's headquarters were in the Wyndham Arcade, St Mary Street, Cardiff. Founded in October 1893 by a group of ex-pupils of Monkton House School, the Wanderers were originally known as 'Old Monktonians', but in 1913 it was decided to change the name to 'Glamorgan Wanderers Rugby Football Club'. The name change was deemed necessary to reflect the wider intake of its membership. The Wanderers grew into their new name well, utilising seven different grounds to host home matches until the Club arrived at its present home, 'The Memorial Ground,' St Fagan's Court, in 1952. This was purchased by raising money via various appeals post World War II. Thus, 'The Memorial Ground' is dedicated to all those players who lost their lives in the two World Wars.

The Wanderers Club in Cardiff's Wyndham Arcade became a famous watering hole from 1923 and many business deals were clinched in the dining room, whilst the snooker room saw many a tense battle, and many famous names, including Wales' greatest ever boxer, Jimmy Wilde, graced the green baize. This was one of the first such clubs to be formed in Wales and its unique atmosphere attracted rugby aficionados from all walks of life and, on International Days, from all over the world! Sadly, the Club in the Wyndam Arcade closed in 1969.

Initially, it had been hoped to incorporate the Rugby Club's name in the name of the new Lodge, but this was not permitted by United Grand Lodge. The Club, being situated in the Wyndam Arcade, was in the ancient parish of St Mary. Consequently, the name 'Llanfair Lodge' was chosen, 'Llanfair' being Welsh for 'The Church of St Mary'. The original St Mary's Church had been situated on the site of the 'Prince of Wales Theatre' (today a Weatherspoon's Public House), but had been swept away by an enormous flood of the Bristol Channel (now thought to have been a tsunami) in 1607.

The second Marquess of Bute encouraged the idea of rebuilding St Mary's Church in Bute Road and he donated the land and £1000 towards the building cost. The Foundation Stone was laid by the Marquess on Wednesday, 8 July 1840 and Glamorgan Lodge No.36, in full Regalia, played a part in the public Ceremony.

It was decided that the Llanfair Lodge Logo should contain a sketch of this second St Mary's Church. A student from the Cardiff College of Art was commissioned to produce a drawing, for which he was paid the princely sum of £2. 2s. 0d (£2.10p). The Motto in Welsh, which surrounds the picture of the Church is *'Heb Dduw - Heb Ddim'* which means *'Without God there is Nothing'*.

The Lodge which Sponsored the Petition for the new Lodge was Harlequins Lodge No.5793. While the WM and Wardens of Harlequin Lodge must have signed the Petition, only one Member, Bro E J Joseph Evans, appears in the list of Founder Members. Twenty-nine Brethren are listed as Founder Members, six of whom were from Glamorgan Lodge, with Dinam Lodge No.4521 providing four Founder Members. Prince Llewellyn Lodge No.2570 provided two Founder Members, one of whom was Bro Geoffrey Malin Ashe. There were two Founder Members from both Llangattock Lodge No.2547 and Trisant Lodge No.1992.

WBro Trevor Phillips, PM Caerdydd Lodge No.3959 was the Founder Primus Master and he became the first Member of the Lodge to become a Grand Officer (PAGDC).

Llanfair Lodge was Consecrated at the Masonic Temple, Cardiff, on Tuesday, 28 September 1954, by RWBro RP St John Charles, ProvGM. Among those assisting were WBro Harold Wilson, AProvGM, 1960-1980, as DC; WBro Vivien Care as ADC and WBro Lance Bailey, ProvGOrg, as Organist. Lance always played the organ at the Lodge's Installation Meetings, right up to the time of his recent death.

St Mary's Church, Bute Road, Cardiff

Immediately following the Consecration Ceremony, the new Worhsipful Master, Trevor Phillips was Installed by RWBro Edgar J Rutter, DepProvGM. Later, Edgar Rutter presented the Lodge with the Volume of the Sacred Law, which is still in use today. The person appointed to act as IPM was WBro David Phillips Rees, PPrSGD, a Solicitor in Cardiff who had been Installed WM of Glamorgan Lodge in 1945. Sadly, David died 6 months later, on 15 March 1955 at 66 years of age.

The first Senior Warden was WBro Percy Cousins, PM St Mildred Lodge No.5078, and the first Junior Warden was Bro Cecil Blockley Boughton of Glamorgan Lodge. Cecil was the Manager of the Wanderers Club in the Wyndham Arcade. Originally from Abbey Lodge No.33, Nice, he had joined Glamorgan Lodge in December 1951. He became WM of Abbey Lodge in 1964 and he was also a Member of Port of Hercules Lodge No.4626, Monte Carlo. He became the third WM of Llanfair Lodge in 1956 and was in due course appointed PPrSGW in the Province of South Wales - Eastern Division.

The Lodge has never held formal Lodges of Instruction, but the Officers have always met on two or three occasions to rehearse the forthcoming ceremony. Rehearsals have been held in numerous places - Glan Ely Hospital, over a Baker's Shop in Whitchurch Road, The Hodge Building, the Tax Offices in Hayes House, Oxford Lane and the Cardiff Masonic Hall. The

Ceremonies have always been of a very high standard and after each one, in the early days, Trevor Phillips (Founder Master) would say '*Phew! Another bloody miracle*'. In 1964, when Bro Brian Cook and Bro John (Poppa) Davies were Raised, the Minute Book records that the Candidates were told that the Traditional History, Tracing Board, Explanation of the Tools and the Extended Signs would all be given at a later date. The reason for omitting so much of the Ceremony was because the Lodge Meeting coincided with the Glamorgan Wanderers Annual Dinner Dance!

From the beginning, it was an unwritten rule that Lodge Members must be members of the Wanderers' Club in the Wyndham Arcade or of Glamorgan Wanderers RFC. It was not permissible to make the Lodge a 'closed shop', but such was the demand for Membership that it was not difficult to enforce this restriction. As time went on, and the demand for Membership declined, the Lodge operated a more open policy, so that today probably only 30% of the Members have the Wanderers' connection.

The fourth Worshipful Master of the Lodge (1957), WBro Cuthbert Banham, was the second Member of the Lodge to become a Grand Officer, with the Rank of PGStB. A Founder Member from Llangattock Lodge No.2547, he was the first Lodge Secretary, an Office he was to hold for many years. He was also an early Member and stalwart supporter of the Cancer Charity, 'Tenovus', established in Cardiff in 1943 by ten businessmen (hence 'ten-of-us') and now invests almost £4 million each year on research, education, counselling and patient care.

Cuthbert Banham was succeeded in the Chair by Geoffrey Malin Ashe, who was first appointed AProvGM, 1976-1977, and then DepProvGM, 1977-1992. He too became a Grand Officer with the Rank of PGSwdB. His biographical details are given elsewhere in this book.

The Lodge's most recent and 4th Grand Officer, WBro Geoffrey William Thomas, was born in Swansea to a Welsh speaking family. Initially educated at Lonlas Welsh Primary School, one of the first schools in Wales to provide an education totally in the Welsh language, he was among one of the first of 69 children admitted to the school when it first opened in 1949. Following the 11 plus examination he went to Dynevor Grammar School, Swansea, before embarking on a career in Banking. He joined Martins Bank (eventually taken over by Barclays Bank) and served in a number of branches in the City of London. In 1961, when the Bank was looking for fluent Welsh speakers to expand their operations in South Wales, he transferred first to Swansea and then in 1965 to Cardiff. Formerly a playing member of Swansea Rugby Club, he joined Glamorgan Wanderers. After retiring from the game, he became one of the Club's administrators, succeeding to the position of Club Secretary, in which capacity he served for fifteen years. In line with many Club members, he was encouraged to join Llanfair Lodge. He was Initiated in 1974 and became Master in 1982 and again in 1991. In Provincial Grand Lodge, he was appointed a Provincial Junior Grand Deacon in 1987 and promoted to Provincial Deputy Grand Director of Ceremonies in 1990. Appointed the Provincial Junior Grand Warden in 1996, he became a Grand Officer in 1998 with the Rank of PAGDC. The following year, he became the Provincial Grand Director of Ceremonies, a position he held until 2004 when he became an Assistant Provincial Grand Master. Promoted in Grand Lodge to PSGD in 2005, he retired as AProvGM in December 2010. A Founder Member of the Wenallt Lodge No. 9082, he was WM in 2008.

In Royal Arch Masonry WBro Geoff was Exalted in Cartref Chapter No. 5772 in 1980. A Founder Member of Hiraeth Chapter No. 8834, he was Installed First Principal in 1993. In Provincial Grand Chapter he was appointed to the Rank of PPrGStdB in 1996 and promoted to the Rank of PPrGReg in 2008.

Mention should also be made of Bro George Strickson, a Member who died before completing the Three Degrees. Nevertheless, he left a sum of money to the Lodge and it was determined that the Lodge would furnish a room at the AEPW Court, Porthcawl, in his memory.

WBro Joe Rooke was another notable Lodge Member and many will remember his renderings of the Traditional History and his own extended version of the Address to the Brethren. Joe was a great believer in the power of honey, so much so that he had his order delivered by the hundredweight!

At the Installation Meeting in 1962, with WBro Peter Fenely in the Chair (Installed 1961), the Lodge met in the Edgar Rutter Temple. When the Provincial party entered the Lodge, RWBro Edgar Rutter suggested to Peter Fenely that being an Installation Meeting, the Lodge should be held in the Duke of Connaught Temple. He went on to suggest that he should 'call off' and then 'call on' again in the main Temple. There was a hurried consultation, and WBro Peter said that the Members were quite happy to remain where they were (nobody knew how to 'call off' or 'call on'!).

The Festive Boards have always been happy occasions and in the early days it was strongly recommended that the duration of a speech should not exceed three minutes. It was usual to distribute song sheets and every Lodge Night included a rendering of 'The Happy Wanderer'. This song has now been replaced with 'When the Coal comes from the Rhondda'. Geoffrey Ashe frequently rendered, from the stage, 'My Bonnie lies over the Ocean', complete with actions. At an Installation, soon after his appointment as AProvGM, it was suggested that he may not wish to sing. 'Certainly I will sing' he replied and went on the stage and said 'You see before you the Assistant Provincial Grand Master'. He then took off his tail coat and in his shirt sleeves said 'Now you don't' and proceeded to sing. Visitors saw Geoff in a different light that evening.

In the early years, the Lodge had a piece of Ritual delivered by the Junior Warden at the Festive Board. He would announce to the Brethren 'This Lodge has After After Proceedings, which take place not far from here and any expert Brother will be pleased to direct your steps'. This of course referred to the Wanderers Club in the Wyndham Arcade, where many would retire for more than a little while.

On 6 December 1967, a notable visitor was WBro Love of the William Massy Ferguson Lodge in New Zealand. He was a Member of the 'All Blacks Touring Party' currently in Wales. At the Festive Board it was agreed that each Lodge would Toast the other at our respective Christmas Meetings. This continues to be done by Llanfair Lodge.

In 2002, it was felt that it would be appropriate to celebrate the 50th Anniversary of the Lodge by commissioning a Banner. The Members of the Lodge each contributed towards the cost, which was approximately £900. The Banner has the Lodge Logo in a central position on a background of stripes of Cambridge blue, black and white. These are the Glamorgan Wanderers Rugby Club jersey colours. The Griffin, which is located in the bottom right corner of the Banner, is the Rugby Club Badge, which, together with the background, indicates the strong connection that the Lodge has with the Club.

The Banner was Dedicated on Thursday, 3 June 2004 by VWBro Peter Frost, DepProvGM. The Regular Meeting date of 31 May (Election Night) was changed by Dispensation, to almost coincide with the 50th Anniversary of the signing of the Lodge's Warrant on 2 June 1954.

Complied by WBro John Hopkins, PPrJGW.

The City of Cardiff Lodge No.7528

Warranted : 1 May 1957

Consecrated : 25 June 1957

Meeting at the Masonic Hall, Cardiff.

On 28 October 1905, His Majesty King Edward VII signed the Royal Charter granting Cardiff the status of a 'City'. This highly distinctive Lodge, Consecrated on 25 June 1957, was so-named to commemorate this historic event. The name was chosen when two of the Founder Members, WBros Charles Price and Gordon Phillips (WM 1963) were returning from London, after registering their intention of Founding a new Lodge, when WBro Gordon spotted a newly erected sign marking Cardiff as a City.

Lodge of Fidelity No.6112 agreed to be the Sponsoring Lodge and it was decided that the Primus Master Designate should be WBro Cecil H Rapport, who had been Initiated into Carmel Lodge No.4774 in November 1936 and Installed WM in 1952. He enjoyed a most distinguished Civic and Masonic career, having served as High Sheriff of South Glamorgan, 1984-1985, and Deputy Lieutenant of the County. He was honoured with a CBE and became KStJ, PPrSGW and PJGD of UGLE. Further biographical details may be found in the history of Carmel Lodge.

Another distinguished Founder Member was the 'larger than life' extrovert Layton Lougher. Born on 18 May 1925 in Llancarfan, Vale of Glamorgan, he was educated at Cowbridge Grammar School as a boarder and graduated in Law from University College, Cardiff. Having been admitted to the Law Society in 1949, he became its President from 1977 to 1979. Well-known in racing circles, he defended a number of jockeys, mostly with successful results, when they were called before the Stewards. He was the youngest Alderman to be elected to the City Council, on which he served for 16 years, and he was instrumental in bringing the successful Searchlight Tattoo to Cardiff. He was Installed Master of City of Cardiff Lodge in 1962 and in Province, he attained the Rank of PPrAGReg. Layton Lougher died on 11 June 2002 and was interred at Michaelston-le-Pit, near his former home in Cwrt Yr Alla.

Also worthy of note was Founder Member, W Francis Thomas, who had been appointed Chief Constable of Cardiff in 1954. He became the second WM of City of Cardiff Lodge in 1958.

The Membership of the Lodge has always been widely drawn from the business community and the professions, with such well known old Cardiff retailers as Lermon's, Roath Furnishings and Rapport's all being owned by Members. Also, many distinguished Barristers, Solicitors, Estate Agents, Police Officers and even the occasional Judge and the Clerk of The Peace, grace our proceedings.

For many years, the senior Lodge Member was WBro Saul Magrill, PPrJGW, WM in 1970, who in 1958 was the Lodge's second Initiate. He served in Algiers during the Second World War as an RAF Volunteer Reserve reaching the rank of Flight Sergeant and was 'demobbed' at the end of 1945. He was awarded five campaign medals and mentioned in dispatches for distinguished service, his name being published in the London Gazette in January 1946. Born in Twickenham in 1914, he began his professional training as a Chartered Surveyor. In 1935, he moved to retail property specialists Dudley Samuel and Harrison in London, where he learned his trade alongside some of the most eminent names in the property world, including Edward Erdman, who sold the Ritz Hotel and shaped the modern British high street by helping WH Smith and Tesco buy their first shops. As a result, Saul Magrill's friends included Tesco founder Jack Cohen. As head of his own property company, Wales and Western, he formed the consortium behind the original St David's Centre in Cardiff, which opened in 1981. Aged 74, he became a commercial consultant with Chris John and Partners Estate Agents in Cardiff and only moved to part-time hours in 2007, when he turned 93. Saul Leopold Magrill passed to the Grand Lodge Above on 23 May 2010, aged 96 years.

Many senior Brethren served with distinction in the Second World War, among them the late WBro Bill Clarke, MBE, TD, PPrJGW, WM in 1973, who served in West Africa, India and Burma, reaching the rank of Major with the Royal Electrical and Mechanical Engineers (REME), subsequently becoming President of The Burma Star Association. WBro Clive Beecher, WM in 1976 and 1984, who passed away in 2001, served with distinction in Malaya and brought all the skills that he learned in the rank of Regimental Sergeant Major to the role of DC, in which he excelled and successfully terrified many of the younger Brethren. A Past Grand Standard Bearer of UGLE, WBro Clive set a wonderful example for subsequent DCs of the Lodge. Lifelong friends, the late WBro Peter G Gregory, PPrAGDC, former Lodge Secretary and Installed Master in 1988 and WBro Vivian Hill, PPrJGW, WM in 1979 and 1990, both served in the RAF, with Vivian eventually becoming President of the Air Crews Association. WBro 'Viv' was Initiated in Duke of York Lodge No.2453 in December 1960 and was Installed as Master of that Lodge in 1974. He was a Founder of Croeso Lodge No.8377, which was Consecrated on 23 July 1971. Sadly, WBro Viv, an Insurance Broker by profession, passed away in December 2009 at the age of 73.

The City of Cardiff Lodge meets four times each year, always on a Saturday, which often conflicts with rugby internationals and may account for the florid complexion of some Members, who have been trying too hard to combine patriotism with loyalty to the Lodge. The Lodge is known as a Dining Lodge and the Brethren like to think that the meticulous preparation of the Festive Board is unmatched in the Province. The Lodge is particularly fortunate to have the Giles family, who have owned Rumney Pottery for more than seven generations, among its Members. They have decorated the Festive Board for many years to a standard similar to that of a civic dinner, with ribbons, samples of their pottery (examples of which are on display in Grand Lodge), flowers, candelabra and other silverware.

The Lodge takes great pride in the quality of its Ritual and has a long list of outstanding Masters, who, over the years, have performed Ceremonies of a very high standard. Many, sadly, are no longer with us. Now, as we move into a new era in Freemasonry, the Lodge has had to reduce some aspects of the formality of its LOIs and LORs in order to encourage the active participation of the new and younger Members, so that they continue to enjoy Freemasonry and see the benefit of making the commitment needed to become worthy Masons.

Idiosyncrasies of the Lodge include the singing of the Lodge Song to visiting Brethren; the Lodge has a 'Snuff Steward' and every Festive Board is closed with 'Auld Lang Syne' performed on the square.

The Lodge Banner was presented in 1969 in memory of the late Bro David Loewenson by his widow and it is now displayed in

503

the Lord Swansea Temple. A second Banner was presented to the Lodge in 1987 by the late WBro Walter Makepeace and this Banner is used for all Regular Lodge Meetings. Depicting the Coat of Arms of the City of Cardiff, the Banner bears the words *'Y Ddraig Goch a Ddyry Gychwyn'* - *'The Red Dragon is ready to wake'*.

This is a very sociable Lodge and over the years many trips to overseas Lodges have been arranged, including those in Florida, Mallorca, France and Gibraltar. Return fraternal visits from these overseas Brethren have also been enjoyed. City of Cardiff Lodge has a particularly close association with Ramon Llull Lodge No.9 of the Gran Logia de Espana, where WBro David Strugnell (WM 1975) is now Acting Provincial Assistant Grand Master. Ramon Llull Lodge is the oldest English speaking Lodge in the Province of the Baleares and was Consecrated in 1982. In 2003, the Lodge enjoyed the company of 13 visiting Brethren from various French Lodges, who came over to see Wales trounced at the Millennium Stadium, making their visit to City of Cardiff Lodge that much more enjoyable!

In common with other Lodges, the Lodge keeps in regular contact with the widows of former Lodge Members and raises funds to take them on an annual outing and to provide for a Christmas gift. The widows are also invited to the regular social gatherings, as well as the annual Ladies' Night.

Compiled by WBro Julian Rosser, PPrJGD.

Coat of Arms of the City of Cardiff

Ystradyfodwg Lodge No.7638

Warranted   :   4 March 1959

Consecrated   :   29 May 1959

Meeting at the Masonic Hall, Pontypridd.

Ystradyfodwg Lodge was Sponsored by Rhondda Lodge No.3979, and the Warrant was granted on 4 March 1959. The Lodge was Consecrated on Friday, 29 May 1959.

WBro Frederick G Hutchings, Founder and the first Master of Ystradyfodwg Lodge, is considered to have been the driving force behind the Lodge's formation. Initiated in Rhondda Lodge in 1925, he became Master of that Lodge in 1939. Appointed PPrJGD in 1946, he was appointed the Provincial Junior Grand Warden in 1960. He was a member of the Committee of Management of the Masonic Benevolent Fund, Eastern Division of South Wales and, in 1962, he became Junior Warden of Hendre Lodge No.3250. In the formation of Ystradyfodwg Lodge, WBro Frederick was supported by 14 Founder Members, three of whom were his sons, Leighton G Hutchings, Derek G Hutchings and F Grenville Hutchings. These Brethren were stalwarts of Rhondda Lodge and other Lodges.

The name of the Lodge has its origin in the ancient upland parish covering most of the valleys of the Rhondda Fawr and Rhondda Fach rivers. With a history going back some 1300 years, the parish is within the Rural Deanery of Rhondda in the Diocese of Llandaff. The name is believed to be derived from 'Tyfodwg' (or 'Dyfodwg') who was a 7th century Celtic Saint, a contemporary of Saints Illtyd and Gwynno. Traditional history provides the Saint with a reputation of being a great evangelist and preacher, and during a persecution of the Church, he was punished by having his tongue cut out, thus preventing him from spreading the word of the Gospel. Ystrad is Welsh for 'Vale'.

The design of the Lodge Emblem was originated by Bro Clifford Gingell, the Borough of Rhondda Architect who became WM of the Lodge in 1996. The Emblem depicts the green hills of the Rhondda Valley forming a background with the ancient Parish Church framed by the Square and Compasses, oak leaves and acorns. The oak and acorn insignia recall the greenness of the valley, when ancient oak galleons of the Royal Navy took their timbers from the now naked hillside. Overall, the Square and Compasses depict, in Masonic terms, both the moral rectitude and the bounds of propriety which this holy and ancient shrine has installed for close on thirteen centuries. The head of Dyfodwg forms the upper part of each compass leg. The one on the left has a protruding tongue, and the one on the right is without a tongue, illustrating the legend of Dyfodwg's punishment.

The Motto: *'Parhaed Brawdgarwch'* was suggested for the Lodge by Bro Francis J Rees, the Vicar of the Parish of Ystradyfodwg. The purpose of all signs and symbols is to *'Let Brotherhood Succeed'* or *'Prevail'* (a free translation of the Motto). The interpretation of the Motto could also read: *'Let Brotherly Love Prevail'*.

RWBro Hywel Davies first visited the Lodge in 1967, many years before he became the ProvGM of South Wales Eastern Division. He attended in support of his Electricity Board colleague WBro H George Davies, who was Worshipful Master at the

the first Worshipful Master by the Installing Master, WBro Harry F Stockwell. WBro L G Bevan was a Chartered Shipbroker, residing at the Old Vicarage, Sketty. He had been Initiated into Talbot Lodge No.1323, in 1935. Frederick Charles Palmer, MC, ProvGStwd, a retired Wholesale Fish Merchant, of West Cross, Swansea, and who had been Initiated into Corinthian Lodge No.4917, was Invested as SW. Bro William George Tucker, JP, a retired Builder, from Horton, Gower, who had been Initiated in Caradoc Lodge No.1573, was Invested as JW.

Distinguished Founder Brethren who were amongst the first Lodge Officers include: Chaplain - WBro Canon Thomas Kenneth Brunsdon, PDepGChap, Installed WM of Lodge of Progress in 1970; Treasurer - WBro Harold Frank Strawford, PJGD, WM of Lodge of Benevolence No.7305 in 1960, ProvSGW in 1954; Secretary - WBro Malcolm H Thompson, Company Accountant, from Newton, Mumbles, Initiated in Beaufort Lodge No.3834, Provincial Grand Secretary, 1967-1990; and DC - WBro Stammers H Alabaster, PJGD, Dentist, Initiated in Indefatigable Lodge No.237 in May 1908, WM in 1922, DC of the Lodge for over 50 years, and the oldest Grand Lodge and Grand Chapter Officer in the Province.

It was resolved that the Consecrating Officer, RWBro R P St John Charles, ProvGM, be Elected an Honorary Member of the Lodge. It was further resolved that £100 be sent to the Swansea Masonic Hall Company for 100 shares in the Company. It was noted that the Secretary had received a proposition form for RWBro Edgar J Rutter, OSM, PGW, DepProvGM, to become a Joining Member.

The Lodge does not have a Banner, but the Lodge Insignia consists of three rungs of an upright ladder, representing 'progress', with the words 'Faith', 'Hope', 'Charity', written in turn immediately above each ascending rung. In front of the ladder is an open VSL. The Lodge Motto: *'Labor est Honor'* meaning *'Labour is Honour'*, is also displayed.

Compiled by WBro Phillip J Morris, PPrGReg, with assistance from
WBro Peter M Davies, ProvJGW, PM Glamorgan Lodge No.36.

Senior Warden's Chair and Organ Loft, Swansea Temple

Aelwyd Lodge No.7982

Warranted : 29 April 1964

Consecrated : 2 June 1964

Meeting at the Masonic Hall, Merthyr Tydfil.

On an icy night in the bleak midwinter of 1963/64, a group of Merthyr Freemasons and their wives gathered around the open coal fire in the saloon bar of the Eagle Hotel, situated in the appropriately named Masonic Street, in Merthyr Tydfil. The purpose of the meeting was to discuss the formation of a new Masonic Lodge in Merthyr. At that time there were only two Lodges, Loyal Cambrian No.110 and North Glamorgan No.4055 in the town. Both Lodges had waiting lists for aspiring Masons of at least five years and also the policy then was to increase the opportunities for active Masons to achieve the Chair of King Solomon. The solution was to form a new Lodge in Merthyr Tydfil.

There are several things about that initial meeting which, less than fifty years later, appear very unusual. The gathering was held in the Eagle Hotel because, although the Merthyr Tydfil Masonic Hall had dining facilities, in those days it did not have a licensed bar. The wives of existing Masons were not only present, but took a full part in the discussions. In those days, Masonic wives purchased, prepared, and cooked all food for the Festive Board, and nothing was going to happen without their input!

In view of the obvious need for a new Lodge, the decision to Petition for one was easily made. When discussion turned to the name for the new Lodge, one of the Masonic wives pointed out that they were all staring at it. 'Aelwyd' is the Welsh word for 'the hearth'. However, 'Aelwyd' means more than just the physical object. It also conveys the warmth, security and friendliness associated with a coal fire blazing in an open hearth. Whilst many current and future Masons may now be unfamiliar with hearths or even coal fires, or even coal, it is no accident that electric and gas fires still attempt to capture the spirit of the hearth with fake coal fire effects. Thus, 'Aelwyd' Lodge, it was to be.

Continuing the theme of warmth and friendship, a PM of North Glamorgan Lodge with a significant Masonic career then still in front of him, WBro Ken Adams Morgan, proposed the Lodge Motto should be *'Yn gytun yn yr un lle'* which means *'with one accord in one place'*. This Motto was taken from Verse 1 Chapter 2 of the Book of The Acts of the Apostles - *'And when the day of Pentecost was fully come, they were all with one accord in one place.'* Unusually for a Masonic Lodge, the Motto was taken from the New Testament.

The Sponsoring Lodge was North Glamorgan Lodge, which then became the Mother Lodge, with Loyal Cambrian Lodge, the Grandmother Lodge. However, the moving spirit behind the Lodge was undoubtedly Ken Adams Morgan, who became its Master in 1966. He can justly be described as the 'Father' of the Lodge. Without his drive and enthusiasm for all things Masonic, it is doubtful if Aelwyd Lodge would have come into existence, certainly not in the form it took.

Once the Petition had been approved and a Lodge number allocated, a Banner was designed by Miss Nan Thomas, a local Art Teacher who, for many years, was regarded as an 'honorary widow' of the Lodge. At the centre of the Banner is the hearth with a blazing open coal fire and an empty armchair placed in front of the fire, symbolising the welcome for visiting Masons. The Banner was sown by nuns living in an English Convent who, unlike many of our own Members, found no difficulty with the Welsh spelling.

The Consecration Ceremony took place on 2 June 1964, at the Masonic Temple in Merthyr Tydfil. The full Provincial team was present led by RWBro R P St John Charles, ProvGM. The Consecration Banquet was a six course dinner, with turkey (in June!) as the main course. In the 1960s, turkey was still a great luxury, reserved for Christmas and other special occasions. Musical entertainment at the Consecration Ceremony was provided by Bros William Arnold Davies ('Bill Baritone') and Haydn Adams Morgan, the father of WBro Ken Adams Morgan.

The Founder Master was WBro Col Reginald Freedman, a local Solicitor and Deputy Lord Lieutenant of Glamorgan. At that time, Col Freedman was virtually blind, and he is still remembered for nearly 'braining' a Candidate during a Third Degree Ceremony!

Over the years, the Lodge has developed its own traditions including a Loving Cup Ceremony. Before the days of health and safety concerns, the cup would be passed around after Installation Ceremonies filled with Malaga wine. At first only the Lodge Founders partook, then PMs and finally all Members. No one knows why Malaga wine was chosen. In those early days of continental holidays, someone probably brought back a bottle from Spain! The closing of each Lodge Meeting is marked with the singing of the Welsh hymn 'Nefol Dad'.

With but few exceptions, Freemasonry tends to be a social activity for the middle classes, and this has always been reflected in the Membership of the Lodge. The history of Aelwyd Lodge over the years is a microcosm of the social history of the middle classes in South Wales during that period. In 1964, many Members were self-employed shop keepers, publicans, and other retailers. The demise of the small retail trader with the growth of supermarkets, together with brewery-owned and later company-owned public houses, has seen a great decline in this type of Membership. Even in 1964, there was a sprinkling of public sector workers, but Membership in this category has greatly increased over the years. Many Members of Aelwyd Lodge, like most Lodges in South Wales, are now Teachers, Local Government Workers, Police Officers, Health Service Workers and other Public Sector Employees. The discouragement, both official and unofficial, now prevalent in the public sector to such employees taking an active part in Freemasonry is obviously having a serious effect upon Membership.

A Lodge with only 45 years' existence cannot claim to have ancient traditions or time honoured landmarks. The Lodge was, thankfully, not around when the World Wars were fought and it has no Roll of Honour and the Members hope never to have one. True to its empty chair placed before the hearth on its Banner, Aelwyd Lodge welcomes all visitors and does not operate a booking system for meals. Any visiting Freemason can turn up at Aelwyd Lodge and take his place in 'the chair before the hearth'. In this way, the Members hope to live up to the Lodge Motto: *'Yn gytun yn yr un lle'* – *'All with one accord in one place'*.

Compiled by WBro Jeff Davies, PPrGReg.

Owain Glyndwr Lodge No.8015

Warranted : 10 February 1965

Consecrated : 13 May 1965

Meeting at the Masonic Hall, Cardiff.

Owain Glyndwr Lodge is the sixth Daughter Lodge of Windsor Lodge No.1754, Penarth, and was closely associated with St Canna Lodge No.6725, from which early Membership was largely derived. There were 21 Petitioners, of whom 7 were Past Masters. The Petition was signed in Windsor Lodge on 4 December 1964. Among the 17 Founder Members were Hadyn Shaw, William George Cornfield, Daniel Gwyn Walters and Lt-Col John Brynmor Davies, OBE, all prominently active Brethren at that time.

The letter accompanying the Petition stated that *'The new Lodge was to serve the Cardiff area, and meet at Penarth. Most of the Petitioners are Members of large Lodges and the new Lodge will enable them to make more progress.'* At the time, Windsor Lodge had 186 Members.

The Lodge was Consecrated on 13 May 1965 at Penarth Masonic Hall by RWBro R P St John Charles, ProvGM. The Installing Master was RWBro Edgar J Rutter, OSM, PGW, DepProvGM, who Installed WBro Hadyn Shaw, PPGW as the first Worshipful Master. Hadyn Shaw, a retired Accountant from Cardiff, was an Initiate and PM Kibbor Lodge No.4364. He was also PM Môr Hafren Lodge No.7194 and in 1963, he had been WM of Hendre Lodge No.3250. Daniel Gwyn Walters, first SW, an Initiate and PM St Canna Lodge, was an Automobile Engineer and Garage Proprietor from Rhiwbina, Cardiff. The first JW, Arthur Stanley Pike, PPrGStdB, an Initiate and PM Sapphire Lodge No.5290, was an Insurance Official from Kittle, Bishopston, Swansea.

The Lodge name was selected in reference to Owain Glyndwr, a national hero and leader of Medieval Wales, whom the Welsh proclaimed 'Prince of Wales'. The Lodge Motto: *'Lux ex Tenebris'* (*'Light from Darkness'*) may also be interpreted as *'to establish enlightenment from ignorance'* or *'hope from despair'*.

At a Regular Lodge on 11 May 1981, it was announced that William George Cornfield (WBro 'Bill') had been appointed a Grand Officer with the Rank of PGADC. He, together with Squadron Leader W N Trimble, were the principal driving forces in the development of the Lodge, as well as being very active in Provincial Grand Lodge matters. It should be mentioned that WBro Bill had served with distinction at Arnhem as a Paratrooper in WWII.

The Lodge Banner was presented to the Lodge by WBro Richard Arnold Drew and was Dedicated by VWBro Geoffrey Malin Ash, TD, PGSwdB, DepProvGM, on 13 December 1982. The Banner depicts the legendry hero, Owain Glyndwr, together with the Lodge Motto. At the same Meeting, a wooden sculpture of the Lodge Logo was presented by WBro Bill Cornfield.

The Lodge is very much involved in 'Freemasonry in the Community' and each year selects 5 local charities to support.

Compiled by WBro Allan J Miles, PPrJGW, Secretary.

The Lodge of Sker
No.8024

Warranted : 10 March 1965

Consecrated : 9 November 1965

Meeting at the Masonic Hall, Porthcawl.

During the years 1961 to 1965, whilst the new Temple in Porthcawl was being constructed, some of the Freemasons in the area were thinking about forming a new Lodge. Venables Llewelyn Lodge No.3756, the only Lodge serving Porthcawl at this time, consisted of over 200 Members. With such a great Membership, Brethren had to wait several years to obtain their first Collar on their progress to the Chair of King Solomon. Another Lodge was needed, and the idea of forming Lodge of Sker was established.

There were 26 Founder Members, of which eighteen came from Venables Llewelyn Lodge. Eight Founder Members had occupied the Chair of the Lodge, whilst a further eight Founders had attained the Chair in other Lodges. The other Lodges were: Lodge of Fidelity No.6112, Cardiff; Afan Lodge No.833, Port Talbot; Margam Abbey Lodge No.5257, Port Talbot; Maesteg Lodge No.6805, Maesteg; Morganwg Lodge No.5084, Bridgend, and Shakspere Lodge No.1009, Manchester.

Unfortunately, one Founder Member, Bro Vivian Barder, did not live to see his ambitions for Freemasonry in Porthcawl fulfilled, as he passed away before the Consecration could take place.

On 25 November 1964, a Meeting of the Founders was held at the Seabank Hotel, Porthcawl. The Deputy Provincial Grand Master was present, and it was agreed that the new Lodge would be known as 'Lodge of Sker' and that the Petition should be presented to Venables Llewelyn Lodge. The Petition was presented to WBro Ben K Michaelson, WM of Venables Llewelyn Lodge, on Saturday, 5 December 1964, when it was duly signed by the Master and his Wardens.

It had been agreed that the first Worshipful Master of the Lodge would be WBro John C Ireland, in recognition of his work as Provincial Treasurer and Treasurer of several Lodges in the Province. The Senior Warden Designate was to be Bro Howard G Griffiths, who had not had the opportunity to progress in Freemasonry due to his professional vocation. The Junior Warden Designate was to be Bro Frank A Railton, who had spent many years in the former British Colonies and Dependencies. With many of these countries becoming independent, he had returned home and was now able to continue with his Masonic career.

One of the points made by the Founders, when agreeing the aims of the Lodge, was that only two Candidates would be Initiated into the Lodge each year, at the September Meeting. The Lodge has been fortunate, to date, in finding two suitable Candidates each year. The Founder Members also agreed that dinner suits and white gloves would be worn at all Regular Meetings. This practice is strictly adhered to.

The Lodge of Sker No.8024, whose Warrant was dated 10 March 1965, was Consecrated in the Masonic Temple, New Road,

Porthcawl. This had recently been completed and had been Dedicated by the Provincial Grand Master on Monday, 27 September 1965.

The Consecration took place on Tuesday, 9 November 1965, and was conducted by RWBro R P St John Charles assisted by his team of Provincial Officers. The Worshipful Master Designate was Installed by RWBro Edgar Rutter, DepProvGM.

Lodge of Sker was the last of 53 Lodges Consecrated in the Province by RWBro R P St John Charles. On 9 February 1966, the Rt Hon the Lord Swansea succeeded him as Provincial Grand Master.

The organising Secretary, WBro C Brian B Richards, ProvGStwd, carried out the research for the naming of the Lodge and in preparing the design for a Lodge Crest. He had been assisted by local historians and also by Professor Emeritus William Rees, who had held the Chair in Celtic Studies at University College, Cardiff. The accepted design for the Banner incorporates the escutcheons and armorial bearings of the Blundell family of Nottage Court, and the Porthcawl Urban District Council. The Blundell family and the Porthcawl Urban District Council both willingly gave their consent for them to be incorporated in the Lodge Crest design. The Crest design is also displayed on the Lodge Banner, which now hangs in the Porthcawl Masonic Temple.

A description of the Badge design is described thus:

'The oval is divided into one half Red (Gules) and one half Green (Vert). The red is derived from the arms of Herbert – anciently and for a long period Lords of the Pembroke Manor. The Green (Vert) is derived from the National Flag of Wales. The Anchor Blue (Azure) extends from base to chief centre with a circlet of escallop shells (Or). The shells allude to pilgrimage in Heraldry and this is relative to the ancient Grange of Sker, when in the possession of the Abbots of Margam and Neath Abbey. The circlet is taken from the badge allegiance incorporated within the new Coat of Arms of Porthcawl. The anchor is charged with a Masonic square and compasses (Argent). The square is in the form of chevron with a chevronell wavy, Blue (Azure) alluding to the seacoast of Sker. The crest is an eagle in Gold (Or) taken from the Arms of Blundell the present Lady of the Manor. The mantle is Argent and Azure, being the same design and form as the Coat of Arms of Porthcawl.*

The Motto: 'Hinc Lucem et Pocula Sacra' may be translated 'From this Source (we draw) Light and Draughts of Sacred Learning'

The first Regular Meeting of the Lodge took place on 21 December 1965. At that Meeting, twelve Joining Members and the first two Initiates were admitted. The Initiates were Mr Peter David Jones, a Lewis, and Mr Colin Phillip Thomas Treharne, whose Grandfather had been a Founder Member of Venables Llewelyn Lodge, the Mother Lodge. Unfortunately, Bro Treharne, a policeman, was killed in an accident whilst on duty, on Monday, 19 December 1966. This was the day before he was due to be Raised to a Master Mason.

The first Emergency Meeting of the Lodge was held on 24 October 1967, when Mr Christopher James Ireland was Initiated. He was the son of WBro John C Ireland, and had returned to Porthcawl from working in Canada. The Worshipful Master, WBro Howard G Griffiths, offered the Chair to WBro John C Ireland, who gratefully accepted the opportunity to Initiate his son into Freemasonry. Bro Christopher Ireland subsequently returned to Canada, and joined Ivanhoe Lodge No.142 in Edmonton, Alberta, where he was Passed on 17 October and Raised on 21 November 1968.

Following the Installation of WBro Henry Burnell in May 1971, WBro Colin S Preedy presented the new Lodge Banner to RWBro the Lord Swansea, for Dedication. The Ceremony of Dedication was then conducted by the ProvGM and his team of Provincial Officers, during which he addressed the Brethren on the Banner's design. At this Meeting, a letter was read from Lord Swansea announcing his intention of naming the new Chapel in The Albert Edward Prince of Wales Court the 'Edgar Rutter Chapel', after one of the Institution's most senior Trustees. At the time, RWBro Edgar Rutter had been DepProvGM for forty years. The Banner was paid for by the generosity of an anonymous donor, who gave £100 towards its cost.

At the Installation Meeting in May 1972, WBro Leonard L Protheroe was pleased to receive a Deputation from several distinguished Brethren, who wished to form a new Lodge in the Porthcawl area. They were anxious that the Lodge of Sker should

to hold two Festival Meetings each year.

Juventus Lodge was formed without any prior knowledge of the existence of the Kindred Lodges Association but, in 1989, Members became aware of a Festival Meeting in Cardiff, to be hosted by Sure and Stedfast Lodge No.8991. WBro Peter Dascombe of Juventus Lodge made enquiries with the Association and as a result Juventus applied to join and were unreservedly welcomed into the Association. WBro Peter was the driving force behind the Lodge's membership of the Association, and was the liaison officer for many years until his sad death in 2005. WBro Bob Voisey then took on that mantle.

Since that Meeting in 1989, Juventus has been privileged to host two of the Kindred Lodge Festivals. The first was in the Spring of 1994 and the second in the Autumn of 2006. In 2006, it coincided with the Installation of WBro Anthony Joss into the Chair of King Solomon. The Ceremony was carried out by the Installing Master WBro P Martin Smart. Over 125 Brethren, together with wives or partners, from around the country attended. As the majority of Brethren attending had been, or were still involved with youth movements, the wearing of uniforms was encouraged. As a result many Members wore Scout, Boys' Brigade or St John Ambulance uniforms. A celebratory cake was made by the wife of one of the Juventus Members, which was ceremonially cut jointly by WBro Stephen Gough, Chairman of the Kindred Lodges Association and the newly Installed Master of Juventus Lodge, WBro Anthony Joss. It was subsequently a very great honour for the Lodge to have received a letter from Her Majesty The Queen expressing her best wishes for an enjoyable occasion.

The Lodge has Sponsored two Daughter Lodges, Lodge of St Andrew No.8934, Warranted on 13 February 1980, and Oriel Lodge No.9023, Warranted on 11 November 1981.

The Lodge Banner was made and donated by Mrs Thelma Tagg, wife of the late Bro Graham Tagg and mother of WBro Huw and Brothers Jon and Ian Tagg. The Banner incorporates a hand holding a flaming torch surrounded by the Lodge Motto in Welsh and surmounted by the Welsh Dragon. It was Dedicated on 13 April 1992 by VWBro Geoffrey M Ashe, DepProvGM, accompanied by the complete Provincial team.

Juventus Lodge believes it is the first Lodge, and it may well be unique in this Country, to receive Dispensation for Mrs Jane Voisey, wife of WBro Robert Voisey, to sing the Master's song at the Festive Board following his Installation in October 2002. WBro Robert commented that it was the first time his wife had acknowledged or even admitted that he was the Master. Mrs Voisey has since sung it at subsequent Installations.

Juventus Lodge continues towards the future with its torch held high and its maxim *'Visions Not Dreams'* guiding its Masonic steps forward.

Compiled by WBro Robert J Voisey, PPrJGW.

John Hussey Hamilton Vivian
4th Baron Swansea
1925 ~ 2005

Provincial Grand Master
1966 ~ 1999

At the beginning of the nineteenth century, Swansea was a port and market town enjoying the prosperity of rapid industrial growth. Copper ores were brought at first from Cornwall, then North Wales and Ireland, then from Spain, Cuba and South America, to be smelted at Swansea. The town became the world centre for nonferrous metallurgy.

John Vivian of Truro (1750-1826) began his involvement in the metal industry acting as agent in Cornwall for the copper smelter, Thomas Williams, and the Cheadle Brass & Wire Company, purchasing copper ore from the mines in the County on their behalf and arranging for its shipment to smelting works in Swansea. He represented the Associated Miners of Cornwall, who had reason to believe that they were not getting full value for their ores from the South Wales smelters. Eventually, the Cheadle Brass & Wire Company set up its own smelting works in Penclawdd and, in 1800, John Vivian became one of the managing partners of the Penclawdd Works. He withdrew his interest from the Company in 1808 and, in the following year, established his own smelting works at Hafod, north of Swansea, going into partnership with his sons Richard Hussey and John Henry. Soon `Vivian & Sons' established itself as a major manufacturer of copper and, by 1829, was the second largest producer of copper in Britain, accounting for about 17 % of national output. By 1811, Vivian had returned to Cornwall to handle the purchase and sales of copper ore in Truro, corresponding weekly with John Henry, who managed the Hafod Works.

John Henry Vivian (1785-1855), was sent to Germany by his father, where he acquired specialised knowledge of metallurgy. He became the greatest authority on copper-smelting during the 19th century. Between 1840 and 1845, he

John Hussey Hamilton Vivian
4th Baron Swansea

developed and patented several smelting processes for zinc, gold, nickel, silver and cobalt. Elected a Fellow of the Royal Society, he was on intimate terms with the leading scientists of the day, including Michael Faraday and Sir Humphrey Davy. Between 1832 and 1855, he sat as MP for Swansea District. In 1817, he purchased the neo-classical villa, `Marino', which had been built in 1784 for Edward King, a Customs Official. He first added rectangular one-bay extensions to either side of the house and, in 1827, work commenced on re-modelling the house in the neo-gothic style, by which time it was known as `Singleton Abbey'. In 1919, the 2nd Lord Swansea sold Singleton Abbey to Swansea Corporation, who in turn sold the house and the nucleus of the estate to the University College of Swansea. Today, the buildings are used to house administration offices for Swansea University.

On John Henry's death in 1855, the management of the Hafod Works passed into the hands of his son, Sir Henry Hussey Vivian (1821-1894). He too studied metallurgy in Germany and in France. He developed a range of by-products from the copper-smelting business and introduced the 'sliding scale' of miners' wages after the strike of 1889. Henry Hussey Vivian served as MP for Glamorgan, 1857-1859, and Swansea, 1885-1893. It was largely due to his efforts that Swansea became a major industrial centre. By 1886, Vivian & Sons employed 3000 people, 1000 of them at the Hafod Works, where they produced copper in bars, ingots, sheets, tube, rod, bolts, circles, sulphate of copper, yellow metal and condenser plates. They also produced naval brass, ferro-bronze, lead ingots, spelter, silver, gold, sulphuric acid, zinc chloride and superphosphate fertilisers! Sir Henry Hussey Vivian was created a Baronet in 1882 and Baron Swansea in 1893. He was succeeded by his eldest son, Ernest Ambrose Vivian (1848-1922), 2nd Baron Swansea, on whose death, the title passed to his half-brother, Otto Richard Vivian (1875-1934), 3rd Baron Swansea, and father of the future Provincial Grand Master, John Hussey Hamilton Vivian, 4th Baron Swansea.

John Hussey Hamilton Vivian was born on New Year's Day 1925 and succeeded his father as 4th Baron Swansea at the age of nine. Educated at Eton, where he developed a talent for rifle shooting, he went up to Trinity College, Cambridge, to read French and German. On graduating, he worked for a land agent and devoted himself to running the family's 11,000 acre estate, Caer Beris, near Builth Wells, which his father had purchased in 1920. There, he bred Welsh mountain ponies, ran a shoot, had a pub and 1,000 yards of fishing on the River Wye. He sold the estate in 1966. He also worked for the publisher, Alvin Redman Limited, London.

Lord Swansea was an outstanding rifleman and a tireless worker for the sport within the National Rifle Association (NRA), of which he was Vice-Chairman, 1989-1992. A founder member, Vice-Chairman and then President of the British Shooting Sports Council (BSSC), an umbrella organisation representing the major shooting associations in the United Kingdom, he achieved international shooting honours for Great Britain and for Wales. Representing Wales, he won a gold medal at the Commonwealth games at Kingston, Jamaica, in 1966, and silver at Brisbane in 1982. He represented Wales 37 times in the short range National Match and 34 times in the Mackinnon long range. In addition, he won the Bisley Grand Aggregate in 1957 and 1960 and the Match Rifle Aggregate in 1971 and 1974, and competed in the Queen's Prize 18 times, coming second in 1958 and 1968. He was one of only five people to have captained their home nation and Great Britain in each of the big five World Championships - the National, Mackinnon, Kolapore, Australia and Palma. Lord Swansea was also an active Member of the House of Lords, until the hereditary peers were removed in 1999. He spoke on Welsh affairs, road safety, his beloved shooting and later, on Freemasonry.

Lord Swansea was Initiated into Alliance Lodge No.1827, London, (Erased 1977) in 1956 and was Installed as WM in 1962. He served as Senior Grand Warden of UGLE in 1965 and, on 9 February 1966, the Patent, appointing him Provincial Grand Master of South Wales, Eastern Division, was signed. His Installation as Provincial Grand Master took place at an Especial Meeting of Provincial Grand Lodge on Monday, 24 October 1966, held at the Sophia Gardens Pavilion, Cardiff. Provincial Grand Lodge was opened at 5.00 pm, and following the call of the Roll of Lodges, the MW the Grand Master, the Rt Hon the Earl of Scarborough, KG, accompanied by Officers of Grand Lodge, were received into Provincial Grand Lodge. RWBro the Rt Hon the Lord Swansea,

DL, PGW, was then duly Invested and Installed. VWBro Edgar J Rutter was once again appointed and Invested as DepProvGM, with WBros Harry F Stockwell and Harold Wilson as AProvGMs.

In the Royal Arch, Lord Swansea was Grand Superintendent of this Province from 1977 until 1999, and appointed Grand Scribe Nehemiah in Supreme Grand Chapter in 1974. While in the Mark Degree, he first held Office as GSW in 1975 and, from 1979 to 1999, was successively Assistant, Deputy and Pro Grand Master. He was Great Seneschal and a GCT in Great Priory and held high Office in the Cryptic, Red Cross of Constantine, Allied Masonic Degrees, Secret Monitor and Royal Order of Scotland.

Such was the Province's affection for him that the 25th Anniversary of his Installation was celebrated with a huge Festival, attended by the Brethren and their wives at Builth Wells. Lord Cornwallis, Pro Grand Master, presented him with an informal portrait, on behalf of the Province.

Lord Swansea served as Provincial Grand Master for 33 years, during which time the Province grew from 109 to 176 Lodges. The first Lodge he Consecrated was Danycoed Lodge No.8127, Caerphilly, on 25 November 1966. The last Lodge was Cwm Rhondda Lodge No.9692, Treorchy, Consecrated on 30 March 1999.

Lord Swansea resigned as ProvGM in 1999. His commitment and service to Freemasonry were recognised by the MW the Grand Master when, on 28 April 1999, he personally Invested Lord Swansea with his Order of Service to Masonry The citation for his OSM concluded with the words: *'For all this, he remains essentially a modest man, who combines reticence with aproachability and deservedly gains the affection of all those with whom he comes into contact.'*

John Hussey Hamilton Vivian, 4th Baron Swansea, died on Friday, 24 June 2005, at the age of 80, at St George's Nursing Home, St George's Square, Westminster, London. Lord Swansea's burial was a private one, and was followed by a Service of Thanksgiving at St Mary's Church, Builth Wells, on Thursday, 7 July 2005. A Memorial Service was held at St Margaret's, Westminster Abbey, on Thursday, 3 November 2005.

On 8 September 2010, The Lord Swansea Chapter No.8364, Sponsored by The Lord Swansea Lodge No.8364, was Consecrated at the Main Temple, Swansea. The 74 Founders were all Installed Principals, and over 160 Companions attended the Ceremony, which was performed by MEComp David Westall, ProvGSupt, and his Officers. MEComp John Taylor, PProvGSupt, was Installed as First Principal; EComp Michael Hoare, PDepProvGSupt, as Second Principal; and EComp Frank Langford, PProv Third Grand Principal, as Third Principal of the new Chapter.

Thus, Lord Swansea is commemorated in the Province by The Lord Swansea Lodge of Installed Masters, and The Lord Swansea Chapter of Installed Principals.

Compiled by WBro Peter M Davies, ProvJGW.

Danycoed Lodge No. 8127

Warranted : 14 September 1966

Consecrated : 25 November 1966

Meeting at the Masonic Hall, Caerphilly.

By the mid 1960s, the combined Membership of the two existing Lodges in Caerphilly, Henry Pendrill Charles No.3769, and St Ilan No.6624, was in excess of 250. Progress up the ladder in both these Lodges was, therefore, very slow. This resulted in a group of Brethren, led by the late WBro Trevor Llewellyn Rees, deciding to investigate the possibility of forming a new Lodge. Their labours were not in vain, and a meeting was called to further this idea, at which 23 Brethren attended with the intention of becoming Founders. An additional 11 Brethren who, due to technical reasons were unable to become Founders, became the first Joining Members.

During this formative period, Caerphilly Freemasons met in a building formerly known as 'Underwood House'. The Founder Master, WBro T L Rees, and some of the Founders lived in the area known as Danycoed. The Lodge name originated from a conversation between WBros T L Rees and L R Bailleux, both of whom lived in the vicinity, while walking to a preliminary meeting of the Founders. 'Underwood', translated into Welsh, is 'Dan-y-Coed' (Under the Wood), hence the new Lodge name was decided upon. WBro Trevor Llewellyn Rees also became known for his 'Danycoed' Ritual!

WBro Lambert Reuben Baillieux had been Initiated in Llangattock Lodge No.2547 in April 1946. He joined Lodge of St Ilan in 1948 and was Installed as Master in 1958. He was the Founder Senior Warden of Danycoed Lodge, became Master in 1967, and for many years he served as Charity Steward and as Preceptor of the Lodge of Instruction. In Province, he was appointed Provincial Grand Steward in 1964, promoted to PPrAGDC in 1965, PPrGReg in 1973 and to PPrJGW in 1979. In 1980, he became a Grand Officer with the Rank of PAGDC.

The Lodge Motto: '*Tragwydd Ein Gwaith*' which translated means '*Eternal Our Work*', was proposed by Bro E C Fry, and subsequently chosen.

On 14 June 1966, Lodge of St Ilan No.6624 was holding an Installation Festival with WBro Donald Lewis Lewis, WM, occupying the Chair. One item on the Lodge Summons was, '*To receive a Deputation of the Founders of a proposed new Lodge and to take any necessary action*'. WBro Harry F Stockwell, AProvGM, entered the Lodge and was greeted in the customary manner, and the WM then invited him to occupy the Chair. WBro H Gethin Davies was invited to occupy the Chair of SW, and

WBro J Powderhill to occupy the Chair of JW. The AProvGM then admitted the Deputation of Founders of the proposed new Lodge. The leader of the Deputation, WBro Trevor L Rees presented the Petition to the AProvGM, who then read the Petition to the Lodge and put the proposal to the Brethren of Lodge of St Ilan. The Petition was accepted unanimously. The AProvGM then outlined the next steps that would be taken and asked the Petitioners to be patient. Thus, Lodge of St Ilan No.6624 became the Sponsoring Lodge for Danycoed Lodge. The WM, WBro Donald L Lewis was then invited to resume the Chair and, as a Founder, was appointed the Acting IPM of Danycoed Lodge.

The Warrant was granted on 14 September 1966 and, on the 25 November 1966, Danycoed Lodge No.8127 became the first Lodge to be Consecrated by RWBro the Rt Hon the Lord Swansea, CStJ, DL, ProvGM, South Wales Eastern Division. He was assisted by RWBro Edgar J Rutter, OSM, DepProvGM, and the AProvGMs, WBros Harry F Stockwell and Harold Wilson.

Plans for a Lodge Banner were drawn up by WBro Donald L Lewis. The designs were taken to Hong Kong by Bro Edward T Griffiths, where a friend of his embroidered the Banner. Bro Ted Griffiths was a Quality Control Inspector at the Nantgarw BOAC Engine Overhaul Unit. He travelled extensively in the Far East and made many Masonic contacts there. The Banner was Dedicated at the 1970 December Meeting by WBro H F Stockwell, DepProvGM.

Earlier that year, the Lodge became the Sponsor of Hamlet of Van Lodge No.8334, which was Consecrated on 25 November 1970.

On the evening of WBro James Cartwright's Initiation in 1974, a number of Brethren from Rhetoric Lodge No.4265, Clerkenwell, London, led by WBro Jim's uncle, WBro Jack Jones, attended the Meeting. This resulted in regular fraternal visits between the two Lodges, which are still ongoing. When Rhetoric Lodge was experiencing difficulties some time ago, a number of Danycoed Brethren became Joining Members, with one, WBro Michael Howell, eventually becoming WM.

Through the auspices of WBro David Chugg, the Lodge has also formed a friendship with Cambrian Lodge No.464 at Haverfordwest. The Officers of Danycoed Lodge conducted the last Ceremony to have been held in the old Haverfordwest Masonic Temple.

Danycoed Lodge celebrated its 40th Anniversary on 19 December, 2006, when it was pleasing to have the company of the first Inner Guard, WBro Trevor Norman Beddoe, and an original Steward, WBro Gordon W Smith. Good wishes were received from the first Acting IPM, WBro Donald L Lewis OBE, who was on holiday in Australia. The first Initiate of the Lodge, WBro Edward G Bolton, was also present.

In 2008, WBro Anthony F Moore, MBE, was appointed DepProvGM of the Mark Master Masons Degree, and was promoted to Grand Lodge in 2009 with the Rank of PGOrg.

Compiled by WBro Dewi Aeron Davies, PPrJGW.

Newton Lodge
No.8261

Warranted : 13 November 1968

Consecrated : 24 January 1969

Meeting at the Masonic Hall, Porthcawl.

The Consecration of the new Porthcawl Temple, on 27 September 1965, prompted the Members of Venables Llewelyn Lodge to search for ways in which to utilize the new building. It was thought that there should be a new Lodge in Porthcawl. WBro Luther Protheroe and WBro Donald (Don) C B Comley were the prime architects for the formation of this new Lodge. They were supported by Members of Venables Llewelyn Lodge No.3756 and other Lodges from Penarth in the east, to Swansea in the west. Venables Llewelyn Lodge was to be the Mother Lodge and it successfully Petitioned Grand Lodge for a Warrant, which was granted on 13 November 1968. There were 20 Founders, of whom 9 were Past Masters. They included WBro E G Harding, PPrSGW, Installed WM of Venables Llewelyn Lodge in 1956, appointed Acting IPM; and WBro J A M Davies, PPrGW, Installed WM of Afan Lodge No.833 in 1964, Treasurer Designate.

Newton Lodge takes its name from the village of the same name. The village was well known to the late RWBro R P St John Charles, ProvGM, who had lived at Newton House for some thirty years, and also to RWBro Edgar J Rutter, DepProvGM, who had at one time maintained a summer residence in the village. At the centre of the village is the Church of Saint John the Baptist, which was established towards the end of the 12th century by the de Sandford family. An image of the church has been adopted for the Lodge Banner and also for the Logo on the front of every Lodge Summons. On the Lodge Banner is displayed the Lodge Motto *'E Comitate ad Pacem'*, which translates as *'Through Fellowship to Peace'*.

WBro Lancelot (Lance) D Bailey, PPrGW, who had been Installed WM of Clive Lodge No.6973 in 1951, was invited to be Master Designate. He was summoned by RWBro Edgar Rutter to the Provincial Office, where he was advised on the formation of the new Lodge. The procedures adopted in Edgar Rutter Lodge No.7196 were recommended as a template, as follows: (i) there should be no music other than that of the Opening and Closing Hymns, 'Fidelity' and the National Anthem; (ii) there should not be a response to the Toast to the visitors. Both these were adopted. The wearing of morning dress, with tail coats being worn by the Officers was another idea introduced by Lance Bailey, and has proved a worthy one. It lends dignity to the Ceremonies, and when the Brethren don their tails, it concentrates their minds and separates the Ceremonies from the everyday events of their lives. He also instituted the quick-fire given after Toasts, though today, not all Brethren like the practice, and it may prove to be one of the traditions that will be abandoned in time.

On Friday, 24 January 1969, Newton Lodge was Consecrated by RWBro the Rt Hon the Lord Swansea, DL, ProvGM, assisted by his Provincial Officers. They included RWBro Edgar J Rutter, OSM, PGW; WBro Harry F Stockwell, PGD, AProvGM; WBro Harold Wilson, PGD, AProvGM; WBro Rev Canon T K Brunsdon, PPrGW; WBro Malcolm H Thompson, PAGDC, ProvGSec; WBro Geoffrey M Ashe, TD, ProvDepGDC. Also in attendance were the Guildford Singers under the Direction of WBro E J Smith, PPrGW. Amongst the Founders and first Officers were: WBro L D Bailey, PGStB, WM; Bro Rev E A Munro Cape, SW; Bro G T Hannaby, JW; WBro Donald C B Comley, Chaplain; Bro David L Protheroe, Tyler. After the Ceremonies, a banquet was held consisting of grapefruit segments with crème de menthe, spring vegetable soup, poached salmon, wild pheasant with roast and boiled potatoes and vegetables in season, sherry trifle, cheese-board, coffee and fresh fruit all served with sherries, a different wine for each course, champagne for the Toasts, port and brandy.

This menu was replicated in 1993, when senior Officers of the Province attended the Lodge to assist in celebrating the Silver Jubilee Meeting. The Lodge was opened by WBro Vyvyan J Price, WM, who, after conducting the Lodge business and opening the Lodge in the Third Degree, invited WBro David L Protheroe, PSGD, to occupy the Chair. He had been Installed WM of Newton Lodge in 1975 and, in 1992, had been appointed AProvGM. A Third Degree Ceremony was then worked. Also present were VWBro Cdr Roy K Hopkin, DepProvGM; WBros Ken Adams Morgan and J Stuart Peters, AProvGMs; WBros Cuthbert L Summers and Samuel Northway, PAProvGMs.

At the Consecration of the Lodge, it was agreed that there should be no more Joining Members. However, some twenty years later, it was agreed that if sufficient reasons could be found, Joining Members would be permitted. Over the years, they have proved useful additions to the Lodge, and many have progressed to become Master.

In the early years the annual subscription was £12, inclusive of the cost of dining and wines. Initially, Members were restricted to one guest, whose name and address was given in advance to the Secretary. He then wrote inviting the guest on behalf of the Lodge. This did not last long; just think of the extra work for the poor Secretary. Beer was not consumed at the Meetings, and alcohol was restricted to sherry, wines, port and spirits associated with the various courses. Meetings finished by 10.00 pm, and most of those attending would retire to the Rock Hotel, run by Founder Member, Bro Idris Davies. Invariably, Bro Elwyn Jenkins, another Founder, would relieve every one present of their loose copper change. After a few years, this copper collection provided for the acquisition of the Lodge Banner.

Three of the Founder Past Masters were appointed Grand Officers, namely, the first Master, WBro Lancelot D Bailey, PGStB, in 1969; WBro Donald C B Comley, PAGDC, in 1975; and WBro Luther Protheroe, PAGSuptWks, in 1978. Also, WBro John Ireland, a Joining PM, who served as Lodge Secretary for many years, was appointed to PAGDC in 1971.

Bro David L Protheroe, Installed WM in 1975, became a Joining Member at the first Meeting. He was Initiated in Talygarn Lodge No.7216. He was appointed the first Tyler. In the Province, he progressed through AProvGDC then DepProvGDC before becoming ProvGDC. In UGLE he was appointed PAGDC in 1988. He also served the Province as AProvGM from 1992 to 1998 and was promoted to PSGD in 1993. His achievements are a matter of pride to the Lodge.

Another Past Master of distinction is WBro Noel O A Alleyn. He was Initiated into Newton Lodge on 20 October 1976 and was Installed as WM in April 1986. He laboured for many years in the Provincial Office and was appointed ProvJGW in 1995. In 1997, he became a Grand Officer with the Rank of PAGDC.

In 1989, the Worshipful Master, WBro W E Terence (Terry) Day, requested that in future, the Brethren should sing the Ode to Absent Brethren at 9.00 pm, every time the Lodge met. One week before the February Meeting, Terry collapsed, and he died on 1 March 1989. Sadly, he never heard his Lodge sing the Ode, and it is with poignancy that those who knew him, carry out his wishes at every Meeting.

Compiled by WBro Degary Nicholas Smith, PPrJGW.

Vivian Lodge No.8267

Warranted : 11 December 1968

Consecrated : 10 March 1969

Meeting at the Masonic Hall, Brecon.

For years the many Swansea Valley Freemasons only had the opportunity of joining and supporting Lodges in Swansea to the south, or Brecon to the north, and so the ideal was always to establish a Masonic Lodge in Ystradgynlais. Unfortunately, there are no records of the initial meetings towards the formation of Vivian Lodge but all those who were involved at the time certainly realised that WBro Tom Walters, an NCB Group Area Mine Manager, who had been Installed as WM of Brecknock Lodge No.651 in 1956, was really earnest in his endeavours to form a new Lodge in his home town. To this end, he sought the aid of several Brethren from various Lodges, all of whom readily pledged their support, initially in a search for a suitable building in which a Masonic Temple could be established.

A local Solicitor and Deputy High Sheriff of Brecon, Bro Roger Thomas, who was also keen on the idea, was enlisted to provide assistance, and he searched keenly for a building which could be readily converted into a Masonic Temple. Initial meetings were held in St Peter's Church Hall, Ystradgynlais, and St John's Ambulance Hall in Crynant, towards forming the new Lodge, with considerable assistance being received from the ProvGSec, WBro Malcolm H Thompson. He attended many of these meetings, advising the Brethren how to proceed but, unfortunately, with the passing of time, it became obvious that there was little likelihood of a suitable building being found in the immediate area.

The tacit approval of the MW The Grand Master to form a Lodge had been provided through the good offices of the RWBro the Rt Hon the Lord Swansea, DL, ProvGM, who had graciously consented to the use of his family name 'Vivian' as the name of the Lodge, and also the family Motto: *'Vive Anima Dei'*, *'Live by the Spirit of God'*, as the Motto of the Lodge.

In October 1968, a Petition was presented to the WM and Brethren of Brecknock Lodge by WBro Tom Walters for the Foundation of Vivian Lodge and to hold Meetings at the Masonic Temple, Brecon. However, this was seen as a purely temporary measure until suitable alternative premises could be found, preferably in Ystradgynlais. It received the wholehearted support of Brecknock Lodge.

It had been accepted that the Principal Officers namely the Primus Master, Senior Warden and Junior Warden had to be experienced Masons and the names of WBro Tom Walters, WBro Islwyn Evans, also PM Brecknock Lodge, and Bro Eurof

Daniel, PM Dyffryn Tawe Lodge No.6056, were readily approved. The remainder of the Founders came from a range of occupations - coal mining, the police, the ministry, teaching, shopkeepers etc.

On 10 March 1969, the Consecration of Vivian Lodge took place at the Masonic Hall, Cerrigcochion Road, Brecon, under the leadership of the Consecrating Officer, RWBro the Lord Swansea, ProvGM, who was assisted by his Officers, together with the Guildford Singers under the direction of WBro E J Smith. Immediately after the Consecration, the ProvGM Installed the Worshipful Master Designate, WBro Thomas Walters, as Master of Vivian Lodge.

Four Candidates and eight Joining Members were subsequently proposed prior to the Lodge being closed, and the Brethren adjourned to the Wellington Hotel for the Festive Board. There were 87 Brethren present. It had also been laid down by WBro Tom that the Wellington Hotel should be host to all Festive Boards and Ladies' Nights!

The Lodge benefitted from a number of gifts before and at the Consecration. Consequently, the Secretary wrote letters of appreciation to RWBro Edgar J Rutter, who had presented the Volume of the Sacred Law, to Bro Walter R Toomey for a Bible Cushion, to Bro W Wheldon for the presentation of both a Sword and a Poignard, and to WBro Stan Mayall for his gift of a frame for the Lodge Warrant. At a somewhat later date Bro Godfrey Thomas received a donation from Mrs Devereux in memory of her husband who had been PM of a Lodge in the South of England, and had frequently visited Vivian Lodge after returning to live in Ystradgynlais prior to his death. The Lodge decided to commission a Roll of Honours Board, as well as purchase Gavels and Wands from the donation. Later again, Bro Wyndham Thomas of Penrice Lodge No.4172, presented a cushion on behalf of his uncle, WBro John Morris of Lodge of St George No.200, Bermuda; and WBro Neville T Walters, an Honorary Member of the Lodge (PM Ithon Lodge No.3320, Llandrindod Wells), had cards printed for the Hymn to Absent Brethren, which he kindly presented to the Lodge.

The first Secretary was Bro David Pritchard, and with WBro Tom and great assistance from the first DC, WBro Lawrie J Hoggarth, set a standard both in the Temple and at the Festive Board, which delighted Lord Swansea. He became a frequent visitor as he lived not far away, in Builth. Tom would insist that Brethren brought visitors to the Lodge and if they failed to do so he would say to them, *'Wus, you haven't got a visitor so I want you to pay for one of the Worshipful Master's visitors – and that will teach you to bring your own visitor to our next meeting'.* Perhaps strangely, this approach worked and led the Members to enjoy their Meetings where attendances frequently exceeded a hundred. With Membership being only around thirty at the time, it now seems rather remarkable. On these occasions and at Installations when numbers well exceeded a hundred, the SW's Chair was moved forward onto the floor of the Lodge so that rows of chairs could be placed behind it. Tom was the first Craft Freemason in Brecon to attain Grand Rank and, so delighted were the Brethren that he had obtained just reward, they resolved to purchase his Grand Lodge Regalia for him.

The first two Initiates were Bro John Evans and Bro Mervyn Morgan, both of whom, unfortunately, did not progress to the Chair of King Solomon, but the third, Bro Alan Rosser Thomas became the first Initiate to be Installed in 1979.

WBro Islwyn Evans, also PM Brecknock Lodge, was a superb Ritualist and made floor work look smooth and elegant. His generosity to visitors was similarly outstanding and ensured visiting Brethren always wanted to come to Brecon.

WBro Eurof Daniel, Managing Director of Blythes, Swansea, President of Abercrave Rugby Club, was 'Mr Fixit', a provider of anything the Lodge needed. He was instrumental in bringing Vivian Lodge to the notice of Swansea Freemasons and very many visited as his personal guests, resulting in a number becoming Joining Members. A goodly number of Members were working for the NCB and so visitors tended to come from Lodges throughout South Wales.

WBro Tom insisted that the Lodge should meet four times a year and that there would be just two Initiates every year and so

Candidates waited up to five years to be Initiated during the Lodge's formative years. All incoming WMs would be presented with a leather bound Bible, and at the Installation Meeting new Master Masons would be Invested as Stewards and would be expected to take part in Ceremonies by learning parts of the First and Second Degree Rituals. This 'Rule' ensured that the Stewards participated in Ceremonies, enabling them to become more accomplished Masons by the time they reached a Warden's chair. It was also laid down that in a Third Degree Ceremony, the WM should always be assisted by a goodly number of PMs in performing the Ceremony.

It was instilled in the Brethren that as the Lodge carried the ProvGM's family name, Ceremonies and the Festive Board should be of the highest order and beyond reproach or criticism. Another of WBro Tom's original 'Rules' was that all the Brethren, not just the Officers, should wear dinner jackets. Our Charitable efforts should also be of the highest order and perhaps rather strangely, considering modern trends, Joining Members should not be encouraged! This was in order to maintain Membership at below 50! However, it must be admitted that in the period between 1960 and 1980, with no less than 48 new Lodges being formed in the Province, many Brethren became anxious that some time would elapse before they had the opportunity of attaining the Chair, and so multiple Membership of Lodges did become very common.

In 1970, the RWProvGM attended the November Meeting in order to Dedicate the Lodge Banner, which had been beautifully made by Mrs V James, wife of WBro Dewi James and daughter of WBro Tom Walters. The Banner depicts a squared pavement, flanked on either side by the two great pillars, on top of which are the celestial and terrestrial globes. In between the pillars, and above the pavement, is the Coat of Arms of Lord Swansea, and Motto. Below the pavement is the Volume of the Sacred Law on which is placed the Square and Compasses. The Banner Dedication Festive Board was held in the Wellington Hotel where there was a Provincial gunroom where all the hospitality was provided by the new Master. WBro Islwyn Evans would always offer two Stewards from Brecknock Lodge, Aneurin Rees and Bill Rees who would serve the drinks ensuring that the gunroom was a total success.

At the Master's own expense, the top table was provided with good claret, white wine, brandy, port and an ample supply of King Edward cigars. The Chief Steward, Bro Trevor Lewis, Director of Dan-yr-Ogof Caves, always had the duty to supply top table guests with their every need, and in distributing the cigars as was his wanton custom; should a visitor decline, he would place it in his handkerchief pocket for further distribution to his friends on other tables.

At another Installation, WBro Sam Francis, Group Electrical Engineer, NCB, and a preacher, had been too familiar with the AProvGM, WBro Cuthbert L Summers when he had addressed him as 'Cuthbert' in the Toast to the Province. Absolute silence prevailed, Sam's etiquette and powers of speech momentarily deserted him, and Tom was not amused.

For all those Brethren returning to Swansea after a rehearsal in Brecon it was the custom, especially during the formative years, to gather in Bro David Pritchard's grocery shop on the Cross in Ystradgynlais. There, gammon and bacon would be purchased to take home, a glass of whisky enjoyed and the evening's Meeting discussed. It was in Bro David's shop that the main business of the Lodge was conducted and where decisions were made as to who was the most promising Initiate to be encouraged to take an active part in a Ceremony- standards had to be maintained!

In 1980, WBro Alan Rosser Thomas Installed Jack Crowther, an NCB Area Mechanical Engineer, as his successor. He (and his late wife, Margaret on her Ladies' Night), had 'The National Coal Board Year' - their visitors coming from all over England as well as South Wales. They held a carol service and buffet in Ystradynlais, a Ladies' Festival in the Cimla Court Hotel, Neath, and a charity race evening at Craig-y-Nos, the former home of Dame Adelina Patti.

Rehearsals have been held mainly in the Masonic Hall, Brecon, and despite early intentions, Festive Boards have been held not only in the Wellington Hotel, but also at the Castle Hotel and the Bishop's Meadow Restaurant. Lodge Carol Services have been held in Trecastle, Ystalyfera and Sennybridge.

The Lodge had been well served by three outstanding Chaplains, namely, Canon Walter James, Canon Griff Lewis and Reverend Mostyn Thomas Williams, who remained for many years the principal after dinner speaker. Mention must also be made of Bro P Gwyn Davies, long serving Treasurer and Bro Richard Henry Jones and WBro David Buallt Jones for their significant contributions when they were Lodge Secretary. Unfortunately, during the 1990s, the Minute Book and records were destroyed in a flood. At that time, Bro Richard Henry Jones, Secretary, kept them at his place of work, the Mond Nickel Works, Clydach, where all the documents were contaminated by chemicals, making the compilation of the Lodge history that much more difficult.

Membership of the Lodge today comes primarily from two distinct groups, one from within and surrounding the Swansea Valley, and the other from the military fraternity surrounding the garrison town of Brecon.

The Lodge maintains a strong tradition of asking Brethren, should they so wish, to perform significant parts of the Ritual in the First and Second Degrees, continuing the original principles. Members still feel that it is an excellent way of gaining an insight into, and an understanding of, the Ritual. Keeping up the tradition established by WBro Tom. PMs continue to contribute greatly in the Third Degree, and they appreciate being involved. If any Lodge today is to continue successfully, Brethren should consider Tom Walters' words: *'Wus, don't tell me what you can't do for this Lodge, don't make excuses, tell me what you can do for this Lodge.'*

Compiled by WBro Alan Rosser Thomas, PPJGW.

The Master's Chair, Brecon Temple

527

Ynys Lodge No.8274

Warranted   :   12 February 1969

Consecrated   :   25 April 1969

Meeting at the Masonic Hall, Port Talbot.

During the 1960s, Freemasonry continued to expand in Port Talbot, in line with the economic growth of industry and commerce in the immediate area. The three established Lodges had large Memberships. Afan Lodge No.833 had 196 Members, Margam Abbey Lodge No.5257 had 181 and Baglan Lodge No.6079, had 146 Members. This resulted in a waiting period for perspective Members of up to six years, which was unacceptable. Senior Brethren were also mindful that RWBro the Rt Hon the Lord Swansea, DL, the ProvGM, was encouraging the formation of new Lodges to reduce the waiting lists of gentlemen wishing to become Freemasons. WBro Edgar M Abraham, PGStB, Secretary of Afan Lodge, with other Members of the Port Talbot, Neath and Swansea Lodges, consequently presented a Petition to Afan Lodge for the formation of a Lodge to be called 'Ynys Lodge'. Of the twenty-two Founder Members, fourteen were Members of Afan Lodge, three of Margam Abbey Lodge, two from Baglan Lodge and one each from Gnoll Lodge No.5057, Neath, and Old Goreans Lodge No.7193, Swansea. At the Regular Meeting of Afan Lodge, held on 2 January 1969, a Deputation of Founders was received, led by the WM Designate, WBro Edgar M Abraham. The Petition was duly signed by WBro Hakim M Sabir, WM, and his Wardens, with the unanimous support of the Brethren.

The Warrant of the Lodge is dated 12 February 1960. The Lodge was Consecrated by the ProvGM at the Masonic Hall, Forge Road, Port Talbot, on Friday, 25 April 1969. He was assisted by WBro John C Ireland, ProvSGW, as SW; WBro Neville T Walters, ProvJGW, as JW; WBro Rev Canon T K Brunsdon, PPrGW, as Chaplain; WBro Malcolm H Thompson, PAGDC, ProvGSec; and other Provincial Grand Officers. Also present were RWBro James Wilfred Stubbs, PGW, Grand Secretary; VWBro Edgar J Rutter, DepProvGM, and WBros Harry F Stockwell and Harold Wilson, AProvGMs. WBro Edgar M Abraham, PM Afan Lodge, PGStdB, WM Designate, was duly Installed as the first WM by the Grand Secretary. Bro W Leonard Stow was Invested as SW and Bro Leslie H Burnett as JW. At the first Regular Lodge Meeting, eleven Master Masons became Joining Members.

The original Banner and Logo were designed and made by Bro David R Morgan, the first Lodge Tyler. In 1982, a new Banner was designed and made by WBro George V Knowles, PPrAGDC, a Founder Member of the Lodge. This Banner was Dedicated by Lord Swansea at a Regular Meeting held on 26 February 1982.

The Lodge Bible was presented by VWBro Edgar J Rutter. The inscribed Square and Compasses were presented by WBro Edgar Abraham, first WM; the Lodge cupboard by WBro A Lyn Jenkins, first Secretary; Wands for the DC and ADC by WBro John K O'Leary, PM, in memory of WBro Maurice M L Watts, his father-in-law, and first DC of the Lodge. Bible markers were presented by WBro William H Ward, PM; Squares & Gavels by WBro Kingsley Bowden, PM; a Poniard by Bro Phillip M Abraham, the first Initiate of the Lodge; and a presentation box for the Working Tools by WBro M Davies and WBro G V Knowles.

Other than the Founder Members, there have been three Members who have become Grand Officers since the Consecration. WBro Dr Arthur Jones, PM, was appointed PAGDC in 1989; WBro M Davies, PM Afan Lodge, appointed PAGDC in 1994; and WBro J Anthony James, PM, appointed PGStB in 1999, and promoted to PAGDC in 2008.

Every Initiate is presented with a Masonic Bible at his Initiation. This tradition, inaugurated by the Founder WM still continues. The 25th Anniversary was celebrated in April 1994 and the Brethren present were given an engraved whisky glass. The 40th Anniversary was celebrated in April 2009, when all Brethren present received an Egyptian cotton table napkin, embroidered with an outline of the Lodge Banner.

The name of the Lodge, 'Ynys', is the Welsh word for 'Island'. Locally, it is the name given to a strip of land situated between Port Talbot and the adjoining village of Cwmavon, around which the River Afan and its tributaries flow, running their course through the old town of Aberavon, now incorporated in the County Borough of Neath and Port Talbot. The name has been adopted synonymously with that of the Sponsoring Lodge, namely Afan Lodge No.833. Leading in the direction of the Ynys and immediately adjacent to Forge Road, where the Port Talbot Masonic Temple is situated, is Ynys Street. Whilst no claim can be made to the name having any historical origin, Masonically quite a number of the Brethren of the local Lodge are actively associated with the Ynys Bowls Club which, again, is located on the banks of the River Afan and very near to the Ynys. Thus, it is more from a feeling of affection than tradition that the name 'Ynys' has been taken as the name of the Lodge, which is logical, bearing in mind that the three earlier Lodges meeting in Port Talbot are named after places of interest within the Borough, namely Afan, Margam and Baglan Lodges.

Compiled by WBro John K O'Leary, PM, PPrSGW, and WBro John Parrv, PM, PPrJGW.

The Senior Warden's Chair, Port Talbot Temple

Kenfig Lodge No.8289

Warranted : 30 April 1969
Consecrated : 20 June 1969
Meeting at the Masonic Hall, Porthcawl.

The formation of a new Lodge at Porthcawl in the late 1960s was the brainchild of the late WBro Squadron Leader D Alun Lloyd, DFC, DFM, PJGD, who was Secretary of the RMBI. As he was closely involved in the building of the Albert Edward Prince of Wales Court, his intention was to engender support for the 'Home' when it became operational. He therefore had to spread his influence further than the narrow confines of Porthcawl. He determined that this would be best achieved by forming a Lodge with a catchment area spreading from Swansea in the West, Pontypridd in the North, and Cardiff in the East – i.e. all within reasonable travelling distance.

Under the guidance and co-operation of WBro Harold Wilson, AProvGM, he approached Venables Llewelyn Lodge No.3756, whose committee agreed to Sponsor such a Lodge. A group of 26 Founders was formed, and it was determined that the Lodge be named 'Kenfig' – the name of an ancient local village. It was also determined that the Lodge would meet four times a year, in the months of March, June, September and November, with the Installation Ceremony being worked at the November Meeting.

Grand Lodge was Petitioned, and a Warrant, dated 30 April 1969, was issued for Kenfig Lodge No.8289. It had previously been accepted that the first Worshipful Master would be WBro Harold Wilson, AProvGM. The Senior Warden would be WBro D Alun Lloyd and the Junior Warden, Bro Dewi Matthews. Together, they selected their team of Officers from among the Founders, covering a wide territorial catchment area. WBro O B Jones, PM Cambrensis Lodge No.6608, was appointed to act as IPM.

The Lodge was subsequently Consecrated at the Masonic Temple, Porthcawl, on 20 June 1969 by RWBro the Rt Hon the Lord Swansea, ProvGM, assisted by RWBro Edgar J Rutter, OSM, PJGW, DepProvGM, and WBro Harry F Stockwell, PJGD, AProvGM, together with their team of Consecrating Officers.

A treatise of the historic village of Kenfig was compiled and delivered at the Consecration by WBro Rev Canon Thomas Kenneth Brunsdon, AGChap, who was also the Consecrating Chaplain. He took his extracts from, 'The Buried City of Kenfig', by Thomas Gray, 1909, and from 'The History of Margam', by Walter de Gray Birch, 1842-1924.

It explained that the ancient City of Kenfig lies buried beneath the sand dunes, three miles West of Porthcawl. Eight hundred years ago, it had been a busy commercial centre, having its regular weekly markets and two annual fairs. It had a navigable river and a large seaport, and was a military station and chartered borough, well governed by a portreeve and twelve aldermen elected by the citizens. However, the great storm of 1607 completed the burial of all of Kenfig save the castle.

The City had its Charter, of which the first is said to have been granted by Sir Leisan De Avene in 1158, which has been lost, though the Charter granted by Sir Thomas Despenser is still extant. The old form of local government, as established by the Despenser Charter, continued until 1886 in spite of sand and foe. However, under the Municipal Corporations Act, the ancient Corporation of Kenfig was at last dissolved, and a board formed to manage the burgesses' affairs.

The meeting place of the Trustees and of the Kenfig Parish Council is in an upper room of the old Guildhall (now the Prince of Wales Hostelry).

The Old Guildhall - The Prince of Wales Hostelry

This was once the seat of Government and is situated on a ridge to the east, out of reach of the sand.

Thus the name of the ancient City lives on and it was thought appropriate that it should also be perpetuated in the name of this new Masonic Lodge at Porthcawl.

Thus, the Lodge was able to be fully functional well before the official laying of the Foundation Stone of the Albert Edward Prince of Wales Court, which subsequently took place on 21 September 1970. The close association of the Lodge with the 'Home' was further cemented on the first week-end following its Official Opening. Two Lodge Members, namely WBro V C Warwick and WBro William J Northway, were appointed to escort groups of visitors on a tour of inspection of the new premises. At the Lodge Festive Board, a collection was made, and donated to the Matron's Social Fund. For the first few years, the Matron and her Assistant were invited by WBro Alun Lloyd to dine with the Brethren after each Regular Lodge Meeting (excluding Installation). Kenfig Lodge continues to support the 'Home' and to date all its Brethren are members of the Friends.

At a Meeting of the Founders, the following procedures were agreed to be adopted within the Lodge:
In the Temple:
1. When processing into the Lodge, the WM will be preceded by the DC who will bear a replica of the Mace used by the ancient Kenfig Borough Council (the original mace is kept in The National Museum of Wales). The Mace will then be placed on the WM's pedestal where it will remain until the WM leaves at the end of the Ceremony. To facilitate the carrying out of this procedure, the replica was made by WBro Horace Durbin of Venables LLewelyn Lodge, who presented it to Kenfig Lodge.
2. The candles will be ignited prior to the entry of the WM and extinguished after he retires from the Lodge.
3. The DC will cease perambulating after the Obligation and Signs.
4. After the first year, the IPM's Collar with Jewel and Apron will be handed down to succeeding Immediate Past Masters
Festive Board:
1. Only wine or spirits will be taken with meals and speeches.
2. Toasts will not be 'fired'.
3. There will be no response to the visitor's Toast, unless we are honoured by the presence of a Masonically eminent Brother.

The WM's Apron was presented to the Lodge by WBro Emrys J Davies, the first Senior Deacon, and the WM's Collar by WBro Graham Bowen (who was not a Founder but later became the Lodge Treasurer). At the end of his term of Office, WBro Harold Wilson was presented with a Past Master's Jewel. He then presented the Collar (with Jewel attached) and the Apron to the Lodge, with the request that it be worn by the IPM at every Meeting.

The wife of Bro Peter Fabian skilfully made the Lodge Banner. Apart from the Lodge name and number, the Banner carries the Lodge Motto: *'Where Concord Reigns'*, as well as the Lodge Crest, as used today.

The Kenfig Mace

The Crests used by the Lodge are shown above. The one on the right is that which was used at the start of the Lodge, and for four years afterwards. After that time, no Crest was used on Lodge Summonses until 1982. The Crest on the left is extracted from the Banner, which was taken and adapted from the original Seal of the City of Kenfig. It was drawn by WBro D E G Wild and was first used on the Summons for his Installation on 12 November 1982, and has been used ever since. It also appears on the Past Master's Jewel.

A set of Gavels was made by a friend of Bro J K Gordon Evans, the first Junior Deacon, who presented it to the Lodge even though he was not a Member. Shortly afterwards, Bro D E Graham Wild presented a wall-mounted display board, suitable for showing the names of Lodge PMs in chronological order.

At a later date, WBro Dafydd Geraint Puw presented a complete set of Working Tools for the Three Degrees, all being housed in a beautiful three-drawer wooden cabinet. This cabinet rests on a ledge to the left of the WM.

The Lodge has been fortunate in having had two Assistant ProvGMs from among its Members. These were, WBro Harold Wilson, the first Master of the Lodge, and WBro Samuel Northway, who was the sixth WM. Also, four other Brethren have received Past Grand Ranks. These are WBros Luther Protheroe, Donald Comley, William J Northway, and Gilbert Hutchings.

Compiled by WBro V C Warwick, PM, PPrSGW.

Hamlet of Van Lodge No.8334

Warranted : 10 June 1970

Consecrated : 25 November 1970

Meeting at the Masonic Hall, Caerphilly.

In 1969, nineteen Brethren agreed to support WBro Robert Cecil O Blundell, PPrAGDC, in forming a Lodge in Caerphilly. It was felt that another Lodge was required in the Caerphilly area to relieve the congestion in local Lodges. The Membership of the four existing Lodges in Caerphilly being 135, 121, 177, and 44.

The Founders unanimously agreed that the Lodge would be named 'St Barrwg's' after the Patron Saint of the 13th century church in Bedwas. The suggested name was duly submitted to Provincial Grand Lodge for approval, but it was rejected for two reasons. Firstly, a St Barruch's Chapter was about to be formed in Barry (Barrwg is the Welsh form of Barruch). Legend has it that St Barruch is reputed to have been a member of an early Monastic Order, which had been established on the island of Flatholm in the Bristol Channel, and therefore quite close to Barry. The second, and most important reason, was that St Barrwg's Church actually lay within the Masonic Province of Monmouthshire!

Further consideration, therefore, had to be given to finding another suitable and acceptable name. Three suggestions were proposed. The first was 'Porset', an area near Bedwas, but actually situated in the County of Glamorgan. The second was 'Rudry', a small village and parish near to Bedwas and Machen, but again in Glamorgan. Thirdly, 'Hamlet of Van', Van being a village on the outskirts of Caerphilly, in an area adjoining both Bedwas and Machen, and situated in Glamorgan.

The first two did not quite meet the original intention of the Founders, who wished to have a much stronger connection with the Bedwas and Machen areas. This paved the way to deciding on the name 'Hamlet of Van'. This name was subsequently submitted to Provincial Grand Lodge, who then approved it. It is believed that there is no other Lodge, under the Registry of the United Grand Lodge of England, with the prefix of 'Hamlet'! (In 1972, the villages of Bedwas and Machen were incorporated into the County of Mid Glamorgan.)

The Petition for Hamlet of Van Lodge was signed by the Master and Wardens of Danycoed Lodge No.8127, at the Regular Meeting on 21 April 1970. There were 19 Petitioners, including 6 Past Masters. The Warrant was granted on 10 June 1970, and the Lodge was Consecrated on Wednesday, 25 November 1970, at the Masonic Hall, Caerphilly, by RWBro the Rt Hon the Lord Swansea, DL, ProvGM, assisted by RWBro Edgar J Rutter, OSM, PGSwdB, PJGW DepProvGM; WBro H F Stockwell, PJGD,

The Columbarium, Van Mansion

AProvGM; and WBro Harold Wilson, PJGD, AProvGM. The Guildford Singers, under the direction of WBro E J Smith, PPrJGW, were also in attendance.

WBro Robert Cecil O Blundell, PPrAGDC, a Funeral Director in Market Street, Caerphilly, Initiated in Henry Pendrill Charles Lodge No.3769 in 1934, and PM St Ilan Lodge No.6624, was Installed first Master. The first SW was Bro Harold Wright (Senior) MM, a retired Valuer of St Martin's Crescent, Caerphilly, who had been Initiated in Emerald Lodge No.5907 in 1958. Terrence William John Hinge, MM, was the first JW. A Lecturer in Engineering, from Llantwit Fadre, he had been Initiated into Teifi Lodge No.4648, Cardigan, in 1955.

The Lodge Banner was presented by WBro R C O Blundell. It was Dedicated by WBro Harry F Stockwell, DepProvGM, and his Provincial Team, on 31 January, 1974. The centrepiece of the Banner depicts the columbarium, large enough to house a thousand doves, which has stood in the grounds of the Van Mansion for nearly five hundred years!

The Lodge Motto is '*Cyfeillgarwch ac Ewyllys Da*', which translated means '*Friendship and Goodwill*'.

Since 1972, the Lodge has enjoyed annual fraternal exchange visits with Royal Albert Edward Lodge No.906, which meets in the City of Bath. A party of 22 Brethren from the Bath Lodge first visited Caerphilly on 22 June 1972. The Caerphilly Brethren usually visit the Bath Lodge in April. The Worshipful Masters of the two Lodges are also guests at each other's Installation Ceremony.

Compiled by WBro M L Clarke, PPrGReg.

Breaksea Lodge
No. 8358

Warranted : 9 December 1970
Consecrated : 1 April 1971
Meeting at the Masonic Hall, Barry.

Consecrated on 1 April 1971 by RWBro the Rt Hon the Lord Swansea, DL, ProvGM, who was also the Installing Master, Breaksea Lodge has, like many others, weathered calm and choppy seas in its 40 year history.

The working plans for the Lodge began, of all places, in Port Talbot Docks, during a previously arranged visit to a submarine. WBro T B Jones, PPrAGDC, first Junior Warden, and one of only two surviving Founder Members, was the Manager of Barry Docks, and both he and another Founder were fortunate to be included in the official party visiting the submarine. It appears that, in conversation, they hit upon the idea of establishing a new Lodge in Barry, with seafaring connections …. 'the strangest things really do happen at sea', as they say. This occurred while they were in conversation with the submarine's Captain, who mentioned that to seafaring men like himself, seeing the light of the Breaksea Lightship always meant 'life'. Hence, the seed was both sewn and watered. That 'light of life' has been translated into the Lodge Motto: *'Goleuni yw Bywyd'*, or *'Light is Life'*. The Breaksea Lightship, anchored in the Bristol Channel, three and half miles south-west of Barry, made the perfect foundation on which to build. The concepts of 'life', allied to 'relief' from the ravages of their sea journey, are a few of the key tenets linking into Freemasonry.

The Lightship is named after Breaksea Point, near Aberthaw, in the Vale of Glamorgan. First established in 1866, it carries a white light which flashes every fifteen seconds, and is visible for some twelve miles. Its diaphone sounds one blast every twenty seconds, and its radio beacon transmits the letters B K. For sailors aplenty, the light clearly brought relief, safety and comfort, that once again, the crew were home among friends.

The Lodge Badge, which depicts the Breaksea Lightship in position at sea, was designed by the late WBro Norman H Andrews, an architect by profession, who was a Founder Member and first Organist of the Lodge.

Following much endeavour, the Lodge found a Sponsor in Vale of Glamorgan Lodge No.3977, with many of its Members becoming Founders. This common Membership has thrived for many years. These inspired Brethren, together with the late WBro Douglas Harries, held their first

planning meeting on 6 March 1970.

Sadly, of the Founders only WBro Tom Jones (now living in Canada) and WBro Vernon Holtam, PPrSGW, affectionately known as 'The Master of Masters', are still with us. Of the other stalwarts, there are a goodly number who merit a mention, amongst whom are WBro Godfrey Holtam, PGStB, and WBro Stanley Michael Mortimer, PGStB.

Without doubt Godfrey and his brother Vernon have been key protagonists in making sure the standards, ethos and culture that the Founders carved out for all to emulate have continued. From the attention to detail in Ceremonies and organisation through the 'Breaksea' way of holding wands, to the high standards of Ritual they predicated, their contribution has ensured the Lodge goes from strength to strength. So much so that today, it is usual for upwards of 20 Members to support LOIs, which is more than some Lodges get at Regular Meetings.

The Secretary's Bench

WBro Godfrey Holtam was Initiated into Vale of Glamorgan Lodge in 1952 and Installed as Master in 1963. He was appointed Secretary in 1967, a post he held until 1983. A Founder of this Lodge, he was Installed Master in 1980. He was appointed PGStB in both Grand Lodge and Supreme Grand Chapter in 1981. WBro Vernon was, like his brother, Initiated in Vale of Glamorgan Lodge in Nov 1960 and Installed as Master in 1970.

WBro Stanley Michael Mortimer was Initiated into Porthkerry Lodge No.6299 in 1956 and became Master in 1964. A Founder Member of this Lodge, he was Installed Master in 1981. He was also a Founder Member of the Provincial Grand Stewards Lodge. In 1987, he was appointed PGStB in Grand Lodge. Stan, together with his Masonic twin, W Bro Alvern Hart, PJGD, were inseparable at Breaksea as well as in other Lodges – some might say they were 'joined at the apron'. Without doubt, Stan's endearing influence, from his time as the first DC, has been mirrored through his son Jeff, who is the current DC. Stan's enthusiasm for Breaksea knew no bounds and was marked by the presentation of an 'Entered Apprentice' or 'Charity' plate to commemorate his memory. WBro Alvern Myron Murray Hart was Initiated into Porthkerry Lodge in 1961 and Installed Master in 1969. He became a Joining Member in 1992, was appointed PAGSuptWks in Grand Lodge in 1988, and promoted PJGD in 1999.

In more recent years, the backbone of the Lodge was WBro Ken Wright, PPrJGW, Secretary for 17 years, who sadly, passed to the Grand Lodge Above on 7 February 2005. Such was Ken's penchant for matters secretarial that the Members saw fit to have a Secretary's bench dedicated in his honour and placed in the Temple for all to appreciate and use.

Bro Haydn Burgess, PPrGStwd, has served two separate terms as Treasurer, amassing over 20 years of dedicated service and with more than 50 years as a Member of the Craft, Haydn has richly deserved his recognition. His dedication to Breaksea has few equals and his 'finger on the pulse approach' to our pennies has enabled the pounds to look after themselves.

WBro Wayne Grant Lewis, PPrAGDC, deserves mention, as his warm and endearing nature was perfect for the unofficial mentoring role he had within Breaksea Lodge. At LOIs, he fostered an environment of learning through commitment, and contrived to mix enjoyment with fun to inspire the rich cocktail that is Breaksea Lodge today. Such was his impact that even after his painful and tragic loss, the tradition he cemented continues. The Festive Board ideas he inspired are legendary - the copious servings of pickled onions, and soon to be new on the menu - spam sandwiches!

The future of Breaksea Lodge is in very safe hands, its light burns ever more brightly, just like the Lightship after which it was named. This nautical theme was further expanded with the Sponsoring of a Daughter Lodge, Lodge of the Seven Seas No.8693, Consecrated on 14 October 1974.

Compiled by WBro Kevin Hearne, PPrDepGDC.

The Lord Swansea Lodge No.8364

Warranted   :   9 December 1970

Consecrated   :   2 February 1971

Meeting at the Masonic Hall, Swansea.

Consecrated as 'The Swansea Lodge' on 2 February 1971 by RW Deputy Grand Master Major-General Sir Allan Adair, BT, KCVO, CB, DSO, MC, DL, The Lord Swansea Lodge No.8364 was the second Installed Masters' Lodge to be created in the Province, but based in Swansea. It was to complement Hendre Lodge No.3250, based in Cardiff.

In his oration to the Brethren at the Consecration, the RW DepProvGM spoke of the dedication of Past Masters committing themselves to Founding the Lodge when they had so many Masonic commitments already. He went on to talk about the name of the Lodge 'Swansea' – 'Never before has this honoured name been given to a Lodge. The place which bears this name is of ancient foundation; it has grown with the Industrial Revolution to become the second city of Wales. It is a community of very diversified economy, of culture, and of learning'. Completing his speech he commented 'this Lodge is founded on the best of bases; it is not to be a kind of club of or for retired occupants of King Solomon's Chair. It is to be a source of an inspiration through each member to Lodges in and around Swansea'.

The Sponsoring Lodge was Penrice Lodge No.4172. There were originally 114 Petitioners for the new Lodge, but shortly before the Consecration, RWBro Edgar J Rutter, OSM, PJGW, passed away, leaving 113 Founder Members, 12 of whom were Grand Officers.

The Membership of the Lodge rose swiftly to just below 200. It remained at around 200 Members until very recently, and has now risen to above 250 Members. The level of attendance is high, the Membership being drawn from Lodges as far north in the Province as Brecon, and as far east as Merthyr Tydfil. The majority of Members are Installed and Past Masters of Lodges in Swansea, Neath and Port Talbot. In 1976, it was agreed that Brethren from other Installed Masters' Lodges in the vicinity should be invited to the Lodge Ceremonies. Reciprocal arrangements have been established between Hendre Lodge, Cardiff; Charles Lyne Lodge No.2964, Newport, Province of Monmouthshire; and Dean Leigh Masters' Lodge No.3687, Hereford, Province of Herefordshire. Four representatives from Lord Swansea Lodge regularly attend the Meetings of these 'sister' Installed Masters' Lodges.

Lord Swansea's Coat of Arms and family Motto have been adopted for the Lodge Insignia. The Motto: *'Vive Anima Dei'*, may be translated *'Live by the Spirit of God'*. The Rt Hon the Lord Swansea was Installed as the first Master of the Lodge, and at the time, he was Provincial Grand Master of South Wales, Eastern Division. It was not until 1991 that the name of the Lodge was changed to 'The Lord Swansea Lodge'. The renaming of the Lodge is significant, not only because it was in recognition of the Lodge's strong affiliation with the Provincial Grand Master, but also because Lodges are seldom named after living Freemasons.

Offices in Lord Swansea Lodge are not progressive, which has allowed many Members to experience Office in the Lodge's short history. Until recently, the Chair of the Lodge was restricted to Grand Officers, who were nominated for election according to a formula which is a closely guarded secret. Past Masters of the Lodge include two Past Provincial Grand Masters, and three Past Deputy Provincial Grand Masters. A full list of Past Masters and their Mother Lodges is given below.

In addition to Installing Members of the Provincial Executive as Masters of The Lord Swansea Lodge, the Provincial Grand Master, Lord Swansea, chose to use Lodge Meetings to Invest Members of his Executive. In April 1976, VWBro Geoffrey Ashe was Invested as DepProvGM, and WBro Cuthbert Summers, PSGD, as AProvGM. In November 1982, WBro Samuel Northway was Invested as AProvGM, and in November 1984, VWBro J Stuart Peters received his first Executive Collar of AProvGM.

Meeting twice a year in the Masonic Hall, Swansea, the Election Night Meeting, which is held on the second Friday in April, traditionally plays host to a variety of lectures and demonstrations. An enactment of the Russian Initiation Ceremony has been performed by a group of Brethren, which included Members of the Lodge. Several presentations were given by WBro Malcolm Thompson, PSGD, ProvGSec, 1967-1980, including one in 1996 on 'The first 25 years of The Lord Swansea Lodge'. More recently, a lecture 'Freemasonry on the Internet', was given by WBro Julian Rees, PPrAGReg, outlining how Brethren are using the electronic age to further their Masonic education.

Looking ahead, The Lord Swansea Lodge will be celebrating its 50th Anniversary in 2021, when it is hoped it will still be a source of inspiration, through its Members, to Lodges in and around Swansea.

Past Masters of The Lord Swansea Lodge

Year	Name	Lodge
1970	RWBro the Lord Swansea, ProvGM, PGSupt	Old Etonian Lodge No.4500
1971	RWBro the Lord Swansea, ProvGM, PGSupt	Old Etonian Lodge No.4500
1972	WBro Stammers H Alabaster, PJGD	Indefatigable Lodge No.237
1973	VWBro Harry F Stockwell, PDepProvGM	Penarth Lodge No.4113
1974	WBro Wilfred Porter, PAGDC, PProvGM (Mark)	Beaufort Lodge No.3834
1975	WBro Llewellyn G Bevan, PAProvGM, PDepGSupt	Talbot Lodge No.1323
1976	WBro E Rhodri Harries, PAGReg	Penllergaer Lodge No.5567
1977	WBro Malcolm H Thompson, PProvGSec, PProvGM (Mark)	Beaufort Lodge No.3834
1978	WBro Frank A Henshall, PPGW	Glan Tawe Lodge No.5378
1979	WBro Kenneth H Robinson, PPGW	Margam Abbey Lodge No.5257
1980	WBro Henry Harries, PPGW	Cambrian Lodge No.364
1981	WBro Leonard D Matthews, PPGW	Corinthian Lodge No.4917
1982	WBro Rev Canon T Kenneth Brunsdon, PDepGChap	Teme Lodge No.4267, Shropshire
1983	WBro Frank Newbury, PPGDC	Caradoc Lodge No.1573
1984	WBro Harold Wilson, PAProvGM	Loyal Commercial Lodge No.2720

1985	VWBro J Stuart Peters, PDepProvGM	Ionic Lodge No.6626.
1986	WBro George Challenger, PPGD	Indefatigable Lodge No.237
1987	WBro C Aubrey Macnamara, PProvAGDC	Corinthian Lodge No.4917
1988	WBro Peter C A Griffin, PProvGD	Beaufort Lodge No.3834
1989	WBro D Hedley Williams, PProvGD	Gnoll Lodge No.5057
1990	VWBro Geoffrey Malin Ash, PDepProvGM	Llanfair Lodge No.7353
1991	WBro Kenneth Adams Morgan, PAPGM	Loyal Cambrian Lodge No.110
1992	WBro Cuthbert L Summers, PAProvGM	Glamorgan Lodge No.36
1993	WBro Islwyn Evans, PJGD	Brecknock Lodge No.651
1994	WBro Gerald Williams, PAGDC	North Glamorgan Lodge No.4055
1995	WBro Lewis Rees, PAGDC	Ionic Lodge No.6626
1996	WBro Thomas H C Quick, PProvAGDC	Dyffryn Tawe Lodge No.6056
1997	WBro D Gwilym Edwards, PGStB	Fforest Lodge No.2606
1998	WBro Peter Glyn Williams, ProvGSec (Mark)	Tuscan Lodge No.7267
1999	WBro B Gwynfryn Hardwidge, PAGDC	Dyffryn Tawe Lodge No.6056
2000	WBro Michael J Hoare, PDepGSupt	Glantawe Lodge No.5378
2001	RWBro Hywel Davies, PProvGM	Aberpennar Lodge No.6354
2002	WBro Brian G Matthews, PAGDC	Windsor Lodge No.1754
2003	WBro Dudley R Brown, PAGSuptWks	Ionic Lodge No.6626
2004	WBro Leonard I Trott, PAGDC	Penllergaer Lodge No.5567
2005	WBro Paul R Clement, ProvGM (Mark)	Corinthian Lodge No.4917
2006	WBro Charles W Penny, PGStB	Corinthian Lodge No.4917
2007	WBro Jeffrey Parry Thomas, AProvGM	Gnoll Lodge No.5057
2008	WBro Andrew McCutcheon, Second Prov Grand Principal	Gnoll Lodge No.5057
2009	WBro Rev Norman Lea, PAProvGM	Aberhonddu Lodge No.8588
2010	WBro E Geoffrey Jenkins, PGStB	Glantawe Lodge No.5378
2011	WBro John H T Aylward, PGStB	Indefatigable Lodge No.237

Compiled by WBro Julian Rees, PPrAGReg.

Croeso Lodge No.8377

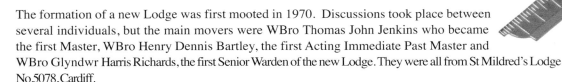

Warranted : 10 February 1971

Consecrated : 23 June 1971

Meeting at the Masonic Hall, Cardiff.

The formation of a new Lodge was first mooted in 1970. Discussions took place between several individuals, but the main movers were WBro Thomas John Jenkins who became the first Master, WBro Henry Dennis Bartley, the first Acting Immediate Past Master and WBro Glyndwr Harris Richards, the first Senior Warden of the new Lodge. They were all from St Mildred's Lodge No.5078, Cardiff.

They were joined by WBro Donald Thomas Richmond, a Past Master of Carmel Lodge No.4774, who became the first Secretary; WBro Charles Kitchener Manley, PM Lodge of Amity No.5823, who became the first Director of Ceremonies; and several other Master Masons from various other Lodges who went on to become Officers at the Inaugural Ceremony. Discussions continued throughout the year and the final arrangements were made at a meeting held in the Globe Hotel in Cardiff on 8 October 1970. By this time, agreement had been reached that the name of the new Lodge should be 'Croeso' and St Mildred Lodge No.5078 would be the Sponsoring Lodge.

The application was duly sent to the Provincial Grand Secretary on 20 January 1971 with the following proposed objectives:

(1) To further the principles of Freemasonry in general and particularly in this Province.

(2) To enable Master Masons to progress to the Chair of King Solomon in a reasonable time.

(3) As friendship is such a vital Masonic principle, a small Lodge would enable all the Brethren to know each other and thus promote goodwill.

The Founders resolved to strive for quality in the Ceremonies, quality at the Festive Board, and above all, to offer a quality welcome to the visitors. Hence, the name of the Lodge 'Croeso', being the Welsh word for 'Welcome', it was hoped that it would reflect one of the most important Principles of Freemasonry, that of Friendship. The Welsh influence continues in the design of the Lodge Crest, which shows the name of the Lodge together with the traditional Square and Compasses over a depiction of the Welsh Dragon.

Happily, the application was accepted and on the 23 June 1971, Croeso Lodge No. 8377 was Consecrated by the then Provincial Grand Master, the RWBro the Lord Swansea and his Officers. WBro Thomas John Jenkins was then Installed as Founder Master.

At the beginning there were 24 Members. The Membership increased steadily to 44 in 1981 to a peak of 50 Members in 1992 on the occasion of the 21st Anniversary of the Lodge. It was decided to celebrate this Anniversary with a Ceremony, where the surviving Founder Members who were still active and regular participants in the life of the Lodge, would be presented with a token of the Members' gratitude. Accordingly, 7 gold rings were commissioned, each with a Masonic blue centre bearing the initial C for Croeso. The Past Masters performed the Ceremony, splitting the larger sections into several parts and taking the floor in groups of three to deliver the Ritual. A commemorative brochure was produced to mark the occasion. The seven commemorative rings were presented to:

WBro Thomas John Jenkins, Founder Master,

WBro Glyndwr Harris Richards, Founder Senior Warden,

WBro Eric John Cross, Founder Senior Deacon,

WBro Donald Thomas Richmond, Founder Secretary,

WBro Francis Thomas Griffiths, Founder Steward,

WBro Vivian Hill, Founder Steward,

Founder's Ring

WBro Charles Kitchener Manley, Founder Director of Ceremonies.

They became known as Founders' Rings and remain the property of Croeso Lodge, to be passed on to Past Masters in order of seniority. As a result, when WBro T J Jenkins, (known as Jack) passed on in January 1994, his Ring was presented to WBro Gary Frederick Cooper, who was Initiated in 1973 and was the first Initiate to attain the Chair of King Solomon. Similarly, when WBro Glyn Richards died in February 1994, his Ring was passed on to WBro Malcolm Harry Argyle PPrJGW, who had been Initiated in 1975, and when WBro C K Manley died in February 1996, his Ring was passed on to WBro Colstan Arthur Hicks, PPrAGDC, who had been Initiated in 1977.

Since then, WBro Francis Griffiths resigned in October 2002 and, likewise, WBro Gary Cooper in December 2006. WBro Eric John Cross passed to the Grand Lodge Above in November 2004, as did WBro Donald Thomas Richmond in February 2006. No doubt, another ceremony will be arranged in the not too distant future to present the Founders' Rings to their new custodians.

In December 2009, WBro Vivian Hill, PPrJGW, Founder Steward, passed to the Grand Lodge Above at the age of 73. An Insurance Broker by profession, he was Initiated in Duke of York Lodge, No.2453 in December 1960 and was Installed Master of that Lodge in 1974. In Province, he had been promoted to the Rank of PPrJGW in 1989.

WBro Roger F Richmond, son of the late WBro Donald Thomas Richmond, (Founder Secretary), was Installed WM in 1990 and in 2005 he became the first, and so far, the only Member of the Lodge to be appointed a Grand Officer. He joined Carmel Lodge No.4774 in 1999 and was WM of that Lodge in 2001 and 2002. He became a Joining Member of Llangattock Lodge No.2547 in 2005. In Provincial Grand Lodge, he was appointed Provincial Grand Steward in 1986 and promoted to PPrJGW in 1999, before serving as Provincial Junior Grand Warden in 2003. In 1999, he was the Secretary of the Events Committee for the 1999 Festival in aid of 'The New Masonic Samaritan Fund'. More recently, WBro Roger was the Secretary of the 2010 Festival in aid of the 'Freemasons' Grand Charity'. He became a Grand Officer, with the Rank of PAGDC in 2005 and was promoted to PJGD in 2011.

One tradition that has lasted over the years is the arrangement whereby the Master of St Mildred Lodge, the Mother Lodge of Croeso Lodge, is invited as a non-paying guest to attend the Installation of each new Master of Croeso Lodge. This arrangement is reciprocated by St Mildred Lodge.

Over the years, Croeso Lodge has enjoyed good attendance, in spite of the numbers falling to a total of 37 today (January 2011). Optimism remains high and prospects for the future seem good.

Compiled by WBro Andrew Davies.

Henry Francis Stockwell
1899 – 1977
ProvGSec 1944 – 1953
AProvGM 1953 – 1971
DepProvGM 1971 – 1977

Henry (Harry) Francis Stockwell was born on 19 December 1899 and spent the first few years of his life at 83, Splott Road, Adamsdown, Cardiff. His parents were from Gloucestershire. Father, William Edward Stockwell, was a Domestic Coachman from Blakeney, and mother, Lena Alice, came from Olveston. They had three children, all boys and Harry was the youngest member of the family. His grandfather, George Stockwell, originally from Cheltenham, was also a Coachman.

In 1925, Harry married Alice David, a daughter of Jonah David, Head Gamekeeper, from Llandough. He was an employee of Edgar John Rutter, who had a Shipping/Coal Exporting Business in Cardiff Docks.

In February 1933, Edgar Rutter opened the first Provincial Office in Guildford Street, Cardiff, part of the Cardiff Masonic Hall premises, and in 1944 Harry Stockwell was appointed Provincial Grand Secretary, a position he was to hold until 1953.

Harry was Initiated into Penarth Lodge No.4113 in June 1921 and he became Worshipful Master of the Lodge in 1932. The previous year he had become a Founder Member of Sapphire Lodge No.5290. When Observer Lodge No.6015 was Consecrated on 11 January 1945, Harry was Installed as the first Worshipful Master. He joined Hendre Lodge No.3250 in 1931, became Lodge Secretary in 1934 and had the privilege to be Installed WM of Hendre in January 1951.

In Province, he was appointed Provincial Grand Steward in 1938, Provincial Grand Treasurer in 1939, Provincial Assistant Grand Secretary 1940-1944 and Provincial Grand Secretary in 1944. He became a Grand Officer in 1945 with the Rank of PAGDC and in 1954 he was promoted to PGD.

He was the Consecrating Officer of Doric Lodge No.5968, Consecrated 12 June 1944 and an Honorary Member of several Lodges, including Doric; Dinas Powis Lodge No.5997; Lodge of Unity No.6030; Duffryn

Henry Francis Stockwell

Tawe Lodge No.6056; Baglan Lodge No.6079 and Lodge of St Illtyd No.6078.

With the Consecration of Lodge of Benevolence No.7305 on 21 September 1953, the 100th active Lodge in the Province, RWBro R P St John Charles, ProvGM, was entitled to appoint two Assistant Provincial Grand Masters. The Provincial Grand Master having been Installed WM of the new Lodge, proceeded to Invest WBros Edgar Lewis and Harry F Stockwell as his Assistants, before appointing and Investing the Officers of the Lodge. Harry was a Founder Member of Lodge of Benevolence and in 1958, as WM of the Lodge, he had the honour of receiving the MW the Grand Master, the Rt Hon the Earl of Scarborough, to an Emergency Meeting on 8 April 1959. The occasion was to mark R P St John Charles's 21st year as Provincial Grand Master. Further details of this important event are to be found in the history of the Lodge of Benevolence.

Harry was also a Founder Member of Lodge of Progress No.7928, which was Consecrated on 30 September 1963.

As a senior member of the Provincial Executive, Harry Stockwell Dedicated several Lodge Banners: Morganwg Lodge No.5084 in 1964; Aberpennar Lodge No.6354 in January 1965; Danycoed Lodge No.8127 in December 1970 and Hamlet of Van Lodge No.8334 in January 1974 to name but a few.

Edgar John Rutter, DepProvGM, died in June 1971. Soon afterwards, RWBro the Rt Hon the Lord Swansea, ProvGM, appointed WBro Harry Stockwell as his Deputy. Also in 1971, he was appointed Grand Superintendent of the Eastern Province of South Wales, an Office he held until his death in 1977. He had been Exalted in Tennant Chapter No.1754 in 1928 and was First Principal of that Chapter in 1937 (the Jubilee year of the Chapter). In 1939, he had been appointed Provincial Grand Director of Ceremonies and in 1945 received the appointment of PGStB in Supreme Grand Chapter.

In 1973, Harry Stockwell became the 4th Worshipful Master of The Lord Swansea Lodge No.8364. The following year, he was Installed WM of Edgar Rutter Lodge No.7196. Also in 1974, he was promoted to the Rank of Past Grand Superintendent of Works, which afforded him the prefix 'VWBro'.

VWBro Harry Stockwell died suddenly on 8 February 1977. The announcement of his death was published in 'The Western Mail' on Thursday, 10 February:

'STOCKWELL - Suddenly on February 8, Henry Francis (Harry) of 4 Pencisely Rise, Llandaff, Cardiff (Steward of Llandaff Cathedral), beloved husband of Alice, devoted father of Gerald, loving father-in-law of Jean and dearest grandfather of Jane and Debbie. Funeral service at Llandaff Cathedral, February 11 at 9.45 am; afterwards, gentlemen only at Thornhill Crematorium. Family flowers only. Donations, if wished, may be sent to Malcolm Thompson, Masonic Benevolent Fund, 7 Guildford Street, Cardiff.'

The Province decided that the late Henry Francis Stockwell should be commemorated by the refurbishment of the St Dyfrig Chapel, at Llandaff Cathedral. According to tradition, a Christian community was established by Saint Dubricius (St Dyfrig in Welsh) at a ford on the River Taff. The first church on the site was founded by St Dyfrig's pupil and successor, Saint Teilo. These two are regarded as the Cathedral's Patron Saints, along with their successor Oudoceus (St Euddogwy in Welsh). In 1980, a Service of Dedication took place in the St Dyfrig Chapel, and a brass plate across the floor of the Chapel records:

'St Dyfrig's Chapel was refurbished in 1979 by the Freemasons of South Wales (ED) In Memory of V.W.Bro. Harry Stockwell, Past Grand Superintendent of Works & Deputy Provincial Grand Master.'

Compiled by WBro Peter M Davies, ProvJGW.

Singleton Lodge
No.8399

Warranted : 8 September 1971

Consecrated : 15 November 1971

Meeting at the Masonic Hall, Swansea.

The first Master, WBro Leonard Cecil Goss, was a Journalist by profession, who for many years had served on the staff of the South Wales Evening Post, Swansea's local daily paper. He was a man of many parts being, for example, well known in the area for the hospitality and assistance which he and his wife extended to the many foreign students who came to study at the University. He was a member of Glantawe Lodge No.5378, and served as Worshipful Master in 1969. Around this time, he left the Evening Post and took up a position as Press Officer of the University College of Swansea. It was he who conceived the idea of forming a Lodge to serve the various academic establishments in the town. A preliminary meeting of interested Brethren was held and the decision was taken to Petition for a Warrant for a new Lodge. The Warrant was eventually granted on 8 September 1971.

It had originally been suggested that the new Lodge be called 'Colleges Lodge'. Apparently, Province was not too keen on this name, since it was rather similar to the name 'Universities Lodge', which was already in existence in Cardiff. It will be recalled that the University at Swansea is built around Singleton Abbey, which at one time had been the home of the Vivian family, the Lords Swansea, until they left the town in 1919. John Hussey Hamilton Vivian, the 4th Lord Swansea, had become Provincial Grand Master in 1966, and it seems that he expressed a wish that the new Lodge should be named 'Singleton' Lodge, thereby combining references to the University and to his own family's connection with the area.

Singleton Lodge No.8399 was Consecrated by RWBro the Rt Hon the Lord Swansea, DL, ProvGM, on Monday, 15 November 1971. It seems that up to that time, his Lordship had never set foot in his family's ancestral home at Singleton; consequently, Len Goss arranged for him to have a guided tour of the old house. Lord Swansea found it a very interesting and nostalgic experience, but he expressed his great delight and relief that he was no longer responsible for the upkeep of that great roof! In 1975, WBro Goss, a Jewish Brother, left Swansea for London, where he took up an important post with The Council for Christians and Jews. He kept up his connection with the Lodge, visiting from time to time as his duties permitted, until his death in 1985.

After much discussion in the early days, the Lodge Committee decided upon a Badge for the Lodge, the design of which was approved by the Provincial Grand Master. The Motto which was adopted was *'Ad Unam Omnes'* which translates as *'One for All'*. This is a highly proper Motto for an organisation which promotes the idea of fraternity and unity, but many Brethren felt at the time that perhaps it had a bit of an echo of the 'Three Musketeers' about it !

At first, various items of Lodge furniture required for the Ceremonies were borrowed from the Mother Lodge, Glantawe. Officers' Collars had already been donated to the Lodge by the Brethren who served in the various Offices during the first year. A beautiful set of Gavels, made out of brass and mahogany, with inset symbols of the WM and the Wardens had been made and presented to the Lodge by Bro George Strickland. In November 1973, the decision was taken to purchase a full set of Working Tools and various other required items. The Lodge was thus now fully equipped, save for the fact that as yet it had no Masters' Board and no Banner - both rather expensive items for a new small Lodge to acquire. Fortunately, the Lodge was presented with a Masters' Board in the late 1970s, through the much appreciated generosity of two Lodge Brethren, Bros T Alfred Stacey and Gerald K Thomas. They were partners in a local firm of builders, and they had undertaken the construction of the Board at their own premises.

The Banner took rather longer to acquire. During the late 1970s, earnest discussions took place as to the prospect of obtaining one, but nothing happened, Banners being very expensive items. However, in 1989, the Lodge was extremely fortunate to be presented with a Banner made by Mrs Judith Holloway, the wife of Lodge Member, Clive Holloway. The Banner was Dedicated by WBro Ken Adams Morgan, AProvGM, with the assistance of WBro the Rev Norman Lea, at an Emergency Meeting held on 30 October 1989. The Banner now hangs above the Worshipful Master's Chair at every Lodge Meeting, and the Lodge records once again its gratitude to Judith Holloway for her generosity.

Memorable events have been the Church Services, held from time to time during the summer recesses. In the early days, these were held at St Peter's Church, Newton, Swansea, where WBro Rev Canon Kenneth Brunsdon, DepGChap, first Singleton Lodge Chaplain, was the incumbent. After the Service, the Brethren would assemble at the nearby vicarage for pre-lunch drinks served by Mrs Essie Brunsdon, and would then proceed to a nearby hotel for lunch. After the Canon's retirement from St Peter's Church, services were held for a number of years at St Paul's Church, Sketty, and on one occasion at St Mary's Church, in central Swansea.

Over the years, social functions, such as Sunday lunches and Ladies' Evenings, have been held at various hotels and hostelries. Popular features of Lodge activities in the early days were the weekend hotel breaks taken at locations in West Wales, including Saundersfoot, St David's and Aberystwyth. Christmas parties have also been arranged for the children and grand-children of the Brethren, at which Father Christmas has never failed to put in an appearance!

Since the Lodge was Consecrated, two Brethren have achieved the distinction of 50 years' Membership of the Craft. Canon Brunsdon reached this landmark in 1990, and a reception was held at the Ivy Bush Hotel in Carmarthen to mark the event. On 12 January 2005, WBro Adrian J Williams, PPrJGW, Founder Senior Warden, also reached the half-century. At the Regular Meeting of the Lodge in March of that year, WBro Anthony Peter Wardle, PGStB, presented him with a certificate on behalf of the Province, and a further gift was presented to him from all the Brethren in the Lodge.

WBro A P Wardle was Initiated into Bexhill Lodge No.4898 in 1961. Founder and first Tyler of Singleton Lodge, he was Installed as WM in 1991. He is also a Joining Member of Tuscan Lodge No.7267 and was Installed WM of that Lodge in 1978. In Province, he was appointed PPrGStdB in 1984, promoted to PPrSGD in 1997, and to PPrJGW in 2001. He became a Grand Officer in 2004, with the Rank of PGStB.

Singleton Lodge is the second Daughter Lodge of Glantawe Lodge. The first Daughter Lodge is Old Goreans Lodge No.7193, Consecrated on 5 June 1952. The three Lodges keep in close contact, and the official reciprocal visits are a notable feature of the Masonic year.

It was originally intended that Singleton Lodge should be associated with the educational establishments of Swansea, although it should be stressed that it was never a closed or restricted Lodge in any formal way. The early Initiates reflected this academic connection, but as time went by, and as the Craft became less popular in the world of education, it became clear that this early intention could no longer be fulfilled. The contact between the Lodge and the academic world has by now been almost entirely lost, and nowadays Initiates come from all walks of life. Like many other Lodges, Singleton Lodge has passed through difficult times, and many Past Masters have had to return to the Chair of King Solomon for a second or third time, and have had to occupy various vacant junior Offices. It is pleasing to report that the Lodge now has a goodly number of new Members. The 25th Anniversary was celebrated in 1996; the Brethren trust that the 50th Anniversary in 2021 will find Singleton Lodge in good heart.

Compiled by WBro Dr Vivian J Phillips, PM, PPrGReg.

Lodge of Harmony No.8414

Warranted : 8 December 1971

Consecrated : 5 May 1972

Meeting at the Masonic Hall, Cardiff.

Lodge of Harmony No.8414, was Consecrated by RWBro the Rt Hon the Lord Swansea, DL, ProvGM at the Duke of Connaught Temple, Cardiff, on 5 May 1972, assisted by WBro A F Randell - Edmunds, PAGDC, ProvSGW, as SW; WBro Cuthbert L Summers, ProvJGW, as JW; and WBro Rev Brynmor Williams, ProvGChap, as Chaplain, together with a full team of Provincial Officers. Music was provided by The Guildford Singers, directed by WBro E J Smith, PPGW, accompanied by WBro E Haydn Lloyd, ProvGOrg. WBro George H C Oughton was Installed as the Primus Master, and Bros W H Hann and W A Isaksson as SW and JW respectively. The occasion was organised by the Founder Secretary, WBro Bernard Frederick Smith, a Member of Lodge of Amity No.5823. The Founder Treasurer was Bro Cyril Aubrey Rees, of Amethyst Lodge No.4026.

Lodge of Harmony was originally Founded for the purpose of giving long serving, older Masons an opportunity to attain the Chair of King Solomon and was Sponsored by Lodge of Amity. Among the 25 Founder Members was Alan Taylor of HTV's 'Mr & Mrs' fame. Everyone was kept 'in check' by Bro James Albert Hargest, who was Governor of Swansea prison. Bro Frank Kiss was a refugee and former pilot in the Hungarian Air Force, who had assisted many Hungarian prisoners to escape. Frank owned a jeweller's shop on the Old Hayes in Cardiff. WBro Walter Aron Isaksson was a former sea Captain whose nautical tales about 'Rounding the (Cape) Horn' kept all fascinated at the Festive Board.

The Lodge name 'Harmony' is derived from the word 'Amity', as indeed the Lodge was formed from Members of Amity Lodge, it having a somewhat similar meaning to 'Harmony'. The Lodge Crest depicts a squared pavement flanked on either side by two Masonic pillars. In the centre of the pavement is a Welsh harp (representing Harmony) with the Welsh Dragon superimposed on its centre.

The Lodge Banner was donated by WBro Trevor ap Phillips, and was handcrafted in embroidery stitch by Mrs Dolly Davies and Mrs W L Davies, the wives of WBro Carlton Davies and WBro James Arthur- Davies respectively, both Founder Members of the Lodge. Bro Fred Barney initially drew the design of the Banner onto the tapestry. He was a local artist and close friend of WBro Trevor. The Banner was Dedicated by the DepProvGM, VWBro Geoffrey Ashe, TD, on 14 November 1977, whilst WBro

Trevor was the WM.

It is interesting to note that the Lodge has a connection with the building of the Ladies' Masonic Temple at the Hawthorns in Llandaff. It was originally an old 'tin chapel', and Mrs Ellen Hyde was one of a group of Ladies that purchased it with a view to setting up a Ladies' Masonic Temple. Ellen was the wife of one of the Founder Members, the late and much revered WBro Charles Hyde. A new Temple was subsequently built on the site. The contractor was Trevor Ap Phillips and the foreman carpenter was WBro J A Davies.

The Lodge is currently a very active Member of a worldwide fraternity, 'The Lodges of Harmony Association', consisting of Lodges bearing the name, 'Lodge of Harmony', which was set up in the Secretary's house of Lodge of Harmony No.7217, Bristol, by 8 Lodges from England and Wales. That figure has now reached 49 worldwide. WBros Anthony Howell and Mike Baker of Lodge of Harmony, Cardiff are the Association's Treasurer and Secretary respectively. Both Members are pioneers of the Association and have presided over this wide and rapid expansion of Membership. Members of Lodge of Harmony, Cardiff, have made a number of visits to other 'Harmony Lodges', principally Bristol, Brighton, Buddleigh Salterton and Plymouth to name but a few! On 5 May 2010, Lodge of Harmony, Cardiff, was the host of the second Meeting of 'The Lodges of Harmony' Association', which meets every 5 years. Lodge of Harmony No.156, Plymouth, in the Province of Devon, hosted the In-augural Meeting in 2005. This Meeting coincided with their Bi-Centenary Meeting, at which a Gavel was presented to Lodge of Harmony, Cardiff. The Lodge retained it until 2010 when in turn it was presented to the next Lodge of Harmony who will then arrange to host the Meeting in 2015. Following the draw, at which all those present had been hoping that Lodge of Harmony, South Africa, Guadalupe or New York, USA, would be chosen, the successful recipient of the Gavel until 2015 was Lodge of Harmony No.9048, Northampton. The Brethren were a little disappointed not to be looking forward to the next meeting on foreign soil, but were immensely pleased to be hosting the next association bash!

The reputation of Harmony Lodge No.8414 has therefore spread abroad, not only via the Association, but also through its Members. In that regard, we have two Brethren from the French Constitution, Christian Uhmann and Jean Claude Vedrine, both of whom hold high Rank in the Grande Loge Nationale Francaise and who, even though they live and work in France, attend our Meetings when they are able.

Early in the 1990s, WBro Anthony Howell discussed the feasibility of raising money for the South Wales Provincial Benevolent Fund with the Provincial Secretary, WBro James R Bevan. This objective was to be achieved by selling photographs taken of Brethren attending the Annual Provincial Grand Lodge Meeting at Barry. These photographs would be based on school-style photographs and would involve those Brethren receiving first Appointments and subsequent Promotions. WBro James Bevan felt that it was a good idea and that the necessary steps should be taken to proceed with the plan. At this point Anthony discussed the idea with WBro John Davies, also a Member of Harmony Lodge. John, who had his own photography business, offered to assist in the venture by printing the photographs that Anthony had taken. This pairing of talents has resulted in a substantial amount of funds being transferred to the Provincial Benevolent Fund each year ever since those early days. This commitment to charitable work within the Province has been greatly appreciated by the Provincial Executive.

Of many notable Past Masters, the late WBro John D Hann, who followed his father, WBro William Hart Hann into Freemasonry, fully deserves inclusion in this history. Initiated into Lodge of Unity No. 6030, on 9 October 1946, he became a Masonic Veteran in 1996, and was appointed a Grand Officer in 1992 with the Rank of PAGDC. He became WM of Hendre Lodge in 1999. 'Jack', as he was best known to all, was the Mandated Officer to Lodge of Harmony and also to Lodge of Unity, until his death in 2006. Jack was also a Member of the Guildford Singers and sang in the choir at the Consecration of Lodge of Harmony. No

Member of the Lodge has yet received Grand Rank in the Craft, but the Lodge was honoured when WBro Anthony Howell attained the Grand Rank of PGStdB in the Mark Degree in 2010.

The Founding IPM, WBro James Arthur Davies, a PM of Lodge of Amity, will forever be remembered for his exacting strictness at LOI in his role as Lodge Preceptor. Woe betided the progressing Brother who forgot his lines or put a foot wrong in the LOI!

A tradition which is possibly unique to Lodge of Harmony, is that the Deacons are directed to instruct the Candidate to advance 'to the Pedestal' by the proper steps and not to 'the East'.

As already mentioned, earlier in our History, the Lodge had a close link with Lodge of Unity. Unfortunately, in 2008 Lodge of Unity surrendered its Warrant and closed for the last time. Six Members of Lodge of Unity decided to bring their support and experience to Lodge of Harmony, and they were very warmly welcomed into the fold.

In the last ten years, the Lodge has experienced mixed fortunes. Membership dropped to less than 20 Members in the period between 2003 and 2007. This was due, in some measure, to the unfortunate loss of older Brethren, who are still greatly missed.

Recently, the Lodge has become a very much stronger unit and Membership now stands at over 30, with new Candidates wishing to partake in Freemasonry. The average age of the Membership is becoming lower and the Brethren look forward to the continued growth of the Lodge with some confidence.

Compiled by WBro G Anthony Howell, PPrJGW, WBro Mike Baker, PPrSGD and WBro Jeff Davies, PPrGSwdB with assistance from WBro Graham Wilcox, PPrGSwdB.

Master's Chair, Duke of Connaught Temple, Cardiff

Lodge of Concord
No.8418

Warranted : 8 December 1971

Consecrated : 18 March 1972

Meeting at the Masonic Hall, Cardiff.

In 1971, a group of acquaintances from various Lodges within the Province decided to form a Lodge of their own, whilst at the same time retaining individual Membership of their respective Lodges. This was for no other reason than to cement their friendships and further their Masonic interests.

Cardiff Exchange Lodge No.3775 was the Mother Lodge and some of the Founders and first Officers were: WBro Harold Freedman, Jeweller, PM Friendship & Justice Lodge No.5830, WM; WBro Reuben Joseph, Garage Proprietor, PM Friendship & Justice Lodge, Acting IPM; Bro Harold Greene, Estate Agent, SW; Bro Anthony W Le Beau, Electrical Manufacturer's Agent, JW; WBro Cecil M Seager, DFC, Wholesaler, PM Lodge of Faith No.141, Clerkenwell Green, London, Chaplain; WBro Solomon Joseph, Barrister, PM Carmel Lodge No.4774, Treasurer; WBro F Stanley Hissey, Newsagent, PM Cardiff Exchange Lodge No.3775, Secretary; and WBro Rex Morris, ProvJGD, Radio Retailer, PM Cardiff Exchange Lodge, DC.

On instigating the proposal to form a new Lodge, much deliberation was given on deciding its name and, eventually, 'Lodge of Concord' was agreed upon, mainly because the dictionary definition of 'Concord' is 'unity and harmony', words that aptly illustrate the chief aims and aspirations of the Founder Members.

The Brethren were asked to submit a design for the Lodge Crest. Subsequently, the one submitted by WBro Glyn Mogford was chosen for its simplicity. He achieved this by incorporating a plain gold band bearing the name of the Lodge, with the Square and Compasses as a centrepiece, the band being joined at its base by clasped hands. The band is topped by a Welsh Dragon. The plain gold band is symbolic of solemnity and unity, the clasped hands of friendship and concord, and the whole is meant to represent a Lodge of Brethren held in brotherly love and concord by the grip of friendship. The Welsh Dragon represents the Members' allegiance to the land of their birth, or which affords them its protection; the ears of corn either side of the clasped hands are emblematic of plenty and signify the wealth of brotherly love and charity. The Square and Compasses are those two great lights in Masonry: *the Square to regulate our actions and the Compasses to keep us within due bounds with all mankind, more particularly our Brethren in Freemasonry.'*

The Welsh inscription, *'Llaw Mewn Llaw'*, means *'Hand in Hand'*, and stands for the hope that the Lodge will be happy and prosperous and that all its Members go hand in hand in concord with each other and the rest of the world.

The Lodge does not have a Banner, although an embroidered Crest on velvet was recently presented to the Lodge by WBro

Allan Davies, for use in the Temple during Ceremonies.

The Lodge was granted its Warrant on 8 December 1971 and it was Consecrated on Saturday, 18 March 1972, by RWBro the Rt Hon the Lord Swansea, DL, ProvGM, assisted by his team of Provincial Officers. WBro Harold Freedman was Installed as the first WM. Following the Installation of the WM and Investment of Officers, each Lodge Member was presented with a Founders' Jewel of the same design as the Lodge Crest, with his name engraved thereon. WBro Harold Freedman died in 1980, and his widow presented the first Master's Jewel to the Lodge, which is now worn by the outgoing WM during his year as IPM.

The Lodge was denominated a 'dining' Lodge and it meets four times a year. The new Master is Installed at the May Meeting. In recent years, the ladies have been invited to the December Festive Board, and in keeping with Grand Lodge's initiative for more openness, non-Masonic guests are also invited.

The Lodge celebrated its 25th Anniversary in 1997 and its 100th Regular Lodge Meeting was held on Thursday, 6 February 1997.

In 1974, the Lodge rose to the challenge of a call for financial assistance from the Edward Prince of Wales Court, Porthcawl. WBros Harold Freedman and Harold Greene chaired a committee to organise a performance of Handel's 'Messiah', by the Welsh National Opera , at the old Capitol Cinema, which at that time was the City's foremost entertainment venue. The performance took place on 16 December, supported by many Lodges and before a full house. The event raised sufficient funds to purchase a new Minibus/Ambulance, which gave the Court many years of service. There was even a surplus which was used to purchase a heated hostess trolley for the use of the Matron. The presentation was made at the Court on 11 May 1975 by WBro Anthony Le Beau, WM.

In the early nineties, the words to the 'Lodge of Concord Chorus', a parody from Gilbert & Sullivan's 'Yeomen of the Guard', were written by WBro Allan Davies. The song has since been sung regularly to the visiting Brethren, with much pleasure and amusement.

In 1996, WBro George Brady, WM, noticed a letter printed in 'The Times' newspaper, submitted by the WM of Lodge of Concord No.4910, Southampton, defending the concepts of Freemasonry. WBro George corresponded with the WM of the Southampton Lodge, and as a consequence, several fraternal visits took place between the two Lodges. WBro David Hodges, who was Installed WM in 2006, even became an active Member of the Southampton Lodge. Through the auspices of the Southampton Lodge, Lodge of Concord No.632, Trowbridge, Wiltshire, was also contacted and occasional fraternal visits have been exhanged with the Trowbridge Lodge.

Only two of the Founder Members remain in the Lodge. The longest serving Founder Member is WBro Anthony Le Beau, PPrSGW, who, having been Initiated in Gwalia Lodge No.4213 on 23 January 1953, is a Masoninc Veteran with 56 years in Freemasonry. He was Installed WM of the Lodge of Concord in 1974 and for over 20 years served as Charity Steward. WBro Anthony is a Lewis. His father, also a Member of Gwalia Lodge, was a bronze medalist in the Olympic Games, held in Stockholm in 1912. Sadly, WBro Anthony is now failing in health and is no longer able to attend Lodge. The next longest serving Member is WBro Glyn Mogford, PPrSGW, who is a Chartered Engineer of the Institute of Engineering & Technology and an Electrical Engineer by profession. He is a Founder Member from Lodge of Amity No.5823, where he was Installed WM in 1970 and was the first SD of Lodge of Concord. He celebrated 50 years in Freemasonry in 2010. WBro Glyn played a very active role in the Lodge, for many years as DC and later as Chaplain. While still regularly attending Lodge, he no longer holds Office. Both WBros Anthony and Glyn could always be counted on to give every assistance and advice to the less experienced Brethren, and in recognition of their loyal and dedicated service to the Lodge over very many years, they were made Honorary Members in 2009. WBro Robert Vincent, a retired Senior Officer in the Fire Service, has been the Lodge Organist since the Consecration, and he also had been made an Honoraty Member.

Since its Consecration, the Lodge has had a fluctuating Membership of between 30 and 40 Brethren, and two Candidates have been Initiated in most years. In this respect, the Lodge is in a relatively healthy position, with a current Membership of 35.

Compiled by WBro George Brady, PPrJGD, with the assistance of
WBros Anthony Le Beau, PPrSGW, and Glyn Mogford, PPrSGW.

Ymlaen Lodge
No.8419

Warranted : 8 December 1971

Consecrated : 24 May 1972

Meeting at the Masonic Hall, Cardiff.

Ymlaen Lodge was Consecrated as the Cathays High School Old Boys' Lodge. The School, with its sister School for Girls, was opened in Sept 1931. It is of particular interest to note that it was built to replace the Cardiff Junior Technical College which had been held in high esteem by both pupils and the commercial and industrial interests in the area.

The first entry into the School consisted of 120 pupils. WBro W (Billy) Douglas, PM Ymlaen Lodge and a Past Chairman (1998) of the Federation of School Lodges, and WBro Gordon B Neilly, one of the first two Co-initiates of Ymlaen Lodge, were in that original entry. The senior forms were made up of those pupils who had been transferred from Cardiff Junior Technical College. WBro Anthony (Tony) Ough started in Cathays in 1937; he was later to become the first Lodge Secretary. Tony left Cathays at the age of 16 to embark on a long and distinguished career with BBC Wales, retiring as their Communications Manager. In Freemasonry, he was appointed the Batham Holy Royal Arch Lecturer in 1991. In the Craft, the Province employed his talents in this direction on a more informal but far more active basis. He was honoured in Grand Lodge, firstly by being appointed PGStB in 1996 and promoted to PAGDC in 2007.

Dr Ellis Lloyd became Headmaster of Cathays High School in the summer of 1944. He was a man of brilliant academic attainment. He left the School in 1949 to take up a similar appointment at Bishop Gore Grammar School, Swansea, and he was destined to become a Founder Member of Old Goreans Lodge No.7193.

In 1946, WBro David B Harries, who was the Founder Master of Ymlaen Lodge, became the second pupil of the School to qualify in Medicine. Much is owed to David, not only for his efforts towards the Foundation of the Lodge, but also for his subsequent considerable contribution. VWBro Roy Keith Hopkin (now a Past DepProvGM of the Province) was also a Founder Member and was the first pupil to gain admission to the Dartmouth Naval College and later to be commissioned in the Royal Navy. A separate biographical profile of VWBro Roy appears elsewhere in this book.

Another Founder was the School's fourth Headmaster, WBro Richard Griffiths, MA. Born in Flintshire and having held teaching posts in North Wales, he left his position as Senior Lecturer in Education at Loughborough College to join Cathays High School.

Among the other Founder Members were WBro David L Crosby, a Consultant Surgeon; WBro Peter Ponsford, a Company

Director; WBro Terry Nolan, a Company Secretary and later a Director of Asteys; and WBro William T Hopkin, a Retired Police Officer (PM Tennant Lodge No.1992) and father of VWBro Roy Hopkin. He was the first Lodge Secretary, holding that Office for just one year, until Bro T J Gwynne Williams succeeded him.

WBro Douglas J Mason, PPrSGW, is another Founder Member to whom the Lodge owes a very great deal. He is the senior Past Master of the Lodge, having been Installed as WM in 1973. He has led a quite distinguished Masonic career perhaps most particularly in the Mark Degree, where he has spent many years as the most respected Provincial DC, which led to him being awarded his first Mark Grand Rank (PAGDC) in 1987. He has since been twice promoted, latterly becoming a Very Worshipful Brother. He has also been honoured with RAM Grand Rank, and is a Mark and RAM Veteran with well over forty year's service in those Orders. WBro Doug proposed the other Co-initiate at the very first Meeting of the Lodge, WBro Jack Jones, with whom he had been managing and coaching Cathays High School Old Boys' Rugby Team for over fifteen years.

Yet another eminent Founder is WBro Stan Williams, an extremely popular PM who recalls *'We can trace the beginnings of Ymlaen Lodge back to an Annual Old Boys dinner held at the Park Hotel in early 1971. It was on this occasion that former classmates enjoyed each other's company over a sumptuous dinner with the aid of one or two drinks! A number of Old Boys found themselves standing next to each other at the bar, when one observed that without exception, they were all involved in Freemasonry. There was silence for a moment, after which it was unanimously agreed that we could form our own Lodge and therefore meet and enjoy each other's company on a more regular basis.'*

WBro Terry Nolan offered to accommodate everyone at one of the Asteys hostelries for a preliminary meeting, and immediately a date was fixed. Subsequently, contacts were made with all known Old Cathaysians who were Freemasons, with extremely encouraging results.

Approximately 20 Old Boys attended that first meeting in what was 'The Globe Inn', at the corner of Womanby Street, opposite Cardiff Castle. A discussion ensued about the future make-up of what was to become Ymlaen Lodge. After a series of further meetings, prospective Officers were nominated, and it became evident that there was an intrinsic agreement to nominate Officers *'in strict order of present Masonic seniority'*. Following this meeting, WBro Tony Ough, Member of Howardian Lodge No.5317, a School Lodge, approached the Howardian Lodge Finance Committee to seek the Lodge's Sponsorship, which was readily agreed.

The Petition was duly signed on 4 November 1971 and the Warrant was issued a month afterwards, with the Consecration taking place on 24 May 1972. The Lodge name had been taken from the School Motto: *'Ymlaen'*, meaning *'Onward'* or *'Forward.'* The School Song, 'Ymlaen Cathays', was also adopted by the Lodge and is always sung at the Festive Board. On one occasion, even Lord Swansea joined in the singing, such was the 'hwyl' created. RWBro the Rt Hon the Lord Swansea, DL, ProvGM, presided at the Consecration Ceremony. His team included WBro Harry Stockwell, DepProvGM; the AProvGMs, WBros Harold Wilson and Llewellyn G Bevan; and WBro Geoffrey M Ashe, TD, ProvGDC.

One of three Joining Members at the first Meeting was Bro T J Gwynne Williams, who was a popular Bank Manager in the Rhiwbina area of the City. He was a Member of Duke of York Lodge No.2453 and was to become the Lodge's long serving Treasurer. Many PMs have WBro Gwynne to thank for his central role in the financial management of the Lodge, and for arranging the very many social evenings, which everyone enjoyed over the years. His unstinting work over 25 years resulted in him being awarded an Acting ProvGStwd's Collar. WBro Chris Parsons has since continued this long tradition of financial stewardship.

Three distinguished Brethren have filled the central role of Lodge Secretary with great distinction. WBro Stan Williams followed WBro Tony Ough, serving fourteen years in that position, with WBro Mike Beynon later serving for over twenty years.

For over forty years, Ymlaen Lodge has achieved and, in recent times exceeded, the targets set for the Provincial Festivals.

This was due in no small measure to the zeal and assiduity of successive Charity Stewards. They number just four, WBro Bill Hopkin, VWBro Roy Hopkin, WBro Peter Ponsford and WBro Graham Wilcox. It must be worthy of note that the Lodge succeeded in contributing almost double the 'target' for the latest Festival in 2010.

Mention should also be made of the tremendous contribution and support provided by WBro Terry Nolan, not only as Chief Steward, but also to the Cardiff Masonic Hall Company. As a Director of many years standing, he was influential in gaining the best terms available in the supply of food, as well as persuading Welsh Brewers to offer the best prices in the supply of beer and spirits. His contribution cannot be recalled without mentioning another very popular and influential Brother, the late Bro Harry (Sandy) Warrener. A former work colleague of Terry's, Sandy, with his wife Gill, were Steward and Stewardess of the Cardiff Masonic Hall Company. For many years they gave friendly and conscientious service, to the enjoyment of all, and were highly regarded.

The Brethren of Ymlaen Lodge were extremely happy to become 'parents', with the 'birth' of a Daughter Lodge, Old Cantonians Lodge No.8875, also a School Lodge, whose Warrant was granted on 14 Feb 1979.

In September 1989, the Lodge hosted the Annual Festival of the National Federation of School Lodges. The Brother overseeing the Festival was the Federation's Secretary, WBro Billy Douglas, who was ably assisted by WBro Gordon Neilly. The highlight and centrepiece of the event, which was held at Cardiff City Hall, was a lecture on 'The History of the Federation of School Lodges', given by our own WBro Stan Williams, which was very well received by the 500 delegates attending.

In common with other Schools Lodges, Ymlaen Lodge hosts a 'Schools Night' once a year when, apart from the other Cardiff Lodges, it is proud to welcome Brethren from Newport (Nioba Lodge No.5264), Swansea (Old Goreans Lodge) and Bristol (Robert Thorne Lodge No.3663). The (unwritten) rules for all such Meetings dictate that *each Brother is expected to pay his own dining fee'*. Gladly, this does not seem to deter Schools' Brethren from visiting each other's Lodges.

Interestingly, a number of blood brothers have taken active roles in the Lodge. WBro Walter Smith, who, as DC, was followed by WBro Gerald Smith in that Office. WBro Gareth Parsons, a Re-joining Member from the Daughter Lodge, Old Cantonians, where he was Lodge Secretary for fifteen years, Installed his blood brother, WBro Chris Parsons, in the Chair of King Solomon in 2007. WBro Jim Parsons, one of the Founders, took great pride in assisting both sons to reach this high Office.

Recently, in May 2010, WBro Bipin V Pitrola Installed his blood brother, Bro Bhupendra Pitrola, as WM. WBro Bipin was made a Freeman of the City of London in June 2005 and was received into the *'Guild of Freemen of the City of London'* in September of that year. He moved to Wales in 2006 and became a member of the Welsh Livery Guild, where he takes an active role as Beadle. As the Ceremonial Officer, he assists in robing, manages the regalia of the Court, and leads the procession on formal occasions.

In 2011, Old Cantonians Lodge found it necessary to seek an Amalgamation with Ymlaen Lodge. Brethren of both Lodges were delighted to be the first in the Province to successfully achieve such an Amalgamation. The event formally took place at Ymlaen Lodge's Installation Ceremony, held on Wednesday, 25 May 2011. The Brethren of Old Cantonian Lodge proudly paraded their Banner into the Temple, and then took their seats as Joining Members of Ymlaen Lodge. In future, their Banner will be placed alongside Ymlaen Lodge's Banner. The Joining Members will wear their own school tie colours within the Lodge and the Old Cantonian Master's Collar will now serve as Ymlaen's IPM's Collar. This truly historic occasion was suitably celebrated afterwards at the Festive Board, in the presence of WBro Wing Cdr John Irfon Davies, CBE, PAGDC, ProvSGW, representing the Provincial Grand Master.

The Lodge is naturally very proud of its background, its Founder Members in particular, and others who have passed through the Chair, many of whom have contributed greatly and are well known and highly respected in South Wales Masonic circles.

Compiled by WBro Graham J Wilcox, PPrGSwdB.

Nottage Lodge No.8452

Warranted : 23 October 1972

Consecrated : 24 November 1972

Meeting at the Masonic Hall, Porthcawl.

Nottage Lodge No.8452 was formed primarily to cater for the ever increasing interest in Freemasonry in Porthcawl. During its 39 year history, the Lodge Membership, originally drawn from the Porthcawl locality, has extended its geographic base to attract Members from farther afield. The Sponsoring Lodge was Lodge of Sker No.8024. There were 22 Founder Members, 8 of whom were Past Masters. Three were Past Masters of Llynfi Lodge No.2965, namely, WBro Herbert Douglas Allen, PPrGW, WM in 1960, WM Designate; WBro Oswald H Lucas, PPrGSwdB, WM in 1968; and WBro W Pitchford, PPrAGDC, WM in 1969. Also, among the PM Founders were WBros A V Huggett, PPrGD, LGR, PM St Peter's Lodge No.476, Carmarthen, and Brentham Lodge No.4980, Beaconsfield, Buckinghamshire; D J Davies, DFC, PPrGD, PM Llangeinor Lodge No.4194; and J R Jones, PPrGD, LGR, PM Graveney Lodge No.5285, Staines, Middlesex.

Nottage Lodge was Consecrated at the Masonic Temple, New Road, Porthcawl, on 24 November 1972, by RWBro the Rt Hon the Lord Swansea, DL, ProvGM, together with his team of 12 Officers. The Guildford Singers were in attendance under the direction of WBro E J Smith. The Primus Master was WBro Herbert Douglas Allen, PPrGW, who had been Installed WM of Llynfi Lodge No.2965 in 1960.

Nottage Lodge originally met four times a year, on the last Saturday in November (Installation), February, and September and the third Saturday in May. It is traditional for the ladies and widows to join the Brethren at the May Festive Board. The February Meeting was moved to January, and a fifth Meeting was introduced in March, to allow for greater flexibility in arranging Ceremonies, and to allow for an occasional Past Masters' Ceremony.

The village of Nottage, from which the Lodge derives its name, is located on the northern perimeter of the seaside town of Porthcawl. A pre-Norman settlement, it consisted originally of a cluster of dwellings situated on a small hillock, near a stream that then flowed southward to the sea. Defence against incursions from the sea was undoubtedly responsible for its compact form. The name is of Old English origin, and was spelt 'Nothashe', in a document signed there in 1351, thought to represent the knotted ash tree marking the central point of the settlement. Nottage was an early centre of Protestant Nonconformity, in which various dissenting denominations were active from the period of the Commonwealth to the end of the eighteenth century. There exists a copy of a Charter, dated between 1147 and 1153, which refers to the gift of Novam Villam (Newton) by William, Earl of Gloucester, to Richard de Cardiff and, the name 'Newton' was established to differentiate it from the old nearby township of 'Nothashe'. The Parish name of Newton-Nottage derives from the amalgamation of the two hamlets. These hamlets now form the eastern and western extremities of the town of Porthcawl, which is reflected in Freemasonry with the two Masonic Lodges, Newton and Nottage, meeting in Porthcawl.

The Lodge Insignia consists of a pollard ash-tree, which signifies the original name of the settlement 'Nothashe'. The tree is situated under the 'All Seeing Eye', flanked to the left and right by the Pillars of Boaz and Jachin, which both stand on the mosaic pavement. This symbolism is encircled by a garland to formalise the design. The Lodge Motto *'Fiat Lux'* has distinct Masonic significance. It translates from the Latin into English as *'Let there be Light'*. The Insignia was designed by WBro William B Harries Baker, a prominent local Architect, who joined the Lodge in 1973 (its first year). The Lodge Banner, which includes the Insignia, was manufactured locally, and now hangs on the western wall of the Masonic Temple, Porthcawl.

It has often been noted by visiting Brethren that the comradeship and fraternal welcome received at Nottage Lodge is one that truly warms the heart and strengthens the bonds within our Fraternity. Indeed, it is fair to say that the Festive Board enjoyed at Nottage Lodge has become a legend in itself. Uniquely, within this Province, is the 'Masonic Firing' of the respective Toasts given in the Porthcawl Lodges. One of the most interesting visits, in the formative years of the Lodge, was from a delegation of Chelsea Pensioners, who dressed in their distinctive scarlet coats, tricorne hats and Masonic Regalia, making for an extremely colourful ceremony. Nottage Lodge is often referred to as 'Maesteg by the Sea', by visiting Brethren from the Llynfi Valley and Maesteg area who frequently attend the Lodge. The link was first made possible by the historic railway connecting the towns. This enabled Porthcawl to become a prosperous seaport, with its world-wide export of coal, transported from Maesteg, via the railway. The railway remained horse-drawn until 1861, when it was finally converted to the 'new' steam technology.

In recent years, the Lodge has attracted a great influx of younger Brethren, eager to take their first steps in Freemasonry. It has also developed fraternal ties on an international basis, notably with Civil Lines Lodge No.310, Delhi, Warranted 21 September 1996; and its Mother Lodge, Jumna No.18, Delhi, Warranted 15 January 1872, both under the jurisdiction of the Grand Lodge of India.

A number of fraternal visits have occurred between Brethren on an individual basis since 2006. A large delegation of Nottage Lodge Members visited the Indian Lodges, on an organised trip in October 2007, further strengthening the ties. During the visit, Brethren of Nottage Lodge attended a Craft Meeting in the presence of the Regional (Provincial) Grand Master of Northern India. This visit was reciprocated by our Indian Brethren in 2008.

Nottage Lodge has been very fortunate in its 39 year history to have had a stable, loyal and active Membership and in recent times has seen a healthy increase in Membership especially from the younger generation.

Compiled by WBro Nigel Jones, PM.

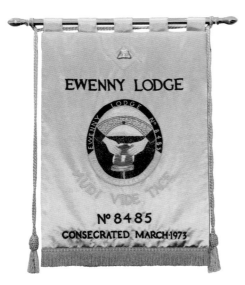

Ewenny Lodge No.8485

Warranted : 13 December 1972
Consecrated : 2 March 1973
Meeting at the Masonic Hall, Bridgend.

The Lodge takes its name from the village of Ewenny (Ewenni), which lies about two miles southeast of the now County Borough of Bridgend. Ewenny is an example of a ribbon village, in which the houses are built along the highway, instead of forming a cluster around the village green. It is thought that the word 'Ewenny' derives from the name of a Celtic Goddess 'Aventi', which suggests there was an ancient Celtic Church near the present Priory. William de Londres, Lord of Ogmore, built the first Church at the beginning of the 12th century. In the year 1141, Maurice de Londres, the son of William, gave the Church of St Michael, Ewenny, to the Benedictine Abbey of St Peter, Gloucester. The Priory remained in existence from its foundation to the dissolution of the monasteries in the reign of Henry VIII, when Sir Edward Carne of Nash Manor bought the cell and the land for £727. 6s. 4d.

The Priory is believed to be the only example of a fortified monastery in South Wales. A Buck engraving of Ewenny Priory in the Royal Institution of South Wales, Swansea, gives a clear impression of a compact fortified monastic enclosure with its splendid Norman Church in the centre, and its setting of the fertile farmlands backed by the highlands beyond.

Ewenny is famous for its potteries, developed here because of the bed of glacial clay in the area. It is thought that the potter's craft was practised by the Monks. From the mid-18th century there have been 15 potteries in the Ewenny area. Now only two remain in existence as commercial undertakings, Ewenny and Claypits. Ewenny is 'the old established pottery in Wales' and has been continuously owned and worked by the Jenkins family since 1785. The present owners, Alun Jenkins and his wife Jayne, with their daughter Caitlin, who are the 6th and 7th generation of the family, are justly proud of their Royal patronage. It is fitting that Bro Alun Jenkins is an active Member of Ewenny Lodge. Let the Bible text which hangs above the heads of the craftsmen as they ply their trade, remind us to leave the future 'In the Potter's Hands'.

Thus, from this historical background, it was decided in 1972 to establish 'Ewenny Lodge', under the Sponsorship of Llangeinor Lodge No.4891, Bridgend. WBros Geraint Jenkins and Ronald B Whittingham, who became an Assistant Provincial Grand Master in 1976, together with a further 19 Brethren, agreed to Petition for the new Lodge. It was agreed that WBro Geraint Jenkins would be WM Designate and that WBro Ronald B Whittingham would be IPM. WBros Walter Kenyon and W Henry

Phipps were appointed Senior and Juniors Wardens Designate, respectively. WBro D B Jones was Chaplain Designate, and WBro Elfyn Thomas, Treasurer Designate. WBro Herbert J Davies agreed to undertake the Office of Secretary, with WBro Alun Griffiths as Assistant Secretary.

Ewenny Lodge No.8485 was Consecrated at the Masonic Temple, Adare Street, Bridgend, on Friday, 2 March 1973 by RWBro the Rt Hon the Lord Swansea, ProvGM, assisted WBro Harry F Stockwell, DepProvGM, two Assistant Provincial Grand Masters and nine other Officers. There were 107 Brethren present for the Ceremony, including the Guildford Singers under the direction of WBro E J Smith. Notice was given that there were two applications for Joining Membership. One was from Bro H George Jones who, having failed to become a Founder Member because he had not been a Master Mason for the required 3 years, was determined to become the first Joining Member. There were also 4 applications for Initiation.

This was an excellent start and during the first three years to 1976, there were 14 applications for Joining Membership and 11 for Initiation; whilst in the first 34 years history there have been 73 applications for Initiation and 24 for Joining Membership. It is very pleasing that for a small Lodge, there have been two Initiates every year, resulting in a constant Membership of around 60, with a broad spectrum of age. With a regular attendance of over 35 Brethren at every Lodge Meeting, the future looks bright '*In the Potter's Hands*'.

This must be attributed to one factor. There has always been a very devoted team of Officers. After the initial years, when Past Masters occupied the Chair, the first Initiate, WBro Peter G Tanner became Worshipful Master in 1980. Since then, only three Past Masters, WBro Basil E J George in 1998, WBro Clive M Davis, OStJ in 2001 and WBro David Lane in 2002, have been called upon to take the Chair for the second time. This was brought about by some younger Brethren being unable to progress, because of business and other commitments. In June 2003, WBro Paul Clement had to withdraw, because he was called to serve in Iraq for six months as a member of the Territorial Army.

The loyalty of Brethren is reflected in the fact that in the first 34 years there have only been three Treasurers, four Secretaries and four Assistant Secretaries, Organists and Directors of Ceremonies. Finally, the Collar of Charity Steward has only been worn by three Brethren.

At the Installation Meeting on 26 March 1974, WBro Ronald B Whittingham, to mark his appreciation of the work done by all the Founder Brethren, presented the Lodge with a case of Working Tools, which was gratefully received by WBro Geraint Jenkins, WM. To commemorate his year in the Chair, the Worshipful Master then presented the Lodge with a photograph of all the Founder Members, which still hangs in the Committee Room of the Masonic Hall, Bridgend.

Only two Brethren have achieved 50 years in Freemasonry. WBro Herbert J Davies, PPrSGW, was Initiated on 18 September 1947 into Merlin Lodge No.1578, Pontypridd. He joined the teaching profession and held appointments at Pontypridd Grammar School for many years before being appointed Headmaster of the Garw Grammar School. On re-organisation, he was appointed the Headmaster of the Ynysawdre Comprehensive School, where he remained until his retirement. Whilst he and his wife, also a Headmistress, took active parts in the community, Herbert had a great love for Freemasonry, especially in the Llangeinor and Ewenny Lodges. He enjoyed playing the organ and did so until he passed to the Grand Lodge Above in 2002, at the good age of 96 years. Bro T Gwyn Davies, PPrGStwd, was also Initiated in Pontypridd, but into Hen Bont Lodge No.4691 on 19 May 1954. He worked in the Magistrates' Courts for 42 years and took appointments at Pontypridd, Dursley and Usk before being appointed Deputy Clerk to the Magistrates at Bridgend on 1 July 1963 until his retirement in 1997. He was awarded the MBE for public service, having been elected an Independent member on the St Brides Major Community Council for 40 years and President of the Court Staff for England & Wales. He also received the Territorial Decoration after serving 16 years in the TA, ending his service by commanding the 53 (Welsh) Signal Squadron at Cardiff. Bro T Gwyn was awarded the Provincial Grand Master's Certificate of Commendation for Services to Masonry on 28 June 1989.

WBro Robert C Burchill, CBE, PPrAGReg, received his honour from the Queen for services as Director of Operations in International Minting at the Royal Mint, where he worked for many years. An Initiate on 25 September 1979, he progressed through the various Offices until Elected Master in March 1989. He remains an active Lodge Member. WBro Gerald W Davis was appointed a Commander of the Order of St John, whilst his brother, WBro Clive M Davis, an Officer of the Order of St John. WBro Alun Griffiths, PPrGSwdB, a Past Master of the Llangeinor Lodge in 1978, is the only surviving Member of the original group of 21 Founder Brethren who attend Lodge regularly. The only other surviving Founder, WBro Michael Hughes, has emigrated to Cyprus.

Of all the applications for Membership, one, on 28 May 1974, was from the youngest person to date, Gerald Walter Davies. Initiated on 27 May 1975, it was not long before he took Office. He moved steadily through all the Offices until, on 22 March 1983, WBro Gerald Walter Davis, CStJ, was Installed as Master by another former young Initiate, WBro John Bressington. WBro Gerald had indicated that when he was Installed as Master, he wished to donate a Banner to the Lodge to make its Consecration complete. This Banner was hand-made and embroidered by his mother-in-law, Mrs Cranogwen Roberts, who was assisted by his wife, Mrs Gaynor Davis, JP. Mrs Roberts commenced making this unique and very special item soon after WBro Gerald's Installation. It took nearly five and a half months of continuous sewing and hand-embroidery before the Banner was completed in the first week of November 1983. It was appropriate that the Banner should be presented and Dedicated during WBro Gerald's year as Master. On Tuesday, 20 December 1983, the Deputy Provincial Grand Master, VWBro Geoffrey Malin Ashe, accompanied by his full Provincial team of Officers, Dedicated the Banner. It was with much pride that, accompanied by his Officers, WM Gerald Davis re-entered the Lodge and presented the Banner to the Deputy Provincial Grand Master.

The Banner is displayed in the Temple at the Masonic Hall, Bridgend. The Ewenny Badge or Crest was designed by the Founder Members in the early 1970s. It illustrates the bridge over the River Ewenny and the Potter's hands working the clay. Masonically, it suggests the Bridge separating Heaven and Earth. The hands suggest that as Freemasons we should endeavour to mold our lives to accomplish our tasks in life in accordance with the high principles of our Order, so that when the final call comes, we may pass over the Bridge of life to the presence of the Great Architect of the Universe. The Banner carries the Grand Lodge Motto: *'Audi, Vidi, Tace'* (*'Listen, Observe and be Silent'*)

On 24 September 1980, a letter from the then Provincial Grand Secretary, WBro Malcolm H Thompson, PJGD, was sent to all Lodge Secretaries, which in brief, outlined Lord Swansea's scheme for creating closer contact between Lodges and the Province. This was to be done by appointing Mandated Officers to each Lodge to provide consultation, advice and improve communications. The first such Mandated Officer to be appointed to Ewenny Lodge was WBro D C B Comley, PAGDC, followed some years later by WBro T King-Davies, PJGD. Then, in early 1990, WBro Ronald Moon, MBE, PAGDC, was the appointed Officer and held office until 2003 when he retired because of ill health. In the meanwhile, at Grand Lodge in April 2001, WBro Gerald Walter Davis, CStJ, was presented with his Grand Lodge Collar of PAGDC by the Grand Master, the MWBro HRH the Duke of Kent. It was very fitting that WBro Gerald, having received such an honour, the first in the Ewenny Lodge, should be appointed to succeed WBro Ronald Moon as the Mandated Officer of his own Lodge. In 2010, WBro Gerald was promoted to the Rank of PJGD.

Compiled by Bro Major T Gwyn Davies, MBE, TD, PPrGStwd, Secretary.

Glanogwr Lodge No.8508

Warranted : 14 March 1973

Consecrated : 11 June 1973

Meeting at the Masonic Hall, Bridgend.

In 1966, the Rt Hon the Lord Swansea was appointed Provincial Grand Master of South Wales, Eastern Division. At the time, there were five Craft Lodges meeting at the Bridgend Temple, then situated in Adare Street, Bridgend. Each Lodge had a Membership waiting list of at least five years, and progression from Steward to Worshipful Master was taking 10-12 years. In order to reduce the waiting times and to allow more Brethren to advance, the new ProvGM encouraged the Brethren to form new Lodges.

With this in mind, a meeting was called on 18 March 1970, with the intention of forming a new Lodge. Brethren from Ogmore, Penybont and Llangeinor Lodges attended the meeting, when it was proposed that the name of the new Lodge would be 'Glanogwr', the name of Lord Swansea's family home in Bridgend. The name is derived from two Welsh words and is generally understood to mean *'Bank of the River Ogmore'*. The meeting agreed on the possible Officers, with WBro Ronald Groom being proposed as WM Designate. His son, Bro R Graham Groom was also a Founder Member and, subsequently, his grandson, Bro Ronald G Groom; his son-in-law, Bro Daniel Thomas; and nephew, Bro Peter Groom, became Members of the Lodge.

Ogmore Lodge No.1752 was approached and agreed to be the Sponsoring Lodge. Little happened until April 1972, when WBro Stanley B Roberts wrote to all interested Brethren after Province had indicated the need for 25 Founder Members. In July 1972, an official letter was sent to the ProvGSec, WBro Malcolm Thompson, with the names of the potential Founders and possible Officers. On 19 December 1972, a meeting was held at Bridgend with all potential Founders and WBro Malcolm Thompson. At this meeting, the names of Officers were proposed. It was also agreed that the Lodge would meet four times a year, on the fourth Thursday in February, March, October and November. The Election Meeting would be in February and the Installation Meeting in March.

On 29 January 1973, WBro Stanley B Roberts wrote to Lord Swansea submitting the Petition for Glanogwr Lodge. It was with delight that a letter, dated 20 March 1973, was received by WBro Stanley Roberts, Acting Secretary, from the ProvGSec, stating that *'the MW The Grand Master had been pleased to accede to the prayer of Petition for the proposed Glanogwr Lodge to meet at Bridgend and the Lodge number would be 8508'*.

The By-laws and music to be used in the Ceremonies were now agreed and Hymn Books were donated to the Lodge by Bro Emlyn Grabham, Organist Designate. Bro Evan Cadwgan, SD Designate, donated a Bible, and Ogmore Lodge agreed that its Working Tools and furniture could be used. The Oxford Ritual, as worked by Ogmore Lodge, was to be adopted, with some minor differences. The dress code was to be dinner suits.

Ogmore Castle

The design of the Banner was left in the hands of Bro D Noel Jones (Junior Deacon Designate) who used Ogmore Castle as the main focus. The Motto of the Lodge was to be in Welsh: *'Mynnwch Fyw yn Ysbryd Duw' - 'Strive to live in the Spirit of God',*

On the 30 May, a letter was received from WBro Malcolm Thompson, ProvGSec, informing the Acting Secretary that the full Provincial Team would be present at the Consecration; then a rarity. The RWProvGM expressed a wish to invite the WM, the two Wardens and the Secretary as his guests for lunch at the Bush Inn, St Hilary at 12.30 pm on the day of the Consecration. The Secretary responded that they would be delighted to accept the invitation, but due to the time limitations, requested permission to arrive in dinner suits (the agreed Lodge Dress), which was accepted. So, at 3.30 pm on 11 June 1973, Glanogwr Lodge No.8508 was Consecrated by RWBro the ProvGM, accompanied by WBro Harry F Stockwell, DepProvGM, and two ProvAGMs, WBros Harold Wilson and Llewellyn G Bevan. WBro L Bailey, ProvSGW; WBro D Comley, ProvJGW; WBro Geoffrey Ash, ProvGDC and WBro Malcolm Thompson, ProvGSec, together with the ProvGChap, Organist, Inner Guard and Tyler were also present. The Ceremony was enhanced by the presence of the Guildford Singers who, throughout the ceremony, added musical responses to the spoken word.

Following the Consecration Ceremony, WBro Ronald Graham Groom, PM Ogmore Lodge, was Installed as Master. He then Invested WBro Alan W Hines, PM Llangeinor Lodge No.4194, as IPM. Bro Idris T Williams was Invested as SW; Bro Neville Ianson as JW and WBro Joseph H Ponsford, PM Penybont Lodge No.6743, as Chaplain. The Founders Elected WBro Maurice A Jubb, PM Ogmore Lodge No.1752, as Treasurer. WBro Stanley B Roberts was the first Secretary and WBro Alfred J Worts was the first DC; both were PMs of Ogmore Lodge. The following Founder Members became WMs: Idris T Williams in 1974, Neville Ianson, in 1975, R Emlyn Grabham in 1976, Ieuan Stenner in 1977 and John A. Gibbs in 1978. Sadly, these Brethren are now deceased.

The first Initiates were Mr Ronald John Dalby and Mr Raymond Thomas Jeynes, who were Initiated at the first Regular Meeting, held on 25 October 1973. At that Meeting there were seven applications for Joining Membership. One, Bro John Matthews became, in March 1979, the first Joining Member to be Installed as Worshipful Master. Mr Ronald D Jones, Initiated on 22 November 1973, was the first Initiate to reach the Chair of King Solomon, in March 1982. In 1974, the Lodge enjoyed its first appointment to Provincial Grand Rank, when the Organist, Bro Emlyn Grabham was appointed PPrAGOrg.

Besides WBro Emlyn Grabham, three further family members joined the Lodge: Bro Arfon Graham and his two sons, WBro Wayne Grabham and Bro Jestyn Grabham.

In November 1978, the Warrant for Glanogwr Chapter No.8508 was issued. EComp Alan W Hines was Invested as the Founder First Principal.

Until 1986, the Lodge was still using the Ogmore Lodge Working Tools. That year, WBro Charles Sydney (Jim) Aston kindly donated a new set of Working Tools to the Lodge. Also, early in 1986, the Foundation Stone of the new Temple at Brackla, Bridgend, was laid and in the October, Glanogwr Lodge held its first Meeting in the new Temple.

The Initial work in the preparation of Founding the Lodge was immense, and the guiding hand was that of the first Secretary, WBro Stanley B Roberts. The contribution of the Founder IPM, WBro Alan Hines, who later became DC and Preceptor, ensured that a high standard of performing Ritual was established. On 25 May 1992, in recognition of their contribution and dedicated service, these Brethren became the first Lodge Members to be made Honorary Members of the Lodge.

In the late 1980s and early 1990s, the Lodge continued to flourish, the high standard of Ritual was maintained and Membership increased steadily. A new Mandated Officer, WBro Keith Brill Lockyer, was appointed in 1996. A Maesteg man, he gave great encouragement to progressing Brethren. His dedication was rewarded in 1998, when he was made an Honorary Member of the Lodge. Two Founder Members and Past Masters, WBros Emlyn Grabham and John Gibbs, were also made Honorary Members.

During the previous 24 years, the original Ritual had been corrupted by the inclusion of parts of other Rituals performed in the Bridgend Temple. In 1997, the Brethren requested the Lodge Preceptor and DC, WBro Raymond C Dickens, to produce a new definitive Ritual, based on the original Oxford Working, as performed by Ogmore Lodge. This extensive work was presented to the Lodge in October 1997 and each Initiate is presented with a copy after his Raising.

The Lodge celebrated its 25th Anniversary in October 1998 with a Banner Dedication Ceremony. However, at the opening, WBro Gwyn Gunner, WM, reported that during the summer recess, two of the Founder Members had passed away namely, Founder Chaplain, WBro Joseph Ponsford and Honorary Member, WBro John Gibbs. The Ceremony then continued under the direction of WBro Paul Clement, ProvDepGDC. The Dedicationg Officer, WBro John Taylor, AProvGM, together with a full team of Provincial Officers was admitted. WBro John Taylor accepted the Gavel from the Worshipful Master and proceeded with the Dedication Ceremony. WBro Alan Hines spoke about the formation and development of the Lodge. Four engraved decanters had been purchased for presentation to the four Founder and Honorary Members, WBros Stanley Roberts, Alan Hines, Emlyn Graham and John Gibbs. WBro John Taylor presented three decanters, but it was decided that the decanter for the deceased WBro John Gibbs be retained by the Lodge. Every year since then, on Installation, the incoming Master fills the decanter with brandy and Lodge Brethren Toast Absent Brethren. On that special evening, all Brethren of the Lodge and the Provincial representatives were presented with commemorative plates displaying the Lodge Insignia.

In March 1999, WBro Anthony Edward Kirkham-Hill was Installed in the Chair of King Solomon for the second time. This Ceremony saw the first appearance in the Lodge of WBro Hywel Davies as AProvGM. In September that year, fifteen Brethren travelled to Builth Wells to see WBro Hywel Davies Installed as the new Provincial Grand Master.

Also in 1999, Bro Ralph Jones, SW, with the approval of the Lodge, applied to Grand Lodge to stage the official Prestonian Lecture in Glanogwr Lodge in 2000. At the Quarterly Communication, held in December 1999, it was announced that Glanogwr Lodge would be one of only three venues for the official delivery of the Millennium Prestonian Lecture. In order to have the full support of the Province, a Dispensation was obtained to confirm the date of the Meeting as Thursday, 19 October 2000. The Lecturer was WBro Richard A Crane, PGTreas, and his thought-provoking subject was entitled 'For therein you will be taught'. There were 147 Brethren in the Temple to receive the Millennium Prestonian Lecture. The Lecturer was accompanied into the Temple by the new ProvGM, RWBro Hywel Davies, together with VWBro Peter Frost, DepProvGM, two AProvGMs, WBro Rev Norman Lea and WBro Robert Nettleship and a full team of Acting Officers led by WBro Geoffrey W Thomas, ProvGDC. On that evening, to mark their 21 years' Membership of the Lodge, WBros Ralph Jones and Raymond Dickens, DC, presented the Lodge with SW and JW Aprons. Commemorative plates were presented to all the official guests and a cheque for £1000.00 was presented to the Grand Charity, which was accepted by WBro Richard A Crane.

A new Mandated Officer, WBro Gerald Davis, CStJ, PJGD, of Ewenny Lodge No.8485, was appointed in November 2002. Well known to the Brethren, and highly respected, he was Elected an Honorary Member of the Lodge in 2005.

It was a unique occasion, when on 27 November 2003, Mr Andrew Hill, the son of WBro Anthony Hill, and Mr Mark Ridgway, the son of WBro Brian Ridgway, were Initiated. The two fathers had been Initiated together in 1984, and to mark this occasion, the Ceremony was performed by the PMs of the Lodge, with WBro Anthony Hill occupying the Chair of King Solomon and WBro Brian Ridgway Acting as SW. The Ceremony was enhanced by the presence of the RWBro Hywel Davies, who presented both Initiates with their Aprons. Subsequently, another son, Mr James Howard Marlow Hill, was Initiated into the Lodge.

At the Installation Meeting in 2006, VWBro Peter Frost, in his capacity as Chairman of the Friends of AEPOWC, Porthcawl, presented the Lodge with a Certificate to mark the Lodge's 100% membership of the Friends. That evening, the youngest ever WM, Bro Dr Barrie John Goode, was Installed at 35 years of age. The following year, he Installed his fellow Initiate, Bro Dr Martin Simon Brunnock as Master, who at 34 years of age, then became the youngest Master of Glanogwr Lodge.

In 2007, Charles Sanders, PPrGSwdB, former Treasurer and Secretary, celebrated becoming a Masonic Veteran with over 50 years Membership of the Craft. Initiated into Glanogwr Lodge on 15 October 1956, he was Installed as WM in 1987. At the Installation Meeting in 2007, he was presented with his Certificate by WBro Geoffrey Thomas, AProvGM, who congratulated him and thanked him for his dedicated service, both to Glanogwr Lodge and to Cyfrinfa Dewi Sant, where he had been the Founder Treasurer and a Past Master.

WBro Dr Barrie Goode was Installed as WM for the second time in March 2009. His SW was Bro David Mark Ridgway, son of the late WBro Brian Ridgway. At the March 2010 Installation, Bro Mark became the first Lewis to occupy the Chair of King Solomon. To mark this special occasion, WBro Dr Barrie Goode invited WBro Anthony Hill to occupy the Chair, as he had Initiated Bro Mark in 2003.

Compiled by WBro Ralph Jones, PPrJGW.

Dinas Llandaf Lodge No.8512

Warranted : 14 March 1973

Consecrated : 22 September 1973

Meeting at the Masonic Hall, Cardiff.

In early 1973, the Provincial Grand Master, RWBro Lord Swansea, indicated that he would like to see more Lodges being formed. Consequently, WBro Julius Hermer, after conversations with WBro Joe Price and Bro Keith Flynn, both of whom lived in Llandaff, undertook to bring into being a new Lodge based on an affiliation with the ancient City of Llandaff. Julius, who had been Initiated into Carmel Lodge No.4774 in 1959, was a Past Master of South Wales Jurists Lodge No.7092 and Joe Price was a Past Master of Carmel Lodge.

At the suggestion of WBro Matt Cohen, father-in-law of Julius Hermer, Observer Lodge No.6015 was asked to become the 'Sponsoring' Lodge and it was agreed that WBro Cohen, PM Observer Lodge, would assume the Office of Chaplain in the new Lodge.

Bro Keith Flynn designed a Lodge Badge incorporating a medieval mitre as a reference to Llandaff's ancient ecclesiastical history.

On 22 September 1973, the Consecration of the new Lodge took place at the Cardiff Masonic Hall in the presence of, and under the guidance of RWBro the Rt Hon the Lord Swansea, ProvGM. VWBro Geoffrey Ashe, DepProvGM, assisted and Installed Julius Hyman Hermer as the first Master of the Lodge.

Founder Members of the Lodge were: Eifion Morgans, Matthew Cohen, Julius Hermer, Joseph Price, Keith Flynn, Gerald Brinks, George Grossman, Thomas Aplin, Frederick Green, Michael Lewis, Stefan Terlezki, George Cronin, John Hodell and Norman Lloyd-Edwards.

The Lodge quickly settled into its stride with enthusiasm and dedication, twin virtues which have obtained to this day. Under the leadership and guidance of WBro Julius Hermer, the Lodge has, over the past 37 years, extended its horizons in the pursuit of Masonic excellence. Emphasis has always been placed on presentation and commitment, both in the Temple and at the Festive Board. Ten years after the formation of the Lodge, in April 1983, the Dinas Llandaf Royal Arch Chapter was brought into being and has since continued to grow successfully. Sadly, WBro Julius passed to the Grand Lodge Above, at the age of 77 years, on Sunday, 18 September 2011.

The Lodge's presentation of Ritual has also been held in awesome regard by many visitors for the high standard of its inventiveness and free interpretation. However, over the years, the Lodge has not escaped well-intentioned comment, in particular with regard to the propensity of its Members to gravitate either to politics or to the law, or both. During the Lodge's history, eleven Members have found their way into politics, both local and national.

Four have served as Lord Mayor of Cardiff: WBros Ron Watkiss, CBE 1981-1982; Captain Norman Lloyd-Edwards 1985-1986; the late Julius Hermer, PJGD, 1987-1988 and Jeffrey Sainsbury, OStJ, PPrAGDC, 1991-1992. Julius also served as Deputy Chairman of Glamorgan County Council 1977-1978.

Three have entered Parliament: WBro Gwilym Jones, OStJ, LGR, PPrJGW, was MP for Cardiff North 1983-1997 and went on to become a Government Minister, and in 2010 he was appointed a Grand Officer with the Rank of PAGDC; Bro Lord Leonard, PPrGStwd, was a Government Minister and Bro Stefan Terlezki, CBE, PPrGStwd, was MP for Cardiff West 1983-1987. Stefan had endured an appalling time as a youth when a slave of the Nazis in the Ukraine during the Second World War, but eventually escaped and after many extraordinary adventures, he found his way to Britain, where he became a successful hotelier. In 1983, he contested the Parliamentary seat of Cardiff West on the resignation of George Thomas (a former Member of Cambrensis Lodge No.6608), who had held the seat for 38 years and had been elected Speaker of the House of Commons. Stefan held the seat for four years until he was defeated at the General Election of 1987 by the Labour Candidate Rhodri Morgan.

Ten Members have made their living in the professional pursuit of justice, either as Barristers or Solicitors, of whom three have received the award of Queen's Counsel. They are WBros Gerard Elias, PPrGReg, Deputy High Court Judge, Recorder and former Leader of the Wales & Chester Circuit, Chancellor of the Diocese of Swansea & Brecon, and appointed on 17 November 2010 as the National Assembly for Wales Commissioner for Standards; Winston Roddick, CB, PPrGReg, Counsel General to the National Assembly for Wales 1998-2003 and former leader of the Wales and Chester Circuit (elected 2007); and Gregory Bull, PPrAGDC, appointed Recorder in 2000, current leader of The Wales and Chester Circuit.

An interesting innovation was introduced early on. This was the purchase of firing glasses with the intention of 'firing' Toasts in the traditional manner at the Festive Board. While the idea was well received and pursued with enthusiasm, the practice fell short of perfect, due undoubtedly to the Members' evident lack of co-ordination and the danger of flying broken glass. In fact, WBro Joe Price almost severed a finger on the first occasion that the glasses were used. The glasses still exist, locked away in a cupboard, but the idea itself wore 'more thin' with every 'firing' until, like many a good idea, with the inevitability of gradualism it faded away.

In the important realm of charity, the Lodge has excelled consistently over the years and, in particular, secured second place in the Province when, in 1975, it raised a considerable sum for the RMBI Festival. Then in 1999, the Lodge again gained second place in the Province by raising another significant amount for the New Masonic Samaritan Fund Festival.

In 1991, WBro Keith Flynn, OBE, JP, PJGD, was appointed the Prestonian Lecturer. This was the first time that a Member of the Province had received such an honour. The Prestonian Lecture is the only lecture held under the authority of the United Grand Lodge of England and, with the exception of the years 1940-1946, regular appointments have been made annually since 1924. The title of Keith's lecture was 'Freemasons at War'. In 1998, he published 'A Province at War' - a record of Freemasonry in the Second World War in the Province of South Wales (Eastern Division) and also in 1998, 'Behind the Wire', a history of Freemasonry in captivity.

Other Brethren, past and present, who have gained distinction, either in their professional pursuits or Masonic activities include: RWBro Captain Sir Norman Lloyd-Edwards, KCVO, GCStJ, RD*, RNR, JGW, ProvGM, Province of South Wales, Lord Lieutenant of South Glamorgan 1991-2008, President of the New Masonic Samaritan Fund 1999-2007. VWBro Andrew Gretton, PGSwdB, DepProvGM, 2007-2011. WBro W George Morgan, PPrAGDC, President of the Welsh Rugby Union, 1987-1988. WBro Sir Paul Williams, OBE, PAGDC, PProvJGW, High Sheriff of South Glamorgan, 2007-2008, former Chief Executive of Bro Morgannwg Trust, Currently Director of NHS Wales, appointed Deputy Lieutenant of South Glamorgan in January 2010.

Compiled by WBro Keith Flynn, PJGD.

Cape St Vincent Lodge No.8524

Warranted : 13 June 1973

Consecrated : 17 September 1973

Meeting at the Masonic Hall, Cardiff.

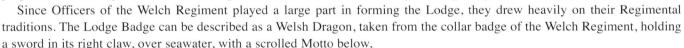

At about the time when the South Wales Borderers and the Welch Regiment merged to form the Royal Regiment of Wales, a group of Welch Regiment Officers met in a room in the Army Recruiting Office in St Mary Street, Cardiff, to discuss the setting up of a Masonic Lodge. Membership was to be drawn from the holders of Commissions in the three Armed Forces. This proposal was developed and Beehive Lodge No.6265 took on the role of Sponsoring Lodge.

Since Officers of the Welch Regiment played a large part in forming the Lodge, they drew heavily on their Regimental traditions. The Lodge Badge can be described as a Welsh Dragon, taken from the collar badge of the Welch Regiment, holding a sword in its right claw, over seawater, with a scrolled Motto below,

'Gwell Angau Na Chywilydd'

'Better Death than Dishonour'

The Dragon is superscribed by a Naval Crown and the date, 12 April 1782, to mark the Battle of the Saintes, a Battle Honour of the Welch. The Battle of the Saintes (known to the French as the Battle of Dominica) took place over 4 days, 9/12 April 1782, during the American War of Independence, and was a victory of a British fleet under Admiral Sir George Rodney over a French fleet under the Comte de Grasse, forcing the French and Spanish to abandon a planned invasion of Jamaica. The battle is named after the Saintes (or Saints), a group of islands between Guadeloupe and Dominica in the West Indies. On either side of the Crown are Masonic Jewels; on the right, the Square and Compasses and on the left, a Setting Maul.

The Lodge is named after the naval Battle of Cape St Vincent (14 February 1797), when a British fleet under Admiral Sir John Jervis defeated a larger Spanish fleet under José de Córdoba near Cape St Vincent, Portugal. A detachment of the 69th Regiment was serving as marines on HMS Captain (The Royal Welsh Regiment is the successor, via The Welch Regiment and the Royal Regiment of Wales, to the 69th Regiment). Having passed between the two parts of the Spanish Fleet with inconclusive results, Jervis then ordered his ships to turn about and *'take suitable stations for mutual support and engage the enemy as coming up in succession'*. Commodore Nelson, who was aboard HMS Captain (commanded by Captain Ralph Miller), interpreted this signal loosely and ordered Captain Miller to *'wear ship and take it out of line'*. This enabled HMS Captain to come alongside the San Nicholas with the San Joseph held fast on her port side. When Nelson ordered *'Boarders Away'*, *'the soldiers of the 69th, with an alacrity which will ever do them credit, led by Lieutenant Charles Pierson were foremost on this service'*. A soldier of the 69th, having broken in through the upper quarter gallery window, was followed by Nelson and others. Having captured the ship, Nelson used it as a bridge to take the San Joseph. This tactic became known as *'Nelson's Patent Bridge'* for boarding enemy vessels. There is a print in the Officers' Mess 3rd Battalion Royal Welsh, depicting Admiral Jervis (later Earl St Vincent) receiving the Spanish Admiral's sword and an oil painting by F S Baden-Powell, illustrating this phase of the battle. For their part in this great victory, the 69th was eventually awarded the Battle Honour 'St Vincent 1797'. This makes the Royal Welsh the only regiment in the British Army to have two naval battle honours.

The Lodge was Consecrated on 17 September 1973 by RWBro the Rt Hon the Lord Swansea, ProvGM, assisted by his Provincial Grand Officers. These included WBro Cecil H Rapport, ProvJGW, and WBro Geoffrey M Ashe, TD, ProvGDC, (DepProvGM, 1977-1992). WBro Colonel Gordon L P Elias, TD, DL, and Past Master of Beehive Lodge was then Installed Primus Master with WBro Colonel Arthur J Lennox as IPM. Bro Lieutenant Colonel John B Davies was Invested as Senior Warden. He became the second WM of the Lodge and later he was appointed to the Rank of PPrSGW. The first Junior Warden and third WM was Bro Lieutenant Colonel Ralph A Tucker, TD, who became a Deputy Lieutenant for the County of Carmarthenshire.

Another Founder Member of note was Bro Lieutenant Colonel Robert Louis Spurrell, who was Invested as the first Junior Deacon. A retired Regular Army Officer, he had a subsequent career as an Electrical Consultant. Bob Spurrell also enjoyed a distinguished Masonic career, which included becoming the fourth WM of the Lodge in 1976 and ultimately PPrSGW in 2001. In 1977, he was a Founder Member of Cape St Vincent Chapter and during 1984 he became First Principal of both Edgar Rutter and Cape St Vincent Chapters. He was honoured with the OBE and was also made a CStJ. Sadly, Bob died on Saturday, 4 April 2009 at the age of 85. At the time of his death, he was the First Principal of Hendre Chapter and PGStB of Supreme Grand Chapter

In 1977, Bob Spurrell was succeeded as WM by Bro Lt Commander Norman Lloyd-Edwards (Appointed ProvGM 2008), who was also a Founder Member and the Lodge's first Inner Guard. Bro Major J Stuart Peters (DepProvGM, 1998-1999) was another Founder Member and he was Invested as a Steward at the Consecration Meeting.

At the first Regular Lodge Meeting, WBro Cecil Rapport became a Joining Member. Later, honoured with the MBE and subsequently the CBE and KStJ, he became a Grand Officer with the Rank of PJGD. Bro Major Revd Ernest H Brown also joined at that Meeting. He became WM of the Lodge in 1980, and in due course was to be known as WBro Major Revd E H Brown, MBE, OStJ, TD, CF, PProvGChap.

The third and final Joining Member at that first Regular Meeting was Bro David Idwal Griffiths, DFC. He succeeded Ernest Brown as WM in 1981, as WBro Squadron Leader D I Griffiths, DFC. The Distinguished Flying Cross, awarded to Flying Officer David Idwal Griffiths (125687) Royal Air Force Volunteer Reserve, No.12 Squadron, Bomber Command, was Gazetted in the Supplement to the London Gazette of 12 November 1943. He was the Navigator of a Lancaster Bomber PH W 4991 Q that flew on numerous raids over Germany and Northern Italy. He was awarded his DFC for exemplary gallantry in the air on one of these sorties. His navigator's dividers, which he used for navigation during and after World War II, are now used in the Lodge, when in the Third Degree, to demonstrate the Working Tools of a Master Mason.

There is a further link between the Lodge and the Battle of Cape St Vincent, provided by Mr C Robert Vincent Norris, who was Initiated into Cape St Vincent Lodge in 1988 and had a Portuguese ancestor. The Portuguese were our oldest allies against

Napoleon, and his forbear fought under Admiral Jervis. When he settled in England, he adopted the English name Saint Vincent. This name was perpetuated through all his male descendents until Bro Norris's father, who dropped 'Saint' from his sons' names.

Freemasonry does not have a monopoly of brotherly love as the following shows: One morning in September 1852, the frigate HMS Dauntless made it into port in Barbados, with officers and ratings so stricken with yellow fever that only one Midshipman and a couple of sailors were left to work the ship. Heedless of infection, detachments of the 69th with their surgeons and orderlies, went aboard and gave all the succour they could. Later, with the approval of the Admiralty, a piece of silver plate was presented to the Regiment. The 3rd Battalion of the Royal Welsh, the current successor to 69th holds this piece, which bears this inscription:

Presented by the Officers of the Royal Navy
and Royal Marines to the Officers of Her
Majesty's 69th Regiment, in grateful remembrance
of the unbounded kindness and
generous aid afforded by them to
the Officers and Crew of
Her Majesty's Ship Dauntless
when suffering and disabled by Yellow Fever
at
Barbados 1852.

The Lodge is privileged to be permitted to display this centre-piece at every Festive Board.

It cannot be denied that Masonry has many Brethren of rank and opulence among its ranks. Cape St Vincent Lodge, a young Lodge with a small Membership, can boast many Present and Past Members of distinction. Below are some of the Brethren who have served the Lodge in many different ways, since its Consecration in 1973.

First and foremost must be the Provincial Grand Master of South Wales (Installed 2008), Captain Sir Norman Lloyd-Edwards, KCVO, GCStJ, RD*, RNR, Lord Lieutenant of the County of South Glamorgan, 1990-2008, who, as previously mentioned, was Founder Inner Guard of the Lodge. He was also a Lord Mayor of the City of Cardiff, 1985-1986, as was Lieutenant Colonel Gareth Neale, CBE, 2006-2007. Cecil Rapport, another Founder Member of the Lodge, was Deputy Lord Mayor, 1970-1971.

Eleven Brethren have been Deputy Lieutenants of the Counties of South Wales and five have been High Sheriffs of these counties. A Member of military distinction was Major General Morgan Llewellyn, OBE, a former General Officer Commanding Wales.

The Cape St Vincent Centre-piece

Compiled by WBro M Roy Scott, TD, DL, PPrGSwdB,
and WBro Howard Worthing, TD, PPrJGW.

Luminary Lodge No.8530

Warranted : 12 September 1973

Consecrated : 13 November 1973

Meeting at the Masonic Hall, Merthyr Tydfil.

The first meeting to consider forming the Lodge was held on 15 January 1972. The Petition was presented to Loyal Cambrian Lodge No.110, the Sponsoring Lodge, on 7 June 1973, and the Warrant was duly granted on 12 September 1973.

The Lodge was Consecrated by RWBro the Rt Hon the Lord Swansea, DL, ProvGM, on 13 November 1973. The Consecration Party consisted of, among others, WBro J William F Batley, PJGD, ProvSGW, as SW; WBro Cecil H Rapport, ProvJGW, as JW; WBro Malcolm H Thompson, PAGDC, ProvGSec, as Secretary; WBro Geoffrey M Ashe, TD, PAGDC, as DC; and WBro E Haydn Lloyd, PPrJGW, ProvGOrg, as Organist. Also in attendance were WBro Harry F Stockwell, PSGD, DepProvGM; WBro Harold Wilson, PJGD, AProvGM, and WBro Llewellyn G Bevan, PJGD, AProvGM.

WBro David Gerald Williams was Installed as Primus Master. He Invested WBro Sidney James Coleman as SW and WBro Idris Roberts as JW. Among the other Founders were WBro Kenneth Bibby, PM North Glamorgan Lodge No.4055, Secretary; WBro Melvyn Jones, PM Kibbor Lodge No.4364, DC; WBro Thomas L Wilson, WM of Fforest Lodge No.2606, ADC, and Bro Gareth Whale, Steward.

Luminary Lodge clearly belonged to the 'new' generation of Craft Lodges in the Province and, in the spirit of the time, its Founder Members were eager to establish a Lodge which increased accessibility and facilitated progress for potential and existing Freemasons. From its conception, it was intended to be a small, friendly Lodge that, by meeting only four times a year and by not requiring wives or partners to play an active part in the catering arrangements (as was the practice of the day), enabled many to reach the Chair of King Solomon, who might otherwise have been deterred from that journey. It was also meant to be a non parochial Lodge and one where an eclectic mix of occupations and interests was to be actively encouraged, when proposing Candidates for Membership. It proved attractive to numerous Joining Members of high standing in the Fraternity and from its beginnings was very popular with Visiting Brethren, who found the welcoming atmosphere on a Friday evening, more than conducive to a productive and enjoyable Masonic experience.

The idea behind the name 'Luminary' was to reflect the enlightened approach inherent in the Lodge's character and 'Light' therefore was to play a central role in the choice of Banner design and Lodge Motto. While there was some deliberation concerning the source of light which would best represent the spirit of the Lodge, it was soon realised that the Volume of the Sacred Law was undoubtedly the most appropriate. This also led to the choice of *'Lux Fiat'* as the Lodge Motto, which alludes not only to the first words of God, *'Let there be light'*, but also to the light of Masonic knowledge, brotherly love, relief and truth which Luminary Lodge, along with every other Craft Lodge, seeks to embody and promote. The Lodge Insignia, which untypically was replicated without any additional embellishments on the Lodge Banner, was designed by WBro Idris Roberts, Founder JW, Installed as WM in 1976. The pleasing symmetry and aesthetic simplicity of his design perfectly matched the Lodge's openness. It has more than stood the test of time in the intervening years.

The Banner was Dedicated by Lord Swansea on 14 November 1975. More than two decades later, in 1999, he Invested WBro Idris Roberts with the Collar of PPrJGW, in recognition of his distinguished position in the history of Luminary Lodge. To those present who witnessed and understood the significance of this act, it evoked fond memories of the promise and optimism of the Lodge during the seventies, which was a feeling no doubt prevalent in numerous other Lodges in the Province at the time.

This optimism was exemplified by the fact that on 10 September 1976, the Lodge received a Petition from the Founders of the proposed Luminary Royal Arch Chapter. The Warrant was granted on 10 November and the Chapter was Consecrated on 3 December.

Another symbolic example of the promise of the early years of Luminary Lodge was the Joint Initiation of two Lewises on 13 May 1977. There was general and genuine satisfaction when Bro Peter John Budd, son of WBro John Budd, WM, and Bro Mark Lloyd Roberts, son of WBro Idris Roberts, IPM, were Initiated together. Both went on to occupy the Chair of King Solomon in Luminary Lodge, the only Lewises of the Lodge to have done so to date. In the 1990s, the need for Past Masters to reoccupy the Chair of King Solomon became a fact of life, but the prevalence of this necessity should not be exaggerated as only five of over thirty WMs served in this capacity.

On 13 November 1998, exactly twenty five years to the day after the Lodge's Consecration, Luminary Lodge held its hundredth Regular Meeting. To mark the Anniversary, WBro John Taylor, AProvGM, was in attendance and his sincere eloquence upon the significance of the event helped to make the evening the highlight in the Masonic lives of many of the Brethren present. WBro Kenneth Bibby, the Lodge's first Secretary and one of the guiding lights in the formation of the Lodge, gave a brief factual résumé of its Foundation. This included the long forgotten detail that the first name agreed for the Lodge was 'Lumine'. However, the RWProvGM had informed the Founder Members that he had been unable to find the word 'Lumine' as a noun in the House of Lords Library and so suggested that the Lodge be called 'Luminary'. The Founders had not realised that 'Lumine' was an Old English verb, now obsolete, meaning 'to light up'. Lord Swansea's suggestion of 'Luminary', a noun, 'a light-giving body', or 'a source of intellectual or moral light', was therefore the perfect solution. This brief, though touching anecdote, conjured up an image of a thoughtful man in high office, who in true Masonic fashion, still found time to be helpful and considerate.

Remaining on the themes of bringing illumination and being helpful and considerate, despite the pressures of high office, it is a tremendous source of pride to the Brethren that RWBro Hywel Davies, PProvGM, is an Honorary Member of the Lodge. He was gracious enough to attend the 2006 Installation of WBro Paul Hughes (his second time as Master), having previously visited Luminary Lodge as AProvGM, when WBro Paul Installed his successor, WBro Mark Lloyd Roberts, in 1999. In addition, the Lodge has been very fortunate to enjoy the frequent support of WBro Brian Eveleigh, AProvGM, who has never failed to enthuse and inspire the Officers, Members and visitors to the Lodge whenever he has attended.

The Grand Lodge Officer for Luminary Lodge is WBro Victor George Watkins, JP, who amply demonstrated his tireless industry and exemplary gift for Ritual when he took the Chair of Luminary Lodge in 2001. He continues to maintain a very watchful eye on the proceedings and his zeal and assiduity remain the stuff of legend.

Regrettably there are just five remaining Founders of the Lodge. Firstly, WBro Idris Roberts, already mentioned and who is now an Honorary Member. WBro Colin Albert Parker, the first Organist and compiler of the musical service for the Lodge, was Installed as WM in 1994. WBro Mostyn John Chapman, first Senior Deacon, became WM in 1978. WBro Tegwyn Havard Jones, who was the first Tyler and WM in 1979 and 1993, and is now an Honorary Member. Bro Glyn Hopkins, first JD, donated the Lodge Banner and subsequently a number of smaller artefacts.

The Lodge history would not be complete without the inclusion of WBro Graham George Allen, who holds a unique place in the annals of Luminary Lodge. He deserves special mention as the Brother who can justly lay claim to being the most conscientious contributor to almost every aspect of the Lodge's business since its inception. He served as Lodge Secretary for a total of seventeen years and was WM in 1987, 2000 and again in 2008. In addition, he was, of course, the Founder WM of Luminary Lodge's Daytime Daughter Lodge, St Tydfil's Lodge No.9753, which was Consecrated so immaculately by RWBro Hywel Davies, ProvGM, on 15 March 2002 and which has so successfully maintained and developed the warm and friendly ethos, so true to the original vision for Luminary Lodge.

Other notable Worshipful Brethren who have played a significant part in the history of the Lodge include: WBro Melvyn Jones, the first DC, who although not WM until 1991, was another guiding light in the formation of the Lodge. WBro Dr Arthur Gruffydd Jones, a Joining Member at the second Regular Meeting on 10 May 1974, Installed as WM in 1983, served as Chaplain for many years, before accepting Honorary Membership for his sterling service to the Lodge. WBro John Charles Wiggins, WM in 1985 and DC for many years, his sense of bonhomie remains legendary to this very day. He formed a great friendship with WBro William Keith Grindle, WM in 1997, who sadly passed away in 2005. They created the best after dinner double act in the history of Luminary Lodge. WBro Dr Arun Kumar Chakrabarti, WM in 1990, has been Charity Steward for as long as anyone can remember. He also took on the role of Chaplain for good measure. WBro Mervyn T Rogers and WBro Norman H Collins who, although not originally Members of Luminary Lodge, have performed the roles of Tyler and Organist, respectively, for so many years and with such success, that good sense and natural justice cried out that they be made Honorary Members.

Compiled by WBro Mark Lloyd Roberts, PPrAGReg.

Lodge of Sincerity
No.8531

Warranted : 12 September 1973

Consecrated : 19 November 1973

Meeting at the Masonic Hall, Swansea.

Lodge of Sincerity was Consecrated on Monday, 19 November 1973 at the Masonic Temple, Swansea, by RWBro the Rt Hon the Lord Swansea, DL, ProvGM.

Earlier in 1973, a small group of Brethren, whose Lodges met in Swansea, had decided that there was room for a new Craft Lodge, a small 'dinner jacket' Lodge, which would meet only four times a year, aim for high standards of Ritual, and dine in style. The objective would be to encourage the introduction and retention of new Candidates; but the admission of Joining Members would be restricted, in principle, to Brethren from Lodges outside the Province.

The proposal found favour when put to the Provincial Office. VWBro Harry F Stockwell, PSGD, DepProvGM, requested WBro William Batley, PJGD, ProvSGW, and a Member of Ionic Lodge No.6626, to assist the intending Founders with the formalities. Under his guidance, a Warrant for the formation of the Lodge was obtained on 12 September 1973.

The Lodge was named 'Sincerity' at the suggestion of the DepProvGM, who explained that 'Sincerity 'came from a Latin word meaning pure, flawless and genuine. It dated back to the potters of Roman times: cracked pottery was repaired with wax but the perfect vase without wax was a genuine and sincere item.

The Lodge has never adopted a Crest or Motto, although several designs for a Crest or Banner were sketched out at the beginning.

There were eighteen Founder Members and the Sponsoring Lodge was Ionic Lodge. The Founder Master was WBro Dudley R Brown, PPrGSuptWks, PM Ionic Lodge. During his year, he Initiated, Passed and Raised a Candidate, who afterwards progressed to JD and then dropped away. After completing his year as IPM, WBro Dudley Brown became Chaplain for a year. He was appointed Almoner in 1980, and continued to serve in that capacity until 1997. For many years, he was also an inspirational Preceptor of LOI. He was appointed to PAGSuptWks in 1997. Since then, he has made his home in the USA. He remained a Member, continuing to support the Lodge and attend whenever he was in the UK, until 2009, when he was Elected an Honorary Member.

WBro Tom Abbott was Founder Chaplain and except for 1975, remained Chaplain of the Lodge until 1984, when he became JW. Throughout this period, he was Preceptor of LOI and noted for his strict but fair insistence on high standards. He was Installed as Master in 1986. The following year, having retired, he moved to the Lake District and eventually resigned from the Lodge.

The Founder Secretary was WBro Terry Short, PM Beaufort Lodge No.3834 and one of the main promoters. It is said that the Lodge was his 'brainchild' and he had been responsible under WBro Batley's guidance, for the formalities leading to the Lodge's formation. He remained Secretary until 1980 and became Master in 1981. He was succeeded as Secretary by another Founder, WBro Alex Milne, a Member and later Master of Talbot Lodge No.1323, who continued as Secretary until 1991. WBro Alex Milne also served as Charity Steward from 1983 until 1995, during which time, the Lodge distinguished itself in the Provincial Festivals of 1986 and 1990. He also laid the foundations for the Lodge's success in the 1999 Festival before ill-health compelled him to retire. He was appointed PAGDC in 1993.

The first Treasurer was WBro V Stuart Hansford, PM Doric Lodge No.5968. He remained Treasurer until 1990, after which he was Chaplain for another five years.

VWBro J Stuart Peters, PM Ionic Lodge, was the first DC and remained in that Office until 1990. He was appointed ProvJGW in 1980 and PJGD in Grand Lodge in 1983. To mark the latter achievement, the Lodge presented him with a regalia case. He was twice promoted in Grand Lodge, to PSGD in 1985, and PGSwdB in 1999. VWBro Stuart Peters was appointed an Assistant ProvGM in 1984 and served continuously in that Office until he was appointed DepProvGM in 1998, retiring on Lord Swansea's retirement in July 1999.

WBro Gwyn Hardwidge, who had been Installed as WM of Dyffryn Tawe Lodge No.6056 in 1977, became a Steward at the Consecration, and continued to serve in that capacity until he was appointed SW in 1984, leading to his Installation as Master in 1985. He was appointed PAGDC in 1992.

WBro Michael J Hoare, who was Installed WM of Glantawe Lodge No.5378 in 1977, became Master of Lodge of Sincerity in 1991. A supreme Ritualist, he delivered the Lecture on the Tracing Board to the Initiate at the first Regular Meeting. His Ritual has since been both an inspiration and an example to all the Brethren. Moreover, he was also the first dining Steward, and retained that important role until he became SW in 1990. Despite that, and subsequent elevation, he continues to the present day to plan and arrange the menus for the Lodge Festive Boards. He was appointed PAGDC in 1993 and promoted to PJGD in 2001. WBro Michael Hoare achieved the further distinction of serving as Deputy Grand Superintendent in Provincial Grand Chapter from 1999 until his retirement in 2005.

WBro Eric Davies was the first JW and became the third Master in 1975. He succeeded WBro Tom Abbot as Chaplain in 1984, remaining in that Office until 1996, returning for a further period as Chaplain from 2000 until 2006, when he was compelled by ill-health to retire. Soon afterwards, he was Elected an Honorary member.

One of the Assistant PGMs present at the Consecration was WBro Llewellyn G Bevan, PSGD, PM Talbot Lodge and also a Member of its Daughter Lodge, Ionic Lodge. WBro Llewellyn Bevan was Elected to full Membership of Lodge of Sincerity on 8 November 1977 and, on 30 January 1978, occupied the Chair of King Solomon to Initiate his son, John L Bevan. At that Meeting, which was held in the Major Temple, 21 Members of the Lodge were present together with 156 visitors, including the RWBro the Lord Swansea, ProvGM, VWBro Geoffrey Malin Ashe, DepProvGM, three AProvGMs, and most of the other Acting Provincial Grand Officers. He occupied the Chair again on 9 May 1978 to Raise his son, but on that occasion there were only 21 visitors. WBro Llewellyn Bevan was Installed as Master of Lodge of Sincerity on 11 November 1980, when the Mandated

Officer was WBro Stuart Peters, ProvJGW. WBro Llewellyn Bevan also became Master of Ionic Lodge in 1982, thus achieving the interesting distinction of having served as Master of three generations of Lodges – Talbot, its Daughter, Ionic, and its Daughter, Sincerity.

It was always the intention of the Founders that the Lodge should remain small in numbers, hold its Meetings in the Minor Temple at Swansea and dine in the Refectory. So it has transpired, with the exception of only three occasions, when the numbers attending were too great to be accommodated in the smaller rooms. The first was the Consecration Meeting and the second the Initiation of John Bevan by his Father. The third was Bro John Bevan's Installation on 29 November 1984. WBro John Evans was Master that year, but at his invitation WBro Llewellyn Bevan assumed the Chair to conduct the Installation of his son in the Installed Board. The Provincial Executive Officer was VWBro Geoffrey M Ashe, DepProvGM, who was accompanied by a full complement of Officers together with four AProvGMs, and there were 77 visitors as well as 22 Lodge members.

The Lodge has stuck quite closely to the original plan to restrict Joining Members. WBro Llewellyn Bevan was a special case. So were WBro Ken Grove and WBro Ray Morgan, who were ineligible to be Founders as they had been Masons for less than three years. They were proposed for Joining Membership at the Consecration Ceremony and Elected at the first Regular Meeting. Ken Grove, PM Indefatigable Lodge No.237 and of Meridian Lodge No.9603, has always made an important contribution to the Lodge as an accomplished Ritualist and in various Offices at different times over the years, including those of Treasurer and Almoner. He became Master in 2004 and was promoted to PPrJGW in 2002.

John Evans, whose Mother Lodge was in Stroud, joined in 1976. He became Master in 1982, took over as DC in 1990 serving in that Office with distinction until he handed over to John Solly in 2004. He has since continued to give inspiration and encouragement to the newer and older Members alike. He was appointed ProvAGDC in 1989 and promoted to PPrGSwdB in 2002.

Another Joining Member from outside the Province was WBro Robert Nettleship, whose Mother Lodge is Stowe Lodge No.9002, London. He first visited the Lodge as an Entered Apprentice on 8 November 1983 and continued to visit regularly for two years, before being Elected to Membership in November 1985. After progressing through the Offices, he was Installed as Master first in 1992 and for the second time in 1996. He was appointed ProvJGW in 1998 and AProvGM in 1999. In Grand Lodge he was appointed PJGD in 2000, promoted to SGD in 2002 and was a member of the Board of Grand Stewards for 2005-2006. WBro Robert Nettleship has been Chaplain of the Lodge since 2006.

At the first Regular Meeting of the Lodge, the first Candidate, who had been proposed at the Consecration Meeting, was Initiated, and was followed by a steady supply of Initiates. A number of then came and went. Those who progressed to the Chair included Tony Hunt, who was the first Candidate to become Master, but moved away from Swansea soon afterwards; Hadyn Morgan, who was the first Initiate to achieve Provincial Rank; Tony Powell, who later resigned because of ill-health; John Moses, who went on to serve as Secretary for several years; John Timothy, who perished in a traffic accident in 2000; John Roach, who has since continued to give devoted service to the Lodge, holding the Offices of Secretary, Charity Steward and Treasurer at different times; similarly Sior Roberts, who has also served variously as Chaplain, Almoner and Secretary for several years, and was reappointed Secretary in 2010; and John Solly, who held the Office of Director of Ceremonies from 2003 until 2011, when he had to step down because of ill-health.

Clive Atkins was Initiated in 1986, became Master in 1994 and again in 2006. He was appointed PPrJGD in 2000. Not only did he serve as Secretary for several years, he has brought in and encouraged the introduction of a stream of further new faces, most of whom have occupied, or are progressing to, the Chair. These include: George Lawrence, Installed as WM in 2000 and

2005, Charity Steward from 2002 until after the 2010 Provincial Festival, now DC and, having been appointed PPrJGD in 2006, was promoted to PPrGSwdB in 2011; Jeffrey Thomas, another accomplished Ritualist, Almoner since 2003, was appointed PPrJGD in 2007; his brother, Vernon Thomas, who served as Secretary from 2006 to 2010, was appointed PPrJGD in 2007; and Ifor Williams, who became Treasurer in 2006, was appointed ProvGStwd in 2009.

Only once has the Lodge been faced with a Ceremony without a Candidate. That was in March 1992, during Robert Nettleship's first term as Master, when a delay in Rule 158 formalities rendered an Initiate temporarily ineligible. The vacancy was filled at the last moment by a request from Stowe Lodge No. 9002 for their Candidate, Rodney Dew, fortuitously the son of Robert Nettleship's proposer into Masonry, to be Raised in Lodge of Sincerity. The Lodge was pleased to comply with the request and it turned out to be a very happy and successful occasion, supported by several visitors from Stowe Lodge.

Lodge of Sincerity takes pride in the fact that, in its comparatively short history, its Membership has included no less than three AProvGMs, one of whom progressed to DepProvGM; one Deputy Grand Superintendent, and four other Grand Officers. In 2000, five Grand Lodge Officers were simultaneously Members of the Lodge.

As intended by the Founders, the Lodge has always maintained an exceptionally high standard of dining and, for this, credit and thanks must go to WBro Michael Hoare for his unstinting efforts in arranging splendid menus, and stimulating the caterers at Swansea to reach ever greater heights. The small Refectory at Swansea provides an intimate and friendly ambience.

After thirty-four years, most of the Founders have moved onwards or upwards, and only WBro Michael Hoare remains a Subscribing Member. WBros Dudley Brown and Eric Davies remain as Honorary Members. The Lodge is, however, in good heart, with a team of young and very competent Officers and some excellent Masons coming through, all of whom it is hoped will ensure that the original dreams of the Founders are fulfilled.

Compiled by WBro Robert J Nettleship, PSGD, PGStwd, PAProvGM.

Y Bont Faen Lodge No.8533

Warranted : 12 September 1973

Consecrated : 4 December 1973

Meeting at the Cowbridge Town Hall.

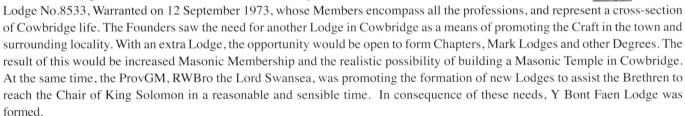

Over the years, Cowbridge has grown from a market town in the Vale of Glamorgan to the thriving town we know today. As Cowbridge has grown, so has Freemasonry. The first Lodge was St Quentin's Lodge No.4778, a Farmers' Lodge, Warranted on 2 September 1925; next came Industria Cambrensis Lodge No.6700, with its connection to Industry, Warranted on 2 June 1948; and finally Y Bont Faen Lodge No.8533, Warranted on 12 September 1973, whose Members encompass all the professions, and represent a cross-section of Cowbridge life. The Founders saw the need for another Lodge in Cowbridge as a means of promoting the Craft in the town and surrounding locality. With an extra Lodge, the opportunity would be open to form Chapters, Mark Lodges and other Degrees. The result of this would be increased Masonic Membership and the realistic possibility of building a Masonic Temple in Cowbridge. At the same time, the ProvGM, RWBro the Lord Swansea, was promoting the formation of new Lodges to assist the Brethren to reach the Chair of King Solomon in a reasonable and sensible time. In consequence of these needs, Y Bont Faen Lodge was formed.

The first Meeting of the Founders took place on 26 February 1973, at the Horse and Groom Public House, Cowbridge. Amongst those present were WBros Sam Northway, John Lock, Bill Northway, Herbert Parry and six other Brethren. At that Meeting, the name 'Pontfaen', was proposed for the Lodge, as it was thought desirable that the Lodge should have a name with a local connection. It was also proposed that the Lodge would meet four times a year at the Town Hall in Cowbridge. Costs were estimated as follows; Founder Member fee, £20; annual dues inclusive of dining, £15. The Officers Designate were proposed as follows: WBro J Lock, ProvAGDC, WM; Bro G Harris, SW; Bro G Edgeworth, JW; WBro B M Griffiths, Treasurer; WBro Sam Northway, Secretary; and WBro W J (Bill) Northway, DC. WBro John Lock was Installed WM of Venables Llewelyn Lodge No.3756 in 1969; the others were all Members of Industria Cambrensis Lodge.

St Quentin's Lodge, probably because it was the senior Lodge in Cowbridge, agreed to be the Sponsoring Lodge. At the next Founders' meeting, the Lodge name was changed to 'Y Bont Faen', after Bert Parry had advised on the correct spelling and translation. The number of potential Founders had increased to 20, but it was discovered that four Brethren were not qualified;

they had not been Master Masons for 3 full years. It was resolved that these Brethren would become the first Joining Members of the Lodge. The Petition was signed at a Regular Meeting of St Quentin's Lodge on 17 April 1973, and the Warrant was issued on 12 September 1973. At the final meeting of the Founders, prior to the Consecration, all the arrangements were in place, and the Borough Coat of Arms was selected as the design for the Lodge Crest.

The Lodge was Consecrated by Lord Swansea on 4 December 1973. For logistical reasons, the Ceremony was held at the Porthcawl Masonic Temple. WBro John Lock, PPrAGDC, Installed WM Venables Llewelyn Lodge No.3756 in 1969, was Installed as the first WM, with Bro Gwyn Harris as SW and Bro Glyn Edgeworth as JW, both being Members of Industria Cambrensis Lodge. The 18 Founders not only came from

The Town Hall, Cowbridge

Cowbridge, but also from Cardiff, Rhondda, Bridgend and Swansea, and they all immediately gelled as a family. Indeed, the Lodge was known as a family Lodge, with the wives of the Officers and Members giving freely of their time to help the Lodge establish itself. Like a family entering names in the family Bible, each Member's name is entered in the Lodge Bible. The Initiate is asked to sign his name in the Lodge Bible on the night that he becomes a Member of the Lodge, which is something unique to Y Bont Faen Lodge.

At the first Regular Meeting, held on 7 February 1974, Louis C Fisher and Bryan Welsby, PPrJGW, became the first Initiates. Since then, 44 Brethren have been Initiated into the Lodge, and 20 Joining Members have been admitted. In 2010, Lodge Membership consisted of 39 Members. WBro Bryan was Installed as WM in 1981.

Any new Lodge needs to have expert Brethren to guide it and set it on the correct course. John Lock, Primus Master, certainly did that. His confidence, superb Ritual skills and warmth of character inspired all the Officers and Brethren to give their very best. WBro Elwyn Lloyd, PPrAGDC, PM Morganwg Lodge No.5084, first IPM, often commented how easy the year was with John in the Chair. John was also Preceptor of the Lodge of Instruction, with Bill Northway and Mansel Griffiths as Vice-Preceptors. Bill Northway, first DC, gave tremendous confidence to all the Brethren involved in the floor work, and he made sure that if a prompt was needed, it was for that Brother and not for the rest of the Lodge to hear.

The organisation and administration of the Lodge were in the very capable hands of Sam Northway, Founder Secretary. Appropriately, Sam, a leading light and driving force behind the formation of the Lodge, was Installed as Master, when the Lodge celebrated its 25th Anniversary in 1998. He had taken the Chair to ensure that the younger Brethren did not proceed through the Lodge too quickly; that they may enjoy each Office and gain the experiences expected of a Brother, who will one day become WM. Other Founders did likewise for the same reason. Bill Northway gave up his usual role as DC to become Worshipful Master in 1990. He was followed by Elwyn Lloyd, Founder IPM, who was Installed in 1991, at the young age of 80. His energy and expertise in the Ritual was an example to the younger Brethren, giving them an excellent role model. The highlight of his year came in October 1992, when he Initiated his grandson, Andrew, into the Lodge with his son acting as SW; the Lodge now has three generations of one family as Members. The other Founder to occupy the Chair was Meidrym Howells, Founder Chaplain, who relinquished the Office to become Master in 1995. Although Meidrym lived in Neath, he never missed a Meeting and demonstrated the commitment of attendance that he would wish of all Brethren. Another excellent Ritualist, he was also Preceptor of Penrice Lodge No.4172, Swansea, where he was Master in 1971.

The 25th Anniversary was celebrated on 15 May 1998, at a Joint Meeting with Industria Cambrensis Lodge, which was celebrating its 50th Anniversary. Each Lodge Member received a special Firing Glass, suitably engraved with the Lodge Crest. The next Regular Meeting, held on 1 October, was another special occasion, when the Lodge Banner was Dedicated in an impressive Ceremony by WBro Rev Norman Lea, AProvGM, together with WBro Rev Canon Huw Mosford, ProvGChap, and other Provincial Officers.

On 1 February 2001, at a Regular Meeting with WBro Barrie Aldridge, WM, in the Chair, the Lodge received a visit from the ProvGM, RWBro Hywel Davies. Bro David Brown, a Marine Supervisor with Associated British Ports, happened to be the Initiate that evening, confirming a subsequent trend of admitting many more Seafarers and former Seafarers into the Lodge. Very sadly, WBro Barrie Aldridge, WM, died in Office on 19 June 2001, at the relatively young age of 56. This was a grievous loss to the Lodge. Barrie had served the Lodge faithfully, actively and vigorously since he was Initiated in 1980. The Lodge was honoured by a further visit from the ProvGM on 6 December 2001, for the Installation of Bro Paul McCann as WM. He was accompanied on this occasion by VWBro Peter Frost, DepProvGM, and a team of Provincial Officers. This was a very memorable occasion, and 70 Members and visitors dined at the Festive Board, held at the Bear Hotel, Cowbridge.

At the Meeting of 6 December 2001, Graham Lloyd stood down as Lodge Secretary, after 18 years of very loyal and conscientious service. He had succeeded Sam Northway in 1983, who had previously served the Lodge as Secretary for the first 10 years of its existence. Sam Northway died on 7 October 2004. He had served the Lodge and Cowbridge Masonry admirably for 31 years.

WBro Louis Fisher, the first Initiate of the Lodge, died on 6 June 2008, after a very long illness. Louis had also been a very prominent Freemason in Cowbridge for nearly 35 years.

Y Bont Faen Lodge has always more than met its commitments to the various Charitable Provincial Festivals held since 1973. In this connection, special mention must be made of WBro Gordon France, who has been Charity Steward since 1994.

On 8 December 2010, in a very impressive ceremony in the Masonic Hall, Bridgend, WBro Gordon France, PPrGReg, Installed as WM in1988, and very active Member of the Lodge, was Invested as Provincial Prior for the Province of Monmouth and South Wales, in the United Religious, Military and Masonic Orders of the Temple and of St John of Jerusalem, Palestine, Rhodes and Malta in England and Wales and Provinces Overseas, more commonly known as the Knights Templar. This very prestigious appointment, equivalent to that of RWProvGM in the Craft, reflects extremely well on Y Bont Faen Lodge.

A long standing tradition of the Lodge is that all Members, on Initiation or Joining , become Life Members of the Friends of the Albert Edward Prince of Wales Court, Porthcawl. The Lodge has been awarded a Certificate for achieving 100% Membership, and this success is mainly due to our very long standing Lodge Liaison Officer, WBro David Gedrych.

Y Bont Faen Lodge has been blessed over the last 37 years with dedicated and enthusiastic Masters, some of whom have had to confront difficult times, but have all helped to build a strong foundation for the future, to which the Lodge can look forward with confidence. The Lodge still meets in the Town Hall, Cowbridge, and the possibility of obtaining a Temple in Cowbridge is, unfortunately, as remote as ever, due mainly to the very high property prices in the very desirable market and commuter town. Nevertheless, our aim should be to complete what our Founders hoped for - a Temple of our own so that we may be masters of our own destiny. They laid the Foundation Stone - let us Tile the Roof.

Compiled by WBro Brian V Thomas, PPrJGW, from notes by WBro W G Lloyd, PJGD.

Lodge of St Theodore No.8536

Warranted : 12 September 1973

Consecrated : 10 December 1973

Meeting at the Masonic Hall, Port Talbot.

By the early 1970s, the older Lodges in Port Talbot, such as Afan Lodge No.833, Margam Abbey Lodge No.5257 and Baglan Lodge No.6079, had a very large Membership, and it was not unusual for a Master Mason to take up to 16 years to reach the Chair. To address this problem, Lord Swansea, ProvGM, made it known that he would welcome the formation of additional Lodges, which were to meet less frequently than the established ones. In consequence, Margam Abbey Lodge decided to Sponsor a new Lodge in Port Talbot, which was to become known as 'Lodge of St Theodore No.8536'.

Originally, it was intended that WBro Kenneth Robinson of Margam Abbey Lodge would be the Master Designate, but this failed to materialize. The reason is unknown, as no preliminary Minutes appear to have been kept before the Consecration Ceremony. The idea was not forgotten, and in the winter of 1972, a Petition was presented to WBro Clifford Jones, WM, requesting the support of Margam Abbey Lodge. The Principal Officers Designate were WBro Lyn Jenkins, WM, Bros T R C Raikes, SW and E J G Parry, JW.

In 1897, a Church, dedicated to St Theodore, was built in Port Talbot to serve the needs of the then rapidly growing population of the town, as the original Chapel of Ease, Holy Cross Church, as it is now called, was proving too small. The Founders proposed the name of 'Lodge of St Theodore', in acknowledgement of all that this magnificent Church had meant to countless people over so many years. It also followed the tradition of other Port Talbot Lodges, which all had long standing affiliations with many of the other churches within the town.

A Warrant for the formation of Lodge of St Theodore was duly granted on 12 September 1973 and it was Consecrated on Monday, 10 December 1973, at the Masonic Temple, Port Talbot.

The Consecrating Officer was RWBro the Rt Hon the Lord Swansea, ProvGM, who was accompanied by the full Provincial team, together with WBro Malcolm Thompson, ProvGSec. The first Master Elect, WBro A Lyn Jenkins, PM Margam Abbey Lodge, was presented by WBro Geoffrey M Ashe for the benefit of Installation, which was impressively carried out by the ProvGM. He also addressed the new Worshipful Master, who then duly appointed and Invested his Wardens. It should also be mentioned that at the Ceremony, the Lodge was honoured with the presence of The Guildford Singers.

It was proposed by the newly formed Lodge that the thirteen Consecrating Officers be Elected as Honorary Members of the Lodge and this was effected immediately. It was also proposed, seconded and unanimously accepted that the Membership subscription be set at £9.00 per Member and that the Lodge would meet five times a year. It would hold its meetings on the second Monday of December, February and April and on the third Monday of October and May, with the Installation Ceremony to take place in the month of February. The Lodge was then closed and the Brethren retired to the dining room, where a Consecration Celebration Dinner was served.

The first Regular Meeting was held on 11 February 1974, when Rev Graham Holcombe became the Lodge's first Initiate. He subsequently resigned from Freemasonry in order to commence theological training for the Church at St Michael's College, Llandaff. The Rev Canon Graham Holcombe, BA, FRSA, OStJ, is now Canon in Residence at Llandaff Cathedral. On 8 April 1974, Bro Edward George Lewis was Initiated and in February 1984 he became the first Initiate to become WM of the Lodge.

Later, on 21 October 1974, Lodge numbers were boosted when five Joining Members were accepted. One of these Joining Members, Bro William Desmond Payne-Jeremiah, who was employed as a Superintendent Radiographer at the Watford General Hospital, Leamington Spa, was unfortunate enough to be walking in Corporation Street, Birmingham, when the now infamous Pub Bomb exploded. Bro Desmond received extensive injuries to his back and legs. Fortunately, he made a good recovery from these injuries.

Initially, it was intended that the December Meeting would be used for Lectures and Demonstrations. However, on 8 December 1975, it was indeed an honour for the Lodge to have Lord Swansea, ProvGM, in attendance. Assisted by the Provincial Grand Chaplain, he Dedicated the Lodge Banner, which had been generously donated by WBro T R C Raikes, Founder Member. At the 1977 December Meeting, a Demonstration of a Russian Masonic Ceremony, based on Tolstoy's book 'War and Peace', was performed, which proved a great success. Then, with increasing Membership, it was resolved that from 1978, the December Meeting would be used for Degree Ceremonies, in order to speed up the progress of new Members into the Lodge.

The Lodge's first Grand Officer, after the Consecrating Honorary Members, was WBro K Robinson. He had been Elected an Honorary Member, in appreciation of the services he undertook in Founding the Lodge.

In September 1980, WBro Tom King-Davies, PAGDC, Senior Warden of Hendre Lodge No.3250, was mandated to represent the ProvGM and was first welcomed into the Lodge on 20 October 1980. Initiated in Llynfi Lodge No.2965 in 1941, he was a Founder Member of Maesteg Lodge and was its Master in 1954. WBro Tom became a frequent and much esteemed presence at the Regular Meetings of Lodge of St Theodore. When, in1984, WBro Tom relinquished his Mandate, all the Members hoped that he would continue to visit the Lodge as often as possible. Such was the Brethren's affection for WBro Tom, that on 20 May 1985, he was Elected an Honorary Member. He was then in his 92nd year, and it is pleasing to note that he continued to visit regularly.

On 16 May 1988, the Petition for the Lodge's Daughter Lodge, South Wales Clerics' Lodge No.9298, was presented and duly signed. The Warrant was granted on 14 September 1988 and the new Lodge was Consecrated on 7 April 1989.

In spite of its short existence, Lodge of St Theodore has taken part in four Provincial Festivals, namely 1976, 1986, 1999 and 2010. Its Members are not only proud to have met their targets for all of the Festivals, but also that the Lodge was amongst the top ten in the Province for donations per capita. Early in the life of the Lodge, it was decided to establish, in addition to Festival Appeals, a totally separate Charity Fund devoted mainly to local Charities. Sponsored by Lodge raffles, by 2010, the Lodge has donated in excess of £15,220 to deserving local causes.

Founding of Grand Lodge. It was, of course, a most memorable occasion, the excellent service being conducted by WBro Rev Norman Lea, ProvGChap, a Joining Member of Lodge of St Theodore. The following year, he was appointed Assistant Grand Chaplain of the UGLE. It was indeed a very proud moment for the Members of the Lodge, when on Wednesday, 18 March 1998, WBro Brian Makinson, WM, escorted WBro Rev Norman Lea into Cardiff Exchange Lodge No.3775 to be Invested as AProvGM by the Provincial Grand Master.

The Church of St Theodore, Port Talbot

On Monday, 14 December 1998, the Lodge celebrated its Silver Jubilee under the Mastership of WBro Brian Makinson. That night, Brethren were treated to a history of the Lodge, very impressively presented by WBro William T L Crompton, PPrJGW, whose hand written notes have provided much of the background to the history of the Lodge. Following the lecture, the Brethren were entertained to the same Festive Board menu as had been prepared for the Lodge's Consecration. It consisted of cream of vegetable soup - paté with brown bread and butter - roast beef with Yorkshire pudding, roast and creamed potatoes, carrots, runner beans and cauliflower cheese - apple tart and custard - a selection of cheese, biscuits, celery and grapes - followed by tea or coffee and mints.

In 1999, Lodge of St Theodore made a commendable contribution to the 1999 Festival, which was held at Cardiff International Arena. The Lodge Tyler, Bro B G Lloyd, volunteered to be a Steward at the Festival and in 2000 he was awarded with Provincial Honours as PPrGStwd. This was the first time that a Junior Member of the Lodge had been so recognised.

Other notable achievements within the Lodges include: WBro Gordon Toms appointed ProvGReg in 1984 and WBro Rev Norman Lea promoted to DepGChap in 2001; together with the following, who became Masonic Veterans: WBros T R C Raikes (1989); Tom King-Davies (1991) and W T L Crompton, PPrSGW (2008).

Compiled by WBro Captain D J M Morris, PPrGSwdB.

Albert Edward Prince of Wales Court

Masonic Home for the Elderly

Albert Edward Prince of Wales Court (AEPWC) stands in extensive, well-kept grounds, situated at the seaside resort of Porthcawl, South Wales, just one mile from the town centre and the promenade.

The 'Home', as it is affectionately known, was purpose-built in 1973, the Architect being Bro Ivan Dale Owen, of Messrs Percy Thomas Partnership. They were assisted by Andrews Wetherfoil Ltd, Consulting Engineers; Roger O A Richards, Esq, Quantity Surveyor; Shepherd Construction Ltd, Building Contractors; and by a Development Committee of nine Brethren. On completion, the Architects were awarded a Gold Medal for Design. In the year 2000, the 'Home' was extensively refurbished.

The Royal Masonic Benevolent Institution, Registered Charity No. 207360, of which Her Majesty the Queen is Grand Patron and His Royal Highness, The Duke of Kent is President, is the Registered Provider of the 'Home'. The land on which it stands was gifted to the RMBI by the Province of Monmouthshire.

Albert Edward Prince of Wales Court was opened at 3pm on Monday, 24 September 1973, by MWBro the Rt Hon the Earl Cadogan, MC, DL, ProGM. He was accompanied to the dais by RWBro James A Terry, PJGW, and Chairman of Management, who gave a welcome address and invited the Earl Cadogan to declare the Albert Edward Prince of Wales Court open and unveil the Commemorative Stone. The Ceremony, which took place in a beautifully lined marquee, was witnessed by over 1800 Ladies and Brethren, including ProvGMs of South Wales ED, Herefordshire, Monmouthshire, Gloucestershire, Middlesex, and RWBro James W Stubbs, PGW, GSec. WBro Rev Preb W R Griffiths, DepGChap, led the assembly in prayer and Dedication of the 'Home'. Prior to the closing, the architect, Bro Dale Owen, presented Lord Cadogan with an English translation of The Mabinogion (Medieval Welsh Mythological Tales), which the Pro Grand Master promised to read. It was a book which he wanted for his library and, as his ancestors were Welsh, he would treasure the gift which would remind him of the warm welcome he had received in South Wales. RWBro Terry then presented a patchwork rug for Lady Cadogan, which had been knitted by a RMBI annuitant aged 92, living in Kent, who performed such work as occupational therapy.

The Edgar Rutter Memorial Chapel at AEPWC was Dedicated a few weeks later, on 14 October 1973. Details and photographs of the Chapel interior are provided in the next chapter of this book.

The 'Home' provides for the needs of elderly Masons of the Provinces of South Wales, West Wales and Monmouthshire, and aims to provide the highest standards of care and attention for its residents.

Over the years, the facilities provided at the Home have

Albert Edward Prince of Wales Court

had to be adapted to deal with sociological changes. When built in the 1970s, the residents' average age was about 63 - 66, and they were able to cope relatively easily with the then long corridors. Today, the average age of the residents is 80 - 83 and, for several, their mobility is rather limited. Such changes necessitated a redesign of the building. The refurbishment of 2000 divided the Home into five house groups, each with its own team of care staff and each having its own comfortable dining room and communal lounge, to cater for the less mobile. Thus, the Home was able to maintain the standards laid down by the various 'Care Standards Acts'. It may be of interest to the reader, that Mrs Evelyn Warman celebrated her 106th birthday at the 'Home' on 15 September 2010. She is the oldest resident at the Home and the second oldest resident in all of the RMBI homes. A further development has been the provision of the

Gardens of the Albert Edward Prince of Wales Court

Dementia Support Unit, Ireland House, opened in August 2010. Although only a small Unit, it offers individual care for people with severe memory loss or dementia. There are ten single rooms with en-suite wet rooms, two lounges, dining room and kitchen.

Within the grounds there are beautiful inner courtyard gardens, consisting of a fishpond, a scented garden and herb garden, for residents to sit and relax and enjoy the outdoor space. There is also a bowling green and Club House in the grounds, where matches are played throughout the season. Residents may participate if they wish.

The whole premise of the RMBI is to create a 'home' rather than an 'institutional style' environment, and it is committed to ensuring that the residents retain the right to dignity, respect, choice and control over their lives.

The Court is home for up to 66 residents, providing 40 residential places, 16 nursing care places, plus a further 10 places in the new Dementia Unit, all in single en-suite bed-sitting rooms and all of which overlook the garden or courtyard area. Rooms are centrally heated and residents may furnish their own rooms if they wish, provided that the furniture meets the required safety standards. In each house group there is bath/shower facilities especially adapted for safe usage so that residents maintain their independence in a safe environment. Kitchenettes are available, where residents can make drinks and snacks for themselves or their visitors.

The fee structure and charging procedures of the RMBI are based on Central Government Fiscal Policy and the Community Care Act, whilst giving consideration to the Charity's remit to assist Masonically eligible people of limited financial means and to use donors' money wisely.

All the Masonic Homes throughout England and Wales are the property of the RMBI but, each has their own Association of Friends organised locally by Freemasons and their families.

The AEPOWC Association of Friends was founded at a meeting held at the 'Court' on Friday, 14 December 1973. WBro Malcolm H Thompson, ProvGSec, Province of South Wales (Eastern Division), now the 'Province of South Wales', opened the meeting. WBro Harry F Stockwell, DepProvGM, and WBro Harold Wilson, AProvGM were both unavailable due to sickness but, WBro Llewellyn G Bevan, AProvGM, was present and was invited to chair the meeting. Malcolm Thompson informed the Brethren of the purpose of meeting and read a suggested 'Constitution and Rules', he also referred to a leaflet, produced by the RMBI, outlining typical social activities for the Home. The Meeting agreed to the formation of an Association of Friends and adopted the name 'Friends of the Albert Edward Prince of Wales Court'. Draft Constitution and Rules with amendments suitable for the 'Court' were adopted, with a proviso that they be submitted to the first Annual General Meeting. WBro Harry F Stockwell was elected first Chairman of the Association and WBro John Clement Ireland first Secretary/Treasurer. Representatives for the various Districts were then appointed and confirmed as members of the Management Committee.

The aim of the Association is to improve the residents' quality of life through activities ranging from individual visits, to group outings to the local shops and other attractions. Concerts by either professional or amateur entertainers are arranged at the Home and suitable vehicles have been acquired to make these activities possible.

Consideration was given to the funding of social activities for the residents and it was decided to set Annual Membership fees at £1.00 and Life Membership fees at £6.00. It was further agreed that Secretaries of all Lodges in the three Provinces would be sent the draft copy of the Constitution and Rules, and encouraged to enrol at least 50% of Lodge Brethren in the new Association of Friends.

The new committee of the Association of Friends of AEPWC then met and decided that Barclay's Bank Ltd be appointed as Bankers for the Association and, that £200 be given to purchase Christmas gifts for the residents and staff. It was also resolved that a trolley be purchased and stocked with goods for sale to the residents, with a rota being set up to man the trolley. Further, flowers would be purchased, every weekend, to decorate the Chapel. It was the wish of the Matron that religious services be held every Sunday Morning and the Church of Wales and other denominations be invited to participate.

VWBro Peter Frost, PGSwdB, PDepProvGM, succeeded WBro Sam Northway as Chairman of the Association in 2000. He has been ably assisted by WBro Geoffrey W Thomas, PSGD, PAProvGM, as Vice-Chairman and a committee comprising of a Secretary and Treasurer, Life Membership Co-ordinator, Fund Raiser, Entertainments Co-ordinator, the three Provincial Grand Masters and their Deputies or Assistants, and the Provincial Grand Secretaries, together with the Home Manager. VWBro Peter Frost retired as Chairman on 25 September 2011, and was succeeded by WBro Alan Gardener, PAGSuptWks, PM Duke of York Lodge No.2453.

The residents of the 'Home' continually rely, for their social and entertainment activities, and for their Christmas gifts, on the subscriptions of the members of the Association of Friends, of which there are about 7000. The subscription is £10 for Life Members and £5 for Ladies. To this can be added annual donations of £50 from most Lodges in the Provinces of South & West Wales, whereas the Province of Monmouthshire makes an annual donation on behalf of all its Lodges.

It is further acknowledged that from time to time many Lodges and Chapters donate substantial sums from fund raising events. The Association of Friends also has an active fundraising programme, which includes a series of 'race nights' held at various Masonic centres in South Wales, as well as the annual Spring and Christmas Fayres which are held at the Home. The Province of South Wales also holds a very successful annual bowls tournament, which hosts the semi-final and finals on the bowls green at the Home.

Compiled by WBro Gwyn Evans, PPrGReg.

'The Last Supper', Edgar Rutter Memorial Chapel

The Edgar Rutter Memorial Chapel

Albert Edward Prince of Wales Court

A plaque in the Chapel records:

'This Chapel and its commemorative windows have been presented by the Brethren in the Province of South Wales Eastern Division in memory of RWBro Edgar John Rutter, OSM, PJGD, and to commemorate his forty years devoted service as Deputy Provincial Grand Master, 1931-1971.'

The first thing that usually strikes a first-time visitor to the Chapel is the aura of peace and tranquillity, more often found in more ancient churches and cathedrals. It is light and airy with seating for approximately 64 people. The Chapel was dedicated on 14 October 1973.

The beautiful stained glass windows bear the Insignia of the Honours held by RWBro Edgar J Rutter:

1. Prime Warden, Worshipful Company of Basketmakers of the City of London, 1969.
2. The Grand Master's Order of Service to Masonry, 1946.
3. Deputy Provincial Grand Master (Eastern Division), 1931-1971.
4. Past Junior Grand Warden of England, 1951.
5. Commander of the Most Venerable Order of St John, 1971.
6. Grand Superintendent of Royal Arch Masonry, Province of South Wales (Eastern Division), 1966-1991.

The light oak furnishings were all donated, as follows:

Altar - presented by the Brethren of Penrice Lodge No.4172.

Lectern - presented by WBro Harry Stockwell, PSGD, DepProvGM.

Altar Rails - presented by the Rt Hon the Lord Swansea, DL, ProvGM.

Kneeling Stands - presented by WBro Malcolm H Thompson, PAGDC, ProvGSec.

Side table - presented by Howardian Lodge Social Committee.

Font – presented by WBroT J Burley, ProvGTyler.

Hymn Board - presented by the Federation of School Lodges.

Pews were presented by:

WBro Frank W E Rutter, PPrJGW.

WBro HH Judge John Rutter, PJGD.

WBro Llewellyn G Bevan PJGD, AProvGM.

WBro Wilfred B Porter, PJGD.

WBro RT Evans, PAGDG.

WBro Morlais J Summers, PAGDC.

WBro L D (Lance) Bailey, PGStB.

Presented in memory of WBro P De Wilde.

The Altar

Presented in memory of WBro P De Wilde.

WBro Harold Wilson, PJGD, AProvGM.
WBro Oscar F Boehringer, PAGDC, Grand Inspector General 33°, S Wales & Monmouthshire.
Mrs O F Boehringer.
WBro Aubrey H Jenkins, PJGD.
WBro E Rhodri Harris, PAGReg.
WBro S Essex Williams, PAGDC.
WBro H L Jackson, PPGW.

Kneelers were presented by:

WBro L (Leslie) H Jeans, PPGW, PAGDC.
WBro J A Cowley, PPGW.
WBro E J Smith, PPGW.
WBro H F Jones, PPGW.
WBro J D Hann, PPrGStB.
WBro W H Hann, PPrGStwd.
Masonic Bellringers: WBro H F Jones, PPrGW and Bro H W Giblen.

On the wall adjacent to the lectern is a plaque depicting the 'Last Supper', illustrated on page 583.

The Provincial Grand Chaplain, WBro Alistair E J Swinford, conducts services in the Chapel most Sundays. At other times services are taken by Canon Godfrey Ball.

In early 2011, the proceeds from collections taken in the Chapel, amounting to the sum of £750, were donated to various charities. New Hymn Books were recently donated on behalf of Mrs Elsie Evans, by her son, Howard Evans, and daughter Mrs Barbara Roberts.

The current Church Warden is Mr Douglas Fussell, who was preceded by Mrs Katherine Evans and Mr Maldwyn Hill.

Immediately on the left, before entering the Chapel is the Vestry. A plaque on the wall in the Vestry bears the following inscription:

The Vestry has been presented by
The Royal Arch Chapters in the Province
of S.W.E.D.
in memory of
Excellent Companion
Edgar John Rutter, OSM
M.E. Grand Superintendent
1966 - 1971

Of the six windows, the five illustrated remain in their original positions in the Edgar Rutter Memorial Chapel. The sixth window is now to be seen in the Vestry, constructed at a later date.

Compiled by WBro James H Cartwright, PPrDepGDC.

Ystrad Mynach Lodge No.8567

Warranted : 13 February 1974

Consecrated : 17 June 1974

Meeting at the Masonic Hall, Bargoed.

The idea of forming a Lodge at Ystrad Mynach was first discussed at a meeting held in the home of the local Undertaker, WBro Evan Richards, PPrGPurs (Mon), PM St David's Lodge No.2226, Rhymney, Province of Monmouthshire. At that meeting, WBro Frank Griffiths, PPrGSwdB, PM Henry Pendrill Charles Lodge No.3769, was Acting Chairman, and Bro Harry Marriot, MM, of Hamlet of Van Lodge No.8334, was Acting Secretary. The following agreed proposals were recorded to be read at the Founder Members' meeting. The title of the proposed Lodge would also be decided at the Founder Members' meeting.

1. The Regular Lodge would be held four times each year either on a Wednesday or Friday night.
2. The Founder Members' fee would be ten pounds and would include the first year's subscription.
3. The proposed Founder Members to be sent a letter asking them to signify their interest and requesting them to attend the Founder Members' meeting.
4. The Acting Secretary to write to the Gelligaer Lodge immediately, requesting them to receive a Deputation at their earliest convenience to discuss the proposed formation of the Ystrad Mynach Lodge, the possibility of using Gelligaer Lodge Temple and adjoining room, and the cost of their use.
5. The Deputation would consist of three Brethren and the following Brethren were Elected: WBro F Griffiths, WBro E Richards, and Bro H B Marriot. However, on the night of the Meeting Bro D R Evans also attended, as he was a Member of Gelligaer Lodge.
6. The Founder Members' meeting would be held at the Beech Tree Hotel, Ystrad Mynach, on Tuesday, 25 September 1973.

The Founders' meeting was duly held at the Beech Tree Hotel, with 20 Brethren present out of a total compliment of 26 Founder Members. The formation of the new Lodge was formally proposed and the name 'Ystrad Mynach' Lodge agreed. It was also agreed that some relevant history of Ystrad Mynach should be incorporated in any future Crest or Lodge Banner. It was also agreed that WBros F Griffiths, E Richards and Bros E A Williams, A M Hopkins and D R Evans meet with VWBro Harry F Stockwell, DepProvGM, to discuss the formation of Ystrad Mynach Lodge.

On 1 October 1973, a Deputation from Ystrad Mynach Lodge was received by Gelligaer Lodge No.6298, which was formally requested to be the Sponsoring Lodge. Gelligaer Lodge willingly accepted, and agreed that the proposed Ystrad Mynach Lodge would have full use of the Temple and all its accessories, free of charge, for a period of two years, to enable the new Lodge to 'get on its feet'.

The Warrant was issued on 13 February 1974, and the Consecration Ceremony took place at the Bargoed Temple on Monday, 17 June 1974. The Consecrating Officer was RWBro the Lord Swansea, DL, ProvGM, assisted by VWBro Harry F Stockwell,

DepProvGM and WBro H Wilson, AProvGM. Also present were WBros J W F Batley, ProvSGW; Cecil H Rapport, ProvJGW; Rev T Douglas Harris, ProvGChap; Malcolm H Thompson, ProvGSec and Geoffrey M Ashe TD, ProvGDC. The Oration was given by WBro Rev Douglas Harris, who enlarged on the truth/legend and origin of the name of Ystrad Mynach.

WBro Frank Griffiths was Installed as the First Master, with WBro G M Phillips as IPM. The ProvGM gave the Address to the newly Installed WM; the DepProvGM gave the Address to the Wardens, and WBro H Wilson gave the Address to the Brethren. The Consecrating Officers were then made Honorary Members of the Lodge

The Regalia of the Lodge was purchased by the Incoming Officers. The musical service for each of the three Degrees was compiled by WBro Iestyn P Evans and Bro David T Hopkins, and the Music Books were donated by Bro David T Hopkins.

A photograph of the Founders was taken at a garden party, where the Founders were guests of Bro John K Mason at his home at Ystrad Fawr, Ystrad Mynach. Founders' Jewels were presented at a buffet tea held in the Church Hall of Holy Trinity Church, Ystrad Mynach, in the summer of 1975.

The Lodge Emblem was designed by Bro Alan M Hopkins and depicts a monk travelling the road towards the setting sun. To the right of the figure is the well-known local landmark, the Penallta Rocks. This is a great sandstone outcrop overlooking Ystrad Mynach. The Emblem is the product of the local belief that Ystrad Mynach means '*the Vale of the Monk*'. Legend has it that monks travelling from the Priory in the Vale of Glamorgan rested at the 'meeting of the waters' at Ystrad Mynach. After their rest they continued on their journey to the Chapel of St Gwladys on the mountainside above Gelligaer.

The Motto of the Lodge is '*Bydded Goleuni*' which means '*Let There Be Light*'.

The Banner incorporates the Lodge Emblem, the name and number of the Lodge, and the Square and Compasses. WBro H R Wilson, PPrGSwdB, wove the Banner, ably assisted by his wife, Lindsay. The Banner was Dedicated on 23 September 1992 by WBro David L Protheroe, PAGDC, AProvGM, supported by WBro J B Hood, PAGDC; WBro W J Northway, PAGDC; WBro Rev Norman Lea, ProvGChap, and WBro P A Gabriel, ProvGPurs.

The 25th Anniversary of the Lodge was held on Wednesday, 12 April 2000, at the Masonic Hall, Caerphilly. The Lodge was opened by Dispensation by WBro T J Evans, WM. The Minutes of the Consecration of the Lodge were read by the Secretary, WBro D C Dean, PPrGStB (Hampshire and Isle of Wight). An Address entitled 'The Founding of the Lodge' was given by WBro D R Evans, PPrJGW (Founder JW).

There were 94 Members and guests present at the celebratory dinner, including 7 Founder Members, and the Mandated Officer, WBro J B Hood, PAGDC. The Official guests were WBros Malcolm H Thompson, PAGDC; Brian Eveleigh, PAGD, AProvGM; the WMs and Wardens of Gelligaer and Henry Pendrill Charles Lodges. To mark the occasion, the Founder Members were presented with suitably inscribed whisky glasses.

WBro Evan Richards was the first Member to receive Provincial Rank, and was also the first Member to receive Provincial Rank in this Province and the Province of Monmouthshire. WBro Alan M Hopkins was the first Member to receive an Acting Rank (ProvAGDC), and WBro D Russell Evans was the first Member to receive Supreme Grand Chapter Rank in the Holy Royal Arch.

The Lodge continues to uphold the excellent traditions established by its forefathers in the performance of Rituals, and by donations to Masonic and non-Masonic Charities.

Compiled by WBro D Russell Evans, PPrJGW, and WBro Hywel Davies, PPrGStB.

Aberhonddu Lodge No.8588

Warranted : 25 April 1974

Consecrated : 18 October 1974

Meeting at the Masonic Hall, Brecon.

The first meeting to discuss the possibility of forming a new Lodge in Brecon was held at the Castle Hotel, Brecon, on 8 January 1974. Many Brethren felt that, as the Membership of the Brecknock Lodge No.651 had increased, the opportunity for taking Office had diminished and the formation of a new Lodge would strengthen Freemasonry in the Town. The following Brethren from Brecknock Lodge, who incidentally were mostly members of The Rotary Club of Brecon, agreed to attend the first meeting: WBros Foster Ball, Installed WM of Brecknock Lodge in 1966, who was to become Primus Master; Richard Griffiths, WM, 1957-1959; Lawrie Hogarth, WM, 1963-1964; Islwyn Evans, WM, 1964-1965; Gwyn Herbert, WM, 1970-1971, Acting IPM at the Consecration; and Kenneth J P Price, WM, 1973-1974; with Bros Kenneth R Anthony, SW Designate; Howard Jones, JW Designate; Dennis Hancox, Mervyn Woodward, Gwyn Angell, Kenneth Thomas, Morley Evans, Glanville Davies, David Morgan and Tony Elston. Apologies were received from Bros John A Parry and Vincent W King, both of whom had intimated that they would agree to any decision taken at the meeting, and who subsequently became Founder IG and Steward respectively. WBro Islwyn Evans was Elected Chairman and Bro Howard Jones took the Minutes of the meeting. The estimated ongoing costs required by Brecknock Lodge were £30 per Meeting, which would include the use of the Lodge building for rehearsals and Committee Meetings. A price had been obtained from Toye, Kenning and Spencer for Aprons, Collars, Jewels and Books totalling £264.75. All present felt that a new Lodge would be a practical proposition, subject only to the approval of PGL, and the Chairman was instructed to approach the ProvGSec, WBro Malcolm H Thompson.

Several names were suggested for the new Lodge and it was finally agreed it should be called 'Aberhonddu Lodge', Aberhonddu being the Welsh name for the town of Brecon. It was also agreed that the Lodge should meet four times a year and that Candidates and Joining Members should come only from within a radius of 25 miles of the town. This rule was dropped in later years to obviate the problem for those who may be living just outside that area. It was agreed that the fees for the Founder Members in the first year would be £30, which would include entertainment of the official guests at the Consecration Dinner; and the Initiation and Joining fees would be £10.

VWBro Harry F Stockwell, DepProvGM, and WBro Malcolm H Thompson, ProvGSec, attended a meeting on 5 February 1974, at which the Brethren were advised of their responsibilities in forming the Lodge. It was agreed that the Sponsoring Lodge would be Brecknock Lodge and that a Brother would be allowed to progress in one Lodge only. This would ensure that Brethren of both Lodges had an equal opportunity to attain the Chair of King Solomon within a reasonable period of time. The Brethren agreed unanimously to the principles and responsibilities, whereupon the Founder Members signed the Petition. On 29 April, a letter was received from the ProvGSec *'I am delighted to inform you that the MW The Grand Master has been pleased to accede to the prayer of the Petition for a new Lodge in Brecon'*.

Several meetings were held prior to the Consecration; amongst other issues to agree was the content of the By-laws, and a tender of £125 was accepted from Mr Harris of Llangasty, for a Past Masters' Board. Regalia and Jewels were obtained and the Lodge Banner was designed by WBro Ivor Elson and made and embroidered by a local lady. Although it had been suggested that £10 be paid by all Founders to cover these initial expenses, all agreed that it should be considered as a loan to be repaid at a later date. However, in 1982, when the question of repayment arose, all the Founder Members agreed that the sum which totalled £180, should be used to purchase a WM's Chain of Office.

Aberhonddu Lodge No.8588 was Consecrated on Tuesday, 18 October 1974, at the Masonic Temple, Cerrigcochion Road, Brecon, by RWBro the Rt Hon the Lord Swansea, DL, ProvGM, accompanied by his team of Provincial Grand Officers. The Guildford Singers, under the direction of WBro E J Smith, were also in attendance. Having performed the Ceremony of Consecration, the ProvGM duly Installed the Master Designate, WBro Foster Ball, who then Invested his Officers. The Consecrating Officers were Elected Honorary Members and two Candidates and three Joining Members were proposed. The Lodge was closed and 123 Brethren retired to the Wellington Hotel, Brecon, for dinner.

Many gifts had been presented to the Lodge both before and at the Consecration Ceremony, and the Secretary was instructed to write to nine Brethren to thank them. Among them were WBro Harry F Stockwell (Lodge Bible), Bro Brian Williams (Gavel and Wands), WBro W Goreman (Tyler's Sword) and WBro Ivor Elson who designed the Lodge Crest and, with his Brother Arthur C Elson, commissioned the Lodge Banner. It bears a representation of the River Honddu running through the town, with Brecon's landmark Castle and the Brecon Beacons in the background.

WBro Foster Ball, Initiated, Passed and Raised two Candidates in the first year, namely Bro Colin R Jones and WBro R D Weller. It has been the practice ever since to Initiate two Candidates each year. Six Joining Members were accepted in that first year, but the Brethren agreed that no further Joining Members would be accepted for the subsequent three years, so that Membership could be kept to a more intimate number. This, however, has long since been abandoned.

The ProvGM, Lord Swansea was again present at the Installation of Bro Kenneth R Anthony in December 1975. He occupied the Chair, and with his team of Provincial Officers, proceeded to Dedicate the Lodge Banner, in the presence of 124 Brethren.

Until 2009, the Lodge was lucky to be honoured with the presence of four Founder Members. Founder Secretary, WBro D Morley Evans, PPrJGW, was Elected an Honorary Member in May 2006 and had moved to Tavistock, Devon. He last visited the Lodge in May 2004, when the then five remaining Founders were presented with an engraved glass to mark the 30th Anniversary of the Lodge. Founder Senior Deacon, WBro Mervyn C Woodward, PPrSGW, Installed as WM in 1977, is now the Senior PM. He remains an active participant in the Lodge and in its affairs. WBro Iswyn Evans, PJGD, Founder Organist, was Elected an Honorary Member in December 2006. He will always be remembered as one of the most important Freemasons to come from Brecon. He was the main driving force behind the formation of the Lodge and the formation of the Brecon Association of Freemasons in 1985 which is one of the reasons for the continuing strength of Freemasonry in Brecon. Lastly, Bro J K H (Ken)

Thomas, PPrGTyler, Founder Tyler, was also a very active Member until relatively recently. He continued as Tyler and it is worth reflecting that there cannot be many of the fifty-nine Initiates of Aberhonddu Lodge who have not been greeted and prepared by him in the 34 years of the Lodge's existence up until his sad demise. So, very sadly, in 2011, WBro Mervyn C Woodward is the only surviving Founder.

These Founder Brethren laid an excellent foundation for Aberhonddu Lodge and since its Consecration over sixty Brethren have been Initiated and forty seven Brethren have become Joining Members, over thirty of whom have been Past Masters of other Lodges. This has led to a number of adopted practices or 'landmarks of the order', which give Aberhonddu Lodge its particular 'feel' or character. During his year as WM, WBro Mervyn Woodward invited the Worshipful Masters of Brecknock Lodge, Vivian Lodge No.8267 and Loyal Wye Lodge No.1807 to present the Working Tools of the Three Degrees during the Installation Ceremony. This practice has continued ever since. Another peculiarity of the Lodge is the delivery of the extended version of the First Degree Working Tools, a practice introduced by WBro Brian Matthews from his Mother Lodge, Windsor Lodge No.1754, Penarth.

Aberhonddu Lodge has been honoured by having several distinguished Brethren as Members. RWBro Hywel Davies, PProvGM, became a Joining Member in February 1982 when his working career with SWEB brought him to Brecon. His Appointment as AProvGM in 1996 was recognised with a celebration dinner at the Bishops Meadow Restaurant, Hay Road, Brecon, which was attended by Brethren from the Brecon, Builth Wells and Llandrindod Wells Lodges. He became ProvGM in 1999 and in a ten year reign was much loved and respected by all. Both then and even now, with enormous demands on his time, he still finds time to attend the Lodge regularly, constantly giving the WM every encouragement and support.

WBro Rev Norman Lea, PDepGChap, PAProvGM, was Initiated into the Lodge by WBro Mervyn C Woodward in February 1978. He was Installed as WM by WBro Robert D Weller on 4 December 1984, and was Elected an Honorary Member on 2 May 2000, to mark his promotion to AProvGM.

The Lodge is also privileged to have a number of Brethren who have been accorded Grand Lodge Honours. Three in number, they are Founder Member, WBro Islwyn Evans, PJGD; WBro Brian Matthews, PAGDC, a Joining PM in 1975, and ProvSGW in 2007; and WBro Barrow Isaacs, PAGDC, a Joining Member in 2005.

Aberhonddu Lodge has always been very proud of its considerable contributions to charity. During the last two Festivals, the Charity Steward, WBro Fred Churchill, PPrGReg, worked tirelessly to maintain a high standard for the Lodge and was duly rewarded by his promotion to PPrJGW in 2011. In June 2006, five Brethren, WBro Nigel Matthews, WBro Garry Davies, WM, Bro Steve Maggs, Bro Peter James and Bro Ian Price, together with Mr Steve Morgan, a potential Candidate, completed a sponsored walk. They climbed Snowdon, the highest peak in the Province of North Wales; Foel Cwm Cerwyn, the highest peak in the Province of South Wales Western Division; and Pen Y Fan, the highest peak in South Wales Eastern Division, raising over £2500 towards the 2010 Festival.

As this History is being updated, the Lodge is looking very healthy, having a number of Candidates waiting to join and, with its background in mind, looks forward confidently to continuing the success laid down by its Founder Members.

Compiled from '200 years of Freemasonry in Brecon 1789 to 1989' by WBro Islwyn Evans, PJGD, with later additions by WBro Nigel D Matthews, PPrJGD.

St Gwynno Lodge No.8599

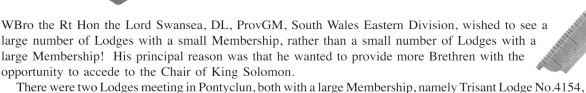

Warranted : 12 June 1974

Consecrated : 7 October 1974

Meeting at the Masonic Hall, Pontyclun.

WBro the Rt Hon the Lord Swansea, DL, ProvGM, South Wales Eastern Division, wished to see a large number of Lodges with a small Membership, rather than a small number of Lodges with a large Membership! His principal reason was that he wanted to provide more Brethren with the opportunity to accede to the Chair of King Solomon.

There were two Lodges meeting in Pontyclun, both with a large Membership, namely Trisant Lodge No.4154, with approximately 160 Members, and Talygarn Lodge No.7216 with approximately 100 Members. Both Lodges independently decided to form a new Lodge, and whilst Talygarn formed Miskin Lodge No.8625, Members of Trisant Lodge formed St Gwynno Lodge No.8599. The Warrant for St Gwynno Lodge was granted on 12 June 1974, and the Lodge was Consecrated on 7 October of that year.

The Lodge name is derived from one of the three Saints associated with the ancient town of Llantrisant (Three Saints). In 'The Lives of the British Saints' the Rev Baring-Gould tells of a St Gwynno, described in the ancient Iolo manuscripts as of the lineage of the mythical Bendigaid Fran, which will be recognised by students of the Mabinogion.

The Lodge was Consecrated by the ProvGM, assisted by WBros Ronald Whittingham, ProvSGW; Frank Newbury, ProvJGW; Malcolm Thompson, ProvGSec; Geoffrey M Ashe, ProvGDC and William Northway, ProvGTyler.

The first Master was WBro Frederick T Upshall, PM Trisant Lodge, a Draper and Outfitter in Ystrad, Rhondda. Bro G Derek Price, MM of St David's Lodge No.366 in Milford Haven, a Passenger Transport Officer in Porth, Rhondda, was the first SW, and Bro Eric Lewis of Trisant Lodge, a Motor Mechanic in Llanharan, Pontyclun, the first JW. They were Installed by the ProvGM, with WBro Colin M Griffin, PPrSGW, of Trisant Lodge, acting as IPM.

WBro Frederick Thomas Upshall, or WBro Fred, as he was affectionately known to all the Members, was Initiated into Trisant Lodge on 5 February 1959 and was Installed as Worshipful Master in 1972. At this time the new Lodge of St Gwynno was being mooted, and he became the Founder Secretary. Master in 1974, he became Secretary in 1976 and continued in that post until 1990, combining this with the Office of Charity Organiser, later changed to Charity Steward. He and his wife Betty were also very strong supporters of the Albert Edward Prince of Wales Court in Porthcawl. He was rewarded for his work by being appointed Past Senior Grand Warden in Provincial Grand Lodge in 1990. He was actively involved in the running of the Lodge until his death in January 1997.

The second Master was WBro G Derek Price, who was appointed Provincial Grand Chaplain in 1980. He was re-appointed in 1981 only to pass to the Grand Lodge Above three days later. This loss was severely felt by the Lodge, and many Members and their families attended his funeral in Cwmbran.

The last Founder to be Installed as Master was WBro Colin M Griffin in 1981. He was Master of Trisant Lodge at the time of the Consecration. He acted the role of the Immediate Past Master for the first year. He was a tireless worker for Freemasonry in Pontyclun and was rewarded by the appointment to Past Senior Grand Warden in Provincial Grand Lodge in 2005.

The Lodge By-laws state that the Lodge will meet seven times annually, with only one change when the date clashes with a Bank holiday.

The Lodge Banner was first mentioned at the Meeting held on 25 October 1977, when Bro John Billet stated that Members had requested that a Lodge Banner be obtained. One year later, on 24 October 1978, the committee recommended asking the Members for donations towards the cost of its production. A design was presented to the committee on 9 December 1978, whereupon modifications were suggested and the final design was re-presented on 9 January 1979. The stone tower, depicted on the Banner, is the remains of a 13th century windmill, known locally as 'Billy Wynt'. It is a well known landmark, being situated at the highest point in the town of Llantrisant. By the early 19th century the tower was in ruins, and in 1893 it was restored as a folly.

Costings for the making of the Banner were obtained at £275.00 and £325.00, and the committee recommended that the higher figure be accepted. The Lodge approved the cost at the Meeting held on 27 March, 1979, upon a proposal made by WBro Colin Griffin, seconded by WBro Derek Price. The Banner was ready by 13 January 1981 and it was Dedicated by VWBro Geoffrey M Ashe, TD, DepProvGM, after the Installation Ceremony on 27 October, 1981.

The first Initiate to become WM was WBro Alun M Thomas, who was Installed in 1982. Now the senior Past Master, with the Rank of PPrGSwdB, he continues to support the Lodge in all its functions. WBro David H Elliott was Installed as Master in 1996 and again in 2004, the only Member to occupy the WM's Chair on two occasions. Both these Masters together with WBro Ronald Williams, Master in1988, were responsible for introducing their respective sons into the Lodge.

At the January Meeting in 1992, a number of Brethren, led by WBro Dillwyn G Enoch, presented a Petition to form a new Lodge in Pontyclun. WBro Douglas J Morgan, WM, invited WBro Frederick Upshall to accept the Petition on behalf of the Lodge, thus the Lodge became the Sponsoring Lodge for Yr Efail No.9502, whose Warrant was granted on 10 February, 1993. WBro Doug J Morgan, PPrDepGDC, who was Initiated into the Lodge in 1981, is the Lodge's long-serving Charity Steward.

Although all the Past masters deserve a mention in any Lodge history, for each brings his own individual stamp to the Office, mention must be made of WBro William Emrys Jenkins, who was Installed as Master in 1995. In Provincial Grand Lodge, he was first appointed to the Acting Rank of Provincial Assistant Grand Director of Ceremonies in 2001, then in 2003 and 2004, Deputy Director of Ceremonies. In 2007, he was appointed Provincial Grand Director of Ceremonies, an Office he still holds. He became a Grand Officer in 2008, with the Rank of PAGDC.

Also, WBro D Keith Davies, who was Initiated in 1983 and became WM in 1992; he was appointed ProvSGD in 1998 and promoted to PPrJGW in 2010. In the Ancient and Accepted Rite, he was appointed District Recorder (equivalent to ProvGSec) and Elected to the 32nd Degree in 2009. Keith's appointment not only makes him District Secretary, but also Deputy in Charge of the Order

From its conception, the Lodge has attracted Candidates of the highest quality, regularly Initiating four new Members each year. This has resulted in competition for Office, which has promoted a high standard of discipline and Ritual of which the Lodge is justifiably proud. The Lodge is proud of its past, and will continue to maintain its reputation as we look forward to the future with great anticipation.

Compiled by WBro Douglas J Morgan, PPrDepGDC.

Discovery Lodge No.8601

Warranted : 12 June 1974

Consecrated : 22 October 1974

Meeting at the Masonic Hall, Cardiff.

As early as 1970, the formation of a new Lodge was being discussed by a small number of Brethren, meeting at various Masonic functions, and when visiting each other's Lodges. The discussions then progressed to one of the favourite 'watering holes' frequented by the said Brethren, one of which was of course, 'The Discovery' Public House in Cyncoed . Another was 'The Three Brewers' in Colchester Avenue, which was being run at the time by Brother Ralph Morgan, who went on to become landlord of the last of the three pubs, namely 'The Butchers Arms' in Llandaff. The decision was then made that the Lodge be called 'Discovery', after the ship in which Robert Falcon Scott made his first expedition to the Antarctic. This was the British National Antarctic Expedition 1901-1904, a joint enterprise of the Royal Geographical Society and the Royal Society, with Scott in overall command.

The Founders and first Officers came from several different Lodges; however, it was the Worshipful Master and Wardens of Observer Lodge No.6015 who signed the Petition, thereby making Observer Lodge the Sponsoring Lodge. A great deal of assistance in the formation of the Lodge was given by WBros Randell Edmunds, Harold Wilson, AProvGM 1960-1980, and Gordon Elias, all very well known and hardworking Masons at that time.

The Master Designate was WBro Robert C Hilton, PPrAGReg, Province of Hampshire and Isle of Wight. He was a PM of Caer Gwent Lodge No.5071, Winchester. (Note that Caer Gwent is the Celtic name for Winchester, and should not be confused with the town of Caerwent, 5 miles west of Chepstow.) His appointed IPM was Founder WBro H D Selway, PM Owain Glyndwr Lodge No.8015. WBro Roy Solomon, SW Designate, was a PM Lodge Roman Eagle No.160, Provincial Grand Lodge of Edinburgh, Scottish Constitution.

WBro Lewis Kenneth Mark Loyns, PDepGOrg (Eastern Archipelago) was JW Designate. Initiated in Centenary Lodge No.7629, Singapore, he became Worshipful Master of that Lodge in 1958. He was also a Member of Aden Lodge No.7652 (now Erased). A Schoolmaster by profession, he taught at Gladstone Junior School, Whitchurch Road, Cardiff. He had joined Glamorgan Lodge No.36 in October 1972, just two years before becoming a Founder Member of Discovery Lodge. He was Worshipful Master of Discovery Lodge in 1977 and Installed in the Chair of Glamorgan Lodge on St John's Day (24 June) 1986. He became a Grand

Officer in April 1993, with the rank of PGStdB, but sadly, died on the 3 October 1993 at the age of 70. His brother, C L Loyns was WM of Discovery Lodge in 1986. WBro H Keith Morris, PPrAGDC, who had been Installed WM of Prince Llewellyn Lodge No.2570 in 1966, was the Founder Chaplain.

Another Founder Member of great eminence was WBro Thomas John Edward Price, PPrDepGSwdB, who had been Installed WM of Themis Lodge No.6355 in 1954. He was the first Lodge Treasurer. 'Eddie' Price, born in Abertillery, Monmouthshire on 18 February 1910, had a Road Haulage Business. He was one of the original ten of 'TENOVUS' founded in 1943. In 1965, the charity set up the Tenovus Institute in Cardiff, which developed Tamoxifen, the drug used in the treatment of breast cancer, and Zoladex, used to treat prostate cancer, and which is now a leading charity in research and treatment of cancer. Eddie was awarded the MBE in 1983. While in Provincial Grand Lodge, he was ultimately promoted to the Rank of PPrJGW. He died at Cardiff on 2 April 2001, a few weeks after his 91st birthday.

Other Founder Members included WBro Morlais James Summers, PAGDC, Funeral Director of James Summers & Son, Newport Road, Cardiff. He was the elder brother of WBro Lionel Cuthbert Summers, AProvGM, 1977-1987. Morlais Summers, Installed WM of Glamorgan Lodge in June 1951 had been appointed Provincial Senior Grand

The Discovery

Warden of the Province in 1971. He was Discovery Lodge's first DC. WBro William George (Bill), WM of Clive Lodge No.6973, was the first Almoner. Born in Bromsgrove, he had settled in Cardiff following wartime service in the RAF. He founded a Motor Vehicle Business in Llandaff, having worked for Lord Austin in the Midlands before the war. He became WM of Discovery Lodge in 1985. WBro Thomas C Fisher, PM Clive Lodge No.6973 was the first Lodge Secretary.

The Lodge was Consecrated by RWBro the Rt Hon the Lord Swansea, DL, ProvGM, on 22 October 1974. The Consecration Ceremony was well attended and the Consecrating Officers included WBro Malcolm H Thompson, ProvGSec, with WBro Geoffrey Malin Ashe, TD, ProvGDC. The latter became DepProvGM, 1977-1992.

The original idea was that Discovery Lodge would be a Dining Lodge and that dinner suits would be worn by all Members. This custom is still adhered to, with very few exceptions.

The first Candidate to be admitted to Discovery Lodge was Bro Alan A Glover, who was Initiated on 17 November 1974 and went on to become Master on 24 March 1981.

In the beginning, Founder Member WBro Ken Loyns brought into the Lodge his experience of the Masonic Workings of the Eastern Archipelago, while later WBro Dennis Protheroe contributed the Emulation Workings of Liverpool. Recently, Bro Henry Montoya, a Master Mason from Cosmos Lodge No.8, under the Grand Lodge of the Philippines, was Installed Master on 23 March 2010. At his Installation, the Lodge was delighted to welcome a number of visiting Filipino Brethren from Manchester, Newcastle, Norwich, Surrey, Hertfordshire, London and Newport.

The Brethren of Discovery Lodge have laboured to sow the seeds of friendship and Masonic good fellowship with Brethren from all around the world, and it is hoped that this voyage in Freemasonry will continue for many years to come.

Compiled by WBros Kenneth Abram, PPrGReg, Secretary, and John Morgan, PPrGSuptWks.

Lodge of the Seven Seas No.8603

Warranted : 12 June 1974

Consecrated : 14 October 1974

Meeting at the Masonic Hall, Barry.

Forming this new Lodge in Barry was not as easy as might first appear, although there were many Brethren who were eager to become Members. The inspiration for the Lodge was WBro Alex R Duff. Alex first intimated to the Barry Masonic Trust Company that he wished to form a *'specialised Lodge'* in December of 1973. The Lodge was to be formed for the benefit of Brethren serving at sea or earning their living from the sea.

The first meeting took place on 21 December 1973 in order to prepare the foundations of the Lodge. WBro Alex R Duff was Elected Chairman and WBro F L Downs was Elected Secretary of this initial Committee. Many informal meetings were held at this stage, and the procedures laid down by United Grand Lodge were, of course, strictly followed. The object of this *'specialised Lodge'* was to give Mariners the opportunity of occupying the Chair of King Solomon. The naming of the Lodge was one of the first hurdles that the Founders had to overcome. The original idea was that the Lodge was to be called 'The Seafarer's Lodge' or 'The Mariners' Lodge'. The oldest Lodge in Barry is Barry Lodge No.2357, which is quite rightly proud of its connection with the Sea, Shipping and Seafarers, and so objected to these proposed two names. Therefore, it was back to the Committee to consider this early setback to their hopes of establishing a new Lodge in Barry. The Founders continued to hold fast to the principle that it was of the utmost importance that the name of the new Lodge should reflect the connection and commitment of its Members to the Sea. It is believed that Alex Duff came up with the perfect solution; the Lodge should be called 'Lodge of the Seven Seas'. Approval was granted by both United Grand Lodge and Provincial Grand Lodge, and there being no objections from other Lodges in the town to the name selected, the Founders' aspirations took a significant step forward. The Sponsoring Lodge was Breaksea Lodge No.8358.

There were seventeen Founder Members who appreciated that with a Lodge restricted to Seafarers, the size of the Lodge would be limited.

The Warrant was issued on the 12 June 1974 and the Consecration took place at the Masonic Temple, Barry, on Monday 14 October 1974. Prior to this Ceremony, a luncheon was held at the Mount Sorrel Hotel, which was attended by sixteen Founder Members. The Lodge was delighted to have the presence of RWBro the Rt Hon the Lord Swansea, ProvGM, accompanied by his Consecrating Officers.

In the history of the Lodge, there is one name that will forever stand out as a leading light, namely WBro Alexander Graham

Duff, known to everyone as 'Alex'. On 25 February 1944, the destroyer HMS Mahratta, 1,920 tons, was torpedoed and sunk by the German U Boat -U.990. On board was Engine Room Artificer, Alex; he was then a young sailor of 24 years of age. HMS Mahratta was one of the ships escorting a Russian Convoy of merchant ships in the Barents Sea, when at 9.15 pm the Mahratta was struck by an acoustic homing torpedo, killing many of the ship's Officers. The crew immediately went to action stations, but at 9.30 pm a second torpedo struck the destroyer's bulkhead. Some of the crew had been preparing a motor and a rowing boat when this second torpedo struck, killing all those working on the boats and both boats themselves were destroyed. At 9.45 pm all members of the crew were ordered to 'Abandon Ship Stations' and it was another 30 minutes, at 10.15 pm that the order to 'Abandon Ship' was actually given. The sea temperature was -14°F and WBro Alex recalled the shock of jumping into the freezing water. When he surfaced, the ship's bows were in the air and the destroyer went down very quickly. Whilst in the water, his trousers became so heavy that he had to remove them. The immediate problem facing him was not the loss of his waterlogged trousers but rather in which direction he should start to swim! He could see nothing, as it was snowing heavily and pitch black, but by good fortune he set out in the right direction, and after a while he saw a small red light on a rowing boat from another accompanying destroyer. This small rowing boat picked up the Engine Room Artificer, and another sailor, who sadly died soon after being rescued. Alex was in hospital at Scapa Flow for many months, but returned to action shortly before D-Day. This story is truly remarkable. Out of a crew of 237 only 16 survived to record this tragic wartime incident. From such an incident was built the character of a Brother, whose foresight and determined leadership led to the formation of Lodge of the Seven Seas.

There was considerable discussion over the design of the Lodge Logo. After numerous meetings, it was finally agreed that it should consist of an Anchor over which is inlaid a Map of the World. The work of designing the Logo was left in the skilful hands of WBro Alvern M M Hart, PM Porthkerry Lodge No.6299. One of his hobbies was the art of penmanship and graphology, and upon whom many demands were placed for illustrating and illuminating the written records of those Brethren attending important dinners etc, in Barry and Cardiff. The design of the 'World' was taken from a school exercise book used by his young daughter. Around this is a 'ship's rope', or 'cable-tow', maintaining the connection between land, sea and Freemasonry; the anchor being based upon a design that WBro Alvern had seen on the Badge of the Royal Marines.

The Lodge Motto is 'Mare Liberum', which refers to 'The Free Sea' or 'The Freedom of the Sea'. This Motto is taken from Hugo Grotuis (aka Hugo de Groot), born in Delft, Holland, 10 April 1583. (Died, Rostock, 28 August 1645.) He worked as a Jurist in the Dutch Republic, and laid the foundations for International Law based on Natural Law. In 'Mare Liberum' ('The Free Seas', published in 1609), Grotuis formulated the new principle that the Sea was 'International Territory' and 'All nations were free to use it for Seafaring Trade'. The Lodge Committee unanimously agreed that this expression of Brotherly Love throughout the Seven Seas, coupled with the view of the Freedom of the Seven Seas was totally and completely in accord with the aims of the new Lodge.

Very early on in the life of the Lodge, the custom of 'Piping the Master' at the Festive Board was established. To explain the procedure: when the Lodge business has been completed, and the Lodge closed, the DC, accompanied by his ADC, takes his position near the door of the Lodge,and then calls upon the Officers to 'take station' to escort the WM. They are called in the following order, Junior and Senior Deacon, Junior and Senior Warden, Secretary and Treasurer, Chaplain and IPM, Officers of the Grand Lodge of England, Officers of Provincial Grand Lodge, Ruling Masters of the Province, Mandated Officer. The Brethren upon being called, form themselves into two columns, leaving a space between the two, in order to facilitate the entrance of the Tyler carrying the Lodge sword, who proceeds between the Pillars until he reaches the Worshipful Master, who by now has descended from the dais. On nearing the Master, he halts and gives a 'court bow', and salutes the Worshipful Master with his sword. In turn, the WM acknowledges this salute, by responding with a 'court bow'. Upon receiving this acknowledgement, the Tyler turns and awaits the arrival of the DC, who upon reaching the Tyler, himself about turns, and announces: 'To Order

Brethren, as the Worshipful Master, accompanied by his Officers retires from the Lodge'. The DC then commences walking between the columns towards the door, immediately followed by the Tyler and the WM. The retiring party then falls in behind the Master. The DC together with his Assistant, the Senior and Junior Deacons, raise their wands to form an arch for the procession to depart underneath on their way from the Lodge. It is also customary for the WM to invite the Brother Initiate to accompany him in the procession. Immediately outside the door of the Temple, the Master, accompanied on his left by his Wardens, and the Initiate, are greeted by the retiring Brethren. The practice of *'Piping the Master'* began at the first Installation Meeting after the formation of the Lodge. When the Master is ready to enter the dining room, the designated person stands with the DC at the entrance. He then produces a *'Royal Navy Boson's Call'* (known to non seafarers as a Boson's Pipe) placing this to his lips he then *'Pipes the Still'*. Upon hearing this shrill whistle, all Brethren cease both talking and movement. It is literally an Order to be obeyed. The DC then requests the Brethren to immediately take their places at table and to *'be upstanding, in order to receive the Worshipful Master'*. As the Master takes his first step forward into the dining room, the piper pipes *'Hands to Dinner'* and continues so doing until the Master takes his place at the dining table.

The Lodge possesses a Ceremonial Sword but not a great deal is known about its history. The Lodge has a copy of a letter, dated 8 February 1983, to Mrs A J Barbrook, thanking her for *'The Splendid presentation to the Lodge of a Masonic Sword, has been thankfully received and will be faithfully applied. Such that our Ceremonies will be enriched by the constant reminder of your dearly departed husband, one of our most Loyal and Faithful Brothers'*. The Sword is still used by the Tyler.

The room in which the Festive Board is held is also a little unusual, in that the walls are bedecked with flags. Each flag is genuine in that it has actually been flown aboard ship. There is, for example, an Ensign that had flown from the stern of the 'Queen Elizabeth'. Two flags or pennants that the Lodge is particularly proud of are from Air Sea Rescue Boats used in World War II. One of these boats had a silhouette in black of a *'Bat'* sewn onto its flag - presumably representing the squadron to which it was attached. Some wag in the Lodge had christened it the *'Flag of the Vampire Patrol'*. These flags and pennants are hung from the four walls of the room and make a very dramatic backcloth to the evening's proceedings.

In 2000, the Lodge was extremely fortunate and delighted to welcome RWBro H W Knapp of the Oso Naval Lodge No.1282, Grand Master of Texas, who was visiting the Lodge Tyler. So impressed was he with his visit, and in particular by the warmth of the welcome the Brethren extended to him, that upon his return to the United States he immediately began work on the fabrication of a Lodge Gavel. The Gavel, for the sole use of the Master, was presented to the Lodge, on 21 February 2001. The Gavel is inscribed *'Made from Texas Living Oak'*. Texas Living Oak being a particularly hard wood, it is envisaged that this gift from the Oso Naval Lodge will assist the Worshipful Master of Lodge of the Seven Seas to maintain order within the Lodge for many years to come.

In the beginning, there was no shortage of Brethren connected with the sea wishing to join the Lodge. However, the shipping industry in the United Kingdom has diminished considerably. Docks have been closed and the land converted to other purposes, both industrial and commercial. Also, it is fashionable to own a flat built in what was once a dockside warehouse. With the resulting decline in suitably qualified Candidates, serious discussions took place as to the future of the Lodge. The Brethren were split into two camps. Some wished to maintain the 'status quo', restricting the Membership to those with Seafaring connections. Others wished to see the Lodge expand by accepting nominations for Membership from Brethren who had no marine connections. It was obviously an impasse, which for the good of the Lodge, had to be overcome. This initially came about by the Brethren agreeing that Lewises were entitled to become Members. Shortly afterwards, it was agreed that the Lodge should be 'open' to all Candidates.

Today, the Lodge is very much back on its feet, and can look forward to a prosperous future, both in terms of the number of Candidates wanting to join and in the quality of its Ceremonies.

Compiled by WBro Trevor G Thompson, PPrGReg.

Miskin Lodge No.8625

Warranted : 11 December 1974

Consecrated : 4 March 1975

Meeting at the Masonic Hall, Pontyclun.

In the early 1970s, a number of Brethren of Talygarn Lodge No.7216 considered that with rising Lodge Membership, the Pontyclun area could support a new Lodge.

The driving forces behind this initiative were WBros Victor Bartlett, George Cronin and D Kenneth Proctor. WBro George Cronin took on the role of Sponsoring Secretary, and he wrote to the Grand Secretary in support of the Petition for the new Lodge as follows: *'The Membership of the Talygarn Lodge having exceeded one hundred, and application for worthy Candidates for Initiation continuing at the rate of six each year, resulting in three 'Double' Ceremonies, it was felt by some of the Brethren that the interests of Freemasonry in general and the interest and Masonic progress of Brethren and future worthy Candidates in particular, could be better served with the formation of a new Lodge.'*

It was further explained that they wished to call the new Lodge 'Miskin', Miskin being the parish adjoining Talygarn, the name of the Sponsoring Lodge.

George Sidney Cronin was an Initiate and PM Talygarn Lodge. Professionally, he was a Company Director, residing in Cyncoed, Cardiff.

The Designated Principal Officers were all Initiates of Talygarn Lodge. WBro Albert Victor Bartlett, PPrAGDC, a Metallurgist from Rhiwbina, Cardiff, was WM Designate. Bro Thomas Arthur Salathiel, a Post Office Telephone Engineer, residing at Llantrisant Road, Pontyclun was SW Designate. Bro Ronald William Frank Cowell, a Method Study Engineer with the NCB, from Tonyrefail, was JW Designate.

The Warrant was granted on 11 December 1974, and the Consecration of the Lodge and the Installation of the first Master took place at the Masonic Hall, Pontyclun, on Tuesday, 4 March, 1975.

The Consecrating Officer was RWBro the Rt Hon the Lord Swansea, DL, ProvGM, assisted by a large number of Provincial Officers. The first WM, WBro Victor Bartlett, was Installed by VWBro Harry F Stockwell, PGSuptWks, DepProvGM. WBro Victor Bartlett was to be a major influence in the Lodge for many years. Not surprisingly, of the sixteen Officers appointed on that occasion, all but eight were Worshipful Brethren, seven of whom were Past Masters of Talygarn Lodge.

The first Regular Lodge Meeting was held on Wednesday, 7 May 1975, at which the principal business was to Ballot for 2 Joining Members, and most importantly to Ballot for the first Initiate, Mr John Rhys Hughes. All 3 Ballots proved successful and Bro John completed his First Degree that evening. He was Passed on 11 February 1976 and Raised on 5 May. He was the first Initiate of Miskin Lodge to become a Grand Officer. He proved to be a first class Freemason, and became WM of the Lodge in 1984. He served the Lodge as Secretary for a number of years, but sadly, he passed to the Grand Lodge Above in February 2004.

A most distinguished Member of the Lodge is WBro Kenneth Proctor, who was WM, 1987-1988. Initiated into Royal Connaught Lodge No.3266, Trinidad, in 1954, his business career brought him to South Wales. He became a Joining Member of Talygarn Lodge in 1966 and WM in 1974. In Province, he was appointed PAGDC and later promoted to ProvJGW. He became a Grand Officer in 1991 with the Rank of PAGDC, and in 2002, he was promoted to PJGD. He also holds high office in Royal Arch Masonry. He was the Mandated Officer for several years and he remains a marvellous source of knowledge, support and encouragement to the Lodge. As a result of the high esteem in which he is held, he was made an Honorary Member of the Lodge over 10 years ago. In addition to having had a successful business career as a Chartered Engineer, WBro Ken served as a Justice of the Peace, on the Miskin Bench, for a number of years.

Not surprisingly for a newly formed Lodge, Initiates were attracted, and within a short period of time the Lodge had grown in both Membership and influence within the Pontyclun group of Lodges.

As with all Lodges, as they establish themselves, important items of Regalia are acquired over time, often as a result of the generosity of either the total Lodge Membership or of individual Members.

In the early 1990s, the lack of a Lodge Banner became a matter of concern and a sub-committee was established to agree on a design. Various ideas were forthcoming and it was finally decided that a depiction of a water wheel in front of a mill would be appropriate. Members remembered Miskin Mill, which is located near Llantrisant, where there has been a water-driven corn mill for most of the last 400 years. Since 1929, the site of the mill and the area around it have been in continuous use by Scouts for camping and training purposes. The Banner was made by a locally based company, and it was Dedicated by VWBro Cdr Roy K Hopkin, DepProvGM, in November 1995.

In February 1996, WBro Gareth A Jones, WM, presented a Master's Collar with silver bars, bearing the names of every WM of the Lodge since its Dedication. Annually, a new bar is engraved with the name of the out-going Master.

The Cuffs worn by the WM, SW and JW were donated in 1988 by the late WBro Mervyn Collins, a regular visitor to the Lodge.

The cushion supporting the Volume of the Sacred Law was made and embroidered by the mother of WBro Gareth J Jones, WM, 2005-2006, and presented to the Lodge in 2007.

In May 2011, WBro John Cross, WM 1998-1999, presented an embroidered cushion on which the Working Tools are displayed in the various Degrees.

Over the years, the Lodge was been blessed with individuals committed to maintaining high standards in the Ceremonies. The Lodge is particularly indebted to the late WBros Cliff Aldridge and Joseph Williams, who were unstinting in their assistance in promoting good Ritual. In more recent times, WBros Arthur Turvey and Ralph Hicks, Preceptors, have carried on the good work. At present, WBro Gareth Jones is both Lodge Secretary and Preceptor.

The Lodge continues to be generous in its support of Masonic Charities, while at the same time it actively seeks out local charitable organisations worthy of its financial assistance.

Miskin Lodge is currently experiencing a healthy and exciting period. New Members are being attracted and the support of the Brethren is strong.

Compiled by WBro G J Jones, PPrGSwdB.

Llanilltud Fawr Lodge No.8644

Warranted : 12 February 1975

Consecrated : 23 June 1975

Meeting at the Masonic Hall, Porthcawl.

The Lodge was formed in the early 1970s by a number of Brethren who were employed in Education. This strong connection has continued, with a significant number of Members still actively involved in that profession.

The Mother Lodge is Universities Lodge No.5461, Cardiff, and there were sixteen Founder Members. The Founder 'Father' was WBro John A M Davies, PPrGW, Installed WM Afan Lodge No.833 in 1964, who was Head Teacher of Llanilltud Fawr Comprehensive School, Llantwit Major.

There were two main reasons for the choice of Lodge name. Firstly, it was originally intended that the new Lodge should meet in the ancient Monastic town of Llantwit Major. However, as there was no Masonic Temple established in the town, the Founders of the Lodge, with due approval, accepted the invitation of the Porthcawl Masonic Hall Company to use its facilities. The Lodge has been based in Porthcawl ever since. Secondly, Llanilltud Fawr Lodge is educationally orientated, with many of its Members being drawn not only from the field of Education but also from other professions, entry to which requires a high standard of formal learning. This has a close connection with Llanilltud Fawr, which was the main seat of learning and monasticism in the 5th and 6th centuries in Wales. Saint Illtyd is described in the 8th century 'Life of Samson', as 'the most learned of all the Britons in his knowledge of the scriptures, in every branch of philosophy, poetry, rhetoric, grammar and arithmetic'. As a teacher, he attracted many students, and St David, the Patron Saint of Wales, was among those who studied under him.

The Consecration Ceremony was carried out on Monday, 23 June 1975 and the Consecrating Officer was RWBro the Rt Hon the Lord Swansea, DL, ProvGM. The Installing Master was VWBro Harry Stockwell, PGSuptWks, DepProvGM, assisted by WBro Harold Wilson, PSGD, AProvGM, and WBro Llewellyn G Bevan, PSGD, AProvGM. WBro John Davies was duly Installed as WM, with Bros W E Thomas and A Higgins as SW and JW respectively. The first Treasurer was WBro F W Dawson, PPrAGDC, who had been Installed WM of Edgar Rutter Lodge No.7196, in 1969. Other Founder Past Masters included, WBro David Herbert Morgan, MBE, WM of Glamorgan Lodge No.36, in 1971; WBro D E Thomas, CBE, WM of Universities Lodge No. 5461, in 1971; WBro E I Davies, WM of Singleton Lodge No.8399, in 1975; WBro P W J Drew, ProvAGDC, WM of St Quentin's Lodge No.4778, in 1971, and who became the first Almoner of Llanilltud Fawr Lodge; and WBro G Waters, PPrAGDC, WM of Llangeinor Lodge No.4194 in 1964. The date of the Warrant is 12 February, 1975.

The Lodge Banner was Dedicated by WBro Samuel Northway, PSGD, AProvGM, on 28 January, 1987. It is pale blue, the colour of the Craft, and has at its head the name of the Lodge. The Crest is a red dragon passant standing on a white Masonic cable tow. The helm is that of an esquire, which is always used for corporate bodies. The wreath of material twisted about the base of the Crest is red and white, the Welsh National colours. The Arms are in the shape of a rectangular shield, which is the format of a Masonic Lodge. At the east and west are eight black and white squares, representing the sixteen Founders of the Lodge, and in the centre of the Banner is the Cross of Illtyd (450-535AD). The Celtic cross is indivisibly linked with St Illtyd, and added to the Cross are four silver Masonic Squares, one at each corner. The Motto is '*Gorau Arf, Arf Dysg*' meaning '*the best weapon is the weapon of learning*'. The Banner was produced by Mrs Gwyther Harris of Merthyr Tydfil, and designed by WBro G Vivian Lewis, a Past Master of the Lodge. The Founders of the Lodge wanted to establish a particular Welsh Celtic identity, and this is summed up in the words of a poem, written in 1975, by WBro W Eirwyn Thomas, the first Senior Warden of the Lodge.

LLANILLTUD FAWR

Embraced by Hodnant's stream on Colhugh's lea
Where history with legend intertwines,
Whence Celtic saintly zealots sailed by sea
To salvage supine souls, myopic minds
Stands Illtud's due domain of yesteryear,
Monastic seat of mystic love and lore
Where faith in God and Man has fractured fear
By Cae Mead's Roman Villa, now no more.
There men were roused to raise aloft their sights
By energetic precept from first youth.
All bidden boldly to belie what blights
Masonic tenets - honour, trust and truth.
Llanilltud Fawr, fan now your flawless flame
For us who vaunt your venerable name.

WBro Leonard Arthur Jones, PPrJGD, a Principal in Technical Education, was the Worshipful Master of the Lodge in 1987 and 1988. He is the only Member of the Lodge to date who has been a Member of the Craft for over fifty years. Initiated in Dr James Griffith Hall Lodge No.3161 on 17 November 1951, he died in 2010. His son, WBro Nigel Spencer Jones, was WM in 2009, and his son-in-law, Bro Paul Jones was Initiated into the Lodge in 2010. This is the first three-generation family in the history of the Lodge.

Various artefacts have been purchased to add to the particular identity of the Lodge. These include Lodge Gavels, donated by WBro Brynley Davies and WBro Paul Thomas; a Bible Fall by Bro Michael Bailey, PAGDC, and a set of Square and Compasses by WBros Andrew Dodd, PPrGSwdB and Peter Jones, PPrGSwdB. In January 2010, to celebrate the 35th Anniversary of the Founding of the Lodge, a chest, containing the Working Tools of the Three Degrees was donated by WBros Anthony Tanner, WM, Keith McCormack and Michael Bailey. It was presented at the Installation Festival, in the presence of the ProvGM, RWBro Captain Sir Norman Lloyd-Edwards.

The Lodge still has a strong connection with Education. and during the Installation Ceremony in 2011, amongst the appointed Officers, eight are active in the teaching profession.

Compiled by WBro G Vivian Lewis, PPrGSwdB, and WBro Andrew J Dodd, PPrGSwdB.

Wings Lodge No.8651

Warranted : 12 March 1975

Consecrated : 10 October 1975

Meeting at the Masonic Hall, Penarth.

Services Lodge No.7139 was the Sponsoring Lodge for Wings Lodge No.8651. The principal Founder Members of the Lodge were WM Designate: WBro Frederick G Hill, PPrGSwdB, (Mon), PM Glyn Ebbw Lodge No.2556, Ebbw Vale and a Member of Charles Lyne (Installed Masters) Lodge No.2964, Newport, and Preswylfa Lodge No.5792; Acting IPM: WBro Thomas J Burley, PM Friendship & Justice Lodge No.5830 and PM of Shir Gâr Lodge No.7339; SW Designate: WBro Vivian C Pitcon, PM Cambrensis Lodge No.6608; JW Designate: Bro Ernest E O Irish of Preswylfa Lodge No.5792. WBro Leonard Roy Evans, PPrAGDC, PM Friendship & Justice Lodge was the first Chaplain and WBro Gurney M Smith, PM Barry Lodge No.2357 was the first Treasurer.

All the Founder Members of Wings Lodge had served in the Royal Air Force and were also Members of the Royal Air Forces Association, whose stated objective is simply, *'To render service to each other'*. This is still the prime reason for the Association's existence. It aims to preserve by charitable means, the memory, the honour and the example, of those who have served in The Royal Air Force and the Air Forces of the Commonwealth. The RAF Association Wings Appeal raises around £2 million each year, dedicated to the welfare of serving and ex-serving RAF personnel and their families. Wings Lodge derives its name from the 'Wings Appeal' Charity of the Royal Air Forces Association. Both organisations are bound by many traditions, but there are two in particular by which they are most closely linked, namely Charity and Friendship. These principles follow in the steps of the great Masonic Charities, and are supported by the Brotherly love which exists in our Lodges. The Motto of the Royal Air Forces Association, *'Not for ourselves alone'*, was adopted by the Lodge and appears on its Insignia.

The Lodge was Consecrated on 10 October 1975 by RWBro the Rt Hon the Lord Swansea, DL, ProvGM. The Installing Master was VWBro Harry F Stockwell, DepProvGM, and the DC was WBro Geoffrey Malin Ashe.

The Founder Members' pledged purpose in forming the Lodge was, *'for having the Prosperity of the Craft at heart and being anxious to diffuse the genuine principles of the Art - to promote the Ethic of Freemasonry throughout the Universe and also that existing within the Royal Air Forces Association, whose Motto is - Not for Ourselves Alone.'*

Bro Edward G Amos, MM of Preswylfa Lodge (later to become Worship Brother), the Founder Secretary, was the driving force behind the formation of the Lodge and without his unstinting efforts, the Lodge would probably never have existed. The idea for the formation of the Lodge was first mooted by Brother Ted at a Meeting of Ystradyfodwg Lodge No.7638, Pontypridd, on 7 June 1969, when several members of the Royal Air Forces Association were present to support WBro Vernon Woods at his Installation. WBro Amos not only worked exceedingly hard for many years in the formation of the Lodge, as Secretary, Worshipful Master and Preceptor, but he also arranged weekend trips, treasure hunts and many other social activities for the Lodge Members and their families. He embodied the spirit of the Lodge and worked endlessly and enthusiastically, not only for Freemasonry, but also in other non-Masonic charitable activities. He raised considerable amounts of money for the Royal Air Forces Association. He was also closely involved with the Royal Air Force Band and a local Male Voice Choir, arranging a concert each year in St David's Hall, Cardiff.

The Lodge celebrated its 25th Anniversary in 2000, when the late WBro Leonard R Evans, who had served as Chaplain since the Lodge's Consecration, was Installed as Worshipful Master.

On 25 May 2006, a Lodge Banner was Dedicated by WBro Geoffrey W Thomas, PSGD, AProvGM, assisted by his team of Officers, led by WBro Ben Smith, ProvDepGDC. The Banner was carried into the Temple by WBro Brian Garner, PPrGReg, the Lodge's Founder IG and an Initiate of Cardiff Exchange Lodge No.3775. He was Installed WM of Wings Lodge in 1985 and again in 2001. The Banner was then handed to WBro Len Evans, PPrSGW, who placed it into a purpose made mahogany stand, ready for the Dedication Ceremony. Well over 100 Brethren attended the Ceremony and Festive Board. A raffle was held, which raised the magnificent sum of £515, which was donated to various charities, including the Royal Air Forces Association.

Wings Lodge follows the Oxford Ritual, and at the Festive Board it is traditional to accompany the Toasts, 'Absent Brethren' and 'The Visitors' in song. It is also customary at the Festive Board to have a display of RAF Squadron shields, which have been donated by Brethren, in racks which run the length of the top table, and to hang prints of paintings of various aeroplanes behind the top table.

When the Lodge was Founded, it had a very strong ex-Royal Air Force Membership, based upon the strong bond formed between ex-servicemen, many of whom had served in the Second World War and suffered the deprivations of that period. However, with the passage of time, the ties with the RAF have weakened significantly and few of the recently Initiated Brethren or Joining Members have a direct RAF connection. Nevertheless, the Lodge still assists the Royal Air Forces Association with regular substantial charitable donations, thus maintaining the traditions established by the Founders.

Compiled by WBro Bill Barratt, with the assistance of the late WBro Len Evans, PPrSGW, and WBro Brian Garner, PPrJGW.

Crystal Lodge No.8713

Warranted   :   10 March 1976

Consecrated   :   21 June 1976

Meeting at the Masonic Hall, Penarth.

It is generally the tradition that Lodges named after Jewels are 'dry'. This one, Crystal Lodge, does in fact partake of the beverage at the Festive Board!

Crystal Lodge was Founded as a result of a conversation between two senior Seafarers, Bros E Prudhoe and J Robson, at a Ladies' Festival in Penarth. They expressed regret at not having attained the Chair of King Solomon in their respective Lodges and so WBro L L Lloyd, who had been Installed WM of Emerald Lodge No.5907 in 1973, suggested the formation of a new Lodge, Sponsored by his own Lodge. This was thought to be a very good idea and the Seafarer who originally suggested it, Bro J Robson, being the younger of the two, agreed to accept the Office of Junior Warden. This was, as it rather sadly turned out, a magnificent gesture as the first Senior Warden, Bro E Prudhoe, passed away during his year as Immediate Past Master. This must have been a very sad and poignant time for the Brother who had stood down to allow him to precede him to the Chair of King Solomon.

Emerald Lodge subsequently agreed to be the Sponsoring Lodge and WBro Lloyd became the Primus Master. There were 6 Past Master Founder Members, of whom 4 were from Emerald Lodge. WBro R M Maurice, Installed WM of Lodge of Unity No.6030 in 1974, was appointed the IPM and WBro D J Pitten, Installed WM of Cardiff Exchange Lodge No.3775 in 1974, was Invested as the first ADC. The Lodge Minutes show that the annual subscription was initially set at £10.00.

The Consecration of the Lodge took place at the Masonic Temple, Stanwell Road, Penarth, on Monday, 21 June 1976. The Consecrating Officer was RWBro the Rt Hon the Lord Swansea, ProvGM. The Installing Master was VWBro Harry Stockwell, DepProvGM, assisted by WBro Harold Wilson, AProvGM. WBro Geoffrey M Ashe was Director of Ceremonies and WBro William J Northway acted as Tyler. The harmony of the Ceremony was enhanced by the presence of the 'Guildford Singers'.

In addition to these distinguished Brethren, WBro Vernon Gordon Allenby Upton, GM, ProvJGW, was in attendance as Consecrating JW. He went on to serve as Crystal Lodge's Mandated Officer for 24 years, and made a truly outstanding contribution to the development of the Lodge. Further, his presence complimented the maritime background of the Principal Founders. Vernon Upton had served as a Merchant Navy Officer during WWII and had been decorated with the George Medal for his gallantry. He was Installed as WM of Emerald Lodge in 1970. In 2004, his magnificent account of life at sea during WWI and

WWII entitled 'Upon Their Lawful Occasions' was published and the net proceeds made a substantial contribution to the 2010 Festival. Sadly, he died on 30 March 2005, but in the full knowledge that he had completed and published his book.

The Lodge's Crest shows a squared pavement, with a winding staircase leading off to the right, and with a window above and to the right. On the left is an ear of corn next to a fall of water. The centre is dominated by a round crystal. The depiction is framed by a pair of white pillars bearing the celestial and terrestrial globes with an arched canopy containing the Lodge name and suspended Square and Compasses in traditional form. The Crest was designed by WBro Derek Scone, PPrGReg, one of the Lodge Founders and its first Director of Ceremonies. He had been Installed WM of Emerald Lodge in 1974. The Founders' and Past Masters' Jewels bear this Crest in an impressive manner, having a solid crystal suspended at the appropriate point. These Jewels have been exclusively produced for Crystal Lodge No.8713, by Toye, Kenning and Spencer Ltd, Great Queen Street, London, since the Consecration. Although there are a number of Crystal Lodges Warranted under the United Grand Lodge of England, this Crest is used exclusively by this particular Lodge.

In recent years, Crystal Lodge has returned to its original maritime background, having a number of current Members with close relationships with the sea; these include a Boat Builder, a professional Sailing Instructor, a Royal Marine, two Officers of Her Majesty's Coastguard and a member of the RNLI.

The Lodge being well established within the Penarth Masonic family, the Brethren later decided to further advance the cause of Freemasonry within Penarth by forming the Lodge's own Royal Arch Chapter. Crystal Chapter No.8713 was Consecrated in 1983, thus joining the two other Royal Arch Chapters already meeting in Penarth, and thereby assisting Brethren to complete their Membership of Pure Ancient Freemasonry.

In addition to being committed to the activities of the Province by providing many Acting Officers, Crystal Lodge has also been greatly involved in the management of the Windsor Penarth Masonic Hall Company. The Lodge has provided two Chairmen, two Company Secretaries, two Maintenance Officers and a Bookings Secretary, to ensure the smooth running of the Hall on behalf of all the Penarth Brethren.

To celebrate its 30 years, the Brethren of the Lodge decided that a Banner should be purchased for display in the Penarth Temple. The Lodge Past Master's Jewel was the template used for the design. On Monday, 30 April 2007, the Banner was Dedicated in an impressive Ceremony, presided over by VWBro Peter Frost, DepProvGM, who gave a very interesting and informative Oration on Lodge Banners in general and the design of the Crystal Lodge Banner in particular.

On Monday, 18 October 2010, WBro Roger Hall, a local Boat Builder and a registered blind Brother, was Installed in the Chair of King Solomon. The Installing Master was WBro Stephen Elworthy, and this significant Installation was graced by the presence of RWBro Captain Sir Norman Lloyd-Edwards, KCVO, ProvGM.

Although a relatively young Lodge, its vibrant and friendly Membership has great hopes for the future. It holds a strong sense of pride in its background, history and traditions, and sets itself high standards of Ritual, practised regularly at LOI.

Compiled by WBro Paul Gallone, PPrJGD, and WBro John Pillinger, PPrSGD.

St Cecilia Lodge No.8748

Warranted : 18 November 1976

Consecrated : 1 March 1977

Meeting at the Masonic Hall, Penarth.

The idea of forming the Lodge arose from 'The Guildford Singers'. They were members of a local Glee Party and various Lodges, which came together in 1960 to provide entertainment for Brethren at the Festive Board. The group made its first appearance at the Installation Ceremony of St Canna Lodge No.6725 in February 1975. Now, only two of the original party are still active.

The conductor was WBro Edward James Smith, FRCO, and the accompanist was WBro Alfred Hill. The choir's title, 'The Guildford Singers', was taken from the name of the street where Cardiff Masonic Hall is situated. It was also, until recently, the location of the Provincial Office. During their first five years, the 'Singers' confined their activities to singing at Ladies' Festivals and Regular Lodge Meetings. In November 1965, however, the Glee Party was invited by RWBro Edgar Rutter, DepProvGM, to sing the Anthems at the Dedication of the new Masonic Hall at Porthcawl, followed by the Consecration of the Lodge of Sker No.8024.

The following year, they were invited to sing at the Installation of RWBro the Rt Hon the Lord Swansea, as Provincial Grand Master of South Wales Eastern Division. In the years following, the Guildford Singers performed at twenty-two Consecration Ceremonies and at the Dedication of the Lord Swansea Temple in the Cardiff Masonic Hall. The year 1967 saw one of the highlights in their career, when they were invited to sing at the Festival of the Royal Masonic Institution for Boys in London. At the Memorial Service for RWBro Edgar Rutter, held in Llandaff Cathedral in 1971, the Choir led the congregation in singing his favourite hymns, which included 'God is a Spirit'. The choir has sung at Masonic functions in London, Bristol and Newport, and also at the Albert Edward Prince of Wales Court, Porthcawl, where they formed the basis of the Choir at the Dedication of the Edgar Rutter Memorial Chapel.

The members of the Choir felt that by entertaining their Brethren, they were spreading the spirit of Freemasonry through the medium of music, which is international and knows no bar to race, creed or colour. The harmonious and Brotherly spirit prevailing among the singers is now transmitted through the Lodge of St Cecilia from generation to generation.

The Lodge is named after St Cecilia (Latin: *Sancta Caecilia*), the Patron Saint of Musicians and Church Music. When she was dying she sang to God, and it is also written that as the Musicians played at her wedding, she *'sang in her heart to the Lord'*. Her Feast Day is celebrated in the Roman Catholic, Anglican, the Eastern Orthodox and Eastern Catholic Churches on 22 November. The Lodge Motto: *'In Perfect Harmony',* is also particularly apt.

The Founders of St Cecilia Lodge approached Edgar Rutter Lodge No.7196 to be the Sponsoring Lodge, which was readily agreed. The Consecration Ceremony took place at the Masonic Hall, Penarth, on 1 March 1977. The Consecrating Officer was RWBro the Rt Hon the Lord Swansea, accompanied by his team of Officers. The First Master was WBro Edward James Smith, PM Lodge of Unity No.6030, and Duke of York Lodge No.2453, PGStB, PPrGW. The SW was Bro. Thomas Frederick Styles Grimshaw, and the JW was Bro Phillip Thomas Cornelius, with WBro H E Patterson, PPrGW, PM Gwalia Lodge No.4213 acting as IPM.

Although Membership is small, the Lodge is very fortunate in having excellent support from its visitors, who often take part in the Ceremonies, if and when called upon. Regular social events are held, which are always well attended, especially the Ladies' Festival, which takes place in mid October, when non-Masonic friends are welcomed. 'White Table' events are also held, where non-Masonic friends are invited to attend and learn something about Freemasonry. It is customary to sing the 'Visitors Toast' at the Festive Board.

At the end of November, it has become a Lodge tradition to visit the Albert Edward Prince of Wales Court in Porthcawl. Gifts of sherry are taken and the Brethren entertain the residents in song. St Cecilia Lodge is fondly known as the *'Lodge that brings the sherry'!*

The Lodge used to make fraternal visits to St Cecilia Lodge No.9341, Wedmore, Somerset, but these visits ceased some time ago, due to the loss of most of the Guildford Singers. It is hoped, however, that these visits will resume in the near future. The Lodge has a connection with the famous Black Dyke Mills Band, through Founder Member, WBro Edward D Andrews, PPrJGW, who has organised a number of fund raising events in Cardiff in the past years.

The Lodge has also helped other Lodges which have had difficulties in Raising their Candidates by performing that Ceremony for them. Three Brethren became Masonic Veterans, WBros John D Hann, James Smith and Bro Ernest Mules. Sadly, all three have now passed to the Grand Lodge Above.

There is an Illuminated Address fixed to the wall immediately outside the Penarth Temple. This is by way of a 'thank you' to the Guildford Singers, for a performance given to a Lodge in Bristol in 1969. It is signed by WBro Reginald Thomas, WM of Tennant Lodge No.1992.

Compiled by WBro John A Taylor, PPrJGD.

Sketty Hall Lodge No.8752

Warranted : 8 December 1976

Consecrated : 4 March 1977

Meeting at the Masonic Hall, Swansea.

The formation of the new Lodge in Swansea commenced with four Brethren, namely, WBro Henry Steele, and Bros Vernon Matthews, Tegwyn Howells and Fitzroy Allen. They gathered together a number of interested Swansea and Neath Brethren, and arranged several preparatory meetings. On 6 September 1976, the four of them met in Cardiff with VWBro Harry F Stockwell, DepProvGM, and WBro Malcolm H Thompson, ProvGSec, when it was agreed that a Lodge would be formed. At that meeting, WBro Henry Steele proposed that the name of the Lodge should be 'Sketty Hall'. The mansion, Sketty Hall, parts of which date from the 1720s, was acquired by Richard Glynn Vivian in 1898, an art lover who gave the Glynn Vivian Art Gallery to Swansea. He was the youngest brother of Henry Hussey Vivian, 1st Baron Swansea, the grandfather of the Rt Hon John Hussey Hamilton Vivian, 4th Baron Swansea, ProvGM of South Wales, Eastern Division. Apparently, the ProvGM had spent much of his childhood days living in the mansion. A representation of Sketty Hall is shown on the Lodge Banner.

Caradoc Lodge No.1573 was the Sponsoring Lodge and the Warrant for Sketty Hall Lodge No.8752, was duly signed on 8 December 1976. Following further meetings, it was eventually agreed that the Consecration Ceremony would be held on Friday, 4 March 1977. The Ceremony was performed by RWBro the Lord Swansea, and WBro Henry Steele was later Installed as the first Master of the new Lodge. Later, at the Festive Board, the WM was presented with a silver tray, inscribed with the names of all the Founder Members, in recognition of his hard work setting up the Lodge.

The first Regular Lodge Meeting took place on Friday, 13 May 1976 with Mr Cyril Norton and Mr Albert Kenneth George as the first Initiates. The latter was Installed as WM in 1986, and in Province, he attained the Rank of PPrAGDC.

Over the years the Lodge has been renowned for organising some memorable trips to London, including visits to Grand Lodge. In the early nineties, visits to a Lodge in Deal, Kent, were arranged by WBro Mayne Price, PPrAGDC, who had been Installed as WM in 1992. The success of these events was due to the hard work put in by WBro Keith Willicombe, PPrSGD, and WBro Andrew Pearce, PPrSGD. They were Installed in the Chair of King Solomon in 1997 and 1998 respectively.

Annual visits to the Mother Lodge, Caradoc Lodge, and Sister Lodge, Beaufort Lodge No.3834, are evenings always looked

Sketty Hall

forward to by the Brethren. Many life-long friendships have been kindled at these evenings, thereby displaying the true spirit and the value of the Craft.

No contemporary Lodge history would be complete without a mention of the contribution made by the first Worshipful Master, WBro Henry Steele, who had been Installed as WM of Caradoc Lodge in 1972. He nurtured most of the Brethren through the Ritual as Lodge Preceptor for many of those years. An exceptional Freemason, respected by all who knew him, he was always ready to help and advise. Those present on the night will never forget his 90th birthday, when he performed a First Degree Ceremony with faultless rendering. Now in the Grand Lodge Above, WBro Henry Steele was a remarkable man and Freemason, whom all Sketty Hall Lodge Members were proud to know.

Compiled byRichard Walters, PM, PPrGReg.

Lodge of Enterprise No.8757

Warranted   :   8 December 1976

Consecrated   :   7 March 1977

Meeting at the Masonic Hall, Cardiff.

The Lodge of Enterprise was formed in 1977 by WBro Harold Greene, PM Lodge of Concord No.8418; WBro Harold Freedman, PPGD (Watch & Clock Importer); and WBro Reuben Joseph. The aim of the Lodge was to bring together like-minded Brethren, who enjoyed good Ritual and a fine Festive Board with good speeches, food and drink. At that time Lord Swansea, ProvGM, actively encouraged the formation of new Lodges in order to enable Brethren who had been in the Craft for many years to attain the Chair of King Solomon. This was an opportunity taken by 10 of the Founder Members. Other Founder Members included WBros Alan J Prescott, PM Lodge of Concord No.8418, Director of Continental Wines; Eric J Cross, PM Croeso Lodge No.8377, Managing Director, Scrap Merchant; Dennis Cantor, PM Carmel Lodge No.4774, Managing Director of Continental Wines; and Clyde C Lewis, PM Cardiff Exchange Lodge No.3775, Postmaster of Sub-Post Offices.

An extract from the Minutes of the Finance, Investigation & Standing Committee of the Friendship and Justice Lodge No.5830, held at the Masonic Hall, Cardiff at 8.00pm on 15 September 1976 states :

'Under any other business, WBro Harold Freedman spoke about a new Lodge to be formed and to be sponsored by Friendship & Justice Lodge, and after some explanation it was proposed by WBro Reuben Joseph, and seconded by WBro M Littlestone that the Lodge would do this. This was carried. As there was no other business the meeting closed at……..'

Why the name Enterprise? It was named to commemorate the coming together of the entrepreneurial spirit of its Founder Members. Of the 19 Founder Members, 17 were self employed businessmen. The Lodge crest and its Motto *'Labore et Honore'* (*'Work and Honour'* meaning *'There is honour in hard work'*) reflects the spirit of the Founder Members.

When I have asked Members of other Lodges what they thought of Enterprise as a Lodge, the results were surprising and fell into two groups.

Group one thought that the Lodge was only for millionaires. Within the Lodge Membership, I can find no evidence of this, excepting at one time eight of the Members drove Rolls Royce motor cars! The Lodge dining fees at that time were priced at £10.00. When adjusted for inflation this would now equal £45.00, whereas the annual subscription was £50.00 equalling some £225.00 in today's terms.

The second group thought that we were a Lodge of shop-keepers, because at that time shops generally closed for a half-day on

Wednesdays in Cardiff. I can find no proof of this. The actual reason for the Lodge being held on a Wednesday is quite interesting. Carmel Lodge No.4774 met ten times a year on the second Wednesday in the month and they gave up their right to four of those meetings, thus allowing Enterprise to utilize them. Masonic cooperation at its best!

Enterprise Lodge was Consecrated in Cardiff on 7 March 1977 by RWBro the Rt Hon the Lord Swansea, DL, ProvGM. The three Principal Officers of the newly Consecrated Lodge were: WBro Harold Greene, Estate Agent, as WM; Bro George W Baker, PProvGStwd, an Electrical Wholesaler, as SW; and Bro Bernard M Schwartz, a Clothing Wholesaler, as JW.

It has always been the custom to present a Past Master's Jewel to the Immediate Past Master. The Past Master's Jewel illustrated overleaf was given to the first Worshipful Master, Harold Greene, PProvJGW, and it is now worn by the current IPM. Woe betide any Member or guest who attempted to carry a pint of beer into the dining room in the presence of WBro Harold Greene; he would demand they left the room and dispose of their glass!

During the Festive Board, Stewards wore a Sommelier's tasting cup suspended from a thin red ribbon around their necks; this enabled visiting Brethren and the less sober Members of the Lodge to be able to quickly identify the person who should be refilling their glass. Members of the Lodge would drink Toasts out of their own silver goblets, but this tradition fell out of favour due to an apparent metallic taste tainting the wine. This tradition was reinstated in 2009 through the generosity of WBro Alasdair King, who donated blue glass goblets, inscribed with the Lodge Insignia, for the use of the Brethren and their guests.

The charity collection was always made at the Festive Board, with the Charity Steward WBro Harold Freedman shouting *'I want to hear crinkles not tinkles'*. This was in the distant days when we had a one pound note, informing the Brethren that a donation to charity must be a minimum of one pound (which equates, adjusting for inflation, to five pounds today.).

In 1980, Lodge Gavels were purchased by the Brethren and dedicated to the memory of Founder Member, WBro Harold Freedman, PPrGW.

On Wednesday, 9 June 1982, a Deputation was received for the formation of a proposed new Lodge to be known as 'Proscenium Lodge'. It was passed unanimously *'that the Lodge of Enterprise should sponsor the proposed new Lodge'*. Harold Greene and Bernard Schwartz were the prime movers in the formation of this Lodge, (as they had been in the formation of Lodge of Enterprise) helped by non- Enterprise Members, WBro Wyn Calvin and WBro John James.

In 1987, Working Tools were purchased by the Members and presented in memory of WBro George Baker, PPrGStwd, the Lodge's second Worshipful Master.

The Lodge Banner was Dedicated on Wednesday, 2 February 1994 by Special Dispensation from the Provincial Grand Master. The Ceremony was presided over by VWBro Cdr Roy K Hopkin, RN, PSGD, DepProvGM, assisted by WBro David Protheroe, PSGD, PAProvGM. The Banner, which now hangs in the Duke of Connaught Temple, and a Lodge Plaque, which is displayed on the wall in the main dining room, were purchased by WBro Ross Cantor and 14 other Brethren.

Siver and Glass Goblets

The Lodge held its 25th Anniversary on Tuesday, 26 February 2002, by Dispensation from RWBro Hywel Davies, ProvGM. At the Meeting, convened at 6.30 pm, the Gavel was proffered by the Worshipful Master to the then AProvGM, WBro Andrew Gretton, PSGD, who graciously accepted and occupied the Chair of King Solomon, and gave a brief history of the Lodge The Festive Board duplicated the banquet served at the Consecration Meeting, including five different wines to supplement each course, together with port and brandy. Interestingly, the catering costs of the original Consecration came to £13.30 per head including wine, the 25th Anniversary catering costs came to £35.00 a head without wine. The champagne, wine, port and brandy for this occasion were donated by Bros Keith Ingram and John Evans.

To commemorate the occasion, a booklet, edited by Bro John Evans, was produced giving a 'tongue in cheek' version of the Lodge history from Members' recollections. Also, a Commemorative firing glass was commissioned by the same two Brethren, and presented to the Founder Members.

The Lodge Membership has included many distinguished Brethren, several of whom achieved high Acting Rank in the Craft. Harold Greene, PProvJGW, was a larger-than-life person, who owned a chain of Estate Agencies in South Wales. On one memorable occasion during the Festive Board at a December meeting, he handed out Christmas Carol sheets and leapt on to the stage playing an accordion in accompaniment to the Brethren's rendition of a carol. When he noticed that most of his fellow Jewish Brethren weren't singing, he stopped and egged them on by saying *come on lads he was one of ours before he went wrong* much to the mirth of all.

Bernard M Schwartz, PProvSGW, another colourful character, was a Major in the British Army. He also had the honour of being Deputy Lord Lieutenant of Glamorgan and President of the Royal British Legion, Cardiff and District Branch. He was universally renowned for his eloquent and humorous after-dinner speaking.

VWBro Andrew L Gretton, PGSwdB, a well respected Member of 30 years, was appointed to Deputy Provincial Grand Master in June 2007. WBro Philip D Stewart, PAGDC, was Invested Provincial Junior Grand Warden in 2000 and subsequently appointed a Grand Officer in 2002 with the Rank of PAGDC. Founder Member WBro Clyde Lewis was a Provincial Steward during 1978, as was Harold Greene the following year. Other Brethren who have honoured the Lodge by their respective Active Provincial appointments include: WBros Eric Cross, ProvGPurs (1980); Dennis Cantor, ProvSGD (1981); Bernard M Schwartz, ProvGSwdB (1985); Graham Humphries, ProvGStB (1997); Gino Rabaiotti, ProvSGD (2001); Denis Tarling, ProvGStB (2004); Ben Smith, ProvDepGDC (2005), and Keith Ingram, ProvGStwd (2006).

The Lodge has always put a huge emphasis on charitable works. At the 1986 Festival, the Lodge became the highest donor per capita in the Province, with a donation of £15,244.00. In 1989, the Lodge donated £2,942.00 to the Cardiff Masonic Hall Company for the refurbishment of the Edger Rutter Dining Room, now referred to as the 'Lodge of Enterprise Dining Room'.

At the 58th Regular Meeting of the Lodge, held on 11 September 1991, the Lodge Charity Steward, WBro Andrew Gretton, reported that the Lodge had donated £15,600.00 to the 1991 Festival and that this was the leading donation from all the Lodges in the Province. Again, for the 1999 Festival, the Lodge of Enterprise made the highest donation of any Lodge in the Province as well as the highest donation per capita, with a staggering donation of £62,500.00.

Charitable funds are generated by the Lodge Members through covenants, charity collections in Lodge, raffles at the Festive Board and more importantly through the Lodge of Enterprise Charity Ball. The Charity Ball was first proposed in 1988 and organised by a number of the Lodge Brethren. It has now become an annual event and continues to be run by an ever-changing committee of Members, currently chaired by WBro Denis Tarling. Since 1988, Enterprise's Charity Events have raised in excess of £60,000.00, which has been shared between Masonic and non-Masonic Charities.

Compiled by WBro T John Evans, PPrSGD.

Lodge of St Martin No.8771

Warranted : 9 February 1977

Consecrated : 6 May 1977

Meeting at the Masonic Hall, Caerphilly.

The Lodge was formed by a group of diverse friends who met regularly at the Masonic Temple, Caerphilly, and who also visited Galen Lodge No.6366, meeting at the Masonic Temple, Cardiff. During 1976, firm plans were made regarding the Founding of a new Lodge, and the Brethren of Galen Lodge agreed to act as Sponsors for the proposed new Lodge.

The Lodge Warrant was granted on 9 February 1977, and the Lodge was Consecrated on Friday 6 May 1977 by RWBro the Rt Hon the Lord Swansea, DL, ProvGM South Wales Eastern Division (the 35th Lodge he had Consecrated), assisted by his Provincial team. There were 19 Founder Members, two of whom, WBro Bernard L Morris, PPrJGW, Installed as WM in 1992, and WBro Peter G Williams, PPrJGD, Installed as WM in 2006, are still Members of the Lodge. The first Master was WBro Clive Lisk, PM Lodge of Unity No.6030. The Acting IPM was WBro Samuel McMillan, PM Galen Lodge. The first Joining Members were Bros Ieuan Jones, John S Davies, Arthur Stonage, Norman Evans, John S Devine and James H Cartwright. The first Initiate was Mr John Gareth Owen, Installed as WM in 1985. He became Lodge Treasurer in 1992 and is still in Office with the Rank of PPrSGD. Much thought and deliberation went into choosing the name of the Lodge. First thoughts were for resurrecting the name of a long defunct Caerphilly Lodge called 'Ancient Britons', or alternatively 'Caerphilly'. During further discussions it was decided not to purchase Founders' Jewels but to donate the cash equivalent to the Royal Masonic Hospital instead. The Royal Masonic Hospital gratefully accepted the donation and presented each of the Founders with a suitably engraved Hospital Jewel, with permission to wear it at all times. This decision paved the way to naming the Lodge after the Patron Saint of Charity, St Martin. Further, the Parish Church of Caerphilly is named St Martin's.

St Martin was born in 316 AD in Pavia, Italy. His father was an Army Officer, and it was always understood that Martin would eventually follow in his footsteps and take up a military career. At the age of ten, however, Martin expressed a desire to enter the service of the Church, and he began by serving at the altar. His father, on the other hand, had other plans for him and at the age of fifteen, and much against his will, Martin was entered for military service in the cavalry! Throughout his military career, Martin's charity, virtue and goodness earned the high esteem of his fellow officers. A prime example of his charity, and the one for which he is most famously remembered, occurred when he was riding at the head of his troops through the gates of the city of Amiens. It was a bitterly cold day and he and his brother officers were approached by an almost naked beggar, blue and trembling with cold, begging for alms. Martin, through his many acts of kindness and charity, had no money to give, but instead he immediately removed his warm cloak, cut it in two with his sword and gave one half to the beggar and kept the other half for himself. This was judged by his fellow officers to be a true act of charity, for Martin had given only what he could afford, and not all that he had at the time. Martin eventually left the army and became Bishop of Tours, devoting the remainder of his life to charitable works. When the Lodge was formed, the Founders were reminded of the life of St Martin and coupled it with the tenets and principles of Freemasonry. Thus the Lodge was so named. There are thirteen Lodges in the English Constitution named after the Saint. The Lodge Motto: '*Friendship and Charity*', is also most appropriate.

The Lodge Banner was made by WBro Michael S Gallacher, PPrGSwdB, WM, 1990-1991, but herein lies a tale. Soon after the Lodge was formed it was suggested that a Lodge Banner would be both welcome and appropriate, and plans were made to organise the making of one. Promises were made, but unfortunately they never came to fruition, and the project was eventually shelved. Many years passed until the idea was resurrected, this time with a firmer commitment to complete the task. But who was there to take on this intricate and time-consuming venture? A volunteer stepped forward in the person of WBro Michael S Gallacher, and the remaining Brethren heaved a sigh of great relief! WBro Gallacher, who is an accomplished artist, especially in watercolours, began the task with great confidence, in the firm belief that all he had to do was paint the scene depicting the Lodge Logo onto canvas and then employ the services of a qualified seamstress to add the border and finish off the other bits and pieces. Fate, however, has a habit of interfering with the best laid plans of willing volunteers. After borrowing a book on Roman military dress (St Martin having been a Roman cavalry officer), he set to work. Tragedy then struck in the form of his wife's serious illness, and this, coupled with pressure of work, put a tremendous strain on him and he found it necessary to put the project on hold for a while. In due time, and conscious of the fact that '*perseverance is necessary to attain perfection*', he took up the task again, and the Banner was completed. Or so he thought! Unfortunately the stitching was found to be inappropriate and the Banner began to fray to the extent that it became beyond repair! It was now a case of 'back to the drawing board', and so he began again from scratch. Once again fate dealt a mischievous hand and, while the painting was acceptable, the person who undertook to do the stitching was clearly not up to the job, and once more the project had to be abandoned. It was at this time that WBro Gallacher decided to apply the famous Welsh rule of 'Three tries for a Welshman', and he set about doing the entire job himself. After a trip to the local library to borrow a book on sewing, he set about the task with grim determination and, at last, the mammoth task was completed. To quote WBro Gallacher: '*It may not be perfection, but it will do until time, or circumstance, can restore the genuine one!*' Friday, 30 March 2007, was a red letter day for the Lodge, being the occasion when, by Special Dispensation to hold an Emergency Lodge Meeting, the long awaited Banner was Dedicated. The Officiating Officer was WBro Brian Eveleigh, PSGD, AProvGM, assisted by WBros Peter Gough, PAGDC, PProvSGW; P M Williams, ProvJGW; Rev Canon D H E Mosford, PAGChap; R W Plowman, ProvDepGDC; DJ Irish ProvSGD; M L Jones, ProvJGD, Lodge Secretary; G N Rosser, ProvGPurs; P D Wells, ProvGStwd; and J Profitt, PAGDC, ProvGTyler. A Lodge Banner Dedication being a rare occurrence at this time, it was no surprise to the Lodge Members that this event was very well attended. It is a fact that there were Brethren present who had as much as thirty years service as Masons, yet had never had the privilege of seeing a Banner Dedication Ceremony, which made the occasion very special indeed. After the WM had opened the Lodge, the Provincial Team, under the direction of WBro Rex Plowman, was admitted and the AProvGM, WBro Brian Eveleigh, occupied the Master's Chair. He began by relating the history of Banners, and their significance throughout history. He then appointed the relevant Provincial Officers to their respective posts, after which the Banner Escort Party retired from the Lodge. This was a particularly poignant moment as two of the Senior Past Masters, WBro Norman Evans, PPrSGD (WM 1982-1983), and WBro D C Pearce, PAGDC (WM 1983-1984) were in wheel chairs! The Banner Escort Party re-entered the Lodge with WBro Peter G Williams, PPrJGD, WM, parading the now unfurled Banner around the Lodge, to the accompaniment of all Brethren singing the hymn, *'Now Thank We All Our God'*. WBro Brian Eveleigh then Dedicated the Banner, after which the ProvGChap offered a prayer. WBro Brian Eveleigh then gave an interesting explanation of the life and times of St Martin. At the conclusion of this colourful ceremony, the WM resumed the Chair, the AProvGM and his Officers retired from the Lodge, and the Lodge was closed in due form. Everyone agreed that it had been a wonderful evening, and public thanks were given to all the Brethren who had worked so hard to ensure its success, especially WBro Michael S Gallacher and WBro Phillip W Davies, PPrDepGDC.

In 1995, Bro Melvyn Jones made and presented to the Lodge a DC's Wand, an ADC's Wand and a pair of engraved Deacons' Wands. They were gratefully received and have since been faithfully applied at every Lodge Meeting. Bro Melvyn was Installed as WM in 2000, and received Provincial Honours in 2006, with the Rank of PPrJGD, and has been Lodge Secretary for several years.

WBro Ieuan H Jones, Installed as WM in 2004, received the unusual honour of having the Provincial Rank of PPrAGDC bestowed on him in 2005, the year that he Installed his successor, WBro Terrence Scarfe, as WM of the Lodge. In spite of a debilitating illness, WBro Ieuan had carried out his duties as Master in an exemplary manner that brought deserved praise from all who witnessed his valiant efforts. Special mention of his appointment was made by WBro Brian Eveleigh, PSGD, AProvGM. Sadly, WBro Ieuan Passed to the Grand Lodge Above in 2008. On 25 June 2010, Mr Lloyd William Davies, the son of WBro Phillip W Davies, was Initiated. He is the 4th generation of his family to become a Member of the Lodge. His father, grandfather and great grandfather have all served as Master's of the Lodge. Sadly, his great grandfather, WBro Leonard Barton, passed away before he received his Provincial honour. His grandfather, WBro John S Davies, PPrJGW, was one of the first Joining Members and was Installed as WM in 1984. His father, WBro Phillip Davies, was Installed as WM in 1996.

The Lodge holds several functions during the year, one being the popular 'Quiz Night', which is open to the families and friends of Members, including their children. The annual 'Social Evening' is usually held in February, and is always well attended. Due to a lack of Candidates applying for Membership in Galen Lodge, several Lodge of St Martin Brethren were Passed and Raised in Galen Lodge. These Ceremonies served to enhance the close affinity that the two Lodges enjoyed. Unfortunately, Galen Lodge eventually found itself to be unviable and it met for the last time on Thursday, 1 April 2010, when it surrendered its Warrant. At the Festive Board that evening, the Galen Lodge Gavels, which had been made by the late WBro Francis (Frank) MacAndrews were presented to the Daughter Lodge, Lodge of St Martin, and accepted on behalf of the Lodge by the WM, WBro John H Butler. Galen Lodge was subsequently Erased from the Register of UGLE in December 2010. With the surrender of the Warrant, the following Brethren were heartily welcomed as Joining Members of Lodge of St Martin: WBros G T Lloyd, PPrJGD; R J Mitchell, PPrGSuptWks; D A Tomlinson, PPrGReg; and Bros G C Burston, R L G Pask, and Bro D G Williams. The Galen Lodge Gavels serve as a constant reminder of the very close relationship that once existed between the Mother and Daughter Lodges.

Compiled by WBro Denis J Woods, PPrJGW.

617

Geoffrey Malin Ashe
1912 – 1993

Deputy Provincial Grand Master
1977 – 1992

Geoffrey Malin Ashe was born in Cardiff on 16 August 1912. His father, James Charles Ashe was from New Cross, County Wexford, Ireland, and in 1901, at the age of 23, was a recently qualified Ophthalmic Optician practising in Keighley, West Riding of Yorkshire. Geoff's mother Beatrice Annie Plumtree, was from Southport, and was qualified in *'sight testing and spectacle fitting'*. She married Geoff's father in 1907 and soon afterwards the couple moved to Cardiff. They resided in Pen-y-Waun Place, Roath, and set up an Ophthalmic Optician's practice under the name of 'Bonner Morgan' in Queen Street and finally moving to Park Place. In 1909, Geoff's elder brother John Byrne was born. Later, when Geoff qualified as an Optician, he joined the family practice, and eventually took over the concern, before his father's death in 1954. He married Sarah (Sadie, born in Motherwell, Scotland) in 1937; Sadie had originally moved to Cardiff in her early childhood when her father moved to employment with GKN in South Wales. WBro Geoff was a keen sportsman, excelling at both cricket and rugby and played cricket for Cardiff, and rugby for Glamorgan Wanderers. He was also an RA Gunner in the Territorials, so he was automatically called up for Active Service on the outbreak of hostilities in 1939.

In company with John Rutter (then a 2nd Lieutenant), Alan Reardon-Smith and Wilf Wooller, he served initially in the 77th Heavy Anti-A Regiment, manning anti-aircraft guns in Cardiff, before finding himself en route for Java aboard the Empress of Australia. The ship docked on 4 February 1942 and within weeks their Regiment was entrained for Soerabaija. However, unknown to them, disaster lay ahead, for during the night, the train was in head on collision with one travelling in the opposite direction. The result was fearful, with twenty-eight men killed and over forty injured, mostly from Cardiff and South Wales. Happily, Captain Ashe was unscathed and when he and Lt Rutter met up, they established that they were the only two Officers unhurt. As the Senior Officer, he set about wresting order from chaos and with John's help, some semblance of order was eventually restored.

Geoffrey Malin Ashe

Upon disembarkation, he was given the acting rank of Major, but it wasn't long before the Company fell into the hands of the Japanese when the country was overrun and he spent almost three and a half years in a prisoner of war camp. It is now well documented that conditions meant that he suffered deprivation and disease as well as starvation. In 1945, however, it was learnt from a home-made radio in the camp, that two atomic bombs had been dropped on Hiroshima and Nagasaki. Apparently, discipline immediately relaxed at the camp and, after great persistence by Capt Ashe, the Commanding Officer had to admit that he had been informed by his High Command that, to prevent further loss of life there was to be no more fighting. Whereupon

Geoff ordered that all the Japanese Officers be summoned to the command post where, assembled around a table, they were confronted by their former prisoners. Still dressed in rags and tatters and wearing his home-made clogs, as Senior Officer, he ordered them to place their swords on the table. They bowed and obeyed without hesitation. Geoff informed them that they were then under his command, and although there was mention of the Geneva Convention, he told them that they would be treated exactly as they had treated their former prisoners. Shortly afterwards, the Commander-in-Chief Far East, Admiral Lord Mountbatten, ordered that he assume the rank of Brigadier, a rank, which apparently he said with typical modesty, he *never bothered to use*.

Less than two years after his discharge, in October 1947, he was Initiated into Freemasonry in Prince Llewellyn Lodge No.2570, thus beginning a long and distinguished Masonic career. He became a Joining Member of Edgar Rutter Lodge No.7196 in 1953. He was a Founder Member of Llanfair Lodge No.7353 in 1954, becoming WM in 1958. In Province, he was made an Acting ProvGStwd in 1964, promoted to ProvAGDC in 1965, and to DepProvGDC in 1967. He became ProvGDC in 1970 and AProvGM in 1976, a position he held for just one year before becoming DepProvGM.

In Grand Lodge, WBro Geoff received his first appointment as PAGDC in 1971 when he was ProvAGDC, and was promoted to PGSwdB in 1978, following his promotion within the Province to DepProvGM.

WBro Geoff was also a Member of Hendre Lodge No.3250, Lodge of Progress, No.7928, The Lord Swansea Lodge No.8364 and SWED Provincial Grand Stewards' Lodge, No.8900. He was the Consecrating Officer and an Honorary Member of Newton Lodge No. 8261, Ynys Lodge No.8274, Kenfig Lodge No.8289, Hamlet of Van Lodge No.8334 and Breaksea Lodge No.8358. In the Holy Royal Arch, Geoff was Exalted into Edgar Rutter Chapter No.7196 in 1968, became its First Principal in 1977. He became a Joining Member of three other Chapters, occupying the Principals Chairs of two of them. He received his first appointment in Supreme Grand Chapter as PGSwdB in 1978 and was promoted to PAGSoj in 1983.

Whilst he was only Chairman of Cardiff Masonic Hall Company for a relatively short period, he was always a prominent and progressive member. He was responsible for finding and appointing Bill Read, who was the 'executive chef' for 25 years. Geoff was a man known for his humour and consideration, who was looked up to, not only with respect, but also with gratitude for his continuing advice and interest, and so it can be said that he had a very great influence in guiding the Province as well as many Masonic Careers.

He died in November 1993 at the age of eighty-one. Such was the respect in which he was held that at his Memorial Service at St Theodore's Church, Port Talbot, in January 1994, the list of those formally participating was nothing less than a 'Who's Who' of Freemasonry in South Wales (Eastern Division). In fact, it was the entire Executive of the Province; led by RWBro the Rt Hon the Lord Swansea, ProvGM, supported by WBro Roy K Hopkin, DepProvGM; the four AProvGMs, WBros Ken Adams Morgan, J Stuart Peters, David L Protheroe and Peter Frost; WBro James R Bevan, ProvGSec; and with WBro Rev Norman Lea conducting the Service.

WBro Geoff did everything with complete assurance and cheerfulness. It was said that he had 'the human touch' and that was why he was so beloved by the Brethren, helping to make the Province a happy and close-knit one. It could be claimed that he coined the saying *once a Steward always a Steward*. Contained in Llanfair Lodge History is an example of 'his human touch', when he was said to have laughed aside a suggestion that he might not wish to offer his usual rendering of 'My Bonnie lies over the Ocean' at the Festive Board, after his Appointment as AProvGM. He apparently divested himself of his tails and sang in full voice with all the appropriate actions.

He was devoted to Freemasonry and to ensuring that correct procedures were followed. He considered the Province to be one of the finest in the country. It was consequently fitting that the Good Neighbours' Housing Association's first development at Cowbridge was named 'Geoffrey Ashe Court'.

Acknowledgements to WBro Keith T Flynn, OBE, PJGD, Author of 'A Province at War', WBro Wyn Calvin, MBE, OStJ, PPrJGW, and WBro Brian E Langley, PGStB, ProvSGW.

Afon Dâr Lodge No.8829

Warranted : 8 February 1978

Consecrated : 22 May 1978

Meeting at the Masonic Hall, Aberdare.

In the mid 1970s, the two Aberdare Craft Lodges, namely St David's Lodge No.679 and Aberpennar Lodge No.6354, were very fortunate in having well over 100 active Members in each Lodge. As it was the policy to encourage the formation of new Lodges at the time, the numbers were thought sufficient to justify serious consideration to actively pursue that aim, if there was sufficient interest among the Brethren. Also, at the time, the Superintendent of Police in Aberdare was Bro Harry Sambrook who was a Member of Vale of Glamorgan Lodge No.3977. He, in company with Bro Hadyn James Parsons of St David's Lodge, discussed the feasibility of a new Lodge being formed. Apparently word spread quickly and a number of St David's Lodge and Aberpennar Lodge Members showed great interest in the idea. The Masonic grapevine spread the word throughout the Province, with the result that even Brethren from Cardiff and Pontypridd intimated their desire to be involved in the venture. A feasibility committee was formed and regular meetings began at the Masonic Hall to establish the numbers required and the procedure that would have to be adopted. Bros Harry and Jim subsequently met with WBro Malcolm Hayes Thompson, ProvGSec, who advised them on the correct course to enable formalities to commence. It was agreed that Aberpennar Lodge should be approached to be the Sponsoring Lodge and also that WBro Henry Edward Sturge, PM Aberpennar Lodge, should be the first Master.

One of the main advantages of forming a new Lodge in the town was that the Founder Members, who were not already Worshipful Brethren, would be able to attain the Chair of King Solomon more quickly than if they had progressed through all the Offices in their Mother Lodges.

There was naturally much discussion about the name and it was finally resolved that due to the proximity of the river Dare, which flows through the town of Aberdare, the Lodge would be called 'Afon Dâr'. It was formally approved and permission was obtained to apply for the Warrant, which was duly received on 8 Feb 1978. The Founder Secretary was informed that RWBro the Rt Hon the Lord Swansea, ProvGM, would Consecrate Afon Dâr Lodge No.8829, on Monday, 22 May 1978.

The Consecration team included WBro G L P Elias, TD, DL, PAGDC, ProvSGW, who acted as SW; WBro Rev F J Rees, ProvJGW, as JW; WBro Malcolm Hayes Thompson, PJGD, ProvGSec, as Secretary; WBro Frank Newbury, PAGDC, as DC; and WBro William J Northway, ProvDepGDC, as ADC. In his Oration, the Provincial Grand Chaplain, WBro Rev Mostyn T Williams, posed the question *'What makes a good Mason?'* Although the answer is to be found in portions and segments throughout our Ceremonies, he summarised his view as *'uprightness of conduct and level steps'*, recommending it anew to all present. He concluded by alluding to Freemasonry having a similarity to the River Dâr, in that its source dates back thousands of years with Solomon, King of Israel, and having continued to flow down through the centuries, as the river does *'with it being stronger today than it has ever been. The Afon Dâr Lodge commences today as a little river - may you gain strength - and others who will follow you - add to its success, may you flourish and expand and continue to flow successfully through the years to come.'*

The Installation Ceremony followed, when VWBro Geoffrey M Ashe, DepProvGM, assisted by the three AProvGMs, WBros Harold Wilson, PSGD, as SW; Ronald B Whittingham, PJGD, as JW; and Cuthbert L Summers, PAGDC, as IG, Installed WBro Harry Edward Sturge as the first WM, as had been previously agreed. WBro Michael George Jones, PM Beehive Lodge No.6265 was Invested as SW; Bro Harry J Sambrook, Vale of Glamorgan Lodge, was Invested as JW; and Bro J Donald Humphreys, of St David's Lodge, as Chaplain; with WBro Glyn D Richards, PM St David's Lodge, as Acting IPM.

During the Risings, Dr Michael Philip Rowlands, was proposed as the first Initiate, to be followed by Malcolm Williams and Christmas Cooper. Three Members of Aberpennar Lodge were proposed as Joining Members, namely Bros James James, Alwyn James and John M Griffiths. Bro Richard George Jones of St David's Lodge was proposed and seconded by his blood brothers, Michael and Gareth, also as a Joining Member. Bro Gareth Jones had earlier been Invested as Founder ADC.

It is interesting to note that among the visitors who attended the Consecration were Bro Hywel Davies, JW of Aberpennar Lodge and Bro Desmond Barnett, SW of Hen Bont Lodge No.4691. Both were to become Provincial Grand Masters - RWBro Hywel Davies, Provincial Grand Master of South Wales Eastern Division, 1999-2008, and RWBro Desmond Barnett, Provincial Grand Master of Mark Master Masons of South Wales, 1996-2008.

Less than two months later, at the Provincial Grand Lodge Meeting at Porthcawl, Afon Dâr Lodge was represented for the first time by not only the WM and his Wardens, but also many of the Brethren. At the first Regular Meeting, when Dr Philip Rowlands and Malcolm Thomas Williams were Initiated, WBro Harry Sambrook presented the Working Tools and WBro Michael George Jones delivered the Charge. Two more Joining Members were proposed, continuing the trend for growth mentioned in the Consecration Oration.

Still with a long list of Candidates in the pipeline, the Lodge assembled on 7 Feb 1983 for a Regular Meeting, with a team of Provincial Grand Officers, headed by VWBro Geoffrey Malin Ashe, DepProvGM, in attendance for the Dedication of the new Lodge Banner. The Banner depicts the Dare Valley through which flows the River Dare, 'Dâr' being the Welsh word for Dare and 'Afon' the word for river. It was made by a School Teacher at Gadlys School, Aberdare, and was designed by Bro Gwilym Evans, a former Headmaster. On this occasion, WBros R C Hilton and M Williams acted as SW and JW respectively and WBro Gwyn George, Provincial Pursuivant. The Banner was escorted into the Lodge, carried by WBro Philip Walters, WM. WBro Rev J E Davies, ProvGChap, then Dedicated the Banner. In his summary of the uses of Banners, VWBro Geoffrey Ashe quoted Psalm 60, Verse 4 *'Thou hast given a banner to those who fear thee, that it may be displayed because of the truth'*. The Lodge, under the Mastership of WBro Philip Walters, went on to perform a Second Degree Ceremony when Bro Denis Whitmore Cotter and Bro Keith George were Passed to the Second Degree. In the Risings, Mr Robert Rowlands, son of Bro Philip Rowlands, was proposed, which resulted in him being the first Lewis in the Lodge.

Not only Regular Meetings but also Installations were very well attended around this time. In the years 1983-1985, the Lodge was very pleased to welcome WBro Ken Adams Morgan, AProvGM, and the DepProvGM, VWBro Geoffrey Malin Ashe, on two successive occasions when Bros Laurence Kahn, Maurice Williams and Alwyn James were Installed as Masters. Unfortunately,

WBro Maurice, IPM, had to resume his duties as Master when WBro Alwyn, WM, had an accident, one which was to trouble him for many years.

All three Jones brothers became Masters of Afon Dâr Lodge and all contributed greatly to its success. WBro Richard was appointed to Grand Rank in 1999, when he was Invested with the Collar of PAGDC, as suitable reward for all his hard work in the Craft.

WBro Henry Sturge presented the Lodge with a Master's Pedestal cloth in October 1992, which is impressively inscribed in gold with the Lodge name and number. Sad to say, in other respects the 1990s saw a reversal in fortune for the Lodge by way of deaths and resignations, necessitating PMs having to occupy the Chair a second and even a third time.

In 2003, the Lodge celebrated its 25th Anniversary, when all the Brethren were presented with cut glass tumblers.

Inevitably, time has taken its toll on the Membership, but the Brethren can look back over the short history of the Lodge to the many memorable events which have been related here; and with circumstances continuing to change in Freemasonry, the Lodge is still able to look forward to more prosperous and fruitful times again, with an influx of Candidates.

Compiled by WBro Denis W Cotter, PPrJGW.

The Senior Warden's Chair, Aberdare Temple

Hiraeth Lodge No.8834

Warranted : 8 March 1978

Consecrated : 9 June 1978

Meeting at the Masonic Hall, Cardiff.

In many instances, the formation of a Lodge arose out of some unusual circumstances, and Hiraeth Lodge was no exception.

WBro Tom Evans, a Manager of the Eagle Star Insurance Company, was Initiated in the Lodge of St Ilan No.6624, Caerphilly, in 1965. Two years after his Initiation, he moved to Cornwall as the Manager of the Truro Office, and became a Joining Member of Phoenix Lodge of Honor & Prudence No.331, Chacewater, Province of Cornwall. In due course, he became the Master of that Lodge.

In 1974, he returned to Cardiff and at a Law Society Dinner, Major Hugh Bartle-Jones enquired about the Masonic Order. (See below.) At that time Bro Sam Richards mentioned that there was a prospect of a Lodge being formed from Members of the Llanishen Golf Club, under the guidance of WBro Eric Cule, a well-versed and distinguished Member of the Craft.

Eric William Cule, a former Local Government Officer, had been Initiated in Kibbor Lodge No.4364 in 1947. He was a Founder Master of Services Lodge No.7139 (WM 1956), a Member of Old Millhillian Lodge No.5752, London (WM 1967), Secretary of the Lodge of Benevolence No.7305, 1967-1975, and WM (1977). In Province, he reached the Rank of PPrJGW (1970) and in 1982 was appointed to the Rank of Past Grand Standard Bearer of the United Grand Lodge of England. In 1974, Eric Cule was appointed Secretary to the Cardiff Masonic Hall Company, a position he was to occupy for 8 years and to mark his retirement the Company presented him with his Grand Lodge Regalia.

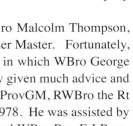

Tom Evans collected the necessary information and met with the Provincial Grand Secretary, WBro Malcolm Thompson, who was very helpful. He suggested that Eric could be the Secretary and that Tom could be the Founder Master. Fortunately, Eric agreed and on that basis he arranged that the Mother Lodge would be Observer Lodge No.6015, in which WBro George Collings had just completed the Mastership. VWBro Geoffrey Ashe, TD, DepProvGM, who had already given much advice and encouragement, put the necessary wheels in motion and the Warrant was signed on 8 March 1978. The ProvGM, RWBro the Rt Hon the Lord Swansea, performed the Consecration Ceremony at the Cardiff Masonic Hall on 9 June 1978. He was assisted by VWBro Geoffrey M Ashe with WBro G L P Elias, TD, DL, PAGDC, ProvSGW, as Senior Warden; and WBro Rev F J Rees, ProvJGW, as Junior Warden; together with WBro Rev E D D Lewis, ProvGChap, as Chaplain; and WBro Malcolm H Thompson,

PJGD, ProvGSec, as Secretary.

Following the Consecration Ceremony, the Installation of the Officers took place, with Geoffrey M Ashe as the Installing Master assisted by the three Assistant Provincial Grand Masters, WBros Harold Wilson, R B Whittington and Cuthbert L Summers. As has already been stated, the Founder Master was WBro Tom Evans, with Bro Sam Richards, SW and Bro Bill Newton, JW. Eric Cule was Invested as Secretary, as was originally planned.

The initial interest of VWBro Geoffrey Ashe was further demonstrated by his suggestion that his son-in-law, Col Douglas Kelly should be one of the Lodge's first Candidates. Consequently, Doug and Hugh Bartle-Jones were Initiated as such on 27 September 1978 and Geoffrey Ashe was present to witness the event. They were both Passed on 22 November 1978 and Raised on 28 February 1979, when Geoffrey Ashe explained and demonstrated the Further Signs of the Degree.

The Phoenix Lodge of Honor and Prudence, No.331, mentioned previously, was Constituted on 25 June 1810. Such an old Lodge has inevitably acquired over the years, unique additions to its ritual, some of which were introduced into Hiraeth Lodge by the Founder Master, Tom Evans. Of particular note are the explanation of the Master Mason's Apron and the unusual method of Installing the Worshipful Master of the Lodge. The additions to the Ritual were always known as the 'Cornish Workings' and variations in the Installation Ceremony have now been seen elsewhere in the Province.

The name of the Lodge was under discussion for some time. Several Members had previously been residing outside Wales and they had experienced that *'feeling of longing to return to the homeland'*. Such feelings are summed up by the Welsh word 'Hiraeth', which was consequently chosen as the name for the Lodge.

The Founders and early Members contributed to the effects of the Lodge. Lord Swansea and VWBro Geoffrey Ashe gave the Volumes of the Sacred Law. The first Officers of the Lodge donated the Collars. WBro Sol Cohen donated the cabinet of Working Tools, the Gavels (modified Golf Club Heads) were donated by WBro Dennis Moore, and WBro Cyril Ellmes donated the Cushion for the presentation of the Apron. The Warrant was framed under the auspices of Tom Evans. The Ballot Box, which is of unique design, has one central opening with an internal divider, requiring careful handing of the Ballot Balls. WBro Col Douglas Kelly, who, in 1986, was the first Initiate to become Worshipful Master of the Lodge, presented the Ballot Box.

The Banner, designed by WBro John Norman and presented by Bro John L Lewis, was Dedicated on 28 November 1983. The main feature of the Banner is a circular arrangement of seven clasped hands, representing 'friendship' enclosing a Square and Compasses.

A major event in the Lodge's history was the formation of a Daughter Lodge, Wenallt Lodge No.9082, (Warranted 9 March 1983). One of the instigators was Sam Richards, who was chosen to be the first Master. Unfortunately, he became ill just a few weeks before the Consecration Ceremony, held on Friday, 3 June 1983. He was called to the Grand Lodge Above shortly afterwards. WBro Thomas Harry Jones, ProvJGD, a retired Building Inspector with British Railways and PM Glamorgan Lodge No.36, WM, 1978-1979, replaced him as the first Worshipful Master.

Regrettably, due to declining Membership the Lodge has recently found it necessary to seek an amalgamation. Fortunately, the Lodge now has an opportunity to join with Wenallt, its Daughter Lodge, with whom it has many special ties.

Both Lodges, Hiraeth and Wenallt, were involved with the formation of the Hiraeth Chapter No.8834 (Warranted 12 February 1986) and with the combined efforts of these Lodges, the Chapter has thrived and now this unique partnership will continue in the Craft as well.

Compiled by WBro Thomas Densel Evans, PPrSGW.

Llangynwyd Lodge No.8854

Warranted   :   8 November 1978

Consecrated   :   12 March 1979

Meeting at the Masonic Hall, Maesteg.

Following his Installation as Provincial Grand Master in 1966, RWBro the Rt Hon the Lord Swansea, DL, was encouraging the formation of new Lodges in the Province. In the late 1970s, a number of Brethren from the two existing Craft Lodges in Maesteg, Llynfi Lodge No.2965 and Maesteg Lodge No. 6805, met to discuss the formation of a third Lodge in the town. The Organising Secretary was WBro Reginald Hugh Lewis, PPrDepGOrg, who had been Installed as WM of Maesteg Lodge in 1962.

The Brethren decided that the new Lodge should be called 'Llangynwyd', after the historical hilltop village, 2 miles to the south of Maesteg. The village is the site of Llangynwyd parish church, the ruins of Llangynwyd castle and Yr Hen Dy (The Old House), reputedly one of the oldest pubs in Wales. Llangynwyd Church was founded in the 6th century by Saint Cynwyd. All that remains of the original structure is the stone socket of a wooden cross, which can be seen in the wall above the entrance. The church was rebuilt in the 13th century and has since been restored several times. The square tower dates from the 15th century and was completely restored in 1893.

Llangynwyd was the birthplace of the local poet and bard, Will Hopcyn, whose tragic ill-fated love of local girl, Ann Thomas, is said to be the basis of the old Welsh legend, 'The Maid of Cefn Ydfa'. Ann was the daughter of the sister of Rees Price, the father of the philosopher Richard Price. (See 'History of the Province in the 18th century - Bridgend Lodge No.33, at the beginning of this book.) According to the story, he had placed his heiress, Ann, in the wardship of Anthony Maddocks, a lawyer of Cwmrisga, who compelled her to marry his own son Anthony. Ann, however was in love with the poet, Wil Hopcyn, who supposedly composed the verses *'Bugeilio'r Gwenith Gwyn' ('Watching the white wheat')* for her. Ann is said to have pined so desperately for her lover that she fell seriously ill. On her death bed she asked to see Hopcyn, and when he arrived she died in his arms. Llangynwyd Lodge Insignia, which also appears on the Past Master's Jewel, portrays the Church of St Cynwyd and the ears of wheat associated with the legend of the Maid of Cefn Ydfa.

Maesteg Lodge agreed to be the Sponsoring Lodge. WBro Thomas King-Davies, PPrJGW, was the WM Designate. Initiated in Llynfi Lodge on 7 April 1941, he was also a Founder Member of Maesteg Lodge and Installed WM of that Lodge in 1954; a

Joining Member of South Wales Jurists' Lodge, he was Installed WM in 1972. In Province, he was appointed ProvSGD in 1959 and promoted to PPrJGW in 1977. He became a Grand Officer in 1980 with the Rank of PAGDC, and in 1990, he was promoted to PJGD. When he died in 2009, he had been a Freemason for 68 years.

St Cynwyd's Church, Llangynwyd

The Consecration Ceremony took place on Monday, 12 March 1979. The Consecrating Officers were RWBro the Rt Hon the Lord Swansea, DL, ProvGM, assisted by WBro F A Henshall, PAGDC, ProvSGW, as SW; W Bro F J V Harverson, ProvJGW, as JW; WBro Rev Elfed Jones, ProvGChap, as Chaplain; WBro Malcolm H Thompson, PJGD, ProvGSec; WBro F Newbury, PAGDC, ProvGDC, as DC; WBro R K Hopkin, RN, ProvDepGDC, as ADC; WBro C Langmaid, PPGD, ProvGOrg, as Organist; WBro John Price, ProvGPurs, as Inner Guard; WBro K Morgan, ProvGTyler, as Tyler. The Consecrating Ceremony was ably supported by the Guildford Singers under the direction of WBro E J Smith, PGStB, PPrGW.

The Installing Master was VWBro Geofffrey Malin Ashe, TD, PGSwdB, DepProvGM; assisted by WBro Harold Wilson, PSGD, AProvGM; WBro R B Whittingham, PJGD, AProvGM; and WBro Cuthbert L Summers, PAGDC, AProvGM. WBro Thomas King-Davies was duly Installed as the first WM. Bro Edward Davies was Invested as JW and he was Installed WM of the Lodge in 1982. He is (in 2011) the Senior Past Master of the Lodge and has been promoted to PPrSGW in the Province. Still active in the Lodge, he is the Lodge Chaplain. WBro David Alan Jenkins, PPrJGW, was the first Secretary of the Lodge and retained this position for many years, until his death in 2008. He was Installed as WM in 1995. Founder Member, WBro Williams Rees Griffiths, was the first Lodge Tyler. He became a Grand Officer in 1998, with the Rank of PGStB.

Of the first four Candidates for Initiation, three are still Members of the Lodge. WBro David F Court, PPrJGW, is now the Secretary and was first Installed as WM in 1993 and again in 1997. WBro Michael R Winn, PPrGSwdB, was first Installed as WM in 1988 and again in 2011. The trio is completed by Bro John A Evans.

The Silver Jubilee of the Lodge was held on Friday, 2 April 2004.

Each year the Lodge holds a charity night, when the ladies provide the refreshments. Over the years, a diverse programme of entertainment has been provided, such as barbershop singers, quiz nights, Old Time Music Hall, and Welsh and country dancing. All the proceeds of these evenings have resulted in many hundreds of pounds being donated to local charities. There are also annual official exchange visits between Mother and Daughter Lodges, namely Maesteg Lodge and Llangynwyd Lodge.

Compiled by WBro David F Court, PPrJGW, Secretary.

Old Cantonians Lodge No.8875

Warranted : 14 February 1979

Consecrated : 18 June 1979

Erased : June 2011

Met at the Masonic Hall, Cardiff.

Canton Municipal Secondary School, as it was then called, was opened in Market Road, Canton, Cardiff, on 21 October 1907. It started with 85 pupils who were transferred from Howard Gardens Municipal Secondary School. In 1933, the name was changed to Canton High School for Boys. This was accompanied by the adoption of the familiar school coat of many colours, and the abandonment of the old 'egg splash' cap, blue with a gold roundel at the crown.

In 1962, and retaining the name 'Canton High', the School moved to new premises at the former School Games Fields in Fairwater. The School had been known affectionately by the locals and other Cardiff Schools as the 'Canton Cowsheds', due to its location on the historic cattle market site. Within eight years, Comprehensive Education had been established in Cardiff and the name of the School had been changed to Cantonian High School. The old school building was sold and is now occupied by the Chapter Arts Centre.

Over the years, many well-known Freemasons, such as WBro Harry Stockwell, DepProvGM, WBro Ben Watson, PPrGOrg, and WBro A C Newsom-Smith, PPrDepGSwdB, had tried to form an Old Boys' Lodge, but without success. An invitation notice, addressed to all Old Cantonian Brethren and posted at the Cardiff Masonic Hall, led to a meeting being held on Wednesday, 15 November 1978. Over 30 Brethren, all Old Boys, attended the Inaugural Meeting, and it was decided that the time was now right to form the Lodge.

WBro Silvin Aster, the Senior Provincial Officer, threw down the gauntlet to the assembly and WBro Jerry Goodman picked it up, allegedly before it had time to reach the table, let alone the floor. A Working Committee was formed immediately, chaired by WBro Silvin Aster and assisted by WBros Jerry Goodman, Robert Preece and Alex Barbrook. Jerry Goodman accepted the challenge with great determination and a nucleus of prospective Officers was proposed from within the number present.

It was agreed that the Lodge should be named 'Old Cantonians' and would apply to become a member of the Federation of School Lodges, once the Lodge was formed. The Federation of School Lodges was the brainchild of WBro Harry T Seymour, PGStB, for the purpose of gathering the School Lodges together into an organisation, which would foster both visiting and fellowship. In 1947, when Post War circumstances allowed, he sponsored the Federation's Constitution and became its first Secretary.

The First President of the Federation was VWBro Edgar J Rutter, PGW, PDepProvGM, a Founder of Harlequins Lodge No.5793. He held that Office until 1958 and thereafter became its Patron, until his death in 1971. With the DepProvGM at the helm, it was not surprising that Schools' Lodges once more began to be formed in the Province - Old Barrians Lodge No.6671 in 1948 and Old Goreans Lodge No.7193 in 1952.

The idea of keeping 'Old Boys of the School' together by forming their own Masonic Lodge dates back to 1898, when Old Masonians Lodge No.2700 was formed entirely of Old Boys of the Royal Masonic School for Boys at Bushey in Hertfordshire. In 1901, Old Boys of Handsworth Grammar School formed Bridge Trust Lodge No.2878 in Staffordshire, but it was not until after the end of the First World War that the next, Hanleinsin Lodge No.3935 was formed in Hanley, Stoke on Trent. Between the Wars a further number of School Lodges were formed in the South Wales area namely, Nioba Lodge No.5264 for former pupils of Newport High School (1931), Howardian Lodge No.5317 - Howard Gardens High School for Boys (1931) and Harlequins Lodge No.5793 - Cardiff High School (1939).

In May 1972, the Consecration of Ymlaen Lodge No.8419 eventually led to the formation of a Daughter Lodge, Old Cantonians No.8875, and to a Granddaughter Lodge, Old Monktonians No.8938. A Schools' Mark Lodge, Ysgolion Lodge No.1487, was also formed and has recently been admitted to the Federation, which had previously been restricted to Craft Lodges. Under Federation Rules, the Mother Lodge would be the last School Lodge Founded in the area and a Petition for Sponsorship was accordingly made to Ymlaen Lodge, which had links with Cathays High School for Boys. Following the acceptance of the Petition, a Warrant was granted to Old Cantonians Lodge on 14 February 1979. The Lodge Crest and tie were designed and approved by Grand Lodge and the musical service transposed and collated by WBro Frank Hamilton-Jones, who became the first Honorary Organist.

The Lodge was Consecrated on 18 June 1979 by the RWBro the Rt Hon the Lord Swansea, ProvGM, together with his Officers as follows: VWBro Geoffrey M Ashe, TD, PGSwdB, DepProvGM, Acting as Installing Master, assisted by the AProvGMs, WBro Harold Wilson, PSGD, WBro Ronald Whittingham, PSGD, and WBro Cuthbert Summers, PSGD. The Guildford Singers added harmony to the whole proceedings and all the Provincial Officers that day were made Honorary Members of the Lodge. There were 17 Founders in total.

Within the first ten years, the Lodge had grown to 37 Members; values had been built upon; the landmarks had been maintained and many traditions established. Four Founders, three Joining Members and three Initiates reached the Chair of King Solomon during this period. The Lodge was now established in the Province in general and amongst the Schools' Lodges in particular. Schools' Lodge tradition at the Festive Board, including the friendly rivalry between the Lodges, has also become accepted, but this rivalry has never been allowed to exceed fraternal humour. The firing of all Toasts is a feature of the Festive Board and the School Song is also sung.

The year 1992 saw the 275th Anniversary of the Founding of United Grand Lodge. The Grand Master of the Grand Lodge of Illinois, MWBro James T Miller, had travelled to Britain for United Grand Lodge celebrations and was the honoured guest at Old Cantonians Lodge Installation Meeting. According to Masonic protocol, the ProvGM, Lord Swansea, was pleased to attend in order to receive him into The Province of South Wales. MWBro Miller responded to the WM's greeting in Greek, the language used at home by the WM's family. This immediately put WBro George Arakas at his ease. A most enjoyable Ceremony and subsequent Festive Board ensued.

The Lodge owes an enormous debt of gratitude to WBro Julius (Jerry) Goodman who passed to the Grand Lodge Above in 1997. He had succeeded, where many before him had failed, in finally establishing Old Cantonians Lodge, guiding its steady growth over twenty years, holding most of the important Offices. He is fondly remembered by Members for his enthusiastic direction of Lodge proceedings from the position of Chaplain.

The following year, in his memory, the Lodge revived the project that had been so close to his heart for many years - the provision of an Old Cantonians Banner. WBro Jerry left a small bequest to the Lodge, and WBro Gareth Parsons, Sec, wrote to WBro Lawrence Goodman, his son, suggesting that the Banner Fund could be a suitable beneficiary of this legacy. WBro Lawrence and Mrs Jo Goodman were both extremely pleased with this proposal and gave their full support to the suggestion. WBro Stephen Lowes, WM, was appointed to oversee the Banner project and he carried out his task thoroughly, with the assistance of the ProvGSec, WBro James Bevan, the Lodge Secretary, the ProvGDC, and the Lodge DC, WBro David Parsons. The Banner Dedication Ceremony was held on 2 May 2001, when many distinguished visiting Brethren were present, none more proud or more welcome than our guest WBro Lawrence Goodman, LGR, who witnessed the Dedication of Old Cantonians Lodge Banner in memory of his father. WBro Andrew Gretton, SGD, AProvGM, conducted the very impressive Ceremony.

The Lodge Crest or Insignia, approved prior to the Consecration in 1979, forms the basis of the Banner design and was taken from the original Canton High School for Boys Badge. It was felt totally appropriate to adapt it for Masonic purposes. WBro Jerry Goodman originally did this, with assistance from WBro Derek Skone of Emerald Lodge, who prepared the drawing for submission. It consists of the chevrons of the Coat of Arms of The Norman Lords of Clare, whose head Gilbert de Clare became Lord of Glamorgan in 1217. These are of red on a gold background and have appeared on various civic and sporting emblems associated with Glamorgan and Cardiff over the years. A similar set of chevrons was traditionally associated with Iestyn ap Gwrgan, the last of the Celtic Princes of Glamorgan. These were silver on red and can be seen held by a Dragon on the Arms adopted by Cardiff when granted City status in 1905. Old Cantonians Lodge chevrons are Gold on Black and are shown on a lozenge, surmounted by the Craft Emblem of the Square and Compasses.

The name of the Lodge and the Motto: *'Semper Sursum' ('Ever Onwards, Ever Upward')* are also displayed at the top and bottom of the Banner respectively. The design is adorned and surrounded by a laurel wreath mirroring the original Badge. The background colour throughout is light blue, the adopted colour of Craft Masonry. When conjoined with the design, the overall colour scheme is blue and gold, which, as explained earlier, were the School colours until 1933 and are still present in the colours of Old Cantonians Association and Old Cantonians Rugby Club.

In 2004, the Lodge celebrated its Silver Jubilee with the Installation of WBro Stephen Lowes as Master for the second time. The Installing Master was WBro Peter Evans. Representing the Province on this occasion was VWBro Peter Frost, DepProvGM. WBro Stephen remained in Office for two years and was succeeded byWBro Richard Whitcombe, again for a second time. Since then, three Initiates, WBros Karl Otto, Robert Clarke and Edward Pearce have attained the Chair of King Solomon together with WBro Mark David, who came into the Lodge to assist. Unfortunately, a shortage of suitable Master Masons willing to progress and a lack of Candidates, brought the Lodge to the situation where it was found necessary to surrender the Warrant. But this was not to be the end, as it has been for several Lodges in the Province which have had to close. The Old Cantonians Motto *'Semper Sursum'* always regarded as *'Ever onward and Ever upward'*, from the words of the school song, prompted the decision to amalgamate with Ymlaen Lodge, the Mother Lodge. Old Cantonians Lodge is the first Lodge in the Province to successfully apply for a Certificate of Amalgamation.

The books have closed, but another chapter awaits within Ymlaen Lodge, where the identity of the Old Cantonians will be retained, and where they will continue to make a useful contribution to Freemasonry in the Province of South Wales.

Compiled by WBro Gareth Parsons, PPrJGW.

Tudor Lodge No. 8886

Warranted : 14 March 1979

Consecrated : 2 July 1979

Meeting at the Masonic Hall, Cardiff.

In the mid 1970s, Provincial Grand Lodge had received numerous enquiries from Brethren engaged in the Civil Service, Banking and Insurance Industries, in addition to those with connections at the University of Wales, who were moving to the Principality, primarily from London and other large cities, and were desirous of joining a Lodge in Cardiff. These Brethren were unfamiliar with the Oxford Ritual, so prevalent in the Province, that WBro J Arthur Cowley was approached on several occasions by WBros Edgar J Rutter and Harry F Stockwell, both former Deputy Provincial Grand Masters, together with Bro Malcolm Thompson, Provincial Grand Secretary, to explore the possibility of forming a new Lodge with these Brethren in mind. Arthur had met Professor Archie Cook, whose Lodge worked West-End Ritual and the seeds were sown. Subsequently, Arthur, who had been Initiated into Lodge of Integrity No.6907 on 6 December 1950, enlisted the assistance of the Members of his Lodge to arrange the formation of Tudor Lodge No.8886. WBro Arthur had been Installed WM of Lodge of Integrity in 1960.

The desirability of forming a Lodge to provide a sojourn for Brethren moving into the Cardiff area from other parts of the country, particularly from London, had been in the minds of the Officers and Past Masters of the 'Emulation Working' Lodge of Integrity for some time. Over the past ten years, a number of Brethren, unfamiliar with the Oxford Ritual, have sought an affinity with, and become Joining Members of, Lodge of Integrity. Many Brethren have attended Lodge of Integrity as visitors, and have joined the Integrity Lodge of Instruction. Whilst some of these Brethren have come from Emulation Lodges, many have been used to other Rituals, such as Universal, West End, Taylor's etc.

The desire of Lodge of Integrity to Sponsor this new Lodge had been encouraged by the Province and the suggestion that it should work M M Taylor's Ritual had also been welcomed. This Ritual, not being well known in South Wales, would therefore be of interest to those Brethren who were keen Ritualists. This would also give those Brethren, who through unavoidable circumstances, had been unable to progress to the Chair of King Solomon in their Mother Lodges, the opportunity to continue to do so within the Ritual by which they were Initiated.

Prior to, and during, the preparations for the Consecration Ceremony, Arthur Cowley advised Lord Swansea, that it was the intention of the Lodge, subject to his consent, to invite their Ladies to the *'After proceedings, following the January and April LodgeMeetings and would that be alright?'* Lord Swansea replied, *'Nothing you do surprises me Arthur, go and enjoy yourselves.'* There was one proviso however, that the Lodge had to write to the Secretaries of those Lodges who met on the same evening, requesting permission for the Ladies to attend. At 3.30 pm precisely, on 2 July 1979, the 19 Founder Members welcomed the Consecrating Officer, RWBro the Rt Hon the Lord Swansea, DL, who having entered the Temple in procession, occupied the Chair and appointed his Officers. Following the Consecration Ceremony, the first Master, WBro James Arthur Cowley, was Installed by VWBro Geoffrey Malin Ashe, TD, PGSwdB, DepProvGM. Also taking part were three Assistant Provincial Grand Masters, WBros Harold Wilson, PSGD; R B Whittingham, PSGD and C L Summers, PSGD, as well as many other distinguished Brethren. The memorable Consecration Ceremony was conducted in an exemplary manner and was followed by an incredible banquet, attended by in excess of 120 Brethren. During the dinner, Brethren were entertained by 'The Guildford Singers', under the very capable direction of WBro E J Smith, PGStdB, PPrGW.

Tudor is the only Lodge working the Taylor Ritual in the four Welsh Provinces, out of a total of 344 Lodges. The main features are the deliberate clockwise perambulations; the squaring of the Lodge Room; the synchronised movements of the Deacons; the Inner Guard positioning himself at the North-West corner of the Squared Pavement when addressing or being addressed by the Master or Wardens; the unhurried manner in which the signs are given and the fact that the Lodge is always closed in full at every Meeting.

An Emergency Meeting of the Lodge was held on 19 July 1986, for the purpose of Dedicating the new Tudor Lodge Banner. The Lodge was opened in due form and with solemn prayer at 11.30 am with a large gathering of Brethren. WBro Cuthbert Summers, AProvGM, and the Provincial Team entered the Temple and the new Tudor Lodge Banner was duly Dedicated. A detailed explanation was given of the history and purpose of Banners throughout the ages by WBro Summers, who concluded his presentation thus: *'You have now been presented with this beautiful Banner through the generosity of your first Master, WBro Arthur Cowley. It is a joint effort, the template designed and drawn by him, whilst the whole of the needlework was undertaken by his charming wife, Doris (Dos). The patience and skill needed for this intricate work can be gauged by the fact that the whole Banner took nine weeks to complete, working as she did, for eight hours per day. In establishing the Tudor Lodge in 1979, one of the stated aims was to provide a sojourn for Brethren moving into the Cardiff area from other parts of the country, particularly, from London. In the furtherance of this aim, the Founder Members were anxious to demonstrate the harmony of the links between England and Wales. After much deliberation, it was submitted to United Grand Lodge for approval in the name of 'Tudor Lodge'. This proposed name acknowledged the achievements of the English Royal House descended from the Welsh squire Owen ap Tudor. Further developing this theme, the Lodge incorporated into the design of its Founders' Jewel, the Tudor Rose. As can be seen from the Lodge Banner, now publicly displayed for the first time today, the Tudor Rose figures prominently between the two classic columns of architecture, which are intended to illustrate the Ionic Order, signifying Wisdom and the Corinthian Order, signifying Beauty and surmounted by the Celestial and Terrestrial Globes signifying Masonry universal. Below the Tudor Rose is a pair of jewelled Compasses to remind us of our obligation to keep us within the bounds of all mankind. These Compasses figuratively rest upon the open Volume of the Sacred Law. Although not visible from where you sit, the needlework has been do designed as to list the individual names of the Founder Members; Consecrating Officers and the Lord's Prayer. Surrounding the overall design are two ears of corn , with which we are all familiar, and which took a total of 22 hours to stitch. I quote Psalm 60 verse 4. Thou hast given a Banner to them that fear thee - that it may be displayed because of the truth. Worshipful Master and Brethren of the Tudor Lodge, in the same way as Banners which are placed in places of worship are symbols of devotion to God's service, so may this new Banner be the symbol of your devotion to the fundamental Principles of our Craft; belief in God and belief in the Volume of the Sacred Law, may it be a symbol of loyalty; of friendship; of good fellowship and of service; may it be the rallying point of all the Brethren and a visible reminder of the duties they owe to Freemasonry in general and to this the Tudor Lodge in particular.'*

WBro Cuthbert Summers concluded his address: *'Worship Master and Brethren; Raise your Banner to the Sky, - let it float there wide unfurled. Bear it onwards- Lift it high.'*

On September 23 1986, WBro Bernard Silver, the first Tudor DC, presented the Lodge with a miniature Third Degree Tracing Board and was warmly thanked by all the Brethren for his generous gift. This particular Tracing Board has been used for the explanation of the Third Degree to Candidates ever since.

At the commencement of 2009, there were six remaining Founder Members. Two, unfortunately, do not enjoy the best of health, namely WBro Eric Davies, Master in 1982 and WBro Dilwyn Cullen, Master in 1985. For their faithful service to the Lodge, they were made Honorary Members. Sadly, Dilwyn Cullen passed away at the beginning of 2011.

WBro Paul Botfield, who was Installed WM in 1994, and is now a Grand Officer with the Rank of PAGDC, remains very active in the Lodge.

WBro Howard Jones, Master in 1984, is the Lodge Mentor and visits the Annual General Meeting of the Association for Taylor's Ritual, in London, thereby ensuring that the Lodge keeps up to date with the Ritual.

WBro Naunton Liles, Master in 1999, has been Lodge Organist since its Consecration.

It is only right and proper that we conclude with WBro J Arthur Cowley, fondly known as the 'Father' of the Lodge. Now in his 96th year, at the December 2006 Christmas party he was presented with the award 'Master Emeritus' - meaning a person honourably discharged from service. He was made an Honorary Member of the Lodge in 2007. Unfortunately, now in failing health, he is unable to attend Lodge and he resides in the Shire Hall Care Home, Overstone Court, Dumballs Road, Cardiff.

The foundation stones of the Lodge were firmly set by the Founders over 30 years ago. The four remaining active Founder Members are delighted with the Lodge's progress to date; to witness the new Members maintaining the high standard of Ritual, and the enjoyment of the social functions; whilst not forgetting the ethos of Brotherly Love, Relief and Truth. The immediate future is in good hands.

Although it is well remembered that, for a short time, the Membership reached 50 some years ago, the average figure has always been in the low thirties.

Recently, the Committee of the Association of Taylor's Lodges has produced a definitive book of Ritual, which sets out in detail the working of the Ceremonies, so that the Lodge Members should have no difficulty in maintaining high standards.

Compiled by WBro Howard Jones, PPrJGW.

South Wales Eastern Division Provincial Grand Stewards' Lodge No.8900

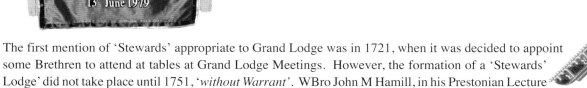

Warranted : 13 June 1979

Consecrated : 2 November 1979

Meeting at the Masonic Hall, Bridgend.

The first mention of 'Stewards' appropriate to Grand Lodge was in 1721, when it was decided to appoint some Brethren to attend at tables at Grand Lodge Meetings. However, the formation of a 'Stewards' Lodge' did not take place until 1751, 'without Warrant'. WBro John M Hamill, in his Prestonian Lecture for 1993 entitled 'The Development of Masonic Charity', states that their main purpose was to look after a central charitable fund. WBro Hamill goes on to state that *'the Lodge, like the Committee of Charity of the premier Grand Lodge, was to be comprised of the Grand Officers and Masters of Lodges in the Cities of London and Westminster. They met formally as a Lodge, the senior Brother present presiding as Master and a Lodge being formally Opened in the 3rd Degree before their deliberation began, and being formally Closed when their work was finished. The Stewards' Lodge was empowered to receive and discuss Petitions and to grant up to five guineas to each case before the matter be referred to Grand Lodge itself. The work of the Stewards' Lodge was very similar to that of today's Report of the Board of General Purposes.'*

The Grand Lodge Directory of Lodges and Chapters shows there are 27 Provincial Grand Stewards' Lodges in England and Wales and 4 District Grand Stewards' Lodges overseas. The oldest Provincial Grand Stewards' Lodge is Cheshire Grand Stewards' Lodge No.3449 which was Consecrated in 1910.

It was not until 1978/79 that the idea of a Grand Stewards' Lodge in this Province was first mooted. The main architect of this conception was VWBro Geoffrey M Ashe, TD, PGSwdB, ProvDepGM, after visiting a Provincial Stewards' Lodge in London. The unique object of the Lodge is to allow Master Masons, who had given invaluable service to our Province and Masonry, to progress to the Chair of King Solomon.

The date of the Warrant is 13 June 1979, and the Petition to form the Lodge was signed by one hundred Founder Members. The Mother Lodge of South Wales Eastern Division Provincial Grand Stewards' Lodge is Lodge of Benevolence No.7305.

The formation of our Provincial Grand Stewards' Lodge came to fruition on Friday, 2 November 1979, at the Masonic Hall in Cardiff, when the Lodge was Consecrated, by RWBro the Rt Hon the Lord Swansea, TD, ProvGM South Wales Eastern Division. There were eighty five Founders present. The first WM was VWBro Geoffrey Ashe. The presence of the Guildford Singers, under the direction of WBro E J Smith, PGStwd, PPrGW, enhanced the solemnity of the occasion.

The first Master Mason to be Installed as WM was Bro L Lawrey, in October 1980.

The Lodge meets twice a year, in October, for the purpose of Installing a new Master, and in May, when a Paper is given. Meetings were held at the Pontyclun Temple from May 1980 until May 1991. Since October 1991, the Lodge has met in the Bridgend Masonic Temple. The venue was changed in order for the Brethren to meet at a more central point within the Province.

It is noteworthy, that during the years since the Lodge was Consecrated, there have been only two occasions when the Chair of King Solomon has not been occupied by an Installed Master of the Lodge. In April, 2005, WBro Douglas Morgan occupied the Chair, and in October 2005, it was occupied by WBro Denzil Powell. Over the years a number of distinguished Brethren have delivered a variety of Papers to the Lodge.

On Saturday, 5 April 2008, the new Lodge Banner was Dedicated by RWBro Hywel Davies, ProvGM, assisted by WBro Rev Alistair E Swinford, ProvAGChap. The ProvGM was accompanied by the ProvAGMs, Officers of Grand Lodge and Officers of Provincial Grand Lodge. Also present were VWBro Peter Frost, PDepProvGM, and WBro Robert Nettleship, PAProvGM. The event was attended by over one hundred Brethren. Before the Dedication Ceremony, the ProvGM gave an address concerning Banners in general and the new Lodge Banner in particular. The Dedication was carried out by the ProvGM and the ProvAGChap, in an efficient and moving Ceremony, that was acclaimed by the Brethren present.

The Banner was designed by WBro Hugh Davies, ADC of the Lodge, and created by Mrs Carol Abraham, daughter of WBro Fred Fox, the Lodge Catering Officer. The design of the Banner includes a Cornucopia, embodied within a set of Compasses, surrounded by the name and number of the Lodge, on a red background. WBro Hugh Davies also designed and printed the Order of Service. Sadly, WBro Hugh Davies passed to the Grand Lodge Above on Sunday, 20 July 2008, after a very short illness. The Banner is a lasting tribute to Hugh and a mark of his dedication to the Lodge and to Freemasonry in general.

The Provincial Grand Stewards' Lodge is a young Lodge, when compared to some of the Lodges in the Province, but long may it continue to enjoy its uniqueness.

Compiled by WBro Hywel Davies, PProvGStwd.

Lodge of St Andrew No.8934

Warranted : 1 May 1980

Consecrated : 16 June 1980

Meeting at the Masonic Hall, Cardiff.

The idea of a Golfers' Lodge was conceived on a Sunday in May 1979, when VWBro Geoffrey Malin Ashe, DepProvGM, and WBro John I Brown were chatting together in the Common Room of Whitchurch Golf Club, Cardiff, and the latter said *'You know, we ought to have a Lodge made up of golfers'* and Geoff replied *'Well, why don't you start one?'*. After a slight pause WBro John Brown said, *'I will, but it will take some time to find Founders, as I do not want a large number of PMs wanting to join as Founders of a new Lodge merely so that they can go through the Chair for a second time, with of course, the exception of the first Worshipful Master and Senior Warden.'*

After a number of potential Founders had shown interest, the first Founders' Meeting took place on 8 July 1979, when the following decisions were made. The Lodge should be called 'Lodge of St Andrew'. A long discussion took place about the name, as the obvious choice seemed to be 'St Andrew's Lodge', but the decision stood. WBro His Honour Judge John C Rutter, PJGD, had been informally approached to become the first Worshipful Master, and he had expressed his willingness, if the other Founders were agreeable. His selection was accepted by all present. WBro F Graham Richardson, PPJGD, PM Cardiff Exchange Lodge No.3775, the Lodge which had agreed to Sponsor the new Lodge, was proposed to be the first SW and, in accepting the Office, he expressed his sincere thanks to his Brother Founders. There were a few subsequent meetings, and some more Brethren expressed interest and joined the Founders. Finally, an application for a Warrant was made, which was subsequently issued by the UGLE on 1 May 1980, some one year after the discussion between Geoff Ashe and John Brown in Whitchurch Golf Club.

The Consecration of Lodge of St Andrew No.8934 took place in the Duke of Connaught Temple, Cardiff, on Monday, 16 June 1980. It was conducted by RWBro the Rt Hon the Lord Swansea, DL, ProvGM, assisted by VW Bro Geoffrey M Ashe, TD, PGSwdB, and a team of Provincial Officers, most notably WBro Harold Wilson, AProvGM; WBro Ronald B Whittingham, AProvGM; WBro Cuthbert L Summers, AProvGM; WBro Malcolm H Thompson, ProvGSec; WBro Frank Newbury, ProvGDC; WBro Cdr Roy K Hopkin, RN, ProvDepGDC, as ADC; and WBro Charles Langmaid, Organist.

Among the Officers Invested by the new WM, WBro HH Judge John C Rutter, were WBro John I Brown as both IPM and

Charity Steward, WBro F Graham Richardson as SW, WBro Brynmor D Jones as JW, WBro L Ken M Loyns as Treasurer and Bro John R F Cripps as SD. At the Festive Board following the Consecration Ceremony, musical entertainment was provided by the Guildford Singers under the direction of WBro E J Smith, PGStB.

David Llewellyn Stevens and Clifford H Morris were proposed as the first Initiates. The former, was a low handicap golfer of Llantrisant and Pontyclun Golf Club and an international player for the Welsh Golf Team. He was Initiated at the first Regular Meeting in September 1980. Clifford H Morris was Initiated at the third Meeting in February 1981. The latter served the Lodge as Secretary from 1997 until 2001.

In September 1980, WBro Robert Ord was Elected to be the first President of the LOI, assisted by WBro Donald A Betty as Vice-Preceptor. A set of Gavels, which is still in use, was presented to the Lodge by WBro John Brown. A game of golf was held at Wenvoe Golf Club in the afternoon before that Meeting, setting a pattern for future Meetings of the Lodge, a pattern which regrettably lasted for only two years. In that time, golf was played at a number of local courses, followed by a Ceremony in the nearest Masonic Hall. The practice had to be curtailed, because Golf Clubs began limiting visiting societies to particular days, which mostly did not fit into the Masonic calendar.

There have been just two Double Ceremonies thus far, the first was on 2 September 1983, when Bro Brian J Mepham and Bro K Phillips were Raised, with WBro Graham Richardson in the Chair. After the Lodge was called off and called on, the WM, WBro Brynmor D Jones, Initiated Bro David K Lo and Bro Anthony L Cullen. At that Meeting, the WM welcomed Bro David Lo's father, WBro C Lo, PM Foochow Lodge No.1912, Hong Kong, a PDepGSwdB. The second Double Ceremony occurred five years later, on 4 September 1998, when the WM, WBro Danny Stone, first Passed Bro Simon Rhys Morgan to the Second Degree and, after the Lodge was called off and on again, Initiated Bro Alan Owen Jones.

At the first Installation Meeting, on 5 December 1981, WBro Graham Richardson was Installed as the second WM. During the Festive Board, he presented trophies for the competitions that had been held during the year, two of which had been borrowed on a long term agreement from Cardiff Exchange Lodge No.3775. These had been laid up by the Lodge for some years. The Cardiff Exchange Cup was won by Bro T A Latchford; the Herbert L Hodge Cup by Bro C H Morris; and the Rutter Putter, which was to be awarded annually by WBro HH Judge John Rutter, was won by Bro M W Evans.

WBro John Brown was Invested as PAGDC by the Grand Master in April 1985, and in the same year the Lodge was pleased to welcome WBro R T Jenkins, Past District Grand Warden of Hong Kong and the Far East, PM Swallow Lodge No.3705, Hong Kong, who was Installed as WM on 5 December 1987. Sadly, he died in 1996, by which date he had been appointed PPrJGW of the Province.

The new Lodge Banner, which had been presented by WBro John Brown, was Dedicated by the DepProvGM, VWBro Geoff Ashe, on 3 December 1988. It now hangs on the west wall of the Edgar Rutter Temple, Cardiff. The date of the Warrant, 1 May 1980, was embroidered on it in error, and not the date of the Consecration as should have been, which was 16 June 1980. The error has of course since been corrected.

In 1992, VWBro Geoff Ashe resigned as DepProvGM, due to ill health. Sadly, some fifteen months later, he died on 5 December 1987. He had always taken a particular interest in the Lodge and had been the visiting Executive Officer at many Installations since Installing Judge John Rutter at the Consecration in 1980.

It is interesting to note that at the Installation on 7 December 1996, WBro John Brown, who had been appointed ProvSGW for that year, was the Mandated Officer, and was welcomed in that capacity by WBro D G Beman, WM.

On 4 December 2004, WBro Simon Rhys Morgan, who had been Initiated on 13 February 1998, was Installed in the Chair of

King Solomon. During his year as WM, the 25th Anniversary of the Lodge was celebrated.

At the Lodge meeting in February 1999, WBro John Brown announced that the Lodge had raised the sum of £9,259.63 for the Provincial Festival in aid of the New Masonic Samaritan Fund, and had earned a gold medal to be worn on the Charity Steward's Collar. On 4 December 1999, he was Installed as WM to mark the Millennium year, when the Lodge was honoured by the presence of the ProvGM, RWBro Hywel Davies, together with his Deputy, three Assistant Provincial Grand Masters, and a very large number of visitors.

In 2004, Honorary Membership was conferred on WBro HH Judge John Rutter, the first WM of the Lodge, and on WBro John Cripps, who was WM in 1983.

Although the Lodge experienced its first resignation early in 1982, it was certainly compensated by Bro David A Westall joining the Lodge. A Barry Freemason, he was first Installed as WM in December 1986, again in 2005 and was Proclaimed for his third year in 2006. He also served the Lodge as DC and Preceptor of the LOI for many years. He had the great distinction of being Invested PAGDC in Grand Lodge in April 2004, when he was already ProvGDC in the Holy Royal Arch. Similarly, David was Invested GStB in Royal Arch Chapter whilst serving to very great effect as Provincial Grand Director of Ceremonies. In 2009, he succeeded EComp John Taylor as Grand Superintendent of the Province. Then, having been promoted to the Active Rank of Deputy Grand Sword Bearer at the 2010 Investiture Meeting of Grand Lodge, he is now a Very Worshipful Brother.

Only two other Brethren have had the distinction of serving more than one year in the Chair. WBro David G Beman, WM in 1990 and then again in 1996, and WBro Philip Curzon who was Installed on 1 December 2001 and Proclaimed WM for his second year in December 2002.

Bro A D Holtham, Founder Organist, continued to serve the Lodge until 1991, when his place was taken by one of the Consecrating Officers, WBro Charles Langmaid, who was Honorary Organist until his death. He in turn was succeeded by WBro Brian Davies, a Member of Cardiff Exchange Lodge.

During its existence, the Lodge has been served by five Tylers, namely WBros Ken Morgan, Julius Goodman, Len Evans, W J Parsons and WBro Ken Vincent, who is the current Tyler.

Like most Lodges in the Province, Lodge of St Andrew has suffered from deaths and many resignations, but having always benefited from a very keen team of Officers, it can look forward to a slow but steady growth in the future.

Compiled by WBro John I Brown, PAGDC, with contributions from
VWBro David A Westall, DepGSwdB, and WBro Philip A Curzon, PPrJGD.

Old Monktonians Lodge No.8938

Warranted : 13 February 1980

Consecrated : 17 June 1980

Meeting at the Masonic Hall, Cardiff.

For many years, prior to 1980, it had been thought a good idea to form a Lodge that would draw its Members from Monkton House School. Indeed, since its founding in 1870, many of its former pupils and staff had been prominent Freemasons. The idea was by no means a new one. In South Wales, Howardian Lodge No.5317, Harlequins Lodge No.5793, Old Barrians Lodge No.6671, Old Goreans Lodge No.7193, Ymlaen Lodge No.8419 and Old Cantonians Lodge No.8875 were already up and running.

Despite there being great rivalry between the Schools, each is linked, not only by a Masonic bond, but also by Membership of the Federation of School Lodges, which brings them into contact with Schools' Lodges all over Britain.

During 1979, a more concentrated effort was underway to bring about Old Monktonians Lodge. By September of that year, regular meetings were being held in the Board Room of Monkton House School. In October, the Secretary (Roy Hopkin) reported that a number of dates had been agreed with the Masonic Hall, Cardiff.

It was also decided that qualification for Founders of this Lodge should be restricted to: former pupild, staff - present and past, parents of boys currently in the school. Other applicants would be considered, in due course, only as Joining Members.

The Secretary reported that he had approached the Master of Old Cantonians Lodge, who had previously agreed to Sponsor the proposed new Lodge.

At the end of 1979 and the beginning of 1980, plans were well in hand, following a visit from WBro Malcolm H Thompson, Provincial Grand Secretary, to one of the meetings at the School, when 'Petition' forms for a new Lodge were left for all Founder Members to complete. Twenty Brethren signed as Founder Members.

At a further meeting, on Tuesday 8 January 1980, it was announced by the secretary that the Petition would be presented to the Old Cantonians Lodge at their next Meeting on Monday, 28 January 1980. Twelve Brethren indicated that they would be present at this Old Cantonians Lodge Schools' Night.

The 17 June 1980 was the date set for the Consecration of the Lodge. The Principal Officers were chosen with WBro Norman Morgan, WM Designate; WBro Alexander Munday, SW Designate and Bro Dennis Parbery, JW Designate. Founder Member, WBro Cecil H Rapport, CBE, DL, KStJ, PJGD, was appointed the IPM. WBro Ken Morgan was to become Tyler and would remain so for the next 21 years.

A Provincial team, led by RWBro the Rt Hon the Lord Swansea, ProvGM, assisted by WBro Geoffrey Malin Ashe, DepProvGM, duly Consecrated the Lodge. During this Meeting, it was proposed by Russell Seale and seconded by Cecil Rapport that Mr Gordon Longmore, Headmaster of Monkton House School, be a suitable Candidate for Initiation. On 9 September 1980, Gordon Longmore was duly Initiated and has been active in the Lodge ever since. Since becoming Master in 1986, he has been Assistant Director of Ceremonies (1 year), Director of Ceremonies (1 year), Charity Steward (10 years), Treasurer (3 years), Organist (14 years), Vice-President of Lodge of Instruction (6 years), plus an extra year as Senior Warden.

Following these promising beginnings, the Lodge suffered its first major 'upset' with the untimely passing of the Senior Warden, Dennis Parbery. Nevertheless, with true 'Old Monks' determination, the Lodge grew, until eventually a number of Members resigned or decided not to take Office. Installed as Master in 1988, WBro Russell Heald remained in the Chair for two years, which gave some stability over the next three years. Between 1993 and 1994, however, the situation was looking very bleak; consequently, WBro Mike Lewis, Installed as Master in 1993, also remained in the Chair for two years. At the Election Meeting on 13 June 1995, the WM addressed the Brethren of the Lodge on the seriousness of the situation. As a result of this discussion, and a Meeting of Past Masters with VWBro Roy Hopkin, DepProvGM, it was decided to admit Joining Members to stabilise the situation.

The first names to be put forward were Edwyn Pritchard and Robert Thorne, who were welcomed into the Lodge on 12 September 1995, and Franco Bottarini, who became a Joining Member on 12 December that same year. The enthusiasm and dedication of these and other Joining Members over the following years, transformed the fortunes of Old Monktonians Lodge. Despite the Lodge now being 'open' to all, its composition as a 'School Lodge' has not diminished. About 45% of the Members still have connections with the School, either as former pupils, parents or staff. Until recently, the last former pupil to be Initiated was Anthony Lewis, in June 1998. He is the son of WBro Mike Lewis. In June 2005, however, the Brethren were delighted to welcome two 'new' former pupils, Andrew Evans and Richard Partridge.

The School is still in existence, but is now known as 'Kings Monkton', following its merger with Kings College. Mr Henry Shewbrooks, BA, who came from Monkton in Pembrokeshire, founded the school in 1870. Once known as 'Shewbrooks' School, it was one of the first to provide advanced secondary education in Cardiff. The School is described in a 1950s prospectus as *'the oldest Grammar School for boys in Cardiff'* and by this time some three hundred and fifty day boys and borders attended. The course of instruction then included mental arithmetic, spelling, composition, writing from dictation, algebra, geometry (theoretical and practical) and oral English, to name but a few!

During the 25th Anniversary celebrations in 2005, a Banner was designed and Dedicated. The original design of the Banner was based on a suggestion made by Phil Sainsbury. It is a simple, uncluttered design, which has at its centre the Monkton House School Badge surrounded by the Square and Compasses, which clearly identifies the Old Monktonians Lodge as a Masonic Craft Lodge.

The School Badge suggests the battlemented tower of Monkton Priory in Pembrokeshire. The torch or beacon behind the tower possibly suggests enlightenment. The Motto that appears on the School Badge: *'Se Accingunt Operi'* (*'They apply themselves to work'*) has not, however, been adopted by the Lodge. The colours of the School were maroon and gold and this has been reflected in the Banner with its maroon background and gold braiding.

The Banner Dedication Ceremony took place on Tuesday, 14 June 2005 and was performed by a Provincial team led by WBro Geoffrey W Thomas, AProvGM. In September of that year, the Brethren were delighted to welcome RWBro Hywel Davies,

ProvGM, and his team to the Installation Festival.

Robert Thorne became Worshipful Master in 1997 and soon entered into the 'spirit' of School Lodges. During a number of visits to the Annual Federation of School Lodge Festivals, he became aware of the existence of Robert Thorne Lodge No.3663, Bristol. When attending the 54th Annual Festival held on 1 September 2001, under the Banner of Robert Thorne Lodge, Robert was treated as an 'Honoured Guest' and so started Fraternal visits between the two Lodges. Robert Thorne Lodge is the only School Lodge in the Province of Bristol and the visits to Old Monktonians Lodge have brought it into regular contact with all the other School Lodges in South Wales and Monmouthshire.

Visits between 'local' School Lodges have been a long tradition with Howardian, Harlequins, Old Barrians, Old Goreans, Ymlaen and Old Cantonians Lodges in this Provincem, plus Nioba Lodge No.5264 in the Province of Monmouthshire, all dedicating one Lodge Meeting a year as 'Schools Night'. These are colourful occasions, with the Brethren being able to wear their school ties to each other's Lodges. Despite the Festive Boards being full of friendly banter, the Ceremonies are conducted to the highest standard, as each Lodge is keen to present itself at its best!

The Old Monktonians Lodge is unique in employing bells instead of Gavels at the Festive Board. A mounted bell is placed before the Worshipful Master and hand bells are employed by the Wardens. The mounted bell used to be on the roof of Monkton House School Assembly Hall and was used to call pupils to assembly. The hand bells were used in the School to bring pupils together at break times.

The following message was received from VW Bro Cdr Roy K Hopkin, PGSwdB, PDepProvGM, Founder, First Secretary and Honorary Member of Old Monktonians Lodge, when Old Monktonians Lodge celebrated its 25th Anniversary:

'There had been many discussions at various Lodge after-proceedings about the formation of an Old Monktonians Lodge, but little or no progress had been made. As Bursar at the school and having access to records and addresses, I was 'volunteered' to set the ball rolling!

Some sixty letters were sent out to old Monktonians who were known to be Freemasons. From the replies, it became clear that there was sufficient support to proceed. In addition to those brethren who wished to become Founders there were many who offered support and donations.

Various prominent brethren were approached with a view to becoming the first Master of the Lodge and it was agreed that WBro Norman Morgan, an Old Monktonian and ProvGM of the Mark Degree would take that Office. WBro H (Bert) Parry became the Honorary Organist and carried out those duties for many years.

Finally, the Consecration took place on 17 June 1980 and the Founders can look at the present Lodge with great pride and satisfaction.'

WBro Norman Morgan was the first Master of Old Monktonians Lodge. In the Mark Master Masons Degree, he was Provincial Grand Secretary, 1969-1974; Deputy Provincial Grand Master, 1974-1978 and Provincial Grand Master, 1979-1983. Biographical details of VWBro Cdr Roy Hopkin are given separately in this book.

Compiled by WBro Michael J Lewis, PPrGSwdB, Secretary.

Sure & Stedfast Lodge No. 8991

Warranted : 11 March 1981

Consecrated : 1 June 1981

Meeting at the Masonic Hall, Cardiff.

The Lodge was Consecrated at the Masonic Temple, Guildford Crescent, Cardiff on 1 June 1981. The Consecrating Officer was RWBro the Rt Hon the Lord Swansea, OSM, CStJ, DL, ProvGM. The Installing Master was VWBro Geoffrey Malin Ash, TD, PGSwdB, DepProvGM. There were 22 Founder Members, all with connections with The Boys' Brigade. Observer Lodge No.6015 was the Sponsoring Lodge.

The Lodge still has two Subscribing Founder Members: VWBro Andrew L Gretton, PGSwdB, PDepProvGM, and Bro Anthony D Vodden, ProvGStwd. The first Master of the Lodge was WBro Michael J Stayt, who is now an Honorary Member. The first two Joining Members were WBro John V Elias, PPrJGW, the previous Lodge Secretary, and the late WBro Don Phillips, who was Master of the Lodge in 1986. The first Initiate was the late WBro Gareth Evans, who was Master of the Lodge in 1994 and 1995.

The words 'Sure and Stedfast' appear very early in the Ritual and are very apt in connection with a Masonic Lodge. The words are derived from the book of Hebrews, Chapter 6 verse 19, (the King James version of the Bible, hence the spelling of 'stedfast'.) *'which hope we have an anchor of the soul, both sure and stedfast'*. These words were chosen by Sir William Alexander Smith as the Motto of The Boys' Brigade, which he founded in Glasgow on 4 October 1883. The first Company in Wales was the 1st Newport Company, formed in 1887 and which is still going today. The Boys' Brigade was the first organised youth movement throughout the world. Sir William always wore an Anchor on his signet ring and we, too, incorporate that Anchor of Hope in the Badge of our Banner.

The Badge on the Lodge Banner consists of three items: The Anchor, The Cross and The Lifebelt. The Anchor, the original emblem of the Boys' Brigade, refers to the Sure and Stedfast hope in the eternal goodness of the Most High and in life after death. The Cross, which was added when The Boys' Brigade and The Boys' Life Brigade merged in 1926, is the emblem of the Red Cross Movement, which is derived from reversing the colours of the National Flag of Switzerland; thus the emblem is symbolic of duty to our fellow men. The Lifebelt is the emblem of the Life Boys, who were for many years the Junior Section of the Boys' Brigade before the name was officially changed to the Junior Section in the 1960s. Its circular form teaches that God is eternal, whilst its unsinkable nature serves to remind us of His ability to preserve us from all ill.

The Lodge Banner was Dedicated on 4 February 2006, with WBro Don Phillips, WM, in the Chair. The Dedicating Officer was VWBro Andrew Gretton, DepProvGM, and the Dedicating Chaplain was the Provincial Grand Chaplain, WBro Rev Canon Huw Mosford, PAGChap. WBro Gareth Jones, OBE, PAGDC, ProvGDC, was also in attendance.

The Founders of the Lodge were deeply grateful to RWBro the Rt Hon the Earl of Elgin and Kincardine, KT, CD, LLD, PSGW, who, as Brigade President, gave permission to use these Emblems on the Lodge Badge. It is often observed that the lifeblood of a Lodge is a flow of Candidates of the right type and outlook. The Boys' Brigade helps us to teach boys to become better men and so that work can only be beneficial to the Craft.

Masonic Charity and Ideals, if they are to be true, should extend beyond the boundaries of our Temples and must be taken into the outside world. The Members of this Lodge try to do this and extend support to all youth organisations. There are six other Boys' Brigade Lodges across the country and Sure and Stedfast Lodge is a Member of the 'Kindred Lodges Association', founding and supporting youth movements.

Members of Sure and Stedfast Lodge have always come from far afield - from the depths of Aberdeenshire, London, Northamptonshire, Anglesey, Portsmouth, Bristol, Weston-Super-Mare, Cornwall, Birmingham and West Wales. It was because so many Members came from such a wide area, that it was decided to adopt the strict Oxford Ritual in the Ceremonies, as rehearsals in the early days were not always practical. However, due to this, the Ritual used by this Lodge became 'tweaked' and it is fair to say that the Sure and Stedfast Ritual is unique, but is always enjoyed by Members and visitors alike. Many Members now live close to Cardiff, so Lodges of Instruction and Lodges of Rehearsal are well attended.

In February 2009, the Lodge merged with Shir Gâr Chapter No.7339, to form Sure & Stedfast Chapter No.8891, operating under the Warrant issued, on 14 February 1962, to Shir Gâr Chapter. In 2005, Shir Gâr Lodge No.7339 surrendered its Warrant, the consequence of which led to the formation of the first Boys' Brigade Chapter No.8891.

It is true to say that after a difficult few years, the Lodge has entered a period of growth and is now going from strength to strength.

Compiled by WBro Michael J Stayt, SLGR (Primus Master).

Pontypridd Lodge No.9001

Warranted : 30 April 1981

Consecrated : 20 October 1981

Meeting at the Masonic Hall, Pontypridd.

The Lodge was formed in response to the Provincial Grand Master's desire (Lord Swansea) that smaller Lodges be formed. He wanted new Members to participate more actively and to progress the Masonic ladder more quickly and considered that this could be achieved in smaller Lodges with fewer Initiates. This view was encapsulated in a letter, written by WBro Leighton Hutchings, PAGDC, Secretary pro tem, to Malcolm Hayes Thompson, ProvGSec. The letter in support of the Petition is dated 22 April 1981 and contains the following: *'Our reasons for seeking permission to form a new Lodge is to further the principles and objects of Freemasonry in the area, to encourage the young Mason to advance in Masonic Knowledge and to undertake the duties of an Officer in the Craft at an early stage in his Masonic career.'*

There were 27 Petitioners, including 13 Past Masters. The Petitioning Brethren were from Merlin Lodge No.1578, Rhondda Lodge No.3979, Hen Bont Lodge No.4691, Craig yr Hesg Lodge No.6724, Ystradyfodwg Lodge No.7638 and Newton Lodge No.8261. Though Rhondda Lodge provided 7 Petitioners, the largest number, the Worshipful Master and Wardens of Merlin Lodge (5 Petitioners) signed the Petition, making this the Sponsoring Lodge.

The Master Designate was WBro Henry James Mars, MBE, JP, PProvGStwd, from Cwmparc Treorchy, PM Hen Bont Lodge. Bro David William Ridgway, Quarry Proprietor of Pontypridd and an Initiate of Merlin Lodge was Senior Warden Designate. Bro David Loxley Hughes, of Ystradyfodwg Lodge was Junior Warden Designate. The Lodge was Consecrated by RWBro the Lord Swansea, DL, ProvGM, at the Pontypridd Temple on 20 October 1981.

Much discussion took place about the naming of the Lodge, a strong contender being 'The Lodge of True Aim'. It was felt, however, that a Welsh name would be more appropriate, and none more so than 'Pontypridd Lodge', particularly as it was to meet at the Pontypridd Temple.

The Lodge Banner was donated by WBro David Melville Morgan. It contains the opening phrase of the Welsh National Anthem 'Mae Hen Wlad Fy Nhadau' - 'Land of My Fathers'. The words of the Welsh National Anthem were written in January 1856 by Evan James and the tune composed by his son, James James, who both resided in the town. Also depicted on the Banner are two figures representing Music and Poetry, designed by the Welsh sculptor Sir William Goscombe John (1860-1952) for the monument to Evan James and James James. The monument, which is in Ynysangharad Park, Pontypridd, was unveiled by Lord Treowen on 23 July 1923. The Lodge Banner was Dedicated by VWBro Cdr Roy K Hopkin, RN, DepProvGM, on 7 March 1997.

It has been the Lodge custom for many years to sing the National Anthem in the Temple, and the Welsh National Anthem at the Festive Board.

The Lodge was intended to be different from the established Lodges that already met in the Pontypridd Temple. It was to meet only four times a year, the Ceremonies were to be as smooth flowing as possible with Minutes being circulated and approved without being read out in Open Lodge. Unnecessary perambulation was frowned upon and the Ceremonies were to be kept as short as possible. The wearing of dinner suits was to be compulsory, with wine and liqueurs being served with the meal in the early years. No beer was allowed at the Festive Board, and the speeches were, and still are, formal with no response from the visitors.

'Music and Poetry' by Sir William Goscombe John Ynysangharad Park, Pontypridd

The first Master was followed by three PM Founders, followed by three Founder Members, with the first Initiate WBro Ieuan Jones becoming WM in 1987. Over the years, the Chair has been held by 9 Founder Members, 5 Joining Members, and 12 Initiates of the Lodge.

The Lodge celebrated its 25th Anniversary in October 2006, with WBro Percy F Hooper, PGStB as Worshipful Master. On this occasion, the Lodge was honoured by the presence of RWBro Hywel Davies, ProvGM. WBro Percy, an Electrical Contractor by profession, was Initiated in Rhondda Lodge in 1974 and Installed as Master of that Lodge in 1985. A Founder Member of Pontypridd Lodge, he first became Worshipful Master in 1990. Sadly, WBro Percy passed to The Grand Lodge Above on 4 January 2011. He was 70 years of age.

Compiled by WBros Ieuan Jones, PPrGR; Ian Bebb Jones, PPrAGDC; and Nicholas Marsh, PPrJGD.

Sir Francis Drake Lodge No. 9008

Warranted : 10 June 1981

Consecrated : 27 November 1981

Meeting at the Masonic Hall, Cardiff.

The Lodge was formed out of the Cardiff Masonic Bowling Association, and was named after that great Admiral from the time of Queen Elizabeth I. Despite making many adventurous voyages, partly for discovery and partly for plunder, Sir Francis Drake is best remembered for his coolness in finishing his game of bowls on Plymouth Hoe in 1588, as the Spanish Armada sailed up the English Channel, before becoming a leading figure, under Lord Howard, in its ultimate defeat. Today there are seven Lodges, under the Constitution of the United Grand Lodge of England, bearing the name 'Sir Francis Drake'. However, only No.9008, meeting in Cardiff, recognises his bowling exploits, as all the other six have Naval connections.

The formation of the Lodge was mainly the brain-child of WBro Lyn D Jones, PPrGReg (Berks), PM Tylehurst Lodge No.6526, Sindlesham, Berkshire and Thatcham Lodge No.8121, Newbury, Berkshire. He was a Joining PM Cartref Lodge No.5772, which subsequently became the Sponsoring Lodge. The idea soon spread amongst the members of the Association, and on Friday, 27 November 1981, the 25 Founders were Consecrated into a Lodge by RWBro the Rt Hon the Lord Swansea, ProvGM, the Warrant having been granted on 10 June 1981.

The first Master, WBro Lyn D Jones, was presented for his Installation by his blood brother, WBro Hubert D M Jones, PM Parirura Lodge No.423, New Zealand, who had travelled especially for the occasion.

During the first year, Lodge Ceremonies were somewhat novel, and warmly referred to by the WM as 'Emulox' working, a cross between his own Emulation and the Oxford Working. Despite this, he Initiated 6 Candidates in the first year, including father and son, Barry and Michael Hopkins, with the latter still giving sterling service to the Lodge; and Passed four Candidates. The following year, WBro John Taylor undertook the mammoth task of holding 4 Double Ceremonies, during which he Raised 6, Passed 4, and Initiated 6 Brethren.

As the Lodge grew, it attracted many of the outstanding bowlers and bowls administrators into its ranks. These included six internationals; John D H (Jock) Thompson (the most capped Welsh Bowler with over a 100 caps), Ellis Stanbury, Lyn Perkins, John Kine, Ray Williams and Ron Pomeroy, with most of them also captaining their country. In addition to the above six, John Taylor, Rufus Jones, Gerwyn Morgan, Edward Durrant, Robert John and John Best all became National Championship winners;

whilst those, in addition to the above, who have represented their County Bowling Associations, are too many to name.

On the Administrative front, the Lodge again excelled in that no fewer than 9 Brethren have served as Presidents of the Welsh Private Greens Bowling Association, with 3 - John Taylor, Jack Parry and Ellis Stanbury, also being honoured with its patronage. In addition, 4 Members have become Presidents of their County Bowling Associations, with James Ireland ultimately becoming President of the Welsh Bowling Association and Ron Pomeroy of the Welsh Indoor Bowling Association.

Although bowls is the main unifying sport, Members have also excelled at other sports, with rugby prominent amongst the Membership with 5 Members - John Taylor, Jack Jones, Alan Barham, Graham Locke and Stephen Stewart all excelling as players, referees or administrators.

The steady growth of the Lodge over the first ten years of its history was brought to an abrupt end in 1990, because problems with the Cardiff Masonic Bowling Association were allowed to spill over into the Lodge. This resulted in the resignation of a number of Members. However, despite this upset, the Lodge quickly settled down, and today it is a happy and contented unit, with around eighty percent of the Membership regularly attending each Meeting.

For its 25th year, its most celebrated Brother, VWBro John Taylor, PGSwdB, became WM for the second time. John was the first Almoner of the Province in 1992, an Office he was to hold until becoming AProvGM in 1998. However, Royal Arch Masonry was his main love and having served the Province as Grand Scribe E from 1993 to 1998, he became the DepGSupt and ultimately MEGSupt from 1999 to 2009.

'Firsts' seem to be a forte of the Lodge, for on Tuesday, 14 November 2006, the Lodge marked its 25th Anniversary by Dedicating a Lodge Banner, simplistic in design but clearly depicting the relationship between bowls and Freemasonry. The occasion was marked in excellent style, with the ladies being present for the first time at any Ceremony within the Craft Province of South Wales Eastern Division. In addition, the Dedication Ceremony was undertaken by VWBro John Taylor, WM, which if not another first in the Province, then one would have to delve back a long way into the history of the Province to find the previous occasion.

Having completed its first 25 years on a high, the Lodge now looks forward to continuing with its excellent service to Freemasonry and the bowling fraternity.

Compiled by VWBro John Taylor, PGSwdB, PAProvGM.

Oriel Lodge No.9023

Warranted : 11 November 1981

Consecrated : 12 March 1982

Meeting at the Masonic Hall, Cardiff.

Oriel Lodge was formed primarily to enhance the ties between those connected with the use, development and conservation of the land. The Founder Members were all connected in some way with surveying, building, mining surveying, engineering, architecture, estate agency and other professions associated with the land. Since then the diversity of Members' activities has widened to include those whose ties are primarily with commerce and business. The Lodge was particularly fortunate to be strengthened in 2006 by three active Brethren who transferred from the former Shir Gâr Lodge No.7339, when that Lodge surrendered its Warrant.

The Lodge was Sponsored by Juventus Lodge No.8105, the Petition being signed by their Master and Wardens in Open Lodge on 17 June 1981. There were nineteen Founder Members - three of whom remain as Subscribing Members in 2009. The Founder Master was WBro Oswald Lucas, PJGD - a much respected Chartered Surveyor then practising in South Wales, who had served with distinction during the Second World War, surviving the evacuation from Dunkirk and later serving in Burma.

Oriel Lodge was Consecrated in the Duke of Connaught Temple by RWBro the Lord Swansea, OSM, GCStJ, DL, ProvGM, with his Provincial team of nine Officers, on Friday, 12 March 1982. Following the Consecration, the Provincial Grand Master and his accompanying Officers were Elected Honorary Members of the Lodge - three remain so in October 2009.

The Lodge can trace its ancestry back to Glamorgan Lodge No.36, one of the oldest Lodges in the Province of South Wales (Eastern Division). The first Daughter Lodge of Glamorgan Lodge was Bute Lodge No.960, Consecrated 30 June 1863. Bute, in conjunction with Glamorgan, Sponsored Tennant Lodge No.1992, Consecrated 10 October 1883. Tennant Lodge had five Daughter Lodges, one of which was Cardiff Exchange Lodge No.3775, Consecrated 17 January 1917. Cardiff Exchange Lodge Sponsored Juventus Lodge No.8105, Consecrated 6 May 1966, and as noted above, Oriel Lodge was Sponsored by Juventus Lodge in June 1981.

The name of the Lodge derives from 'Oriel' - a window which projects from the upper stories of a building to let light into an otherwise dark room behind. The Founders were inspired by the hope that lessons learnt from their Ceremonies, combined with the prudent use of their charitable donation, would not only encourage them to be good citizens, but also help to enlighten some dark places beyond the Lodge. The Lodge has always been served by a conscientious and dedicated Charity Steward and (for a small Lodge) its record of charitable giving has been most commendable.

The Lodge Badge was carefully designed primarily by the late WBro Peter Powell, PPrGSuptWks, a distinguished Architect and Founder Member, who sadly died in 2001. It is explained as follows: *'The overall shape is an elongated 'O' for 'Oriel', being a pleasant perimeter 'non - heraldic' shape. Contained within this overall shape is a symbolic 'Oriel window' - a polygonal formation corbelled with squares. As it will symbolize a Welsh Lodge, the Badge reflects the Welsh element (however subtly) through its symbolic representation of the 'Owain Glyndwr' helmet. Seen simplistically, the Badge is designed to represent 'a single ear of corn'. This symbolizes a new Lodge which from small beginnings and with an element of faith and enjoyable effort, will be fruitful and multiply in the quality of its members and in the strength of its friendships. The Compasses and Squares form part of the design and are symbolic of the roof and window brackets respectively.'*

The Lodge Banner substantially replicates the Lodge Badge, completed with the requisite tassels and includes the Lodge's Welsh Motto: *'Bydded Goleuni' ('Let there be light')*. It was designed by WBro W A M ('Bert') Jones, CBE, PPrGStwd. It hangs above the Senior Warden's Chair in the Lord Swansea Temple, Cardiff, where most Lodge Meetings take place. This Banner was presented to the Lodge on its 21st Anniversary by the Founder Master (WBro Oswald Lucas, PJGD) and Dedicated on 19 February 2003 by WBro Brian Eveleigh, PSGD, AProvGM, assisted by Provincial Officers.

On 19 April 2001, (19 years after the Consecration) the Lodge was honoured with a memorable visit from RWBro Hywel Davies, ProvGM, accompanied by his Provincial team of eight Officers. It was the Provincial Grand Master's desire to attend any Installation where one of his active Officers Installed his successor - on this occasion, WBro Bryan Thomas, ProvSGD, was also completing his second term as Master.

Another significant event occurred on 21 April 2005. To mark the 90th birthday of the Founder Master, all the surviving Past Masters, together with the Ruling Master, WBro Howard Thomas, PPrJGW, and his Wardens in Office, together subscribed to present WBro Oswald Lucas with a Master's Collar inscribed with the names of all the Masters who had preceded him and with spaces available for the names of future Masters. The Collar was presented to WBro Oswald by VWBro Peter Frost, PGSwdB, DepProvGM, an Honorary Member of the Lodge. WBro Oswald immediately donated the Collar to the Lodge and Invested the incumbent Master with it. As this was an Installation Meeting, WBro Howard had the pleasure of Investing his successor, WBro Roy Piggott, PPrJGD (Staffs), with this Collar. Sadly, WBro Oswald Lucas passed to the Grand Lodge Above in June 2007.

The Oriel Lodge Ritual is essentially based on the 'Oxford' version, with some variations introduced at the time of Foundation. It was produced in booklet form by the Lodge's first Secretary, WBro Philip Williams, PPrGSuptWks, who, after serving the Lodge in that capacity for thirteen years, retired from the Secretary's appointment to become Master in 1996. The Lodge Ritual was revised and reprinted during the years 2002-2004 through the determined efforts of the late WBro Michael Traynor (Master 2003) and WBro William Thomas (Master three times - 1993, 1998 and 2001). An updated and more comprehensive version of the Ritual was then produced, which is presented to all new Members on the occasion of their becoming Master Masons (or Joining Members). Sadly, WBro Michael Traynor, an enthusiastic and committed Member of the Lodge since his Initiation in 1996, and Ruling Master when the Lodge Banner was presented and Dedicated in 2003, died at a relatively young age in 2005; the 'Lodge Ritual' will prove a lasting legacy from him to the Lodge.

A long-standing tradition of the Lodge is that all Members, on Initiation or Joining, become Life Members of the 'Friends of Albert Edward Prince of Wales Court' - a home for the elderly and infirm at Porthcawl. The Court is usually open for visits by Brethren on many occasions during the year, and over the years, most Members of the Lodge have enjoyed such visits.

Oriel Lodge meets four times a year on the third Thursdays of October, December, February (Election Meeting) and April (Installation Meeting). Meetings have always been held at the Masonic Hall, Cardiff - usually in the Lord Swansea Temple, except for Installation Night which is normally held in the Edgar Rutter Temple.

Since inception, the December Meeting has always been associated with Christmas celebrations, with Members encouraged to invite their ladies and non-Masonic guests to a traditional dinner following the Meeting, after which a Carol Concert and Charity raffle are held.

The Lodge has been in existence for almost 30 years and the current Membership (2011) stands at 20 Subscribing Members.

Compiled by WBros Vivian Morris, ISO, PPrSGW, Secretary;
William Thomas, PPrDepGDC, and Bert Jones, CBE, PPrGStwd.

Princes Lodge No. 9036

Warranted : 10 March 1982

Consecrated : 4 June 1982

Meeting at the Masonic Hall, Caerphilly.

The Lodge gained its name from the situation of the Masonic Hall, which is located in Princes Avenue, Caerphilly. It was formed to encourage and support all Brethren, who employ their own particular talents in the service of Freemasonry, to achieve the Chair of King Solomon. The Lodge was Sponsored by Lodge of St Ilan No.6624, the Petition being signed by the WM and his Wardens in Open Lodge on Tuesday, 9 February 1982.

The Lodge meets four times a year on the first Tuesday in the months of March, May, October (Installation) and December.

The Lodge Logo is bounded by two Masonic Pillars, respectively capped by Terrestrial and Celestial Globes. The upper capitols of the pillars support an arched bridge, which bears the name and the year of the Consecration of the Lodge. The centre represents two hands clasped together, each presenting an olive branch encompassed by two circles, signifying Freemasonry Universal and Freemasonry Indivisible, encapsulating seven stars. The concentric circles are supported by a scroll with the Motto in Welsh: *'Brawdgarwch'* signifying *'Brotherliness'* or *'Brotherly Love'*, one of the fundamental Principles of our Order.

The Lodge was Consecrated by RWBro the Rt Hon the Lord Swansea DL, ProvGM, South Wales Eastern Division, accompanied by his Provincial Team of Officers, on Friday 4 June 1982.

The first WM was WBro Donald Lewis Lewis, PM St Ilan Lodge No.6624, PPrAGDC. WBro Donald, who was the Preceptor for 21 years, was born in London and came to Caerphilly in 1940 to work for a local firm. He joined the RAF in 1942 and saw distinguished service as a navigator in Bomber Command, serving in Lancaster and Stirling Bombers. He was wounded in action and invalided out in 1945. He was Initiated in Lodge of St Ilan in 1953 and has given distinguished service in a number of other Lodges and Degrees. He was awarded the OBE for services to the Builders Federation of Great Britain, becoming their Chairman in 1986. He holds Grand Rank in both the Craft and Royal Arch. In his spare time, WBro Donald was, for many years, Chairman of the Production Committee for the Wales Festival of Remembrance, held annually at St David's Hall, Cardiff. On Monday, 9 June 2003, a dinner was held to celebrate the 25th Anniversary of the Lodge, and also to mark WBro Donald Lewis's 50 years in Freemasonry. A number of Founder Brethren have also given long and distinguished service ranging from 22 to 25 years!

The Lodge has always striven to maintain a high standard in both Ritual in the Temple and at the Festive Board, where six course meals were the norm, together with good wine and vintage port, accompanied by live music and later by entertainment.

Ladies of Princes Lodge Brethren have always taken an active interest, attending both the Christmas and St David's Day Festive Boards. This is not unusual today, but it was a cutting edge innovation twenty five years ago!

The Lodge is considered to be a 'Family Lodge'; inasmuch as it has had five sets of fathers and sons, soon to be six; five sets of fathers and sons-in-law; three sets of blood brothers and one uncle and nephew among its Members.

The Lodge Banner was made by Mrs Anne O'Neil, the wife of WBro Arthur O'Neil. Mrs O'Neil was looking for a project when the idea of a Lodge Banner was first mooted. When she saw a full size drawing of the proposed Banner, she decided that she would make it, on the understanding that she would do all the cross-stitching, but the actual Banner would be made up by someone else. Together with her husband, she went to a firm called 'Photostitch' in Cheltenham, which specialises in producing embroidery charts from photographs. There, they purchased all the materials necessary, with everything sorted, cut and arranged on a work station, for £85. However, due to the size of the Banner they also had to purchase a large free-standing embroidery frame. This they bought while on holiday in Yorkshire! The frame was set up in their spare bedroom and Anne worked on it for two years, during which time she was hospitalised twice to undergo major surgery. The task took 700 hours, exactly 304,452 cross-stitches and approximately one and a quarter miles of thread! Before being finally made up, it was put on display. This was just as well, as a closer examination revealed that due to the magnifying of the drawing in order to make one of the charts, one of the hands was found to have 5 fingers! Fortunately, this was easily rectified. Mrs O'Neill acknowledges that without the help of the drawing made by WBro Edward Bolton, PPrJGW, and the expertise of 'Photostitch', she would have been unable to complete the task. The Banner was Dedicated on Saturday, 21 June 1997. The Ceremony was performed by VWBro Cdr Roy Hopkin, RN, DepProvGM, and his Provincial team.

The Lodge Organist is Founder Member WBro Anthony F Moore, MBE, who, at the time of writing, has served the Lodge as such for more than 22 years! WBro Tony received his MBE for service to Music and Musical Education. Initiated in Danycoed Lodge No.8127 in 1974, he was WM of that Lodge in 1985. He is well known in the Province, having first been Provincial Grand Steward in 1991, promoted to PPrSGD in 1995 and to PPrJGW in 2004. He became a Grand Officer in 2007 with the Rank of PGOrg. He was appointed Deputy Provincial Grand Master in the Mark Degree in 2008.

Compiled by WBro F T Williams, PPrJGW.

Senior Warden's Chair, Caerphilly

Wenvoe Lodge No.9038

Warranted : 10 March 1982

Consecrated : 24 May 1982

Meeting at the Masonic Hall, Barry.

The idea of a Masonic Lodge for the village of Wenvoe had long been envisaged by Freemasons who had been born and bred within the area. Over many years, Brethren who were Members of Cardiff, Barry and Penarth Lodges, discussed the idea, whilst engaged in church and social activities and at various Masonic Meetings.

During the 1970s the idea became a reality, when WBro Gordon Clement Bedford, PPrAGDC, PM Porthkerry Lodge No.6299 together with WBros Joseph Henry Mills, Alvin Hart, Jack Peers Broadbent and Bros John Lloyd, Roger Browning, Brennig Powell, Philip Morant, Michael Thomas, Sidney Donald Richards, Alan Fry, Prosser Rees, Anthony Jones, Roy Wright and Clive Williams got together at the local public house, The Wenvoe Arms, to further this enterprise. At the time, The Wenvoe Arms was under the stewardship of Bro Stuart Perrot. He and his good lady Nancy allowed the use of the upstairs lounge for the meeting, which is still used for committee meetings to this day. Between 1978 and 1981, this initial meeting was followed by many such gatherings, which were held in St Mary's Church Hall and in the homes of several Brethren. At later meetings, Bros Charles Rush, Douglas Maplestone and Peter Ball joined the group. It was then discovered that Roger Browning was not quite eligible to be a Founder Member, nevertheless, he became the senior Joining Member and, in February 2008, the Worshipful Master of Observer Lodge No.6015.

Following a series of meetings with the various Trust Companies of Cardiff, Penarth, and Barry Masonic Halls, the Founders decided to hold the Regular Lodge Meetings at Barry. They also decided that there would be 4 Meetings a year, inclusive of an Installation Ceremony. During 1981, a few social events were held in the upstairs lounge of The Wenvoe Arms. All the Lodge furniture was purchased, the Gavels were donated by Bro John Lloyd (Senior Warden Designate) and Bro Anthony Alan Jones (Barry Lodge No.2357) and Bro Brennig Powell donated the Hymn Books. A draft Ritual, adopted from Môr Hafren Lodge No.7194 was prepared and scrutinised by WBro Alvern Hart, who became the first Lodge Preceptor.

WBro Alvern also designed the Lodge Crest, which incorporates an illustration of the Parish Church of St Mary's, Wenvoe, with a history going back some 600 years. Alvern spent many hours at the church with his sketchpad, causing many of the residents to question why this 'strange man' was making short appearances outside the church at night! This design is also featured in the Past Master's Jewel. At this time, the Junior Warden Designate, Bro Clive Williams, stood down and Bro John Joseph Claude Hewitt (Porthkerry Lodge) was nominated for that Office.

It had been decided to approach Dinas Powis Lodge No.5997 to act as the Sponsoring Lodge. WBro Gordon Bedford, who by now was nominated Primus Master, and Bro John Thomas Lloyd (Lodge of Unity No.6030), nominated Senior Warden, presented the Petition at the Dinas Powis Lodge Installation Meeting in February 1982 which was duly signed under the Mastership of WBro Derry Moore. On 10 March 1982, the Warrant for Wenvoe Lodge No.9038 was granted. It should be recorded that the Provincial Grand Secretary, the late VWBro Malcolm Thompson, afforded the Brethren a great deal of assistance in their endeavours to obtain the Warrant.

St Mary's Church, Wenvoe

The Consecration took place at the Cardiff Masonic Hall on 24 May 1982 with the Provincial Grand Master, RWBro the Rt Hon the Lord Swansea, DL, as Consecrating Officer, assisted by his team of Officers, which included WBro R K Hopkin, AGDC, ProvGDC, who was eventually to become Deputy Provincial Grand Master, 1992-1998.

The Installing Master was VWBro Geoffrey M Ashe, TD, PGSwdB, DepProvGM, assisted by WBro RB Whittingham, PSGD, and WBro Cuthbert L Summers, PSGD, Assistant Provincial Grand Masters. Also present were seven Brethren from Dinas Powis Lodge, including the IPM, WBro Derry Moore, who had received the Petition. In total, 157 Brethren attended the Ceremony and 147 the Consecration Banquet.

The first Regular Meeting of Wenvoe Lodge was held at Barry Masonic Hall on Monday, 27 September 1982, when 70 Brethren attended a First Degree Ceremony, conducted by the Worshipful Master, WBro Gordon Clement Bedford. Mr Desmond James White and Mr Robert William Harrhy were the first two Initiates. The First Mandated Grand Lodge Officer was the late WBro Godfrey Holtham, PGStB, PM Vale of Glamorgan Lodge No.3977. It was under his guidance that WBro John Lloyd revised the Wenvoe Lodge Ritual, which was formally adopted by the Lodge in 1991.

On Monday, 28 February 1983, Mr Alun Stephen Arthur was Initiated into the Lodge and in 1988, Alun became the first Initiate of the Lodge to become Worshipful Master. It had been the aim of the Founders that Brethren from the village of Wenvoe and the surrounding area should progress to the Chair and Alun was also the first Brother to achieve this distinction. Since then, other villagers have followed, namely WBros Glan Reston, Eric Williams, John Custance and Andrew Carnell. Andrew is now the Secretary of Vale of Glamorgan Lodge and in 2008 he was honoured in Provincial Grand Lodge with the Rank of PPrJGD for services to Wenvoe Lodge.

The Lodge Banner was Dedicated at the Barry Masonic Hall in 1985 by the Deputy Provincial Grand Master VWBro Geoffrey M Ashe. The Banner, in tapestry, depicting St Mary's Church, Wenvoe, was made by Mrs Gladys Wright, the wife of the late WBro Ken Wright, who had served as Secretary. In 2007, it was decided to make Ken an Honorary Member of the Lodge in appreciation of his and his wife's services to the Lodge. Ken was aware of this decision, but sadly, he passed to the Grand Lodge Above a few weeks later.

Also, in May 1985, a Roll of Honour Board was presented to the Lodge by WBros John Lloyd and Anthony Alan Jones, which now hangs in the Barry Masonic Hall.

A short time later, the first Mandated Officer, WBro Godfrey Holtham, passed to the Grand Lodge Above and was succeeded by WBro Kenneth Withers, who was originally from the Province of Nottinghamshire. Following Kenneth's demise, WBro Alvern M M Hart, PJGD, PM Porthkerry Lodge No.6299, succeeded him. Since 2004, the Mandated Officer has been WBro Ralph Alistair Hopper, PGStB, PM Afan Lodge No.833. Alistair, as he is affectionately known, guides the Lodge in a quiet and unassuming manner, and he is highly respected by all the Brethren.

In 2005, the Lodge was honoured when the Provincial Grand Master RWBro Hywel Davies, the Deputy Provincial Grand Master VWBro Peter Frost, the Assistant Provincial Grand Masters, WBros Norman Lea, Andrew L Gretton, Brian Eveleigh, and Geoffrey Thomas; together with WBros Akram Baig, PAGDC, WM, 2009-2010; James R Bevan, PJGD, ProvGSec; Alistair Hopper, David A Westall, Grand Superintendent; Vernon Holtham, PPrSGW, PM Breaksea Lodge No.8358 and blood brother of the late Godfrey Holtham; and Normand Bullock, PAGDC, PM Vale of Glamorgan Lodge No.3977, all accepted the Lodge's invitation to become Honorary Members.

Special mention should be made of WBro David Tilley, PAGDC, PM St Quentins Lodge No.4778, who also became an Honorary Member of the Lodge in 2005. As Provincial Grand Almoner, he served in this Office with great distinction until illness curtailed his work. Sadly, in 2010, WBro David lost his battle with illness and passed to the Grand Lodge Above. David was a great supporter of Wenvoe Lodge and had only missed three meetings since the Consecration. He was an inspiration to all.

Since its Consecration, the Lodge has Installed or Proclaimed 28 Masters, 12 of whom were Initiated into the Lodge. At the time of writing, there are only 5 Founder Members still in the Lodge. Two Members have served as Master on three occasions, namely WBro John Thomas Lloyd, PPrGSuptWks, the first WM Installed at Barry, and WBro Jeffrey Coates, PPrGReg, who is also an Initiate of the Lodge. John is currently Vice-President of LOI, Almoner, and Home Charities Representative, and Jeffrey is the DC, Treasurer and President of LOI.

Compiled by WBro John Thomas Lloyd, PPrGSuptWks.

Clyne Lodge
No. 9049

Warranted   :   9 June 1982

Consecrated :   3 September 1982

Meeting at the Masonic Hall, Swansea.

The origin of Clyne Lodge has its roots in the Mother Lodge, Dr James Griffith Hall No.3161. A number of Brethren from that Lodge, which was Consecrated in 1906, together with like-minded Brethren from other Lodges, wished to Found a new Lodge which would, among other aspirations, have *'a very high standard at the Festive Board'*.

This concept was promoted by WBro Hayden Jones and his father-in-law, WBro Stanley Morgan who, together with WBros Peter Glyn Williams, Ronald Luxton, Phillip Davies, Hensley Davies, William Floyd, and Bros David Rothwell, Alexander Hannan, Noel Wood, Rhoslyn Thomas and Gerald Thomas, attended the first Founders' meeting at Swansea Masonic Hall, on 24 February 1982.

At this meeting, it was proposed, and unanimously carried, that the name of the new Lodge would be 'Clyne Lodge'. The Lodge is named after Clyne Castle, Swansea, built by the Carmarthenshire land-owner Richard Phillips in 1791. 'Clun', or in local parlance, 'Clyne', was the name given to the slope of woodland and meadow which rises from the western foreshore of Swansea Bay; Clyne Forest being a prominent landmark when the first Normans arrived in Gower. Clyne Castle was bought by William Graham Vivian in 1860, and remained in the Vivian family until 1952, when it was acquired for use as halls of residence for the then new University of Wales, Swansea. In 2004, Clyne was sold for conversion into luxury apartments.

The Insignia of the Lodge is a representation of Clyne Castle, which also appears on the front of the Lodge Summons, and on the Past Masters' Jewels, which also bear the date of each Past Master's ruling year.

At the first Founders' meeting, it was also agreed that the new Lodge would meet four times a year, and that no more than two Candidates would be admitted in any one year.

On 11 March 1982, a Deputation met with RWBro the Rt Hon the Lord Swansea, DL, ProvGM, and WBro Malcolm H Thompson, ProvGSec. At a second Founders' meeting, held later that same day, Brethren were informed that the formation of the Clyne Lodge had met with the Provincial Grand Master's approval. At the same meeting, it was unanimously resolved that all Lodge Members and guests would wear dinner jackets, with no exception. In addition to usual items of Lodge furniture purchased by the Founders, six silver candlesticks and sixteen flower holders were also bought, and these have pride of place at the Lodge's Installation Festival every September. A further Founders' meeting was held at the Caswell Bay Hotel, Swansea on 24 June 1982, when all the Founder Members were introduced to each other and arrangements for the Consecration Ceremony agreed.

Clyne Castle, Swansea

Clyne Lodge was Consecrated on Friday, 3 September 1982 by the Provincial Grand Master, assisted by WBro Rev Canon T K Brunsdon, PDepGChap; WBro Malcolm H Thompson, ProvGSec; and WBro Cdr R K Hopkin, AProvGDC.

VWBro G M Ashe, DepProvGM, then Installed WBro Peter Glyn Williams as the first Master of Clyne Lodge. Among others appointed and Invested were: Bro A J E Hannan as SW, Bro A Davies as JW, WBro D S Morgan as Treasurer, WBro H E Jones as Secretary and WBro P H Davies as DC.

Clyne Lodge has Initiated two Candidates nearly every year since its Consecration. Lodge Membership has been steadily maintained at around 40 Brethren.

On Friday, 31 January 1986, the Deputy Provincial Grand Master again attended Clyne Lodge to Dedicate the Lodge Banner.

Clyne Lodge's first Worshipful Master, WBro Peter Glyn Williams, later served as Grand Secretary of the Grand Lodge of Mark Master Masons and other Orders administered from Mark Masons' Hall, from 1986 to 1997. WBro Williams is Supreme Grand Ruler of the Order of the Secret Monitor, and also holds Grand Rank in a number of Masonic Orders throughout the world.

Clyne Lodge's first Mandated Grand Officer was WBro Neil Howard Matthews, DepGSuptWks, of the Order of Royal and Select Masters; Deputy Great Marshall of the United and Religious, Military and Masonic Orders of the Temple; and Past Deputy Provincial Grand Supreme Ruler in the Order of the Secret Monitor. On 16 September 2010, WBro Matthews was succeeded by WBro D G Rowbottom, PAGDC, as Mandated Grand Officer.

It is also noteworthy that, in 2001, WBros D S Morgan, H E Jones and P H Davies retired as Treasurer, Secretary and Director of Ceremonies respectively, after nineteen years of sterling service to Clyne Lodge. Their successors as Secretary and Treasurer, WBro Ron Slater, PPrDepGDC, and WBro Paul Davies, PPrGSuptWks, respectively, retired in 2009 after eight years dedicated service.

Clyne Lodge celebrated its 25th Anniversary and 100th Meeting on Wednesday, 5 September 2007, having maintained its reputation for the stylish Festive Boards, as well as its high standard of Ritual.

Compiled by WBro David J Rees, PM, Secretary.

Proscenium Lodge No.9059

Warranted : 8 September 1982

Consecrated : 22 November 1982

Meeting at the Masonic Hall, Cardiff.

By the early 1980s, the Capital of Wales boasted two national television centres, the internationally renowned Welsh National Opera, two leading classical orchestras, the Welsh College of Music and Drama, several strong music societies, and a number of leading performers and entertainers. It was against this background, that a group of distinguished Cardiff Freemasons were keen to form an 'entertainment' Lodge. They included WBros Harold Greene, PPrJGW, and Bernard Schwartz, PPrSGW, who later became a Deputy Lieutenant for the County of South Glamorgan. Together with the enthusiastic encouragement of Brethren such as Wyn Calvin, MBE, PPrJGW; Tony Moore, MBE, PPrJGW; Phillip Felman, PPrJGW; Wayne Warlow, PPrJGW; John T James, PPrJGW; Rex Plowman, ProvDepGDC; David Ronson, PPrSGD.; Malcolm Lucas, PPrGStdB, and Malcolm Brooke, PPrSGD, and several others, they formed the Founder core of the proposed new Lodge. They did not enjoy those Masonic Ranks in 1982 but after twenty-five years of diligence in the Craft, they had been well earned.

The Mother Lodge that was to give birth to this new creation was Lodge of Enterprise No.8757, Cardiff, of which WBros Harold Greene, Bernard Schwartz and Harry Williams were Members.

The first proposed Lodge name, put forward by Harold Greene, was 'The Lodge of Orbit'. Harold Greene was the first Secretary of Orbit Theatre, Cardiff, which had been formed in 1968. The Founders included Bro Frank Wooles as Producer/Director with Bro Ivan Sadka as Honorary Musical Director. They, together with several other members and friends of Orbit Theatre became Founder Members of Proscenium Lodge. Bros Frank and Ivan staged some twenty major productions at the New Theatre and Sherman Theatre, Cardiff. These included Welsh Premières of West End show releases, Oliver, The Sound of Music, Half a Sixpence, Fiddler on the Roof, Annie, Gigi and Cabaret.

Bro Frank Wooles was the longest serving Area Representative and Honorary Life Member of the National Operatic and Dramatic Association (NODA) for over 50 years. He was also responsible for 24 Amateur Musical and Dramatic companies in South East Wales and Rhondda areas. In recognition of his services to Proscenium Lodge for over 27 years, he was given the Provincial Rank of Master Mason in 1999.

Bro Ivan Sadka is a Solicitor, who supported his legal studies by playing piano professionally in and around London, until qualification. He fronted as Conductor over 40 major musical productions mainly at the New Theatre, and other times at the Sherman Theatre, Cardiff. At the request of the American Conductor, Robert Mandell, he formed the Orbit Chorale, which for many years was part of the Melachrino Strings concerts at St David's Hall, Cardiff. Upon retirement from Orbit, Ivan was able to devote more time as a freelance pianist. He formed his own jazz quintet, performing in the Czech Republic, London and in Cardiff. For over 25 years, he has been the Organist of Proscenium Lodge. At the annual Meeting of Provincial Grand Lodge at Barry in 2009, he was honoured the accolade of Provincial Grand Lodge Rank of a Master Mason.

The name 'Lodge of Orbit' did not entirely suit the professionals in the business and the name 'Proscenium' was introduced instead by Wayne Warlow, and was readily accepted by all the Founder Members. There were, however, two other Lodges with that name, one in Cheshire and the other in London. The Provincial Secretary, Malcolm Thompson gave this proposal his support, Lord Swansea later endorsed it and the Warrant was signed on 8 September 1982. John James was responsible for the Motto: '*Omnes Partes Agimus',* with its twin meaning, '*We play all parts*' or '*We all play our parts*'.

Thus, the curtain went up with the Consecration of Proscenium Lodge No.9059 on 22 November 1982, since which, in its 29 years' existence, it has played to full houses and given outstanding performances. The Consecration took place in the Duke of Connaught Temple, Cardiff, under the superintendence of RWBro the Rt Hon the Lord Swansea, ProvGM, accompanied by the full retinue of Provincial Grand Lodge Officers. A splendid dinner followed, consisting of saumon fumé, consommé xérès, sole Veronique, followed by baron de boeuf with emperor pineapple for dessert. Coffee, brandy and port wine completed the menu.

Martin Greene, son of Harold, was the first Master of the Lodge, with Wyn Calvin, SW, and Wayne Warlow, JW. After Martin Greene's year in the Chair, he emigrated to Florida, USA, where he carved out a new career selling cars. Harold, as a successful businessman, continued his Estate Agency Business on Churchill Way in Cardiff. He was truly a flamboyant character, full of energy, drive and to a degree, eccentricity. His great joy was to dress in his 'Black Tie' on Orbit Theatre's opening nights at the New Theatre. He loved the theatre in general, having travelled as a performing youth in Music Halls throughout the country. Theatre was in his blood. His other delight was to drive his beige coloured Rolls Royce, displaying the registration plate 'HOU5E', when visiting Lodge. He was undoubtedly a 'one off'; he well lived up to his nickname 'Mr Producer', and he loved his involvement with the Variety Club of Great Britain.

WBro Wyn Calvin was Initiated into Thalia Lodge No.5177, London in 1973. He became a Freeman of the City of London and, in 1991, became King Rat in the Grand Order of Water Rats. In 1989, he was Invested by Her Majesty as a most noble Member of the British Empire. Throughout 28 years and 100 Meetings, Wyn, in his wonderful and inimitable style, has proposed the Toast to the visitors on all but three occasions. This is a statistic that could not be excluded from the Lodge history. He well knows that the first syllable of fund-raising is FUN. That sense of good humour and often hilarious laughter may explain part of Proscenium's popularity with visitors and its fine reputation for generous Charity Collections. Over the years many 'House Full' signs have been put up whenever Proscenium has met, the attraction largely being WBro Wyn.

WBro Wayne Warlow was Initiated in Hen Bont Lodge No.4691 in 1967 and became its Master in 2005. An extremely talented professional musician, he has worked and travelled all over the World and recently had his arranged works performed by the Boston Pops Orchestra at Symphony Hall, under the baton of John Williams. He is a Past Provincial Grand Organist and his achievements and recognition to the Side Orders of Masonry are distinguished. Suffice it to say, he has been an accomplished and valuable Founder Member of Proscenium Lodge. In the year 2010, Wayne achieved the unique distinction of being honoured by United Grand Lodge of England by being given the year to present the series of Prestonian Lectures. In 2011, he was further honoured by becoming a Grand Officer with the Rank of PGOrg.

The first Regular Meeting after the Consecration was attended only by Founder Members, visitors made their entry at the following Meeting. Wayne Warlow recalls that *the singing of 'There's No Business like Show Business' to accompany the Visitor's Toast just happened of its own volition. Nobody suggested it beforehand, and I've always regarded its introduction as being a very happy and spontaneous accident*. The songs 'Just one more Chance' and 'The Bells of St Mary's' are just two delightful traditional additions that enhance the Lodge's Festive Board. It may, however, not be coincidental that these songs are performed at the Grand Order of Water Rats festive occasions of which Wyn Calvin is, of course, a Past King Rat and Preceptor of the Order.

It has been a tradition at Proscenium Lodge that the Charity Steward acts as the Director of Ceremonies at the Festive Board. Currently (2011) this is WBro Gareth Morgan, PPrSGD, who is also a Police Officer. He controls the proceedings with fun and with his Officer's hat on. However, the first DC at dinner was the charismatically wonderful and sadly missed Bernard Schwartz. He was a successful businessman and a retired Army Major. His claim to fame being that during his army career in the Middle East, he had the distinction of being the only Jewish Officer to lead and be seconded to the Arab Legion. He lit up the dining hall for more than 22 years, merging his own presence with Wyn Calvin, and together they made a formidable double act. Bernard's cousin, Alan Schwartz, PPrAGDC, also a Member of the Lodge, was awarded the MBE in 2003, for his services to multi-faith co-operation and co-ordination in the City of Cardiff.

Visitors at the Lodge today are likely to be greeted by the Tyler, WBro Phillip Lloyd, PPrSGD, whose familiar face may be seen more frequently at the BBC's 'East Ender's Queen Vic Pub'. One of the Stewards, Terry Dyddgen-Jones is a Past Head of BBC Wales Drama and also a Director of the longest running soap opera, ITV's 'Coronation Street'. While another, (Phillip Madoc) may be recognised as the face of David Lloyd George, or the German Naval Officer who wanted Pike's name in the comedy series, 'Dad's Army'. Phillip regularly attends Lodge from his home near London. The Organist can create solemn and sacred sounds, which conceal Ivan Sadka's talent as a fine jazz musician.

The Lodge Secretary since 2002, Kelvin Jones, PAGDC, ProvDepGReg, has been seen frequently touring South Wales in several Pantomime roles with Bro Owen Money. This, however, does not conceal the volume of work he has undertaken in the Province of South Wales. Initiated in Hamlet of Van Lodge No.8334 in January 1978, he became a Joining Member of Proscenium Lodge in 1987 and was Installed Worshipful Master of Proscenium in December 1995. In addition, he is the Secretary of Hendre Lodge No. 3250, was Worshipful Master of St Mildred Lodge No.5078 in 2007 and is the first Scribe E of the newly Consecrated Proscenium Chapter (May 2006). In 2008, he achieved the remarkable distinction of being appointed Acting Provincial Junior Grand Warden, an accolade well worthy of his Masonic input over the years.

A PM Services Lodge No.7139 and one of several great contributors to the Lodge was Hugh Johns, PPrSGW, who was the voice heard by millions commentating on the 1966 World Cup. Hugh went on to become a much loved and greatly respected sports commentator and journalist well past the year 2000. For many people, the mere mention of his name evokes fond memories of ITV's Sunday afternoon football programmes 'Star Soccer' and London's 'The Big Match' in the 1970s, when he regularly commentated on matches from the East Midlands. In recent years, Hugh was also the Province's External Communications Officer, responsible for dealing with the press and with Public Relations issues. This too was a busy role, particularly in the light of the then deliberations of the National Assembly for Wales on the issue of Freemasonry. His 11-year tenure as DC of the Lodge ended in 2004, when he left as his legacy a remarkably detailed synopsis on all points of procedure concerning the formal side of the Craft. His death in 2006 led to quite a remarkable funeral. It was truly a special occasion when the cortège drove from his house in

Radyr to the Church, just a few hundred yards away, flanked by five Past Masters plus the ruling Master at the time, WBro Lee Gilbert. The procession was preceded by a Caribbean Jazz Band, reminiscent of a scene from the James Bond film 'Dr No'. Having seen the film many years before, he instructed that that was exactly what he wanted. Many Sports' Journalists and Broadcasters attended the service including the Head of Sky Sports, who delivered Hugh's eulogy.

Proscenium Lodge is still managing to attract new performers into Freemasonry – Owen Money, Rupert Moon, thingy and whatsisname – to name just a few. There are also backstage workers and musicians, all of whom are grateful to the Founders for setting the high standards in both the Lodge and at the Festive Board, which have made the Lodge unique in the Province.

In 2006, after two years of demanding and skilful work, John James, PPrJGW, turned his hand to another craft. Not only had he been Lodge Secretary for the first 20 years of its existence, but he also created a Banner for the Lodge, which he had begun in 2004. The design was taken from the original Lodge Logo designed by Haydn Morgan, PPrGSuptWks, Monmouthshire, when he worked as a graphic designer for HTV in 1982. The Banner took more than 6,000 hours of work and consists of half a million cross-stitches with the use of more than 30 different coloured cottons. The Banner depicts the original Logo of the Lodge, using the proscenium arch of the theatre as its centrepiece. On 4 September 2006, the Banner Dedication Ceremony was held at the Duke of Connaught Temple in Guildford Crescent, Cardiff. The Ceremony was presided over by VWBro Peter Frost, DepProvGM, and this Banner now hangs in the North West corner of that Temple. The Director of Ceremonies for the Banner Ceremony was Rex Plowman, ProvDepGDC, Founder Member.

In 2007, another milestone was recorded in the Lodge's history, when WBro Tony Moore, a Founder Member, was promoted to the Rank of PAGOrg of the United Grand Lodge of England. He is also the Assistant Provincial Grand Master of Mark Master Masons of South Wales. He has been associated with education all his working life and in 2006 he was Invested by Her Majesty as a most noble Member of the British Empire, for services to Music and Education. When Proscenium Chapter was formed in 2006, he became its first 'Z'.

On Thursday, 6 May 2010, Past Master WBro Wayne Warlow, SBStJ, PPrJGW, Prestonian Lecturer for 2010, gave one of the official presentations of his Lecture in Proscenium Lodge. The Lecture, entitled 'Music in Masonry and Beyond', examined examples of music and Masonry in combination and included playing numerous recordings of music ranging from the classical repertoire of Mozart, Bach, Brahms and Sibelius to the lighter Gilbert & Sullivan, George Gershwin, J P Sousa and Louis Armstrong.

It can truly be said that here is a Lodge that will long face the Sun and leave all its shadows behind.

Compiled by WBro Rex Plowman, PProvDepGDC.

Dewi Sant Lodge No.9067

Warranted : 10 November 1982

Consecrated : 1 March 1983

Meeting at the Masonic Hall, Bridgend.

Dewi Sant Lodge was Consecrated on 1 March 1983. However, in order to get the complete history in perspective it is necessary to go back eight years to 1975, when WBro Brian Sparks, being very keen to improve his spoken Welsh, thought that joining a Welsh speaking Lodge would help him considerably. He very soon realised that no such Lodge existed, and it was at this point that the notion of a Welsh speaking Lodge materialized. The first enquiry to Provincial Grand Lodge regarding the formation of a new Lodge able to perform Ceremonies in the Welsh language was on 13 December 1975. The reply indicated that Province was neither for nor against the formation, but urged patience in the matter. You will come to appreciate the word 'patience' as it permeates the Lodge's 29 year history!

The intended name for the new Lodge was 'Yr Hen Iaith', 'The Old Language'. A steering committee was formed and WBro Dafydd Walters was given the onerous task of translating the three Craft Degrees of the Oxford Ritual into Welsh. This done, the steering committee held meetings with Welsh language rehearsals in the old Bridgend Temple in Adare Street. Before long, this committee had formed a demonstration team, capable of performing the First and Second Degrees in Welsh.

Like all the best stories, days, months and even years passed, and the request for patience was still the order of the day. This situation took its toll on the morale of the steering group and the number of Brethren attending meetings and practices dwindled. Eventually only three Worshipful Brethren, Brian Sparks, Moelwyn Llewellyn and Dafydd Walters were present at one rehearsal, and with frustration gathering momentum, it was these three Brethren who were instrumental in forging ahead and applying for a Warrant to form a new Lodge.

Provincial Grand Lodge stipulated four areas in which the new Lodge would need to comply. Firstly, it had to show the support of 50 Masons of Installed Master Rank, all of whom would support the intended Lodge. This was very quickly achieved. Secondly, the proposed Lodge name of 'Yr Hen Iaith', - 'the Old Language', was deemed unacceptable, being considered to be too contentious. It was felt that something like 'Dewi Sant' would be more appropriate and acceptable. This was a great disappointment to the Founders, but in order to achieve the greater goal, it was reluctantly agreed. It was felt that the ultimate aim of a Lodge conducting its business in the Welsh language was more important than having the intended name challenged. Thirdly, the quality of the original Welsh Ritual by Dafydd Walters had to be examined to ensure its accuracy. The Welsh translation of the First Degree Ceremony was sent to Provincial Grand Lodge and subsequently to Grand Lodge, to be examined by WBro Perry, HMI of Schools. He commented that there was nothing in the Welsh translation to cause any concern, and that it was an excellent effort. Finally, the new Lodge would have to Initiate, Pass and Raise Candidates in the English language. In order to use the Welsh language, the Lodge must first 'call off', demonstrate the Degree in Welsh, then 'call on', and revert to English. This was much more contentious, and several 'would be' Founder Members decided at this stage to withdraw. The majority, however, felt that this was a move forward, and given time, it may still be possible to achieve the original aim.

In October 1982, the WM and Wardens of Penybont Lodge, No.6743, signed the Petition, thus Penybont Lodge became the Sponsoring Lodge. Dewi Sant Lodge was subsequently Consecrated on 1 March 1983, with WBro Brian Sparks Installed as Primus Master, Bro Ellis M Williams as SW and WBro John Mathews as JW. Dewi Sant Lodge requested seven Meetings a year, one for each of the three Degrees, to be demonstrated in Welsh and subsequently worked in English. The seventh Meeting was for the Installation Ceremony. Both the Election night Ceremony and the Installation Festival would be held in the English language. The Lodge was welcomed by the Maesteg Lodges into their Temple.

Of the 27 Founders, only seven are still alive with just one, WBro Charles Sanders, remaining a Member. The new Lodge raised a few eyebrows amongst some Brethren in the Province, and was often referred to as '*Oh, the Welsh Lodge!*' At times it felt like being a stranger in your own land but, nevertheless, the Lodge had arrived and Cyfrinfa Dewi Sant was well and truly active. In October 1983, the first two Candidates were Initiated, namely, Bro Warren Davies and Bro Roger Thomas. In March 1989, Roger Thomas had the honour of becoming the first Initiate of Dewi Sant Lodge to occupy the Chair of King Solomon.

Between March 1983 and September 1992 seven requests were made to conduct the Ceremonies in Welsh. This was a difficult time, because no one knew when it might be appropriate to make further enquiries, and while wanting to keep the issue alive, the Brethren did not wish to make a nuisance of themselves. In retrospect, it was a 'no win' situation.

In October and November 1992, acting on information received, which proved ultimately to have been misleading, or at the very least to have been misinterpreted, it was decided by the Membership to conduct two Initiation Ceremonies in the Welsh language, without 'calling off'. This, as history shows was a big, big mistake! In December 1992, the ProvGM, the Rt Hon the Lord Swansea, suspended the Lodge for a period of 5 years, for failing to comply with the remit that the Lodge was given prior to, and at its Consecration. As you can imagine, this decision had a profound effect on the Brethren. Every attempt was made to maintain morale by meeting regularly, but the whole business was proving too traumatic for some and inevitably there were resignations. In August 1993, Cyfrinfa Dewi Sant appealed to UGLE for a reduction in the period of suspension given by Lord Swansea. The Lodge was represented at Grand Lodge by W Bros Roy Jones, Charles Sanders, Byron Davies and Richard George Jones. The meeting was successful. UGLE congratulated the Lodge representatives, particularly Richard George Jones, who led the appeal, on the very professional way in which they had presented their case. Grand Lodge reduced the suspension to two years and, subsequently the ProvGM, reduced the suspension to one year.

Thus, in 1994 the Lodge was up and running again but, unfortunately, not without problems. The four Candidates who had been Initiated in the Welsh language had to be re-Initiated. This was personally disappointing for the Candidates as well as for the Lodge Members. Two of the Brethren concerned, Arwyn Reynolds and Roy James, are now PMs of the Lodge. The other two Brethren, however, resigned within a very short time of completing their Third Degree, never really recovering from the disappointment of having to repeat their Initiation. Ironically, it was decreed that the original date of the Welsh Initiation Ceremony was to remain the official date of Initiation!

The Grand Secretary, in a letter to the Lodge Secretary in May 1994, stated that despite all that had happened, if Dewi Sant still wished to seek permission to use the Welsh language in Open Lodge they should make a formal request to the ProvGM, but should wait at least two years before so doing. On 9 October 1995, an application for a bilingual Lodge was once again sought, but on this occasion, the answer was an unequivocal 'NO'. Membership again fell because of further resignations and an inordinate number of deaths. Indeed, so poor were the numbers that, not only were there difficulties in filling the Offices, there was no one to act as a Candidate. At this stage, Bro Huw Jenkins, a visitor from Llynfi Lodge No.2965, stepped in and acted as Candidate for five First Degree, three Second Degree and four Third Degree Ceremonies. Huw was presented with a signed copy of the Welsh Ritual to thank him for his efforts.

Always wishing to support a wider audience, in 1996, Cyfrinfa Dewi Sant sponsored the first prize of £300 for the 'mixed under 40 in number choir' at the National Eisteddfod, held in Bridgend. This was much appreciated by all those concerned with the Eisteddfod. In a small way, this also promoted Welsh Freemasonry in a positive light to the general public.

In September 1999, Lord Swansea retired as ProvGM, and his successor, RWBro Hywel Davies, made inquiries of the Lodge about its future intentions. A meeting was arranged with VWBro Peter Frost, DepProvGM. WBro Roger Thomas, Secretary, emphasised that the Lodge wished to be completely bilingual, and use the Candidate's preferred language. No one would be prevented from joining or progressing in the Lodge because of a language issue. Moreover, it was emphasised that there was no linguistic apartheid whatsoever, indeed, some of the PMs, Brian Sparks, Charles Sanders, Kerry Jones and Stephen Harries, all only spoke English, but without whom Dewi Sant Lodge would not exist. There were also English speakers learning pieces of the Welsh Ritual, and doing so with great expertise.

In November 2003, with no further progress being made towards its bilingual goal; with no Candidates; no Joining Members; further deaths and only 10 Members regularly attending Lodge; it was decided by 90% of the Brethren that the Lodge could no longer remain viable, and they offered their resignations with effect from 31 December 2003. The Lodge Secretary advised involving WBro Geoff Thomas, Mandated Officer, who, after consultation with the ProvGM, called a Special Meeting of the Lodge. He stated in no uncertain terms the seriousness of handing back the Lodge Warrant. He felt that there was an untapped number of Masons who would willingly become Joining Members. There was a promise of at least 10 Joining Members, who had a particular love of the Welsh language. Consequently, in March 2004, 14 Brethren were Balloted for and accepted as Joining Members and, as a result, all resignations were withdrawn. It is worth noting that several of these new Brethren were not Welsh speakers. This is regarded as a key point in the history of the Lodge, particularly when one considers its subsequent progress.

From October 2004, the number of Regular Lodge Meetings was reduced from 7 to 5. The Meetings in May and September had been found to be very poorly attended. The Brethren of Dewi Sant Lodge coming from such diverse areas, it was felt that Bridgend would be a much more central and convenient venue. So, in 2006, the Lodge moved from Maesteg to Bridgend, with the last Meeting in Maesteg being held in April and the first Ceremony in Bridgend taking place in October. At the initial Bridgend Meeting, the first Initiation Ceremony since 2002 was held, with WBro Stephen Harries in the Chair of King Solomon.

The Lodge has demonstrated Welsh Ceremonies at St Elli Lodge No.3942, Llanelli; Aeron Lodge No.7208, Aberaeron; Penrice Lodge No.4172, Swansea; and Gnoll Lodge No.5057, Neath. Several such Ceremonies at St Elli Lodge have raised an amount in excess of £1000 for charity. The Lodge has also taken part in two television performances focusing on Freemasonry in Wales, with particular emphasis on the Welsh language.

WBro Elfan Jones became WM in 2007. By now, it had become increasingly evident that the excellent translation of the Ritual by Dafydd Walters appeared rather dated, and WBro Elfan Jones was asked to update it, which he did with great expertise. The new translation was used throughout 2007, with Dafydd's original Ritual being delivered by the 'old timers', who had previously learned it. All in all, 2007 proved to be a very successful year in re-establishing Dewi Sant Lodge as a viable force in Welsh Masonry.

From 1983 to date, there have been 20 Worshipful Masters, five of whom have been in the Chair of King Solomon twice, namely, Brian Sparks, Richard George Jones, Roger Thomas, Iorwerth Morgan and Roy James.

In just over 25 years, 33 Brethren have been Initiated, despite the difficulties; however, of those 33, only 11 remain as Members.

Cyfrinfa Dewi Sant has always prided itself on offering a very warm and fraternal welcome to all of its visitors. A strong fraternal bond has been established with Wenallt Lodge No.9082, with which annual reciprocal visits take place. The Lodge is also renowned for the music played and sung both inside the Temple and at the Festive Board. Any excuse for a Gymanfa and the Brethren and visitors are ready and willing to oblige.

Who knows what the next 25 years will bring. Hopefully, the language element will move forward and we shall achieve our bilingual goal.

Compiled by WBro R Thomas, PPrGReg.

Wenallt Lodge No.9082

Warranted : 9 March 1983

Consecrated : 3 June 1983

Meeting at the Masonic Hall, Cardiff.

Ah, Paris, city of romance, the Folies Bergère, the Eiffel Tower and, well let us be honest…..rugby. The reason that a particular group of men had gathered at the restaurant L'Atlantique on the Boulevard Magenta in 1981 was the Wales v France Rugby International. This was by no means the first trip, nor had the diners only known each other for five minutes. These were in fact members of 'The Must-get Beers' (TMB) on tour; they were all close friends, who had known one another for a long time. In a casual aside one observed that *'there are six Brethren from six different Lodges at this table, indeed we could even seriously consider forming our own Masonic Lodge'*. My goodness, what oaks grow from such little acorns.

On their return from Paris, a meeting was organised with WBro Malcolm Thompson, ProvGSec, who was to provide vital support, advice and assistance in the coming months. Every new Lodge has to be Sponsored and, as they were Members of the same Lodge, WBro Sam Richards and WBro Geoffrey William Thomas, who had made that comment in Paris, decided to approach Hiraeth Lodge No.8834, which was delighted to act as the Sponsoring Lodge.

To have the germ of an idea about forming a Lodge and to succeed in seeing it through to its Consecration, is no small feat. It is an onerous, time consuming and complicated process. Most of this work was undertaken by WBro Jeff Sainsbury (WM 2005) and WBro Geoff Thomas (WM 2008). The Brethren of Wenallt Lodge are truly grateful to both for the effort and hard work applied to ensure success in creating the Lodge.

One early, though naturally important question - what name to select? A name was needed which would give some idea of the background of the Lodge as well as its Founders. In the end, the choice proved relatively straightforward. It had to be 'Wenallt', as the Wenallt hill in north Cardiff dominates that part of the city and most of the Founders had grown up, and indeed were still living, in the area. The name also gives a very strong flavour of the Lodge's Welsh roots. Wenallt is derived from the Welsh 'Gwen-Allt', 'Gwen' meaning 'white' and 'Allt' meaning 'hill'. Wenallt is an inversion of 'allt wen' ('white hill'), with 'gwen' mutated to 'wen'. The Wenallt, Cardiff, is so-named because of the whitethorn bushes on the hillside.

The Warrant was issued on 9 March 1983, and the Lodge was duly Consecrated on Friday, 3 June 1983, at the Masonic

Temple, Guildford Crescent, Cardiff. The Consecrating team was headed by RWBro the Rt Hon the Lord Swansea, DL, ProvGM. He was assisted by WBro Malcolm H Thompson, PJGD, ProvGSec, as Secretary; WBro Cdr Roy K Hopkin, PAGDC, as DC; WBro Keith Tod Browning, ProvDepGDC, as ADC; and WBro Ken Morgan, ProvGTyler, as Tyler.

Following the Consecration, the first WM of Wenallt Lodge, WBro Thomas H Jones, was Installed by VWBro Geoffrey Malin Ashe, TD, PGSwdB, DepProvGM. He was assisted by the four AProvGMs, WBros Ronald B Whittingham, PSGD; Cuthbert L Summers, PSGD; Ken Adams Morgan, PSGD; and Sam Northway, PJGD. WBro Tom Jones appointed and Invested Bro E Haydn Jones as SW and Bro Ron Sainsbury as JW. Among other Founders taking Office were WBro Norman Lloyd-Edwards, PM South Wales Jurists' Lodge No.7092 and PM Cape St Vincent Lodge No.8524, acting IPM; Bro Bernard Weare, Treasurer; Bro Jeff Sainsbury, Secretary; WBro Geoff Thomas, WM of Llanfair Lodge No.7353, DC; WBro Gwilym H Jones, JD; and Bro Paul Turner, IG. The Guildford Singers, under the direction of WBro E J Smith, PGStB, added to the atmosphere of celebration and enjoyment at the Festive Board.

Sadly, not many weeks before the Consecration, WBro Sam Richards was called to the Grand Lodge Above. Sam was to have been the Founder Master, and would have joined his son Ken in the new Lodge. It was most fortunate that WBro Tom Jones was able and willing to assume the mantle and go on to become a hugely influential force within the Lodge during its formative years.

If fate had not so cruelly intervened, Wenallt Lodge would have begun life with an amazing total of five pairs of fathers and sons. With the death of Sam Richards, his son Kenneth Richards, who was Installed as WM in 2000, was unable to enjoy his father's companionship in Lodge. However, Tom Jones was a Member with his son David C Jones (WM 1986); Ron Sainsbury (WM 1985) was a Founder Member together with his son Jeff Sainsbury (WM 2005); whilst Haydn Jones (WM 1984) and his son Gwilym Jones (WM 2004), were able to enjoy each other's company. WBro Maldwyn Davies was delighted to assist at the Initiation of his son, the very first Initiate of Wenallt Lodge.

Those strong family links within the Lodge continue to grow. Honorary Member, WBro Andrew L Gretton, PSGD, PDepProvGM, assisted when his son James was Initiated. Likewise, WBro Geoffrey W Thomas assisted at the Initiation of his son-in-law, WBro Michael Jones (WM 2002). It is also worthy of note that WBro Merrick Jones (WM 2003), the grandson of the Primus Master, WBro Tom Jones, became the third generation of his family not only to become a Member of the Lodge, but also to be Installed in the Chair of King Solomon. Everyone was delighted when WBro David Jones occupied the Chair to Install his son; a father-son scenario, which was repeated when WBro Paul Marshall (WM 1992) occupied the Chair to Initiate his son, David. Being able to propose his blood brother into Freemasonry, as well as assist at his Initiation, was a particular joy to WBro David Franklin, PPrAGReg (WM 1996).

Indeed, family traditions have continued unabated. It was a very special night when, on 22 November 2010, the WM invited WBro Malcolm Kidd to occupy the Chair and, in the presence of RWBro Captain Sir Norman Lloyd-Edwards, ProvGM, and a very full Duke of Connaught Temple, he proceeded to Initiate his son, Ian James Kidd. It was a most memorable occasion for father and son and indeed for all those present. At the following Lodge Meeting, in February 2011, yet another Member's son was Initiated. This was Andrew David Jones, the son of Bro Michael Jones, IG. Incredibly, Bro Andrew became the 11th Lewis of Wenallt Lodge, which elevates it to a rather unique position within the Province and perhaps in Freemasonry as a whole, considering that all were admitted within a thirty year period since the Lodge's Consecration.

Perhaps the first major event following the Consecration, however, was the evening in 1990, when the Lodge's second Initiate, Malcolm Kidd (who was made a Mason on the same evening as Hugh Davies), was Installed in the Chair of King Solomon. Malcolm had a very strong, long-standing connection with the Scouting movement. Having acted as ADC to the Chief Commissioner of Scouting in Wales, it was natural for Malcolm to invite the Commissioner to his Installation. It just so happened that the Commissioner was RWBro the Rt Hon the Lord Kenyon, CBE, DL, ProvGM for North Wales. The attendance of such a personage required that our own ProvGM, Lord Swansea, should also attend. Coincidentally, this was also the last night that WBro Geoff Thomas acted as DC before becoming ProvDepGDC. It was a truly momentous and memorable evening for all those lucky enough to have been present.

The 100th Meeting of the Lodge, which also marked the Lodge's 25th Anniversary year in 2008, was also a momentous event. WBro Geoff Thomas PSGD, AProvGM, was Installed into the Chair, the last of the Founder Members still in the Lodge to receive the honour. The occasion was enhanced by the presence of RWBro Hywel Davies, ProvGM, who was accompanied by his successor designate, RWBro Captain Sir Norman Lloyd-Edwards, himself a Founder Member of the Lodge, together with a full Provincial team. WBro Geoff retired as AProvGM in 2010 after serving almost seven years in that Office.

Various members of the Lodge have risen to positions of prominence. Outstandingly, RWBro Captain Sir Norman Lloyd-Edwards, KCVO, GCStJ, RD*, JP, RNR, has of course, risen to considerable eminence, being not only a Past President of the Masonic Samaritan Fund, but was also Lord Lieutenant of South Glamorgan. In 2007, he was appointed acting Junior Grand Warden of the United Grand Lodge of England and, in 2009, he became Provincial Grand Master of South Wales.

At the time of the Consecration, WBro Gwilym Jones (WM 2004) was the MP for Cardiff North. WBro Paul Marshall (WM 1992) was awarded the OBE for services to Commercial and Industrial Development in Wales, and also appointed Provincial Grand Treasurer as well as PAGDC. Then, in March 2011, he was Invested as AProvGM. In 1999, WBro Geoff Thomas was appointed ProvGDC and in 2004 he became an AProvGM.

Three Members of the Lodge became Lord Mayor of the City of Cardiff. RWBro Captain Sir Norman Lloyd-Edwards, WBro Jeff Sainsbury (WM 2005) and WBro Tim Davies (WM 2001). They would have been joined by another Member, Bro Clive Milsom, a Joining Member from his Mother Lodge, Ymlaen Lodge No.8419, had he not been called to the Grand Lodge Above.

The Lodge has also been honoured to have had a number of Brethren promoted to acting Provincial Rank: WBro Malcolm Kidd (WM 1990), WBro Paul Marshall OBE (WM 1992) and WBro Hugh Davies (WM 1997) all became ProvGStwds. WBro David Jones (WM 1986) became ProvGSwdB and WBro Martin James (WM 1995) a ProvJGD. WBro Malcolm later became Provincial Grand Tyler.

Whilst many Brethren have contributed much to the Lodge, WBro Hugh Davies (WM 1997) has done so in two profound and meaningful ways. He not only manufactured and presented the Lodge with a Sword, but he was also instrumental in the design and production of the Banner.

'The Wenallt' is depicted on the Banner as a wooded hillside in the background, with an oval ball as well as the Welsh Dragon below. These allude to the common interest of the Founders, who travelled to Dublin and Paris in support of the Welsh Rugby team. The Welsh Motto *'Byddaf Yna'* translates to *'I will be there'*. The Lodge name and number are shown at the head of the Banner, the Date of the Consecration is at the foot. The two pillars are surmounted by the terrestrial and celestial globes, signifying Freemasonry universal, and are positioned alongside the chequered pavement, on which lies the Volume of the Sacred Law upon which the Square and Compasses are displayed; the whole being on a light blue background with gold trim. The Banner seeks to incorporate, as far as possible, the common interests and bonds of friendship that unite the Founders, as well as the majority of the other Brethren of the Lodge.

The Banner was Dedicated in an impressive Ceremony on 30 March 2004 by WBro Brian Eveleigh, PSGD, AProvGM. The evening was another really outstanding event with many distinguished Brethren of the Province taking part. Amongst them were

The Wenallt Lodge Sword

the late WBro Julius Hermer, PJGD, as SW; WBro Roger Richmond, PProvJGW, as JW; WBro Rev Canon Hugh Mosford, PAGChap, as Chaplain; and Lodge Member, WBro Geoff Thomas ProvGDC, as DC.

The Lodge's treasured Sword took WBro Davies some twelve months to manufacture in his workshop at home. Modelled on the sword traditionally used by midshipmen in the Royal Navy, the blade was fashioned from sprung steel, grooves having to be ground on each side. The D shaped guard with cross hilt was manufactured from a piece of brass plate, before being brazed to the blade. Before proceeding any further, the blade was brought to a high and permanent polish through the good offices of WBro M N James (WM 1995). Once this stage had been completed the handle was bound with leather and secured with copper wire. To complete the project, WBro Hugh constructed an oak box, lined with blue baize, left over from a ceremonial presentation cushion, which WBro Hugh had previously presented to the Lodge.

The TMBs still go on tour and for many years the 'Pick and Shovel' song *('When the coal comes from the Rhondda ,,,,,,, I'll be there!')* has been part of their repertoire. It was therefore natural that Wenallt should adopt the song as its Lodge Anthem and it is sung immediately prior to the response to the visitors' Toast at the Festive Board.

A close Fraternal relationship has developed with Dewi Sant Lodge No.9067, Consecrated on 1 March 1983, just three months before Wenallt Lodge's Consecration, on 3 June 1983. As a result, several Brethren have become Joining Members of Cyfrinfa Dewi Sant.

Through the Lodge's connection with the Holy Royal Arch, many of the Brethren have been Exalted into Hiraeth Chapter No.8833, with several progressing to become Principals.

The acorn having been sown, an oak has grown. Whilst Wenallt Lodge might not yet be a mighty oak, it is certainly beyond the sapling stage, having young vigorous growth and deep sturdy roots.

Compiled by WBro A Paul Turner, PPrJGW, assisted by
WBro Geoffrey W Thomas, PSGD, and WBro David C N Franklin, PPrAGReg.

Celtic Eagle Lodge No.9132

Warranted : 12 September 1984

Consecrated : 18 January 1985

Meeting at the Masonic Hall, Port Talbot.

In the autumn of 1983, enquiries were made amongst Freemasons employed by Barclays Bank in South Wales, with regard to forming a 'Bank Lodge', which would serve the Masonic interests of employees who were Freemasons. It was intended that the new Lodge would embrace Membership from the Provinces of Monmouthshire and both the Eastern and Western Divisions of South Wales. Port Talbot was selected as the most convenient place to meet. Dialogue continued for some twelve months, and after alleviating many concerns, a Petition was presented to the Master, Wardens and Brethren of Afan Lodge No.833, on 2 February, 1984.

The name chosen for the new Lodge was 'Celtic Eagle', the Eagle being similar to the emblem of Barclays Bank and Celtic reflecting the Welsh connections. Upon receiving sound advice from senior Provincial Officers, it was decided to maintain an open list for prospective Members. Today, some twelve of the Brethren have Barclays Bank connections. For the first few years discretion was exercised with choice of Ritual. It was found that Brethren used at least three different workings in their Mother Lodges, with many local customs included. Eventually, Celtic Eagle Lodge settled on the Oxford Workings and the Lodge has also developed a few customs particular to the Ritual carried out.

The Lodge was Consecrated on 18 January 1985 by RWBro the Rt Hon the Lord Swansea, DL, ProvGM. The day was marked by the arrival of the first heavy snow of winter. About 50 percent of expected Brethren failed to journey through the snow, especially those from West Wales. Consequently, WBro Sam Northway, AProvGM, kindly agreed to occupy the Chair of SW, and WBro J Stuart Peters, AProvGM, the Chair of JW. WBro Ken Adams Morgan, AProvGM, acted as IG and WBro Cdr Roy Hopkins was the DC. The Installing Master was VWBro Geoffrey M Ashe, DepProvGM.

The first WM was WBro Gareth Whale. He had been Initiated in North Glamorgan Lodge No.4055, in 1965 and was Installed WM of that Lodge in 1976. In Province, he was appointed ProvJGD in 1980 and was promoted to PPrJGW in 1990. Bro William Vaughan was Invested ast SW and Bro Elvan Rees as JW. Bro Bill Vaughan was Installed as WM in 1986 and Bro Elvan Rees was Installed in 1987 and again in 1992. WBro Ken Mabe was appointed Chaplain, WBro Eric Morris Elected Treasurer, W Bro Chris Bates was appointed Secretary and WBro John Richard appointed Director of Ceremonies. The absence of so many Celtic Eagle Brethren gave the newly Installed Master a problem and visiting Brethren helped willingly to fill the vacancies. WBro Ken Adams Morgan, AProvGM, described it as a Merthyr takeover!

The Lodge Banner was Dedicated on 12 March, 1981 by a Provincial team led by VWBro Geoffrey M Ashe, DepProvGM. The evening was well supported by some ninety Brethren. The Banner featured the aforementioned Eagle, with similarity to the Barclays Bank version, and a Welsh Dragon. It was designed, painted and produced by WBro Viv Knowles of Afan Lodge.

In September 1992, WBro Gareth Whale was honoured by United Grand Lodge with the Rank of PAGDC. In 1996, WBro William Porter Vaughan was honoured by United Grand Lodge with the Rank of PGStdB. The Brethren received the news of these appointments with much joy and celebration.

In January 2006, the Lodge celebrated twenty one years since its Consecration. The Brethren were at the same time saddened by the untimely death of Founder WBro William Porter Vaughan in the previous month. During the Lodge Meeting, the newest Member, Bro Robert Nicholls, played music from the Magic Flute by Masonic Brother Wolfgang Amadeus Mozart. The Lodge Brethren also subscribed to the purchase of a set of Working Tools in loving memory and considerable affection for the outstanding skill and leadership shown by WBro Bill in Founding the Lodge.

Despite some setbacks during its history the Lodge continues to prosper under the guidance of WBro Elvan Rees, who has held an Office since the Lodge was Consecrated, together with the help of many other hard working Officers. It continues to play its part with the other Lodges which meet at Afan Masonic Temple, Port Talbot. The Lodge has been fortunate to have had many excellent Worshipful Masters, including three who have filled the Office twice; namely WBro Ieuan Walters, WBro Steven Lewis and WBro Lee Howard. In displaying its usual warmth and friendliness, the Lodge continues to attract new Initiates and many visiting Brethren.

Within four years of Consecration, Celtic Eagle Lodge had welcomed some one thousand visiting Brethren, and the Lodge is pleased to record that a similar level of support has continued. Visiting Brethren and their Ladies also fully support the Ladies' Nights. The Lodge has also been able to support both Masonic and non-Masonic Charitable causes throughout its existence, and Celtic Eagle Brethren also express thanks to their many friends from other Lodges for the excellent support they have always received.

Six Founder Brethren remain Members; namely Bro Geoffrey Evans, WBro Elwyn Moseley, WBro Graham Phillips, WBro John Richard, WBro Elvan Rees and WBro Gareth Whale. Celtic Eagle has also seen an encouraging influx of new and younger Masons and is well supported at Lodge Meetings.

Compiled by WBro Gareth Whale, PAGDC, and WBro Elvan Rees, PPrJGW.

Loyal Sportsman Lodge No.9197

Warranted : 1 May 1986
Consecrated : 29 October 1986
Meeting at the Masonic Hall, Bridgend.

A small group of sporting friends regularly met at Barry Rugby Club to support and encourage the Barry teams. This group of friends, with the foresight, inspiration and zeal of Dai Sam Davies, all equated with the purest ideals of both sport and the Fraternity of Freemasonry. The talk on these occasions was about the enjoyment of sport, the camaraderie amongst sportsmen in general and how it would be an ideal situation if they were able to meet in 'friendly union', on occasions other than on home fixture dates. The most notable amongst the friends was Ronnie Boon, and as the discussion progressed, it soon became apparent that there were amongst the number, fellow Freemasons. When these individuals came together, the talk turned to the formation of a sports' orientated Lodge. Not only did they have enough Past Masters and Brethren to fill the necessary Offices, but there was also a pool of like-minded non-Masons available to recruit.

The name of the new Lodge was debated, with many suggestions made, but these were rejected as being too specific to one particular sport. Eventually, the name 'Loyal Sportsmen Lodge' was agreed, but Provincial Grand Lodge advised that names had to be in the singular and specific, so the name was amended to 'Loyal Sportsman Lodge'.

It was decided to approach Barry Lodge No.2357 to be the Sponsoring lodge, as the majority of the Founders were Members of that Lodge. Sponsorship was gained, the Petition submitted, and the Warrant was granted on 1 May 1986.

The Lodge Insignia, which is incorporated into both the Founders' and the Past Masters' Jewels, is an Olympic flame, surrounded by laurel leaves, which is the universal emblem for sport played in peaceful harmony. The Lodge Motto: *'Audi, Vide, Tace'*, meaning *'Hear, See, be Silent'*, is from the UGLE Coat of Arms of 1815.

The Past Master's Jewel has been designed to replicate the Founders' Jewel, to remind each Past Master of the Founding Principles of the Lodge. Each Jewel is engraved with the name and year of the Past Master to whom it was presented. It is hoped that many of these Jewels will be recycled in future years, and form part of the traditions and furniture of the Lodge.

The presentation of the Petition to Barry Lodge on 11 March 1986 is here described by an extract from that Lodge's Minutes:
Visiting Brethren were admitted and welcomed by the WM, WBro Russell Jones. After the visiting brethren were seated, the Founder Members of the proposed Loyal Sportsman Lodge entered, the three Principal Officers Designate, WBro Ronnie Boon,

PPrSGD, PM of the Old Barrians Lodge No. 6671; WBro Dai Sam Davies, PPrAGStB, PM of the Barry Lodge No. 2357 and WBro Gordon John Watkins, WM of the Old Barrians Lodge No. 6671 remained in the West. WBro Ronnie Boon addressed the Worshipful Master and explained the principles and objectives of the Loyal Sportsman Lodge and asked if the Barry Lodge would support their petition to the Grand Master.

Bro John Wyndham Lemon, SW, proposed and Bro. Neville Terence Batten seconded the proposal that The Barry Lodge supports the Petition, as presented. A ballot was held and Russell Jones, WM, then informed Ronnie Boon and the other Founders present that the ballot was in favour of the Proposition and offered both his good wishes together with those of the Past Masters, Officers and Brethren of the Barry Lodge to the new Lodge. Ronnie Boon then thanked the Worshipful Master and Brethren of the Barry Lodge.

The acting DC, WBro Kenneth George Bennett, then escorted WBro Gordon Watkins, organising Secretary and JW designate, to each of the Principal Officers of the Barry Lodge, who duly signed the Petition.'

The Primus Master, WBro Ronald Boon, known as 'Ronnie' to his friends and colleagues, was one of Welsh Rugby's great characters of the 1930s, whose catch phrase, which he used until his departure for his retirement in Australia, was *'have no fear, Boon is here'*. He played for Wales in the 1930s, with his first match against Scotland, following which he made eleven other appearances, the most notable of which was against England at Twickenham in 1933, scoring a try and a dropped goal to assure a 7 - 3 victory over the 'old enemy', the first time Wales had won at Twickenham. He played his club rugby at Cardiff, where he scored 76 tries in 98 matches and was considered one of the best wingers in Britain at the beginning of his international career. He also made eleven appearances for Glamorgan Cricket Club, and was an outstanding athlete, winning the 200 yards title at the 1929 Welsh Sprint Championships. In 1931, he went to Dunfermline, Fife, to study Physical Education, and then played the majority of his rugby in Scotland. He was invited back to Cardiff to play in their 'big' games and, in 1931, played against the Springboks and scored a try with a scintillating run of 45 yards. In 1933, Ronnie suffered an injury which sidelined him for the season and, partly due to his taking up a teaching post in Scotland, he never played for Wales again. His teaching career encompassed posts in Scotland, London and North Wales, before he returned south to take up the Chair of South Glamorgan Education Committee. Ronnie was also responsible for the musical accompaniment at the Ceremonies, adapting many of the standard 'odes' to be sung to patriotic tunes, such as Calon Lân for the closing hymn. In 1996, Ronnie emigrated to Australia, to spend his final years with his beloved grandchildren but, rugby was never to be far from his mind. He joined the local rugby club and took an active interest in their games. Ronnie is never far from the thoughts of the Brethren of Loyal Sportsman Lodge, as each time we join together to sing within our Ceremonies, his music reminds us of a really great sportsman and a dependable Brother.

WBro David Samuel Davies, affectionately known as 'Dai Sam', had been Initiated into Barry Lodge in November 1957, and attained the Chair of King Solomon in 1972. 'Dai Sam' was one of the prime movers in the formation of Loyal Sportsman Lodge, and was the first SW. He was first elected Master in 1987, and again in 2004. He was a keen supporter of the Lodge from the outset. He proposed a great many of the current Brethren into the Lodge, and has encouraged them to participate in the Ceremonies and enjoy their Masonry to the full. In November 2007, 'Dai Sam' completed fifty years in Freemasonry. He was also a Member and Installed WM of Breaksea Lodge No.8358 in 2002. He was active in many other Degrees within Freemasonry, his greatest love being the Mark and Royal Ark Mariner Degrees, in which Orders he attained Grand Lodge Rank. Regrettably, in 2008, 'Dai Sam' passed to the Grand Lodge Above, and the feeling of loss within the Lodge, his sports clubs and local church was immense. They had all lost a 'true friend'.

WBro Glynne Holmes, Installed WM in 1994, could be called the Past Master who never was! He was placed in the unenviable position by his employer, Barry Town Council, of having to choose between his job and Freemasonry. At that time, many Local Authorities, as well as the Police Force and other government backed organisations, were under the misconception that Freemasonry had an unfavourable influence on its Members, and went against the standards to which their employees were expected to adhere. After a lot of thought and negotiations, WBro Glynne felt bound to resign from the Lodge, and he didn't even complete his year as Master. The Provincial Office ruled that his name could not be included on the Lodge's Past Masters' Board.

Part of the traditions established at the Foundation of the Lodge was that the February Meeting be designated as 'Founders' Night' and that the Festive Board must have a 'sports' theme, with an invited guest to deliver a talk on his particular sport. Over the years, the Lodge has invited a number of notable guest speakers as well as Brethren from within the Lodge to talk about their love of sport. Amongst the guest speakers have been the world boxing champion, Jack Peterson; the Olympic athlete, Dame Tanni Grey Thompson; and the Welsh Olympic archery coach, Digby Mansel Edwards, to name but a few. Other speakers have told fascinating stories from sports commentating, motor sports, professional cycling, sailing before the mast, rugby, etc.

On Founders' Night in 1999, to celebrate the 1999 Rugby World Cup, visiting Masonic rugby supporters from around the world were invited to attend a Second Degree Ceremony, during which the ProvGM, the Rt Hon the Lord Swansea, gave an explanation of the Second Degree Tracing Board. This was a proud moment and a highlight, not only for the Candidate, but also for the WM, WBro Derek Peplow, who organised the celebration.

Following a number of lean years, the Lodge is at last on the way up, thanks mainly to 'Dai Sam' Davies, who spent hours extolling the virtues of Freemasonry in general and the benefits of the Loyal Sportsman Lodge in particular. Due to his efforts and with the assistance of the rest of the PMs, the Lodge has built up a reputation, both for the high standard of its Ceremonies and an entertaining Festive Board.

The Lodge owes a deep debt of gratitude to Barry Lodge, as Sponsoring Lodge, for supporting the Founders and assisting in many of the organisational tasks required to bring Loyal Sportsman Lodge into existence, Thanks also go to the Founder Brethren of the Lodge and the Barry Rugby Club members, who were the catalyst for the Lodge, with Ronald (Ronnie) Boon, Primus Master; David Samuel (Dai Sam), Davies, first SW; and Gordon Watkins, first JW. These two Wardens became the second and third WMs of the Lodge, and subsequently filled various other Offices. True appreciation must be accorded to WBro Arwel Powell, whose administrative skills ensured the Consecration Meeting was so successful.

Compiled by WBro S G Evans, PPrGReg.

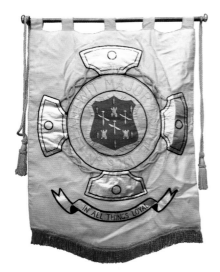

Llantwit Major Lodge No.9241

Warranted : 30 April 1987

Consecrated : 16 October 1987

Meeting at Llantonian Hall, Boverton, Llantwit Major.

The Founding of a Lodge in the Vale of Glamorgan town of Llantwit Major was largely due to the inspiration of WBro M D M Thomas, known to all as 'Mel'. He had been Installed as WM of Porthkerry Lodge No.6299 in 1981. First appointed a Grand Officer in 1992, with the Rank of PGStB, he was promoted in 2004 to PAGDC. His intention was to provide a Lodge for the use of the many Freemasons already resident in the town and its locality, and to attract new Members from this area.

There had previously been an attempt to establish a Lodge at Llantwit Major in the early 1970s. This resulted in the formation of Llanilltud Fawr Lodge No.8644, Warranted 12 February 1975. Due to the lack of suitable premises in Llantwit Major, a recurring theme in this history, Llanilltud Fawr Lodge has always met in Porthcawl.

A series of preliminary meetings were convened early in 1987, at which the first Officers were proposed, with Mel Thomas as Primus Master; WBro Gordon D Sweeting as SW Designate; and WBro M Rees Evans, as JW Designate. Porthkerry Lodge agreed to Sponsor the Petition, and the Llantwit Major Town Council agreed the use of the town's Coat of Arms for the Lodge Badge, which is set inside a Celtic Cross. Underneath is the Lodge Motto: *'In All Things Loyal'*. The Master Elect presented his team of Officers, which included Rev Dyfrig Lewis as Chaplain, and Bro D S Price (Dai) as Tyler. Sadly, both these great characters have now passed to the Grand Lodge Above. By-laws were agreed and the annual subscription set at £25.

Llantwit Major Lodge was Consecrated at the Masonic Temple, Barry, on Friday, 16 October 1987, with RWBro the Rt Hon the Lord Swansea, DL, ProvGM, as the Consecrating Officer.

Initially, Lodge Meetings were held in a former oast-house, at the rear of The White Lion Hotel, East Street, Llantwit Major, from November 1987 until September 1999. Since the oast-house was used for public purposes as well as Lodge Meetings, the Temple furniture was assembled immediately prior to the Meeting, and packed away again when the Meeting finished. In its place, dining tables were assembled prior to the enjoyment of the Festive Board. Although this practice entailed much hard work for both Members and visiting Brethren alike, this unusual and rustic venue proved very popular with all, and the room was often full to capacity.

Sadly, due to increasing difficulties with the Hotel management during 1999, an alternative venue had to be sought. Directly across the street from the White Lion Hotel was a building known as Compton House, which traded as a restaurant by day. This was where the Lodge found its new home, and the first Meeting was held there in November 1999. Once again, the Masonic Meetings and Festive Board took place in the one room, which required the same work in assembling, dismantling and storing of furniture. This situation again proved successful, and Lodge Meetings were enjoyed at Compton House until June 2002. In 2002, the proprietor of Compton House made arrangements with another restaurateur to utilize the premises as an Indian restaurant. The new business would occupy the building by night and day, so once again a new venue had to be found.

During 2002, negotiations were held with the management of the Llantwit Major Social Club. The Club had been in decline for many years, and was keen to receive the Lodge's custom and an extra forty plus new Club members. This resulted in a five year lease being drawn up, allowing the Lodge the use of a disused room on the top floor of the building. The room had been neglected for many years and required a great deal of refurbishment. This included lighting, heating, painting and decorating and equipping the room to act as a permanent Temple. In addition, emergency lighting and fire safety measures had to be installed as a condition of occupancy. In order to accomplish these requirements, time and effort were provided by the Members, who also freely donated the necessary finances. This meant that by September 2002, for the first time in the Lodge's history, it had a purpose built Temple that did not have to double-up as a dining room. The Lodge's 'bijou' Temple at the Social Club could hold no more than 55 people, so it appeared full on many occasions. Three more years passed, but unbeknown to the Lodge Members, the Social Club had amassed large debts, which resulted in the electricity supply being cut off. As a result of their financial situation, the Social Club closed, and with it the Lodge's occupancy ceased.

For the next year, the Lodge became itinerant and met in a number of local Masonic Halls, such as Bridgend and Barry, but most often in the Cowbridge Town Hall. This was probably due to the fact that the Members missed carting furniture about, a necessary task in Cowbridge. The inconvenience of this situation did not diminish the enthusiasm of the Lodge Members, but visiting Brethren had to be alert to find the Lodge!

Since November 2006, the Lodge has been re-established in Llantwit Major. The Meetings are now held in Llantonian Hall, a Community Hall situated at the rear of Llantwit Major Rugby Club car park. The Festive Board is undertaken at the Rugby Club. Once again, the Temple has to be assembled before the Meeting takes place, and disassembled upon completion. As there are no storage facilities at Llantonian Hall, the Lodge furniture is transported to the Hall prior to Meetings taking place, and taken away again following the Meeting.

The first twenty years of the Lodge have been challenging and great fun for the staunch and resourceful Lodge Members, who have had to overcome many obstacles. Optimistically, it is hoped that the Lodge can continue to meet in Llantwit Major and offer visiting Brethren a unique experience,

WBro Roger Edward Walden Andrews, Initiated in Crystal Lodge No.8713 in 1978, but resigned in 1983, became a Joining Member in 1994. He was Installed as Master in 2000, serving that Office for two successive years, and is currently the Lodge Secretary. On 13 May 2011, he was invited to take the Chair of King Solomon, and had the pleasure of Initiating his son, Richard, into the Lodge. Roger, a renowned sculptor was commissioned by the WRU to sculpt a statue of the late Sir Tasker Watkins, VC, a war hero who became an eminent Judge and also President of the WRU. Sir Tasker had been a Member of South Wales Jurists' Lodge No.7092, 1951-1961. The statue now stands at the entrance to the Millennium Stadium in Cardiff and was unveiled by his daughter, Lady Mair Griffith-Williams on 15 November 2009.

Compiled by WBro R J Williams, PPrGStB.

Adare Lodge
No. 9247

Warranted : 10 June 1987

Consecrated : 6 November 1987

Meeting at the Masonic Hall, Bridgend.

The first Bridgend Masonic Temple was founded in 1891 and was situated in Adare Street, Bridgend. The Foundation Stone was laid by VWBro Marmaduke Tennant, DepProvGM. By the 1980s, the Temple was becoming too small, and when parking restrictions were implemented along with limited access, it became clear that a new venue and Temple had to be found.

Shortly after the sad news that the Temple would close, a group of Past Masters, along with a group of developers, got together to find an alternative site. Land became available on the present site, Coychurch Road, Bridgend, and plans for a new Masonic Temple were drawn up. With the prospect of wonderful new facilities and ample parking, the building work began. The Foundation Stone was laid by RWBro the Rt Hon the Lord Swansea, DL, ProvGM, on Tuesday, 1 April 1986, using the same Trowel that was used to lay the Foundation Stone for the Old Temple in 1891. This Trowel is now displayed in a glass case, situated above the visitors' book in the New Temple.

In 1986, whilst the new Temple was being constructed, a number of Brethren from various Lodges expressed an interest in forming a new Lodge, which would ease the waiting time for those Brethren anxious to progress in the Craft. It would also enable many more Brethren to participate specifically and generally in the life of the new Lodge. Further, it would provide for a greater and much needed financial contribution to the new Temple, Masonic Charities and Freemasonry in general.

A meeting was convened in June 1986 for those interested in Founding a new Lodge, and a Steering Committee was formed. By January 1987, planning had reached an advanced stage and the blessing and support of the Province had been received. At the suggestion of VWBro Geoffrey Malin Ashe, DepProvGM, Ogmore Lodge No.1752 was asked to Sponsor the new Lodge. At a separate meeting, Ogmore Lodge agreed to the Sponsorship, therefore becoming the Mother Lodge. The old Masonic Temple in Adare Street had been the home of Freemasonry in the Bridgend area for well over a hundred years, so to commemorate this connection, the new Lodge was named 'Adare Lodge'.

Because of the long history of Lord Dunraven's ancestors with the name Adare, it was decided to seek the permission of the present Lord Dunraven to allow his family Coat of Arms to be incorporated into the design of the Lodge Banner. (The Earl of Dunraven and Mount-Earl is styled Viscount Adare.) Permission was granted, thus, the Banner bears the Dunraven Coat of

Arms, a replicate of Dunraven Castle along with a raven, which of course alludes to Lord Dunraven. The Motto, in Latin, *'Quae Sursun Volo Videre'*, translates literally as *'I wish to see that which is above'*, or *'I wish to see heavenly things'*. An alternative interpretation is: *'That To Which I Aspire Is On High'*. The Banner was made by a seamstress from Bridgend, and was Dedicated on 5 April 1991. The Banner was presented to Adare Lodge by the late WBro Hubert Charles Martin.

At a meeting on 2 September 1987, it was announced that the Consecration Ceremony would take place at 3.30 pm on Friday, 6 November 1987. It was also announced that the Lodge number would be 9247, and that £80 was to be forwarded by the Treasurer to Grand Lodge for the preparation of the Warrant of Constitution (which was granted during the Consecration Ceremony). Also at this meeting, it was reported by WBro Peter Williams that a whisky tumbler, engraved with the Lodge name and date of Consecration, would be given to each Brother attending the Festive Board. Additional tumblers would be obtained to be given to future Initiates and Joining Members.

The Consecration Ceremony took place on 6 November as announced, and was conducted by the RWBro the Rt Hon the Lord Swansea, DL, ProvGM, accompanied by his Provincial Officers. The Installing Master, VWBro Geoffrey M Ashe, TD, PGSwdB, DepProvGM, was assisted by WBro Ken Adams Morgan PSGD, AProvGM; WBro Samuel Northway, PSGD, AProvGM; WBro J Stuart Peters, PSGD, AProvGM; and WBro Cdr Roy K Hopkin, RN, PAGDC. WBro Thomas H Pugh, WM Designate, was duly Installed as the first WM. Bro H C Martin was Invested as SW and Bro H Lloyd was Invested as JW. WBro R Hart was appointed acting IPM; WBro P Williams, PPrGStwd, was Invested as Chaplain; Bro B Davies was Elected as Treasurer and the first Secretary was WBro K Roberts.

Adare Lodge uses the Oxford Ritual with no deviation from text. The Mandated Officer is WBro J Andrew McCutcheon, PGStB. The Lodge is also linked to Adare Chapter No.9247, which was Consecrated in the Bridgend Temple on 14 September 1993.

In 1994, WBro Norman J Davies, WM, conducted the Ceremony of Installing WBro Billy Riddler, SW, who went on to Install his co-associate, WBro Eric Hiscocks. They were the first Initiates of the Lodge. Both Brethren had gone through their Masonic careers together.

Although Adare Lodge has a short history compared with most other Lodges, its ideals and charitable contributions are second to none. During the calendar year, various functions are carried out, including a Ladies' Night. During these events, visiting Brethren from near and far are received with a warm welcome from the WM, and are made to feel part of a very special evening. All this is to raise money for various charities, local and otherwise.

Compiled by WBro Norman J Davies, PPrSGD, and Bro Mark D Goodridge.

South Wales Clerics' Lodge No. 9298

Warranted : 14 September 1988

Consecrated : 7 April 1989

Meeting at the Masonic Hall, Port Talbot.

Any student of history will know events occur for a variety of reasons. Sometimes there is social pressure, sometimes there is a righteous cause and sometimes there is anger and frustration at being misunderstood. Such were the beginnings of South Wales Clerics' Lodge.

The main stream Churches had throughout the years found no conflict with what their male members did in their Masonic Lodges and what they expected of them on a Sunday. Many Clergy were prominent and recognizable Freemasons, both on the national scene and in the Provinces throughout the land. Bishops and Archbishops were Grand Chaplains and the majority of Lodges had Clergy as their Chaplains. This close association was free of suspicion and distrust and had an element of mutual support about it. Clergy found Freemasonry a natural outlet for men of faith, based as it is on Biblical precepts and stories, and with its sense of due order, but with the advantage of being outside the formal church environment. In the late sixties and seventies all this began to change.

What brought about the change is difficult to chart accurately. Did society as a whole need to find scapegoats for all its ills, and what better place to look than at a so called 'secret society'? The Church likewise followed suit. Clergy were now being actively discouraged from being Freemasons and less than subtle hints were dropped that promotions and appointments could, and would be, compromised by an association with the Craft. But the pressures ran deeper than that. Many Clergy were lampooned and ridiculed for being Freemasons, while the question of lack of orthodox belief, thought to be inherent in being a Freemason, was never far away and was personally destructive to those who had given a life time of service in the cause of the Christian Gospel.

It was obvious to a few Clergy that something had to be done to show firstly, that there was no conflict between orthodox Christian belief and Masonic ideals, and secondly the need for embattled Clergy to find a place to mutually support each other in their quest to maintain the age long association between the Church and Freemasonry.

This was the background that gave rise to the formation of South Wales Clerics' Lodge. Ironically, the idea first began to germinate during a Clergy School held by the Diocese of Llandaff in the University of Exeter back in the early eighties. Two clergy at the School, the Rev Norman Lea and the Rev Bob Jones, both Freemasons, became more and more determined in the face of so much unfair and unfounded hostility, to do something about it. They had the support of a quite remarkable man, who was both a deeply committed Churchman and an outstanding Freemason – the late WBro Malcolm Thompson, who at the time just happened to be the Provincial Grand Secretary and a Churchwarden.

Malcolm embraced the idea of a Clerics' Lodge with typical enthusiasm and drive. The ProvGM, RWBro the Rt Hon the Lord Swansea, eagerly supported the prospect of a Clerics' Lodge without a second thought, and offered his wholehearted and unflinching encouragement. The groundwork needed to Found such a Lodge was undertaken by Malcolm, but before anything could get off the ground officially, Clergy willing and able to join had to be found. The most obvious first step was to approach the most senior Clergyman and Freemason in the Province, WBro Rev Canon Thomas Kenneth Brunsdon. He had been Initiated in Teme Lodge No.4267, Knighton, Province of Shropshire, in November 1940, and was Installed as WM in 1955. He was a Member of Loyal Wye Lodge No.1807, Edgar Rutter Lodge No.7196, and a Founder Member of Lodge of Progress No.7928, where he was Installed WM in 1970. He served as ProvGChap, Province of Shropshire 1964-1967, and in 1967 he was appointed ProvSGW.

At first, strange though it now seems, Ken was not all that enthusiastic. His long and distinguished association with Freemasonry was in some ways an obstacle to him fully appreciating the need for such a Lodge as South Wales Clerics'. Those of us who were privileged to know Ken also knew how to handle him, and so with subtle and not so subtle argument and discussion, he finally accepted the need for such a Lodge and consented to become its first WM.

Once Ken was on board, the task of finding enough Clergy Freemasons to establish a functioning Lodge was made a great deal easier. Ernest Brown, SW Designate; Alun Petty, JW Designate; John Workman, Denzil and Huw Mosford, Dafydd Edwards, Don Lewis, Mostyn Williams, Roy Luther Thomas, to name but a few were approached and all agreed to become Founder Members of this new Lodge. We were able to draw prospective Members from the three South Wales Provinces and thus offered Clergy, who were Freemasons, the opportunity to enjoy Masonic fellowship without recrimination or embarrassment. It looked as if the Founding of the Lodge was slowly becoming a reality. The next major question, where was it going to meet? From the very outset, the Brethren in Port Talbot had offered unconditional support, and the decision for the new Lodge to meet there has never been regretted. The Lodge of St Theodore No.8356 agreed to be the Sponsoring Lodge and the Petition for South Wales Clerics' Lodge was duly signed at the Lodge's Regular Meeting on 16 May 1988. That initial support and encouragement has never faltered over the years; it has in many ways become stronger. New Freemasons in Port Talbot carry on where their predecessors left off and give, without question, their support to South Wales Clerics' Lodge.

There were 15 Petitioners, and when the Petition was submitted to Grand Lodge, the supporting letter stated: *'It is not intended, at this stage, to admit Candidates for Initiation. It is intended that the Meetings, other than the Installation will be used to receive appropriate lectures and to promote discussion. So there can be no suggestion that the Lodge is being used as a means of recruiting Members of the Clergy.'*

The Lodge was Consecrated on 7 April 1989 by RWBro the Rt Hon the Lord Swansea, DL, ProvGM, assisted by WBro C H Rapport, MBE, PJGD, ProvSGW, as SW; WBro E Williams, ProvJGW, as JW; VWBro Rev Canon Richard Tydeman, OSM, PGChap, as Chaplain; WBro M H Thompson, PJGD ProvGSec, as Secretary; and WBro D L Protheroe, PAGDC, ProvGDC, as DC. The four AProvGMs, WBros Ken Adams Morgan, PSGD; Samuel Northway, PSGD; J Stuart Peters, PSGD and Cdr Roy K Hopkin, RN, PSGD, were also in attendance. The Consecration completed, the DepProvGM, VWBro Geoffrey M Ashe, TD, PGSwdB, Installed the Master Designate, the Rev Canon T K Brunsdon, PDepGChap. WBro Rev Ernest Harry Brown, MBE, OStJ, ProvGChap, from Swansea, was Invested as SW. Initiated in Dr James Griffith Hall Lodge No.3161, in 1975, he was PM Cape St Vincent Lodge No.8524. Rev Alun John Petty, of Baglan, Port Talbot, Initiated in Sapphire Lodge No.5290, in 1974, was Invested as JW. WBro Rev Chancellor Ilar Roy Luther Jones, PProvGChap, of Swansea, was Invested as Chaplain. Initiated in Ithon Lodge No.3320, he was PM Teme Lodge No.4267, Knighton, and PM Lodge of Progress No.7928. WBro Rev Robert William Aplin Jones, PProvGChap, Rector of Cowbridge, was the first Secretary. Initiated in Bute Lodge No.960, Installed WM in 1979, he was also PM Old Cantonians Lodge No.8875. The Ceremonies of Consecration and Installation were followed by a sumptuous banquet held at the dining room of the Masonic Temple, Forge Road, Port Talbot. The annual subscription at the beginning was £25.00.

Clerics' Lodge lost its first WM in late 2003, on the death of WBro the Rev Canon Kenneth Thomas Brunsdon, a former Vicar of Llandegley, Builth and St Peters Church, Newton, Swansea, and former Canon of Brecon Cathedral. He took his leave of this world peacefully at Albert Edward Prince of Wales Court, Porthcawl, on Monday, 22 December 2003 after a short illness. He was distinguished in Freemasonry as Past Deputy Grand Chaplain of the UGLE and Past Deputy Grand Superintendent of the Province of South Wales Eastern Division in the Royal Arch.

Another man and Mason, amongst many, who has left his mark on Clerics' Lodge is the Rev Huw Mosford, PSGD, PProvAGM, WM in 1994. Vicar of St Mary's Church, Clydach, 1986-1996; Vicar of St Catherine's Church, Gorseinon, 1996-2009; he has also worked in Ystalyfera and in Luca, Jamaica. Huw left South Wales to take up a new role in London, as Director of Chaplaincy of Ministry for the Mission to Seafarers, in January 2010.

Mention must also be made of Rev Alistair Swinford, PAGChap, who joined South Wales Clerics' Lodge in 1994, becoming WM in 2004. He is currently Lodge Almoner and Charity Steward, was appointed AProvGChap 1992-1993 and 2006, ProvGChap in 2007, and PAGChap in 2010. Another man and Mason of the Lodge who must be mentioned, despite his modesty and feeling that he need not be so highlighted, is the Rev Norman Lea, PDepGChap and PAProvGM. Installed WM of Clerics' Lodge in 2005, he was the first Lodge Treasurer. Initiated in Aberhonddu Lodge No.8588, in 1978, he was Installed as WM in 1984. In Province, he was appointed ProvGChap in 1989. In 1992, he was asked to contribute to the Conference held at Freemasons' Hall, in celebration of the 275th Anniversary of the Founding of Grand Lodge. The Provincial Church Service to mark the 250th Anniversary was held at his Church, St Theodore's, Port Talbot. He is still a very active Member, and affectionately regarded and respected throughout the Province of South Wales, as indeed he remains thus by former Parishioners of his Church, St Catwg's in Cadoxton, Neath, from which he retired in 2010.

What then, has been the contribution of South Wales Clerics' Lodge to Freemasonry in this Province? It has never been, nor will it ever be, numerically a large Lodge, yet its very existence speaks volumes in the debate about Freemasonry and Christianity. In a purely outward and visible contribution to the Province, it has provided it with two Assistant Provincial Grand Masters and five Grand Lodge Officers, a Deputy Grand Superintendent plus a galaxy of Provincial Grand Chaplains both in this Province and in the other Provinces.

Perhaps the greatest contribution of Clerics' Lodge has been its unique character as a Lodge solely for those Ordained into the Ministry of the main stream churches, and to make the outward and visible sign that those commissioned to preach the Christian Gospel see no conflict with their association or their relationship with Freemasonry. Long may that outward and visible sign continue.

Compiled by WBro Rev D Brian Thomas, PPrJGW (SWED), PrGChap (SWWD), and WBro Rev Norman Lea, PDepGrandChap, PProvAGM.

Roy Keith Hopkin

Deputy Provincial Grand Master
1992 - 1998

VWBro Roy K Hopkin has led a very interesting and active life, both inside and outside Freemasonry. A born leader, he has proved inspirational in every sphere in which he has become involved.

Roy Keith Hopkin was born in 1929, in the Canton area of Cardiff. Educated at Cathays High School for Boys, he became Head Boy, 1946-1947, and captained the School at rugby, cricket and athletics. In 1948, he obtained a scholarship to Dartmouth Royal Naval College, where he commenced his long and distinguished career in the Royal Navy. Initially, he served on the training cruiser HMS Devonshire, then on HMS Illustrious as a Midshipman. It was not long before he was promoted to the rank of Lieutenant, after which he spent two years in South East Asia involved in the Korean conflict. Later he became a Staff Officer at Plymouth, and achieved further sporting distinction by playing rugby for the Navy against the most prominent first class clubs of the time, including Llanelli, Cardiff and Newport. After a spell in Sri Lanka there were further tours of duty, which took him to other exotic places such as Hawaii, Fiji, Tahiti and Panama. After becoming Secretary to Michael Le Fanu, who only a little later was Knighted and became Admiral of the Fleet, Roy went on to do service in Londonderry, where he was Supply Officer. Somewhat nearer home for a change, there was a spell at Brawdy. He completed 25 years of distinguished Naval Service as Fleet Security Officer under Commander-in-Chief Fleet, at Northwood.

VWBro Roy Keith Hopkin

Meanwhile, VWBro Roy had been Initiated into Tennant Lodge No.1992 on 10 April, 1952. He was proposed by his father, Bro William Thomas Hopkin, who was later Installed as WM of the Lodge in 1963. As a serving Officer in the Royal Navy and serving in Korea, he was not Passed until 2 July 1954 at a Lodge of Emergency, and was Raised at another Lodge of Emergency held on 30 July that same year. He rose through all the Offices to become WM in 1971. His first Provincial Collar was that of Acting ProvAGDC in 1977. He was promoted to DepProvGDC in 1978 and, in 1981, achieved real distinction when he was again promoted to ProvGDC.

However, he had not been altogether happy at being retired and, now in civilian life, in 1975 he took on the onerous post of Bursar at

Monkton House School. He says that he spent 17 very happy though challenging years at the School, during which time they took over new premises – a major headache for a School Bursar!

In his Masonic career, he was likewise extremely active, quite apart from his literally Active Offices in the late 1970s. Whilst WM in his Mother Lodge, he became a Founder Member of his School's Lodge, Ymlaen No.8419 in 1971, playing a prominent part in taking that forward. Then, in 1980, he played a large part in the Founding of another School Lodge, Old Monktonians No.8938. This occurred within months of him being similarly involved in the Founding of Llanfair Chapter No.7353.

In United Grand Lodge, the Grand Master was pleased to appoint him Acting AGDC in 1982. In 1988, immediately following his appointment as AProvGM, he was promoted to PSGD. Having absorbed both the feeling and needs of the Province in carrying out his many active rolls, this appointment also marked his most creative period right into the early 1990s. He was then appointed to succeed VWBro Geoffrey M Ashe as DepProvGM, subsequently being promoted to PGSwdB. This was also the year that Roy became WM of Hendre Lodge No.3250.

In 1989, a new Masonic Charity was created and chaired by Roy. Based at Cardiff Masonic Hall, it was called 'Masonic Feed the Homeless', and has flourished and grown over the years. Towards the end of 2008 the Charity was replicated in Swansea and that has also proved successful. Both are continually looking for ways to ease the pain of the single homeless in the region. That same year began the Christmas Party for less fortunate children, inspired and organised by Roy. This event continues to this day and has been copied all over the Province. Then, after currying support over a period of time, the new Provincial Magazine, 'The Guildford Gazette' was 'born' in January 1993. That too has flourished and has grown into a real presence, not only in the Province, but throughout Freemasonry in England and Wales. It was renamed 'Y Dalaith' in January 2007.

Apart from achieving distinction in Royal Arch Chapter, Mark Masonry, Royal Ark Mariners and Rose Croix, VWBro Roy was Editor of the Masonic Year Book, a Member of the Royal Masonic Institution for Girls and Boys, a Member of the Appeals Committee of the Royal Masonic Hospital, President of Cardiff and Caerphilly Good Neighbours and Chairman of the Masonic Housing Association. Interestingly, Roy was also concurrently Chairman of the Wales National Festival of Remembrance and Cardiff Masonic Hall Company, during which time it was a common feature for those involved in the Festival, often numbering 400, to dine at the Masonic Hall.

It was with sadness and very deep regret that VWBro Roy felt it necessary, for very personal reasons, to resign his post as Deputy Provincial Grand Master in 1998. It was indeed equally sad for the Brethren of the Province. He will always be remembered for his sincerity, his involvement and his leadership.

Compiled by WBro Brian E Langley, PGStB, ProvSGW.

Yr Efail Lodge No.9502

Warranted : 10 February 1993

Consecrated : 21 June 1993

Meeting at the Masonic Hall, Pontyclun.

A casual remark one evening, during the Festive Board in the winter of 1980, at Talygarn Lodge No.7216, led to the formation of Yr Efail Lodge No.9502. Several Brethren present were former pupils of Tonyrefail Grammar School and WBro Dilwyn Enoch, who had been WM of St Gwynno Lodge No.8599 in 1984, was asked to make tentative enquiries as to whether a new Lodge would be viable. It could not be a 'closed' Lodge restricted to the former pupils of the school and, therefore, Brethren living in Tonyrefail, or who had links with the village, were invited to attend meetings to ascertain the feasibility of establishing such a Lodge.

The appeal aroused great interest among the Brethren, and after convincing the ProvGM that a new Lodge would be viable, work began in earnest, with WBro Dilwyn Enoch undertaking the task of Petitioning Secretary. He was subsequently nominated to become the first WM of the Lodge, with Bros Raymond Bishop and Ivor Stuckey being SW and JW respectively. Although Talygarn Lodge was initially suggested as the Sponsoring Lodge, it was in fact, St Gwynno Lodge that assumed that honour.

The process took almost two years, the Warrant being finally granted on 10 February 1993. The Lodge was due to be Consecrated by RWBro the Rt Hon the Lord Swansea, on 17 May 1993. Tragedy, however, struck just two days before the Ceremony, when Janice, the wife of the Master Elect passed away unexpectedly. The Consecration Ceremony was therefore postponed for five weeks. This will explain the anomaly of Saint Catherine's Lodge No.9503 being Consecrated on Monday, 17 May, before Yr Efail Lodge No.9502, which was Consecrated on Monday, 21 June 1993.

Bro Colin Edwards presented the Lodge with several ornaments linking Yr Efail with local history. A miniature anvil, a miner's lamp and the last piece of coal mined from the Coedely Colliery, Tonyrefail (closed 28 November 1986), now grace the top table at every Festive Board. These objects remind the Brethren of 'Ton-yr-Efail', the mining village from which the Lodge name is derived. Mr John Williams, Teacher of Welsh at Tonyrefail Grammar School, used to emphasise to his pupils that the name, 'Ton-yr-Efail', may be translated as 'The Sound of the Smithy' or even as 'Waves of the Anvil'.

At the first Regular Meeting, held in September, a large number of Joining Members were admitted. Also, at that Meeting, the Lodge Initiated its first Candidates, Bros Nicholas Cocco and Colin Smith. WBro Nicholas is the son of WBro Sabatino (Gino)

Cocco. Both Brethren have distinguished themselves as Masters of Yr Efail Lodge, Gino in 1997 and Nicholas in 2000. WBro Nicholas was subsequently promoted to PPrDepGDC.

The Lodge Banner was designed and painted by Founder Member, WBro Sidney Robling, PPrDepGDC. The Banner, painted in the traditional manner of earlier Banners, was completed in readiness for the Regular Meeting in May 1996. WBro Sid Robling was a part-time teacher of sign writing and design at Bridgend Technical College, his speciality being Heraldic Work. He is now the senior Past Master of the Lodge and became the second WM in 1994, instead of Bro Ray Bishop, SW, who died from cancer before realising his dream. In 2007, Sid became a Grand Officer with the Rank of PAGDC. His description of the Banner design is as follows: *'The Charge of the Banner is Anvil Argent on a field Vert which represents the town of Tonyrefail, and is symbolic of the Lodge. The Smithy is reputed to have played an important part in the capture of Edward II at Pant-Y-Brad near Tonyrefail, and the horseshoe theme is continued on the super-scroll. At the apex of the scroll containing the name of the Lodge is the 'All Seeing Eye' within a Square d'or and Compasses argent. Its position at the zenith reminds us that the Great Architect of the Universe is central and Supreme to our Order.'*

Edward II is reputed to have hidden in an oak tree to avoid capture and this is represented by a tree inset with the Plantagenet Crown surmounting the anvil. Dexter and sinister Badges of daffodils refer to the Welsh connection of Edward II as Prince of Wales. The inscription *'Nid Dysg Heb Foes'*, which means *'No Learning without Culture'* is taken directly from the Motto of the Tonyrefail Grammar School, the Alma Mater, or place of work, of many Lodge Members. The scrolls of the Banner are predominantly green and white, suggesting former school uniform colours.

A translation of the Public Records document relating to the capture of Edward II states: *'In the year of our Lord 1326, on 16 November, on the Feast of St Edmund, the Archbishop; a great storm arose in the middle of the night and continued for the whole of the next day, with horrible thunder and lightning, rain and hail, accompanied by a vehement howling wind. And the same day the Lord King Edward, who was a fugitive in Wales, was captured by the Welsh and taken to the castle at Llantrisant near to Neath in Wales. The Lord Hugh Dispenser, the Younger, was captured close by hiding in a small wood. Also Robert de Baldock, the King's Chancellor, Lord Thomas Withers and John of Beck, Knights J le Bennet, T le Smale, B Holdene, Simon of Reading and numerous others were captured and taken to Hereford.'*

The captives were taken first to Llantrisant Castle from whence the King was subsequently taken to Berkley Castle, where, after being forced to abdicate he was put to death in a particularly horrific manner.

Near Tonyrefail is situated the tiny hamlet of Pant-y-Brad, which translates as *'The Hollow of Treachery'* or *'The Hollow of the Betrayal'*. According to popular belief it was near this place Edward II was discovered hiding in that tree. Contemporary chronicles disagree about the precise location of Edward's capture.

The Banner Dedication took place on 23 May 1996 and was performed by VWBro Cdr Roy Hopkin RN, PGSwdB, DepProvGM. The Banner was borne into the Lodge by WBro Ivor Stuckey, WBro Sid Robling's brother-in-law, and who succeeded him as the third WM of Yr Efail Lodge.

Compiled by WBro Dilwyn G Enoch, PPrJGW.

Saint Catherine's Lodge No. 9503

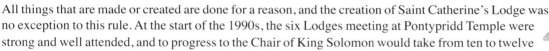

Warranted : 10 February 1993

Consecrated : 17 May 1993

Meeting at the Masonic Hall, Pontypridd.

All things that are made or created are done for a reason, and the creation of Saint Catherine's Lodge was no exception to this rule. At the start of the 1990s, the six Lodges meeting at Pontypridd Temple were strong and well attended, and to progress to the Chair of King Solomon would take from ten to twelve years. While acknowledging that progression through every Office gives one more fulfilment as a Mason, there were Brethren, who had been Masons for ten to twenty years, who had not progressed due to family, health or work commitments. For such Brethren to start progressing from the bottom was not always acceptable. There were also young Past Provincial Officers who felt at a loose end for, in most Lodges, Offices such as Secretary or Treasurer were occupied for long periods.

Three of the Past Masters of Craig-yr-Hesg Lodge No.6724, having discussed over a period of time, the possibility of forming a new Lodge, now agreed to find out what support there would be for such a venture. The response was immediate and, with confidence they approached WBro Henry J Mars, who was a Grand Lodge Officer and a much respected Mason, to be the first Master of the new Lodge.

The next step was to agree to a name for the Lodge, and accepting that the Founder Brethren came from all districts around Pontypridd, it was considered more acceptable to have a name associated with the area. The choice fell to the prominent Parish Church in the centre of the town, namely Saint Catherine's. To ensure that it was in order to name the new Lodge 'Saint Catherine's', the PProvGSec, WBro Malcolm H Thompson, was approached and he informed the Founder Members that this name was acceptable as there were already a number of Lodges named Catherine. (Note – the name of the Pontypridd Lodge is written as 'Saint Catherine's Lodge', and not 'St Catherine's Lodge', according to the Warrant and the UGLE Directory of Lodges & Chapters, and is the only such named Lodge under the UGLE, though St Catherine's is used on the Lodge Banner.)

Before a new Lodge can be formed it must have a Sponsor and Craig-yr-Hesg Lodge No.6724 was approached, and the Petition signed on Thursday, 4 June 1992. Grand Lodge accepted the Petition and No.9503 was allocated to Saint Catherine's Lodge.

The twenty nine Founders met to establish the number of Meetings to be held each year, the dress code and to formulate the

By-laws. The latter would be based on those of the Sponsoring Lodge, Craig-yr-Hesg. All Toasts, whenever possible, would be formal ones. In keeping with tradition, every Founder Brother donated his Collar to the Lodge. The Merlin Masonic Hall Company was then approached by the Founder Brethren, who requested permission to use the Pontypridd Masonic Temple for the Meetings. This was agreed.

When it had been established that a new Lodge was being formed in the Pontypridd Temple, the six existing Lodges between them presented the new Lodge with Entered Apprentice and Fellow-Craft Aprons, Wands and a comprehensive set of cased Working Tools, which was made by Bro A Wall. When combined with the Regalia provided by the Founder Brethren, the new Lodge was in the position of being able to perform all the Ceremonies.

The Warrant of the Lodge was signed on 10 February 1993, and the Consecration Ceremony took place on 17 May 1993, under the direction of the RWBro the Rt Hon the Lord Swansea, DL, ProvGM. The first Master was WBro Henry J Mars, MBE, DL, PAGDC, PProvJGW, who was Installed by VWBro Cdr R K Hopkin, RN, PGSwdB, DepProvGM.

The Consecrating Ceremony was also attended by two Ruling Masters of other St Catherine Lodges; unfortunately, their names are not known.

The first milestone in the Lodge's history was the Dedication of a Banner, donated by WBro Dr Vad Bali. On the Banner is a depiction of St Catherine's Church, with the Lodge Motto: *'Nid Cadarn ond Brodyrdod'*, which may be translated as *'Not Force but Fellowship'*, which could be interpreted as *'Not Mighty but Upright Brethren'*. The Dedication Ceremony was held, by Dispensation, on 18 November 1988, and was conducted by WBro John Taylor, AProvGM, and his team of Provincial Officers. This was followed by the taking of a photograph of the Dedication Team and the Officers of Saint Catherine's Lodge. The ladies joined the Brethren for the Festive Board.

Once Saint Catherine's Lodge was established, a number of the Brethren presented the Lodge with candelabra for the Festive Board. These are always used at the Christmas Lodge Meetings, and combined with representatives of the Mid Rhondda Brass band playing carols, have ensured that the Temple is always full on these occasions.

Since the Lodge was Founded, WBros Desmond Barnett, Michael Eveleigh, John Profitt, Percy F Hooper, David G Hackman and Brian Eveleigh have attained Grand Rank, with WBro Brian Eveleigh holding the Rank of AProvGM, 1999-2010, and WBro David G Hackman appointed his successor as AProvGM. WBro D Barnett holds the Rank of ProvGM in the Mark Degree.

The Worshipful Master's Chair has been occupied by nine Founder Brethren.

The success and health of the Lodge are indicated by the fact that during the past two years, double Ceremonies have been worked and on two occasions Dispensations have been obtained to hold additional Lodges. Ladies have attended the Festive Board at these additional Meetings.

There are, in fact, seven other Lodges on the register of UGLE bearing the name Catherine. St Catherine's Park No.2899, London; St Catherine's Lodge No.3743, London; St Catherine's Lodge No.5393, Durham; Lodge of St Catherine's No.6823, Warwick; St Katherine's Lodge No.7051, Bristol (Note: this the only one spelt with a K); St Catherine's Priory Lodge No.7960; and St Catherine's No.8577,Wrexham. The only one with the title Saint in full is Saint Catherine's No.9503 in Pontypridd, which makes this Lodge unique.

Compiled by WBro Terrence Thomas, PPrJGW, Founder Member.

Hafan Deg Lodge No.9520

Warranted   :   9 June 1993

Consecrated   :   23 November 1993

Meeting at the Masonic Hall, Barry.

In the early nineties, an increase in absenteeism and resignations among the more elderly Brethren became evident and, in many cases, this was directly attributable to reluctance on the part of these Brethren to venture out on dark and oft inclement nights. To stem the loss of these otherwise dedicated and able Masons, and to provide them with a more suitable forum in which they could practise their Masonry, it was to decided to form a dedicated 'Daylight Lodge', the first in the then Province of South Wales Eastern Division. The name chosen for the Lodge was 'Hafan Deg', which loosely translated from Welsh means 'Safe Haven'. Consequently, the Lodge Crest depicts a sailing ship, with sails furled, lying peacefully at anchor in the calm waters of a break-watered harbour, untroubled by the rough seas without. Several possible meeting places were considered before it was decided to opt for Barry, with its close proximity to both rail and road links.

The Sponsoring Lodge was Penybont Lodge No.6743. The Lodge was Consecrated on 23 November 1993 by the Provincial Grand Master, RWBro the Lord Swansea, following which WBro James Richard Bevan, PJGD, ProvGSec, was Installed as the Primus Master by VW Bro Cdr Roy K Hopkin, PGSwdB, Deputy Provincial Grand Master. WBro James R Bevan was Initiated in Lodge of Endurance No.6729 in 1978 and was Installed as Master in 1986. WBro Akram Baig, PAGDC, and WBro Normand Hayes Bullock, PAGDC, were appointed and Invested respectively as Senior and Junior Wardens. WBro Akram Baig was Initiated in Vale of Glamorgan Lodge No.3977 in 1981and was Installed as Master in 1990. WBro Normand Hayes Bullock was Initiated in Vale of Glamorgan Lodge in 1953 and was Installed Master in 1964.

The Lodge benefited from 24 Founders, of whom no fewer than five were Grand Officers, and it was their aim not only to provide a place of comfort for more senior Brethren, but to assist those who were Master Masons to attain the Master's Chair. Although the original expectation was that the Membership would be increased by Joining Members, this did not prove to be the case. In the first 14 years, the Lodge took in no fewer than 14 Initiates ranging in age from 27 to 77 years.

The first Master Mason Founder to be Installed as Master was WBro Brian L Whitaker, PPrAGDC, in 1998, and he was followed, in 1999, by the late WBro Ronald M Davies, PPrSGD. At the time of his Installation, WBro Ron Davies was aged 82, and had been a Master Mason for 46 years!

In 2002, the Lodge obtained approval for a Banner which, in the main, replicates the Lodge Crest. The Banner was ably designed by WBro Alvern Myron Muray Hart, PJGD, PM Porthkerry Lodge No.6299, and donated to the Lodge by WBro Akram Baig, PAGDC.

Hafan Deg Lodge continues to attract high attendances from both Members and visitors to its three Meetings each year, with the Ladies joining the Brethren for lunch at all but the Installation Festival.

Compiled by WBro James R Bevan, PJGD, ProvGSec.

Keystone Lodge No.9521

Warranted : 9 June 1993

Consecrated : 3 December 1993

Meeting at the Masonic Hall, Aberdare.

The Members of this special Lodge have strong associations with the Mark Degree in that they are all Mark Master Masons. The aim of the Keystone Craft Lodge is to promote and elevate Mark Lodge Past Masters, who are still Craft Master Masons, to the Chair of King Solomon. The Keystone is a Mark symbol, and aptly describes the function of the Lodge, in that it supports and locks together Craft and Mark Freemasonry.

Keystone Lodge No.9521 is still a fairly young Lodge, formed in 1993 as a Daughter Lodge of Morganwg Lodge No.5084. The original idea came from WBro Malcolm A Thompson who, as ProvGM of South Wales Provincial Mark Lodge, was surprised by the number of Dispensations he was asked to sign for Mark Masters Elect, because they had not passed through the Chair in the Craft. A subsequent investigation revealed that there were Mark Provincial and even Mark Grand Officers who had not been Installed as Masters in the Craft. The Lodge has indeed been successful in solving the problem and has therefore remained true to its original objectives.

RWBro Hywel Davies, PProvGM, was one of the more active Founder Members of the Lodge and, in fact, it was he who presented the Petition at Morganwg Lodge in the spring of 1993, when WBro T R Monoghan was WM. The Warrant was duly granted on 9 June 1993 and the Lodge was Consecrated by RWBro the Rt Hon the Lord Swansea, ProvGM, in Bridgend Masonic Temple on 3 Dec 1993. The Lodge meets twice a year, on the second Saturday in September, the Installation Meeting, and the third Saturday in February. The Lodge originally met in Bridgend, but in 2000, following an Extraordinary Meeting of the Lodge, a move to the Aberdare Masonic Hall was approved. The first Regular Meeting in Aberdare was held in February 2001.

The Lodge is unique in that the Membership includes two PProvGMs (One Craft and one Mark), one DepProvGM, one AProvGM and two ProvGSecs. Initially, the Lodge sought Membership only from South Wales Eastern Division as it then was, but it was soon able to invite Membership from West and Mid Wales. As a result, both the Membership and the lists of Fraternal visitors are representative of Lodges far and wide. In this, the Lodge acts as an interesting and perhaps an essential link across the Principality.

Keystone Lodge has so far not built up any collection of Banners, Mottos, treasured possessions or special Rituals. It prides itself in the very deep knowledge of, and loyalty to Freemasonry found in its Members, with each individual Brother being dedicated to rising to the highest possible levels in the Craft. This is reflected in the names of the Founders and those who have subsequently joined the Lodge and who have since risen to the highest Ranks.

The list of Founders could be from 'The Who's Who' of Freemasonry, and principally includes WBro Malcolm Hayes Thompson, PProvGSec, PAGDC, PProvGM Mark Master Masons of South Wales; WBro Vernon G A Upton, GM, PJGD; WBro Harry J Mars, MBE, DL, PAGDC; WBro Keith Tod Browning, PAGDC; and RWBro Hwyel Davies, PProvGM. Those who have subsequently attained Grand Rank include WBro Des Barnett, PJGD, Immediate PProvGM (Mark); WBro Jeff Clarke, PAGDC, ProvGSec (Mark); WBro Anthony Francis Moore, MBE, PGOrg, DepProvGM (Mark); and WBro Noel O A Alleyne, PAGDC, PDepProvDC (Mark).

Other distinguished Freemasons numbered among the Founder Members are WBros Tom Halliday; Richard G Jones, first Charity Steward; W J Lewis Groom, first Tyler; Alan W Hines, Alan Ford Thomas and Gordon W A Stowe. Two Brethren, WBro Eric W Cule and Bro Arnold Williams were admitted as Joining Members at the Consecration on 3 Dec 1993.

The Consecrating Officer was RWBro the Rt Hon the Lord Swansea, DL, ProvGM, and he was assisted by, among others, WBro D Gerald Williams, PGStB, ProvSGW as SW; WBro Len I Trott, PProvJGW, as JW; WBro the Rev Norman Lea, AGChap, ProvGChap, as Chaplain; WBro James R Bevan, PAGDC, ProvGSec, as Secretary; WBro William J Northway, PAGDC, ProvGDC, as DC; and WBro Andrew Lindsay Gretton, ProvDepGDC, as ADC. After an Address from the ProvGM, the Secretary read the Warrant, an Oration was given by the Chaplain, and the Invocation led to the uncovering of the Lodge Board.

As is customary, the Installing Master was the DepProvGM, VWBro Cdr Roy K Hopkin, RN, PGSwdB, who, in turn was assisted by the four AProvGMs, WBros Ken Adams Morgan, PSGD, J Stuart Peters, PSGD, David L Protheroe, PSGD and Peter Frost, AGSwdB. The DepProvGM duly Installed WBro Malcolm Hayes Thompson, PSGD, as Master, and he, in turn Invested Bro I R Harfoot and Bro T N Halliday as SW and JW respectively. The appointment and Investiture of the remaining Officers was followed by the Election of a long list of distinguished Masons as Honorary Members, headed by RWBro the Lord Swansea and VWBro Cdr Roy Hopkin.

After the Consecration in December 1993, the Ladies were invited to join the Brethren at the Festive Board and this became a custom of the Lodge at the September Installation Meeting. It is very satisfying and pleasing to note that the Lodge is continually blessed in having very many visiting Brethren, who in recent years often average 50 in number, and come from Lodges near and far. The unique nature of Keystone Lodge continues to be its strong link with Mark Masonry, together with the distinguished nature of its Brethren.

Bro Howard Thomas, who was Installed as the 4th WM of the Lodge, designed the PM's Jewel, which uniquely incorporates the 'keystone', the very symbol of the Mark Degree. The Jewel was presented to the first Worshipful Master, WBro Malcolm Hayes Thompson, on completion of his year in Office and, at his request, it has become a tradition of the Lodge for this Jewel to be presented to the Immediate Past Master at every Installation Meeting. The Lodge will maintain this tradition and, in so doing, will be remembering WBro Malcolm Hayes Thompson and the other Founder Members.

Compiled by WBro Arnold Williams, PM, PPrJGD.

687

Lodge of Round Table No. 9549

Warranted : 9 March 1994

Consecrated : 3 June 1994

Meeting at the Masonic Hall, Cardiff.

The Lodge of Round Table was formed by WBro Dr Akram Baig, PAGDC, together with a number of like-minded Masons, to bring together Members of the Round Table Movement and Freemasonry, to 'Adopt' the principles of Freemasonry, to 'Adapt' them to the friendship of Round Table, and to 'Improve' their lives by this combination.

The name of the Lodge is derived from the Round Table Movement in the British Isles and Ireland, (RTBI), of which every Member of the Lodge is, or has been, a Member of the Round Table Movement. The Mother Lodge is Vale of Glamorgan Lodge No.3977.

In August 2010, the Lodge had 31 Members, and although it is not a closed Lodge, all the Members, past and present are, or have been, Members of the Round Table Movement.

The Consecration Ceremony was held on Friday, 3 June 1994, at the Duke of Connaught Temple, Cardiff. The Provincial Grand Master, RWBro the Rt Hon the Lord Swansea, CStJ, DL, was in attendnece, together with WBro D G Williams, PGStB, ProvSGW; WBro L I Trott, ProvJGW; WBro Rev Norman Lea, PAGChap, ProvGChap; and WBro James R Bevan, PAGDC, ProvGSec. The DC was WBro W J Northway, PAGDC, ProvGDC and the ADC was WBro Andrew Lindsey Gretton, ProvDepGDC.

The Installing Master was VWBro Cdr Roy K Hopkin, RN, PGSwdB, DepProvGM. He was assisted by the four Assistant Provincial Grand Masters, WBros Ken A Morgan, PSGD; J Stuart Peters, PSGD; David L Protheroe, PSGD and Peter Frost, PAGSwdB.

The Founder Principal Officers of the Lodge were: WBro Dr Akram Baig, PM Vale of Glamorgan Lodge No.3977, WM; WBro Cuthbert L Summers, PSGD, PAProvGM, PM Glamorgan Lodge No.36, Acting IPM; WBro Brian R Densley, PPrJGD, PM Shir Gâr Lodge No.7339, SW; and WBro John M Steward, PPrGSwdB, PM Beehive Lodge No. 6265, JW. WBro David A Westall, PPrAGDC, was the first DC.

There were 22 Founder Members, of whom 9 where Past Masters. Five Founder Past Masters have already been mentioned. The other four included WBro L John Collins, PM Services Lodge No.7139, who was the first ADC and was Installed as WM of the Lodge in 1997. He was later appointed to the Rank of PPrAGDC. WBro Malcolm J Hackman, PPrAGDC, PM Ystradyfodwg Lodge No.7638 was the first Almoner. He was Installed as WM of the Lodge in 2006 and has been promoted to the Rank of PPrJGW. WBro Allen J Oliver, PM Barry Lodge No.2357, was the first Secretary and WBro Elfan W Jones, PM Universities Lodge No.5461, was the first Organist.

Following the Installtion Ceremony, 7 Brethren were proposed as Joining Members. The first Joining Member to beome WM was Bro David J Lewis, who was Installed as such in 1999. He now has the Rank of PPrSGD.

The Lodge is very proud to have two Grand Officers, WBro David A Westall, DepGSwdB and WBro Dr Akram Baig, PAGDC. WBro David Westall was appointed ME Grand Superintendent of the Provincial Grand Chapter of South Wales, on 28 September 2009, a great honour for both WBro David and the Lodge. The Lodge also has its own Chapter, the Chapter of Round Table No.9549, which received its Warrant on 12 November 2003.

The Lodge Banner was designed and presented to the Lodge by WBro Dr Akram Baig and was made by his mother. The design is a combination of the Round Table Rondel and Motto: *'Adopt - Adapt - Improve'*, and the Masonic Square and Compasses. The Banner Dedication Ceremony was held on 26 March 1999.

There are Biennial Meetings of Round Table Lodges, there being 46 such Lodges in England and Wales. In July 2006, Lodge of Round Table hosted the weekend in Cardiff. In 2008, the weekend was hosted by Round Table Lodge of South Cheshire, No.8787, in Chester and, in 2010, the weekend was held in the City of Lincoln, hosted by Round Table Lodge of Lincolnshire No.8240.

A tradition of the Lodge is that prior to the Tyler's Toast, at the end of the Festive Board, the Masonic Tablers' Toast, *'To Freemasonry and to the RTBI'* is given.

Compiled by WBro David Lewis, PPrSGD, Secretary.

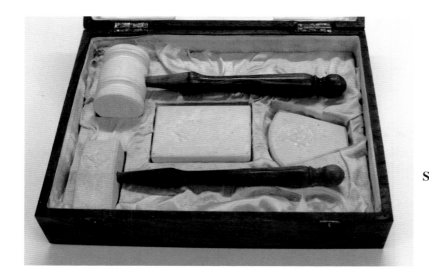

Gavels presented by
WBro Malcolm N Thompson PJGD
Cardiff Masonic Hall
Wood from the forests of Lebanon
Stone from King Solomon's Quarries, Jerusalem.

Geoffrey Ashe Court

During the latter part of the 1980s, the Province of South Wales Eastern Division decided to explore the possibility of establishing sheltered housing accommodation for Freemasons and / or their dependants. Accordingly, a parcel of land at Cardiff Road in the historic market town of Cowbridge in the Vale of Glamorgan was identified as being suitable for the purpose. In order to proceed, it was necessary to register the name of the Association with the Registry of Friendly Societies, a legal requirement under the Provident Societies Act 1965. This was finalised on 2 February 1989, its Registration Number being 26445R. The name of the Association was agreed to be the 'The Good Neighbours (SWED) Housing Association Ltd.'

It was necessary that the initial seven Members and the Secretary of the Society be listed on the application. They were WBros James Stuart Peters, Geoffrey Malin Ashe, Malcolm Hayes Thompson, Roy Keith Hopkin, Noel Orville Arrindell Alleyne, George Sydney Cronin and interestingly, Mrs. Mildred Patricia Thompson, the wife of WBro Malcolm H Thompson, the then Provincial Grand Secretary. The return was signed and submitted by the Secretary, WBro Clive Beecher.

The Board of Management was then strengthened to twelve in number by the addition of RWBro the Rt Hon the Lord Swansea, DL, ProvGM, WBro Kenneth Adams Morgan, AProvGM, WBros Julius H Hermer, Donald L Lewis and John I Brown.

While the official title of the Association is 'The Good Neighbours (SWED) Housing Association Ltd,' it is more popularly known as 'The Geoffrey Ashe Court', in memory of VWBro Geoffrey Malin Ashe, who served this Province as an Assistant Provincial Grand Master, 1976-1977, and as Deputy Provincial Grand Master, 1977-1992.

The objects of the Association are to provide a high standard of housing accommodation and associated amenities for elderly Freemasons or dependants of Freemasons, who are, or were Members of the English Constitution.

The complex was built by Northway Bros, a well established firm of local building contractors, owned by two well known senior Freemasons in the Province, namely Sam and Bill Northway. WBro Sam Northway, AProvGM, 1982-1993, also served as Second Provincial Grand Principal in the Royal Arch Degree in the Province for several years.

The construction work being completed, the complex was officially opened on 25 March 1994 by Geoffrey Malin Ashe, accompanied by the previously mentioned Members of the Board of Management. The fulfilment of this scheme was only made possible by the award of a substantial grant from the Freemasons' Grand Charity, with the balance being borrowed from a leading Bank.

The Housing development consists of sixteen one-bedroom flats and one two-bedroom flat. The flats were built to the highest standard and each one boasts a fully fitted kitchen and bathroom complete with bath and shower. Each has fitted carpets throughout and the bathrooms and kitchen have vinyl cushion flooring fitted as standard. Heating is by Economy 7 system (electricity). Consideration was given during the initial design and construction to enable the bathrooms to have sufficient room to accommodate wheelchair access. A large furnished Residents' Lounge, with facilities for tea/coffee making, is available for communal use and where residents may entertain their guests. This lounge was furnished with the generous support of the South Wales Provincial Grand Lodge of Mark Master Masons. The Manager's office is adjacent to this facility. The complex is set in its own grounds. The gardens, lawns and surrounding hedges are maintained by a part-time gardener, Mr Alan Keates, who takes great pride in providing the residents with a beautiful outlook and wonderful colours throughout the growing seasons. A secluded patio area, complete with garden furniture and barbeque are also provided.

All flats have an emergency call system in operation when the Manageress, Mrs Julia Keates is not on site, and each of the first floor flats have stair lifts for safe, easy access.

As a Management energy conservation policy, and for the comfort of the residents, in the spring of 2009 the Board authorised the installation of the latest specification of pvcu windows.

Over the period of twenty years since its inception, the Society has had four Chairmen and two Secretaries. The former Chairmen were VWBro James Stuart Peters, 1990-1992; VWBro Cdr Roy Keith Hopkin, 1992-2002; and WBro Donald Lewis Lewis, OBE, 2002-2006; while the present Chairman is WBro Victor George Watkins, JP, who was appointed in 2006. WBro Clive Beecher served as Secretary from 1990 to 1995, and was replaced in 1995 by the current Secretary, WBro Geoffrey William Thomas, PAProvGM.

Whilst over the twenty years there have been many changes in the membership of the Board of Management, the Provincial Grand Master has always been the Honorary President. Naturally the current Provincial Grand Master, RWBro Captain Sir Norman Lloyd-Edwards continues the tradition and regularly attends the Board Meetings. Sadly, of the original Board of Management, the last surviving member, WBro Julius H Hermer, MA, passed to The Grand Lodge Above on Sunday, 18 September 2011. The present Board of Management (2011) consists of:

Honorary President	:	RWBro Captain Sir Norman Lloyd-Edwards, ProvGM
Chairman	:	WBro Victor G Watkins, JP, PAGSuptWks
Vice - Chairman	:	WBro Gordon D Evans, PAGDC
Treasurer	:	WBro David Davies, FCA, PGStB
		WBro James R Bevan, PJGD, .ProvGSec
		WBro Neil H Matthews, PDepGSuptWks
		WBro John T J Davies, PAGSwdB
		WBro George C Royle, T.D, PAGDC. ProvGAl
		WBro Byron F Butler, DL, JP, PPrGReg
Secretary	:	WBro Geoffrey W Thomas, PSGD, PAProvGM.

The Board of Management meets on a regular basis at its Registered Office, The Provincial Office, at 128 Newport Road, Cardiff, CF24 1DH. More importantly, rota visits are made by two Board Members to the Geoffrey Ashe Court on a monthly basis. In so doing, the Board can be kept abreast of the feelings and needs of the residents, and are in a position to report back to the Board any topics or comments that may have been raised during such visits. A Manageress is employed at the Court, and she is required to make reports on the health and well-being of the residents to the two-monthly meetings of the Board of Management. Further, the Chairman is in very regular contact with the Manageress and any day to day issues may be quickly resolved on his authority.

Compiled by WBro Victor G Watkins, JP, PAGSuptWks.
WBro Geoffrey W Thomas, PSGD, AProvGM.

Meridian Lodge No.9603

Warranted : 13 September 1995

Consecrated : 20 February 1996

Meeting at the Masonic Hall, Swansea.

Following a conversation between WBro Michael J Hoare and WBro Ken D G Grove, the latter mentioned that some 5 years earlier, he had suggested the formation of a Daylight Lodge, but due to a lack of encouragement the idea was shelved. WBro Hoare thought the idea had merit and agreed to pursue it further, which resulted in a successful proposal being put before the Provincial Grand Master.

The first full meeting of the Founders took place in September 1994. WBro Kenneth David George Grove, PPrJGD, Treasurer of Lodge of Sincerity No.8531, was appointed WM Designate. An Initiate of Indefatigable Lodge No.237, he was the Managing Director of a Polythene Manufacturing Business. He was Secretary pro tempore, during the process of setting up the new Lodge. Bro Thomas Howard Williams, a Pharmaceuticals' Sales Manager and also an Initiate of Indefatigable Lodge, was SW Designate. The JW Designate was Bro William Stanley Norman Merriman Williams, retired School Teacher. He had been Initiated in St David's Lodge No.366, Milford Haven, and was a Member of Indefatigable Lodge and Singleton Lodge No.8399. WBro David Eric Thomas Davies, PPrAGDC, retired School Teacher, was appointed as acting IPM. An Initiate and PM Carmarthen College Lodge No.3280, Southgate, London, he was also PM Lodge of Sincerity and Treasurer of Singleton Lodge.

Lodge of Sincerity agreed to be the Sponsoring Lodge, and the Petition was duly signed by the WM and his Wardens at the Regular Lodge Meeting on 14 May 1995. There were 19 Petitioners, of whom 13 were Past Masters. The Petition was sent to RWBro Cdr M B S Higham, RN, PJGW, Grand Secretary, with an accompanying supportive letter from WBro James R Bevan, ProvGSec, dated 14 July 1995, as follows: *'The name of the Lodge reflects the desire of the Petitioners to hold their Meetings during the hours of daylight, which they feel will be beneficial to older Brethren who are reluctant to attend Lodge in the evening.*

My PGM is particularly supportive of the Petition, as he feels that there is a need for such a Lodge in Swansea.

The formation of Hafan Deg Lodge No.9520, Barry, at present the only 'Daylight' Lodge in the Province, has been a great success and a similar Lodge in the west would, Lord Swansea thinks, meet with equal support.'

The name, 'Meridian', was suggested by Bro T H Williams, as it meant 'midday', from the Latin 'meridianus', and was considered most appropriate for a daytime Lodge. It was agreed that the Lodge would meet on the 3rd Tuesday in April, September and November, with the Installation Meeting in February. It was also agreed that the ladies should be encouraged to hold their own lunch while the Brethren were attending Lodge, and a combined social lunch would be held in the months between Lodge Meetings. As a daylight Lodge consisting mainly of retired Members, the aims of Meridian Lodge are to foster friendship through Masonic and social activities, and to assist Brethren, who might have difficulties with the Ritual, to have the opportunity of reaching the Chair of King Solomon.

The Consecration took place on Tuesday, 20 February 1996, and should have been conducted by RWBro the Rt Hon the Lord Swansea, CStJ, DL, ProvGM, but, unfortunately, he had fractured his arm and was unable to attend. The duties of Consecrating Officer fell on the able shoulders of VWBro Cdr Roy K Hopkin, RN, PGSwdB. Following the Consecration Ceremony, WBro Kenneth David George Grove was duly Installed as Primus Master. He Invested Bros Thomas Howard Williams and William Stanley Norman Merriman Williams as his Senior and Junior Wardens respectively. John Hughes Dallimore, PPrJGD, an Initiate, PM and Treasurer of Penrice Lodge, was Invested as Treasurer. William Leslie Richards, PPrAGDC, an Initiate, PM and Almoner of Penrice Lodge No.4172 was Invested as the first Secretary. WBro Harry Edward Richards, PPrGO, PM and Organist of Tuscan Lodge No.7267, was Invested as Lodge Organist. All the above Officers, together with WBro David Eric Thomas Davies, acting IPM, are named on the Lodge Warrant.

The large gathering, which had already witnessed an impressive ceremony, then enjoyed an excellent repast at the celebratory Festive Board. The Brethren of Meridian Lodge presented the Founder Master, WBro Ken Grove, with a beautiful crystal decanter, engraved with the names of all the Founder Members. At the first Regular Meeting on 16 April 1996, the decanter was suitably filled, and its contents enjoyed by the Brethren. It continues to be used at every Installation Festive Board.

It was most appropriate that WBro James R Bevan, Provincial Grand Secretary, was the Mandated Officer at the Installation Meeting in February 1977. He had played a major part in the formation of the Lodge and was the Primus Master of the first daytime Lodge in the Province, Hafan Deg Lodge. At the Installation, Bro Thomas Howard Williams, SW, became the first Elected Worshipful Master, and he Initiated Mr C Clement, the Lodge's first Initiate on 15 April 1996. The Lodge suffered its first loss that year, with the sudden and unexpected death of the first Treasurer, WBro John Dallimore. His passing was announced at the November Meeting, and a tribute was paid by the Chaplain, WBro T O Murphy, who had proposed WBro John Dallimore into Freemasonry.

On 16 January 2001, WBro Rev Norman Lea, AProvGM, Dedicated the Lodge Banner, which had also been designed by WBro H Bidder. He also designed the Past Master's Jewel. Both Banner and Jewel include the Lodge Insignia and Motto *'In Luce Lucens'*, meaning *'In the light shining'*. The Banner was presented to the Lodge by Bro Paul Dallimore in memory of his late father, WBro John Dallimore. It was accepted with appreciation and pride on behalf of the Lodge by WBro I J Loveluck, WM. A memorial lectern was presented by Penrice Lodge, WBro John Dallimore's Mother Lodge.

The Lodge has been well blessed with visits from senior Provincial Officers. On 20 February 2001, RWBro Hywel Davies, ProvGM, accompanied by his Provincial Officers, attended the Installation of W Bro Keith Daniel. During his year, WBro Keith Daniel Initiated his son, Simon Daniel, who was to become the first Initiate to reach the Chair of King Solomon. While, during his year in Office, WBro Simon Daniel Initiated his son-in-law, Mr Ian Urquhart.

The Worshipful Master's Collar was presented by WBro Richard Evans, PM West Glamorgan Lodge No. 5291. Unfortunately, he was unable to become a Founder Member, as West Glamorgan and Meridian Lodges meet on the same evenings. At the Regular Meeting on 18 September 2001, WBro Clive Carroll presented the Lodge with an impressive silver chain, which had been attached to the Worshipful Master's Collar.

Meridian Lodge can also boast of having its own opening and closing hymns, both written by WBro Kenneth J Hutin. The former is sung to the tune 'Llef', and the latter to the tune 'St Clements'. WBro Cecil Chriswick donned the mantle of 'Lodge Photographer', and as a result of his skills, the Lodge has an impressive portfolio.

Compiled by WBro Ken Grove, assisted by WBros I J Loveluck, Archivist, and WBro S Roberts, Secretary.

United Services Lodge No. 9605

Warranted : 13 September 1995

Consecrated : 19 January 1996

Meeting at the Masonic Hall, Bridgend.

The concept of establishing a Services Lodge to embrace all branches of the Armed Forces was that of WBro Colin Mogg, PAGDC. The seeds were sown following a visit to a Service Lodge in 1994, an occasion he enjoyed very much and where he found the camaraderie to be very similar to what one would find in a Military Mess. Having received a favourable response from fellow Brethren who were ex-servicemen, an article was placed in the Provincial magazine, 'Guildford Gazette', now named 'Y Dalaith'. In addition, some twelve hundred letters were circulated resulting in a positive response from sixty Brethren.

Colin joined the Royal Horse Guards in 1953, serving in both the Mounted and Armoured Car Regiments, before leaving in 1962 to become a full time Staff Officer in the Territorial Army. From there he embarked on a career with the Automobile Association, working mostly with the Patrol Force, before retiring in 1991. In Freemasonry, he was Initiated in Ogmore Lodge No.1752 in 1982. He was a Founder Member of Hafan Deg Lodge No.9520, Warranted 9 June 1993, and became Master in December 1996. In 2002, Colin began planning a daylight Lodge, which was to become Lodge of Contentment No.9763, the Daughter Lodge of United Services Lodge, and of which he was the Primus Master at its Consecration on 10 March 2003. In Grand Lodge he was appointed PAGDC in 2006.

The planning committee first met in June 1994, and the Petition was Sponsored by Ogmore Lodge at a Meeting in April 1995. During the meetings of the Founders, it was agreed that although priority would be given to Candidates who had served, or were serving, in the Armed Forces, applications would be considered from other suitable gentlemen or Brethren. In its short history, only one Member had not undertaken military service. It was also agreed that an appropriate Service tie could be worn by Members and visiting Brethren during Lodge Meetings, together with miniatures at the Festive Board following the Installation Ceremonies.

As the Lodge was established to embrace all arms of the Military, it had been agreed that its name would be 'United Services Lodge'. The Warrant was signed on 13 September 1995. The Lodge was subsequently Consecrated in accordance with Antient and Established custom on Friday, 19 January 1996, by RWBro the Rt Hon the Lord Swansea, DL, ProvGM. There were twenty-four Founder Members. The Primus Master was WBro Glyn G H Miller, PGStB, with WBro G C Royle as SW. Originally, Brother Gordon D Pengelly had been designated Junior Warden, but unfortunately he died before the Consecration. Having signed the Petition, his name appears on the Warrant as being the Founder JW, but an addition has been made to indicate that Bro Frederick P Hannan was the holder of that Office.

The first two Candidates proposed for Initiation at the Consecration Meeting were Mr John Davies, a Financial Officer with the Ford Motor Co, and Mr Stephen Robinson, a Civil Servant. Following his Initiation on Thursday, 11 April 1996, Bro John Davies progressed to become the first Initiate of the Lodge to be Installed as WM, in November 2001.

WBro Glyn G H Miller, Primus Master, was Initiated into Freemasonry in Penybont Lodge No.6743, on 21 September 1962, and Installed as Master in 1978. He was also a Member of Hendre Lodge No.3250. He attended school in Croydon and later entered Teacher Training College. During WWII, he served with the Royal Corps of Signals in the Far East, particularly in Burma. He later commenced teaching in Ogmore Vale and became Headteacher before he retired.

On returning to his native Wales from Essex in 1994, Bro George C Royle PAGDC, RRC, TD read the advertisement in the Guildford Gazette for interested servicemen or ex-servicemen to join the proposed United Services Lodge. In November 1996, he became the first Elected Master. Initiated into Freemasonry in Lodge Orion in the West No.415, London, in September 1990, he became WM in July 1997. As an old boy of Barry Grammar School, he joined Old Barrians Lodge No. 6671 in 1997, and was Installed as Master in 2002. A Founder Member and first SW, he was Master of Lodge of Contentment in May 2003. He is also a Joining Member of Proscenium Lodge No.9059 and Hendre Lodge. George is the Right Worthy Grand Preceptor of the Commemorative Order of St Thomas of Acon. A retired Director of Nurse Education and Lt-Col RAMC(V), George was awarded the Territorial Decoration in 1987. He was further honoured with the Royal Red Cross, a personal honour from the Queen, for Military Nurses, in 1990. In the Province of South Wales, he was appointed Provincial Grand Almoner in 2006.

Bro Frederick P Hannan, first JW, was Installed as Master in November 1997. He subsequently became the Almoner, an Office he held for several years. He was Initiated into Freemasonry in Clyne Lodge No.9049 in 1986, and became a Joining Member of Penllergaer Lodge No.5567 in 1989. In Province, he was appointed PPrSGD in 2003 and promoted to PPrJGW in 2009. He was a former Regular Soldier serving with the Royal Corps of Engineers, and a retired Civil Servant. Having been a member and regular supporter of the Royal Engineers Association for 52 years in the year 2000, he was appointed Vice President of the Swansea Branch. He was further honoured in 2006 with the award of Badge of Merit. WBro Fred's son, David, a Member of Clyne Lodge, became a Joining Member in 1998 and progressed to become Master in 2004.

Early in 1998, discussions commenced with respect to the design and subsequent purchase of a Banner. Requests were made for Members to produce an example of a suitable design for consideration. It was agreed that it should depict all three of the Armed Forces. Contrary to all the training he had received as a soldier, *'never to volunteer for anything'*, Bro William Lightfoot agreed to design something suitable. The Ornaments of the Banner are really self explanatory. Two pillars with the Square and Compasses to represent Craft Freemasonry; the Eagle to represent the Royal Air Force; the Anchor to represent the Royal Navy and the two Swords representing the Army. Some Members with a Royal Air Force background felt that the eagle's wings were more attributable to a seabird. A leaflet was procured showing the RAF eagle design, and with this image being used to replace the original one, the amended design was accepted. Approval was sought from UGLE, but it was turned down, with the suggestion that the background colour be changed from green to blue. Following re-submission the Members were delighted to learn that it had received approval. The Banner was Dedicated on Thursday, 16 March 2000 by VWBro Peter Frost, PGSwdB, DepProvGM, assisted by other Acting Provincial Grand Officers. WBro Alan Hopkins was WM, Bro William Lightfoot was SW and Bro John Davies was JW. It is of interest to note that Bro William S Lightfoot was the very last Master Mason to receive the honour of PPrGStwd from Lord Swansea, before his retirement as ProvGM in 1999. Bro William acceded to the Chair of King Solomon in November 2000, and was promoted to PPrSGD in 2006.

It was whilst visiting Comrades Lodge No.2740, London, early in 2001, that WBro Colin Mogg first learned of the 'Circuit', even though the President was VWBro J Stuart Peters, PGSwdB, PDepProvGM of South Wales Eastern Division. The main aim of the Circuit of Service Lodges is simply to promote comradeship and fraternal contact between Military Masons. It began in 1993, when RWBro Sir James Stubbs, Grand Secretary, a Member of Certa Cito Lodge No.8925, London, the Royal Corps of Signals Lodge, felt that it would be advantageous for Lodge Members to be exposed to London Masonry. A Prestonian Lecture given at that time and entitled 'Masonry at War', set the wheels in motion. The die was now cast, and the concept of an organisation for Brethren having a Service background to meet together in Masonry was launched. Although there were 73 Lodges identified in London alone with a military background, many had merged with other Lodges, and only a few had a current membership of Brethren who were serving, or had served, in the Armed Forces. Half a dozen Lodges were keen enough to take part in the inevitable round of Meetings, but this number was reduced to four, when the Constitution drafted for the Circuit of Military Lodges (as it was initially called), restricted Membership to those Lodges whose Membership consisted entirely of serving or retired Servicemen. The criteria have now changed, and provided there are 50% serving or retired servicemen as Members, a Lodge is eligible to apply for Membership of the Circuit. There are currently 20 Lodges in the Circuit, 15 of which meet in London, with United Services Lodge being the only one in Wales.

The issue of the Lodge joining the Circuit was subsequently put to a Lodge Committee meeting and wholeheartedly supported. United Services Lodge was welcomed as the tenth Lodge in the Circuit. The rest, one might say, is history. WBros George Royle and Colin Mogg attended their first meeting as representatives of the Lodge in October 2001. Since that time, Brethren of the Lodge have taken the opportunity of visiting other Military Lodges throughout the country. Many Members will be seen to sport a small blue lapel badge, depicting the body and head of a lion carrying a horizontal sword, a wing on its back and a fish's tail at its rear. These represent the three branches of the Armed Forces, but the cynic might say it is the strength and power of the Army, with the Air Force winging it, and The Navy bringing up the rear!!!

The United Services Lodge has done well in attracting serving and retired Servicemen from the three branches of the Armed Forces, both as Initiates and Joining Members. Inevitably there have been losses due to death, and resignations for a variety of reasons. Nevertheless, the Lodge has maintained a healthy Membership, with an average of 43 Members during the first decade of its existence.

Compiled by WBro George C Royle, RC, TD, PAGDC, Provincial Grand Almoner.

Ancient Britons Lodge No.9672

Warranted : 11 February 1998

Consecrated : 16 June 1998

Meeting at the Masonic Hall, Caerphilly.

The first Masonic Lodge in Caerphilly was Ancient Britons' Lodge No.126, Constituted on 16 December 1807. The Lodge appears to have ceased working in 1814 and, on 5 March 1828, it was Erased from the Register of UGLE. An account of this first Caerphilly Lodge is given at the beginning of the book. It was not until the Consecration of Henry Pendrill Charles Lodge No.3769, on 23 August 1916, that Freemasonry was revived in Caerphilly. With the Consecration of Princes Lodge No.9036, on 4 June 1982 the number of Lodges meeting in the town had risen to seven.

Towards the end of the 1990s, a number of Caerphilly Brethren met to consider the formation of a 'Daylight' Lodge. Foremost among them was WBro Donald Lewis Lewis, OBE, PAGSuptWks. A Retired Company Director, who had worked in the Construction Industry, he had been Initiated in Lodge of St Ilan No.6624 on 10 February 1953 and Installed as Master in 1965. He was also PM Princes Lodge and a Founder Member of Danycoed Lodge No.8127, Caerphilly, Consecrated on 25 November 1966. In 1990, he became a Grand Officer with the Rank of PAGSuptWks and, in 2003, he was promoted to PJGD. At the first meeting of the Founders, it was agreed that WBro Donald L Lewis would be WM Designate. At that meeting, he strongly recommended that the name of the first Caerphilly Lodge should be resurrected, and that the new Lodge should be known as 'Ancient Britons' Lodge.

Henry Pendrill Charles Lodge agreed to be the Sponsoring Lodge, and the Petition was signed in Open Lodge on 7 January 1998. There were 25 Petitioners, of whom 19 were Past Masters. The Petition was submitted to WBro James Bevan, ProvGSec, on 20 February 1998, followed a week later by an explanation for the selection of the name 'Ancient Britons', and supported by a comprehensive paper, prepared by WBro Denis Woods, charting the history of Ancient Britons' Lodge No.126, and the contribution it had made to Freemasonry in South Wales. (WBro Denis Woods, PM Lodge of St Martin No.8771, Caerphilly, had developed a reputation as a Masonic Historian and, incidentally, is one of the editors of this Provincial history book.) The Warrant was granted on 11 February 1998, with the Grand Secretary noting on the Petition, *'The original Ancient Britons Lodge was formed in 1807 and is seen as the Mother Lodge for so many in the South Wales Province. (174 Lodges)'*. Note: of the 174 Lodges in the Province at this time, 112 are descended from the original Ancient Britons' Lodge.

The Lodge Badge has at its centre a cromlech, or standing stones, which represent the achievement of prehistoric man in successfully devising structures which have endured throughout the ages. The Motto *'Gosod y Sylfaen'*, translates as *'Setting the Foundation Stone'*, and combines the cynghanedd of Welsh poetry with the illusion of the skilled Mason setting the Stone correctly. This is fundamental to our Order, for if the Stone, representing both Lodge and Initiate, is not set correctly, the Masonic superstructure will ultimately fail. The Badge is enclosed in a circular cord, binding that which had been broken with the cessation of Ancient Britons' Lodge No.126 (1807-1828) and re-joined in 1998 with the Consecration of Ancient Britons Lodge No.9672, thereby demonstrating the enduring quality of Freemasonry. The design of intertwined chains is to be found on ancient relics and represents continuity and longevity, whilst in the smaller circles are depicted the 'All Seeing Eye', the Volume of the Sacred Law, and the Square and Compasses. The Lodge Motto can also be translated as 'Resetting the Foundation Stone, and refers symbolically to the name of the new Lodge, which after a period of 170 years, had reset the honourable title of 'Ancient Britons' once again in Caerphilly.

Ancient Britons Lodge was Consecrated in the Caerphilly Temple by RWBro the Rt Hon the Lord Swansea, DL, ProvGM, on 16 June 1998. He was assisted by WBro N H Bullock, PAGDC, ProvSGW, and WBro Brian Eveleigh, ProvJGW, who, in 1999, was to become AProvGM, an Office he held until 2010. WBro Rev Canon D Huw Mosford, ProvGChap, was also present, and he became AProvGM, 2007-2009. The DC was WBro Andrew L Gretton, PAGDC, ProvGDC, who was to be DepProvGM, 2007-2011.

The Installing Master was WBro J Stuart Peters, PSGD, DepProvGM, who duly Installed WBro Donald L Lewis as Primus Master. WBro Edwin William Ellis, PADepGDC, Printer & Stationer, Monmouth House, Trethomas, PM Princes Lodge, was Invested as SW. WBro Arthur O'Neill, PProvSGD, Retired Insurance Inspector from Bedwas, PM St Ilan Lodge, was Invested as JW.

It is interesting to note that the Installing Master was assisted by WBro Peter Frost, PSGD, AProvGM, later DepProvGM, 1999-2007; WBro Hywel Davies, PSGD, AProvGM, later ProvGM, 1999-2008; WBro Rev Norman Lea, PAGChap, later AProvGM 1998-2007; and WBro John Taylor, PAGDC, AProvGM, later Grand Superintendent, Royal Arch Freemasons of South Wales, 1999-2009.

Seven Founder Members are named on the Warrant, the three Principal Officers already mentioned and four others: WBro Colin Howell, PPrJGW, Retired Electrical Engineer from Waterloo, near Machen, ProvGDC and then Deputy Grand Superintendent in Provincial Grand Chapter from 2004 to 2010, PM Henry Pendrill Charles Lodge, was Invested as the first DC; WBro Philip Ernest Redman, PPrAGReg, Retired Lecturer from Maesycwmmer, PM Hamlet of Van Lodge No.8334; Royston David Roberts, PPrAGDC, Retired Mechanical Engineer from Caerphilly, Initiated in Henry Pendrill Charles Lodge, PM Danycoed Lodge & Princes Lodge; and WBro Charles Bertram William Chard, PPrJGD, Local Authority Management Services Officer from Bargoed, PM Gelligaer Lodge No.6298, who was Invested as the first Almoner.

Another Founder Member of note is WBro Anthony Francis Moore, MBE, PGOrg, PM Danycoed Lodge. Tony, a retired Deputy Head Teacher, was awarded the MBE in January 2001 'for Services to Music and Education in Wales'. In 2008, he was appointed Deputy Provincial Grand Master of Mark Master Masons of South Wales. He was Invested as the first Organist of Ancient Britons Lodge, and has continued as such ever since.

One of the reasons for forming Ancient Britons Lodge was to enable Brethren who for various reasons were unable to proceed to the Chair of King Solomon in their respective Lodges, to attain that honour. Among them was the late Bro Brian 'Tug' Wilson, who was Installed as WM in 2002. Another such Member is Bro Roger Bidgood, the first Tyler, who was Installed as WM in 2003 and has since been appointed to the Rank of PPrJGD.

Compiled by WBro Donald L Lewis, OBE, PJGD, and WBro Peter M Davies, ProvJGW, with acknowledgement to WBro Denis Woods, PPrJGW.

James Stuart Peters

Assistant Provincial Grand Master
1984 - 1998
Deputy Provincial Grand Master
1998 - 1999

James Stuart Peters was born on 10 April 1928 in Sketty, Swansea. He had an older sister, Margaret, sadly, now deceased, and he has a younger brother, David. Educated at Swansea Grammar School, he joined the Army on leaving school in 1946, serving initially for a few months in a camp for German POWs in Dorset, before being posted to the Far East. He first served in Singapore for 2 months, before being posted for a period of 18 months to Hong Kong. He was demobbed in November 1948 and, in January 1949, he became Articled to Thatcher & Payne, Chartered Accountants, Swansea. In 1952, he qualified as a Chartered Accountant

and, in 1953, he was admitted a Member of the Institute of Chartered Accountants in England and Wales. Initially employed as Assistant Accountant with British Anthracite Company Limited, 1952-1955, he commenced his own Chartered Accountancy practice in Walter Road, Swansea, in 1955, which he sold upon his retirement in 1985.

On returning to Swansea after National Service in 1948, he joined Swansea Uplands Rugby Football Club on its re-formation after the War. In 1939, with one exception, the members of Swansea Uplands RFC had joined up en bloc in the Welch Regiment and formed the Machine Gun Platoon. The one exception joined the Royal Navy. J Stuart Peters also played rugby for the 53 (Welsh) Division TA. He ceased playing rugby in 1960 and became Secretary of Uplands RFC for 4 years. His other sporting interest was golf, and he became a member of Langland Bay Golf Club in 1953. He remained a member until 1996, when he resigned due to injury.

In 1950, he joined 16 Battalion the Parachute Regiment TA. When they were disbanded in 1954, he transferred to the 4th Battalion, The Welch Regiment, where he remained for 4 years, retiring as Major Commanding 'C' Company in Swansea.

He married Joan Davies in Swansea in July 1954. They have four children, William, John, Henry and Sarah.

James Stuart Peters

VWBro James Stuart Peters, PGSwdB ranks among the most Masonically decorated and distinguished Members in the history of the Province. Initiated into Ionic Lodge No.6626, Swansea, in 1957, he was first Installed as WM in 1969 and again in 1993. His brother, David Peters, PPrSGW, was also Initiated into Ionic Lodge. Stuart Peters is a Founder Member of The Lord Swansea Lodge No. 8364, which was Consecrated on 2 February 1971; he became WM in 1985. He was a Founder Member of Lodge of Sincerity No.8531 and of Cape St Vincent Lodge No.8524; and a Joining Member of Edgar Rutter Lodge No.7196. In addition, he was a Joining Member of Hendre Lodge No.3250, and became WM in 1998. He is also a Founder Member of Pegasus Forces Lodge No.9393, Farnborough, Province of Hampshire and Isle of Wight, and was Installed as WM in 2010.

In Provincial Grand Lodge, Stuart Peters was appointed ProvSGD in 1975, and promoted to ProvJGW in 1980. He was appointed Assistant Provincial Grand Master in 1984 and became Deputy Provincial Grand Master in 1998.

He holds the unusual distinction of becoming a Joining Member of the Province's Grand Officers' Lodge, Lodge of Benevolence No.7305, before being appointed a Grand Officer! This is all the more extraordinary because in those days the Lodge Membership was limited to 50 and there were many Grand Officers in the Province waiting to join the Lodge. This unusual situation came about due to the sudden passing of the auditor of the Provincial Benevolent Fund, WBro Brynley Bowen, in 1973. WBro Malcolm Thompson, ProvGSec, contacted Bro Peters on a Monday morning, requesting that he audit the accounts to be presented to the Benevolent Fund Committee on Friday of that same week - which he did! Senior Members of the Province commented that this task was the usual task of a Grand Officer, and one Senior Mason even went as far as to say *You'll be a Member of Lodge of Benevolence next!'* This remark was made in the hearing of VWBro Harry Stockwell, DepProvGM, and WBro Llewellyn Bevan, AProvGM. Bro Stockwell remarked *'Indeed he will, - and I will propose him'*, to which Bro Bevan added, *'and I will second him'* – hence VWBro J Stuart Peters became a Member of a Grand Officers' Lodge when still a Provincial Officer! He was Installed as WM of Lodge of Benevolence in 1991, but has since resigned from the Lodge.

In due course, Stuart Peters was appointed PJGD in UGLE in 1983 and promoted to PSGD in 1985. In 1999, he was promoted to the Rank of PGSwdB with the title of VWBro.

In Royal Arch Masonry, he was Exalted into Doric Chapter No.5968, Swansea, in 1964, and Installed as First Principal in 1975. He is a Founder Member of Ionic Chapter No.6626 and was First Principal in 1994. He is also Founder and First Principal of Cape St Vincent Chapter No.8524, Consecrated in 1977. In Provincial Grand Chapter, he was appointed to the Rank of AProvGSoj in 1978 and promoted to PProvGSN in 1984. In Supreme Grand Chapter, he was appointed to the Rank of PAGSoj in 1985.

In the Mark Degree, Stuart Peters was Advanced in Talbot Mark Lodge No.179 in 1967. He was a Founder Member of Sir Frederick Alban Mark Lodge No.1455 and Master in 1979. He was also a Founder Member of De Cymru Mark Grand Officers' Lodge No.1606. He is a Joining Member of the Grand Stewards' Lodge of Mark Master Masons. In Mark Provincial Grand Lodge, he was appointed PPrGJO in 1982 and promoted to ProvGSW in 1984. In Grand Lodge of Mark Masons, Bro Peters was appointed GStwd in 1985, promoted to PGJD in 1991, PGJO in 1993, PGMO in 2004 and to PGJW in 2008. In the order of Royal Ark Mariners, he was Elevated in Abertawe Lodge RAM No.179 in 1970 and Installed as Commander in 1980. He is a Founder Member of Sir Frederick Alban RAM No.1455, and was appointed to Provincial Royal Ark Mariner Rank in 1985. In 1990, he was appointed to Royal Ark Mariner Grand Rank.

In the Ancient and Accepted Rite, he was Perfected in Morganwg Chapter No.70 in 1965 and Installed as MWS in 1977. A Founder Member of Gwyr Chapter No.870, he was Enthroned as MWS in 1986. He is a Joining Member of Sir Frederick Alban Chapter No.625 and was MWS in 1998. In Supreme Council of The Ancient and Accepted Rite, he attained 30° in 1978, 31° in 1984 and 32° in 1995.

In the Order of the Royal and Select Masters, he was Received and Acknowledged in the Merthyr Tydfil Council No.120 in 1986. He is a Joining Founder of Cartref Council No.169 and was Master in 1992. He is a Joining Member of Euston Council No.4. In the District Grand Council of South Wales, he was appointed Cryptic Divisional Rank in 1995. In Grand Council, he was appointed PAGDC in 1997 and promoted to Past Grand Lecturer in 2010.

In the Order of The Red Cross of Constantine, he was Installed in Dewi Sant Conclave No.185 in 1974. He is a Founder and was First MWS of Merlin Conclave No.402 in 1989. In Grand Conclave, he was appointed GTreas in 1992, an Office he retained for some ten years. He was promoted to Knight Commander Constantine in 2010.

In The Order of The Allied Masonic Degrees, Stuart Peters was Admitted to the Principality Council No.53 in 1970. A Founder of Gower Council No76, he was Master in 1977. He is a Joining Member of Stewart Council No.16. In Grand Council, he was appointed PGStB in 1981, Divisional Grand Prefect for the Severn Division in 1986, and Deputy Grand Master in 1992, a position he held for ten years.

In The Order of The Secret Monitor, he was Inducted into Cymru Conclave No.207 in 1970. He is a Founder of Dyfed Conclave No.233 and Tawe Conclave No.238 and was Installed as Supreme Ruler in 1973. He is a Joining Member of Summus Conclave No.3 and The Supreme Rulers' Conclave No.123. On the Constitution of The Province of South Wales and Monmouthshire, he was appointed Deputy Provincial Grand Supreme Ruler in 1975, and continued in that office for six years. In Supreme Grand Conclave, he was appointed GStB in 1975 and promoted to Past Grand Visitor in 1979. He was appointed DepGDC in 1986 and promoted to GDC in 1988, an Office he held for some twelve years. In 1990, he was promoted to Grand Guide. In 2009, he was appointed to the prestigious continuous Active Office of Grand Chancellor, an Office that ranks below the Deputy Grand Supreme Ruler but senior to Provincial Supreme Rulers.

In the Royal Order of Scotland, he was Advanced in the Chapter of the Provincial Grand Master of South Wales in 1983, and promoted to ProvSGW in 1989.

VWBro J Stuart Peters is a Founder of The Ancient and Masonic Order of The Scarlet Cord and was appointed Past Grand Chancellor when the Order was inaugurated at Freemasons' Hall, London, in July 2010.

Compiled by WBro Roy Woodward, PSGD, AProvGM,
and WBro Robert Nettleship, PSGD, PAProvGM.

Cwm Rhondda Lodge No. 9692

Warranted : 10 February 1999
Consecrated : 3 March 1999
Meeting at the RAFA Club, Treorchy.

In the latter part of the 20th century, much discussion took place among Rhondda Freemasons, emphasising the fact that there had never been a Masonic Temple actually in the Rhondda. Every Rhondda Freemason had to travel to Pontypridd, Cardiff, Pontyclun, Penarth or Treharris to attend Lodge Meetings. Another important point, that due to business pressures, the younger Brethren, and possibly Candidates, mostly finished work at 6.00 pm and found it impossible to return home to change and arrive at those Temples in time for the 6.30 pm start. The idea that the new Lodge could meet in a Temple in Upper Rhondda Fawr was formulated, and further discussion took place to examine its feasibility. The concept was received with great enthusiasm and much excitement. The early motivation came from a Grand Lodge Officer, WBro Desmond Barnett, who was to become the Primus Master, and WBros Thomas Griffith Horton (First Treasurer), John Kerson Mathias (Organising and First Secretary), Leo Douglas Wynne (First DC), and a number of Past Masters from the Rhondda. Early Meetings with Provincial Grand Lodge went very smoothly, and the Lodge received the fullest support.

The venue presented a particular challenge, and with great creativity a small room in the Griffin Inn, Pentre, was selected and later transformed into a mini Temple. Expert craftsmen were generous with their expertise and the Lodge was fully furnished and carpeted to a top quality standard. The Lodge Room had returned to the early days of Freemasonry, with peripatetic furnishings and meeting at an Inn. However, with the possibility of over 30 Founder Members, and with the room only able to hold 60 people, space would present a limit to both the number of Members and to the number of their visitors able to attend. Later, the size of the room proved to be impractical, and the Lodge was fortunate to arrange accommodation in the Royal Air Forces Association (RAFA) Club in Treorchy. Here, the room selected proved to be very suitable, both for Lodge Meetings and for dining.

The name of the Lodge, 'Cwm Rhondda' was a very early suggestion and it was received with unanimous acclamation. The Lodge received much support from Hen Bont Lodge No.4691, which was proud to become the Sponsoring Lodge.

The Lodge Warrant was granted on 10 February 1999, and the Consecration Ceremony took place on 30 March 1999 in the

Masonic Hall, Cardiff. The Consecrating Officer was RWBro the Lord Swansea, CSJ, DL, ProvGM. He became ProvGM in 1966, and during his term of office he Consecrated 67 Lodges, with Danycoed Lodge No.8127 being the first, and Cwm Rhondda No.9692 being the last. The only Lodge not Consecrated by him was Lord Swansea Lodge No.8364, in which he was Installed as Primus Master. The Consecration of Cwm Rhondda Lodge was an impressive event with many prominent Freemasons attending, many of whom, although Rhondda born, were now living away from Wales.

Cwm Rhondda Temple, RAFA Club, Treorchy

It was particularly poignant for the ProvGM; he was carrying out his last Consecration Ceremony in the Province. His New Samaritan Fund Festival was to be held in Cardiff on Friday, 16 April, and he would preside over his last Provincial Grand Lodge Annual Meeting on Monday, 18 June. He retired as ProvGM on Friday, 31 July 1999.

While the Consecrating Ceremony was taking place, a large number of beautiful bouquets of flowers were delivered to Lady Swansea at her London home. This 'Cwm Rhondda' gesture was greatly appreciated by Lady Swansea, as she was able to share in the great joy being experienced in Cardiff.

In the first year, the Lodge Ritual was fully discussed and established. The hymn 'Cwm Rhondda' would be sung at every Meeting and the Visitors Toast at the Festive Board would end with the Members singing 'We'll keep a Welcome'.

Each year the Lodge has Initiated 2 Candidates, who are very carefully selected. These are actively encouraged to take part in the Lodge Ceremonies, and the Lodge is very proud of the progress made by the Initiates, who enrich every Ceremony with their efforts. The Lodge had only been able to accept 5 Freemasons as Joining Members whilst at the Griffin Inn, because of the size of the Lodge Room. These 5 did not qualify as Founder Members, as at the time, they had not been Master Masons for the minimum required period of three years. They have since become valuable Members of the Lodge.

With the move to Treorchy, the Lodge was able to accept more Joining Members; WBro Harry J Mars, MBE, DL, PAGDC, was made an Honorary Member, and he graces the Lodge with his presence at most Lodge Meetings. His experience and advice is much appreciated by all the Members.

Each WM has stamped his own personality on the Lodge; whilst WBro Leo Douglas Wynne, as DC in the first seven years, ensured that the Ritual and ceremonial, agreed to in the first year, were maintained to a very high standard. The Treasurer, WBro Thomas Horton, ensured that the Lodge flourished and fulfilled both the vision and the objectives of the Founders.

The Lodge has an annual Ladies' Night, which has proved very successful, with many friendships being formed as a result. The Lodge is very grateful for the help and support it receives from the Ladies.

In January 2011, the Lodge Membership stood at 45, with excellent attendances at Meetings, and with all Members proactive in the Lodge. Each Meeting also welcomes a goodly number of visitors, who enrich the ambience of the Meeting.

Compiled by the late WBro Thomas Griffith Horton, PPrSGD,
and WBro A Turner, PPrJGD.

Hywel Davies

Provincial Grand Master
1999 – 2008

Hywel Davies was born and brought up in Llanelli. He studied Electrical Engineering at Llanelli and Swansea Technical Colleges. His studies were briefly interrupted for a period of two years while he served in the RAF as an Officer/Navigator. After National Service, he enjoyed a successful career with the former South Wales Electricity Board. Commencing as an Engineering trainee, he qualified as a Chartered Engineer and, in due course, he became District Manager for Mid Wales and, in 1998, Chief Personnel Officer at Head Office.

In his youth, Hywel met his future wife, Rhianydd Aurwen James, whom he married in Llanelli in 1959. In December 1979, they moved to Brecon, where they continue to reside. They have two daughters, both graduates of Exeter University. The elder, Suzy, is a Solicitor, a Welsh Assembly Government Member, and a farmer's wife with two sons. The younger, Hilary, is a successful Civil Servant with the Ministry of Communities and Local Government in London.

Hywel's sporting interests have included terms as Vice-President of Brecon Cricket Club, Brynmawr Rugby Club, Welsh Charitables RFC, Shareholder and Patron of Llanelli Scarlets, membership of Edinburgh Wanderers Rugby Club, Brecon and Caradoc Golf Clubs.

A well filled diary also had at one time: Life Member of RAFA, Governor of Pencoed and Rumney Schools, Director of Powys Enterprise, Welsh Office Member of the founding NCVQ, Member of the Board of Powys FHSA, as well as Past President of Brecon Rotary Club, and Past Chairman of Brecon Probus Club; all of which would seem to leave little time for Freemasonry - but read on!

Hywel was Initiated into Aberpennar Lodge No.6354, Aberdare, in 1968 and was Installed Master in 1979. He joined The Lord Swansea Lodge No.8364 and was WM in 2001. In February 1982, he became a Joining Member of Aberhonddu Lodge No.8588, Brecon, and was Charity Steward for five years. He joined Lodge of Benevolence No.7305 and Hendre Lodge No.3250 in 1993, and was WM in both in 2000. He was also a Founder Almoner of Keystone Lodge No.9521 in 1993. In Province, he was appointed PPrAGDC in 1985 and promoted to PPrGRreg in 1989. He became

Hywel Davies

Provincial Junior Grand Warden in 1990 and, in 1992, he became a Grand Officer with the Rank of PAGDC. In 1996, RWBro the Rt Hon the Lord Swansea, ProvGM, appointed him AProvGM, and the following year he was promoted to PSGD in UGLE. He was Vice-Chairman of the successful 1999 Festival and President for the first five years of the equally successful 2010 Festival. He was also a Founder Board Member of the New Masonic Samaritan Fund, on which he served for some nine years, and was the second Chairman of the newly formed Association of Brecon Freemasons for 9years, of which he was the Founder Secretary.

In Royal Arch Masonry, he was Exalted in the Loyal Hay Chapter No.2382 in 1981, its Scribe E for 8 years, and Installed First Principal in 1986. He became a Joining Member of the Gloucestershire and Hereford Chapter of First Principals in 1987 and First Principal in 1999. He is now an Honorary Member of both. He joined Brecknock Chapter No.651, in 1990, and was its Scribe E for 7 years. He joined Hendre Chapter No.3250 in 1997, and was Founder IPZ of The Lord Swansea Chapter No.1914 in 2010. After being appointed to Provincial Rank in both Provinces, he was appointed to the Active Ranks of Grand Sword Bearer in 2006 and Grand Scribe N in 2008.

In Mark Masonry, he was Advanced in Arthur Lewis Mark Lodge No.585 in 1970 and was Installed as Master in 1980 and again in 2008. He became a Joining Member of South Wales Installed Mark Masters Lodge No.1201 in 1981 and WM in 2003. He was Organising Secretary, Founder Master in 1994, and Secretary for 3years of Brychan Lodge No.1725. He joined De Cymru Lodge No.1606 in 1997, and was Founder Registrar of Marks, for Cyfrinfa Marc Dewi Sant Rhif 1914 in 2010. In the Province, he was appointed ProvGStB in 1983, ProvGMO in 1987, and PPrGJW in 1995. In Grand Lodge he was appointed PAGDC in 1997, GSD in 2002 and PGJO in 2007.

In Royal Mark Mariners, he was Elevated in St Illtyd's Lodge No.785, in 1985 and became a Founder Guardian of the Arthur Lewis Lodge No.585 in 1986, being Installed as Commander in 1991. He was Founder Commander of Brychan Lodge in 1998, and joined South Wales Installed Comanders Lodge No.1201 and was Founder IPZ of De Cymru Lodge No.1606 in 1999. He was appointed to ProvRAMGR in 1998 and RAMGR in 2000.

In the Royal and Select Masters, he was Received as a Member in the Glyntaf Council No.40 in 1985 and was its Master in 1993. He was appointed District Grand Master for South Wales, 1998-2003. He was Installing Officer at the Consecration of Giraldus Cambrensis Council No.225 in 2000; and Founder Steward for the Keith Hind Council No.260 in 2005, and then Deputy Master in 2009. He was Founder Deputy Master of Ambat Zaphan Council No.287 in 2009 and its Master in 2010.

In the Ancient and Accepted Rite, he was Perfected in St Alud Chapter No.799 in 1984, was its MWS in 1994, and joined Sir F J Alban Chapter No.625 in 2002. He was appointed to 30° in 1995, 31° in 2002 and 32° in 2006. RWBro Hywel was also a Member of the Royal Order of Scotland for many years.

The obvious highlight of Hywel's Masonic career was his appointment, on 31 July 1999, as Lord Swansea's successor as ProvGM. RWBro Hywel Davies was Installed as such at an Especial Meeting of Provincial Grand Lodge, held at the Royal Welsh Showground, Builth Wells, on Thursday, 16 September 1999. It proved to be an ideal location, being able to accommodate the 1,200 plus Brethren who had assembled to witness the event. The Deputation from UGLE was led by the Deputy Grand Master, RWBro Iain Ross Bryce.

On 15 June 2000, RWBro Hywel had the honour to welcome the MW the Grand Master HRH Prince Edward, Duke of Kent to the Province. The Grand Master visited the Albert Edward Prince of Wales Court, Porthcawl, to re-dedicate the Home on completion of the work in converting it into six house groups.

During his period as ProvGM, Hywel Consecrated two 'Daylight' Lodges: St Tydfil's Lodge No.9753, Merthyr Tydfil, on 15 March 2002; and Lodge of Contentment No.9763, Bridgend, on 10 March 2003. Sadly, two Lodges were also Erased from the

Register of UGLE: Shir Gâr Lodge No.7339, on 24 April 2005; and Lodge of Integrity No.6907, on 10 December 2008. Thus, the number of Lodges in the Province remained unchanged, at 176 Lodges. Also, during this time, he attended 199 Installations, having previously represented the ProvGM at 4 Installations while ProvJGW, and at 81 Installations as AProvGM.

When Hendre Lodge celebrated its Centenary on 25 January 2008, RWBro Hywel Davies was the Master and welcomed the Right Worshipful Assistant Grand Master, RWBro David K Williamson, to the Province. This was the first time in almost a quarter of a century that one of the Rulers had attended a Private Lodge in this Province.

Hywel is President of the Bridgend Masonic Golfing Society, a very successful 'Charity Venture', which was formed in response to his 'Freemasonry in the Community' initiative. Founded in May 2002 by WBro Ralph Jones, PPrJGW, PM Glanogwr Lodge No.8508 and WBro Phillip Aubrey, PPrSGD, PM Ogmore Lodge No.1752, it was decided to invite the ProvGM to become Life President of the Society, which he readily accepted. Since August 2002, an annual open tournament has been held at Pyle & Kenfig Golf Club, which is a major fund raising event. For many years, RWBro Hywel entered a team from Brecon and until recently played in the team. In 2003, he presented the Society with a magnificent silver trophy to be presented annually to the Society Champion, and he always attends to present the President's trophy to the winner. Since its formation, the Society has donated over £34,000.00 to local good causes with over £24,000.00 going to non-Masonic charities. In 2008, Hywel presented the Society with a Past Captains' Board, which is displayed on the wall at the entrance to the bar at Bridgend Masonic Hall.

Another of Hywel's major initiatives was the inauguration of the Provincial Church Service on 25 May 2001, at Llandaff Cathedral. Since then, this important event has taken place annually and was held at Brecon Cathedral, where Hywel worships, for the first time on 23 November 2003. It was held again at Brecon Cathedral on 22 October 2006, having been at St Catherine's Church, Gorseinon, in December 2004, and Llandaff Cathedral in October 2005. Following a visit to St Mary's Church, Swansea in October 2007, and Llandaff Cathedral again in 2008, the Service was held for the first time in a non-conformist church, Pisgah Baptist Church, Pyle, in October 2009.

Not only has the Christian faith been recognised, but on Saturday, 11 August 2007, a party of around a hundred Masons, their wives and families, attended a special service at Cardiff's Sikh Gurdwara in the City's Roath district. The party was led by Provincial Grand Master, Hywel Davies, accompanied by Mrs Davies.

The following year, on Sunday, 24 February 2008, the ProvGM, accompanied by the DepProvGM, the AProvGMs, and around 120 Brethren and their wives, attended a thanksgiving service at the United Synagogue, Cyncoed, Cardiff. They were welcomed by Rabbi Mordecai Wollenberg and the keystone Address was given by WBro Elkan D Levy, PJGD, PAGSoj, Hon Grand Almoner (Israel), Metropolitan DepGChap.

During his memorable and distinguished nine year period as Provincial Grand Master, Hywel became much loved and well known to all the Brethren, and visited all the 176 Lodges then in his Province. During his period in Office, the Provincial diary, and the Provincial tie were also introduced.

Since his retirement as ProvGM, RWBro Hywel is still a very active Freemason, but now without the pressures of active high office, he enjoys his interests in the many Lodges and Chapters he attends, and continues to encourage younger Masons with his friendly and relaxed manner.

Compiled by WBro B G Matthews, PAGDC.

Peter Frost

Deputy Provincial Grand Master
1999 – 2007

Peter Frost was born in Penarth and educated at Penarth Grammar School. He was born in an era where the sight of people in military uniforms was not unusual, it being the time when National Conscription was in force. The only uniform that really impressed him, however, was that of the Glamorgan Police Force.

He became a Police Cadet and in due time was conscripted and served in the Corps of Royal Military Police. On completion of his military service he achieved his ambition and became a Constable in the Cardiff City Police Force. He rose quickly through the ranks, attaining the rank of Sergeant in 1965 and Inspector in 1967. On the formation of the South Wales Constabulary in June 1969, he became a Detective Chief Inspector at Police Headquarters in Bridgend, and was promoted to Superintendent in 1972. He was later seconded to the Home Office as Chief Superintendent of the National Crime Prevention Centre, during which time his duties required him to travel the world advising various countries on crime prevention and security measures. During his career in the Police Force, he received 18 commendations for his work in connection with all kinds of crime, including the most serious kind. At the time of his retirement in 1988, after completing 34 years, he was the Chief Superintendent and Divisional Commander of Bridgend Division.

Peter is married to Maureen and they live in Cowbridge. They have five grown up children and twelve grandchildren. Three of his sons have followed their father's career and are serving Police Officers. He was a keen and active sportsman, with rugby, swimming, including water polo, diving and golf featuring high on

Peter Frost

his list of activities. He qualified as a Welsh Rugby Union Coach, served on the Welsh Council of the British Boxing Board of Control, the Welsh and British Amateur Swimming Associations, and the Commonwealth Games and Olympic Committees. In addition, he is a past Chairman of Cowbridge Probus Club and past President of Cowbridge Rotary Club.

Peter's Masonic career began on 21 September 1962, when he was Initiated into Caerdydd Lodge No.3959. He became WM of the Lodge in 1974 and occupied the Chair of King Solomon again in 1999, taking the Lodge into the new millennium. He was made an Honorary Member of Caerdydd Lodge in 2002. Peter joined Hendre Lodge No.3250 in 1980 and was WM in 2003. He joined Lodge of Benevolence No.7305 in 1994, and was WM in 2005, and he is also a Joining Member of Industria Cambrensis Lodge No.6700.

Appointed ProvGSwdB in 1979, Peter became ProvJGW in 1992 and, in April 1993, he was appointed to the Acting Rank of AGSwdB in United Grand Lodge. In June 1993, he was appointed AProvGM, and promoted to PSGD in 1995. Appointed DepProvGM in July 1999 and, in April 2000, he was promoted to PGSwdB, with the title Very Worshipful Brother. He served as DepProvGM until 2007. That year, he became the President of the Deputy Provincial Grand Masters' Mess for England and Wales.

In Royal Arch Masonry, Peter was Exalted in Sir George Elliot Chapter No.960 in 1965, and became First Principal in 1989 and again in 1990. He was appointed ProvGSwdB in Provincial Grand Chapter in 1991, PGStB in Supreme Grand Chapter in 2001, and promoted to PGSoj in 2009.

In Mark Masonry, he was Advanced in Cowbridge Lodge No.1573 in 1982, and became WM in 1990. In Provincial Mark Lodge, he was appointed ProvGSwdB in 1992, promoted to PPrGSW in 2000, appointed PAGDC in Grand Lodge of Mark Master Masons in 2004, and promoted to the Acting Rank of GSwdB in 2011.

In Royal Ark Mariners, Peter was Elevated in Dunraven Lodge No.950 in 1990, and became Worshipful Commander in 2002. A Joining Member of Cambrensis Lodge No.1528, he was appointed Provincial RAMGR in 2007 and, in Grand Mark Lodge, promoted to RAMGR in 2011.

In 1989, he was Perfected in Cowbridge Chapter of Rose Croix of Heredom No.985 and became MWS in 1995. He was promoted to the 30th Degree in 1996 and to the 31st Degree in 2006. He joined Powys Chapter No.406 in February 2011.

Finally, in 1998, he was Advanced in the Royal Order of Scotland.

St Tydfil's Lodge No.9753

Warranted : 14 November 2001

Consecrated : 15 March 2002

Meeting at the Masonic Hall, Merthyr Tydfil.

WBro Graham G Allen worked long and hard on the concept of a Daylight Lodge in Merthyr. He, with a number of likeminded PMs cooperated to Found St Tydfil's Lodge, essentially to answer the perceived demand in the north of the Province. It is primarily intended to attract retired Freemasons, and therefore meets during the relative safety of daylight hours. Wives and partners are encouraged to attend the Festive Board when appropriate, and the Lodge is already renowned for its friendly and supportive ethos.

The Founders were all Brethren whom WBro Graham, the Founder Master, had known for a number of years. They were delighted to join him in the formation of St Tydfil's Lodge. The Lodge meets in the Merthyr Temple, within easy travelling distance for Brethren living in the Aberdare, Rhondda, Rhymney and Bargoed valleys, the Members being drawn from all these parts.

The first meeting to discuss the Lodge's formation was held on 17 April 2001, with WBro James R Bevan, ProvGSec, in attendance. His participation and advice were greatly appreciated. Then, at a full meeting of the Founders, held on 31 May 2001, the seven Petitioners whose names were to appear on the Warrant were chosen: WBros Graham G Allen, Victor G Watkins, J Donald Humphreys, A Desmond Jones, and Bros Bryn E Lewis, Arthur E Smith and W Leighton Nelson. The Musical Service was compiled by WBro Norman H Collins, who chose the Hymns for their suitability for a Daylight Lodge.

As WBro Graham had been WM of Luminary Lodge No.8530 on two previous occasions and, since many of the Co-founders were also Members, it was deemed appropriate to invite Luminary Lodge to be the Sponsoring Lodge. Luminary Lodge generously agreed and it takes considerable pride in the success of its Daughter Lodge. Naturally WBro Graham was the Founder Master with Bro Emlyn Lewis, SW Designate; Bro Arthur Smith, JW Designate and WBro Don Humphrey, PM St David's Lodge No.679, as acting IPM. Among other Founders taking Office were WBro John Wiggins, PM Luminary Lodge, Chaplain; WBro Vic Watkins, PM Gelligaer Lodge No. 6298 and PM Luminary Lodge, Treasurer; WBro Colin Butler, PM Loyal Cambrian Lodge No.110, Secretary; WBro Mervyn T Rogers, PM Aelwyd Lodge No.7982, as DC; and WBro D Gareth Gait, PM St David's Lodge No.679 and PM Cwm Rhondda Lodge No.9692, Charity Steward.

From the outset, WBro Graham had in mind 'St Tydfil's', as the most suitable name for the Lodge, and the other Founders unanimously agreed. According to legend, St Tydfil was slain in the 5th century AD for refusing to betray her principles. All

Masons will immediately recognise the legend's Masonic connotation and appreciate the appropriateness of the name for a Masonic Lodge. Further, Merthyr Tydfil, where the Lodge meets, means the 'Shrine of St Tydfil'.

WBro Graham's vision of a Banner and PM's Jewel was realised by the designs of WBro Mark L Roberts, who by happy coincidence is the son of WBro Jesse Roberts, the designer of the Banner of St Tydfil's Mother Lodge, Luminary Lodge. At the centre of the Banner is the figure of St Tydfil standing before the image of a bright sun. The sun symbolises both the metaphorical warmth of the Lodge and the fact that it is a Daylight Lodge. Surrounding this motif is a circular band of Masonic pale blue, containing the Lodge Name, Number and Motto.

The Motto: *'Diogelwch a Chynhesrwydd,'* literally translated means *'Safety and Warmth'*. This sentiment conveys both the safety advantages of a Daytime Lodge, especially for older Brethren and the warmth and friendship that St Tydfil's Lodge seeks to embody and promote. On each side of this central emblem is a golden Masonic Pillar surmounted by a Globe. The Pillar on the left-hand side is of the Ionic order representing King Solomon and Wisdom. This pillar supports the Terrestrial Globe, which symbolises the temporal and material world and also the universality of Freemasonry. The Pillar on the right-hand side is of the Corinthian order representing HA and Beauty. This Pillar supports the Celestial Globe, which, in turn symbolises the eternal and spiritual world to which we all aspire. The Pillars and Globes are joined at the top and at the base by two paler blue curved bands, the one at the top has 'Merthyr Tydfil' on it to indicate the location of the Lodge and the one at the bottom, the date of the Consecration of the Lodge. The Square and Compasses surmount the centre of the upper band to clearly identify St. Tydfil's Lodge as a Masonic Craft Lodge and to remind its Brethren *'to regulate their actions and to keep within due bounds with all mankind'*.

The Lodge was Consecrated on 15 Mar 2002 by RWBro Hywel Davies, ProvGM. It was the first new Lodge in the Province for three years, and the first Lodge to be Consecrated by the ProvGM. None would have realised it from the immaculate manner of the proceedings. The ProvGM was assisted by WBro Stanley M Mortimer, PAGDC, ProvSGW as SW, WBro David G Hackman, ProvJGW, as JW; WBro Canon Rev D Hugh E Mosford, ProvGChap, as Chaplain; WBro James R Bevan PJGD, ProvGSec, as Secretary; and WBro Geoffrey W Thomas PAGDC, ProvGDC, as DC.

The Installing Master was VWBro Peter Frost, PGSwdB, DepProvGM. He was assisted by all four AProvGMs, WBro Rev Norman Lea, DepGChap; WBro Andrew L Gretton, PSGD; WBro Brian Eveleigh, PSGD; and WBro Robert J Nettleship, PJGD. WBro Graham George Allen, PPrGReg, was duly Installed in the Chair of King Solomon, and he Invested Bro Emlyn Lewis as SW and Bro Arthur E Smith as JW.

Subsequently, on 15 October 2004, at a Regular Lodge Meeting, the new Banner was expertly Dedicated in a most impressive Ceremony by WBro Brian Eveleigh. He was ably supported by a strong Provincial team and, of course, the Banner Escort was provided by the Lodge, appropriately led by the Ruling Master, WBro Arthur Smith. WBro Brian Eveleigh paid tribute to the Founder Master's foresight and the creativity of WBro Mark L Roberts, when he read his description of the Banner. Among those assisting WBro Brian Eveleigh were WBro Phillip T Humphreys, PAGDC, ProvSGW; WBro H E Roy Woodward, PPrJGD, ProvJGW; and WBro Gareth Jones, OBE, PPrGSwdB, ProvGDC.

A landmark, which has to be recorded, is that the second Initiate into the Lodge, Bro Norman Parker, son-in-law of WBro D Gareth Gait, became the first Candidate to occupy the Chair of King Solomon, being Installed as WM in June 2009.

The Lodge is proud that it has always been able to attract the very strong support of visiting Brethren. The PProvGM, RWBro Hywel Davies has been the Executive Officer at two Installations and in common with many of the Consecrating Team, most predominantly WBro Brian Eveleigh and WBro Robert Nettleship, likes to attend the Lodge whenever other commitments allow.

Particularly in the current climate, the Lodge is also proud that it continues to attract new Members and Joining Members, so that despite inevitably having lost many to the Grand Lodge Above, Lodge numbers are steadily growing.

Compiled by WBro Mark L Roberts, PPrAGReg.

Lodge of Contentment No.9763

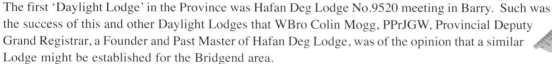

Warranted : 11 September 2002

Consecrated : 10 March 2003

Meeting at the Masonic Hall, Bridgend.

The first 'Daylight Lodge' in the Province was Hafan Deg Lodge No.9520 meeting in Barry. Such was the success of this and other Daylight Lodges that WBro Colin Mogg, PPrJGW, Provincial Deputy Grand Registrar, a Founder and Past Master of Hafan Deg Lodge, was of the opinion that a similar Lodge might be established for the Bridgend area.

During the early part of 2002, WBro Colin discussed this possibility with a number of Bridgend Brethren, and it was agreed to form a committee with him as its Chairman. Within a short time, a sufficient number of Brethren had shown an interest in the formation of a Daylight Lodge. Colin led a Deputation to United Services Lodge No.9605, petitioning Sponsorship for the way forward in the planning of the new Lodge, to meet at the Masonic Hall, Bridgend. At the time, Colin was Secretary of United Services Lodge. Subsequently, the Petition was signed by 30 Brethren, seven of whom were Members of United Services Lodge.

Further meetings ensued, and it was decided to name the Lodge 'Lodge of Contentment'. It was further decided that the Lodge would meet twice a year, on the first Thursday in October and on the third Thursday in May, the latter being the Installation Meeting. Once these decisions had been made, draft By-laws were drawn up for submission to the Provincial Grand Secretary. The Founders agreed to pay for the Officers' Collars and WBro Colin purchased and donated the Honours Board for recording the list of Past Masters.

The Consecration of the Lodge was performed on Monday, 10 March 2003, conducted by RWBro Hywel Davies, ProvGM, assisted by VWBro Peter Frost, PGSwdB, DepProvGM, together with the Assistant Provincial Grand Masters, WBros Rev Norman Lea, DepGChap ; Andrew Lindsay Gretton, PSGD; and Robert J Nettleship, PSGD. Immediately following the Consecration Ceremony, the Deputy Provincial Grand Master conducted the Installation Ceremony, when WBro Colin E Mogg, Master Designate, was Installed as Primus Master. WBro George C Royle, PPrGStwd, (who was appointed Provincial Grand Almoner in 2006), was Invested as Senior Warden and WBro Brian C Ridgeway, PPrSGD, was Invested as Junior Warden. The Provincial Assistant Grand Chaplain, WBro Rev Canon John C Buttimore, PPrJGW, was Invested as the first Lodge Chaplain, with WBro Martyn L Daley, ProvAGSec, as Inner Guard.

Since its Consecration, the Lodge has progressed from strength to strength and whilst only meeting formally twice a year, it nevertheless meets on far more occasions for social events.

The Lodge Banner, designed by WBro Alvern Hart, PJGD, and donated by WBro George Royle, was Dedicated at the Masonic Hall, Bridgend, on the morning of 7 June 2007 by WBro Rev Norman Lea. Also in attendance were the Provincial Grand Master, the Deputy Provincial Grand Master and the other three Assistant Provincial Grand Masters. WBro George Royle had the honour of parading the Banner around the Temple at the beginning of the Ceremony.

During the Ceremony, Rev Norman Lea gave an Address on the history of Banners in general and then on that of the Lodge of Contentment in particular. He described the design of the Banner as skilful, with the centrepiece consisting of the Phoenix rising from the flames. This being a mythical bird that depicted new life, continuity and new beginnings, he considered it to be a most appropriate symbol for the newest Lodge in the Province. The Phoenix is bounded on one side by the Square and Compasses, which are well known as the two Great Lights in Masonry, and on the other, by the Blazing Star or the Star of David. One interpretation of the latter is that one Triangle looks up to God, whilst the other looks down to the real world, but as they are both intertwined they form a whole, uniting both the divine and the temporal.

The Lodge Motto: *'To Help - To Suffice'*, appears below the centrepiece. This can sometimes bring as much confusion as enlightenment, but Rev Norman Lea felt that to offer help when needed and to offer that help to the utmost, will and does bring in its train *contentment*. He also added that it had a very pleasing and practical look and, with a background colour of blue, it signified an association with Craft Masonry, thereby depicting Truth and Fidelity.

Prior to the actual Dedication of the Banner, Rev Norman Lea said that he was delighted to have been chosen to conduct the Ceremony, as it marked his last official engagement as an Assistant Provincial Grand Master before retirement.

Compiled by WBro Colin E Mogg, PAGDC.

Andrew Lindsay Gretton

Deputy Provincial Grand Master
2007 - 2011

Andrew Lindsay Gretton was born in the Canton area of Cardiff and grew up in Victoria Park. He points out that the two benefits were the park, 10 yards across the road, and the famous Clark's pie bakery, 15 yards from his back door. He was educated in Lansdowne Road Primary School and Fitzalan Technical High School, where he came into contact with several Members of the Craft, who were to influence him in later years. The Headteacher, Harold C Eyre, was a Past Master of Harlequins Lodge No.5793; the Technical Drawing Master, Geoff Hancock, was a Past Master of Ymlaen Lodge No. 8419; and another teacher, Ivor Lodge was Organist in many Cardiff Lodges. Andrew Gretton has spent all his working life in Cardiff; one of his early jobs was that of Clerk at W H Hancock's Brewery Ltd, in Crawshay Street. He describes this as the best job in Cardiff because *'you got two bottles of Five Five Export Ale every day'*. The Chief Clerk at Hancock's at that time was WBro Ken Atkins, Treasurer of Caerdydd Lodge No.3959. After many years in employment, Andrew started a janitorial supplies company, Gremer Chemicals UK Ltd, in partnership with Bro Brian Merrick of Clive Lodge No.6973. Later, in 1985, he was involved in the opening of Kiwi's Bar on the site of 'The Old Wine Shoppe' in the Wyndham Arcade, Cardiff. Andrew retired from business life in 2005.

In 1971, Andrew married Gaynor, and they have three children, Claire, James and Simeon. James was Initiated into Wenallt Lodge No.9082 in 2001. Over the years, VWBro Andrew developed a love of National Hunt Racing, and became the owner of a horse, which he named 'Observe', after the Observer Corps, as was Observer Lodge No.6015, Founded in 1945, and which his father had joined in the mid 1950s.

As a Lewis, Bro Gretton was Initiated into Observer Lodge, Cardiff, in 1975, and Installed as Master of that Lodge in 1983. Andrew was a keen member of the Boys' Brigade; he is a Founder Member of the Lodge that bears their Logo, Sure and Stedfast Lodge No.8991, Warranted on 11 March 1981. A Joining Member of Dinas Llandaf Lodge No.8512, he was Installed as Master in 1993. Also a Joining Member of Hendre Lodge No.3250, he was honoured with being Master of that Lodge during its Centenary year in 2007. He is also a Joining Member of Lodge of Enterprise No.8757, South Wales Eastern Division Provincial Grand Stewards' Lodge No.8900 and Lodge of Benevolence No.7305.

In 1980, Andrew was Exalted into Edgar Rutter Chapter No.7196 and Installed as First Principal in 1992. He is a Founder Member of Dinas Llandaf Chapter No. 8512 and was Installed as First Principal of that Chapter in 1994. He is a Joining Member of Hendre Chapter No. 3250, and was promoted to the Grand

Andrew Lindsay Gretton

Rank of PGStB in 2011.

In Provincial Grand Lodge, he was appointed Provincial Grand Steward in 1989, promoted to ProvDepGDC in 1992, and appointed ProvGDC in 1995.

In Provincial Grand Chapter, he was appointed ProvAGSoj in 1995 and promoted to PProvGReg in 2008. He was the Year Book editor with responsibility for the Royal Arch for a number of years.

In Mark Masonry, he was Advanced in Cambrensis Mark Lodge No.1528 in 1992, and Elevated as Royal Ark Mariner in that Lodge in 1993.

During his four years as ProvGDC, WBro Andrew set a very high standard of communication and ceremonial, upon which many others have modelled their ceremonial bearing and demeanour. He was instrumental in the success of the Grand Gala Dinner which culminated the 1999 Charity Festival. On 16 September of that year, he assisted in overseeing the arrangements for the Installation of RWBro Hywel Davies as Provincial Grand Master, and the Installation of Ex Comp John Taylor as Grand Superintendent, at Builth Wells. That day, he was appointed Assistant Provincial Grand Master, and just a year later was charged with the responsibility for promoting the Province's 'Freemasonry in the Community' initiative. This involved planning and implementing policy decisions over the next two years. The Community Programme was an unprecedented success and resulted with a historic joint venture involving the four Welsh Masonic Provinces exhibiting at the Royal Welsh Show, Builth Wells, in 2002.

In 2006, Andrew was invited onto the Council of The Freemasons' Grand Charity (FGC) by the MW the Grand Master, HRH the Duke of Kent. A direct result of this prestigious appointment was the historic occasion when a general meeting of The Freemasons' Grand Charity was held for the first time in the Province. The Vice Grand President of The Grand Charity, Lord Lane of Horsell, welcomed over 500 delegates and their wives from South Wales and other Provinces to the meeting, held at the City Hall, Cardiff, on 23 October 2007.

In 2007, WBro Andrew was appointed Deputy Provincial Grand Master and the following year he was promoted to PGSwdB, thereby becoming VWBro Andrew Gretton. The very successful 2010 Festival in support of The Grand Charity was in large part due to his leadership and guidance as Executive Chairman of the Festival. It resulted in a remarkable donation of over £4M to the Grand Charity.

On 31 July 2010, Welsh Installed Masters Lodge No.9857 was Consecrated in the Grand Temple, Freemasons' Hall, London. Founder Member, VWBro Andrew Lindsay Gretton, was Installed as Primus Master.

VWBro Andrew Gretton describes the highlights of his Masonic career as his Initiation, at which his father was present, and which he still remembers vividly; and being appointed to the best job in the Province, Director of Ceremonies, *'hiding uncontrollable giggles when things go wrong, as they invariably do'* .

He lists one of his greatest concerns as the preservation of the old standards and modes of conduct, which he feels are in danger of erosion due to excessive ambition. VWBro Andrew's considerable Masonic experience has certainly benefited the Province of South Wales. His readiness to assist, advise and help the Brethren has contributed to the ongoing development of Freemasonry in South Wales, and whilst he has always been careful to avoid unnecessary innovation, he is always conscious of the importance of maintaining the basic tenets of The Craft, and the high social and personal standards of its Members in South Wales.

Compiled by WBro Roger Richmond, PJGD.

Robert John Nettleship

Senior Grand Deacon
2002 ~ 2003
Grand Steward
2004 ~ 2005

Robert John Nettleship was born on 30 January 1936 in Peshawar, then the North West Frontier of India, where his father, George, a Dentist from Perth and an Officer in the Royal Army Dental Corps, was stationed. Robert's mother, Nancy, née Stevens, was one of five children of a Swansea Solicitor. There were four daughters and a son, all of whom became lawyers. Before her marriage, Nancy practised for a short time as a Solicitor. She was one of the first lady Solicitors in Wales, while her sister, Robina, became the first lady Barrister in Wales.

In 1939, when war with Germany seemed unavoidable, Robert and his mother returned to her family home in Swansea and shortly afterwards, his sister, Rosemary, was born.

Robert grew up in Swansea but, at the age of eight, he was sent as a boarder to Northaw Preparatory School, near Shrewsbury. The School had been evacuated from Ashford, Kent, for the duration of the War, and returned to its original home in 1946. After Northaw, he continued his education from 1949 until 1953 at Stowe School in Buckingham. On leaving school, he served five years' Articles with Andrew, Thompson and Partners, Solicitors, Swansea. During this time he continued to live at home, apart from two periods of six months each at Law School in London and Guildford. He qualified and was admitted as a Solicitor in July 1959.

His National Service had been deferred during his Articles but, on qualifying, he made arrangements to apply for a short service commission in the RAF Legal Department. However, by that time National Service was about to be abolished altogether, and he failed the medical because his eye-sight/vision was not quite 20/20.

Following employment as an Assistant Solicitor in Swansea for a short time and seven years as a Junior Partner in a firm of Swansea Solicitors, in November 1967, he set up in practice on his own in St Mary's Street, Swansea. Two years later he merged his practice with that of Peter Landers Thomas, PM Dr James Griffith Hall Lodge No.3161, under the name of 'Geo L Thomas, Nettleship & Co'. Mr Landers Thomas died five years later, and Robert, with one other partner, continued the practice under the same name until, in 1998, they merged with the Cardiff firm of 'Morgan Bruce and Hardwickes', to become 'Morgan Bruce'. Robert retired from

Robert John Nettleship

the practice in April 1994, and shortly afterwards became a consultant with John Morris, Solicitors, Cardiff, in which capacity he continued until he finally retired in 2007.

On leaving school, Robert joined the Swansea Uplands RFC, where he first met VWBro J Stuart Peters, as he later became: they have remained close friends ever since. He played for the Uplands in the First XV and, later, the Second XV until January 1961, when he had to retire due to a leg injury sustained during a match against Glyncorrwg. He has since remained a member as Vice-President of the Club.

In 1955, he joined City of Swansea Swimming Club, and served as Vice-Chairman for two periods, 1960-1962 and 1979-1983. During the 1970s, he was Club Secretary for seven years and also represented the Club in gala competitions and water polo, until forced to retire after eye surgery in 1980. He was made a life member of the Club in 1979.

While still in Articles, Robert met Judy, née Moulson, in 1956. They became engaged in December 1959 and were married at St Paul's Church, Sketty, Swansea, on 15 July 1961. They have two daughters, Kathy, who is married and lives in Penclawdd and is a freelance Television Line Producer, and Mary, who is a Solicitor and General Counsel and Group Secretary in a group of public companies and lives in London.

Since 1984, Robert has been a chorister at St Mary's Church, Swansea. It is a commitment to which he attaches increasing importance and which is a source of great joy to him.

In 1980, Robert was approached by an old school friend who told him that Stowe Lodge No.9002 was about to be formed and suggested that he might be interested in becoming the first Initiate. For better or for worse, he agonised about the decision and it was only after three reminders that he decided that Freemasonry was definitely for him, by which time he was to be the Lodge's third Initiate. He was Initiated at an Emergency Meeting at Stowe School on 2 September 1983. WBro J Stuart Peters was present. His Passing and Raising took place in the Lodge's regular meeting place in St James's, London, in the following February and June. He progressed yearly through the Offices and was in the Chair of King Solomon when the Lodge celebrated its 10th Anniversary in 1991.

In the meantime, he had also begun to pursue his Freemasonry in South Wales, joining Lodge of Sincerity No.8531 in 1984 and South Wales Jurists' Lodge No.7092 in 1988. He was Master of the former in 1992 and 1996 and of the latter in 1994 and 2000. In due course, he also became a Joining Member of The Lord Swansea Lodge No.8364 and of Hendre Lodge No.3250.

In London, he joined Lodge of Peace and Harmony No.60, a Red Apron Lodge, in 1987 and, on being its Master in 2003, served as a Grand Steward 2004-2005. He joined the Public Schools Installed Masters' Lodge No.9077 in 1990 and served as its Master, 2006-2007. In 1998, he was appointed to London Grand Rank, and was promoted to the Active Rank of Senior Grand Deacon in UGLE in 2002.

Back in South Wales, Robert's first Provincial appointment was Junior Grand Warden in 1998 and the following year he was appointed Assistant Provincial Grand Master, in which capacity he served until June 2004. On achieving the Rank of Past Junior Grand Deacon in 2000, he became a Joining Member of Lodge of Benevolence No.7305. In June 2011, he became Master Elect and was Installed as WM of that Lodge on 21 October 2011. On each of the eight occasions that WBro Robert Nettleship has been Installed in the Chair of King Solomon, the Address from the West has been given by VWBro J Stuart Peters, which truly must be a record.

WBro Robert is also active in other Orders. In the Royal Arch, he was exalted in Ionic Chapter No.6626 in 1987, Installed as First Principal in 1998, appointed ProvGSoj in 2001 and promoted to PPrGReg in 2008. In Mark Masonry he was advanced in Sir Frederick Alban Lodge No.1455 in 1991, Installed as Master in 2001, appointed PPrGSD in 2004, promoted to PPrGJW in 1998, and appointed PAGDC in 1999. In Royal Ark Mariners he was elevated in Sir Frederick Alban Lodge No.1455 in 1996, and was Installed as Commander in 2001. He was promoted to Provincial Ark Mariners Grand Rank in 1999. In the Ancient and Accepted Rite, he was Perfected into Gŵyr Chapter No.870 in 1986 and Enthroned as MWS in 1998. Finally, he was Elected to 30° in 1999 and to 31° in 2008.

Captain Sir Norman Lloyd-Edwards

Provincial Grand Master
Installed 24 July 2008

Captain Sir Norman Lloyd-Edwards was born on 13 June 1933 at Aberfan, Merthyr Tydfil, where his father, Evan Stanley Edwards, was a Dentist, and his mother, Mary Leah Lloyd, a School Teacher. It was in those early years that he developed a lifelong love for music and drama. After his early education at Monmouth School for Boys and Quaker's Yard Grammar School, Treharris, he continued his education at Bristol University, obtaining his Degree in Law, and remaining in the city to complete his Articles.

Working as a Solicitor, he became the Senior Partner and Consultant with Cartwrights Adams and Black, Cardiff, and was President of the Cardiff Law Society in 1995.

Sir Norman joined the Royal Navy Volunteer Reserve in 1952 and served his National Service in the Royal Navy from 1958 to 1960, after which he joined the South Wales Division of the Royal Navy Reserve. He was awarded Reserve Decoration in 1971 and Bar in 1980. He was appointed Commanding Officer of HMS Cambria in 1981 and promoted to Captain in 1982. In 1984, he was appointed Naval ADC to HM Queen Elizabeth II, serving as such for a year. He was also Honorary Colonel of Second Battalion Royal Regiment of Wales (TA), 1995-1999 and became Honorary Colonel of the newly formed Royal Welsh Regiment, 1999-2003, later Honorary Colonel of 160 Brigade (Wales) 2007-2011. Previously, he had been Chairman of Glamorgan Territorial Auxiliary & Volunteer Reserve Association (TAVRA), President of Reserve Forces' and Cadets' Association (RFCA) Wales, 1999-2005, and President of No.1 Wing Air Training Corps.

In his civic duties, he served on Cardiff City Council, 1961-1967; was Deputy Lord Mayor, 1972-1973; and Lord Mayor 1985-1986. He was appointed Deputy Lieutenant of South Glamorgan in 1978, Vice Lord Lieutenant in 1986 and, in August 1990, he was appointed Lord Lieutenant by Her Majesty the Queen, after being recommended by the Prime Minister, the Rt Hon Margaret Thatcher. In an interview at the time of his appointment, Sir Norman said: *'There was no ceremony, no hand-over. I went to bed one day an ordinary chap and woke up the following day with a sort of cap on my head.'* As Lord Lieutenant,

Captain Sir Norman Lloyd-Edwards

he has been involved in setting up Royal visits as well as carrying out functions on behalf of the monarchy. He retired from the Lord Lieutenancy on his 75th birthday in June 2008.

Sir Norman, a very keen churchman, was Chapter Clerk of Llandaff Cathedral, 1975-1990, and is now President of the Friends of the Cathedral and for the Parish of St John, central Cardiff and of St German's Church, Adamsdown. In 1983, he was made an Officer of the Order of St John, promoted to Knight in 1988, and, in 1996, he was promoted to Bailiff Grand Cross, the highest grade in the Order. He was Prior for Wales, 1989-2005, and Deputy Lord Prior, 2005-2011, as one of the Great Officers, governing St John Ambulance worldwide and the St John Eye Hospital in Jerusalem.

He is also President of many organisations, including: Cardiff Branch National Trust; Community Foundation in Wales; George Thomas Hospice; Wales Committee of Duke of Edinburgh's Award (having been Chairman 1981-1996); Cardiff Branch of Sail Training Association Schooners; King George's Fund for Sailors; United Services Mess, Cardiff; He is also Vice-President of The Royal Welsh College of Music and Drama; and a former President of South Glamorgan Scouts, Wales Book of Remembrance and Wales Festival of Remembrance and a former Governor of the English Speaking Union.

Sir Norman was appointed Honorary Doctor of Laws, University of Wales, and Honorary Doctor of University of Glamorgan in 2010; Fellow of the University of Wales Cardiff Institute in 1995 and, in 2002, Fellow of the Royal Welsh College of Music and Drama.

He is Chairman of the National Youth Orchestra of Wales and of the Welsh Chamber Orchestra He was Chairman of the National Rescue Training Council, 1987-1995, Founder Master of the Welsh Livery Guild for Arts, Science and Technology, 1993-1995; Chairman of Gwerin (Royal British Legion) Housing Association, 1991-1996 and was for some years Chairman of the Cardiff Festival of Music and a former member of the Welsh Arts Council and of the BBC Council for Wales.

In the New Year's honours List, 2007, it was announced that Captain Norman Lloyd-Edwards had been appointed Knight Commander of the Royal Victorian Order by Her Majesty Queen Elizabeth II. The Royal Victorian Order is an order of chivalry in the Commonwealth realm, established by Queen Victoria on 21 April 1896. The Monarch is the Sovereign of the Order and appointments are in her personal gift. Membership is conferred on those who have performed personal service to the Sovereign.

Captain Sir Norman Lloyd-Edwards first became involved in Freemasonry when he was Initiated into Loyal Cambrian Lodge No.110, Merthyr Tydfil, (his father's Lodge) on 3 May 1956. He was Passed on 8 November 1956 and Raised on 4 April 1957. Work commitments resulted in a move to Cardiff, when, reluctantly, he resigned from the Lodge but he rejoined in 2006. He was a Founder Member of Cape St Vincent Lodge No.8524, Cardiff, Consecrated on 17 September 1973, and was Installed as WM in 1977. He was a Joining Member of South Wales Jurists' Lodge No. 7092, and became WM of that Lodge in 1979. In addition, he is a Founder Member of Dinas Llandaf Lodge No.8512, Consecrated on 22 September 1973, and of Wenallt Lodge No.9082, Consecrated on 3 June 1983. In 2005, he became a Joining member of Castle Lodge of Harmony No.26, Duke Street, London and, in 2007, a Joining Member of Royal Alpha Lodge No.16, London. He is also a Joining Member of Lodge of Benevolence No.7305 (October 2008) and The Lord Swansea Lodge No.8364 (March 2009).

In Grand Lodge he was appointed JGD in 1986; President of the New Masonic Samaritan Fund, 1998-2007; PJGW in 2006; Acting JGW in 2007. He has been a member of the Grand Master's Council since 2000.

In Royal Arch, he was Exalted in Cape St Vincent Chapter No.8524 on 21 January 1978, and was Installed First Principal on 20 October 1990. In Grand Chapter, he was appointed GSoj in 2000, promoted to GSwdB in 2005 and to PGScribeN in 2009.

In Rose Croix, he was Perfected in Landav Chapter No.700 on 18 April 1987. He joined Morning Star Chapter No.33 on 9 January 2009 and St Dyfrig's Chapter No 788 on 14 September 2011.

At a Regular Meeting of Loyal Cambrian Lodge on 1 June 2006, he was presented with his Masonic Veteran's Certificate, marking the 50th Anniversary of Initiation into Freemasonry, by RWBro Hywel Davies, ProvGM.

Appointed Provincial Grand Master for South Wales with effect from 1 July 2008, RWBro Captain Sir Norman Lloyd-Edwards was Installed ProvGM of South Wales at the Memorial Hall, Barry, on Thursday, 24 July. The Special Meeting of Provincial Grand Lodge was opened by VWBro Andrew Lindsay Gretton, DepProvGM in Charge. The Installation Ceremony was conducted by RWBro Peter G Lowndes, Deputy Grand Master, assisted by the Grand Director of Ceremonies, VWBro Jonathan Spence, (now Pro Grand Master and Deputy Grand Master respectively). Also in attendance were thirteen Provincial Grand Masters and other Officers of UGLE. During the Ceremony, the Patent of Office was read to Provincial Grand Lodge by VWBro Graham Redman, Deputy Grand Secretary. The Ceremony was followed by a splendid luncheon at Cowbridge Leisure Centre.

On his appointment as Provincial Grand Master of South Wales, Captain Sir Norman Lloyd-Edwards was presented with the 'Kent Cube', a personal gift from the MW the Grand Master HRH the Duke of Kent, KG, and given to each new ProvGM. The cube, of clear perspex, contains a round gold 'coin', bearing the Arms of the United Grand Lodge of England on one face, and the facsimile signature 'Edward GM' on the reverse.

Captain Sir Norman Lloyd-Edwards was Advanced to Mark Master Mason on 20 February 2009, and given the secrets of Master in De Cymru Mark Grand Officers Lodge No.1606 and promoted to PGSD in June 2009. He was Elevated in Cambrensis Lodge No.1528, of Royal Ark Mariners on 12 November 2009 and given the secrets of Commander on 10 February 2010.

On 4 February 2010, he was Installed as WM of his Mother Lodge, Loyal Cambrian Lodge, for the Lodge's Bicentenary Year. The Bicentenary was celebrated on Wednesday, 22 September 2010, at the Rhydycar Leisure Centre, Merthyr Tydfil. Among the distinguished guests were MWBro Peter G Lowndes, Pro Grand Master, VWBro C Nigel R Brown, Grand Secretary and VWBro Thomas J Caplin, Deputy Grand Director of Ceremonies.

In October 1981, Captain Sir Norman Lloyd-Edwards had become a Joining Member of Hendre Lodge No.3250 and, on 27 October 2011, he was Installed as the 104th Worshipful Master of that Lodge.

Gareth Jones, OBE

Deputy Provincial Grand Master
Invested 14 March 2011

WBro Gareth was born and brought up in Rumney, Cardiff and was educated at Rumney High School and Llanrumney High School. He read Economics at Bristol University and afterwards joined the Civil Service. Whilst he was Private Secretary to Lord Young, Secretary of State for Trade and Industry in the Thatcher Government, he got rather bored commuting on the train back and forth to Kent, so he studied modern history to pass the time and obtained an Open University degree as a consequence. He played rugby for Cardiff High School Old Boys RFC, hence his link with Harlequins Lodge No.5793 and he was Initiated into this Lodge in February 1984 and, after serving in all the Offices, he was Installed into the Chair of King Solomon in May 1993. He was subsequently accorded the honour of being appointed to the Active Rank of Provincial Grand Sword Bearer in 1999, his first Office in Provincial Grand Lodge.

Highly thought of, he was appointed Provincial Grand Director of Ceremonies in 2004, an Office he held for three years. In 2005, he became a Grand Officer with the Rank of PAGDC and was Invested as such by the MW the Grand Master, HRH the Duke of Kent, KG, at the Grand Lodge Meeting in April of that year. Then, in 2007, he became the first Initiate of Harlequins Lodge to be appointed an Assistant Provincial Grand Master. In 2008, he was accorded the privilege of serving United Grand Lodge as an Acting Senior Grand Deacon, during which time he was fortunate enough to escort the new Pro Grand Master, MWBro Peter Geoffrey Lowndes, and Deputy Grand Master, RWBro Jonathan Spence, at their respective Installation Ceremonies. WBro Gareth was promoted to Deputy Provincial Grand Master in March 2011. His Investiture as DepProvGM took place at a Regular Meeting of his Mother Lodge on Monday, 14 March, when the Provincial Grand Master, RWBro Captain Sir Norman Lloyd-Edwards, accompanied by a full Provincial team Invested WBro Gareth as his Deputy. Immediately afterwards, the ProvGM Invested WBro Paul Marshall, OBE, ProvGTreas, PAGDC, as Assistant Provincial Grand Master. Very

Gareth Jones, OBE

interestingly, the Provincial Grand Master had accepted the Gavel that evening from the Acting WM, WBro Peter Jones, PProvJGW, (now PAGDC), the blood brother of WBro Gareth.

WBro Gareth is a Joining Member of five Lodges: Hendre Lodge No.3250; Lodge of Benevolence No.7305; The Lord Swansea Lodge No.8364; Dewi Sant Lodge No.9067 and the new Welsh Installed Masters' Lodge No. 9857, Consecrated on 31 July 2010, in London. He is also an Honorary Member of no less than eighteen other Lodges in the Province.

He was responsible for the introduction and establishment of the 'Universities Scheme' within the Province of South Wales. Having been a member of the organising committee of the 1999 Festival, he was appointed Chairman of the 2010 Festival Event Committee by RWBro Hywel Davies, ProvGM. It can clearly be seen that WBro Gareth does nothing by halves!

WBro Gareth holds Grand Rank in Holy Royal Arch and in the Mark Degree and is a member of the Ancient and Honourable Fraternity of Royal Ark Mariners, the Ancient and Accepted Rite and Royal and Select Masters.

In private life, he is married to Susan, a Primary School Headteacher. They have two grown up children, Lucy, who is a Secondary School Teacher, and William, who is working for a Merchant Bank in London. WBro Gareth has a fairly active interest in most sports, has played team tennis and rugby at a high level and now enjoys skiing. Apart from that, his sporting life now revolves around watching William play rugby, who has represented Wales at every level up to and including Under 21s and gained rugby blues at Cambridge University.

In his working life, WBro Gareth has been a Civil Servant for over thirty years and has mastered many demanding roles. As Private Secretary to Lord Young, he undertook the role of Director of Operations for Wales during the Foot and Mouth outbreak in 2001, and spent 5 years as Director of Environment and Agriculture for Wales. He is presently Chief Executive of Companies House and Registrar of Companies for England and Wales. In consequence of his role as Director of Operations for Wales, he was awarded the OBE in 2003 for *'services to the National Assembly for Wales'*.

Compiled by Peter Jones, PAGDC.

The Masonic Halls of the Province of South Wales

The Temple - Aberdare

The Temple - Bargoed

The Masonic Halls of the Province of South Wales

The Temple - Barry

The Temple - Brecon

The Temple - Bridgend

The Temple - Builth

The Masonic Halls of the Province of South Wales

The Temple - Caerphilly

The Duke of Connaught Temple - Cardiff

The Masonic Halls of the Province of South Wales

The Edgar Rutter Temple - Cardiff

The Lord Swansea Temple - Cardiff

The Masonic Halls of the Province of South Wales

The Temple - Town Hall, Cowbridge

The Temple - Llandrindod Wells

The Temple - Llantonian Hall, Llantwit Major

The Temple - Maesteg

The Masonic Halls of the Province of South Wales

The Temple - Merthyr Tydfil

The Temple - Neath

The Temple - Penarth

The Temple - Pontyclun

The Temple - Pontypridd

The Temple - Porthcawl

The Masonic Halls of the Province of South Wales

The Temple - Port Talbot

The Temple - Swansea

The Masonic Halls of the Province of South Wales

The Temple - Treharris

The Temple - RAFA Club, Treorchy

The Provincial History Book Committee
2006 – 2011

WBro Jim Cartwright
PPrDepGDC
Danycoed Lodge No.8127
Editor

WBro Peter M Davies
ProvJGW
Glamorgan Lodge No.36
Chairman & Final Editor

The Late WBro Morris C Fish
PPrSGW
Cambrian Lodge No.364
Editor

WBro Roger Gale
PProvSGD
Lodge of St Illtyd No.6078
Editor

WBro Anthony Howell
PPrJGW
Lodge of Harmony No.8414
Photographer

WBro Don Jones
PProvSGD
Preswylfa Lodge No.5792
Editor & Graphic Designer

The Provincial History Book Committee
2006 - 2011

WBro Brian Langley
PGStB, ProvSGW
Beehive Lodge No.6265
Secretary & Editor

WBro Douglas J Morgan
PPrDepGDC
St Gwynno Lodge No.8599
Editor

WBro Peter T Morgan
PPrAGDC
Morganwg Lodge No.5084
Editor

WBro David M Murphy
PPrJGD
Glamorgan Lodge No.36
Proof Reader

WBro John K Pillinger
PPrSGD
Crystal Lodge No.8713
Editor

WBro Ken Pontin
PPrJGD
Adare Lodge No.4127
Editor

The Provincial History Book Committee
2006 – 2011

WBro Edward Llewelyn Thomas
PPrJGD
Lodge of Progress No.7928
Editor

WBro Graham J Wilcox
PPrGSwdB
Ymlaen Lodge No. 8419
Treasurer & Editor

WBro Denis J Woods
PPrJGW
Lodge of St Martin No.8771
Editor